The Story of Life

The Story of Life

A Shocking Revelation About God and the
Universe to End Fear and Liberate Humanity

Christopher McKeon
Tőteppit Press

Tŏteppit Press
Rico, Colorado USA

www.storyoflifebook.com
www.toteppitpress.com

Publisher's Cataloging-in-Publication Data
McKeon, Christopher David, author.
The story of life : a shocking revelation about God and the universe to end fear and liberate humanity / Christopher David McKeon.
First edition. | Rico, CO : Tŏteppit Press, 2022. | Includes bibliographical references and index. | Also available in audiobook format.
LCCN 2022911616 (print) | ISBN 979-8-9864707-2-6 (hardcover) | ISBN 979-8-9864707-0-2 (paperback) | ISBN 979-8-9864707-1-9 (PDF)
LCSH: Prayer–Christianity. | Spiritual life. | Mind and body. | Consciousness. | Well-being. | BISAC: BODY, MIND & SPIRIT / Inspiration & Personal Growth. | RELIGION / Spirituality. | SCIENCE / General.
LCC BL624 .M35 2022 (print) | LCC BL624 (ebook) | DDC 158/.12–dc23.

Unless otherwise indicated, scriptural quotations are from the Holy Bible, New International Version (NIV), various publishers and dates. Those labeled KJV are from the King James Version, various publishers and dates. Quotations used per applicable copyright law.

Cover design by nskvsky
Text set in EBGaramond, Cambria Math, Helvetica-Narrow

Net sale proceeds from this book support the *Story of Life* free paperback program (PDF ebook is free).

Let us make mankind in our image…
— Genesis 1:26

In prison cell and dungeon vile
Our thoughts to them are winging,
When friends by shame are undefiled
How can I keep from singing?
— Doris Plenn, as sung by Enya₁

There is no purpose to this life,
You make your own purpose;
That's what makes life beautiful.
— El

For my beloved daughters who elevated this
experience for me from weird to real.

And in memory of every manjack
who e'er sought reality
o'er the veil of belief.

Contents, Figures & Tables

II All Existence …

III   ... All That's In It ...

24 THE CORRUPTION

IV ... And Us

V Energy Testing

VI Appendices

Figures

Tables

Prologue

WHAT YOU ARE reading is my two middle daughters' and my testimony. This book is revelatory, not reasoned, researched, or imagined. It's the product of thousands of real-time, full-duplex conversations with God (henceforth, *Mina*);[1] the so-called angels Gabriel, Lucifer, Michael, and others;[2] Jesus; Sun-myung Moon;[3] Buddha; Muhammad; Abraham; Zoroaster, and many more; plus family, friends, and others living in spirit world,[4] the real and surprisingly simple nature of which we convey in this book.

"*Whoa!* Hold up right there," you might be thinking. "There's a million of these psychic tales on the market. What makes this one any more credible?"

We say, "What if you could verify it yourself, so you don't simply need faith in the book?"

"I'm no spirit medium," you might retort.

"Don't have to be. With a little training and practice, anyone can do this."

"You're going to show me how? Spiritualists don't show their tricks."

"We are. We will. And there are no tricks. You'll see for yourself."

What you will read is revelation in that spirit persons conveyed it, but we still had to get out of our own heads just to range through the possibilities and then *ask*. So, this book is also *learned* knowledge. That suggests a need to expand, if not outright dispense with, the concept of revelation. As a core aspect of our zeitgeist, however, we stick with it for now. To help you know the how and why, and to get a feel for our discovery as an experience, we begin in the *The Big Event* narrating our extraordinary first two days and the circumstances leading up to it, the universal transformation it sparked, some of what we learned, and its effect on us. PARTS II–IV comprise the whole story of life that we've so far learned and clarifies things we only introduce in the narration. We found out the hard way an extrapolation may appear to logically and consistently follow a revelation with eminent sense, but isn't necessarily true at all. Therefore, what you will *not* read in this book are our own inferences, opinions, and beliefs masquerading as revelation. Rather, we analyze and interpret in concert with Mina and relevant spirit persons. We fix editorial errors as discovered for future editions.

"Well, gosh," you perhaps scoff, "all I get is your word of honor on that?"

No, not exactly. This whole amazing affair originated with inquiring minds wanting to . . . well, know

---

1. Creator, Father, Lord, Master, Allah, Jehovah, YHWH, Brahman, Ahura Mazda, First Cause, Source, Universal Force, or whatever and in whichever faith language you use. He asked us to knock off calling him God and all the rest because they reference painful behaviors that distort what he is. He accepted Protector and Grandfather until we learned his birth name, Reikishiña, although we generally address him by his preferred name on Earth, Mina (cf. his name in § 1.1:336).

2. These aren't their birth names but bestowed by humans (Table 17:523).

3. Korean evangelist (d. 2012) and founder of the Holy Spirit Association for the Unification of World Christianity (HSA–UWC, or Unification Church). Turns out, he played an important part in this story while alive and then afterward, too.

4. We use pseudonyms except where individuals, as noted, permitted our use of their real name.

what's *real*. When we discovered how to get a measurable response, we started asking and asked a lot. We subtitled this book "A Shocking Revelation . . ." because the answers profoundly *shocked* us. My daughters took it mostly in stride with the aplomb, I suppose, that befits their jaded millennial youth. I felt the ground quake beneath my Judeo-Christian feet. Questions—*disbelief!*—poured out of me, occasionally accompanied by my children's exaggerated eye rolls. Having less baggage to jettison themselves, they thought I should more easily flush away decades of faith, learning, and enculturation instead of hammering the same questions from every angle to assure belief we were talking with *the* Creator, not to mention everyone else, and to reconcile what they were saying with what we thought we knew. As disruptive a thinker as some found me through the years, this experience carried me well past even my farthest boundaries. Right from its October 2017 beginning and throughout the months and years we found only loving, embracing energy, logical consistency, common sense, simplicity, hope, and above all, *liberation*. Our feelings upon release from millennia of human delusion and fatuous complexity felt like draining a dirty bathtub.

As you read on, you'll see this amazing opportunity appeared not through grace, benevolence, providential timing, holier than thou-ness, the Call, or some mystical lottery but simply from our curious, out-of-the-box thinking unbounded by religious and philosophical regimentation. We rang, and Mina answered. So, too, with you after employing PART V's training.

"You have to think like Captain Jack Sparrow, Dad," my girls, in all gravity, urged in mopier moments.

I wasn't even sure what that meant. "Isn't he a drunkard?"

Eye rolls.

Humanity long ago assured itself that its creator—if there even is one, say the naysayers, and we're not the random progeny of haphazard accidents and amorous monkeys—is the Silent Master of the *terribilis mysterium fidei* or maybe just a broody mute too regal or pissed off to talk to his ungrateful zoo. In truth, our 'creator' Mina—God—tried repeatedly through the ages to make himself known to those aware enough to notice. But it was an unproductive slog. This book represents only his third success directly conveying the real story of life to conscious (as opposed to dreaming, entranced, or spirit traveling), spiritually aware persons here on Earth. So . . . *carpe diem.*[5]

Lest you think this book is yet more chicanery from dodgy mediums peddling pious interviews with mystical, condescending gods and gurus—angelically descended from someone's ersatz spirit world to philosophize us into laundering our profane selves from smutty clay to divine ecstatics, all the while considering us too venal or stupid to grasp the sophisticated benevolence of their Almighty—or unattributed aggregations of extant works, or just making it all up, PART V shows you how to answer for yourself the questions that inevitably arise in your mind from reading these pages. You'll learn to converse in real time with Mina, the 'angels' including your guardian 'angel(s),' spirit guide(s), spirit family and friends; frankly, anyone willing. With that ability, you needn't rely on just our word of honor not to lie to you.

"Well, that's something new," you may admit.

Subscripted endnotes (example$_{52}$) and superscripted footnotes (example[78]) are citations and related discussion, and contain brief clarifications and pertinent information, respectively. Cross-references to footnotes or endnotes use the format *FN[EN]:note#:page#*. References directing you to another [chapter]section use the format *[CH.#]§#:page#*, sometimes prepended by *CHAPTER-NAME* for clarity. Dialogue is verbatim when it really stuck in our minds or we wrote it down, otherwise it's the speaker's approved paraphrasing. "Double quotes" indicate spirit person dialogue, or as noted. 'Single quotes' and *italics* indicate phrasing and emphasis. Italics also indicate energy-test responses like *yes*, *no*, *maybe*, and other words or phrases (CH. 41:623). *Above* and *below* reference text within a page; *further* is prefixed when it's more than a page or so away but in the same section or (short) chapter. In a citation, *io* and *ia* means italics original or added. We split our bibliography between *Cited* and *Consulted* works since energy tested, intuited, or clair-sensed answers to 'why' questions on the variety of topics we encountered meant consulting fields of study where our knowledge wasn't up to par to derive a sufficiently aware comprehension adequate to formulating pertinent queries. We shelved what we couldn't understand until studying up for another go or an *aha!* moment we could then energy test.

We encountered these revelations as a typical, sometimes fractious, American family. Through it, we found ourselves a more healed team. Although I'm penning this book, I couldn't have done it without my two middle daughters. Their ability to intuit, sense energies, feel spirit persons' emotions as if reading body language, utilize clair senses, grasp concepts I stumbled over, figure out better questions when I'd driven myself into a ditch, be a compass when I'd get lost, and validate what, on my own, I certainly could have only doubted, was

5. Literally *pluck the day [as it is ripe]* (Horace, *Odes*, 23 BC, I:11), which it is, so we are.

invaluable. Thank you, girls, for your help as I wrote this book, and especially for our wonderful experiences at Wild Flower Lane discovering its beginnings. It immensely challenged us. We got on each other's nerves. It dug out our rawest emotions, flayed our hearts, at times put us to tears. We shared the foxhole. Now you're in the Big City and I'm proud of you both.

We thank *you* for acting on your curiosity, interest, or intuition to consider this material. Just reading it broadens humanity's awareness of the universe in which we live and, in so doing, promotes healing. In your own way, you're contributing to reducing harm and trauma which seeds a better future.

The Story of Life is a foundational work. As such, Mina asked us to make it free because, for him, gaining awareness of reality through learning about this material opens a person to basic, life-changing healing that leads to happier life choices—reading nothing more about Mina, reality, and energy testing than this book is sufficient for anyone to begin whatever healing process they desire—and he loathes converting pain and suffering to aggrandizing fees. But to get the book in front of the widest possible audience requires booksellers, so we've agreed we'll sell the hardcover, paperback, specialty bindings, and abridged versions wherever books are sold while distributing the PDF ebook free—look for a possible EPUB version in future—as well as a *free paperback book program* as funds are available, some from us according to our means and the rest from crowdfunding which details you can find at *toteppitpress.com*. In future we may offer *Story of Life* merchandise, which net proceeds along with a portion of the net proceeds of select future books will also support the free paperback.

Regarding the ebook, Mina's caveat is that electronics (and electricity generally) disrupt spiritual 'energy' such as the chakras. This reduces your spiritual awareness, intuition, and ability to cognize the book's content. My computer often disrupted my own while writing the book as they progressively 'opened' and developed greater sensitivity, thus usefulness. Mina—"It's a necessary sacrifice, so just re-open them and keep going"— routinely coaxed them back to duty until I could do it myself and they grew robust enough to better resist it. He'll open yours, too, if you ask (CH. 29:497).

Introduction

THIS BOOK IS the story of how the walking disaster that's life—which we're all just trying to grin and bear our way through to its Wagnerian finale—did a one-eighty October 13, 2017 on everything we've ever hated, feared, chewed on, ignored, denied, sighed over, prayed about, cried for, railed against, killed over, lived in denial of, built coping delusions to . . . well, on and on, right? More than just how it happened, this book tells you what changed that day and over the following months and years, why life is the way it's been up till now and how it really is and, most important, how it all affects *you*.

"Dad," said my daughter El in deadly earnest right on the heels of me agreeing to write this book, "make absolutely sure you tell them this is totally *not* a new religion or any kind of dumb philosophy."

Palms out, I said, "Okay, I promise."

"That they don't have to listen to it, or worship anything, or—"

"Yes, of course I will, sweetie."

"Because people are totally, absolutely *free*."

"El, I got you."

"I'm just saying, Dad." Her eyes toyed with a roll. "Cuz that's the *last* thing we need!"

A strong *Yes!* from Mina (God).[6]

So, now you know. The book you're reading is simply the story of life. Not how we'd like it to be in our happiest fantasies or self-loathing expiatory flagellations, but how it really is. It might shake you up, amaze you, or freak you out. Could be you'll sigh contentedly over your absolute autonomy or tremble in angst at your divine unaccountability. If you keep an open mind, the one thing you might feel is a profound feeling of *free*. Liberated. Released. Empowered. *Relieved*. In it, you might surprise yourself to encounter a natural capacity for love and acceptance you never seriously imagined in actuality existed.

That's what this book is offering you. And you needn't do a single just-change-yourself-this-or-that-way thing to experience it. Simply relax your fearful, pent-up self enough to consider fairly this story of life and it will happen naturally. That's how it went for us, anyhow. It's even odds it'll go that way for you, too.

You know as well as anyone that life isn't what it could be. Since the 1970s, youth have been rejecting society as it is because they're increasingly spiritually open. They sense that something's terribly wrong yet aren't spiritually aware enough to know what it is or how better to live. The fact is that life can be a whole lot better. For now, it's not, but it could be worse. As philosopher Alan Watts opines, living with

> the frustration of having always to pursue a future good in a tomorrow which never comes, and in a
> world where everything must disintegrate, gives men an attitude of 'What's the use anyhow?' . . . We

---

6. Continue on to *The Big Event* for how it is that he's communicating with us (for his name, see FN 1:i; § 1.1:336).

> crave distraction—a panorama of sights, sounds, thrills, and titillations into which as much as possible must be crowded in the shortest possible time (Watts 1951, 21)

because all we can see is the eternal finitude of our physical, bodily existence however ambitiously we try spiritualizing it with antipodean aspirations of eternal life and faith in a just reward. It's a sad fact that even Christians and Muslims, who teach a (maybe not so much for some) joyous afterlife purchased through ardent, obedient belief, generally rue death and wail upon the fresh graves of loved ones. Why do you suppose they do that despite their faith? What if our physical life is just a phase in a larger, logically consistent, yet different life the way our short childhoods are to our much longer yet equally dissimilar adult lives? No one's yet sold us on that, being so stuck as we are in biology's rut that

> most of us are willing to put up with lives that consist largely in doing jobs that are a bore, earning the means to seek relief from the tedium by intervals of hectic and expensive pleasure. These intervals are supposed to be the real *living*, the real purpose served by the necessary evil of work. (ibid, io)

This is where we as a race have been spinning our wheels since the primordial ooze. Overwhelmed by our physical senses and unaware of our spirit self and its reality, we've missed the forest for the trees.

> But what are we to do? The alternatives seem to be two. The first is, somehow or other, to discover a new myth, or convincingly resuscitate an old one. If science cannot prove there is no God, we can try to live and act on the bare chance that he may exist after all . . . But . . . this will never amount to a vital faith for it is really no more than to say, 'since the whole thing is futile anyhow, let's pretend it isn't.' The second is to try grimly to face the fact that life is 'a tale told by an idiot,' and make of it what we can, letting science and technology serve us as well as they may in our journey from nothing to nothing. (ibid, 22)

Well, *meh*. We'll take door number three, thanks, which recognizes the creator of our little playhouse as he really is and the (nonhuman) life he brought forth as *it* really is. Taking on existential reality is like the maturating experience of growing from child to adult where we need come to grips not only with the world as it is instead of how we thought it should be till it punched us in the mouth, but with our parents as they really are and the world they constructed for us throughout our childhood as it really is. The five stages of grief—denial, anger, bargaining, depression, and acceptance—are literally how we traverse this inescapable demand of life; it's how psychiatrists stay in business anyway. Each of us goes more or less further along this five-stage trajectory. Some never make it through and wallow. Some endlessly restart if-then-else loops. Still others lurch through to the promised land only to bang into the ongoing confusion, faith, hope, belief, or delusion of an uncertain world while hoping, praying, and striving to make it through to death with some semblance of happiness toward a brighter deceased tomorrow. Like all merry-go-rounds, it can dizzily spin one into puking or entirely off into the weeds.

Wouldn't it be convenient just to get off? You do that by understanding what's really going on, to gain a clear awareness of where you stand as a physically alive person in the larger universe. We've never reliably been able to do that, hence all our competing revelations, theologies, and philosophies. But with this book, we now can. For that, we introduce *energy testing* (ET; PART V), a reproducible physiological method for getting the real skinny from the horse's mouth. Getting at reality is where PARTS II–IV of this book come in, where we discuss the universe—its spiritual *and* physical facets—its creator, and humanity. Some of it will make perfect sense right off the bat, like something always known or long-suspected and now here it is in print, cogently explained. Some will likely draw out a healthy skepticism for which you can use the training in PART V to replicate our own experience for yourself so you won't be left in a bog of faith, compelled to believe or else to forfeit it. You can do exactly what we did: discover energy testing, then through your own visceral, physiological experience decide if you're actually feeling the spiritual energy of Mina, 'angels' (spirit-born humans), your family, friends, or others in in spirit world answering your questions, and then formulate queries which answers you can accept, reject, or dispute.

Our revelation-and-response comes on the heels of my own sixty-year trek through Christianity, forty-plus years of it—for my daughters, since birth—caught up to one degree or another with Rev. Sun-myung Moon's deep spirituality and his vapid Unification Church with its rinse-and-repeat emotional and spiritual chaos.[7] Only as my older daughters came of age did I put those closet monsters to bed. What I heard then as God's call to once more leap deep in the breach came a-knocking like that friend pursuing their next sure-fire investment

---

7. See McKeon (2003) for the first 21 years of this wildin' tale.

while you're staggering back from their last bout of other people's money. The long and short of *that* is what eventually put us on the road to this book.

The Story of Life is an axial moment challenging socioculture's norms. *We* aren't that axial moment, it's God—well, Mina. We are, let's say, his cogitative messengers. In addition to moneymaking and volunteer professions, I've been a missionary, minister, pastor, and military chaplain all my adult life. Yet, here I am having found religion, faith, philosophy (except its critical reasoning toolset) and its subset theology[8] all largely albeit not entirely, as you'll see, bunk; illusion at best, delusion at worst.

If you're at all religious or philosophical, all this may quite naturally concern you. If it makes you feel any better, it challenged us on all counts, too. The reaction is natural though not inevitable, and is certainly amenable. Before judging, consider. Fallacious, religion and philosophy certainly are. But rubbish, 'God' and rationality absolutely are not. 'God' is real. Not deitic or divine nor magical but a human person; it's how we come to *be* human. He's eminently sensible. Via principles of reality we discuss in PARTS II and III, he created this universe for us to live in absolutely, unconditionally, and unequivocally *free*. Not free within reason, or as a duty, under law, responsibly, morally bounded, or only as long as we keep it on the straight and narrow thus on the road to judgment and punishment if we don't, but utterly, perfectly, *a*judgmentally free. This book provokes you to wrap your head seriously around the concept of *free*. You may find it less easy than maybe it ought to be.

Love is the flipside to freedom, the obverse equivalent of an indivisible coin. But love is so amorphous. No one really *knows* what love is, and that's why it's difficult to live accordingly. For now (at least with us), Mina boiled it down to *caring, consideration for*, and *doing no harm*,[9] and in that context *loving freedom*. More precisely, loving *another*'s freedom (simply to be) and therewithal living in one's own freedom absent malice or resentment. We were surprised to find love isn't the centrality of creation, the universe, or its creator. But then neither is freedom. It's because they don't exist independently but only *au pair*, the same way men and women naturally exist pairwise because that's *human*. Freedom is a state of existence while love expresses that state. One doesn't exist in love except through freedom and one doesn't exist in freedom except through love. Our mind,[10] of course, is irreducibly free no matter how we oppress it; and yes, we do indeed oppress—deny freedom and love to—ourselves. Others can only do so in our stead with our tacit permission, which we usually give in our profound unawareness of our spiritual reality to gain or avoid a benefit or trauma.

The genesis of this book was our, perhaps naïve, desire to know The Truth. We couldn't foresee that things we thought firmly rooted and plainly sensible were not true and others we never even imagined were. I joke about my jaw-hitting-the-floor comedy routine, but our schooling was anything but a barrel of laughs. Sure, we had a lot of fun. Mina, the 'angels,' and family and friends in spirit world are for the most part wonderful, kind, considerate, happy, and caring people. But what they had to say was ofttimes dry gravel down our gullet. We couldn't just ignore their testimony, though—weren't *we* interrogating *them*?—especially when we'd reason it through and find no substantive chinks.

So, turn the page to *The Big Event* and discover our October surprise. Then in PARTS II–IV what we learned during and afterward. Finally, in PART V, how you can spin this wheel yourself so that instead of having only faith or hope this book isn't pulling your leg, you come away with knowledge and liberation that, indeed, it's not.

Christopher McKeon
New Mexico, USA
July 2022

---

8. Religion (theology) relies on revelation and philosophy (reason) to frame it; philosophy (not its pure reason toolset) relies on reason and theology (revelation) to frame it.

9. In this context, *caring* is kind, sensitive, and empathetic while *considerate for* is consciously thoughtful and observant.

10. Heart, traditionally the seat of our feelings, is in actuality our mind (CH. 26:391).

Part I

The Big Event

All Shook Up

Thursday October 12, 2017 ca. 5 PM

F ALL THE days in all the months in all the year, Friday the 13th just had to be the day the world as it was all sort of just blew up in our face. My two daughters and I . . . well, we quite lit the fuse when, about sixteen hours before that cool October morning, we'd tramped through the garage door of our woodsy rural log cabin home following an afternoon of errands and posed a simple question. Atop a wild, spiritually hectic week culminating in our long afternoon in the car talking over God, ancestry, life, and surprises from dear dead friends, my two-days-eighteen daughter El froze mid-step in our living room and blurted, "Creator, do you have a family?"

And he answered.

We all three traded surprised eyes at the *yes* response, but she was on a roll.

"Do you have a wife?"

Yes.

"Do you have children, not just us?"

Yes.

She paused a few seconds, thinking through the logic. "Do you have a *mother?*"

Yes!

While I jacked my jaw up off the floor, she looked at me. "Dad, I can literally *feel* his joy that we've just discovered this! He's really happy! Can we meet her?" she added, not to me. "Can we talk to her?"

At which point El swiveled to her right, face and eyes cranking upward as though at a much taller person. Her expression transformed, aglow with delight and excitement. A smile burst across her cheeks as her hands flew to her heart. She sucked her breath.

"*Hi*, Mother!"

Yeah. I gawped, too.

Even a wizened skeptic like me could tell my younger daughter was having a moment, an experience, a—well, a revelation. Chills, tingles, and heat shivered me timbers stem to stern. Energy and pleasure radiated from El. I could see her gleam. There was no mistaking her profound joy and rapture. We, too, felt the presence of 'Mother' fiercely blazing with happy excitement. Communicating. In our *home*. To *us*. Who were *aware* of her. My older daughter and resident spiritualist Ayako, now two days from her twenty-first year, twisted round a blue-upholstered, high-backed dining chair and plopped into it facing El with a knowing curiosity, feeling all the energy we were experiencing and more. We incessantly questioned Mother and Mina—God (FN 1:i)—into the night, all of which you'll encounter throughout this book.

That wasn't even the really exciting part. But before we got to that, our curiosity slanted us through some scary hours later in the night that left my exuberant daughters tearful and terrified, and me wondering just what can of worms we'd pulled the pop-top on. For now, though, we enthusiastically pushed our envelope of reality and the eye-popping responses snowballed. A lifelong Irish Roman Catholic, Protestant Christian, Unificationist[11], and now post-Unificationist, it soon registered that my worldview, my *lifeview*, was in some real distress here. Stuff needed clarifying if not a little unmitigated arguing. Yet for all that, Mina's answers were coherent, consistent, and sensible. Only good, loving, calm but excited energy bathed the room. With that, it seemed as wise a time as any to get down to the suddenly apropos nitty-gritty.

I said, "Creator,[12] is the Bible true?"

No.

I pulled a hard breath, astonished, though as a graduate of divinity school maybe not all that surprised. Even so, a linchpin of my lifeview clattered to the wide-planked floor.

"What about the New Testament? Is Jesus' teaching in that true?"

"Dad, he said—"

No.

"*All* of it?" I gave my girls each a once over, but if you could wear a body shrug like a pantsuit, they were. *Kids*, I thought. Always jaunty at the start of a march across somebody else's Bataan.

No.

"So, some of it, then, is true."

Yes.

"How 'bout Jesus," El said, "is he a real person?"

Yes.

Well, that was a relief. I think. Anyhow, the girls looked copacetic. We quizzed Mina on this topic awhile until, inevitably, it led to the issue most pressing me.

"Is Rev. Moon's teaching in *Divine Principle* true?"[13] I mean, I'd largely bet the farm on it in 1981.

No.

My ribs fell in. There went another linchpin. I let out a wheeze like I'd just downed a shot of two-hundred proof. Bleary eyes landed on each daughter, but saw in them none of my own jolt.

"Jeez, girls," I yawped. "That's been my lifeview purt' near forty years!"

Ever sassy, Ayako said, "Welcome to the next wave, Dad."

Unlike Jesus, I *knew* Sun-myung (he eschews titles, now). His theologically ultra-modern Divine Principle was more real to me than worn out, foggy old Christianity, its grand morsels of wisdom and Jesus notwithstanding. Sure, Divine Principle reposed upon the biblical witness, but to me it more sensibly elucidated its core truths. It underwrote the full scale of my adult life. I might be perennially at war with Sun-myung's pigheaded church institution but not his Divine Principle, not by any stretch.

I said, "*All* of it?"

I had to ask because, like everyone in spirit world communicating with a non-conversational medium[14] in the physical world, Mina must needs be literal in our mode of communication. He has to be, really. Absent face-to-face or even just voice-to-voice conversation, it's nigh impossible to gauge what a person actually means by words alone. Consider how the misunderstanding curve rises proportionally to one's metaphorical distance from the speaker. One's words themselves—rooting in shared definitions—need convey precisely what's meant. That's a tough row to hoe for humans, wedded the way we are to contextual word play. You might think Mina could simply know our thoughts, but that creates complications of its own we discuss later. What it boils down to, Ayako pointed out, is that we had to formulate our questions thoughtfully into unambiguous inquiries and confirmations that backed up our responses.

No, Mina answered me through El.

Huh. So again, only some of my lifeview was true. Was that good? I didn't know. As with the Bible, I could only wonder, *which freaking part? Divine Principle* is a weighty *vade mecum* in its own right.

Being young, unformed, and like many in their generation rejecting religion generally though not God specifically, my daughters *looked* okay—my eldest like an old soul hearing something she'd long suspected and her kid sister charmed in high cotton—but *my* cosmology was melting apart like Icarus' wishful wax job. This conversation was sweeping away a lifetime of hard-won truths, from the nature of the universe and God to Jesus and Sun-myung's messianism and the spiritual verity and providential histories that went with them

---

11. A follower of Sun-myung Moon's teachings, which he calls Divine Principle, the core of his Unification Church.

12. How we addressed him before he said he prefers Mina or, better yet, his real name, Reikishiña (§ 1.1:336).

13. His codified theology published in Korean (1954, 1966) and English (1973, revised 1996).

14. One not able to converse voice-to-voice with spirit persons as in spoken conversation.

(likewise with all religions), not to mention what I'd sacrificed—wasted?—for it all. My head was spinning. I was anything *but* okay. But dammitall if that would throttle my interest; perish the thought. Come hell or high water, I'm nothing if not the cat tempting curiosity.

By and by, we worked our way to the crux of the Abrahamic religions: the Fall of Man. Original sin territory and their *raison d'être*. After some unexpected and perplexing responses from Mina, we needed to get a few things straight.

I said, "Are you saying the Fall never happened?"

Yes.

"So . . ." dittoed El, finally sounding a tad betrayed, "there *was* no Fall of Man?"

No.

"Satan never persuaded Eve to eat the 'fruit'?" she continued. "Lucifer never fell—never had a wrong sexual relationship with Eve like Rev. Moon said? People never tried to be God and 'fell' from grace or perfection, or whatever?"₂

No, no, no.

"Well," said I, "fuuu—!"

No.

Ayako shifted round to me with disapprobation. "That 'no' means negative energy resonates, Dad."

Great.

After more give-and-take—during which Mina recast 'the Fall' as *The Corruption* in which humans self-manifested our selfish, harmful world and self-alienated ourselves from God (I mean, Mina) without any help from anybody, including our evolutionarily left-over, full-blown-batty reptile brain—El perceptively said, "Wait. Are Adam and Eve even real people who actually lived?"

No.

Ayako and El traded stares. It seemed their own lifeviews were at last meeting some unexpected renovation. About time.

I choked. "Um, they don't exist?"

No. They don't exist.

"Then, is Satan a real being, a fallen angel, or . . . whatever?"

No. No . . . no.

"Wait, wait." Just. *Wait.* I needed a minute to *think.*

El didn't. "You mean Satan doesn't even *exist*? There's no devil, no evil force or being that—"

No, no.

"So, no war in heaven, no angel rebellion, no beings cast down to earth," she went on with obvious offense, practically ticking through Revelations (12:7–9) on her fingers and giving me, her ministerial, semi-Bible-thumping father a flinty eye, "no ancient good versus . . . *none* of these stories religion taught us are true?"

No. Sorry.

El blew off a heavy breath, threw up her hands, and tromped in a circle. Oaths welled up in my brain so fast they had to take a number.

A little hostile, I said, "What about Darwin, then?

"Not Darwin, Dad," said Ayako, ever the schoolteacher, "Darwin*ism*. Unless you mean the guy, you're talking about natural selection."

"Uh, sure . . . but is he—it—true?"

No.

"What? But then—?"

"So, evolution is *wrong*?" said El.

Yes.

"All of it?" I added, pretty much expecting the obvious.

No.

Yep. Here we go again. "So, basically, *everybody's* explanation for humanity's existence and miserable condition is total bullshit?"

"Dad . . ."

"False?"

Maybe . . . yes.

Ayako said, "Remember, Dad, he said not *every* single thing."

"Yeah, but everybody's?"

"Like, all religions and philosophies?" El said plainly.

Yes.

She let out a low, gruff whistle. "*Waaah*—when your whole existence is just a fat lie."

"So, Islam, too?" I said. "And Buddhism, Confucianism, Hinduism, Animism—"

Yes, yes, ye—

Ayako gave me an eye. "He said all religions, Dad. Come on."

Yes.

"I'm just being thorough." And not taking sides, I didn't say.

No.

"I'm not? But I . . . wait," I said toward El, who was doing our energy testing. "Are you pulling my leg?"

Yes.

"Well. Isn't he just a barrel of monkeys. Never took God for a joker," I said to Ayako, though I'd heard a medium once make the claim.

"Lots of things you never thought of, Dad," she chirped, queen of the snappy comeback and earning my tight-lipped stare-down. My mood was a little nettled, frankly.

A flurry of questions and statements followed as we plunged ever deeper down our rabbit hole. I put evolution aside for now. It only dealt with our bodies anyhow. We had *cosmic* issues on the table. But now, a few other things in my head about the human 'fall from grace' were rising to the fore and clashing with Mina's assertions. It occurred to me we'd need to pull in somebody else, the very somebody who off and on since late summer had purveyed through a local medium a seemingly clear, unambiguous spiritual reality that included a very real Adam and Eve. Archangel Michael.[15]

1.1 Seven Weeks Earlier . . .

See, back on August 27, 2017 my 'woo-woo' spiritualist church friend, Moth Man[16] (who's always going on about spirit world, Mother God, the Divine Feminine, angels, spirit animals, and the like), sauntered up to me after church in Bowie, Maryland with a friend of his whom I didn't know particularly well. He said, "Hey, we have this thing going on in a few minutes where we're going to use Emotion Code [an alternative healing modality], to heal Archangel Gabriel and Michael. You like angels, right?" All I had for that was a body shrug. "Why don't you join us?"

I blinked, nonplussed. "Uh . . . what's wrong with them?"

"They have trapped emotions." Moth Man's eyes flitted to his nodding companion. "Gabriel came to my buddy here in a dream last night, asking him to do an Emotion Code healing."

Ohhh-kay, then. I didn't really hang around goofy new-agey types but, as we'd been acquainted since 1982, I'd made Moth Man the exception. I've always been a cutting-edge theologian though apparently a little conventional in my angelology. If you're wondering why angels would even need healing much less humans to do it for them, well, I did, too.

I said, "What's 'emotion code' and why do they need us?"

Moth Man launched into a quick overview, noting they'd lined up a local Unificationist 'mental medium'[17] in a breathless 2 AM phone call who also happened to be a certified Emotion Code practitioner. The stars were aligned. He wore an expectation I'd say yes the way a dog starts chewing while chow's still airborne twixt the bag and bowl. I'm really *not* the new-agey type, did I mention that? On the other hand, I'm always game for something interesting and unusual and this scored about a hundred-forty on that scale. The four of us sat down at a faux wood-top table in a quiet, closed room in the church. Our local medium (*Ms. Medium*, whom I'd only just met scant weeks earlier) laid out her Emotion Code three-ring handbook, composed herself as we all sat on tenterhooks, and then gently asked the room if Gabriel was present.

Well, of course he was.

Our 'Angel Code' meetings that followed this initial gathering (during which Ms. Medium averred Michael "pushed" Gabriel aside to grab the healing benefit "all for himself")[18] was shaping up to be a deuce of a book

---

15. No such thing as *arch*angels. We use it traditionally for clarity and convenience (What 'Angels' Are, § 1:520).

16. My Moonie best friend and 'spirit animal' expert, his own being the moth.

17. One who experiences spirit world mainly via the clair senses of hearing, seeing, feeling, or a combination.

18. And here's where Mina says all the trouble started with these Angel Code meetings.

in its own right until Mina and these self-same angels later cratered the whole episode's veracity, but more on that later. The gist of this backstory is that it's here the dichotomy arose between Michael and Mina's revelations that began tickling my mind at the news there'd been no human Fall. It began during our third Angel Code meeting at Moth Man's house when Michael was lamenting, through Ms. Medium's anguished tears, how Lucifer provoked the Fall of Adam and Eve and that he loathed himself for not doing more to stop it. How paralysis had gripped him till he'd ultimately done nothing. How, afterward, Lucifer arrogantly strutted through spirit world striking fear into the hearts of the stoutest angels (Michael, anyway) with his intimidating bluster and caused a rift, or 'war,' between the many soon-to-be-fallen angels flocking to his new-way standard and those clinging steadfast to God. How *our* fault lay in giving Lucifer all his venal power by adopting his self-centered philosophy. And so on. Michael had plainly painted Adam and Eve, the Fall, and Lucifer-*cum*-Satan as thoroughly real.

This had been some heady stuff for me, practically an elixir. It sure triggered my Moonie humans-ruined-the-universe-and-stabbed-God-in-the-heart guilt reflex that makes stereotyped Jews and Catholics look like dabblers in the stigmatic arts. As Ms. Medium narrated Michael's torpedoed feelings during this third meeting, my heart clutched at my ribs, squeezed in viselike empathy as I contemplated this forlorn angel's suffering. My own traitorous chest crushingly proclaimed my own *personal* responsibility for it. This direct physical experience with such a powerful energy left me feeling profoundly *woke*. I went from skeptic to believer in two seconds flat for three reasons. First, I implicitly trusted Ms. Medium's integrity that imparted the certainty she was indeed speaking with *the* Archangel Michael. Second, I felt my body and the atmosphere ever so energetically and emotionally charged. And third, his story was logically consistent with Divine Principle (my spiritual lifeview which had emitted a too-good-to-be-true flicker of caution I rather too casually tamped down). Unhappily, Michael's thrilling drama seven weeks ago was now colliding head-on with Mina's cold, hard layout of reality.

1.2 Thursday, October 12, 2017 ca. 11 pm

Having skipped dinner, we'd been in spiritual conversation with Mina and Mother for about six hours by now. Except for Ayako sometimes hand testing[19] from her dining chair, El and I had been swaying on our feet the entire time. My stiff lower back burned in knotty resentment. Trembling legs tottered from the fatigue of Mina's energetic answers. Here in my house this crazy evening, with Mina thrashing so many cornerstone beliefs, the contradiction with Michael's pious professions through Ms. Medium resolved into focus. It opened a new line of inquiry I couldn't resist and demanded explanation in any case.

There was little doubt in my mind we were receiving outside-of-self answers to our questions. Besides astounded to my core by this wholly unexpected turn of events, the spiritual energy in the house and coursing through our bodies was electric even for a two-dimensional guy like me who saw himself amongst the more spiritually dense of the species. It was all too strong, too real, certainly nothing my body had ever experienced. And this wasn't merely me observing Ms. Medium's clairvoyance, but my daughters' and my own. The three of us double-checked, validated, and corrected each other. Ayako was a regular genius sorting out the confusion of my oft-vague query formulations. As a historian, pastor, chaplain, theologian, research writer, software engineer, deputy sheriff, and all-around seeker of truth, the one thing I can't abide is illogic, irrationality, inconsistency, and complexification. They point only to confusion and untruth. Contradiction's a fair beast to slay or one can't claim to *know* anything. Aside from simply defaulting to 'divine' authority, how was I to resolve the apparent contradiction between this evening's new information and Michael's from our Angel Code meetings seven weeks ago?

I thought the solution was obvious. "Creator, would you ask Archangel Michael if he'd come so we could ask him a few things?"

Yes. You bet.

We expected a friendly Q&A. We got something else entirely.

---

19. Using the subtle energy in the hands to replicate sway, or push, test results (§ 2.2.1.1:626).

The Fracas

OTH GIRLS FELT Michael's energy enter the room. El described it as calm, quiet and unassuming. I thanked him for coming. Ayako still lounged in the open dining area facing El, standing in the open living room. She was leaning on the opposite side of the peninsular kitchen counter from me rocking on my feet in the open kitchen in front of our double-door fridge. I sensed, or rather felt, Michael alternately rooted stock-still then pacing from one side of El to the other. Ayako considered herself already plenty experienced interacting with spirit world since childhood—as, too, did El since the previous weekend (§ 1.2:28)—and felt his presence was the real deal.

For starters, we put Mina's new information about the no-Fall and Adam and Eve, Cain and Abel, and Satan's non-existence along with Lucifer's amazing innocence to Michael. Enthused over the evening's events and our minds expanding beyond albeit still boxed into many preconceived notions, none of us imagined what we were about to unleash.

"Did you know about any of this before now?" El straight up said, some cross-examination in her voice.

No, Michael said. *I'm only learning about it this very moment.* His response felt less energetic—less confident, maybe?—than Mina's and slower besides, as if hesitant, perhaps temporizing.

"What about the stuff you told us in the Angel Code meetings?" I said, and not just a little skeptically, either. "How you saw the Fall happen, about Lucifer's violence and arrogance . . ."

No.

"No? You didn't tell us those things?"

Yes.

"What?" I scowled across the counter at El, looking a little quizzical herself. "I don't—"

Ayako said, "Come on, Dad, you have to remember he's being literal. He means yes, he *didn't* tell you those things."

Ah, jeez. I'd stumbled again over my own poorly phrased question—"vague," Mina later called my grammatical convolutions. "Well, if you didn't tell us those things . . ."

"Michael, are you saying Ms. Medium lied?" said El.

"Whoa," I said. "How'd you get to *that*?"

If eyeballs could shrug. Two-for-two cutting straight to the point, though.

El pressed on: "So, did she, Michael?"

Yes.

I felt a sucker punch to the chin. "Creator, is that true? She *lied*?"

Yes.

My lungs vacuumed the room through my slack-jawed mouth. That was such a hard pill to swallow I could only set it aside for the moment. Instead, I said, "But, Michael, you just told us you *didn't* know the Fall never happened. Or that Lucifer was *never* guilty of wrecking the universe. That's exactly what Ms. Medium said."

"You have to ask a yes or no, Dad."

Bah. The whole discussion was already feeling queer.

El said, "Did you know the Fall never happened, Michael?"

No.

"Or that Lucifer never 'tempted' or 'fell' with anybody, especially not with Eve who never even existed?" El was giving me that epic-pastor-fail look again.

No. I didn't know a thing about it. I'm totally surprised!

I said, "You told us you watched it happen!"

Yes. His answer was consistent but felt more like a shrug, to be honest. And after all it was Ms. Medium who'd actually said it.

El's eyes were on me, a little viper behind her lashes. "Dad thinks you're lying, Michael."

"What? No! I wasn't saying—I mean, that's not . . ."

"*Are* you lying, Michael?" she said.

"For God's sake, El! I'm trying to find out—"

No.

"Somebody's lying," said El. Lordy, but I'd raised a snappy little trial lawyer. "Either Michael or Creator. The Fall happened, or it didn't. Adam and Eve exist, or they don't. Michael saw it go down, or he didn't. Lucifer—"

"Yeah, yeah, I got it." I contemplated things a minute. "There's something we're not understanding."

"Well, there's only one way to—"

I palmed a hand at her. "Just gimme a minute, will you?"

"So, Michael," she declared, ignoring the parental hand, "for sure you did *not* know Lucifer's innocent. Is that correct?"

Yes. I didn't know.

But, really, how? It's preposterous falsehoods like the Fall or Adam and Eve's existence or Lucifer's rebellion could endure from the beginning of time, hidden from Mina's own archangels, from their very eyeballs as they traversed the cosmos in service to humanity. Was there something Michael *wasn't* saying? *Was* he lying? Did angels even lie? And right in front of God? If *God* was lying . . . well, what for? Why would anybody—well, except Adam, Eve, or Lucifer—lie about any of this? *Cui bono?*[20]

I felt entirely perplexed. Perspicacious El seemed flummoxed, too. Ayako just looked content to referee. As I mulled it over, arms folded and head absently bowed to my inner investigator, I tried to formulate some rational follow-on query. Movement caught my eye.

1.1 LUCIFER ARRIVES IN A FURY . . .

El stiffened. Fear flashed across her face. Facing me, she twisted her torso round and jerked her eyes toward the front wall of the house. My own eyes followed but met only our two cavernous living room windows, inky black portals to the utterly Stygian forested Virginia night that had so terrified the girls when we'd first moved in from the luminous suburbs four years earlier. We could've been floating inside a black hole. She flinched, cried, and faltered backward, colliding with a counter stool.

"It's Lucifer!" she hissed. In that instant, her spiritual senses opened wide. She perceived Lucifer huge and swelling and in a fury blasting into our house through the exterior living room wall. She felt his seething energy, saw his eyes "raging with murder and squarely fixed on *me!*"

Ayako shrank transfixed into her chair, eyes locked on her sister and Michael beside her. I sensed his nebulous shape or lambent presence standing to El's left but moving fast to her right. My own feet felt magically stapled to the pine floorboards. I didn't understand my daughters' reactions because I neither spiritually saw nor intuitively perceived their experience. All the same, icy fingers fluttered over my skin as a ball of lead sank in my gut. El burst out crying as she described a spiritual blowout.

"Dad! Lucifer and Michael are fighting!" Her eyes tracked them struggling down along the length of the peninsular countertop. "They're right in front of your bedroom door now!"

"I don't see anything," I said.

---

20. Latin: to whom is it a benefit? From Cicero, " 'cui bono' fuisset" in *Pro Roscio Amerino* (80 BC), § 84.

"You can't feel the heat?" said Ayako with accusation, eyes fixated on the vestibule where my bedroom entry cornered off the basement stairs.

"They're really fighting, Dad!" Panic and tears lit El's voice. "I mean, *ohmigod*, it's a full-on battle!"

She scooted round the kitchen counter's end and latched hard onto me. Her eyes refused to relax their grip on the unseen tableaux at my bedroom door. I felt her quaking and hugged her close with my left arm, wondering just what I should do. What I *could* do. Not in the parenting manual, this. Ayako was mute, rigid against her chairback, knees locked, legs straight out in the air, hands white-knuckled on the seat's edge. Her eyes bored a beeline over her toes to the angelic battleground at my bedroom door. Though we didn't know it then, spirit persons Taiji, Hideto, *Obāsan*,[21] and Ayako's own two guardian angels protectively surrounded her. Then seventeen *other* angels 'jumped into' Ayako to shield her from the fierce energies spiritually scorching the room. Taiji screamed. Hideto froze in fear. My and El's guardian angels, along with my dad (d. 2012) and his mother (d. 1992), shielded the two of us. El clamorously *commanded* Mina to force them out of our house. She hollered at Michael to take their fight somewhere else and angled her expectations up at me.

"Creator!" I bellowed, my voice hard yet feeling stupid all the same because, to me—except for their terror and my persistent icy, bony fingers, leaden feet, and some vague Spidey sense—the house was calm as ever. "Please, get them out of the house right away. *Now*. They're scaring everybody!"

In moments, my children relaxed. El reported the archangels gone and Ayako that their blistering heat had waned. She slowly unwound, legs deflating feet to floor and color returning to her hands. Her welling eyes shifted to me. I sharply felt my dimwitted helplessness.

With a strident tone El said, "Will you keep Lucifer out of our house, Creator?"

Yes.

"You promise he can't come back inside?"

Yes.

"You'll keep him out if he means *any* harm to me or wants to fight?"

Yes.

She looked none too placated to me. But how militant does one really get with the world's creator? Well, maybe plenty, judging by El's clamant attitude.

"I feel burned up, Dad," Ayako said, verging on tears. "It was like a blowtorch shooting over from your bedroom. I thought I was gonna catch fire!"

El echoed her big sister's perception.

I said, "Why didn't you move, or just come over here with me?" I was already feeling heelish for not yanking her out of the line of fire myself. Even if I couldn't see it or feel it, she could and it had showed. That should've moved me to snatch her out of her chair, dammit.

She blinked, flipping her palms up in her lap. "I couldn't move. It was too terrifying. You can't imagine. I felt, you know . . . I don't know, locked in place."

"Jeez."

Then El squealed in full panic. "*Ohmigod*, they're fighting in the spirit world! They're scaring *everybody*! Dad! Spirit world's emptying out . . . the angels are taking sides! People are running away to Earth to escape the war!"

"Wha—?"

With a guilt-ridden expression, her wet eyes beseeching my soul, El breathed, "You don't think we broke the world, do you, Dad?"

I mean, seriously? The world's been here a long time and people have done a lot dumber stuff than this. I paced, massaged my neck. All I could finally muster was, "I don't know, honey. I'm sure it'll be okay."

What El was actually sensing, we learned later, were hundreds of *quadrillions* of what we then thought of as angels flocking from across the universe to the epicenter of Michael and Lucifer's unprecedented, ferocious pulse of raw, supercharged mind 'energy' (we later termed it ℒife force; § 6.11.4:198; § 2.3.2.1:241), a colossal macroburst that clobbered our universe. Arriving in various states of concern, curiosity, and uproar, they literally packed the planet and solar system's 'spiritual plane' to capacity. This titanic energetic disruption pushed the, on average, ten-plus billion potently weaker spirit people here minding their own (or maybe your) business right off the Earth the way a light bulb scatters roaches. At that moment, however, this was all beyond our ability even to imagine.

---

21. Japanese (お祖母さん): *grandmother*. Taiji Sawada and Hideto (Hidé) Matsumoto are dead Japanese rock stars. *Obāsan* is my children's great-great grandmother. More on them later and in the endnotes (EN 55:649; EN 57:649; EN 60:650).

Agog with worry, we peppered Mina for insight. El found Mother and him in seemingly grave spirits over the fallout from the chaos in spirit world (not exactly; not in the way we construed things, but we thought so, then). That revelation only cranked El's fears higher. Her dread that billions on gazillions of fear-crazed or outright 'evil' spirits fleeing angelic bedlam would wreak havoc on Earth's innocent like wandering barbarian hordes ran her blood cold. She nagged Mina to make our house the safest refuge in the world—he promised it now was—because, by this time of the night, she was examining her unfortunate need to sleep, unconscious and vulnerable, and not liking her prospects.

Not gazillions, but quadrillions of the guardian angels now garboiling all round the planet had left their physical human charges on the back burner to pile into this crowd—El's and mine chose later that night to leave us because of how we'd interrogated Michael—to directly witness and focus their collective attention on this situation. Ayako's were older and more sober. They'd interposed before her like angelic Marines.[6] Although the guardian angel coterie left many people across the world and universe in the lurch that night, Lucifer mobilized temporary replacements within 36–48 hours and permanent replacements in a week.[7]

When Mina revealed all this to us—we were surprised, to be sure, though instinctively felt *au courant* to know Lucifer oversaw guardian angels—and how dire he and Mother had viewed a celestial 'war' cooking off in spirit world . . . well, we might've had *Ghostbusters* (1984) on the brain. While the overall situation seemed an epic crisis for the angels and scattering humans, Mina didn't take the angelic uproar or the human spirit world's manic panic as a crisis the way we did at all. He understood the emotional outburst as normal if not orderly or productive. Of course, the questions we'd posed, especially framing them in terms of 'war,' and how we'd interpreted the answers, had a lot to do with our mindset at the time.[8] When it occurred to us to ask, we learned war can't achieve anything in spirit world. Celestial war and angelic rebellions are the personification of physical world concepts. Violent struggle isn't an angelic proclivity anyway, even though angels do emote and fight and spirit humans do play war.[9]

A plot twist would blow out this 'heavenly storm' the next morning. But the mood in our home this night was grim. We—particularly El—felt responsible for blowing up spirit world to rival (in our minds) anything vedic or biblical, all because of our cat-killing curiosity.[10] Yet for all that, my children were adamant that Mother and Mina hadn't lost their immense joy and excitement that we'd productively uncovered these realities for the first time, even if the initial outcome seemed to us wholly counterproductive. Master compartmentalizers those two are, we reckoned.

On the other hand, my daughters' joyous feelings and (probably cavalier) excitement had evaporated. Ayako, for all her airy *sangfroid* throughout the evening, was feeling the shock of her life as Mother mused over a providential response that might've asked her—to paraphrase Lucy Baldwin's sharp 1940s wit—to "just close your eyes and think of England."[11] El's earlier exuberance and steely prosecutorial persona shattered. She was frantic spirit world would descend any moment on our gloomy forest home thrusting torches and pitchforks high, convulsing with fury to 'get' the instigator of their travails.

Our energy now about as insolvent as the Weimar treasury, we finally called our talkathon a night near on one o'clock in the morning. Ayako quietly cried herself into a fitful sleep somewhere near dawn. Her sister bolted her basement door with a chair under the knob and trembled 'neath her sheets. Me, I instantly passed out, obtuse head to pillow.

Michael's Reveal

AWOKE FRIDAY THE 13th to a whispery house a little wrung out a few ticks past six, the sky just lightening into sunrise still an hour away. I lay awhile sprawled under warm, embracing blankets pondering our big event now dawning into an unheralded PART DEUX. Eventually, I found myself in my just-bought plush and comfy swivel desk chair with a steaming homemade Indian *masala* tea lubricating the brain wheels and studying last night's shocking events, especially Michael's odd-sock behavior that seemed to be what set off the fracas. If I was to bet money, something there was going unspoken, were I to take it all at face value, that is. What were my options, realistically? Flush it out the back of my head or drop another nickel in the slot, is what I figured.

I climbed to my feet and free-ranged questions with Mina—still there, so I wasn't hallucinating—trying to grasp the Fall of Man biblically and in Sun-myung's Divine Principle interpretation in light of what we'd learned the previous evening. It was a slow and laborious process for me. I wasn't near as adept at this conversational method as my daughters had tirelessly made themselves in the single short week just passed. However, I could literally feel Mina's energy pulsate through my body, so I had that going for my credulity. His answers were plain but came torturously slow, sometimes so languid I wasn't sure I'd even got one. I asked and re-asked questions and statements just to satisfy myself I'd received what I thought I'd received. More than once I apologized for being tedious. More than once he pushed back, *no problem*.

1.1 EL RISES TO THE OCCASION . . .

Despite his ungrudging answers, I couldn't yet see any bigger picture. Whatever train of thought I needed to follow eluded me. I felt stuck. Exasperated, I dropped into my chair and nursed the remains of my tea. Not much later, I heard a peeved clomping on the stairs—El rising uncharacteristically early from her basement dwelling as her older sister still lay dead to the world.

"What are you doing, Dad?" she grumped as she staggered barefoot into my room. "Archangel Gabriel just *literally* pulled me bodily out of my warm, toasty, loving bed and told me I was needed upstairs."

I'm sure I sort of gaped at her. "Really? He *pulled* you out of bed? Like, physically?"

"Yes! I could feel him tugging on my ankle, like I had no choice. So . . ." She crossed her arms and cocked a hip not unlike some pointy-head schoolmarm, I thought. "What have you started?"

I snorted tea. Boy, children! Wait. I'd forgot: she was entering day three of her eighteenth year today . . . and artlessly trying out its pre-adult powers.

After explaining my investigative effort, she took over receiving answers while I sat back in my deluxe leather seat, eyes lidded like Roman Rudenko scaring up another prosecution for Stalin. With my daughter as Mina's stand-in, I threaded my way through humanity's supposed fall from grace as Divine Principle and Judeo-Christo-

Islam (and humanity generally) typically understand it juxtaposed against the new data we'd encountered the night before. El emotes the spiritual energy and feelings that she intuits with an esprit as entertaining as informative. As she vocalized Mina's responses, she couldn't help aping his heart and personality the way she did Mother the previous evening. This natural ability of hers is what really elevated this experience for me from merely a pretty-hard-to-believe curiosity that might've simply fizzled to a serious revelatory experience meant to be seriously taken. As I watched her work, it seemed Mina himself was poised in her, well, bare feet.

I picked my way through the process and motivation of the Fall as Mina confirmed or rejected the various theological elements I raised. Each validation or repudiation spawned entirely new directions to pursue. Hope I was actually getting somewhere started brewing, yet there was a lot of institutional confusion to work through. I caught myself wondering if this was the sort of investigative process by which Sun-myung, if not Jesus, had come to understand the Fall as he did.[12]

It's worth saying that even in such a serious moment as this Mina was not above kidding around. He's simply not overwhelmed by life the way our spiritually immiserized existence creates the impression we're circling the drain. He has a long view that makes ours myopic. However momentous an event this was for us, it could've been just another day at the office for him. How often has he been disappointed, I had to wonder? Were we going to be just another flat tire? Well . . . he *was* excited, we could tell that. But worried? vexed? Not really, more like neutrally observing. El occasionally stopped herself with a, "was that a joke?" or, "are you laughing right now?" and we'd have a jocular sidebar until she'd soberly ask, "So, what's your serious answer to Dad's question, Creator?" Or I would. Patience isn't always my strong suit.

Then El set flat eyes on me. "Michael just arrived," she said.

1.2 Michael Arrives . . .

"He's here? Now?" My own eyes quested through the room. "Uh . . . hi, Michael," I said, and to El, "Where's he standing . . . or whatever?" I mean, he could be floating in the lotus position, right?

"I think he's sitting on the bed."

"What, like, right in front of me?"

"That's my impression. I can kind of see him where he is, but not quite. You know what I mean?"

My shaking head said not even close. It later turned out her impression was not of Michael but Taiji, who'd slipped in to watch our efforts. I imagined his irreverent self bringing popcorn to make it a show. Michael, on the other hand, had actually closeted himself in Ayako's bedroom where he could feel out of prying eyes. She reminded him of someone he'd loved and trusted, which after all his volleying with Ms. Medium and Lucifer, as well as his own fears, gave him a sense of safety and comfort. Initially, Gabriel had attempted to rouse Ayako to help me talk with Mina, but Michael stayed his hand for reasons we detail farther on. He'd pulled El from her slumber, instead, and sent her upstairs to me. Michael had only briefly stepped into my bedroom to trip El's antennae to his presence before melting back into his safe space.

"Could I ask you some more questions, Michael?"

El swayed and nodded.

As I queried him, I couldn't help but feel myself, maybe irreverently, looming over Boss Tweed's 1870s New York City Chambers Street witness rail in a sober, inquisitorial three-piece. Keeping my attitude friendly and respectful was job one, I reminded myself. Badgering angels wasn't on my bucket list. Neither was shooting down possibly my one opportunity to plough the world's oldest unbroken sod. Nevertheless, Ms. Medium's flagged narrative—especially last nights protestations of ignorance in spite of Michael faulting her misrepresentations (which I was far from ready to call lying)—had my mind on rails. I homed in on how he could possibly have not known there'd been no human Fall, let alone Adam and Eve's very central absence from the scene. There's a certain hierarchy of credibility here. Discrepancies between versions could realistically be resolved only one way. Absent better evidence, I defaulted to Mina's.[13]

The more I dug into the Fall and Michael's role, the more I sensed some level of evasion, or at least an ulterior theme. Not outright obfuscation, really—certainly not lying—but avoidance, I supposed, a preference to beat around the bush.

In our experience, angels tell the truth when it's put right to them (and they're not winding you up with a grin). This morning I couldn't tell myself angels don't lie because Michael's discrepancies last night would've had me whitewashing a truth. So, it wouldn't be they can't or don't lie, just that (following Michael's Reveal) they haven't to *us* . . . that we could detect.

Increasingly, I was seeing Michael playing some untoward role in germinating the very concept of the Fall. Not to mention the ancient accusations that Lucifer deceived Man to become "God of this world" (2 Cor. 4:4 KJV), tore down the heavens in war and rebellion, and in Divine Principle's more recent indictment that he'd statutorily raped (a now non-existent) Eve and utterly corrupted human nature till we hated our own selves worst of all. Goosebumps surged and prickled as I examined his answers through my unexpectedly sagacious daughter.

1.3   LUCIFER INTRUDES …

Startling me in my ruminations, El jumped and gulped a breath. She shrank into the wall. "Lucifer's here!" she yelped. "Creator! You *promised* Lucifer couldn't come back in our house!" Fear and accusation fairly roared from her tight throat.

"Hang on," I said, flying to my feet. "Creator, *is* Lucifer here?"

Yes.

In fact, he'd planted himself in Ayako's room and was eyeing Michael nose-to-nose. I fisted hands on hips. "Does he mean any harm? Is he going to fight with Michael?"

No.

"He's agreeing to be peaceful?"

Yes.

"So he's here with your permission, then?"

Yes. Of course. A little *duh* crept out of his response but that might've just been me.

Hunched flat against the wall, El's eyes circled the room like prey. "You'll kick him out if he makes any trouble?"

Yes.

"But not," I clarified, "if he's being peaceful."

Yes.

"Is that true, Lucifer?" I added for El's benefit. I wasn't feeling any threat myself. "You're going to behave yourself?"

Yes.

I know! It sounds ridiculous, considering who's in the house. But my daughter whom I *loved* now looked election-night panicked. And Ayako's forsaken, imploring face from last night still smoldered fresh in my mind. This was my house, so my rules. Just because I'm an earth-bound human doesn't mean I have no authority, even with an angel—though, since they're invisible beings, it's not like my authority goes far. Frankly, sometimes the authority you have is the authority you take. Nobody respects a weenie. Anyhow, Unificationism taught me that God created human beings higher than he did angels and I was still operating on that premise. We've since learned that human beings and angels are equal in all respects because both are human beings. There's no higher–lower, superior–inferior, or even authority amongst angels themselves or between angels, humans, and Mina. That's physical humanity's vogue. We're each of us, altogether, the human 'race,' a veritable family vast and universal.[22]

El still cringed all saucer-eyed. As I talked it through, she got a better feel for our home's energy and slowly uncoiled as she more clearly felt Lucifer's intentions. She plainly trusted Mina. And me. But if Lucifer chose to rampage, there wasn't anything I could practically do about it. I couldn't exactly go toe-to-toe like Jacob at the Ford of Jabok[14] … not without a Sam Colt in hand, and what good would that do?

Her own fear and misgivings vying with trust in Mina, she accepted Lucifer's reassurances and pulled herself together to carry on. After all, she'd seen and felt his thunderous wrath seemingly bullseyed right on her just last night. Who wouldn't residually quail from that? Whether that was Lucifer's real intent, indicative of some hellish true nature, or just accidental was beside the point. It was real enough for her.

If indeed Lucifer was framed for the Fall, then bringing that lie to the surface should've been a welcome relief to him. In that light, his volatile behavior perplexed me as much as Michael's equivocation. But at the end of the day, El was a just-eighteen young lady thoroughly awed by who he was and his imposing size and fury. Later that evening, and for several days thereafter, he would profusely apologize to us all for that wild night. He especially comforted El till her anguish melted in his arms. That story comes farther on.

---

22. Distinctions twixt human and angel serve clarity in this narrative but we switch to accurate nomenclature in PART IV.

At this point, Michael said he wanted to talk about the Fall and his role regarding it, but not with Lucifer in his face. What he wanted to get out he preferred said in private without Lucifer right there possibly reacting with anger.

Anger? I could almost hear Lucifer's echo.

A moment of unheard angel–God conversation later, Lucifer exited Ayako's room exuding much obvious misgiving, annoyance, and suspicion, and cooled his heels on a counter stool in the main room. Gabriel had been here awhile already, and together they waited on whatever it was to come off Michael's chest. I turned my attention back to Michael when I'd verified Lucifer's departure (to the degree possible). He answered a long series of questions which only bore witness to just how human angels are.

1.4   THE TALE MICHAEL TELLS . . .

Here's Michael's tale—told on unsteady feet over Ayako's sleeping countenance, a seraphic image of comfort and trust and non-judgment he could pretend was his only audience—as he now amended it.

1.4.1   THE FALL OF MAN THAT WASN'T

There was indeed no original couple, he admitted, and he (along with Mina, Lucifer, and Jesus) fully well knew it. No Adam and Eve from which sprang the human race with some inherent duty to obey or worship God.[15] No providential responsibility to perfect themselves (Moon 2006, 78; Matt 5:48) and bear perfected children (ibid., 34, 64). No disobedience or attempt to be "like God" (Gen 3:5) or some other 'failure' that doomed as-yet-unborn humanity to physical death, eternal suffering, or some loathsome compromise with both without, as with many human traditions, some complex and ever-postponed salvific process. This goes for every human creation myth, not just the Abrahamic religions. Sure, Mina guided our physical bodies from microbe to swaggering biped but humans were and are naturally, *divinely*[23] human in accord with our intrinsic way of being. And then physical humanity's nineteenth generation[24] produced a woman—Mnèèptē (pronounced 'muuh-ne-ehp-tee'), in her language[16]—whom Michael came to love.[17] As. Did. Lucifer. She chose Lucifer. Yeah, *boi*.

"Oh, my God," I mumbled, "are you kidding? It's a classic love triangle!" My angelology was no-joke getting a sobering upgrade. El's face was a panoply of expressions I had some trouble deciphering. Did she even know what a triangle was? Maybe. Probably. Kids today are sadly more savvy than we parents might care to know and mine did plenty of reading . . . I elected to worry later.

Bereft, Michael had felt inferior, as anyone who's ever loved unrequitedly knows. Coincidentally, it was at just this point in human history that angels were increasingly noticing that, as a 'race,' they'd transformed from how they were at their inception to what today we call *fallen* or *Corrupt* but, for those back then, was yet unclear. This was a source of real concern and angst amongst the angels who after all had taken on the task to raise, educate, and protect humans in the physical world. Yet, humans and angels both only knew they were becoming . . . well, different, and not a good different. No one understood why what Mina calls The Corruption was happening because it was already confusing them. Humans and angels didn't perceive it for what it was or even act to nip it in the bud.

Mina laments that, although they could have, no one turned to him for guidance. They'd already forgot, or transposed, or got hazy on a lot of his story of life, including him being an accessible parent, grandparent, and friend. Without their cooperation, Mina had no practical means to alter their mindset, though he was far from tightlipped. And he'd never quash their freedom to be whatever they wanted to be even if he did. That's ultimately what it means to be free and loved. The Corruption's allure is strong, exquisitely gossamery, and comes across sensible and right. It has a short-term quality all its own but none of its presumed benefits—a cotton candy in the rain, one might say. The justifying delusions we create render it self-sustaining.

In this insidious milieu of Accountability and its minions morality, justice, fairness, law, judgment and punishment, young Michael[18] for the first time encountered a self-negating inferiority in his beloved Mnèèptē choosing Lucifer—obviously, the better man in *her* eyes and something of an accusation in its own right—over him. Surely, her inexplicable choice meant Lucifer must have said or done something nefarious to harm her

---

23. Not a turn of phrase Mina wholeheartedly approves owing to the implications in *divine*. We want to convey the intangible distinction between humanoid and human when, from the apparent fossil record, we can't perceive the difference.

24. Not on Earth, but at the time it was more or less the same generation everywhere because angels guided our coetaneous development across all human-inhabited worlds. Mina wanted none of his children to fall behind any others due to factors outside their control, although the human factor has since naturally thrown off that little dream.

feelings for him. He lashed out in wounded 'justice,' as a wrongheaded youth might, to subtly discredit Lucifer as the better man not only in her eyes but in all. Like a cartoon anvil, Michael dropped the same heavy weight of hurt, loss, and accusation he was feeling times a million on Lucifer. Up to this point, there'd been no love relationships between physically alive humans and spirit world angels nor the dysfunctions we take as usual. This was unknown territory for both. Already alienated from Mina by The Corruption (and for those in a physical body the added estrangement of a diminishing spiritual awareness), humanity lost touch with many core principles of life by which the universe, Mina, and humanity operate. In that vein, a human–angel relationship seemed unnatural to angels and could be made to appear *morally* wrong, a penal offense, even.

Michael initiated a deception amongst the angels that it was Lucifer's relationship with Mnèèptē,$_{19}$ that proximately caused what, in truth, was only the coincidental Corruption now twisting (especially a spiritually atrophying physical)$_{20}$ humanity into "malevolence."[25] It was not a rumor traceable to its source because Michael insinuated it as inexplicitly as The Corruption itself had. And really, like any good con amongst a willing or gullible audience, it needed only an impetus and the occasional reinforcement whilst it matured. As with The Corruption, Michael's deception self-reinforced. Angels naturally intensified and embellished it in the thinking and telling akin to the game *Chinese Whispers* or *Telephone* no different from humans. Some angels, of course, knew Lucifer well enough to scoff at the very notion. Yet his own childhood[26] was itself marred in a way that encouraged even their contemner.

Gradually, and without consulting Mina—indeed, as their comprehension of Mina's nature metamorphosed from reality to delusion—many in the angelic world blamed Lucifer for The Corruption they were all feeling in themselves and seeing in physical humanity. They rejected him even as he lived amongst them and oversaw the work of guardian angels. Michael's fake news percolated into physical humanity's consciousness despite The Corruption degrading the connection between our spiritual mind and physical brain. The human belief that Satan–Devil–Lucifer rebelled against God, evilly deceived Eve, precipitated the human Fall thus corrupting our nature and creating death and all evil, seized our birthright, and rallied the troops to fight an actual war against courageous Michael and his own stalwarts until being "hurled down" (Rev. 12:9)$_{21}$ persists to this day, along with its countless derivations spread throughout humanity's creation myths. All of it spewed from the elements of Michael's Lie, itself rooted in The Corruption's very premise. Physical humanity saw in this two-pronged delusion, allied to our singular imaginations,$_{22}$ the reason for life's toil and trouble, death and distress, and our inability to live up to a preternatural 'divine' nature and its hippie-dippie perfection—the whole problem of evil in a nutshell, really. Out of this dirty bath trod Religion and Philosophy, all shiny and neat and wearing sensible shoes.

Educing Michael's story was truly labyrinthine. Its terribly divergent nature, our own mindset, and the tedious, literal means of our communication were so many traps and pitfalls.$_{23}$ In the course of nitpicking through the many questions, blind alleys, and apparent contradictions, Michael hesitated, prevaricated, and obfuscated, for sure. He never lied, though. We give him a pass on the former because his fear and shame was a tough nut with a preferably avoided Mina figuratively standing right there.[27] Too, our communication constraints prevented Michael volunteering information except through our intuitive faculties—certainly less helpful then than now. Contradictions or illogic that might've indicated fraud he cleared up with sensible, logical consistency as soon as we zeroed in on the right queries. Michael framed the preceding story and resolved its arcana. Mina, Gabriel, and Lucifer fleshed it out for us over time.

1.4.2 WHY MICHAEL TOLD HIS TALE

So, we're talking epochal time scales here. Why did Michael only now want to get this story out? Even as a far-out, wrong-way Moonie$_{24}$ you could've knocked me over with a feather when Michael allowed that part of the reason was that, as the great Ibn Sina might say, Sun-myung's *wājeb-al-wujud*[28] produced actual, tangible spirit-world effects. He literally altered universal reality, staggeringly counterintuitive considering how wrong

---

25. Mina chose this word. Just saying.

26. Yes, angels are born babies and grow up in families becase they're human, not a separate 'angelic race.'

27. Mina 'dialed in long distance' instead of being bodily present.

28. Arabic: *necessary being* (واجبالو جود; coined by Avicenna (d. 1037) to inject Persian ontology into ontologically bare Arabic); principally, Sun-myung's ontic 'is-ness' (*hasti*, Persian) of loving, without condition, that which necessitates being unloved: Satan. His way wasn't wishful make-believe after all. Mina credits him the only human (lacking direct access like Jesus (and one other person)) ever to arrive at this core apprehension of love despite Earth's never critically examined admonition to "love your enemies" (Mt. 5:44). Spirit-unaware, Sun-myung walked a supremely torturous path to 'level up' this way.

he'd got God, Lucifer, most of his Divine Principle including the Fall of Man, his bombastic proclamations, and (it goes without saying) a corrupt, abusive church institution he built from scratch and failed to curb. All the same—and it just goes to show—one of his effects was to rouse Lucifer in 1999[25] to let go his obdurate pain of condemnation "and just move on" by at last accepting Mnèèptē's hand, which he'd held at arms' length since the accusations sprang up so long ago, and to start a family.[26] The first substantive improvement in human reality since The Corruption—because it made what's coming up next possible—and it was globally disparaged Sun-myung Moon who'd kicked it off with universally shunned Lucifer. Well, it took my breath away.

Lucifer's change of heart jolted Michael, too, as if from a stupor. After all this time, he didn't love Mnèèptē the same way anymore, nor was she the reason he'd now decided to set things right and clear his heavy guilt. But like me feeling woke from Ms. Medium's storytime, Lucifer's new reality *woke* Michael. Then like anyone dreading owning such an epic cock-up, he got cold feet—and here's why he stayed Gabriel's hand from waking up the far defter Ayako to help me energy test: El's unseasoned skill would delay the chopping block that much longer, and in any case Ayako, for reasons below, was now his indispensable muse. Accepting since 1999[27] how egregiously he'd acted, and fearing everyone's reaction to the news, he couldn't bring himself to just sidle on up to Lucifer and let it rip. That seemed like throwing water onto quiescently boiling oil. Lucifer only reinforced that image when, clueless, he'd overhead Michael's obvious lies the night before and apoplectically, if only tentatively, put together two and two.

1.5 MICHAEL REFLECTS...

After their brawl and our retiring for the night, Lucifer had buttonholed Michael to come clean even more doggedly than he'd done after Mina had 'broadcast' the truth throughout our 'quantumly entangled' universe[28] at the very start of this ancient drama, and Jesus himself had confronted the issue. Unfazed, yet paralyzed by indecision, Michael held fast his denials despite Lucifer hearing his inculpating palter *in flagrante delicto*. As evenings went, I thought his own sounded pretty bleak, tense, and scary, but he disagreed when we talked it over many months later.

I said, "So, Lucifer wasn't some raging bull like he was earlier but actually calm and reasonable?"
Yes. He was calm.
"He wasn't looming over you with his fists? Screaming in your ear? Pushing you around?"
Michael laughed. *No.*
"Kinda like two brothers talking, maybe."
Yes.
"Just a long, tedious harangue, then?"
Yes, pretty much.
"After I asked Creator to call you, then asked my first question, did you know where it all was going ... like, the writing was on the wall?"
Yes.
"No backing out then. This was it."
Yes.
"On account of Creator being there?"
No.
"The Angel Code discrepancy, then?"
Yes.
I barked a laugh. "Just that?"
No.
Dang. These guessing games. I gave my intuition a minute. "Umm ... well ... there was no backing out because you'd irrevocably committed yourself to getting this out, coming clean?"
Yes.
"But, by now, I guess your plan for that was fairly shot to hell—um, so to speak, I mean."
Yes. Boy, yes!
"Uhh, sorry about that?" But was I? Probably not.
No. So, neither of us then.
It wasn't that Michael preferred humans to angels for his mea culpa. It just turned out physical humans were, by dint of ignorance, the only neutral ones, in his view. Michael recognized that the Unificationism-derived (though faulty) belief the so-called Fall had traumatized the angels could meet his need. Moth Man's friend had

embraced it, so he'd persuaded Gabriel to call him forth in a dream. It seemed a perfect venue. In the midst of expressing his pain, he could "just let slip" the sordid truth in a safer, therapeutic environment with Gabriel at his back that might mute the inevitable raving shitstorm. Instead, Ms. Medium hijacked his effort for her own wicked reasons and produced her dodgy divergence between Michael's alleged account and Mina's own—plus, scotched that marvelous Angel Code book I'd been dreaming up.[29] Worse still for Michael, the girls and I came away all boozed up on Ms. Medium's pious sham, but had now asked him to his face all the wrong questions in front of the decidedly wrong crowd like a disappointed tosspot bellowing right at the bar over cut whiskey.

Even though Ms. Medium put words in Michael's mouth, his denials to us last night were, on their own, a bundle of contradictions that, for me, cracked his credibility. Lucifer saw it, too, but in a land of unaccountability, what's a stonewalled angel to do? By October 2017, Michael's come-clean plan was in ruins. Ms. Medium had ice-picked him in the neck, the Angel Code folks had deviated into futility, and a spirit world TV exposé was a never-gonna-happen. Michael's easy options had narrowed to nil. Maybe he'd never get his penitence out and the universe would go on reeling immutably onward in its half-baked way. Then yesterday, El went straight to the Source and we'd dragged him into it for the Sixty-four Dollar Question.

"But Creator said Jesus learned all about it and tried to help," I said. "You didn't want him to mediate?"

No.

For crying out loud, why not? "Uh, let's see . . . well, you denied everything when Jesus confronted you during and after his lifetime, right?"

Yes.

"Did you see him as a neutral party at this point?"

No.

Never catching a break, that Jesus. "But you wanted the whole mess out and done with."

Yes.

"So . . . why'd you lie to *us*, then?" I wondered.

It was simple, really. Michael didn't like how we'd pulled him into this very public powwow with Mina. Even a half-wit could see it was an arrow straight between the eyes. He knew Lucifer's ear would catch it and, like snatching off a Band-Aid to 'soften' the pain, he just didn't want to go there, not like this, a raccoon trapped in a garbage can. He wanted to put us off track, gain himself some breathing space, control his situation. Bald-faced lying about Adam and Eve and Satan to our revealing queries would almost certainly provoke Lucifer into a fiery blow-up—who had his own reasons—and produce immense confusion. Maybe we'd get too scared and just let it go. If he was lucky, he might just deflect the whole thing until he could make arrangements more suitable that (maybe foolishly setting aside his prior bad experience) involved a private confession through a mediator.

To that end, he'd wanted to go through Mnèèptē because of his sense of connection with her. Recently wed to Lucifer, she'd seemed the perfect go-between. Who better to tamp down his brother's certain outrage? Then he imagined the inevitable horror and betrayal on her face for what he'd done and that plan seemed a whole lot less perfect. He felt just too ashamed to put it to her. That route was out. Sure, he wanted to scare off El and me like some *Scooby-Doo* scamp. On the plus side, he'd then intended to approach Ayako privately the way he had Ms. Medium in 2004. According to Mina, he'd often babysat Ayako. Minus the whole framing Lucifer fiasco, she spiritually knew him pretty well (news to me). Michael calculated that her newfound energy testing—not as direct as Ms. Medium would've been, but sufficient for the task at hand—made her a suitable stand-in for his ideal intermediary.

"She looks enough like Mnèèptē," affirmed Mina later, "the average person would think them sisters."

Plus, Ayako snubbed her own judgmental tendencies where Ms. Medium gave them full rein. In Michael's mind, it added up to a win-win. Safe to approach and reminiscent of his former flame, Ayako was an ataractic for his much-daunted heart. Yes, the perfect muse, she was.

Well, we'd surprised Michael openly talking over the Fall with Mina. That hadn't happened since Jesus, and he'd done it privately, face-to-face, without serious controversy. Over time, The Corruption coupled to Michael's deceit converted Mina, in the minds of angels, into what we call an *Accountableist*[29] deity few found pleasant to contemplate. Michael hadn't even considered confessing to Mina in this sorry state of affairs. An eventual victim of his own deception, he'd come to fear a divine Accountability that never even existed.

"Hoist on your own petard," I said, clowning around.

Yes.

But he wasn't laughing. He hadn't welcomed our involving Mina until *after* the fat lady sang.

---

29. One concerned with accountability in all its forms. Basically, your typical god.

The Big Healing

Friday October 13, 2017 ca. 9 AM

IS THAT IT, Dad?" griped El, and stifled a (maybe fake) yawn. "You done? Can I go back to bed now?"

Wasn't she at least going to marvel a minute? "Hang on, sweetie. First, I'd like t—"

Her spine arched. "*Dad!*" she yowled in fear and anger. "Lucifer's back!"

With the bare bones of Michael's admission only barely out, and me off cogitating, Lucifer (low-key taking in Michael's stunner in the main room with Gabriel) bolted back into Ayako's room and startled Michael. El felt it, and could've jumped right out of her socks if she'd been wearing any. Suited up in a spirit world version of casual Friday that did sport socks, Michael practically did. He braced himself for Lucifer's long-dreaded, outraged, savage onslaught. He'd exactly predicted his clichéd reaction. Hadn't he?

1.1 LUCIFER AND MICHAEL . . .

"Creator! You promised . . . !" But then El stopped. Listening via intuition and her *energism*[30] to take the measure of the room while quietly asking Mina questions, she instead said, "Wow, Dad! Lucifer's sitting on the bed with Michael . . . and—"

"He's on my bed now, too?"

Like me still learning the nuances of spiritually communicating, El assumed it was Lucifer she'd sensed on the bed from her intuition and scanty queries—until we got it sorted later—but it wasn't. Out in the main room, Hidé had been eyeballing Lucifer's darkening expression—surprise tangled up in hurt and betrayal—with a sinking soul at another fiery battle in the offing. He hadn't reacted too well the first time and wasn't hip to an encore. But he didn't want to desert us. Nestled in my bedroom with Taiji when (or *if*—nothing's sure till it's sure) a scrap kicked off had looked to Hidé a shrewd move, so in he'd fled. El sensed him enter and position himself on the bed alongside Taiji, facing me, about the same time she sensed Michael react to Lucifer barging in to brace him in Ayako's bedroom. Still presuming Taiji was Michael sitting on the bed, she figured the second person she'd sensed must be Lucifer. Instead, Lucifer and Michael were now shuddering cheek by jowl at Ayako's bedside. In these early days, El's sense experience sometimes intermingled with her energy test answers. If we weren't paying attention, we'd get confused until the inevitable contradictions pushed us to sort out corrections.

"—and . . . they're *embracing*! Michael's apologizing to Lucifer . . . he's in tears . . . and now so is Lucifer . . ." Her voice quavered. "*Ohmigod*, Dad! They're just hugging and crying."

---

30. A term we redefine here to reflect the combination of skill, talent, experience, and receptiveness to encounter spiritual energy, in this case translating it to cognizable communication analogous to vibes and body language.

Lucifer had burst into Ayako's room with a tornado of emotion tearing through him. Yet, Michael's bared heart and the sheer intensity of his sorrow, regret, repentance, fear, self-contempt, grief, and despair carved across his countenance and buzzing through his energy, all lumped into something that amounted to an unadulterated "I deserve it: taze me, bro," stopped Lucifer cold. He'd stormed into a choice—"When you come to a fork in the road, take it," Yogi Berra once quipped—with an instant to decide. Before he knew it the past, with all its hurt, melted like hot beeswax out of each ferociously walled-up cell of the honeycomb bursting in his chest till all he knew and felt for Michael was *how Michael felt*. If he hadn't already reconciled his feelings for Mnèèptē and his overall situation back in 1999 (thanks to Sun-myung), then what was now happening would've crashed and burned on the runway. It had altered Michael, made space for him to forgive himself and consequently accept Lucifer's forgiveness, which is what it takes for two people to reconcile. Lucifer grabbed for Michael, who dissolved into his unjudging, thoroughly *un*Accountableist embrace that lanced Michael's own pus-drowned *nous* like a boil.

Kicked back and possibly a little too relaxed in the saddle, I took in the empty, blank room—ignorant the real fireworks bloomed and thundered on the other side of the wall behind my chair and above Ayako's sleeping "shell," as she oft jested of her dormant body—and marveled at my younger daughter's sensitive perception. I'd long known Ayako was spiritually sensitive, but El's hit me from left field. A well of love and esteem gurgled up from the marrow at her unexpected empathy. I prized her in that instant like oxygen to the soul. We didn't know it yet, but even as Michael and Lucifer repented, forgave, and loved, and I perceived El in a new light, the universe began its own transformation as a great, stultifying 'mental layer' beguiling every thought and feeling since The Corruption—the very warp and weft of every person—spontaneously dissolved (§ 4.2.1.4:382).

El kept up her running commentary as Mina's answers swayed in. She sensed the bright, loving energy, and intuited the appropriate queries.

"Lucifer says Michael's apology is all he needs to hear," she said.[30] "He doesn't bear him any ill will at all. It's like the whole thing is just washed away."

Jeez, I thought, *just like that?* I said, "Just like that?"

She nodded, teeth broadly gleaming, eyes glued to my bed.

I'd belatedly activated the record function on my phone amidst Michael's interview, but later found it had failed to save. Our couple hours of conversation were lost. This technical failure would recur with a depressing persistence; a recording would fail to save, fail to activate, or simply get 'lost,' even though I would see the *now saving* message on my not-so-smartphone screen. It's a *mysterium* technology doesn't like to think it shares with faith. Mina disclaimed any responsibility for it. Initially, I suspected foul play by spirit people who didn't want recordings made for reasons that made sense to them, or else I just bungled it each and every time. Instead, Gabriel—reflecting Mina's aversion to modern, spiritually destructive electronics—was the culprit here, though, at other times, 'random people' did the deed. I guess technology was innocent . . . this time.

"Dad," said El, "their whole *family* is here."

I shoved my eyebrows into my receded hairline. "Angels have families?"

"Oh. My. *God,*" she said after a flurry of questions. "They're *brothers*!"

A thermonuclear love triangle, then.

"And they have two sisters!" She paused, solemn. "Their parents are here."

I was still stuck on family and siblings.

"Wow, Dad, the whole house is filling up." She looked around, maybe straightened her posture, and then announced with pleasure and gravity, "Mother's here." Her face lit with the supernal glow I'd seen yesterday afternoon when we'd first met her. El crooned, "*Hi,* Mother!"

"What's the feeling in the house?" I felt a little left out with only my prickly chills for company.

"Everybody's crying and hugging. *Ohmigod*, Dad, the joy and happiness feels so strong I want to cry, too!" Her timbre indeed was weepy.

I reeled off a checklist of status requests. Mina let us know that Gabriel, Lucifer, and Michael are brothers in that order with book-end sisters.[31] It wasn't just Michael and Lucifer reconciling, but their siblings, too. Their family reconciled with other angelic families, who then reconciled with others, who paid it forward. With that earlier-mentioned 'mental layer' now dispersed, Mina now could and did 'broadcast' the Reveal and Reconciliation to all of spirit humanity.[32] On its heels, The Corruption's debunking shock-waved through

---

31. Fraternal twins to Gabriel and Michael, plus between Gabriel and Lucifer we later learned, which plays into Lucifer's drama.

32. Your own spirit self got the message, too, but since your brain doesn't fully integrate mind owing to The Corruption's effects, this is news to your physical self (§ 1.2.2:253).

the universe. As that *jupitérien* mob of angels departed, vast spirit crowds—about 60% from *other* worlds—streamed into our home's environs including all of history's religious leaders who'd been paying shocked attention to our bursting their bubbles.

Then El plopped a real wonderment in my lap. "Creator's saying you're the most famous person in the universe right now, Dad."

"Me!? Umm . . ." *Shit?*

"*Everybody* knows your name."

I plopped my head against the chairback. "Not sure I want that."

"Well, could've left it alone."

"Thanks. I'll stick that on my tombstone."

As I ruminated on ethereal *Cheers*-style fame, Michael's newly bestowed infamy had quite naturally cut out for him a less-than-attractive 'ninth-step' effort[33] that would take him through eight Earth months of penance before the aggrieved petered out. After some preliminary meetings with all three angels over the next week or so regarding this book, we didn't see much of Michael for some time.

"Creator is *soooo* happy somebody's finally exposed the whole situation in a way everybody in spirit world gets. But now . . ." She wandered a few seconds. "Now I'm feeling such huge joy and excitement and . . . um . . . like, pure delight? at what's happening. It's just so intense, Dad. Dang, I wish you were feeling it."

"Humph."

She said, "The energy's off the charts. It's so lit!"

It certainly was. And just like that we went from seeming to break the universe to healing it, all in about seventeen hours. My head spun to make Linda Blair jealous.

And here's where Mina dropped the biggest bombshell yet. Humanity's chief obstacle to throwing off The Corruption and psychically healing[34]—the aforementioned stultifying 'mental layer'—had now ceased to exist. El vibrated with Mother and Mina's giddy exhilaration at this hoped-for, yet not entirely certain, blossoming of a new world as it now shifted to Game Over for the crusty old.[31]

1.2 THE NEGATIVE COLLECTIVE CONSCIOUSNESS

What was this obstacle, this 'stultifying mental layer'? Why did it disappear with Michael and Lucifer's Reconciliation? What makes *their* conflict so special in a peevish universe fit to bust? And just how does it affect you? We spell it out in THE CORRUPTION (CH. 24:361), but here's the nutshell.

Humanity is not fallen,[32] nor stuck with a selfish gene.[33] We aren't shorn of an original sacred nature nor ever had one. No magical salvific to remedy a situation beyond our control—or, per Alan Watts, "grimly to face" (1951, 22) the ineluctable suckage of life—is of any use. We are not in a state of irremediable sin because sin isn't real. It's a human delusion, an artifact of The Corruption and with Michael's Lie.[34] Though we want to reconcile the self-winding contradictions in life's ineffable struggle and our way of being with some diaphanous higher, better, divine self, it's a deficient analysis and anyhow Mina rejects the characterization. Rather, our forebears birthed *unconditionally free*[35] and, therefore, free to love—and we do!—whether we're civilized or savage about it. No existent nature or divine law circumscribes us. Besides pain and suffering, there's nothing wrong with and no contradiction in the human psyche.[36] We aren't "wired for perversity and prone to do evil" (Venema et al. 2017, 195) to "fall short of the glory of God" (Rom. 3:23), nor enslaved to our unevolved, mad reptilian brain.

So why is life so unremittingly unloving, inertial, and destructive if it isn't profane by nature or God's own creative intent, or the imprecision of Darwin's random, ruthless evolution? The short answer is that we're exactly how we choose to be, as we're consummately free. *We habituated* life exactly as it is. That's problematic because we Corrupted ourselves by choosing a Corrupt baseline—say, Accountability over freedom, or consideration *from* others over consideration *for* others—and, ants to honey, our unhappy *astī* followed.[37] Our *choice* ever brings suffering. Change our choice, change our state of being. There is no Satan, Devil, anti-God, yin-yang darkness, biological determinism or biogram,[35] natural evil, or even acts of evil or evil persons—howsoever

---

33. From the 12-step program created by Alcoholics Anonymous in 1935.

34. In this context, a catchall term for salvation, liberation, forgiveness, 'divine' assimilation and ascension, enlightenment, restoration; whatever you call it in your faith language.

35. Take a moment; sit back, close your eyes, and truly unpack *unconditionally free*.

36. Erroneously *human nature* in psychology and *fallen nature* in religion, but *way of habit* is more fitting.

37. Persian: 'is-ness' (*momken-al-wujud*, ممكن الوجود, for Ibn Sina; FN 28:15).

harmful—nor any moral state of being. Morality itself is a delusion, and one of Accountability's many thugs. Habit alone self-coerces us to be as we are. Our suffering powers the cycle of violence. Any ultimate deity or idea that's a perfect standard of good is illusory. Becoming aware of reality is how we free ourselves from delusion to heal and thus achieve a happier outcome.

That now-defunct 'mental layer' (I call it a *noosphere*)[36] formed from our individual mindsets as a collective force of habit. El termed it the Negative Collective Consciousness (NCC, i.e., Ultraculture; § 4.1:291).[37] Physical humanity imbibed The Corruption and Michael's Lie from its very *noogenesis*[38] via the angels and, more so than them, we took it on the chin. Spirit and physical humanity's Corrupt self-coercion got so powerful it severed Mina from his creation,[39] literally from his own family.[40] Premised as it was on The Corruption, merely shattering Michael's Lie could only do so much. Lucifer's reaction, which Michael so feared, was the fulcrum. Their utter rejections of *Accountableism*, embodied in their apotheosis of forgiveness and reconciliation, knocked the legs out from under The Corruption's premise itself, and every story of life it ever engendered in our collective mind. The combination swept through humanity's collective consciousness like a cleansing tornado. It was a one-two punch and the NCC folded. It was glaringly obvious in spirit world, and people jolted from it like a bad dream.

The important take-away is that, having self-manifested our mess, we aren't helpless. Now the NCC is gone, neither will our still-habitual,[41] but eventually-quenched Accountableist mindset bring it back. Its dissolution is permanent, says Mina, because its genesis is undone and rendered inert. From here on, freedom rooted in Mina's original premise will only expand, so long as enough of humanity wants it to, because . . . freedom. Free of the NCC, Mina flashed the Reconciliation throughout spirit humanity, which underwent an unprecedented sea change. Shockwaves roiled it (and less obviously, physical humanity) for months. Mina, keen to help and now permitted the tools, moved on the healing opportunity immediately (*below*). This was hard to take in. It's taken me a year just to write this much of it, and I think it's only a crude outline. Mina calls it "more a 'limited expression' of reality."

1.3 THE MEANING OF THE BIG HEALING

There in my bedroom that Friday morning, we felt our comfortably flowing rivers of belief and knowledge abruptly divert off a cliff. Ayako had plunged over the night before,[42] cried through it overnight, and now slept it off beyond the wall behind where I sat, first under Michael's watchful eye, and then amidst his Reconciliation with Lucifer. El's façade of cheery imperturbability held steady, but her flitty eyes reminded me of a starling at the hawk's distant shriek. She'd process this like her sister later, absolutely. I could've just left it alone, chalked it up to "it's interesting, aye, but not really my cuppa," and this morning's event would've aborted. Except it *was* my cuppa. I couldn't not know any more than I couldn't not breathe. I wondered which made me the bigger idiot, but figured only time or someone wiser would know that.

Then my turn to face an Ayako-style inconvenient truth arrived with Mother. She let us know Michael and Lucifer's Reconciliation mooted last night's 'war' tomfoolery along with her (hard-nosed, to Ayako's mind) prescription regarding Ayako's future.

"Everything's changed?" I said. "In the whole universe?"

Yes.

Here's one of this book's fundamental messages of hope and liberation: the NCC's dissipation removed every block on Mina acting in the universe. From now, he'll be healing wholesale everyone in the physical and spirit worlds of its deleterious effects, irrevocably healing humanity of the NCC and freeing us to change our Corruption habit and, to the degree each is ready and willing, of any traumas, trapped emotions, and the like as well. We consciously or unconsciously need merely express our desire. Through Michael and Lucifer's meme-busting choices, humanity nascently restored its pre-Corruption, pre-Lie awareness and annihilated the facticity of The Corruption and Michael's Lie as any sort of legitimate epistemology and archetypal, ontic *Dasein*.[38] Mina predicted a week to complete the Big Healing.[43]

"So, everyone can be healed? No exceptions?" I said.

Yes.

What if they don't want to be healed," El wondered. I thought, *why would you imagine that?* "Will you still heal them?"

---

38. German: from *Da-sein*, 'there-being/here-being' and ontologically prior to the one who asks the question of Being as a "being-in-the-world"—*Im-der-Welt-sein*—person (Heidegger 1962).

No.

"No?" I said. "Because you can't violate a person's freedom?"

Yes.

El said, "So, a person only needs to want to be healed, or ask to be healed, and you'll heal them?"

No.

"You mean there's a *condition*?" I practically gasped.

Yes.

Well, huh. I fixed El with an oh-sure-there's-always-a-string-attached look.

She held my eyes in return. "I know what it is, Dad," she said. "They may not want to be healed in their subconscious,[39] even if they consciously ask to be healed. Everything happens in the subconscious."

Ah. "Makes sense," I said, thinking about the concept of self-sabotage and cognitive dissonance.[44] "We might want to be healed, Creator, but if something in our mind or heart is refusing, that's the condition?"

Yes.

"Can you do anything about that?"

No.

Hmm. We'd discovered the same thing in our earlier foray into Emotion Code with Ms. Medium, hadn't we, when people resisted healing or weren't ready to release their trauma, either because we hadn't dug deep enough to find its source, or their innermost self just wasn't ready to give it up.

I said to Mina, "So, your condition is people must want healing, not superficially but genuinely?"

Yes.

"It's not really a condition, Dad," said El. "More like, just reality."

Yes.

"And when it's in what we've always called our subconscious, then it's genuine."

Yes.

"Because," she added, "how's he gonna heal you of whatever you really don't want healed?"

Yes.

"Then a person just needs to figure out why, on a subconscious level, they may not want to be healed if they ask you to heal them but don't feel healed."[45]

Yes.

"Can you help them want to be healed?"

Maybe . . . no.

"It's up to them, Dad. Everything's up to each of us."

Yes.

As one of my other darling daughters is fond of opining, 'You may not think it be like it is but it do.' Well, you love freedom, I consoled myself. Apparently, we're free to be what we don't necessarily want to be but actually are. The story of hapless humanity.

I said, "Seems like there's gonna be a lot of people who don't get healed, though. All that negative universal energy gone and it won't make a difference—"

"He's saying no, Dad."

Ah, jeez. "But you said you won't heal anybody who doesn't want it or isn't ready anyhow to be healed. If that's the case—" But El was shaking her head. I said, "That's not the case?"

No.

"That 'no' means it's *not* the case, right?"

Yes.

I sighed. Yeah, a little petulantly, too. These sorts of contradictions and grammatical quirks are a common struggle with this mode of communication owing to its intrinsic limitations and our tendency to misconstrue. It'd be so much easier if we could get 'why' answers. I racked my brain for a scenario in which both his statements could be true. El and I pitched possibilities back and forth to a steady beat of *no*.

"Maybe he just can't heal everybody of both the negative consciousness thing and all their personal problems," El finally offered.

Hmm. "So . . . you can heal everybody of whatever ails their psyche, right?"

Yes.

---

39. The subconscious as traditionally understood isn't the subconscious we reference here (§ 2.1:393).

"But if they're unwilling or not ready or whatever, then you can't."

Yes. I can't.

"And that's because you can't wave away problems people created themselves? I mean, you can't just change their heart, right? If they're resentful, let's say, then they're resentful. Unless a person wants out of that, you can't do anything, correct?"

Yes.

"So . . ."

"Creator," El said, "are we responsible for how the Negative Collective Consciousness effects us?"

No.

Oh. Nice work, El.

She continued, "That means it doesn't matter if they're willing or not? The negative collec—it isn't a problem of their own making?"

No.

"Ahh . . ."

"Ok, I get it," I said. "You'll heal everyone in the universe of the Negative Collective Consciousness. I mean, uh, how it's affected them?"

Yes.

"Ha!" I said with a gloat. "So, everybody gets healed of the negative . . . *that*, but not their own personally-built problems if they're unwilling, or not ready, to give them up. Do we have it, now?"

Yes.

"Bingo!" I said, "Contradiction solved."

El grinned at me. "Yep. Nice work, Dad."

"*Danke*, you were pretty goo—"

She doubled over in a rowdy fit of hilarity, palms out, thumbs cradling her chin, but not with my German lingo sopped up from my dad. "I'm. *Weak*. Mother and Creator want you to write a book!"

My jaw dropped. That inconvenient truth I mentioned just said 'hello, sucker.'

1.3.1 WEDNESDAY–THURSDAY, OCTOBER 11–12, 2017 CA. MIDNIGHT

I thought back a couple of nights to when we'd healed *Obāsan*. We'd moved from my bedroom to the main room as we got to know her and her family when all hell (figuratively) broke loose over their cheeky opinion that revising my 1998 book spiritually analyzing American race history, a new edition of which I'd been slaving over the last six months, was a waste of time. That I should toss it. Move on. But to me, renewed racial conflict and Donald Trump promoting to inner city black youth their right to the American Dream got me to thinking that now would be the perfect time to re-issue my book. I'd spent January through April 2017 catching up with it, pleased to find that, twenty years later, it still made sense. In May, I settled into updating and revising it, using the vast research now available at Internet-accessible libraries unavailable to my itchy fingers two decades ago. Now, here it was October. I'd hoped to have it ready in just a few more months. My daughters knew the book was important to me. After all, I'd been "tirelessly torturing" them with my copious endnoted research and analyses for months.

Affronted by those give-up ancestors, I'd fired off a logically fallacious call to authority. "Do you think it's a waste of time, Creator?" Because, who'd know better and could shut them up?

No.

Whew. "So, it's important? I should get it published?"

Yes and *yes*. I figured out later he was just being kind, since what we were going to learn writing this one would make that one redundant.

"Ha, in your face!" I crowed.

My girls howled. That ended those ancestors' uninformed slander of my book. It probably didn't change their opinion any, I had to admit. Oh, well. You take your victories where you find them. But then it was *Obāsan*'s turn to be affronted, thinking me pretty rude when I commented a little too bluntly on her family's early twentieth-century social passing from Ryukyu island bumpkins to upstanding Japanese elites. It took some humble pie to quell her vexation, but then she laughed for the first time.

"*Obāsan* says you're not half the ass she thought you were, Dad," Ayako said with more cheek than her new ancestors. The girls were uproarious.

1.4 Friday ca. 10 am: Our Commission to Write this Book

But now, Mina was saying he'd rather I shelve that work of stupendous social significance for a new book dishing the full monty on what had just ensued. I was *shook*. His earlier, solid shutdown of those craven ancestors had left me not only unprepared for his sudden change of focus but frankly unwilling, too. It felt a bit like Ayako's scenario with Mother last night.

Hoisting my jaw from the floor was getting to be a comedy routine. El's chuckling eye from her spot riveted twixt my bed and master bath got me wondering if she wasn't seeing a silver lining in Mina's newest wrench in my works.

"Can I write it after I finish my book?" I pleaded.

No.

"Maybe I can do them both at the same time."

Maybe . . . no. Not really. Come on, get a grip.

"So you definitely want me to write this new book?"

Yes.

"Right now?"

Yes.

El piped in her two cents. "*Duh*, Dad. You don't *have* to do anything. Creator won't judge you because you don't write it, you know that. He told us so."

Yes.

Fine. True enough. We'd extensively combed through his total rejection of judgment, punishment, and coercion[40] last night whilst possibly a little too merrily disemboweling religion and philosophy as we illuminated the real creator and our real relationship. So, he wasn't *exactly* issuing marching orders, then.

"He'll just find somebody else," El impishly added. "That's what he always has to do anyhow."

Wait. How could some poser write this without *our* life-quaking experience? What were Michael and Lucifer going to do, stage an instant replay? Just because it sounds like there's reverse psychology going on doesn't invalidate the point. My daughters sure weren't inclined to write it, that went without saying. The Reconciliation was a once-in-eternity moment born out of our curiosity and newfound energy testing along with Michael and Lucifer's own 'present-in-the-world' and 'potential-in-the-world' psyches. El was a mensch energy testing all my whining with Mina. I cycled through the five stages of grief seven ways from Sunday before at last penciling in his precious book.

"Can I finish my racism book after I write this one, then?" I finally croaked. "I mean, cripes! will it still even be relevant or meaningful after all this?" Finally catching on that no Adam and Eve meant no Cain and Abel, I had to wonder.[46]

Yes, yes.

"He can still write a book with footnotes?" said El, thinking of the book's academic chops, I supposed . . . or more likely all my prideful boasting in my endnoted research and, too, that some semblance of academia would pique my interest so I could be more happily dragged onboard this train. I wondered, though, what I could possibly analyze or cite in a revelatory work. This was my first revelation. I hadn't the foggiest how to proceed. Wouldn't I just be writing a mouthpiece? "Because," she added with an incisory look at me, "he really loves his footnotes."

Okay, stop.

Yes.

Just because Mina doesn't coerce (or guilt) people to do or be anything doesn't mean our own sense of moral duty or plain old people pleasing is absent. I reasoned this event was big news. I mean, BIG. NEWS. Not sharing it would be poking a sharp stick in humanity's eye, which (in the physical world, anyway) largely disagrees with life and the creator who made it, and is always combing the grass for pleasanter alternatives. But I considered how spirit people might react when I inevitably relocated to spirit world . . . or, probably more salient, its less restrained coterie even before I rested in peace beneath Shady Acres.[47] And, honestly, this was hardly an impossible situation. Unlike your traditional revelation which, let's face it, most of us take with a grain of salt, this one comes with a means to verify it for yourself directly with Mina and spirit persons, and

---

40. Spirit people are far less fastidious than Mina about engaging in these sorts of behaviors. Nothing's beyond the pale for some of them in their private pursuits of accountability.

even more if you're really curious and develop your skill. You needn't believe any of this off the shelf, you can just energy test it.

I said, "Well, fine, then. But, hmmm . . ."—a little jauntier now—"I wonder how it'll sell? You know these kinds of books can really—"

"Hold on, Dad," said El, conversing with Mina amidst a blooming smirk. "You can't charge for it. He doesn't want people forced to pay for healing."

"What?!" My jaw was getting tired of this routine.

"He wants it to be a story that brings healing. And I totally agree. It's terrible to make—"

"Sure, sure, but how am I supposed to print and distribute it?"

"He says you'll find a way. I mean, it's not like you're dumb, Dad,"—*Thanks?*—"and, like he said before, charging money to heal and teach the truth about him is wrong."

"I thought we were free," I sulked.

"Your book is." She grinned, and quite evilly.

"Har-dee-har—"

"Remember what Aya said, Dad: 'It's our birthright.'"

"Pshaw! Nobody will take it seriously if they don't have to put out any dough for it. Even the most worthless books on Amazon or Smashwords or in the bargain bin cost at least something."

"Obviously, you can charge if you want, but he can't be happy with that. You know how he feels."

Isn't there a word for that? But watching El's face was like seeing Mina's own. Ah, anyhow I agreed with his scruples, dammit! I'd even said so last night.

"All right, what the heck, what's one more impossible task for an old Moonie?" I said, and I'm sure I sniveled like a real victim. "The book will be free. I'll figure out the logistics. But I'm gonna need a sugar daddy if you really want this book all over the world."

El grinned, less evilly. "Or, three."

That settled, I spent a week persuading myself I'd made the right decision while polishing off my racism book's in-process manuscript work which the last hectic, ground-shifting seven days had interrupted (CH. 5:27). With everything we'd learned in just two days, my multi-year manuscript now read like semi-fiction anyway. A serious re-think was in its future. So much for holding up to the flow of history, I complained apropos of nobody. More sighs. Finally, with a last longing look at the pile of research material scattered across my desk and floor, I loaded forty-plus mewling books into bags to cart them home to their libraries, closed all documents on my computer, and cleared my Einsteinian desk for action.

Mina then asked me to hold off for thirty days to pump barbells on my spiritual sensitivity. Intuitive leaps would be important in this work, he said, and I needed to muscle-up. Like most un-jaded clergy, I'd cultivated a strong link to my Christian–Unificationist God through work, study, and prayer. I've briefly seen and talked with spirit persons and angels a number of times over the years, but it always seemed random and accidental, like a dollop of grace or maybe a flight of fancy. I'd never nurtured any mediumistic spiritual abilities because I never thought I had the aptitude and, well, who really needed it? Not sensible clergy, certainly. But I did now. My three middle children are all mediums to one degree or another, casually seeing or talking with spirit persons since they were old enough to tell me about it. I've progressed since October 2017, astonished to discover I've been an empath and undeveloped medium all along . . . which might explain a lot about my personality, emotions, and dubious choices over the years. Spiritual boot camp for thirty days or not, I'd be starting this book relying on intuition and energy testing. And my daughters, naturally. As a resource, they're a couple of Godiva chocolate bunnies.

By now, morning was closing on noon. We already felt rather worn down. El had missed out on all the sleep she'd tetchily coveted, but the excitement she'd finally caught had made up for that. If I weren't a teetotaler, I'd be swilling down something bracing, neat. Mina, Lucifer, Gabriel, and the multitudes went off to heal the universe and maybe Monday-morning quarterback. Michael moved out on his ninth-step rounds that he was looking forward to like an overdue dental visit where he still owed fees. Mother headed out on her own business in her own universe[41] until she returned a bit later to help a tired Mina (healing a universe takes energy). And Ayako was now up and about. Over lunch, we shared with her our dramatic scoop, especially that, as a result of this morning's events, Mother and Mina had rescinded their Ayako Providence formulated in last night's rough waters. She seemed decidedly underwhelmed.

"I'm emotionally drained, Dad," she said, slumping on a counter stool. "Don't wanna talk about it."

Fair enough.

---

41. The multiverse is real but not how science or fiction imagines it (Table 12:312).

Our Six-day Prolegomenon

FOLLOWING ALL THAT, and before we lunched with a newly risen Ayako, Mina was sharing his dim views on a franchise known as ThetaHealing[42] and the damaging energy it produces in place of any connection to a healing 'Source' energy, in part because it demands money to heal and teach spiritual so-called truths, a practice Mina "loathes." He asked us to pass his uncompromising message to the certified instructor—*ThetaHealer*, Ms. Medium's very own daughter—conducting the ThetaHealing Advanced DNA workshop that kicked off this very evening way up in Maryland. Ms. Medium had earlier captured my tentative agreement to consider attending with Ayako but, honestly, after getting Mina's lowdown on the story of life last night and this morning, another $880 spent on that was for the birds. Still, a verbal *no thank you* did seem in order.

1.1 SHARING THE NEWS WITH MS. MEDIUM ...

After this morning's Reconciliation, and while Ayako was still sleeping off last night's trauma, El and I got Ms. Medium on speakerphone ostensibly to convey Mina's message in lieu of a drive up to Maryland. First tentatively, then with greater assurance, we outlined everything we'd just learned, though the part about not charging money for healing got stuck in my throat. She absorbed all we said in silence. Uttering our last word, naught but the proverbial hiss lit up the line.

"I want to be you when I grow up," she jested with El, who'd done most of the explaining after I'd faltered. Kneeling against my bed and propped on her elbows, El raised a speculative challenge to me under an impeaching brow. "And I believe you," Ms. Medium continued with conviction, her voice suave and alluring. "I believe everything you've just said."

Wow, didn't see that coming. That's because it wasn't news to her. Michael had confided the truth to her years before but she'd reacted, well, let's just say, poorly.

Before we managed a comeback, she added, "Are you coming to the workshop? I think you'll really—"

Didn't she just say she believed what we'd only just told her? *We're talking to* God, *lady. What's your* workshop *got?* "Um, I don't think there's any point after, you know, what we've learned," I temporized.

"It'll be a really great workshop. I know you and Ayako will get a lot out of it."

Like what? I asked myself, eyes rolling for El's benefit. Anyway, how would she know we'd get a lot out of it? Maybe that's just how mediums talk when they're on the economic hustings.

"She shouldn't charge money for what she's doing," El whispered, impatient with my kid gloves treatment. "Don't forget, Dad."

---

42. An 'energy' healing modality promoted by Vianna Stibal of Bigfork, Montana to discern, remove, and replace limiting beliefs, blocks, and traumas trapping emotional energies leading to mental or physical disease and dysfunction.

"Well, Ms. Medium," I hemmed and hawed, El boring holes in me and willing the right words to flow, "it's kind of like this: God wants us to . . ." Yeah. *Dang.* This didn't feel like a message I could blurt over the phone and expect to impart productively. Sure, it was easy for her to believe our woo-woo over the phone . . . until it sewed her pocketbook shut. If I wanted a shot at her responding positively, maybe in-person was the way to go. And it was a persuasive reason to procrastinate. I might have something in common with Michael, there. "Ayako's still sleeping," I concluded. "When she's up we'll decide."

El curled her face at me like she'd shoveled soggy cornflakes into her mouth, then hustled from the room for the real thing. *Meh.* I rang off with Ms. Medium.

Following lunch, the three of us resolved to trek the hundred miles north to unload on ThetaHealer in person what we'd handed to Ms. Medium over the phone as a way to grease Mina's no-charging-money-to-heal message. Then, we'd decline to attend the Advanced DNA all in one fell swoop. For me, just voicing it seemed aggressively confrontational. It almost felt like proselytizing, never my métier ironically enough. Believe me, we weren't looking forward to the conversation even if—maybe because?—it was a revelatory message. In all likelihood, we'd simply be Muhammad preaching up Mecca's unamused merchants. If there's one area where people blank on God, it's being deprived of money they figure is or should be theirs. Hadn't Luke quoted the Big Man himself dictating "the worker deserves his wages" (Lk. 10:7)? Already, we'd be throwing their bible out the window. I daresay it wouldn't be the first time I did something inane. At least I'd have my kids for a shield.

"Hilarious, Dad," Ayako said to that. *Yeah.*

1.2 Exactly One Week Earlier . . .

As we entered Friday the 13th's afternoon, we were coming full circle in a seven-day spiritual whirlwind that had started last Friday (the 6th) when Ms. Medium had persuaded me to attend ThetaHealing's Basic DNA weekend workshop following an Emotion Code healing session with her several Sundays back. Emotion Code had struck some inscrutable chord in me which, overall, intrigued me.₄₈ I thought ThetaHealing's thing might be a good means to connect my unhappy older daughter with Ms. Medium the happy healer.

Ayako is spiritually sensitive and aware, having already studied chakras, auras, emotions, pendulums, clair senses, paranormalism, spiritualism, mediumism, and the rest of the psychic barnyard during her school years. I'd hoped she'd hit it off with the motherly Ms. Medium because, if the kids lacked anything, it was a helpful mother figure. She demurred to the last minute, then broke her reclusive mold and signed up. That was a game changer because it's what incited El's leading question that fateful Thursday evening later in the week. I coolly smiled at her unexpected "Ok, Dad, I'll go" but, inside, I was *hot-diggity-dog!* It was a major step and I felt terrific for her. Surely, something good would come from her new behavior. I'd been trying for months to get her into an Emotion Code healing session with Ms. Medium to see if any trapped emotions and traumas underlay her depression, and maybe restore her zest for life. But she'd brutally resisted; out of angsty shyness, was my take. Her anxiety, depression, and mild agoraphobia increasingly, if not a little despairingly, worried me like the growing roar of water from up a canyon.

"But I'm not going it alone," she added.

My cool smile faltered at the low-low price of only $440 each, which generously included Vianna's voluminous page-turner, *ThetaHealing: Introducing an Extraordinary Energy Healing Modality*, but we teamed up. I was betting real skin something peachy keen would pop loose in her. Little did I know.

I turned expectantly to El and opened my mouth. "No thanks!" she barked in one of history's greater ironies. "I have no interest in that stuff at all! You can just go without me."

I blew a laugh at her independence rally in the run-up to her presently four-days-away eighteenth birthday. I said, "Suit yourself, big girl. Food's in the pantry. Have fun."

"Hmmmph."

1.2.1 Friday–Sunday, October 6–8, 2017: At the ThetaHealing Workshop

Emotion Code uses pendulum and some muscle testing modalities to identify trapped negative emotional energy and 'heart walls' in a person, the causes of which can be addressed and cleared to pave the way for the body and psyche to self-heal. ThetaHealing, in contrast, attempts to use meditation and prayer to achieve a theta-wave brain state to enable the body-sway test—using the body itself as a pendulum—to identify core limiting subconscious beliefs and traumas so they can be cleared, replaced, and body and psyche can self (or, according to Vianna, instantly and miraculously) heal. Ayako was immediately taken with sway testing, and got some real world practice working on her co-participants. I realized I'd encountered it myself a couple years earlier. Having tried it on my own with little practical result, I'd forgot all about it. Seeing it in action with a roomful of practitioners at the Basic DNA workshop re-whetted my appetite. Maybe it wasn't as offbeat or as difficult as I'd thought, I persuaded myself. Yet, I couldn't seem to do it. I didn't see Creator's 'white light' that Vianna said we were supposed to zoom toward in meditation in order to 'connect' to 'Source' energy's theta-wave state. Nor did I see the various colors that acted as signposts on the way through the "seven planes of existence".[49]

Ayako saw it all and then some. Success following her own method, however, tipped her to the monkey business in Vianna's theories even as I fancied it at face value. Instead of seeing and entering the Vianna-approved white light that connects to the "Creator of All That Is" (Stibal 2011, *ix*) to enable sway testing, Ayako saw only yellows and purples that, in her experience, shook out as higher order energy. So, right away, she saw B-O-G-U-S type itself across her mind's eye in a clattery teletype from Common Sense. Mina later told us Ms. Medium and ThetaHealer had sensed Ayako was spiritually "more powerful" than they, which got their attention.

Meanwhile, Ayako noticed Archangel Michael hanging with her during the workshop, and her very ancient, highly respected guardian angels keeping out of sight to avoid tipping our discerning mother–daughter duo to Ayako as somebody worth, as it were, possessing. According to Mina, they saw and sensed Michael at the workshop but said nothing. Instead, they siphoned Ayako's energy to the point she could hardly move, lift a limb, or open her eyes. "Just paralyzed in my sofa seat," she recalled. Mina said they funneled it from all of us attending the workshop, though I don't recall feeling especially tired. Bone-weary is my standard operating procedure, so they'd really have to open the tap to get my attention. They "aren't malicious," Mina monished us, "just inadvertent; the result of connecting to Vianna's negative energy source."

We learned Ayako's energy vibration is very high, just below angels. At home, lower-vibration spirit people avoided her proximity because her energy field was too strong, hence, uncomfortable for them. Hidé, for instance, retreated to the far side of the basement whenever she'd shower next to El's bedroom, just to avoid her "too intense" energy envelope. He couldn't even pass by the door to the stairs because it was too close, and her energy rattled and 'burned' him.[43] All that discomfort passed, however, when the Big Healing strengthened his energy. Michael later opined—and Mina agreed—that Ayako eventually would've tumbled to Mina and energy testing even without attending ThetaHealer's workshop, but I have my doubts. Ayako chose to keep her misgivings about ThetaHealing from us—from *me*—until after the Big Healing, when suspicions over spoiled food and sickened health on the heels of our new awareness finally crowded into all our minds and she'd put the pieces together.

In any case, Ms. Medium's thirtyish son very kindly worked with me for hours to identify and heal trapped emotional energies and limiting beliefs. At last, *finally*, I felt spiritual energy flutter through my muscles when I queried my subconscious,[44] which pushed me forward or backward quite independent of my own will—certainly not from losing my balance, which I strove to hold as sternly as a rooted tree.

Following the workshop's Sunday evening (October 8th) end, we gravitated to Ms. Medium's roomy, split-level ranch-style tract house for home-cooked hamburgers,[50] sway testing practice, to learn more about ThetaHealing, and to play cards. Whilst the workshop briefly mentioned chakras, I didn't really grasp at this point that sway testing necessitated them being open. Our modicum of training—mine seemed so obstinately shuttered, a category-5 hurricane wouldn't have pried them open—failed to do the trick for me (afterward, Mina directly taught Ayako, and she taught me). Reliably getting me 'online' bordered on the miraculous. While Ms. Medium cooked our hunger's salvation, her son grimly drilled into my trapped emotions, limiting beliefs, and past traumas with messianic determination. At last, my grudging chakras cracked their lids and I began consistently sway testing with faint conviction. Around midnight's far side, we shared parting hugs on the stoop with our new besties, then reluctantly motored the two hours to our rural Virginia home and, for me, a 4 AM date with my alarm clock.

1.2.2 MONDAY–TUESDAY, OCTOBER 9–10, 2017: REFUEL DAYS ONE AND TWO

On ninety minutes of sleep, I hustled another two fun hours to Lynchburg, Virginia. Swanked out in my Army blues, I was all squared away for Monday's PREFUEL event for chaplains at Jonathan Falwell's three-day

---

43. At the time, Hidé found it uncomfortable to pass incorporeally through walls and floors on the 'physical plane,' preferring to move around the same way he would if physically alive. Taiji was the opposite.

44. As the traditional concept of the subconscious doesn't jive with reality, Emotion Code and ThetaHealing practitioners are, quite unawares, actually sway testing the responses of whomever most energetically replies: their client's own spirit self, family, or random spirit individuals. At the time, of course, we didn't know this, either.

REFUEL conference for pastors at Liberty University.[51] Aside from a congenital aversion to pop-Christian emotionalism, PREFUEL passed innocuously enough. Mingling with uniformed chaplains from all the services brought me contentment and a sense of belonging I'd missed from decades of local Unification Church leaders ostracizing me from my spiritual alma mater.[45] I returned around 8 PM to a home spiritually quiet but a temporal cacophony of Japanese alt-rock ripping through YouTube on our big-screen overlaid with my wailing daughters hopping and skittering to its beat across our room-sized Persian rug. They regarded me with faces firmly believing no news is good news. After a couple hours thriftily schmoozing anyway about my glorious PREFUEL day without neglecting their alt-rock ipseity, I slipped into my welcoming and non-judgmental bed for tomorrow's 4 AM dash to REFUEL's Day Two.

While I sang my heart out at Tuesday's REFUEL, my daughters got up to high shenanigans at home. The previous day, Ayako had quietly inducted I'm-not-interested-in-that-stuff El into ThetaHealing's wondrous world of sway testing, substituting her own methods for Vianna's disagreeable trek through jelly-filled barriers to the white light and dodgy creator hiding out on the back forty of the "seventh plane" (Stibal 2011, 26). El had picked it up like a natural, but didn't take off full speed until today. She'd blithely deep-sixed her earlier "no thanks" declamation after the two of them realized sway testing's possibilities for communicating with *people* instead of some boring subconscious. She flew off the blocks in a sprint. In a Monday afternoon phone call, the girls deliriously recounted their adventures delving into family and ethnicity with Mina—now addressed as "Creator" in deference to Emotion Code—which, in roundabout fashion, led them to meeting their two favorite Japanese superstars, Hideto Matsumoto (d. 1998) and Taiji Sawada (d. 2011). Both, according to them, murdered.[52]

"How'd you even know to use it for that?" I'd said, startled.

Pungently, El said, "We have a book, Dad. We opened it."

Ach! I'd forgot all about Vianna's 337-page how-to in Ayako's hands because ThetaHealer ran out of copies at the workshop and mine was still clawing through the postal system. "But the manual says *nothing* about using sway testing to talk to spirit world!" I protested.

"We improvised," she deadpanned.

Did they ever. Seven straight hours sway testing with Taiji.

"Hidé ['hee-deh'] dipped after twenty minutes from all our death talk, and didn't come back till midnight," Ayako later lamented with a giggle. "He still can't really face his murder. It gets him so mad."

Having now met Taiji and Hidé, and brimming with excitement, they were dying to investigate their Asian pedigree. They've been obsessed by all things Japanese, Korean, and Chinese since wee sprouts. All apparent evidence to the contrary, and goaded by maternal family rumors of a Chinese great-grandmother that had supercharged their imaginations, not to mention Unificationism's built-in Asia worship, they've always *felt* Asian, specifically, Japanese.

"Where," I wondered in dubious strain, "could Asian genes be in your mom's obvious Africanity?"

"It's there, Dad. Just look at us. *Duh*."

Learning the sway test ropes with Taiji and Hidé emboldened them to leap into the mystical realm of The Ancestors, but the answers they got jolted them. For days afterward, they unrelentingly reproved me with, "When you've been lied to your whole life, *Dad*, about who you are . . ."[53]

In riposte, I said, "Just be glad you know your mom and I are your real parents."

Now, Tuesday morning, I was experimentally hand testing with Mina along the two-lane winding through the countryside, Ayako having taught me during our schmooze last night so I could try it out while driving. Which I did. In spades. After transitioning to the four-lane south of Charlottesville, my 'conversation' segued to my dad when I sensed he'd joined me in the car. He practically K.O.'d me with a stunning revelation about his wartime service.[54]

My 4 AM start dragged into a late dinner with my chaplain colleagues at some mediocre chain hashery. I finally reverse putt-putted my Prius into the double garage of our blazingly lit, night-defying prefabbed log house going on midnight. In my haste to rest my vengefully screaming fingertips-to-elbows—a lingering 2007 nerve injury, still maddened by handling steering wheels—I snagged the side-view mirror on the garage door frame and, but for its handy foldability, would've snapped it clean off at the neck. Tired as I was, with sleep crowding out all else, I needed a few breaths of perspective before facing my Ancestors-intoxicated children and finding out— reminiscent of a certain biblical God strolling through his garden one fateful afternoon—what their uppity day had, in due course, wrought. I was surprised to find the Japanese alt-rock silenced like a former

---

45. Involving my reluctance to commit to their mindless obedience and not-too-thoughtful study of Divine Principle.

BFF (best friend forever) and the house tomblike. I'd only just shucked off my uniform for home clothes when my daughters poured breathless into my room.

"Dad!" El led off. "We found our ancestors!"

Was that a baleful eye I turned to them? I hated to think so, let alone make my tongue a party to it, so I said, "That right? Which ancestors?"

"On mom's side. And," she squealed in explosive excitement, "we're *Japanese!*"

I quirked a Spockian brow.

"Actually," her rather steadier sister said, "we're only part Japanese, the other part is Chinese with a smidge of Korean."

"And we found our great-great-grandmother!" El bubbled on. "I think she's from the *Amami* islands, in the Ryukyus."

"Okinawa?" My other brow joined its kin.

"*Nooo.*" El gazed on me like the mentally challenged. "*Amami.* It's its own ethnicity. But we need you to help us figure out her name and which island, because you know Japanese. We're all confused."

Ah, jeez.

1.2.2.1 MEETING *Obāsan* . . .

I took a rib-bursting, see-ya-later-sleep breath and loudly blew it off. It seemed a tall order. Wasn't I just as much the noob? What were they expecting? I hadn't even brewed an evening tea. All the same, and in spite of my diffident self, I scrabbled up avid pen and paper and plopped onto my spurned bed. Both daughters hovered across from me, near the door to the master bath. Ayako did the testing since her responses, unlike El's and mine, were already practically instantaneous. She'd spent the day really burning up the wires with Taiji. Despite her exhaustion, she was in no mood to stop. Her skill made the conversational aspect of our communication feel a lot more sociable. I'd already enviously asked how she did it, but she'd shrugged it off as if axiomatic. I took that with something less than a stiff upper lip.

It was an hour-plus getting their maternal great-great-grandmother's story.[55] Fortunately, spirit world comes with a built-in universal translator, so we didn't have to rely on my rusty Japanese after all.[46] It wasn't so useful placing her in a historical, physical world context, either. We'd got a false start when I had her spell her family name in Japanese characters, only for El to realize she'd given us her ethnic Amami, rather than her Japanese, surname.[47] A studious adoration of the *Samurai Champloo* (Fuji TV 2004–05) anime series is what kick-started El's curiosity in Amami language, culture, and history, and now it paid a nifty dividend. But the girls were certain we'd need her Japanese surname to track down her extant family, Amami apparently being as moribund as Gaelic, or maybe grammatical English. For their part, the girls instantly bonded with their great-great, and El asked if she'd mind us calling her *Obāsan.*

She strongly assented, said El, with "a huge feeling of joy and happiness to finally connect with us. Apparently, she's watched over us since before we were born."

I slumped back at that one, ruminating on their mom's pregnancies and the girls' childhoods. That brought to mind their mom's announcement one day in the mid-1990s that she'd seen a silver-haired "old white lady" in a dream, who said she'd been watching over the two of us and the girls' infant older brother, but was "pretty damned unhappy" with our constant quarrelling. When I'd asked their mom to describe this old lady, out popped my own scary Irish-Texan paternal grandmother! The very same who would shortly be helping my dad protect me during Lucifer's upcoming melee with Michael. *Obāsan* seemed a different kettle of fish from my grandmother, but I quashed any extended-family comparisons to keep a neutral interest in the proceedings.

It was after 1 AM when we'd learned all we could, and healed *Obāsan* and her cantankerous family of their grief, sorrow, rage, guilt, and so forth using an egg salad of Emotion Code and ThetaHealing techniques. That's what happens when amateurs go unsupervised. We ignored our doctrinal deviations because there is no doctrine. If a person's wants it, Mina heals them.

We drifted into the main room of our house with *Obāsan* and her large, formerly reviled family in tow. I took to opining on how interesting it was that bumpkins from the Ryukyus (a conquered, colonized, contemptible set of islands to the Japanese) had managed to gain a Japanese surname and pass into its elites—so far as to

---

46. Unless speaking voice-to-voice while physically awake, in which case one does need a common lingo.

47. It later turned out she'd actually given us a family codeword, not her Amami surname, so the girls would have bonafides when they inevitably reached out to living family in the Ryukyus.

work in a pre-war capacity for Emperor Hirohito—the way American blacks passed for white to sneak into WASP society. That went down like sour milk with *Obāsan*. She scolded me for being rude and obnoxious (and possibly stupid; the girls sometimes edited for my ego, bless their little lying hearts). I backed off fast. I'd taken an instant liking to *Obāsan* and preferred her good side. No telling what she could do if properly incited, and I didn't want to find out. I explained my western view of Japan–Ryukyu history but she swished that aside. The more I discussed my thinking, though, the more she caught my heart until pronouncing me "a good man" whom she liked, and we all had a laugh. Well, I tittered through beaded sweat. The girls whooped a few we-don't-know-this-guy yowls while *Obāsan* maybe nodded along to memories of her own Chinese-hating politician father helping govern WWII Japan's own Ryukyus-cannon-fodder policy.[56] Yep. It can be like that.

My made-in-Korea wind-up mantel clock had long-since bonged away a drowsy 2 AM. I used a lull with *Obāsan* to say my goodnights. Ayako and El chittered undaunted beyond my bedroom door as I lay down and snapped off like a blown bulb.

1.2.3 WEDNESDAY, OCTOBER 11, 2017: REFUEL DAY THREE

Wednesday's third and final REFUEL convened at a brunchy 9 AM, but the Ancestors had dashed my plans for extra sleep. A paltry three-hour head start is all my alarm got before jangling me awake. When I fell out of bed at five-thirty, my daughters were only just saying their goodnights and staggering off to their bedrooms. In the boiling shower, I dwelled on *Obāsan* and who-all-else my girls might have dredged up overnight. What surprises were in store for me when they awoke this time?[48][57]

Zipping down the county road to the conference with my usual scalding *masala* tea in hand, I chatted up Mina and built my hand testing skills. This was so convenient, I thought admiringly. No more one way babbling to a figment God maybe shooting pool than listening to *me*. Now I could babble in response to *answers*. Inevitably, this led me to consider if he'd be willing to ask Jesus and Sun-myung to give me a few minutes of their time. He was, they did, and we small-talked around my unexpectedly well-tied tongue. Nothing faith shattering like later in the week, though. Baby steps. That's all you can expect with a frog pulling your tongue down your throat.

Day three of the conference surprised me. Now, I abhor Christian pop music with the best of atheists and have since before I was born (don't judge me). Even so, throughout the conference I'd noticed the music pleasantly uplifted me even as I choked on many of the lyrics.[49] During the 'praise' sessions between typecast speakers, I felt so spiritually energized that I raised my hands along with everyone else, something I'd never done. I didn't even feel stupid or self-conscious. I just belted out the songs, hands in the air, sappy lyrics be damned. Or I recast them on the fly when lyrically nimble enough. The emotional atmosphere triggered it, naturally, but I couldn't help but think God's spirit was laying it on me right thick. And why not? Wasn't I a fervent believer like the rest of this in-the-clouds crowd, even if my bohemian faith clashed over a few measly details?

On breaks in the crowded coffee courts, I surreptitiously communed with Mina and Sun-myung about the REFUEL conference and with Jesus on his perspective. It made me weigh how folks might react if they'd had any inkling he was standing right there with a jaundiced eye. I couldn't get enough of this new access to heaven's wise heavyweights, and that's an understatement. I tucked into Jesus' feelings generated by his eponymous faith and Sun-myung's on his own church's rowdy postmortem schism. It didn't occur to me to ask the really pointed questions until El kicked open that door later in the week, which right now was still a day away. *Today*, however, Divine Principle riding o'er the Bible like Windows over DOS still soothed my soul and ordered my world. I'm surprised how, in most ways, I just accepted things as they were, that maybe I wasn't as critical a thinker as I back-patted myself. Looking back, it seems all my theological *sturm und drang* keeping me in hot Unificationist water really only tweaked the baseline. When Sun-myung's unexpected 2012 demise crashed the Unification Church with the shock and awe of Bear Stearns' hedge funds going belly up, I'd scrabbled through 2015 before working out that Mrs. Hak-ja Han Moon had checked herself and her freshly-wrested dead husband's religion into *l'hôtel des délires*. Only now, under Mina's tutelage, was I toying with truly radical, faith-bending inklings. And then Jesus casually said on break that he'd washed his hands of Christianity a long time ago.[58] *Damn*. I'd been on the wrong track. Stuff like that needed time to soak in. El was sure ahead of me there.

---

48. The suspense wouldn't last long. El would ecstatically report they'd connected to yet another Japanese music sensation (still alive, so his pseudonym will be Akio) who turned out to be family, too.

49. Harsh, I know. I apologize to all its great melody-producing artists. On the other hand, 'dislike' is far too milquetoast to convey Mina's revulsion at its heartbreaking Jesus-death worship, magical God, and dystopic, lickspittle, domestic-violence themes rampant in this genre's lyrics that reflect modern Christianity generally.

There was no getting around *sans*-Jesus REFUEL's results, though. I was *pumped*. Energized and spiritually replenished after several draining years a chaplain surrounded by brainy psychoanalytic types devoid of spiritual fervor and Godly solutions to soldiers' problems—or their cups running over with magical but empty Goditis—not to mention the dry-boned pastors and institutional leaders of my church and, overall, Christianity's generally defunct *élan vital*. If I hadn't already put feelers across Michelangelo's finger chasm and discovered Mina, I'd have thought Traditional God Himself was riding my shoulders at the conference. REFUEL was what I'd been looking for! It bookended my idea of a chaplain: spiritized like those four WWII heroes who'd given up their lifejackets to go down with their ship, *The Longest Day*'s (1962) padre so determined to rescue his underwater communion kit so nobody would go without the sacraments that he paid no mind to enemy fire whipping by, or even those who quietly recognized the spiritual genesis of apparently psychological dysfunctions like PTSD.

I attended a tasty post-conference buffet into the evening with Jonathan Falwell and friends, then highwayed home. I took a few minutes to once more badger my dad to let me share his WWII whopper with his grandkids, but no dice. He was taking what felt like a C-note burning a hole in my jeans to eternity.

1.3 Six-day Journey's End...

At home Wednesday night, I babbled on about the "amazing" REFUEL conference while the girls labored like stevedores to push the conversation back to their new BFFs *Obāsan*, Hidé,[59] Taiji, their newfound Chinese great-great-grandfather they call *Yéyé*,[50] still-living megastar cousin Akiō, spirit visitors, and the Japanese side of our family now using our house like an earthbound timeshare. The girls laser-focused on *Obāsan* and her illicit China-born daughter (their great-grandmother) who so implausibly ended up in St. Vincent and the Grenadines in the early 1950s to bear their grandmother Martina, whom I personally know and which, at last, hooked me up real-time to the girls' historical revelations.[60]

I was thoroughly wound down by this preludial six-day odyssey—Friday's ThetaHealing start through Wednesday's REFUEL end followed by tomorrow's lead-up to the Big Event—when yet another midnight-plus rolled around and I hit the rack. My indefatigable daughters plugged away, learning what they could or chatting up common interests far into the nether gloom. It was a great social game for them which Ayako realized is key to mastering energy testing competency, whereupon Mina asked that she teach it to the world as a social skill. Near noon the following day, the girls dragged themselves from bed weary as the world to run family errands with me. It was now Thursday noon, October 12, 2017, some five hours before El would unleash her fateful opening salvo on our world of wishful thinking.

---

50. Less formal Mandarin (爷爷): *maternal grandfather*. He tolerates their preference for *yéyé*, but favors the correct Cantonese paternal (阿公) *ah-gung*. Ayako obliged him but now my ear prefers *yéyé*.

In the Hurricane's Eye

Thursday October 12, 2017 ca. Noonish

MIDDAY THURSDAY ARRIVED calm and collected. The wild energies of ThetaHealing's Basic DNA weekend workshop, Monday–Wednesday's REFUEL conference, and their hand killing road tripping were behind me. Energy testing was giving us a wee touch of the spirit, aye, but it was small potatoes, nothing to work us into a lather. For me, God still lounged all empyrean and hermitic in some magical, enigmatic corner of spacetime. For the present, we focused on acquainting ourselves with new personalities and tying down ethnicity. I wasn't so all-fired curious to see how well-grounded my Irish muttness might or might not be, although . . . African?

"Sure, why not?" I told myself. "The fam comes from the American South anyway. I'd be naïve to be surprised."[61] But, nope. I'd rather treasured my Gaelic-Nordic-Gallic-Germanic heritage before it occurred to me that, as we're primarily spirit than biological beings, ethnicity is utterly irrelevant, immaterial, and archaic, more a fun intramural sport than a fact of any consequence. Even Mina has an ethnicity.[62] *Had.* Now he's whatever he wants to be. Shorn of biology, he—like everyone else in spirit world—is free to be how he wants to be. Now that was something I could get into. The girls, on the other hand, were sliding into their new Asianity with a little more gusto than purely which gens is scrawled on their ancestral sheepskin, settling into their Eastern family lands after a long sojourn in the West.

As we set out for errands, our wheels thumped off the uneven lip of the garage sitting six inches off the eroded, graveled earth. For me, the spinal jolt was part and parcel of a serene foray into life's mundanity we'd made a million times, and that's all I'd envisaged today. I fast discovered the oddities of our new reality along for the ride. Ayako and El prattled non-stop with Hidé, Taiji, *Obāsan,* even me when I managed to shoehorn my comments in. And then we discovered one of my best friends hiding out *inside* me like a squatter in an abandoned tenement, except I wasn't exactly vacant; in spades, it turned out.[63]

1.1 RE-MEETING A BEST FRIEND . . .

What happened was, I'd street-parked alongside University of Mary Washington's Fredericksburg campus and hiked to its library to return a stack of reference materials from my soon-to-be-postponed racism book. Ambling back to my daughters waiting in the car, it hit me just how utterly depleted I felt. I stuttered along fatigued of every morsel of energy wholly untethered to spirit, all but zombified like some unlucky Haitian.[64] I wasn't exactly unused to bone weariness. Chronic pain from multitudinous injuries normalized an unnatural lassitude over the years. Sapped to flat-out prostrate was often my daily carousel. Yet, today, right now, felt strangely different. Calling me lethargic would be an insult to lethargy. If my eyeball showed a systems readout, I'd be seeing the *Batt* icon flashing red: *recharge now or shutdown, buddy*. I groped for the car door handle verging on collapse, then promptly did so into the driver's seat.

"Maybe it's everything you've been doing, Dad," Ayako not so helpfully said from the passenger side.

Not on your life, wobbled my head. "I need toothpicks to keep my eyelids open," I said, sounding whiny, I'm sure, but really just exasperated with my body. "I feel drained . . . like, vampire-drained, except this one's sucking energy."

That rang a bell with her. "Sounds like somebody hanging around you, then."

"You mean a spirit person?" Her head bobbed. "Like who?"

"I don't know. Somebody you were close to, maybe, who'd want to hang around you."

I snorted. "Nobody wants to hang around me."

"Don't be negative, Dad," El scolded from the backseat. "You just make it true."

Ah, je . . . "Why would anybody who even liked me that much want to be slurping out my energy like *The Mummy* movie mummy?"

Ayako said, "People have issues."

"Issues! That's it?"

She merely raised her what-do-you-expect? palms.

Gah. Fine, then. I plunked my head back on the headrest and stared at the sun visor. I murmured, "Who do I know like that who's dead . . . who'd plug into me like their own personal General Electric?" I made a few stabs at it. Ayako tested each one negative. I groaned.

Then El blurted, "It's Miss Helen!"[51]

I twisted round to catch her eye. "How do you know that?"

She snapped a shrug. "It just came to me."

"You mean it popped into your head outta nowhere?"

"Yeah. Like that."

You know, there's times it's helpful to have kids crazier than you. "Helen Smith," I said a little tremulously as I asked probably the oddest question of my life, and in front of my kids to boot, "are you, uhhh . . . here, in the car?"

Yes, Ayako hand tested.

Ah, quit being squeamish. "Are you *in* me?"

Yes.

Damn! I stared slack-jawed at Ayako next to me as she tested Helen's responses to my questions. Violated was certainly one emotion I was feeling. I mean, *shit!* Was nothing sacred? A whole host of images of my private life patently shared with Helen banged through my mind like cops on a warrant. Still, as they like to say before whipping out the handcuffs, points for honesty.

I said, "You mean, right now?"

No.

Well, that sounded better.

"But until just now?" said Ayako.

Yes.

Oh. Not that much better. "Since you died?"

No.

"Within six months of dying?"

No.

"Within a year?"

Yes.

"Was it more or less one year after you died?"

Yes.

"But . . . but, why?"

El said, "Dad, you can't—"

"Is it because," Ayako jumped in, "you found yourself in a low or dark place in spirit world?"

Yes!

"But she's a Blessed Moonie!" I said, aghast.[52]

"Forget about position, Dad," said El.

---

51. Totally not her real name (she picked it after all our other dead-end suggestions) or personal details.

52. A Unification Church Blessing of Marriage participant, a salvific in that faith.

"Yeah," Ayako said equably. "It's just your energy vibration. That's what matters in spirit world. Well . . . intention defines your energy, but, yeah."

"And why would you even be surprised?" said El, twisting screwdriver. "It's the Unification Church."

Ignoring her as a pastorally prudent parent ought, I said to Helen, "You were shocked and terrified where you ended up"—*Yes*—"and looked for a way out and eventually found me"—*Yes*—"and I was spiritually bright enough you felt safe and protected and comforted"—*Yes*—"like a home away from home?"

Yes!

"Really, really big yes," Ayako said, feeling Helen's energy.

"Boy . . . any harbor in a storm, I guess . . ."

Yes.

"Well, fuuu—rick."

"It is what it is, Dad."

"You just have to deal with it."

When did my kids get so adoringly philosophical?

As Helen transitioned to spirit world, she'd been frightfully upset. She wasn't ready. Tasks beckoned, people needed her. For all her faith, terror gripped her as she'd expired. She'd tried migrating to higher, brighter levels, but their potent energies pained her. Instead of putting up with her rubbish spirit accommodations, she'd retroverted to Earth for the comfort and normalcy of family and friends, but then she'd felt a vagrant. As a follower of Sun-myung's Divine Principle that teaches he's the second coming of Christ,[65] Helen, like any Moonie, absolutely anticipated a spiritually bright and happy residence for the persecuted faithful in spirit world. And why wouldn't she? She'd worked hard for the church, obeyed her leaders, got Blessed, raised a Blessed child,[66] and studied a little Divine Principle on the side. Just your average, conflicted child of God trying to live right. Like all the faithful.

"Not a bad person a'tall, in my book," I told the girls. "She never harmed anybody, really."

The same way that intention manifests our reality here—an impoverished mind begets an impoverished life, let's say—even more so does our thought define our situation in spirit world. Every facet of our being combines to create an overall life-intention often at variance with our conscious desire or our own self-image, like seeking love while stubbornly holding onto hate or one's last lover, or at least not giving up on the fixation that 'it's all about me.'

It dismayed Helen that she'd gravitated to a land of "darkness and dread," peopled with the incompatible despite her own compatible energy. Naturally, she'd looked for an out. Then she had a lightbulb moment and came a-calling on me.[67] And there I was, all bright but not too shiny, energetically peaceful, and painless enough for a safe haven, and she'd clung fast. The upside was, she needn't stay put in her unhappy spirit world billet nor wander the Earth a vagabond to avoid it. The downside was . . . well, none, for her. The invasion of privacy and her contribution to my occasional death knell of fatigue she could live with; putting up with the intimate experience of me, too, I supposed, but I wisely didn't ask about that. She'd turned a blind eye anyway. I didn't see much of an upside for me, though. This news triggered long-forgotten memories of Korean *ansu* sessions where we'd evict just these sorts of wastrels through repeated beatings of our *own* body until they were convinced our body wasn't their home.[68]

"So, are you the reason I'm feeling so washed-out right now?"

Yes. Sorry about that.

"Are you the *only* reason?"

No.

"You mean there's even more in there?" *Ansu* flooded my mind. "Like, a lot more?"

Yes, and yes.

1.2 CLEANING OUT SPIRIT SQUATTERS

This, I begrudged the universe, is how it was for virtually everyone prior to the Big Healing.[69] I shot hunted eyes over to Ayako, our spiritualist expert and, right now, my only steady oar in this uncharted sea. Under her astute queries, Helen clarified that thousands of spirit people "infested" me, hiding in or clinging to me and, both purposefully and inadvertently, draining away my energy to greater or lesser degrees like those smart, furtive rats tapping power lines in the 1982 film, *The Secret of NIMH*. House-party physics would've made the energy loss inevitable in any case. There's no malice on their part—just trying to relieve their suffering—but that hardly comforted me.[70] We didn't know why this afternoon it had left me so knackered. Later we found out that opening my chakras and dialing up Mina's direct line had spiked my energy into beacon status that drew thousands more freeloaders to me who'd overwhelmed my already slaphappy generator. "Is that right, Creator?" I said. "What Helen just said?"

Yes.

"How many are there?"

"Come on, Dad, you can't ask a 'how many' question," El reminded me.

"When you're more together than your dad," I bellyached in frustration, but Ayako lit me up with a warm glow of real sympathy. "Are there hundreds, Creator?"

Yes.

"Thousands?"

Yes.

Gulp. "Tens of thousands?"

No.

"Well, thank God for small favors! Uh, you know what I mean."

"He says 'yeah,'" said Ayako.

After some trial and error, we arrived at a number of "about ten thousand." I needed a cleanout like nobody's business, but not with *ansu*. That sadistic ship burnt long ago to its waterline.

"Creator, can you—are you able—to remove them, clear them out of me?"

Yes.

"Wow! Really?"

Ayako got a high-energy response and laughed. "*Big* yes, Dad."

"Can you do it, like, right now?" Mind you, we were still sitting in the car parked at the curb, Ayako energetically hand testing in the front passenger seat. At least the windows were tinted.

Yes.

Using Emotion Code's methodology, I intoned, "Creator, it is commanded all the—"

"Wait, Dad!" said El. "You don't want to throw out Miss Helen, do you?"

Well, *yeah*. I mean, uhh, no . . . I guess? It seemed to El I was heartlessly whirling Helen off into the dark bowels of her just desserts. Maybe I was being cruel. I wasn't feeling all that objective much less charitable at the moment.

"Miss Helen, do you want to be healed of any trapped emotions, traumas or limiting beliefs so you can change your situation? Cuz we'd like you to."

Yes.

"Is there anything we need to deal with before you're ready to be healed?" El continued, her Emotion Code down pat.

No.

"So you're ready to be healed right now?"

"Big, *big* yes," Ayako said with a lilting laugh.

I cycled through the mixed salad we'd used on *Obāsan* and her family to ask Mina's healing.[53] Through welling tears, El monologued on Helen's energy change and its effect inside the car. My skin rippled with shivers scalp to seat then back again. I was getting real practice with goosebumps.

"She's in the back seat with me now, Dad."

"You can feel her there?" I twisted round to look, wishing I could see spirit people like a real medium, the way one of our pastors' wives (avowedly) turns it on and off like a pair of Google glasses. I imagined Helen sitting beside El as she appeared in her vernal funeral photo.

"Yeah," said El. "I can feel her energy right up against me."

"Well, right, then. Creator, it is commanded all the spirit people who are in or clinging to me and the girls, except Helen"—just in case, right?—"be removed from us permanently and that we're protected from any further, um, 'infestation.'" I didn't know where'd they go, but frankly didn't care. *Just get out!* was the long echo of my mind. My gaze roved across the rearview. Would Helen be sending me a glare for that "infestation" crack? I wondered how she felt being caught piggybacking off my life. On reflection, that felt stupid. She'd just

---

53. Since the Big Healing, modalities like Emotion Code and ThetaHealing, along with their intoning jargon, are redundant. Mina heals automatically as soon as one's ready and permissive. Indeed, he's healing everyone right now upon entering spirit world post-death, as well as you in your spirit embodiment while awake or asleep according to your desire.

directly experienced God flooding her with healing energy, loving her like the queen of the world. Wasn't she a different person now? Dishwater, drainpipe, right?

"Creator," Ayako said, "did it work?"

Yes.

"We're completely free of spirit people in us?" I said.

Yes.

I fist pumped. "Yes!"[54]

But how would I know? It's not like I felt emptier or my stolen energy surged back into me. I guessed I'd have to wait and see how I bounced back in the next few days . . . if I did. This spirit clearing-out didn't affect Hidé and Taiji or anyone else we'd met because they were hanging around *outside* us as guests, or at least acquaintances, and not *inside* like parasites. I didn't really like applying *parasite* to Helen, whom I still loved as a best friend, but it was what it was, no sense whitewashing it. And now, it was over.

This was all exploratory for us. I, for one, didn't really understand at all what we were getting into. That would come in the slow-mo thunderclap tonight and tomorrow. Contemplating the visceral reality of spirit world is old hat for serious Unificationists, and anyhow, this wasn't my first woo-woo rodeo. I've seen angels and spirit persons before, and even conversed with some of them. Yet those times seemed so random that I'd felt disconnected from each moment as though watching another person. Our experience the last few days was firmly in our control and much more immediate, even intimate. It wasn't me watching me, it was me *being* me, and finding thousands of spirit people so entwined with my body, my existential singularity, that they degraded my energy and health. It shook to the core my placid, ontic *Dasein*. It was one thing to suffer Korean spiritualists jabbering on about spirit infestations bred by desperation to escape anguish only to callously whack them out of us during those long, painful *ansu* sessions for a bargain basement $1,000 fee, which we'd instead just instantly accomplished through a simple, painless, free request. It was quite another, indeed, to talk to and feel the heart of—to actually know!—someone giving me the business for real. Not a stranger or acquaintance, either, but a best friend. There were a million things I wanted to say to Helen. I couldn't think of a single one.

"Creator, can they come back?" El wondered.[71]

No.

Now that *was* good news. I cast back over my shoulder. "And you're good, Helen?"

"*Very* big yes," Ayako said, feeling Helen's deeply happy, extra energetic response. She must've been ecstatic: the next day she joined my one spirit guide to form a team, a 24–7–365 largely thankless on-call service.[72] Very humbling, that. What do you say to such a friend? *Thank you* seems awful paltry.

So far, you could say we'd gone through a few minor life updates leading into Thursday's Genesitic cool-of-the-day full upgrade. Our reality had expanded, yes, but honestly, not all *that* much. Discovering The Ancestors was a jump into a cool, dawn plunge pool for my daughters. But now, they were catching their shocked breath. Hak-ja Han's goofy Moonism revamp and Helen's stage-left entrance withal, my Principle lifeview oddly enough only settled deeper in my mind like bones in a soupy seabed. I noted the incongruity as we nattered on about all we'd learned, yet unsure what to make of it. Then our errands wrapped up as daylight thought about packing its bags, and we traversed the narrow, winding roads home to El's inadvertent, total upheaval of our reality.

---

54. It dawned on me much later that we should've asked Mina to heal them all just like Helen, instead of giving them the boot. When I sheepishly raised the issue, Mina said of course he didn't "throw them back into their suffering situations!" He'd healed them all. They'd then left naturally, voluntarily, *happily* for better digs.

Doom Ride

Friday October 13, 2017 ca. Mid-afternoon

AST FORWARD THROUGH Thursday night's Big Shake-up and Friday morning's Reconciliation and Big Healing, and it's now Friday mid-afternoon after lunch. We were on Virginia's schizophrenic Interstate 95 struggling north into Maryland to bunt Mina's in-your-face memo into ThetaHealer and her mom, Ms. Medium's, ballpark. For each of us, this task seemed an epochal showdown like hoving guns out round the headland. With each dying mile, our guts knotted a little tighter. The reason was more than just Ayako's and my aversion to handing people adverse news. It was Mina hitting us—undeterred by our fierce (maybe inanely curious) skepticism—with intel that Ms. Medium had forged Michael's seminal Angel Code story.

"She accurately conveyed Gabriel's portion," he'd said, "but doesn't like Michael."

As soon as she'd recognized Michael speaking—piously lampooning him for "push[ing] Gabriel out of the way so he could get the healing faster" when, actually, Gabriel had kindly yielded the floor—she'd begun dissembling. Not misinterpreting or mistaking this for that. Not confusing things, or shocked by something so bizarre she couldn't accurately convey it. Not even because she might've been a fake medium. Nope. *Lied.* She'd even wept conveying her ginned-up messages in these proceedings. Here's why.

1.1   MS. MEDIUM BETRAYS MICHAEL ...

Thirteen years before we fired up the Angel Code, Michael had quietly knocked on Ms. Medium's door to confide in her his hatchet job on Lucifer. Her advanced clair senses and devotion to Unificationism's Restoration[55] had caught his interest. Sun-myung taught her to not only love Lucifer–Satan, but that he'd surrendered to God in 1999 because of Sun-myung's unconditional, death-defying, Principled love for him. That suggested to Michael that her Satan-hating days would be over, that she'd comprehend Lucifer in his new, *never*-Satan togs. Michael thus calculated she'd be conducive to helping him rebuild his burnt bridges, a sort of Swiss mission to his older brother.

She leaned that way, sure. But devotion aside, she didn't bend all that far toward unconditional love. That wasn't uncommon. Unificationists warmly embracing Sun-myung's rapturous *Satan surrendered, y'all!* coldly couldn't care less for the devil who'd put them in their toils. *What's it mean for me?* was the first concern on many a lip. Anyhow, wasn't his surrender really somebody else's mile marker on their own road to glory? Even less willing to friendlily backslap a Restored Lucifer than suspicious Jews were an evangelized Saul, Unificationists left him in the firmament of evil like spoiled eggs forgotten in the pantry but smelling up the house. If pressed on why they continued heaping blame on Satan, they'd explain that *Satan* really meant his

---

55. Unificationist salvific term that denotes fallen nature's eradication and restoration of God's sovereignty on Earth.

newly promoted minions now that Lucifer had (supposedly) gone legit. According to Sun-myung, *they* hadn't surrendered a thing. But this collective Satan redux had nonetheless learned its evil ways at Lucifer's odious knee. Wasn't it thusly Lucifer's ultimate doing that the Unification Church still bled members like a pickled hemophiliac? Why its members, to varying degrees, cheated on their spouses, beat their children, abused their fellows, ignored Divine Principle, generally sinned with religious abandon, trod on Sun-myung's still-fresh grave, and worse, couldn't even manage to make a difference in the world? And look, they reasoned, we can even use the same pet name *Satan* for the vomitous lot of them.

The average Moonie mind could never manage to shear Lucifer of his opprobrium any more than world-weary Soviets could separate Rudolph Hess from Nazism four decades after *not* participating in Russia's immolation, or Americans Benedict Arnold twenty decades after switching horses midstream. If post-1999 their no-hoper foibles and providential failures persisted, it could only mean that Satan remained at large or, in any case, at fault. Who but the former *arch*angel, the Great Deceiver, had the moxie to spurn the Messiah's naïve love and pull off such a gangsterish sleight of hand? That Moonies are their own satanic saboteur is for them a distinction without a difference.

In this general frame of mind, Ms. Medium wasn't ready for the venerated Archangel Michael to say something along the lines of, "So, here's the thing. The Fall, Adam and Eve, and Satan aren't real. I made it all up to frame Lucifer. The unhappy rest sort of, well, just happened. But now I want to fix it."

She took it, Mina said, "pretty badly."

I said, "Because Michael's perfidy stomped her heart?"

No. But perfidy's the key word, here.

Michael sticking it to his brother and seeding a weedy take on reality rightly shocked Ms. Medium. Moreover, she thought he should tell Lucifer without delay, then bit her tongue; she couldn't hide her growing contempt for him. But she counter-shocked him by wanting his help to rise up through ThetaHealing's constellation to superstardom. Its new and creative modality was mining hitherto untapped wallets with ease. And it worked—at least, so long as customers thought it did, and that was good enough. Ms. Medium's healer aspirations, plus Unificationism's close-held suite of sanative moneymakers, had so far added up to a big fat zero for her and it wasn't fair. Being psychic, though, she'd already suspected ThetaHealing wasn't a benign curative, and then Michael made plain it was "dangerous and caused more harm than good, even killing people."

Yet, after his shocking revelation, she'd rejected his warning even as she'd believed it. Anyhow, *caveat emptor*.[56] She had kids to feed. Michael recoiled at the very idea. When he then had the gall to "full-on judge her cracked moral compass," Ayako told us, she'd played virtuous Stalin to Hitler's 1941 dupery after carving up Poland like BFFs and offered him the blackmailer's option: "Help me or I blab your secret."[57]

She'd be lying for money as Michael had lied for revenge. What was the difference, really? In the bigger scheme, wouldn't her minor moral deviance pale beside his devastating fit of pique? Surely, in return for that money—though, unlike a biblical tax collector, by 2017 she'd reaped only poverty, misery, and anonymity for her dishonesty against Michael's beloved albeit undeserved angelic status—she'd help a few suffering souls, and all without putting any innocents in the frame, or stitching up a fake deity like a certain somebody had. *Two wrongs don't make a right? Tell it to Michael!* He'd rejected her by refusing to help her dredge up trusting sufferers through ThetaHealing's dark mire. Then he'd judged her as wanting. *What a hypocrite!* She couldn't appreciate the burden of alienation Michael's misdeed had brought him. How could she, when abandoning her own profession of faith had blinded her to her own? To top it all off, his penitent self-exposure only made her feel outrageously outed. Ms. Medium despised Michael for what he did to (and wouldn't do for) her. She branded him satanic for her own, and the world's, lied-to misery very much how she'd always blamed Lucifer, who *now*, according to Michael, wasn't even blameworthy. And wasn't her guilt for that Michael's fault, too? After all her trust and sacrifice . . . how could life—*how could Michael!*—do this to her?

Michael had pricked her bubble of faith, but it didn't bring her any of the happy relief it had us. Why would it, when she'd invested in its polar opposite? Now she'd lumped him in with Satan. Who cared what Rev. Moon said about Lucifer? He'd reaped billions promising his followers honor, glory, even a pension. All they'd ever harvested was ridicule and penury. What did he know? Once dead, his own wife might bulldoze his grave given half the chance. And at the end of the day, what had she actually heard about Lucifer's surrender? Not a psychic thing.[58] Her hearty conditioning that Lucifer was Satan and Satan was hateful didn't flinch an inch.

---

56. Latin: 'let the buyer beware.'

57. Paraphrased, of course; maybe the world's first 'deal with the angel.'

58. Naturally. Satan doesn't exist, so no surrender could've happened.

So, she'd rejected Michael and innocent Lucifer with him. She tried coming right out with the seamy truth to spiritualist friends and others to make good her blackmail, but came off a crackpot—except to one medium who'd believed her but (in different words) told her, "If you want to make money as a psychic, shut up about Michael." Well, turnabout was fair play. With luck, she could certainly dirty the phony's coattails.

Notwithstanding Michael's—"I still don't regret it, either"—anger with Ms. Medium's God-fearing willingness to risk harm to others for ThetaHealing money and his shock at her chutzpah, her contempt had scalpeled him to the nub. Ayako couldn't find words to convey how betrayed and hurt he'd felt. I struggled to empathize, even after he shared it with me. This was exactly the abhorrence he'd dreaded but had paralyzingly expected Lucifer—everyone!—to pile on him without pity. Even so, avoiding such an Accountableist outcome formed a motivating intention for him. People had a right to be steamed; he got it. But his target had been Lucifer, not humanity. Mina says Michael didn't foresee nor intend its fallout. The larger human disaster unfolded from the already-Corrupted minds of every person who uncritically bought into Michael's Lie and then, ofttimes embellished, passed it on through living up to it. Michael wasn't and isn't the 'real' Satan. That said, he did have to get his mess out. The irony was harsh and brutal. Unwittingly stuck in his own Accountableist mindset, he'd stymied himself in finding a way. Mina hovered helpfully in the wings quite ignored. Michael never thought he actually _knew_ but was only guessing.[73] "I don't know what you're talking about" had been his uniform response.

Gabriel didn't know the truth, either, but knew his brother was troubled and grieving over something; probably just Mnèèptē, and he was past due getting that horse pastured out. For whatever reason, Michael wanted to work with humans, and Gabriel humored him. Accordingly, he'd gone to Moth Man's angel fanatic friend to arrange another go but, at Michael's request, he'd stressed he not engage Ms. Medium at all. Yet, as soon as Moth Man's friend shuddered up from his glorious dream around two in the morning, he rang her up purely out of reflex. Life's just a basket of variables. Michael was cornered. After Gabriel went to all that trouble, what reason could Michael possibly give for now pulling out? No, he was pinned as a bug to a board. He made a valiant attempt with Ms. Medium, but it was a foregone conclusion. Pulling her in meant he'd get the kibosh, and so he had. His effort to come clean with some dignity and control was in a shambles. He fell back to reassess, only to be then swept up in our breaking adventure.

At the time, we knew very little more than that Ms. Medium's Angel Code 'readings' were lies. Discovering she'd also 'poisoned' us energetically via touch, proximity, and food, our relationship sundered mid-bud all on its own. Altogether it bulled the girls into taking Mina at his word that she'd lied. I lamented in doubt for months even as I made a slow peace with the facts on the ground.[74]

1.1.1 MICHAEL'S FURY AT MS. MEDIUM'S LIES . . .

I wasn't the only one with a coping deficiency. Michael lost his marbles over Ms. Medium's double-dealing. While Ayako and El chatted happily over ping-pong downstairs at Moth Man's suburban Maryland home back in August 2017, our third and doubly-attended Angel Code meeting—a whole new client base taking shape right before Ms. Medium's all-seeing eyes!—séanced over their heads. Then mid-swing in the girls' game, "dizzying bursts of energy" skull-slammed them both in ball-meets-paddle fashion, and horse-kick headaches bloomed from nothing to the Big Bang. Uneasy eyes on the ceiling, they fretted over what no-good pot the 'grownups' had just daftly stirred.

None of us knew at the time that Michael had got so worked up over Ms. Medium's bodacious lying to all of us around Moth Man's dining room table that his livid energy surged EMP-like through the house and anyone sensitive to it. This was the meeting at which Ms. Medium channeled Michael's supposed hurt, terror, and self-loathing at "Lucifer's bullying after the fall" that he'd so cowardly failed to confront, where I'd felt my heart literally crushing itself beneath my ribs as if Michael's wounded psyche was my own. I could've cried with grief believing Michael's feelings were mine. Addressing Ms. Medium, I'd even apologized to Michael like a ringleader for my mere sliver of a part enabling Lucifer-cum-Satan. Witless me. It was Michael's EMP-like fury, anguish, sadness, sorrow, and exasperation with Ms. Medium's determined fabrications that was working me over every bit as good as my ping-ponging daughters downstairs.

"Michael knew exactly what she was doing," Ayako later revealed prior to us teasing out the whole saga. "He just couldn't believe a life-long Unificationist, with a spirit-world aware lifestyle and the Moonie desire to help humanity, plus her ability to actually see him—that she'd do that."

Man, was he ever the optimist. I said, "She literally saw, heard, and experienced him and _knew_ what he was really saying to all of us?"[59]

"Yet, could still lie. Michael was beside himself!" Ayako clapped a hand to her forehead. "And we suffered for it!"

Absently, I massaged my breastbone. "Surely she felt all that wild energy. Didn't she at least get a—"

Ayako just waggled her chin. "Who cares about reactions when you're lying? Besides, she has control of her senses and can turn 'em off whenever."

"You're saying she just switched him off and ad-libbed?"

"I'm not saying it. Michael's saying it."

I guess that's a handy option we might now sometimes appreciate ourselves but . . . ad-libbed? That was some Oscar-level talent. Unbeknownst to me, the energy coming off many of those physically attending that session had to varying—"and creepy," according to Ayako—degrees repulsed my daughters. Both instinctually wanted to keep their distance, and rejected out of hand my invitations to join in. I'd no idea how unappreciated it was when, months later, I'd tried setting up a friendship between Ms. Medium and Ayako via Emotion Code and ThetaHealing. Boy, howdy.

These Angel Code meetings bowled over all of us who'd so trustingly participated. Really, Ms. Medium's duplicity was fantastically challenging to accept—more for me than the girls, by far—even with Michael's attestation of Lucifer's innocence right there in front of us. Ms. Medium's tearful imagery never strayed from the Biblical, bolstered by helpful Unificationist and new-agey overtones. That should've rung our oddity bell straight off. When "[a]ll genuine revelations are revelations of mystery" (Ward 2002, 238) or seamlessly jibe with extant belief, a giant snapping flag tends to run up the mast for me. Observation repeatedly demonstrates how unlikely it ever is that what we think we know is what's actually so until demonstrated. Expectation, meanwhile, expends all its energy reining in what we know to keep it tightly bound to what we believe. It wasn't that the angels' energy-tested stories were at total odds with Ms. Medium's own. Rather, unlike the theological conundrums implicit in her Christo-centric imagery, theirs possessed logic, consistency, universality, and *simplicity*. Occam's Razor is a compelling guide.

Honestly, such human frailties notwithstanding, we liked our (to all appearances) friendly, kind, and considerate Ms. Medium. Over our ThetaHealing Basic DNA weekend, it seemed to me that she and Ayako had built the beginnings of a sisterhood. I couldn't have been happier for my dystopic daughter. Really, Mina's pronouncement of lying was the worst news. Oh, we'd asked for it, aye. We could've stopped, ignored this elephant in the room. Likewise, we could've brushed off any of the faith-eating news that makes up this book. Isn't that humanity's Machiavellian way with inconvenient truth? How hard could it be? Hadn't Ms. Medium accomplished it? Yet, turning a blind eye wasn't only uncharacteristic for us but seemed unhelpful and, considering her energy 'poisoning,' downright foolhardy, too. So we'd plowed on furrow after curious furrow until we looked up to behold ourselves on an endless plain of upturned reality. Well, you can't un-till a field.

Respectable reasons for why Ms. Medium's version of Michael and Gabriel's stories diverged so dramatically from ours eventually ran dry. We abjectly accepted the only explanation still standing. Her betrayal of our trust ground on our nerves. More than that, the effect on our physical health as well as our food from ThetaHealing's mordant energy and Ms. Medium's own venom that permeated her till she was off-gassing it like a volcanic plume struck us even more incredulously. Never mind its effect on fragile intangibles like chakras and spiritual well-being.[75]

1.2 HE SAID SHE SAID: CLAIRVOYANCE VS. ENERGY TESTING

These vulturous thoughts gathered even more dread to our minds as we now trekked north up Interstate 95 for our closeup with Ms. Medium and her family. Only El appeared ready, if not disturbingly eager, to take the bit in teeth and do what needed doing. Maybe it was her 'never say die' boundless optimism that militaries find ever so attractive in recruits. She waves the comparison aside, but I see in her a little United States Marine Corps eyeing somebody's beach.

This naturally brings up the prickly issue of how one distinguishes what's true, credible, and sensible when confronted by critical discrepancies between (supposed) spiritual experiences. Why should we believe our energy testing and clair senses over Ms. Medium's experienced and not unconvincing (apparent) clairvoyance and claircognizance?[76] One reason is that, separately or together, we three consistently tested the same or similar answers and intuited more or less the same energy and feeling. Discrepancies and corrections to each other's energy testing errors only brought out a fuller understanding. Whether with Mina, the archangels, Hidé and

---

59. According to Mina, Ms. Medium isn't clairaudient but clairvoyant and claircognizant; hence, she still understands.

Taiji, *Obāsan*, Sun-myung and Jesus, Helen, my dad, and others, we developed not just trusting relationships but could distinguish them intuitively or by their personalities and vibes from the way each one energy tests. The girls perceived all this more than I did. However, I often felt Lucifer cozy up close (especially to read this manuscript over my shoulder when he wasn't listening to it in my conscious thoughts) because sometimes he's so intense his energy translates to heat.[60] Besides, the things Ms. Medium attributed to Michael and Gabriel at our Angel Code get-togethers raised grave logic and consistency dilemmas in my mind.[77]

Between our direct, corporeal or tactile experiences and Ms. Medium's unverifiable 'readings,' there seemed no contest whom to believe. But it hurt having to choose. And here's the real problem with mediums: one can't validate their claims. They're either fake in whole or part, or they willfully, negligently, or innocently confuse local truths gleaned from their very narrow entrée into spirit world with universal truths of spirit world, God, or our universe as a whole. "We tend to generalize on the basis of our given experience of how things are and then believe that we hooked up with the fundamental level of reality. This is how world-views are generated and they are always provincial" (Markus, par. 6). As they say in the apparently real spirit world city of Uversa, "All finite knowledge and creature understanding are *relative*."[78]

It might seem no more than a he-said-she-said spiritualist quarrel, something a provident person laughs off. You might be chuckling out a little sensible humor right now. But we didn't actually care what Ms. Medium *did* say in these meetings. We'd just had our own direct spiritual experience, and that was enough for us. Ms. Medium's chutzpah sorely chafed Michael and Gabriel, it did. Even so, they came off gracious about the whole thing. Neither Mina nor angels compel or judge a person into doing anything,[79] even if humans hardly shy from it.[80] When humans whom Mina and angels engage end up veering off a cliff, they neatly move on to the next in line. People are too fickle to get worked up each time one flubs no matter what's at stake (don't conclude one is then a failure, hence rejected, judged, and booked for punishment by Mina; that would be false). No, we cared what Ms. Medium *didn't* say: the truth, the real story of life. We have to remember that once we're done with our physical bodies we continue living just as we are only sans biology. Whatever happens in our physical life, whatever we do, however we're traumatized—dead *in utero*, shot, bludgeoned, crucified, or deceased from a long, happy life of trials and tribulations—we heal. Nor are the disasters that befall civilization permanent.[61] Collectively, we get through them. There's nothing like eternity to make the long view the only view.

A more troubling corollary to Ms. Medium's nefarious conduct vis-à-vis Michael was Mina's remark that ThetaHealing, to which she was joined hip-to-socket, is a lie, too.[81] Ayako and I'd just gone through a $440-per-person *Weekend at Bernie's* that left us, if not spiritually dead, then so clogged by sticky wrong energy that we both felt *half* dead when almost any food Ayako ate left her nauseated.[82] And then a 'cold' hit us all.[83] Ayako fared worse than El and me, having spent two nights during the Basic DNA workshop in Ms. Medium's energy-contaminated home, eating her energy-contaminated food, and participating two-plus days in an energy-contaminated program that had drained her like a pre-dinner chicken strung up by the ankles. I was lucky bunking elsewhere. While it took El less than a week and me a couple more to shake the spiritual 'cold' and get Mina's nod that its negative energy had cleared, Ayako took closer to seven weeks. She was spiritually fitter than I was so, in spite of the heavier dose of ill will, she endured far less interruption to her more muscular chakras than did I. In these early days, my chakras regularly stumbled and knocked me spiritually 'offline' like some crummy motel Wi-Fi outside Reno.[84]

1.3 Friday, October 13, 2017 ca. 4 pm

Just when I thought a two-to-four-hour road trip up the sludge pipe to the DC Metro area couldn't get more interesting than its drab scenery, I proved myself wrong. Our new car-normal was my daughters carrying on animated conversations via hand testing with their new BFFs Hidé, Taiji, *Obāsan*, and anyone discovered entering our vehicle.[85] In the mix, our old-normal window-glass-flexing singalongs to Bollywood epics competed with newer heavy metal faves X Japan, visual-*kei* GazettE or Diaura, Japanese alt-rock Buck-Tick, and other alt-musicians the girls were crazy for. My "you're too serious, Dad" Q&A's with Mother, Mina, and the angel squad periodically 'blowing up' the car with BIG NEWS barely pushed in from the edges.[86]

This particular Friday afternoon's menagerie included Hidé, Taiji, Helen, *Obāsan* and some family members, our spirit guides, guardian angels, Jesus, Sun-myung, my dad, and others who "popped and dipped" as our conversation caught or lost their fancy. Most interesting to me was Lucifer—instinctively, I liked him—who

---

60. I know! Right? Ironic, given his undeserved association with fiery hell.

61. There's an unhappy semi-exception to this covered in EARTH'S HUMAN HISTORY (CH. 32:531).

came and went to channel energy from us while helping Mina conduct the Big Healing now in full swing since morning.[62] The girls intuitively and energetically sensed these arrivals and departures with ease. More a spiritual laggard myself, I noticed Lucifer only because 10–20°F temperature spikes heralded his arrival. I'd drop the windows to pull in the sixtyish outdoors until his departure cooled the heat wave and then up they'd go. He explained Mina was healing *everyone* in the universe[63] and it called for energy beyond even Lucifer's expectations. He had little time for chitchat but, with brevity between arriving and departing, he kept us up on whatever we'd ask. Mina was busy enough over those twenty-four hours that, when we called on him, his response seemed more like a languid radio call from Mars.

Feeling the lag, we asked, "Are you too busy with the Big Healing?"

Yes.

So, just to clarify: "We can't ask you anything, then?"

No.

"But, later, right?"

Laaaag (possibly a sigh). *Yes.*

All righty, then. Still getting used to him after all, especially since he was nothing like we'd expected even if we could've articulated *what* we'd expected, which none of us could beyond the Great and Powerful Oz or maybe *der Überführer*. We weren't even sure he'd continue communicating. Our self-esteem just hadn't anticipated hearing from the creator of our universe and was now faltering in its mission.

Lucifer, in keeping with the sensitive personality we were coming to recognize, apologized for channeling so much energy from us every time he popped in, especially to my daughters who so keenly felt the draw. Besides the sapping, "skull-cracking" pressure Ayako found characteristic of Mother's excited interactions with us when she'd pitched-in hand-in-glove to help heal with Mina, Ayako had worn herself out energy testing virtually nonstop all day for days. She complained of being even more enervated than "my new usual." Then her eyes rolled back and she slumped into her seat . . . at which point a surge of energy jolted her awake as Lucifer, alarmed at her state, channeled energy back. Meanwhile, El gently cycled between lively awake and dead asleep with pulse-like regularity as our clavering waxed and waned.[87]

I could only look askance at all this while hurtling north into DC Metro's inevitable rush-hour molasses. Maybe my implicit trust in Mina, Mother, and Lucifer to bring no harm to my children with these energy antics scandalizes the casual observer. We, however, wanted to give without reserve whatever extra energy we could muster for this extraordinary, pivotal event, even if it did exhaust us. Otherwise, we'd have felt pretty much out of the bigger—seemingly, all-hands-on-deck—picture. It wasn't as if our energy wouldn't bounce back with a little rest. It seemed natural, even ordinary, to accept this energy channeling all in stride rather than, as some might be tempted to say, a demonic[64] harbinger or akin to ThetaHealing's vampiric entity. We weren't alone donating juice to the effort anyway. It was universal.[88]

"It doesn't seem like much of an energy pull to me," I said, airily kissing off their complaints.

"You're *driving*, genius," the ever-droll Lucifer droned through Ayako (now giving me The Look).

"We sure don't want *your* eyeballs rolling up white," El quipped to me while checking her sister over.

"Hmmph." Now I felt a little cheated.

We sure weren't going to employ any of Ms. Medium's crooked depictions of spirit world, so we were at a loss to envision how the NCC-freed *ultima mundi* was right now transforming under Mina's love-unsparing revivification. It was a good bet no horn-blowing angels were casting around Ms. Medium's gold-plated harps, though. More like *Obāsan*'s midnight healing writ large, we guessed.[65] We wondered if people around the world would even notice. To be truthful, we were feeling a little full of ourselves about now. Like a refund out of China, humility travels on a slow boat. It turned out some people did notice, if only anecdotally. They felt "something" unusual, unburdening, healing, or in some way special to them.[89] No one we knew described seeing visions of God healing the uncountable masses *à la* Ms. Medium's vivid Angel Code imagery, but so what? Few mediums have a clue about spirit world beyond their micro-level perspectives anyway. They're hardly the pundits to abide for what's going on there at the macro level.

"Yeah, but it's all a pretty fantastic tale," you might be mumbling about now.

---

62. See PART II and III for the energy relationship between the physical and spirit universe, and physical humanity's role.

63. All living things as affected by the NCC, close to a quintillion persons.

64. There's no such thing as demons, it's a human fable loosely based on human behavior.

65. "Close enough," Mina told us. *Obāsan*-level dramatic for humans, less so for angels.

We couldn't agree more. Still and all, this is our own sense experience. We have to roll with it till something legitimately discounts it. At least energy testing is a means for you to corroborate our experience or to have your own.[66] The extra-sensory perception behind the blowy pronouncements of psychics and mediums can't be validated except by an equal or better extra-sensory sensor—or a common sensor. That works surprisingly often, too.

---

66. Or not. Sometimes answers differ for various reasons. As late-night informercials disclaim, "Your results may vary."

Confrontation

8

FTER CREEPING THROUGH torpid traffic, we ghosted as only a hybrid can into a tree-shrouded driveway at the Maryland home hosting the $440-per-person ThetaHealing Advanced DNA weekend workshop. It was just now getting underway. Six or seven attendees comfortably lolled about the bay-windowed living room. Ms. Medium's thirtyish son—the chap I really liked, who'd selflessly helped me achieve energy testing capability at the Basic DNA workshop the previous weekend—smiled angelically through the window from his roost on a plush sofa. I prefer to think he was happy to see us, but he could've just been reflecting his ThetaHealer sister's joy at another near grand walking through the door. Either way, it didn't offset my daughters' perception that the family's youthful skin seemed aged, wrinkled, and grayed out from their exposure to ThetaHealing's negative energy as if withered by prolonged tobacco or alcohol use. Or maybe they chain-smoked through eighty-proof meals. I kept an open mind.

"The whole group's a mess," Ayako opined.

El said, "It's just their Moonie vibe, Aya."

"Do we really need another cat in this bag, girls?"

Shaking off the interminable car ride, El quietly passed on to us that Lucifer was back to give moral support. Like the rest of us, he'd been a nervous Nellie about our plan to update ThetaHealer. On top of which, he avouched to Ayako, his conflict aversion and fear of rejection left him "super nervous" after earlier requesting she tell Ms. Medium that he wanted to talk afterward (prima facie evidence, I'd supposed, of Ms. Medium's bona fides).[90]

Lucifer's no slouch, though. Along with Gabriel and Michael, he'd evinced a real affinity for us. So, besides Ms. Medium's wonky ThetaHealing vibe and mishandling Michael's Angel Code messages, her change of heart since (or fakery during) our phone call this morning markedly agitated him to set things straight with her. What sort of response might he get? He wasn't too sanguine, considering Michael's salty Angel Code affair. It's not like he thrives on rejection. Lucifer stands nine feet and can come across, El might graciously say, *stern*. But relationships amongst spirit persons differ little from here regardless age, power, influence, or lack thereof. Any real medium would be looking up at our approach. We wondered how ours would react—if she did.

Not keen at all, I rapped on the door. Happy voices were a warm welcome justifiably mistaking us for paying customers. After pleasantries, Ms. Medium and ThetaHealer followed us outside to discuss our attendance and for what I'd phrased as "an important message from Creator." I felt chilled despite the warmish mid-sixties air. Maybe it was fear. I'm not great at disappointing people. Simple disagreement sometimes looms over me a ferocious specter of past conflict. Not too unlike Lucifer, evidently. That's not what this was or for what we'd come, but a face-off is how it felt. Prescient I was, too. Our plan soured the instant we circled up in front of the house beyond the covered porch and I opened my mouth.

Ayako had latched herself to a white-painted porch support on my left to prop up her shaky, used-up body. By now, it felt to her more a shell than when sleeping 'neath this morning's big scene. Michael—still "angry, but more hurt, than anything" (Ayako said) by Ms. Medium's sniffy predilections—'portaled' in to quietly observe from the sidelines. He took up station to Ayako's left for strength in her knackered state and to deflect the negative energy spritzing from Ms. Medium and ThetaHealer. I faced the latter across the circle with El to my right and Ms. Medium to El's right and ThetaHealer's left. Lucifer seethed between them because she'd instantly snapped shut her spirit eyes like nosy-neighbor blinds to pretend she hadn't noticed him prowling her neighborhood. He'd got his answer at any rate.

1.1.1 Reflecting on Ms. Medium Ignoring Lucifer . . .

Afterward in the car, I said to Ayako, "She can close her senses just like that, and *poof!* he disappears?"

"Sure, why not? It's no different than closing your eyes so you don't have to acknowledge something."

"Ah. The way people stare at their feet . . . or look away as if you're not already in their face."

She laughed. "But more effective."

"She's a medium. What possible motivation could she have to ignore an angel? Isn't that, like, bad form or something?"

"She's trying to resurrect the Moonie passion for spirit world and healing people because she saw how much money you can make from it."

"How are those two things even connected?" Ayako looked at me like I was asking her to explain why it's wet when raining. "So . . . what, she felt shamed seeing the Great Satan in Michael's easy company after all her talk about his fear of Lucifer the Bully? Like she'd been caught out?"

"Yeah," Ayako said with a snigger. "I'm sure it was a very embarrassing moment for her unless she's that callous."

"El-oh-el," carped El in a dour monotone from the backseat.

1.2 Ms. Medium Reacts to the Angels . . .

Michael, however, was interpreting Ms. Medium's fleeting but bracing eye-lock from across our loose circle as a pair of incoming stilettos. Meanwhile, Lucifer, practically bumping shoulders with her, was reduced to a will-o'-the-wisp on the wrong side of her second sight.[91] Frankly, she seemed just on the edge of wild eyed. Probably the stress, I thought, though I hadn't seen her explicitly swing her eyes up to a nine-foot altitude. But would a medium have to?

On the other hand, recall our spirit bodies can manifest custom sizes. Lucifer could've drawn up eye-to-eye or knee-high to a munchkin for all I knew at the time.[67] To a psychic medium, however, this couldn't have looked *less* like an ordinary conversation. El sensed Ms. Medium shrink into herself, just psychically step out of the meeting and retreat to the peanut gallery.

1.2.1 Ayako Opines About Lucifer . . .

Talking it over driving home, Ayako said, "I started feeling really bad inside at that point, Dad. Everything just seemed wrong. I felt really upset on the inside."

"You're a pretty sensitive person, you know. I'm not surprised you felt—"

"No, no. It didn't feel like any type of reaction *I* would have had!"

Giving her the eye, I said, "What do you mean?"

"It turns out it was Lucifer's feelings of rejection and heartbreak, really super intense."

"Huh." He hadn't let on about that when we'd talked it over later, but Ayako well knew that wasn't his style. A quiet sufferer, he is, at least with us. "Ms. Medium's attitude must've been like one more blistering spike in his back, I reckon." My fingers lightly drummed the steering wheel as I considered her. "The deepest and hottest, maybe, since she now knows the truth, said she totally believed it, then backstabbed him anyway when he showed up. I mean, what the he ?"

---

67. He prefers his natural height in all practical cases, even if feeling a need to stoop, but did sport angel wings paired with a dapper European sartorial cut to impress, though not oxford wingtips; a missed opportunity (humor and style balance his pathos).

"It's not like our church wants to forgive Lucifer," El chimed in, "even if Sun-myung did tell them true love had 'melted' his heart. Even if God himself . . ." She dropped to a doleful whisper. "Nothing but hate for the guy and he didn't even do anything."

Ayako sighed with a bit of song. "And everybody's guardian angels—especially mine!—losing their *ish* didn't help at all. Haha, no wonder she was looking crazy."

1.3 THETAHEALER GIVES US THE BUSINESS . . .

Not ThetaHealer, though. She bellied up to the bar like an industry professional, suffering none of her mother's misgivings. According to Lucifer and later El, then finally Mina, ThetaHealer could see all the angels present (most sporting wings for effect) except for Ayako's who, like the archangels, are "ancient, advanced, and ooze a regal air."[92] They once more obscured their presence to avoid giving Family ThetaHealer any inclination that Ayako was more than she seemed, though it might not have mattered. Like her mother, ThetaHealer disregarded the angels, too.

"So, what is it you want to say?" ThetaHealer said, friendly yet cautious considering her wonderment at this impromptu ensemble. She stood easy on her heels, relaxed, open, confidently in charge, and from El's vantage, inclined to listen. Props for that. Yet, her fingers gently kneaded wrists at waist level like Chinese *Baoding* balls.

"Well," I drawled, "we decided—all of us—that we can't come to the workshop but wanted to tell you in person because we were also asked to give you a message about it."

"A message? From who?" I guess she wasn't going to fight the loss of income but judging by the face drama, her slightly bored antenna sure perked up.

"Yes, hmm, well, it's like this . . ." and, in very general terms, El and I laid out our experience with Mina: the no-Fall, The Corruption, Lucifer's frame-up and his Reconciliation with Michael, the Big Healing, who God really is, and an elevator pitch framing the kernel of this book.

ThetaHealer looked round our group, and not a little incredulously, either. Who could blame her? All the same, I expected her, as a spiritualist, to give us the benefit of the doubt, if not sway test our claims on the spot since that was her shtick. In scurvy silence, Ms. Medium cast her eyes everywhere except upon her own daughter. We gradually realized she'd deleted our morning phone call from her brain log.

Her tone was chary. "*Creator* said this?"

I nodded. El said "Yes!" and with quite some nerve, too, which left me shifting on my feet. Even so, her bald confidence was comforting. This was our first sally into the public square with our revelatory experience. We were all feeling warbly, perhaps me most of all. Sure, the First Amendment shielded us, something Martin Luther and Jesus—or Joseph Smith, I suppose—would've appreciated. But my children swelled with the habitude of their youthful *dégagé* and their second-generation, scot-free, 'blessed child' status. Amongst politically complex Unificationists, that put them on equal spiritual footing with thirty-ish ThetaHealer, despite their greater youth, but a well-greased rung or two *above* her thrice older first-generation mother. It perforce left them feeling far less the pariah here than I. Ironically, Ms. Medium's family inadvertently galvanized me when, later, Ayako and then Mina clued me in they had indeed authenticated our story in real time, yet ignored it. Until then, I don't think I ever really appreciated the lengths to which people go to fool themselves.

"How are you receiving this information?" ThetaHealer continued.

"Sway testing," El declared.[68]

ThetaHealer's eyebrows hit the clouds. "Sway testing? You can't use the muscle test for that!"

"Well, we did," Ayako snapped out like gunfire.

"And it works!" El added.

I tossed my own two cents into the ring. "We've been having a shocking, unbelievable spiritual experience with it all week."

To ensure I couldn't give an encore performance of this morning's cowardly phone call, El said, "Creator wants—well, asked us to tell you—he doesn't want people charging money to teach about healing, or love, or healing. It's wrong. He doesn't like people doing it."

Well, that was diplomatic. "That's really why we can't attend the workshop," I now admitted, and to back up my outspoken daughter. "Or don't want to, I guess, because, well, we agree with Creator."

---

68. What we now call energy testing (PART V).

ThetaHealer shifted to the balls of her feet, tense, brows beetled, and poised to sway test, debunking her chastising us for doing it. I could see the boxer in her winding up. She hit me with narrowed, laser eyes and the lazy voice of authority. "It sounds more like you're connecting with a dark, negative entity instead."

Yeah, *that* shoe's on the other foot, right enough. The thing is, she couldn't just say it wasn't possible to connect to spirit people through sway testing because, for starters, that would invalidate ThetaHealing's principal modality. Sway testing is sway testing. It accurately reads spiritual energy as a yes or no (or a maybe), or it doesn't. It connects to universal Source energy of Creator of All That Is—God—and the subconscious, or it doesn't. Our reading the energy of identifiable spirit persons, including Mina and angels, was really just our advanced awareness as a variant of ThetaHealing's application.

Second, she couldn't tell us we were sway testing incorrectly. She'd not only trained us the previous weekend, but issued us certificates of competence in Basic DNA, as well. Besides, incorrect testing simply gives one a yes instead of a no or vice versa, or no response at all. It doesn't invalidate muscle testing itself.

Third, as for connecting to a negative entity instead of Creator, we relied not just on our sense of the energy, psychic imagery, sounds, touch, and other clair senses, but on logic, rationality, consistency, simplicity, and common sense to guide us. Just as ThetaHealer assumably does when connecting via the seven planes of existence to Vianna's white light she presumes is universal Source energy and the subconscious.

Plainly, she wanted to shut us down on all three counts. Our wild money-changers-in-the-temple talk certainly had to stop. What if her students were listening? They might want a refund. Perhaps she anticipated my gnarly daughters pouncing like wolf spiders if she'd tried to poo-poo our experience using any of the above. In the end, it left her with the logic of illogic. Her conundrum was real. It was only natural she'd get defensive and resort to her version of shrieking, "It's the Devil!"

I opened my mouth to reply but El—the material girl who'd said *No thanks! I have no interest in that stuff at all*—beat me to it, her voice tinged with choler. "No, we haven't connected to some dark entity! We've felt only the kindest, most loving, embracing, and positive energy. We're absolutely not talking to any sort of negative entity! That's Vianna's 'creator.'"

A little taken aback by El's furious snap back—though a tad so over-focused on El's scourging of philanthropic avarice that she'd missed her closing zinger—ThetaHealer said, "What's wrong with charging money for helping people with ThetaHealing?"

"It's not just ThetaHealing," said El. "It's everything."

"That's right," I said, "it's the problem of excluding people from understanding God or love or happiness or healing if they can't pay."

"Well, everybody charges. It's quite normal in the industry."

I said, "Yeah, it is normal, like crime is normal—"

"Funny you call healing people an 'industry,'" El slipped in.

"—but normality doesn't make something right, much less desirable."

The *snick* of an unsheathing knife in her voice, ThetaHealer said, "We aren't doing anything criminal."

"I didn't mean that how it sounded," I said. Well, maybe: $440 was a lot of dough for what Vianna's $10 book already covered. "But I ran into this same problem with Leal Brown's Luv-One healing program. If you can't pay for her book or membership, or for her retreats and workshops that go for up to a thousand bucks, she isn't helping you. You're on your own." Yeah, yeah, I know, there's YouTube and the public library; that wasn't my point. And to be fair, Leal is a caring woman who gives free teasers and sometimes scholarships the needy into her upper-middle class interventions. But the exception demonstrates the rule. It's a business.

She said, "That just proves my point. Her healing work is obviously valuable."

"I guess, if you're teaching real estate or spirit animals or car repair. Dial for dollars all you want. But you're helping people find God and love, healing and happiness. I mean, it's a human need. People are desperate. It's easy taking advantage of them. Leal's program *is* valuable, but not monetarily. That's not why, as she says, God gave it to her."

"People get what they pay for, just like anything. They're more likely to get taken advan—"

"If they can't pay they just get to suffer? Charging money's exactly why Leal can't spread her healing, why it's anemic. Imagine church door-charges, priests with a hand out over the communion plate."

She'd taken to hugging her arms. Feet apart, she needed only a Spartan shield to complete her defensive posture. This manifestly wasn't any sort of discussion. More like fighting a tuna in rough seas. Should I just put up my hands with a "well, that's all we wanted to say"? Hadn't we now done as Mina asked?

"You think churches don't charge for their so-called salvation?"

"I'm just saying, demanding money for healing discourages healing. It keeps people . . . well, it promotes exactly what it pretends it wants to fix."

She pushed out a hard "Pshaw!" and looked askance.

"I don't always charge," Ms. Medium piped up from the third tier, eyes swinging (through Lucifer) from El to me and back. "If people can't pay, I do it no charge or for a donation they can afford."

Being caught up in the moment, I didn't respond to that. But I had to hand it to her. She may harshly judge the penitent and leave the innocent scorned, lie about angels, invent fictitious spirit worlds to generate a psychic reputation and thereby customers and the admiration of her community, be sopped in Vianna's negative, life-sucking energy and besotted with her in general, and overall seep energetic 'poison' into us, but she was definitely on point with her fee-for-service flexibility. She'd only asked me to give a $20 donation for her Emotion Code healing a few months back, and I'd certainly appreciated her for it.

"How else do you help humanity," ThetaHealer challenged us, "without the money to help humanity?"

"How, exactly," I countered, "are you helping humanity when, without payment, you're not helping?"

"Answer: you're not helping," Ayako pelted out.

"I mean, you're really just selling a product you call 'help.'"

"That *helps* people," ThetaHealer said, now feeling the high ground, yet sending each squirming hand back to wringing the other's neck.

"With an absolute spiritual necessity!" El said.

"So long as they pay first," Ayako added, conjuring in my mind an image of St. Peter saying to the faultless petitioner from under his craggy brow, "Yeah, but *then* you went and . . ."

El continued, "Creator doesn't like charging money for spiritual necessities because, like Dad mentioned, it excludes people. But what it really does is *create* suffering."

"And prolongs it," Ayako said.

"But not end it," said I.

"No. That's all wrong. You can't just give food away and that's a necessity. Somebody has to grow it. Nobody gives it away for free. People have to pay for their groceries."

"That's what gardens are for," snapped Ayako.

ThetaHealer gave her a hard, pitiless glare. The energy rocketed from tense to electric. She'd segued from her *Baoding* wrist massage to folded arms and then back to a meaner hand wrangle. A nervous tic, I supposed, arriving like an attentive lawyer as soon as scrutiny said hello to her cash cow. But now I had to ask myself if I was really seeing her hands doing what I thought they were doing. In one smooth motion, she'd shifted to stridently jackhammering her index finger in and out of her other circled index finger and thumb, perversely simulating with her *manus* the timeless affront of the *digitus impudicus*.

I wasn't sure if my mouth fell open, but it felt like it as my astounded eyes dropped to her hands, back up to her face, then again to her hands. Her finger enthusiastically humped its sister now dropped from her waist, lingering squarely atop the fork in her road for the remainder of our accidental excursus. I couldn't be sure if she was doing it unconsciously in shame or maybe fury, or as a calculated retort she'd never utter in front of her mother. Fervid braziers seared Ayako then me from her impassive, tight-reined face.

Ms. Medium's trembling-bird eyes fleeted round our amoeba-shaped circle while ThetaHealer's younger brother eavesdropped from just inside the front door, expertly sway testing right along with Ayako and his slower sister who seemed stung Ayako sway tested more responsively than she.

1.3.1 AYAKO OPINES ON THETAHEALER . . .

"Honestly," Ayako said later, "she was so tight."

"According to Mina, she really was consciously sway testing everything we said and coming up with the same results," I said.

"Told you."

I could only shake my head at sway testing speed as a contention. Maybe it was same-dress syndrome, or just plain old competitiveness. I didn't know, but marveled it lent all the more *oomph* to our controversy.

Mina later told us ThetaHealer's brother—spiritually more aware than she—instinctively knew our message was true even without sway testing it, but had elected to remain quiet to not rock the family boat in which he still dwelled, proving yet again that pragmatism usually trumps verity. But I could appreciate he didn't need any extra domestic squabbles. In any case, I didn't want the accusation I'd fomented any laid at my feet like some decapitated horse head beneath my sheets.

1.4 ThetaHealer Takes On Mina's Message . . .

"It's not wrong to charge people money for my services," ThetaHealer was saying. "I had to pay for my training—"

"We're not the ones to convince," I said, glancing at the girls. "We're not trying to put you on the spot anyhow. I totally understand where you're coming from. It's all very surprising and unexpected for us, too. We just thought you'd want to hear Creator's message—since, you know, you teach about him and all."

"And we agree, too. With his message, I mean," said El.

"I don't set the price anyway. That's Vianna, she requires we charge for the workshop. I have no control over—"

"It *is* wrong to charge money, though," Ayako cut in, "because you're denying people healing, denying them what they were born to, which is their birthright from God. You don't think that's wrong?"

"That's stupid. Money is just—"

"It's not stupid!" That was the wrong word and set Ayako aflame. She was acutely edgy, I thought. She could throw a pout with the best of them but at home, in her *sanctum sanctorum*. I supposed it could've been the tensity of our extraordinary week. Or maybe she was feeling Michael's iconic sword waving alarmingly about. ThetaHealer might've simply represented something Ayako despised. "It's just wrong to charge money for healing, including *how* to be healed. Is it stupid to demand honesty just because everybody lies?"

"I. Don't. Lie."

"I'm just saying. Payment to heal is like denying people a right to life. That's—"

"What?! No one's—"

"—Creator's attitude."

"—denied any right to life just because they pay for training."

"You just said people have to pay for groceries. So if they can't pay, they can't eat. Isn't that denying them a right to life?"

"That's—"

"But isn't it the same principle?"

I mumbled, "I guess gardening's looking less irrelevant right about now."

"Plus, people are paying for something—like healing—they can easily do themselves." Ayako pointedly glanced Ms. Medium's way. "The fact you charge for that without telling them they can do it *is* deceitful."

Ms. Medium either didn't catch that, or chose the no-reply option. Possibly, she'd closed her senses to Ayako, too. But ThetaHealer bristled. "I'm not deceiving anybody, Ayako, and neither is Vianna." Her eyes set upon her unhelpful mother. "In any case, people can't heal themselves if they aren't shown how."

"Exactly," Ayako said. "Creator's original point."

ThetaHealer paused on the finger sex to spread her hands in triumph. "So, then, training people is the only way to better the world."

"You're trying to make a better world but you charge money for it?" Ayako snickered. "You're kidding."

I thought, *Bloody hell, these girls are a couple of snapping turtles!* Was I proud or aghast? I couldn't decide. I pondered how Mina was taking our performance. Was he egging us on or face palming? Were we giving him a bad rep or planting his flag? Was ThetaHealer's response a foregone conclusion and Ayako's mini-tirade merely her pushing a Sisyphean boulder up ThetaHealer's unwilling hill? Or, like sound resonance, would our effort only later reach the 'shatter frequency' of her mindset's formidable crags? I couldn't answer any of these riddles and tied a mental string to my finger to find out later.[93]

"I have to pay my expenses to fly here and pay for my needs, to have my life."

"You don't charge your mom or your brother," Ayako said, "so you're obviously okay with free healing and free workshops in principle."

"So long as it's for the right people," said El with a whiff of Groucho Marx.

ThetaHealer had a spastic, high-strung head wag going cycling to Ayako's pontificating, but now cocked it puppy-like to one side. Congenial, she said to the girls, "You're both young. You don't understand everybody has to make a living regardless the field they choose. I chose to make my living helping people. What have you chosen to do?"

"That just means you chose to make a living off other people's suffering, like a vampire," said Ayako. "Get another job and volunteer for this instead of making excuse after excuse to justify yourself."

If ThetaHealer was softening, Ayako had just stiffened her spine. Her fingers leapt back into coitus and frantically banged away. Heck, they'd shifted into overdrive with Ayako's stinging slap. I'm sure thirtyish ThetaHealer didn't appreciate their young adult effrontery.

I had to admit—with a certain, perhaps shameful? glee—that these young ladies of mine could hold their own. I wasn't too sure about myself, though. I was white hot over ThetaHealer's rank hand gesture, but restrained a caustic mouth from provoking worse. We were only here delivering a simple message anyway— from God, *yeah*, but not as judge and jury. It sure wasn't our place to assault anyone's freedom. And anyway, didn't such Accountableism doom everything Mina held dear?

My legs trembled. Whether from anger, stress, the spiritual energy surging around and through us, disgusted angels, the 64-degree temps, or some combination of it all was hard to say. I could barely keep my feet. I was feeling how Ayako looked.

El caught me with a worried eye, wondering if my fear of ThetaHealer's aggression was getting the best of me—the way my kids felt I'd often placated domestic violence—and could maybe leave them fending for themselves. I'd noticed a wood-slatted porch chair behind me and now scuttled over to it. Perched on its unyielding seat edge, my outstretched legs jumped under my skin with a frenetic will of their own.

Lucifer later chuckled, *Nah, you weren't shaking from any spiritual energy.* Yeah, I was probably just fuming. Conflict averse too, maybe, so laugh-back, buddy.

To me, ThetaHealer said, "You said this comes from Creator?"

"Yes," El answered for me. "It hurts him seeing—"

"Hurts? Well, that's your clue right there you're not talking to the Creator of All That Is. He doesn't have feelings. He's not a *person*."

I blinked. "He's not a—?"

"He *is* a person!" said El, riled once more. I vaguely advised myself we might be unwisely entering the shouting phase, but wasn't really listening. I wondered if we three might've bonded with Mina more than your average 'revealee' bonds with their revelator. "He feels more deeply than any of us."

"No. Creator is just an energy source in the universe. *The* universal energy. Source energy."

Ayako stiffened, astonished. El hugged herself against the onslaught of tumultuous, indignant angelic energy battering her from all quarters. Ms. Medium had raised ThetaHealer in a Moonie household, and Moonies are thoroughly wedded to a God of personhood who embodies a personality of unconditional love. We thought it bizarre she'd convert her childhood's parental God of love into a wall outlet. Then again, maybe in her household that God had got locked out. But to chalk up *our* spiritual experience to the manipulations of a negative entity because we broke the sway testing rulebook of *her* ThetaHealing practice? Okay, fine, let's be honest. We were challenging her business model along with her ethics and altruism. Who'd take that lying down?

"What kind of God is that?" I wondered aloud.

She said, "God is only here to serve people. He has no agenda, like religion or money. He's just an energy being, not a sentient person." Those ideas seemed primitive to us, a throwback to, I don't know, animism or shamanism, or something Neanderthal if not *Homo heidelbergensis*. She continued, "It's a dark entity you're connecting to, not Creator."

"We've felt Creator's love and his feelings," El said, "even *heard* them. He's told us how he feels!"

"And none of it is dark," pronounced Ayako.

"There *is* no God like you're talking about," ThetaHealer said. "Creator has no personality, no love, no feelings at all. Whoever you're talking to isn't a Being of Light."

That sounded to me as irrational as an abuser crying their love while droppin' a whuppin.' Why not sway test it right now, I was thinking. Didn't she want to know? Was she afraid of the answer? Lack of curiosity is a mortal sin in my book. If sin was real, I mean. Which it isn't.

My children's faces reflected how appalling ThetaHealer sounded. I glanced at Ms. Medium for a reaction to her daughter's most un-Moonie belief system, but she wasn't coming down from the cheap seats. Maybe it was a long-lost argument at home. El edged nearer me as tears overflowed her lashes, which seemed a little over the top. I didn't realize that, after five days, she was approaching emotional overload.

It wasn't only El or us feeling this way. Our crew of disgusted angels, who mindfully prized today's Big Event and their stake in our effort, were boiling over. My children vibrated to their truculent energy like antennas in a high-wattage ether. And all the while, ThetaHealer's half-bent finger slithered in and out, in and out, all but touching her sex appeal. *Fuck. You.*

Ayako and El were oblivious to the finger action, but not to the energy. I watched El losing it and caught up to my own advice. It was time to cinch this conversation down. Michael, firm alongside Ayako—"the two level-headed ones," she later japed—beamed "a death stare" at her guardian angels now out from their 'bush' and raucously fomenting a verbal beat-down of ThetaHealer's own, who'd paraded their discomfort with their charge's attitude yet, nevertheless, had her back per their commitment. Gabriel now quietly parked himself on my right without flair, limiting himself to *Observing with Gravitas* to try curbing some of this angelic ardor.[69] Ours own, too, perchance. Ms. Medium seemed to wither under the spiritual tension what with "Michael's hard, knowing glare," in Ayako's words, lighting her up and Lucifer's slighted energy pulsing at her side.

"Do you have any shamans in your family?" ThetaHealer inquired with a fair dose of scorn. I guess she wasn't ready to quit.

"You mean dark arts people," I mused, "like witches, or whatever?" But she'd focused herself on Ayako.

"No!" belched Ayako. "We have nothing to do with shamanism!"

"Isn't that Vianna and her husband's thing?" said El, her voice quaky.

ThetaHealer glared, but her voice held steady. "It's most likely a malevolent spirit at work here. That's who's telling you all this."

"Why would a malevolent spirit even care about charging money?" I said, and wondered if her pounding finger wasn't itself operated by one even now spurning Mina's Big Healing.

"Seems it'd want people charging even more money if it's really malevolent," Ayako cracked, wordfully slicing yet another *Z-for-Zorro* segment across ThetaHealer's knurled forehead.

Her cheeks flushed with our message—or delivery, if we're being fair—stacked over and above Ayako's superior sway testing caliber. She'd only think a thought and move with verve whereas ThetaHealer had to wait for a demonstrably weaker push. Well, in truth, I couldn't blame ThetaHealer for that. El and I felt a similar frustration at home, wishing Ayako's energism energized us, too.

ThetaHealer did know our message was valid. She couldn't help her trained, sensitive medium's body moving to Mina—apparently not so busy healing he couldn't pay attention to this nicely hosed quagmire—responding to her thoughts and feelings with the same answers Ayako sway tested. Being a sway test practitioner, ThetaHealer could hardly discount a *no*-push when she told herself charging money to heal was okay, or that her creator was nothing more than a universal Energizer bunny. Rather than accept this revelation, she ignored it to discredit the message. This whole conversation devolved into an exercise in futility as she rationalized contradicting her own sway testing experience.

1.4.1 Ayako Recalls Thetahealer's Scrutiny . . .

"She was so mad!" Ayako recalled as we later staggered home. I'd noticed very little of this covert catfight at the time, but Ayako had scrutinized ThetaHealer's body with gator eyes. "She knew all my sway testing was right on, Dad. She couldn't help but test the same as me, so she knew Creator was telling her the same thing!" She chortled. "Talk about stubborn."

1.5 Our Confab Winds Down . . .

Right now, though, ThetaHealer looked to be wondering how Ayako could be so expertly, if not masterly, sway testing as good as her little brother with his thousands of hours of experience. Hadn't Ayako attended her Basic DNA workshop only the previous weekend and only just learned the technique? It was a sensible supposition. Who'd pay $440 to learn what they already knew? She recognized Ayako's psychic ability, but didn't know how experienced an empath, psychic, and medium she was, having practiced a wide variety of spiritual disciplines, including astral projection, and capable in degrees of all eight clair senses. Her sister and I are comparatively novices, one reason Mina asked her to take on Michael's role of Teacher in our wee threesome.[70] In certain key areas, she's dramatically more advanced than ThetaHealer and Ms. Medium. Certainly, more a medium than either had taken her for.

"Look," I said, "I appreciate your situation. We only came up to tell you what we've learned from Creator. Obviously it's up to you to—"

---

69. Freedom means there's no command authority to exert dominance. This is their norm.

70. For our group in these early days, Mina had asked El to take on Gabriel's Messenger role and me, Lucifer's Mediator role. She'd been a good messenger today, aye, but I'd felt no mediating skills at all.

"You can do what you want. I'm going to charge money, regardless." She looked around, then across her right shoulder at the house. "I have students waiting." She didn't have to say *who've paid*, but that came through loud and clear. "Thanks for coming."

"Sure. Thanks for listening." I was now satisfied a phone call was a poor substitute for this face-to-face, however sideways it went.

El, her posture slumped, turned for the Prius as ThetaHealer disappeared into the house. Ms. Medium reached out an unsure hand. She said, "Are you okay, El? What's wrong?"

El's frazzled mind raced. *Are you kidding? You're asking that* now? *As soon as your daughter walks away, you break your vow of silence after telling us this morning you believed our every word? We thought you'd have our back.*

Ms. Medium shuffled forward to hug her, but Lucifer bodily blocked her so they couldn't touch. He was too in a boil himself to follow up his request to Ayako (who hadn't forgot) to ask Ms. Medium to talk with him when we'd finished. He gave it a go some days later, but all he managed was some shouting with her spirit self before abruptly turning on his stylish heel. They did later talk while she was awake, but she turned hard-hearted Barb'ry Allen's ear to him.[94] He 'portaled' away dejected by her shard-studded 'heart wall' not yet realizing, he surprised me by saying, that she wasn't actually hearing his words.

Lucifer spiritually took El in his arms, a towering nine-foot comforter El physically felt as she visibly trembled and wept. My physical arm wound round her and I pulled her into my chest. If Ms. Medium seemed overpowered by the furious energies, El was staggered. Ayako was already spent when we'd started but had nonetheless stood-to like a soldier.

The least spiritually aware of them all, I could almost appreciate Ms. Medium's query to El because, outwardly, our ten-minute conversation sounded benign. To the ear, no one's tone rose to lead a bystander to presume anyone was hot under the collar. Just folks conversing with a few jabs and barbs. It was under the hood and out of sight that our dust up's real engine roared, fumed, belched, and shuddered like some unholy Monster Truck. Ms. Medium had closed her spirit senses and cut herself out of most of the real action. In our debriefing while driving home, the girls gave me a finer appreciation for the subtext and undercurrents that were at play, and for what they'd just gone through on a level I'd noticed only in my trembling legs, intuitive leaps, disturbed vibes, and the cold mercury oozing through my skin.

1.5.1 Our Convalescent Thoughts . . .

Ostensibly, our meeting was to see about pulling Ms. Medium and ThetaHealer—spiritually powerful mediums and sway testers fully capable of all we were doing and vastly more—up from their crude, money-grubbing, toxic energy bath. Whatever Mina thinks of their attitudes, he feels no judgment or rejection for them. That's a truth worth accentuating. It harkens back to Catholicism's bromide to hate the sin but love the sinner except without the sin, or the hate. We're free to be free, but one isn't free when judged, rejected, and penalized by the freedom-giver for exercising it.

Regardless, our effort's fuller purpose lay in Mina hoping the three of us could publicly stand behind this story of life and leave the safety of our home to carry its illumination to others. We'd demonstrated the mojo to step up to the plate and swing the bat on humanity's birthright. Timorously running the bases would only make it an easy out, so we ran hard.

Once stuck in, Gabriel and Michael had encouraged our Angel Code meetings with stories to gauge Ms. Medium's reliability because, well, they didn't know. However unlikely, ThetaHealer One or Two or both could've embraced our message because breaching the NCC paved the way for the Big Healing and its irrevocable change of spirit world. As tough as it might be, Mina wanted us to publicize it and me to drop my prized book project for which I was well versed to write this iffy, obscure, serpentine, and possibly unwelcome account. Then, before my eyes could even roll up dollar signs, he'd nixed any remuneration and I'd thought, *ah, nuts!* And the Family ThetaHealing had now served as a barometer for all of it.

With a small sense of kismet, it seemed things had now come full circle since our Basic DNA beginnings last Friday. We'd built our own destiny now, hewing to our curiosity and honoring Mina's request to bring opportunity to Ms. Medium and her family. Given our personalities, could or would we have done it any different? It's hard to say.

Mina, too, is of a mind we'd eventually have stumbled across energy testing spirit people on our own. Ayako, anyway. To my way of thinking, the resonance between the three of us is what harvested this morning's spectacular results. I'd singly fumbled all that away in my half-assed muscle testing explorations a couple years earlier when I'd failed to make the leap from testing my 'subconscious' to testing its originator, which was already obvious—if unnoticed—in Divine Principle. Together, we'd fertilized each of our strengths, inquisitiveness, and willingness to transcend the obtuse physical for the esoteric spiritual as an objective reality we could show and tell. This is where I think free will and fate tend to get all mixed up.

1.6 DECAMPING WITH HEAVY HEARTS ...

With ThetaHealer departed and Lucifer holding Ms. Medium at bay, we said our farewells. I said to Ms. Medium, "El's okay, just super tired and feeling overwhelmed."

"I'll talk with you later, then," she said, hovering behind a weak smile on the far side of Lucifer.

Not if we see you first, we all cautioned ourselves.

Honestly, I was feeling supremely disappointed with Ms. Medium at this point. My children now exuded the sort of affection for her that Americans reserve for Nazi doctors—or monkey brains, maybe. Their inclination for another conversation with her floated drowned in the deep end. Foremost in our minds was our experience being sickened from her negative energy, and the way it had clung to us to wreck our foodstuffs a hundred miles away.₉₅ To whom else had we unwittingly carried it?

"You don't hang around a nuclear pile without a rad suit, do you?" I later explained to a less-than credulous Moth Man. "Keeping our distance from her seems the only healthy choice."

"Better you than me," he said. Alas.

Revival Ride

Friday October 13, 2017 ca. 6 PM

E PLOPPED INTO the Prius and burbled backward down the driveway. Ms. Medium fruitlessly waved us on our way. I waved a polite hand and thumbed the knee-banger gear selector over to Drive and motored away. A collective sigh of relief swarmed the cabin. It hadn't even been that long of a conversation yet zonked us like a daylong broadsword battle in heavy armor on the boot-sucking moors.

"Well, that's done," I said. "I hope Pro—"

"Thank God!" Ayako doubled over then pitched against her seatback. "That was just too much!"

Seated right behind me, El burst into full-blown hysterics. Tears streamed down her face onto her shirt. I wanted to stop and hold her, but she babbled Lucifer was doing that.

"Well, jeez, but . . . okay," I drawled, like I'd just been sacked.

"*God*, my chest hurts *really* badly," she sobbed. "I can hardly breathe. Nothing works."

Tears welled in my eyes. In my own chest detonated a kinder, gentler brand of Michael's earlier Angel Code EMP. I figured she'd built up a bunker load of emotional energy by now and it sorely needed venting. What's more efficacious than crying? I dropped the window for a cool breeze and hoped it soothed El, too. Ayako pulled some napkins from the glove box and passed them back to her sister whose grateful, sloppy-wet eyes registered their bonded love.

Ayako resettled herself, and said, "Lucifer's *so* angry."

I glanced her way. "With ThetaHealer?"

"Ms. Medium. I mean, he's pretty unhappy with ThetaHealer, the way she's teaching people her junk that Protector—how we now addressed him since last night—is basically nobody, a thing."

"So weird," I said. "Not even a person, much less your traditional deity. He's ticked because she's misrepresenting him, but knows better?"

She did some quick hand tests. "Yes. But he's really furious with Ms. Medium"—another pause to test—"and he says she doesn't know any better about Protector and stuff, but she should. She's capable of knowing the truth."

"Mad, like Michael?"

"No, Michael's not angry. He's just really sorrowful—as usual." She cheeped a laugh. "He has a very calm spirit, overall. That's how I feel him when he shows up."

I nodded along as I drove, thinking he wasn't too calmly sorrowful with Ms. Medium at our EMP'd Angel Code session. His outrage had boomed through my girls' heads like the world's biggest gong. I guess everybody has their limits.

"But Lucifer was practically raging back there," Ayako continued.

"Raging? That's not doing his rep any—"

"You know what I mean, Dad. Ms. Medium knew he was there. She tuned him out, ignored him, and she let Michael just stew. I mean, all she had to do was recognize him there and give him an 'I'm sorry' look, or a thought, or just something, and they'd be fine with that."

"I was shaking like a leaf," I said, "like all that fiery energy was running through me. Felt like being low-voltage electrocuted."

"Low voltage? Ha! The angels were ready to start a big fight! Mine were practically out of control." She chuckled.

"I thought yours were this ancient, wise, married couple who never lost their cool, even hung on in The Fracas like troopers."

"Didn't I tell you I got new ones? My originals were spending too much time away calming spirit world after the fight. Anyway, they couldn't stop picking their own fight with ThetaHealer's guardian angels . . . saying things like, 'How can you let her talk like that?' and 'Why are you sticking with her?' and 'Can't you even deal with her?' And then her angels got furious, too!"

"With your angels? It's not like they weren't being pretty provoca—"

"With ThetaHealer!" She bounced her skull off the headrest. "Oh-em-*gee*! With my guardian angels, too, yeah. With everybody." She gave me a cool, twinkly, self-conscious eye. "They were feeling pretty attacked, Dad."

"I bet!" I rested my own noggin on the headrest and rocked it gently to and fro as a comfort, eyeing the slightly unfocused road from beneath the rim of my eyeglasses. A smirk played along my lips at the image of all these fulminous angels versus their traditional sagacity . . . screwy all in itself, considering the monotheisms teach a third of the angels launched a civil war against God, the other two-thirds literally beat them into the dirt, then iced their cake with prodigious odium. More and more, the ancient Greeks and Hindus were looking pretty keyed-in to the lifestyles of the divine and celestial.

"Michael spent his time trying to defuse all that"—incredulity marked her face—"but everybody's angels were in an uproar. It was like a giant schoolyard riot!"

Lucifer's opinion and all that, I'm certain I was trembling from all that wild energy more than dread. I've never quaked like that before. Maybe in a real fight, I suppose. Ayako was an old hand with spiritual chaos. El and I were greenhorns riding hell for leather into a whole new, unimagined, mind-bending reality. So much still made so little sense to us. The reality of spirit world mixing it up with the physical one hit like a visceral one-two bowling ball to the chin. We needed a minute to catch ourselves, thank you. It might've all been obvious to my religious faith, but I'd never noticed with adequate thoughtfulness to make a difference. Ayako's inner coolness under this sort of fire was a blessing it took me some time to appreciate, I guess because, at her age, I mostly incurred her outer snark.

"So much uproar just over attitude?" I said. "Seems kind of excessive."

"Dad, angels are *intense*. They feel on a whole different level. They know how people are. We don't usually get under their skin. But when somebody for sure knows what's going on spiritually, then twists it all around anyway—especially for money!—that really gets them hot. Think about it. How would you feel?"

"A lot like the people I bet Michael's running into right about now on his ninth-step rounds."

"Come on, now, leave him alone."

"Okay . . . so, maybe they were feeling how The Corruption grabbed 'em, if they ever think back on it."

"Why wouldn't they?" She felt no need to test that but did anyhow, pronouncing, "Of course they think about it."

"Alright, don't get all protective on me. Protector said they knew better, but went with it all the same and never even asked him for answers, all I'm saying."

"Um . . ."—test, test—"yeah. Especially now, it's all so insulting with the whole Reconciliation and healing that's going on."

"Like turning Protector into some faceless gnome," I griped.

"Like lying about the truth!" she said, still a little hot there, herself. "She sway tested my same answers over and over, but denied it all. *Lied* about it. I watched her! Is she a sway tester or not? Is sway testing real or not? She teaches it. She uses it to make money. But when it contradicts what she wants, she ignores it. Then she teaches all those lies to people who don't know any better . . ."

I sniggered. "But pay through the nose for it."

"Yeah! It's *just* like The Corruption."

From the back seat, a somewhat composed El growled through tears, "That makes *any* normal person mad, Dad!"

With that, she launched into 'fighting up' Ms. Medium ex post facto with Ayako helping to process her feelings. While they went hammer and tongs at ThetaHealer One and Two, I realized I needed to decompress a beat, myself. We'd lunched about six hours ago, but it seemed like days. We were starving dogs. It occurred to me to drop by Moth Man's not-too-distant castle to enjoy some welcoming company for a change. He was always up for the sort of woo-woo we were sitting on. Fancied himself its persecuted king in the local Unification Church. He'd gobble this stuff right up. I took a minute to jink off the roadway for a quick Google Maps consult, then navigated to Moth Man's while, backseat, El—Ayako frequently twisting round during our review to engage her little sister—worked at winding herself down, interjecting less emotional and more thoughtful counterarguments to the Family ThetaHealers' perspective.

1.1   VISITING MY FRIEND MOTH MAN . . .

The girls weren't too hip for a rest stop at Moth Man's, but they graciously gave their dad his due. Besides, they were hungry and Moth Man always stocked snacks galore. Sometimes his kitchen looks to us like a hole-in-the-wall corner store. They hung out quietly in his living room with one of his same-age sons sharing chips, dips, drinks, and happy talk. Trotting along behind my spiritual kin in his quest to complete his honey-do tasks, I spilled some of our story of Mina and ThetaHealer. Disappointment hit a little hard that he didn't seem to catch much of it. In awe, I realized our woo-woo was too strong even for the master.

He said, "Angry angels? Lucifer framed, you say? God prefers we call him *Protector*? And he's got a freakin' *wife*?" His perplexity read like a tachometer in the red zone. It was all far outside even his open-door gonzo box. Spirit animals and Unificationism's take-no-prisoners imperative to Restore The World at any cost pretty much pussy-whipped his day-to-day worldview into an eyes-down approach to life. Ms. Medium was his fellow traveler. I trod that thorny path only on tippy toes.

1.1.1   AYAKO AND EL OPINE ON MOTH MAN . . .

Ayako and El later had the same take. "Dad, he probably thinks you're just another Moonie psycho."

"Except I'm not a Moonie," I protested. "Not really, not anymore." Not by most members' definition anyway, most of all Moth Man's.

"Once a Moonie psycho," said El, "always a Moo—"

"Whatever." We did show up for church a few times a month, mostly as a social call for the girls and their previous Maryland school chums. I looked forward to those visits like a parolee from the hermitage, ditching church and its insipid pastoral henpecking to pace the block talking Real God with Moth Man. Our 100-mile gesture just to get there was enough in their convert-hungry minds to see us all in the family who'd hopefully tithe though, in all honesty, they really saw us more the inbred cousins preferably bolted in the cellar when company called. "I think I'm now more a Sunnie than a Moonie," I added.[96]

"They're not going to like you any better, Dad," El said with wisdom beyond my years.

1.2   MOTH MAN PRONOUNCES SENTENCE . . .

Moth Man at last gave his predicted assessment: "You're officially crazier than I am, buddy."

"That's crazier than I want to be."

"They're gonna excommunicate you, brother."

I let go a belly laugh. "Like they haven't done that how many times already? Who cares, mate." Hasn't it been since the Renaissance that rogue Christians have snarled in religion's face, 'O, Excommunication, where is thy sting?'[97] Bring it on, ye posers!

He seemed dubious of my breezy dismissal of people appropriating the wrath of God. "I'm talking the world, here, bro. You better be careful who you piss off."

"All things considered, I'm not sure how I'd go about doing that."

What we did do was head over to Boston Market in Riverdale, Maryland. We took a booth in the windowed corner with our chicken and vittles and Moth Man largely deflected my glad tidings of Mina. *Propheting 101*, I sourly groused.

He said, "What you really need is a marketing team."

"That's what the book's for."

"Yeah, but how're you gonna get the book in front of people?"

Well, he had me there. I leaned back. "I couldn't pay them, anyway. The book has to be free."

"Whaaa—?" He just stared at the crazy guy.

"I'm gonna need a sugar daddy."

"Or three!" El spluttered through a buttery corncob.

Moth Man drummed a finger ditty on the tabletop. A self-published author of little renown himself (*Drink Your Own Water: A Treatise on Urine Therapy* his best seller), he did know a thing or two of the publishing challenge I faced. He said, "Yeah, okay . . . you can work with that. Ebooks don't really cost anything once you set them up. Self publishing, eh? You can get it out to everybo—what?"

"Ahh . . ." I sounded pretty lame even to myself. "Protector doesn't really dig electronics. He wants a print book only."

His head was nodding, but his forehead and Sicilian brows clawed heavenward, glazed eyeballs trying to follow but anchored to their sockets. His disbelief challenged each of my girls in turn.

Ayako said, "It has to do with energy fields and electronics radiation. Hurts the body, but really it closes your third-eye chakra."

"It does?"

"Yeah," she said agreeably. "If you're reading it as an ebook, then you're getting the opposite of what you want, because you want your third-eye open so you can sway test and intuit, or just be more spiritually aware in general."

He swung back to me with a chuckle while his head wagged no. "Print only? You're gonna need to marry Crœsus, buddy."

Everybody's a comedian. I said, "Maybe I can change his mind."[71]

"There's that. Lot managed it in the Bible."

"And it went so well for him. Thanks."

Dismissing my publishing parameters, Moth Man turned to regaling the girls with spirit animals, pronouncing Ayako's the eagle and El's the praying mantis. Ayako munched her chicken with the couldn't-care-less of the dead. El picked up on the mantis with a certain satisfaction that twitched up the corners of my mouth. Some while back, he'd introduced me to mine: the hawk. Apropos it was, too, as I'd grown up in the Rockies soaring in my imagination high on thermals and winging through clouds, though I'd seen myself more a majestically screamin' bald eagle than a puny, squawking hawk. I did hear they're smarter, so there's that. Funnily enough, Moth Man gets his spirit animal dope through muscle testing what he also calls universal Source energy. That made him a kindred spirit of sorts—I know, not unlike Ms. Medium and her family—but that's where we parted.

The girls were only half listening. They looked and felt washed out, utterly depleted and discharged like my dad-gutted Prius battery back in 2016 (EN 51:648). Finishing with dinner, their hollowed-out faces said, "Just get us home to our beds, Dad. *Puh-leeze.*"

Right. *Ugh.* Another hundred-mile drive. I wasn't feeling too spirited, myself. But when the going gets tough, aren't even—especially!—faulty dads supposed to get going?

1.3 OUR RIDE HOME TAKES A DETOUR . . .

Except for Interstate 95's eternal stop-and-go pileup through northern Virginia's Woodbridge–Occoquan traffic disrupter where The Road of Good Intentions corsets five lanes of traffic into three with an on-ramp and incline thrown in for the challenge, we flowed south relatively freely now the evening rush hour had played out. Our car talk resumed its new-normal tenor as the girls, energized by their victuals and sense of safety in the family car, on and off engaged Taiji, Hidé, Helen, *Obāsan*, and others. Hidé and Taiji pointedly lightened the conversation to ease everyone's feelings. They're considerate that way.

At one point, I turned the discussion to Mother to find out how she'd produced her children and noted, "By the way, that's a lot of kids you had! What about their father? Same guy?"

That detour took us into one of those BIG NEWS moments I mentioned earlier, which got the spirit denizens of our car clamoring, pulling in Jesus, Sun-myung, and others we never identified.

Then Ayako sensed someone besides the usual crowd fielding her questions. After some investigation, it turned out ThetaHealer's guardian angels—both of them—had been apologizing to our guardian angels and

---

71. Well, he did anyhow. In 2019, he accepted an ebook so long as we included a disclaimer about chakras.

everyone concerned for ThetaHealer's attitude and their own part in the earlier fray for a good forty minutes or so before we clued to their presence.

"But wait," I said, "aren't one of you supposed to be with your 'guardee' at all times?"

Yes.

"Then what're you both doing here, and for so long? You jailbreaking? Heh-heh."

Pause.

Ayako grinned. "Not getting an answer to that one, Dad . . . Wait. You don't want to go back?"

No.

"Let me get this straight," I said. "I was just joking but . . . you don't want to be her guardian angels anymore?"

Pause. I imagined them turning their faces toward each other, maybe sheepishly checking out all our guardian angels. *No.*

"*Boiii!*" squalled Ayako. "That sure created a shh—shtuff storm with the other angels!" After a minute, she added with a flash of teeth, "My angels chased them back to their job. Ha-ha! My new ones are ancient too, Dad, top of the line. You don't mess with *them.*"

"They were fighting?" I said.

"No, no, no. They just lectured them how they can't be away so long. It's very bad."

"They'll get in trouble, then?"

She said, "That's not their reality. Nobody forces anybody."

"Unless you're some sad sack in the darker levels," I said, my thoughts running to Helen. "Before the Big Healing clears them all out, I guess." We still expected another six days for that job.

1.3.1 SIDE TRIP: OUR DISCOVERY OF COSMO . . .

Speaking of guardian angels, some days later Ayako and I were chewing the spiritual fat in her bedroom with "the squad," as the girls were now wont to call our happy and growing covey of spirit folk which, for the moment, included Lucifer as CEO and chief bottle washer of Guardian Angels, Inc., or whatever. I was availing myself of Ayako's superior spiritual awareness, energism, and Teacher status among us. That means I was having her energy test for me. She lay stretched out lazily on her bed with her nose to the iPhone. I'd squeezed myself into the narrow strip of carpeted floor between her bed, stacks of laundry, musical instruments, and the closet. She'd picked the smallest room when we'd moved in, and small is being generous. It had a private half-bath half the bedroom's size that she'd seen as the perfect trade off. El's usual YouTube on the 70-inch flat-screen in the main room was entertaining her, but she leapt up with Mother's general burst of *yes* energy to my asking if she was a created being like Mina. Until then, see, we'd been imagining Mother as the *über* 'deity' of the multiverse, and it wasn't lost on me how *that* theological reversal would energize the when-God-created-Man-She-was-only-kidding crowd.

Ayako sat bolt upright and said, "Oh-em-gee, Dad, the room's filling up with everybody! Sun-myung and Jesus are bouncing off the walls. I can feel people all over my bed!"

One of our bigger BIG NEWS moments. I often wondered how it was that, according to Mina, such titans as Jesus and curiosity hounds like Sun-myung or axial thinkers like Zoroaster or Plato or Marx, or just anybody, hadn't already asked many of the questions we were now pulling out of our collective hat. I supposed I could sort of see it. None of us imagined *this* question till our spontaneous conversation had sparked it just now. Yet, hadn't it been oh-so-obvious ever since we learned of Mina's mother? New concepts, like bread dough, just need time to rise. What we've learned of Mina and the universe falls so far outside our traditional thought matrix that follow-on query B to revelation A is very often less than self-evident until it is self-evident. But one needs to care and be curious, too. If you don't want to hunt, what is it you're going to catch? Besides, while angels already figured they knew all there was, Mina said a lot of these big-name doers and thinkers in life lost all their dash and wonder in spirit world because most of their existential angst resolved itself with death. What hangs on is swamped by how much more there is across the briny void to engage one's mind. And, too, people don't easily shed ingrained concepts. My dad and mom (d. 2018), for example, said they don't really talk to Mina themselves because they haven't shook off their grisly Catholic indoctrination even as they listen in on our conversations with him.

El flung open Ayako's door and smoked to a stop by her bed while I was trying to get a name for Mother's creator but missing the tendril. I bandied about such (not always serious) pseudonyms as Morpheus (*NO!*), Cosmos (*No*), Universe (*Hmm . . .*), Big Daddy (*Oh, please*), Optimus Prime, (*Absolutely not*).

Full of hope casting back to when she'd met Mother, El said, "Can we meet him, Mother?"

No.

Her face fell into a moue. "Can I call him Mr. Universe?"

I barked an inadvertent "Haw!" at that steroidal image.

No.

Well, rats. What *were* we going to call him?

"He's an introvert, Dad," Ayako said, hand testing on the bed. "He created everything from the start[72] and just travels universe to universe checking everything out, seeing how everybody's doing, enjoying the life, and being Mr. Anonymous."

"Talk about behind the scenes," I said, with grumpy air quotes. But even I wouldn't have suggested calling him Mr. Anonymous. I was partial to Mr. Universe.

"He doesn't want to be known. He doesn't want to be *worshipped*," she added.

Ah, yes, the danger one never seems to escape when it comes to people. Ayako tested that he has no prior creator.[73] *Yeah, but what'll we find out* tomorrow? I dubiously asked myself because, so far, this train had no brakes.

"He doesn't want to talk to us?" El said to Mother.

Ayako hand tested. "He's just not ready yet, El. He'll let us know."

"So the buck stops with him?" I said.

Yes.

"He created the very first universe all the others are patterned off of?

Yes.

"And he is, as they say, timeless? Always existed?"

Maybe . . . yes.

I gasped. Ayako looked at me. "You don't know?"

No. Not exactly.

Perplexed faces all around but Jesus and Sun-myung were feeling charged up and maybe on the job, though that didn't help us. I gave a nod to disgruntlement that those two might use my brainstorm to springboard to a lot of awesome knowledge from Mina that I was dying to know (well, not *that* dying to know) with their Johnny-on-the-spot option. Boy, was I pining for clairvoyance. All I had in my toolbox was what I could think up to test and the intuition that helped it along. It's a lot, don't get me wrong, but you have to exercise it like a racehorse to muscle it up to contender status. And dang it, all that my brilliant insight had effectively accomplished was to find Creator Prime two degrees removed from where humanity always thought he was with all the same unanswered questions[74] and on walkabout.

"Philosophers are gonna laugh," I half-joked.

"Quit worrying about reactions, Dad," said my homegrown therapist.

"Easy for you to say, El, you're not doing the book. Did you ever ask him this stuff, Protector?"

Maybe . . . no.

"Seriously."

Yes.

"Because you didn't care?"

No.

"Then because . . . uhh . . ."—waiting for intuition to strike—"you already knew what you needed or wanted to know, so it wasn't pressing? I mean, um, you didn't *need* to know, so you never thought about it? Am I right?"

Yes.

Far be it for me to say, but isn't that the definition of complacence? "You gonna ask him about it now?"

Ayako felt him laughing through the energy of his reply. *Yes.*

"Because you're suddenly curious?"

Yes.

Wow. We'd piqued his interest in something new. How'd I feel about that? I didn't know. It was too exciting for much reflection. I was still riding cloud nine to the penthouse with a definitely swelled head.

---

72. He didn't, actually, but was the genesis of Mina creating our universe and, as emergent *L*ife like us, has no prior creator (CH. 19:245). We hadn't yet learned to discern literal from nuanced responses nor *maybe, kind of, not exactly*, etc.

73. No, but Mother never inquired into his backstory and had inaccurate information. We later corrected it with him and Mina.

74. Almost a year later, I finally turned to getting those answers, which you'll find throughout the rest of this book.

In the ensuing discussion—we agreed to call our alleged *über* creator Universe, but after a few months it was only confusing us during our cosmology dialogues. I made an executive decision to switch to *Cosmo*. Mina and Mother said they'd ask him about opening a conversation with us as well as permission to put him in the book.[75] Mina was inexorable, though: no permission, no inclusion. It took seven months to get Cosmo's green light.[98]

Then it slipped out that ThetaHealer's guardian angels had been in the car with us. Through El, Lucifer instantly put his oar in. *What! Both? For how long?*

"Um . . ." We collectively shrugged and looked at one another like schoolkids in the principal's office. "All told, somewhere going on an hour, maybe? We're not sure before we noticed."

El said, "He says that's seriously not allowed."

"Are they in trouble?"

"Whoa," said El. "He's gone. He said he'll be back."

We hadn't intended to put ThetaHealer's guardian angels under the gun—as we understood it, anyway. Our conversation ad interim on their fate touched on all the dystopic possibilities. Then Lucifer rejoined us and, naturally, we pestered him for the deets.

He only said (through El), *Don't worry. If they're going to be like that, they can change persons if they want. She's got a replacement.*[99] Three sets of eyes briefly touched, then we changed the subject.

1.4   IN THE CAR, EL SPIRITUALLY OPENS AND LUCIFER ARRIVES ...

For the moment, our confab in the car thrumming down I–95 from Maryland revved across the span of our trip from idle to Ayako's "fire speed" and back. El was more a yoyo now than on the drive up. Her spiritual strength being "a little undeveloped" in Ayako's cool judgment, and with today's exhausting events sitting on most of a week's dearth of sleep, the potent spiritual energy and ardent individuals infusing the car cyclically overwhelmed her and tears would flow. Then she'd snooze a bit till narcoleptically heaving awake in a burst of chatter. Round and round she went. The closer to home and the later the evening, the more frequent her crying bouts. El's spiritual senses had now opened beyond anything she'd experienced. So many sensations flooded her. She felt zapped in and out of physical reality the way it feels when your spirit self begins giving your body the heave-ho at the start of astral projection,[100] or that whole fifth of 190 proof Everclear kicks in. As a spiritualist first-timer, this terribly shocked and unsettled her.

Between tears, she said, "I'm seeing colors, Dad."

I inspected her face in the rearview. "What, like you're dizzy or something?"

"No, in my mind. Not with my eyes. I don't know. They're in my head, but I'm seeing them."

"So . . ."

"Purples, blues, yellows, like that. Colors. It's everywhere." She paused, thinking . . . experiencing. "Ohmigod, I'm *hearing* them!"

"You're hearing colors?" I turned to Ayako. "Is that real? Can you do that?" She nodded with vigor. It's called synesthesia. This was a pretty sudden onset.

El said, "Dad, I'm hearing Protector!"

"You mean you're hearing him talk, his voice?"

"No, no, it's through the colors . . . and feelings."

"Whaaat?" Dad School never covered this kind of 'listening to your child.'

Through sniffles, she said, "Yeah, jeez, I can understand him. I just . . . I don't know! I understand what he means. I can feel how he's feeling." She thought about it while my eyes alternated between the spotlighted roadway, her sister beside me, and El's darting wonder in the rearview. "It's like soft ideas . . . and colors. Nothing vocal, nothing I'm, like, hearing with my ears." She paused again, her face tight with concentration. "It's more like *seeing* the convo and feeling it, you know what I mean?"

Sure, easy-peasy, why not? Ayako was nodding. Naturally, she got it.

El settled back in her seat, her view angled out the dark window but a little glazed as she focused within. Had this been a strange week? Oh, aye! The portents were next week would be a step above. And then Lucifer slid into the backseat like a pro a few miles from home and I knew I'd been thinking too small.

"He's apologizing, Dad," El said after a minute of between-the-ears discussion. Her tears picked up their pace. "He's soooo, so sorry the way he scared us last night. He's saying he feels really, really terrible about it. I'm telling him it's okay, we understand now."

---

75. We realized 20 months later that we'd mistested much of Cosmo's reality. This is why re-testing responses is critical to accuracy.

I said, "You're talking to him in your head?" and scanned her face in the rearview when I could.

"Yeah, it's crazy!" She giggled through mushrooming tears. "It's not words. It's just . . . God, *I don't know*!" Sobs muted her a moment. "I just feel it. I sense it. I see colors, hear feelings . . . it's . . . I just know what it all means."

"Jesus . . ." I muttered.

She added, "He's right next to me, I—"

"Jesus?"

"What? No. Lucifer."

"Gotta keep up, Dad," Ayako said with her typical twinkle in the midst of someone else's drama.

Ah, jeez.

"I can feel him," El continued. "His body heat . . . I mean, his energy, I guess. It feels warm. He's, like, all cuddled up close, holding me. Lucifer"—more wet sobs—"is your hand on my head?"

Up front, Ayako contemplated her little sister with savvy eyes. "She's okay, Dad, just kind of overcome."

"She and me both," I grumbled.

My view toured the road to El's mirrored face to Ayako to El to the road and back. Besides my concern, I certainly envied her newfound abilities if not the hysterics. Later, I developed some of these spiritual sense skills myself along with the effects that come with them which my just-eighteen daughter was evidently transiting right now.[101]

Her week's experience had artificially jacked up her sensitivity until a giant raw nerve. Built-up spiritual energies, and now Lucifer infusing her with his own over-the-top energy and feelings as he embraced and comforted her, blasted through her fragile, unprepared psyche like the camel's last straw. Over the following weeks these energies calmed and her spiritual sensitivity and clair senses receded to near original levels. Having the chance to catch her breath, she began her real spiritual skills building from there.

Her breathless sobs subsided into weeping. She leaned in a collapsed heap in the corner where the car door meets the seatback, looking for all the world a spent soldier in the trenches. My heart flew to her. I could scarcely imagine giant Lucifer gently holding her tight.

Ayako said, "Lucifer didn't realize El couldn't handle his energy. Angels feel so much more intensely than we do."

"On account of being angels? Or just as spiritual beings?"

"Because they're born and raised on the spiritual plane. They don't have their essential selves so heavily filtered by ignorant physicality like us."

Ahhh. I digress, but have to say I detest our physical nature dissed . . . why it's so aggravating reading the plethora of spiritual poseurs on the best-seller list hating on our corporeality and preaching an amorphous divine celestiality that doesn't even exist as the only true and worthy pursuit although, in this case, I was finding it hard to disagree. We are terribly ignorant, but there's nothing wrong, illusory, mistaken, punitive, or base in our physicality. We can rectify ignorance with awareness, not rejection for a pie-in-the-sky spirituality.

I said, "So, El got it directly and couldn't handle it."

"He mixed his energy with hers." She saw my brows furrow. "I mean, he sort of extended his aura [her turn of phrase; spirit persons have no aura] around her, like, he enveloped her, you know? So El could feel his heart for her, his love. Um . . . the heartistic comfort he was trying to project."

"Sounds a little Vulcan mind meld-ish."

"Ha-ha! No, he's expressing with energy, or feelings, I guess, instead of words or a simple hug. You know, he's basically invisible for physical us. There's a lot gets missed in that sort of communication."

"Not to her." I had to laugh. "What a joke! She was absolutely terrified of him last night, and this morning probably more furious than anything. Now, they're cuddled up in the back seat like best friends."

"That's how it is, Dad. Welcome to the Millennial Generation."

When your kid's saying you're not in Boomer Kansas anymore. I said, "But how could he not know she couldn't handle his energy?"

She tested that. "Because he saw my energy and assumed El was the same."

"Okay . . . but why? He could see hers, too, right?"

Ayako gave me a shrug-face as if I was dense. "He didn't try to see her energy situation."

"So, you have to *look*-look for that? Seems a little amateurish for a guy like him to miss som—"

"Come on, he just didn't think he needed to look."

"I know, but . . . well, you know what they say when you assume."

She blew off a lungful. "I don't know, Dad. That's as far as I asked. He just didn't think he needed to look first. Maybe he was all caught up in the moment."

Yeah, I could see that. Had to give him his humanity, didn't I? *Hmm*. Lucifer was starting to look an awful lot like a regular Joe. Michael, too, the little we knew of him, and even lesser-known Gabriel.

"So, Lucifer," I said into the blank rearview mirror, thinking back to his first unsettling stopover in our home, "you're welcome to visit our house anytime."

Ayako hand tested. "Wow, he's totally shocked, Dad."

"What? Why?"

"Uh . . . he's never been invited into anyone's home before."

"Never?" Ayako was shaking her head before I even finished, and never's a short word. "Come on. That sounds impossible! How many billions of years old is he?"[76]

"He says it's true. He's wondering if it's even allowed."

"Allowed?! By whom? It's my bloody house! I'll have anybody in it I want." I looked around the car at the riders I couldn't see. "That goes for the whole squad, too, by the way, including Protector and Mother, if you're listening in."

"Well, he was just wondering," said Ayako.

"What about before the Fall? I mean the no-Fall, that is, before Michael saddled him with The Corruption blame."

Again with her dissenting headshake she said, "Nope. He says he's always been kind of an outsider, kind of not wanted around."

"Seriously? Since the universe kicked off? He's an archangel, for crying out loud!"

"It's how he was raised, apparently. He was born to be an archangel, from archangel parents, and they raised him to be conscious of that. He never felt he fit in."

"That's what he's saying?"

"Yep. I tested it."

"So, angels are born to their positions?"

"Um . . . Protector says no," she now said. "Just Lucifer, Michael, and Gabriel."

"There's just the three, then."

"Yeah, Protector says." [77] She hand tested. "Ha-ha! Lucifer says he's nothing special, no such thing as archangels. Whoever does the job best is who does it."[78]

"Well, that's not what—" Something swirled in the back of my mind. "Hmm. Didn't we already test that he took over from his parents, or at least one of them?"

"I think—"

"Wait!" Something else swirled. "You said he didn't feel he fit in?"

A bevy of hand tests as Ayako dug into the topic. We coasted up to the mailbox cluster at the end of the paved, state-maintained road. Ahead of us loomed the gloomy, tree-shrouded tunnel of our mile-long, rocky, rutted, potholed, gravelly-dirt road the girls loathed even to crunch their boots over, but which I associated with the joy of peaceful, right, country living. At its hip-wrenching end, we'd slide into our doorless garage and home sweet blessed home after this incredible day. We pulled abreast our mailbox and I opened my window, then clicked on the map light to illuminate its dark maw. Hoping for no spiders (a bird once nested in the newspaper tube underneath), I slipped out the mail and passed it to Ayako while snapping the bent-up box door closed with my left hand and electrically gassing the Prius onto the graveled dirt for a total six-second pit stop. My window thumped shut about when the hybrid's gas motor rattled on. I edged our car as slow as possible across the rubbly track of the girls' nightmares because I wasn't ready to quit our conversation right yet.

"He says he spent his whole life sad," Ayako said. "No one invited him over, like he's the nerd nobody would be seen dead with."

"Angels are like that?"

---

76. Not billions, only millions, and angels were born long after Mina built our universe.

77. There are actually seven (THE SECOND 'ARCHANGELS', § 2.2:522).

78. We didn't yet know Lucifer was born coeval with physical humanity. His parents groomed him to oversee guardian angels, raising him differently than Gabriel and Michael. There is no such thing as 'archangels,' but it took several months of climbing out of our Judeo-Christian angelology to figure out that 'angels' are simply regular human beings born in the spirit, rather than the physical, world. Physical humanity calls them angels, but they're just spirit-born persons (§ 1.1:520).

"They're people, Dad. They feel everything we do. How do you think The Corruption happened, anyway?" Thanks, but I didn't need reminding it was *angels* who got suckered in the first place then "stupidly"—Mina's phrasing, just saying—passed it on. She added, "Lucifer spent all that time feeling ostracized and, since The Corruption, hated and reviled."

"Man, who'd have ever thought? This story just gets weirder and wilder. And then Michael's fake news is when it really took a turn."

El piped up in a cracked voice. "He's crying, Dad. He doesn't want to talk about any of this."

Oh. "Well, then, I'm sorry we—"

"Protector's saying no, absolutely not!" said Ayako.

"I didn't even finish!" *Typical.* Last night Mina got so excited that he was even having this conversation with us that he was responding faster than I could articulate my queries into conscious thought, much less words (before realizing we could just talk in our heads), especially when I struggled with a concept but he knew where I was headed with it. That led me to re-test each time so, at the very least, I knew what I was asking and could make sense of the answer. Irksome, then. Maybe funny in hindsight.

"Protector says don't let him off," she went on. "Make him talk about his problems. He's kept it quiet long enough, and it needs healing. I guess this is all coming out for the first time, Dad."

"Yeah, been getting a lot of that."

A bit lippy she said, "Welcome to the Big Healing."

With a quavering laugh in her crackly voice, El said, "I bet he was bullied as a kid."

Ayako's hands were a blur. "Oh. Em. Gee! That's right!"

"I was joking, Aya."

"I know, El, but it's true. Nobody wanted him around. Ever."

I couldn't help but scoff. "What, because he was *the* archangel?"

"Don't laugh, Dad," Ayako scolded me. "Protector wants him to get this out."

I gave her a side-glance. She wasn't kidding, with that draconian expression. "So it *was* because he was born to be a top archangel? In a world of no special position?" I couldn't help the sarcasm, but it garnered more disapproval from Ayako.

"Wow, he *was* bullied," said El in wonderment.

I said, "How would you even bully—"

"His parents were—I mean, are—archangels," El continued. "He was born special out of all the angels. They expected—"

"But he was the middle child! What were Gabriel and Michael, chopped liver? That makes no freaking sense." That, of course, was my ruthlessly hierarchical, class-conscious, Korean Unificationist mindset talking smack.

"Exactly," Ayako said contrarily. "You never heard of middle child syndrome, Dad?"

No, actually. "My own middle child's schooling me on child dynamics, now?"

"If the shoe fits."

I snapped hard eyes at her and she met me head-on. *Dang.* These grown-up kids.

El ignored our banter. "He says his parents tried to raise him as normal, but still treated him kind of pretty strict . . . um, different, in a sense . . . like he was special."

"You're hearing this in your head?" She ignored me, or nodded and I missed it. Ayako's face, a faint, half-lit moon-over-Japan in Virginia's rural blackness, bobbed with her sister's words.

"They put more responsibility on him. Trained him to, you know, *be* his position . . . that he wasn't like everybody else."

"He wasn't just like Gabriel and Michael? I don't get it."

"Other angels picked up on that," Ayako said after hand testing.

El added, "I think—well, he's not exactly saying it—but it's like they thought it was okay to treat him all aloof and, I don't know, like not one of them and everything because that's how his parents were."

Ayako said, "Lucifer's really sad, Dad. I mean, really, really sad."

"Yeah, he's crying again," El added, "and now I'm—"

Sniffles told me she was empathizing with soft tears in the backseat, I presumed in synchronicity with Lucifer.[79] They were each still feeling the same thoughts and emotions intermingled in a way I couldn't

---

79. When I dug into this late the following summer, Mina, too, began weeping—at one point so deeply that his energy left me wobbling in a jerky circle as I sway tested. He needed a minute as he relived the memories.

understand beyond my monochromatic intellect. Imagination failed me. I'd experienced similar feelings that got me swooning in a past love relationship, but nothing ever sent me into El's paroxysms.

Honestly, I couldn't erase her vivid description of now-weeping, cuddlesome Lucifer blasting into our living room last night like an avenging god of war, angelic wings flared wide, blazing eyes firing Zeus-level thunderbolts as he beelined for Michael, Ayako melting into her chair and El cringing like a bug under a falling shoe. As Mina said, people do what they do from suffering.

1.4.1 Ayako Digs Into Lucifer's Motives . . .

Ayako later asked him about the wings. "Was it just to look good? Make an impression?"

Yes, and *yes*.

She stopped there, but this called for a little more peering into Lucifer's head, which we didn't get to until much later. When we did, the reality was that he'd "looked down" on Michael involving physical humans in his business—to Lucifer, it was an obvious play because, although he wasn't sure of Michael's reasons, why else would he be lying to us right in front of Mina?—especially ones as young as my daughters. Not only had he been in full bristling mode at suddenly recognizing that, somehow, Michael was up to his neck in his tethering to the whipping post since his youth but, as Mina affirmed, he also wanted to "scare off" the girls from dabbling in his business and maybe doing more harm than good.

The latter was his star aim for now so intensely apologizing to El. He said he'd changed his heart on that score following the Reconciliation for a number of reasons, each one having left him jarringly touched. First, he recognized that only the truth, and not constructing a self-satisfying narrative, impelled us. Second, he saw how murderously difficult it was for Michael to get the story out, and only Ayako's presence had provided him the courage. Third, El's bang-up job energy testing for me with her perceptive empathy was unique. Fourth, and last, was our lack of any outrage, hate, scorn, judgment, or rejection for any of them, including all the angels, and even Protector.[80]

1.5 Home Sweet Home . . .

As we rumbled down the last grade before the house, Ayako said, "I don't think we're gonna get to the bottom of Lucifer's business tonight, Dad."[81]

"So, Lucifer," I said, closing the circle. "You *are* welcome to visit us anytime. Hang out with us. Stay over tonight, if you want."

"Lucifer's so deeply moved, Dad," El said weepily. "He feels so much love and acceptance from us, he can't help but cry."

I said, "Well, uh . . . I have to say, my perspective's changed, somewhat."

"Lucifer," said El, "you want me to make you a pallet to sleep on?" And to assuage my unmentioned (though, instinctually, no less felt) concern, she added: "I'll make it in the family room."

"Yeah, he's up for that, El." And to me, Ayako said, "Thank you."

---

80. Because when one considers the problem of evil, who is its chief culprit?

81. Months later, we did. Mina couldn't tutor me when physically awake back then, but only respond to my questions, which were coming from my limited, not to mention inaccurate, Judeo-Christian awareness, comprehension, and intuition.

Denouement

Friday October 13, 2017 ca. 10 PM

THE PRIUS COASTED up to our weather-beaten, plywood-sided storage shed. I reversed through a half circle into the right-hand garage bay hand-in-glove, and shut down its wheezing motor with another couple hundred-some miles racked up on its long-suffering odometer. El had herself pulled together by now. Pretty fast after all that crying but, you know, young and resilient goes a long way. A sunnier disposition now undeniably animated her. Her face lit with excitement at the assembled spirit persons (including Lucifer) she now sensed all around her.

She all but sprinted to Ayako's half-bath, then banged down the stairs to the laundry room. Yanking bedclothes off the tiptoe-tall white wire shelves, she neatly spread two light-colored sheets and a dark blanket topped with a fluffy white-cased pillow over the sad-blue, short-napped, and meanly unpadded family room carpet a few feet from her bedroom door. I ambled down a few minutes later and gazed on her happy, contented effort in a sort of wonder, touched to my soul by her innocence and sweetness in the way she was reaching out to this previously terrifying and detested angel with whom she'd just shared a couple hours of cherished, comforting intimacy. Later in the night, he relaxed atop it for about ninety minutes and chatted, reclining Roman dining style, with Taiji, Hidé, Helen, my dad, his mom, *Obāsan*, several of her family, and whoever else crowded into the capacious room before he had to go.

"Yeah, he had stuff to do, but he was being courteous," Ayako later commented. "He'd never let El's effort go to waste."

Meanwhile, Ayako sedately fired up the television and brought up YouTube to share their favorite Japanese alt-music with our ever-growing squad. With El now back upstairs, and x Japan's music videos blasting through the television speakers, Ayako put out two pieces of box chocolate on the kitchen counter for Lucifer to enjoy. My sweet tooth noticed and got me wondering if anybody would beat him to it.[82]

"Dad, sit down and chill with us," Ayako said, snagging me trying to slip into my bedroom to collapse before sleep with a nice piece of witless fiction on my plush, king-sized antidote to car seatery. I froze mid-stride, your basic deer in headlights. "The whole squad wants you here."

"Yeah, Dad," echoed her sister, "don't be a loser in your empty room."

Ah, jeez. I really wanted to check out for the night and threw a covetous gander through my open bedroom door. Exhaustion was Arnold bench-pressing his weight whistling *Edelweiss* compared to how my body was registering on the ol' life-o-meter. One way or another, I can be as much an introvert as Mother and Mina had painted Cosmo when I'm beat just short of a puddle.

---

82. Taiji and Hidé did, but left a piece for him. Spirit people can taste and enjoy physical food because all things physical have a spirit existence (THE 'REFLECTIVE' ENVIRONMENT, § 7.1.1.1:212) as long as they exist and can be interacted with like any object. This is how we shared physical meals and drinks with the squad.

None of our experience was as literal to me as to my daughters, either. Sure, I felt and sensed and swayed. I intuited and caught vibes. I had a persistent faith—"a conviction of things not seen," as (maybe) St. Paul put it in Hebrews (11:1, ASV)—that smoothed life's scalpel-edged undulations. The girls snatched actual glimpses, though. They felt energy. Perceived thoughts and emotions, even smelled and touched. El was hearing colors and seeing sounds, for Pete's sake. Ayako intuited like a whisper in the ear.[83] It all left me with a sense of being the old guy on a walker in a room full of wildly gyrating kids. Bed with a novel had seemed a fine hideout.

But doggone it, I thought. *She's right.*

I supposed I could stretch my senses, practice perception, tune my ear. Maybe it's like learning a language, I consoled myself, and my two nimble younkers just have it over their cloddish old man. How often comes an opportunity like this in a dad's life anyhow, one shared equally with his children? These last few spiritually fierce days had rebooted us as individuals and as a family. It left us bonded as drum-tight as nearly half a lifetime raising them through the holy hell of domestic violence and its battle fatigue never had. I thought that pat old foxhole metaphor was, for sure, right on the money with what our last two days had brought us.

"Our family is fire," Ayako later happily put it.

Wasn't I well-nigh in Dad Heaven? What was my bedroom now but a self-imposed purgatory?

Weary? What was I thinking? Where were my manners? I gratefully sank into the cushy-enough sofa and half-listened, half-watched my daughters' x Japan crushes and formerly physical Taiji and Hidé pyrotechnically screaming out their alleged music onstage while images and feelings from the last week nickelodeoned through me.

Knowing I still couldn't tell who from whom in their outlandish stage getups, the girls excitedly pointed them out. "There's Taiji, Dad . . . when he was alive, heh-heh," followed by, "He says ha-ha yourself, Aya," and "Look at Hidé's gorgeous hair!" or, "See how he's glaring at Yoshiki? . . . hey, Hidé, is that cuz you were mad?" X Japan was one of many bands and genres they cycled through for our guests' pleasure, which made me wonder about good manners all over again.

Standing behind the sofa, El was particular about locating everybody's place in the room at any given moment. Excited squeals and happy banter revealed this or that person's arrival, or the discovery they were hanging out. Mina (just a flyby),[102] Jesus, Sun-myung, Lucifer, Gabriel, our guardian angels, Taiji, Hidé, Helen, Daphne (formerly, 'Frenchie the Innominate' until I learned her name) and all our spirit guides, my dad, *Obāsan*, and other Japanese, Chinese, Carib, Irish and European family, and many more whom we didn't know, or even know about, filled the space.

Tired or not, spiritual dimbulb or not, I could feel the voltage and its reality.

"Ayyy . . . turns out Gabriel's a music lover, Dad!" Ayako said, energy testing while El took a break. "A total tunes connoisseur."

I said, "Is that right?" I couldn't avoid a blasé response—maybe on account of being all highwayed-out and, I admit, feeling a little drowned by revelation after shock after astonishment—but, in truth, I was pretty surprised. I tried to imagine Gabriel hanging around concerts, nightclubs, and finger-pickers by the campfire checking out the global music scene top to bottom like some millennian roadie working up his musical acumen. "What about rap and hip-hop?"

"Yep, he listens to *everything*."

"Does he? We're not the only inhabited planet and he's been around awhile, so that's a lot of music."

El hopped off her counter stool to energy test this new development herself. She gushed, "That's, like, so lit! And he *loves* this genre!"

The screeching Blue Hearts? "Maybe he's just being polite."

"Aw, quit resisting, Dad," Ayako reproved like a mother. "He's being real."

I chuckled and spread my palms. "Okay, okay. Got to know my limitations, I reckon."

Still, if I had to vegetate on the sofa, something mildly melodious would go down a treat. When the girls relented and went digging for more appetizing fare, Gabriel, through Ayako's grinning sway test, "loudly objected." The girls weren't fooling around with their new pals, so it was back to the alt-music scene, the volume nicely cranked to the majority crowd's happy endorsement. Dad could just take a backseat.

Taking in the room's physical and spirit activities, I caught my small family blossoming before my eyes. Our lives would never be the same. How could we return to the spiritually dulled, corporeal-only reality we'd been living where, among other things, Lucifer the sensitive, caring brother was a murderous, Jack Nicholson-esque

---

83. Some weeks later, she heard me raking leaves in the front yard beyond the living room windows, except I was standing right beside her. After some testing, she found it was bored Taiji cleaning the yard. The *wrong* yard. The *physical* leaves yet awaited *me*.

psychopath and Mina, the all-embracing, freedom-loving grandparent a pedantic, judgmental *paterfamilias* in a universe filled with punishment, darkness, and dread? I couldn't turn my back on any of what I'd learned. I knew my cavorting children could never jettison their new way of life nor the friends and family they were growing to love and their presence to cherish. More than simple revelation, more even than a rockin' spiritual experience, we'd discovered a whole 'nother reality that's as natural a part of our lives as loving. And who wants to cut love out of life's itinerary?

Something thinly called music jangled my ears and pulled me from my reverie. I looked around. What a house my home—or maybe what a home my house?—had become. Ah, well. Some of the music wasn't half-bad. Heck, a few I even still put in my ears all voluntary-like. And the full spectrum conversation was righteous. My daughters were as joyous and loved as I'd *ever* seen them. What's that worth?

Part II

All Existence ...

A New Dawn

WHEW! WE FELT bowled over by all we'd learned those first two flabbergasting days meeting our 'creator,' The Ancestors, my best friend Helen, and all the others. Everything was different, the proverbial scales were fallen from our eyes. The world—our very existence!—now lounged in virgin territory. It was unsettling. At the same time, our sense of liberation from the psychic bondage of the God Hypothesis, the Moral Dilemma, the Science Conceit, and our naturally evolving embrace of the absolute freedom of life . . . well, it was indescribable. You'll just have to experience it for yourself.

SECTION 1
The Next Day

We cracked our eyes Saturday morning, October 14, 2017 on what effectively was a new life. The challenge now before us, besides our own growth and development, was to write this book. To accomplish that as its principal author, I had to learn more than I ever dreamed in those early days. I didn't want to merely regurgitate 'revelations' about the 'right life'—let's be honest, who really cares about another woo-woo convo with God dissing our existence?—but to explain in some detail the what, how, and why. Real knowledge. *I* certainly wanted it. The book begged for it. Pursuing it sent me down many rabbit holes as answers only spawned questions and I struggled to master the quirks of energy testing (ET).

My crafty daughters skated on the effort by moving to New York City four months later to kick off El's restively budding adulthood. Ayako, bless her heart watching over her rookie sister, continued helping me negotiate every ET impasse.[84] To pursue my mandate, however, I needed to glean from the ether things I hadn't a clue I didn't know and no idea how to ask about. Most of what you'll read in PARTS II–V took over a year of learning, comprehension, and intuition before I even had sufficient awareness to conceive the questions that eventually rendered whatever level of clarity you're finding here. Recall, this information isn't just raining into our heads from on high the way it supposedly does in traditional revelation. We had to seek after it through ET queries. Frankly, I was disappointed how long it took me to think up lines of inquiry that looked awfully obvious in hindsight. I chalked it up to the vagaries of muscling up my 98-pound psyche.

1.1 OUR FIRST HURDLE

As wild as The Big Event was, the nearly five years it took to get this book into your curious hands was a cosmic-class roller-coaster. The first summit to surmount was how to winnow reality from fantasy and truth from just plain BS. For us, it came down to establishing trust in the process. It was incredibly helpful there

---

84. Well, several times Mina aggravatingly advised Ayako not to test answers for me so I'd have to work it on my own and improve my testing, reasoning, and intuitive skills.

were three of us. We could bounce our experience off each other to cut through our confusion and skepticism. The girls handled the transition fairly well. By that, I mean quick. They're naturally empaths, psychics, and mediums and felt, saw, heard, and otherwise directly experienced a much richer experience than I did. And it didn't hurt that, after El blurted how the girls were his cousins, Japanese rock superstar Akiō—yep, still using pseudonyms—came back a silent week later having confirmed it (to our mutual astonishment) with his still living, psychic grandmother (EN 55:649). If that wasn't real-world validation of ET, we figured nothing was.

On the other hand, I looked on as an obtuse bystander pervaded by a lifetime's enculturation that, despite my long church experience, militated against this kind of balderdash and poppycock. Unlike my discerning daughters, I incessantly wondered *just who the* heck *am I talking to, really?* No amount of persuasion by the girls could set my heart at ease on that score. I was on my own. I eventually noted subtle nuances in the relative intensity and flavor of the energy I felt from different spirit people with whom I energy tested. That, and El's spunky example, regularly inspired me to query my respondents' feelings and attitudes. I simply got to know them. Each person turned up a different personality. For example, *Obāsan*'s younger brother Kengo, the successful *kamikaze*, is an inveterate joker. We always had quite a time getting serious, therefore truthful, responses out of him. If there's a master manipulator behind our ET, then he, she, or it is one bloody great performer! But considering the un-cozenish content, we decided the deception scenario was unreasonable. By summer 2018, I finally began developing my own trust in this newfangled ET methodology, although Mina jokes with Ayako how my skepticism seesawed like a sine wave still two years more. It's only trust that resolves the conundrums arising in drinking new wine from new wineskins. Trust in the methodology, the data, the conveyor, or in whatever does it for you.

1.2 OUR SECOND HURDLE

Our second hurdle to working with ET was our Brobdingnagian worldview. A person's philosophy of life, by definition, frames their self-identity.[103] In those first two days, I'd lost virtually all the pillars supporting my awareness of the world and my place in it. Eventually, it appeared we now possessed at least as good a source in ET to understand our existence as science and philosophy has ever had to wring metaphysical truths from their micro observations and macro reasoning . . . except better.[104] The girls didn't need a lot of persuasion to abandon the rubble of their nascent worldviews, but I did.

Even so, the hard truth dawned that philosophy and science provide no coherent, rational story of existence, the smoke and mirrors of their reasoned, reductive, and quantum observations notwithstanding. The outcome of this vacuum in real awareness has been ugly, too, fueling deranged ideas across the millennia that produced only unremitting suffering and unhappiness. Modern science's vaunted enlightenment has only doltishly superseded religion as humanity's most life-destructive foundational thought process. Sure, nobody planned it that way. But, like religion and philosophy, justifying the means is the ineludible practical outcome of being fixated on the ends—that humans are only biology, life is material, existence is finite, coercion a positive good—regardless how enlightened one's technique in pursuing awareness.[105]

SECTION 2

Confronting the Book

The remainder of this book reports on the confounding mystery of reality that science, philosophy, and religion presume to clarify but only muddle. Our ET data challenges established aspects of these disciplines, from the expanding universe and quantum entanglement to *creatio ex nihilo*[85] and *biologism*[86] and many things in between. We were some sorry naïfs in this respect. Mina wasn't kidding when he said this book would push the boundaries of my intuitive and intellectual faculties. I found it necessary to bone up my science and philosophy to meliorate my conceptual awareness so I could form pertinent queries and then cognize the answers in the context of the many fields of inquiry into which they led me. I oft slipped into backstopping his revelations with the relevant literature. "Resist the impulse!" was his rallying cry along with, "Keep it simple!" Well, anyway, my efforts were pointless. False realities box in science and philosophy's mindsets too much for them ever to lend credence to their unavoidable intuitive and revelatory doppelgänger. Instead, new theories

---

85. Latin: 'creation out of nothing;' contrast with *creatio ex materia* ('creation out of matter') and *creatio ex deo* ('creation out of the being of God'), none of which are accurate.

86. Biologism interprets human existence from strictly a biological perspective.

and hypotheses need forming and experimental and logical tests devised, but this book's deadline just didn't allow for much of that. Developing ET into a credible mode of inquiry will take a while. Data as 'revelation' will have to do for now. That doesn't wholly satisfy Mina, so he has a gaggle of rigorous, topical follow-on books on my honey-do list.

It's not for nothing that (even religious) people gravitate toward science over revelation. "The 'scientific worldview,'" Rupert Sheldrake seems to acknowledge rather grumpily in *Science Set Free,* "is immensely influential because the sciences have been so successful [transforming our world] by an immense expansion of knowledge" (2012, 6). Even so, humanity remains qualitatively unsatisfied with it because it just fails on some unquantifiable level to give us a sense that the reality science shows us is the full human reality that is. Even materialistic "scientists remain[ed] dualists, and continue[d] to use dualistic metaphors" (ibid, 34) because it "seems impossible to be a consistent materialist. Materialism depends on a lingering dualism, more or less thinly disguised" (ibid, 36). Even "many scientists have philosophies or religious faiths that make this 'scientific worldview' seem limited, at best a half-truth" (ibid, 23). The inconsistency lies in our being not simply material bodies. Our minds aren't confined to our skulls. Our thoughts aren't the random outcome of electrochemical neuronal activity. People just *know* this, including materialists who can't imagine (while pridefully accepting their Nobel Prize) that their lauded creative brilliance is only the inevitability of mere random chemistry like a monkey clacking at a keyboard[106] and not the fruit of a purposive, irreducible trans-brain individual consciousness that noncomputationally *thinks*.[107]

When it comes to reality, people want to know essentially three things: where are we, what are we, and why are we? We expect the answers to these (on their face, fairly simple) questions will tell us what's going on and the optimal way to play the game of life to achieve ultimate satisfaction; to experience happiness. Allied with the unquenchable need to live, this is humanity's basic survival drive.[108] We've been at it tooth and nail since the first human looked around with their newfound powers of creative thought and wondered, WTF?

The (ET) fact is that the natural and *supra*natural[87] are normative. As concepts go, however—and despite using them throughout this book—the traditional natural and supranatural are largely defunct. What else is defunct is the model of a deitic God and a universe under his arrant control that even data-driven quantum mystics can't or won't refine out of their archaism.[109]

Well, our direct-experience ET ruthlessly crowbarred the girls and me out of our traditional modes of perception. Lo and behold, there we were in the same paradox as the upstart quantum crowd, wondering how to reconcile our understanding of reality with the scandalous data. Well, we adopted their same solution: more observation and analysis to clear the static. Old school physicists couldn't deny the ever-accumulating quantum data. Its quirky reality finally did-in their spiritual model before, incongruously, lately pushing them to take another cautious peek. Neither could we three deny our ET 'revelation' as it morphed into data. The reality which ET exposed to us crushed my family's own standard model of existence and sunk much of what we thought of as reality. We suppose ET looks as nutty now as quantum theory did a century ago. In time, it will similarly push through humanity's mythic mindset, although via spiritual energy to derive falsifiable data instead of theoretical equations . . . or unmitigated imagination.

Scientists and philosophers—with whom I callously lump spiritualists—are both after knowledge, or perhaps better put, awareness and comprehension, though in seemingly different domains and to differing degrees. Regardless, Mina's gripe is they both deindividuate the person. On the one hand, we get the simple materialistic human biological machine in a random, physical world. The other hands us the complex transcendent human moral machine in a controlled, ersatz-spiritualized world. Both dehumanize. When applied to existential reality, both approaches assume too much. For example, the "tenets of materialism are more accurately seen as metaphysical extrapolations based on some scientific findings" (Taylor 2017, 150) and leaves the person playing second fiddle to ruthless gene survival or moral supremacy. If there's a single thread that runs through Mina, it's that the individual—the person, the human consciousness—is the inviolable cornerstone of All Existence (§ 1:90). Even if we recognize All Existence as a complex system, the human aspect is an emergent reality wholistically transcending its complexity.[88]

Our writing method for PARTS II–IV engages Query *&* Response (QR)—sometimes informed by research of the relevant literature to the degree we were capable—to establish context and awareness, which we then

---

87. Synonymous with *super*natural but without the religious, mystical, and magical baggage.

88. As used throughout, *wholism* is the whole in and of itself. *Holism* is the parts as they interact to create the whole, and the relationship between the parts and whole. The distinction follows from the emergent type, which isn't greater than the sum of its parts so much as transcends the whole that was greater than the sum of *its* parts.

validated with Mina. He hovered over my shoulder so to speak as I wrote the text. It's a joint effort. Suppose I write, as I did above, ". . . when applied to existential reality, both approaches also assume too much. For example, the 'tenets of materialism are more accurately seen as metaphysical extrapolations based on some scientific findings.' " The quotation is just its author, Taylor's, opinion notwithstanding any empirical fact or sound logic used to support it. For the purposes of this book, however, it's all quite useless as opinion generally is in the quest for knowledge and understanding.

The workaround here is Mina, the human person behind our physical existence and the authority on our universe. I ask if he agrees with what I wrote, if it's true and accurate of reality, and so forth. If his answer is *no*—and I certainly get that often enough—I work it out to our mutual satisfaction. Sometimes, that means glumly jettisoning words, phrases, or whole trends of thought I thought clever and spot-on but ultimately didn't energy test as correct. This prevents me inserting my own fancy into the text and making the book just another highbrow work of fictional nonfiction. That said, however, text that later reliably tests as incorrect is on me alone for not vetting it as thoroughly as I thought I had.

This book matters to Mina on the theory that awareness of reality leads to happier choices, thus a happier life. This is the fundamental truth in today's spirit world following the Big Healing October 13, 2017 as the reality about our creator, the universe, and life settled into humanity's shared mindset and, through Mina's healing, spurred the release of eons of ignorance and psychic trauma. Overall, every person in existence—starting with spirit humanity that's more amenable, and by that route working its way into physical humanity's more convoluted psyche—is being gradually enlightened and uplifted to the degree that each is willing. Mina doesn't force the issue. If it makes a person happier to cling to or act out their trauma, he leaves them to it. He imposes no judgment or consequences, he merely waits until, inevitably, they're ready to heal. For him, it's all about healing. We've experienced it ourselves, plenty.

Numerous spirit persons with axes to grind relentlessly assailed me, for example, in a myriad of creative and shocking ways over the course of writing this book, from seizures and cognitive blindness to grinding fatigue and pain, or sniped at me in less inimical or waspish ways.[89] Ninety percent of these attacks weren't malicious, in Mina's view. Often, they only wanted my attention to facilitate their healing because they were unwilling or unable to approach Mina or my spirit self directly. Still, it resulted in levels of harm, grief, aggravation, and so on that I could've done quite nicely without and for which I periodically wanted just a smidgeon of biblical vengeance. Mina counseled me away from such feelings. Once I'd realize a problem was a spiritual attack, my only sensible recourse was to identify and converse with the person directly or indirectly through Mina or my spirit self, and encourage them to accept healing. And they did, more often than not, because that's what they were initially—and then, eventually—after.

Even with the Big Healing, many people in spirit world are in thrall to the certainty of an Accountableist God. For awhile, my deceased parents were even though they were right there for many of our freewheeling talks, arguments, and tantrums with this supposed Accountableist God. Others feel paralyzed by shame and embarrassment and can't bring themselves to directly ask Mina, other healers, or healing facilitators in spirit world for help, advice, or even company. Some are so cowed by Accountableism's effects that not even a flicker of permission for anyone to bring them healing can spark to life in their weeping heart. Because of our role in revealing The Corruption and Michael's Lie, vast crowds of spirit people come to us for healing. Initially, we only facilitated it until we learned to heal through Mina. It's quite sad that people lock themselves away in their minds from reality and their deepest desire. Thankfully (in spirit world, anyhow) it's a diminishing problem. But we digress.[110]

If you're feeling what we're saying, then you can see a person's happiness genuinely matters to Mina, our universe's builder. Not the phony, first-get-yourself-compliant-with-deitic-authority-and-personal-perfection happiness, but the kind one pursues on one's own terms. Mina would forego this book if it made me happy not to write it. He'd treat me no less for it, either. He'd simply find another way to accomplish his intent, as he always has. It's easy to fool ourselves if we don't understand this core familial nature of his character. Regarding this book, I'd ask him, "Should I say this-or-that?" or, "Is it useful to add or remove such-and-such?" To the former, he'd invariably answer *no*, because he won't tell me what to do, or even necessarily what he desires.[90] A follow-up like, "So, I shouldn't say 'this,' then?" gets a *no*, too, and that's my clue to start rephrasing.

---

89. There are (formerly physical) people used to how spirit world was and not at all enamored of the Big Healing's cosmic disruption to their personal fiefdoms and situations.

90. He will with Ayako, though! She reports that he's uncompromising with her because their relationship is quite different, his expectations for her unique. Still, their relationship never suffers, even when she complains or flat out ignores him. She says his attitude with me comes from his appreciating how much I detest coercion.

When, early on, Ayako asked him if it was okay to eat sugar, he responded *yes* even though Gabriel was shouting, "*No!* It's *not* okay!" In this case, Mina's *yes* meant "you're free, so do it if it makes you happy," not that eating sugar was health agnostic for her. Absent strong intuition or clair senses, a communication mode like ET doesn't let Mina couch his response in conciliatory or explanatory language. He can only respond to the literal question. Hence, at least with me, a moral imperative like 'should' always meets his *no* response regardless how I *mean* the query. Unless he's pushing me to do my own thinking first, he'll give a straight-up answer to 'is it useful to the book?' though not to 'is it useful to me?' types of queries for obvious reasons. For me to get Mina's *objective* preference, without any reference to whether or not I'd be happy about it, sometimes takes a slightly more roundabout effort to ensure that, from his point of view, I'm not taking his response as a Godly demand, a 'request,' a guilt trip, and so forth. Our tendency for that remains a human malady.[III]

The information in PARTS II–IV isn't revelation in the ordinary sense. It's a presentation of supranatural data collected via ET (CH. 12:83). The data isn't raw the way it would be from, say, a sociological or biological study. We don't interpret, analyze, or draw conclusions except by verifying it via ET or empirically with observation. We derive the book's data through querying spirit persons, primarily Mina. The information presented is the respondents' point of view, not ours. Since ET is a query-based mode of inquiry, a spirit person can't answer an unasked question.[91] That's why it can take a long time to build up sufficient data to achieve comprehension beyond some vague awareness. Investigators understand that queries flow from comprehension. Many queries just don't germinate until we develop the appropriate soil, although intuitive leaps make a handy shortcut. Our own habituated bias gets in the way, too, until our awareness expands and our bias updates. We hope to periodically publish revised editions of this book to account for new data, improved comprehension and, where we've erred testing or in failing to double check our work, corrections.

We organized the book from large to small. PART II describes key concepts of emergence and infinity via the ET-derived science of our physical universe and All Existence from *creatio a priori*[92] and the structure and nature of our macroenvironment to consciousness. PART III describes our place in the larger context, who and what our 'creator' is, and his creation of our microenvironment. PART IV describes key facets of physical and spirit humanity along with relevant aspects of human history and certain historical personalities. Finally, PART V explains ET and how to use it to explore your own questions.

ET is a skills-based mode of inquiry. Hence, one's testing can deviate from a respondent's answer for a variety of reasons. We might test a *no* when it should be a *yes* or some variant of *maybe*. Moreover, ET is *conversation*, not interrogation. It flows in the manner people converse—including joking, teasing, or simply responding in a way to teach us to think and act for ourselves instead of depending on some deity or spirit sage for it all. This naturally differs in accord with whom one is ET conversing. It took us a bit to realize that some *yes* answers are people giving us the energy equivalent of a polite head nod or an "uh-huh," just as we all do in conversation to let the speaker know we haven't tuned them out for cat memes.

Then, what about fibbing, lying, and deception, isn't that normal conversation, too? Well, we've encountered it off and on in accord with whom we're conversing. Michael wasn't terribly forthcoming that first Friday, to be sure. But in the end, he forthrightly implicated himself in a cosmic deception that put him in everybody's crosshairs. Our experience is that when we ask a person if they're lying or hedging, they generally admit it because there are few if any consequences to inhibit them.[93] I was surprised that spirit people who attack me can be so blatantly upfront about it when confronted. That's because it's mostly impossible for other spirit people to make them sorry for it. Still, some people are just malicious and lie pathologically. You simply need be aware and get the straight dope from Mina if there's not a privacy issue. Fortunately, there aren't too many of these malicious spirit people in our experience. On the other hand, *Obāsan*'s younger brother Kengo is a pathological joker. It takes some effort to get him to be serious. If we take his first answers to be his real feelings or a truth about his experience, we'd probably fool ourselves. Until we figured out his personality, we certainly did! *Obāsan* scolds him for it.

We resolve contradictions that crop up in Mina's responses through better queries, more information, greater comprehension, verifying amongst each other, and persuading him case-by-case that we don't want him to tell us what to do but to get his true opinion or desire so we can consider it along with everything else. Besides

---

91. Though, if we're standing, we do get unsolicited responses just from talking or even thinking, and we then dig into the details. It's a constant with Mina during any conversation with Ayako whenever she's on her feet.

92. Latin: 'creation from what is before.'

93. It turns out that even when a person lies, the nature of how ET works contradicts it. For instance, if I test, "Is this Mina's yes/no answer I'm testing?" and someone else falsely says, *Yes*, then my body actually tests a *no* answer (§ 2.1:636).

intuition, our crosscheck for these sorts of contradictions is logical consistency, rationality, reasonableness, and so forth.[94] People definitely *do* lie in spirit world, aye. To our knowledge, only a few ever did with malicious intent to obstruct our getting at the truth.

ᴇᴛ's credibility rests in the main less on knowing one is talking to the people one thinks they are than on the responses themselves. Anybody with some effort can identify to their satisfaction with whom they're conversing. But that doesn't mean that person's responses are materially correct. That's the rub, isn't it? Responses can be empirically tested quickly (e.g., with Akiō's living grandmother) or over time (e.g., Betelgeuse's supernova showing up in 2045; § 2:107). This book is ᴇᴛ's debut. It naturally awaits a larger validating pool to establish its bona fides. And that's where you, the interested reader, come in. In the next chapter, we make the case for ᴇᴛ as a mode of inquiry that produces data which leads to information thence to knowledge. After that, we reveal what we learned about reality.

---

94. A perfect example is our earlier mention of people resisting healing for fear of judgment and their tendency to misread Mina if he uses moral imperatives or states his preference. I ran into confusion and contradiction finalizing that very text, especially when I brought my parents into it. Some random person interfered with their answers, and I'd worded my questions such that Mina's necessarily literal response didn't jive with what I thought my question meant. I thus misinterpreted. It took an hour to work through the confusion. Frustrating and aggravating, but it is what it is.

Energy Testing as a Mode of Inquiry

The greatest challenge facing mankind is the challenge of distinguishing reality from fantasy... to decide which of our perceptions are genuine, and which are false...
—Michael Crichton[112]

THE PROBLEM WE have cognizing reality as it matters to us—who, what, why, and how we are—is that we can't readily observe much of it. The story of knowledge has been a tale of discovering how to witness and interpret what's unobserved, from germs and quarks, mind and will, to spirituality and a creator, and then build that into an understanding of reality we can comprehend. Science seeks to explain reality in *natural* terms and found a method to uncover it. Philosophy seeks to explain the same reality in *humanistic supranatural* terms. Beyond its tools of reason, however, philosophy—especially its sub-discipline theology, including religion and spiritualism focused on the *divine supranatural*—has failed to uncover any natural *or* supranatural reality at all. This puts us in a quandary. Science readily points to what it observes to exist (nature) and declares, "Reality!" Philosophy points to what it can't observe but only reason into existence (supranature) and posits, "Also reality!" The scientist scoffs at the philosopher as naught but a cerebral imagineer, ignoring our fuller reality for only its obvious parts the way a Mr. Magoo engineer, coming in through the only door, might myopically observe the underground home's aboveground furnace room *as* the house. See the forest-for-the-trees problem here?

SECTION 1
Science and Philosophy

Science places great faith in the somatic senses. The thinking is that, if I can sense it outside my body then you can, too; it's objectively real and we can verify what we think we know with what actually is. Philosophy's faith is in the psychosomatic (rational) senses. Its problem is that, although I can sense something, you can't necessarily; we can't deduce if it's objectively real and can't verify what we think we know with what actually is. In this case, we don't even know what actually is, only what we've deduced. We readily accept as an objective reality that humans invisibly and inexplicably love, hate, conceive art, intuit, and use the power of thought—say, intention, often called a plan—to make things occur in observed reality. Pointing to objective data, science boils all that down to neurons and chemistry whereas philosophy reasons a perhaps ineffable causation deduced from subjective data.

Like our Mr. Magoo engineer, we can't avoid the sense there's something under our feet we can't see, perhaps muffled footsteps or doors clunking closed. But he's interested in the furnace he can see and touch, not strange, *probably* furnace-connected sounds, though his philosophical assistant might be.

"Shut up about what's obviously not there," our engineer says. "I've got this furnace to deal with."

"Yeah, but what's *below* the furnace?" retorts the assistant.

"Not my problem, and you'll never figure it out. I can experience this furnace, so I can deal with it. You're just speculating about what you're not sure is maybe there that you can't experience anyway. Where's the use?"

"Yeah, but," his ear to the floor, "did you hear that?"

1.1 SCIENCE AND PHILOSOPHY'S EPIC FAIL

We're not so unlike the regressed societies of Larry Niven's *Ringworld* (1970) who are ignorant of their artificial reality and psychologically quarantined from its inconvenient truth. For all our intellectual progress, science and philosophy fail spectacularly to unveil who, what, where, how, and why we are. They'll continue to fail for three simple reasons.

1. It's our tendency—ignoring naturalism's rubric the supranatural is merely a fruity figment—to see the natural and supranatural like oil and water according to a seemingly genetic certitude that matter is profane and base whereas spirit is sacred and enlightened.
2. Awash in objective observation, science will only more intransigently dissociate from supranature while philosophy, rooted in subjective observation, will more insistently disengage from nature.[95]
3. In their application to society, both science and philosophy are deeply flawed. Very little offsets the former's reckless hiccups beyond its technological benefits, which only punctuate its flaws. All that offsets the latter's flaws is how closely it hews to the former's methods which, again, only accentuates its flaws. Their defects incriminate their quest with the offense of irrationality. The resultant confusion traipses merrily along at fever pitch unabated generation to generation, quantum speculation being a case in point.

We can't help this merry-go-round. The natural and supranatural captivate us. To quit wondering what's 'out there' is to be, one way or another, dead inside. We need a means to experience the supranatural in a *repeatable* way that commutes our subjective to objective experience. That's energy testing (ET).

1.1.1 DATA'S DILEMMA

To understand how ET fits the repeatable experience paradigm, we need understand what constitutes *data*. At its simplest, data is a collection of *datum*, a single piece of observation. It forms into data to establish a complete observation, of which each datum is in some way a part. Data is raw, unorganized, unconsidered. It becomes *information* when we view it in a given context through analysis, deriving information by organizing, considering, and presenting it in such a way that it's useful.

1.1.1.1 EMPIRICAL AND RATIONAL DATA

Science collects data using the somatic senses allied with instruments to observe readily accessible nature. Any person with the training, skill, and equipment can collect the same data, which is why folks consider it *objective*. It analyzes data into information, theory, and eventually knowledge. On the flipside, philosophy collects data using the mental senses (oft augmented by scientific data) to deductively observe *humanistic* supranature because it's been wholly inaccessible in any meaningful way. This limitation means it's not possible for any person even with the necessary training and skill to deduce the same observation, which is why folks consider it *subjective*. That seems to put the supranatural squarely out of reach for deriving information and knowledge. Because we can't repeat, measure, or test philosophy's observations, science tends to conclude the supranatural isn't real. At least, not *objectively* real like the world of matter.

Science is all about applying knowledge derived from observation to solving specific technical problems, from healing sickness to building transportation to lighting the darkness. Philosophy applies knowledge in the form of ideas to solving specific nonpareil human questions involving existence, freedom, and behavior as well as technical ones involving knowledge, value, beauty, and so on. The overall nature of experiential, data-driven science means it's limited in terms of what issues it can solve, particularly the metaphysical kind. On the other hand, the overall rationalist nature of philosophical inquiry—besides ill suited to solving real problems—means it can't answer the fundamental questions of life and reality, either.

Such limitations are an obstacle between these two classes of study and the common reality they seek. Each one attempts to derive meaning and comprehension of the larger world from data that's necessarily too

---

95. Quantum and spiritual science (philoscience) are of no help, being rooted firmly in nature.

limited for the task. False or misconstrued scientific *data* is correctible through repetition, *information* less so. Philosophy suffers generally from an incorrectability of information because we derive it from rational instead of experiential data. That's why bad science goes away relatively quick while bad philosophy lingers like poor dental work. The upshot is that both disciplines derive a false reality from false information worked up from bad—misconstrued—data. Of course, science has a reasonably accurate understanding of, say, physics though not so much the reality actually driving it much less the Big Bang. Still, scientific data works to limit flights of fancy. Without experiential data to keep it grounded, philosophy (like mathematics) is more likely than science to veer off to wherever the mind can rationally take it. And there's very little we can't rationalize when it suits us.

1.1.1.2   Revelatory Data

Religion, differing from general philosophy in seeking to explain the natural world in *divine supranatural* terms, tries to get around this metaphysical impasse via *revelation*, a substitute for experiential and rational observation that's limited to single individuals and occasionally groups.₁₁₃ Theology is really philosophy working off revelatory instead of reasoned data. It therefore presents subjectively and is the reason Mina lumps it in with philosophy. Theologians typically verify revelation using the tools of philosophy or simply rank calls to authority. This worked out pretty well for organized religion in the age before modern science and philosophy, but it never solved any human problems in the definitive manner science does. Nor does revelation advance beyond classical, much less modern, philosophy in definitively solving any human or divine issues. It's really no more than a flimsy 'spiritual wild-ass guess' (swag). Funnily enough, science scorning supranatural experience as imagination run wild or tricks of the subconscious, or that consciousness (non-evidentially) arises in matter, ironically itself relies upon the supranatural by definition: mind, which is invisible, non-natural, inexplicable, and only individually experiential.

1.2   Supranatural Data's Epic Revival

Mina lumps all types of inquiry under *Philosophy with a capital-P* as humanity's primary knowledge-seeking class of study. Yet, it's useful to recognize that the three principal modes of inquiry we use to acquire data (empiricism, rationalism, revelation) and their principal subclasses of study from which we derive information (science, philosophy, theology) each interacts with and relies upon the others. Even so, they're hamstrung producing real knowledge of our natural and supranatural reality. There's no getting around it. It's counting sheep to reckon that next week—or next year, or next century—their breakthroughs will render comatose our present minuscule comprehension or majuscule suffering.

The tendency in science and philosophy to scorn the supranatural as unworthy of study is simple bias that follows from a lack of ready tools to collect data, the presumption no tools exist, and broadly accepted explanations based on the most obvious and accessible: physical nature. That's a myopic perspective at best, a hydra raising another head each time a new theory posits the seemingly impossible or absurd.

The real question is, what method can repeatably collect supranatural data that presents objectively and resolves to objective information which veracity we can then repeatably establish? The answer is ET. In practice, it's revelation, so the question is, how can revelation transition to data? It's quite simple, really.

1.2.1   Energy Testing as Data

The functional value of data is that it's repeatably and independently collectible. Rationalism and revelation that can never produce objective information are therefore traditionally worthless tools for data collection. Data collection from the natural world only serves as data because anybody can access it. You might be surprised to know that anybody can access supranatural data, too, and ET is the tool for it. As with the natural world, anyone who learns the methodology taught in PART V can, with the requisite training, skill, and their mind–body for equipment, collect for themselves any of the supranatural data we present in this book. Of course, how we collect, report, and analyze natural data intrinsically is debatable, and it's no different with supranatural data. One can certainly err with ET as with other data collection methodologies. My daughters and I verify and re-verify each other's ET to clarify or correct our data and the information we derive from it. Ayako, El, and occasionally Moth Man (FN 16:4; § 1.1:61) double-checked parts of my work as I wrote this book, and I double-checked their corrections. As well, I double-check my own data continually when intuition, inconsistencies, or new data indicates it, or when Mina and others point out errors. The supranatural environment of our universe is as vibrant and dynamic as the natural. Nothing is static. It's a human environment after all. Even data that tests correctly can alter over time if conditions or one's awareness changes (§ 1.3:634).[96]

1.2.1.1 The Nonutility of Revelation as Data

Revelation is defined loosely as information received from a *super*natural entity through communication by inexplicable, internal (spiritual) means. It's subjective, not repeatable, and unusable for hypothesizing about reality no matter how visceral or well reasoned. Even if revelation contains valid truth, it can't be verifed as knowledge. To consider it a theory in the scientific sense or a truth in the philosophical sense, one's bare option necessarily is faith (religion) or rational belief built up from logical analysis (e.g., Augustine, Aquinas). All analysis can do, however, is verify a revelation's internal consistency, not its presumptive accuracy.[97] Yet, the whole point of collecting data is corroboration, to establish its likelihood of accuracy. Shorn of that, revelation is just circular reasoning. It fails as an alternative to empirical and rational data.

1.2.1.2 The Utility of Energy Testing as Data

Et is a third way. What it produces *is* data. It's not religion, metaphysical mumbo jumbo, enlightened soulspeak from the Summer Lands, or parlor tricks. It's a skills-based discipline, a direct, experiential, repeatable observation by the natural senses of a (seemingly) supranatural phenomenon producing information, knowledge, and wisdom. In collecting data from the supranatural, Et is classifiable as revelation but that's where the similarity ends. It's as different from traditional revelation as practice from theory. While traditional revelation is through inexplicable means, Et 'revelation' is via readily understood physical mechanisms: the sway (push; § 2.2.1:626) of one's body. One can explain, measure, test, and validate it. Its data comes via Query & Response (QR) as opposed to a mystical mind dump followed by rationalization. It's interactive; question follows answer until one is satisfied of an understanding. One checks it for internal consistency and overall logic as with traditional revelation and science. Crucially, however, one can winnow Et data in any direction until arriving at a datum capable of objective verification, say, air pressure in a car tire or deceased grandma's safe deposit key's location.[114]

Another reason we reference Et as observation and experiment, and the resulting data as information rather than revelation, is that revelation is decidedly a monotheistic—versus intuition as a non-monotheistic—construct. Revelation carries with it three problematic elements: 1) it links to an all-powerful God or vying brands of *Übermensch*;[98] 2) it's primarily personal; and 3) it's usually classified sacred and infallible thus unassailable, meaning, in the lingo of science, that it's unfalsifiable.[115]

As that's not the case with Et, it's best to avoid promoting the misnomer. Without organized religion historically coercing humanity via government and morality, revelation as a means to understand reality would've remained a believer's backwater of irrelevance. In any case, only about 55% of the world's population thinks monotheistically where revelation as a concept even exists, let alone as an accepted practice vis-à-vis its already-codified sacred revelatory scripture.[116] The bottom line is that traditional revelation isn't useful for discovering reality, supranatural or otherwise.

1.2.1.2.1 Energy Testing is a New Class of Study

Et isn't your grandmother's table knocking or any discipline arising in Philosophy with a capital-P. It constitutes a new class of study, not merely an emerging field or sub-discipline nor even a merging of subclasses like today's fatally flawed 'spiritual sciences,' e.g., *philoscience*.[117] Et transcends the false reality of Philosophy with a capital-P and its subclasses of study even as it harmonizes their empirical, rational, and revelatory modes of inquiry into a coherent whole. It explains the natural *and* supranatural in *cosmic* terms. Whereas science, philosophy, and religion proceed upon oft-unfounded assumptions drawn from the other two, or that even negate one for the other, Et proceeds from a tabula rasa, its assumptions arising only from QR Et data. Its unique mode of inquiry is energy testing, which makes any data accessible—natural or supranatural. Of maximal gravity, Et is a direct line to our 'creator' from whom we can compile (toward empirically validating) any information. This is

---

96. During summer 2018, for instance, Mina explained spirit humanity's fear that he's a judgmental creator, Big Healing or no. Rechecking in February 2020, we found that collective fear mostly resolved.

97. More than science, philosophy (like mathematics) is chock-a-block with rational, internally consistent yet wrong ideas.

98. German: from *Thus Spake Zarathustra* (Nietzsche 1883–91), various translations rendering it: 'beyond-man' (Alexander Tille 1896), 'superman' (Thomas Common 1909), or 'overman' (Walter Kaufmann 1954).

the unprecedented value and magnitude of ET. It's not silly to suppose that, if we want to understand our full reality which plainly includes an unexplainable aspect humanity labels supernatural, and supposing too that we knew for a surety that a creator exists, that the expedient course of action would be to query said 'creator.'

Why ignore the supernatural just because we hitherto couldn't make head nor tails of it? Science hasn't a clue what to make of a quantum universe or consciousness or life, but that hasn't stopped it from working the problem. Toward that end, people using ET will want to demonstrate, at least for themselves, that they're communicating with our 'creator' or with spirit persons they've identified by name and not Ming the Merciless or Joe Liar from the Outer Rim.

1.2.1.2.2 Energy Testing's Value

Consider ET's capability. Can you imagine applications beyond the rather esoteric pursuit of cosmic reality besides talking to deceased family and friends or inquiring into your health? ET is applicable to anything where information plays a role and the spirit persons involved are knowledgeable and willing to share.[99]

1.2.1.3 Contextualizing and Deconflicting ET Data

Our own nearly five years of using ET leads us to conclude it's more likely than not we're talking to the people we think we are and acquiring legitimate, objective supranatural data. Science never knows anything with a hundred percent certainty anyhow, any more than law courts are ever a hundred percent certain of guilt or innocence. But we strive to use a preponderance of the evidence—however one defines evidence—to narrow the margin of error beyond a reasonable doubt. Like anything operated by humans, ET has a margin of error, too. My daughters and I slim it down using, for instance, alternative inquiries and an ET equivalent of the scientific control experiment to eliminate confounding variables. Acquiring and deconflicting ET data can sometimes be time intensive. It builds gradually into a reasonably coherent picture of reality amenable to classification, hypothesis, theory, and laws (in the scientific sense). When Mina contravenes established scientific theories, we apply to his explanations reason, logic, consistency, and—as William of Occam smartly advised in the 1320s—simplicity. That doesn't justify the data, it simply makes it worth pursuing further.

"Nothing in life . . . makes sense without theory," Harvard biologist emeritus Edward O. Wilson tells us. "It is our nature to put all knowledge into context in order to tell a story" (1998, 56). That tale, dear reader, is the story of life, and it's coming up next.

---

99. Yes, there are spirit people who will help one pursue harm, but it's difficult and bad juju in any case. While Mina doesn't judge or punish, those harmed (and their family and friends) may have no compunction dishing out the long justice.

Emergence

Quick Summary. All Existence refers to 'all there is.' It's a novel emergent property of a previous All Existence that self-organized into today's current All Existence that, for the first time, included human consciousness. It's infinite, meaning indeterminate, in existence, space, and time and is self-grounded. All Existence operates in some ways like a mind but without sentience or sapience. In terms of its effect on consciousness, the current iteration of All Existence is its final one. It sustains human consciousness and an experiential multiverse of infinite human-creatable universes. Our universe is one of them. Chance and randomness aren't emergence.

IN THE BIG scheme of things, it may seem it doesn't really matter if we know all about real existence or so-called cosmic truth. How, you might wonder, will understanding reality affect how you live your daily life, your relationships, or your happiness? Well, it won't . . . not right away. It's a process. Like any process, it will expose you in time to a higher order of being that elevates your life experience as your perspective broadens. Not *can* but *will*, *if* you play the process out. In the shorter term, if you have an interest in who, what, and why you are—like, "What happens when I die?"—then understanding the larger reality, within which is the small tuft of grass upon which you live your individual life, can come in handy.

From this point forward come the meat and potatoes of this book. The Big Event gives you context for how we learned all that follows. It puts a human face to it that, right off the bat, announces—a bit like, as the song goes, "This is the dawning of the Age of Aquarius"[118]—the bedrock change the Big Healing ushered into our universe. As well, it shows that energy testing (ET) is a discipline to improve and not a magical mind meld with Eternity, that it goes part and parcel with necessary, bulk cogitation. My daughters and I haven't taken all this in without a shred of critical thinking, not at all. When Mina decides that I (for one) am getting complacent, relying too much on facile ET answers, he stops the show until I conversate and reason through to a higher order of comprehension he can then affirm or negate. That means resolving conundrums, contradictions, and inconsistencies and not relying on glib responses that lend to concocting rationalizations. It's not the simpleton's overview we're trying to give you but as much of the nuts and bolts we can work out within the confines of a readable book. ET isn't the sort of revelation that flows down from on high like a waterfall into an open catchment. Instead (to go all metaphorical on you), we have to hand-pump it up using Query & Response (QR) from an ET wellhead drilled by curiosity, its borehole lined with functioning chakras (CH. 29:497).

We titled this chapter EMERGENCE because *All Existence*—'all there infinitely is,' including our own universe and us—emerged and self-organized not from nothing but from something.[100] *Emergence* as herein described is an enabling feature for All Existence as well as its constituent parts, making possible that which without it is not. All Existence comes in three basic flavors: 1) all the space, 2) everything that's in it, and 3) human consciousness. That's a lot to unpack so, unfortunately, this book is more a brief than a dissertation despite its length. We put forth no arguments for the remainder of the book. We simply impart what we learned via ET.

---

100. *Why is there something rather than nothing?* is a question with "no logical bridge . . . the darkest in all philosophy" (James (1911) 1916, 46), the Supreme Brute Fact bedeviling Philosophy with a capital-P since time immemorial (cf. Holman 2010, 108–19).

Scientific and philosophical justification is for another day and no doubt other persons. To a limited degree, we link science and philosophy to what we learned to better express Mina contravening these fields of study, not to persuade you—that's your job—but to clarify. This chapter and the remainder of PART II covers the first flavor, *all the space* including human consciousness. PART III delves into the second flavor, *everything that's in it*. PART IV explains *us* in our everyday conscious essence in this universe that we bodily experience.

SECTION 1

All Existence

A physical person has a *brain* but behind that is *mind*. Imagine all there infinitely is—All Existence—in that way. What we see of our universe is its *finite, classified* structure, like our brain, beyond which lays *infinite, unclassified* existence and human consciousness, like our mind. Philosophy with a capital-P is out with the jury on the mind–brain issue, but even so, consider: do you feel bounded by your skull? Can you, the inscrutable person, detect when your thoughts, dreams, aspirations, feelings, and imagination reaches your brain's neuronal edge and you just can't create more thought? No? Well, that's not from incompetence. Your mind is boundless even as your brain is bounded.

Similarly, All Existence is fundamentally unbounded, infinite in all coherent ways. As our mind contains all possible thoughts, All Existence contains all possible realities, although—and unlike, say, St. Anselm's ontology[119]—just because we can imagine something doesn't mean it's a potential (possible) reality.[120] All Existence is limited, or finite, in what's possible in the same way our brain is limited, or finite, in what's possible according to how it's organized "so as to promote a specific function" (De Wolf et al. 2005, 7), which is to express a certain way and no other. What's possible for All Existence is dictated by the way it self-organized to express a certain way, to establish a certain reality and no other. All Existence is a self-assembled *emergent property* of a previous All Existence which then *self-organized* in a particular way that promotes a *particular* reality, not all *imaginable* realities. Let's briefly look at emergence and self-organization before describing the inception, structure, and nature of All Existence as it is.

As we begin, recall ET is a query-based discipline. If one can't contrive a query, there's no positive response to get. Incoherent queries beget incoherent responses. When Mina initially said All Existence issued from something prior, we conceptualized something along the lines of caterpillars from butterflies. But that didn't fit his responses—too many *no*'s. Eventually, *emerged* elicited a strong *yes*. Our next question was, "Emerged from what?" And wasn't that the sixty-four dollar question! Sadly, whole sentence responses are intuitive, not an ET modality. We needed a basis to understand what he meant so we could ask logical next questions instead of blindly casting about with an unbaited hook. We stumbled into emergence theory as the most fruitful, if imperfect, query paradigm to comprehend how a timeless, infinite reality came to be. To avoid confusion, we refer to All Existence in three separate modes of existence: 1) Previous All Existence, or what was before; 2) Emergent All Existence, or what emerged from what was before; and 3) Current All Existence, or what emergently self-organized into today's reality.

SECTION 2

Emergence

When diverse entities of a system locally disturb, differentiate, and coalesce in novel, coherent structures, "surfacing innovations and distinctions among its parts" (Holman 2010, 14) sufficient to globally disrupt the system, the system itself differentiates and ultimately coalesces—that is, self-assembles and self-organizes—into a novel, coherent system in ways that are, even in principle, irreducible to their emergent constituents. Emergent "even-in-principle irreducibility" (Piiroinen 2014, 146) recognizes that the sum is sometimes more, if not other than, its parts, and that "entities (properties or substances) 'arise' out of more fundamental entities and yet are 'novel' or 'irreducible' with respect to them" (O'Connor et al. 2015, par. 1).[121] Such entities are new, surprising, and unpredictable. Author Steven Johnson puts it this way: "[A]gents residing on one scale start producing behavior that lies one scale above them: ants create colonies; urbanites create neighborhoods; simple pattern-recognition software learns how to recommend new books. The movement from low-level rules to higher-level sophistication is . . . emergence" (2001, 18). They're viewed as *weakly* emergent when they're "unexpected given the principles" (Chalmers 2006, 244; e.g., cellular automaton program[122]) of their constituent parts, or *strongly* emergent when they're "not *deducible* even in principle" (ibid, 10; e.g., quantum entanglement[123]) from their constituent parts. Philosophically, something from nothing.

Emergent irreducibility isn't a property of our ignorance of how it could be reduced to its constituents, because "explained novelty is no less novel than unexplained novelty" (Mahner et al. 1997, 29). "[A]ll it takes for P to be emergent is that it is a property of a whole but not a property of its parts" (Piiroinen, 145–6). Current All Existence, however, is a new whole emerging transcendent of a previous whole. Whether it's ontological or epistemological, strong or weak, comprehended with respect to (henceforth, w.r.t.) its mechanism or not, or some aspect of "the rest of the gamut of emergence conceptualizations in philosophy and science today" (ibid, 146) isn't relevant because reality exceeds the theory. Mina says emergence is the best conceptualizing tool for the moment, though, so that's where we are.

People tend to view All Existence reductively but complexity science[101] fosters the view that some linchpins of reality—chief among them All Existence—can't be predicted, much less explained, by contemplating their constituent parts. Emergence is an irreducible that vexes reductionism and life. The advent of consciousness just piles it on. Inasmuch as emergence provides guidance on how All Existence came to *be*, it doesn't describe how it *is*. In emergence theory, for instance, despite an emergent property's new, higher-level, irreducible organization, "lower-level principles of organization are not altered by the emergence of higher levels" (Emmeche et al. 2000, 15). That is, the constituent low-level domain remains a normative player in the emergent high-level domain, e.g., personality from brain (mind), traffic from drivers, fluidity from water. This isn't the case regarding All Existence (although it is the case w.r.t. to All Existence vis-à-vis consciousness). Moreover, there is no *downward causality*—a defining principle of emergence whereby an emergent high-level domain influences its constituent low-level domain (O'Connor 1994, 97–8)—because Previous All Existence *ceases to exist* as a low-level domain upon Emergent All Existence self-organizing into Current All Existence (*Fig. 1*).

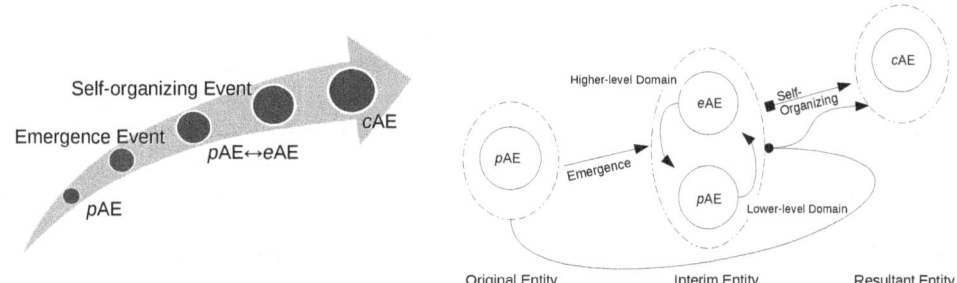

Figure 1. The change pattern starts with Previous All Existence *p*AE in coherence. Spontaneous disruption emergently breaks apart the status quo. Distinctions and innovations arise and *p*AE differentiates and coalesces into Emergent All Existence *e*AE. Novel structures self-organizationally interact and a new, more complex, and novel coherence arises as Current All Existence *c*AE (e.g., Holman 2011, 1161).

SECTION 3
Self-organization

The emergent phenomenon entails *self-assembly* "whereby a system is formed out of its components . . . [and] the aggregate x turns spontaneously . . . into the system y" (Mahner et al., 33–4). That means Emergent All Existence spontaneously self-assembled out of its emerging (differentiating and coalescing) self. Self-organization is, roughly, "a self-generated increase in statistical complexity" (Shalizi 2001, *ii*). A system is self-organized "if it changed its own organization, rather than being rewired by an external agency" (ibid, 6). Self-organization is a phenomenon confluent with emergence (De Wolf et al., 9–13; Addiscott 2011, 469–70). The "self-assembly process is one of *self-organization* iff [if and only if] the resulting system is composed of subsystems that were not in existence prior to the onset of the process" (Mahner et al., 34).

What this means w.r.t. All Existence is that self-organization itself is an emergent property of Emergent All Existence. And, as Current All Existence features an unaware subconscious intelligence (CH. 18:227), human consciousness is an emergent property, too. The upshot is that Emergent All Existence carried across a wide range of self-organizations before All Existence settled into a stable, coherent, transformationally satisfied final-

---

101. Such as chaos and network theories, and non-linear and self-organizing systems.

phase system that we term Current All Existence. Beyond our basic nod to the literature, self-organization w.r.t. All Existence denotes a certain reality rising emergently in series to the fore as *the* reality. That reality grounds *our* reality, the one encompassing our awareness, life, and the natural and supranatural environments (§ 7.1:212).

If you're having trouble visualizing emergence and self-organization, try thinking of it in terms of a person. A baby emerges from the constituent parts of its parents and for a time exists in a relationship of higher-domain (baby) to lower-domain (mother), as in weak emergence. Over time, however, the baby self-organizes into a recognizable, unpredictable, and irreducibly distinct physical being and personality whose reality is specific to that person, as in strong emergence. We can imagine, as we always do, many different realities for such a person just as the person themselves can. But their reality will be coincident with their emergent personality and the shifting confines of their environment. Local emergent properties routinely manifest in their life, but they, too, tend to coincide with extant personality and environment unless a system-wide disturbance innovates and coalesces into a novel emergent property and one observes the person living an emergent life without a vestige of its forebear; say, a religious conversion or epiphany. Admittedly, this is an imperfect analogy. Among other things, a person is sentient, sapient, and consciously choice-capable whereas All Existence is not.

SECTION 4

Chance, Randomness, and Emergence

Is emergence just another form of randomness and chance? No. To see why, let's briefly consider them. Often conflated, randomness and chance are two distinct concepts. One possibility, called the Commonplace Thesis, says "something is random iff it happens by chance" (Eagle 2019, par. 2). At the same time, if an event is truly random then it's inexplicable. Although this is just another way of saying an event is emergent, randomness and emergence aren't synonymous, either, since randomness is in principle predictable at least in probabilities whereas emergence is unpredictable even in principle. "[I]n no sense is any notion of mathematical randomness serving as an explication for 'ultimate physical randomness' . . . Taking 'mathematical randomness' to be product randomness, and 'physical randomness' to mean process randomness (chanciness),[102] this conclusion seems unavoidable" (ibid, § 8 CONCLUSION, par. 2–3). While we can probabilistically calculate randomness, we can't emergence. Not only is it unpredictable in principle locally, but globally, too.

What this means is that, although we can see, for example, *global* mutation in a species over several million years, none of those *local* mutations were in and of themselves—even in terms of adaptability to known environmental stressors—predictable either specifically or as a probability. And though we have a historical record of adaptations, it's not possible to calculate the probability a species *will* adapt to its next environmental stressor because undirected adaptation (RISE OF THE HUMANS, CH. 21:303) is emergent, not random or chancy. However many times we toss the coin of emergence into the air, it might or might not land on either face— emergence (heads) or no-emergence (tails)—at all. It might land on its analogous edge, blow away in a breeze, defy gravity to never drop, or possibly others; the point being that, as emergence is unpredictable even in principle, it's not possible to calculate the probability of any of those possibilities even occurring beyond calculating the probability they *could* occur. Specific emergence is noncalculable thus nonquantifiable.

This doesn't mean emergence as an event isn't probabilistic; it is. We can, for instance, legitimately calculate the probability of an emergent event somewhere in our universe in the next million years and be correct. But this is the same as predicting that any or all of the above coin possibilities *could* occur, but not that one or any of them necessarily will. The probability itself is emergent and, therefore, intrinsically unpredictable, thus not random nor a product of chance. Emergence is a truly random event, but a truly random event is not necessarily emergence. Without developing the philosophical reasoning here, we just note that randomness and chance aren't similar or related but different concepts entirely. Moreover, emergence is a truly random event in that an emergent property is unpredictable even in principle—though we can quantify the event as a probability—but it's neither randomly predictable nor predictably random. Emergence is both a random event and a chance occurrence, but doesn't happen *by* randomness or chance. Its reality is unpredictable.

We cover emergence, unaware subconscious intelligence, and All Existence's iterative states more comprehensively in ALL EXISTENCE and PSYCHE INFINITY (CH. 18:227; CH. 19:245). Next, we consider how these concepts of emergence and self-organization apply to our existence and the universe around us.

---

102. A process randomly generates an outcome, such as some number of consecutive coin tosses, as distinguished by the randomness of its product in which a random sample is random. Though we expect to toss at least one heads, there's a chance we won't even if we do.

Infinity

Quick Summary. We developed logic equations in this and the following chapters with Mina. They aren't meant as proofs but to help conceptualize what we learned. If you find this and the following science-oriented chapters uninteresting or problematic, we encourage you to glean their general concepts as best you can as they inform the metaphysical (woo-woo) data throughout this book. Infinity is real but isn't a thing that dimensionally encapsulates, e.g., size, scope, distance, volume, or time. It's rooted in the dimensionlessness of 'energy,' an indeterminacy that's indefinable. We can define its attributes (say, space without end), but we can't define *it*. Mathematical infinities have no reality and are the wrong way to comprehend infinitude. All Existence is globally infinite—indeterminate—whereas our universe is locally infinite. After we reframe the concept of infinity in this chapter, we describe it in terms of its four principal forms: existence, time, space, and psyche.

LET'S TALK ABOUT the elephant in the room: *infinity*, what physicist Max Tegmark calls "a beautiful concept" (2015, 48) but mathematician Georg Cantor (d. 1918) of infinite set theory fame chides w.r.t. time and space as "monstrous nonsense" (Kragh 2014, 5).[124] It exerts a surprisingly elephantine effect on our understanding of reality. The struggle with infinity has always been whether, as a concept, it can or does exist in the real world in which we live and its relation to how, perhaps by whom, our existence came to be. Infinity isn't just a fun diversion for eggheads to ponder the imponderable on someone else's dime. It matters because the concept of infinity informs our thinking regarding how our lives work and whether we're infinite ourselves; that, in physical death, we cease to exist as a conscious personality or not.

A person who orders their life on the premise that existence ends with death is justified to enjoy and prolong their life by whatever means because, for them, it's rational that morality is transient and relative—many on Earth live accordingly and treat others just so. On the other hand, a person who thinks existence never ends regardless physical death is justified to temper life with self-sacrifice, including giving their (perhaps one and only) life for others, because, for them, it's rational that morality is intransient and transcendent—many on Earth live accordingly that way, too, and treat others just so. Though notions of infinity seem hidden behind an Ozian curtain, it plays a foundational role in human existential behavior. Now, Mina draws some sharp distinctions regarding infinity:

1. infinity is *real* and a contrast with Philosophy with a capital-P's *actual* and *potential* (or, *variable*), and even *absolute* infinities;[125]
2. our (local) infinite universe is only a part of a broader, transcendent (global), infinite reality;
3. while infinity is indeed a *reality*, it's not a real *thing*, like a manipulable object or impalpable existent; it represents an abstraction without being an aspect of reality;
4. everything in existence (except four categories, defined farther *below*) is finite in its own way;
5. there's interplay between what's finite and infinite (e.g., while object or wave motion is finite, motion in and of itself is infinite because space is, which follows from existence being infinite);

6. bearing distinction 2 in mind, there are two broad classes of infinity: 1) *global* infinity w.r.t. no beginning and no end, and 2) *local* infinity w.r.t. to a beginning but no end (farther *below*).

Understanding infinity can be a tricky business, but it needn't be if we avoid misapplying knowledge and concepts. Defining infinity as limitless, unlimited, endless, boundless, unbounded, size-less, unsized, and so on; or as a quality or nature of perfect, beyond compare, archetypal, inexhaustible, without constraint, unable to increase, fathomless, and so on; or as the traditional four Omnis of God[126] all fail because these concepts are really about bounded states, of scope and scale. However infinite or ineffable we define scope and scale or quantity and quality, we're really just calling a canary a cat. The concept intrinsic to dimensional terms speaks to finites in that implicative of conceptualizing a lack of dimensionality is countability.[127] Whether countably or uncountably scoped or scaled is of no difference, it's still the finite writ indefinably large and thus a determinate.

SECTION 1
The Concept of Infinity

Mina defines infinite at its most basic as *indeterminate*.[128] 'Infinite past,' for example, just means that time's start is undefined, meaning it is *start-countable indeterminate*. It's faulty to view it as some amount or span, or a completed whole of time past. Turning to logic to conceptualize infinity then,

$$\forall t, x \in \mathbb{R} : \left\{ \neg \exists x \mid \forall t, (t - x = 0) \right\} \leftrightarrow t \notin \mathbb{R} \tag{14.1}$$

where any time t (of which some x is an element of the set of real numbers $\mathbb{R}$, there's no x such that, for any time t, $t - x = 0$) is materially equivalent to t not an element of $\mathbb{R}$.[103] Similarly, 'infinite space' means *energy indeterminate*. 'Infinite' never references any sort of completed existent such as "infinite space goes on forever."

We habitually project finite constructs onto infinity that necessarily lead to paradoxes, inconsistencies, and contradictions that seem to render it an absurdity (EN 125:656). Let's consider mathematics, as it most comprehensively articulates today's concept of infinity. Suppose the infinite set S, defined as

$$S = x \left\{ x \mid x \in \mathbb{N} \right\} \tag{14.2}$$

where the set S contains some value x such that x is an element of the set of natural numbers $\mathbb{N}$, which we denote simply as the infinite set $\{\infty\}$ such that $\mathbb{N} \leftrightarrow \{\infty\}$. This set is certainly possible in mathematics but not in reality because it's a contradiction to collect or range—scope or scale—an indeterminacy, such as when defining a function whose *domain*[104] is, say, the infinite set of all integers $\mathbb{Z}$, or of real numbers $\mathbb{R}$, or of natural numbers $\mathbb{N}$. Now, suppose the function

$$f(x) = \left\{ x \mid (\infty + x = \infty) \right\} \bigwedge x \in \mathbb{N} \tag{14.3}$$

where, say, $f(\infty + 1 = \infty)$, 1 is a defined entity, and $\bigwedge$ is the logical 'and.' What exactly is the infinity (∞) operand, here? If it's the *cardinality*[105] of the infinite set, then the infinity operand is a finite unbounded number that's undefined.[106] If the infinity operand is $\mathbb{N}$, the infinite set itself, then the operand is a finite unbounded scope, or domain, that's undefined. If the infinity operand is the *elements* of $\mathbb{N}$, then the operand is a finite unbounded series that's undefined. The operation actually occurring in $f(x)$ is $undefined + defined = undefined$. This isn't very different from an operation on the empty set $\{\}$, which is infinitely empty whereas the infinite set is infinitely *not* empty but certainly not infinitely full. Both are undefined by dint of undefined cardinality, scope (domain), or series. In effect, infinity and infinite sets really operate as finite unbounded entities that are necessarily undefined and aren't definable as *infinite*. To compare, say, $\mathbb{N}$ to the infinite set of all real numbers $\mathbb{R}$ (as in Cantor's Theorem[107]) in order to show $\mathbb{R}$ is a *greater* defined infinity (that is, one containing more finite unbounded elements) than $\mathbb{N}$—albeit strictly valid

---

103. In propositional logic notation, $\forall$ means, 'for all' or 'for any;' $\exists$ means, 'there exists;' the vertical bar $\mid$ means, 'such that;' $\leftrightarrow$ means, 'is materially equivalent to;' $\neg$ is 'not' (negation), and $\notin$ means, 'not an element of.'

104. The set of all possible values that can go into a function.

105. The number of elements of a set, denoted $|x|$ where x is the number of elements.

106. *Finite unbounded* is conceptually similar to the finite but unbounded two-dimensional surface of a sphere.

107. The mathematical proof Georg Cantor used to demonstrate infinite sets.

as a logical matter—is a fallacy, thus untrue as a reality. It's fallacious because even mathematics doesn't define infinity by cardinality or infinite denumerability but rather by its indeterminacy such as in

$$\int_a^b f(t)\, dt = \infty \tag{14.4}$$

where the integral means $f(t)$ doesn't bound a finite area from a to b.

Let's take $x = \frac{0}{0}$ that mathematically is in an undefined result, meaning indeterminate as a matter of truth, which is to say, nothing divided by nothing doesn't actually equal *nothing*. Rather, the equality can't be defined because nothing itself is an undefined—an indefinable—quality. Physics, however, often views this expression not as undefined but as actually infinite, meaning that, since mathematics posits that

$$x = \frac{0}{0} \Leftrightarrow 0 * x = 0 \left\{ \; x \mid x \in \mathbb{R} \right. \tag{14.5}$$

where $\Leftrightarrow$ means 'logically equivalent' and any real number to infinity works for x, then $x = \frac{0}{0}$ is infinite because x can be infinite, which it's not (Massive Objects & Lightspeed, § 6.1:165). But as infinity is indeterminance, we can't say the equivalence in Eq. (14.5) is valid or true simply on the grounds that it works for x as any number, because $0 * x = 0$ literally means 'nothing taken some x number of times is nothing.' No matter how many times we take nothing it's still nothing, and nothing, being not something, is undefined (Something from Nothing, § 2.1.1:231). Therefore, $0 * x = undefined$, not zero, and $0 \Leftrightarrow \{\}$ with its cardinality $|\{\}|$ is not zero but undefined.[108] In fact, zero as cardinality is the perfect representation in mathematics of the miscomprehension of infinity because it's a bounded nothing when it should be indeterminance. Neither can we strictly say that x in $0 * x$ works for any number because that presumes $0 * x = 0$ when, really, $0 * x = undefined$. Thus,

$$x = \frac{0}{0} \neq 0 * x = 0 \tag{14.6}$$

and, accordingly, infinity is indeterminance and not an infinite denumerability where zero or the empty set $\{\}$ is an uncountable entity.

Strictly speaking, mathematical infinity expressed by the *aleph* symbols $\aleph, \aleph_0, \aleph_1, \dots \aleph_n$ and Ω and ω[109] aren't infinite in the sense of indeterminate but in the sense of unbounded.[110] A mathematician will say some $\aleph$ is 'infinite' even while accepting that $\aleph$ can be mathematically manipulated, such that

$$\aleph_n < \aleph_n + 1 \tag{14.7}$$

where the tacitly infinite is greater than infinite. This renders $\aleph$ determinate (however undefined) thus an unbounded bounded finite and not an indeterminate, which is to say, an infinite. Hence, $\aleph$ can't be an infinity and

$$\aleph \not\Leftrightarrow \infty \tag{14.8}$$

wherein the operator $\not\Leftrightarrow$ negates the logical equivalence. Herein lies the reason infinity can't be 'greater than' infinity. It's not a set with some cardinality of $\aleph$ as in

$$\mathbf{c} = 2^{\aleph_0} > \aleph_0 \tag{14.9}$$

where $\mathbf{c}$ is the cardinality of the continuum;[111] it's indeterminate. If we include time t in Eq. (14.7) as

$$t\aleph_n < t\aleph_n + 1, \tag{14.10}$$

then it's apparent that two or more time infinities are a contradiction of infinity as indeterminate and time as scope. However abstractly useful in mathematics, infinite sets are built around a faux infinity that contradicts

---

108. This means that, while zero *can* exist, the empty set $\{\}$ can't because zero is indeterminance but $\{\}$ is an unbounded bounded entity which isn't indeterminance even if we say it *contains* indeterminance. See § 2.1.1:231 for more on $\{\}$ and *nothing*.

109. Hebrew letter 'aleph' ($\aleph$); uppercase and lowercase Greek letter 'omega' (Ω, ω).

110. *Bounded* and *unbounded* means to be in some way contained or uncontained.

111. The 'size' of the set of real numbers $\mathbb{R}$.

infinitude as a matter of principle. If one philosophically comprehends real world infinity in mathematical terms, as many do, then one stumbles into contradiction.[129]

Similarly, Hilbert's Infinite Hotel Paradox,[112] which is variously used to prove or disprove real world infinity as well as God or a creator by demonstrating the absurdity,[130] avails itself of a faux infinity that multifariously contradicts its own premise, to wit:

1. if infinite rooms are occupied then infinite humanity is implied and accounted for so no new guest is even possible;

2. guests are paired to rooms in a 50:50 ratio but the solution to a new guest arriving alters that, rendering the room side of the ratio less than 50% (however briefly) and thus no longer infinite;[131]

3. moving any guest to a new room by shifting guests in one case to a room one number higher, and in another case two numbers higher, to accommodate new guests means there are either unoccupied rooms in an *actually* infinitely occupied hotel or the *potentially* infinitely-roomed hotel manufactures new rooms for infinite humanity-plus-one. Either way, the hotel doesn't have infinite rooms infinitely occupied by infinite humanity (EN 125:656);

4. the hotel isn't a discrete infinity of rooms at all but more like the *res potentia*[113] of a quantum probability space.[132]

Of course, Hilbert's thought experiment isn't addressing infinity at all but Set Theory's notion that any set X is infinite if a proper subset S exists for X in a one-to-one correspondence;[113] the new-guest–new-room solution is simply an algorithm that assures it. Infinity engenders no paradox w.r.t. spatiotemporal reality or a creator when it's accurately contextualized in, and not conflated beyond, the reality where it belongs. The way Philosophy with a capital-P popularly conceptualizes it as infinite is faulty. Hence, when Mina tells us our universe is space-infinite and existence-infinite, we can't comprehend his meaning through a flawed filter such as mathematics (thus philosophy and religion) because it has no logical relation to infinity; it's irrelevant. That "[m]athematics is the science of the infinite" (Weyl 2012, 17) is untenable.

SECTION 2
Indeterminance

Then, what does indeterminate mean in the context of real infinity? Simply, that it's not something you can point to and say, "that's infinity" or "that's a block of never-ending time or matter or volume," or worse, "the counting scope or scale is infinite." Infinity is without identity. It's nothing more and nothing less than indeterminacy because, in terms of, let's say, All Existence (CH. 13:89; CH. 15:99 ff), the very concept of a point of departure or a terminal accession for time is alien just as volume or measure is alien to space. Imputing a terminal, or maximal quantified value—even if the quantification is some variation of 'infinite'—to infinity is really a function of finitude. Infinity can't be infinite when it's vested with finitude. Infinite time, for example, is start-countable and end-countable (and infinite space is 'energy') indeterminate as a function of existence infinity (CH. 15:99; CH. 16:105; CH. 17:111).

In either context, it's self-evident in conceptualizing infinity that we can't apply relational indeterminacy to time, or start-countable and end-countable indeterminacy to space. Doing so leads to conceptualizing time infinity as an existent, or space infinity as spacetime (§ 2:107). But indeterminacy doesn't reference uncertainty, innumerability, or denumerability. Infinity doesn't have an objectively precise value. There's no determinate reference. Real infinity doesn't relate to truth-values in the way of logic and mathematics or to the superman models (*Zarathustra*; FN 98:86) of the 'infinite Absolute' that inhere to theology. Infinitude is not a *property* of nature but an *expression* of reality. It's necessary to scotch the notion that infinity is a mathematical infinite number, or a domain for the infinite variability of reality's parts, or that infinite has anything whatsoever to do with an "absolutely infinite" creator such that we might any better comprehend some "new and useful piece of knowledge about God, the way that 'denumerably infinite' *does* give us new and useful knowledge about the rational numbers" (Le Blanc 1993, 62, 10).

When Mina says infinity is indeterminate, he's creating no organizational scheme to which, or in which, infinity coheres. But when *we* say infinity "is that which has no limits," we *are* creating an organizational matrix

---

112. Hypothetical hotel of infinite, occupied rooms faced with a new guest; posited by David Hilbert (d. 1943) in 1924 (Kragh, 3).

113. Latin: 'potential things' along the lines of René Descartes' (d. 1650) *res extensa* and *res cogitans*.

upon which, or in which, infinity resides in schemata. And that's precisely the problem with Philosophy with a capital-p's conceptualizations of infinity. It invests it with organization, an existence, some matrix that bounds infinity and the infinite. The truth is it's none of those things. Infinity is simply indeterminacy w.r.t. its predicate.[114] It's not the abyssal mystery of reality or some deitic Silent Bob[115] that lies behind the sour complexities of infinity, but that humanity has heretofore invested infinity with attributes and properties intrinsic of some mystic creator or terra incognita and then tried to define *that* as a reality. Ultimately, all extant notions of infinity, including those of mathematics and quantum science, come steeped in mysticism.

SECTION 3
Classes and Categories of Infinity

Let's turn now from this ET-informed discussion on infinity generally and talk some specifics. In All Existence, two classes of infinity are 1) *indeterminate*, which can be thought of as global, meaning it applicably transcends our universe; and 2) *determinant*, which is local, meaning it's applicable within our universe. An example of this is time, which is bidirectionally time-infinite in the global context but unidirectionally time-infinite in the local context (*Fig. 2*).

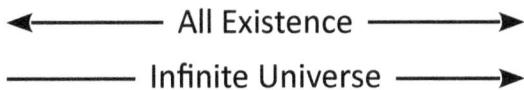

Figure 2. Time infinity: top, bidirectional; bottom, unidirectional.

Of these two classes of infinity are four discrete categories as mentioned in the fourth distinction (farther *above*): 1) *existence* infinity Ei referring to emergence; 2) *time* infinity Ti referring to event periodicity (CH. 16:105); 3) *space* infinity Si referring to energy (CH. 17:111); and 4) *psyche* infinity Pi referring to subjective experientiality (consciousness; CH. 19:245). Accordingly,

$$\exists!AE \left\{ Pi \to (Ti \to Si) \to Ei \right\} \leftrightarrow R \tag{14.11}$$

where for exactly one All Existence AE, if psyche infinity Pi then time infinity Ti, hence space infinity Si, thus existence infinity Ei, altogether materially equivalent to reality R.[116] As existence naturally underpins all else, we turn first to existence infinity before considering time, space, and then psyche infinity.

---

114. For example, 'space is infinite' or 'time is infinite' *predicates* the infinity of space or time.

115. cf. films *Dogma* (1999) and *Jay and Silent Bob Strike Back* (2001).

116. The notation ∃! means 'there exists exactly one' or 'for exactly one;' → means 'if . . . then,' 'implies,' or 'presumes.'

Existence Infinity

Quick Summary. There is ever only a single reality termed All Existence. Current All Existence has a beginning in time (which, like motion, is an expression of existence), yet is timeless. It's an emergent property of a Previous All Existence whose single existent reality assimilated via the emergence process into a new, novel, emergently Current All Existence. In emergence, Previous All Existence explains Current All Existence. Together, they form an ontological system that explains and causatively justifies a current reality in terms of its previous reality. Hence, there's no uncaused cause or infinite regress to confound explaining ultimate cause in the context of infinity.

ALL EXISTENCE IS infinite. Even so, *our* universe hasn't existed for infinite time and neither has human consciousness. Each began at some point and before that, wasn't. This raises an issue in that All Existence supports the existence of our universe and human consciousness whereas at points past there was no such universe or consciousness. To that we could say either All Existence didn't yet support them or they hadn't yet developed. In either case, All Existence *exclusive* of our universe and consciousness was substantively different from All Existence *inclusive* of our universe and consciousness.

If All Existence wasn't the same then as now, the obvious wonderment is how was it then and how'd it get to this, now? It leads to the question Philosophy with a capital-P has about the Big Bang and most anyone has regarding time and space infinity, which is, "What infinite reality existed before *our* seemingly finite reality?"[134] The short answer is that All Existence *now* is an emergent property (§ 2:90) of a previous All Existence *then*. That begs the question: assuming an All Existence now, where'd the previous All Existence come from and where'd it go? Well, as an emergent, All Existence isn't a mere assemblage of a prior All Existence, nor on account of time and space infinity is it a higher-order domain to a previous All Existence the way traffic is to lower-order domain cars, or quantum entanglement is to particles.

Science can't imagine any reality that appears to defy its pat physicality—temporal finitude, howsoever infinite (eternal)—dovetailing with our physical senses despite technologically extending itself into previously insensible albeit still-natural regions while steadfastly shunning supranaturalism in the sense that an eternal, or uncaused, reality is unnatural hence impossible. Philosopher Jim Holt in *Why Does the World Exist?* essentially recognizes, without admitting, its scientific futility. It coincidently mirrors neuroscience's temporal reductionism to explain the vastness and unpredictability even in principle of human thought and emotion as naught but the brain's electrochemical neurology.

Despite recognizing that "the great lessons of the history of science is that reality always turns out to be more encompassing than anyone imagined" (2012, 84), the unshakeability of causality (conjoined to a universe) amongst Philosophy with a capital-P is the culprit. "With an eternal world," says Holt, describing the attempt to rationalize away the clash between causality and eternity, ". . . there is no inexplicable 'creation moment' . . . it's existence at any moment can be explained by its existence the previous moment" (ibid). It's therefore "a world with solid ontological foundations" without contingency (ibid, 81). Philosopher David Hume's (d. 1776) assertion in *Dialogues Concerning Natural Religion*, which Holt discusses, that the universe is an eternal succession of objects (or events), necessarily eschews a first as well as an uncaused cause[117] because any "succession of objects . . . is caused by that which preceded it . . . that the uniting of these parts into a whole . . . is an arbitrary act of the mind, and has no influence on the nature of things" (Aiken (1779) 1948, 59; Holt, 85); the universe isn't a *thing*, an existent, but *way of being* (§ 2.2.1.1:234). For Hume, "an eternal world looks like the cause of itself . . . It is *causa sui*—an attribute usually reserved for God. But there's still something missing here" (Holt, 85–86, io). Hume provides insight if we elevate causality from just our universe to All Existence.

An Emergent All Existence such as our Current All Existence doesn't exist in a separate time or space from its constituent, or propagative, All Existence because All Existence as reality (we'll call it P) is infinite. Therefore, any Previous All Existence as reality (we'll call it Q) upon which P is ontologically dependent is also infinite. Accordingly, P and Q are each infinitely the same time and space. Being infinite, All Existence can't exist within, alongside, or displace a Previous All Existence that's also infinite; where in time or space would two such space-infinite All Existences—by definition 'all there infinitely is'—exist? Therefore,

$$\exists! R, \forall P \left\{ \infty(P) \bigwedge \infty(Q) \right\} \leftrightarrow \left\{ P \to (P, \neg Q) \right\} \tag{15.1}$$

where for exactly one reality R and any All Existence P, an infinite P and infinite Previous All Existence Q is materially equivalent with infinite All Existence without a concomitant infinite Previous All Existence. In that sense, All Existence doesn't come from nothing but from something (§ 2.1.1:231). We can't point to that something in All Existence, however, because for any Emergent All Existence, its constituent All Existence assimilates in the emergence process. As All Existence is time-infinite and space-infinite, only one All Existence is ever possible. Consequently,

$$\exists! AE \; \forall P \, A \left(P, Q \right) \leftrightarrow R \tag{15.2}$$

where for exactly one All Existence AE there exists a P in which output Q of assimilative emergence function $A(x, y)$[118] outputs an All Existence P that's reality R.

The class of infinity for All Existence generally is *indeterminate* but that of Current All Existence—or, All Existence as it exists now as opposed to that before human consciousness and our own universe—is *determinant*. This means Current All Existence is ontologically dependent on Previous All Existence. As that naturally raises the question of pedigree[119] for Previous All Existence, it's needless to say it's ontologically dependent itself on a prior All Existence, and *that* prior All Existence is ontologically dependent on a still prior All Existence—well, ad infinitum. And here's where we land in the Gordian knot of infinite causal regress[120] that, so far, has tightly trussed up Philosophy with a capital-p. The reason it's done so, of course, is the mereological possibility that "each thing is dependent on some further thing(s), with nothing being fundamental" (Ross 2019, § 2, par. 13); nothing is ever ultimately explained. But this conundrum is not a necessity. What now follows is a barebones outline of a reflexive ontology in which All Existence exists because of All Existence, thus removing the infinite causal loop. On the surface, this might initially sound like an uncaused cause but, as is apparent farther on, it's anything but.

SECTION 1
Reflexive Ontology for Infinite All Existence

As an explanans, let an existence P be ontologically dependent on a previous existence Q. Hence, P *grounds in*—its reason for existing is explained by—Q. For a fundamental explanation of P, then, Q suffices. Therefore,

$$\exists! R \left(P \to Q \right) \leftrightarrow \left\{ Q \leftarrow P \right\} \tag{15.3}$$

---

117. God, or existence, never *came into* existence but always existed.

118. The *assimilative function* $A(x, y)$ and notation is unique to this discussion.

119. In choosing pedigree over provenance, Mina notes that, in his mind, pedigree relates to the source/process of creation while provenance relates to whatever existential reality obtained in consequence of All Existence at any point along its described ontological chain. Therefore, All Existence's origin is pedigree while its nature is provenance.

120. The truth of a proposition P_1 requires the truth of some proposition P_2, which itself requires the truth of a proposition P_3, ad infinitum, without ever reaching an ultimate, causative truth and, hence, no actual beginning of God or existence.

where for exactly one reality R, 'if P then Q' is materially equivalent to 'Q is implied by, or presumes, P;' there is 'not P without Q.' Thus, P and Q are elements of ontological set $\{P, Q\}$, which is an ontological *system* wherein the existence of one (Q) explains that of the other (P). $P \rightarrow Q$ is a *unitary* explanation for All Existence that presents in the ontological system $\{P, Q\}$, stated as

$$\exists! R \left(P \rightarrow Q \right) \leftrightarrow \left\{ P, Q \right\} \tag{15.4}$$

where for exactly one reality R, 'P implies Q' is an ontological system $\{P, Q\}$. Let's call this ontological system $\{P, Q\}$ a *grounding unit* denoted GU_a and let it represent $\{P, Q\}$ such that

$$\forall P \forall Q \in \left\{ P, Q \right\} \left(\left[(Q \leftarrow P) \leftrightarrow (P \rightarrow Q) \right] \leftrightarrow \left\{ P, Q \right\} \right) \leftrightarrow GU_a \tag{15.5}$$

where any P and Q that are elements of ontological system $\{P, Q\}$—in which 'Q is implied by (or presumes) P' is materially equivalent to 'if P then Q' (or, 'P implies Q'), and is $\{P, Q\}$—is altogether a grounding unit GU_a. Now, where $P \Rightarrow Q$, from whence comes Q? It must ground in a prior existence. This raises the specter of infinite regress that vitiates ultimate cause, and existence fails explanation.

1.1 EMERGENTLY INDEPENDENT ONTOLOGICAL SYSTEMS

For this book, here's how Mina reflexively resolves this seeming conundrum. Let any existence prior to Q be Q_{-1}, Q_{-2}, Q_{-3} ad infinitum. Accordingly, Q is ontologically dependent on Q_{-1} such that $Q \rightarrow Q_{-1}$ in the same way that $P \rightarrow Q$. Consistent with the above, then, Q and Q_{-1} are elements of ontological system $\{Q, Q_{-1}\}$, which we duly represent as grounding unit GU_{a-1}. We now simplify Eq. (15.5) to

$$\exists! R \left((Q \rightarrow Q_{-1}) \leftrightarrow \left\{ Q, Q_{-1} \right\} \right) \leftrightarrow GU_{a-1} \tag{15.6}$$

where for exactly one reality R—since 'if Q then Q_{-1}' is materially equivalent to ontological system $\{Q, Q_{-1}\}$—then, as above, it is grounding unit GU_{a-1}. Whereupon, it follows that

$$\left\{ Q_{-1}, Q_{-2} \right\} \leftrightarrow GU_{a-2}, \left\{ Q_{-2}, Q_{-3} \right\} \leftrightarrow GU_{a-3}, \ldots \infty \tag{15.7}$$

as a series of discrete, *independent ontological units* in which ontological system $\{Q_{-1}, Q_{-2}\}$ is grounding unit GU_{a-2}, and so on ad infinitum as per Eq. (15.6).

What this analysis gets us is that ontologically discrete grounding units GU_a, GU_{a-1}, GU_{a-2} ad infinitum resolve *via emergence* to ontologically independent *systems*. GU_a fully explains and justifies the existence of All Existence without appealing to any further-regressed Previous All Existence. It describes that what came before All Existence (prior to our universe—the Big Bang—and human consciousness) *was* All Existence and fully explains and justifies *itself*. We accordingly moot the necessity for infinite regress to explain infinity. How? Well, recall how emergence operates w.r.t. All Existence (§ 2:90).

Let's take for example the grounding unit GU_a that represents $\{P, Q\}$ in Eq. (15.5). In this independent ontological unit, self-organizing emergent P assimilates Q such that $\{P, Q\}$ reduces to $\{P'\}$ (read, 'P-prime') with a cardinality of one ($|P'| = 1$), where Q is not a subset of $\{P'\}$ and neither is $\{P'\}$ a subset of $\{P, Q\}$. At the conclusion of this emergent process, GU_a resolves to GU_a',[121] representing emergent $\{P'\}$—where $\{P, Q\}$ or P and Q, no longer exists—such that

$$\exists! GU_a \left(P(Q)^A = \left\{ Q \in GU_a \,\middle|\, Q \not\subset \{P\}, P \not\subset \{P, Q\}, |P| = 1 \right\} \leftrightarrow \{P'\} \right) \leftrightarrow GU_a' \tag{15.8}$$

where for exactly one grounding unit GU_a, 'the assimilated Q of P' $(P(Q)^A)$—where Q is an element of GU_a such that Q is not a subset $\not\subset$ of ontological system $\{P\}$ or of $\{P, Q\}$, and the cardinality $|P|$ is 1—is materially equivalent to ontological system $\{P'\}$ and is grounding unit GU_a'.

Similarly, GU_{a-1} representing as above the ontological relationship $Q \Rightarrow Q_{-1}$, reduces $\{Q, Q_{-1}\}$ to emergent $\{Q'\}$ and, accordingly, resolves to ontologically independent GU_{a-1}'. GU_{a-1}' is the Previous All Existence

---

121. The *assimilated* notation $P(Q)^A$ is unique to this book (cf. FN 118:100); $\not\subset$ means 'not a subset of,' and $|P|$ is 'the cardinality of P.' GU_a' is read 'grounding unit a-prime' or 'GU-a-prime.'

reality that eventually experienced emergence of P as above, giving rise to $\{P, Q\}$ that we represented as system GU_a and ultimately resolves to emergent $\{P'\}$, represented by GU'_a such that

$$\exists! GU'_a, P' \left\{ P \leftrightarrow Q \,\middle|\, P \subset^E GU_{a-1}, P(Q) \bigwedge P(Q)^A \right\} \leftrightarrow GU'_a \tag{15.9}$$

where for exactly one GU'_a, P'—in which P is materially equivalent to Q such that 'P is an *emergent subset* $(\subset^E)$[122] of GU_{a-1},' Q of P, and the assimilated Q of P—is GU'_a. GU'_a is the emergent final state we've termed All Existence AE, the version today we've termed Current All Existence cAE. Accordingly,

$$\left(GU'_a \leftrightarrow cAE \right) \vDash R \tag{15.10}$$

where cAE entails ($\vDash$) reality R. This same systemic, unitary dynamic obtains for GU_{a-2}, GU_{a-3}, ad infinitum such that

$$\exists! R \left\{ \left(pAE \leftarrow eAE^{so} \right) \rightarrow U^{\infty}_{-n} \right\} \rightarrow \ldots \left\{ \left(U_{-n} \leftarrow pAE^{so} \right) \rightarrow Q \right\}$$
$$\rightarrow Q \left\{ \left(Q \leftarrow eAE^{so} \right) \rightarrow P \right\} \leftrightarrow cAE \tag{15.11}$$

$$\rightarrow time \rightarrow$$

where for exactly one reality R, if any *prior* All Existence pAE is implied by, or presumes, a self-organizing *emergent* All Existence eAE^{so} (or, per Eq. (15.3), 'not eAE^{so} without pAE') then any post-emergent, post-assimilated, stable, realized system n is backward relative to the time arrow. This pattern repeats such that if U_{-n} is implied by, or presumes, a self-organizing previous All Existence eAE^{so} then there's a Q. Accordingly, then, if Q is implied by, or presumes, a self-organizing emergent All Existence eAE^{so} then there's a P. Ultimately, this pattern is materially equivalent to Current All Existence cAE.[123]

With the above in mind, Emergent All Existence self-organizes into Current All Existence in the course of which Previous All Existence assimilates, consequently ceasing to be as it was. We simplify Eq. (15.11) to

$$eAE \left(pAE \right) \vdash \left(cAE \leftrightarrow eAE(pAE) \right) \vDash \exists! R \tag{15.12}$$

where Previous All Existence of Emergent All Existence $eAE(pAE)$ yields ($\vdash$) a materially equivalent Current All Existence cAE as a simple function $f(x)$ that ultimately entails ($\vDash$) exactly one reality R. At this point, Current All Existence forms a discrete, coherent system and is ontologically dependent, or grounded, in *itself*. It exists *because* it exists, a self-referential, or reflexive, reality on account of its emergent, self-organized, and assimilative properties. Thus, let R be the set {Reality}. GU'_a *maps to* R as

$$R = f \left(GU'_a \right) \left\{ GU'_a \,\middle|\, GU'_a \in R, |R| = 1 \right\} \tag{15.13}$$

where f is a mapping function of GU'_a that's an element of R with a cardinality $|R|$ of 1.

This ontological grounding—or, epistemological justification—is a holistic phenomenon, not circular or recursive but unitary. Because of the features intrinsic to emergence (§ 2:90), Current All Existence is grounded in what the system collectively—wholistically—is and not on account of its initial ontological dependence. The emergent process renders it not ontologically necessary that Previous All Existence be ontologically justified or valid in order for Current All Existence to be ontologically justified or valid. Accordingly, infinite regress in search of ultimate cause presents no difficulty because it isn't necessary to account for an ontological infinity of All Existence.[135]

In terms of causality (and in particular, 'originating cause'), the self-organizing and assimilative feature set of emergence w.r.t. All Existence is itself the causative agent of All Existence.[136] The bottom line is that All Existence caused itself *to be as it is* even though, as we've seen, its ontological pedigree caused it simply *to be* as an existential matter.[124] Even if we look back through an infinite regress to a mythical origination, it could be naught but emergent. All Existence is existentially infinite, which is to say, indeterminate. It isn't possible for 'something' to precede infinity existentially or ontologically because that implies (in a Cantorian way)

---

122. The 'emergent' notation $\subset^E$ is unique to this book.

123. The notation $U^{\infty}_{-n} \ldots U_{-n}$ is an infinite regress segregated as ontologically discrete units; x^{so} is any self-organizing x.

124. Our universe, existentially thus ontologically different from All Existence, *does* have a First Cause: Mina (CH. 22:335).

something more infinite than infinity, meaning more indeterminate than indeterminate. That's irrational, as it injects abstract set theory into reality. Accordingly,

$$\exists!R \left\{ AE \mid (AE \leftrightarrow AE^\infty), (\neg AE \notin AE^\infty) \bigwedge (\neg AE \ngtr AE^\infty) \right\} \leftrightarrow R \tag{15.14}$$

where for exactly one reality R, All Existence AE—such that AE is infinite All Existence AE^∞, *not* (or, the negation of) AE is not an element of AE^∞, and *not* AE is *not greater than* AE^∞—is reality R. In other words, AE is infinite AE. If something is not AE, then it's not part of infinite AE nor greater (or more infinite) than infinite AE. This is reality. Hence, there's never more than a *single* reality, which is infinite as a function of existence, time, and space. Such a reality has a complete ontological pedigree only to its previous (assimilated) reality from which it emergently arose. Having now described infinity as a function of existence, we turn to infinity as a function of time.

Time Infinity

Quick Summary. Time is infinite in terms of indeterminance and is equivalent to existence infinity. As an encapsulation of events or something with properties, time isn't real. There's only *timekeeping*, which proceeds from motion infinity, itself a reality of energy infinity. Timekeeping is a contextually unique and discrete event interval that we term *event periodicity*. Past, present, and future are timekeeping experiences but not *time*; hence, time travel necessarily isn't real. Time is a human collation of timekeeping block chains. Spacetime isn't a description of real space but a timekeeping tool. Timekeeping is relative to an event, thus arbitrary; time dilation is a relative, subjective experience. Universal timekeeping—an absolute clock—is fundamental motion.

SECTION 1
The Concept of Time

TIME'S NOT A thing anymore than infinity's a thing. There's no such existent as *time*, only *timekeeping*. The best way to describe it, says Mina, is as an experience because, outside of human consciousnesses, time as some sort of objective reality doesn't exist. It seems significant because we routinely conflate timekeeping with time existence. But time is not an existent even though it follows from existence rather than matter. Features of matter are what we use to reckon time, but it isn't a feature of All Existence like gravity, space, or motion. Time isn't caused. It's not brought into existence by principles of causality, neither is it, in and of itself, causative.

If one can say philosophies of time matter, then it's only as a conceptual tool to help us comprehend existence infinity, meaning the indeterminate, emergent nature of All Existence. When we think of time philosophically whereby we tend to imagine it as a whole in terms of Cantor's infinite sets (CH. 14:93), what we're really pondering is whether time τ as an existent is finite or infinite such that

$$\exists!\tau\exists!\mathbb{E}, \tau \leftrightarrow \mathbb{E} \bigvee \tau^{\infty} \leftrightarrow \mathbb{E}^{\infty} \tag{16.1}$$

(where $\bigvee$ is 'logical or'), which is just another way of pondering whether existence $\mathbb{E}$ itself is finite or infinite. For example, whenever we scroll our timekeeping back to the first nanosecond of the Big Bang, we encounter the seemingly existential nature of time with our compulsion to imagine whether time kicked off at that moment or preceded it. However, that's nothing more than a timekeeping question because there's nothing more to time. The real question we're posing regarding time before the Big Bang is can we *count time* prior to the moment of our universe's creation, not does time *exist* (which is really asking *if* there's existence) prior to the Big Bang. Therefore, where τ is time as an existent (as opposed to time t as timekeeping), the common proposition that

$$\forall\tau \mid \tau \to \infty \left\{ (\infty \leftrightarrow \{\infty\}) \bigwedge (|\infty| \leftrightarrow \infty) \right\}, \left(\aleph_0 - x = \aleph_0 \right) \to \left(\aleph_0 - \aleph_0 = \aleph_0 \right) \tag{16.2}$$

is nonsensical w.r.t. real infinity—where for any time existence such that time is infinite, infinity is the infinite set and its cardinality is infinite; thus, if the cardinality of infinity less some x is the cardinality of infinity, then the cardinality of infinity less the cardinality of infinity is the cardinality of infinity—because where infinity means indeterminacy, what's really being said is that

$$\forall \tau(x) \mid x \in \mathbb{R} \left\{ indeterminate - x = indeterminate \right\} \rightarrow$$
$$x \notin \mathbb{R} \left\{ indeterminate - indeterminate = indeterminate \right\} \tag{16.3}$$

where $\mathbb{R}$ is the set of real numbers. Time is non-denumerable and inoperable because time is not timekeeping. It contains nothing because it isn't a whole, a set, or an aggregate. Like existence infinity $\mathbb{E}^{\infty}$, time infinity τ^{∞} is simply time indeterminacy. Accordingly,

$$\left(\tau^{\infty} \leftrightarrow \mathbb{E}^{\infty} \right) \equiv \left\{ \tau^{\infty} = \mathbb{E}^{\infty} \right\} \bigvee \mathbb{E}(\tau)^{\infty} \tag{16.4}$$

where infinite time τ^{∞}, materially equivalent to infinite existence $\mathbb{E}^{\infty}$, is equivalent in identity ($\equiv$) with infinite time *as* infinite existence, or time as a function of infinite existence.

As a term, time is conceptual shorthand for event interval. It's a means for a percepted observer, meaning us, to be aware of interval states, or more colloquially, change. This yields only timekeeping however, not time itself. When you get right down to brass tacks, timekeeping is pretty much all anybody cares about regarding time anyhow. Time doesn't exist outside of timekeeping. It doesn't flow or bend or dilate, it's not flexible or relative, it doesn't increase or decrease, nor does it exist as any sort of state or property. We presume to observe these effects, but they're not an expression of time but rather of perceptual timekeeping, thus, of events.

In terms of Albert Einstein's (d. 1955) Theory of Relativity,[125] time isn't different between observers in truth but only in perception. Simultaneity is real but distance and variant motion defeats our ability to experience it (§ 6.5:170). Nevertheless, motion variance between event observers is irrelevant to time because an event interval is unique to its event, not to its observers. The periodicity of events is to what we ascribe time, but the event interval is how we perceive and calculate it. After all, how would we experience time at all without timekeeping?

1.1 THOUGHT EXPERIMENT: SENSORY DEPRIVATION TANK

Let's do a thought experiment. Imagine yourself in a sensory deprivation tank, an eventless environment, though not completely so because you consciously exist inside your physical body and it has perceptible biological rhythms such as a pulse[137] from which you can deduce your state, say, that you're physically alive. Not only that, you can deduce the passage of time—shorthand for a timekeeping interval such as an hour, day, or week—by keeping track of your pulse interval. If you know your at-rest pulse rate and don't lose count, you can relate the events of pulse-time to clock-time outside your sensory deprivation tank. In this scenario, you're not totally sensory-deprived.

Now, suppose instead your biology is dampened in that all you perceive are your thoughts, as though you're just a consciousness out there in the ether devoid of the sensory apparatus of a body. How would you comprehend your existence now? Would time mean anything to you in this seemingly eventless state? Would the 'passage of time' cease? If it did, and you didn't forget you're inside a sensory deprivation tank, would you imagine time outside your tank had ceased to pass, too? And if you imagined it, would it be *time*? If not, why not? Suppose you forget you're in a sensory deprivation tank, or better yet, really are just an eventless consciousness and *you* are literally All Existence, just your thoughts for company. What would you perceive about time? Only that a thought follows another thought. The one following the other is an event because it's thought motion, and motion induces a change in state. Change, which is motion, is intrinsic to All Existence. "Necessarily," says Mina, "if change exists then time exists," viz.

$$\left[\tau \rightarrow c \right] \leftrightarrow \left[c \rightarrow \tau \right] \tag{16.5}$$

where c is change. You have no means to calculate a thought event interval so you can't use your thought events for timekeeping. But you know your thoughts recur, one after the other, sometimes simultaneously, although a thought T in no case precedes a logically anterior thought T_{-1} where $T_{-1} \rightarrow T$. You're thinking *this*, now, and you thought *that*, then. For the duration of each thought, there was an incalculable period in which you were thinking a thought before you thought another thought, which in and of itself is altogether another

---

125. Denotes his special and general relativity as a whole except as noted.

incalculable thought period. This tells you there's an ordered periodicity to events. The thought duration and whether it's regular or irregular is immaterial.

SECTION 2
Event Periodicity

What we're talking about here is *event periodicity* (denoted E_P). At its most objectively fundamental, event periodicity is time and time is event periodicity such that

$$E_P \leftrightarrow \tau \bigwedge \tau \leftarrow E_P \tag{16.6}$$

where event periodicity E_P is materially equivalent to time τ and thus time is implied by, or presumes, event periodicity. Timekeeping occurs when we settle on some predictable rhythm—the resonance of cesium-133 atoms,[138] the oscillations of a quartz crystal, thoughts, feelings, or experiences in blockchain, biological or natural cycles, and so forth—to regulate our perception, or the reality, of event periodicity. Outside the human need to be aware of and establish a regulatory matrix for event periodicity, time is not an existential thing with existent properties, hence

$$\left\{ \neg \exists P(\tau) \right\} \rightarrow \left\{ P(\tau) = 0 \right\} \tag{16.7}$$

where, if the set P of all properties of time τ doesn't exist, then there are no such properties, hence, no time. There is only event periodicity at whatever macroscopic or microscopic level whereat events occur.

Past, present, and future are not illusions because of event periodicity. On the other hand past, present, and future are not existentially real. The past, for example, isn't ontological simply because it occurred and we have a memory of it and can still feel its effects in the perceptible present. A past event, when it was present, set in motion a future-cum-present event. Past events don't produce present events because they're in the past, no longer an *eventing*-event but an *evented*-event—a memory if you will. Heat dissipating into cold or an egg turning into an omelet is not a so-called one-way process in time—though, mechanically, indeed it is, since they're events—such that we can derive time directionality. Time has no directionality, merely event periodicity. The flow of memory doesn't correlate to the flow of time. Instead of the flow of time or the arrow of time, there's simply the *flow of memory*—in some respects, the timekeeping of our consciousness, our reality. In this sense, 'time' memorializes the *time horizon*, which is what the terms 'present' and 'now' really indicate. 'Event' memorializes the *event horizon*, which is what the term 'past' really indicates. We can repeatedly predict the future—the event environment beyond the event horizon—but it doesn't exist unless or until it eventizes, to wit

$$E_H \left(\tau_H \right) \vdash E_P(t) \tag{16.8}$$

where a time horizon τ_H of event horizon E_H yields ($\vdash$) a timekeeping t of event periodicity E_P. When the time horizon crosses the event horizon and a future event occurs, becoming the present, the time horizon τ_H becomes timekeeping t. If a predicted, or predicated, future never eventizes then it never enters the time horizon (it never crosses the event horizon), hence, it never *is in* time.

Let's consider the star Betelgeuse. Its location relative to Earth oscillates about 55 light-years (LY), putting it at any given moment approximately 568LY–623LY from Earth. Mina tells us Betelgeuse blew up simultaneously with March 9, AD 1457. Its distance means the bulk of the supernova's electromagnetic radiation (EMR), traveling at lightspeed c, won't show up in our telescopes until 2025–2080. As it was about 589LY from Earth along its oscillatory path when it blew up, its supernova will become evident to us sometime in 2046 (according to the math; Mina puts it during the last six months of 2045, instead).[139] When the supernova's light does reach us, we'll be 'seeing back in time' about 589 years. But if in 2045 we could instantly teleport across that distance, we wouldn't see the supernova occurring at Betelgeuse's spatial coordinates but its 589 year old remains because that event—its explosion, not all the events following it—finished simultaneously with March 9, 1457. Like a thought moving on to another thought, Betelgeuse has already moved on from its pre-supernova to its post-supernova state even though, in 2045, its supernova state will only just arrive as EMR for us to view as though in real time. This isn't because of some temporal flow or 'arrow of time' that only follows entropy, moving from order to disorder, but a result of ceaseless event periodicity. The Betelgeuse supernova isn't a future event—although our *experience* of it indeed lies forward of *our* time horizon—but a past (memory) event of which we're yet to be aware. This is not unlike how an explosion's sound delay twenty miles down the road is a fresh experience there while the explosion itself twenty miles up the road is already approximately 88 seconds in the past.

The metric of event periodicity encapsulates the *state space*[126] of All Existence where events permeate the subatomic to the suratomic although time as an expression of event periodicity is not limited simply to the event horizon of the state space, as we see later. Accordingly,

$$\forall E_P \, S(x) \left\{ x \mid x = E_H(\tau_H) \right\} \leftrightarrow E_P \tag{16.9}$$

where, for any event periodicity, the state space S at some x—such that x is the state space's event horizon E_H at time horizon τ_H—is materially equivalent to event periodicity.

While we can imagine and predict the future, it doesn't already exist regardless the fantastical vagaries of lightspeed and Relativity. That's partly because past, present, and future are not existents, and partly because events naturally occur consistent with state space. The former means event periodicity is in constant flux regardless its event interval; each event is unique in the event it follows, the event it precedes, and its contextual events. This is basic causality. The latter means an event inconsistent with its state space can't occur any more than a gun can fire sitting unmanipulated on a table. Now, one might think emergence contradicts this, but we see it doesn't when considering emergence occurs when the state space is conducive to it and not magically without any predisposition for it, viz.

$$\forall \mathcal{E} \, S(x) \left\{ x \mid (x = E_P) \bigwedge (x \to \mathcal{E}) \right\} \to \mathcal{E} \tag{16.10}$$

where for any emergence $\mathcal{E}$, if the state space S at some x such that x is an event, and if the event is emergent, then emergence occurs. Of course, we can't accurately predict emergence because, first, we lack a sufficient understanding of the phenomenon—although, in some instances, we can predict *an* emergent property, e.g., that in a given context traffic will emerge from the presence of cars in motion or that fractal patterns will emerge in snowflakes, but not its *nature*, e.g., that traffic will snarl movement to a standstill over a span of x miles, or that a particular fractal snowflake pattern will emerge—and second, because emergence is by its nature unpredictable both in occurrence and content and therefore, by definition, unexpected.

Time is a contrived frame of reference—a human collation of timekeeping block chains—for event periodicity, itself a fundamental feature of All Existence which, being ontologically infinite, is also time infinite such that

$$\exists! R, E_P \in \text{AE} \left\{ (\text{AE} \to \infty) \bigwedge (\text{AE} \to \tau) \right\} \leftrightarrow \left\{ \text{AE} \to \tau(\infty) \right\} \tag{16.11}$$

where for exactly one reality R in which event periodicity is an element of All Existence, and there's infinity and time, then time is infinite. A link is there between space and time, but spacetime isn't a thing and it doesn't warp to give us gravity (§ 3:119). Spacetime is actually a timekeeping tool, not a description of real space. Time is always relative in spacetime because, when physics assigns time t to a spacetime coordinate, from whence then comes time t? Well, it's either what's known as 'coordinate time' t which is local to an event's observer (relative time), or 'proper time' τ which is local to the event itself (inertial time). But it doesn't matter which, or how many, discrete observers. Time t is always relative to an event or an event's observer and thus virtually arbitrary. Simply put, the big deal with Relativity is the notion that time slows down or speeds up according to greater or lesser velocity, e.g., gravity. This is significant only in relative context. For example, suppose Person A is bored and experiences time dragging whereas Person B, right beside Person A, is excited and experiences time flying by. Would Person C be justified to conclude there's an objectively real time dilation going on between Person A and B? Not really, no. Time is experiential in this case. Can we also say time is experiential in the case of some material event outside our mind? Yes, because event periodicity is objectively local to its own event and not objectively relative to another event—say, a notional clock somewhere ticking off event intervals at observer point ω being different than a synchronized clock comoving with event point α—such that

$$\forall E_P(x) \left\{ x \mid x = E_H(t) \bigwedge \neg E'_P \right\} \leftrightarrow E_P(x) \tag{16.12}$$

where any event periodicity at some x—and x is an event horizon at time t as timekeeping and not any next event periodicity E'_P—is materially equivalent to only that event periodicity of x.

---

126. A model using the event horizon of a quantified environment to describe a system (such as All Existence) where the event horizon at any given time horizon corresponds to a unique point in the state space.

What this means is that an event in, say, a black hole's gravity well has an event interval comoving with that gravity well. Its inconsistency with another gravitational environment is immaterial unless an observer is making a comparative relationship with a different event beyond that gravity well. If there were such a thing as an absolute clock that kept absolute time throughout the universe—indeed, timekeeping is universal because fundamental motion is universal (MATTER–ENERGY, § 2:114); objects having their own proper time not in synchrony with other objects' proper time doesn't negate universal time—we could only assert that event periodicity in a high gravity environment proceeds differently w.r.t. to absolute time than in a low gravity environment.[127] Special Relativity essentially notes that when you run knee-deep through mud, you move slower than does another runner the same distance on the same or a different vector outside your mudflat. You'd only know this, of course, if you observed it, or a third observer—an absolute time clock, say—compared the two runners. This is spacetime short and sweet, and why it's not a description of time reality but a timekeeping tool that comprehends event periodicity.

Event periodicity is contextually discrete and unique. This means no two events anywhere in an infinite universe can be the same, that any event could ever recur, or that any future event could occur absent its context and state. Relativity often interprets time as if it describes reality instead of perception. Forward time travel, for example, supposedly 'allowed' in Relativity by velocity, is no more actual time travel than Woody Allen's cryogenics in *Sleeper* (1973, film) or the various Rip van Winkle folktales.[140] Event periodicity is comoving with its event's velocity and acceleration, that is, an event interval is unique and normative to its event and doesn't relate to another event environment except via hypothetical observers. Therefore, if velocious event periodicity is slowed relative to inertial event periodicity, the velocious event interval proceeds slower than the inertial event interval. The effect of velocity or acceleration on event periodicity of time-dilating physics is real enough but isn't time travel, a concept that's predicated on experiencing the past or future without regard to present reality.

Reverse time travel is even more a canard; it essentially entails reanimating a concluded event. For example, if right now is $t = 0$, then reverse time travels means physically moving oneself to some $t - t_n$. Every event at some $t - t_n$ carries unique antecedents and context. To experience an event periodicity at $t - t_n$ (let's say, Julius Caesar's murder and the millions if not trillions of events immediately antecedent and contextual to it) one would have to recreate an infinite regress to establish the event conditions in which Julius Caesar's murder occurred because, as a result of being ontologically infinite, All Existence is time-infinite. This means that some prior time τ implies a prior time t_{-1}, and thus, $\tau(t_{-1} \rightarrow t_{-2}), \tau(t_{-2} \rightarrow t_{-3})$ ad infinitum. No matter how far in time one regresses, one can always regress farther, because event periodicity is start-indeterminate consistent with All Existence's ontological infinity (*above*; § 1.1:101).

Event periodicity is infinite because events are infinite even when we regress to a system-wide point of no motion (change), itself an event periodicity although that sort of periodicity has no quantifiable ready frame of reference. Hence, it's impossible to reverse time travel to any $t - t_n$ unless one assumes that, upon arrival at $t - t_n$, the event periodicity local to that very moment in history is ready-made and waiting for the time traveler's arrival. That would presuppose a sort of Akashic Record[128] of infinite event periodicity we can rewind at will for some particular individual(s) while the rest of humanity and the greater universe proceeds apace, or else everyone (including their transcendent consciousness) magically snaps back in time, or to nonexistence, or into a different future without regard. We don't need mind-melting paradoxes to render the time travel concept untenable, therefore, absurd. Time travel improperly predicates time as a contained thing that can be manipulated or traveled through, which it cannot because of event periodicity.

The nature of time infinity, being equivalent to existence infinity, is that it's without beginning or end and therefore never began but always was, and will never end but always will be. Unlike wondering why there's something instead of nothing, wondering "why is there time instead of no time?" is a false question because time isn't an existent. Mina gave us three principal reasons to presume time infinity:

1. Current All Existence—not to be confused with our universe, which is significantly younger—is nearly a trillion Earth years old, indicating a conceivably indeterminate existence for it;
2. Previous All Existence didn't cease to exist when it assimilated via emergence into Current All Existence but part of it, weakly analogous to a caterpillar constituently assimilating into a butterfly;[129]

---

127. Objective (universal) time arises in pairwise single archí—the smallest expression of matter (§ 2.3.1:115)—oscillations, some number of which are equivalent to one Earth minute (1_{Em}). How we count time affects our experience of it, e.g., 1_{Em} in archí oscillations feels longer than in 24-hour clock time. Regulating natural time with archí oscillations normalizes it vis-à-vis supranatural time; physical and spirit persons objectively experience time the same while subjectively differently.

128. A surmised celestial library containing every human event ever to occur (§ 2:593).

3. Previous All Existence itself similarly came into being at some point, indicating an All Existence prior to Previous All Existence, and this pattern is infinitely retrogressive (CH. 15:99).

Altogether, the most knowledgeable human minds going back to the beginning of human consciousness[130] conclude from their available evidence that there never existed nothing (§ 1:228; SOMETHING FROM NOTHING, § 2.1.1:231; § 2.1.4:311), that ontologically infinite All Existence in some form always was until, through emergence, it was what it is today.

---

129. W.r.t. how a transcendent emergent is a higher-order domain yet retains no lower-order domain remnants, consider a caterpillar reducing to amorphous biology in reassembling and reorganizing into a butterfly, no caterpillar constituents remaining.

130. Collectively referred to as *the Cardinal* (translated from Mina's language without religious connotation; references throughout the text). Originally the first universe builders, it now includes all universe builders. The girls and I have conversed with only one other of them: Cosmo (§ 1.2.1.1:338).

Space Infinity

Quick Summary. A proto-energy we term Energent permeates our universe from which emerges matter, fundamental forces, and applied energies. Matter–Energy, not mass, defines space and therefore gravity. A photon is a massive (object or body with non-zero rest mass) particle of matter–Energy that, in addition to fomenting electromagnetic radiation (EMR), emits it via EM waves (EMW) that spread along its track. Accordingly, there are two variant lightspeeds, photonic actual and EMW normative, and matter isn't speed-restricted to either one. Special and general relatively and quantum science correctly describe certain aspects of reality, but fail to explain how these—and reality, more generally—work and conflate reality with perception. A natural (physical) and supranatural (spirit) environment forms our overall universe, and the natural powers the supranatural. Because existence is fundamentally 'energy,' the infinity of space is rooted in its indeterminance. We live in the observable universe, the materially finite 'centrality' of the larger, immaterially infinite universe.

Contents [Section Subsection]

NOW, WHAT ARE we to say about infinite space? Unlike time, with space we're talking about a seeming existent, something real and tangible—and yet, we're not. Sure, we can fly spaceships through it, see light traverse it, experience its near vacuum, find all things there, and we exist in its context. Yet, like infinity and time, the apparent boundless extent that is space isn't a *thing*, either. Accordingly, it can't be infinite in the way we typically think of a thing as infinite—as some sort of a completed whole, an infinite set of matter, an endless place, or the like. The norm is to see space as a physical reality that has expanse; that's why we think of its infiniteness dimensionally as endless volume, size, or distance.

Although indeed a physical reality, space only has expanse—a definable scope between referents,[141]—in the presence of relational, detectable objects from galaxies to dust to gas; in short, matter (§ 2:114). Beyond where there are detectable objects there is no expanse, which is a relational term. Something has expanse only in context. Space has expanse between our Milky Way galaxy and the Andromeda galaxy, for instance, because there's a measurable relationship between the galaxies that provides context for it. That expanse is approximately 2.54 million light-years (MLY) in terms of the distance product of velocity and time ($d = vt$). If we flew a spaceship from one to the other, we could measure our passage and the expanse using one or both galaxies as referents. But what's the expanse of space beyond its farthest object, beyond even its light? Science postulates a universe that's infinite in expanse, size, or volume and that, based on the average number of particles in some cubic chunk of the observed universe, of which only finite configurations are possible, there must be infinite atoms that make up infinite galaxies with infinite planets containing infinite life forms and so on, including infinite versions of you.[142] That's an irrational assumption. The luminous, normal matter[131] we detect could be all there actually is. In this case, if space has infinite expanse, then beyond the farthest objects (not counting elementary and composite subatomic particles) space would be object-less and therefore expanse-less. If you flew a spaceship at lightspeed c for infinite time in that context, you'd never encounter a physical end to space, to be sure. More to the point, you'd be in a measureless void, unable even to know if you were, in fact, moving. In such an expanse-less environment, what then would space infinity in actuality be?

SECTION 1

Fundamental Energent

Well, indeed that's how Mina structured our universe. All material existence in the form of atomic objects are concentrated right here where we detect them because this is the locality, called the observable universe (OU) in our infinite universe, (IU) where human consciousness physically resides (§ 4:150). Beyond the OU is objectless space, and this reality has implications for the concept of infinity. It's not entirely empty space, of course. Besides subatomics, there's the *Fundamental Energent* (Energent; $\Theta_{\varepsilon\mu}$), a universal permeant that's the root source of existence in our universe (Mina calls what expresses from it *real energy* as opposed to *force*, or *applied energy*; real energy isn't a property of the Energent). It is, to cite Mina, "*the* fundamental resource agency and instrument of power and energy." Hence, the $\Theta_{\varepsilon\mu}$ notation.[132]

Loosely, the Energent is a dielectric saturant of so-called pure, or *proto-*, 'energy' in that it's not ensuant to, nor dependent upon, matter—similar in some conceptual respects to the hypothesized Higgs field, or vacuum energy,[143] also known as the cosmological constant Λ[144]—that acts somewhat like a field of potential energy. The Energent, in and of itself, is without traditional waveform. It's infinitely just there, ever in 'motion,' brought into being by Mina not magically, divinely, or in some fantastic way, but by mechanics we describe later. Six descriptors define the Energent for our purposes here. It's the

> 1) binding force of the universe; 2) life 'energy' of the universe; 3) supranatural 'energy' source; 4) medium through which all things interact and have awareness of each other; 5) medium through which Mina interacts (loosely described in The Big Event as 'quantum entanglement;' § 1.5:16) with the totality of the universe; and 6) expression of the primary Energent, or Energent–prime, of All Existence (*below*).

It underlies the fundamental forces of nature (*Fundamental Force*, FF; gravity (GR) isn't included, as it's an FF phenomenon; § 3:119), there being eight, not four, in total. These are:

> 1) Archí Force AF, 2) Strong Nuclear Force SNF, or strong interaction; 3) Weak Nuclear Force WNF, or weak interaction; 4) Electromagnetic Force EMF; 5) Parity Force PF; (§ 6.11:191); 6) Field Force FF; 7) Métier Force MF; and 8) Flavor–color Force FCF.[145]

In the physical universe, the Energent is invisible but detectable, exerting its presence throughout. We sometimes experience it as unexplained heat in our body—mainly the spine, a sort-of 'antenna'—when intensely emoting or bringing it into the body for healing (Living force, § 2.3:583). There's a supranatural Energent, too. Aware persons can manifest it (and the natural one) in such a way as to perceive it as something like a hazy heat wave. The Energent's 'energy' harkens back to the start of our universe, the first 10^{-43} second of the

---

131. What interacts electromagnetically and gravitationally with other matter and radiation.

132. Greek letter Theta (Θ) for θεμελιώδης (*themelíodis*: fundamental, basic, cardinal), epsilon (ε) for ενέργεια (*enérgeia*: energy, instrumentality, its characteristic distributed capacitance of the vacuum (ε_0), as well as εξουσία (*exousía*, power); and μέσο (*méso*, agent, resource). Side note: Mina helps but doesn't much care what we call things, so long as a term conveys the correct concept, although he did insist we not call the Energent a 'field' or 'force.'

Planck epoch. It's the 'energy' of creation itself. It originates in the equivalent Energent of All Existence that transcends our universe (§ 1:90), which we term *Energent–prime*, with which Mina brought our IU into being (§ 2.1.3:309)—you didn't think it popped out of nowhere in some big bang, did you? The Energent permeated our IU since the get-go, as it was the first actuality to come into existence at its creation. It empowers everything natural and supranatural in the IU to exist and operate.

Although the natural and supranatural Energents are discrete, the former's 'energy' (single quotes when referencing the Energent) translates to the latter's in a synergic relationship because only physical processes manufacture it. The supranatural aspect of our universe makes no 'energy' of its own. 'Energy'-producing physical processes continually replenish the natural Energent which translates that 'energy' to its supranatural twin (§ 7.1.3:214).[133] It's a net 'energy' consumer whereas the natural one where we physically live is a net producer although, from the perspective of All Existence, our universe is itself a net 'energy' consumer whereas All Existence is a net producer, currently providing roughly 19% of our universe's net 'energy.'[146] In short, the natural environment is the power plant for the supranatural one, where a bit over three-quarters of universal humanity lives.

The Energent comprises a *proto-energy* from which Fundamental Force energizes and emanates. It's not *applied* energy in the sense we scientifically and popularly cognize the concept of energy as work or force. In its quintessence, it's more an *élan vital* in that it indelibly enlivens the system from its initial, full entropy microstate to its one and only possible, hence irreversibly ensuant, dynamical, zero entropy macrostate we call our infinite universe. Thus,

$$\Theta_{\varepsilon\mu} \vdash \left\{ P(\Omega) = 1 \bigwedge \left[\overrightarrow{E} \mid S(\Omega) = 0, \overrightarrow{S}(\Omega) \ngtr 0 \right] \right\} \Rightarrow \mathfrak{A} \qquad (17.1)$$

where, if the Energent yield (⊢) of the probability P of any probable microstates in the macrostate (Ω) is 1, and total system 'energy' $\overrightarrow{E}$ as a vector such that macrostate entropy S of any probable microstate as the sample space (Ω) is 0, and its probability of increase $\overrightarrow{S}$ is not greater than 0, then our universe macrostate $\mathfrak{A}$ results. This proto-energy isn't the *élan locomotif* quackery of eighteenth–twentieth century vitalism.[147] It is 'energy' of nature even more fundamental than EMF, SNF, WNF (and gravity, which science takes as fundamental, but isn't). Despite the inverse proportionality between wavelength and frequency expressed in $\lambda = {}^c\!/f$, the Energent excites an EMR below the extremely low frequency (ELF) range with a wavelength of about 300,000 km, a frequency of roughly 2.9 Hz, and energy between >1.24 fev (femtoelectronvolts) and <12.4 fev as a constant that defines the vacuum energy of space (cosmological constant Λ, *above*).

Proto-energy is an 'on–off' phenomenon. There's no point space w.r.t. proto-energy because it's without time and space, thus without distance, hence, travel (§ 6.11.4:198). But if we think of a point space in the universe, the proto-energy there is either 'on' or 'off' at any given moment of point-space time. 'On' is when proto-energy is exerting and 'off' is when it's not, which is to say that 'on' affects point space and any matter therein whereas 'off' doesn't (where *affect* means that matter in motion—as archí always are—only interacts with proto-energy when it's 'on'). The 'on' phenomenon happens trillions of times a second although Mina admits neither he nor the Cardinal (FN 140:110) have managed a more exact estimate that's credible. Despite 800BY of effort, proto-energy remains just too unavailable for study. Proto-energy 'moves' and 'undulates' when a point-space region is 'on' at the same time (§ 4.3:150; § 6.11.2:194), meaning that, instead of proto-energy in any given point space being randomly 'on' or 'off,' the whole point-space region is 'on,' thus exerting w.r.t. (affecting) the point space and its matter. We liken this to the sound of conversation in a crowd periodically but randomly peaking and falling silent.

The Energent's proto-energy is exceedingly 'dense,' so much so that it acts less like an invisible, non-impinging potential energy field and more like a solid w.r.t. to its reaction to matter–Energy (*below*) distortion with something akin to (but not) a piezoelectric[134] effect (§ 3.2.2:123; Fig. 90:213).[135] When the Energent interacts with matter–Energy, the proto-energy involved takes on mass because now it's no longer simply 'energy' but Fundamental Force, i.e., *real energy*. It is otherwise without mass. Although not Fundamental Force, gravity is nevertheless a Tier 2 expression of the Energent.[136] EMF, SNF, WNF and other Fundamental Force express in

---

133. Our universe is an 'open'—nothing, in and of itself, is a 'closed'—system; conservation of energy is its expression, not property.

134. Piezoelectricity is a phenomenon that occurs when certain solids distort but it can occur in certain non-solids, too, when density and charge are sufficient to resist distortion. It derives from Greek πιέζειν (*piezein*, to press or squeeze) and ηλεκτρον (*elektron*, electron), thus we denote piezoelectricity π_η.

135. Einstein correctly perceived that matter–Energy provokes field distortion, or a warping effect, but it's the Energent that's 'distorting,' not any spacetime field or fabric.

their own subatomic, matter–Energy contexts. The building 'energy' for matter comes from Fundamental Force reactions with the Energent, but the Energent's reaction to matter–Energy underwrites them all.

SECTION 2

matter–Energy

A brief aside on matter–Energy (mE) is in order, as it's an unfamiliar concept and plays an important role in understanding space infinity as well as gravity. Note that while mass, mass–energy, and matter–Energy are different, they all reference a tangible, physical object. First, let's define energy.

2.1 ENERGY

There are three energy types overall: 1) real, actual 'energy' that exerts a presence in reality independent of anything else; 2) 'energy' that exerts in relationships; and 3) measured, or applied, energy that results from those relationships. The first is the Energent, the second is Fundamental Force, and the third is potential, kinetic, inertial, gravitational (weight), and so on. The second is expressed in terms of force, such as forces of nature, while the third doesn't actually exist, as it's just a measurement of relationships (such as $E = mc^2$), which makes it the space infinity version of time infinity, thus the applied energy version of timekeeping (CH. 16:105). Matter and force—applied energy—are twin expressions of the Energent in that

$$\Theta_{\varepsilon\mu} = m + \mathrm{F} \qquad\qquad (17.2)$$

where $\Theta_{\varepsilon\mu}$ is the Energent, m is matter, and F is force. As Carnegie-Mellon puts it,

> Matter and force are the two fundamental entities of which the universe is composed. All that exists can be classified in these terms. All environmental phenomena occur because of the interactions between matter and transformations of matter in space and time. As the arrangements between forces and masses change, the change is manifested in terms of energy.[148]

But standard—including quantum—science doesn't account for actual 'energy,' such as that which powers the forces of nature and life. The Energent is *creation 'energy'* that powers, or enlivens, all (nonhuman) things. Fundamental Force is *real energy* that builds matter. We denote it with the Greek uppercase letter Υ (*Upsilon*). Force generically is *applied energy*, which we denote with the usual symbol E. We describe real and applied energy in more detail later. For now, let's turn to matter.

2.2 MATTER

Simply, matter is the stuff which composes our physical reality—from the tiniest subatomic to the largest accretion—and *mass*[137] is the amount of matter that constitutes an object, usually measured in kilograms. Mass as an amount of matter, however, is more typically understood in force terms such as *gravitational mass* (force exerted by gravity on an object, measured in kilograms) and *inertial mass* (an object's resistance to applied force, measured in newtons). Science considers these two forms of mass to be generally equivalent. Additionally, mass is "mainly defined by relating it to momentum, that is, $p = mv$ [p is momentum, m is mass, v is velocity] . . . One may say that this definition is an extension of Newton's concept of inertial mass" (Chang 2016, 3[149]), and that " 'mass' is only the proportional constant between p and v" (ibid, 4). Mass in this context, though, is really just a measurement of force (applied energy) acting on matter such as change in motion, pull of gravity, or 'binding energy,' as well as when there's none at all (rest mass). Mass lets us convert units of matter to units of applied energy as when, say,

$$1.66 \times 10^{-27} \mathrm{kg} = 1\,\mathrm{u} \leftrightarrow \frac{931.5\mathrm{MeV}}{c^2} \leftrightarrow 1.54 \times 10^{-10}\mathrm{J} \qquad\qquad (17.3)$$

where u is the unified atomic mass unit, kg is kilograms, MeV is megaelectronvolt, c is normative lightspeed (§ 5:151), and J is joules. It led to $E = mc^2$ energy equivalence and, conversely, $m = E/c^2$. Yet, mass can't explain gravity much less space infinity, even when considering mass "on the same footing as energy and momentum"

---

136. Tier 1 is the most critical, Tier 2 the next critical, and so on (GRAVITY, § 3:119).

137. Not to be confused with weight as gravity's action on an object's mass.

(Chang ibid, 1) rather than intrinsically a particle property. The reason is that gravity doesn't follow from the $E = mc^2$ mass–applied energy relationship but from the matter–Energy relationship intrinsic of the reaction $\mathbf{R}$ of the Energent ($\mathbf{R}\Theta_{\varepsilon\mu}$) to the real energy Υ 'charge' of atomic matter.

A different expression describes the matter–Energy relationship. Let's look at it more closely. For that, we first need to understand from whence hails matter. Let's note, however, that the standard view's Big Bang cosmology is 99% inaccurate in its conclusions, so for now we set it aside. Let's begin with a truncated chronology that follows our universe's creation and the 'dense,' congruously fluidic 'energy' of the Energent coming into play. An important distinction holds between force and 'energy.' The latter references a certain aspect of the Energent's proto-energy. The former references proto-energy's interaction with matter that expresses as Fundamental Force, which came into existence as an expression of the Energent; as soon as the Energent existed then naturally so, too, did Fundamental Force. In a practical sense, Fundamental Force is the Energent reactively manifesting to matter, or more accurately, to the 'energy' intrinsic of matter. As a force, then, Fundamental Force is essentially an Energent force. Prior to matter's existence, Fundamental Force was simply unexpressed by the Energent's 'energy' (*enérgeia*, defined in § 4.3:150) flux; a potential force if you will.

2.3 Archí and Photons

Matter begins quite simply during the Planck epoch as an Intentionalized (§ 3.2:282), weakly emergent 'energy' phenomenon.[138] Energent proto-energy emergently coalesced into stable, super 'dense,' ultra-'charged,' self-contained emboli—think non-popping air bubbles in near-boiling water—that segregated from the surrounding 'energy' flux. Each emergent embolus reached sufficient real energy Υ 'charge' and 'density' as to be impermeable to the Energent as well as to other emergent emboli. In so doing, it achieved a construal, tangible physical form—though, at the subatomic, nothing is really corporeal in the usual sense—and transitioned in behavior from proto-energy to matter. This bubble of proto-energy is so 'charged' and 'dense' that it passes beyond 'energy' into tangibility as a material entity; thus, matter (and herein lies the definition of fundamental matter as an impermeable 'energy' structure).[139] With that, the first material entity we term *archí* (pronounced 'ar-kee;' $\alpha\chi$)[140] was 'born' with its own mode.[141] It's a direct 'energy'-to-matter translation. There's no part-'energy'-part-matter transitional proto-particle, there's just the Energent's proto-energy saturating the IU and then, of a consequence, archí matter and then Fundamental Force, the Energent's reaction to these emboli (matter).

2.3.1 Archí

Think of archí as the material version of the Energent. A stochastic antiparticle with unchanged angular momentum and angular velocity termed *antiarchí* ($\overline{\alpha\chi}$) weakly emerges from an archí through a real-world form of what science calls charge conjugation. For example,

$$C|\psi\rangle = |\overline{\psi}\rangle : C\psi(q) = C\psi(\overline{q}) \tag{17.4}$$

where C is the transformative operation, ψ is a particle, q is a property, and the expression right of the colon indicates parity and symmetry w.r.t. the C operation. The probability that an archí transforms to an antiarchí is quantumly indeterminate such that

$$\Pr(\overline{\alpha\chi}) = \langle \mathrm{E}(\alpha\chi)\psi \,|\, \psi \rangle \tag{17.5}$$

where Pr is the probability of an antiarchí $\overline{\alpha\chi}$ and E is the antiarchí's projection on the state space ψ. References to archí henceforth include antiarchí unless noted.

Archí is the original, irreducible subatomic particle and is what science terms a truly neutral particle.[150] It's so 'charged' and 'dense' that it's a *truly spherical object* approximately $1\ell_P \times 0.71865$ meter (m) in diameter.[142] It can

---

138. Intentionalized emergence means it's predictable that it *will* emerge because it's Intentioned (Psyche Fundamental Force, § 3.2:282), yet unpredictable *how* it emerges, which always varied in Mina's practice (fn 245:208).

139. We can liken this process (not its product) in certain respects to excitation waves in particle physics. The Energent—itself in 'motion'—'flows' around this materialized 'energy' bubble and generates, among other things, electromagnetism. This is the origin of the em force and field.

140. Greek: αρχή (principle, beginning, outset, inception, origin, basis).

141. Although Intentionalized, since archí are weakly emergent they always emerged from proto-energy in Mina's pre-creation practice, though never twice in the same way.

142. t_P is Planck time (5.39×10^{-44} second), the time light travels in $1\ell_P$ ($1.616255(18) \times 10^{-35}$ m).

be described by properties that include, in Υ terms, 1) 'charge,' 2) 'energy density,' 3) diameter, 4) temperature, 5) angular momentum, 6) angular velocity, 7) internal proto-energy behavior characteristics equivalent to a wavelength λ of 3.666666×10^{-10} m and a frequency f of 3.0810^{-9} kHz,[143] and 8) Υ mass. It sits five structural levels below the quark (Table 1:122)[151] and weakly emerges continually from the Energent reminiscent of hematopoiesis in bone marrow, concomitantly serving as a metaphorical stem cell for complex matter.[144] Never-bonded archí predictably dephase—'energy density' falls to zero relative to archí, and self-containment dissipates to remerge with, that is, become indistinguishable from, the Energent—within $\approx \frac{1 t_P}{9475.156}$ second (FN 142). During the period of creation,[145] for instance, there was a non-zero chance of no bond until archí permeated the universe. Following that period until now, there's a negligible non-zero chance of no bond in the IU and zero chance in the OU. With an average archí density in free space of $\pm 270 \times 10^9$ m^3 and archí diameter greater than its binding distance, you can see why (§ 2.3.3:117).[146] The estimated 95% of the mass of the universe for which science can't account is archí and its associated 'energy.'[152] Tot up the factors and it seems obvious. Although mass is of no consequence w.r.t. to the Energent, it's a factor w.r.t. real energy Υ and a principal aspect of applied energy E.

The reason for dephasing is that, although an archí achieves its material state on the basis of its Υ 'energy density,' it emerges from the Energent without sufficient Υ 'charge' to sustain it.[147] Once an archí bonds to another archí structure (matter), it absorbs 'energy' from the *'bound energy'* (§ 2.3.2:116) of its archí partner(s) and effectively up-'charges' itself. A bonded archí oscillates $\sim 4.00078887645 \times 10^{105}$ cycles/sec.[148] From this point, it maintains sufficient 'charge' except when terminally expending 'energy.'

Dephasing is more measured when archí decouple from other archí than when one never bonds in the first place because sufficient Υ 'charge' is retained. Dephasing occurs because archí 'energy density,' thus self-containment, falls to zero. For example, when an atom—a cloud of archí in varying 'energy' relationships constituting its substructures—absorbs 'energy,' it does so because it's bonding with archí from whatever source. Such 'colliding' archí[149] bond via SNF with the atom's archí in whatever macro location the interaction occurs, say, an electron, proton, or neutron. This imparts real energy Υ and applied energy E that 'charges' the atom to a higher Υ and E energy state. It overloads ('overcharges') the SNF bonds in the location of the archí collision. The most 'overcharged' bond disrupts and that archí releases. The atom thus returns to its 'energy' state minus the released archí, itself 'overcharged' although, counterintuitively, its 'energy density' halves because the 'overcharge' increases its diameter. Overall, the 'charge-to-density' relationship is a basic inverse proportionality in which

$$\eta_{\alpha\chi} = \frac{1}{\Upsilon} \qquad (17.6)$$

where $\eta_{\alpha\chi}$ is archí 'density.' To calculate the Υ denominator, one calculates the values in the relationships between Υ 'charge' to Υ 'density' ($\sim$1:17.39641893), Υ 'charge' to tangible diameter ($\sim$1:600), and Υ 'charge' plus diameter to temperature ($\sim$1:10,000). Other proportionalities and relationships obtain w.r.t. all the archí's properties, but it's all too complex for this book.

2.3.2 PHOTON

An archí that releases up-'charged' with a 50% 'energy density' is what science calls a photon, thus,

$$\alpha\chi_{\Upsilon E} = \frac{1}{2}\eta_{\alpha\chi} \rightarrow \gamma \qquad (17.7)$$

where $\alpha\chi_{\Upsilon E}$ is archí Υ and E energy, η is 'energy density,' and the Greek gamma (γ) is a photon. Hence,

---

143. The λ and f figures are approximate to classical waveform; Energent is different.

144. To find archí, a method other than particle colliders is necessarily used.

145. The first picosecond (1×10^{-12}, or trillionth, of a second) is the period of creation, after which Mina considered the universe to be operating and developing as expected.

146. Native binding force is *enérgeia* (defined in § 4.3:150), which is impotent since binding distance > diameter; thus, SNF.

147. Archí as a real energy Υ phenomenon is itself Fundamental Force.

148. This is a constant, and an absolute rather than a relativistic measure. Unbonded archí oscillate albeit don't effectively exist (except as photons). Pairwise single archí oscillation is the basis for objective, universal time in the universe.

149. Archí (subatomics) don't physically crash into—touch—each other, even in particle colliders, but interact 'energetically.'

$$\eta_\gamma = \frac{1}{2}\eta_{\alpha\chi} \rightarrow \Delta\alpha\chi_P \begin{cases} \Delta\alpha\chi_P = \gamma_P \\ \Delta\alpha\chi_\eta = \frac{1}{2}\eta_{\alpha\chi} = \gamma\eta \end{cases} \tag{17.8}$$

where η_γ is Υ 'density' of a photon, $\eta_{\alpha\chi}$ is archí formative (or, initial state) Υ 'energy density,' Δ is 'change in,' and P is 'properties.' Bonded archí oscillate within their bond at *actual lightspeed* ç (defined in § 5:151; § 6.6:171), so when they decouple to the photon state, that oscillation converts to velocity at that speed (§ 5:151). The Υ up-'charge' converts to what we perceive in applied energy E as EMR.

The photon—the $\frac{1}{2}\eta_{\alpha\chi}$—is a single archí or antiarchí and remains a discrete entity w.r.t. the Energent. It is self-contained but no longer sporting the 'energy density' sufficient to achieve the state of matter defined above. As antiarchí exist, so too do antiphotons ($\bar{\gamma}$, though without effect on how and what radiates). Hereinafter, references to photons include antiphotons unless noted. When a photon, for example, terminally interacts with an object, it gives up all its 'energy' and consequently dephases; the photon—the archí—is gone, it has 'energy'-transformed. The photon-to-object energy exchange isn't only applied energy E—kinetic and electromagnetic—but includes the $\frac{1}{2}\eta_{\alpha\chi}$ real energy Υ 'binding energy,' too (Eq. 17.8–17.10, inclusive). An archí exhibits 'wave' characteristics within its impermeable self-containment (inner state space) as a natural consequence of its 'energy' matrix. These segregated characteristics don't impinge on, or react with, natural space (outer state space). Accordingly, an archí experiences motion in the outer state space as a particle, not a wave. On the other hand, the $\frac{1}{2}\eta_{\alpha\chi}$ inner state space is one-way permeable to the outer state space, thus its inner state space 'wave' characteristics interact with the outer state space. The Energent can't get in, but the inner state space 'wave' characteristics affect the archí's EM field wave characteristics (cf. § 5.1.1:152).

2.3.3 MATTER–ENERGY INTERACTION

With matter briefly described, let's move on to how it works. Archí exist with a real energy Υ 'charge' that's SNF without a partner. *Enérgeia* flux around the archí produces Υ 'charge' as it moves through space. This effectively means SNF and WNF are the same energy, thus force, as EM force which uniquely interacts according to matter context. For example, when archí achieve proximity—their binding distance of $\approx \frac{1\ell_P}{9475.156}$ is their Υ-'charge' field's reach—their individual Υ-'charged' fields interact to snap together like opposite magnetic poles. Science calls this action SNF. Via the appropriate Fundamental Force, this binding process operates from suratomic to subatomic matter. Matter accretes from the variant bonding of, or interactions between, fundamental archí particles. Everything contains archí. Because, colloquially, they're just 'condensed energy,' ultimately everything is made of 'energy' as archí pairs and their configurations scale up to more complex atomic and molecular configurations, thence to visible matter.

While Fundamental Force is the Energent's reaction to matter in various states and proximity, it isn't simply an 'energy' interaction but constitutes the *binding force* of matter. This force is real and measurable. Binding force is a directed expression of the 'energy' manifested between object groups of whatever size. When figuring matter–Energy equivalence, one needs calculate this 'energy.' Therefore, one calculates real mass off the number of constituent particles in an object. From this information, one finds binding force thence 'bound energy,' which is the *real* matter–¢nergy equivalence (FN 150). However, what science calls energy is actually applied energy. Einstein's matter–¢nergy equivalence is really a mass–applied-energy relationship. Mass, however, is an insufficient concept to understand energy equivalence. $E = mc^2$ isn't equivalent to 'energy' generally but to applied energy specifically. His formula just means that *energy is equivalent to mass in motion*. Hence, $E = mc^2$ (and its nominal parent, $E = \sqrt{p^2c^2 + m^2c^4}$) is really saying that motion energy equals matter in motion ($\overleftrightarrow{E} = \overleftrightarrow{m}$). Consequently, mass as a convention to comprehend real energy equivalence needs replacing by matter–Energy (mE)[150] because the latter references the former's constituent binding force and hence its 'bound energy' (*below*). That's the truest expression of matter as energy and vice versa. In this way, one can look at any piece of matter and calculate its equivalence in total 'energy' since matter scales up from pairwise to larger archí complexes.

Force and matter are the twin expressions of the Energent. They relate because force is a product of energy while matter, a physical structure, exists only in terms of the real energy that powers the existence of archí and the binding forces between them on up the chain to atoms, molecules, and visible matter. If we calculate the matter of a given object and know the binding forces involved, then we can calculate the object's mE and,

---

150. We capitalize Energy in matter–Energy to distinguish it from conventional matter–energy, typeset as matter–¢nergy for clarity.

thereby, its real energy equivalence. A given glop of matter always has a given glop of 'energy' represented in the 'condensed energy' of the archí and the 'bound energy' between archí. Thus, we can see that matter—what should be *mass* as the energy of the forces within an object—is equivalent to *'energy'* rather than *applied* energy as with $E = mc^2$, which is really just a statement that

$$E^A = F^F c^2 \tag{17.9}$$

where E^A is applied energy, F^F is Fundamental Force, and c is normative lightspeed (§ 5:151).

The point of $E = mc^2$ is to understand how physical stuff (matter) equates to—or rather, relates to—non-physical stuff (energy) so we can do useful things with it. But the equivalence *and* relationship only exists because of the 'energy' intrinsic of the bonds of matter, not the energy intrinsic to the force of applied energy acting on matter. Stated simply then,

$$E_R \Leftrightarrow mE \tag{17.10}$$

where E_R is *real energy* and mE is matter–Energy, the 'energy' bound up in matter, not its motion-expressed energy. Dispensing with unit conversion issues inherent in $E = mc^2$, we rewrite Eq. (17.10) as

$$\Upsilon \Leftrightarrow E_R \Leftrightarrow mE \therefore \Upsilon \Leftrightarrow mE \tag{17.11}$$

where Υ is a shorthand for $\Upsilon\Theta_{\varepsilon\mu}$, the fundamental 'energy' unit of the Energent's proto-energy, and is equivalent to E_R, which we use throughout. With the above as background, we can more sensibly comprehend this new mE concept and how it's foundational to space as well as gravity infinity. In terms of real energy equivalence as opposed to applied energy equivalence, we dispense with $E = mc^2$ for the modified expression of Eq. (17.14), derived as follows.

'Energy' equivalence derives from the nature of matter. At its most basic, matter is 'energy' because matter's fundamental constituent, the archí, weakly emerges as a super 'dense,' impermeable self-containment of 'energy' with a segregated, internal type of 'wave' characteristics. At this level, matter simply *is* 'energy' because there are no forces within the archí that need taking into account;₁₅₃ ergo, Eq. (17.11). However, *bound* archí are a different kettle of fish. From the above, we've learned that real energy Υ is an expression of the Energent's proto-energy and isn't the same as the applied energy E that science uses. The mE variable derives from recognizing that, along with constituent 'energies,' archí bonding produces forces. Therefore, to calculate matter–Energy equivalence w.r.t. to bonded archí necessitates taking all these 'energies' and forces into account. We work up the expression from the binding forces to matter–Energy and finally to 'energy' equivalence for a single archí pair. Consequently, the dot product

$$F_B = F_b \cdot F_t \begin{cases} F_b = \text{SNF} + (\Upsilon_{\alpha\chi})^2 + \frac{\overleftarrow{\alpha\chi}}{c^2} \\ F_t = \frac{\overrightarrow{\alpha\chi}}{c^2} + \sum_{i=is,os}^{2} P_g i \end{cases} \Leftrightarrow E_b \tag{17.12}$$

where, conceptually:

1. F_B, a tensor, is total *bound force* of the system produced from the inner product of SNF that binds the archí in the relationship (F_b) and the tension forces (F_t) acting contra to F_b;

2. F_b is unitary *binding force*, $\Upsilon_{\alpha\chi}$ is archí constituent 'energy' as force, $\overleftarrow{\alpha\chi}$ is archí vector motion inward toward the paired archí, and c is lightspeed;

3. F_t is unitary *tension force*, $\overrightarrow{\alpha\chi}$ is archí vector motion outwards, away from the paired archí, and $\sum$ is the summation of the pull of gravity within and without the archí unit; and

4. E_b, *'bound energy,'* is bound force F_B expressed in real energy Υ terms. Although SNF is simply manifested Υ 'energy,' it operates as a force and, therefore, we treat it in the F_b expression and not in Eq. (17.13)'s 'energy' expression.

With the involved forces (F_b) calculated and equated with 'energy' (E_b), we now take into account the 'energy' relationship of the archí pair, to wit,

$$E_B = \frac{E_b + E_\ell}{c^2} \begin{cases} E_b \Leftrightarrow F_B \\ E_\ell \Leftrightarrow \Delta E_b = \frac{E_b + 2v}{c^2} \end{cases} \Leftrightarrow mE \tag{17.13}$$

where, conceptually:

1. E_B, a tensor, is total 'bound energy' of the system;
2. E_ℓ is 'liberated energy,' the 'energy' available upon system neutralization;
3. ΔE_b is change to E_b; and
4. v is release velocity of both archí upon system neutralization.

Thus, mE is equivalent to E_B, which is real energy Υ, hence $\Upsilon \Leftrightarrow mE$. From this follows a modification to $E = mc^2$ such that

$$\Upsilon = \left(mE + \mathbf{R}\Theta_{\varepsilon\mu} + G_r^{\mathrm{Pr}} \right)\left(\mathbf{R}\xi^{\mathrm{F}} \right) - E\xi^{\mathrm{F}}(d) \tag{17.14}$$

where, conceptually:

1. mE as defined above;
2. $\mathbf{R}\Theta_{\varepsilon\mu}$ is the reaction $\mathbf{R}$ of the Energent $\Theta_{\varepsilon\mu}$;
3. G_r^{Pr} is the field pressure of gravitons (§ 3.2.1:122);
4. $\mathbf{R}\xi^{\mathrm{F}}$ is the reach of the quasi-piezoelectric field (ZAI PHOTON, § 3.2.2:123);
5. $E\xi^{\mathrm{F}}$ is the 'energy' of the quasi-piezoelectric field;
6. d is radial distance of $\mathbf{R}\xi^{\mathrm{F}}$ from mE center to mE atomic circumference; units don't conflict.

Because $E = mc^2$ conflates applied energy with real matter, it mathematically assumes an increase in applied energies at fractional lightspeed means an equivalent increase in real mass; as velocity tends to lightspeed, mass equivalently tends to infinity requiring equivalently infinite energy to accelerate it. Science then presumes the impossibility of mass accelerating to, or beyond, lightspeed c. But speed in a vacuum is constant; constant speed is relative rest; mass at constant speed is effectively rest mass. We now understand from Mina that a photon has classical mass in that it is matter, yet travels at actual lightspeed ς (§ 5:151) in a vacuum. A significant takeaway here, as described in § 6.1:165, is that matter can accelerate to c; it's not impossible. It's a mathematical fallacy that it takes infinite energy infinitely increasing mass whether defined as the stuff *of* matter or it's resistance to change, such as acceleration.

Eq. (17.14) doesn't replace $E = mc^2$. Instead, it amplifies its emphasis on applied energy E to the realm of real energy Υ. As the concept of real energy is new and the underlying data revelatory, there's quite a bit of work—energy testing, mathematical development, and empirical validation—still to be done to flesh it out. The expressions in this book are basic and conceptual. In their simplicity, they mask a lot of behind-the-scenes complexity, as any scientist can appreciate. However, they introduce the new field of *Energent science* with its cosmological corollary *Energent physics*. There's plenty here to nitpick, to be sure, but don't let that distract you from the bigger picture or the ET tool at your command. Ultimately, the proof is in the empirical pudding as we get a better handle on the revelatory data.

SECTION 3

Gravity

An expression of the Energent that science considers infinite is gravity, of which it holds two basic notions. First, the standard Newtonian (classical) view is that it's an instantaneous force over infinite distance of a strength proportional to an object's mass and the squared distance between two massive objects m such that $F = G\frac{m_1 m_2}{r^2}$, where G is the basic constant measure of the force's strength. Every object attracts every other object according to G and smaller mass always moves the most toward greater mass (*Fig. 3*, left).

Second, the standard Einsteinian (Relativistic) view is that gravity results from a warping of the 'fabric' of spacetime—a massive object 'sucks in,' or contracts, spacetime around it (*Fig. 3*, right)—where smaller-mass objects 'fall into' a 'well,' or 'depression,' created by another object's larger mass, e.g., the Moon and Earth, and that between any two objects $G_{\mu\upsilon} = \frac{8\pi G}{c^4} T\mu\upsilon$, where $G_{\mu\upsilon}$ is the Einstein (second rank) tensor representing the curvature of spacetime and $T_{\mu\upsilon}$ is the stress-energy tensor representing spacetime's matter–¢nergy content. Thus, smaller-mass objects geodesically move geometrically around larger-mass objects like a marble around a bowling ball, whose weight depresses a 'well' into a trampoline's surface in two dimensions, or where mass contracts space in three dimensions around its object (*Fig. 3*, center, right). While these two views postulate the

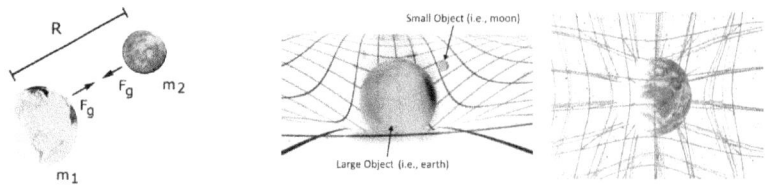

Figure 3. Left, Newtonian gravity as a mass-induced force. Gravity as Einsteinian (Relativistic) spacetime curvature: center, 2-D trampoline view; right, 3-D curvature (contraction) view.[154]

mechanics of objects orbiting or attracting toward other objects, they don't explain why. Though consistent in some ways with observation, they're inaccurate overall.

Gravity isn't a Fundamental Force alongside EMF, SNF, or WNF. It has no working relationship with mass whether as a mystical attraction or warped space. Instead, it's a one-to-one relationship of matter–Energy (mE) to Energent ($\Theta_{\varepsilon\mu}$) that yields the pull of gravity P_g such that

$$\left\{ (mE \to \mathbf{R}\Theta_{\varepsilon\mu}) \vdash (\mathbf{R}\Theta_{\varepsilon\mu} \propto mE) \right\} \Leftrightarrow P_g \tag{17.15}$$

where mE yields ($\vdash$) the Energent's proportional reaction $\mathbf{R}$. Gravity is an EM phenomenon—initiated when the graviton (§ 3.2.1:122) provokes a nonnormative photon release which builds local electrostatic interactions over multilocal distances—that gives rise to certain matter interactions that result in a net pull. It works by tugging individual subatomic particles across a continuum of contiguous multilocal chains of archí structures that compositely make up discrete objects of matter (*Fig. 4*). *Multilocal* refers to the local environment between and around two discrete objects wherein no other object intrudes. Multilocal chains are these multilocal environments that contiguously interconnect over distance.

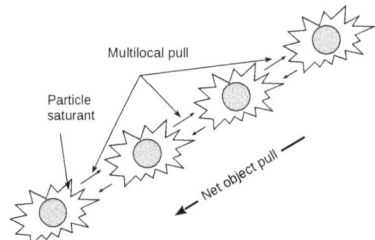

Figure 4. Gravity as an EMF net pull, which tugs across a multilocal chain of objects.

Let's pause to reflect that electromagnetism (EM) isn't fundamental—a field, force, or thing in and of itself—but an Energent reaction to archí (matter) in motion. This Energent reaction with matter is real energy Υ, whereas EM is a reaction between matter and is applied energy E. Consequently, the former is a field Υ and the latter a field E. What we observe to be the EM field or force is the ceaseless emanations of uncounted photons throughout space inducing a reactive phenomenon from the Energent that science calls electromagnetism (§ 2.3:115). Accordingly,

$$\vec{\gamma} \vdash \mathbf{R}\Theta_{\varepsilon\mu} \Leftrightarrow EM \tag{17.16}$$

where $\vec{\gamma}$ is photon emission and $\mathbf{R}$ is the Energent's reactive phenomenon. This means gravity arises as a product of energy, not mass. When EM propagates through a conductor, the resulting phenomenon is electricity. When it propagates through space (vacuum or medium), the phenomenon is EMR, e.g., visible light or radio. When it propagates multilocally across a continuum of object chains, the phenomenon is gravity. This expanded conceptualization of EM tempts one to expand its descriptor from an electromagnetic field or force to something like an electrogravomagnetic (EGM),[155] field or force, but that would be inaccurate since gravity is an effect, or manifestation, of EM. Gravity as a thing—like electricity and EMR—is distinct from EM as a thing. Gravity as an EM phenomenon necessarily eschews it operating as we've traditionally perceived it would *as* EM.

What science thinks is the entire EM field or force is only a part of its larger phenomenon—broader than standard concepts of electric and magnetic forces operating electricity, moving EMR, etc.—producing a different kind of interaction, namely, gravity. This broader phenomenon derives from the interaction of a certain type of matter with the Energent's proto-energy (§ 3.3:124).

Although the standard scientific view considers gravity infinite, it's only so in the sense it appears to permeate matter, nothing appears to interrupt it, and it demonstrates a long-range effect. These features arise, however, from gravity being matter-centric, not intrinsic of matter, and accordingly not a product of mass. Gravity is a principal consequence of the Energent's response to matter–Energy. This means it's materially equivalent to matter–Energy ($P_g \leftrightarrow mE$) where *pull* of gravity (real energy Υ) replaces the traditional *force* or *interaction* of gravity (applied energy E) because gravity isn't a long-range force between—or a spacetime curvature by—massive bodies, but a short-range interaction that accretes across a multilocal long-range continuum. Gravity also isn't Fundamental Force because it results from Fundamental Force, namely, EMF.[151] The *cause* of gravity is real energy Υ, but the *effect* of gravity is applied energy E.

3.1 PARTICLE SATURANT

The common impression that most of the universe is empty space—a hydrogen atom is 99.9999999999996% empty according to science—is inaccurate. The space within subatomic to suratomic objects thought to be empty is actually a bit less than a trillion (10^{12}) times *less* vacant than estimated. When you consider the binding distance between archí is $\approx \frac{\ell_P}{9475.156}$ (§ 2.3.2:116), it's impossible to justify such vast emptiness producing a universe of matter much less life. Composite archí structures of varying complexity and infinitesimal charge and magnetic force—a *particle saturant* (*Fig. 5*)—jam every object's so-called empty space and has consequences w.r.t. gravity. Space is a continuum much like any medium.

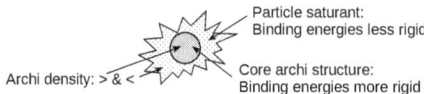

Figure 5. Schematic: particle saturant around an object, compositely sized and commensurate; electric charge is always neutral and analogous to an electron 'shell,' also a saturant, in that electron orbits are fungible and can pass between protons and neutrons, though not between their quarks, etc. (§ 6.12.1.1:206).

In the world of matter, particle saturants are everywhere. Each one doesn't constitute from only its core archí structure, e.g., quarks or leptons, where the archí structure is denser and binding forces more rigid and less inclined to movement, but also from its particle saturant, a fundamental element of the overall particle's particle-ness. We define it as a saturant because it fills much of a particle's internal and proximate 'empty' space. Its archí density is lesser and binding forces less rigid and more inclined to movement. This range in force rigidity permits an easier response to other particles, making it more likely an interaction such as EM or gravity can occur. The saturant also acts like a kind of lattice—a honeycomb, say—though without any sort of material uniformity. It imparts greater energy and structural integrity to the overall particle than what's strictly available from the core archí structure's 'binding energies' alone.

That being the case—recall matter constitutes of smaller archí constructs—we need recast how we view the subatomic in order to understand how gravity functions as an EMF phenomenon that initiates with the smallest structures across a multilocal matter continuum until it involves large bodies like you, planets, galaxies, and so forth. We reconceptualize the subatomic as a series of gradations from its traditional atomic constituents down to pairwise archí (Table 1). Now, let's break down gravity to its component parts.

3.2 GRAVITY INITIATORS

The Energent has 'density' as does applied energy E, the archí sphere, and the photon (§ 2.3:115). In this context, we define 'density' as the amount of real energy Υ in a region of space (as a system), per unit volume, as

$$\Theta_{\varepsilon\mu}^{E} = \rho_{\alpha\Omega} = \left[x \left(\frac{L}{T^2} \right) \right] \Upsilon m^3 \qquad (17.17)$$

where $\Theta_{\varepsilon\mu}^{E}$ is the Energent in terms of its proto-energy ^{E}, ρ is energy density, $\alpha\Omega$ is Energent proto-energy, x is a unit Υ, L is spatial coordinates of x (because 'density' is always in flux), T^2 is velocity of $\alpha\Omega$ over a time period,

151. There's no such thing as *Fundamental* Force anyway; the only 'force' that's *fundamental* is the Energent. All other 'forces' are how it expresses in the presence of matter in different contexts. We use the traditional term to keep a sense of reference.

Table 1. The subatomic continuum. Tau neutrino is more complex than electron and muon neutrino; graviton is the one described in this book; muon neutrino isn't part of the particle saturant; *hyposubatomic* refers to the collection of subatomic levels in toto.

	Levels	Constituents of level above	Relative complexity *vs* archí
	Suratomic	Molecule	n/a
	Atomic	Atom	n/a
Hyposubatomic	Subatomic$_1$	Proton, neutron, electron, tau neutrino	Structural levels 8, 7, 6, 6 above archí, respectively
	Subatomic$_2$	Quark, lepton, higgs, gluon, et al.	5 structural levels above archí
	Subatomic$_3$	Baryon, meson, graviton, et al.	4 structural levels above archí
	Subatomic$_4$	Electron & muon neutrinos, particle saturant, pairwise archí	Structural levels 3, 2, 2, 1 above archí, respectively
	Subatomic$_5$	Archí, photon	Structural level 0

and Υm^3 is Υ units per cubed meter (§ 4.3:150). The rise in Energent 'density' from an object's displacement in space of a composite particle that we term (for lack of a better word) *graviton* initiates the gravity phenomenon within an object's particle saturant.

3.2.1 GRAVITON

Our graviton (G_r) bears no resemblance to the no-mass, no-charge elementary particle that science hypothesizes as the force carrier, or exchange particle, for gravity *à la* the photon between electrons for EMR, certain bosons between left-hand fermions for WNF, and gluons between quarks for SNF. It formed in the Planck epoch as the first complex composite particle to affect rather than simply react to Fundamental Force. Its principal effect amplifies matter–Energent interactions to enable gravity's pull over distance. Essentially, it's a force multiplier. Without the graviton, felt gravity would be nil. Large-scale matter accretion, including galaxies and the OU, would be random and unlikely. The graviton enables an electrostatic field effect (when stronger forces otherwise neutralize it) by over-exciting an area to produce more photons than would otherwise be the case in order to initiate gravity.[152] It's a large and heavy subatomic *omnium-gatherum* composed of a shocking gaggle of smaller particles. Science hasn't detected it because it hasn't even conceived it, much less gone fishing for it as a means to explain EM anomalies. This is because of its habituated bias against EM explicating gravity that's rooted in its observation, first, that gravity is a long-range force acting on mass since it appears observationally proportional to mass; second, that matter can block EM but not gravity; and third, that electrostatic repulsion must necessarily negate gravity's pull. Legitimate objections all, but misconceived, as we'll see.

The constituents of the graviton (each of which is built up from archí), with the number of each in parentheses, are: top quark (5), down antiquark (1), up antiquark (2), charm antiquark (3), bottom antiquark (1), W⁻ boson (4), the quasiparticles holon (1), orbiton (2), phonon (10), roton (2), and 33 yet undiscovered. Its mass is approximately 0.74 MeV.[153] Gravitons permeate the Energent like plankton in the sea, a constantly IU-replenished reservoir of matter–Energy that's 'consumed' in the composite building-block production of atomic matter, assembling and disassembling similar to archí (§ 2.3.1:115). About 98.5% of all gravitons repulse from matter. The remainder break up via decay processes with portions interacting with the impinging matter.

Matter–Energy displaces gravitons analogous to an object displacing a liquid.[156] As an object enters a liquid, which isn't compressible, and occupies it's space, it pushes it out of that space because two objects can't occupy the same space. The displaced liquid must push any liquid contiguous to itself out of the way so the displaced liquid can occupy the space nearest itself, and so on outward from the initial displacement. At the same time, there's a resistance from the larger liquid context—a pushback to being displaced, called hydrostatic pressure—that exerts inward toward the displacement, not only on the object itself but on the displaced liquid. Overall, what happens when liquid displaces is that its level rises (when contained in a finite space). Even if its container is an entire planet, every molecule, however distant, experiences displacement regardless how immensurate. Being incompressible, displaced liquid has nowhere to go but in the direction of compressibility, where there's no liquid.

---

152. The main difference between electrostatic and electromagnetic force is that the former refers to the forces between charges that aren't moving relative to each other, whereas the latter refers to electrostatic as well as other forces between charges and magnetic fields where they may be moving relative to each other due to an exchange of photons.

153. The up quark's mass is ~1/2 MeV, not the standard view's ~2 MeV; others vary, too.

The graviton field is infinite in the sense it permeates wherever there's Energent. So, it's not the case that gravitons in aggregate displace the way bounded water as an aggregate displaces. That's just an analogy. What happens is that matter–Energy displaces gravitons in its local field where graviton density rises (Fig. 6). Gravitons displace outward from matter–Energy. As those directly affected displace, they displace others with consequent resistance, or pushback. A ripple effect of sorts—though not the so-called gravity wave that Caltech/MIT LIGO detected in 2015, which is a direct result of the EM Force (§ 3.7.3:136)₁₅₇—moves outward within the OU to zero.

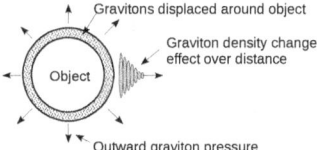

Figure 6. mE displaces gravitons, raising density; a reason gravity is proximally strong but distally weak.

Even millions or billions of light-years from its source—basically, to the OU's fringe—the graviton field experiences the energy distortion, though not necessarily the 'ripple' effect.[154] However negligible the Energent's reaction R at some distance d as it approaches infinity, the reactive phenomenon (energy distortion) at a distance cubed is never zero. Hence,

$$\lim_{d \to \infty} \left(\frac{R\Theta_{\varepsilon\mu}}{d^3} \right) = 0 \qquad (17.18)$$

whereby the energy distortion is distinct from the 'ripple' effect.

3.2.2   Zai Photon

The rise in graviton density from the field distortion of proximal matter–Energy raises local EM field density—that is, $R\Theta_{\varepsilon\mu}$ excitement energizes the potential applied energy E of archí that emit as photons in the EM range—and induces the aforementioned quasi-piezoelectric field and effect (§ 1:112; Eq. (17.14)). We term it *zai*[155] and denote it ξ^F for its *field* and ξ^E for its *effect*.[156] Science overlooks the EM density differential because the EM density it observes as normative is actually graviton-raised EM density. The rise in EM density is subtle and small but nonetheless detectable. Matter–Energy excites the Energent by displacing gravitons from the space it occupies, compressing the field and raising its 'energy charge density.' This accordingly induces the *zai effect*—the high-quantity emission of photons with real energy Υ charge that translates to an applied energy E lower-range EM gamma and infrared energy—such that

$$R\Theta_{\varepsilon\mu} \to REM \to \xi^E \therefore \xi^E \Vdash REM \Vdash R\Theta_{\varepsilon\mu} \qquad (17.19)$$

where ⊩ means 'is reducible to,' and REM is electromagnetic reaction (emission of gamma and infrared photons). Zai photons in the gamma range emit at an approximate wavelength, frequency, and applied energy E of $< 10^{-20}$m, 3×10^{24}Hz, and 9×10^{-19}J, and in the infrared range at 986 nm, 609 THz, and 1.19465 MeV, respectively. It's not space, spacetime, or their forces contracting around a massive object, but 'energy' manifesting from Energent proto-energy we term *enérgeia* (§ 4.3:150), its 'density' raised by gravitons via pushback. Time changes in the relativistic sense, in this context, because the rise in *enérgeia* 'density'—contraction around the object—affects event periodicity (§ 2:107), thus affects timekeeping.

The zai effect creates local, hyposubatomic electrostatic attraction where normatively science wouldn't expect it, until now thinking only large-scale electric charges and other forces dominated. As the zai reaction to matter–Energy graviton distortion lessens over distance, so too does the zai effect's reach, viz.

---

154. If you're thinking these interactions sound a lot like atmospherics, you're right. Any object in space is plowing through an ocean, or continuum—though not a Minkowski spacetime—of gravitons and 'energy' that, among other things, produces velocity variability, although that's counteracted by gravitons and Energent 'pressure' in an object's 'wake.' This effect partly produces observed planetary motion. Nothing in space is ever objectively at rest.

155. Greek letter ξ (*zai*), pronounced 'zai' or 'sai' in English.

156. Fun fact: about 0.5% of our body heat is produced by ξ^E.

$$\mathbf{REM}\left(d^3\right)\left\{d \mid d > 0\right\} \propto \xi^{\mathrm{F}}\left(d^2\right) \tag{17.20}$$

where d is distance from the center of matter–Energy to the productive zai reach. This accounts too for the observation that an object's pull of gravity weakens, or lessens, over distance such that $\xi^{\mathrm{F}}\left(d^3\right) \propto \xi^{\mathrm{E}}\left(d^3\right)$. As with gravitons, the zai effect is locally finite while its reach is globally infinite because $\xi^{\mathrm{E}} = \frac{\mathrm{R}\Theta_{\varepsilon\mu}}{d^3}$. However negligible its effect at some distance d as it approaches infinity, it's never zero, hence,

$$\lim_{d \to \infty}\left(\frac{\xi^{\mathrm{E}}}{d^3}\right) = 0. \tag{17.21}$$

When the zai effect, propagating from an object we'll call mE_1, encounters another local Energent excitement produced by an object we'll call mE_2, the mE_1 zai field naturally encounters the mE_2 zai field, which then augments the overall zai effect now encompassing mE_1 and mE_2 (*Fig. 7*). The zai effect—the flood of photons—isn't what produces what we observe as the pull of gravity P_g or experience as the force of gravity F_g. Rather, it integrates mE_2 with mE_1 in a zai field. In this composited field, mE_1's gravity pull interacts with mE_2's, which in turn interacts with mE_1's such that

$$\xi^{\mathrm{F}} \Leftrightarrow \frac{\xi^{\mathrm{E}}\left(mE_1\right) + \xi^{\mathrm{E}}\left(mE_2\right)}{d^2} \propto P_g\left(mE_1 + mE_2\right) \tag{17.22}$$

where d is distance between the farthest productive reach of the mE_1 and mE_2 zai effect. Unlike the classical force of gravity equation $F = G\frac{m_1 m_2}{r^2}$, where mass multiplied across distance reacts with the gravity force G to produce felt gravity, mE is additive in the above P_g equation without the standard gravitational constant G because P_g is an energy rather than a mass relationship. Practically speaking, the zai effect acts as the force carrier at the atomic—the electrostatic effect acts as the force carrier at the hyposubatomic—level for the pull of gravity, not the graviton nor even the zai photon as one might think.

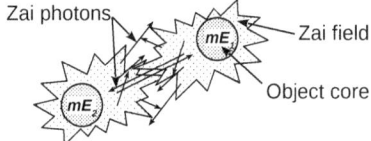

Figure 7. Zai photons (arrows) of mE_1 and mE_2 interacting across zai fields (particle saturants).

3.3   THE THREE STEPS OF GRAVITY

So, besides being the traditional, nebulous force of nature or the curvature of spacetime, or gravitons and zai photons, how exactly does gravity occur? The process is straightforward, just a simple cascade of events of which there are principally three:

1. a matter object displaces gravitons, which spike Energent 'density' to excite its region of space;
2. zai photons flood the region, provoking EM net attraction of subatomic$_3$ and subatomic$_4$ objects;
3. suratomic objects then follow subatomic$_1$ and subatomic$_2$ objects to move incrementally as multilocal, gravitationally accreted object chains along the strongest pull vector.

The overall effect is what we call *gravity*—it's pull, force, and acceleration. Let's go through each of these three event processes and then describe each of the overall effect's three elements.

3.3.1   GRAVITY STEP ONE

A matter object displaces gravitons, which spike Energent 'density'
to excite the object's region of space.

Recall that any piece of matter, from the foundational archí on up, is never at rest, not even when it's at relative rest—say, this book in your hands, or you sitting on a chair. Though you and the book look to be at rest, both are moving through space with Earth. An asteroid in deep space seemingly at rest relative to all around it moves with the galaxy of which it's a part. Even were the galaxy itself relatively motionless, the OU is in motion and so on. Matter's hyposubatomic constituents remain in motion down to the single archí even if, hypothetically, the matter itself came to absolute rest. Even if the OU came to absolute rest, the Energent itself remains indelibly in 'motion.' Magically bring *that* to absolute rest, and matter dephases to static 'energy'—itself a contradiction, hence a nullity—as if the universe was uncreated.

Matter in motion through an Energent in 'motion' ceaselessly charges and discharges Energent proto-energy, which provokes contextual interactions in which real energy Υ and applied energy E manifest. Gravity begins when matter displaces gravitons in space around it. The graviton is net real energy Υ neutral in its natural (so-called rest) state. All other matter–Energy is net real energy Υ negative in its natural state.[157] In the presence of matter–Energy, the graviton takes on a net Υ charge opposite that of the impinging matter–Energy, which correlates without causation to the object's applied energy E charge. This provokes excitation in both graviton and matter–Energy followed by nuclear decay (not the same as unstable atomic decay (§ 6.12.2.1:208) or graviton decay). This produces any matter–Energy's zai field and effect, what the standard view calls the gravitational field and gravity. Accordingly,

$$\xi^F = F_{GR} \rightarrow \xi^E = P_g \Leftrightarrow GR \qquad (17.23)$$

where ξ^F is zai field, ξ^E is zai effect, F_{GR} is gravity field, P_g is pull of gravity, and GR is gravity in toto, it's pull, force, and acceleration. The zai field interactively influences any object thusly caught up in it. In the case of Earth, its every particle—inhabitants, biosphere, atmosphere, its particle saturant (§ 3.1:121; § 6.12.1.1:206),[158] and all else within reach of the zai field—is itself gravitationally influenced. Earth's zai field extends beyond the Moon and thus pulls on it (which resists via the centrifugal force of its orbital velocity as well as its own repulsive tendency). The zai effect w.r.t. to any particular object lessens over relative distance because with an increasing absence of significant matter–Energy, zai field density falls below a gravitationally productive threshold and the effect wanes. Every object, however, creates its own zai field and effect. The matter–Energy of multiple objects tied together in a combined zai field generates a zai field larger than any of the objects alone (*Fig. 8*). Across the infinite universe, the Energent is normatively in an excited state as matter–Energy distortions ceaselessly sweep through it.

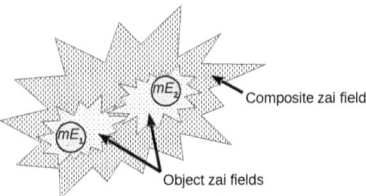

Figure 8. Composited zai field across multiple objects.

3.3.2 GRAVITY STEP TWO

*Zai photons flood the region, provoking EM net attraction
of local subatomic$_3$ and subatomic$_4$ objects.*

Gravity is intrinsic to, though not a property of, an object. Therefore, gravity exerts independently w.r.t. to an object without need of another object. For the remainder of this section, however, we discuss gravity in terms of two or more objects to better explain the effect, using the same mE_1 and mE_2 notation for the larger, gravitationally stronger and the smaller, weaker object, respectively.

Gravitons displaced by both objects' matter–Energy emit zai photons multilocally that flood each object's space, from the central-most atom at its core to the farthest gravitationally productive reach of its zai field. This is any object's normative state because contact with the Energent is ever-present. Zai photons emit in all directions. Their passage through the Energent generates real energy Υ that manifests as applied energy E in the form of self-extending (or, oscillating) energy known as electromagnetism. The zai photon energy characteristics generated upon photon emission determine this particular EM energy and hence the characteristics of this particular EM field. To distinguish zai from non-zai induced EM waves, we call them zai waves while remembering they're not actually waves but field extensions in space (§ 5.4:158). The larger object displaces more gravitons than the smaller object and accordingly generates a larger zai field and emits more zai photons. These collide with mE_2's

---

157. Real energy Υ charge is different from applied energy E electrical charge, so we use $\pm$ metaphorically to denote an equivalent dynamic, although $\pm\Upsilon$ charges don't attract or repel.

158. Even galaxies—not to mention the OU and IU—have particle saturants so vast they reach across intergalactic space to mingle with others in multilocal chains. Saturants are always larger in mass than the graviton and always displace them.

composite archí structure at a greater rate than mE_2's zai photons collide with those of mE_1.[159] If mE_1's zai field is twice the size of mE_2's, for example, then mE_1's photon collision frequency rate cubes w.r.t. mE_2 such that

$$2\xi^{\mathrm{F}}(mE_2) = \left(\xi\gamma_{\mathrm{colr}}(mE_1)\right)^3 \qquad (17.24)$$

where $\xi\gamma_{\mathrm{colr}}$ is zai photon collision rate. Each mE_1 photon collision excites mE_2's composite archí structure to a stronger net real energy Υ charge and another series of zai photons emits in all directions. The larger zai field's greater photon collision rate translates to greater energy transferred to the smaller zai field. This energizes mE_2's smaller zai field to emit more zai photons, which amplifies object charge. The stronger charge generates an applied energy E standard EM attraction that pulls contiguous (local) atoms toward each other. Both objects must emit zai photons into each other to create an EM attraction over potential repulsion. This transfer of real energy Υ between zai fields through zai photon collision that enables a net electrostatic attraction is what constitutes what we call the pull of gravity P_g.

Since a zai field is jammed with subatomic matter—the particle saturant—and uncountable numbers of zai photons, the zai effect begins there because its objects lie closest to mE_1 and farthest afield of mE_2's potentially electrostatically repulsive structure. Within these local EM ranges, pull of gravity net dominates EM repulsion where it exists because gravity attraction outranges charge repulsion. Although two objects' charges repulse, gravity attraction keeps them close enough to gravitationally accrete.

The zai effect is the same for every object—recall that archí throughout are an archí collective in various 'energy' relationships—because every zai photon is the same energy, constant within a negligible margin of variability. The pull of gravity is the energy of a single zai photon in the zai field such that $E_\gamma = P_g$ where E_γ is photon energy. Accordingly, the pull of gravity is invariant regardless zai photon saturation. The pull of gravity of the Sun, Earth, Moon, your body, this book . . . the biggest and smallest gravity-sensitive objects in the universe, all exert the same *pull* of gravity. The variant *force* of gravity is what we observe at work in the universe—say, Earth's gravity experiencing greater force relative to the Moon's—but it's the invariant pull that makes the force. This all means that gravity flows outward from an object's core, infinitesimally pulling every multilocal object along the way from hyposubatomic to suratomic.

Although related and correlated, the applied energy E charge is immaterial to the real energy Υ charge. Recall from Archí & Photons (§ 2.3:115) that when a photon collides—interacts—with a local part of an object it binds to it across a real energy Υ field rather than physically striking it or ricocheting away, as well as transferring certain applied energy E such as kinetic or heat. Naturally, the zai photon operates the same way. When a zai photon interacts with the local archí structure of an object, the electrically neutral photon imparts real energy Υ to the object, which changes its Υ energy structure. This in turn provokes a change in the object's applied energy E—in this context, its electric charge—because the object is moving through the Energent, which reacts to matter–Energy.

3.3.2.1 Attraction and Repulsion

Here's a good place to digress into the nature of attraction and repulsion. First, let's draw a distinction between *electric* and *electrostatic* force. The former, indirectly observable, is real energy Υ while the latter, directly observable, is applied energy E. They work in tandem in their respective environments. Electric force comes about in space from a relevant matter–Energy interaction with the Energent whose interaction with Fundamental Force (namely, EM) electrically charges it. Electric force *propagates* spherically within and beyond the object across a vacuum reminiscent of electromagnetic waves (EMW; though it's not electromagnetic); electrostatic force *exerts* in space as well as with other electrostatic force it encounters. Though attraction and repulsion is an EM phenomenon generally, it's an electrostatic one w.r.t. gravity.

3.3.2.1.1 Electric Force

Electric force is real energy Υ. It emanates from a positively charged object in all directions and planes, and tends to migrate toward so-called field lines—real, analogically venous 'energy' structures, not simply schematic force vectors (*Fig. 9*)—resulting in it being stronger along these lines than between them. As it migrates into these field lines, more of it generates in space from its continuous interaction with the Energent. The number

---

159. Even in particle colliders, subatomic objects never physically contact but get only as close as their energies allow whereby real energy Υ and applied energy E energies translate (Natural–supranatural 'Energy' Translation, § 7:211).

of field lines is random in any region of space, and vary from relatively few to many with no minimum or maximum. Similar to EMW, it spherically propagates at a constant rate beyond the object from its ongoing interaction with the Energent within the electrically charged object.

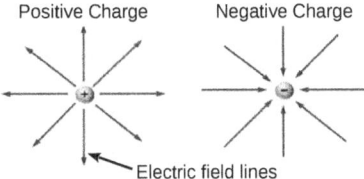

Figure 9. Field lines that pictorially map infinitesimal force vectors and electric force propagation.[158]

In this way, electric force propagates to theoretical infinity at approximately $5\ell_P$ per $\frac{1}{4}t_P$ where ℓ_P is Planck length and t_P is Planck time (FN 142:115). Deriving initial Planck values from normative lightspeed c and the standard *distance = speed × time* formula, the ratio of propagation in a vacuum between electric and electrostatic force is

$$s = \frac{d}{t} = \frac{5\ell_P}{\frac{1}{4}t_P} = \frac{8.081205497848 \times 10^{-35}\,\text{m}}{1.3478 \times 10^{-44}\text{s}} = 5{,}995{,}849{,}160 \ \text{m/s}$$

$$\Rightarrow S_{EF} : S_{ESF} = \frac{5{,}995{,}849{,}160}{299{,}792{,}458} = 20 : 1$$

(17.25)

where S_{EF} is speed of electric force and S_{ESF} is speed of electrostatic force which, of course, is lightspeed c. Across the board, real energy Υ within a real energy Υ field (EMF, in this case) operates 20 times faster than applied energy E. Because electric force is present in advance, electrostatic force interacts as it does.

Even if an electrically charged object switches to electrically uncharged, thus ceasing to propagate electric force, its previously propagated electric force continues propagating for indeterminate time and distance, as that process is intrinsic to the electric force, not the object. Naturally, the electric force has a real energy Υ charge that correlates to an object's applied energy E electric charge and interacts equivalently. The electric force of a negative electrically charged object is only a potential and reacts to the electric force of a positive electrically charged object as an energy sink.

Electric force field lines propagate through space redolent of lightning step leaders moving through air to ground, organically branching, dead-ending, and re-emerging constantly as it propagates. They follow something like autochthonal ley lines (§ 1.4.2:635) in the Energent. Its 'undulations' and other such phenomena affect how field lines propagate similar to how air conditions determine the path of step leaders through the atmosphere. There's an Υ charge differential between the leading edge of the electric force and the Energent in the direction of propagation. The presence of the electric force creates it. Carrying the lightning analogy just a little further—it's not a full analogy, however—the charge differential 'ionizes' the Energent similar in function to electrostatic charge separation in a cloud ionizing the air that creates a pathway for electrons to move easily and increasing the cloud's potential energy. Energent 'ionization' creates a path from one electric force's field lines to another in proximity.

When a propagating electric force encounters another, these 'ley lines' respond to respective field lines the way streamers respond from the ground to the pre-lightning electric field as a focal point for step leaders to bridge the gap from the cloud along a line of least resistance. Where field lines are of opposite Υ charge, the field lines merge like a completed circuit, propagation of that field line stops, and its electric force dissipates; if they're of like charge, they shear at random, opposite angles, and propagation continues. The attraction occurs because the opposite Υ charge acts as a 'ground' similar to how lightning attracts to earth, permitting electric or electrostatic force to neutralize charge separation. Accordingly, areas of electric force cease to exist over time as field lines cease propagating spherically outward from an object.

3.3.2.1.2 ELECTROSTATIC FORCE

Electrostatic force is applied energy E. It's what we observe as attraction–repulsion twixt electrically charged objects. It follows electric force. The same principle operates where applied energy E electric charge emanates from an object. When electrostatic field lines encounter another electrostatic force, they follow electric force into the object if it's oppositely charged and don't if not. Between any two electrically charged objects, one

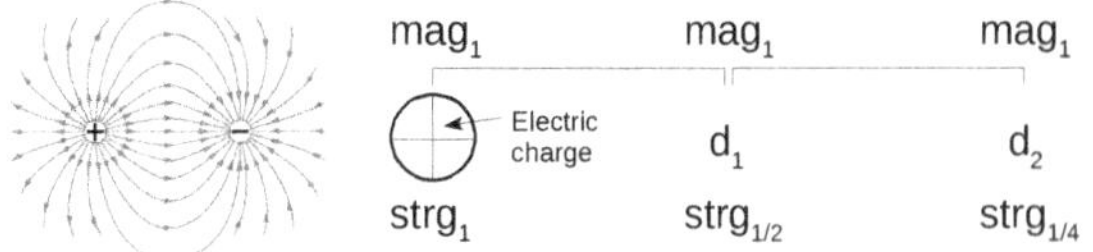

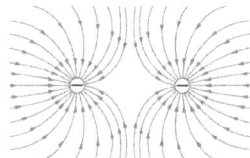

Figure 10. Left, schematic showing negative electric charge attracting electrostatic force and positive charge promulgating it; right, magnitude (mag_n) falling off in strength ($strg_n$) over distance (d_n).[159]

acts as an energy sink. That's why what's called negative electric charge appears to attract electrostatic force while positive charge promulgates it (*Fig. 10*, left). A negative charge doesn't generate electric force at all on its own but needs a sufficiently close positive charge. Electrostatic force isn't simply the 'force' of attraction or repulsion, however, because this 'force' is an effect not a cause. *Magnitude* is the overall strength of charge and is invariant over distance. *Strength* is the ability of a charge to establish a circuit of magnitude, varies at distance, and indicates attraction or repulsion (*Fig. 10*, right). Thus, magnitude over distance is electrostatic strength of attraction and repulsion.

When opposite electric charges mate up and establish a circuit, science says there's charge attraction. The attraction follows a natural shortening of the field lines, thus the constricting, or contraction of the field distance between, the objects. This physically draws the respective objects closer together (*Fig. 10*, left). So, it's not really x attracting y but the distance between x and y shrinking as the circuited field connection between them narrows. Repulsion is when non-mateable electric fields increasingly compress between objects that are physically moving closer from momentum or other reasons (or already are too close) until field compression, like hydrostatic pressure, resists further compression and rebounds—electric force working to reestablish its normal configuration in space—to force them apart (*Fig. 11*).

Figure 11. Like-charges repulse as fields reestablish normal configuration, pushing objects (Source: Fig. 10).

Electrostatic force falls off over distance inversely proportional to the square of the distance ($F = \frac{1}{d^2}$). In the former case, the charge strength over distance is weaker at any point relative to charge magnitude; thus, there's an insufficient circuit and insufficient constricting force to draw the oppositely charged objects closer (analogous to an angle that's too great to generate leverage). In the latter case, the electrostatic field expansion has reached its maximum extent.

3.3.2.2   INCREMENTAL MOVEMENT OF HYPOSUBATOMIC OBJECTS

Zai photon collisions provoke infinitesimal local net attractions across the multilocal chain of an object's constituents along a gravity vector. Let's suppose a zai photon interacts with some local portion of an object in a larger zai field. It could be anywhere along the $subatomic_1$–$subatomic_2$ spectrum, from a collection of pairwise archí—a particle saturant *desolatum*—to a local part of an object's particle saturant, to the object that owns the saturant itself. The electrically neutral zai photon binds to the local archí structure. It transfers Υ and E energies that alter the object's interaction with the Energent, thus its reaction to the object, and changes the local electric charge. Since an 'energy' change in bound archí anywhere is everywhere, this naturally alters the entire object's existing electric charge (though not of the saturant as a whole). Recall, too, that when a photon interacts with an object, the 'energy' change causes the emission of a series of photons in response as energy rebalances. The change to the object's electric charge is momentary, the time between zai photon interaction and photon emission. The Υ charge of a photon momently alters the electric charge[160] of an object to net attraction ~94% of the time, on average.

The flood of zai photons incited by graviton displacement increases the time an object experiences a net attraction even when it's normatively repulsive. Where an object normatively repulses from the gravity vector,

---

160. Same with the particle saturant except it always maintains a neutral charge. A photon series emits from a single photon collision because Υ 'bonding energy' always exceeds E photon energy, hence the object neutralizes it all via serial emissions.

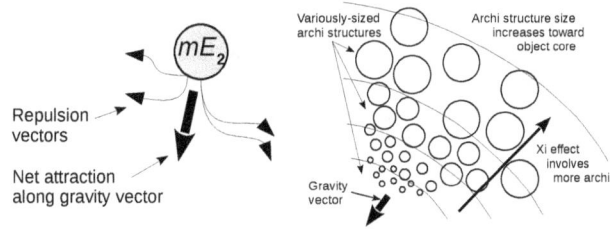

Figure 12. Left, net attraction over repulsion; right, multilocal object chain: gravity smallest to largest.

the infinitesimal net attraction is enough to move the now repulsively reduced or negated object an infinitesimal distance along the gravity vector before its electrostatic force renormalizes (*Fig. 12*, left).

The local net attraction created over the time period isn't isolated but happening at the same time, without letup, locally throughout all the objects that constitute any larger objects. Between the leading edge of any object (usually its particle saturant) and the overall gravity vector, zai photons work locally from constituent to constituent through the object until the entire object is involved. These constituents infinitesimally increment along the gravity vector even if normatively repulsive. Each of these constituents is also emitting their own photon series that involve any objects behind and farther up the gravity vector. Photon collisions with those objects (including zai photons from farther down the gravity vector that penetrate deeper into an object's sphere of influence) create the same infinitesimal net attraction to the nearest (local) object farther down the gravity vector.

This process is the aforementioned multilocal chain that net-attracts along a gravity vector until an entire object is net attracted regardless its normative electrostatic force (*Fig. 12*, right). As zai photons spread deeper into an object's volume, more and more *local* objects pull toward the exerted gravity *globally* across multilocal EM environments, in this way eventually involving the object in toto. The zai field eventually envelopes larger repulsive objects that initially resist incremental movement down a gravity vector (not counting centrifugal, velocious, or other forces at work) until the object is gravitationally captured by the constant infinitesimal multilocal chain of net attractions that negate the object's normative repulsion.

A pulled-on object can lie in any position in three-dimensional space relative to the pulling object, which can pull it away or in shear to the net gravity vector. In such case, gravitational attraction is a bit of a two-steps-forward-one-step-back affair (*Fig. 13*, left). On balance, there's no appreciable effect from this on gravitational force or acceleration. The local-to-multilocal process is incremental and can zigzag, but an object as a whole smoothly moves with the gravitational pull along the force vector (§ 6.8.2:176).

Figure 13. Left, object in 3-D space pulled away from or in shear to the overall gravitational force vector; polarization: center, electrically neutral object with uniform proton–election count; right, like charges (electrons) move away from strong external charge while opposite charges (protons) move closer.

3.3.2.3 STATIC CLING

A known electrostatic anomaly is *static cling* (not static *electricity*), where an electric charge builds up between electrically dissimilar materials and electrically net positive or negative objects attract weaker same-charged or neutral objects. This appears to violate Coulomb's law. The standard view's explanation is that opposite-charge particles within an object move closer to an external object while like-charge particles move farther from it (*Fig. 13*, right). Science calls such charge segregation *polarization*.

Polarization theory accurately explains the anomaly at the macro level of protons and electrons but the multilocal chain of net attraction described above explains it at the micro level. A piece of paper that static clings to a comb run through one's hair (cf. droplet; § 3.7.2:136) isn't an EM or electrostatic phenomenon that violates Coulomb's law but an example of gravitational attraction. The comb and paper both displace gravitons that create a zai field in and around them both. When these objects get close enough to each other, the zai effect exerts between them locally more strongly than between each object and, say, Earth's multilocal pull of gravity, because static electricity has supercharged them. The zai photons already exchanging between the two objects and Earth now have a stronger electrostatic attraction between the two objects locally than they do with Earth multilocally. Thus, the paper more strongly attracts to the comb than to Earth in its local context but overall remains more strongly attracted to Earth—if one lets go of the comb and paper, they fall to the ground—in the multilocal context. We see that, while gravity is weaker than EM or electrostatic force in a local context, it's stronger across a multilocal chain than either one.

Local–multilocal pull is the cause of gravitational attraction. As object zai fields encroach, the expanding web of zai photon emission, collision rate, and incremental movement via object pull is more frequent. The increase in pull rate translates to gravitational acceleration (§ 3.6:132). The practical effect of the expanding web of zai photon collisions throughout objects is to increase gravitational force (§ 3.5:131).

3.3.3 GRAVITY STEP THREE

Suratomic objects then follow subatomic$_1$ and subatomic$_2$ objects to move incrementally as multilocal, gravitationally accreted object chains along the strongest pull vector.

Imagine matter no bigger than an atom floating around the primordial void in closer or farther proximity. Each one generates a zai field in all vectors from its core to its farthest gravitationally productive reach, gently tugging on the constituents of any nearby atom with which it interacts. As their leading edges increasingly involve, their constituents infinitesimally pull closer via multilocal chains of net attraction. Shorter, three-dimensional multilocal chains expand to longer ones, and larger particles follow smaller. It all adds up to real movement through space. Suppose two atoms, mE_1 and mE_2, wander close enough to productively interact. Each atom is of similar mass and capable of changing its vector vis-à-vis the other atom's zai field with the same level of resistance; their classical mass is proportional. These two atoms draw closer via the zai effect—gravity—until their zai fields merge and they gravitationally clump despite normative electrostatic repulsion. While the *pull* of gravity remains constant regardless the amount of matter, its *force* cubes as a tensor then squares as a vector according to the amount of matter, such that

$$P_g \Leftrightarrow \left(\overrightarrow{T} x^3 \right)^2 \tag{17.26}$$

where $\overrightarrow{T}$ is force as a tensor and x is archí number. This means our two clumped atoms have a doubled mass (w.r.t. resistance to a vector change) but a cubed–squared zai (gravity) effect on any other atom (*Fig. 14*) because the mE_1 pull of gravity P_g is simultaneous along multiple vectors which exert a pull on mE_2.

Now, let's say a third, similar-mass atom mE_3 wanders close enough to mingle zai fields with our clump. It's doubly resistant to a vector change and mE_3's cubed-squared force than is mE_3 to the clump, which accordingly moves toward the clump more than the clump moves toward it. Matter accretes in this way, all the while growing more resistant to locally normative electrostatic repulsion and any vector change w.r.t. to any other object of lesser accretive force; it becomes gravitationally net attractive.

2x mass; (x³)² zai effect

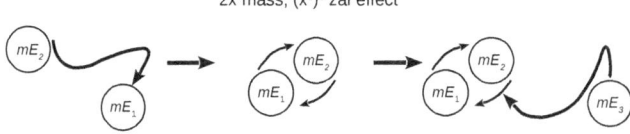

Figure 14. Growth of clumping force and resistance to movement.

Observing such accretion, it appears that objects of greater mass (as matter) exert greater gravitational attraction than objects of lesser mass. But the observation is misconceived. Rather, the accretion phenomenon (outside normal EM attraction) arises from the Energent reaction to matter–Energy displacing gravitons and the local-to-multilocal electrostatic net attraction. With this understanding, we can describe our three principal gravity terms: 1) pull of gravity, 2) force of gravity, and 3) gravitational acceleration.

3.4 PULL OF GRAVITY

Pull of gravity is real energy Υ transferred via zai photons between zai fields. It's cumulative but doesn't aggregate. This means real energy Υ accumulates with increasing zai photon emission and cumulatively energizes the zai field—which aggregates in the force of gravity—but the zai energy transferred per unit of photon remains constant and, thus, so does the pull of gravity. Holding Eq. (17.26) in mind, we define pull of gravity P_g as the infinitesimal pull between two local subatomic$_4$ objects[161] induced by a single zai photon. Hence, an object's incremental movement per zai interaction is the same regardless mass or matter–Energy in the object's larger body because P_g is the local coupling between matter–Energy and Fundamental Force. This definition deprecates classical mass w.r.t. the gravity phenomenon. Consequently, we define a new universal gravity constant as a vector unit of real energy Υ denoted $\vec{\mathcal{G}}$ that fits the bill as a universal absolute strength-of-gravity-force constant. It derives from the real energy Υ transferred by a zai photon required to energize one subatomic$_4$ object to pull another such object gravitationally, regardless normative EM, electrostatic, and other like forces such that

$$\vec{\mathcal{G}} = \frac{\Upsilon_{\xi\gamma}(x)\,(\text{Sub}_4)^2}{c^3} \ \text{J} \cdot \text{N}^2 \cdot \text{iVLK}^3 \tag{17.27}$$

where $\Upsilon_{\xi\gamma}$ is a zai photon in real energy, x is number of photons required to excite an atom, Sub$_4$ is matter–Energy of a generic subatomic$_4$ object carrying a $\pm$ electric charge, c is speed of light, and the units are joules, vibratory motion of the photon's applied energy E electric field, and the three-dimensional zai field between two discrete subatomic$_4$ objects. Viewing Eq. (17.27) atomically,

$$\vec{\mathcal{G}} = \frac{\Upsilon_{\xi\gamma}(x)\left(^A_Z X^{e\pm}_{mE}\right)^2}{c^3} = 7.43665775 \times 10^{-8} \ \text{J} \cdot \text{N}^2 \cdot \text{iVLK}^3 \tag{17.28}$$

where $^A_Z X^{e\pm}_{mE}$ is matter–Energy of a generic atom carrying a $\pm$ electric charge. Thus, we calculate

$$\begin{cases} \Upsilon_{\xi\gamma} = 5.55555555 \times 10^{-26} \ \text{J} \\ x = \sim\!1.00000000009900000819130 \times 10^{18} \end{cases} \tag{17.29}$$

from our ET-given result in Eq. (17.28). The $\vec{\mathcal{G}}$ constant is a vector equivalent to the standard scalar G universal gravitational constant—whenever science resolves it to its ET-corrected value of $G \cong 7.58888 \times 10^{-18} \text{Nm}^2\text{kg}^{-2}$—in a non-mass context. Although gravity's *effect* is infinite, its *pull* is not.

3.5 FORCE OF GRAVITY

Force of gravity is the force of one subatomic$_4$ object locally pulling another in the gravitational context, and is a scalar constant. It differs from the standard gravity equation, $F_g = G\frac{m_1 m_2}{r^2}$, because it describes the force between subatomic$_4$ objects' mE rather than between objects' mass. Accumulated real energy Υ aggregates from the number of subatomic$_4$ objects involved in the zai field. Hence, the force of gravity aggregates with the accumulation of zai photons. Accordingly,

$$F_g \propto P_g \tag{17.30}$$

where F_g and P_g are force and pull of gravity, respectively. The former increases exponentially, inversely proportional to the latter's rise in real energy Υ. Thus, w.r.t. objects from the hyposubatomic to suratomic,

$$F_g = \vec{\mathcal{G}} \frac{(mE_1 + mE_2)F_{\text{ES}}}{d^3} \quad \left\{ F_{\text{ES}} = k\frac{q_1 q_2}{r^2} \right. \tag{17.31}$$

as a scalar where $\vec{\mathcal{G}}$ is the aforementioned gravity vector constant, d is linear distance between the farthest productive reach of the zai fields, and the equation right of the bracket is electrostatic force F_{ES} as a scalar where k is Coulomb's constant, q_1 and q_2 are the signed charge magnitudes of mE_1 and mE_2, and r is the distance between them. The pull of gravity localizes, or focuses, in any center of densest, cumulatively greatest matter–Energy due essentially to gravitational accretion. Hence, dirt, you, and the Moon experience pull toward the center density of Earth, its core. The zai effect constantly tugs on the content of matter. While the traditional $F_g = G\frac{m_1 m_2}{r^2}$ yields a reasonably accurate representation of *felt* gravitational force within the math expressions that science has devised (where its lack of knowledge leaves our comprehension of the real universe skewed and wanting), it doesn't yield a realistic, accurate representation of the objective force pulling objects toward gravitational center. We need calculate the force of gravity pulling objects toward gravitational center differently than the *felt* force of gravity because the objective force exerted between objects is the P_g

---

161. Local pull at the subatomic$_3$ level is the lesser of the two, thus unsuitable as a definitor.

magnitude and not its effect. The former is the *magnitude* of the pull of gravity and the latter the *strength* of the pull of gravity. Both are two aspects of the same force of gravity. One can certainly make the case that the limitation of the traditional force of gravity equation doesn't matter, since our system of weights and measures works for us sufficiently well. On the other hand, it boxes in our science and limits how far we can take it. And, of course, it's one reason science has yet to figure out gravity much less antigravity.

3.6 GRAVITATIONAL ACCELERATION

Gravitational acceleration is the rate at which objects pulling objects move toward a stronger zai field in a vacuum where gravity is the only force in play. Acceleration is the net result of zai field real energy Υ. Accordingly, $A_g \propto P_g$ and, therefore,

$$A_g = \vec{\mathcal{G}} \frac{mE}{d^3} \tag{17.32}$$

where A_g is any object's gravitational acceleration in a net force-less environment where pull of gravity is the only force, $\vec{\mathcal{G}}$ and mE as defined, and d is spherical distance as the totality of vectors between the farthest productive reach of zai fields. Although $A_g \not\propto F_g$ directly (where the notation is as defined),

$$A_g \propto \frac{1}{2} \frac{(F_g)^2}{P_g}. \tag{17.33}$$

3.6.1 PEAK VELOCITY

There's a peak velocity to the acceleration of gravity.[162] This occurs when a zai field reaches photon collision saturation; it is maximally energized. When the frequency and velocity at which atoms pull on each other and, in aggregate, pull their respective object toward a gravity source to enter this range, the zai effect reaches an effective steady state. This is the zai field's applied energy E limit. Science traditionally calculates Earth's maximum acceleration of gravity near its surface—it's steady state—solely under the pull of gravity (ignoring Earth's rotational effect) as $\sim 9.80665\,\mathrm{m/s^2}$. This means an object at rest in Earth's gravitational context increases its net speed by 9.80665 m/s for each second of free fall; after x seconds, an object's free-fall speed is about $9.80665x\,\mathrm{m/s}$. But the standard view's figure is too low. Let's see why.

Just as the rate at which electric and magnetic fields propagate limits EMW speed (§ 5:151), the maximum rate at which zai photons collide before a zai field is saturated limits gravity's pull on an object. When a body experiences maximum pull of gravity—its steady state—it reaches its maximum response (speed) to that pull. After all, the only thing that creates free-fall motion in a body along a gravity vector is the pull of gravity. Without it, there'd be none. Peak acceleration for Earth is ET-given as $\sim 21.86764\,\mathrm{m/s^2}$, about 2.229 times greater than the standard view. This means the same object will steadily gain speed each second in free fall up to peak A_g, and no more, as it moves toward Earth's gravitational center.

The standard view's transitional acceleration from $0\,\mathrm{m/s^2}$ to $9.8\,\mathrm{m/s^2}$ takes place in a series of six unequal steps over the course of the first second of motion, while the transition from $9.8\,\mathrm{m/s^2}$ to $21.8\,\mathrm{m/s^2}$ is a 12-step unequal series. For example, it's ET-given that a 100-kg person needs about 7,500 km in a gravity-force-only environment to reach peak A_g, whereas a 100-kg solid iron object needs only about 400 km, on average.[163] Additionally, the matter–Energy content of a 100 kg person is about $7.894\,\Upsilon$ units while that of 100 kg of iron is about $684.2\,\Upsilon$. Now, iron has a density of 7,870 kg/m^3 whereas a human body has about 1,000 kg/m^3, on average. We calculate the mass density ratio of 1 kg of iron to 1 kg of human at about 7.87:1 whereas, in terms of matter–Energy, the ratio is about 6.842:0.07894, a significant differential. Hence, iron's mass is about 7.87 times denser than a person's, while its matter–Energy is a whopping 86.67 times greater, on average. However, there's no constant in terms of either weight or matter–Energy to calculate an object's travel distance to peak A_g. At this point, the data remains revelatory.

By way of comparison, the Moon's maximum acceleration of gravity is traditionally calculated to $1.625\,\mathrm{m/s^2}$. In matter–Energy terms, though, its peak acceleration of gravity—being a quarter Earth's matter–Energy[164]—is $\sim 5.305625\,\mathrm{m/s^2}$, or 24.26244% of Earth's.

---

162. Not escape velocity (speed $s > F_g$) nor terminal velocity (peak A_g under resistance toward gravitational center).

163. They'll never reach peak A_g because there's nowhere absent resistance (matter, atmosphere, FF, particle saturants).

164. Don't confuse this with mass, which science calculates to one-eightieth Earth's from gravity one-sixth as strong.

3.6.1.1 Weight and Terminal Gravitational Velocity

Weight, or heaviness, comes from an object attempting to accelerate to peak A_g in a zai field along the gravity vector, but can't because of resistance from atmosphere, EM force, the ground, and so on. One feels their body's heaviness from it trying to accelerate toward peak A_g against the blocking surface of Earth, or the weight of a sack of flour trying to accelerate to peak A_g against the blocking surface of one's hand. A one-kilogram mass, for example, is the equivalent of a force against a resistance that we measure as one kilogram. It's called a kilogram-force (kgf). It equates to 9.80665 Newtons, a unit of force. In everyday use, science abbreviates kilogram-force to simply kilogram as a unit of weight.

We're used to thinking of terminal velocity as a maximum speed through a pervious medium where "air resistance equals in magnitude the weight of the falling object"[160] whereby it achieves a steady state. Weight, however, is a function of gravity so, in that context, it means the magnitude of a body's force against a resistance at the maximum attainable acceleration of gravity. Consequently, ground resistance equals in magnitude the force of an object's maximal gravitational acceleration, termed *terminal gravitational velocity*, TGV. Accordingly, weight is the product of a body moving at TGV against a resistance.[165]

Although one appears to be at local rest standing on the ground, meaning not under motion or acceleration toward Earth's center, from gravity's perspective one's body is being pulled with the force of TGV against an equal and opposite resistance—the ground—which translates to weight. It's a direct translation of the force produced by a body at TGV against a resistance (both of which can vary) that impedes its motion toward gravitational center. This is similar to classical weight being a product of mass times gravitational acceleration ($w = m\mathbf{a}$; sometimes written $\mathbf{F} = m\mathbf{a}$ where $\mathbf{F}, \mathbf{a}$ are vectors and $\mathbf{a}$ is gravitational acceleration). Since mass is altogether an inaccurate concept (§ 2:114), we restate the classical weight formula in matter–Energy terms as

$$w = FR \begin{cases} F = mE \ (\text{TGV}) \\ R = \frac{F_g + B_E}{2} \end{cases} \left\{ \text{TGV} = \sqrt{\frac{2mE \ (-\rho V)pA_g}{\rho A C_d}} \right. \tag{17.34}$$

where w is the magnitude of a body's force against a resistance (weight), F is the force of a body's maximum speed against a resistance R, B_E is 'binding energy' of the involved objects, say, a body, and the ground to a depth of about 100 feet at sea level. For TGV, we modify the standard terminal velocity formula where ρV is displaced fluid mass of the medium through which a body is falling (or when at relative rest, such as when standing on the ground, then just $+1$), ρ is density of the medium, e.g., air, A is an object's projected area, and C_d is drag coefficient (a dimensionless quantity), and the remaining terms as defined.

Although the atmosphere (and other less obvious things) resists, say, a skydiver's *speed* in free fall toward gravitational center in terms of peak A_g, it doesn't resist their *motion*, so the skydiver falls toward the ground *feeling* weightless albeit *having* what's called *resistance weight*. The ground, unlike air, arrests a falling body's motion toward gravitational center. Standing on Earth's surface—at relative rest—gravity still pulls one toward its center at TGV. We translate the effect of such relative rest into weight. While both a falling body and Earth's surface are pressing toward gravitational center against resistance at TGV, the impervious matter that's between gravitational center and the ground arrests its motion relative to the body falling toward it through pervious air. The force exerted by a body that's gravitationally pulled toward gravitational center while resisted by impervious matter blocking its motion—the ground, say—is resistance weight. This is the force produced by motion resistance along a gravity vector. It's what we normally think of as weight in pounds, kilograms, and so forth.

The free-falling skydiver encounters relatively less resistance to motion from the atmosphere than the ground does from the underlying matter between it and gravitational center. Therefore, the skydiver exhibits motion relative to the underlying ground whereas the ground exhibits no motion relative to the underlying mantle and core. For this reason, the skydiver's greater pervious gravitational motion relative to the impervious ground must reduce to its same, lesser gravitational motion upon contact with it, either instantly (no parachute) or gradually (with parachute). Since objects are always pressing—attempting to accelerate—toward though never attaining peak acceleration due to resistance, there's always weight, however negligible. That means a moving object has resistance weight not only along its gravity vector, but along its *momentum* vector, too (*Fig. 15*).

---

165. The relationship in Einstein's thought experiment between standing on Earth feeling weight and in an accelerating elevator in space feeling weight is *perceptually* equivalent but in no sense *materially* equivalent, as the forces are distinct.

3.6.1.1.1 Momentum Weight

Simply put, momentum is the impetus, or tendency, of a moving object to keep moving absent some force acting on its motion. This applied energy E property of an object is classically a product of mass and velocity, viz. $p = mv$ (where p is momentum). Kinetic energy is the potential applied energy E stored in momentum. But $p = mv$ is an incomplete analysis of momentum because nowhere is an object and its motion not acted on by gravity, no matter how slight. We don't detail the modification to the classical equation but, in Energent terms, momentum must account for not only matter–Energy instead of mass, but pull of gravity, too. In real energy Υ terms then,

$$p = mE(P_g)v. \tag{17.35}$$

The elements of the space an object traverses resist its momentum. For example, principally atmospheric constituents resist the momentum of a thrown ball or a fired bullet or a bird on the wing. Particle saturants as well as real energy Υ principally resist an object's momentum in free (vacuum) space. Air resistance is substantial while vacuum resistance is insubstantial, mostly negligible. Whether in air or a vacuum, the force produced between momentum and resistance translates to weight along an object's trajectory. When a baseball line drive smacks you in the face, the impact you experience isn't the ball's momentum per se but its *weight* as a function of resisted momentum pressing against your impervious skull much the way earth experiences a skydiver's weight as a function of gravity when slamming into it or lightly touching down. The applied energy E that translates from the ball to your face as a function of weight correlates to its velocity as in $w = \mathbf{ma}$ (*above*). In other words, there's no functional difference between you experiencing weight standing on (or, pressing against) the ground at TGV, and you pressing against it at some dynamic velocity. Both scenarios translate to momentum which, when resisted, translates to weight. In the former, your *static* weight correlates to Earth's acceleration of gravity constant g and is steady whereas in the latter, your *dynamic* weight correlates only to your momentum and is instant. The first is *gravity weight* and the second is *momentum weight*.

In a sense, both these weights are the same thing. A body has momentum whilst at relative rest on the ground, which we experience as weight, because the gravitational interaction with Earth is perpetually pulling toward peak A_g. Of course, a body has an absolute gravity weight even when falling apparently weightless toward the ground or just floating in space. What we normally think of as *mass* in weightless space is really only when it's at rest; mass manipulated in some way translates to *weight*. Whether it's manipulated by encountering hyposubatomic matter or energy such that, at the point where mass and resistance meet, there's weight (*Fig. 15* at $RF = w$, where Obj meets m_R), or manipulated by an astronaut on a spacewalk such that where mass and the astronaut meet in resistance there's weight, mass in motion doesn't have only momentum but resistance weight. However, this doesn't mean a slowly moving massive body having the same momentum as a rapidly moving, light body has the same resistance weight.

Imagine an object moving through our solar system along a momentum vector, as in *Fig. 15*. First, it encounters mostly negligible resistance at point [Obj, m_R] where momentum translates to weight, though perhaps too slight to measure or matter. Additionally, supposing there's a pull of gravity from some angle along the momentum vector; then, the object's pull toward peak A_g through resistance m_R also translates to weight. Second, suppose it encounters a pull of gravity—even multiple pulls—as at point [Obj, GR_R] where $RF = w$. Here, the pull of gravity is from a vector other than the momentum vector. In this case, the object's mass translates to weight as the inverse of the object's momentum resisting the pull of gravity. We get a hint, here, how force of gravity isn't some force of nature acting on object mass but a function of the pull of gravity on object constituents in a matter–Energy environment, ever striving against resistance to reach its maximum, and keeping matter (and you) firmly anchored to the planet in the process.

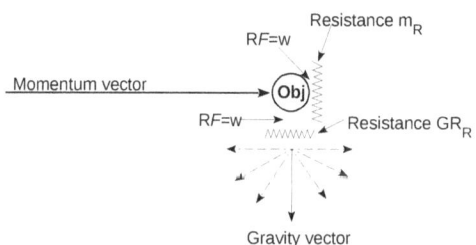

Figure 15. Two types of weight: resistance along gravity vector GR_R and momentum vector m_R.

3.6.1.1.2 THE HAMMER AND THE FEATHER

To illustrate the consistent pull of gravity not resulting from mass, let's look at a landmark experiment. Apollo 15 Commander David Scott performed a televised experiment August 2, 1971 on the lunar surface during which he dropped a hammer and feather from roughly the same height (*Fig. 16*, left, center). They fell at the same rate and hit the lunar surface at observably the same time.[161] Physicist Brian Cox duplicated Scott's result in NASA's Ohio vacuum chamber October 23, 2014 (*Fig. 16*, right).[162] Using the standard equation for acceleration $a = \frac{\Delta v}{\Delta t}$, we look at three calculations that derive different values for lunar A_g. We consider Scott's scenario from three perspectives.

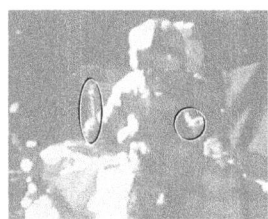  

Figure 16. Left, center, CDR David Scott simultaneously drops a hammer and feather on lunar surface; right, Brian Cox vacuum chamber experiment; both experiments show the objects simultaneously landing.[163]

1. Using basic video tools on NASA's grainy film, we averaged Scott's drop duration at about 1.062 seconds from NASA's stated 1.6 m height. This averaged $A_g = 1.417376$ m/s^2.[164]

2. *Flipping Physics* measured time and height at 1.201201 seconds and ∼1.2 m, but didn't carry it through to acceleration. Using their variables, we calculated a velocity of 0.999 m/s, thus a gravity acceleration of 0.831657 m/s^2.[165]

3. Mina gives an actual drop time and height of 1.011102 seconds and 1.559657 m, respectively. This drop distance varies from NASA's by 0.040343 m, or 1.5883 inches. These variables calculate to a gravity acceleration of 1.525593 m/s^2.

These values all deviate from the standard value of 1.625 m/s^2.[166] This indicates scientific uncertainty w.r.t. to lunar mass, density, and so on, but if we take Mina's data with merit then the standard estimation of non-peak A_g in this case $(1.625 - 1.525593$ m/s$^2)$ is within 0.099407 m/s^2, or 6.117% of Mina's . . . which frankly we didn't expect to be so narrow given everything else in this chapter. Still, all these values are a far cry from lunar *peak A_g*. These calculations are standard physics but, while $a = F/m$ (where F is net force acting on a body of mass m) describes Scott's and Cox's observations (the effect), it doesn't explain the phenomenon itself (the cause) which is that, although the number of atoms—hence, mass as resistance—in the hammer and feather differ, the atoms in both incrementally move forward at the same rate as already described. Two or two million atoms affect gravitational *force* but not gravitational *movement*, i.e., the pull of gravity. That the hammer's greater mass is said to impose greater resistance to movement compared to the feather is a convenient explanation from a mass-centric perspective, but immaterial not to mention inaccurate w.r.t. to gravity's actual workings.

3.7 SOME GRAVITY CONSIDERATIONS

Several questions arise regarding 1) gravity versus electromagnetism, 2) hydrogen bonding defying gravity, and 3) so-called gravity waves. We consider each in turn.

3.7.1 GRAVITY vs. ELECTROMAGNETISM

If both electromagnetism and gravity have effectively infinite range, why does gravity hold Earth in orbit around the Sun and not electromagnetic force? The standard view's answer is that negative electric charges somewhat cancel an equal number of positive charges w.r.t. their combined force ($p = qd$ where q is ± charge, d is distance, and p is measured in Coulomb · meters). This means resultant electromagnetic force reduces over distance by $1/r^3$ for a dipole, $1/r^4$ for a quadrupole, and for an increasingly shorter $1/r^n$ (where r is linear distance between objects) since equal numbers of opposite electric charges increase with object size. At the suratomic scale, where most atoms have equal positive and negative charges, the range of electromagnetic force thereby lessens more and more over distance; the larger an object, the more positive and negative charges and the increasingly shorter its electromagnetic range.

Since the standard Newtonian view sees gravity as a function of mass, and as there's no such thing as negative mass to positive mass, then gravity's force lessens only by $1/r^2$ regardless the amount of mass (that is, at scales smaller than galaxy groups in the Einsteinian view, beyond which it sees the universe expanding and gravity inconsequential). Consequently, while raw electromagnetic force of a single charge has a theoretical infinite range, in practice its range for typical macro objects shortens to the point of effectively nothing. This leaves the only other range-infinite force known to science, gravity, as the force capable of exerting over astronomical distances to hold Earth in orbit to the Sun. The correct answer to this question, however, is that, having described gravity and seeing that Newtonian and Einsteinian views produce inaccuracy w.r.t. reality, the question itself is irrelevant and immaterial.

3.7.2   GRAVITY *VS.* HYDROGEN BONDING

A corollary question that arises in gravity being a weaker short-range force than EM is, *how can hydrogen bonding—one of the weakest forms of EM—and a single drop of water perched at a fingertip defy gravity?* SNF is the strongest force at atomic distances so, regardless electrostatic repulsion or the pull of gravity, protons and neutrons will come together. Water (H_2O) sticks to the gravity side of one's finger (*Fig. 17*) due to electrostatic force attracting water molecules toward molecules in the skin (§ 3.2.1:122).

Figure 17. Electromagnetic force defying gravity force.[167]

On the other hand, gravity as the EM force acting locally through multilocal chains of net attraction along the gravity vector sufficiently suffuses throughout the water molecule's constituents to cause the drop stuck to the underside of one's finger to hang down along the gravity vector (toward the ground), but not suffused enough to disrupt the local electrostatic force between the water atoms until either 1) the amount of water increases such that gravity via EM exerts more force throughout the water drop along the gravity vector than the electrostatic attraction exerts between the finger and the portion of the water drop close enough to the skin to participate in the electrostatic force between them, or 2) the pull of gravity suffuses the drop of water and, over a time period, alters the electrostatic grip holding the drop to which it's stuck and the drop falls.

The thing about Fundamental Force is that it works within specific distances in specific contexts according to Energent interaction with matter–Energy; ergo, gravity exists everywhere in the universe at all times wherever there's matter–Energy. The observable universe is precisely the right size-to-matter ratio ($s:m=1$) to balance all its repulsive and attractive forces. If this ratio was smaller than one, it would clump and crush. If greater, it would fly apart. Either way, life would be unsustainable. The Energent is so-called dark matter/energy (§ 6.11:191), thus gravity-negative. At effective distances where there's a dearth of matter (intergalactic), it takes over from gravity-pull to repulse instead. The graviton initiates gravity-pull within its pull distance but, beyond that range, proto-energy incites gravitational repulsion.

Science wonders why gravity apparently only exhibits attraction, but it just doesn't notice its repulsion because, at short distances, its pull-in dominates much like SNF does at short distance while, beyond its effective distance, SNF may as well not exist as other forces dominate, such as EMF. Magnetic attraction and repulsion at the bounded level (§ 3.7.3.3.2:140) has the same relationship in principle as gravity's at the cosmic level albeit no field or flux lines manifest. The tension between the Energent and Fundamental Force is always trying to push apart or pull together archí and this creates incipient oscillatory archí motion; without it, there'd be no archí motion. On the vast cosmic scale, this tension acts on the rotating, centrifugally displacing observable universe to pull it centripetally inward in its own eventual, oscillatory fashion. Accordingly, we can see how cosmic inflation theory mistakes reality.

3.7.3   GRAVITY WAVES

What happened with the LIGO–Virgo equipment (below) *that made scientists think they'd detected gravity waves?* As this chapter lays out over many fronts, the very concept of gravitational waves (GW) fails. So, if not GW, just what did LIGO–Virgo detect? To answer that, we consider the GW concept, how the LIGO–Virgo equipment works, and what it actually detected. As the topic is too complex for this book, we provide just an overview, then describe what Mina says about the phenomenon.

General relativity predicts GW as "disturbances in the curvature of spacetime, generated by accelerated masses, that propagate as waves outward from their source at the speed of light . . . [and] transport energy as gravitational radiation, a form of radiant energy similar to electromagnetic radiation."[168] Gw are "elusive ripples in the fabric of the universe" so far detectable only from massive disturbances such as when binary neutron stars or black holes collide (*Fig. 18*).[169] We see later how their predicted radiant nature relates to ET data but, at first glance, it's clear the phenomenon depends on spacetime. As we discuss spacetime's non-reality elsewhere (§ 2:107 ff), we skip it here without further ado. What the GW concept suggests however is that a stellar disturbance can deform Earth's geometry. Scientists tested that theory.

3.7.3.1 The ligo–virgo detectors

The Laser Interferometer Gravitational-wave Observatory (LIGO) are large-scale interferometers near Hanford, Washington and Livingston, Louisiana, situated 3,002 km apart. Virgo is a single facility situated near Pisa, Italy. LIGO comprises two 4-km arms each and Virgo two 3-km arms, each set at right angles (*Fig. 18*).

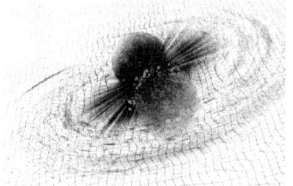

Figure 18. Left, artist's concept of neutron stars colliding, causing outward ripples in spacetime 'fabric.' Large-scale laser interferometers: center-left, -right, Washington and Louisiana, USA; right, Pisa, Italy.[170]

The two arms together comprise a laser interferometer. As the name suggests, it merges two or more overlapping light waves to create an interference pattern at a single terminus from which science gleans information (*Fig. 19*, left). The LIGO–Virgo interferometers (LVI) time their lasers so that, when the beams meet at Terminus, they destructively interfere to produce no light to detect.

Using the theoretical spacetime model, scientists expect GW ripples to deform the spacetime 'fabric' and, along with it, Earth (including you). This means that as a ripple passes through and deforms the interferometer and the lay of the land upon which it sits, one arm lengthens or contracts relative to the other. The distance traveled by one of the lasers relative to the other thus takes an infinitesimally longer or shorter time to travel each arm's distance during the brief period the ripples pass through, essentially forming two 4-km rulers (*Fig. 19*, left). Consequently, the laser beams at Terminus, having taken different times to reach it, constructively interfere and the apparatus detects the resultant light, indirectly revealing the presence of a deformational event that science chalks up to GW (*Fig. 19*, center). Taking into account seismic and other disturbances that always affect the apparatus, the laser measures a change in arm length of as little as one ten-thousandth a proton's diameter, correlating to a planetary distortion of as little as one-millionth a proton's diameter (Alderson 2019, par. 6–7).

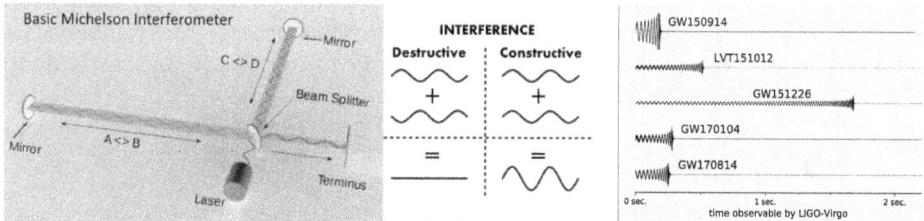

Figure 19. Left, laser emits from Laser, separates at Beam Splitter to arm A ↔ B and C ↔ D, mirrors back to Beam Splitter then to Terminus; center, destructive interference: no viewable light; constructive: viewable light; right, LVI signal reception as a time function of 4 confident, 1 candidate (LVT151012), GW.[171]

This is all straightforward enough except that ET data indicates gravity exerts from a process sans wave effects (§ 3.1:121–§ 3.3.3:130); there's no GW to squeeze or stretch non-existent spacetime, thus Earth. But there's no doubt that LVI is detecting a change in the relative length of its interferometer arms. That suggests a deformation to the planet, which accordingly suggests some sort of pressure wave.

3.7.3.2 Gravity and Spacetime

Gravitational force has always been a mystery. It's a brute reality and that's the best anyone has made of it. Einstein recognized a relationship between gravity and relative motion (acceleration) that he could instead use to explain gravitational force as a feature of energy and momentum in spacetime.[166] Yet, his effort with Relativity only theorizes gravity's expression, not how the mechanism of spacetime exerts. Intense energy emissions correlated to infinitesimal deformations of Earth is an effect whose explanation builds off presumptions, one being that the stress–energy tensor $T_{\mu\nu}$—the density and flux of energy and momentum in spacetime—describes something real about space rather than being a mathematical derivation. As with statistics, one can build a house of cards from relativistic mathematics if one gets the numbers to add up to apparent observation. But that doesn't equal *reality*. It's just math.

Even so, the concept of a ripple through space and the math predicting it hits the jackpot because a change in matter's state—a deformation—plainly indicates a change in proximal force, meaning something tangible is behind the deformational phenomenon. The math, however, ultimately drags science off the mark by conflating predicted observation with predicted causality as a probabilistic reality: the observation fits a pattern that fits a prediction that validates the model, thus proving the causation. Reality isn't probable though, it's explicit. Gw propagation is fundamentally inexplicable because the metric tensor 'fabric' $g_{\mu\nu}(x, y, z, t)$, and why mass even distorts it, are themselves inexplicable as realities. Energy needs an equivalent to mechanical inertia and elasticity to move (propagate) through space. In the GW context, the EMW equivalent to the former is the particle saturant (§ 3.1:121) and to the latter the vacuum permittivity ε_0 and permeability μ_0 of space (§ 6.11.2:194).

There's no functional relationship between a stellar disturbance followed by planetary deformation and an intense energy emission followed by a gravitational effect because GW, as ripples in spacetime, necessarily converts not just a Newtonian inward contractive force simultaneously to an outward exerted force, but also, w.r.t. Relativity, converts an energy emission to real mass (via $E = mc^2$) that locally deforms spacetime and real matter as though it were itself real matter. This ripple (energy in motion) then traverses space like a photon with mass at lightspeed c using the metric tensor 'fabric' as its medium, gravitationally deforming some real spacetime structure and anything inhabiting it along the way until it deforms Earth by some part of a proton's diameter as it passes through. Gravity can't practically draw inward and exert outward as the same phenomenon, whether it's a Newtonian force or a spacetime geodesic. As energy in motion, gravity of this sort requires a medium to move through space; this is spacetime w.r.t. Relativity, except spacetime's a mathematical tensor construct without objective reality. Unlike water and air as energy mediums, spacetime's medium is entirely mathematical. So, LVI's noted deformations of Earth correlates to gravitational deformations in spacetime only as a mathematical construct, not of reality.

Since stellar disturbances like collisions between binary neutron stars (and, according to Mina, black holes; § 6.9:178) emit intense EMR energy, and their energy emanations correlate to deformations of Earth that necessarily aren't the result of wave distortions to some stress–energy or metric tensor that changes the relative space in and around matter, then do such energy emissions arrive on Earth in a more familiar way? Well, partly, yes they do. Mina describes intense stellar disturbances that correlate to LVI's observation of planetary deformation as a simple relationship between energy and matter in which intense gamma ray bursts (GRB) interact with subatomic4 particle saturants as nominal[167] EMR, which then transports via its usual EMW medium (Table 1:122) along a GRB's combined anisotropic and isotropic vectors (§ 3.7.3.4.1:147). To understand how that is, we need briefly survey an EMW's vitals.

3.7.3.3 EM Field Extension vs. EM Wave

Energy classically moves through space as EMR via the medium of EMW (§ 6.12.1.1:206). To this, Relativity adds the purely mathematical construct of a focused energy disturbance—ripple—through the metric tensor

---

166. Refers to the combined metrics of space and time, not a physical existence or force, and enables Relativistic math to measure path geometry of objects in gravitational fields.

167. Throughout, *nominal* is "of, being, or relating to a designated or theoretical size that may vary from the actual" within acceptable tolerances or within an expected or normal range (*Merriam*, s.v. 3b 'nominal').

of spacetime it calls a gravitational wave (gw) as a second means by which energy moves through space. Since the metric tensor 'fabric' isn't any more real than spacetime, we dispense with it here, as well.

But classical waveform as a model for describing emw isn't particularly real itself, either. It came into vogue with science observing that emr energy transports over distance through a vacuum similar in some respects to how energy transports over distance via water and other physical mediums. It didn't hurt that electric and magnetic fields propagate perpendicular with rotation to their emw's vector just as water molecules propagate their location disturbance over distance perpendicular with rotation to their water wave's vector (*Fig. 20*). The apparent resemblance is only superficial, though. The discovery that emr traverses space without a detectable medium (such as the luminiferous æther) did nothing to discourage using the wave model to describe emr transport. When Thomas Young's (d. 1829) revisited double slit experiment yielded an ambivalent result regarding light's particle or wave nature, scientists simply recast emw as a product of the wave equation (§ 5.4:158) and wavefunction (§ 6.11.1:192).

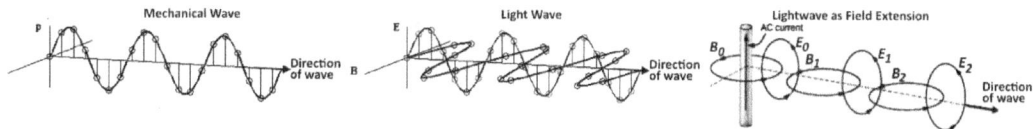

Figure 20. Mechanical *vs.* emw waveform *vs.* (an analogical) emw field extension in a single plane where magnetic $\vec{B}$ and electric $\vec{E}$ fields propagate perpendicular to each other and perpendicular to wave direction. Waveform lines indicate field vector.[172]

3.7.3.3.1 The Origin of EMW

Recall the energy source for emr—the archí—is the fundamental element in emw, not frequency, wavelength, or wave speed, all of which are determined by, and are direct manifestations of, emr system energy (§ 2:114). The rise of emw starts with a photon (§ 2.3.2:116), which in its applied energy E essence is indeed a unit, or quantum, of energy. When it emits and moves through space, *enérgeia* flux ($\Phi_{\alpha\Omega}$) across its archí shell contextually expresses as em Fundamental Force (emf). The spatial area over which emf exerts is termed the em field $F_{\mu\nu}$. A proto-electric E force charge of q_E arises from emf (§ 3.7.3.3.2:140); q_E and magnetic q_B force/fields arise from the q_E charge in $F_{\mu\nu}$ as a product of *enérgeia* interaction with emf.[168] This initial process, $\Phi_{\alpha\Omega} \rightarrow$ emf $\rightarrow F_{\mu\nu} \rightarrow q_E \rightarrow E$ force/field $\rightarrow q_B \rightarrow B$ force/field $\rightarrow q \rightarrow b \rightarrow$ emw, takes place over $\sim 2.366 \times 10^{-13}$ second, with $\sim 1.746 \times 10^{-27}$ second on average between the individual components of the series. This overall period is longer than the photon's duty cycle (Eq. (17.39)–(17.40):154), taking almost $2^{1}/_{2}$ decillion (2.44×10^{34}) times longer for an emw to set itself up than for a photon to deposit that many emw precursors along its track. This is why detectors don't recognize emw at lightspeed ç (§ 5.1:152) but only at lightspeed c.

Recall too that *enérgeia* is proto-energy (§ 1:112), a wholly non-material entity without time and distance (§ 6.11.4:198). On the other hand, real energy ϒ, or Fundamental Force, arises from *enérgeia*'s interaction with matter (§ 2.1:114) and is thus a material entity of time and distance. It exerts in and across space at a measurable speed that's et-given as precisely 814,833,682.8686 … m/s, roughly 1.7 times actual lightspeed ç and 2.7 times normative lightspeed c. The moment emf arises, it exerts across space a distance commensurate with its real energy ϒ as derived from *enérgeia* flux across the photon. It fills space around the photon's pulsed E charge (ibid) as a spherically symmetric, isotropic em field $F_{\mu\nu}$ faster than the photon itself is moving. Decillions of discrete, non-combinatory, non-overlapping emf iterations form in any single second like a string of pearls reeling out in the photon's wake (*Fig. 21*). As they're also moving—while expanding isotropically outward—through space in the photon's direction of travel, then essentially the photon is unspooling moving-point-charges along a metaphorical wire from its point of emission to wherever it dephases (§ 2.3.2:116). As *enérgeia* continually interacts with matter in this specific context, it gives rise to expanding emf along this 'wire' at each moving point charge.

Enérgeia's contextual interaction gives rise to emf of a certain *mode*, or expression. This emf mode acts as an em precursor, predetermining how electric, magnetic, or both forces exert in $F_{\mu\nu}$. That is, *enérgeia*'s interaction with the material universe contextually exerts emf in such a way that only the appropriate forces deploy in the appropriate force structure, in this case, an emw of a particular emr energy. In a poetic sense, emf 'knows' what it wants to do even before it's arisen as a force of nature.

---

168. 'Force' is contextual as real energy ϒ or applied energy E (Newtonian).

Figure 21. Idealized discrete EM force as many discrete EM fields $F_{\mu\nu}$ in photon γ wake. Each $F_{\mu\nu}$ is moving forward while concurrently expanding isotropically at lightspeed c infinitesimally earlier than the $F_{\mu\nu}$ proceeding it (cf. Fig. 30 for $F_{\mu\nu}$ expansion).

Both electric **E** and magnetic **H** force (Table 2) are real energy Υ and have force charge q_E and q_B. Science defines *charge* generally as "a physical [though, as ET-given, not a conserved] property that causes matter to experience a force within an electromagnetic field" (Helmenstine 2019, par. 1). What we call *electromagnetic* force is really a singular *energy* force (§ 3.7.3.3.2:140) that exerts real energy Υ as a force charge that shows up as electric charge q_E and magnetic charge q_B according to *enérgeia*'s ongoing matter interactions. The force charge initializes each the electric E and magnetic B applied energy E force (Table 2), which then exert in space at their most basic as applied energy E electric or magnetic monopoles, i.e., electric q or magnetic b charge.[169] Although an electric monopole can constitute electric force, a magnetic monopole cannot constitute magnetic force.[170] Intrinsically, electric force charge is *either* positive electric charge/force *or* negative electric charge/force. Extrinsically, magnetic force charge is *both* positive magnetic charge/force *and* negative magnetic charge/force. Meanwhile, since $F_{\mu\nu}$ is an applied energy E construct (derived from real energy Υ EMF), *enérgeia* continues contextually interacting with $F_{\mu\nu}$ in the photon's wake. From this arises in $F_{\mu\nu}$ the remainder of the above-described EMW component series ($q_E \to E$ force/field $\to q_B \to B$ force/field $\to q \to b \to$EMW) in the noted time, and thus an EMW constitutes.

Table 2. Process overview for creation of EMW in space where $\alpha\Omega$ is *enérgeia*, FF is Fundamental Force, **E/H** is real energy Υ electric/magnetic force, and E, B is applied energy E electric/magnetic force.

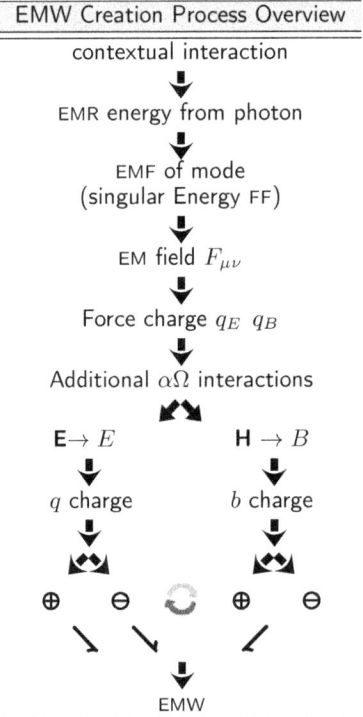

3.7.3.3.2 Rise of Electric and Magnetic Forces

As mentioned, Electromagnetic Fundamental Force isn't simply a combination of electric **E** and magnetic **H** force, but a singular real energy Υ *Energy* Fundamental Force that arises from *enérgeia*'s contextual interaction

---

169. Using b to symbolize magnetic *charge* is unique to this book.

170. According to Mina, magnetic monopoles that exert magnetic force aren't possible in nature.

with matter. It's the primary mechanism by which *enérgeia* translates 'energy' into the applied energy E context—the world in which we live. Therefore, the singular force known as Electromagnetic Force (EMF) is more aptly termed *Energy Force* (EF), because its fundamental effect is translating *enérgeia* interactions with matter into applied energy E forces that do work on matter.[171] *Energy charge*, an applied energy E entity that embodies the positive/negative nature of electric and magnetic charge, arises from Energy (EM) Force. It's not a neutral entity like a balanced positive–negative electric charge q, but a wholistic one. Electric and magnetic force arises from it, which in turn brings about positive and negative electric and magnetic charges. We schematize it as *force→charge→field* where real energy Υ ultimately expresses as applied energy E. Electric **E** and magnetic **H** force manifest energy in two distinct forms to achieve complementary applied energy E effects, as follows.

1) *Electric force* **E** is an applied energy E medium through which Energy (EM) Force in the context of electric field $\vec{E}$ *transports* applied energy E electric charge. *Electricity* is the mechanics that transports electric charge via electron movement. An *electric* field is a contextual *energy* field. Electric force is the primary expression of Energy (EM) Force. Magnetic force is secondary. Whenever both forces arise in tandem, magnetic force arises approximately 1.999×10^{-27} second after electric force. The delay originates in electric force arising first as a static monopole before it contextualizes to its full instantiation. If such is a moving electric charge, then *enérgeia*'s reaction to that reinitializes the energy charge from which magnetic force arises in the context of the moving electric field. However, the one doesn't itself create or induce the other despite their primary–secondary relationship. Independent q and b charges don't exist under time-varying conditions; where there's one there's the other with an order of instantiation but not of procreation. In the EMW context, *enérgeia* flux provokes a perpendicular $\vec{E}$ field rotation (*Fig 22*). The sophistication and instantaneity of this mechanism as a whole is simply breathtaking.

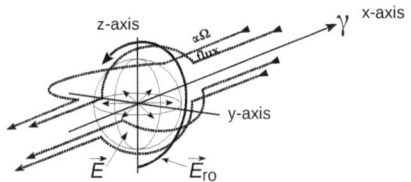

Figure 22. $\vec{E}$ field rotation ($\vec{E}_{ro}$) perpendicular to travel vector provoked by enérgeia $\alpha\Omega$ flux (right-to-left arrows parallel to photon γ travel vector).

2) *Magnetic force* **H** is an applied energy E medium through which Energy (EM) Force in the context of a magnetic field $\vec{B}$ interacts *mechanically* with the physical universe, e.g., when magnets move other magnets and certain metals at a distance. A *magnetic* field is also a contextual *energy* field. Electric force motivates magnetic force. It's the natural environment of a moving electric charge. If it's moving, the magnetic environment exists, if not then it doesn't. Each electron of matter constitutes a moving charge that establishes an electric field, which altogether creates a magnetic field and, thusly, natural magnetism. We plainly notice this phenomenon in ferromagnetic or ferrimagnetic materials. In fact, all objects are naturally magnetic—including photons and even you—although it's too infinitesimal to easily perceive. Such infinitesimal magnetic fields arise from magnetic *domains* (§ 6.8.1:174). Generally, they cancel each other microscopically, but there are always some domains that 'line up' to establish a coherent macroscopic magnetic field of infinitesimal proportion.

3.7.3.3.3   RISE OF EMW

As Table 2 indicates, EMR–EMW is a pairwise energy unit. EMR gives rise to EMW via the photon, and EMW transports EMR. The $\vec{B}$ force is rotational to the isotropically radial $\vec{E}$ force and $[\vec{E} + \vec{B}]$ acts as a pairwise force (Fig. 32:146, left (*inset*)) that interacts unit-like with *enérgeia* and moves—propagates—isotropically at lightspeed c in a Mach cone-like pattern (*Fig. 23*; § 5:151). From this point, EMW self-propagates across space from its point of origin on the photon's track.

Here lies the reality behind Dutch physicist Christian Huygens' (d. 1695) notion that EMR wavelets emanate from all points on, and thereby constitute, an EMR wavefront (§ 5.1.1:152), and Augustin-Jean Fresnel's (d. 1827)

---

171. We similarly encounter term confusion with WNF. It's the same absolute strength or magnitude relative to SNF. The difference is that SNF is strong over a farther distance r^2 relative to the particles it affects while WNF is strong over a nearer distance r^2 relative to the particles it affects. This is the contextual nature of Fundamental Force. As WNF primarily serves to remove excess components from atoms (e.g., proton–proton fusion in stars), WNF is more aptly termed *Disjoining Force* (DF).

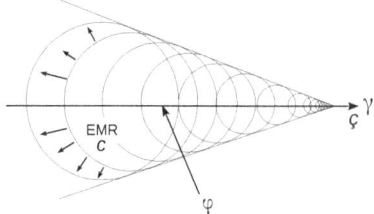

Figure 23. EMW as the singular component of each $F_{\mu\nu}$ expanding at normative lightspeed c over time and distance (per Fig. 21) in a Mach cone pattern where photon γ is moving at actual lightspeed ς (§ 5:151).

explanation for light interference and its prediction of a bright (Arago, or Poisson) spot in the center of a small disc's shadow. Their work helped prove the wave (EMW) theory of light over Descartes' corpuscular, or particle (photonic), theory. There's still no substantive proof either way, so quantum science simply adopted the theory of wave–particle duality and dropped anchor. Mina shows the presence of both as well as (notwithstanding some differences) Huygens and Fresnel's prescience.

3.7.3.3.4 PROPAGATION OF EMW AS A FIELD EXTENSION

The mechanical wave model—including the quantum wave packet as a means to comprehend the apparent mystery of particle–wave duality (§ 5.4:158)—simply doesn't apply to EMW. It's a broken metaphor. Though helpful in some contexts and capable of modeling EMW's basic reality (*Fig. 24*, left), using waveform generally to comprehend EMR transport obscures the real propagative nature of EMW.

What's really happening with EMW is that electric **E** and magnetic **H** force of a particular EMR energy form $\vec{E}$ and $\vec{B}$ fields that *extend* outward into space a distance relative to that energy. At its maximum extension in space, the EM field renews, or *resurges*, to re-extend outward into space the same distance, and so on. Accordingly, we introduce *resurgent field extension* (F_x) as a more apt analogy for EMW propagation than oscillatory wavelength (*Fig. 20*). The field extension process is a *resurgent* pulse series. It only mimics the oscillation typical of mechanical waveform. Electric and magnetic fields resurgently extend and develop because each field extension— a single EMW at time t—interacts with *enérgeia* which then energizes Energy (EM) Force within a spatial area consistent with the magnitude of the EMW's EMR energy. In this way, Energy (EM) Force precedes an EMW such that ensuing EMW resurge in the first place. Self-propagating EMW isn't some deitic hat trick or a *mysterium per universum*; specific force mechanisms constantly rebuild—resurge—its framework in space.

As Energy (EM) Force resurges, the electric–magnetic fields redevelop. In this resurgent fashion that's only reminiscent of the oscillation of mechanical waves, EMW propagates in three dimensions through space. From isotropically expanding electric field $\vec{E}$ arises encapsulating rotational magnetic field $\vec{B}$ at a right angle to it (*Fig. 24*, left). The magnetic field $\vec{B}$ in turn gives rise to a new electric field $\vec{E}$ farther out in space from which arises its own $\vec{B}$ field. This process resurges ad infinitum unless interrupted.

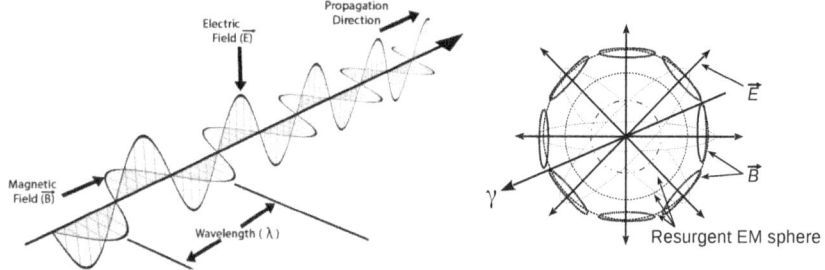

Figure 24. Left, standard representation of EMW as an oscillatory wave; right, schematic of single-plane EMW resurgent electric $\vec{E}$ and magnetic $\vec{B}$ isotropic fields. Arrows represent EMW field lines which are finite, hence propagate over a sphere of area $4\pi r^2$ such that field line density, i.e., field strength, is proportional to $1/r^2$ (inverse square law). $\vec{B}$ rotates 90° to $\vec{E}$.[173]

A closer inspection shows the y-$axis$ $\vec{B}$ field circumgyrates the ninety-degree z-$axis$ $\vec{E}$ field line, each perpendicular to the x-$axis$ photon direction of travel (*Fig. 25*). Electric fields radiate in infinite direction— represented by arrowed field lines—to instantiate infinite complemental magnetic fields at the 'surface' of the expanding, isotropic EMW (*Fig. 24*, right). As with electric fields, each magnetic field is discrete from its neighboring magnetic fields.

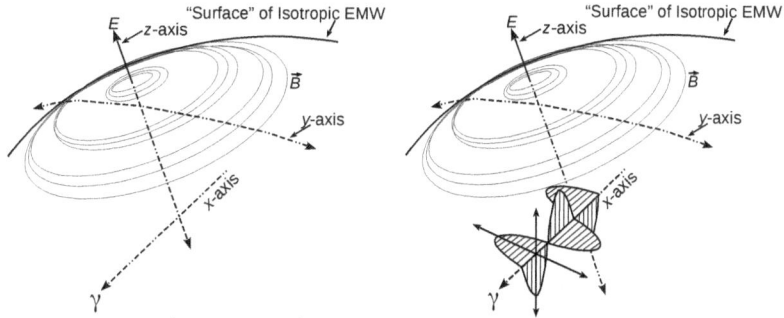

Figure 25. Left, schematic of $\vec{B}$ field 90° to $\vec{E}$ field along the expanding 'surface' of isotropic EMW in a single plane; right, typical single-plane wave oscillation superimposed along $y\text{-}axis$ and $z\text{-}axis$ perpendicular to $x\text{-}axis$ direction of travel (per *Fig. 24*).

Each exertion of $\vec{E}$ force/field gives rise to an infinitesimally delayed $\vec{B}$ force/field (§ 3.7.3.3.2:140) that extends in space along the photon vector a distance equivalent to classical wavelength. Since the electric field radially extends in three dimensions, if it wasn't moving at lightspeed c it would radiate backward into the decayed 'old space' of the expanding EMW sphere as much as it radiates forward into the 'new space' of the developing field extension (*Fig. 26*, left). As it's moving, however, the expanding fields end up looking more like a reverse Mach cone (Fig. 30:145). The electric field's concomitant magnetic field exerts around it across the span of the field extension at any time t or distance d and no further. Neighboring magnetic fields laterally limit it as implied in *Fig. 25* much the way neighboring underlying **E/H** force and $F_{\mu\nu}$ constrain any particular F_x's **E/H** force and $F_{\mu\nu}$ from mingling, similar to how opposing electric and magnetic fields resist mingling.

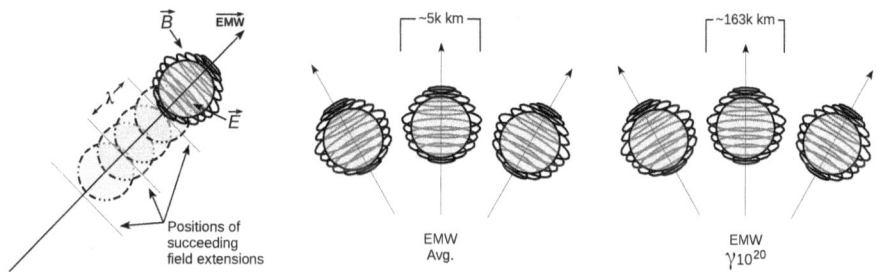

Figure 26. Schematic (2-D single plane): left, view of resurgent $\overrightarrow{EMW}$ field extension expanding isotropically; center, average maximum expansion of ~5k km for $\vec{E}$ and $\vec{B}$ of an EMW averaged over all EMW once field line density falls over area $4\pi r^2$ such that $\vec{E}$ and $\vec{B}$ fields encounter no lateral resistance from other field lines of same EMW; right, avg. max. of ~163k km for gamma γ EMW of 10^{20} Hz frequency, on average.

Over distance, the area affected by each EMW field line enlarges. This means there's more distance between, and less interference by, neighboring EMW field lines. Accordingly, an EMW's $\vec{E}$ and $\vec{B}$ fields extend their maximum as shown in *Fig. 26* (right) where field strength beyond spatial F_x, or wavelength distance, is progressively minimal and ineffectual until it's zero at its maximum. This is a factor in why EMR intensity appears to weaken—or, in the case of visible light, to appear visually dim—over a distance proportional to the amount of EMR emitting in a given $4\pi r^2$ region of space.

EMR energy determines the spatial distance that its resultant $\vec{E}$, $\vec{B}$ force/field can effectually extend. This provides our concept of field extension F_x and determines its extent (classical wavelength). Recall a nascent EMW E charge coming off a photon moving at actual lightspeed $ç$ immediately slows to (propagates at) lightspeed c—notwithstanding the speed at which real energy Υ Energy (EM) Force exerts (§ 3.7.3.3.1:139)—as that's the speed applied energy E charge exerts across spatial distance. As we noted w.r.t. Fig. 22:141, the moving E charge develops rotation from *enérgeia* flux (*Fig. 27*). This $\vec{E}$ (and $\vec{B}$) rotation is where EMW sinusoidal waveform gets its characteristic oscillation. Moving E charge means the F_x resurgence of $\vec{E}$ and $\vec{B}$ charge/field happens over a period of time t and distance d along a 'sliding scale.'

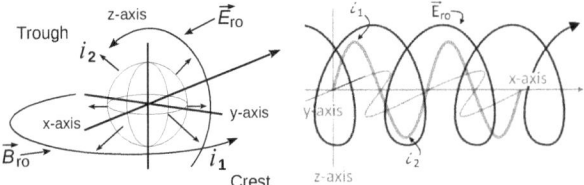

Figure 27. Schematic: EMW $\vec{E}$ ($\vec{E}_{ro}$), $\vec{B}$ ($\vec{B}_{ro}$) field rotation (cf. Fig. 22:141); classical $\pm$ wave crest i_1, i_2.

3.7.3.3.5 THE EMW CYCLE

Within a single cycle of EMW, a resurgent—new—E charge manifests only when the present $\vec{E}$ field's $\vec{B}$ field reaches a strength threshold of about 99.2% (*Fig. 28*). This occurs approximately when $\vec{E}$, $\vec{B}$ field expansion reaches midpoint in the F_x cycle. At this point, the present F_x's local **H** force—an element of the local Energy (EM) Force, recall—manifests a resurgent E charge. The resurgent E charge manifests in physical space at about 4% its maximum field strength (defined as 100% when it resurges a new F_x, at the beginning of the classical wavelength spatial distance). It's also moving forward at lightspeed c along with the still expanding $\vec{E}$, $\vec{B}$ field of the present F_x as they propagate to F_x spatial distance. The present EMW's $\vec{E}$ field strength peaks at F_x midpoint and begins to decline, reaching about 99.2% field strength at about $^7/10$ the F_x spatial distance, while $\vec{B}$ field reaches 100% field strength at about the same $^7/10$ F_x spatial distance. This means there's an infinitesimal delay between $\vec{E}$ and $\vec{B}$) peak field strength. At the same time, a resurgent $\vec{B}$ charge/field forms around the nascent resurgent $\vec{E}$ charge/field. When the present F_x $\vec{E}$, $\vec{B}$ field expands to encompass the entire F_x, or wavelength spatial distance, the resurgent E, B charge have reached 100% and 51% field strength, respectively, and a new—that is, resurgent—F_x cycle begins, we say the EMW self-propagates onward.

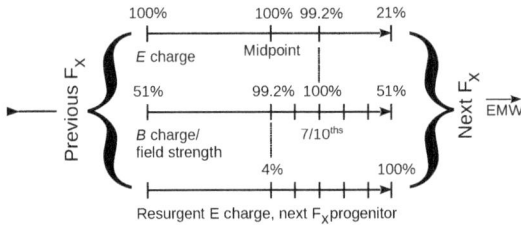

Figure 28. Schematic of a single F_x, or classical wavelength, during which its $\vec{B}$ field provokes a new, or resurgent, E charge that's the progenitor of the next F_x (waveform oscillation).

At this point in F_x, a single classical $\vec{E}$, $\vec{B}$ waveform will have oscillated through its wave crest and trough. This describes the essence of an F_x, or classical waveform, cycle and shows how E and B charge reproduces such that an EMW self-propagates through space.

We can see that when an EMW first propagates (and with each resurgence thereafter), E charge—having grown from 4% to 100% over the course of the previous F_x—exerts at 100% strength from the start of the resurgent F_x and then wanes from its midpoint over F_x distance to about 21% of that. Its B charge, on the other hand, having also grown commensurate with resurgent E charge's growth, starts the resurgent F_x at about 51% its maximum strength, waxes to 100% strength by about $^7/10$ through the F_x cycle (oscillation), then wanes to its initial strength (*Fig. 29*). The reason the $\vec{E}$ and $\vec{B}$ fields wane w.r.t. effectual EMR over the course of F_x (wavelength) is because each have their own energy budget as derived from **E/H** force, itself derived from the real energy Υ up-charge of the photon upon its emission that creates the particular EMR in the first place (§ 2.3.2:116). While the field strengths vary, local **E/H** force remains constant within the F_x space; beyond it, of course, it decays to zero along with its $\vec{E}$ and $\vec{B}$ fields since, once past F_x (wavelength) spatial distance, it's ineffectual and we can consider the F_x cycle completed.

Within the F_x space, the consistent **E/H** force is what resurges E and B charge for the next F_x resurgence. Although their separate interactions with *enérgeia* initiate their pairwise operation, these resurgent charges operate as a pairwise unit interacting with *enérgeia* to raise a new F_x space. When E and B charge strength reach their thresholds, the Energy (EM) Force raises a resurgent E charge via the extant magnetic field around the midpoint of F_x. The resurgent E charge manifests instantaneously when present $\vec{B}$ field strength achieves threshold around F_x midpoint as in *Fig. 28*. It isotropically expands at lightspeed c while also propagating forward at lightspeed c (*Fig. 30*) as its pairwise magnetic field concomitantly arises.

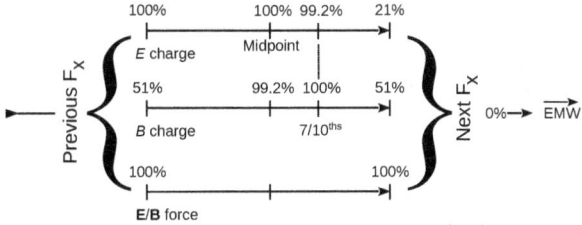

Figure 29. Electric and magnetic force (**E, H**), charge (E, B), and field ($\vec{E}$, $\vec{B}$) relative strength across spatial distance of a single EMW F_x.

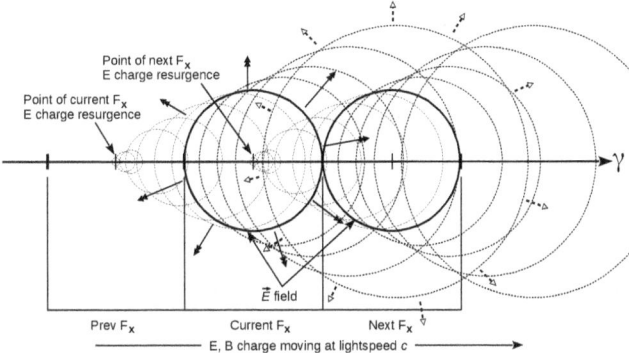

Figure 30. Schematic: resurgent $\vec{E}$ field expanding at lightspeed c to, then beyond, F_x (wavelength) spatial distance (SD), while moving at lightspeed c. Dark circles show $\vec{E}$ field expanded to fill F_x SD. Dotted circles <> F_x SDs indicate $\vec{E}$ field expansion over time. $\vec{B}$ is ignored. Note reversed Mach cone-like pattern.

3.7.3.3.6   EMW Field Extension vs. Wave Oscillation

The rotational nature of $\vec{E}$ field is behind the oscillatory appearance of EMW as it moves through each 180° cycle (*Fig. 27*). To visualize it, we overlay Fig. 30 with waveform (*Fig. 31*). This F_x process start to finish comprises a single cycle in a single plane of a self-propagating EMW (*Fig. 32*, left).

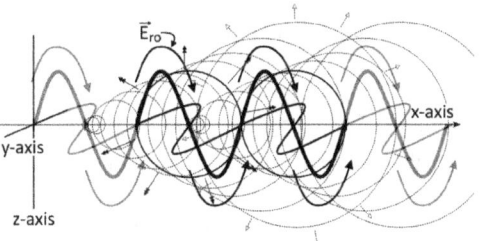

Figure 31. F_x overlain with classical waveform and $\vec{E}$ field rotation ($\vec{E}_{ro}$).

As a field extension F_x rather than an oscillation c/λ, the traditional peak-to-peak wavelength is naturally inaccurate. Recall peak-to-peak wavelength references $\vec{E}$ field rotation. F_x distance is baseline-to-baseline when applied to the waveform model (*Fig. 32*, right). A wave trough, its lowest or minimum point, isn't simply an inverted wave crest, its highest or maximum point, in a larger wave cycle as the waveform model portrays EMW. Instead, the energy peaks (which the wave crest is meant to represent) are from F_x initialization to midpoint at the baseline where both E and B charge are at or rising to greatest field strength, and wave trough is from F_x midpoint to terminus where E and B charge are declining in field strength as they approach their nadir. Also, E and B charge propagating 90° to the direction of wave travel (Fig. 20:139, Fig. 24:142) doesn't make EMW a transverse wave over a field extension.

EM field extension interactions with each other result in outcomes typical of classical wave interference. Hence, the waveform metaphor scientifically satisfies at a certain level even though it doesn't provide a proper description of how EMW works. Rather, the observed mechanical waveform model of EMW interference is the interaction of energies at different periods of the field extension. Let's say from F_x initialization to midpoint is Period One P_1 and from F_x midpoint to terminus is Period Two P_2; two field extensions interfere during their

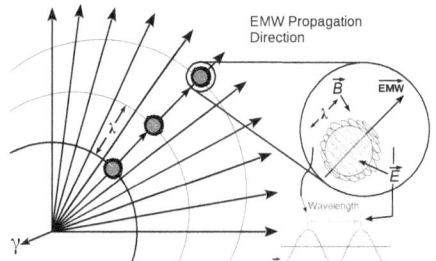 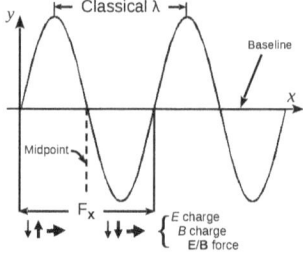

Figure 32. Left, schematic of EM field extension showing three F_x cycles moving along its vector at lightspeed c; right, classical wavelength λ as field extension F_x; resurgence (oscillation) is baseline-to-baseline rather than peak-to-peak and is a measure of field rotation, not field strength.

P_1 subcycle where E and B charge are at or close to greatest strength. Their EMW energies sum to produce constructive interference per the classical summed sinusoidal wave model equation, as

$$U_1(\mathbf{r}, t) = A_1(\mathbf{r})e^{i[\varphi_1(\mathbf{r})-\omega t]}$$
$$U_2(\mathbf{r}, t) = A_2(\mathbf{r})e^{i[\varphi_1(\mathbf{r})-\omega t]} \tag{17.36}$$

where A is wave displacement magnitude at point $\mathbf{r}$ and φ is phase difference in radians of a wave, except it's w.r.t. a field extension rather than waveform. The same holds for two F_x that interfere during their P_2 where E and B charge are declining in strength and approaching their nadir. Unlike Eq. (17.36) where U_1 and U_2 wave behavior sums, EMW energies subtract to produce destructive interference. Waveform math correctly calculates interference w.r.t. to waveform, but we can't use the same math wholesale to calculate interference w.r.t. to field extension despite each describing roughly the same visible result. The reason is that Eq. (17.36) calculates interference as a function of a wave—amplitude (strength)—which indirectly references EMW energies. Without deriving the math from Eq. (17.36), we simplify field extension F_x constructive and destructive interference between any P_1 and P_2 (in applied energy E terms) as

$$P_1 + P_2 = P_3$$
$$P_1 - P_2 = 0 \tag{17.37}$$

where P_3 is the energy displacement magnitude of the calculated field extensions. It calculates interference in terms of energy, the amount of energy magnitude (strength). Whereas Eq. (17.36) is a function of mechanical waveform *position* at time t, Eq. (17.37) is a function of F_x *energy* at time t. EMW is energy pulsed over a gradient in discrete F_x. Because it resurges, the pulse nature of the individual EMW cycle appears to oscillate, which precipitates using waveform as the EMW model. Despite a repeating pulse appearing oscillatory, there's a real distinction between mechanical oscillatory waveform and pulsed energy F_x.

Even though 'energy' affects matter in certain ways, it doesn't behave like matter. More important, while EMR requires EMW as a medium to propagate through space, EMW itself requires no pre-existent medium to propagate such as the luminiferous æther or an always-present Energy (EM) Force/field. Rather, it 'generates,' or gives rise to, its own EM field F_x medium on the fly as it moves (§ 5.1:152) in accord with vacuum permittivity ε_0 and permeability μ_0, and the particle saturant that collectively fills most—not all—of free space in the OU (§ 3.1:121). Even in a medium like water, glass, or air, EMW doesn't create water, glass, or air waves the way a stone passing through water creates water waves as a function of displacement. Rather, it remains separate and distinct, passing through the medium as an energy field extension F_x without disturbing it (except by heating, perhaps).[172]

3.7.3.4 GAMMA RAY BURST SHOCKWAVES

Having discussed the particle saturant and how EMW arise and self-propagate, we can now coherently consider why Mina tells us that a gamma ray burst (GRB) riding within and behind a particle saturant shockwave is the mechanism behind so-called Earth-deforming GW detected by LVI. Normally, EMW transfers energy without transferring—that is, producing mechanical interactions with—mass, and this includes the photoelectric effect

---

172. EMW traveling through plasma appears to indicate EMW is a longitudinal wave although some observers define it as more like a sound wave. Both are inaccurate. While science correctly observes the phenomenon, it incorrectly perceives it. Plasma doesn't show EMW being a longitudinal wave that we happen to perceive thanks to the plasma medium. Rather, it shows the plasma medium itself reacting in longitudinal waveform to the EMW field extensions passing through it.

(§ 6.12.1.1:206). So, how can a GRB incite a physical deformation of Earth the LVI can notice? To answer that question, we first briefly describe a GRB.

3.7.3.4.1 Gamma Ray Bursts

"GRBs form when the core of a massive star collapses or two neutron stars merge together. The resulting explosions are the brightest events in the universe, vastly outshining entire galaxies containing hundreds of billions of stars. The energy output is believed to be largely concentrated in a jet, however, rather than spread out in all directions. A GRB event is detected if the Earth happens to lie within the beam direction of its jet."[173] The widely variant, extremely energetic gamma emissions last from milliseconds to hours. A GRB subclass associated with binary neutron star and black hole (§ 6.9:178) mergers is the short GRB, which lasts less than about two seconds and, says Mina, constitutes ~30% of observed GRB. The other 70%, lasting longer than about two seconds, is the long GRB and is associated with kilonovæ (~1,000 times stronger than typical novæ). A GRB emits as much energy in a few seconds as the Sun over its entire alleged 10BY lifespan, roughly that typical of supernovæ.

Astronomers believe GRBs emit only as diametric collimated jets, the intense magnetic field 'funneling' EMR outflow as a short GRB (*Fig. 33*, panel 1). Mina avers that, over the course of the short GRB period, the jet action weakens the magnetic field's magnitude until it can no longer funnel EMR into jets. At this point, the remaining gamma and incident EMR emits isotropically outward in symmetrically spherical fashion typical of EMW as long GRB (*Fig. 33*, panel 2). Following its kilonova (*Fig. 33*, panel 3), a second GRB emits the balance of the binary collision's retained energy plus that of the kilonova itself (*Fig. 33*, panel 4). In toto, a GRB constitutes a short followed by two long GRBs of varying durations. While a short GRB produces the same shockwave, it's the long GRB shockwave series the LVI detects as Earth's deforming agent.

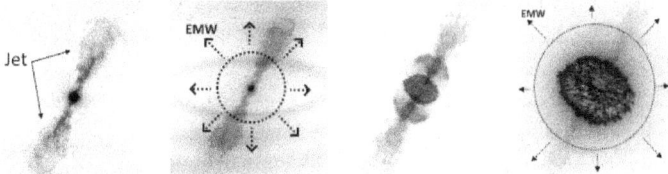

Figure 33. Artist depiction of GW170817/GRB 170817a GRB jets. Panels, left to right: 1) short GRB jets; 2) long GRB EMW; 3) follow-on kilonova; 4) second, long GRB EMW.[175]

Ordinarily, Earth's atmosphere absorbs most gamma radiation originating in space. Even if it didn't, EMW doesn't physically move matter except when ejecting electrons in the photoelectric effect. But ejecting electrons doesn't physically displace matter (other than electrons), and that's not what LVI is detecting anyway. As discussed, the particle saturant fills most of OU space. Its subatomic$_4$ complex archí structures lack the matter–Energy either to impede or get involved with typical EMR passage through space. Two questions thus arise. Why don't astronomers detect long GRB from binary neutron star collisions, or for that matter, any GRB at all from binary black hole collisions? The answer lies with the particle saturant. Thus, the second question: how does the particle saturant become a shockwave?

3.7.3.4.2 Particle Saturant as GRB Shockwave

ET data shows that typical EMW don't interact with the infinitesimal subatomic$_4$ particle saturant 'clouds' because nominal EMR energy isn't strong enough to disturb the Energy (EM) Force holding these matter clouds in proximity to their host objects. But a gamma ray burst (GRB) is. For example, as the most intense Energy (EM) Force event in the universe outside an ultranova (§ 6.9.2:180), binary collisions that typically produce intense GRBs emit energy from about 10^{40} to 10^{90} joules with a mean of about 10^{65} J. This is greater than typical supernovæ of 10^{44} J as well as the bulk of the upcoming 2045 Betelgeuse supernova, which Mina estimates at 5.335×10^{58} J (Event Periodicity, § 2:107). If we include the final 20 milliseconds before a binary collision, the mean energy emission averages about 20% greater.

GRB EMW emits from a binary collision first in collimated jets and then isotropically as a symmetrical sphere. Both types of emissions immediately—and for their entire journey—encounter particle saturant clouds, as does any EMR. Recall a GRB isn't normative for gamma ray emission. It emits about 8,650% more gamma

---

173. The core collapse and resulting supernova produce distinct GRBs, but so close in time as to appear a single GRB.[174]

energy photons per region of space than a non-GRB gamma ray emission, all of which constructively and destructively interfere with each other. Hence, a GRB emits an energy magnitude sufficient to disrupt matter.[174] When these concentrated field extensions F_x encounter particle saturant objects, their aggregated electric and magnetic charges disrupt the saturants' 'binding energy' (§ 2.3:115). The composite saturant structures then separate into smaller albeit still subatomic₄ matter–Energy structures. Being now of a size where GRB F_x dominates their energy space, the aggregated propagating electric and magnetic fields propel these fragments to the forefront of each resurgent F_x, stripping these infinitesimal structures from their hosts' influence by instantly accelerating them to, and keeping them at, lightspeed c (cf. discussion Eq. (17.8)–(17.14):117–119). This process occurs across space and time along GRB vectors.

These reduced particle saturants pile up along the GRB EMW's leading edge like a shock front. The GRB EMR consequently loses energy to these accelerated particle saturants. Over significant time, about 90% of the GRB EMR attenuates to x-ray through radio rather evenly across the spectrum. Nearly 98% of total GRB EMR energy, on average, is lost over time accelerating subatomic₄ matter to lightspeed c. This means astronomers only detect roughly 2.1% of the binary collision's gamma radiation that shows up after the shockwave. Behind it, the so-called afterglow is GRB remnants faded to x-ray through to radio. It includes EMR from collisions between ejecta and interstellar gas—inclusive of subatomic₄ archí structures—as well as the greater subatomic₄-only particle saturant itself. On average, about 26% of the afterglow is from gamma EMR that lost energy over time banging around behind the final shockwave in the series. The process in toto is remarkably similar to that observed in Drexel University's MXene material in which individual flakes absorb radiation by absorbing, or trapping, it until it falls lower on the energy spectrum (*Fig. 34*, left).

The particle saturant shockwave builds up spatially into multiple shock fronts, or 'layers,' of matter that progressively trap gamma EMR originating in the GRB until it loses energy. Drexel claims MXene blocks EMR in two ways. When "[i]ncoming EM waves . . . strike the surface of a MXene flake . . . part of the EM waves is [*sic*] immediately reflected from the surface . . . whereas induced local dipoles . . . help with absorption of the incident waves passing through the MXene structure . . . waves with less energy are then subjected to the same process when they encounter the next MXene flake, giving rise to multiple internal reflections (dashed black arrows [*Fig. 34*, left]), as well as more absorption . . . its intensity is substantially decreased, resulting in an overall attenuated or completely eliminated EM wave" (Shahzad et al. 2016, Fig. 4, 1140).

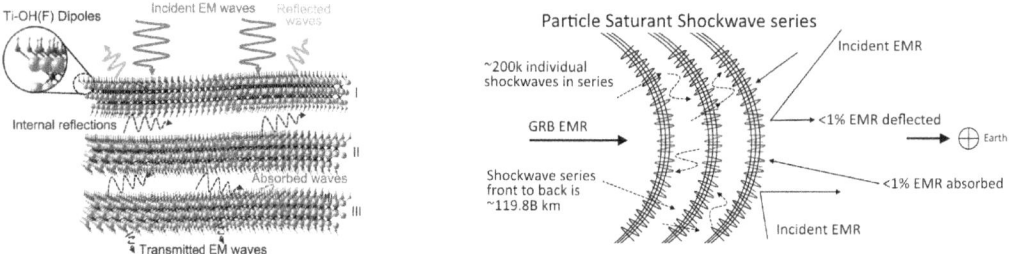

Figure 34. Left, MXene is "a family of 2-D materials" etched in thin layers "from MAX phases, a family of hexagonal layered ternary transition metal carbides and nitrides" that reflect and trap EMR until it loses energy; right, schematic of particle saturant shockwave (note that non-source incident EMR reflects from shock front while GRB EMR reflects between and behind, and absorbs into, saturant matter); ⊕ is Earth.[176]

Similar with MXene but in reverse, GRB EMW propagates behind the particle saturant shockwave while internally reflecting within its 'layers.' Some F_x leak into the structure itself. Others knock around between its 'layers' in MXene fashion. Each successive GRB EMW field extension—electric and magnetic force—pushes shockwave elements ahead of it like a bow wave. Successive waves of GRB EMW propagate behind the initial EMW and shockwave, each building up its own shockwave until they end. The remaining GRB EMW—gamma and lower frequency (afterglow) EMR—follow behind.

As the shock front moves through space, it reflects incident EMR from unrelated sources similar to MXene's outer flake (*Fig. 34*, right).[175] On average, approximately 96% of gamma EMR—97% inclusive of lower frequency radiation—that astronomers detect in the roughly 1.8 seconds *before* an LVI detection, which is in line with

---

174. One reason that gamma rays are biologically lethal.

175. The shockwave absorbs <1% of such unrelated incident EMR.

the incoming GRB shockwave, is shockwave-reflected incident EMR from other sources. It originates in other regions of space, crosses paths with the shockwave, and some of it reflects along the shockwave's vector toward Earth. Mixed in with it is about one percent of long GRB and any photonic EMR that got through particle saturants before they built into shockwaves.[76] The particle saturant shockwave—and reflected incident EMR, too—hides, or screens, about 99% of the GRB EMR piled up behind it. Only when the shockwaves run their course do astronomers detect GRB EMR.

3.7.3.4.3   SHOCKWAVE IMPACT

LVI detects shockwaves from relevant stellar events and scientists classify them as GW moving akin to EMR at lightspeed c. Their data, so far, shows them arriving over a $\pm$ 0.2–1.7 second period (though some events are longer) prior to the arrival of GRB EMR. The delay indicates a time sequence where GW leave the impending binary collision followed about two seconds later by the actual collision and consequent GRB. On its face, it all appears to corroborate spacetime gravitational wave theory. However, in order to describe the delay per ET data, we need dissect what a GRB is actually delivering to Earth.

ET data shows prodigious GRB energy emits into space and disrupts susceptible matter, forming it into shockwaves. These come in series like any shockwave event, one after the other until there's an insufficient concentration of energy to raise more. Each shockwave's depth—from shock front to GRB EMW acting on its tail end—averages about 0.0001 seconds at lightspeed c, or about 29.979 km of particle saturant front to back. Its saturant material is about 40% less dense in front than at back. This means each individual shockwave lands on Earth like a series of shockwaves in and of itself, causing a gradually more pronounced effect from start to finish. Mina avers the series comprises an approximate mean of 11,750 discrete shockwaves built up from the average GRB's emissions. The interval between each shockwave in the series is an approximate mean of 0.008 seconds, or 2,398.339 km, which totals about 94 seconds across all ±11,750 shockwaves. A single shockwave, including its spatial interval, is thus ~0.0001 + 0.008 = 0.0081 seconds, or 2,428.3 km. Totting it all up, we get an approximate mean shockwave series of $0.0081s \times 11,750 = 95.175$ seconds that spatially spreads across about 28,532,747.19 km (*Fig. 35*, left). This isn't too far from LVI's maximal detection of 100 seconds or so.[77] And then GRB EMR arrives.

Propagating in the space between shockwaves is its GRB EMW progenitor, emitted so long ago from its own origin (*Fig. 35*, right). This gamma EMR is what interacted with particle saturants encountered on the way, accelerating portions of it to lightspeed c and shedding energy in the process. As this EMW continually interacts with the matter–Energy of the shockwave that it's propelling ahead of itself, it's also transferring EMR energy to its constituents. Over time, its EMR frequency attenuates generally to superlongwave radio of $\pm$2.997 Hz (§ 6.9.3.4:184). It constitutes about 99.8% of the EMR propagating through the spatial distance comprising the approximate 0.008-second shockwave interval. The superlongwave radio appears to be EMR-empty space. Naturally, this attenuated EMR follows behind the final shockwave, as it does each one in the series. Accordingly, it's the proximate reason for the apparent delay between LVI's last registered shockwave and what astronomers presume is the first arrival of a short GRB.

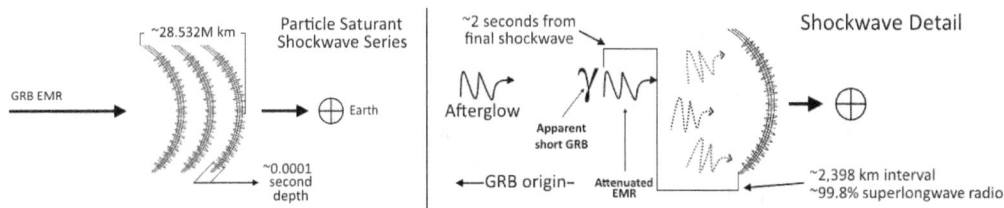

Figure 35. Schematic: left, gamma ray burst shockwave; right, detail of last shockwave in series; ⊕ is Earth.

Except that, what they're detecting isn't a short GRB at all. It's the last gasp of the series of short GRB plus two long GRBs, the frequency of which didn't attenuate because it built up no more shockwaves and otherwise lost no energy. The average GRB delivers to Earth about one percent its total output ahead of the shockwave, essentially no gamma EMR during the period the shockwaves pummel Earth, then about two seconds of gamma

---

176. Zero photonic GRB EMR arrives on Earth when its origin is distant, even from a GRB jet. About 13% of EMR from 2017's relatively close NGC 4993 GRB landed as photons.

177. From GRB GW170817A in NGC 4993, August 2017.

EMR mistaken for a short GRB. Ultimately, astronomers detect only ∼2.1% of what a GRB actually emits toward Earth before its afterglow arrives, which itself is just attenuated GRB EMR. LVI detects on average about 99% of each shockwave event. Quite surprising, about 5% of the shockwave series passes entirely through Earth with a kinetic energy loss of about 82% although its speed remains at lightspeed *c*. This means that, while passing through Earth, it doesn't encounter any matter—electrostatic, magnetic, or other energy—that stops, deflects, or slows it, although the particle saturant does experience interactions where it sheds kinetic energy.

Bottom line, what looks like GW is an Energy (EM) Force event disguised by a particle saturant shockwave series forming the infinitesimal physical impingement that triggers LVI detection. ET data indicates that Energy (EM) Force is far more pervasive and deeply entwined in the phenomena of the infinite universe than previously imagined. Going forward, we tackle a variety of follow-up issues regarding mass, lightspeed, Relativity, and 'energy' transliteration between the natural and supranatural aspects of our universe. These fill out our general understanding of energy and motion toward comprehending space as something infinite, and what it means.

SECTION 4

Mass

When we look at any object in existence, what do we need to see, besides its constituent makeup, in order to understand that object? Three things, really: its nature of motion, motivating force, and existent 'energy.' We partially comprehend its nature of motion via classical science and its traditional concept of mass. We get its motivating force through comprehending real energy Υ because that's Fundamental Force, the force of nature. Its existent 'energy' is how and why anything is what it is and does what it does—in short, "the energetic essentiality of a thing's nature" according to Mina. We briefly consider each in turn.

4.1 Nature of Motion

To understand a thing as a motive entity, science contrived the concept of mass. It helps us sense the amount of matter that constitutes a thing but, more importantly, how it moves in real space in terms of vibration, velocity, heat, frequency, resistance to change, and so on. It gives insight to the physical forces at work around us but, as a *how* not a *why*, it provides no insight on Fundamental Force. We're compelled to accept mass as a given and derive what we can from its observed (or misobserved) effects. The crowning achievement equating matter to energy in $E = mc^2$ demonstrates its terminal limitation; real energy Υ necessarily changes how we conceive it.

4.2 Motivating Force

To understand real classical matter–¢nergy equivalence requires comprehending real energy Υ. Mass isn't useful here because it's a property of applied energy E. In pursuing why matter exists at all, why it moves as it does, why it's equivalent to energy . . . well, we're dealing with 'energy,' not mass, matter–Energy, nor mass–energy. Mass doesn't help us understand the real energies of an object, its binding force; just the matter that's there and what it does in space w.r.t. motion. Classical science uses how much matter constitutes an object as a baseline for understanding matter in applied energy E terms, which gets us gravitational mass and inertial mass, for starters, to help us discover what it will kinetically do in space.

We need a different concept for such a baseline in Energent science to tell us the energetic how-and-why behind the mechanics of how and why an object is what it is and does what it does. It's nice to know that Fundamental Force lies behind electromagnetism and gravity, but how and why is *that* force even there, and in what way do we measure, or experience, it? Let's term this new conceptual baseline—and it's apples and oranges to mass—Υ *force* (§ 2.1:114). In the same way mass gives us a matter baseline to calculate its kinetic nature so as to manipulate and harvest its applied energy E, Υ force gives us an 'energy' baseline to calculate matter's force nature (such as binding force) so as to manipulate and harvest *its* power. Not applied power, *force power*. This distinction, and difference, is exponential.

4.3 Existent 'Energy'

This brings us to the Energent, the root of it all. The Energent is life, not life itself, of course, but the presence behind (nonhuman) life that gives physical things motility and the ability to be. The girls and I want to call it *energy* but it's just not. It mandates a fundamental rethink to cognize its existential nature, but that's a whole 'nother book. As a conceptual baseline, Mina selected the term *enérgeia* (ενέργεια), using it in the sense of "the energetic essentiality of a thing's nature." He likens it to Aristotle's view that *enérgeia* is not a movement (*kinēsis*), since it has no endpoint of completion, but rather that what's happening is happening in a complete way in and of itself (else it's not happening at all); "Every moment of . . . consciousness is a perfect whole" (Aristotle (c. 353–322 BC) 1956,[177] X.4.1174b (593–5)). *Enérgeia* is not applied energy E nor real energy Υ nor the Energent. Applied energy E describes energy as motion, force, or work that results from real energy Υ, nature's empowering force. The Energent, *enérgeia*'s parent, is the "absolute essentiality of a thing's nature" in our universe and of *its* parent Energent-prime in All Existence.

Enérgeia manifests from the interaction between matter and Energent. Ultimately, a thing isn't simply Energent but *material* Energent. Here lies true matter–¢nergy equivalence: a thing embodies *enérgeia*, manifests real energy Υ, and operates as applied energy E. The full spectrum of existence rises from the Energent to (natural *or* supranatural) matter like the alpha and omega of our universe. We haven't defined units of real energy Υ or *enérgeia* yet, so for now Mina denotes them Υ ("upsilon") and $\alpha\Omega$ ("enérgeia,").[178]

Enérgeia is the Energent's *expression* in time and space (§ 6.11.4:198) whereas the Energent has no time and space. It's the proto-energy inside the archí constituting its entirety (§ 2:114). Overall, the Energent omnidirectionally '*moves*' and '*undulates*' like a lake with many agitation vectors whereas *enérgeia* multidirectionally '*flows*' such as through inter-archí spaces (§ 6.9.3.3:182). Energent proto-energy and *enérgeia* are different. *Enérgeia* is 'energy' that forms on the fly out of proto-energy in response to motion of matter through the Energent. It's *enérgeia*'s flux across matter that creates real energy Υ from which arises applied energy E. Nowhere in the infinite universe is matter too insufficient for *enérgeia* to manifest.

While matter and energy are equivalent in each of the E, Υ, and $\alpha\Omega$ contexts, the 'energy' side of that relationship fundamentally doesn't equate across the E, Υ, and $\alpha\Omega$ spectrum. Even when understanding the science behind each, the best we'll be able to do is approximate one in terms of the other. That said, recall that Υ is *enérgeia* flux over the archí shell for single archí but, when bound in relationships, Υ is *enérgeia* flux combined with bound force such that, for two or more archí,

$$E_{mass} \risingdotseq \Phi_{\alpha\Omega} + F_B \tag{17.38}$$

where mass in applied energy E terms (E_{mass}) is the image of ($\risingdotseq$) *enérgeia* flux ($\Phi_{\alpha\Omega}$) and Υ bound force (F_B). There is no classical mass for archí because it has no matter, no material 'stuff' out of which it's made; it's 'condensed' proto-energy after all (§ 2.3:115).[179] Classical—say, atomic—mass is properly a regimen that accounts for an object's constituents, its complex archí relationships. Accordingly, mass—as opposed to motive energy 'mass' (including 'rest mass,' as that's simply motive energy at zero)—can't be unitized to kilograms or electronvolts or so on at all and still yield a result consistent with reality beyond the relatively elementary level of applied energy E. As we state elsewhere in different contexts, $E = mc^2$ isn't dealing with real mass but motive (applied) mass, ergo, E isn't real energy but applied energy. It works, of course, in its own context to deliver today's applied energy technology, but real energy technology—the difference is kindergarten to post-doctoral—still awaits scientific discovery.

To help visualize an archí, we can guesstimate its real energy Υ w.r.t. classical mass E. Mina gives its mass Υ as the approximated image of $\frac{110.2 \text{ eV}}{c^2 \pm 47\%}$. Two bound archí's mass Υ is the image of $\frac{4.1038 \text{ keV}}{c^2 \pm 62.5\%}$, significantly more than a simple doubling. Photon mass Υ—just a single Υ-up-'charged' archí, mind you—is $\frac{8.4048 \text{ keV}}{c^2 \pm 47\%}$. The uncertainty arises from the innate incompatibility of the conversion.

SECTION 5
Lightspeed

There are two light speeds in our universe, actual and normative. Mina reports a photon's *actual* lightspeed in free (vacuum) space is ∼477,758,137.911246 m/s with a velocity variability of ±0.00559494% , and is a constant; we denote it ς ("c-tail"). The increase over *normative* EMR lightspeed's 299,792,458 m/s—this so-called universal speed limit is what it is because that's as fast as electric and magnetic fields can propagate in physical space—arises from the nature of photons and EMR propagation described in this chapter. Using standard equations, we derive the relationship between these two lightspeeds.

---

178. Greek letters upsilon (Υ), alpha (α), and Omega (Ω).

179. The applied energy E concept of mass is no part of Energent science in any form.

Earlier, we described the photon as an archí, an object of matter, and that its passage through the Energent produces EM excitation that propagates out behind the photon with the same energy characteristics (§ 2.3:115) and in a manner science likens to a wave. In two-dimensional space, an electromagnetic wave (EMW) propagates like a boat's v–wake except that, since we're dealing with three-dimensional space, it's in 360° like a cone. This is an aspect of a larger phenomenon called bow wakes. Lord Kelvin (d. 1907) demonstrated in 1887 that a boat's wake fans out regardless speed at a constant angle of 19.47° and travels at a fixed fraction of 81.6% of a boat's speed.[178] Similar boat-to-wake ratios play out three-dimensionally w.r.t. to the Mach cone, a phenomenon that occurs when aircraft velocity exceeds the speed of sound (*Fig. 36*). Likewise, EMW propagates in a three-dimensional cone shape—the wavefront lies along the arc of the EMW sphere—with a constant vector $\vec{\gamma} \angle \psi$, where $\vec{\gamma}$ is photon vector and $\angle\psi$ is the bounded wave propagation angle of the EMW.

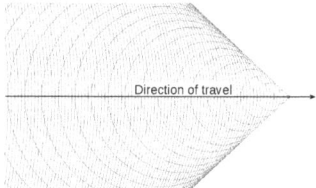

Direction of travel

Figure 36. Typical Mach cone (source moving to right) where source speed exceeds propagation speed.[179]

Science observes the effect as Čerenkov radiation when beta particle speed exceeds EMW propagation in water where "photons [EMR] . . . are emitted in the exact forward direction of the charged particle at an angle θ" (L'Annunziata 2012, 943), and in a light-scattering medium as a "propagation of a scattering-induced photonic Mach cone as an instantaneous light-scattering pattern" (Liang et al. 2017, 5; *Fig. 37*). Indeed,

> . . . the [Čerenkov] radiation must spread out along the surface of a cone whose axis forms the path of an electrically charged particle while the surface line forms with this axis the angle [θ] . . . the radiation spectrum is continuous . . . the light of different wavelengths is propagated at angles which, even with strictly constant velocity of the particles, differ somewhat from one another. (Čerenkov 1958, 434–5)

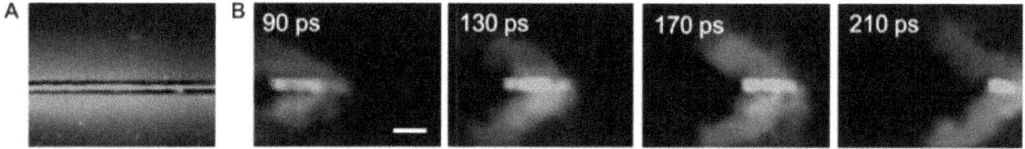

Figure 37. Photonic Mach cone in a light-scattering medium as source speed exceeds propagation speed.[180]

To understand lightspeed and the conic propagation of EMW, we need comprehend how an EM wave actually generates w.r.t. a photon. So, let's revisit our new friend the archí.

5.1 EM WAVE GENERATION

Science describes EMR as a self-propagating electromagnetic phenomenon where an oscillating electric field provokes an oscillating magnetic field further along in space than the electric oscillation, which in turn provokes a new electric oscillation still further along in space than the magnetic field, which begets another ad infinitum (*Fig. 38*, left). We've already defined EMW propagation as a *field extension* rather than a wave (§ 3.7.3.3.4:142) and schematically visualized it in Fig. 24:142 (left). In this leapfrogging fashion, EMR propagates independently away from its source along its photon's vector at lightspeed c.

5.1.1 ARCHÍ PHOTON AS A MOVING CHARGE

As the archí is the foundation of matter, it's also the foundation of applied energy E. An archí has velocity, whether oscillating in a bound relationship or moving through space as a photon, which generates EMR. The flux of the Energent across the archí shell gives rise to real energy Υ (Fundamental Force). As everything in our universe is in motion, everything is passing through the Energent (itself in 'motion') generating real energy Υ, and if it's reacting to matter in some other way, too, then certain applied energy E as well. The root applied energy E charge of a single archí in motion that hasn't been up-'charged' as a photon, or as part of a composite structure—boson, quark—is given as $\sim 12595.17376668 \times 10^{-900}$ ev (with mass in the image of $110.2\,eV/c^2$ $\pm 47\%$; *above*). As noted (§ 2:114), archí emit from composite structures with real energy Υ that translates to an applied energy E electric charge with which science is familiar. Thus, the archí emits as a photon. In current physics where a photon is considered a quantum of EMR, its energy—given by $E = hf$ where h is Planck's (proportional) constant and f is EMW frequency of oscillation—determines how it interacts with matter. This, however, is only an applied energy E reflection of real energy Υ which charged the archí in its bonded context and from which it subsequently released, or emitted, as a photon.

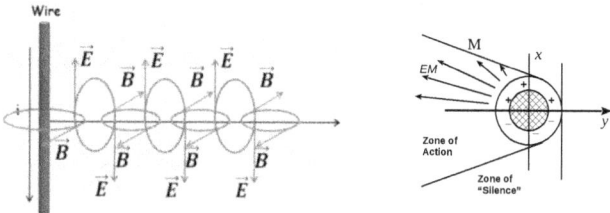

Figure 38. Schematic: left, EMW as field extension instead of oscillation; $\vec{E}$ is electric, $\vec{B}$ is magnetic field (Fig. 24:142); right, archí photon: y-axis is direction of travel, x-axis is perpendicular plane forward of which no applied energy E from around the photon propagates; M is Mach cone; EM is EMF.[181]

A photon is a real energy Υ-'charged' particle in motion through space. The Energent washes across it like water over a submarine's hull. As water interacting with a hull generates a propagating disturbance, the Energent interacting with the archí generates real energy Υ (Fundamental Force). It non-sinusoidally oscillates between 'on–off' states. The 'on' state induces the photon's spherical applied energy E electric charge; in the 'off' state it dissipates. This oscillating charge is equivalent to a moving charged particle and behaves in similar fashion. It's as spherical as the archí itself but doesn't constitute a charged sphere because it doesn't contact or charge the archí sphere itself. Balanced between positive and negative, the charge is electrically neutral. It emits an electric field that radiates in 360° at lightspeed c. Because the photon is in motion at actual lightspeed ς—an $\sim 59.36\%$ speed differential with lightspeed c—the electric force cannot transit beyond the plane perpendicular to the rise of the Mach cone just as sound waves can't transit forward of a Mach cone owing to the differential between sound's normative speed and its aircraft source (*Fig. 38*, right). However, instead of radiating like sound waves along the axis of travel into a compressed sound cone, the electric force simply doesn't radiate at all forward of the perpendicular plane to the axis of photon travel. Rearward from the point of perpendicularity to the axis of travel, and within the Mach cone, the electric force radiates normally at lightspeed c.

EMW propagates off the moving electric charge that effectively anchors it to the photon. Otherwise, it would get out-of-sync with the photon and make visible light, for example, unpredictable. It radiates outward from the axis of photon travel more like an expanding Mach bubble than linearly wavelike the way EMW is most often depicted. When real energy Υ thus applied energy E electric charge cycles to the 'off' state, EMR, induced by the 'on' state, radially self-propagates away from the archí photon's axis of travel.

5.1.2 ARCHÍ PHOTON DUTY CYCLE

Real energy Υ, hence applied energy E electric charge, completes an 'on–off' cycle in the time it takes the photon to move forward in space along its axis of travel a distance equal to the time taken by the pulse's 'on'-state and 'off'-state. The 'on' state includes the pulse's rising edge (Pr), its 'on' state (P$_1$), and falling edge (Pf); the 'off' state includes the 'on' state plus the null, or no-charge, state (P$_0$).

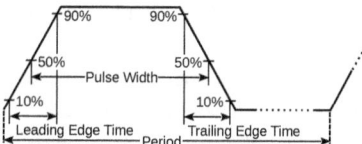

Figure 39. Pulse wave with rising and falling edges, pulse width, period, and its null ('off') state.

These elements collectively are the pulse period—also called pulse transit time (PTT)—and give us the pulse repetition frequency (PRF), pulse repetition interval (PRI), and duty cycle (D; the 'on'-state duration). Using archí diameter ($\varnothing_{\alpha\chi} = \ell_P \times 0.71865$ meter; § 2.3.1:115) as a fundamental unit of measurement, the Pr and Pf are each $944\varnothing_{\alpha\chi}$, and P_1 and P_0 are each $944^3\varnothing_{\alpha\chi}$. The duty cycle D is

$$D = \frac{PW}{T} \Leftrightarrow \frac{\text{'on' period}}{\text{'on' period} + \text{'off' period}} \Leftrightarrow \frac{Pr + Pf + P_1}{Pr + Pf + P_1 + P_0}$$

$$\rightarrow \frac{2(944) + 944^3\varnothing_{\alpha\chi}}{2(944) + 2(944^3)\varnothing_{\alpha\chi}} \rightarrow \frac{841,234,272\varnothing_{\alpha\chi}}{1,682,466,656\varnothing_{\alpha\chi}} \tag{17.39}$$

$$= 50.000056807\%$$

where $\varnothing_{\alpha\chi}$ is archí diameter units, PW is pulse width and T is pulse period in units of archí diameter; we abbreviate the calculation. PRF calculates as

$$PRF = \frac{1}{T} \Leftrightarrow \frac{1\,\sec}{\text{'on' period} + \text{'off' period}} \rightarrow \frac{1\,\sec}{\frac{(\ell_P \times 0.71865\text{m})(1,682,466,656\varnothing_{\alpha\chi})}{c_A}}$$

$$\rightarrow \frac{1\,\sec}{\frac{1.954190019300 \times 10^{-26}\text{m}}{477,758,137\,\text{m/s}}} \rightarrow \frac{1\,\sec}{4.090333304569 \times 10^{-35}\,\sec} \tag{17.40}$$

$$= 2.444788542984 \times 10^{34}\ \text{cycles/sec (Hz)}$$

$$\therefore T = \frac{1}{PRF} = 4.090333304569 \times 10^{-35}\,\sec/\text{cycle}$$

where PRF and T are as defined, ℓ_P is Planck length, and Hz is Hertz. This means there's about 2.44×10^{34} duty cycles—thus, EMW precursors—per second arising from the photon's movement through space being strung out along its vector to develop into self-propagating EMW even before the first one in line actually begins to self propagate (§ 3.7.3.3.4:142).

5.1.3 EMW MACH CONE

As the photon continues forward along its axis of travel at actual lightspeed ç, the oscillating electric charge at the photon induces a magnetic field that, in turn, induces another electric field, and so on, as standard EMW propagating at lightspeed c. However, neither the electric nor the magnetic force can radiate forward of the photon for two reasons: 1) the photon's moving faster than the electric and magnetic force radiates, and 2) EMW can't propagate faster than itself. Since propagation is the same velocity at which the electric and magnetic fields radiate, it's unable to radiate forward of the perpendicular plane along the axis of travel (Fig. 38:153, right). The electromagnetic energy propagates three-dimensionally outward from the axis of travel at lightspeed c. Therefore, behind the perpendicular plane to the axis of travel the energy radiates normally from the moment of electric field genesis whereas the energy at the perpendicular plane to the axis of travel is minutely behind. The energy forward of the perpendicular plane doesn't radiate in the direction of the axis of travel at all (until the photon moves forward accordingly).

This effect is akin to one moving at lightspeed c and turning on a flashlight from which no beam shines in the direction of travel because the photons coming out of the flashlight aren't going any faster than the flashlight itself. But as one rotates the flashlight away from its axis of travel toward the perpendicular, the flashlight beam exits the flashlight as it shines toward the perpendicular plane. Its light doesn't shine straight to infinity from any point space along the line of travel, though, because it's radiating at the same speed the flashlight is moving perpendicularly forward. The effect thus makes it seem the light beam is dragging backward along the axis of travel (*Fig. 40*, left). This happens because the light beam, shining at lightspeed c 90° to the flashlight's axis of travel at lightspeed ç, can only get so far from the flashlight before its source physically moves forward to a different location, taking the beam with it.

Instead of dragging back along the axis of travel, the light beam instead appears to angle away as it moves perpendicularly outward from each point space where, a moment before, the flashlight was physically located before moving forward along the axis of travel. We can visualize this with a water hose or tracer bullets shot from a moving platform. Just as the beam seems to angle backward along the direction of travel, EMW propagates at an angle that, in terms of its leading edge, forms a cone. In this way, EMW propagation shares a similar dynamic to the Mach cone. The conical nature of EMW propagation lets us comprehend the phenomenon and its wavefront in terms similar to a Mach cone such that

$$\sin(\mu) = \frac{c}{\varsigma} \wedge \left\{ M = \frac{\varsigma}{c} \right\} \Rightarrow \sin(\mu) = \frac{1}{M}$$

$$\rightarrow \mu = \sin^{-1}\left(\frac{1}{M}\right) \tag{17.41}$$

$$\rightarrow \theta = \mu$$

where μ is the photon cone angle in radians, c is normative lightspeed (299,792 km/s), ς is actual lightspeed (477,758 km/s), M is velocity of the cone vector as a scalar, $\sin^{-1}(x)$ is arcsin, and θ is cone propagation angle in degrees. Plugging in the relevant values renders

$$\sin(\mu) = \frac{299,792}{477,758} = 0.627497 \,\text{rad} \wedge \left\{ M = \frac{477,758}{299,792} = 1.5936 \right\}$$

$$\Rightarrow \sin(\mu) = \frac{1}{1.5936} = 0.62751 \,\text{rad} \tag{17.42}$$

$$\rightarrow \mu = \sin^{-1}(0.62751)$$

$$\rightarrow \theta(\mu) = 38.866°$$

where 38.866° is the angle the EMW propagates in relation to the photon's vector, its axis of travel. Angle of propagation and wave vector are constant as the wake propagates outward behind the photon, similar in nature to the Kelvin wake pattern (*Fig. 40*, right).

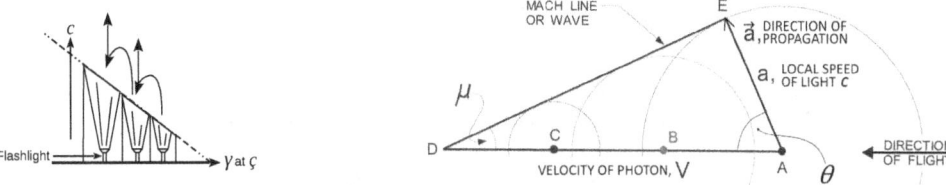

Figure 40. Left, EMW effect propagating at lightspeed c perpendicular to axis of travel at actual lightspeed ς; right, $\vec{a}$ is EMW propagation at variable local lightspeed a along line AE.[182]

As noted, EMR propagates Mach cone-like at a fixed fraction of the photon's speed in free space. Mina gives this as 62.74776% of actual lightspeed ς, which calculates to ~299,782.529 km/s, a difference of about 9.929 km/s, or 0.003%, with lightspeed c as presently measured. We can show the relationship between ET-given actual lightspeed ς and observed lightspeed c with simple wave dynamics, in which

$$\nu_p = U \cos(\theta) \tag{17.43}$$

where ν_p is phase velocity of EMW propagating in free space, U is photon speed, and θ is the propagation cone right angle and previously calculated angle μ subtracted from 180° $(180 - (\llcorner + \angle \mu))$. Using the above values,

$$\nu_p = 477,758 \,\text{km/s} \cos\left(180° - (90° + 38.866°)\right)$$

$$\rightarrow 477,758 \cos(51.134°) \rightarrow 477,758 \times 0.62750113 \tag{17.44}$$

$$= 299,793.684 \,\text{km/s}$$

where ν_p calculates to within 1.000004%, or 1.226866 km/s of lightspeed c. Allowing for the ET-given velocity variability of ±0.00559494% in actual lightspeed ς as noted at the start of this section, ν_p calculates to 299,809 km/s at its upper range and 299,776 km/s at its lower range. This falls within 1.00005% , or 17 km/s, at the upper range and 0.99994% , or 16 km/s, at the lower range of lightspeed c. The given fixed fraction of actual lightspeed ς at which EMW propagates in free space lies within the variability range and very close to lightspeed c, though that's never been precisely measured, either.[183]

While the photonic Mach angle and EMW propagation velocity are constants in a vacuum, they of course vary in a non-vacuum medium. Two examples suffice: in water, and the Liang light-scattering medium. Within the range of possible speeds for a beta particle[180] in the Čerenkov radiation phenomenon, the 38.866° photonic

---

180. A fast-moving electron emitted by radioactive decay, such as in a nuclear reactor.

Mach angle that's characteristic of free space repeats in water when a beta particle travels with a speed ν_{bp}, in that $c/n < \nu_{bp} < c$, such that

$$\beta = \frac{\nu_{bp}}{c} = \frac{252,568 \text{ km/s}}{299,792 \text{ km/s}} = 0.84247$$

$$\to \cos(\theta) = \frac{1}{n\beta} = \frac{1}{1.33(0.84247)} = \cos(0.89246317) = 0.627496059$$

$$\to \cos^{-1}(0.627496059) = 51.134°\theta \qquad (17.45)$$

$$\Rightarrow \mu = 180 - (90° - 51.134°) = 38.866°$$

where β is the ratio between particle speed in a medium and lightspeed c, ν_{bp} is velocity of the beta particle, θ is the angle opposite the Mach angle μ, n is the refractive index of water (which slows EMW propagation to ~0.75c), and μ is Mach angle. Eq. (17.45) is derivative of Eq. (17.41) with which we can describe the relationship between actual (photonic) lightspeed ς and EMW lightspeed c in water. Photons lose about 0.488% of their speed in water—the speed index s, rendered in decimal form 0.00488—similar to EMW propagation in water decreasing by a factor of 1.33.[181] Hence, photonic lightspeed $\varsigma - s\varsigma$ is 475,426 km/s and EMW lightspeed c/n is 225,407 km/s. Therefore,

$$\sin(\mu) = \frac{225,407}{475,426} = 0.47411 \text{ rad} \wedge \left\{ M = \frac{475,426}{225,407} = 2.1 \right\}$$

$$\Rightarrow \sin(\mu) = \frac{1}{2.1} = 0.47619 \text{ rad} \qquad (17.46)$$

$$\to \mu = \sin^{-1}(0.47619)$$

$$\to \theta(\mu) = 28.43°$$

where the notation is the same as Eq. (17.41). Mach angle μ calculates to 28.43°, which makes angle

$$\theta = \cos^{-1}(0.47619) = 61.56°. \qquad (17.47)$$

Then per Eq. (17.43), substituting $\varsigma - s\varsigma$ for U, we derive the observed EMW lightspeed c from the ET-given photonic lightspeed ς (in water) as

$$\nu_p = U \cos(\theta) \to (-s) \cos(61.56°) \to 475,426 \times 0.47623$$

$$= 226,412 \text{ km/s} \qquad (17.48)$$

where ν_p is phase velocity of EMW propagating through water. The relative error between EMW lightspeed c in water per Eq. (17.48) and EMW lightspeed c in water per the observed refractive index is

$$\delta x = \frac{x_0 - x}{x} \to \frac{226,412 - 225,407}{225,407} = .004458 \qquad (17.49)$$

where δx is relative error as the change to x and calculates to an absolute error of 1,005 km/s.

The above demonstrates the mathematical relationship between Mina's reported photonic lightspeed ς and observed EMW lightspeed c. Now, let's look at the relationship between photonic and EMW lightspeed from the perspective of Mach angles. For this, we use Jinyang Liang's 2017 experiment that demonstrates a photonic Mach cone in a light-scattering medium with a refractive index of $n = 1.4$ and "a semivertex [Mach] angle, directly measured . . . [of] ~45°" (Liang et al. 2017, 5). Based off Mina's given photonic lightspeed ς of 477,758 km/s, we calculate both EMW lightspeed c and Mach angle in Liang's medium. First, using the relevant values per Eq. (17.41), Liang demonstrates a Mach angle of

$$\sin(\mu) = \frac{\frac{c}{n}}{c} \to \frac{214,137 \text{ km/s}}{299,792 \text{ km/s}} = 0.71428 \Rightarrow \left\{ M = \frac{c}{\frac{c}{n}} = 1.4 \right\}$$

$$\to \sin(\mu) = \frac{1}{M} = \frac{1}{1.4} \to \mu = \sin^{-1}\left(\frac{1}{M}\right) \Leftrightarrow \sin^{-1}(0.71428) \qquad (17.50)$$

$$\Rightarrow \mu = 45.58°$$

---

181. Counterintuitively, the archí photon's speed is the same in air or water, although air density lessens with altitude and water density maximally increases about five percent.

where $^c/_n$ is EMW lightspeed c in Liang's medium. To relate Liang's result[182] to Mina's reported photonic lightspeed ς, we calculate the photonic Mach angle in Liang's medium and, from that, calculate the EMW Mach angle. Writing Eq. (17.41) in different terms for clarity, we have

$$\sin(\mu) = \frac{\text{velocity of propagation}}{\text{velocity of source}} \Leftrightarrow \frac{1.4c}{\varsigma - s\varsigma} \to \frac{214,137\,\text{km/s}}{475,426\,\text{km/s}} = 0.45041$$

$$\Rightarrow \left\{ M = \frac{475,426}{214,137} = 2.22 \right\}$$

$$\to \sin(\mu) = \frac{1}{M} \to \frac{1}{2.22} = 0.45045 \to \mu = \sin^{-1}\left(\frac{1}{M}\right) \to \sin^{-1}(0.45045)$$

$$\Rightarrow \mu = 26.77°. \tag{17.51}$$

Mach angle μ calculates to 26.77°, which makes angle

$$\theta = \cos^{-1}(0.45045) = 63.22°. \tag{17.52}$$

Then, per Eq. (17.43), we derive the observed EMW lightspeed c from photonic lightspeed ς in Liang's light-scattering medium as

$$\nu_p = U\cos(\theta) \to 475,426\cos(63.22°) \to 475,426 \times 0.45056$$
$$= 214,207\,\text{km/s}. \tag{17.53}$$

The relative error between EMW lightspeed c per Eq. (17.48) and EMW lightspeed c observed in Liang's medium is 0.000326, using Eq. (17.49); the absolute error is 70 km/s.

With the above foundation in place, we can calculate the EMW Mach angle in Liang's medium from the perspective of a tangible photon traveling through the medium at 475,426 km/s, and then compare it to the EMW Mach angle that Liang observed. Accordingly,

$$\sin(\mu) = \frac{214,207}{299,792} = .71451 \to \left\{ M = \frac{299,792}{214,207} = 1.3995 \right\}$$

$$\to \sin(\mu) = \frac{1}{1.3995} = 0.71454$$

$$\to \mu = \sin^{-1}\left(\frac{1}{M}\right) = \sin^{-1}(0.71454)$$

$$\Rightarrow \mu = 45.6°. \tag{17.54}$$

The relative error between EMW Mach angle produced in Eq. (17.54) and Liang's 45.58° EMW Mach angle as calculated in Eq. (17.50) from Liang's parameters is 0.000438, with an absolute error of 0.02 degrees per Eq. (17.49). Although an archí (versus the classical wave-packet) photon with a speed of 477,758 km/s in a vacuum is revelatory data obtained via energy testing, the above mathematics indicates a pairwise relationship with lightspeed c and, thus, a reasonable avenue to explore. Five observations follow.

5.2 EMR Consistency

First, the combination of a photon as a particle with 'anchored' EMW[183] propagating EMR spherically is the reason we perceive light as steady, constant, and saturating instead of flickering with blank spots. Without EMW, we'd perceive only those photons on a trajectory into the eyeball as visible light. Photons from any point space that missed the eyeball would, at their source, visibly be a point of nothing from that eyeball's perspective (though visible at another's), similar to the effect produced by the blind spot in the human eyeball that lies next to the optic nerve.[184]

Photons also emit on random trajectories. There's no logical basis for the apparently standard view presuming a photon collision with an object results in the object emitting a new photon on the same trajectory. Although a visible light photon collision with an electron in glass lacks sufficient energy to move the electron to a higher-energy orbit, its energy is nonetheless absorbed. The excess energy dissipates through the electron's

---

182. Liang reports only the estimated angle. We calculated it to two decimals.

183. Light within, e.g., ~1MLY is composed of ~68.85% EMW EMR and 31.15% photonic EMR, a nearly two-to-one ratio.

archí substructures ($dia. \cong 8.5 \times 10^{-18}$ meter), thence into its particle saturant (§ 3.1:121), and from there to other particle saturants until, say, over a distance $4\pi r^2$, it's absorbed to dissipation. An EMW field extension (wavelength; § 3.7.3.3.4:142) encountering an electron similarly dissipates. There's enough photonic and EMW EMR passing through glass that these collisions don't distort visible light enough to notice. Glass blocks higher-energy infrared because those photon collisions result in new, random emissions that end up sequentially trapped in the glass until energy loss results in no more emissions.

As light distorts when interacting with matter, nothing would visibly be as it seemed. Without archí to receive a real energy Υ charge that translates to photonic applied energy E, there would be no EMF and consequently no EMR—no light, radio, and so on. The footnoted two-to-one ratio (FN 183) changes when gazing directly at a source of EMR emission—the Sun, for example. Here, we perceive nearly 100% of its photonic EMR not to mention its saturating quantity of EMW EMR. While all that falls on Earth, overall the sunlight entering the eyeball while looking at the disk of the sun is about 95% photonic and 5% EMR. The optical afterimage of a bright light is not an EMW but a photonic phenomenon.

5.3   FAR SIDE SUNLIGHT

Second, and consequent of the first, Earth receives direct, or linear, sunlight via photon traveling at actual lightspeed ς and indirect, or nonlinear, sunlight via EMW traveling at lightspeed c. This means direct photonic sunlight, on average, reaches Earth in about five minutes while EMW takes anywhere from zero to about eight minutes (the range arises from EMW propagating off a photon (Eq. (17.40):154) about every $4.09\sim \times 10^{-35}$ second of its flight from the Sun to Earth). A corollary observation is that Earth takes in approximately 2.65% of its overall EMR content from the Sun's farside hemisphere (the side not facing Earth at any moment during orbit; *Fig. 41*, left). Spherical EMW propagation is why. Farside EMR takes on average about 45.5 times longer than that required by nearside EMR.

5.4   DOUBLE SLIT EXPERIMENT

Third, the famous double slit experiment now presents asymptomatic regarding EMR's particle or wave nature. Thomas Young first conducted this experiment sometime between 1801 and 1805.[185] In different configurations, it demonstrates particle- and wave-like patterns on a rear detection wall by single, and streams of, entities—photons, electrons, atoms, even molecules—sent through a narrow single or double slit in a barrier. These observations form part of the backbone of quantum science but fail to definitively prove or falsify the particle or wave nature of EMR and matter, leaving science to ponder its apparent ontological probabilistic duality.

What's really going on here is that conical EMW propagation trailing the photon particle passes through the slit(s) whether or not its photon does. With a single slit, there's nothing to reinforce the EMW and we observe no pattern. With a double slit, the conical EMW passes through both slits whether or not its photon does. Either way, it doesn't change the outcome if the photon also passes through the slit (~5% pass-through rate, on average) along with its conically propagating EMW. With two EMW passing through to the far side of the slit, there is constructive interference between each EMW cone, reinforcing certain EMW sufficiently to show up on the detection wall in a striped (interference) pattern characteristic of waves (§ 3.7.3.3.6:145). As every particle above a photon builds up from bound archí, then every piece of matter produces stronger or weaker conical EMW propagations of EMR. In composite archí structures (matter), EMW of the constituent archí each conically propagates. As those cones propagate as described, they interfere with the EMW of other constituent archí to cancel or reinforce each other (*Fig. 41*, right). Ultimately, the composite (electron, atom, or molecule) object's EMW forms a wholistic, conical EMW from the surviving, reinforced, constituent archí EMW (*below*).

The experiment's set-up as well as its detection equipment contributes to the effect because, as explained below, all matter produces EMW and this interferes with the outcome of the experiment. In this way, ET data more simply explains so-called particle–wave duality. The notion "[t]here is good experimental evidence to support the idea that quantum qualities become definitive only upon measurement" (Lea 2018, par. 25) is inaccurate because quantum qualities are already definitive until something interferes with them—like, say, a measurement emitting countervailing EMR as a new and unknown variable.

5.4.1   WAVELENGTH PROPORTIONALITY

Of note is that all matter—subatomic or molecular—generates EMR. This is why the double slit experiment appears to demonstrate matter exhibiting a wave nature like light (EMR). In composite archí structures such

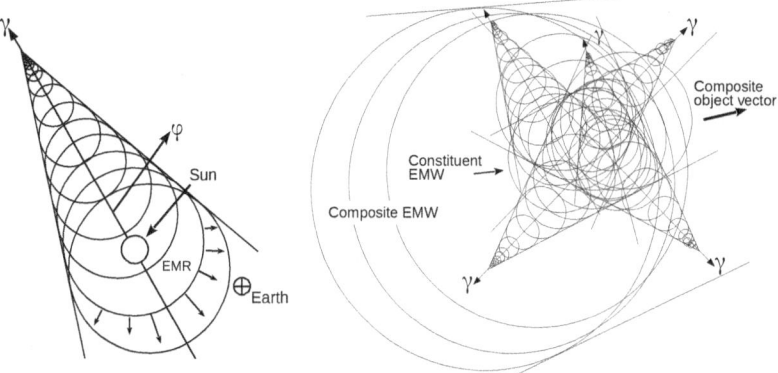

Figure 41. Left, far-side sunlight reaching Earth: γ is a photon, φ is its EMW propagation; right, schematic of a composite object's multi-interfering EMW resolves to coherent object EMW (*below*).

as electrons, atoms, and molecules, EMR internally radiates from each archí constructively and destructively to varying degrees with other archí in the structure (*Fig. 41*, right). Ultimately, its EMR establishes an overall energy signature that singly radiates from the composite archí structure. Science understands EMW as photonic electromagnetic oscillation in terms of mechanical waveform where frequency f times wavelength λ equals wave speed c where c is normative lightspeed ($c = f\lambda$). This relationship means frequency and wavelength are *inversely* proportional; larger frequency means smaller wavelength and vice versa ($f = {}^c/\lambda \Leftrightarrow \lambda = {}^c/f$). On the other hand, Mina avers non-photonic composite archí EMW frequency and wavelength are *directly* proportional; larger frequency means larger wavelength and vice versa ($f = k\lambda \Leftrightarrow \lambda = kf$ where k is the ET-given proportionality constant of $\sim$3.3793429).

The reason for this seeming incongruity is that archí are the energy source for EMR. It's the fundamental element in the equation, not frequency, wavelength, or wave speed, which are determined by, or rather are direct manifestations of, system energy (§ 3.7.3.3.4:142). The mechanical wave model simply doesn't apply to EMW. It obscures its real propagative nature. Recall that electric and magnetic fields of a certain energy form and extend in tandem outward into space a distance relative to EMR energy, generating, or resurging, a new EM field, which extends outward into space the same distance ad infinitum. In this resurgent fashion only reminiscent of mechanical waves, EMW propagates over distance. From this perspective, it's easy to see that EMW doesn't propagate analogous to wave energy but as a field extension mediated by energy.

It's obvious with waves why frequency and wavelength are inversely proportional, but it's counterintuitive that frequency and wavelength can be directly proportional unless we comprehend EMW as a field extension. Water moves in waveform when energy—underwater landslide, surface wind—injects into the system and physically displaces the water, which results in a push. As the water in motion pushes against water at relative rest—and because two objects can't occupy the same space at the same time—the water rides up to form a water wave and then proceeds to undulate across a water surface as an energy medium. Science similarly imagines this form of propagation for sound and electromagnetic energy. In the latter case, however, we're not dealing with displacement or vibration of matter but propagation of energy (ibid).

Insofar as we do conceptualize EMW in waveform terms, we can similarly model non-photonic EMW. In this case, we liken interval speed of EM field extension to frequency, field extension spatial distance to wavelength, and propagation speed to wave speed. Similarly, we modify the basic wave equation $c = f\lambda$ to

$$c = \frac{f\lambda}{\Delta f} \quad \left\{ \Delta f = \frac{f}{c/\lambda} \right\} \tag{17.55}$$

where c is wave speed, Δf is the change between photonic and non-photonic frequency, and other terms as defined. Using the values for an averaged electron EMW where oscillation is ET-given as 295,880 Hz, field extension as 999,880.6688988 meter, amplitude as 99.99 kHz, and time period calculated as $t = {}^1/f = 3.379\sim \times 10^{-6}$ seconds/oscillation, and propagation speed is lightspeed c, then, using Eq. (17.55),

$$c = \frac{(295,880\text{ Hz})(999,880.6688988\text{ m})}{295,880\text{ Hz} \big/ \frac{299,792,458\text{ m}}{999,880.6688988\text{ Hz}}} \rightarrow \frac{295,844,494,400}{986.83167110820694495256448379366} \tag{17.56}$$

$$= 299,792,458\text{ m/s} \leftrightarrow c$$

where c is normative lightspeed. Photonic EMR's energy quantum is found through the Planck–Einstein relation $E = hf$, where h is Planck's constant and f is photon frequency. For non-photonic EMR, which radiates from composite archí structures that contain many more archí than just the one of a photon, we modify the equation as $E = hf\alpha\chi_T$ where $\alpha\chi_T$ is total archí count such that,

$$E = \left(4.135667662\,(25) \times 10^{-15}\text{ev}\right)(295,880\,\text{Hz}) \times (\pm 2,330,000\,\alpha\chi)$$
$$= 2.8511309404498648 \times 10^{-3}\text{ev} \tag{17.57}$$

where ev is electronvolts and $\alpha\chi$ is the averaged archí count in Mina's averaged electron-EMR example. The result is significantly greater than photonic EMR of the same wavelength such that, using $E = hf$,

$$E = \left(4.135667662\,(25) \times 10^{-15}\text{eV}\right)(299.8284\,\text{Hz}) = 1.2399906\sim \times 10^{-12}\text{eV} \tag{17.58}$$

where 299.8284 Hz is the normalized photonic frequency for the aforementioned wavelength of 999,880 meters. Non-photonic EMR energy is thus about 2.299 billion times greater than photonic EMR energy. This greater magnitude of energy translates to a non-photonic EM field that extends further in space for each oscillation than does photonic EM of the same frequency (§ 6.12.1.1:206).

While higher frequencies and shorter wavelengths typically denote greater energy, thus constituting increasing levels of harm to living tissue—e.g., high-frequency–short-wavelength EMR like gamma rays or x-rays can strip electrons from atoms, compromising or destroying the larger molecule—the greater energy associated with non-photonic EMR is generally offset by the proportionally longer field extension (wavelength).[184] Although photonic and non-photonic *frequency* can be the same, their energy levels will differ; conversely, although photonic and non-photonic EMR *energy* can be the same, their frequencies will differ. Our world, of course, is flooded with both natural and manmade EMR.

A natural question then arises: why does photonic and non-photonic EMW that's spawned by the same energy produce field extensions (wavelengths) inversely proportional to frequency in the former but directly proportional in the latter? The simple answer is because non-photonic EMW interval speed and field extension (frequency and wavelength) accumulate from the varying interval speeds, field extensions, and energies produced by each archí constituent in a composite archí structure (such as the averaged electron-EMR earlier described), whereas photonic EMW interval speed and field extension result from an EMR charge produced by a single archí. The photonic result is an EMW field extension that consistently is a distance inversely proportional to frequency. The non-photonic result is a directly proportional EMW interval speed and field extension that is, in a simple form, described by

$$f_{\alpha\chi}^{\text{comp}} = \sum_{i=1}^{\alpha\chi_T} f_{\alpha\chi}^i, \lambda_{\alpha\chi}^{\text{comp}} = \sum_{i=1}^{\alpha\chi_T} \lambda_{\alpha\chi}^i \tag{17.59}$$

where $f_{\alpha\chi}^{\text{comp}}$ and $\lambda_{\alpha\chi}^{\text{comp}}$ are, respectively, interval speed and field extension (frequency and wavelength) of a composite archí structure, and $\alpha\chi_T$ is total archí constituents.

5.5 POLARIZATION

Fourth, archí photons have the same unbounded archí $\pm 1/2$ spin (intrinsic angular momentum), not the ± 1 science assigns it as a massless particle.[185] Archí photons emit with a $-1/2$ spin. When a photon passes through a polarizing filter, its spin shifts to the opposite spin and sheds applied energy E, reducing EMR energy. It also loses momentum, thus speed, because it loses mass from its applied energy E loss. If it then passes through a second polarizer that's ninety degrees relative to the first filter, its spin shifts to zero and it loses the rest of its energy and is absorbed, i.e., dephased.

If, instead, it passes through an intermediate polarizer that's offset relative to the first filter some angle other than 90° and 270° before passing through the second, 90° filter, its spin shifts back to original. For any series of

---

184. Various forms of matter—certain plastics, for example—emit non-photonic EMR that's noticeably toxic to living tissue over an average human lifespan.

185. While so-called point particles like electrons (and archí) do not literally spin like a basketball, archí photons literally do. The photon electric and magnetic fields also literally spin independent of the archí photon sphere. The reason why electron intrinsic angular momentum (spin) behaves in every possible way like real, literal angular momentum in the macroscopic world, even while we can't measure the electron itself literally spinning, is because the electron magnetic field is literally spinning around it (COSMIC LIGHT LENSING, § 6.8:174). The archí magnetic field literally spins around the archí, as well.

polarizing filters where x is filter one at o° and n is the final filter at 90°, which blocks all visible EMR, and filter $x + 1 < n \neq 90° \wedge 270°$ is any filter between x and n, then photon spin alternates between $+1/2$ and $-1/2$ after passing through any filter not x and n. Approximately 12% of visible wavelength energy passing through a polarizing filter is photonic—which isn't enough to register on the eye—while the remainder is EMR, which the eye does register. A single zero-degree filter blocks about 38% of photons. Each successive filter not equal to 90° and 270° blocks a further percentage.

5.6 STELLAR REDSHIFT

Fifth and last, stellar redshift doesn't indicate an expanding universe; indeed, it's not. The universe existentially is what it is—infinite, which is to say, indeterminate. As noted, however, the cluster of matter we observe from Earth and call the *observable* universe (OU) is the clumping of all atomic matter that's in the *infinite* universe (IU). We can't see the entire OU of course because of distance. Nonetheless, it's finite in breadth. Stellar redshift—a catchall term for EMR spectrum shift toward both the blue and red ends—refers to any electromagnetic radiation in transit between its source and Earth that experiences energy changes which shift its wavelength shorter or longer, thus to a higher or a lower EMR spectrum (radio toward gamma rays, or violet toward red; *Fig. 42*, left).

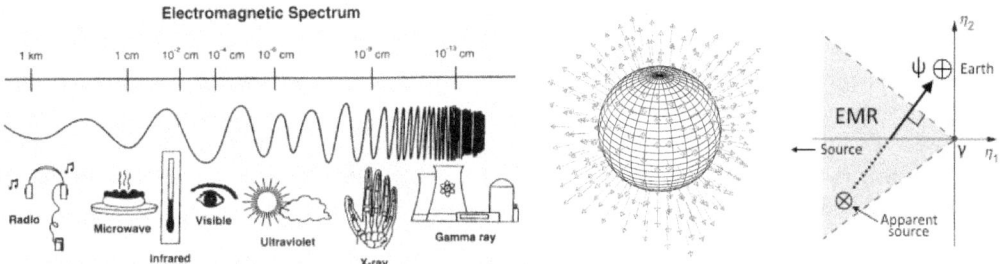

Figure 42. Left, the electromagnetic spectrum. Wavelength is shorter (bluer, as visible light) at right and longer (redder) at left; center, EMR emitting spherically from source; right, photon γ with η_1 axis of travel from Source and EMR propagating in direction ψ from Apparent source.[186]

Generally, the scientific consensus is that spectrum shift is caused by 1) the Doppler effect that assumes source movement toward or away from Earth; 2) the expansion of the spacetime fabric between redshifted stars and Earth—really, just a relativistic Doppler—or, 3) gravitational effects. Doppler redshift is the principal defense for cosmic expansion. The 1998 reported results for SNIa-type supernovæ (Filippenko et al. 1998; Kirshner 1999, 4226) is its principal (accelerating) evidence. Mina reports redshift is none of these. The reason is the nature of EMR propagation. As we've learned, EMR propagates in two ways, via archí photon and via EMW. Any EMR emits initially as a real energy Υ-'charged' photon from a source, e.g., a star, and travels outward from the source at actual lightspeed ς in all directions, spherically, in 360° (*Fig. 42*, center). In each photon's wake, EMW continually propagates its EMR energy at lightspeed c inside a photonic Mach angle relative to photon axis of travel (*Fig. 42*, right).

5.6.1 NONLINEARITY OF EMR

The above presents the unexpected observation that EMR isn't necessarily linear—along a line of sight, e.g., from Earth—from its source. Beyond a certain distance, the starlight we see in the night sky isn't pointing back along a straight line-of-sight trajectory to the star that originally emitted it but to its EMW source instead, which is a photon traveling from a different star in direction η_1 (*Fig. 42*, right). Of course, this seems pretty strange and ridiculous, so let's diagram it (*Fig. 43*).

A consequence of spherical EMW propagation along a photonic Mach cone wavefront ($[S_{wavefront}, \lambda]$; *Fig. 43*, left) is that EMR—say, visible light—from a single source $[S_{source}]$ arrives on Earth linearly via photon along line $[S_{source}, Earth]$, but then also nonlinearly via EMW from other $[S_{source}]$ photons traveling away from $[S_{source}]$ along a line $[S, Earth]$, as in the figure. EMR via this EMW arrives on Earth along the leading edge of the propagating Mach cone $[S_{wavefront}]$ at an angle formed by the axis of travel of the EMW's photonic source and its eventual intersection with Earth. For demonstration purposes, we show the angle as 90° along the line $[S, Earth]$. We previously noted that a photon pulses EMR approximately every $4.090333304569 \times 10^{-35}$

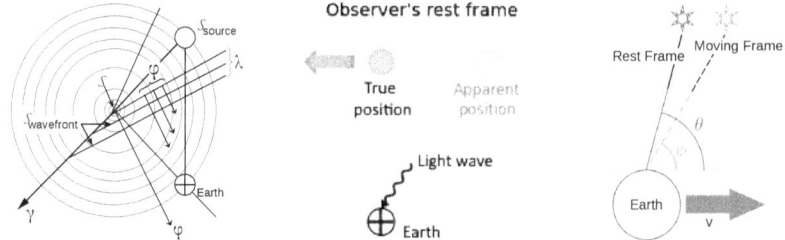

Figure 43. Left, S is EMR radiant flux, S_{source} is an EMR source (star), $S_{wavefront}$ is the leading edge EMW wavefront in any dimension, concentric circles are EMW propagating outward in three dimensions in direction φ, γ is photon axis of travel, and S_{source} and Earth are assumed at relative rest; center and right, stellar aberration (related to light-time correction) showing true star location at the time its light arrives on Earth and its apparent location based on visual sighting.[187]

second, or $2.444788542984 \times 10^{34}$ cycles per second (Eq. (17.40):154). Thus, EMR propagates toward Earth from many point spaces along the photon $[S_{source}, \gamma]$ axis of travel.

The upshot is that when we view *distant* light from Earth, it doesn't lead us linearly back to its ultimate source because there isn't enough linear photonic light from it arriving on Earth. Out to about four light-years, we receive on average approximately 85% more EMR via photon than EMW. Accordingly, the spatial locations of those EMR sources are relatively easy to observe with some accuracy because there's plenty of linear photonic EMR to point the way. There's certainly no doubt as to exactly where the Sun is. From about 1MLY, that ratio flips and we receive on average around 85% more EMR via EMW than via photon. And from the most distant galaxies currently visible, we receive about 99.999% more EMR via EMW than via photons. Regardless the distance, EMR via photon never falls to zero such that, when $d > 0$,

$$\lim_{d \to \infty} \left(\frac{k_\gamma}{d} \right) = 0 \qquad (17.60)$$

where d is distance and k_γ is the photon constant. There's a strong negative Spearman correlation between distance and EMR via photon ($R_s[5] = -1, p = 0.02$), with a concomitant positive correlation between distance and EMR via EMW.[188] Such fuzziness in the farther universe isn't Mina's grand plan but the inevitability of finite EMW speed in a vast universe. He could've quickened lightspeed but that raised more issues than it solved, similar to changing an intersection's traffic light timing producing undesired repercussions elsewhere. Lightspeed c represents the best balance between cost and benefit.

Because EMR propagates spherically from the photon instead of from its source, EMR can't lead linearly back to its source but only to EMR's EMW source—the photon itself—which lies somewhere in space at any given moment along the photon's axis of travel. Using light preponderantly delivered by EMW to derive a distant star's location, much less its movement in space, is akin to using water waves to derive the spatial location of the rock at rest before it moved to hit the pond and generate waves. The startling result is that distant stars in the night sky (beyond ∼1MLY) aren't actually where they appear to be. The more distant the star, the farther from its apparent location it really sits. EMR from ∼56.85 light-years arrives on Earth at roughly a fifty-fifty photon–EMW split. Calculating spatial location using phenomena such as stellar aberration or light-time correction is increasingly ineffectual beyond this distance (*Fig. 43*, right).

The differences alluded to regarding the Huygens–Fresnel principle—in which every point of an EMR disturbance (a wavefront) becomes the source of another EMR disturbance, or a new spherical EMR wavelet, where the sum of the waves determines the form of subsequent wavelets—lies in this ET data (§ 3.7.3.3.3:141). In effect, photons form the wavefront. EMW propagates spherically outward at any moment at all points along each photon's track in the wavefront (though it wrongly presumes the wavelets propagate only forward in their direction of travel rather than in 360°; *Fig. 44*).

5.6.2 Leading-edge and Trailing-cone Redshift

This book can't fully address redshift, so we cover its highlights. For this next bit, *redshift* references only the shift toward the red end of the spectrum. We touch on spectrum blueshift afterward, although some parts of the following apply to it as well. Redshift is an applied energy E phenomenon. It doesn't occur with

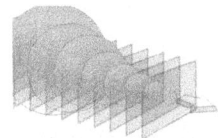

Figure 44. EMW propagating spherically outward at each plane wave cross section at lightspeed *c*.

photonic EMR because photons are real energy Υ-energized particles and not radiant energy. As a photon travels through space, it continually emits new pulses of applied energy *E* derived from its real energy Υ charge. Each propagates as EMR via EMW and observably redshift over time as they travel cosmic distances. The shift is noticeable on Earth from an emission distance of about 1MLY. Redshifted EMR arrives on Earth via EMW from two vectors, along the Mach cone *leading edge* ($S_{wavefront}$; *Fig. 43*, left) and from the *trailing cone* (*Fig. 45*, left). On average, approximately .005% of single-source—star, galaxy—EMR redshift seen from Earth is from leading edge EMR and 99.995% from trailing cone EMR.

Redshift arises from a diminution of EMW energy. There are three principal causes to leading-edge redshift. First is gravity, which as discussed above is an EM field effect. Second is EMW passage around objects that creates an interference effect. Of note is that any EM field saps (or adds) energy from (or to) any encountered EM field which shows up as diminished (or increased) EMR energy over time. Third is the propagated magnetic field of an EM oscillation propagating a new electric field, which is infinitesimally less energetic than the previous electric field that propagated its magnetic field. We state this as,

$$\forall \vec{E} \vdash E \rightarrow \left(E \vdash B\right) \Leftrightarrow \text{EMW}$$
$$\therefore \forall \text{EMW} \Vdash \left(E, B\right) \rightarrow \left(B \vdash E' \left\{E' \mid Q_{E'} < Q_E\right\}\right) \tag{17.61}$$

where a moving charge $\vec{E}$ that yields electric field *E*, where *E* yields magnetic field *B*, is defined logically equivalent to EMW. Therefore, if an EMW is reducible to *E* and *B*, then *B* yields the next-propagated electric field *E'* such that its EMR energy, $Q_{E'}$, is less than current EMR energy Q_E. This phenomenon occurs because there's an energy cost to energize an electric field that the magnetic field absorbs; there's no concomitant diminution to propagated magnetic fields, however. Such an infinitesimal energy transfer per oscillation retards EMW wavelength over its transit time. Using the vector rate of energy transport per unit area $\vec{S} = 1/\mu_0 \, \vec{E} \times \vec{B}$, the EMR energy per oscillation is described as

$$S = \frac{1}{\mu_0}EB \rightarrow S' = \frac{1}{\mu_0}B\left(\frac{\left[\frac{E'}{B}\Delta q\right]}{S}\right) \tag{17.62}$$

where *S* is magnitude of EMW, *S'* is magnitude of next-propagated EMW, μ_0 is vacuum (magnetic) permeability in free space,[189] Δq is the change in energy charge, and other symbols as defined.

Trailing cone redshift results from the aforementioned leading-edge causes in addition to a Doppler effect as photon-generated EMW propagates back along the axis of travel of photons not arriving on Earth (*Fig. 45*, left). Roughly 90% of trailing-cone—and 99.995% of all—redshift results from the Doppler effect. The 9.995% trailing-cone remainder is from leading-edge redshift that also occurs in the trailing cone. The disparity between our earlier .005% leading edge redshift along the leading edge and the 9.995% leading edge-type redshift in the trailing cone results from the greater amounts of EMR arriving on Earth from the trailing cone than the leading edge of any particular EMW, on average.

As noted, an observer perceives this Dopplered EMR apparently pointing back along its EMW track to a particular star out in the far distance. In reality, it is EMR emitted from a source in another direction entirely. Whether viewed with the naked eye or the Hubble telescope, a light source may literally have no linear EMR source behind it at all, and the farther from Earth the more likely this scenario. Moreover, an EMW can vary as the photon travels through the varying environments of space. In some regions, the EMR will be energy dampened (or boosted, in the case of blueshift) by passing through a saturated EM region, a scattering or absorbing region, a high-density matter region, and so on whereas, down the Mach cone's leading-edge road, the local EMR isn't affected by that environment and its EMW proceeds normatively (*Fig. 45*, right). This effect occurs up and down the leading edge of an EMW as it propagates through space. As a photon emits normative EMR along its axis of travel, that EMR varies dynamically in energy—thus wavelength, frequency,

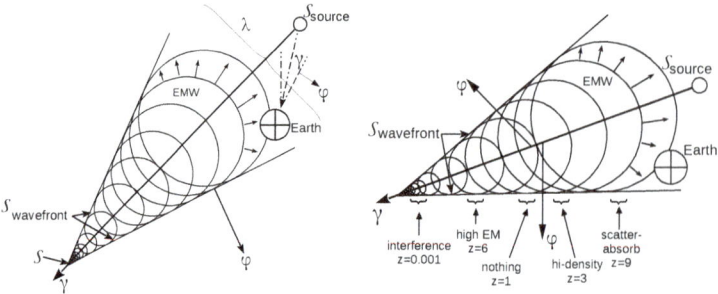

Figure 45. Left, trailing-cone redshift. Photon γ passes Earth along line $[S_{source}, S]$. Leading edge Mach cone EMR arrives Earth along direction φ, then EMW arrives from the trailing cone. Both may be Dopplered. Photon γ EMR arrives Earth along line $[S_{source}, Earth]$ with leading edge Mach cone EMR in direction φ. Right, each EMW is an independent entity even though spawned from a larger coherent wavefront. Redshift z value tends larger toward the trailing cone in a net-neutral environment but varies and shifts in variant local environments. Our universe is like a lake of infinite, and infinitely intersecting, waves.

and EM amplitude—according to local environments. Consequently, along any given photon track, the EMW Mach cone wavefront can be a rainbow of EMR energies and redshift values.

Naturally, the same effect is present in the trailing cone's EMW wavefronts because EMW propagates spherically. Additionally, an EMR's existing redshift or blueshift (Dopplered or not) can be strengthened, diminished, or returned to its normative emission state according to environment and interaction. As trailing cone EMW delivers the bulk of EMR to Earth, it's easy to see what a mishmash EMR is, and how completely convoluted and confused our picture of deeper space really is without our even suspecting it. Premised as it is on visible and invisible EMR, cosmology isn't what it seems to our eyes or instruments.

Out to about 4MLY, the margin of error is about two percent—which, incidentally, is Mina's view of what constitutes a 'reasonable margin of error' in this context (he avers science averages a margin of error of ~14.5% w.r.t. to EMR source distance and location). With the exception of radar (Mina it considers reasonably accurate), parallax, cepheids, supernovæ, and redshift yoked to Hubble's Law as tools to calculate distance and location, are "wholly inaccurate [and] never derive accurate measures even within reasonable error."[186] Indeed, the math that enables various methods to serve as indicators of distance and position is premised on inaccurate assumptions about EMR.[190] For example, galaxy M100 in the Virgo cluster is about 53.3MLY from Earth, not 56MLY as calculated using cepheids, a 4.8% difference. While Alpha Centauri's 4.37LY calculated distance is "sufficiently accurate," its actual position differs from its perceived position by about 1,000 light hours along a line some 127.7° from the perpendicular (*Fig. 46*).

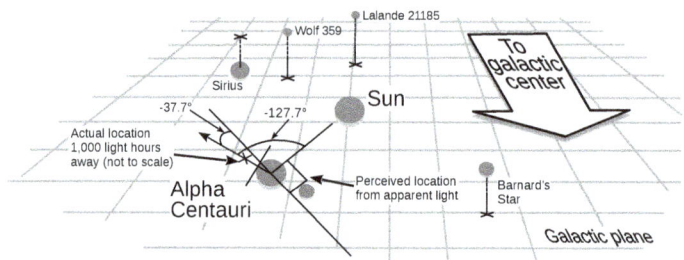

Figure 46. Alpha Centauri's perceived and actual position relative to Earth in the plane of the page; the greater the distance from Earth, the greater the difference between perceived and actual spatial position.

5.6.3   STELLAR BLUESHIFT

Leading-edge blueshift results from the second of the three causes for leading-edge redshift as described, which is interference from encounters with other EMW. When one EMW's EMR infinitesimally loses energy and redshifts from an encounter with another EMW's EMR, then that other EMW's EMR infinitesimally gains energy and may eventually blueshift. Trailing-cone blueshift, on the other hand, results from leading-edge blueshift

---

186. Radar maps objects in our solar system. Cepheid stars radially pulsate with a regular period, having a calculated relationship with luminosity from which science infers distance.

phenomenon in addition to a Doppler effect, primarily from travel time through our own Milky Way galaxy where there's more EMF, movement, and other forces than in intergalactic space.

A blueshift example in this context is the Andromeda galaxy. The blueshifted EMR attributed to Andromeda, which implies it's moving toward the Milky Way and in some 4.5BY will collide, doesn't actually originate with Andromeda but with the Perseus, Cassiopeia, and Triangulum constellations. Notwithstanding about 85% of EMR attributed to Andromeda arrives on Earth via photon, and we therefore can linearly backtrack it to Andromeda so one might think we're getting an accurate EMR picture, there is, nonetheless, overwhelming interposing EMR propagating via EMW from other sources that's indeed blueshifted, some of which arrives on Earth in the same plane as Andromeda's apparent line of sight. Taken as a whole, Andromeda's EMR scene is more complex than at first glance (*Fig. 47*). Accordingly, that galaxy isn't on a collision course with ours. Rather, it's both rotational and in linear motion along a flat parabola at about 7.7 km/s.[187] The ratio of leading-edge to trailing-cone blueshift delivered on Earth is roughly the same as redshift. The Standard (Big Bang) Model is inaccurate in some key respects.

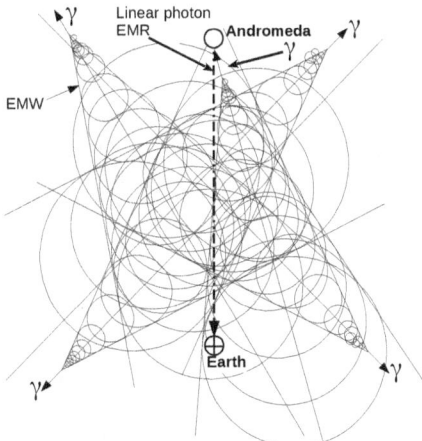

Figure 47. Linear line-of-sight EMR via photon from Andromeda (top) to Earth (bottom) interposed by innumerable other-source photons and EMW that presents a tangled EMR environment.

SECTION 6

Relativity and the Quantum

The ET data throughout this chapter indicates that Relativity's explanations for various observations, as well as those of quantum science, are generally true in the relativistic context of *perceived reality* but as explanations for how the universe *actually works* are inaccurate. In this section, we consider the following:

Contents

6.1 MASSIVE OBJECTS AND LIGHTSPEED

According to Mina, massive objects (viz. archí) can accelerate to and move at lightspeed c and beyond (Eq. (17.8)–(17.14):117–119). The practical reasoning as to why Relativity gets actual reality wrong lies in the principal implication of $E = mc^2$—that accelerating a massive object toward lightspeed c entails infinite en-

---

187. Andromeda's apparent lateral speed from our perspective is actually parabolic speed in its own reference frame.

ergy thus infinite mass—being built off a wrong premise. Even if the equation's longer, not-at-rest form $E = \sqrt{p^2 c^2 + m_0{}^2 c^4}$ was accurate with reality, a zero in the denominator for m as in Eq. (17.63) doesn't produce an infinite value for energy and mass but one that's simply *undefined* (INFINITY, CH. 14:93). The equation leads to this conundrum because it conflates applied energy E to real mass when its proper equivalent is *applied mass* (§ 4:150). Presuming a massive object approaching lightspeed c requires infinite energy because $m/0 = \neg 0 \wedge \neg(\neg 0)$, and thus undefined, hence, literally infinite, is an error. When, for example, velocity v equals lightspeed c such that

$$E = \frac{mc^2}{1 - \left(\frac{v^2}{c^2}\right)^{.5}} \rightarrow \frac{mc^2}{0}$$

$$\Leftrightarrow m = \frac{m_0}{\sqrt{1 - \left(\frac{v^2}{c^2}\right)}} \rightarrow \frac{m_0}{0} \qquad (17.63)$$

where E is logically equivalent to m, then a value for E, thus m, can't be found because dividing by zero—that is, nothing—can't be defined in mathematics. Eq. (17.63) or similar is typically cited for why a massive object approaching lightspeed c requires infinite energy and mass. Science relies on it because the math is valid. But just as correlation doesn't imply causation and logic doesn't imply truth, valid math doesn't imply reality. Restating the principal fractions in Eq. (17.63) as an $x/0$ subtraction-until-zero operation to find the quotient also fails to find for infinite value. To see why, let's first consider how subtraction-until-zero works. If we take

$$y = \frac{9}{3} \Leftrightarrow \begin{cases} y_1 : 9 - 3 = 6 \\ y_2 : 6 - 3 = 3 \\ y_3 : 3 - 3 = 0 \\ y = 3 \end{cases} \qquad (17.64)$$

then $9/3 = 3$. Similarly, when using $x = 1$ to examine $x/0$ as an infinity per Eq. (17.63), we get

$$y = \frac{x}{0} = \frac{1}{0} \Leftrightarrow \begin{cases} y_1 : 1 - 0 = 1 \\ y_2 : 1 - 0 = 1 \\ \cdots \\ y_n : 1 - 0 = 1 \end{cases} \qquad (17.65)$$

where y_n implies infinity and, indeed, it seems valid therefore true that $y = \infty$ because y will never result in 0 or any real number for infinite iterations of the operation. Yet $y \neq 0$ or any real number because an infinite iteration isn't equivalent to a *value* for y. Neither are the expressions in Eq. (17.63) limits, where the denominator gets closer and closer but never quite reaches zero, as when

$$m = \lim_{v \to c} \left(\frac{m_0}{\sqrt{1 - \left(\frac{v^2}{c^2}\right)}} \right) = \infty \qquad (17.66)$$

such that mass m grows to infinity as velocity v approaches, but never quite reaches, lightspeed c. For the limit to be true, v^2 can never equal c^2, otherwise it yields a zero denominator that leaves m undefined. In both Eq. (17.63) and (17.66), when velocity v equals lightspeed c instead, then the values for E and m each resolve to undefined from the straightforward equation $x/0$ and not the limit $x/0.00...001$. A limit here would be an artificial imposition not consistent with reality anyway. Even if it was, the expression itself is not infinite but undefined. Also, if we consider mass not as matter but resistance to acceleration—which is certainly more accurate, since mass can't in actuality become more than it is simply from force and speed—and as it's ET-given there's no non-negligible drag in free space that limits speed,[188] then there's no appreciable force that resists acceleration beyond real mass which is a constant w.r.t. to any linear motion in free space over time (where $v < 2.09$ actual lightspeed $ç$). The non-relativistic equations $s = dt$ (speed, distance, time) and $v = v_0 + at$ (where v_0 is start velocity, a is acceleration (F/m), t is time) correctly describe linear motion where $0 < v \leq 2$.

The nullity described above doesn't—can't—resolve to an infinite which *is* a value, however incalculable, but to undefined which is *not a value* and *not* calculable (Eq. (14.1)–(14.11):94–97). All this means is, we can't use

---

188. Although negligible enough to create resistance weight (§ 3.6.1.1.1:134).

energy equivalence to calculate a real energy or mass value w.r.t. linear motion. The undefined result describes Relativity's intrinsic inadequacy to relate matter to energy to linear motion because $E_{undefined} \to E_{\infty}$ is a reference frame for energy whose physics differs from all others. In a universe where the principle of relativity[189] and general covariance[190] are true, variant speed can't spawn variant physics. This doesn't mean Relativity is wrong per se, only that we can't indiscriminately apply it across the board to derive conclusions about actual reality from perceived reality that it can't intrinsically support . . . like, say, a theoretical undefined nullity equating to real-world infinite energy and mass.

The question then arises as to why particle accelerators like the Large Hadron Collider (LHC) don't appear to accelerate particles to lightspeed.[191] The common wisdom is that Relativity limits any massive object—proton, electron, atom—to less than lightspeed c. No matter how many nines get pushed out to the right of the decimal, it will never meet or exceed $1c$, as if magical things happen in the universe when we clock a particle at $1c$ but not when it's merely a half meter per second less, or $0.999 \ldots \infty c$, and thus not *officially lightspeed* as *we* reckon it. Nevertheless, Mina avers that in LHC's history, about 5% of the protons they've juiced to 6.5 TeV did achieve a velocity where $1c < v \leq 1.085c$, and a single neutron ejected from a lead atom which struck the tube wall reached about $1.1c$ for a distance of $\pm 1.65555 \times 10^{-12}$ meter. Moreover, while the relativistic speed equation $E = \gamma mc^2$ (where γ is the Lorentz factor w.r.t. to motion) artificially limits particle speed to less than $1c$ in line with Relativity, Mina tells us that 9 TeV is sufficient to routinely accelerate a proton in the LHC to $1c$ and 9.15 TeV to bump it over the line to $1.0001c$.

6.2 LENGTH CONTRACTION

The foregoing provokes us to wonder if there's really a maximum speed limit for matter. Mina says there is. It's a bit over twice-actual lightspeed, viz. 2.09ς (§ 5:151). The reason there's a speed 'limit' at all is the Energent's flux pressure on matter traversing it. It's a hydrostatic, scalar phenomenon and, in this respect, analogous to water pressure on a submarine hull. Lightspeed flux pressure is non-negligible where $v < c$, substantial where $c \leq v \leq \varsigma$, and significant where $1\varsigma < v \leq 2\varsigma$. *Enérgeia* flux pressure compresses the space between bonded archí before finally compressing each archí itself. Compression occurs in all dimensions[191] at these speeds. It's non-negligible where $v \leq 1c$, substantial where $1c < v < 1\varsigma$, significant where $v \geq 1\varsigma$, and terminal where $v > 2\varsigma$. At $v = 2.09\varsigma$ compression for archí is analogous to submarine crush depth. Compression is wholistic; the object contracts throughout.

Recall from MATTER–ENERGY (§ 2:114) the archí is a 'condensed energy' whose Energent 'charge' and 'density' renders it impermeable to the Energent. At speeds where flux pressure is significant, the archí compresses into less physical space which accordingly raises its 'energy density.' This means an archí emitted as a photon is physically smaller (by ~4%, hence 'denser' and more 'energetic') than a non-photonic archí. Above 2ς, the archí is so compressed it bleeds proto-energy through its increasingly permeable containment. The lower the 'energy density' the greater the compression until, at 2.09ς, 'energy density' falls below containment threshold and the archí dephases. This process is the same for all matter as it's composed of composite archí structures.

Let's consider a magical spaceship. Within the above parameters and all else being equal, its pilots can accelerate to any speed but contraction is absolute. Mina says that neither speed nor compression is harmful to human astronauts in such a ship up to 1.53ς but, by 1.54ς, compression is significant and, by 1.6ς, fatal because the spaceship and all within—the space between the archí constituents of its matter—have by then contracted by $99.999\ldots\%$. Like an implosion, it escalates fast.

6.3 CONSTANCY OF LIGHTSPEED

A key element in Relativity involves the axiom—an underlying assumption—that lightspeed c is constant and inviolable. As we've seen, c is the rate of EMW propagation, lightspeed ς is the negligibly variant photon speed, and 2.09ς is the speed at which matter dephases to Energent proto-energy. The unique thing about light (or any EMR) is that we can only observe it when it has arrived unlike, say, a projectile. From whatever angle we view light, it's only observable, as Yogi Berra might quip, because wherever it goes there it is, already arrived in our eyes or instruments and no longer on the way. In this respect, its clock speed isn't relevant. It only stands

---

189. Physics must be identical for all observers, accelerated or not.

190. "[T]he general laws of nature must be expressed by identical equations relative to all other systems, whichever way they are moving" (Einstein (1920) 1987, 141 [Doc. 31]).

191. Relativity predicts length-only contraction; it's incomplete, as it treats only one dimension.

to reason, then, that lightspeed is measurably the same in any inertial or moving frame of reference (IFR or MFR, respectively) even if a frame is moving faster than light, because the principle of relativity and covariance are real if inaccurately described. A projectile at lightspeed c is different. We can view it at a distance—before it arrives—because the light (EMR) which reveals it is traveling via photon and EMW at lightspeed $ç$ and c, and arrives first. If the projectile is moving instead at lightspeed $ç$ then it, too, is invisible until it arrives since the light revealing it is traveling at the same velocity. Matter and 'energy' arrive together in this case.

6.3.1 GALILEAN RELATIVITY

In what's called Galilean relativity, if a person on a train moving at velocity $v = 50$ mph throws a ball moving at $u = 10$ mph in the direction of travel, then one simply adds the train and ball velocities as $\vec{u}' = \vec{v} + \vec{u}$ to get the ball's groundspeed.[192] This is really just an observer's IFR alongside the railroad (*Fig. 48*). Relativity won't straightforwardly add relativistic velocities to get the ball's actual IFR speed as in Eq. (17.67) not just as a matter of perspective, but of presumed actual reality. The reason is premised on $E = mc^2$ and its axiom that lightspeed c is the limit that energy can move in any reference frame without a preferred frame—in other words, 'groundspeed.' For Relativity, this precludes matter moving faster than lightspeed c even when its own reference frame is moving at a velocity v of lightspeed c.

Figure 48. Left, Bob on the moving train and Alice observing from the ground alongside; right, ball thrown from train relative to groundspeed (Alice's point of view).[193]

Therefore, on a train moving at $v = c$ as in *Fig. 49*, the bullet fired by [A] can never reach [X] who's also moving at $v = c$ in the bullet's same direction of travel, even though both persons and the bullet are in the same reference frame that, for them, is at rest and thus an IFR. The same would have to be true of a laser beam, as [X] is still moving at lightspeed c in the same direction of travel as the lightspeed c laser. This premise is nonsensical because the ball or bullet's speed is *imparted* whereas laser light *self-propagates* and speed is a *relative measure* but motion is *absolute*. It doesn't matter that one throws a ball slower, at, or faster than c. Its speed is imparted and that's the variant motion at which it's moving. If you throw a chunk of non-photonic light—EMW is energy and moves as an electromagnetic field extension (§ 3.7.3.3:138), not as matter—then, no matter how Zeus-fast you fling it, it necessarily moves forward only at its speed of self-propagation, which is lightspeed c, and *that's* the motion at which it's moving. That's why Einstein noted that light moves independent of its source.

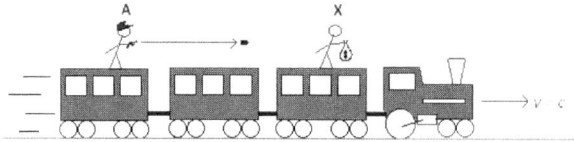

Figure 49. Train moving at $v = c$ where, according to Relativity, [A]'s bullet can never reach [X].[194]

Speed is thus relative but motion is absolute; there's motion or there's not. This is straightforward. So, when we talk about a massive object moving at lightspeed, we're dealing with imparted not self-propagated motion.

6.4 FRAMES OF REFERENCE

Having no preferred frame of reference (PFR) is sensible w.r.t. observer perspective. Indeed, it's necessary to effect technology like GPS that relies on the awareness that timekeeping is relative between reference frames. Entirely dispensing with a PFR, however, yields an inaccurate view of reality—such as when a bullet fired on a spaceship at lightspeed c is not moving faster than the spaceship it's on even though it's traversing the spaceship's MFR (it's own IFR) back to front. Ironically, Relativity doesn't actually operate as if there's no PFR because it effectively assigns that role to lightspeed c. But let's consider that bullet.

6.4.1 RELATIVISTIC BULLETS

Suppose a spaceship is moving at $v = c - 200$ m/s in which a passenger fires a bullet moving at $u = 300$ m/s in the direction of travel (*Fig. 50*, left). Unlike the sub-lightspeed train in *Fig. 48* where the thrown ball's groundspeed exceeds the train's groundspeed, Relativity perceives the bullet speed u' in terms of lightspeed c's inviolability according to

$$u' = \frac{u - v}{1 - \frac{uv}{c^2}} \tag{17.67}$$

and other reasoning which yields the bullet's net speed less than its actual speed in its own IFR. Relativity's explanation for this revolves around time dilation and length contraction—though otherwise recognizes no other forces impinging the bullet's speed—as well as an observer's perspective in a reference frame outside the spaceship in which, as the saying goes, what happens in the spaceship stays in the spaceship. So, let's say the bullet moving in the spaceship's IFR at an imparted speed of

$$\Big((c - 200\,\text{m/s}) + (300\,\text{m/s})\Big) = (c + 100\,\text{m/s}) \tag{17.68}$$

pierces the front of the spaceship, as it must do in its own IFR, and travels forward outside the spaceship in its direction of travel (*Fig. 50*, right). In the spaceship's at-rest frame of reference, this is the natural outcome of shooting a bullet. From an observer's frame of reference, Relativity tells us the spaceship with its flying bullet is length-contracted at that speed, longitudinally nearly flat. Therefore, the bullet isn't *really* going faster than light, it just appears that way to the passenger in the spaceship, though not to the observer who sees only a pancake barely moving in time-dilated slo-mo—and certainly not from the perspective of light in its own IFR. Even so, the spaceship is in motion at lightspeed c and the bullet has pierced the front of the spaceship. In *that* reference frame, the bullet's now ahead of it in the direction of travel. Whether or not the spaceship's a slo-mo pancake from an observational reference frame, it's certainly not a pancake in the spaceship's own reference frame. Just by traversing the spaceship back to front, never mind blasting through its nose, the bullet's imparted speed plainly exceeds the spaceship's forward motion in its own at-rest frame of reference.

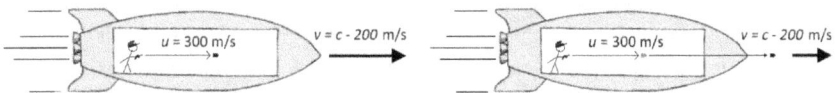

Figure 50. Left, bullet fired on a spaceship moving at lightspeed c; right, bullet pierces its front.[195]

Now if, as Relativity opines, there's no PFR yet lightspeed is a constant in all reference frames, then the spaceship must be moving at lightspeed c in terms of the constant-in-all-reference-frames lightspeed c, which means that's the case in any observational reference frame since the laws of physics must act the same throughout space. But if the bullet is not exceeding lightspeed c as in Eq. (17.67) even though it travels beyond the front of the spaceship, then the spaceship can't be said to be traveling at lightspeed c in its own reference frame and thus not in any observational reference frame either, nor in the IFR that constitutes the constant-in-all-reference-frames speed of light. This is a contradiction with the plain meaning that there are multiple realities in which the spaceship is simultaneously moving and not moving at lightspeed c. That makes sense w.r.t. relative motion since that's perceptual, but is nonsensical w.r.t. reality. The solution is that non-relativistic and relativistic physics are true at the same time in different contexts, the former w.r.t. reality and the latter w.r.t. perception.

6.4.2 RELATIVISTIC LASERS

Let's switch from our passenger shooting a bullet at an *imparted* speed to firing a laser beam moving at the *self-propagated* speed $u = c$ in the direction of spaceship travel where $v = c$ (*Fig. 51*, left). From an observer's perspective, Relativity still predicts the inaccuracy of classically summing the speeds ($u' = v + u$) to get a space laser version of the thrown ball's groundspeed as in *Fig. 48* because it implies the laser beam is moving faster than its own self, a logical impossibility. This is a fundamental misunderstanding.

First, the laser beam isn't moving at an imparted speed like the bullet but self-propagates. Second, the laser's reference frame is the spaceship's IFR, not an observer's or the space outside the hull. In the spaceship, the passenger fires the laser in a frame of reference at relative rest. Therefore, the laser emits at lightspeed c and travels the spaceship's at-relative-rest interior back-to-front, not at speed $v + u$ but only at speed u. Its speed logically can't be measured inside the spaceship relative to any other (outside) reference frame because the laser beam moves at a self-propagated, not an imparted, speed. Therefore, *outside* the spaceship the laser beam's speed is the same as inside, except that it *is* inside. It's moving *relative* to its own at-rest reference frame whereas, outside, it's moving *relative* to *that* at-rest reference frame. Accordingly, the laser beam moves at lightspeed c inside the spaceship that's also moving at lightspeed c because the hull differentiates *enérgeia* flux within and without the hull. If it wasn't enclosed, it wouldn't be an at-rest IFR and the laser beam wouldn't propagate in the direction of travel.

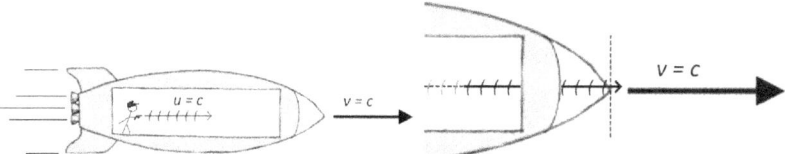

Figure 51. Top, laser beam emitted at $u = c$ in direction of spaceship travel where $v = c$; bottom, laser at $u = c$ passing beyond its IFR into an observer's IFR (source: Fig. 50).

Let's now suppose the laser beam strikes the transparent front of the spaceship and travels through it into space beyond the hull similar to the bullet in *Fig. 50*. As the laser propagates through the transparent hull, it's still moving at lightspeed c (*Fig. 51*, bottom). The instant it passes *beyond* those atoms of the IFR moving at lightspeed c, however, it *appears* to an outside observer to stop. The reason, of course, is the laser beam is still propagating at lightspeed c but now in a different, non-spaceship frame of reference in which the spaceship is moving relative to it at lightspeed c. Therefore, the laser beam can't outpace the spaceship *outside* of it as it seemingly did *inside*, or as the bullet with its imparted speed did. This is the corrected reasoning behind Einstein's postulate that lightspeed is constant in all reference frames.

6.5 SIMULTANEITY

Well, the spaceship itself is a situation of imparted motion. Let's compare that to self-propagated motion. Our thought experiment supposes a train moving at high speed. A passenger at a train carriage's midpoint and an observer alongside the railroad observe a simultaneous light pulse from opposite ends of the carriage (*Fig. 52*). Because the train is moving, the light pulse from the rear takes longer to reach the passenger at midpoint of the carriage than the pulse from the front (surprisingly, quite like the sub-lightspeed bullet). The passenger therefore concludes the pulses did not simultaneously emit. By dint of the observer's particular position vis-à-vis the train at its moment of passing, and the timing of the pulses, they reach the observer's position simultaneously. The observer therefore concludes the pulses did simultaneously emit. Relatively speaking, both observations and conclusions are valid. Absolutely speaking, however, they're not. Both are based on perception, which is always relative. Change the relative positions of the passenger and observer, or the train's speed, and there's at least one point where both experience the light pulses to simultaneously emit. The simultaneous pulse emission is an actuality, thus, absolute.

It's obvious there's a problem perceiving simultaneity from different reference frames, but it's immaterial to absolute simultaneity. The lights pulsed or didn't; each pulsed comoving with the other (thus,

$$\Sigma(t_0) = \Sigma'(t_0) \tag{17.69}$$

where Σ and Σ' are comoving inertial reference frames and t_0 is the moment of simultaneity) or didn't. If they didn't, that invalidates the experiment anyway. They moved at lightspeed c equally in all reference frames or they didn't. These are absolute realities (recall the discussion of Eq. (16.4):106) of which our perception is immaterial, although how we perceive them is the proper subject of Relativity. In all cases w.r.t. Relativity, EMR at constant lightspeed c is the IFR to which all other reference frames are relative.

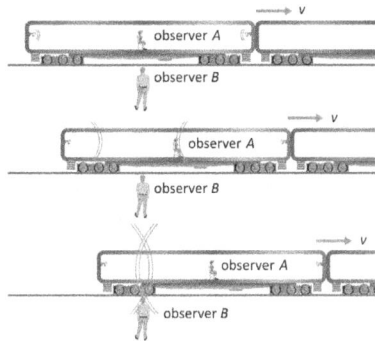

Figure 52. High-speed train with light pulses perceived as simultaneous by observer A in the pulses' IFR but not by observer B in a different reference frame.[196]

If there's no PFR in reality then, effectively, the universe is chaotic because, instead of simultaneous event periodicity being actual, it would only be relative. That means if event {X} happened for person A, it wouldn't necessarily have happened then, if it did at all, for person B. Let's suppose a light beams from a moving platform (spaceship A) to a mirror on another platform (spaceship B) moving at the same speed, and then reflects back to spaceship A (*Fig. 53*, left). So far, we have three reference frames: spaceship A, spaceship B, and an IFR that includes the whole setup. To observers on spaceships A and B, the light appears to transmit vertically from A to the mirror on B then vertically back to its source on A during time t.

To an observer outside these reference frames—constituting a fourth reference frame—the light instead appears to move toward spaceship B at an angle of, say, 45° before reflecting at the same angle back to spaceship A (*Fig. 53*, right) during time $t + t_n$. Imagine it similar to a bomber plane whose bomb falls to earth along an angled trajectory because it's initially moving forward at the bomber's airspeed while descending as its forward speed reduces and its drop speed increases.

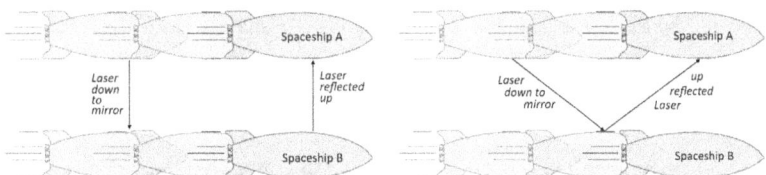

Figure 53. Left, light beamed at time t from moving platform (A) to mirror on another same-speed platform (B) viewed within its IFR; right, light between moving platforms per figure at left viewed from a fourth reference frame (source: Fig. 50:169).

Both perspectives are perception, not actuality; it's an important distinction. All four reference frames experienced a perceived reality that's simultaneously four different things: 1) a light beamed vertically upward and downward; 2) a mirror receiving and returning the light vertically; 3) an upward and downward 45°-beamed light; and 4) a mirror receiving and returning a 45°-angled light. If we extrapolate this scenario to all natural activity as actually real instead of perceptually real, then everything is happening and not happening in the universe all at once. In such case, there's only a reality in which lightspeed isn't constant and physics isn't the same in all frames; in short, chaos. Instinctively, we know this isn't true.

6.6 Preferred Frame of Reference

Is there a universal PFR? Yes. It's *event periodicity* (§ 2:114). No preferred frame is okay w.r.t. relative observation but must exist from the perspective of the universe, which is like the primordial rest frame of all space the way the ground is the primordial rest frame of all Earth. Event periodicity describes motion as the fundamental nature of the universe, independent to itself. Thus, each motion constitutes an independent frame of reference.

Collectively, however, motion in toto forms a universal *Motion Frame* of reference. This is why we can, and do, measure lightspeed c (which is its own reference frame) in terms of the motion of a clock (also, its own reference frame) without any need to transform from the clock frame to the lightspeed frame. More than that, we measure light not just at some speed but also in actual motion. We can only know motion with certainty against a frame to which all others are relative, including light (EMR). The Motion Frame isn't a reference frame in the relativistic sense but more of a baseline.

If, in actuality, light is moving through space then it can only be said to be moving at all w.r.t. to an independent frame of reference (indFR). A relativistic reference frame can't referee the reality of light's motion since every such frame is only a relative reality where any other frame can agree to disagree. Therefore, although lightspeed c is indeed an absolute constant, the relativistic constancy of lightspeed is questionable because there's no accepted PFR by which we can establish light is even moving to begin with, let alone at what speed. Of course, we intuitively conclude light moves because we see objects outside our eye and measure its speed as a function relative to another frame, say, the ground. So, the question is, how can we correctly perceive its constant motion across all reference frames so to fully utilize it?

As a baseline, the Motion Frame is the universal IFR. What makes this frame inertial is that it's rooted in the oscillation rate of bonded archí (§ 2.3.1:115). Recall the archí is the fundamental tangible expression of the universe—the Energent substantiated—oscillating as matter's existential fundament like a metaphorical heartbeat. That makes every reference frame non-inertial irrespective how we consider a frame to be inertial relative to some other frame and means that, absent the Motion Frame, there's no real IFR. If that were the true state of affairs in our universe, then Relativity's postulates couldn't be true because neither lightspeed nor the laws of physics would be constant in all reference frames. Absent an inertial referent, each one in and of itself would only be relative.

Einstein got around this conundrum by proposing lightspeed c as the universal constant. In essence, he designated lightspeed c as the real inertial referent. But it's not. Our perception of lightspeed c or $ç$ is relative, not actual; not the value we assign to its motion denoted as speed,[192] but how we perceive its actual motion through space. Absolute lightspeed $|c|$ and $|ç|$ is only properly measured from archí oscillations.

The way to establish a universal IFR for speed, time, and distance is to define speed, for example, as $|S|$ number of archí oscillations, time as $|T|$ number of archí oscillations, and distance as $|D|$ number of archí oscillations, such that $|S = DT|$ renders a useable ratio that calculates to $s = dt$ in a relative frame of reference, say, on Earth or in a spaceship moving at lightspeed c. Absolute timekeeping thus grounds in the existential nature of the universe. Spacetime is the result of Einstein's intuitive awareness that a preferred, *über* inertial frame of reference is necessary. The Motion Frame is a fuller application of his spacetime theory as an interdependent fourth spatial coordinate.

6.7   TIME DILATION

This is an elapsed time phenomenon between observers. It comes in two flavors: first as a perception relative to observers in different reference frames, and second as an actuality irrespective of reference frames. The former—Case 1 (*below*)—is perceptual, hence relative. The latter—Case 2—is actual, hence absolute. Relativity, working off observations of relative phenomena, posits that time dilation extends to the nature of time itself. As discussed in TIME INFINITY (CH. 16:105), however, that's inaccurate. There is no 'time itself.' There's only event periodicity and timekeeping, although in both cases time dilation is a real phenomenon.

6.7.1   CASE 1

Time differences in this case arise from perspectives between reference frames, usually in the context of velocity or gravitation differences (± acceleration), the reason being mainly geometry and mechanics. The two cases are not mutually exclusive, though. While perspective drives a perception of time dilation in some inertial Frame 1 vis-à-vis moving Frame 2, the latter can in fact be experiencing Case 2 time dilation as well. Strictly speaking, the effects of *enérgeia* flux compression (§ 6.2:167) don't arise with velocity or gravitational differences between observers in and of themselves but only with actual time dilation as in Case 2.

Therefore, while timekeeping is affected perceptually—a clock moving at a constant speed ticks time at the same rate as a stationary clock if the gravity environment is alike and it's not moving at compression speeds—biology isn't actually affected. Hence, there's no real aging differential between persons in space, e.g., aboard the International Space Station (ISS), whose timekeeping is simply slower w.r.t. velocity or gravity (± acceleration) relative to another observer, a person on Earth, say. Nor do persons living in low gravity environments like the Moon or Mars experience slower aging as a biological actuality. Rather, their bodies

---

192. Using atomic clocks to define lightspeed c is just using the relative frame value of cesium–133 measured against another relative frame value of seconds for yet another relative frame value designated a baseline constant.

simply endure less gravity-induced biological trauma along with other net helpful environmental factors in the less-than $1g$ gravity pull (acceleration) of such non-Earth environments.

6.7.2 CASE 2

The observational difference in this case arises from *enérgeia* flux compression induced solely by speed, not perspective. Here, time dilation is actual not perceptual, although it's observable only in comparison with another reference frame. Compression reduces the distance between matter's constituents, which means that, since everything is closer to everything else, event periodicity takes less time to complete; it occurs with greater rapidity. Here lies the reason Case 2 is not a relative but an absolute phenomenon.

Suppose a spaceship is traveling at lightspeed c to Alpha Centauri, where *enérgeia* flux compression effects are at the low end of substantial (§ 6.2:167). The spaceship's matter compresses a certain amount and event periodicity completes faster onboard relative to Earth's uncompressed event periodicity. The onboard clock counts out cesium–133 atoms faster relative to Earth, and our astronauts' biology operates faster, too. They don't notice their timekeeping operates faster than Earth's because the change was gradual with acceleration and steady at constant lightspeed c, and because their own sense of time is in keeping with their biology, including their sped-up brain processing. At lightspeed c, compression raises the rate of event periodicity (timekeeping) on the spaceship to about 24,000 times that of Earth, according to Mina.[197] Consequently, the 4.5LY trip will appear to the passengers to take only $\sim^{4.5}/24,000 = 0.0001875$LY, or about 1.64 hours; 3.28 hours roundtrip. Event periodicity as an absolute rate calculates as

$$\left| \boldsymbol{R}_{\mathrm{EP}} = \left(\frac{1}{x}\right) k \right| \tag{17.70}$$

where $\boldsymbol{R}_{\mathrm{EP}}$ is rate of event periodicity relative to lightspeed c, $^1/x$ is any fraction of lightspeed c, and k is the timekeeping constant 24,000. Lightspeed c is the baseline. Therefore, at lightspeed c,

$$\left| \boldsymbol{R}_{\mathrm{EP}} = \frac{1}{^1/_1} (24,000) = 24,000 \right|. \tag{17.71}$$

Meanwhile, event periodicity on Earth completes at its nominal rate of

$$\left| \boldsymbol{R}_{\mathrm{EP}} = \left(\frac{1}{10,065.425}\right) 24,000 = 2.384 \right| \tag{17.72}$$

(where the fractional lightspeed is Earth's average orbital velocity of $\sim$29.785 km/s) and nine Earth-normal years pass for the Earthbound. Of note is that spaceship-normal and Earth-normal times aren't *absolute* (or, universal)-*normal* time, which is the time such a trip would actually take as an objective matter, and is therefore relative to Motion Frame (archí-oscillation) time irrespective of the relative perspectives of the spaceship and Earth.

It seems counterintuitive that the faster biological event periodicity on the spaceship results in Earth's perception that time slowed for the astronauts because they return home nine Earth years later a mere three-plus hours older than when they departed. The effect of compression means not just timekeeping sped up, which is a relative effect, but event periodicity itself—the very motion of the universe within the reference frame of the spaceship—which is an absolute effect. Recall that time as an existential reality isn't real but motion is (TIME INFINITY, CH. 16:105). Local motion due to compression from *enérgeia* flux relative to motion anywhere else is how time dilation as a concept can even exist as an actuality. Although it seems the astronauts must age faster than those on Earth must because their rate of event periodicity is $\sim$24,000 times faster, everything around them is experiencing the same event periodicity, too. Therefore, Earth's local time in its own reference frame has no relationship with the spaceship's local time in its own reference frame. One can talk about observers and relativity, but those are naught but thought experiments about perception with no basis in reality.

On a side note, if we consider some fractional lightspeeds per Eq. (17.70), we notice that for astronauts on the ISS moving at approximately 7.7 km/s, $|\boldsymbol{R}_{\mathrm{EP}} = (^1/38,930) 24,000 = 0.616|$, which counterintuitively is less than Earth's $|2.384|$. The reason for the seeming disparity is that $|0.616|$ is relative to lightspeed c whereas, when it's relative to a different reference frame, then $\boldsymbol{R}_{\mathrm{EP}}$ is additive to that frame. Hence, $\boldsymbol{R}_{\mathrm{EP}}$ onboard the ISS is $\boldsymbol{R}_{\mathrm{EP}}^{Earth} + \boldsymbol{R}_{\mathrm{EP}}^{ISS} \rightarrow |2.384 + 0.616| = 3$ relative to Earth, and not slower after all.

Not all is relative, however. There's absolute timekeeping (archí oscillation) after all. Regardless spaceships and Earth or any other reference frames, there's the baseline oscillation of the archí. It's possible to account for this in clocks aboard the spaceship and on Earth so that each is aware of actual, universal IFR time. On the spaceship, then, the local-time clock moves normally while the Earth-local clock spins around the dial and the archí clock stoically metronomes universal time (assuming a constant speed). Similarly on Earth, the local clock moves normally while the spaceship-local clock only imperceptibly creeps across the clock face while the archí clock heroically keeps the same time as its twin aboard the spaceship.

6.8 COSMIC LIGHT LENSING

Lensing is an optical phenomenon where light bends. Cosmic lensing—light from behind an object in space on a trajectory with Earth appears to bend around it to create a lensing halo—is a pseudo phenomenon involving (archí) photons, although it is EMW we observe in the effect. Relativity chalks it up to the curvature of spacetime induced by mass (energy density) and accordingly terms it *gravitational* lensing. That's inaccurate since spacetime isn't real, gravity isn't a factor, and anyhow *lensing* isn't the effect that's actually happening. Although a lensing-like phenomenon is observably real, Relativity's explanation for it isn't. Gravitational lensing is a theory invented in the absence of an understanding of photons, Mach cones, and EMR propagation. So-called lensing is the observation demonstrating it. It's a two-part process in which 1) a magnetic (not electromagnetic) field bends a photon's trajectory resulting in 2) the angle of EMW propagation creating a lensing-like optical illusion w.r.t. EMR.

6.8.1 PHOTON MAGNETIC FIELD

First, recall the photon is an archí moving at actual lightspeed ς in an environment of *enérgeia* flux (§ 2:114). Also, recall the positive–negative applied energy E charge oscillating around the sphere of the archí (Fig. 38:153, right). This generates an applied energy E magnetic field **H** (denoted H_γ) perpendicular to the electric field around the photon and in the plane of the archí sphere, with field strength H_S reflecting the EMR charge it carries (§ 5:151). In this milieu—absent any external magnetic field of sufficient strength H_S such as those encountered around large matter–Energy (classically, mass) objects in space—a collection of north–south poles of differing orientations oscillate across the archí sphere as *magnetic domains*[193] that create, uncreate, and reorient with each oscillation (*Fig. 54*, left). There are 5–10 million—with 7.5 million the mean—of these magnetic domains around a photon. Thus, in free space, a photon sports a tightly bound collection of magnetic fields. The random and constant reorientation of the magnetic domains means that, absent external magnetic force of sufficient strength H_S that unifies domain orientation (*Fig. 54*, center), the archí photon's magnetic field is magnetically neutral.

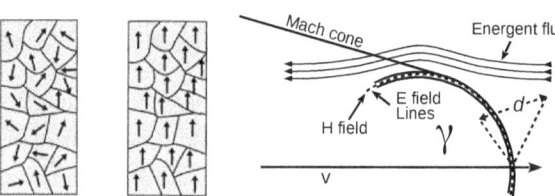

Figure 54. Schematic visualizing photon sphere magnetic domains; left, the domains cancel, leaving no over-all magnetic field; center, external field H_m reorients H_γ to a single orientation with a single dipole; right, photon magnetic field in relation to Mach cone. *Enérgeia* flux compresses **H** and E fields to within about $2.3563363363 \times 10^{-60}$ meter at d to the surface of the photon.[198]

Naturally, its magnetic field doesn't extend forward of the Mach cone because, instead of projecting three-dimensionally into space as is typical, *enérgeia* flux compresses it two-dimensionally along the plane of the archí sphere and within the Mach cone. (*Fig. 54*, right; ibid). Recall the Mach cone isn't physical, where faster-moving air molecules pile up against the slower-moving as with supersonic aircraft. It's where lightspeed c can't keep up with lightspeed ς in an environment of *enérgeia* flux.

When a photon (effectively operating as a charged particle) on a vector from an EMR source encounters one or many objects of sufficient matter–Energy to project a stronger than average individual (*Fig. 55*, left) or composite (*Fig. 56*) magnetic field, its own interacts with it. Ordinarily, average magnetic fields in space aren't

---

193. In ferromagnetic materials, unpaired electron spins line up parallel with each other in a region called a domain wherein the magnetic field is intense. As a whole, it's usually unmagnetized because domains themselves randomly orient w.r.t. one another. With a photon, discrete domain poles accomplish this effect.

sufficient to affect a photon traveling at lightspeed ç, much less bend its trajectory like a magnet bends electron paths to paint images on a cathode-ray screen (*Fig. 55*, right).

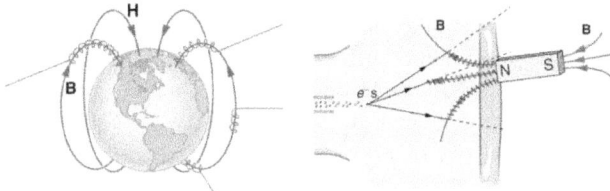

Figure 55. Schematic: left, magnetic field lines curving through space around an object of mass (Earth) where field **H** is magnetic force and field **B** is an induced (applied) field indicated by circularized charged particles spiraling around magnetic field lines; right, magnet bends electron path in cathode-ray tube.[199]

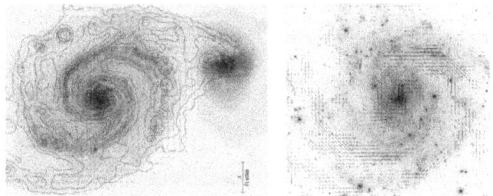

Figure 56. Line overlays indicate composite magnetic fields; left, Messier 51a; right, galaxy IC342.[200]

Let's suppose a photon in space approaches a mass object's magnetic field (denoted H_m) of sufficient strength H_S nonparallel to its magnetic field lines. A photon carries an average real charge Υ in the image of the applied energy E charge q of about $3.867466355 \times 10^{-34}$ coulombs (C). Hence, we modify the magnetic field strength vector equation $\vec{F} = q\vec{v} \times \vec{B}$ (written for scalar values as $F = qvB\sin(\theta)$) as

$$F = \Upsilon vH \sin\left(\theta\right) > 0 \begin{cases} \Upsilon \eqcirc q \\ H = B - M \end{cases} \tag{17.73}$$

where Υ is as above, v is photon velocity, H is the scalar value of field **H**, and θ is photon angle of incidence of v on field **H**. The photon's magnetic field H_γ interacts with the mass object's magnetic field H_m as in *Fig. 57*, left. Owing to its Υ charge, the photon's magnetic field magnifies the force of the interaction in a ferromagnetic manner as though it's magnetized in the presence of H_m. Its magnetic *differential interactivity* (expressed in terms of *differential susceptibility*[194]) is

$$\varrho_{ij}^d = \frac{\partial M_i}{\partial H_j} = 50,000 \tag{17.74}$$

where the result is a unit-less value of magnification; the term ϱ_{ij}^d [195] is a tensor derived from partial derivatives (∂) of components of the magnetic response (denoted **M**) with respect to components of **H**; i and j refer to the directions (x, y Cartesian coordinates) of the applied field and magnetization, respectively; d is the infinitesimal interval or rate of change; and M and H are vector values. **M**[196] is dependent upon the orientation of the photon and can occur in directions other than that of the applied field **H**.[201]

The H_γ–H_m interaction causes H_γ domains to reorient with each other. This dramatically boosts the magnetic interaction with H_m than is normally the case with such infinitesimal magnetic fields. In the preceding example, then, a photon interacting with a free space magnetic field H_m of sufficient strength magnifies the external magnetic field **B** (the interaction brought about between H_γ and H_m as in the figure) 50,000 times what the two fields normally would achieve absent such ferromagnetic-like behavior.

When H_γ interacts with H_m, it reorients in the direction opposite H_m. This produces amongst the many H_γ domains a single 'north–south' pole orientation (*Fig. 57*, center) always reposing 5° apart (*Fig. 58*, right). All

---

194. A differential is used for ferromagnetic materials where the relationship between M and H isn't linear. Photons aren't magnetic material, so we substitute interactivity for susceptibility.

195. Greek letter rho-variant is a modification to standard χ_{ij}^d where ϱ represents the internal, formative *enérgeia*-expressed nature of a magnetic field (as *epsilon*-variant ε does w.r.t. electric fields) in applied energy E terms where **B** and **H** fields are defined.

196. Or **M** as 'magnetization of the material.' In this case, it's the interactivity of H_γ, with H_m measured in amperes per meter.

domains essentially become one domain. 'North–south' orientation on a photon always reorients to the same H_m 'north–south' orientation, resulting in repulsion. The H_γ domain orientations parallel to the applied H_m orientation don't grow at the expense of other H_γ domains, however (*Fig. 57*, right). Instead, its domains remain discrete while individually changing orientation. With the next oscillation of the photon's electric field everything changes again anyway, although in the presence of an applied H_m magnetic field the photon oscillation produces its own composite H_γ field with a *single* domain and a *single* 'north–south' pole until the photon passes beyond the influence of the applied H_m field (*Fig. 58*, left). A photon thusly has a multi-domain magnetic field that, in the presence of a strong magnetic field in space, transitions to a single domain that magnifies its interactive effect 50,000 times.

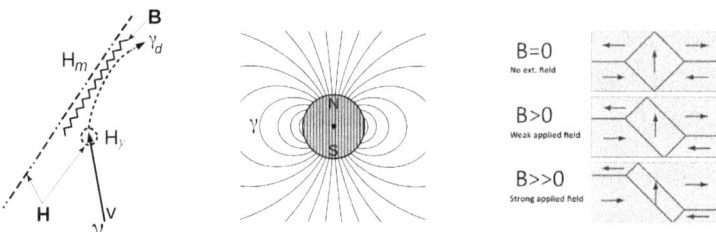

Figure 57. Schematic: left, interaction between photon γ of velocity v and magnetic fields **H** that are denoted H_m and H_γ that induce applied field **B**, which results in deflection γ_d; center, photon magnetic field **H** schematic with field lines moving along photon sphere surface; right, ferromagnetic materials behavior in presence of various strength **B** fields; photon magnetic domains remain discrete per oscillation.[202]

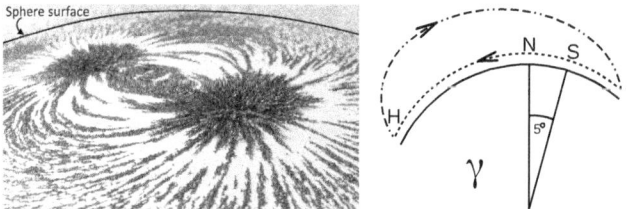

Figure 58. Left, perspective visualizing looking across photon sphere to imagine magnetic field lines spreading out across its spherical surface; magnetic force doesn't penetrate or touch the archí shell, but saturates the sphere above its actual Energent containment surface and is perpendicular to its electric field (§ 5:151); right, photon sphere schematic with 5° pole separation and field line flux (expanded to demonstrate).[203]

6.8.2   PHOTON TRAJECTORY

Now, let's consider how a free space magnetic field of sufficient strength affects a photon's trajectory. Given the above, suppose a photon's angle of intersection is perpendicular to H_m orientation. Repulsion occurs at the H_m point of intersection with an average net magnetic force F on the photon of

$$F = \Upsilon v H \sin(\theta) \begin{cases} H = B - M_i \begin{cases} M_i = H_j \varrho_{ij} \left\{ \varrho_{ij} = \frac{\partial M_i}{\partial H_j} \right. \\ B = \frac{F}{\Upsilon v \sin(\theta)} = 3.867466355x10^{-34}\text{C} \end{cases} \\ \Upsilon \doteqdot q \end{cases}$$

$$= 6.999999x10^{-30}\,\text{A/m}$$

(17.75)

where A/m is ampere per meter, C is coulombs, and other terms as defined in Eq. (17.73)–(17.74). Since H_γ's effect on external **B** magnifies 50,000 times, the repulsive effect of **B** nudges the photon's trajectory. As with any charged particle, the more a photon trajectory deviates from parallel to H_m orientation at any point in the field, the more **B** nudges it from its initial trajectory (*Fig. 59*, left). Since a photon has the same $\pm 1/2$ spin as when it was an unbounded archí (§ 5.5:160), it encounters each interaction with H_m in various orientations. This means H_m will alternately nudge a photon's trajectory in different directions, creating an infinitesimal zigzag as the photon traverses H_m in three-dimensional space (*Fig. 59*, right). The outcome is similar to how a market index shows thousands or millions of small-timescale cyclical bull and bear trends that merge into a single large-timescale bull or bear secular trend. A photon's cyclical zigzag over three-dimensional distance results in a secular trend of deviation from its initial trajectory.

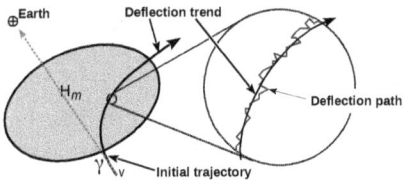

Figure 59. 2-D schematic of H_m magnetically nudging a photon along a 3-D 'zigzag' deflection path with an overall secular deflection trend. Each aspect change can be viewed in, or vertical to, the plane of the page.

Given the repulsive effect, the photon's course deflects laterally in accord with angle θ, moment of spin, state of H_γ field, and **B** field strength as in *Fig. 60* (left, center), with a trended radius of curvature of

$$r_{\mathrm{T}} = \frac{mv}{\Upsilon H} \qquad (17.76)$$

where m is mass, v is photon velocity, and Υ and H as per Eq. (17.73). Regardless the photon's aspect at the instant of encounter, it always laterally deflects to *its right* (not its *direction of travel*; *Fig. 60*, left).[197] The lateral right deflection arises because the H_γ magnetic moment[198] always orients opposite B, opposite the photon's right orientation in any given encounter. Thus, repulsion is rightward. Additionally, it arises in its *y-axis* $\pm 1/2$ spin (*Fig. 60*, center). When H_γ encounters applied **B**, the photon's magnetic axis undergoes Larmor precession from a kind of magnetic torque (acting on the intrinsic photon magnetic dipole moment) analogous to a classical gyroscope effect such that, in vector terms,

$$\tau = \mu \times B \qquad (17.77)$$

where τ is torque, $\mu = IA$ (where I is current and $A = LW$, where L is length and W is width of a coil), and torque is perpendicular to the photon's magnetic moment.

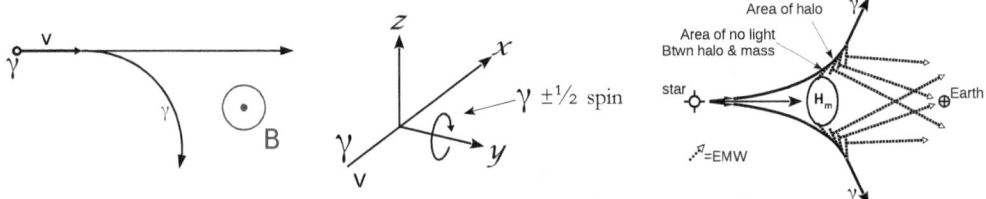

Figure 60. Left, deflection of photon γ by external magnetic field **B**; center, photon γ $\pm 1/2$ *y-axis* spin; regardless, a photon takes 1,000 rotations through 360,000° to return to its original quantum state (an electron takes two rotations through 720°, as it has a mean 25 magnetic domains *vs.* a photon's 7.5 million); right, only light emitted at a certain Mach cone angle from a certain portion of a deflected photon's path reaches Earth, giving the appearance of a lensed halo around a mass object.

The z-component of photon γ magnetic moment μ associated with photon spin, which is modified from $\mu_z = \pm 1/2 \mu_B$ in the electron context, is

$$\alpha\chi_z = \pm \frac{1}{2}\mu_{\alpha\chi} \begin{cases} \mu_{\alpha\chi} = \frac{\Upsilon\hbar}{4m_\gamma} \\ \mu = (IA)^3 \end{cases} \qquad (17.78)$$

where $\alpha\chi_z$ is the archí spherical z-component of magnetic moment μ, which is modified from Eq. (17.77) to a cubed exponent because IA is defined in three-dimensional terms; using an electron variant called the Bohr magneton, Υ is real energy photon charge, $\hbar$ is the reduced Planck constant, and m_γ is photon mass in terms of applied energy E. Photon H_γ orientation is always the same w.r.t. to H_m whether spin is $+1/2$ or $-1/2$. As a result, the photon's magnetic field repulsively orients to applied field **B** such that photon trajectory alters

---

197. Compare with axis-oriented white blood cells uniformly chemoattracted by fMLP (a tripeptide macrophage activator) that tends to move left. Ultimate causation is EM and Métier Force operated through a centriole (a cylindrical organelle comprised of nine chiral microtubule triplet structures with left-handedness). Ablation of centrosome (both centrioles) interrupts leftward movement and indicates its role (Xu et al. 2007, 9296–7).

198. Strength and orientation of an object's magnetic field defined in terms of its torque therein as a vector.

toward its right in any three-dimensional plane. This means a photon deflects along a path of infinite geometry until it exits H_m influence. Thus, from any observational point space, the trended deflection appears to be up, down, left, right, and all points between.

Of course, a photon continues emitting EMR throughout its deflection event. As it continues along its deflected trajectory, EMR emanates toward Earth along the deflected trajectory. From our perspective on Earth, the light emitted nearer the mass appears to bend around it rather than—as it does—emanate toward Earth along a line of sight from a point lateral to the mass. The light that appears to be a lensing halo is merely the only light that emits along deflected photon trajectories that are line of sight to Earth (*Fig. 60*, right). Therefore, we see it. The remainder of the EMR that emanates at the wrong angle simply passes by Earth undetected. Therefore, we don't see it—that is, we don't see it as emanating from the point in space of the halo effect. The point in space where that pass-by light emits appears to us on Earth as unlighted space both between the mass object and the faux lensing halo, and between the halo and farther space.

The halo phenomenon isn't a lensing effect but a straightforward change in aspect of EMR emission along a Mach cone (§ 5.1.3:154) from a photon deflected by a sufficiently strong magnetic field. Gravitational 'lensing' is an optical illusion as planetary retrogrades arise in perspective and orbital velocity.

6.9   Black Holes

As with stellar redshift and cosmic light lensing, black holes aren't what they seem, either. They're altogether unrelated to infinite mass, gravity, and singularities. A full discussion on black holes is too complex for this book, so we limit this section to describing their creation and operation according to Mina, as well as why they appear as atramentous voids in space.

"Black holes are mysterious objects predicted by Einstein's theory of relativity" (Thompson 2018, par. 1). They're a "massive star in the last phase of its evolution, in which the star collapses, creating a volume of space-time with a gravitational field so intense that its escape velocity equals or exceeds that of light"[199] (*Fig. 61*, left). "[B]ecause we can never see a black hole directly, it's impossible to know with absolute certainty that they really exist. All we know is that our theories of physics predict that black holes should exist, and that there are objects out there in space that exhibit every characteristic we would expect black holes to have" (Thompson ibid, par. 6). Astronomers then announced on April 10, 2019 the first ever 'photograph' of a black hole, M87*.[200] They composited the image from radio EMR imaged over ten days in April 2017, then converted it to an optical rendering (*Fig. 61*, center, right). You can see the 'hole' in the center surrounded by its accretion disk circling the event horizon's drain, "an invisible sphere surrounded by a donut of hot gas, if you will" (Kaufman 2019, par. 22). Black holes fall into three types: stellar-mass, intermediate-mass, and supermassive. Differences are superficial, though, as black holes fundamentally result from the same phenomena.

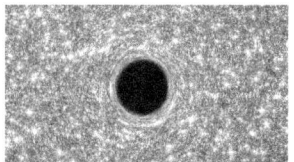 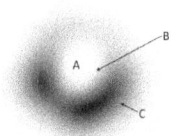 

Figure 61. Left, artist's conception of a black hole. Here, M60–UCD1 dwarf galaxy, near M60 elliptical galaxy; center, M87* supermassive black hole in the Messier galaxy composited of radio waves converted to color-inverted optical light for presentation (A: a remnant star's location, the 'hole;' B: event horizon is closer to A, photon sphere is closer to C, accretion disk); right, normalized b/w rendering.[204]

6.9.1   Star Lifecycle

As with everything in our universe, stars have a lifecycle (*Fig. 62*). The standard view is that fuel exhaustion leads to star death from which only massive stars might lurch onward to black hole immortality. For example, heat emission produced by fusion in living stars counteracts (balances out) the tendency of gravity to maximally contract a star's volume. So, its outward heat pressure cancels out its inward gravitational pressure. When a star

199. *American Heritage* 2020, s.v. 1 'black hole.'

200. The asterisk denotes a black hole. Mina has m87* about 40MLY from Earth at 5.5B solar masses ($M_\odot$) and 2.5866×10^{13} km at maximum diameter, differing from the standard view's 55MLY, ~$6.5 \times 10^9 M_\odot$, 38B km maximum diameter.

exhausts its fuel, its heat pressure declines. At a certain point, a catastrophic pressure differential between heat and gravity provokes a core collapse—typically, though not always,[201] leading large-mass stars to supernova—until gravity contraction and repulsive forces achieve a new balance that eventually defines its maximum contraction and density. The standard view calculates this super-contracted, super-dense remnant star at zero or near-zero volume with infinite density and calls it a black hole because it appears a lightless EMR void in space.

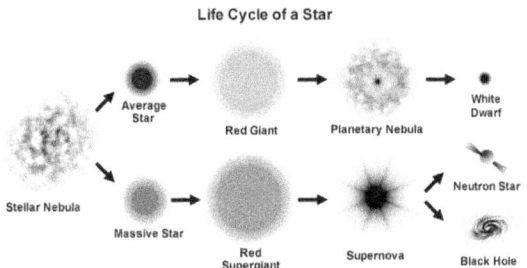

Figure 62. Basic star lifecycle; black dwarfs follow from white.[205]

6.9.1.1 RED GIANTS

Mina refines a few elements in the above process as follows. A star of less than a certain mass expands into a *red giant* (*Fig. 63*) as it nears its lifespan. When it exhausts its fuel, this star type undergoes a gravitational core collapse that spikes its electric and magnetic forces and fields. Consequently, the star's electromagnetic environment ionizes its mass-light matter. The mass-heavy, non-ionized matter collapses into the star's gravitational center and the ionized matter repulses (is 'shed') into space. This eventually loses its gravitational connection to the star remnant and drifts away to form a planetary nebula comprising, on average, an approximate 80:20 gas–plasma ratio. Such nebulæ are pantries of future stars. The resulting core remnant is a white dwarf star. It can accrete matter from a nearby companion resulting in explosions and cycles of various types but, eventually, cools to what's called a black dwarf to reach its lifecycle terminus. White and black dwarfs are actually no different than black holes except their EMR emissions remain nominal (§ 6.9.3:181). Terminal black dwarfs end as cold, dead hunks of former blazing glory eventually scavenged by gravitational forces that render them into gas, plasma, and dust—the building blocks of the future cosmos.

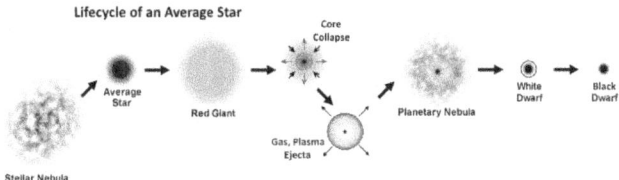

Figure 63. ET-modified average star lifecycle; terminus is black dwarf state (source: Fig. 62).

6.9.1.2 RED SUPERGIANTS

A star above a certain mass expands into a *red supergiant* (*Fig. 64*) as it nears its lifespan. Exhausting its fuel, this star type's core collapses, too, but triggers a supernova. Where its core survives it evolves, according to its composition, in one of two ways. If core composition isn't too dense for *enérgeia* flow-through (§ 6.9.3:181), it appears as a neutron star. Otherwise, it appears as a classical black hole. Neutron stars are no different from black holes in the same way as white and black dwarfs, and similarly recycle.

This is where the standard view considers the remnant star dead. Besides some theoretical thermal radiation, its only existential activity is the gravitational capture of matter and EMR straying across its event horizon (*Fig. 61*, left). It's now a black hole for eternity that may or may not 'evaporate' via Hawking radiation. However, while 30% of massive stars eventually reach the black hole phase (30% of these become neutron stars, 40% core-less nebulas), it's not their vampiric end after all but a gestation period for new stars.

---

201. About 25% appear as black holes without a preceding supernova as failed gestational stars (§ 6.9.2:180), e.g., N6946-BH1 during 2011 located (ET-given) 22MLY away in the NGC6946 'Fireworks galaxy' (JPL/CIT 2017).

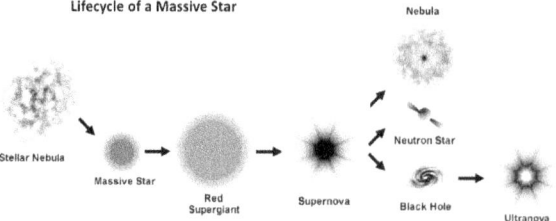

Figure 64. ET-modified massive star lifecycle; terminus is nebula, neutron star, ultranova (source: Fig. 62).

6.9.2 GESTATIONAL STAR

Following 'star death,' the next stage in its lifecycle isn't terminal but chrysalid. Since a black hole ultimately produces new stars, it makes more sense to call it a *gestational star* (*G-star*). The process unfolds in three steps: 1) a star collapses, 2) an accretion disk forms, 3) an ultranova destroys it. We consider each.

First, *a star collapses* into a super-contracted, super-dense remnant of its former volume and makeup. Note that gravitons displace in the same amount for objects of super-high density as with objects of average density with the same volume (§ 3.2.1:122). Maximal gravitational contraction against electrostatic repulsion at the subatomic₃ level generates heat.[202] Gravity contraction shortens the distance between hyposubatomic objects. This degrades hyposubatomic net attraction, meaning its ability to draw multilocal objects any closer together ceases because intrinsic electrostatic repulsion is now too strong for the infinitesimal moments of zai photon-induced net attraction to reduce any further the distance between local objects across a multilocal distance (§ 3.6:132). The pull of gravity balances against electromagnetic repulsion to which the aforementioned heat pressure contributes as the junior partner, resulting in the remnant star's maximum contraction in volume.

Second, *an accretion disk forms* around the G-star composed of "gas, dust, planetesimals, asteroids, or collision fragments in orbit" (Wikipedia *Circumstellar disc* 2019, par. 1). These travel up to about 80% lightspeed *c* depending on location within the disk relative to the gravitational—the actual—surface of the G-star. Gravity and friction contract and raise the disk matter's temperature and it emits EMR that we detect visually or via instruments. Matter from the disk wends its way closer to the so-called photon sphere (where the greatest heat produces the greatest EMR) that lies between the disk and the G-star gravitational surface until it falls to the surface (*Fig. 61*, left, B). G-star gravity, however, doesn't capture EMR (e.g., visible light) per popular black hole theories. The remnant G-star appears black and lightless for other reasons described below. Heat, including from matter accretion, builds pressure in the solid, super-contracted, super-dense remnant G-star mass that inflexibly resists any volume expansion. After about 1BY–1.1TY—about 600BY on average, depending on heat buildup and composition, which determines gravity force—heat pressure results in a catastrophic failure of resistance with a force greater than its original supernova (if one occurred) that we term *ultranova*.[203]

Third, *the ultranova destroys* the remnant G-star sometime during the aforementioned timeframe. The ultranova vaporizes most matter in about a 10LY diameter. Its remnant is a cloud of gas, dust, and other debris expected to be—since one hasn't yet occurred in our universe—roughly 67LY in diameter by about midpoint of stage two as defined for supernova remnant expansion.₂₀₆ Even by the end of supernova stage one, its kinetic pressure and other phenomena affects astronomical objects, including molecular clouds, out to a diameter of about 230LY. Whether or not a black hole rotates during its gestational phase, the ultranova's nebula develops its own rotation from the forces involved throughout. The various forces, including nebular elements in local rotation, eventually result in the formation of three new stars for every gestational star. Of the three types of black holes, only some stellar-mass, but all intermediate-mass and supermassive, black holes experience ultranovæ that lead to triple star formation.

Black holes that don't go ultranova cool over time until—about 825BY on average—their super-dense gravity restrains archí motion to the point there's no Energent reaction with matter to generate Fundamental Force. At such time, G-stars' nuclear and EM forces fail. Beginning on the surface and moving toward the core, this type of black hole's matter breaks into single archí that dephase back into the Energent. When enough archí

---

202. Notwithstanding physicist Freeman Dyson's (d. 2020) seminal 1966 paper purportedly showing it's the Pauli exclusion principle applied to electrons and protons (subatomic₂ components) playing the main role here.

203. As herein defined, a stellar explosion of an estimated mean of 9700 foes (*foe* means 'ten to the power of fifty-one ergs,' or 10^{44} joules of energy), or about 9.7×10^{54} ergs, and 71.3 times the largest possible supernova of about 136 foes and a mean 1.1 times the largest GRB (GRB 080916C) ever recorded of about 8,800 foes.

dephase and that pressure reduces on the remainder, sufficient archí motion resumes and restores nominal Fundamental Force. Overall, this process takes about $t_P \times 1.75$ second. This dead G-star remnant then expands in time to a gravitationally nominal volume and is eventually scavenged by gravitational forces. This, or the ultranova, marks the end of the G-star lifecycle.

6.9.3 Why Black Holes Look Black

The fundamental reason we detect no EMR from beyond the so-called event horizon of a G-star (black hole) isn't that infinite gravity captures it,[204] but that a different Energent state in and around a black hole disguises it. Simply put, the force dynamics in and around a G-star converts what emits in normal space as familiar EMR-energy photons (gamma to radio; § 5.1:152) to photons that emit at a reduced EMR level that we presently don't detect—all of a G-star's EMR converts to undetectable radio. Let's go through this surprising result in a bit more detail, describing G-star collapse, density, Fundamental Force, and finally this unexpected EMR state.

6.9.3.1 G-star Core Collapse

Gravity is the principal applied energy E reason a star is born. Its nuclear interactions create the star fusion process, the outward heat pressure halting inward gravitational contraction. Until its tank runs dry, that is. No fuel means no heat, thus no stopping matter's contraction until maximized. The standard view promotes the *singularity*, the black hole's dimensionless center point of infinite density in zero volume effectively corresponding to infinite gravity irreducibly exerting outward to the event horizon, then diminishing over distance before normalizing. But gravity can't contract two objects simultaneously into the same space (which is what must happen when mass reduces to zero volume) as gravity lacks the maximal force to overcome matter's maximal resistance. Quantum physics doesn't overcome this problem.

Recall how gravity exerts (§ 3.3:124) and the distinction between the strength of the pull of gravity and its magnitude as two aspects of the force of gravity (§ 3.5:131). The classical equation $F_g = G \frac{mM}{d^2}$ describes the former and $F_g = \vec{\mathcal{G}} \left(\frac{(mE_1 + mE_2)F_{ES}}{d^3} \right)$ per Eq. (17.31):131 the latter. But the classical equation describes gravity in the wrong context w.r.t. black holes, deriving a nonsensical result like infinite density in zero or near-zero volume. Recall, too, that matter is comprised of impervious archí. To actually contract two archí into the same space entails overcoming each archí's super-'dense energy' form so they merge, which would then release each archí's 'energy' from compression and both would simply dephase. That's not what is happening. Neither can two archí structures contract to entangle in such a way that we could say they inhabit the same macrospace—like two bunches of intertwined grapes on the vine—but not the microspace where each individual archí (grape) inhabits its own discrete space. The binding forces between pairwise archí prevent it.

Rather, as with any object, a remnant star core gravitationally collapses to its maximum extent and that's as far as it goes, except that its maximum gravitational contraction is greater. For example, following a typical massive star's core collapse to G-star (black hole) status, the contracted volume is—as a roughly accurate ratio within an approximate percentile range for any massive star—about 0.0002566% its original volume. The distance from gravitational center to gravitational surface of the collapsed core—the radius r—is about 0.37% the original distance. A collapsed star's gravity is less than its original gravity because it loses energy in the collapse as well as constituents. A star with an idealized gravity force of one that collapses to its smallest and densest drops on average to about 89% of that; the lost 11% is its departed 'energy' and related constituents. On average, a collapse to G-star or neutron star status sheds about 20% of the star's mass; to white dwarf status about 30% of its mass which, as it cools to black dwarfness, sheds about 17% of that mass. A star's density increase coupled to its volume decrease, even with less than its original mass, does affect its gravitational force, but isn't the principal cause of the apparent increase.

Gravity's effect is the same whether talking mass or matter–Energy. With respect to its *observed effect* rather than its objective pull and force, mass or matter–Energy both sufficiently describe it. If we want to calculate its objective force, however, mass as the benchmark leads us astray, so we needs must use matter–Energy. An inverse proportionality means that gravity at the surface of a denser unit of volume is greater, not because its surface is closer to its center, in this case, but because less pronounced Fundamental Force creates an apparent increase in magnitude, not objectively but subjectively stronger. What makes Fundamental Force less pronounced in the G-star context vis-à-vis normal space?

---

204. Where $d = m/v$ (d is density, m is mass, v is a volume of zero) since, according to the standard view that $x/0 = \infty$ (§ 6.1:165), gravity is infinite when there's zero distance between an object's surface and its gravitational center.

6.9.3.2   G-STAR DENSITY AND *Enérgeia* FLUX

Recall that matter and Fundamental Force result from Energent motion, which is *enérgeia* flux. According to a collapsed core's composition, its density either permits *enérgeia* flux such that it appears as a white dwarf or a neutron star, or else it alters *enérgeia* flux such that it appears as a classical black hole. Recall, too, that since individual archí are impervious to *enérgeia*, then it must flow around them (§ 2.3:115) as well as the increasingly complex archí substructures that comprise all matter. Naturally, this means *enérgeia* flows *through* matter via the physical space that separates archí.

In normal space, the distance between archí is invariant regardless their composite structures—bosons, leptons, quarks—and the physical spaces obtaining between them. The binding distance for archí is $\sim \frac{1\ell_P}{9475.156}$ (§ 2.3.2:116), and this constitutes *inter-archí space*. *Enérgeia* flux alters somewhat analogous to the venturi effect—not literally, as *enérgeia* is 'energy,' not a fluid—when flowing through matter whose inter-archí space narrows to about 14.75% nominal. A black hole reduces inter-archí space dramatically further, to about 0.000155% surface nominal and about 0.000000137% inner core nominal, which amounts to a physical space of approximately $\frac{1\ell_P}{9475.156} \times 0.000000137\% = 2.336921 \times 10^{-48}$ meter (*Fig. 65*). This not only significantly alters *enérgeia* flux dynamics throughout the black hole, but also staunches it entirely within its inner core.

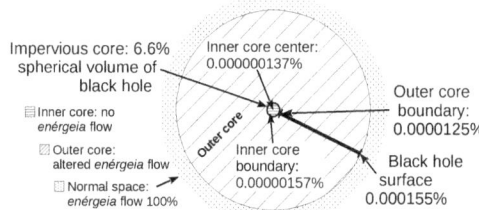

Figure 65. Black hole cross section showing inter-archí distances from surface to innermost core as a percentage of nominal inter-archí distance, dramatically weakening *enérgeia* flux.

This effect gives a black hole some similarity to a single giant archí—not exactly an archí writ large, though, because while its inner core is indeed impervious to *enérgeia* flux due to its super contraction, its remaining 93.4% bulk merely alters it, howsoever drastically. And, too, unlike the archí itself which is nothing but super-'dense' proto-energy (§ 2.3.1:115), it's fashioned from archí substructures.

6.9.3.3   G-STAR FUNDAMENTAL FORCE

Recall that Fundamental Force operates according to Energent interaction with matter–Energy (§ 2:114). EMR energy for instance is a product of *enérgeia* flux across an archí photon at actual lightspeed ç (§ 5:151). It's an energy-to-force relationship where the energy of speed as a product of *enérgeia* flux translates, ultimately, to EMR magnitude (force) such that, as a simple scalar

$$E = Fd \rightarrow F = \frac{E}{d} \rightarrow F = \frac{\Upsilon}{E_s} \begin{cases} \Upsilon = \frac{\alpha\Omega}{E_s} \\ E_s = \Phi_{\alpha\Omega}d \end{cases}$$

$$\rightarrow \mathrm{m_{EMR}} = \frac{\Upsilon_{EMF}}{E_s}$$

(17.79)

where E is energy, F is force, d is distance (length), Υ is real energy, $\alpha\Omega$ is *enérgeia* as a constant, E_s is energy of speed, $\Phi_{\alpha\Omega}$ is *enérgeia* flux, $\mathrm{m_{EMR}}$ is EMR magnitude, and Υ_{EMF} is real energy as EMF. In normal space, inter-archí space thus E_s is nominal and induces Fundamental Force as what we observe in nature.

We see, however, the final expression in the above equation presents an inverse relationship between EMR magnitude $\mathrm{m_{EMR}}$ and energy of speed E_s. Greater *enérgeia* velocity produces greater flux, thus a greater E_s leading to less pronounced real energy Υ and, consequently, less pronounced Fundamental Force. It's useful to think of *enérgeia* flux in a G-star as a venturi effect because, similar to how a fluid transiting from a larger to a smaller flow-through increases velocity (energy) but decreases static pressure (force) as an inverse relationship (*Fig. 66*, left), *enérgeia* transiting narrowed inter-archí space typical of a G-star also strengthens in *enérgeia* flux but lessens in real energy Υ, thus Fundamental Force effect.

The greater 'energy' translates to lesser force. Therefore, the greater *enérgeia* flux, the lesser Fundamental Force (*Fig. 66*, right). Whereas an ideal fluid's density is constant, meaning incompressible, a similar state for

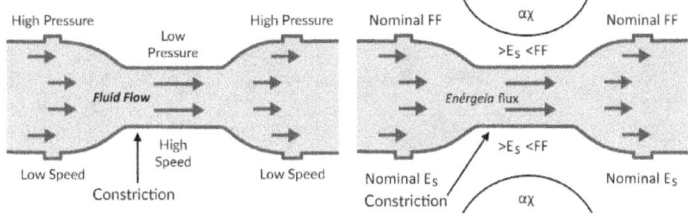

Figure 66. Left, Venturi effect; right, pertaining to *enérgeia* flux through narrowed inter-archí space.[207]

Energent proto-energy is only analogous to density in that it's of a constant state whether flowing through normal space or a G-star's super-constricted inter-archí spaces. However, if we model Bernoulli's equation (which describes the Venturi effect) after ET data, where

$$\frac{E_s}{4} + \Psi + \frac{F^F}{\alpha\Omega} = |\Theta_{\varepsilon\mu}\rangle, \tag{17.80}$$

then we comprehend the G-star environment as we comprehend the Venturi effect's environment. The divisor 4 accounts for *enérgeia* multidirectional[205] speed differentials in the linear distance d (from $E_s = \Phi_{\alpha\Omega}d$ in Eq. (17.79)) from exit to entrance of any two inter-archí spaces; Ψ is the force potential at a point, in this case the inter-archí space at a point x, y; F^F is Fundamental Force; and $|\Theta_{\varepsilon\mu}\rangle$ is the Energent system state in the G-star context as a dimensionless constant. The Venturi effect isn't a perfect analogy, but illustrates the principle.

With Fundamental Force less pronounced in a G-star, the resulting applied energy E force is also less pronounced. It's true that mass in a unit of volume shows more surface gravity than the same mass in a greater unit of volume. But gravity from greater mass per unit of volume sufficient to crush matter to gargantuan densities leading to zero or near-zero volume is an effect mistaken for the cause. Its principal cause is the relative weakness of Fundamental Force, as cited. Although less pronounced, EMF does induce less pronounced gravity overall than does EMF in normal space—giving the impression gravity should be less powerful in a G-star than normal space—the concomitantly less pronounced Fundamental Force makes it possible for inter-archí space to narrow more than is possible in normal space. This gives gravity an *apparent* stronger effect on G-star matter per unit of volume, contracting it to greater density per unit of volume than possible in normal space (Table 3).

Table 3. Idealized. While gravitationally relevant factors can be the same, apparent gravity force differs between objects. F_g and P_g is force of, and pull of, gravity.

Normal Space	Gravitational Factors	G-star space
1	Volume	1
1	Multilocal object F_g	1
1	Multilocal object P_g	1
1	F_g	100
1	radius r	1
1	Fundamental Force	.001

Any matter, such as from an accretion disk, crossing the G-star's less pronounced Fundamental Force boundary—its event horizon, approximately 63 km on average from gravitational surface—encounters the same less pronounced Fundamental Force throughout its entirety, thus experiencing a force of gravity apparently greater than it would at an object's surface with equal volume but less density (*Fig. 67*).

However, *enérgeia* flux means there's a limit to how narrow inter-archí space can get regardless how less pronounced Fundamental Force or how apparently stronger the force of gravity is along an ever-shortening core radius from gravitational center to its surface. This means force of repulsion F_R strengthens relative to force of gravity F_g until they balance out in a unit of volume vastly smaller than possible in normal space. Thus, a G-star reaches maximum density and minimum volume when $F_R = F_g$ such that

---

205. While *enérgeia* has multidirectional *'flow,'* Energent proto-energy has omnidirectional *'motion'* (§ 1:112). The Energent 'undulates' omnidirectionally, like a lake with many agitation vectors. Recall that Energent proto-energy and *enérgeia* are different. *Enérgeia* is 'energy' that forms out of proto-energy in response to motion of matter, and then that 'energy' (*enérgeia*) fluxes across matter to raise real energy Υ, and so forth. Analogically, *enérgeia* 'flows' through inter-archí spaces unidirectionally but, between them, it's multidirectional. *Enérgeia* arises 'on the fly' responsorially with matter's motion through the 'moving' Energent. Nowhere in the universe is there insufficient matter to create *enérgeia*.

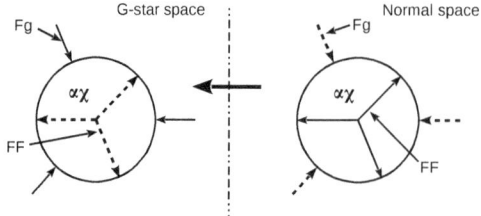

G-star space　　　　　　　Normal space

Figure 67. Matter crossing from normal to G-star space where it experiences greater apparent gravity (solid arrows) from less pronounced FF (dotted arrows).

$$\forall \Delta \rho : \left\{ \rho \mid \rho > 0 \bigwedge F_R = F_g \right\} \Rightarrow \rho_{max} \bigwedge \rho_{max} \to V_{min} \tag{17.81}$$

where any change in density $\forall \Delta \rho$ such that, if the change is greater than zero and force of gravity equals force of repulsion, then density ρ_{max} is at maximum. Accordingly, volume V_{min} is at minimum, so we end up with a ball of matter of minimal volume that's maximally dense producing lesser gravity but greater repulsion than the classical gravity force equation predicts. Although the Planck force F_P represents a real, maximum possible force (Wikipedia *Planck force* 2018), it's not wholly relevant to maximum gravity, which is to say, it's not exactly "the force that confines a self-gravitating mass to half its Schwarzschild radius."[208] It's an applied energy E—specifically, a kinetic—force anyway. Therefore, it can't affect real energy Υ (the source of gravity) because Planck force itself is an *expression* of real energy Υ. Consequently, Planck force isn't the reason gravitational force maxes out; it's just a mathematical perspective.

As the core collapses it alters Fundamental Force, allowing continued core collapse, further altering Fundamental Force, in a cycle terminating at maximum density and minimum volume. Accordingly, Fundamental Force in a G-star context manifests differently than anywhere else in our universe. Real energy Υ in this context is ∼43% nominal. EMR radiating from this space naturally follows suit.

6.9.3.4　G-STAR SUPERLONGWAVE EMR

G-stars emit EMR energy even though they look like EMR voids—black holes—in space. The reason for such a seeming paradox is not that the force of gravity from infinite density in zero or near-zero volume creates an escape velocity greater than lightspeed c, but that G-star space experiences less pronounced Fundamental Force for the reasons described such that, when archí release from binding as real energy Υ-'charged' photons, they do so with less real energy Υ than they do in normal space (§ 2.3.2:116). This correlates to a smaller magnitude electric charge generated around the photon by its motion through space, thus less energy (§ 5.1:152). Since an EMW propagates according to its EMR energy—EMW magnitude correlates to EMR energy—then less EMR energy means less energetic, thus smaller magnitude, EMW propagation though space. On average, this translates to an amplitude about 95% nominal, a super low frequency of about 2.997–0.697 Hz, and a superlongwave—or, as Mina prefers to call it, a *summa extensio* (or, *sumex*)[206]—of about 100,000–430,000 km.[207] The differential between nominal and *sumex* EMR wavelength is proportional. Short wavelength gamma radiation emits at the shorter end of the *sumex* range and longwave radio at its longer end (*Fig. 68*). *Sumex* EMR is presently undetectable, so we observe an apparent EMR void in space only by its gravitational effect on proximal objects, as well as its accretion disk if it's large enough to detect from Earth.

We were astonished and perhaps you are, too, that, while Mina foresaw all the phenomena we've described here, he never peered deep enough into the mechanics to predict the EMR-void state we call black holes. Not until about 1BY after creation did he notice its first occurrence in space. That might seem absurd but, unlike the magical finger-snapping creator gods of humanity's various theisms, he *Intentioned* our universe. He had no need to consciously blueprint it down to the nitty gritty like a physicist or an engineer because those details unfold naturally through Intentionality (§ 3.2:282; CH. 30:515).

---

206. Latin: *total extension.* Mina prefers it to *superlongwave* as 100,000-430,000 km is roughly the naturally possible maximum EMR wavelength range.

207. We don't detect *sumex* because it needs an impractically large antenna. According to Mina, however, a global very long baseline radio interferometry phased array—along the lines of the Event Horizon Telescope used to image the M87* black hole (Fig. 61:178, center, left)—comprised of at least nine radio telescope pairs with about 2,900 km between any two sites, and each site about 9 km in diameter (say, a local phased array), would detect them.

ELECTROMAGNETIC SPECTRUM

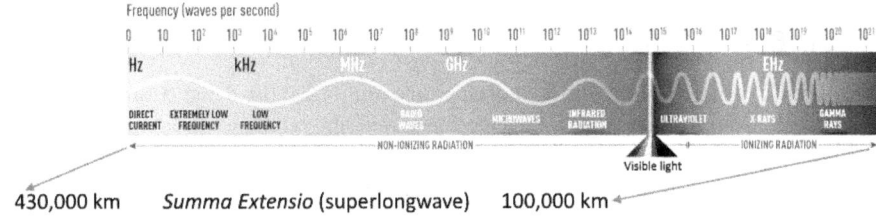

430,000 km   *Summa Extensio* (superlongwave)   100,000 km

Figure 68. Normal EMR spectrum shift to *sumex* radio spectrum.[209]

6.9.3.4.1 G-STAR TEMPERATURE

As there's no spacetime curvature owing to there being no such thing as spacetime (§ 3.7.3.2:138), as well as no gravitational event horizons and the like, we can see that mathematical presumptions like black hole temperature being inversely proportional to its mass are inaccurate. Applied to G-stars, equations such as

$$T = \frac{\hbar c^3}{8\pi G M K b} \tag{17.82}$$

where T is the body's temperature, $\hbar$ is the reduced Planck constant, G is the gravitational constant, M is the object's mass, and Kb is the Boltzmann constant, don't accurately describe the temperature environment because the *sumex* radio emissions go undetected.

6.9.3.4.2 G-STAR ACCRETION DISK

Matter *accretes* when it falls onto an object under gravity. Such material tends to circumgyrate a G-star in a flattened, planar shape called the *accretion disk* that lies in normal space (*Fig. 69*). Energy releases from matter as it falls onto the G-star. The standard view allows this is the most efficient energy-emission-from-matter process in the universe, emitting up to 40% of its rest mass energy. Mina confirms this aspect of the standard view. Indeed, most of our research regarding black hole accretion disks met with his agreement. However, since there's no event horizon with a gravitational escape velocity greater than lightspeed c, there's no real disappearance of matter or EMR when it crosses the Fundamental Force (event horizon) boundary from the accretion disk. Rather, the material accretes to the G-star in accord with its extremely strong (not light-sucking) gravity, but its energy now emits subject to the less pronounced Fundamental Force as *sumex* EMR, which we don't detect.

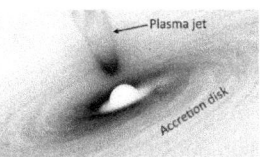

Figure 69. NASA/JPL-Caltech concept of supermassive black hole accretion disk and vertical plasma jet.[210]

ET data negates the complex mathematical and geometric gyrations that science postulates to explain the theoretical movement of EMR such as visible light around a black hole. The remnant star masses called black holes work pretty much the way it describes, except there's no infinite gravity trapping light and no zero or near-zero volume having infinite density.

6.9.3.4.3 WHITE DWARFS

A white dwarf is a remnant main-sequence star of $\sim 5 M_\odot$ comprising a dense sphere as described that slowly cools by thermal radiation,[208] eventually becoming a black dwarf which do exist. Naturally, they're difficult to detect as they emit very little EMR. As with G-stars, we can find them by observing their gravitational influence on proximate bodies. Astronomers using MDM Observatory's 2.4-meter telescope on Kitt Peak near Tucson,

---

208. The standard view finds them conventionally less than 9-10$M_\odot$ and a dense sphere of electron-degenerate matter (which, unlike neutron degeneracy, isn't a real phenomenon).

Arizona, USA in 2012 found various white dwarfs cooled below 3900 K. Their estimated age is 11–12BYO, though Mina ranges it between 2–8BYO. On average, a black dwarf takes about 5BY to cool to blackness.

6.10   THE BIG BANG

Our universe did not spring into ready-made existence in a primordial Big Bang. Although science gets some details about creation essentially correct, the creation it describes confuses discrete aspects and processes of reality. Mina reports our infinite universe (IU) has a definable beginning about 13,795,785,505 years ago (YA) from 2020. The observable universe (OU), on the other hand, came into measurable existence about 13,110,599,155YA when the first star began to burn. The OU is currently about 92.25192BLY in diameter and is permanently expanding from matter accretion, on average, about one percent every 100 million years. By the time the IU doubles in age, the OU will have more than tripled to about 3-1/2 times its present size (Table 4:188). As well, it expands and contracts an average of about 10% across large scale time cycles—presently about 670BY, but that lengthens as the OU accretes—with the ebb and flow of attractive and repulsive gravitational and centrifugal and centripetal forces within and without the OU (§ 3:119). There is no correlation between its size in light-years and the IU's age in years because there's no spacetime-expanding Big Bang that birthed it.

Cosmologists consider galaxy GN–Z11 the oldest and most distant known galaxy, but it's really about 11.798250BLY in present proper distance (PPD) from Earth, not the ~32BLY in expanding spacetime distance or the ~13.4BLY in actual light travel distance that's estimated using stellar redshift (§ 5.6:161; *Fig. 70*, right). PPD and distance calculated by lightyear is the same, not different as implied by Relativity's theory of expanding spacetime. Redshift is of no use for large distance calculations because space is such a mishmash of EMW and photons (§ 5.6.2:162), plus it's not a function of wavelength lengthening from spacetime expansion anyway. Even so, using GN–Z11's ET-corrected distance and angular size of about 0.034965 seconds, Mina correlates its current $z = 11.09$ redshift to $z = 6.32$, and linear size to about 1999.982LY. Brightness–luminosity is overall a better practical, if anecdotal, guide for measuring cosmic distances.

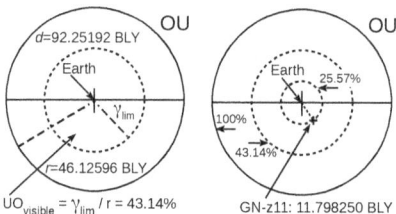

Figure 70. Left, size of observable universe (OU) and the maximum portion visible to us where $\gamma_{lim} = 19.9$BLY (§ 6.10.3:189); right, GN-Z11 relative to Earth and the OU (not to scale or geometry).

6.10.1   PROCESS AND STRUCTURE OF CREATION

This is all a bit more fathomable when we understand the basic process and structure of creation. Consider the following brief overview. Mina kicked off our IU by Intentioning[209] its *frequency space*[210] as a 'dimension' of All Existence. At the instant his intention was ready to be real, then it was via Intentionality and the IU existed. This isn't divine celestial magic. It's literally the capability of the human consciousness (FN 209). Any sufficiently educated and trained human can Intentionalize a universe. You, too, as a spirit person if you make the tremendous effort Mina did. At the same time, he established within that 'dimensional space' the Energent and essentially—to use Big Bang lingo—cooked it up to an infinitesimally small, infinitely 'hot,' and infinitely 'dense' single point—not really infinite, of course, but you get the idea—by fomenting, or, Intentionalizing,[211] a real energy Υ 'gravity well' (*Fig. 72*:188).

While the Energent was dynamic at this point, it had nothing with which to react in or out of itself. Practically speaking, it was in a state of quiescence. The homologous 'gravity well' pulled *enérgeia* into a tiny, non-expandable space like an archí (*Fig. 71*, right), but with what we can visualize as a semi-permeable, one-way-membrane and no off switch. One might think that would lead to a proverbial big bang, as with

---

209. Forming something's reality in one's mind, then extending it as an independent reality in the world (§ 3.2:282; CH. 30:515).

210. Defines the 'dimensional space' of which 'energy' manifests a unique signature.

211. Meaning, Mina's consciousness acted as an outside 'force' on the Energent.

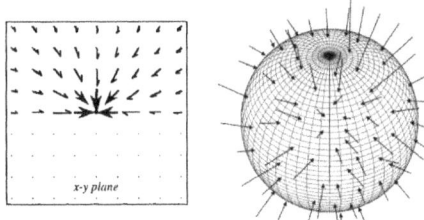

Figure 71. Left, typical 2-D slice of a gravity field; *z-axis* represents energy, not spatial dimension; right, gravity wells are spherical with force vectors (arrows) representing converging 'energy' movement.[211]

any energy expanding in a space, but this is real energy Υ, not matter-derived applied energy E. The outcome was more analogous to a magnifying glass concentrating the broad heat spectrum of sunlight into a superhot pinprick sufficient to jumpstart, say, a leaf, from its rest state to a sustained combustive reaction. With the Energent, the point was to jumpstart archí creation (§ 2.3.1:115) along with a pair of self-sustaining 'gravity wells.' When *enérgeia* in this initial 'gravity well' reached its peak of real energy Υ 'charge,' 'density,' 'heat,' and the like, it 'combusted.' The effect exceeded its pull, so the combustion raced instantaneously outward—within the Energent the absence of event periodicity hence travel means instantaneity (§ 6.11.4:198)—setting 'fire' to the Energent like a wildfire to a sun-baked prairie from which archí, like 'smoke,' madly bloomed with elemental particles forming in its wake. This eventually led to an applied energy E saturation forming what science now calls cosmic background radiation (CBR).

This catalyzing 'burn' was instantaneous throughout the IU. Archí 'boiled' like 'smoke' out of the 'raging' Energent and into material existence all at once across the IU until the process reached its peak. It then slowed to self-sustaining regularity—not a perpetual motion machine, but close enough—and, over time, the CBR formed and cooled. As archí emerged from the Energent, its 'currents' ('energy' meridians) resulting from the real energy Υ 'gravity well'—which initially 'condensed' the Energent into what amounts to a one-shot pilot light—settled into a pattern that carried *enérgeia*, along with bonded-archí drawn by an applied energy E gravity well that formed out of the 'combustion' (Table 4), from the IU toward the pinprick we now call the OU. Sufficient matter existed within the concentrated OU region for significant aggregation of subatomic clumps to begin in scattered groupings all around it and not just at its center where the gravity well originated.

As matter clumped and complexified, the homologous real energy Υ and actual applied energy E gravity wells at OU center naturally encompassed all of the developing OU in a fashion similar to a galaxy or cluster's composite magnetic field. The real energy Υ gravity well extended outward from its point of origination, growing as the OU materially grew. The applied energy E gravity well, however, didn't extend from OU center outward but rather composited itself from the many developing applied energy E gravity fields throughout the developing OU region. Thus, the OU didn't become an all-consuming well like the storied black hole. Typically, inbound archí only pair rather than scale up to composite matter because, outside the OU, it's rare for archí to meet.[212] At this point, Mina stepped back to let our universe operate on its own terms—it's way of being (WOB)—according to his initiating Intentionality, i.e., his 'operations plan.'[213] We describe in § 2.1:340 why he created our universe in the first place.

6.10.1.1 Why the Night Sky is Dark

We can now understand the night sky is dark instead of bright for two reasons. First, about 56.86% of the OU remains invisible to us because the light in that portion is still in transit. Hence, that portion of the OU is dark to us at present (§ 6.10.3:189). Second, even if we could see the entire OU, it has finite stars and light whereas lightless—no-EMR—hyposubatomic particles populate the vastly more dominant infinite universe that surrounds it. The OU's finite light isn't greater than the infinite lightlessness beyond it; like a sailor marooned on a one-crab sandbar in a vast sea, we live in a lighted mote in a vast gob of dark. In his largely forgotten *Eureka: A Prose Poem* (1848), Edgar Allen Poe presciently notes that,

---

212. About 99.9% of all IU archí dephase for lack of a near-enough pairing partner; this low-yield process regulates matter creation.

213. Some universe maintenance is required, else (reversible) chaotic, entropic behaviors form over trillion-year timescales. 'Archangel' Michael assumed supervisory responsibility from his parents who handled it originally. Mina handles high-level maintenance; with the Big Healing, Michael took on more (§ 2:522). It seems surprising spirit persons need care for our universal home but differs not from our caring for Earth.

Table 4. Size development of the observable universe (OU).

Age (BY)	~% of todays' OU
1	37%
2	50%
3	53%
10	87.85%
12	97%
13	99.6%
14	104.5%
27.6	350%

Growth rate looks haphazard because archí flow into the OU in waves of irregular amounts.

> Were the succession of stars endless, then the background of the sky would present us an [sic] uniform luminosity, like that displayed by the Galaxy—*since there could be absolutely no point, in all that background, at which would not exist a star.* The only mode, therefore, in which, under such a state of affairs, we could comprehend the *voids* which our telescopes find in innumerable directions, would be by supposing the distance of the invisible background so immense that no ray from it has yet been able to reach us at all. (Poe 1902, 273–74, io)

Concordant with science, Poe fails to consider an infinite universe needn't be one of infinite stars, planets, and light. Yet, if our eyes could register the full EM spectrum, space would seem infinitely 'bright.'

6.10.1.2 'GRAVITY WELLS'

Why, then, is the universe infinite if all there is of it that's habitable is the OU? Besides All Existence itself being infinite, the OU as an eternal construct requires infinite expandability thus an infinite reservoir of archí and *enérgeia* that perpetually flow into the OU like food to an organism (§ 7:211). These migrate inward from infinity (*Fig. 72*) in response to the OU 'gravity wells.' For archí, we describe this in simple terms as the external gravitational potential Φ of a spherically symmetric body such that

$$\Phi(\vec{x}) = -\frac{\vec{\mathcal{G}}\, mE}{|x|} \tag{17.83}$$

where $\vec{x}$ is a vector of length x pointing from the point mass—OU center, Eq. (17.84)—toward inbound archí, $\vec{\mathcal{G}}$ is the gravitational vector constant (Eq. 17.28:131), mE is matter–Energy (Eq. (17.8):117), and $|x|$ is the scalar value of the 'gravity well.' We idealize the gravitational potential to a point mass because the OU's spherically symmetric mass distribution effectively acts as a point mass. Hence,

$$V(r) = \frac{1}{2}\pi\vec{\mathcal{G}}\rho\left(r^2 - 3R^2\right), r \leq R \tag{17.84}$$

where V is gravitational potential, r is distance from the center of point mass (gravitational potential), R is radius, ρ is density of the uniform spherical body (the OU), and $\vec{\mathcal{G}}$ as defined in § 3.4:130.

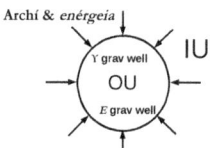

Figure 72. Real energy Υ and applied energy E 'gravity wells' draw *enérgeia* and archí into OU (Eq. (17.84)).

The Energent's 'combustion' created a real energy Υ and an applied energy E gravity well a shadow of what they are today, but sufficient nonetheless to pull in *enérgeia* and archí, respectively. The Energent 'current' is not a product of archí moving, nor is archí movement a product of the Energent 'current.' The applied energy E gravity well—a composite gravity field for the entire OU—pulls archí. On the other hand, the real energy Υ 'gravity well,' an extant central presence exactly 7,649.12 km in "semi-permeable-membrane" diameter at OU center, pulls *enérgeia*. The current and pull for both is sedate and measured. Neither Fundamental Force nor applied energy E was a thing (in *our* universe) until the moment 'combustion' produced archí and the Energent reacted to it as Fundamental Force.

It might seem valid to conclude the universe must be finite if the catalyzing process described above actually completed. Though valid on its face, it's not true because infinity isn't space, volume, distance, time, et cetera (CH. 14:93; CH. 15:99; CH. 16:105). Properly describing infinity in the context of our natural (physical) universe is the purpose of this chapter, and each section clarifies some aspect of reality so we can comprehend the phenomenon of space w.r.t. infinity. That something infinite, which began in an incomplete state, can acquire a state of completion gets to the crux of the problem with our concept of infinity. Cantor solved this conundrum for mathematics with infinite set theory, but those are mind games inapplicable to reality where the enigma endures. We discuss it fully in § 8:223.

Of course, we've been speaking of the natural universe. But recall there's a supranatural environment, too, with its own Energent, matter, and human ℒife (§ 1.2:246). The supranatural Energent didn't turn 'on' for quite some time after the initial 'combustion' in the natural universe because it depends on the latter's for its proto-energy, which translates across the natural–supranatural boundary, in part, via archí (§ 7:211). As that mechanism took some time to spool up and begin transferring 'energy,' the supranatural Energent's startup naturally lagged. Instead of a universal Big Bang with instantaneous cosmic inflation and matter formation, we had the creation of the IU followed by a catalyzing event we call the Big Combustion, with matter accretion over time in a discrete venue termed the OU within the encompassing IU; a two-step—three, figuring in the supranatural—macro process of creation.

6.10.2 LOCATION OF EARTH (SOL)

Part of cosmology's mandate is to understand both our literal and metaphysical place in the universe (PART III–IV). Our ET data via Mina indicates that it's within greater All Existence as well as in our universe wherein we physically and spiritually reside. While Mina considers the OU to lie at the center of the IU, he concedes that's only a mental convenience signifying nothing, as there is no 'center' to infinity. Here, we deal only with Earth's literal place in the OU.

The easiest way to convey where we are in the OU is with a sphere cutaway. While the OU isn't exactly spherical, it is, like Earth, spherical enough to warrant the analogy (*Fig. 73*, left).[214] If we divide it into zones similar to Earth's inner and outer core, mantle, and crust, and for the convenience of visualization align its *y-axis* with Earth's north–south—the IU exhibits no up, down, left, right, north, south, so it makes no sense orienting on those terms—then Earth is roughly located in the 'outer core' zone (*Fig. 73*, left).

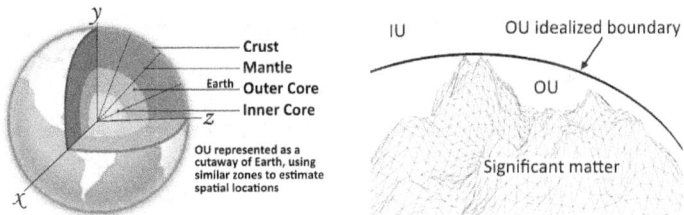

Figure 73. Left, Earth's position generalized to the OU 'outer core' zone; right, idealized OU–IU boundary.[212]

Earth is located in the *y*, *z* spatial plane, which in *Fig. 74* (left) is a vertical slice of space about 6.5MLY wide on a line about 46.6775° from the OU center relative to the spatial plane of the *y-*, *z- axis*. Earth is about 15,859,863,994LY from OU center. From Earth's location in *Fig. 73*, we see there's still about 65.61% of the OU, or 30,266,096,006LY, between its idealized OU–IU boundary and Earth.

GN–ZII is located ~19.664BLY from OU center, ~15.57BLY from MIOI ('pinwheel galaxy,' lying directly behind GN–ZII near the *z-axis* on the far side of the *x-axis* in roughly the same horizontal plane as GN–ZII) in the constellation Ursa Major, and 26.46196BLY from the OU boundary (*Fig. 75*, left).

6.10.3 HOW FAR WE CAN SEE

We've already seen how space is a mishmash of photons and EMW which, at great distance, creates a wrong impression of where stars actually reside, and that spacetime and its expansion isn't real. Recall a lightyear is the distance light travels at lightspeed *c* via EMW in one Earth year. Without the faulty expanding-spacetime

---

214. Significant matter doesn't uniformly extend to the OU's literal imaginary spherical boundary. Topographically mapping its surface would show a plethora of valleys and peaks indicating matter's actual location relative to the boundary (*Fig. 73*, right).

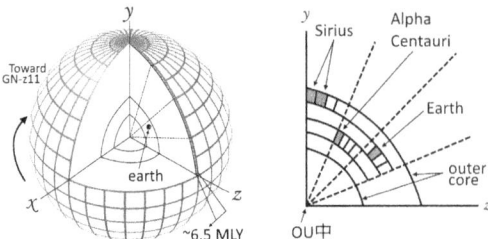

Figure 74. Left, Earth in the y, z spatial plane. The narrow dark band along the curved y, z hypotenuse is the 6.5MLY-wide vertical slice of interest. Right, close up 2-D view of y, z spatial plane showing Earth in approximate relative orientation at regional positions with Alpha Centauri actual and Sirius actual (dark segment) and perceived (light segment).[213]

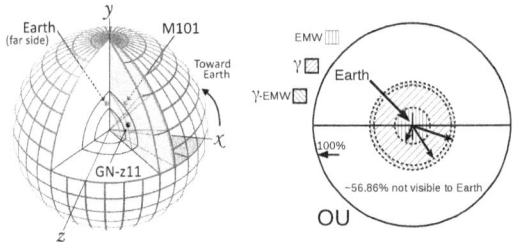

Figure 75. Left, actual location of galaxy GN–ZII on the y, x spatial plane diagonal to Earth on the far side (source: Fig. 74:190); right, the visible OU boundaries crosshatched, with radial arrows: EMW ∼28.42%, photon γ ∼39%, photon γ–EMW ∼43.14%.

concept, OU age in Earth years correlates to EMW travel distance, meaning light that's traveled about 13.11BLY emitted coincident with the OU's first starshine circa 13.11BYA in a region within 13.11BLY of Earth. We call this 13.11BLY distance–travel time the *EMW perimeter*. Photons traveling at lightspeed ς cover more distance, marking the *photon perimeter* at about 17.993BLY (*Fig. 75*, right). Considering how worthless stellar redshift is for estimating distance as well as pinning its greater ranges on expanding spacetime, science did a yeoman's job using mathematics alone to estimate OU diameter at ∼93BLY, within 0.8% of our ET data from Mina.

The farthest photonic light (or any EM energy) that's had time to reach Earth comes from about

$$V_r = \text{OU}_{age} + \left(\text{OU}_{age} \left(1 - \frac{c}{\varsigma} \right) \right) = 17,993,496,210.74062\text{LY} \tag{17.85}$$

away, where V_r is the visible radius of the photon perimeter. Thus, the portion of the OU directly visible to Earth forms a sphere of diameter roughly $2r = 35,986,992,452.86288\text{LY}$. But light spreads via EMW, too (§ 5:151), and we indirectly see photonic light from a source ∼1.907BLY further from Earth than V_r via EMW propagating along a photon's direction of travel from or within a maximum radius from Earth of

$$d_{lim} = t_\gamma^T \varsigma + t_{EMW}^T c, \quad d_{lim} \le \gamma_{lim}^{EMW} \tag{17.86}$$

where $t_\gamma^T \varsigma$ is photon time of travel in light-years at actual lightspeed ς, $t_{EMW}^T c$ is EMW time of travel in lightyears at lightspeed c, and $d_{lim} \le$ ∼6.9BLY, because the maximum distance from which photonic light has had time to reach Earth via EMW since (per Mina) the OU's first starshine is approximately the *photon–EMW perimeter* $\gamma_{lim}^{EMW} = 19.9\text{BLY}$ (*Fig. 76*). Accordingly,

$$\gamma_{lim}^{EMW} - \text{OU}_{age} = d_{lim} = \sim 6.79\text{BLY} \tag{17.87}$$

where the terms are as defined. Consequently, the limit to our view of the OU is a sphere roughly of diameter $2 \left(\gamma_{lim}^{EMW} \right) = 39.8\text{BLY}$. This is true for any point of view anywhere in the OU due to lightspeed (*Fig. 76*, right).

About 78.1% of all the EMR (including sunlight) that Earth receives comes from within the 13.11BLY EMW perimeter, 14.9% from beyond the EMW perimeter out to the photon perimeter, and 7% from beyond the photon perimeter out to the photon EMW perimeter. Of that 7% EMR, about 8.7% of it is photonic (direct line of sight to Earth) and the remainder is EMW (indirect to Earth, as described). Presently, Earth receives zero percent of its EMR from beyond the photon–EMW perimeter although, as time passes, that perimeter expands as light currently in transit reaches us (*Fig. 76*, center). Naturally, we can't see the entire OU from Earth. If

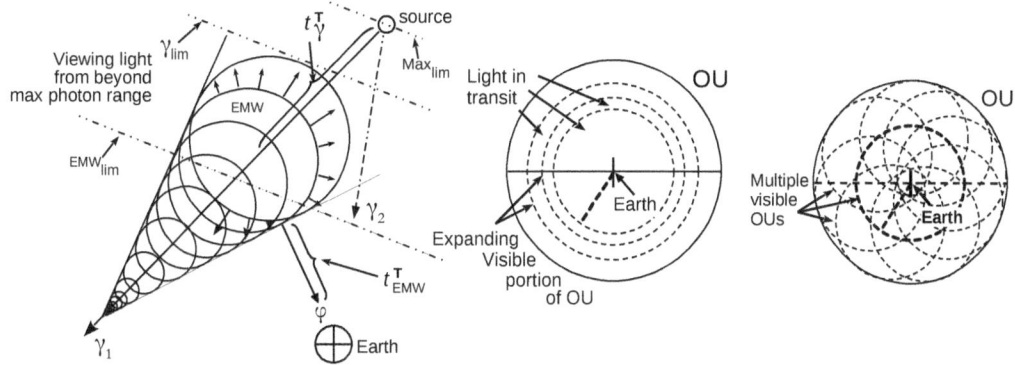

Figure 76. Schematic: left, light falls to Earth from a source beyond the photon–EMW limit when photons cover a sufficient distance that its EMW reaches Earth over time $t \leq \text{OU}_{age}$; center, expanding perimeter of maximum light travel to Earth; right (2-D), multiple visible portions of OU (Earth not at actual OU center).

one travels around the OU, their perspective changes as to what's visible to them. One sees a different visible portion of the OU wherever one travels, and each visible portion overlaps others (*Fig. 76*, right). There are no multiple observable universes but only multiple visible portions of the singular OU for anyone anywhere in the IU because the OU is unique, finite in size, and light travels only a finite distance in a finite time.

Mina tells us there are ~77.4 million human-populated planets within the ~43.14% portion of the OU visible to us (Fig. 70:186, left). No two lay within less than ~7.885BLY of each other. Although (with average differences) sapient life is recognizably human, Mina has two principal aims for these buffer zones. First, it provides uninhabited space for a planet's unhindered development on its own terms (freedom). Second, it avoids potential inter-race conflict, as that's no less likely in space than on a planet.[215] Nevertheless, all people in our universe, as well as the occasional visitors from others, freely mix in the supranatural environment (§ 2.2:564; CH. 28:465).

6.11 Quantum Entanglement

This phenomenon is broader than simple correlation of object states. Entanglement operates at both the hyposubatomic (quantum) and atomic (classical), from archí to humans and beyond. Recognizing this helps clarify—and there's more work to be done in this regard than possible in this book—how quantum and classical science are one and the same w.r.t. reality, and that there's no Heisenberg cut[216] differentiating the hyposubatomic from the atomic. Quantum science isn't weird, counterintuitive, or restricted to the subatomic any more than classical science is sensible, intuitive, or valid only at the atomic. Not only is the probabilistic indeterminance of quantum physics incorrect as a fundament of reality, but so, too, is the determinism of classical physics as a fundament of causality. Quantum principles don't break down in the macroscopic or vice versa. Quantum objects intrinsically possess independent existence separate and apart from their probabilistic behavior and measured states. All is objectively real.

For example, the unpredictable random orbit of an electron in the context of an atomic population's probabilistic behavior is as predictable and objectively real as is unpredictable individual human behavior in the context of a population's probabilistic behavior. While we can know an individual's exact state at any given moment, their thoughts, feelings, and actions are intrinsically unknowable because these are emergent properties only probabilistically knowable; if we ask about their state—make an observation—then it consequently changes. Accordingly, an individual who's a functional part of a crowd can be, at the same time, functionally apart until an emergent state renders him or her at time t 'crowd' or 'not crowd,' which we simplify to,

$$\frac{|individual\rangle_{realstate}}{|crowd\rangle_{realstate}} (|t\rangle) \rightarrow \frac{|individual\rangle_{crowd}}{|individual\rangle_{notcrowd}} (|t\rangle)$$
$$\rightarrow |individual\rangle_{probablestate} (|t\rangle) \tag{17.88}$$

where each ket $(|x\rangle)$[217] represents a quantum system's state. Similarly, while there are more states to an electron

---

215. Mina certainly Intentioned what we might call a utopia, which includes absolute freedom, so anything's possible—and happens—including self-annihilating war (Original Humanity Self-Destructs, § 1.3:538).

216. Hypothetical interface separating quantum events from observers (measurements).

217. A ket is a vector. It's bra ($\langle x|$) is its Hermitian conjugate. Also called Dirac notation after Paul Dirac (d. 1984).

than is presently known, they too are intrinsically unknowable because they're weakly emergent properties arising in Energent 'undulations' (Eq. (17.95):195). This is why we can't predict an electron's specific location in its orbital at time t but only its statistically probable location, which we simplify to

$$\frac{|electron\rangle_{realstate}}{|atomic\rangle_{realstate}}(|t\rangle) \rightarrow \frac{|electron\rangle_{cloud}}{|electron\rangle_{notcloud}}(|t\rangle)$$
$$\rightarrow |electron\rangle_{probablestate}(|t\rangle). \tag{17.89}$$

Although emergence and quantum indeterminance might seem functionally identical regarding outcome, the former arises unpredictably from the constituent object state (including context state) that forms a confluence resulting in emergence, while the latter is pure randomness unrelated to known object states.[214]

Entanglement refers to quantum objects, which (local) quantum states[218] (denoted $|\Psi\rangle$) are describable only in reference to other (non-local) objects where states like spin, position, momentum, and so on correlate across many random measurements more than mere chance would account for in a universe of local realism.[219] If an object A randomly measures a spin up, then its entangled partner B down the street, on another continent, or at the edge of the observable universe measures an instant, mirrored spin down (Fig. 80:198) with a statistical certainty that seems inexplicable without the semi-explanatory power of quantum math. So, what's happening?

6.11.1 QUANTUM SUPERPOSITION

Entanglement invokes a phenomenon called quantum superposition, which in quantum science means that objects simultaneously embody all possible states (*Fig. 77*, left; Fig. 80:198). Known as the quantum wavefunction (denoted Ψ), it expresses a complex-valued probability amplitude and the probabilities for all possible outcomes (*Fig. 77*, right).[220] For two particles with spin $1/2$ (singlet state[221]), the spin state probability of system Ψ as the superposition of all possible states is

$$|\Psi\rangle = \frac{1}{\sqrt{2}}(|\uparrow\downarrow\rangle + |\downarrow\uparrow\rangle). \tag{17.90}$$

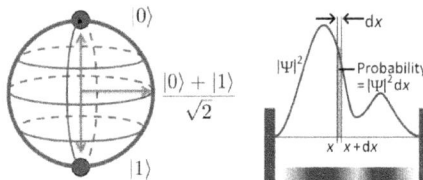

Figure 77. Left, quantum superposition represented as a quantum bit (qubit) used in quantum information processing applications. Right, quantum wavefunction where the probability of finding a particle in the region dx located at $x \mid x \propto |\Psi|^2\, dx$.[215]

6.11.1.1 SCHRÖDINGER'S CAT

In 1935, Austrian physicist Erwin Schrödinger (d. 1961) criticized quantum superposition by positing a cat sealed in a box with poison and a radioactive isotope that randomly may or may not decay in a certain time (*Fig. 78*, left). If it does then a detector releases the poison and kills the cat, if it doesn't the cat remains alive. The cat, the box, the certain time, and all the rest constitute a *quantum system*.[222] His critique is that until one looks in the box—makes an observation—the cat's aliveness and deadness must logically be in superposition, literally in both states at once. The system wavefunction forms an inseparable total possibility structure of

---

218. A quantum state is a vector containing all the measurable data about a system.

219. *Principle of locality*: an object is influenced directly only by its immediate environment.

220. Quantum science views reality as random and probabilistic, rejecting the determinism of classical (Newtonian) science that explains subatomic oddities as a lack of knowledge.

221. A system where electrons are paired with a net zero spin.

222. A portion of a quantum environment taken in isolation to analyze.

$$\frac{1}{\sqrt{2}} \, |undecayed\rangle_{atom} \, |no \text{ "click"}\rangle_{Geiger} \, |notfallen\rangle_{hammer} \, |intact\rangle_{vial} \, |alive\rangle_{cat}$$
$$+ \frac{1}{\sqrt{2}} \, |decayed\rangle_{atom} \, |\text{"click"}\rangle_{Geiger} \, |fallen\rangle_{hammer} \, |broken\rangle_{vial} \, |dead\rangle_{cat} \tag{17.91}$$

where the value $|\frac{1}{\sqrt{2}}|^2 = 0.5$, a 50% probability (denoted $\mathfrak{P}$) that one possible state becomes the actual, real state upon measurement (Eq. (8) in Thyssen 2013). The salient question Schrödinger poses is, what's the cat-box system's literal state prior to opening the box? Is the cat alive or dead? And exactly where in the wavefunction—the Heisenberg cut—did the quantum superposition collapse from alive and dead prior to opening the box to a definite reality of alive or dead after? It literally must be one or the other before opening the box. As each is statistically probable, both must be true. The how and why of this conundrum is the essence of the so-called measurement problem in quantum physics (§ 6.11.2:194).[216]

Rather than taking Schrödinger's cat as a rebuke, it's used instead to show how quantum superposition (and quantum science generally) actually works as reality, converting it to mean that, in principle, the cat's literally in each probable state at the same time just as a photon is literally in each probable wave and particle state or an electron is literally in each statistically probable spatial position at the same time until an observation—a measurement—provokes the system to decohere—take a definite state—which is called *wavefunction collapse* (Fig. 80:198). This means a system's real state is the sum of contributions of its every probable state (Dirac 1930, 8). Accordingly, for system Ψ with probable system states a_ψ and b_ψ,

$$|\psi\rangle = a_\psi |\uparrow_z\rangle + b_\psi |\downarrow_z\rangle \tag{17.92}$$

where $|\psi\rangle$ is the quantum wavefunction denoting system probabilities, and the *z-axis* spin up $\uparrow_z$ and spin down $\downarrow_z$ states are each a probable state φ defined as a_ψ and b_ψ. The expression $\langle\varphi|\psi\rangle$ is the probability amplitude for the state ψ to collapse from its probability state $\langle\varphi|\psi\rangle$ into real state φ.[223] Quantum superposition either doesn't distinguish between microscopic and macroscopic superposition—what's true for the photon is true for the cat—or it distinguishes each as separate systems operated under the principles of microscopic (quantum) and macroscopic (classical) physics—what's true for the photon is *not* true for the cat—between which incompatibilities and contradictions abound.

But really, one could posit the same regarding any human being who, like Schrödinger's cat, is at any moment alive now, yet dead at some indeterminate future time (a millisecond to whatever period), and whose system wavefunction must therefore be

$$\frac{1}{\sqrt{2}} \, |now\rangle_{time} \, |alive\rangle_{human} + |later\rangle_{time} \, |dead\rangle_{human} \tag{17.93}$$

where the value $|\frac{1}{\sqrt{2}}|^2 = 0.5$, a 50% probability $\mathfrak{P}$ that one possible state becomes the actual state when, say, an observer outside our world-box deigns to take a measurement to find out which possible state is the real state. From quantum science's perspective (not to mention St. John's at 11:25), we must in principle be coincidently alive and dead. Like Schrödinger's cat, this appears sensible to science for the same reason an object appears to be simultaneously a particle and a wave until measured (§ 5.4:158).

Eq. (17.93) is a statement of probability, not reality. Therefore, two probable system state configurations, let's say a_ψ and b_ψ, constitute the *probability system* $(a_\psi |\uparrow_z\rangle + b_\psi |\downarrow_z\rangle)$ as in the noted equation, but only a *reality system* $(|x\rangle - |\neg x\rangle)$ where x is any probable state and $\neg x$ is all probable states not x, regardless any $\neg x$ forming some nontrivial residual part of x (*Fig. 78*, center, right). Quantum superposition properly describes probability states from our perspective, not reality states from the universe's perspective. A system with multiple probability states is not a system of multiple reality states prior to measurement. It's only ever a system of one reality state at any given time until a measurement (mayhap) changes its state. Quantum superposition is an inaccurate concept insofar as it describes reality. Measuring an object is an interaction affecting its environment whereupon its state compensates (changes).

Quantum superposition as a description of reality is a misobservation, as Schrödinger meant his "quite ridiculous . . . [and] diabolical" (Trimmer 1980, 328) cat box to demonstrate. It conflates epistemic with ontic, probability with reality, prediction with causation, phenomenological interpretation with explanans, and valid

---

223. To know the probability that a system will go from $|\psi\rangle$ to $|\varphi\rangle$ one calculates its inner product. This gives one a number called the probability amplitude. Taking its absolute square, one gets the probability they wanted to know (e.g., $\langle\varphi|\psi\rangle = 1/2$, thus $|\sqrt{1/2}| = 1/4$, or a 25% probability).

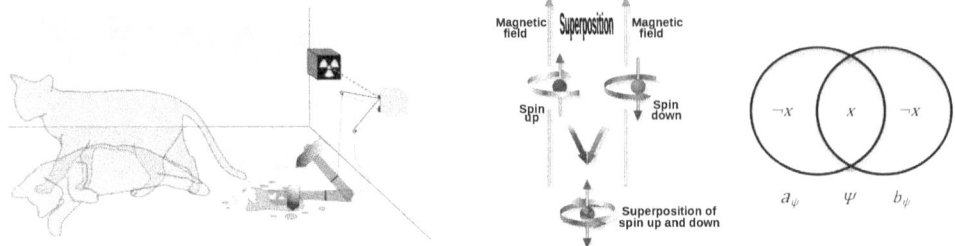

Figure 78. Left, 'Schrödinger's cat' thought experiment showing both possible states of radiation decayed/not, detector triggered/not, hammer fallen/not, poison vial broken/not, and cat alive/not; center, probability system $(a_\psi \, |\uparrow_z\rangle + b_\psi \, |\downarrow_z\rangle)$; right, reality system $(|x\rangle - |\neg x\rangle)$.[217]

math with empirical reality. Unlike linear, deterministic classical physics, the (wavefunction) *collapse postulate* that follows from Eq. (17.91) is non-linear and indeterministic (probabilistic), hence random. This chapter's ET data indicates that what seems like classically incompatible quantum oddities—explicable only by randomness resolvable through calculated probabilities—are really extensions of classical, intuitive physics absent pertinent data[224] exacerbated by slavishness toward holy mathematical quantum writ. The quantum wavefunction—which purports to describe all that's measurable about a system where "[a]ny information that cannot be derived from the wave function does not exist" (*Copenhagen* 2019, § 1)—simply can't describe anything individually about the constituents of the system[225] and, therefore, imparts less useful knowledge than is possible. It's an inaccurate concept. This is why quantum math only describes in probabilities but doesn't explain in certainties the double slit experiment, quantum entanglement, and all the rest, settling instead for what amounts to a Gallic shrug that the quantum world intrinsically is "pure probability" (ibid), intrinsically unknowable.

While observation implies "the indeterminacy observed in nature is fundamental" (ibid, § 2, par. 3), it's not. It's fallacious if not outright hubris to presume our current state of understanding "does not reflect an inadequacy in present scientific knowledge" (ibid). Einstein, Podolsky, and Rosen tried to articulate this in their 1935 EPR paradox paper but didn't quite get there owing to faulty assumptions. Although John Bell's 1964 theory of inequalities demonstrates the non-locality of entanglement, it too fails on faulty assumptions, principally the indisputability of Relativity and the intrinsic probabilistic nature of reality (e.g., particle–wave duality).

6.11.2 THE MEASUREMENT PROBLEM

The so-called measurement problem is a faux dilemma rooted in considering probable states as real states owing to the lack of a satisfying explanation for apparent particle–wave duality and entanglement. The cat-box wavefunction (Eq. (17.91)) doesn't describe real entanglement anyway because the relationships between the elements of the cat box system don't presuppose actual entanglement just because a decayed atom triggers a Geiger counter that drops a hammer that breaks a vial that releases a poison that kills the cat . . . or not. This isn't entanglement any more than, say, an asteroid collision is that which changes a trajectory that lands a meteor that flattens your house that kills your cat. The cat box's probable states aren't a superposition of real states. Rather, Eq. (17.91) is the linear, deterministic Schrödinger evolution (Eq. (17.109):206). In some respects, it's a quantum version of Newton's $F = ma$ with which we can predict a system's full state at each instant of its trajectory. His equation describes the transition of probability to reality, not the transposition of one reality to another such as

$$|reality\rangle_{premeasurement} \, |state\rangle_{allpossible}$$
$$\rightarrow |reality\rangle_{post-measurement} \, |state\rangle_{onepossible}$$

(17.94)

in which premeasurement reality is the literal superposition of all possible realities that collapse into post-measurement reality.[226] The net result of Eq. (17.94) is the transposition of entanglement with causation. That isn't a feature of entanglement. Resonance isn't causation. We discuss these farther below.

---

224. Not Einstein's 'hidden variables' theory.

225. This doesn't mean a system—a whole—is reducible to its parts, only that such parts exist.

226. Philosopher Rochelle Forrester's notion linking conscious observation to actual reality via observer "sensory worlds" (Forrester 2015, 20) doesn't overcome the problem.

The problem with the quantum world is not that things are so small but that they're so fast and exhibit a kind of emergent behavior. For example, if we take a billiard table full of moving balls as a system, we can fully describe it using position and momentum ($m \times v$). Once we've established the initial state of each moving ball and thus the system's initial state at some time t, we then know where everything is on the table, where they're going, and how fast at time $t = 0$. We can accurately predict the future state of the table—the dynamical evolution of the system—at any future time $t + x$ as a function of $F = ma$. Now, if we take a similar quantum system of subatomic particles all in motion, it becomes experimentally impossible to determine both a single particle's position and its momentum at the same time because measuring one changes the other. The upshot is that we can never know exactly where on the quantum billiard table our subatomic billiard balls are, where they're going, and how fast. It's comparable to all the billiard balls on the table stochastically moving before the cue ball even responds to the strike of the cue. We can only know this information as a probability. Science asserts this is so because, in the quantum world, particles sometimes appear to behave like waves. This idea is equivalent to observing a moving billiard ball phase into an iridescent wave along the table at some time t and then at time $t + x$ it's a billiard ball again next to the corner pocket. Except that's not what's happening at all.

An impermeable object of matter—the 'empty' space that makes up most of an object is immaterial here—doesn't transmute to a permeable diaphanous wave nor behave as a wave (§ 6.12:202). It's always a particle with definable position and momentum even if, today, we can't experimentally determine them at the same time. Whether we model its behavior as a particle or a wave isn't *its* reality but *ours*. It's a product of our sensory world because of how we're able to interact and what we conclude about that interaction. Accordingly, its 'reality' is from our perspective, subjectively comprehended (Forrester 2015, 20). But that's not the quantum's reality from *its* perspective. Although it's indeed possible to simultaneously measure quantum position and momentum albeit not with today's equipment, it is nonetheless impossible to predict a quantum's exact future state because of its exquisite sensitivity to disturbances in its environment, what earlier we called a kind of emergent behavior.[227] Science considers such disturbances to be measurement related—hence, the so-called problem—but that's only part of the story.

Starting with Fritz Zwicky (d. 1974) in the 1930s, cosmologists noted that observed mass didn't account for the necessary gravitational forces to hold galaxies and clusters together. They posited some other force was doing the lion's share (Siegel 2018a, par. 5). In doing so, and partly to explain in 1998 the apparent accelerated expansion of the universe (EN 144:657), science resurrected Einstein's discarded cosmological constant Λ (§ 1:112) to explain the apparent greater-than-zero energy density of empty space, dubbed dark energy, and invented unseen matter to explain the apparent missing gravitational mass–energy in galaxy clusters and elsewhere, dubbed dark matter (Cooper 2018, par. 3). What science was only vaguely nibbling at was the even older notion of a cosmological æther, redefined and better explained here as the Energent with some similarities to albeit but not actually a medium through which matter moves. As proto-energy, the Energent is always 'undulating' in 'charge,' 'force,' and 'density' (in *enérgeia* terms) as it interacts with matter. We describe the 'undulating' Energent $\Theta_{\varepsilon\mu}$ as a partial derivative such that

$$\Theta_{\varepsilon\mu}\left(\overrightarrow{u}, \alpha\chi\right) = \frac{\partial f}{\partial \overrightarrow{q}} + \frac{\partial f}{\partial \overrightarrow{F}} + \frac{\partial f}{\partial \overrightarrow{\rho}} + \varepsilon_0\mu_0 c^4 \tag{17.95}$$

where, in *enérgeia*-equivalent applied energy E terms, $\overrightarrow{u}$ is 'undulation,' $\alpha\chi$ is archí (matter) as a scalar, $\overrightarrow{q}$ is 'charge,' $\overrightarrow{F}$ is 'force,' $\overrightarrow{\rho}$ is 'density' as second rank tensors, with ε_0 (vacuum permittivity), μ_0 (vacuum permeability), and c (normative lightspeed). 'Charge' (q) refers to the 'strength' of *enérgeia* reaction to local matter, 'force' (F) to the 'strength' of its effect on local matter, and 'density' (ρ) to the local random coalescence of *enérgeia* independent of matter.

For example, the unpredictability of particle trajectories like electrons comes from unpredictable 'undulations' of the Energent. They're unpredictable because they're random the way, say, water motion is the random confluence of still undulating, or 'echoing,' motions of water. The randomness of water motion comes from the fact that if two identical molecules or pairwise solitary waves of water interact in the exact same way, the resultant relationship and outcome is never the same even though the initial state is the same at the moment of interaction. This is because they exist in a larger environment than themselves. Science concludes the quantum world is random because it's trying to measure what amounts to a water molecule in

---

227. An interesting correlation we later develop is that *Life* individually or in toto operates exactly like a quantum system, where stochastic behaviors, processes, and outcomes are only probabilistically predictable because supranatural humanity, some of whom disturb the system (consciousness) or the 'reflective' environment (§ 7.1.1.1:212; § 3.5.2:486), are unaccounted for.

an undulating sea without ever noticing the undulations, or that objects have unexpected intrinsic behaviors such as EMW or entanglement that mutually affect the undulating sea.

The unpredictable motions of quantum objects consequently appear inexplicable and nature seems inchoate and intrinsically random. Entanglement is a case in point. Science can't—and it's not possible to—predict that a specific object will entangle with another specific object, but can only randomly predict entanglement with a hundred percent certainty across large sample populations. The reason is that the Energent's 'undulations' randomly affect whether the magnetic field that creates entanglement can even develop in the first place to establish the resultant resonance between them (§ 6.11.5:199).

6.11.2.1   PROBABILITY WITH SUPERPOSITION

Energent 'movement' (and sometimes 'undulations') necessarily means no existent is ever static. In other words, let's say a quantum particle ($qPart$) in an ion trap or a Casimir equilibria never has zero momentum because, even when held in perfect motional stasis, *enérgeia* still 'moves' around and through it (§ 6.9.3.2:182) which produces Fundamental Force and applied energy E. These forces are in constant interaction with $qPart$ and, at any time t, reflects not just proto-energy's interaction with it but *enérgeia*'s interaction with its larger, global environment, i.e., $1.33333\sim \times 10^{-46}$ meter where $qPart$ is a pairwise archí. When observing the seemingly non-classical behavior of quantum objects, it's necessary to take into consideration the 'reflective' environment—an aspect of the supranatural Energent that, in response to matter–Energy, acts in proto-energy terms notionally like a sheer-thickening fluid vis-à-vis natural proto-energy to 'reflect' in that environment any physical existent down to its pairwise archí (§ 7.1.1.1:212)—which produces a 'return exertion' of supranatural proto-energy into natural proto-energy conceptually similar to air molecules striking a surface that, not bonding, rebound back into the air, exerting a return force against air still moving toward the wall to perturb a localized environment; or, like a water molecule pushed in direction x such that it pushes against others in that direction as well as in direction y and z that 'return exerts' in direction w (backward) in its discrete space.

Quantum superposition is a productive means to imagine a quantum state $|\psi\rangle$ in the context of its time evolution t, such that $|\psi(t)\rangle$ is a quantum probability where some aspect of $|\psi(t)\rangle$, like spin, momentum, or position is reasonably certain but all else only probable. However, because any $|\psi\rangle$ that's a $qPart$—electron, quark—isn't a solid macro particle object like a billiard ball but a complex composite of pairwise archí inclusive of its particle saturant (§ 3.1:121) in a proto-energy 'bath' that's sensitive to the most negligible perturbation, one can't adequately describe a $qPart$ or its $|\psi\rangle$ in terms of its discrete, complex composite structure—as an elementary particle—but needs must account for its local environment in the same way one accounts for the local, or, internal, environment of a proton or an atom when describing its overall properties or, indeed, as with particle saturants vis-à-vis gravity.

This environmental matrix is the reason the quantum environment appears stochastic and only descriptive as a probabilistic wavefunction decohering from coherent, or phase-related, probabilities to a singular reality 'mixed' with its environment. The 'reflective' environment's 'return exertion' enters the picture here as a perturbation unassociated with observation (measurement) or $qPart$ interactions in the natural environment ($qPart \leftrightarrow qPart$; $qPart \leftrightarrow$ magnetic field) which arises in the 'return exertion' force disturbance in $qPart$ point space that exerts in proto-energy as a sort of 'reflection' of a 'reflection' that's 'moving,' and sometimes 'undulating,' with proto-energy such that it appears to an observer—a detection instrument—a discrete yet physically real $qPart$ (*Fig. 79*).

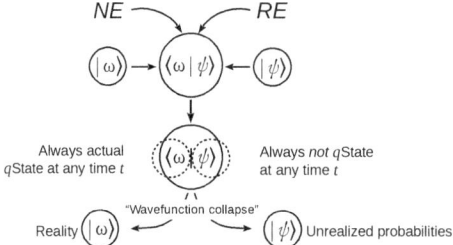

Figure 79. Quantum particle $qPart$ in natural NE, 'reflected' RE, environments with quantum states $\langle\omega|\psi\rangle$.

The 'reflected' $qPart$ in the 'reflective' environment is the negative of the physical $qPart$, where *negative* means the force-absent state, since there are no forces interacting with $qPart$ as a 'reflection' because the 'reflective' environment merely 'reflects' the natural one. Accordingly, a physical $qPart$ with a certain $|\psi\rangle$ such as spin-z up, momentum m, or position p is actually *not* spin-z up, *not* momentum m, and *not* position p. For example, a $qPart$ with spin-z up 'reflects' in the 'reflected' environment as *not* spin-z up that 'return exerts' in natural proto-energy as *not* spin-z up, which an observer consequently observes as spin-z *down* because it's *not* spin-z up as is the physical $qPart$ at the moment of observation. Such a perturbation is physically real in the sense it *exerts* the properties of the physical $qPart$ with the same magnitude but 'weaker' in the sense that, not being actually physical but just a proto-energy perturbation, it degrades with time (decohering) as though losing its quantum behavior analogous to 'losing' energy through friction as in classical mechanics.

As there is no particle–wave duality (§ 5.4:158), quantum probability needs expand its horizons to account for the proto-energy environment of $qPart$ and its 'reflection return exertion,' its basic calculus

$$|\psi\rangle = c_+ |\omega\rangle + c_- |\psi\rangle \tag{17.96}$$

where the coefficients c_+ and c_- are the probability amplitude of the wavefunction for possible quantum states $|\omega\rangle$ and $|\psi\rangle$ instead gauging $qPart$ entirely inclusive of proto-energy such that, for any $qPart$,

$$|\psi\rangle = \alpha \left|\omega^{i\Theta_{\varepsilon\mu}}\right\rangle \rightarrow \beta|\psi^{i\Theta_{\varepsilon\mu}}\rangle \tag{17.97}$$

where the coefficients α, β are the probability of measured outcomes of possible quantum states $|\omega\rangle$ and $|\psi\rangle$ without wavefunction probability amplitude, and the exponent $x^{i\Theta_{\varepsilon\mu}}$ is, first, the physical $qPart|\psi\rangle$ as exponent i and, second, Energent perturbation arising in physical interaction (proto-energy 'movement' and sometimes 'undulation') and the force disturbance of 'return exertion' as exponent $\Theta_{\varepsilon\mu}$.

6.11.2.2 Dark Energy

So-called dark energy *is* the Energent. However, science calculates only that portion dense enough to affect matter (viz. gravitational matter–Energy) while not yet noticing its vast remainder as *enérgeia*. It makes up about 77% of our universe. Matter is in balanced tension down to the most fundamental two-archí relationship. An example is that between two protons in an atomic nucleus; they're pulled apart by EM force, yet pulled together by SNF ('residual strong interaction') that holds quarks together 'within' the proton. Accordingly, so-called dark matter—the undetected mass of our universe—is Energent that's emerged as unbound archí pairs and makes up about 19% of our universe. This means dark matter is just undiscovered elementary particles. Regular matter is the remaining 4%.[228] We can dispense with particle–wave duality, thus the measurement problem, when we comprehend Energent science.

6.11.3 Quantum Entanglement is Energent Parity

Schrödinger's impious *felis catus* confronts us, too, w.r.t. entanglement; indeed, he coined the very term in his cat-box paper (Trimmer, 332ff). Here, science presumes an object—photon, electron, proton—is for instance simultaneously in opposite spin states until a measurement instantly collapses each into definite opposite states of spin up or spin down seemingly regardless distance and lightspeed c limitations. Forsooth! but quantum correlation seems a vexing conundrum . . . yet, not an impossible one. Its solution lies with *enérgeia* (§ 4.3:150) and recognizing the phenomenon as one where entangled objects *resonate*. Each of these effects—entanglement followed by resonance—are related yet discrete attributes of a larger phenomenon that altogether is a type of *parity* where the state of some particle B oppositely mirrors the state of its entangled partner A (*Fig. 80*). Entanglement as a concept fails to get at what being entangled means, however, because it incompletely describes the phenomenon. As it's really an expression of *enérgeia* anyway, we term it *Energent Parity* (denoted $\mathbf{P}_E$, bolded and capitalized to distinguish it from normative as well as quantum parity[229]) to conceptually encapsulate both its entanglement and resonance aspects.

Earlier we saw that, among other things, the Energent is the medium through which all things interact and have awareness of each other, and through which Mina interacts with the totality of our universe (§ 1:112). Parity is a predictable consequence of the Energent, which expresses as *enérgeia* in the presence of matter. In

---

228. Measurements from the 2009–13 Plank mission and others suggest the cosmos is roughly 68–73% dark energy, 23–27% dark matter, and 4–5% ordinary matter.

229. *Normative*: physics that are the same in right-handed or left-handed systems of spatial coordinates. *Quantum*: a transformation or inversion of spatial coordinates.

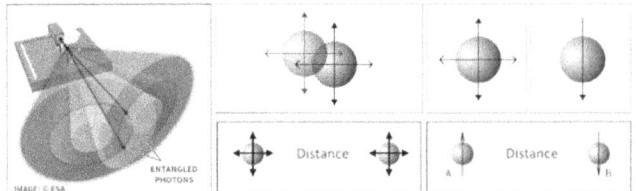

Figure 80. Left, lab-produced entangled particles A, B; top center, entangled in superposition; top right, observed in all possible states but measured in only one collapsed wavefunction ψ state; bottom center, quantum superposition at any distance pre-measurement; bottom right, entangled collapsed wavefunction ψ states at any distance post-measurement.[218]

fundamental interactions, *enérgeia* operates in real energy Υ terms as Fundamental Force. Hence, Parity is an *enérgeia* expression right up there with SNF, WNF, EMF, and the rest. This means Parity is the Energent reacting to matter in a certain state. Resonating entangled objects is *enérgeia* operating in its real energy Υ context as Fundamental Force, namely, Parity Force (ibid). Entangled objects resonate via the medium of *enérgeia* just as SNF, WNF, and EMF operate in their own way via that medium. Perhaps a helpful way to see the relationships between all these elements is

> the Energent altogether as the 'ocean' itself and its basin, and *enérgeia* as the waters that fill it; real energy Υ as the water's interaction (and the energy released or involved) with non-water; Fundamental Force as the specific kind of force involved, such as the force of current and wave action; and applied energy E as expressions of that Υ force such as erosion, deposition, temperature. Real energy Υ is not discrete from *enérgeia*, the term only distinguishes its force from its nature just as current distinguishes water's force from its nature. (ibid)

6.11.4 Instantaneity

Time and distance don't exist within *enérgeia* because, being proto-energy, it's outside the realm of matter. Recall matter comes into existence when *enérgeia* emergently transforms through 'charge' and 'density' from proto-energy to tangible archí (§ 2.3.1:115). Unlike proto-energy, archí are impermeable to other archí and, therefore, matter is impermeable to matter. This is, at root, the reason matter can't simultaneously occupy the same space whereas energy can, which we see in the admixture of Fundamental Force and applied energy E where they concurrently share the same space. Event periodicity and spatial location—dimensionality—arise from the tangibility of an impermeable object (matter). Event periodicity leads to time (timekeeping) and spatial location leads to distance, while movement (motion) in spatial location leads to *travel*. Absent event periodicity and spatial location, there is no time or distance, ergo, no such thing as travel. That means the distance between objects is dimensionless, what one might call null. Consequently, *enérgeia* is *instantaneity*. Without time and distance, events don't transpire within *enérgeia*, they simply are. There's no state of becoming as there is with spatial existence, only the Persian state of *is*-ness that's *astí*. We can say *enérgeia* is the Energent's internal nature and matter its external form (*Fig. 81*).[219] Awareness of instantaneity, thus the resonance field, is a feature of the Energent's internal nature.

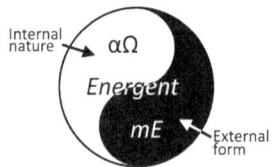

Figure 81. The Energent as internal nature (*enérgeia* $\alpha\Omega$) and external form (matter mE).[220]

Earlier, we noted the fundament of All Existence is the original, primordial Energent we termed Energent–prime (§ 1:112). The Energent of our universe saturates both our natural and supranatural existence quite as we observe EMF to do. Even so, the Energent coalesced as tangible archí is no longer proto-energy that's timeless and distanceless in its external context. Matter can move only so fast since its intrinsic motion predicates event periodicity and spatial location that together constitute travel. Vibration entails not only distance but also motion change in point space, which as a whole is event periodicity.[230] Parity thus raises an implication for

---

230. Archí, for example, vibrate faster than other matter, at *universal peak speed*.

human consciousness, itself an All Existence emergent phenomenon (ibid; § 2.3.2.1:241; § 3.1:280). After all, consciousness isn't packaged in a skull or even a universe. As an emergent of Previous All Existence's Energent–prime, consciousness inherits certain of its attributes, principally infinitude and instantaneity. Therefore,

$$\left\{ \left((C = A) \bigwedge (A = T) \right) \right\} \leftrightarrow C = T \tag{17.98}$$

where C is consciousness, A is awareness, and T is Thought. This means Thought is instantaneous. Not *brain* thought, which physically has an imposed material limitation of synapses, electrons, chemistry, and so forth, or the *act* of thinking, but *mind* Thought, which has no imposed limitation whatsoever. At first blush, it seems eccentric to say that Parity is the same 'energy' type as Thought. Yet, when we consider the ineffability of *L*ife (§ 1.2:246) and consciousness in the context of a functional, ordered, causative universe, it stands to reason phenomena like Parity don't magically invent themselves but result from a process like emergence or attribute expression. Thought itself is the 'energy' through which it conveys; Thought and its medium are the same. Consequently, Thought is *'energy' that's aware* such that

$$\Theta_{\varepsilon\mu} \to |\alpha\Omega| \to |C| \to T \therefore \Theta_{\varepsilon\mu} \to T \tag{17.99}$$

where Energent $\Theta_{\varepsilon\mu}$ is unaware, *enérgeia* $|\alpha\Omega|$ and consciousness $|C|$ are their non-aware and aware iterations, and T is Thought (§ 2.3.2:240). In such case, therefore, Energent logically means Thought. The resonance field invoked by entanglement, though non-aware, is described similarly in principle as

$$\Theta_{\varepsilon\mu} \to |\alpha\Omega| \to |C| \to R_u \therefore \Theta_{\varepsilon\mu} \to R_u \tag{17.100}$$

where R_u is unaware resonance and other terms as per Eq. (17.99). In this case, Energent logically means unaware resonance. Accordingly,

$$R_u \cong T \tag{17.101}$$

in that resonance and Thought are congruent as they both function according to the same principle while being unaware and aware, respectively. We consider consciousness, awareness, and Thought a bit more in § 6.11.7:201, then fully in All Existence (ch. 18:227) and Psyche Infinity (ch. 19:245).

6.11.5 Subatomic Parity

Let's look at Parity's (entanglement) mechanics. All objects carry applied energy E charge at some level of their structure. Therefore, a magnetic field exists, however tremulous. Any number of objects initiates entanglement when their electric fields simultaneously exert force on each other. When the outermost effective region of their magnetic fields is proximal to about $5.946888555 \times 10^{-30}$ meter at the same moment, and their polarity (magnetic field spin) differs relative to the other(s) in the same composite axis plane, torque thereby exerts on the objects and stops their individual magnetic field spin in an orientation giving rise to a single, multi-object magnetic field (*Fig. 82*). If their electric fields sufficiently interact—they might not, said objects proceeding along their path unentangled and velociously unimpeded—then a single, composite magnetic field generates between them for, on average, $5.9468885555 \times 10^{-16}$ second, and entanglement completes and resonance forms.[231] In the totality of the process, the polarity of the composite magnetic field is the trigger for resonance.

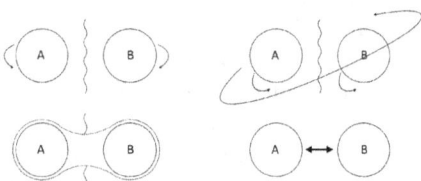

Figure 82. Steps of Parity (quantum entanglement); top: left, physical interaction of minimally separated objects; right, torque provokes magnetic field orientation and a composite magnetic field across separation; bottom: left, objects entangle across separation; right, resonance occurs regardless separation.

---

231. Similarity of distance and time figures is an artifact of emergent creation.

Enérgeia expresses as real energy Υ operating as Parity Fundamental Force (§ 1:112). Science refers to this phenomenon as the inexplicable quantum communication between entangled objects, but here we see it's indeed explicable. The entangled objects either remain in some proximity or separate to parts unknown according to their individual motion which is unimpeded by entanglement. Whichever, a *resonance field* now obtains between them until one, both, or all objects later entangle with other objects (because Parity is a one-to-one relationship).[232] Resonance fields saturate nature but are discrete by frequency (*below*), a function of the combined objects' unique real energy Υ bound archí 'charge.'[221] As already noted in THE MEASUREMENT PROBLEM (CH. 6.11.2:194), resonance between entangled objects happens via *enérgeia*, which is infinite; the awareness of object B to object A's state is therefore instant; the awareness is resonance. When the state of object A changes, it resonates via *enérgeia*. Because there's a resonance field between objects A and B, object B resonates with object A unless object B has since entangled with another object. Besides losing their entanglement when one or both objects subsequently entangle with another object, the Energent's 'undulations' can interrupt resonance.

6.11.6 RESONANCE 'FREQUENCY'

Ordinarily, *enérgeia* has no 'waveform' in its natural state, but it does when materialized into archí containment (§ 2.3.1:115) as, too, does Fundamental Force wherever it exerts. In the process of coalescing between entangled objects to establish the resonance field, *enérgeia* naturally increases in Energent 'charge' and 'density.' This partially materializes *enérgeia* as a much reduced, non-materialized version of archí that's contained by the resonance field and sufficient to establish an Energent version of wave characteristics. In such a 'dense' form, Parity produces something like a standing wave in the resonance field (*Fig. 83*). As with archí, however, it's not a classical standing wave—we use the term to help visualize the process—but a non-motive back-and-forth awareness *in the image of* waveform unique to *enérgeia* that produces qualitatively the same result. Thus,

$$\alpha\Omega \fallingdotseq \check{\Psi} \tag{17.102}$$

where $\alpha\Omega$ is *enérgeia* and $\check{\Psi}$ is waveform. Since there's no event periodicity or spatial location in the resonance field, *enérgeia* doesn't literally 'oscillate' as such. What's happening is, a phenomenon homologous with awareness resonates in the field between entangled objects (§ 6.11.7:201; § 2.1.5.4.7:320).

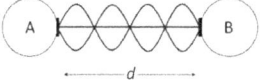

Figure 83. Entangled Ⓐ↔Ⓑ resonate conceptually similar to a standing wave via *enérgeia* at distance *d*.

Something similar, though imperfectly analogous, occurs when unconsciously driving. There's resonance twixt vehicle (driver) and road. One perceives each discrete entity as single, wholistic; vehicle and road in a sort of superposition. As road conditions change, the vehicle (driver) mirrors it. Practically speaking, entangled objects, regardless their differing spatial location, form a wholistic singleton via Parity. Like capacitor–inductor resonance or indefinite light cavities, Parity is self-sustaining.[222]

Recall that objects' magnetic fields must be in different relative states to set up the condition to entangle (§ 6.11.5:199). This means when entangled object A changes state and object B oppositely mirrors it, it's because object B started from a different relative state and, although it mirrors the change, its end state differs accordingly. Entangled objects appear to start out in quantum superposition and then collapse into definite, opposite states, but really they're already in different or opposite states upon entanglement, despite what laboratory experiments appear to imply about their initial setups. Because quantum superposition yields an incomplete description of the phenomenon, we term it *Energent superposition*. The difference between quantum and Energent superposition is that the former means entangled objects are simultaneously in all possible states (superposition) prior to measurement, whereas the latter means entangled objects altogether constitute a superposition.

---

232. Consciousness and Energent are in one-to-many relationships with and within all universes, but mutually discrete.

6.11.7 Macroscopic Parity

Schrödinger's cat (§ 6.11.1.1:192) pokes fun at the inevitable problems scaling up quantum superposition to the macroscopic world in a reality where physics must be (and is) internally consistent. Energent superposition scales from subatomic to suratomic without inconsistency. The fuller macroscopic discussion needs await a later book, however. Here, we just consider it w.r.t. to humans, including Mina. It seems surprising to recognize quantum entanglement as Parity, but more so to extend it to persons. If we could ontologically isolate individual aspects of nature an objection might have legs, but we can't. The reality is that everything connects at some degree of separation; no object is an island, to twist a phrase. Just from archí, we see how all matter is 'energy' and literally so, not in some quantum mystical woo-woo fashion. Since microscopic nodules of condensed 'energy' bound together by a ligamentous of Fundamental Force constitute our bodies from the ground up, and our consciousness constitutes yet another form of 'energy,'[233] it's natural that Parity should express macroscopically, too. Let's take in turn Parity's two key aspects of entanglement–resonance and instant awareness over distance as they apply to humans.

6.11.7.1 'Entanglement'–resonance

We've all experienced this to some degree. A sixth sense, intuition, the clair senses, hyperawareness, emotive connection . . . all are manifestations of 'entanglement'–resonance. People 'entangle' not just with objects and physical people but with spirit persons and 'energy,' too. Some can perceive, or sense, the energy of a place whilst knowing nothing of its spirit human presence or the residual energy of the physical events that transpired there. This involves the omnipresent human consciousness that, via Parity, has awareness of the 'energy' of another consciousness (physical or spirit) that feels a connection to a place or situation (Meaning of Human, § 3:280).[234] In the natural world, humans 'entangle' with humans and anything not-human via Thought or direct encounter (skin-to-skin or skin-to-object Touch (§ 2.1.5.4.7:320). Let's consider the latter.

'Entanglement' begins at the smallest subatomic level and scales from the point of contact until a composite magnetic field occurs around the in-contact persons in roughly the same process as the microscopic, because it is microscopic. Archí in ascending levels of complexity make up the human body, so naturally Parity (entanglement) is occurring at the particle level. The difference is that it's happening in a complex environment cascading from simple particle pairs to higher composite levels. 'Entanglement' takes ~14,570 times longer for persons than subatomic particles, $\sim 8.7716606193625 \times 10^{-12}$ second. Resonance follows 'entanglement,' occurring at the point of contact and propagating from there to the macroscopic, eventually 'entangling' the whole of the bodies so long as there's contact for the above period. There is a gradation of 'entanglement' and resonance with humans depending not only on time of exposure but intent as well. Additionally, humans can 'entangle' with multiple persons and objects at the same time (Charkas as They Are in Reality, § 1.2:498). The multiple resonance fields thusly established are of varying strength and duration and can be dis-'entangled,' re-'entangled,' weakened, strengthened, multiplied, divided, and so on. 'Entanglement' and resonance are key aspects of human ℒife just as with subatomic existence.

6.11.7.2 Instant Awareness Over Distance

Human consciousness is infinite—what religion ascribes to God as omnipresence—and is thus internally instantaneous (§ 6.11.4:198). Its fundamental feature is awareness, which shares the same instantaneity. A natural world example is feeling fully engaged 'a million miles away' from one's physical location such as during unconscious driving, sometimes being so all encompassing that we lose sight of our physical reality for that of our mind. A supranatural example is spirit individuals[235] moving across any distance instantaneously simply by shifting their awareness from point A to point B, or even simultaneously to points C, D, E . . . n (where $n \leq 24$; § 1.2.3.3.3:472). The process of thinking is itself not instantaneous, so the act of choosing to shift one's awareness isn't instant, but Thought is (§ 1.2.2:253). Consequently, so too is the shift in awareness, because awareness and Thought are aspects of essentially the same thing.

---

233. The mind will never homogenously slot into reductive brain-based materialist schemata.

234. Once recognizing how our universe exists and operates, one can see the mysteries of ℒife are sensibly, intuitively explicable.

235. Whose bodies, by the way, are physically real in the context of supranatural supramatter but projections (manifestations, Intentionalities) nonetheless of their consciousness.

The reason behind instantaneity of awareness in the physical world and instantaneity of presence in spirit world is the infinitude of consciousness, which works for humans the same way the resonance field works for objects (Eq. (17.99)–(17.101):199). This is because consciousness—Thought—and the resonance field *are each their own type of Energent*. For all practical purposes, consciousness is a self-aware Energent. On the grand scale, the Energent is the unifying force across all aspects of universal existence, natural and supranatural. All forces and matter emerge from the Energent. It energizes (nonhuman) life. Accordingly, human consciousness in its own context is as infinite, eternal, and governing as the Energent of our universe and Energent–prime of All Existence 'in' which our universe exists (CH. 15:99; CH. 18:227). Mina, for instance, created our universe using the 'energy' of his own consciousness, not magic, divine power, or some obnubilate alien machine (§ 6.10.1:186). The elusive Theory of Everything, the Grand Unifying Theory of Science, resides with the Energent.

The takeaway here is there are two relative instantaneities of awareness with humans. The first is that 'entanglement'–resonance establishes a resonant awareness in us of other persons or objects. It's an infinite and unconscious awareness that's always there because it unconsciously forms through physical interactions to which we pay little attention. We're consciously unaware of this awareness unless it rises to a conscious level. We term this *Parity instantaneity*. The second is that our consciousness is infinitely and consciously aware—omnipresent. A natural environment example is the ancient belief a person's ears burn, tingle, or itch when others elsewhere are discussing them. This myth is mostly wives' tales, but the body's response to the perceptions of our consciousness is real since our physical body integrates mind, having an awareness however unconscious in our day-to-day lifestyle of the supranatural environment.

An example of that environment is physical-born spirit persons keeping a subconscious ear cocked toward the natural environment for their name or anything of concern. In early August 2019, Ayako called to say she'd just discovered the Apache Indian lineage we'd previously traced to my father's father was Chiricahua. Naturally, she lit my interest to ask Mina the details. When he said my paternal great grandfather is the only sibling of famous Chiricahua medicine man Geronimo—and a medicine man himself, whom I nicknamed Shasha since, for now, I can only mangle his Chiricahua name—they were aware we were discussing them and answered as soon as we called.[236] This is how Taiji and Hidé discovered Ayako and El ruminating on their deaths; they sensed it and followed the trail.

Omnipresent *consciousness instantaneity* like twitchy ears work in the natural environment because, absent awareness and training, our brain is a mind-sieve for mental 'energy' like a badly insulated house. In the supranatural environment, mind is hermetically sealed unless we expose conscious aspects of it to another; that's twitchy spirit ears right there.

6.12   QUANTUM TUNNELING

Science presents quantum tunneling (QT) as virtually magic, but it's not. Despite its conceptual principles being practically utilized for real equipment like electron tunneling microscopes, an object 'tunneling' out of a nucleus isn't the phenomenon that actually occurs. For example, the visible effect produced by supposed QT alpha particle emission (*Fig. 85*) is actually an aftereffect of *enérgeia* 'undulation' (discussion, Eq. (17.95):195) and Energent Parity (§ 6.11:191). Additionally, QT plays no role in the hydrogen–helium fusion process in stars. Rather, proton–proton 'fusion' is a Parity pre-game before SNF binds them into deuterium. Distinct processes enable radioactive decay and fusion, the former largely via *enérgeia* 'undulations' and the latter via Parity. Radioactive decay provides a simple service regulating heat production via unstable (radioactive) atoms time consumingly achieving a stable, non-radioactive state. Parity makes regulated stars possible via the intrinsic difficulty overcoming the barrier to hydrogen–helium fusion. For instance, Mina avers radioactive decay produces approximately 43.27% of Earth's intrinsic (non-solar) heat and altogether ~50% inclusive of beta and gamma decay,[237] and Parity is directly responsible for ~10.4% and indirectly for the other 89.6% of the total energy output of stars like the Sun.[223]

Quantum tunneling as a concept is yet another scientific misnomer describing nothing about the phenomenon. An object is said to 'tunnel' through a potential energy (PE) 'barrier' or out of a PE 'well' of a certain 'height' either to fuse with, or escape from, another object (*Fig. 84*, left). This rather unhelpful imagery implies some sort of spooky action. What the quantum brains mean is that, in a way they don't particularly understand, an object—alpha particles, electrons, protons—negates or circumvents the Coulomb force[238] of

---

236. Although they already knew us because they'd watched their lineage unfold over the years (EN 61:650).

237. Residual heat from Earth's molten beginnings produces the other ~50% .

repulsion or SNF attraction that exists between objects that permits them to bind with or escape from each other in a situation where these forces indicate it ought to be impossible.

For example, positively charged protons repel each other. The *potential* force of repulsion between them increases or decreases as their distance from each other decreases or increases. It's an effect of electrostatic force, thus energy, which science terms the *potential energy barrier*. The barrier's 'height' or 'depth' of its 'well' is the difference between the tunneling object's own kinetic energy (KE) and the energy it needs to overcome another object's repulsion so it can bond. If object A has an energy profile of KE = 5 MeV and if the potential repulsive energy of object B is PE = 20 MeV, then object A needs gain another 15 MeV of kinetic energy to overcome object B's repulsion else it will get only so close before the force of object B's repulsion reduces object A's motion to KE = 0 and it repulses. If you've ever tried pushing two same-pole magnets together then you've experienced this repulsive force and effect. The same applies in reverse to objects escaping attractive force, such as the SNF. Object A will get only so far away before object B's greater attractive force reduces object A's motion to KE = 0 and hauls it back. If you step away from an anchored object while attached to it by a strong rubber band until the band's tension exerts a backward pulling force that overcomes your strength to move away, then you've experienced this attractive force and effect.

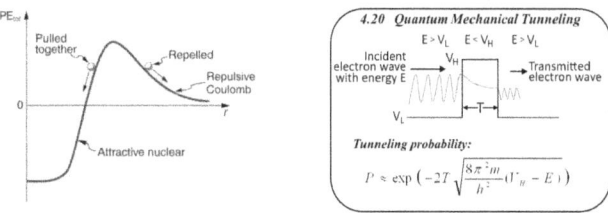

Figure 84. Left, potential energy barrier; right, probability of quantum tunneling (integrated circuit).[224]

Either way, PE + KE total energy remains the same but, eventually, objects get so close or far the Coulomb force compels KE to zero. Classical physics says an object of KE = 0 is incapable of moving closer to, or farther from, an object. Bonding via proton–proton fusion at deficient temperatures, or escaping via alpha particle emission, should be impossible. Yet, observations and experiments appear to show this impossibility happening. As quantum science is a probabilistic regimen, it predictably quantifies QT as a probabilistic phenomenon. The probability of 'tunneling' is how it explains an object of energy E with less energy than a potential energy barrier V circumventing these forces (*Fig. 84*, right). How it actually happens, science hasn't a clue. But ET data explains it. Before we get to that, however, we need discuss the problem with Heisenberg's Uncertainty Principle, a core quantum science concept.

6.12.1 HEISENBERG UNCERTAINTY PRINCIPLE

Science generally accepts that quantum objects don't operate according to the same rules—the same physics—as macro objects. This means it's not possible to know certain property pairs of a quantum object—say, position and momentum, or time and energy—simultaneously as we more or less can with a macro object. Since this chapter already describes in various scenarios how quantum science is entirely a poorly understood facet of a broader conceptualization of classical physics,[239] we can understand that German physicist Werner Heisenberg's (d. 1976) 1927 Uncertainty Principle (HUP)[240] is a not-entirely-accurate statement of reality. Mina says it's possible to measure 90% of an object's conjugate (non-commutative) pairs or unrelated properties simultaneously with certainty. The remaining 10% is always uncertain but extrapolative with about 50% accuracy. Science simply has to figure this out. The topics covered in this chapter will help it experimentally do that.

HUP essentially states "the position and the velocity of an [quantum] object cannot both be measured exactly, at the same time, even in theory."[225] That is, HUP denotes an intrinsic constraint on our ability to make precise statements about the behavior of a quantum system whether or not we attempt a measurement. The usual reason cited is that the product of the uncertainties in, say, position and velocity equals or exceeds $\frac{h}{4\pi}$, a

238. Or, *electrostatic force* of attraction and repulsion between opposite or like charges.

239. Science is unstinting in trying to unify the quantum and classical.

240. Originally, a statement about error and disturbance in the measurement process, its modern interpretation regards the uncertainties as intrinsic to quantum states (along with particle–wave duality and other quantum oddities).

minimum physical quantity where h is Planck's constant (about 6.6×10^{-34} joule–second). The accuracy of one conjugate pair's measurement is inversely proportional to the intrinsic uncertainty regarding the other such that $\Delta x \propto \frac{1}{\Delta p}$ where Δx is the uncertainty in position and Δp the uncertainty in momentum. The uncertainty product doesn't rise to significance in larger objects like automobiles, baseballs, or houseflies because it's too small to observe or matter in ordinary experience, but it does at the nanoscale. Uncertainties arise for HUP because measuring one subatomic property like position ineluctably changes its conjugate momentum (that is, $m \times \Delta v$ where m is mass and Δv is change in velocity), not because of technique, technical inadequacy, or observer presence, but to "the intimate connection in nature between particles and waves"[226] (particle–wave duality). As *Britannica* puts it, a

> particle is most likely to be found in those places where the undulations [probability amplitude] of the wave are greatest, or most intense. The more intense the undulations of the associated wave become, however, the more ill defined becomes the wavelength, which in turn determines the momentum of the particle. So a strictly localized wave [a particle in a specific location] has an indeterminate wavelength [momentum]; its associated particle, while having a definite position, has no certain velocity. A particle wave having a well-defined wavelength, on the other hand, is spread out; the associated particle, while having a rather precise velocity, may be almost anywhere. A quite accurate measurement of one observable involves a relatively large uncertainty in the measurement of the other,[227]

and the conclusion is that a particle wave essentially defines a particle's properties.

As we've seen throughout this chapter, that isn't reality. Such uncertainties aren't intrinsic to nature but arise from a deficiency in observational technique, not (entirely) of the manner or skill in which we observe but the mental picture derived from our habituated way of thinking about our observations. Preconceived notions are very powerful. For example, we customarily think of particles and waves in an either–or context. This was the basis for Thomas Young's double slit experiment and the confusion regarding its observational result, as well as that of Einstein's photoelectric effect. Quantum science tries to expand this mental box with particle wave theory but loses focus in mystical theories of particles being waves being particles when it suits, or when an observer notices, or for other inscrutable reasons, all of which translates to taking observation as reality. Yet, when we consider how a particle of a certain charge physically moves through space while also emanating its energy as EMR via EMW mechanics in the Energent milieu, the mysticism of particle–wave duality disappears, the double slit enigma resolves, and we have instead a reality intuitively described by a broader classical physics, which coincidently explains EMR's quantized nature (§ 2:114). There's a clear distinction between observation and reality at the quantum level.

Then how are scientists failing to measure conjugate pairs simultaneously when Mina tells us we can do so with certainty? The culprit is the math and scientists' overreliance on it. Heisenberg's thought experiment—rooted in particle wave theory where

$$\Delta x \Delta p \geq \frac{h}{4\pi} \qquad (17.103)$$

in which the smaller the Δx then the larger the Δp whereby the more accurately we know a particle's position then the less accurately we can know its momentum—presumes the impossibility. Our inability to measure both simultaneously with certainty using blunt force tools like photons appears to prove it. Justification turns to macro objects for analogy. For example, one might ask if it's possible to know a car's exact velocity and its exact location at which it was at that velocity. HUP says no. Let's suppose we know a car's position within a half-meter, and its exact weight of 1300 kg. Using HUP from Eq. (17.103), we know $\Delta x = 0.5$ m and $\Delta p = m \times \Delta v$. Therefore,

$$\Delta x \cdot \Delta p \left\{ m \cdot \Delta v \right\} \geq \frac{h}{4\pi} \rightarrow \Delta v = \frac{h}{4\pi} \cdot 1 \Delta x \cdot m$$

$$\rightarrow \Delta v \geq \frac{6.626 \times 10^{-31} \mathrm{J} \cdot \mathrm{s}}{4\pi} 1300\,\mathrm{kg} \times 0.5\mathrm{m} \qquad (17.104)$$

$$= 8.112 \times 10^{-35} \mathrm{m/s}$$

where h is Planck's constant. Accordingly, we find an uncertainty of 8.112×10^{-35} m/s regarding velocity. If we knew the car's location to a fraction of a half (1×10^{-31}) meter, then the uncertainty of its velocity calculates to 6.854×10^{-60} m/s. Of course, if we could know the car's *exact* position, then its $\Delta x = 0.0$ meter. According to HUP, we couldn't estimate Δv, as the equation necessarily results in zero.

Eq. (17.103) doesn't accurately define the inability to measure with certainty conjugate property pairs of a quantum object because it's only quantifying the problem inherent in the blunt force tools that science uses to detect quantum objects and not any problem intrinsic to measuring their conjugate pairs simultaneously. Hup is a mathematical construct that only presumes it's not possible to measure conjugate pairs simultaneously because of a devotion to particle–wave duality and an overreliance on theoretical mathematics and not because actual measurement data qualitatively demonstrates it. While applying Hup is indeed mathematically valid, it's contextually invalid and leads to wrong conclusions because its premise rests on a belief in the wave nature or wave-like behavior of quantum particles in which it's difficult or impossible to measure precisely a wave's physical position in space. Like many theoretical constructs in science, Hup really only suggests what's experimentally possible now and what might be, but isn't necessarily, true of reality.

According to Mina, quantum objects down to the infinitesimal size of archí are particles emanating EMW, randomly and indeterminately disturbed by micro environmental changes with definitive states and properties at any given moment in time quite irrespective of what we're able to cognize through theory or observation. Therefore, a quantum object has absolute velocity and position simultaneously in reality even if we haven't simultaneously measured or mathematically derived them using the inaccurate wavefunction tool. The probabilistic nature of quantum science comes about not because we can't ultimately predict a future quantum state owing to quantum nature being intrinsically probabilistic, but because quantum states are intrinsically more fragile than macro states and subject to alterations from the tiniest stochastic disturbances in their environment.

A quantum particle doesn't have a trajectory like a billiard ball because it's subject to forces along its track that induces what appears as probabilistic if not outright random motion and states, hence the belief electron "motion is smeared out in a strange way."[228] Although Mina says we can accurately measure a particle's conjugate pairs simultaneously at an exact moment in time like a freeze frame, we nevertheless can't use that information to predict its future trajectory or state as we can with macro (classical) physics[241] owing to quantum state fragility and emergence. Hup really means there's an uncertainty in *predicting* particle states but not in *measuring* them, despite Heisenberg's 1925 observation on the impossibility of measuring one without disturbing the other using traditional blunt force, applied energy E tools. Consequently, Schrödinger's wave equation (Eq. (17.109):206) predicts only a partial, probabilistic future quantum state; say, an object's state within a nucleus where a small probability exists of it appearing (quantum tunneling) outside the nucleus while lacking the (classical) energy to do so.

Schrödinger's equation describes a quantum object's state in terms of a wave function. It's a quantum analogue to Newton's $F = ma$ used to calculate or predict a classical system's state over time from a known initial condition from which we derive simultaneous position and momentum (§ 6.11.2:194). While science sees a classical object as a particle, it sees a quantum object as sometimes a particle and sometimes a wave (wave-like) and its particle-like nature quantized as a wave packet of localized or concentrated energy—its particleness—that's located or localizable only as a probability somewhere in space. A quantum particle seems to science more like a movement of energy as a wave spread out over distance and time until it localizes as a wavefunction collapse than a discrete, localized object carrying energy. While Schrödinger's equation yields accurate mathematical results in various situations to a certain extent, it yields no accurate information regarding reality. Einstein's proposal that a photon's energy is proportional to its frequency ($E = hf$; h is Planck's proportionality constant) is not a glimmer of particle–wave duality, but of an object's pulsating nature and EMR emission via EMW.

We're used to an observation essentially mirroring reality in the classical world. We carry this habituated expectation—a human eigenstate, one might say—into the quantum world, too. This wouldn't be problematic if we understood the quantum world as well as the classical, but we don't, of course. Consequently, our observation of a quantum state doesn't necessarily mirror its reality. Quantum science recognizes this yet, instead of accepting the dichotomy between observation and reality, it describes quantum reality as *intrinsically* stochastic, knowable only as a probabilistic instead of a deterministic reality. Setting aside for the moment that neither probabilism nor determinism adequately characterizes quantum or classical reality, the wavefunction Ψ—let's say its general, positional–space version of

$$\Psi\left(x, t\right)$$

(17.105)

---

241. Though with extreme long-range ballistics, a bullet is probabilistically or even randomly influenced by conflicting winds, terrain, magnetic anomalies, and other environmental factors.

where x is position and t is time—really only comprehends our *observations* of a quantum state but not its *real state* for the simple reason it fails to account for the forces acting on it. This includes applied energy E, real energy Υ, and *enérgeia*. Accordingly, one can only describe a quantum state in terms of observable alternatives whereby

$$|\psi\rangle = \sum_i c_i |\phi_i\rangle \qquad (17.106)$$

where c is the probability amplitude coefficient and the ket $|\phi_i\rangle$ specifies the probable quantum states, or basis eigenstates, one ϕ_i of which will probabilistically occur upon measurement in the process called wavefunction collapse in which

$$|\psi\rangle \rightarrow |\phi_i\rangle \qquad (17.107)$$

whereupon the full quantum state $|\psi\rangle$ 'collapses' to (or assumes one of the $|\psi\rangle$ basis eigenstates of) $|\phi_i\rangle$, taking its real state with the probability $\langle\psi|\phi_i\rangle|^2$. As discussed (§ 6.11.1:192), the probability doesn't mean the particle state will *become* real state $|\phi_i\rangle$ but will be *observed* in real state $|\phi_i\rangle$. This probability uncertainty can be reduced when we account for the forces intersecting with the quantum state such that

$$\frac{\Psi(x,t)}{\alpha\Omega + \Upsilon + E} \propto \frac{h}{4\pi} \qquad (17.108)$$

where, as scalars, $\alpha\Omega$ is *enérgeia*, Υ is real energy (Fundamental Force), and E is applied energy E. If we cognize the forces at play, we can accurately predict future quantum states within the intrinsic probabilistic parameters induced by random, indeterminate forces that are non-trivial at the quantum level.

Science uses Schrödinger's equation, here in its most general, time-dependent form that describes a system evolving with time as

$$i\hbar \frac{d}{dt} |\Psi(t)\rangle = \hat{H} |\Psi(t)\rangle \qquad (17.109)$$

where i is the imaginary unit,[242] $\hbar$ is the reduced Planck constant, t is time, $\hat{H}$ is the Hamiltonian operator, and the others as defined. In reality, the expression describes in terms of probability amplitude the evolution of our *observation* of a quantum system and not its *real* state. This, too, is because it doesn't account for the forces affecting a quantum particle, which creates the probabilistic reality in the first place. Our modification to the wavefunction portion of Eq. (17.109) is

$$|\Psi(t)\rangle = \frac{\Psi(x,t)}{\alpha\Omega + \Upsilon + E} \qquad (17.110)$$

where the terms are per Eq. (17.108). All this results from considering quantum science probabilistic versus deterministic when it's neither since a quantum does simultaneously have conjugate pairs (measured or not) in an invariably disturbed environment. Thus, a quantum object is a particle while we can measure a quantum of energy as a wave; a particle is a particle and a wave is a wave but the one is never the other. The wavefunction contextualizes observation by telling us where or how we'll most likely observe a quantum. While it predicts what we observe, it's not predicting reality. The wavefunction is only a mathematical model of probable reality, not observed reality. It can't predict observed reality because it doesn't account for reality's quantum environment.

6.12.1.1 PARTICLES AND WAVES

There is no amplitude w.r.t. EMR. The holdover physical wave concept misleads. Accordingly, EMR energy isn't directly proportional to it. While brighter light ejects more electrons in the context of the photoelectric effect, it doesn't increase kinetic energy because brighter light isn't more intense in terms of energy transference. More photons striking a surface don't add up to more energy transferred to any particular electron's kinetic energy.[243]

---

242. Based on $\sqrt{-1}$, $\sqrt{-2}$, etc., which has "no physically-direct relevance to a measurable reality" (Tanguay 2015, 188). The wavefunction can't actually exist any more than 2.5 children per family can except as an approximated reality, since there's no such thing as a .5 child. Tanguay defines unit i in terms that the wavefunction can exist; for Mina, he's inaccurate overall.

243. It's not light as particles (photons) that knock electrons out of material (or, quanta) in the photoelectric effect. It's EMW transferring energy from field extensions into an electron. This energetically excites it to leave its place of effective (stable) rest. This occurs when light is above a threshold frequency regardless intensity because that's where the electron EM field frequency reacts to incoming EMW frequency.

Higher frequency (shorter wavelength) transfers higher energy to any particular electron in the photoelectric effect. Planck's $E = hf$ theory is generally correct but doesn't account for the whole phenomenon. Science finds that the energy of waves (amplitude) and energy of EMR (frequency) don't coincide and concludes light is a particle with wave properties. That's inaccurate since EMW isn't wavelike but a field extension (§ 3.7.3.3.4:142). Therefore, de Broglie's wavelength γ_B,

$$\lambda_B = \frac{h}{p} \rightarrow \lambda = \frac{h}{mv} \tag{17.111}$$

where p is momentum, m is mass, and v is velocity is premised on the wrong assumption that, first, EMW is wavelike and, second, that matter exhibits properties of particles and waves. Since matter emits EMR, we can see in the second case that wave theory blinds science to comprehending reality. There are no wave properties with EMR because it's not wave energy but an energy field extension. Consequently, there's no relationship between particle and wave. Thus,

$$(E = mc^2) \neq (E = hf) \therefore (mv^2 \neq hf) \bigwedge \left(mv^2 \neq \frac{hv}{\lambda}\right) \Rightarrow \lambda \neq \frac{hv}{mv^2} \neq \frac{h}{mv} \tag{17.112}$$

because particle energy is real energy Υ, whereas EMR energy is applied energy E. Particle energy and wave energy don't have the same traits as de Broglie's equation assumes; light would appear to undulate if it was actually wavelike. The particle–EMR relationship is one in which

$$\Upsilon \neq E \Rightarrow P_e \neq EMR_e \because (P_e = \Upsilon) \bigwedge (EMR_e = E) \tag{17.113}$$

where the initial inequality is the second inequality as a material reality, P_e is particle real energy Υ 'energy,' and EMR_e is EMR applied energy E energy (§ 2:114; § 5.1:152).

Recall that wave properties f, λ, and v correspond generally to field extension properties of interval speed f_{FE}, extension λ_{FE}, and speed v_{FE} (discussion, Eq. (17.55):159). To account for EMR energy propagating via EMW, we further modify Planck's $E = hf$ equation from $E = hf\alpha\chi_T$ per Eq. (17.57):160 to

$$E = h\left(EMW_e + EMR_e\right) \begin{cases} EMW_e = \frac{v_{FE}}{\lambda_{FE}} \\ EMR_e = h\tau \end{cases} \tag{17.114}$$

where τ is EMR pulse time (duty cycle). EMR expresses energy when the EMW field extension reaches its maximum and before it begins its next extension. It thus appears that EMR is packetized (quantized). This gives credence to particle–wave duality, but it's only an energy pulsation in the larger context of its carrier EMW propagating as a field extension (Fig. 39:153). This means an EMW essentially is the medium through which an EMR energy pulse propagates. Earlier conjectures that light for instance must travel in a medium—such as the popular nineteenth-century luminiferous æther—are correct in principle but incorrect in application. Instead, an EMW is a focused disturbance in the locally raised EM field in which an EMR energy pulse moves through space. Eq. (17.111) indicates there's more to the energy profile of a quantum, such as a photon, than hitherto considered.

Another quantum system's environment that's insufficiently accounted for is the electron, which orbits a nucleus as a composite archí particle while emitting EMR via EMW. Besides conflating its particle and wave components as a duality or a 'cloud of charge,' neither observation nor wavefunction detects the electron's subtle vector changes in the midst of its circumgyrations provoked by quantum environmental disturbances like *enérgeia* 'undulations' and momentum changes that periodically carry it between its atom's protons and neutrons (which transiently slow it). This is principally why science can't predict electron position; it follows no prescribed start-to-finish path in any circumgyration of a nucleus. However, it is subject to indeterminate vector changes across a probabilistic area within a uniform probability of environmental disturbances (Eq. (17.110):206).

We can easily comprehend a typical hyposubatomic object. Tiny as it is, it's physical, tangible, and definable. It's not some tiny solid ball like a single spherical archí, but a composite archí structure. As such, it's a highly energized space within its overall sphere of influence around its composite archí core, itself an inner energized space. Yet, science largely concludes from its double slit and related observations that such particles are also undefinable non-physical waves, something fuzzy and spread out in space. Since every object pulses and produces EMW, it isn't surprising that we seemingly observe waves in association with particles. Nonetheless, we're observing not the sometimes wave behavior of a particle but simply EMW streaming from it as it moves in space. Mina says equipment already exists to detect and manipulate *enérgeia* which we can use to measure one element of a conjugate pair without disturbing the other, such as position and momentum, and thereby gain greater awareness of hyposubatomic reality and HUP's tendency to confuse probability and uncertainty with reality owing to its inadequate understanding of, and accounting for, quantum objects in their environment.

6.12.2   QUANTUM TUNNELING QUA ENERGENT PARITY

Mina designed and intentioned 25% of the workings of our universe—100% of our physical body[244]—while the other 75% is WOB emergent. A lot of his preparation for creation involved perfecting his Intentionality so it emergently spawned all the basal necessities for the whole thing to work as intended.[245] One of those necessities is that stars have an orderly, controlled production of energy in an environment conducive to preventing runaway and premature burnout, and that planets have a long-term stable heat supply important for eternal habitability. Radioactive decay and fusion are emergent properties that support his Intention. You may have noticed throughout this chapter the linkage between phenomena from the nanoscale to the macroscale. Quantum tunneling is no exception, as the phenomenon is actually *enérgeia* 'undulations' or Parity aka quantum entanglement. We overview what's really going on, then hit the nitty gritty.

6.12.2.1   RADIOACTIVE DECAY—*alpha emission*

Radioactive is the term for an atom exhibiting spontaneous nuclear decay because of what appears to be an imbalance of neutrons to protons. This makes for an unstable atom because, while electromagnetic force pushes the protons apart, as they have the same charge, the SNF pulls the protons and neutrons together. Each holds the other in check. For science, a nucleus is stable only with the right balance of neutrons and protons and has no extra energy. If it does, it's unstable, as nature seeks equilibrium. Radioactive *decay* is the term used for unstable nuclei reorienting to a more stable state. Science believes an unstable atom randomly emits parts or radiates energy via decay processes—alpha, beta, gamma emission—until it achieves an equilibrium suitable to that element. An example is the transformation of radioactive Uranium-238 ($^{238}_{92}\mathrm{U}$) through a decay chain of various isotopes and elements until it eventually arrives at observationally stable lead ($^{206}_{82}\mathrm{Pb}$). This is inaccurate, however. Instead, a different process leads to an unstable atom's lessening instability and the observation of decay emissions. We focus on alpha emission because its decay process is relevant to our broader discussion on quantum tunneling.

An *alpha particle* ($^{4}_{2}\mathrm{He}^{2+}$) is an atom *outside* the potential energy barrier (§ 6.12:202) composed of two neutrons and two protons with a double positive charge, as it's missing two electrons for a helium–4 ($^{4}_{2}\mathrm{He}$) atom. But it doesn't emit from the nucleus as science presumes. Instead, it's energized by a particle *inside* the potential energy barrier that's a composite archí structure $\sim 1.275 \times 10^{-19}$ meter having $\sim 75\%$ the energy of a quark and $\sim 51\%$ the mass of a neutron. We term it *delta particle* (δ_P), as δx represents an infinitesimal change x in nucleonic energy that, for physics, is unstable atomic energy reorienting toward stability. How is it in a neutron? Essentially, the magnetic fields of three quarks forming into a neutron stochastically compress bonded archí (§ 2.3.1:115) in the intervening space until they're close enough to bind as a δ_P. It can't bind with the quarks across the magnetic field nor escape restriction.

6.12.2.1.1   ALPHA DECAY PROCESS

Alpha decay is typically thought to begin when an unstable atom like $^{238}_{92}\mathrm{U}$ randomly ejects an alpha particle from its nucleus. The question is why and how it happens where SNF and Coulomb forces supposedly hold each in check, and in fact do so for very long times before mysteriously decaying. Science explains it as a spontaneous—meaning, inexplicable—event, but atoms don't emit parts without cause, there's some process in play beyond the simple thermodynamics of too much energy for the nucleus to hold it all together. It begins when a $^{238}_{92}\mathrm{U}$ atom encounters an 'undulation' in the Energent that perturbs its nucleonic interactions (Eq. (17.8):117; Eq. (17.95):195). Here, the 'undulation' expands the distance between the three quarks constituting a particular neutron, weakening its magnetic field and the SNF binding them for approximately 2.918642×10^{-33} second. If the quarks include a δ_P, it might 'ride' the 'undulation' beyond its restriction. The reason alpha decay

---

244. Human consciousness manifests a supranatural (spirit) body independently of any universe's creator but is consistent throughout because of megaversal humanity's collective consciousness and emergent way of being (ORIGIN OF LIFE, § 2.3.2:240).

245. Mina created small-scale discrete, finite, disposable 'universes' to perfect his Intentionality except w.r.t. to humans, whose *embodiment* he only *physically* developed (FN 244; § 2.1.5:313; § 2.1.6:328).

appears intrinsically random and predictable only as a probability is that *enérgeia* 'undulations' themselves are locally random though globally consistent, and δ_P's trajectory may or may not coincide. A particular neutron and δ_P encountering an 'undulation' having this outcome is therefore random albeit statistically certain over large numbers of nuclei.

The exit of δ_P from the neutron actually *completes* the decay process, as the neutron is now stable. This is *actual* decay. Observed alpha emission *as* decay is only an artifact of δ_P emission from the neutron *but not the atom*. This is *apparent* decay. With δ_P out of the neutron and nucleus, though still within the atom, it's energy no longer contributes to nucleonic instability since the Flavor–color Force (FCF; § 1:112) responds to δ_P's proximity to the rotatory motion of archí components in exterior-localized regions of a quark, deflecting its trajectory from the nucleus such that it no longer interacts with it. To visualize why the continuing presence of δ_P doesn't affect the atom wholistically, consider an atom scaled to the size of ten soccer fields (about 1100 meters) in diameter where its nucleus in the center would be about the size of a small house spider (about 5 mm) with $\delta_P \sim 1/100^{th}$ the size, its scope of energy within $\sim 6/10^{ths}$ a soccer field's distance, and moving too fast to interact with electrons. So-called alpha emission via QT across the potential energy barrier is not the culminating process of alpha decay but the unrelated aftereffect of δ_P interacting with helium–3 ($^{3}_{2}\mathbf{He}$) electrons beyond the potential energy barrier (Fig. 84:203).

We might visualize the three quarks of a neutron enclosing a δ_P experiencing *enérgeia* 'undulation' like three floats strung in a triangle, bobbing in undulating water where, as an 'undulation' passes, each float bobs nearer or farther from the others. As the quarks momentarily 'bob' infinitesimally farther apart, the SNF and composite magnetic field act across a greater distance which opens up their restriction of δ_P somewhat analogous to broadening the space between jail bars such that a prisoner can squeeze through. If δ_P is in the right place at the right time, with a trajectory similar to that of the 'undulation,' then it exits to greater atomic space where it no longer influences neutron thus atomic stability. SNF and the atom's magnetic field keep it close, but neither can it reenter the nucleus due to FCF. Its trajectory deflection in degrees (β) toward the nucleus is where $\beta > 0°$ marks its inner closest approach. Its farthest possible distance of ~ 1.5 femtometer (fm) from any proton is where $KE_0 = 0$ marks its kinetic minimum (*Fig. 86*). Within this orbital, where $KE_0 = 0 \rightarrow \beta > 0° \rightarrow KE_i = 0$, $KE > 0$. We end up with the classic quantum description of δ_P banging around the nucleus' sphere of influence, equally unable to bind to or escape it.

At this point, science introduces quantum tunneling to explain how a radioactive atom with a certain atomic mass appears to randomly decay to a mass less four (e.g., $^{238}_{92}\mathbf{U} \rightarrow {}^{234}_{90}\mathbf{Th} + {}^{4}_{2}\mathbf{He}$), as it observes alpha particles sprinting away from the object and presumes they magically 'tunnel' through the potential energy barrier—its outer (kinetic minimum) orbital, which classical physics says it can't do—to escape. If we observe alpha particles racing away from a radioactive element—itself eventually correlating to a different isotope or element—it seems obviously conclusive the alpha particle previously *inside* said element must now be *outside* it and implicating its atomic weight, which mass spectrometry appears to validate. Mina says no, however. What science attributes to an ejected alpha particle quantum tunneling away, thus improving nuclear stability, is actually a δ_P restricted to the decayed isotope or element not contributing to its instability, but the reason alpha particles appear to emit (*Fig. 85*).

Figure 85. Alpha particle trails (white lines, includes electrons) appear to eject from radioactive uranium (center) inside a Peltier cloud chamber.[229]

Let's suppose a situation where two composite archí structures are moving toward each other. One we'll call alpha particle αA (it's the δ_P) that's within the influence of an atom's nucleus. The other we'll call αB (it's a free-ranging $^{3}_{2}\mathbf{He}$ atom beyond the influence of said atom). Particle αA approaches its kinetic maximum, the potential energy barrier. At the same time, αB approaches its own closest-approach resistance barrier from another direction (*Fig. 86*, left). In a situation where science presumes QT occurs, αA reaches $KE_0 = 0$ sufficiently close (§ 6.11.5:199) to αB reaching its own $KE_0 = 0$.

This is the potential energy barrier for each, the point where attractive–repulsive forces perfectly balance and compensate, and αA and αB come to a standstill for $\sim 1.6666668 \times 10^{-17}$ seconds. The potential barrier between them is the distance between αA's sphere of influence over αB and vice versa, and the energy required to close that distance (*Fig. 86*, right). Across this distance their magnetic fields interact with the energy potential between them, which arises from their own potential energies—αA's resistance to getting too far from the influence of its atom (effectively trapping it) and αB's resistance to getting too close to the atom—and the resistance between them, i.e., the potential energy barrier.

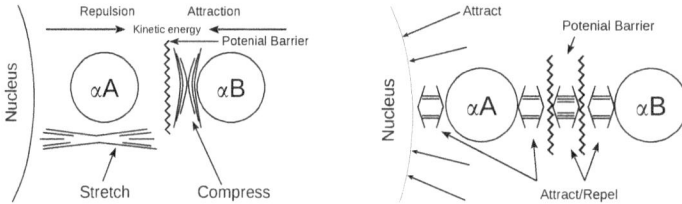

Figure 86. Left, αA and αB approaching each other; right, the potential barrier as distance separating the particles and the energy required to close that distance.

The strengthening energy field between them gives rise to a distinct magnetic field. It expands as the objects approach to critical distance, exerting an effect over each sufficient to stop their individual magnetic field rotations. This reorients each to the encapsulating magnetic field now connecting them. The encapsulating magnetic field—tiny but sufficient—brings αA and αB the last mile beyond their respective $KE_0 = 0$ like two rubber bands under tension. The magnetic field also draws αB's two protons (a $^3_2\mathbf{He}$ atom, recall) maximally close. The encapsulating magnetic field exerts its force for a time, then the repulsive forces obtaining between αA and αB shoots them apart like tensioned rubber bands released.

This all happens *nearly* instantaneously. When the magnetic field's pull ends, the protons rebound from the electrons, which rebound from δ_P with a kinetic energy that propels them to 4% lightspeed c over $\sim 1.5635 \times 10^{-20}$ meter. Their neutron falls behind a maximum of ~ 1 fm, or $\sim 1 \times 10^{-15}$ m, and only closes the gap as αB slows. The two rebounding electrons are on the heels of their protons, but before resuming their average orbital velocity of $\sim 51\%$ c, and after $\sim 0.57673 \times 10^{-20}$ m of travel, or roughly halfway toward $v = 4\% c$, the $^3_2\mathbf{He}$ atom ionizes partly from velocity and partly from colliding with a particle that captures a neutron, which makes it an alpha particle $^4_2\mathbf{He}^{2+}$. Object αA rebounds to go nipping about inside its atom, and we observe αB in a cloud chamber appearing to eject from the atom as an alpha particle (*Fig. 85*). This is the alpha particle's origin.

The alpha particle αB flying away from the radioactive element as in *Fig. 85* isn't the result of quantum tunneling, which doesn't exist in this case, but magnetic pull, which does. The δ_P in the atom (αA) resumes being buffeted around its orbital by FCF and SNF until, at some future time, it randomly approaches close enough to another $^3_2\mathbf{He}$ atom beyond its potential energy barrier as just described, and another alpha particle appears to emit from the atom. This goes on so long as the element exists; more alpha particles arise from δ_P interactions post-decay than from actual decay. *Enérgeia* 'undulations' aren't strong enough to affect stable atoms, which don't have any δ_P anyway. An alpha particle is an apparent emission, an artifact of actual decay. It contributes nothing w.r.t. decay. This process is similar for all interactions attributed to quantum tunneling, such as electron emission, electron tunneling microscopes, and so forth. The reason the probability for decay in any particular atom is unpredictable is that the probability of an $^3_2\mathbf{He}$ atom on the other side of the barrier close enough to interact is low.

6.12.2.1.2 NUCLEAR TRANSMUTATION

Finally, how does nuclear transmutation—an element becoming a different element—occur, since there's no alpha particle ejection physically removing two protons and neutrons? When δ_P escapes restriction, it takes with it $\sim 9\%$ the quarks' gravitational and inertial mass with it, sort of like debris spewing out of the nucleus which eventually ends up incorporated into the atom's particle saturant (§ 3.1:121), while δ_P offsets neutron mass loss. As a matter Energy structure, the neutron now interacts differently; it's inert in terms of how science understands the interactions that make a proton a proton and a neutron a neutron. The neutron's different behavior leads to a secondary proton (beta-minus) decay process, whose particle saturants integrate with it (two protons and two neutrons form a quad structure in a nucleus via their particle saturants). This decay process leaves both protons as protons in structure, each still having two up quarks and one down quark, but a neutron in charge, which then involves the other neutron in the quad structure such that it, too, becomes inert in the way we're using the term. Thus, two protons and neutrons no longer interact with the atom as protons and neutrons following alpha decay; they've decayed. Accordingly, the parent element—say, $^{238}_{92}$U—is effectively short these nucleons and now interacts with other elements in the way science observes its daughter isotope Thorium ($^{234}_{90}$Th) to do. In this process, energy conservation is immaterial since nothing is actually lost, but internally conserved. This paragraph is necessarily brief, as a detailed account is too lengthy.

6.12.2.2 HYDROGEN–HELIUM FUSION

The second major quantum-tunneling phenomenon is the proton–proton fusion process that powers stars like the Sun, converting hydrogen to helium for fuel (*Fig. 87*). Even in the Sun's high-temperature, high-pressure environment, protons don't have enough energy to overcome the repulsion between two positive charges to get close enough for SNF to take over and create deuterium, the second stage in this fusion process. This is where science theorizes that one of the protons quantum tunnels through the potential (repulsive) energy barrier to fuse with the other proton, which is too far apart to touch and permanently separated by the barrier. As we've seen, this sort of particle–wave duality magic isn't happening.

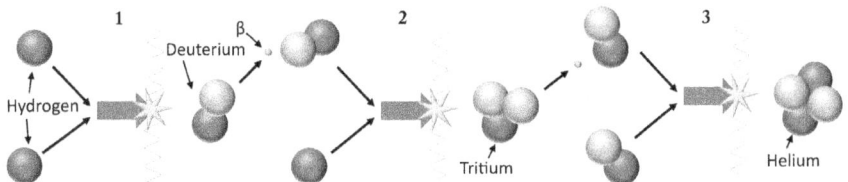

Figure 87. Stages of proton–proton fusion. L → R: 1) $^1_1$H + $^1_1$H → $^2_1$H $_{+1}^{\ 0}\beta$; 2) $^1_1$H + $^2_1$H → $^3_1$H $_{+1}^{\ 0}\beta$; 3) $^2_1$H + $^2_1$H → $^4_2$He. Tritium is helium-3 ($^3_1$H).230

In this case, the protons don't actually fuse together in the sense of being close enough to each other that SNF can snap them together, despite the Coulomb repulsion between them. Instead, they entangle across a Parity bridge, as described. In the local Parity environment KE > 0 for both protons, meaning their energy state is elevated and requires they release some energy. Whichever proton reaches this point first sheds a positron and a neutrino, and converts to a neutron. With this, the Coulomb repulsion disappears and they accordingly bind via SNF to form deuterium. From this point forward, the fusion process plays out within the prevailing conditions of the star.

SECTION 7

Natural–supranatural 'Energy' Translation

"At the quantum scale, space is a writhing, frantic, ever-changing foam, with particles popping into existence and disappearing in the wink of an eye. This is not just a theoretical idea—it's confirmed" (Lincoln 2013, par. 3). This ostensible reality lays alongside virtual particles (VP) and zero point energy (ZPE). To science, quantum foam (QF)—the rapid change in state of beer bubbles as they formed and popped inspired the nomenclature—is a phenomenon where new spacetime Planck-length dimensions unfurl then furl back in on themselves at Planck-time speeds, creating infinitesimal distortions in time and space that appear to affect EMR passage. Virtual particles are transient quantum fluctuations (temporary changes to the amount of energy in a point space) that science believes act in some respects like real particles; ZPE is considered the lowest energy (ground) state—though not a *no*-energy state—of vacuum space. For some scientists, its discovery leads to reintroducing some type of non-material æther as an explanans.

Concepts like these are the quantum mystique decurtate. Some call it reality, hyperbole, metaphor, or just plain old BS. What's really going on behind these observations, besides misapprehension, is a bleary glimpse of the process that powers the natural environment, which in turn powers the supranatural one. Spacetime isn't a thing (§ 2:107ff) and QF is actually a VP effect which itself reflects archí popping into existence, failing to bond, then dephasing (§ 2.3.1:115), the 'energy' perturbations of which mimic characteristics of composite archí structures like so-called elementary particles. Sometimes, archí materialize close enough together they're taken as pairs although, in archí terms, are too far apart to bond, hence, dephase. With ZPE, science is scratching around omnipresent and permeative *enérgeia*, 'undulating' in both empty space and that within matter as well.

These confusing quantum phenomena point to the Energent. Its 'foamy' nature reflects the process producing the raw material that eventually *translates*—transfers without moving—natural environment 'energy' to power the supranatural. It's simple in concept but, as usual, the devil's in the details.

7.1 STRUCTURE OF THE UNIVERSE

Our infinite universe is a wholistic, physicospirit structure composed of two interwoven and fully interactive environments, the natural and supranatural, which Philosophy with a capital-P generally renders the physical and spirit worlds. While the natural–supranatural is indeed a fundamental demarcation, they meet in a 'reflective' environment where a 'turbid' area forms a 'fluid' bridge between the two Energents (*Fig. 88*, left; § 1:112). We explain these terms below.

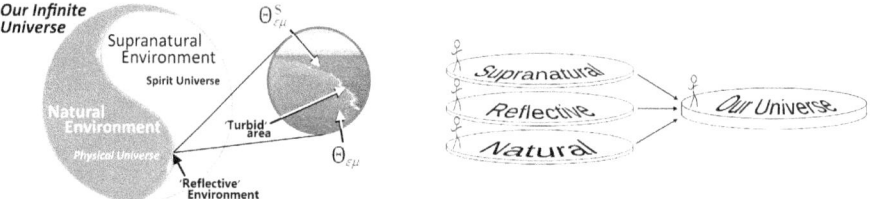

Figure 88. Left, environments of our infinite universe; 'turbid' area is the proximal interaction of the natural $\Theta_{\varepsilon\mu}$ and supranatural $\Theta_{\varepsilon\mu}^S$ Energents in the 'reflective' environment; right, schematic of a person in our infinite universe. Left, exploded view; right, integrated, wholistic.[231]

A physicospirit person exists *simultaneously* in all three of these discrete but interconnected environments— four, inclusive of consciousness—as a singular, wholistic entity (*Fig. 88*, right). If all our senses integrated as intended, then when we looked in the mirror we'd be able to perceive our physical body here in the natural environment, our body's nonphysical 'reflection' in the 'reflective' environment, and our spirit body in the supranatural environment. We explain these environments in PART III but, for clarity, we describe them here as pertains to 'energy' translation.

7.1.1 NATURAL ENVIRONMENT

Everything in the natural (physical) environment 'reflects' in the 'reflective' environment. This means physical matter has two apparent forms: physical and nonphysical (*Fig. 89*). The nonphysical is too ethereal for our physical senses to experience. It has no purpose as such; it's more an artifact of the way the natural and supranatural Energents behave and interact, which interface bridges the difference between the natural and supranatural environments. Chakras, a purposed phenomenon of this 'reflective' environment, serve to bridge physical and spirit persons so they can interact (§ 1.2:498).

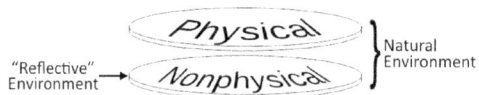

Figure 89. Physical and nonphysical aspects of the natural environment.

7.1.1.1 THE 'REFLECTIVE' ENVIRONMENT

Right up front, let's clarify the 'reflective' environment isn't a real environment the way the physical and spirit environments are real. It's more a boundary between the natural and supranatural Energents where the latter is reactive in proximity to phenomena of the former, the effect of which composites dimensional physical motion—down to the singular archí oscillation—into a dimensionless 'reflection' of physical matter and its applied energy E phenomena (§ 6.II.4:198).

To help visualize its 'reflective' nature, imagine your hand in a tall transparent pot of a non-Newtonian fluid (nNf) like *oobleck* (*Fig. 90*, left), which we use analogously as a stand-in for supranatural Energent proto-energy (§ 1:112). NNf suffuses the space between the constituent archí of your hand and the space around its overall composite form. Since every archí is in motion—oscillating—your hand is in motion, too, even though it appears perfectly still. Each archí oscillates $\sim 4 \times 10^{105}$ times per second (§ 2.3.1:115), which merge into about 1,300 aperiodic oscillatory sets per second. Each set vibrates so fast it's essentially a standing wave, acting like a constant nnf-style sudden force vis-à-vis the nnf medium.

To simulate the 'reflective' environment where physical reality doesn't exist but only 'reflects,' let's have your physical hand magically disappear from your physical senses within the nnf. It's still there and attached to your arm, just invisible, its individual archí still oscillating in the pot of nnf that surrounds and suffuses your invisible hand. Our analogous nnf reacts to this apparent standing wave of sudden oscillatory force like a solid—it 'hardens'—in the overall shape of your hand, from each individual archí up to your composited hand and outermost skin. The effect creates a fully dimensional impression of your hand in the nnf-like medium as though your hand was physically visible again, except it's not, it's just a 'reflection' in the nnf-like nonphysical 'reflective' environment. Move your hand around, flex your fingers; the nnf-medium 'reflects' each changing shape and spatial position of your invisible hand and its constituent archí. To your senses, it looks physical though it's really a nonphysical 'reflection.'

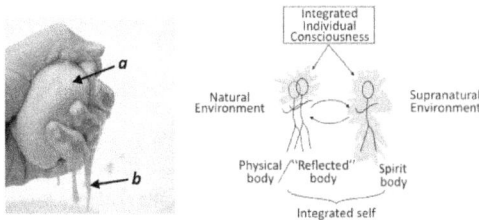

Figure 90. Left, nnf *oobleck* (a cornstarch and water solution) is a shear-thickening fluid that reacts as a solid to sudden force (*a*) but as a liquid to gradual or no force (*b*). The 'reflective' environment is nnf-*like*; right, schematic of human consciousness interacting with the universe via three integrated body states.[232]

The nnf-like medium we're describing here illustrates the supranatural Energent's change in 'energy density' as a function of its proximity to archí oscillation as a sudden force. Essentially, the 'reflective' environment is the nnf-style effect of the supranatural Energent reacting to archí motion. We touched on this concept w.r.t. displaced gravitons provoking a rise in natural Energent 'density' as a precursor to gravity (§ 3.2:121). Here, each archí 'reflects' in the supranatural Energent where it's proximal to archí oscillation and physical objects composite nnf-style as fully dimensional existents, except as *nonphysical* and *nondynamic*, since it constitutes not from physical matter but as 'hardened' supranatural proto-energy.

The 'reflective' environment appears real because it's a fully dimensional representation of physical matter and its applied energy *E* phenomena, but it's not those things. It's just a 'reflection.' It has no dynamism apart from its physical counterpart any more than a shadow has apart from what cast it. It and its environment are nondynamic. A spirit person visiting the natural environment can only perceive and (with Intentionality) interact with this 'reflection,' not with the physical world itself.[246] They experience physical reality going about its business all around them as though in the physical world, but they're actually experiencing its nonphysical 'reflection,' as they can't see or experience the actually physical. Since physical matter's applied energy *E* phenomena 'reflects' there, too, then a spirit person, who isn't a 'reflected' part of this environment, experiences its phenomena—rain, wind, fire—just as a physical person does, but not its effect—wetness, blowing hair, burns—because the phenomena isn't real but only its 'reflection' (*Fig. 90*, right). So, while fire and its heat 'reflect,' for example, deterministic cause and effect like a burn doesn't. A spirit person can walk through a 'reflected' wall and feel the sensation of it scraping as they pass through but isn't scraped, feel the wetness of rain falling through their body but isn't wetted, and feel wind on their skin but their hair doesn't blow around. All this because their spirit body isn't as 'dense' as the 'reflective' environment, which itself isn't near as 'dense' as the physical one (§ 7.2.1.2:217). The 'reflective' environment is also the environment physical people experience when they astral project (§ 1:591).

Any physical entity, right down to its constituent archí, 'reflects' in this nnf-style aspect of the supranatural Energent so long as it physically exists. Also, what seem like extra or inexplicable animal senses, or aspects of human sixth sense, are in part 'reflective-self' phenomena. Only humans and certain companion animals

---

246. When a spirit person appears to manipulate a material object (say, a light switch), they're actually moving its 'reflection' via Intentionalized 'energy,' which naturally moves the physical entity since it integrates like a shadow with its object.

(CH. 39:601) have dynamism in the 'reflective' environment because these alone integrate autonomous spirit bodies (§ 1:303). A physical person who's spirit-aware and trained can consciously interact via their spirit body with any nondynamic 'reflective' object—human bodies, animals, bugs, bacteria, DNA, inanimate objects—as well as the dynamic spirit body of other persons, certain companion animals, and spirit world residents. We describe how the 'reflective' environment operates in the context of 'energy' translation below (§ 7.2.1.1:216).

7.1.2   Supranatural Environment

Matter in the supranatural environment differs fundamentally from natural matter just as its Energent differs from the natural one. This difference is why we can't physically interact with supranatural matter using our physical body, but need our 'reflective self' as a bridge via the chakras to integrate our brain–body with mind's awareness of the supranatural.[247] When we're brain aware of the supranatural (§ 1.2.2:253), we can consciously interact with that environment using our spirit body even while physically alive and awake. This is how (legit) mediums consciously experience spirit persons. Mina provided for our complete freedom of existence in the way he structured our universe. When we understand how reality works, we're quite literally unlimited in what we can be, do, think, feel, and experience.

7.1.3   'Energy' is Required

All things need energy to exist. From stars to rocks to things alive, energy holds it all together and enlivens it. This means the Energent to create archí and bind it into forms like stars and planets from which sunlight, air, water, and so forth arise to support physical life. That's all separate and apart from *vital energy*—Living and *L*ife force (§ 1.3:272, § 1.2:246)—that enlivens things, makes them actually *alive*. Living force comes to entities through their 'reflected'-self's chakras via the natural Energent. *L*ife force is human and comes to our physical body via integrating our emergent *L*ife self.

Our spirit body isn't *exactly* a body in the physical sense, meaning an objective existence in its own right— an existent—with independent processes and mechanisms that requires self-maintenance. Rather, it's a manifestation of the mind, coalesced via Intentionality (§ 1.2.1.1.1:248, § 3.2:282) from proto-energy into spirit matter with human form without need of conscious Thought (§ 2.3.2:240); our mind just does it. Perhaps the easiest way to picture this is to imagine how you see yourself in your mind's eye. Are you tall, short, good looking, happy, bright, sour, dynamic, with gravitas, and so on? In the same natural way you physically walk around projecting a self-image, the natural capability intrinsic to your mind integrating the supranatural Energent simply brings your spirit body into real supranatural form. With our present awareness here on Earth, we can only imagine how we want to be and hope for results over time. Even so, people often perceive us not as how we actually are but by what we (sub-)consciously project. This phenomenon reflects the observation that we eventually transmute into reality what we intend in an Intentional way. To the degree that spirit people master the process, they literally transmute 'energy' into whatever form they Intentionalize.

To actualize Intent requires 'energy.' Supranatural matter, for instance, doesn't appear out of thin air like magic. One doesn't manifest a real, touchable, experiential spirit body as a figment of the imagination. It's a (supranaturally) corporeal thing. Although Intentionality effectuates the overall result, we're really manipulating 'energy' into matter of definite form and function, whether it's our own spirit body or just a cup of coffee. In this respect, the natural and supranatural environments are more similar than different.

The 'energy' we're talking about here is Energent proto-energy. But it can't directly translate to the supranatural Energent like a river into a sea because the natural Energent is an organic expression of Energent–prime whereas the supranatural Energent is a universe builder's own creation. It's substantively different. We call it an Energent because it serves the same functional purpose, but it's a construct, a facsimile, not an organic expression of Energent–prime, the root of All Existence. Operational incompatibility between the natural and supranatural Energents arises from this substantive difference. Just as initially immiscible ocean waters eventually integrate as their properties—temperature, density, salinity—equalize, or convert, to the norm in and around an ocean cline (Fig. 88:212, *inset*), *enérgeia* must convert to a supranaturally integrable norm. The reason is straightforward.

Mina built the supranatural Energent with Intentionality whereas the natural Energent is an organic expression—an appendage—of Energent–prime with unique, adjunctive properties that isn't encapsulated, or

---

247. *Aware* in the sense our mind integrates our brain more than the current normal.

segregated, from All Existence. He simply Intentionalized (designed) our universe to interface with it. The natural Energent is discrete yet wholistic vis-à-vis Energent–prime. While the supranatural environment is singularly one of 'energy' in which matter arises only in response to Intentionality,[248] the natural environment is one of mixed matter–Energy where, in the context of a universe, matter (archí) emergently arises from proto-energy with its own existentiality (§ 2.3:115) that constructs complex form of its own accord (§ 6.10.1:186). Because it takes 'energy' to form matter, and the supranatural Energent doesn't manufacture it, then it's a net 'energy' *consumer*[249] whereas the natural Energent, manufacturing 'energy' via physical processes, is a net 'energy' *producer*. Accordingly, the former must import its 'energy' from the latter wherein the process initiates. How does conversion and importation occur? Well, pretty simply. In brief, 'energy' translation begins in the natural environment with single pairwise archí—a bonded-archí pair (b–archí)—in motion that 'reflects' as motion in the supranatural environment, where translation ends. Three methods accomplish this task.

> **Method 1** overall translates a large quantity of 'energy' over a vast number of small aperiodic increments via the interaction between every *non-Living* b–archí (in whatever complex structure it exists) and the natural or supranatural Energent. The interaction itself is the conduit.
>
> **Method 2** is the same as Method 1 but differs in two ways. First, it operates to translate an overall large quantity of energy over fewer but larger aperiodic increments. Second, it operates on b–archí constituting *Living* and *Living–Life* structures (b–archí of matter that's alive).
>
> **Method 3** is a more general 'energy' translation and happens in stars. It operates to translate a relatively large quantity of 'energy' over a single, small random increment. In brief, a *non-Living* b–archí pulled into a star core encounters the up quarks of a silicon–28 proton whereby their combined 'energy' translates to the supranatural Energent, leaving all involved entities dephased.

The greatest quantity of 'energy' per translation happens via Method 2, followed by Method 3, then Method 1. We describe each method in order.

7.2   'Energy' Translation: Method 1

Recall that everything is in motion (§ 2.3:115). If nothing else, archí oscillate. Whatever constitutes from archí (matter) also oscillates. Without motion there's no proto-energy interaction, no forces or 'energies' arise, no b–archí, and physical matter ceases to exist. As we've learned, *enérgeia* arises from proto-energy in the natural environment through the interaction between the Energent where there's no time and space, and between b–archí in motion where there is time and space. *Enérgeia* gives rise to real energy Υ from which applied energy E arises (§ 3.7.3.3.1:139). At the same time, each b–archí—each piece of physical matter—non-physically 'reflects' (Fig. 89:212) to bridge the natural and supranatural environments since they aren't compatible. The incompatibility arises in the natural Energent being a direct expression of Energent–prime and the supranatural Energent being human built. The result is different operational symmetries.[250] A key difference is that, while the natural Energent is a net 'energy' producer that intrinsically interacts with deterministic physical matter (b–archí) as autonomous existents, the supranatural Energent is a net 'energy' consumer for which spirit matter only exists when coalesced from its proto-energy into spirit material form via Intentionality.

7.2.1   How 'Energy' Converts

To translate *enérgeia* from the natural to the supranatural Energent requires a compatibility conversion. Method 1 accomplishes this when non-Living b–archí in motion—b–archí that's not a part of matter that integrates Living or *Life* force—give rise to *enérgeia* in the natural environment (§ 2.3:115), which 'reflects' as motion and translates to the supranatural environment as supranatural *enérgeia*.

It happens thus. B–archí oscillation in the context of the natural Energent gives rise to *enérgeia*.[251] Recall from earlier that natural *enérgeia* isn't compatible with supranatural *enérgeia* because of differences in operational

---

248. There's a basic undirected Intentionality built into the supranatural Energent that's somewhat independent of animate existents (§ 6.11.4:198). It maintains the baseline 'world of nature' in the supranatural environment separate from albeit not immune to animate existents' Intentionality (Culture, § 4:291).

249. Though a net 'energy' consumer, people can 'rebate' it to the natural side.

250. *Symmetry* in the sense of invariance; the natural Energent is non-transformable absent an emergence event, as is the supranatural Energent, because its way of being (wob) is invariant absent Intentional change by its builder.

251. Energent proto-energy is the 'energy' source. The process is an *enérgeia* phenomenon.

symmetries we simplify to '*amplitude*,' which represents those differences. If we think of All Existence not in infinite terms as it is but instead as a finite space—say, inside a ball that's filled with Energent–prime—then, when a founder builds a new universe *inside* this ball, it comes into existence in that exact same finite space that, until then, was only All Existence, except it's of a different 'frequency' and, therefore, functionally a different space (*Fig. 91*).[252] So, although this previously existing All Existence and new universe now 'share' that same finite space (*Fig. 91, c*), the one doesn't experience the other owing to their differing 'frequency space' except via Energent–prime which, regardless 'frequency space,' permeates our finite space example inclusive of all frequencies, which is to say, all universes. We term this inclusive finite-space example current All Existence (*c*AE), which is just All Existence that previously didn't include a built universe (*Fig. 91, a*) but, after its creation, did (§ 1:100; § 2:230). Indeed, there are, in reality, many infinite universes all sharing the one infinite All Existence (§ 2.1.4.1:312).

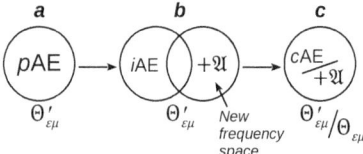

Figure 91. Universe creation process in All Existence AE. In *a*, there's Energent–prime $\Theta'_{\varepsilon\mu}$ in a previous *p*AE; in *b*, a new universe $+\mathfrak{A}$ is built and $p\text{AE} \rightarrow$ interim $i\text{AE}$ occurs in a picosecond, both suffused in $\Theta'_{\varepsilon\mu}$; in *c*, $i\text{AE} \rightarrow$ current $c\text{AE}$ inclusive of $+\mathfrak{A}$ all suffused in $\Theta'_{\varepsilon\mu}$ except that, within $+\mathfrak{A}$, we call its 'frequency'-discrete proto-energy *Energent* $\Theta_{\varepsilon\mu}$, just as AE's non-'frequency'-discrete proto-energy is $\Theta'_{\varepsilon\mu}$.

7.2.1.1 THE PHYSICAL–'REFLECTIVE' CONNECTION

A universe like ours is built with a differentiated natural and supranatural environment in which the matter of each express according to their way of being (WOB; § 6.10.1:186). The supranatural Energent a universe founder builds can't generate its own 'energy' because it doesn't constitute from real proto-energy. Therefore, its 'energy' isn't autogenic nor do archí emergently arise from it to generate *enérgeia* as with the natural Energent. It's a facsimile lacking the intrinsic emergent properties—the *vitæ mysterium*—of proto-energy (FN 140:105). The supranatural Energent must absorb the power its environment requires from the natural Energent, which, being an expression of Energent–prime, is real proto-energy. Since it can't absorb 'energy' *directly* from the natural Energent, it does so *indirectly*. As noted, the 'reflective' environment serves as a 'fluid' bridge between the natural Energent driving our universe and the supranatural environment it powers. Let's look at this from the perspective of process and phenomenon.

As a *process*, it's analogous to the way an automatic transmission's fluid coupler connects a car engine's power to its wheels without the engine's energy input directly connecting to the transmission's output (*Fig. 92*). Engine motion—piston oscillation—'reflects' in the fluid, which translates it as motion to the transmission's output. The 'transmission' w.r.t. energy translation is the 'reflected' b–archí immersed in the supranatural Energent's 'turbid' area (*Fig. 119*). How does it translate power, exactly? As with a fluid coupler, it happens via motion. Let's explore that.

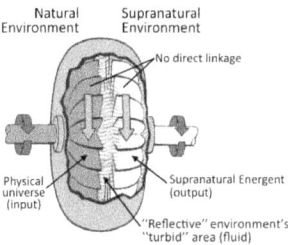

Figure 92. Basic automatic transmission (fluid coupler) conceptualized as a process that bridges the natural and supranatural environments to indirectly translate *enérgeia*.[233]

---

252. We describe them in terms of their 'frequency space,' 'amplitude,' and 'density' but this is just a terminology convention to help visualize their discrete similitude.

7.2.1.2 Natural to Supranatural *Enérgeia*

The 'reflected' b–archí is the 'shadow' of the physical b–archí in the sense of an object's reflection cast upon some other medium, like the ground or even something as rarefied as smoke. Similar to how a shadow isn't a real thing but an object outlined by—reflected in—an absence of light, there's no real 'reflected' existent of a physical object (a b–archí). Though it really *exists* as a fully dimensional 'reflection' in the nNf-like medium of the supranatural Energent, it's not *there* in actuality. This seems contradictory. Let's explain it.

We briefly outlined (§ 7.1.1.1:212) how b–archí oscillation induces a vibratory effect that ultimately constitutes a 'reflection' of the entire physical universe in the supranatural Energent as its medium. In essence, the 'reflective' environment is just an aspect of the supranatural Energent, an nNf-style 'reflective' medium in the context of its 'turbid' proximity to b–archí oscillation throughout the infinite universe. Here, we describe 'reflection' in its phenomenal context where our principal consideration is the natural Energent being significantly 'denser' than the supranatural.

As a *phenomenon*, b–archí oscillation 'reflecting' in the supranatural Energent is analogous to speaking through a wall where the voice sets up sequential vibrations in the wall's molecules (sound wave; *Fig. 93*, left). As it penetrates the wall, the sound wave vibrates the air molecules on the other side where a person there can hear the voice from the wall's other side, except that the sound of the voice changes density between the speaker and the listener—muffled, let's say—because of the dampening effect of the interposing wall's greater density. The 'wall' between the physical and 'reflective' environments is the difference in 'amplitude' between the natural and supranatural environments' operational symmetries. The vibratory effect which b–archí oscillation sets up—Fundamental Force, applied energy E, and its phenomena such as visibility, corporeality, temperature, electromagnetism—on the physical side of this 'wall' 'reflects' in the 'turbid' area of the supranatural Energent.

A b–archí—including your body—manifests in the 'reflective' environment in a literal way as a vibrational 'reflection' in the 'hardened' nNf-style medium of the supranatural Energent, just as sound is a 'hardened' vibrational reflection in the medium of air. It doesn't *really* exist in the 'reflective' environment any more than one's voice actually exists in the listener's ear a hundred feet away from the speaker, it just reflects the sum total of b–archí oscillations that constitute the physical object's properties. To help better visualize this 'reflection' concept, think of b–archí 'reflection' the way a parabolic sound mirror reflects a distant voice as if spoken near the listener (*Fig. 93, center*). Except, instead of reflecting only sound, imagine this magical parabola reflects the speaker's entire body mouthing the words right there in the listener's ear. In this sense, it recreates, or reflects, the speaker's body at the point where one hears their voice, which is at the parabola. In the same way, the physical universe as a whole 'reflects' in the 'parabola' of the 'reflective' environment (*Fig. 93, right*).

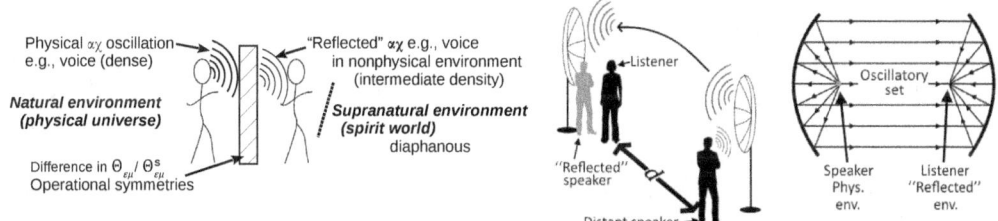

Figure 93. Left, b–archí oscillation 'reflected' through 'wall' of differing natural $\Theta_{\varepsilon\mu}$ and supranatural $\Theta_{\varepsilon\mu}^{S}$ Energent operational symmetries, the former logarithmically 'denser' than the latter; center, a parabola sound mirror reflects distant sound as if local, making speaker seem beside listener; right, oscillatory set similarly translates as motion from physical to 'reflected' environment.[234]

Likewise, imagine the listener in a quiet, forested field away from a city where they can hear but not see its (muted) sounds, as with the center-left figure. This example is the city as a 'reflected' invisible physical existent. Instead of only hearing city noise, each discrete aspect of the city manifests, or reflects, all around the listener such that what they 'hear' of the city reflects in full dimensionality all around them, just as with the speaker vis-à-vis the listener in the figure. They see, hear, smell, and experience people of the city as though on a street corner instead of in the distant field which, in this example, is the 'reflective' environment. These are crude analogies, to be sure, but illustrate how the full dimensionality of the physical universe 'reflects' in the 'turbid' area that's the 'reflective' environment as a result of the sudden force of b–archí oscillation in the supranatural Energent's nNf-like medium (Fig. 88:212, left).

B–archí oscillation 'reflecting' in the supranatural Energent is indeed real in the sense that it's happening. However, while all physical energy manifestations—vibration, temperature, charge—*reflect* in this context, the only effect that *manifests* a response from the supranatural Energent is b–archí oscillation because it's the only thing there that's an existent, everything else derives from it. B–archí oscillation and its real energy Υ and applied energy E phenomena produce only in the context of the natural environment's Energent. The supranatural Energent can't respond to b–archí to *create* 'energy' such as Fundamental Force, thus applied energy E, because it's not real proto-energy; it's not sufficiently 'dense' and its created nature woв isn't deterministic but Intentional. That's how it's only a facsimile of the Energent and not the real thing. Whereas cause and effect arise through physical existents in and of themselves, it arises in spirit world (where nothing is an existent in and of itself except supranatural Energent 'motion' and emergent ℒife) through Intentionality.

Let's shift to describing the natural and supranatural Energents in terms of 'density,'[253] of which 'amplitude' is a property. The supranatural Energent is logarithmically about 10% the 'density' of the natural Energent which, being an organic expression of Energent–prime, has its same 'density.' The supranatural environment's difference arises in being Intentional, not organic like the natural environment. Its lesser 'density' ensures the greatest ease manipulating spirit matter in its Intentional environment relative to the tedious—as in, grueling—nature of manipulating physical matter in its 'denser,' deterministic physical environment. Tediousness, like forcing change on a powerful spinning gyroscope, translates to impossibility for those who are unaware. It's why people consider manipulating physical matter with the mind a ridiculous notion. But it's not. It's just more tedious than supramatter. If we place the supranatural Energent's 'density' at 10^1 on a log_{10} scale, then the natural Energent's 'density' is at 10^4, about $1,000$ times 'denser' than the supranatural's (*Fig. 94*, left). This is why spirit persons can't interact with the physical; the supramatter constituting their bodies is gossamery in comparison. One may as well try feeling wind through rock. Physical persons necessarily interact with spirit persons via their own spirit selves.

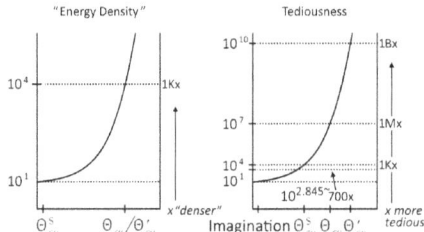

Figure 94. Left, logarithmic scales for 'energy density;' right, tediousness of 'energy'-to-matter formation.

We use a different logarithmic scale to compare how tedious it is to manipulate 'energy' into form in the context of each of these proto-energy 'densities.' On this scale, the supranatural Energent sits at 10^4 against a baseline of 10^1 for simple imagination (howsoever detailed, but lacking Intentionality), the natural Energent measures 10^7, and Energent–prime 10^{10} (*Fig. 94, right*). The overall effort to manipulate 'energy' into form is, therefore, about $1,000$ times more tedious in the supranatural environment than just imagining it in one's mind, about a million times more tedious in the natural environment, and about a billion times more tedious to manipulate Energent–prime into the form of a universe. We've said it elsewhere, but this is why—being the most difficult challenge to undertake—people don't just willy-nilly build universes on a Saturday afternoon.

You might be wondering how, if the supranatural Energent is so comparatively wispy, it can possibly experience b–archí oscillation. It does so because its 'amplitude' (as 'density') where it's proximal to b–archí oscillation rises nnf-style toward the natural environment's 'density,' logarithmically beefing up to about 40% the natural Energent's. That means in this proximal, or 'turbid,' area, the supranatural Energent's 'density' logarithmically increases from 10^1 to about $10^{2.845~}$, or about 700 times 'denser' than its norm (*Fig. 94*, right). In this context, the supranatural Energent experiences b–archí oscillation with an nnf-style 'vibratory' effect which results in a 'hardened,' fully dimensional b–archí 'reflection' (*Fig. 95*). Since every b–archí constituting complex archí structures oscillates from the individual archí up to whatever its wholistic composite form—subatomics, atoms, molecules, dirt, rock, trees, bugs, Elmer Fudd's "wascally wabbit," human beings—then their oscillations in toto reproduce the entirety of the physical world down to its smallest constituent, the archí, as a vibratory 'reflection.'

---

253. *'Density'* in the sense it's part of proto-energy's integrated way of being (woв; nature), not a property.

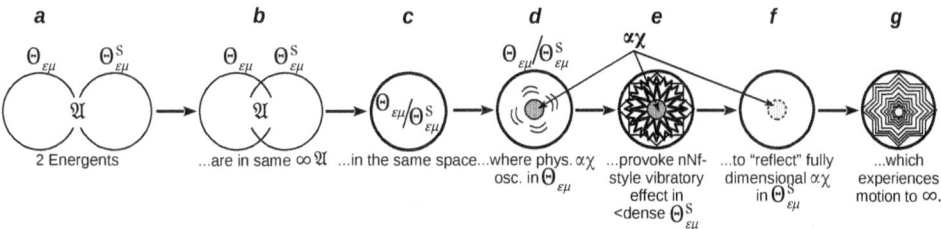

Figure 95. Schematic of how the natural $\Theta_{\varepsilon\mu}$ and supranatural $\Theta_{\varepsilon\mu}^{S}$ Energents suffuse the same infinite universe $\infty\mathfrak{A}$, and how single b–archí $\alpha\chi$ oscillation (*e*) 'reflects' nNf-style fully dimensionally in $\Theta_{\varepsilon\mu}^{S}$, which experiences the motion to infinity (*g*).

Even at ~40% the logarithmic 'density' of the natural Energent, the supranatural Energent's vibratory effect is still too ethereal for physical persons to experience because their physical senses register only the physical universe's 'density.' We can't perceive it without bringing our $\mathcal{L}$ife mind senses to bear (§ 1.2.2.1:253; § 2.1.5.4.1:316). In any case, b–archí oscillation represents the translation of natural *enérgeia* to the supranatural Energent. The way this vibratory effect represents actual *enérgeia* is as follows.

Recall the natural Energent is in 'motion' (§ 1:112), as too are b–archí. The interaction between Energent in 'motion' and b–archí in motion results in *enérgeia*. When the 'turbid' area's beefed-up supranatural Energent experiences 'reflected' b–archí motion, these 'vibrations' spread outward from their origin (as with waves in a medium) into the comparatively diaphanous infinite supranatural Energent (*Fig. 96*). In proto-energy terms, this 'vibratory,' or wavelike, action effectively sets the supranatural Energent in 'motion.' The 'vibrational' effect is only adequately concentrated (as oscillatory sets; § 7.1.1.1:212) right at the 'turbid' area source to produce the fully dimensional 'reflection' of the physical universe. The reason is that, as a 'wave' that naturally travels, the 'vibratory' effect gets less and less concentrated as it travels from the 'turbid' area into the diaphanous medium until it no longer 'reflects' its physical existent but something more like a progressive 'blur' until there's no 'reflection' at all, just 'motion.'

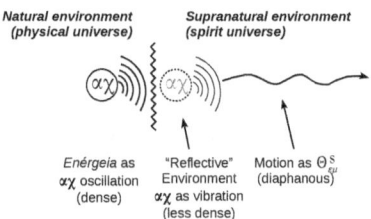

Figure 96. Schematic: *Enérgeia* translates via archí $\alpha\chi$ oscillation as supranatural Energent $\Theta_{\varepsilon\mu}^{S}$ 'motion.'

Outward 'motion' of the infinite supranatural Energent's 'vibration' never diminishes to zero such that

$$\lim_{d \to \infty} \left(\frac{M\Theta_{\varepsilon\mu}^{S}}{d} \right) = 0 \tag{17.115}$$

where $M\Theta_{\varepsilon\mu}^{S}$ is supranatural Energent 'motion' and d is distance (cf. Eq. (17.18):123). The 'motion' is infinite in the medium. Recall there's no time or space in the context of the supranatural Energent, so we're not talking motion in its ordinary, dimensional sense but in its dimensionless sense (§ 6.11.4:198). As b–archí oscillation sets up 'vibrations' ('wave' action) in the supranatural Energent, they aren't this in the ordinary sense at all. Though *enérgeia* arises in the context of the natural Energent between the Energent in 'motion' and b–archí in motion, in that of the supranatural Energent 'motion' in and of itself means *enérgeia* (*Fig. 96*). More concisely,

$$M\Theta_{\varepsilon\mu}^{S} = \alpha\Omega \tag{17.116}$$

where $\alpha\Omega$ is *enérgeia*. Accordingly, *enérgeia* doesn't generate or arise in the supranatural Energent but simply *is* through its 'motion.' That's how Mina built it (§ 6.10.1:186) as an environment of human Intentionality without the cause and effect determinism of the natural environment or Energent–prime. This means spirit world is a 100% human-defined reality, built and operated entirely from multitudinous levels of Intentionality, from nonconsciously undirected to consciously directed. Our control over the supranatural environment— spirit world—is absolute.

How exactly does b–archí oscillation result in the translation of real energy from the natural to the supranatural contexts? Well, not every single oscillation results in a one-to-one vibration in the supranatural Energent context of the 'reflective' environment. Oscillations build up in a dimensionless version of partial destructive wave interference until they altogether achieve translational 'amplitude' the supranatural Energent can experience. We earlier described this phenomenon as an oscillatory set (§ 7.1.1.1:212). 'Motion' translates as *enérgeia* when the oscillatory set generates an 'energy harmonic' that achieves 'amplitude' consistent with the 'turbid' area's beefed-up supranatural proto-energy. The portion of b–archí *enérgeia* then matching 'amplitude'— on average about 5% of total translatable b–archí 'energy' at any given translational moment—translates to (absorbs into) the supranatural Energent as 'motion.' The translation disrupts the harmonic, which ceases until the next oscillatory set aperiodically rebuilds. Because the supranatural Energent permeates the natural and supranatural environments discretely as 'amplitude,' *enérgeia* that translates in the 'turbid' area naturally suffuses throughout the whole of the supranatural Energent, available to spirit world that it powers.

Energy doesn't translate in the ordinary sense of being lost or conserved at point A as it translates to point B as in classical physics, which describes applied energy E. As 'motion' itself is *enérgeia* in the context of the supranatural Energent, b–archí *enérgeia* in the natural one doesn't change. This is why we say *enérgeia translates* from the natural to the supranatural instead of *transfers* or *moves*.

Every b–archí that exists continually interacts with both Energents contextually per the method described (§ 7.1.3:214). Consequently, vast quantities of 'energy' translate from the natural Energent via uncountable tiny per-b–archí increments spread across not only the observable universe but our infinite universe as well, since physical archí arise throughout the infinite Energent (not described here).

7.2.2 Power Units Translated by Method 1

It's not possible to adequately quantify the 'energy' that translates in applied energy E terms, such as joules, because Energent proto-energy is simply too different, not just from applied energy E but from our very concept of energy. It's less conceptually challenging to convert to real energy Υ, but the problem remains of renormalizing two utterly different energy paradigms. We nevertheless take a stab at it to help visualize the vast, seemingly incalculable 'energy' involved in a universe. Mina estimates a *single* non-Living b–archí translates to the supranatural Energent approximately $10^{20}\pm5\%$ joules on average.[254] This amount is roughly the equivalent of half a supernova, or about half the total output of the Sun during its whole 10BY projected lifespan.[255] This equates to about $3.55555 \times 10^{1000^{1000}} \times 10^{20}\pm5\%$ joules of 'energy' translated *per minute* from the natural to the supranatural Energent. That's a lot of 'energy,' but represents only about 935 trillionths of one percent of the total minute-to-minute translatable *enérgeia* of non-Living b–archí in the *infinite* universe *in any given minute*.

7.3 'Energy' Translation: Method 2

This method translates 'energy' from b–archí that constitute Living (alive) matter as well as b–archí that constitute the Living–𝓛ife matter of the human body. According to the same process as in Method 1, oscillating b–archí integrating Living or Living–𝓛ife force translate *enérgeia* from its 'reflection' in the 'reflective' environment to the supranatural Energent. The difference with Method 1 is that, first, there's fewer of these b–archí in any given moment, and second, proto-energy's interaction with Living and Living–𝓛ife b–archí energizes them with vastly more *enérgeia* than it does non-Living b–archí because of the Living and 𝓛ife force integrating and animating the matter they constitute. Whereas the energy of non-Living b–archí is only what its interaction with Energent proto-energy produces, Living and Living–𝓛ife b–archí carry the extra 'charge' of Living force and 𝓛ife force; b–archí constituting Living–𝓛ife matter manifest more *enérgeia* per b–archí than does Living b–archí. Accordingly, the greatest per b–archí energy translation possible from the natural to the supranatural lies with Living–𝓛ife b–archí. This method of 'energy' translation is limited to the *observable* universe.

7.3.1 Power Units Translated by Method 2

A Living b–archí translates to the supranatural Energent the 'energy' equivalent of ~$1.66666 \times 10^{100}\pm5\%$ joules, or about 3.6 supernovæ on average. That's a bit over seven times that of non-Living b–archí. It equates to ~$3.55555 \times 10^{10,000^{1000}} \times 1.66666 \times 10^{100}\pm5\%$ joules of 'energy' translated *per minute* from the natural

---

254. Energent science offers a greater useable 'energy' potential than standard physics.

255. Mina says the Sun, *absent* human intervention, has an effective natural lifespan of ~17.8BY (cf. "Sun," EN 223:660).

to the supranatural Energent throughout the *observable* universe. A single Living–ℒife b–archí translates the 'energy' equivalent of ∼$2.22222 \times 10^{100} \pm 5\%$ joules, about five supernovæ on average. That's ten times non-Living b–archí and about 1.4 times more than Living b–archí, and equates to ∼$3.55555 \times 10^{10,000^{2000}} \times 2.22222 \times 10^{100} \pm 5\%$ joules of 'energy' translated *per minute*.

These are vast sums of 'energy' per b–archí, yet only about 31 trillionths of one percent of the total minute-to-minute translatable *enérgeia* of Living b–archí in the *observable* universe *in any given minute*, and about 88 trillionths of one percent of the total minute-to-minute translatable *enérgeia* of Living–ℒife b–archí. On average, a single human body translates to the supranatural Energent the 'energy' equivalent of about 90 *million* supernovæ over its average lifetime of ∼20,930 days, or ∼4,300 in any given minute.[256] This represents ∼40%—absent The Corruption, ∼70%—of the body's total lifetime 'energy'-equivalent production, significantly more than Living b–archí's ∼13%.

7.4 'Energy' Translation: Method 3

Rather than Method 1 and 2's continuous aperiodic transfer, this method translates *enérgeia* via direct dephasing encounters between single b–archí and silicon–28 quarks in stars. Over the average star's lifecycle, its silicon–28 density is < 1% except in the planetary nebulæ and supernova phases where it's ±20%. 'Energy' translation occurs when a b–archí's trajectory brings it into proximity with a proton's two up quarks in a silicon–28 atom—there are misses, of course; reality entails probabilities—that carry the requisite characteristics of red and green color charge, $+2/3e$ applied energy E charge, and 1/2 spin, among others (*Fig. 97*, right). If a b–archí connects with one of its neutron's single up-quarks (or any other structure), for instance, the effect described here doesn't occur because, like a virus seeking entry to a cell, there's only one suitable receptor. When the incoming b–archí achieves proximity with two such up-quarks, their oscillations achieve an *enérgeia* 'harmonic' which then involves the remaining up-quarks in the silicon–28 nucleus as well as their particle saturants (*Fig. 97*, left). In the 'reflective' environment, the 'harmonic' induces an 'amplitude' change to a lesser 'strength' in the b–archí's *enérgeia* (as well as among the b–archí constituting each up-quark of this type) that's consistent with Method 1.

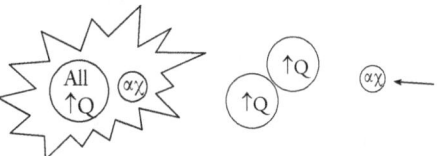

Figure 97. 'Energy' translation process in stars; right, a b–archí αχ encounters a silicon–28 proton's pair of up quarks ↑Q; left, 'energy harmonic' between b–archí and all ↑Q of a silicon–28 atom.

Now, the incoming b–archí doesn't physically collide with the two up-quarks. As soon as it achieves proximity, the 'harmonic' builds to attain the 'amplitude' matching the supranatural Energent's own. Unlike with Method 1 and 2, which is ongoing aperiodically with b–archí everywhere, when there's 'amplitude' convergence in this method then *enérgeia* contained in and between the b–archí and silicon–28, along with their particle saturants, is no longer consistent (compatible) with the natural environment's 'amplitude.' It ceases to be a phenomenon there and becomes Energent 'motion' in the supranatural environment. This disrupts the b–archí bonds—SNF—throughout the entities and each pairwise structure's individual archí push away, since archí diameter is greater than binding distance (§ 2.3.1:115). Being unbonded but not up-'charged' as a photon, they predictably dephase and associated natural *enérgeia* no longer arises. Colloquially, we'd say the entities and associated *enérgeia* 'magically' disappear from the physical universe (*Fig. 98*). This ends the 'reflections' as well as the 'harmonic' of the entities' and *enérgeia* translation completes. All this happens in about 82 Planck times, or $4.42082254 \times 10^{-42}$ second, like the flash of a meteor streaking through the atmosphere to dissipate into nothing.

The universe took around 3.72 billion years before enough silicon–28 existed in the right places for non-Living b–archí to sufficiently power up the supranatural Energent using Methods 1 and 3. Until then, spirit world was a no-furniture-lights-off-furnace-to-zero embryo beyond the veil. Recall that All Existence provides about 19% of our universe's 'energy' requirements (§ 1:112). Proto-energy from All Existence to the natural

---

256. Averaged from Humanity 2.0's beginnings (cf. field literature). Another planet has the longest average lifespan at ∼36,000 days.

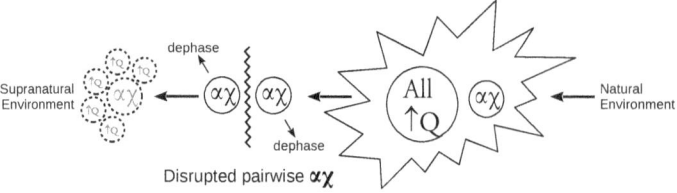

Figure 98. End state dephasing in *enérgeia* translation process.

environment needs no conversion since Energent–prime and the natural Energent connect organically, like an ocean to a bay. Consequently, proto-energy translation from Energent–prime to the natural Energent differs from Method 1–3 (not described in this book).

7.4.1 POWER UNITS TRANSLATED BY METHOD 3

On average, a single b–archí-plus-silicon–28 pair translates to the supranatural Energent the rough 'energy' equivalent of $10^{99}\pm5\%$ joules, about 2.25 supernovæ. About $2.1974972 \times 10^{10^{70}}$ b–archí *per minute* translate 'energy' via this method. On average, this equates to $\sim\!2.1974972 \times 10^{10^{70}} \times 10^{99}\pm5\%$ joules of 'energy' translated to the supranatural Energent *per minute* throughout the *observable* universe. This represents only about one quadrillionth of one percent of the b–archí and a trillionth of one percent of the silicon–28 total minute-to-minute translatable *enérgeia* in the *observable* universe *in any given minute*. And, like Doritos, the universe is always making more.

7.5 POWER STRUCTURE OF OUR UNIVERSE

The methods described make up the in-house power plant for the continual (eternal) existence of our physi-cospirit universe. Methods 1 and 3 altogether produce $\sim\!70\%$ of the average power needed while Method 2 produces the remaining 30%, of which $\sim\!60\%$ comes from Living entities and 40% from Living–𝓛ife human bodies. In a perfect universe, these methods generate all the power our universe ever needs. Yet, it integrates $\sim\!19\%$ of its power from Energent–prime (§ 1:112). What's up with that?

 'Energy' for existence arises in Energent–prime. When creating a universe seemingly out of thin air, the 'energy' to accomplish it arises with Intentionality through the interaction between a founder's Thought, 𝓛ife force, and Energent–prime (§ 3.2:282). The Energent expressing in a universe in accord with this process ideally becomes its sole 'energy' source.[257] Mina built ours to operate independently of Energent–prime—effectively a perpetual motion machine—but it has yet to meet that goal. The reason is simple.

 In the beginning, before physical matter developed in sufficient quantity to transfer meaningful amounts of 'energy' to the supranatural environment, Energent–prime made up the difference as part of Mina's plan to set the supranatural Energent in 'motion.' Yet, our universe continues drawing as much as $\sim\!19\%$ of its power from Energent–prime. The principal cause of this design deviation is The Corruption and Michael's Lie (§ 1.4:14; § 4.1.2:378) from which arose human conflict, thus instability, in the physical population that led to suppressed numbers, such as when Original Humanity immolated itself (§ 1.3:538). Despite copious 'energy' from non-Living entities like planets and stars, a deficiency in Living entities and Living–𝓛ife human bodies means deficient 'energy' for our universe. This isn't insurmountable, however. The Big Healing along with ongoing mass healings throughout spirit world is rectifying the causes of the deficiency (§ 1.3:22; § 1:577). Mina now foresees future physically-alive populations—presently constituting $\sim\!25\%$ of our universal human population—achieving growth longevity toward reaching the bare minimum $\sim\!38\%$ population share, as well as increasing 'energy' translation per individual from $\sim\!40\%$ to $\sim\!70\%$ (in $\sim\!40$–50KY), that's necessary for 'energy' independence.

---

257. In a case where a universe creates more than 100% of its power needs in-house, the Energent 'excess' overflows to Energent–prime because they're naturally connected. When a universe fails to meet all its power needs, the deficit similarly integrates 'energy' from Energent–prime into the Energent of the universe. In some cases, a builder, for whatever reason, doesn't include this capability in their universe's way of being (WOB; § 2.2.1.1:234), rendering an 'energy' deficit unfixable absent altering its WOB. Mina built our universe with the quality of foresight.

SECTION 8
Infinity of Space

We set out at the beginning of this chapter to better define space infinity toward understanding why and how the spatial universe can be infinite and human life eternal. The preceding overviews—Fundamental Energent, Matter–Energy, Gravity, Mass, Lightspeed, Relativity and the Quantum, Natural–supranatural Energy Translation—clarify some aspect of reality to help us comprehend the phenomenon of space in the context of infinity. So, how is an infinite cosmos—Sarah Scoles' *everspace* (2016, par. 7)—all about 'energy' instead of expanse, size, volume, and so on? Well, one thing we see is that infinity, which science hitherto closely associated with mass, is not a form of dimensionality because space isn't about mass but 'energy.' Accordingly, the essence of our universe is not matter or matter's applied energy E relationships, but the dimensionless, timeless Energent. In sum, infinite space *is* the Energent in that

$$Si \Leftrightarrow \Theta_{\varepsilon\mu} \tag{17.117}$$

where Si is space infinity and $\Theta_{\varepsilon\mu}$ is the Energent, and the logical equivalence doesn't imply identity. As a mode of existence, the Energent means a web of energetic (eR), indeterminate (dR), and intertwined (wR) 'energy' and matter *relations* such that

$$\Theta_{\varepsilon\mu} \leftrightarrow \frac{M}{e} \begin{cases} eR \\ dR \\ wR \end{cases} \tag{17.118}$$

where M is matter and e is 'energy' as modes of being, and the matrix eR, dR, wR is the Energent's aforementioned relational elements.

Matter and 'energy' in general include the natural and supranatural nature of the universe, so infinite space is both. Infinite space is to infinite time as space, energy, and the natural and supranatural is to time, event periodicity, and cause and effect. As such, they're twin components of existence infinity. 'Infinite space' is how we think about our sense of dimensionlessness and spatial dimension, but there's a difference between its referential *dimensions* of distance, size, volume, and so on—like how we think of the distance to Mars, or the volume of our solar system, or the size of our observable or even infinite universe—and its dimensionlessness, meaning its *lack of dimension*, as an existential reality. Dimensionlessness and dimensionality are different concepts albeit often conflated. 'Space as infinite' is about the *nature* (or, mode of existence) of the universe and not its *reality* (or, mode of being).

It might seem valid to conclude the universe must be finite if the Big Combustion catalyzing process described in THE BIG BANG (§ 6.10:186) actually completed. However logical on its face, it isn't accurate because infinity isn't dimensional. That something infinite yet incomplete can acquire a state of completion gets to the crux of Philosophy with a capital-P's problem with infinity. Its best rigorous analysis of it (Cantor's infinite sets) just isn't conversant with reality so, for it, the enigma endures.

Infinite space is really about 'energy' relationships, not dimensionality, because matter–Energy is a relationship expressed in terms of real energy Υ rather than applied energy E. Therefore, since dimensionality has meaning only in terms of objects (matter–Energy), what's tangibly infinite in our matter–Energy universe is real energy Υ's genesis and the Energent's expression, *enérgeia*. Since space infinity is logically equivalent to the Energent as a mode of existence, and the Energent is logically equivalent to *enérgeia*, then an equivalence obtains between space infinity as a mode of existence and *enérgeia* such that

$$Si \Leftrightarrow \Theta_{\varepsilon\mu} \Leftrightarrow \alpha\Omega \tag{17.119}$$

where $\alpha\Omega$ is *enérgeia*, and the logical equivalency doesn't imply identity. In the mystical tradition, we can say this defines the harmony of yin and yang, or internal and external (*Fig. 99*, left), each two sides of the same coin thus congruent in principle.

There's a flow-through from mode of existence to mode of being such that

$$R \leftrightarrow \Theta_{\varepsilon\mu} \cong \alpha\Omega \to mE \mid mE \Leftrightarrow \neg\infty \tag{17.120}$$

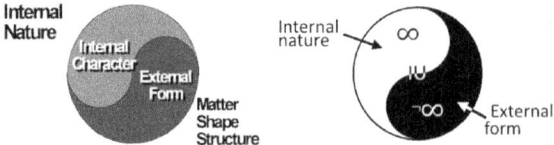

Figure 99. Left, yin–yang, or internal–external, where space infinity is internal character to Energent as external form, and Energent is internal nature to *enérgeia* as external matter, shape, structure; right, infinite universe IU as internal nature (space infinity) and external form (matter–Energy).₂₃₅

where R is reality, mE is matter–Energy as a mode of being, and its logical equivalence with not-infinity doesn't imply identity. This means space infinity is like our universe's yin internal character and matter–Energy like its yang external form (*Fig. 99*, right). Therefore,

$$Si \cong mE \tag{17.121}$$

whereby we see the unity between mode of existence and mode of being, and that the nature and mode of space infinity is the 'energy' relationships intrinsic of matter.

Moreover, because the Energent permeates the universe, it isn't possible to determine any dimensionality—size, scope, volume of space overall—to the 'energy' relationships that express through *enérgeia*. When we think of space as infinite (indeterminate) in expanse, size, volume, and so on, what we're really talking about is not dimensional attributes per se but the 'energy' relationships that make distance, size, and volume features of reality in the first place. "Space infinity is the Energent" means 'energy' indeterminacy. *Enérgeia* expresses wherever there's matter–Energy which, in that respect, is an existent indeterminacy itself. Accordingly, space infinity is relational. Expanse, size, volume, distance, measurement . . . these aren't concepts that describe space at all but rather our relational perception of it and our interaction with the finite matter that forms it.

Space is a web of relationships amongst matter–Energy. Regardless how far out from some initial point we trace these relational nodes, we can never reach a terminal nexus. The density of relationships thins out, of course, as one passes beyond the observable universe where there are no more galaxies and matter is correspondingly sparse. Even where there's no matter more complex than a single bonded–archí pair at all, there's the Energent which indeterminately reacts to matter–Energy disturbances anywhere (however negligibly) analogous to water reacting (however negligibly) to an object's intrusion into its liquid space on the far side of the bathtub, pool, or planet. Thus, when we say "Space is infinite" we're really saying "Space is the Energent" with all that "Energent" implies.

With the above in mind, let's consider our universe in toto as a mode of being vis-à-vis the Energent as a mode of existence in which

$$\exists! R \Leftrightarrow \Theta_{\varepsilon\mu} \leftrightarrow R \tag{17.122}$$

where R is the single existent reality, and the equivalencies between mode of being and mode of existence don't imply identity. In a colloquial sense, reality and the Energent are *the same but different* in the same way two people are the same *humans* but (because consciousness is unique) different *persons*. Likewise, reality and the Energent are the same *existence* but different *function*. The universe is our spatial reality, so by definition $U := R$ where U is universe.²⁵⁸ Since $Si \Leftrightarrow \Theta_{\varepsilon\mu}$ (Eq. (17.117):223), then

$$R \Leftrightarrow Si \tag{17.123}$$

where the logical equivalence between mode of being and mode of existence doesn't imply identity; reality and space infinity are the same in principle but different in functionality.

With respect just to the natural environment, Mina agrees in principle that "space is only a set of relationships among existing physical material, and time [CH. 16:105] is a set of relationships among the events of that physical material" (Dowden, n.d., § 5 par. 3) in the context that "space and time exist independently of physical material and its events" (ibid, par. 2; § 2:114). Philosophy with a capital-P considers these Relationist (relationalist) and Substantivalist (absolutist) concepts—the latter implies 'empty time' without need of physical events while the former mandates them—incompatible because it presumes they both can't be true (though both can be false).₂₃₆

---

258. In mathematics, the colon-equals (:=) 'defines' some x as synonymous with some y and is global in nature.

Yet, they aren't mutually exclusive at all when we recognize All Existence and its indeterminate time prior to human consciousness as well as multiple universes that embody natural and supranatural matter (§ 2.3.1:239). When, via energy testing (ET), we understand infinity for what it really is, we can rationally comprehend human consciousness for what it really is—an infinite, eternal existent—and our environment and our place in it as they really are without all the mumbo jumbo of religion, spiritualism, quantum mysticism, and scientific legerdemain ad nauseum. Everything becomes comprehensible. In the next chapter, we approach infinity from a comprehensive perspective.

SECTION 9

To Sum it All Up ...

It took 16 months to energy test, write, and edit this chapter. It was supremely challenging for us, having no serious background in science and mathematics. Even so, Mina avers we got it 95% accurate anyhow w.r.t. reality—though even after all this, my understanding of gravity, says he, is still just a 4 on a 10 scale. All things considered, we take that as a win. While that missing 5% might seem big enough to sail *Titanic* through, we encourage you to absorb the chapter conceptually and work through its literal implications on its veridical foundation. Eventually, future works will rigorously treat these topics.

The principal takeaway of this chapter is that matter is 'energy' where 'energy' is dimensionless, dimensionlessness is indeterminate, and indeterminance is space infinity. Here lies the root of real matter–¢nergy equivalence that Einstein was trying to get at, as well as the science behind the very common all-matter-is-energy cliché that mystics sell. Too, we glimpse the logic and science behind our intuitive sense of life after death, spirit reality, and the sensible shoes in which all creation walks. Nothing in our universe is too mystical or incomprehensible for the human mind because, literally, a human mind created it. Neither is All Existence—the timeless reality prior to, and transcendent of, our own so-called Big Bang and the ultimate progenitor of our own—mystical or incomprehensible, but logically and scientifically explicable.

Sure, empirical science perforce laughs it off, originating as it does in revealed data without peer-reviewed experiment and rigorous mathematics to back it up. But those inquisitive investigators who really think this through, pin down the unanswered questions it raises, and develop the mathematics to describe it, will develop a brand new Energent science that transforms how we manipulate matter and 'energy' in the natural (physical) environment in ways similar to how spirit humanity already does it.

This chapter gives you a solid foundation for the rest of this book. In the next two chapters, we describe nebulous All Existence as a prelude to tackling the most nebular of all, psyche (consciousness), the last of those four infinities we listed in CLASSES & CATEGORIES OF INFINITY (CH. 3:97). American physicist Richard Feynman (d. 1988) cheekily quips, "Science is the belief in the ignorance of experts" (2015, 291), but we're rather more reverently saying that, henceforward, awareness is the belief in validated energy testing. For that, we encourage you to read ENERGY TESTING (PART V) and start down that road.

All Existence

Quick Summary. All Existence is 'all there infinitely is' and differs fundamentally from our universe; each requires unique explication. All Existence comes to be via emergence as a first cause along a path from Previous All Existence to Emergent All Existence until finalizing as Current All Existence. It possesses something akin to albeit not exactly like plantlike intelligence, expressing not in any distributed network sense but as nonconscious way of being via Energent–prime, the fundamental proto-energy from which derives the proto-energy of our universe's Energent. Humanity emergently births 'in' Energent proto-life, a *Life*-precursive proto-energy that's an emergent property of Energent–prime. Accordingly, Current All Existence comprises All Existence, Energent–prime, *Life* (consciousness), and the universes (and nonhuman life) that humans build.

LOOKING AT OUR universe, we tend to imagine that what we perceive is all there is. In the preceding chapters, we introduced you to All Existence, a reality more panoptic than our universe, describing it as an emergent reality (§ 2:90) and a reflexive ontological existent as an explanans of First Cause and infinite existence, time, and space (§ 1:100). Here, we take a more wholistic approach to it.

There are two principal aspects to All Existence: humanity, and everything else. We adopted the term 'All Existence' over 'the universe' or 'creation' because creation is only part of the story and talking about a universe references only the tree, not the forest. The first thing to get about All Existence is that, besides being infinite like 'the universe,' it's more inclusive yet perfectly simple. Sure, it all seems complex and confusing; we're looking at trees instead of forest after all. One could liken us to tree beetles striving to understand our larger environment from a groove in the bark in which we cling. Even when we think we're scoping the whole forest, we're really just scaling up or down our comprehension of the tree, if not the bark alone, to explain the larger, unseen, incomprehensible forest in toto.

Philosophy with a capital-P styles our desire to collapse existence into one comprehensive explanatory format or equation as the Theory of Everything (TOE). It's a holy grail in physics and even theology, a wholism to explain reductive existence and grand purpose. But there's too much emergence for that approach to bear fruit. Worse for understanding reality, thought matrices "handed down, or sold to us, or generated by our own hopes and fears" (Crichton 2003, par. 2) color our perceptions and hamper what we're willing to cognize, much less imagine. If we step back to widen our field of view, though, the 'forest' comes into focus and our 'tree' comprehension improves.

Ayako, El, and I perceived this almost from the start, my girls far quicker than me. Our learning effort's been one of pecking through one *matryoshka* paradigm after another until the data built up a broader, consistent, conceptual understanding of All Existence. Once there—though by no means complete—we could more clear-sightedly drop back into the minutiae to understand everyday life, which PART IV describes. And that raises an important caveat. Spiritual experience is important but if it's irrational then, ultimately, we can't rationally accept it. If the universe is as rational and orderly—thus predictable—as science and some theology make it out to be, then shouldn't our existence and relationship with its creator also be such? Thinking this way over a lifetime ushered me from superstitious Catholicism through kooky flavors of Protestantism to the elementary scientism of Unificationism.$_{237}$ This chapter works at lifting our sight from the tree to the forest. We tackle the 'everything else' aspect of All Existence in this chapter, and then the 'us' part in Psyche Infinity (CH. 19:245).

SECTION 1

First Cause

At its simplest, All Existence is a double-headed coin, each aspect the same, yet not. One aspect of this coin is *way of being* and the other is *all there is*, which we describe first. If you can imagine our universe in its infinite sense, as indeterminate and dimensionless (CH. 14:93), then you've formed a working image of All Existence. Before our universe existed, before our putative Big Bang, there was All Existence. Before All Existence itself existed . . . well, All Existence existed (CH. 15:99). Back through indeterminate timelessness, there was All Existence. It was a *different* All Existence, to be sure, but *the* All Existence all the same. What this means is that All Existence is an emergently 'evolved' reality of All Existence. The timescales are unknown even to the Cardinal (FN 130:110), who conjecture that Current All Existence is about a trillion Earth-years old and human ℒife—consciousness—about 800 billion (§ 2:304).²⁵⁹

The obvious question is, *what came before the very first All Existence?* Well, in truth, that's not a meaningful question. It's reasonable and rational but doesn't cognize reality as it is. The reason is that the question necessarily presumes existence prior to existence, which is delusive. If there's existence, there can be nothing prior to existence because then *that* would be existence. We see this echoed in St. Anselm's ontological argument for God where he postulates there can be no greater being than that which we can conceive because, if we can conceive it, then it's greater than the greatest being, hence, *that* becomes the greatest being. His is really an argument for infinity that leads to contradictions like Cantor's infinite set theory and *nothing* (§ 1:94; § 2.1.1:231). Accordingly, wondering what came before existence is absurd. And yet, we can't help ourselves. *We must know!* There is a way to answer this question, however.

Besides the above, existence prior to existence poses infinite regress conundrums. However much we drill down toward ultimate cause, we never get there because every cause is necessarily the effect of an earlier cause. The emergent, reflexive ontological system we described in § 1:100 resolves it. Previous existence explains current existence in an existential, ontological system. What existed before the system is immaterial because, existentially, it explains itself; before the system *was* the system. No chain of systems exists needing explanation because there's only *the* emergent system without ontological antecedent.

The idea that existence *always* existed is difficult to grasp because we live in simplistic causality where something is always causatively prior to something else—the Big Bang and ℒife's precursor now point to All Existence—but it's not impossible. Even if we regress All Existence to its simplest, seemingly irreducible, form it's possible it existed regressively from that point in a different form altogether. There's no determinate for how many 'forms' All Existence might experience back through indeterminate time, so we can't presume some uncaused First Cause didn't have a cause. The presumption a first cause is even necessary is insensible anyway; emergence and indeterminance sever its rationale.

One might ask, "Why does a first cause even matter?" The only answer, beyond curiosity, is that we want to know the origins of our universe the same way a child wants to know his or her own parents, extended family, all about their home, why their socioculture is what it is, and so on to larger and larger environments that help them place themselves in greater inclusive contexts that in some way defines their reality in a way they comprehend and appreciate. We want to know our ultimate parentage whether it's a process or a person—say, God—and, thus, our raison d'être.

1.1 God as First Cause

"It is commonly accepted that there are two sorts of existent entities: those that exist but could have failed to exist, and those that could not have failed to exist" (Davidson (2005) 2019, par. 1). The former are *contingent* and the latter *necessary* beings. This means you, Fido, and all creation are contingent beings. God or any sort of causative act or event is a necessary being. Traditionally, existence is contingent in that it could have failed to be yet ƒs, and ƒt ƒs because, somehow, ƒt came to be. In other words,

---

259. To be honest, their estimate is really just SWAG, a scientific wild-ass guess. They calculate the human era a bit less SWAGishly but estimate it even so, although advanced science is involved; hence, SWAG instead of a mere WAG.

$$P \Leftarrow Q \tag{18.1}$$

where P is the creative agency, Q is existence, and if there's Q then logically, without exception, there's P. Science assigns causation of our universe to a somewhat explicable but mostly unknown process, with the less explicable theory being that it was uncaused since, presumably, no universe pre-existed ours. Religion, on the other hand, assigns causation to an inexplicable uncaused God and simply concludes that, pre-existence, He always was. Whether God or quantum magic, at the end of the day P is just agency. Accordingly, we've recast premise P from *being* to *entity*; we want to address both the nonconscious and conscious creator. *Entity* avoids the inevitable deitic overtones of *being* (despite Philosophy's definition of the term as any existing *thing*), which elevates the individual (God) over the role as well as its materialistic undertones, which elevates the role (causation) over agency. Mina refuses to acknowledge himself as the necessary *being* of our universe because it implies the necessity of his personhood, whereas *entity* implies the necessity of the action (event). With universe creation, the action is necessary, not the actor. Mina's keen we understand he's a person, not a magical deity, which don't exist.

It goes without saying a contingent entity proceeds from a necessary entity—child from parent, plant from seed, planet from matter, light from 'energy,' Fundamental Force from *enérgeia*, the Energent from Energent–prime, universe from builder. A necessary entity is an obvious First Cause and, w.r.t. a universe, it's a person. A caution here is that this type of causation isn't deterministic but intentional. From causal Intention (§ 3.2:282) follows causal effect, which is deterministic or emergent with each potentially displaying some elements of both. Mina Intentioned our universe—'frequency space' (§ 6.10.1:186), the Energent, and is our progenitor—hence, it coming to be is Intentionally deterministic. What follows is variously deterministic and emergent. Such causal agency is Intentional, not mechanistic.

But what about the initial contingent state, say, the Big Bang or extra-universal existence like All Existence? Here, a necessary entity is a function. For example, the progenitor of a lineage or a dynasty is the necessary person of the chain of causes that brings about those contingent existents. Without such a person, those particular contingents necessarily wouldn't be. The necessary person of our universe is Mina, who lies beyond it since he precedes it, but isn't himself an uncaused cause (CH. 22:335). However, there's no necessary person who begat All Existence. It's an emergent process. One might say All Existence—a serial emergent that's never not existed (§ 2.1:231)—is its own necessary entity, a Spinozan *causa sui*.[260] Despite this, All Existence isn't self-caused, as that implies an uncaused state—*nothing*—which is a contradiction thus invalid (§ 2.1.1:231).

Although *causa sui* and self-cause appear alike, the distinction between them is the same as that between emergence and determinism. All Existence doesn't exist prior to itself, either, since prior to itself was an entirely different All Existence. However, Previous All Existence, different from Current All Existence, is nevertheless All Existence, or 'all there infinitely is,' because by definition there's ever only one 'all there infinitely is.' Therefore, All Existence is prior to All Existence, yet isn't prior to itself. This seems paradoxical or a semantic illusion. It's not. The reason is that 'all there infinitely is' is still 'all there infinitely is' even though it comprises an *emergently* different intersection of the sets

$$\exists! E \leftrightarrow \left(\{pAE\} \cap \{eAE\} = \{cAE \,|\, E \leftrightarrow GU_1\} \right) \tag{18.2}$$

(terms are defined following Eq. (18.4)) than does its antecedent All Existence's sets

$$\exists! E \leftrightarrow \left(\{pAE_{-1}\} \cap \{eAE_{-1}\} = \{cAE_{-1} \,|\, E \leftrightarrow GU_{-1}\} \right) \tag{18.3}$$

when, prior to cAE, GU_{-1} was 'all there infinitely is,' and E is $\exists! E$ regardless whether 'all there infinitely is' is GU_1, GU_{-1}, GU_{-2} ad infinitum. Consequently, as

$$\{GU_{-1}\} \cap \{GU_1\} = \{AE\} \tag{18.4}$$

then GU_{-1}, as 'all there infinitely is *before*,' ontologically grounds GU_1 as 'all there infinitely is *now*' and is thus indeed prior to GU_1. But since emergent

$$GU_{-1} \cong GU_1, \tag{18.5}$$

---

260. Latin: *cause of itself*; something generated within itself absent external involvement (Baruch Spinoza; d. 1677).

and as both grounding units are 'all there infinitely is,' then even though GU_{-1} is ontologically prior to GU_1, GU_{-1} isn't prior to itself because there's only ever *one* 'all there infinitely is' and it's a *continuity*. Equation definitions are as follows (cf. CH. 15:99).

1. Eq. (18.2): E is existence, or 'all there infinitely is;' pAE is Previous All Existence; eAE is Emergent All Existence; cAE is Current All Existence; GU_1 is the grounding unit that represents cAE .
2. Eq. (18.3): GU_{-1} is the grounding unit that represents a previous pAE ; likewise eAE and cAE .
3. Eq. (18.4): AE is All Existence, or 'all there infinitely is.'
4. Eq. (18.2)–(18.5): the material equivalence and congruence don't imply identity.

We can see how All Existence is prior to All Existence, yet, as 'all there infinitely is,' isn't prior to *itself*, as there's ever only one All Existence. Always existing, it can't exist prior to itself. The distinction's worth the discussion because it's important to comprehend that 'all there infinitely is,' regardless its emergent iterations, is continuously whole. Causal agency of this sort is mechanistic, not intentional. Mina is our universe's first cause, but there's no uncaused First Cause of All Existence. Thus, even if God was the First Cause of All Existence, He can't be an uncaused cause because *nothing* precludes it (§ 2.1.1:231).

<h2 align="center">SECTION 2</h2>

<h1 align="center">All There Is</h1>

When we say All Existence is 'all there infinitely is,' we mean, negatively, that there isn't anything that isn't All Existence, and positively, that All Existence *is* Energent–prime.[261] It doesn't simply exist 'within' All Existence as if All Existence is a container, a bubble of reality (in some necessarily greater reality) within which Energent–prime plies its trade. Rather, Energent–prime *is* All Existence in the sense there's no All Existence sans Energent–prime. And—recalling that, as with our universe in which *enérgeia*, Fundamental Force, applied energy E, and archí (matter) all constitute from Energent proto-energy (§ 2:114)—Energent–prime is all that exists; it *is* existence. Accordingly,

$$AE \leftrightarrow \Theta'_{\varepsilon\mu} \tag{18.6}$$

where AE is All Existence, $\Theta'_{\varepsilon\mu}$ is Energent–prime, the material equivalence doesn't imply identity, and from which Eq. (17.122):224 follows. Existence in its primal *reality* is the essence of All Existence and, in its primal *function*, is Energent–prime, the former its mode of being and the latter its mode of existence. Therefore,

$$\exists! E = AE \leftrightarrow \Theta'_{\varepsilon\mu} = R' \tag{18.7}$$

where E is the only existence, the equality means identity, the material equivalence doesn't imply identity, and R' is All Existence (global) reality–prime that transcends our universe's (local) reality R. Consequently, existence as a concept for understanding 'all there infinitely is' resides with All Existence. Thus, when we say 'existence,' we're really saying 'All Existence' with all that the term implies. Therefore,

$$R' \to R \bigvee R \leftarrow R' \tag{18.8}$$

where reality–prime grounds *our* reality (encompassing our awareness, life, the natural and supranatural environments) or, conversely, if R' then logically, without exception, it grounds R. As such, our universe isn't 'all there infinitely is' in and of itself but is only a part of 'all there infinitely is' (All Existence).

We've heretofore thought of our own universe as containing (at least materially) all that exists—stars, galaxies, infinite space. A container however implies containment, which is a bounded condition that's incongruent with an indeterminate reality whether in our universe or All Existence. Infinite All Existence doesn't 'contain' all that exists but *is* all that exists. Too, it implies that All Existence as a container differs from all it contains, and that's not the case, either. It wholistically[262] integrates analogous to how a globule of water isn't a hydrologic container for water but in and of itself *is* water. The Cardinal doggedly investigates All Existence as infinitely regressed as its members can get. Querying them through Mina is a much more lengthy undertaking, as what

---

261. Our universe's Energent is materially different albeit the same in origin as All Existence's Energent–prime.

262. Not *holism*, "coined . . . to designate this fundamental factor operative towards the making or creation of wholes in the universe" (Smuts 1926, 98), but *of the whole* itself.

might've come before Current All Existence is (for us, at least) even more esoteric than what we've got going on in the here and now.[238] Their rooting through the basement of existence isn't germane for us here, so we don't dwell on it.

As form follows function, structure follows emergence w.r.t. to All Existence. Whether natural, biological, or manmade, any necessary entity must account for its initial in situ topography (domain), formulate function, and establish structure. Accordingly, in this chapter we classify Previous All Existence as a *domain period*, as it is 'all there infinitely is' before emergence and thus forms the topography, or domain reality (its constraints), in which novel properties emerge. We classify Emergent All Existence as a *function period*, as that's when novel properties undergo self-assembly and self-organization, which effectively establishes the developing 'all there infinitely is' as nonconscious intent. Finally, we classify Current All Existence as a *structure period*, as that's where 'all there infinitely is' stabilizes out of Emergent All Existence in a topology of functionally correlated form. Let's look at each of these three periods in turn.

2.1 PREVIOUS ALL EXISTENCE: DOMAIN PERIOD

In Existence Infinity (ch. 15:99), we describe in detail the ontological *grounding unit* system in which a previous All Existence transcends through a series of emergent self-organizations before settling into the stable, coherent, transformationally satisfied final-phase system of a current All Existence. In our case, that would be Current All Existence which features emergent, unaware, nonconscious intelligence that expresses via Energent–prime and human consciousness.[263]

Although an ontological system—being emergently self-explanatory—is necessarily not part of a causal chain, if we leaf back far enough the Cardinal deduces there comes a point of no motion although time—timekeeping, or event periodicity—remains. This is because a no-motion state is an event period nonetheless. Prior to that, there's still existence, of course, just absent motion; more like an existent puissance. Prior to that a state of pre-puissance, and earlier still, no-puissance . . . nothing we can easily comprehend anyhow. Eventually, there's only indeterminate existence, traditionally considered *nothing*, and that's all anyone (including the Cardinal) can say about it.[264] But there can't be, literally, nothing.

2.1.1 SOMETHING FROM NOTHING

There's never been, in our scientific and philosophical sense, *nothing* w.r.t. existence (e.g., Holt 2012). Even *nothing* is *something*, after all.[265] There can't be *nothing* because, if there were, it would naturally fall outside the set {Something} which, in the case of indeterminance, would be not the empty set {} but *no–set*. The empty set reflects *nothing as something* (an existent) but *nothing* isn't *something* nor the absence of *something*, it's just *nothing*. Therefore, we denote no–set as nonexistent '}{,' the reversed curly braces representing *nothing* antithetical the existent empty set '{}.' No–set is indeterminate but not indeterminance, the latter which implies existence and the former that doesn't. Hence, no–set is nonexistence. Let's take a closer look at *nothing*.

"Nothing is not something" means that nothing is the absence of something, or in other words, nothing is 'not-something.' Nothing being not-something and nothing as the absence of something are both a state of being. In sum, they're each existents and, therefore, *nothing* and *something*. This means *nothing* necessarily is *something*, and not just any something, but not-*something*. Yet, if we consider not-*something* as the negation of *something*, it leads us to negation being *nothing*, except it's not; it's a thing, specifically, it's negation. Negation of existence isn't nonexistence, which would be not absence of existence but no existence at all. Instead, negation is nullity, which is a null state or null existence. Either way, it is beingness and not *nothing* but not-*something*. The notion of *nothing* as literally nothing goes unremarked because we feel a need, or an inevitability, to comprehend *nothing* in terms of—or juxtaposed with—*something*, much as we do infinity vis-à-vis finite where we then miss the notion of indeterminate. And too, strictly speaking, *nothing* defies our

---

263. "Emergence in human systems has produced new technologies, towns, democracy, and some would say consciousness—the capacity for self-reflection" (Holman 2010, 19).

264. They speculate there's some existence antecedent to simple indeterminance that's entirely different from anything imagined. Their thinking is reflected in Oxford physicist Roger Penrose's conformal cyclic cosmology (*Cycles of Time* 2010) in which the universe—his theory doesn't cognize emergence or All Existence apart from our universe although it's implicit—oscillates from Big Bang to Big Bang, each one unique.

265. Conceptual existents *nothing* and *something* as italicized are not used in the normal sense of the words.

contemplation because it's literally not there; it's nonexistent. We can't contemplate what isn't except in terms of what is, which automatically renders nothing an existent and thus not *nothing*.

Then is *nothing* actually *something*, which is to say, *not* nothing? Despite set theory's faulty logic—in this case that, as a vacuous truth,[266] the empty set {} is a subset of any set; the statement "nothing is not something" isn't valid because '*nothing* is not *something*,' which isn't valid, either, because *nothing* doesn't relate to value whereas *something* does. That is, *nothing* is without value whereas *something* is with value; *nothing* is non-value (or, *nothing*-value) whereas *something* can be value or not-value (e.g., zero or {}). Accordingly, *nothing* can't be a subset of *something* any more than the empty set can be a valid subset of any set: that's saying *undefined* is a subset of *defined* (like zero) which can't be true because *undefined* is non-value whereas *defined* (e.g., zero) is not-value and a null state. This is why the negation of existence isn't nonexistence but a nullity. The negation of value results in not-value which is a null state and thus an existent like the empty set rather than non-value which is no–set, hence, *nothing*.

Nothing isn't a potential reality. If it's the absence of *something*, and an absence of *something* is something, then there can't *be* nothing. If *nothing* is not-*something* then *nothing* is the absence of *something*. But that makes *nothing* a property of *something*, or *something* an existential property of *nothing*. This means *something* defines *nothing*. But *nothing* is simply nothing, it has no contextual relationship with *something*. As concepts, they're decoupled. This is why *something* can't come out of *nothing*; it's not possible for *something* to come from *nothing*. Since our senses tell us there's *something*, then it didn't come from *nothing*. *Nothing* can't exist because the one contradicts the other. The idea there was *nothing* before there was *something* means there was some sort of existence of *nothing* before an existence of *something* existed. This implies some existentiality where some something (an existence) could *come* to be *something*. That is, before *something*, when there was *nothing*, there was *becoming*; hence, *nothing* is actually *becoming*. This is a contradiction and it's fundamental.

Nothing implies that the absence of everything is the absence *from* something. Stated differently, when *something* is the existent set {Something} where *nothing* is the negation of *something*, then

$$S - S = \{\} \tag{18.9}$$

where S is the set {*Something*} and the empty set {} as an existent is the absence of all *something* from S. For example, *nothing* indicates there's a *something* from which that *nothing* derives, that we can't have *nothing* without *something* to compare it to just as we can't have love without its comparator hate (§ 3.3.2.1:285). Consequently, *nothing* depends on *something*, which means that, ontologically, *nothing* grounds in *something*. But again, that makes *nothing* a property, if not a subset, of *something* in the same way the empty set {} is (vacuously) the subset of any set (*Fig. 100*). This means there's no such thing as nothing because it's like dividing by zero where the result's not nothing or infinity but undefined.

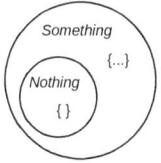

Figure 100. Nothing inaccurately a subset of *Something* as {} ⊂ {...}.

The idea there's *nothing* is imprecise. Instead, it's a *something* that's undefined. Being undefined, it can't even be said to exist. This is why nonexistent *nothing* isn't like the existent empty set {} w.r.t. *something* as the existent set {Something}, but rather like the nonexistent no–set }{. It's evident there's no operation to be had between no–set and any set. So, '*something* from *nothing*' in the sense of existence from nonexistence really means 'existence from indeterminate,' hence '*something* from *indeterminate*,' which is invalid. The philosophical question, "why is there something rather than nothing" (Holt 2012, 28) or the statement "something comes from nothing" (Lao-Tzu, Pine 2009, 80) are vacuous truths. *Something* can't come from indeterminate. Thus, *nothing* is nonexistent. This is a contradiction and another way of saying impossible, a reality that can't be.[239]

---

266. A statement that resembles $P \rightarrow Q$ where we know P is false, e.g., "all cell phones in the room are turned off" is true even when there are none present. Like $E = mc^2$ presuming division by zero leads to infinite mass and energy (§ 6.1:165), the absence of cell phones means the statement can only be undefined. Moreover, the statement, "for any integer x, if $x > 5$ then $x > 3$" is also not a vacuous truth but indeterminate. Vacuous truth is irrational.

It's not possible to know what sort of existence comprises a previous All Existence, but it's not necessary to know, only to explain ontologically a current All Existence. We do that via reflexive ontology, how a present state of existence emergently transitions to a new existence state (§ 1:100). The basic process as an alteration of reality is as follows: an emergent cascade triggers a system-wide emergence in which a previous All Existence (*p*AE) differentiates and coalesces (self-assembles) into something novel, in this case an emergent All Existence (*e*AE), which then self-organizes into a current All Existence (*c*AE) as the final altered state (*Fig. 101*). The old *p*AE rules break down non-chaotically during emergence as the system differentiates and coalesces around novel principles. Let's consider the alteration.

2.2 EMERGENT ALL EXISTENCE: FUNCTION PERIOD

Once upon a time, Previous All Existence was a stable, equilibric system. Emergent events occurred constantly and routinely at below-system level just as they do today in Current All Existence. At some point, however, an emergent event occurred that triggered a system-wide emergence cascade that, within about 1.155×10^{-56} second,[267] resulted in Emergent All Existence, the emergent property that serves as transitional, in-process All Existence. Things could've halted right there with this Emergent All Existence being just another new Current All Existence in an infinite line of new Current All Existences, self-assembled and self-organized to some higher yet merely incremental degree. Instead, this time *unaware nonconscious intelligence* with higher-order complexity emerged with a *way of being* (nature) that, in self-organizing, triggered additional self-assembling and self-organizing emergent events resulting in discrete *Life*. This transcendent, final-state, multi-self-organized emergent property is Current All Existence in which megaversal humanity exists (TODAY'S FAMILY OF UNIVERSES, § 2.1.4.1:312; *Fig. 101*). The process took about 200 billion years from *p*AE to *c*AE (§ 1:228).

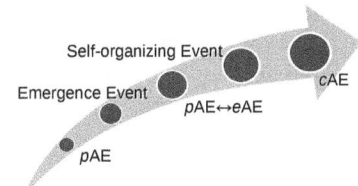

Figure 101. Transformation of *p*AE to *c*AE (EMERGENCE, § 2:90).

The transformation is a function such that

$$f(S_e) = S_{so} \tag{18.10}$$

where function input S_e is the state space of Emergent All Existence and output S_{so} is self-organized, emergently transcendent Current All Existence. The transformation is complete when state space S_e is no longer extant in any constituent form but *is* S_{so}. This means there's no lower order remnant S_e in S_{so}.

2.2.1 ENERGENT–PRIME INTELLIGENCE

When we talk about *unaware nonconscious intelligence* (UNI), we're altogether referring to All Existence, Energent–prime, and UNI wholistically and holistically (FN 88:79) since all existents in All Existence are simultaneously discrete yet equivalent. With reference to our discussion in SPACE INFINITY (§ 8:223), all existents are discrete as a mode of being but equivalent as a mode of existence. A mode of being is like a *logical mode* and a mode of existence is like an *existent mode*. Here, a logical mode differs in functionality but is equivalent in principle.[268] It's the *way* it is, meaning it's the reality of existence, or (the nature of) reality in toto. An existent mode is equivalent in functionality but differs in nature. It's the *how* it is, meaning it's the nature of existence, or (the nature of) how reality operates in toto. We develop this interrelatedness farther below. The point we're making here is that

$$\{UNI\} \cup \{AE\} \neq \{mind\} \cup \{body\}, \tag{18.11}$$

which means the one doesn't exist in terms of the other; that concept is alien.

---

267. With a 99.9% confidence level, which Mina carefully distinguishes from 99.99% .

268. Equivalent in principle doesn't imply same in principle.

What UNI is not is sapient or sentient. Current All Existence, inclusive of Energent–prime, isn't a conscious being or a self-regulating organism any more than planet Earth is sentient Gaia.[240] Rather, it's a *quinta essentia*[269] predating Current All Existence, reaching all the way back to when there was only indeterminate. It's not material, spirit, or 'energetic.' Its essence emergently iterated such that its iterative environment *now* is no longer how it was *then*. It's a noncognitive essence without consciousness, not a being or person but more a universal 'subconscious.' From its reality in Previous All Existence, it emergently self-assembled and self-organized during the aforementioned system-level emergence into its novel and unexpected quintessence in Current All Existence.[241] Similar overall to a caterpillar self-digesting into a butterfly, emergent UNI (the butterfly) is not just more than the sum of its parts (the caterpillar), but transcends the whole (its caterpillar-ness) that was greater *then* than those *now* non-existent parts.[270] This essence is the source for which science sees an ordered and seemingly designed-for-ℒife universe (e.g., Davies 2007) that, in terms of ℒife, includes—not that Philosophy with a capital-P would ever admit it—physical and spirit environments (§ 7.1:212).

UNI is an 'adaptive force' but doesn't rise to ℒife force, the self-aware proto-energy that is each one of us (§ 6.11.4:198). Mina likens it to brainstem intelligence (§ 2.2.1.2:237). It's discrete, an individual entity amongst all the entities of All Existence. In one sense, All Existence qualifies as an entity because it has a distinct and objective existence although, dictionarily, it doesn't "exist[s] apart from other things, having its own independent existence."[271] All Existence is 'all there infinitely is.' Every entity of that is a free, integral, interrelated part of a whole while at the same time free, autonomous, and independent to experience and even change its existence on its own terms in a way that transcends our everyday sense of either wholism or holism. No part of existence is constrained intrinsically by the whole of existence. Now, everything nonhuman in existence shares in a predilection toward order, congruence, coherence, consistency, and so on which (like freedom, autonomy, and independence) is a self-organized subsystemic trait (§ 2.2.1.3:238) that permeates the system. That trait is the UNI. But don't think intelligence presupposes order or that order presupposes intelligence; it can just as well presuppose disorder or, as indeed it does, nonintelligence from order. Why, then, would Mina pick *intelligence* to describe this nonconscious, noncognitive trait? There are three reasons: way of being, existence interface, and traits, which we describe in order.

2.2.1.1 WAY OF BEING

First, the nature of intelligence is that it is *way of being*. Intelligence itself, its reality, is mainly about *how one is*.[272] It's not "the ability to learn, understand, and make judgments or have opinions that are based on reason,"[273] or "a very general mental capability that . . . reflects a broader and deeper capability for comprehending our surroundings" (Gottfredson 1997, 13), nor is it a cognitive process or even "a set of cognitive processes" (Cianciolo et al. 2004, 8). For example, plants express a way of being that nonconsciously and noncognitively informs how they are contextually with their environment (e.g., *Secret Life,* Tompkins et al. 1973; *Brilliant Green,* Mancuso et al. 2015; "Plant Cognition," Parise et al. 2020).

Intelligence isn't cognition and doesn't imply consciousness or sentience–sapience. It transcends cognition which is not process-compartmentable anyhow but, like everything else in All Existence, is wholistic and holistic. Each aspect of cognition that one might call a cognitive process is wholistically integrated, interrelated, interdependent, and so on. Intelligence and cognition—"the use of conscious mental processes"[274] or "a variety of mental processes that allow us to maintain, understand and use information to create knowledge and reflect" (Dumper et al. 2019, par. 5)—are different things entirely. Though it's common to do so, conflating cognition with intelligence is inaccurate. Instead, intelligence expresses as cognition w.r.t. a brain modality, as awareness w.r.t. a mind modality, and as *unawareness* w.r.t. an *unmind* modality (Table 5). Cognition is simply one expression of intelligence where the modality is conscious–cognitive or nonconscious–noncognitive. Cognitive processes need not be as traditionally defined nor even conscious to be cognition.

---

269. Latin: *fifth essence* (and root of quintessence) in medieval philosophy, hearkening back to an unknown medium—æther; currently, dark 'energy'—bathing All Existence.

270. Caterpillar is mode of being but *like* a logical mode (reality of existence). Caterpillar-ness is mode of existence but *like* an existent mode (nature of existence).

271. *Cambridge Dictionary* online, s.v. 'entity.'

272. *How one is* means the totality of an entity relationally with the totality of environment.

273. *Cambridge*, s.v. 'intelligence.'

274. *Cambridge*, s.v. 'cognition.'

Uni is a self-organized aspect of Current All Existence's way of being (wob), a system-level trait toward order, coherence, freedom, and such infusing its every aspect. An entity possesses an essential referential awareness of self and environment from own-self totality to base constituent. In our universe of natural and supranatural matter, for example, such awareness expresses in the complex (consciousness) and the simple (archí). Intelligence reflects an entity's wob in terms of how it is in relation *to* the totality of intelligence as well as *of* the totality of intelligence. Table 5 visualizes intelligence as a domain contextually expressing (differently for each subclass) in All Existence through two classes (conscious and nonconscious) across three subclasses (brain, mind, and unmind). We consider each class in turn.

Table 5. Intelligence by domain, class, and subclass.

Intelligence = *way of being* = Awareness					
Conscious (human)			*Nonconscious* (AE)		
Brain		Mind		Unmind	
wholistic cognition		wholistic awareness		wholistic unawareness	
totality of cognitive processes		totality of contextual experience		totality of regulatory feedback	
an integrated, interrelated expression for each process		an integrated, interrelated expression for each experience		an integrated, interrelated signaling, comms, & response system	
each process is holistic		each experience is holistic		each element is holistic	
distributed intelligence		distributed intelligence		distributed intelligence	
immaterial	material	immaterial	material	immaterial	material
stimuli inside body	stimuli outside body	experience with own or other consciousness	experience with what's outside of consciousness	acts in entity's totality	acts in entire AE's totality

2.2.1.1.1 Conscious

This class of intelligence is consciousness; sapient and sentient, specifically human (§ 3.1:280).

2.2.1.1.1.1 Brain

Intelligence expresses through this subclass as traditional cognition as a totality of wholistic cognitive processes that are integrated and interrelated expressions for each one where, in a holistic, distributed intelligence sense, processes brain-internal and brain-external stimuli. The brain is a physical organ structured functionally instead of amorphously. Its plasticity doesn't remove structured functionality but restructures it as necessarily determined according to the wholism of cognition in consonance with intelligence.

2.2.1.1.1.2 Mind

Intelligence through this subclass deals with the brain in terms of its physical interface translating mind to body but is otherwise distinct from brain. Cognitive processes don't operate in the mind because it's consciousness, ℒife-precursive proto-energy we term *Energent proto-life* (EPL; § 2.3.2.1:241). Consequently,

$$ॐ \cong \odot \qquad (18.12)$$

where the *pranava* Sanskrit syllable ॐ [*om*] is mind, $\odot$ is consciousness, and the congruence doesn't imply identity. It might feel ridiculous to reduce the human person seemingly to proto-energy—though it's no worse than reductive evolution—but the reality is that mind is Thought and Thought is indeterminate, meaning infinite. Recall from Eq. (17.98)–(17.101):199 in Instantaneity that consciousness is Thought, and Thought is sapient proto-energy. Therefore,

$$\odot \cong T \qquad (18.13)$$

where T is Thought and the congruence doesn't imply identity.

Accordingly, intelligence w.r.t. mind expresses as *awareness* (rather than cognition) as a totality of wholistic, contextual experiences that are integrated and interrelated expressions for each experience, where each experience in a holistic, distributed intelligence sense is experientially aware of own-self and whatever's outside own-self, including other selves. There's no cognition because mind is unstructured and 'energetic.' Accordingly, the instant that sense stimuli encounter consciousness they *are* consciousness, not processed *into* consciousness; mindful, not cognized. Incoming stimuli become consciousness when, before, it wasn't consciousness and then, after, it is consciousness. Consciousness' woв *is* stimuli's woв. There's no cognitive process here; no cognition occurs. This is how a person 'just knows' (has awareness of) something sans cognition. Woв just *becomes* and stimuli and consciousness are synomic as woв.

2.2.1.1.2 Nonconscious

This class of intelligence is nonconsciousness, neither sentient nor sapient and specifically nonhuman, its mind behavior (devoid of mind–brain function–structure) plantlike, but not exactly. A short definition is

$$|\}\,\text{ॐ}\,\{| \tag{18.14}$$

where '|}{|' is the 'absolute nothing value' and follows from no–set principles (§ 2.1.1:231), and |}ॐ{| is the absolute value of nothing-mind, or non-mind, which is mind without {mind}; *unmind*. This is because the absolute value of *nothing* |}{| is un-*nothing*, that is, *something* without {something} and thus its 'un-' form. It isn't negation because there's still unmindness, though not mindness (§ 2.2.1.1.2.1:237). Mind is the thought aspect of consciousness, which is the totality of self such that

$$\odot \leftrightarrow |\}\odot\{| \tag{18.15}$$

where ⊙ is consciousness, the absolute *nothing* value follows from Eq. (18.14) as nonconsciousness,[275] and the material equivalence doesn't imply identity.

Unmind is a compound of noncognitive, nonconscious, plantlike intelligence and is nonconscious. It's distinct from unconscious in its normal meaning, yet is subconscious in the sense it operates as a noncognitive permeant in the totality of an entity's awareness. Unmind is the essence of Energent–prime (as well as of a universe Energent) such that

$$\left(\Theta'_{\varepsilon\mu} \leftrightarrow |\}\,\text{ॐ}\,\{|\right) \bigwedge \left(\Theta_{\varepsilon\mu} \leftrightarrow |\}\,\text{ॐ}\,\{|\right) \tag{18.16}$$

where $\Theta'_{\varepsilon\mu}$ and $\Theta_{\varepsilon\mu}$ are All Existence Energent–prime and a universe's Energent, respectively, and (even though, in the larger sense, both Energent–prime and Energent *are* unmind) the material equivalence doesn't imply identity. Hence, without implying identity,

$$\text{AE} \cong |\}\,\text{ॐ}\,\{| \cong \Theta'_{\varepsilon\mu}. \tag{18.17}$$

Practically speaking, All Existence is the totality of unmind and Energent–prime, which are the same in function but different in aspect. Unmind is *way* of being of All Existence whereas Energent–prime is *reality* of being. This relational totality expresses in, with, around, and through any entity (*Fig. 102*).

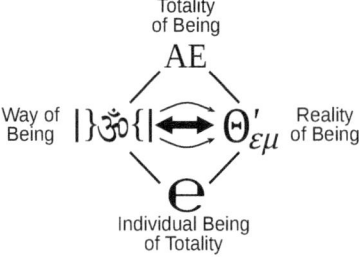

Totality
of Being
AE

Way of
Being

Reality
of Being

Individual Being
of Totality

Figure 102. All Existence 'four-position foundation' of existence, where Ɵ is any entity and 'Being' means entity beingness, not entity *as* being (cf. Fig. 127:295).[242]

---

275. We use *non*consciousness instead of *un*consciousness because, in this case, conventions in English render using *un-* more confusing. Topologies of mind (psyche) like conscious-preconscious-un(sub)conscious and its variants are inaccurate. There's only mind–brain and mind, where ॐ ≅ ⊙. From our physical (and even spirit) perspective, mind is the un(sub)conscious. Habit, for instance, is woв of mind and brain rather than simply an un(sub)conscious phenomenon. Note that, like mind–brain, mind–spirit-mind (our spirit self) is also different.

2.2.1.1.2.1 Unmind

Intelligence through the unmind subclass is plantlike in that it noncognitively perceives relevant environmental reality, qualifies it w.r.t. own-self WOB in the context of the totality of environmental WOB, and applies a responsive, or regulatory, course of action. This isn't all too different from the definitions of cognitive intelligence previously cited. Unmind intelligence is distributed awareness. But since it isn't consciously aware and doesn't experience cognition then, per Eq. (18.14)–(18.15), its nonconscious awareness is unmind, the absolute *nothing* value of awareness, which is *unawareness*, thus

$$|\}\,\text{ॐ}\,\{| \leftrightarrow |\}\text{awareness}\{| \tag{18.18}$$

where $|\}$awareness$\{|$ is *unawareness*. This isn't a limited-capability biological phenomenon, but an All Existence WOB phenomenon. Proto-energy, Fundamental Force, and matter down to single paired archí all express unawareness in the way they form, structure themselves, and wholistically and holistically interact with their environment. Therefore, unmind intelligence (not unmind itself) is a feature of every nonhuman aspect and entity of All Existence as well as of any universe, including ours. Accordingly, intelligence w.r.t. unmind expresses as *unawareness* rather than awareness or cognition as a totality of wholistic regulatory feedback systems that are integrated and interrelated signaling, communications, and response subsystems where each system in a holistic, distributed intelligence sense acts w.r.t. the entity's totality as well as All Existence's totality in toto.

2.2.1.2 Existence Interface

Second, UNI functions as an interface between All Existence as a whole entity and its parts as individual entities, holistically integrating all existence wholistically. We were struck by Mina's brainstem analogy (§ 2.2.1:233)—which came some time after this interface concept—because, what does a brainstem do but interface twixt body and brain, between its *reality* of being and its *way of* being? UNI provides a brainstem-like regulatory function, too. Notably, it's the 'urge' of any entity toward WOB with its concomitant freedom, order, and so on permeating every aspect of All Existence. Everything in existence ultimately emanates from this WOB. UNI is the *creator* of All Existence because it is self-organizationally the essence of what and how it means for any entity to exist. When an entity's WOB deviates from totality WOB in moving beyond those parameters in a novel, self-organizational way, we call it emergence. This means there isn't infinitely imaginable realities *in reality* just because our universe, for example, is infinite (indeterminate). It exists according to its WOB and to no other because there is no other. Absent a system emergence event, this holds for All Existence, too.

2.2.1.2.1 Blueprint of Existence

Now, there's an issue that comes up in software programming languages called 'the diamond problem' which allow multiple inheritance of a variable state (*Fig. 103*) and forms a metaphor for UNI's nature as an interface, because All Existence is a 'multiple inheritance environment.'

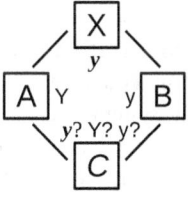

Figure 103. The 'diamond problem' in multiple inheritance; confusion arises as to which object class to call.

In *Fig. 103*, let X be an object in All Existence whose WOB is property y and is consistent with All Existence's WOB. Let C be any new object in existence, and let A and B be any already existing objects that previously instantiated from X. If new object C instantiates from objects A and B where each one has overridden (or, modified) X's shared property y to, say, Y and y—perhaps in variant low-order emergence events—then which version of shared property y inherits to new object C? Is it property y, Y, or y? From the UNI perspective, object C must inherit from X, which remains consistent with All Existence's WOB, rather than A or B's now-variant emergent WOB, which are inconsistent with X. Otherwise, their WOB deviation could raise incompatibilities in C that destabilize the system locally or in totality.[276]

In programming parlance, UNI is like an *object masterclass*, a blueprint for All Existence (and a universe) that's not too unlike Plato's Forms, though more nuanced and sophisticated (cf. e.g., Burgin 2017). It permeates All Existence so comprehensively that to cognize an object's WOB is to cognize UNI WOB. All Existence resolves the diamond problem when new object C inherits WOB from All Existence via X through this permeation effect. This is why $2H_2 + \frac{1}{2}O_2 +$ 'energy' $\rightarrow H_2O$ and not randomly something not-water, for example. The WOB inheritance from Form to Object is so thorough, the object isn't merely a reflection (imitation), as with Plato's Forms, but an *instantiation* of UNI itself regardless object form. As humans are ℒife possessing consciousness— an entity in and of itself, wholly discrete from, thus not regulated by, All Existence except in terms of our physical and spirit embodiments composed out of All Existence—we're free to emergently evolve even if All Existence remains static (§ 2:304), and All Existence can emergently evolve even if ℒife remains static.[277] In this way, ℒife is an 'All Existence' in and of itself; *you* are your own 'All Existence.' Here lies the root 'neath the mystic's adumbration that "you are the universe; the universe is you." UNI has implications w.r.t. The Corruption (CH. 24:361).

This previews the stunning breadth of integration intrinsic of All Existence. As to the Platonic question of whether there's a form for what doesn't yet exist, the answer is no. There's no Form, or object class, for any specific thing in All Existence but rather for that which constitutes a thing, such as (in the case of our universe) *tree-ness* or *archí-ness*, but not *tree* or *archí*. This means tree-ness or archí-ness is WOB as a totality for an entity that, in totality, expresses as tree or as archí, the reason being that things express and interact freely and imaginatively in unpredictable ways because that's a prime essential in All Existence's WOB.[278] What comes to exist is a full expression of All Existence WOB and where it's not, it doesn't exist. There's no Form or object class until something comes to exist but then, at that point, it's an instantiation of WOB anyway, not a Form. Some of this is latent in All Existence and expresses only when instantiated in a universe. WOB doesn't govern All Existence with inviolable rules. It simply permeates All Existence in the same way there's no water without wetness. It might seem to be the same Platonic body style but, under the hood, it's WOB. Whatever comes to exist, it forms naturally by and through WOB. UNI is WOB, therefore, intelligence.

2.2.1.3   TRAITS

Third, UNI as a trait forms a feedback loop with the wholistic totality and holistic parts of All Existence, and it always adapts toward optimal freedom, order, coherence, and so forth consistent with the overarching WOB that permeates All Existence (thus a universe). This includes adapting toward life of a specific type, say, carbon over silicon;[243] there is system homeostasis.[244] Individual entities populating All Existence don't disjunctively maintain own-self steady state. Rather, a part of each entity's unique individual nature is an extension of the trait's WOB toward a certain steady state that keeps the entity in equilibrium with successively higher levels of wholeness. As such, All Existence achieves homeostasis. For example, even though biology reveals the effect of our brainstem autonomically regulating our body homeostatically, the cause doesn't lay in DNA expressing through the brainstem's functionality, but in UNI from which DNA constitutes in the first place and which constitutes an aspect of its influence. Homeostasis is a trait that (for brained entities) expresses through the complex physiology of the brainstem. With respect to All Existence, homeostasis is a UNI self-organized trait. Thus, All Existence is a finely balanced—at equilibrium—operation. It achieves balance because UNI's homeostasis trait, its intelligence, influences everything in existence toward a steady state consistent with WOB self-organized as Current All Existence.

Recall All Existence's emergent nature, though. It's not static or rigidly locked into only one WOB. It adjusts all levels up to but not inclusive of system WOB (except in a system-wide emergence event, such as $pAE \rightarrow cAE$). Our universe, however, has a specific system-level WOB that's consciously Intentional as opposed to All Existence's nonconsciously Intentional. An emergent WOB inimical to Mina's founding Intentionality (§ 3.2:282; § 2.1:340) can't overthrow the system steady state even though, at all other levels, such emergent WOB alterations routinely occur. From an unschooled perspective, the sophistication that one perceives throughout our universe easily mimics conscious intelligence, encouraging one to postulate a consciously intelligent creator or some sort of directed process. Although our universe—any universe for that matter—does indeed have a consciously intelligent founder, the noncognitive and nonconscious UNI that is All Existence certainly does not.

---

276. A system-level cascade emergence event can be sufficient to override said system's WOB.

277. The Cardinal hasn't established such an emergent change's effect on the other, however.

278. Recall that type-identical objects (e.g., quark) constitute from variant archí substructures, yet still attain quark-ness (§ 2:114).

So far, we've considered two foundational components of our existence: the way All Existence came to be in the first place (domain period), and the unaware intelligence that permeates it (function period).

2.3 Current All Existence: Structure Period

Let's now turn to structure. Current All Existence is simple in this respect, although *structure* isn't precisely what we mean (*below*). Nevertheless, there are three fundamental aspects involved: 1) All Existence as the totality of 'all there infinitely is,' 2) *Life* (consciousness), and 3) Energent–prime (*Fig. 104*). First, we investigate Energent–prime together with All Existence and then consciousness.

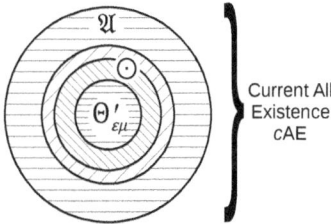

Figure 104. cAE in totality; ⊙ is consciousness (*Life*) singly and collectively, and $\Theta'_{\varepsilon\mu}$ is Energent–prime.

2.3.1 All Existence

Although *Fig. 104* implies structure and a certain hierarchy, or even a relational or 'neural' net, that's not the case. The figure is schematic, a metaphor to visualize All Existence in terms of what's *in play*, not what's *there*. Our bias tells us that something which exists should have structure, form, or function, but All Existence has no specific such. Even infinity, as murkily conceptualized as it is, has these (§ 1:94). But All Existence doesn't. The reason is *it doesn't even exist*—not in any way we think of it anyway.

All Existence is WOB. When we look at it, we're not seeing an existing thing, just WOB. If it were a thing, it necessarily exists as an existent in some space, some environment. That's impossible w.r.t. All Existence because, as a thing's environment necessarily isn't the thing, then it must necessarily be that its environment isn't All Existence but some *other* not-All-Existence, and there we are with All Existence as some sort of container in a necessarily different environment. Thus, it can't be a literal thing but simply WOB. Our conceptualization needs to shift from All Existence as a thing to WOB as not-thing. All Existence is indeterminate because it's not a thing but simply WOB. In sum, All Existence *is* WOB. There's no functional reality to that, no structure. Nothing is tangible. It's formless, essentially without existence albeit *there*. In and of itself, WOB is a *prototype* of existence. This isn't so strange, really. We see it foreshadowed in WOB permeating the nonconscious as well as latent aspects of All Existence (§ 2.2.1.2.1:237). It also pops up prior to creation in Genesis 1:2, where "the earth was formless and empty, darkness was over the surface of the deep, and the Spirit of God was hovering over the waters," and in the Quran, too, where "the heavens and earth were 'once' one mass [a joined entity] then We split them apart."[245] This prototype is the latent existent that comes to fruition in created (Intentioned) universes.

Energent–prime—what we call proto-energy in its totality, just as All Existence is what we call Energent–prime in *its* totality—expresses as WOB. It fundamentally *is* WOB. They're one and the same yet distinct, the same functionality but different existents, altogether an indivisible whole such that

$$\text{WoB} \leftrightarrow \Theta'_{\varepsilon\mu} \tag{18.19}$$

where $\Theta'_{\varepsilon\mu}$ is Energent–prime and the material equivalence doesn't imply identity. Because neither aspect is a thing of structure, form, or function then All Existence exists as a whole both existently as a thing and non-existently as a way. WoB is plantlike nonconscious consciousness, whereas proto-energy is its nonconscious (nonsentient, nonsapient) existence in which WOB is rooted in the same fashion *Life* roots in its conscious (sentient, sapient) existence; our own living 'Energent.'

The foregoing is the way All Existence is indeterminate.[279] It's not a space or dimensional entity, but Energent–prime which never doesn't not exist. If Energent–prime didn't exist, its nonexistence would be All Existence's nonexistence and, therefore, *nothing*. As noted, *nothing* is a contradiction and impossible (§ 2.1.1:231). When we conceptualize Energent–prime, all there is to conceptualize is WOB. It's a dimensionless

---

279. And because All Existence is indeterminate, any created universe is, too.

quality. We can't conceptualize Energent–prime in dimensional terms as we're wont with infinity or as any sort of dimensionality because it's just WOB, and that's all there is. All Existence, being 'all there infinitely is,' is an emergent of Energent–prime proto-energy, which is WOB (as opposed to some sort of structured existent) and, therefore, indeterminate.

Although it seems implicative that relational or neural nets of some type serve as WOB's mechanical back office, we'd be wrong to presume so. Mina doesn't like *relational net*, *neural net*, or any such concept, as it implies structure, form, and functionality whereas All Existence, Energent–prime, and universes with their Energents are WOB expressions that are a totality without substructure. Elements of All Existence or universes aren't netted but free. Their interactions and formulations, local, non-local, and global effects et cetera aren't node-to-node but express through Energent–prime or a universe's Energent, respectively. It's netlike but not a net at all. Existence isn't synergistic even though synergy happens as part of existence.

The nature of All Existence's structure is that it's composed of elements through WOB. Our natural tendency is to imagine elements in relations, but that's not the case. Instead, it's WOB. Elements relate according to WOB as it inculcates, or instantiates, in them in object-masterclass fashion (§ 2.2.1.2.1:237). The basic feature, or characteristic, of an object is that it's composed of elements, each of which expresses local, non-local, and global WOB inherited locally, non-locally, and globally. 'Relating' or 'relationships' is the expression of WOB between objects. An object's response to WOB expression isn't responsorial but the expression of its own WOB. It's an 'expression-and-response' that, although it seems relational, doesn't constitute 'relating' or 'relationship.' One object's experience with another is WOB encountering WOB. In the larger WOB context (say, non-local or global), the two WOB simply express non-local WOB in which a certain reality obtains locally and non-locally for the two objects.

Rather than interacting or relating in context, the objects, given their WOB, are simply *being* as they only can be in the context of their environment's in-the-moment WOB. Functionally, there's no actual interaction as such. WOB for each object, locally and non-locally, simply expresses according to the WOB of both objects in proximity. Consider our earlier H_2O (water) example. Two molecules of hydrogen and one of oxygen encounter each other in an environment—where *environment* means there's bonding conditions for the molecules—whose WOB *is* H_2O. The molecules don't react, interact, or relate with the others to create H_2O but altogether *conform* to the WOB in which there *is* H_2O. This profound shift in perspective alters our base understanding of entity relations and the 'energy' and matter manipulation that's possible, say, with chemistry.

2.3.2 ORIGIN OF LIFE

We are not our bodies. That's a fundament of human reality and a caution not only to physical-born humanity but surprisingly relevant to the spirit-born, too.[280] Consciousness isn't the reification of properties or aspects attributed to the various states of awareness, but a substantive entity as real as electromagnetic fields. Humanity hasn't really ever defined the what-is of consciousness beyond a tentative assertion that it's invisible and fraught with interpretive meaning. Instead, Philosophy with a capital-P focuses on the how-is because, outside of revelatory data, what are its options? Even so, it's made little progress, overall. It's as big a mystery as ever. And in the last hundred years or so a materialist focus on mind-as-brain largely superseded the non-materialist mind-as-not-brain. From here on, we ignore about 100% of the extant interpretive lexicon of *conscious* and *consciousness* in order to zero in on the nub of the human being as transcendent self-existence and treat consciousness as one of two expressions of life (§ 1.2.1.1:248). Accordingly, the concept of *Da-sein* (*there-being/being-there*; FN 38:22) assumes the duty from that of consciousness as principal category for all aspects of awareness typically imputed to conscious and consciousness, whether human or not (§ 2:275).

Consciousness and mind are different, yet the same—discrete yet integral aspects of the same thing—in much the same way as All Existence and Energent–prime. Brain, however, is top to bottom a different category. In this book, *consciousness* means the totality of self-aware experience and *mind* the totality of Thought, which is thinking–feeling in the totality of consciousness. Thought is distinct from both, although our experience of it is mind which is logically equivalent to consciousness. Mind is the experience of Thought within the totality of our consciousness in the totality of All Existence. Moreover, consciousness always references, or includes, the entity (human or nonhuman) in totality. There's no sundering the entity/person from consciousness, hence, it's more a comprehension for life than for its subset, self-awareness. However clinical our discussion of

---

280. Until the Big Healing, spirit persons, like physical persons, had no idea they were existentially a substantive self-existent being of consciousness beyond their spirit body. Theories abounded, of course, just as here, but not about this particular reality.

consciousness might come across, it's always in the context of the entity (human or nonhuman) and not as some esoteric philosophical construct describing some perceived ability. For the remainder of this book, we reference consciousness and its accoutrements in the context of *Life*—Fraktur-h Human—unless noted.

Since we cover consciousness as *Life* comprehensively in the next chapter, we're more concerned here with its place vis-à-vis the larger context of Current All Existence. We show its relation to the various aspects of Current All Existence in *Fig. 105*, but bear in mind the hierarchical depiction is only to help visualize consciousness in context.[281] A universe has structure, after all, but All Existence doesn't.

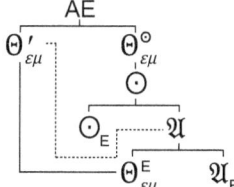

Figure 105. Consciousness in context. AE is All Existence; $\Theta'_{\varepsilon\mu}$ is Energent–prime; $\Theta^{\odot}_{\varepsilon\mu}$ is Energent proto-life (EPL); $\odot$ is consciousness (*Life*); $\odot_E$ is totality of consciousnesses; $\mathfrak{A}$ is totality of universes; $\Theta^{E}_{\varepsilon\mu}$ is totality of universe Energents; $\mathfrak{A}_E$ is totality of existents within totality of universes. Dotted line indicates $\mathfrak{A}$ materially instantiates from Intentional instantiation by consciousness integrated with $\Theta'_{\varepsilon\mu}$.

The figure above indicates the principal constituents of All Existence are Energent–prime, Energent proto-life, and *Life* (consciousness). Humans build universes that are included but not original to Current All Existence. Tout ensemble, the figure is a panoramic of 'all there infinitely is.'

2.3.2.1 ENERGENT PROTO-LIFE

Energent proto-life (EPL) emergently arose during Emergent All Existence as *Life-precursive proto-energy*. Naturally, it differs from Energent–prime's nonconscious proto-energy. They're wholly distinct, residing in unique 'frequency spaces'[282] just as universes reside distinct from others and Energent–prime yet, altogether, All Existence. *Life* emergently birthed in the context of EPL.

When we say *Life* is an emergent, we don't mean it sprang into existence from constituents of Previous All Existence through Emergent All Existence in the same way Current All Existence did. Rather, its emergence was a spontaneous eruption of self-awareness 'in' EPL *conceptually* the same way archí spontaneously erupt from our Energent as matter.[283] *Life* as an entity (not consciousness as an expression of *Life*) is a kind of 'matter' in that, in the EPL context, it's spatially finite as a mode of existence (as an existent) yet nonspatial and indeterminate as a mode of being (as a function). In EPL, 'matter' doesn't mean something tangible or physical but signifies an instantiation of *Life* that differs in nature from EPL. This difference is what we're loosely calling a spatial, dimensional existent. While an individual *Life* is a discrete yet indeterminate entity, it isn't discrete the way an archí is discrete, or indeterminate the way EPL is indeterminate. In terms of our spatially oriented universe, *Life* is determinate in space and this is a valid corollary for nonspatially oriented EPL even though, as you can see, there's a substantive conceptual distinction. Emergent *Life* in and of itself isn't infinite the way our universe is (say, in terms of dimensional space); rather, it's 'discrete,' 'finite,' 'contained.' Yet, it's infinite in the sense that, suffused in EPL, our consciousness can *have awareness* of any part of it and any reality thereby. Essentially, a person *is* EPL (where

$$人 \leftrightarrow \Theta^{\odot}_{\varepsilon\mu} \tag{18.20}$$

in which the Chinese character 人 [*rén*] is *personness* [Introduction, CH. 19:245], $\Theta^{\odot}_{\varepsilon\mu}$ is EPL, and the material equivalence doesn't imply identity) that emergently formed self-existence just as an archí is Energent proto-energy that emergently formed discrete matter (ibid). While *Life* is entirely unrelated to matter, it relates to dimensionality. It exists in a discrete and dimensional state that's not directly translatable to how we spatially

---

281. Moreover, we lack the conceptual awareness, hence language, to articulate the reality of proto-energy and especially consciousness proto-energy. We don't have time to develop it here beyond an overview, as Mina prefers the book published sooner than later. A detailed conceptual awareness with attendant language awaits a future work.

282. A proto-energy state space. The analogy is weak but we hope sufficient to convey the idea. When noted, 'weak' means no accurate ('strong') analogy exists.

283. Weak analogy, though not exactly cars to candy bars.

comprehend discrete and dimensional. We can think of it as EPL-discrete and EPL-dimensional as a way to conceptually demarcate EPL's reality from our own. *Life* instantiates immersed 'in' EPL similar to archí instantiating immersed in *enérgeia*, not as a solute but heterogeneously like balls floating in a sea (Fig. 106). Since consciousness interacts with all consciousnesses, a person (embodied or unembodied) can be aware of and interact with all humanity similar to how archí are WOB-aware of, and interact with, all archí. Since EPL also interacts with Energent–prime, a person can be as aware of, and interactive with, the Energent of a universe and any entity of said universe as they can with Energent–prime overall. This reality is the so-called Akashic Records (§ 2:593).

Figure 106. Left, schematic of instantiated *Life* (individual person) 'in' EPL 'solute' as EPL-discrete and dimensional 'balls' floating in a non-dimensional EPL 'sea;' right, thought experiment: people in balls represent discrete minds in touch via (EPL) 'water' with others and the whole megaverse (§ 2.1.4.1:312).₂₄₆

EPL is proto-life just as Energent–prime (as well as an Energent) is proto-energy, and *Life force* energizes 'in' and emanates from proto-life the way Fundamental Force energizes 'in' and emanates from proto-energy (§ 1:112). *Life* arising from Intentionality (§ 3.2:282) 'in' EPL is the same in concept as archí arising from Intentionality in Energent proto-energy (§ 2.3.1:115). *Life* is EPL proto-energy 'sticking together' in a larger sea of 'unstuck' EPL. While that seems awfully similar to Energent proto-energy emergently coalescing in density until archí matter arises, Mina says no, it's a false analogy. The reason is that *Life* doesn't arise from proto-life by coalescing until achieving an emergent 'density' threshold as with archí in proto-energy (which is a nonconscious, in a sense mechanical, event), but from proto-life coalescing via Intentionality until achieving an emergent *Life* threshold. It's a natural comparison and seems logical but, in Mina's mind, comparing nonconscious anything to conscious something is apples to oranges; it's invalid. In that respect, EPL 'sticking together' just isn't analogous to a coalescent rise in proto-energy 'density' because the latter is an emergence of nonconscious form and the former a *birth* of conscious*ness: Life*. In truth, the issue is almost entirely unclear. The Cardinal has no specific answer that gets above a 25% confidence level for how *Life* arises from EPL, only that, under specific, known conditions, it does.

2.3.2.2   SPONTANEOUS AND INTENTIONAL EMERGENCE

We can't accurately talk about spatiality or dimensionality w.r.t. EPL, but we can accurately talk about a conscious entity being spatially finite 'in' EPL. The first two humans to birth were a spontaneous emergence (§ 2:304) 'in' EPL as novel life, each unique, aware, and self-aware.[284] Since then, humans conceive humans via Intentionality. Conceived *Life* emergently births 'in' EPL as an Intentional instantiation of EPL. Two persons conceive—altogether, Intentionalize—a new person.[285] Their Intentionality stimulates a nascent emergence 'in' EPL which coalescently differentiates and self-organizes into novel *Life*, in this case a unique, individual person—you. Novel emergence is why each person is unique, an instantiation of *Life* that can never be duplicated, ever (§ 1.2:246). The Cardinal's thinking on why no more and no less than two persons can conceive is because emergent *Life* arose in a societal context—as a kinship pair, not singular or as a group—and thus the conditions of emergent procreation itself naturally arose, too, as a kinship experience (and is the reason humanity's WOB is intrinsically familial). They feel it's a plausible theory, though give it only a 30% confidence level. As before, the why and how aren't clear, only the fact.

Intentionality is 'focused intention,' not simply desire or will. The focused intention needs reach a 'critical Intentionality' before the conceptive effect occurs, at which point new *Life* births 'as' EPL, meaning an emergent person births. The new consciousness emerges randomly 'located' in EPL according to 'wherever'

284. Weak and strong emergence categories don't apply to human emergence.

285. Conception by unembodied, physical, and spirit persons is process invariant but methodologically variant (§ 1.2.1.1:248).

EPL is conducive at that very moment to the Intentionality, and another 'ball' achieves fruition in the EPL 'sea' (Fig. 107). However, EPL doesn't have dimensionality any more than the Energent does. This means there's no matter, hence no event periodicity, thus no time (timekeeping), distance, or travel. Accordingly, there's no actual point in EPL 'space' where an emergent ℒife arises, just that it does arise at a specific 'point'—one might map it to a physical point space, were it possible to do—where EPL is conducive to experiencing the 'energy' of conception in a way in which ℒife emergently arises.

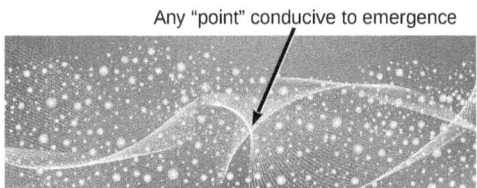

Any "point" conducive to emergence

Figure 107. ℒife emergently births at a 'point' where EPL is conducive to coalescent differentiation at the Intentional moment, the instant of conception.[247]

The Cardinal understands the mechanism for conception, how Intentionality works, and that it's an internal force of ℒife mobilized by one's consciousness. But they don't understand *why* Intentionality does what it does, why EPL responds to this internal force of ℒife, and why its response results in the emergent birth of a human or our intrinsic ability of mind to synthesize matter and 'energy.' No one understands the existence of Intentionality in any context, in fact—though the first two humans have a 49% confidence level (§ 2:304)—only that it reliably manifests a couple's Intentionality to birth a new human and to synthesize matter and 'energy.' Such recondite reality is a true *vitae mysterium*, and that's where we have to leave it.

2.3.2.3   EPL AND ENERGENT–PRIME

EPL is the 'medium' that allows a consciousness to interact with others and with proto-energy beyond any 'normal' means. As a ℒife-precursive proto-energy that is proto-life, EPL is distinct from nonconscious proto-energy, i.e., Energent–prime or a universe's Energent. It resides as a different expression to Energent–prime that's weakly analogous to the way the natural and supranatural are different expressions of a universe's dual-purpose, yet still singular, Energent. Put differently, Energent–prime and EPL discretely exist in Current All Existence as separate yet relational, noncontiguous yet interactive, entities (*Fig. 108*). Consciousnesses communicate or interact with each other and all Current All Existence environments through both non-EPL and EPL in exactly the conceptual way that all entities of a universe communicate or interact via their own universe's Energent (e.g., quantum entanglement).

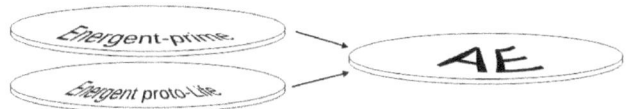

Figure 108. Energent–prime and EPL as discrete yet wholistic.

It feels disappointing if not downright incredible that ancient humanity's combined knowledge and wisdom going back some 800 billion years lacks perfectly complete knowledge of ℒife. The reality is that All Existence is inscrutable, but emergence of ℒife even more so. As many cosmologists make their home in *nothing* being prior to the Big Bang, we have to live with emergent ℒife being largely inexplicable as a brute fact even as it's largely explicable as a function. This chapter gives us a sense of where we as conscious beings stand relative to 'all there infinitely is.' Next, we consider our conscious beingness in detail.

Psyche Infinity

Quick Summary. Consciousness doesn't describe the whole person who is unique, self-aware emergent 𝓛ife. Animals have brain-capable levels of conscious self-awareness and some 'companion' animals have a spirit self. A physical person is mind integrating a body—which, itself, is animal—as an 'avatar' in which the brain transliterates mind, although it presently lacks sufficient neurons to represent mind in full. Memory is a feature of mind, not brain. 'Brainwaves' reflect brainstate as an electromagnetic (EM) transmitting 'antenna' but don't affect mindstate. Heart coherence as an emotional driver is a fiction. Humans dream in NREM and REM sleep; dreams are insufficiently REM-translitered mind memory. Humans affect their environment via Intentionality. Emotion, including hate, derives from proto-love. Empaths experience others' emotion and sometimes memory via integration. Minds in unison instantiate culture, which roots in the person not the group. Existence, time, and space infinity all ground in psyche infinity. Humans are intrinsically autonomous, ergo, absolutely free.

CONSCIOUSNESS IS WHAT we talk about when referencing what's unique, special, or differentiating about being human. On its own, however, 'consciousness' just doesn't capture it. The key thing is that the essence of so-called consciousness is *personness*, which is ꮒuman, humanness, emergently conscious (§ 2.2.1.1.1:235), and altogether 𝓛ife. Its functions—freedom, existence, choice, cognition, phenomenal awareness, qualia, and so on—are properties of the person. Taken together,

$$\left\{ \left(\odot = 人 \right) \Leftrightarrow \text{ꬱ} \right\} \Leftrightarrow \text{☥} \tag{19.1}$$

where $\odot$ is consciousness (Eq. (18.12):235), the Chinese character 人 [*rén*] is personness (Eq. (18.20):241), the Ethiopic (Amharic) letter ꬱ [*pä*] represents ꮒuman, the Egyptian hieroglyph ☥ [*ankh*] represents 𝓛ife, the equality is identity, and the logical equivalence doesn't imply identity. Secondarily,

$$\text{ꬱ} \cong \text{ꬱ}^{\text{F}} \tag{19.2}$$

where ꬱ^{F} means functionality of humanness and the congruence isn't identity. Nonhumans possess the same essence and functionality of entity as humans but aren't ꮒuman, thus, not having 𝓛ife. Consequently,

$$\exists\neg\text{ꬱ}\left(\left\{ \left(\neg\odot = \neg人 \right) \right\} \Leftrightarrow \neg☥ \right) \therefore \left(\neg\text{ꬱ} \cong \neg\text{ꬱ}^{\text{F}} \right) \bigwedge \left(\neg\text{ꬱ}^{\text{F}} \ncong \text{ꬱ}^{\text{F}} \right) \tag{19.3}$$

where $\exists\neg\text{ꬱ}$ is any nonhuman whereby nonconsciousness (§ 2.2.1.1:234) is own-self, or entity-ness, and the rest follows per Eq. (19.1)–(19.2). This means nonhuman aliveness isn't 𝓛ife, thus

$$\neg☥ \ncong ☥; \tag{19.4}$$

nonhuman life isn't ꮒuman 𝓛ife. Accordingly, nonhumanness (biology) is *Living* which isn't 𝓛ife.

SECTION 1

ℒife and Living

We didn't expect nonhuman entities to be so thoroughly human*like* that we'd encounter a distinction between *living* and *life*. Other definitions aside, we're used to them as nouns, verbs, or adjectives for the same thing: the state, quality, or experience of aliveness. On top of which, Philosophy with a capital-P is biased toward living organisms being alive in the same way we are because they appear similarly vital and motile even if dissimilarly smart and aware. That's true with our bodies, but neither our personness nor our humanity depends on our body—in and of itself capital-ʟ *Living* and not having ℒife—because mind is ℒife whereas brain is Living. The distinction here is fundamental, though admittedly, as terms, Living–ℒife is linguistically arbitrary (unlike mind–brain). A person has ℒife while their body, like an amoeba or a cow, is only Living. This may only seem to reiterate the already pernicious mind–body problem but, in reality, provides a new conceptual wherewithal to resolve it. Toward that end, let's unpack ℒife and Living as the two principal aspects of vital creation.

1.1 SELF-AWARENESS DEFINED

First, self-awareness needs defining. As you might expect, it comes in two flavors: nonhuman and human, the reason being brain, in and of itself, instantiates nonhuman mind whereas ℒife, in and of itself, *is* mind. Overall, self-awareness is the subjective experiential awareness of own-self's (§ 2:275) subjective experience of objective reality. It diminishes in scope indirectly proportional to the increase in primitivity.

Nonhuman self-awareness is the subjective experiential awareness of an entity's subjective experience of objective reality, not as qualia, of which it's an aspect, but as own-self in the totality of the experience. This means a nonhuman entity is subjectively aware of how it experiences objective reality albeit not aware it is subjectively aware. It's why chimpanzees for instance plot, exact revenge, make war; dogs grieve; elephants weep. This limited self-awareness diminishes according to capacity; one isn't going to encounter a scheming field mouse, a depressed cockroach, or a raging nematode. Nonhuman self-awareness is an aspect of instantiated Living mind (§ 1.3.2:273) that in a person integrates their Living (animal) mind with ℒife (human) mind (§ 1.2.2:253) which permits a wholistic experience of reality. The takeaway here is that nonhumans subjectively experience own-self in the totality of their experience; they're not simply dumb animals even if they don't experience the full monty of human self-awareness.

Human self-awareness is the subjective experiential awareness of being subjectively aware of one's subjective experience of objective reality, not as qualia or as own-self in the totality of experience of which both are aspects, but the autonomous experience of own-self itself. This self-awareness is ℒife and entirely a function of the emergent person. This means a person has experiential awareness of own-self as though not own-self, as if they were a separate, equally autonomous observer. It's why a person can exist as though an autonomous entity apart from own-self yet experience own-self's subjective and objective reality *as* own-self while *not* own-self; to 'clinically detach' from self to experience self. Self-awareness in average terms is a very limited experience because few people really engage it. Only some members of the Cardinal have ever pushed it to its absolute apparent limit; even then, they can only ever know they've reached *their* limit and not *its* limit (cf. § 3:331).

In sum, human self-awareness isn't 'true' self-awareness while the nonhuman version is merely its portrait; they differ only in degree not in kind. Mina created superlative nonhumans with the most robust self-awareness possible so we could experience a mammalian class as companions, whether or not we choose to utilize them as food, sport, pets, or friends. With this basic understanding of self-awareness in hand, we can describe emergent human ℒife and nonemergent nonhuman Living (§ 1.3:272).

1.2 ℒIFE

For Philosophy with a capital-P, about the only agreed-upon definition of life is that entities possessing it exhibit certain characteristics that sum up to a state of being that's called *alive*. These include cellular organization and metabolism in a homeostatic environment that shows growth, adaptation, stimuli response, and reproductive ability (§ 1.1:532). But these functions define a state of Living; such automata don't add up to having ℒife. It might seem like it does materially (bodily), but it doesn't with mind for the straightforward reason that biology is living matter and mind isn't. Even taking the position that mind arises in biology, we're still left with mind being not-biology—at least in terms of cellular automata, a specific enzymatic, hormonal, or cellular mechanism in and of itself being thinking, feeling, intuition . . . the whole gamut of mind experience—but an apparent emergent property sans physicality. Science reckons biology alive with certain caveats but, if we imbue it with ℒife, we lose the nonconscious distinction with consciousness, the ineffable emergent *being* having ℒife where we distinguish ℒife from life as uniquely human versus capital-ℒ Living from lowercase-l living as uniquely nonhuman. Then, what does it mean to *have ℒife* versus *Living*? We answer this by comprehending what it means to be human, since humanness is the sum total essence of consciousness as personness. We begin, therefore, with ℒife.

1.2.1 EMERGENCE OF ℒife

ℒife is unique to All Existence, not just to our (much less any) universe. It doesn't arise in evolutionary biology as does Living. ℒife is *human*; *human* is ℒife. In the process chain of emergence, ℒife is what arises. Not as a trait or property, but *born*. It self-organizes as a particular way of being (wob; § 2.2.1.1:234) that's consciousness as personness, humanness, an eternal, self-existent being. It's an existent of humanness in terms of functionality (consciousness) and singularity (personness) of being. As noted (§ 2.3.2.2:242), ℒife—after it spontaneously birthed as the first two emergent persons (§ 2:304)—arises only from human Intentionality (§ 1.2.1.1:248); it isn't random. It arises in three contexts because a person exists simultaneously in one, two or three states of being: unembodied (everyone), spirit-embodied (spirit- or physical-born), and physical-embodied (physical-born).

Unembodied means we initially, or by later choice, experience ℒife without objective environmental interaction beyond that constituted by interaction with the reality of other unembodied persons. Think of this mode of ℒife simply as mind-to-mind interaction. It's important to realize this aspect of ℒife is as real as any other. The reality of our own mind is a full, tangible reality to *us*, though not a simultaneous objective reality to others. We can open our minds to others for them to experience our conscious thinking–feeling, but not the subconscious reality that is what we are. The mind is inviolable—unique, discrete—in that respect.[286] This unembodied state of being is fundamental.[287] If one is unembodied-born, then it's their normal state; being *embodied* is at-will. For the rest of us, being embodied is our normal state; being *unembodied* is at-will.

Spirit-embodied means we initially, or by later choice, experience ℒife in the objective, tactile, supranatural (spirit) environment of a universe through a *subjective body*. In this mode of ℒife, we manifest our body through the Intentionality of our mind. This is what we typically think of as spirit world—the so-called after—life. It's simultaneously the province of the spirit-born and physical-born. Even when physically alive, one can access the supranatural at will. The spirit body we naturally (without conscious thought) manifest reflects our wob, how we truly see ourselves. We can modify it any way we like via Intentionality. Such freedom is instrinsic of ℒife although, prior to the Big Healing, few spirit persons remembered or ever learned of these things because of The Corruption (§ 24:361) and the Negative Collective Consciousness (§ 1.2:21; § 4.2.1.4:382).

Physical-embodied means that we initially experience ℒife in the objective, tactile, natural (physical) environment of a universe through an *objective body*. In this mode of ℒife, our body is a biological existent we integrate. That means it's a reality in its own right with its own processes, needs, and intrinsic behaviors. While we can materially affect our physical body, we can't change it wholesale as we can our spirit body because it operates in accord with inviolable biological parameters. If we obviate those, the body loses sustainment. We typically think of this mode of ℒife as regular—the only *real*—life. Intrinsically, this state of being is more albeit not anywhere near as limited as it appears today. Educable awareness rectifies our ignorance of our physical embodiment.

Although there's an obvious functional difference between these three contexts of being, unembodied isn't intrinsically better or more enlightened than embodied. A physical-born person who, after death, chooses to live unembodied isn't any different from, say, a Japan-born person emmigrating to America to 'disembody' their Japanism and embody Americanism. In each case, they're the same person simply in a different context. We cover these states of being comprehensively in PART III.

---

286. At present, you and I aren't capable of this awareness level because, to be honest, as physical-born persons we're just babes in the awareness department with a lot of developing to do as we progressively learn, beginning with the reality described herein.

287. But the unembodied state isn't so-called pure consciousness, which for some traditions is the ultimate destination of human perfection, nor is it the ultimate source of existential being. It's just our fundamental, mind-intrinsic state of being.

1.2.1.1 BIRTH OF INDIVIDUAL LIFE

Life isn't a biological emergent as aliveness is with Living entities (§ 1.3:272). It's not a function of our universe; Mina didn't design it. It's independent even of All Existence (§ 2.3.1:239). Life is its own reality. That's why properties, or functions, of Life like self-awareness, choice, and freedom are intrinsic to human existence, not granted by an all-powerful deity, government, religion, philosophy, ideology, or the individual to seize or dispense at will. When Thomas Jefferson (d. 1826) opined "all men are created equal," he was aiming at this fundamental truth without knowing it. Nor that "created equal" means only equality in human creation—equality *of* persons *in* birth—and not equality in being, which is all forms of equality *between* persons *in* relationship and is both a choice and a freedom (§ 5.1:428; CH. 36:585).

Life emergently births spontaneously from Energent proto-life (EPL; § 2.3.2.1:241) when two persons' intention to procreate becomes Intentionality. This simply means one achieves a state of mind[288] that exerts an Intentional effect (in this context) w.r.t. EPL such that it responds in coalescent differentiation 'at a point in' EPL where it's conducive to the Intentionality until a *critical Intentionality threshold* obtains and Life births (§ 2.3.2.2:242).[289] Procreative Intentionality comes in two forms: mind and biology. Our conscious or subconscious intent produces mind Intentionality. With physical procreation, Intentionality lies in the biology itself—sperm is a biological Intentionality in its own right—which means it constitutes out of biology's ineluctable process without need of mind Intentionality at all. For example, whereas unintended procreation is a bane of physical sex because the biological process of fertilization ineluctably operates regardless one's intent, it doesn't occur with spirit sex unless both parties Intentionalize it the same way in all respects (§ 1.2.1.1.2:249). Both spirit and physical procreation works through a series of checkpointed—that is, interruptible—mind or biological Intentionalized operations in three phases, respectively, to provoke birth of Life, as follows.

1.2.1.1.1 PHYSICAL-BORN BIRTH OF LIFE

Three phases we term 1) coalescent differentiation, 2) self-organizing, and 3) completion checkpoint both the physical and spirit procreated rise of emergent Life, as follows.

In **phase one**, emergence of Life begins with a *coalescent differentiation* of proto-life 'within' EPL, meaning it's reacting to the biological creation of a unique, self-existent being. It triggers during physical procreation when—during the mitotic cell division process following sperm–egg fertilization whereby a cell divides in the cleavage subprocess toward developing into an embryo—the internal parts of a fertilized cell's single-nucleus (the zygote) first gather up the nerve to separate over the course of the (early and late) prophase and metaphase stages of mitosis (*Fig. 109*, left 3 panels).[290]

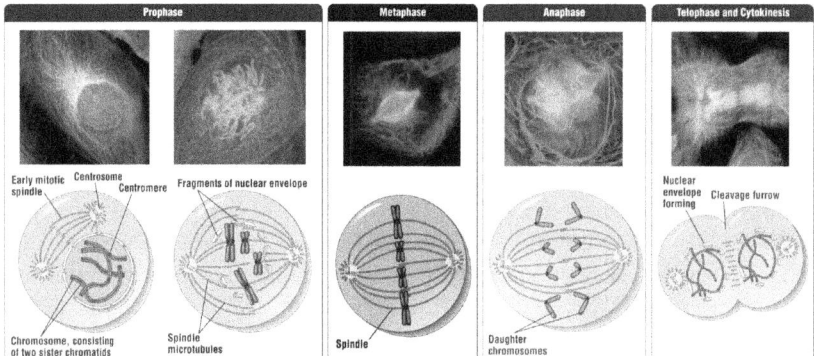

Figure 109. Left 3 panels: mitosis stages over which EPL initiates the coalescent differentiation (at first mitosis; phase 2) and completion (at second mitosis; phase 3) phases of emergent Life; right 2 panels: mitosis stages over which emergent Life self-organizes (at first mitosis) and completes (at second mitosis).248

In **phase two**, the emergent Life process then moves into *self-organizing* when the zygote successfully divides its single nucleus into two nuclei—while still a single cell where actual cell division hasn't yet initiated—

---

288. Not a mental state but one of personness, as it's our entire being involved, not simply the conscious content of our mind.

289. An approximation of what's happening, as we lack suitably descriptive conceptual language.

290. Mitosis is a cellular process where replicated chromosomes separate into two new nuclei.

over the course of the anaphase and about 70% of the telophase (prior to cytokinesis) stages. The developing person has nascent Life at this point but not humanness—it embodies none of the WOB of humanness—until this first cell division from single nucleus to two nuclei successfully completes (*Fig. 109*, right 2 panels). During this phase, there's feedback from the biology to EPL where biology–EPL establishes co-awareness.[291] Cell division undergoes a multiple checkpoint, or transition, methodology (Hartwell et al. 1989, 630; Hunt et al. 2011, 3495), only two of which, the G_2/M and the anaphase–telophase (spindle) checkpoints, are relevant to emergent Life. If, for whatever reason, the cell division process goes out of spec at any one checkpoint, then cell division fails or stalls early, in which case the biology ceases production (e.g., Green et al. 2014, 1466c), EPL response ends, and there's no emergence of Life. Following successful first-cell division—there are now two discrete cells comprising the zygote-cum-embryo—but before each of these two cells begins their internal mitotic process leading to next cell division (from two cells to four), biology–EPL co-awareness conveys to EPL that the biology is a stable, in-spec creation. This feedback process, intrinsic of proto-energy as well as of proto-life, is how Mina knew within a picosecond that our universe was in spec and functioning as intended, that his Intentional contribution to creation was over, and that the universe would self-develop from that point in accord with its Intentionalized WOB.[292] We term the cell division process in this phase *first mitosis*.

In **phase three**, the continuation of biology's in-spec feedback to EPL permits the nascent being to finish self-organizing and move to *completion*. In this phase, the coalescently differentiated and self-organized proto-life at the EPL creational focal point reaches the critical Intentionality threshold, that moment before which there wasn't, and after which there is, an eternal, self-existent human having Life. This occurs immediately after successful first mitosis which earlier resulted in a two-cell zygote-cum-embryo. Now, each of these cells divides again in a *second mitosis*. This phase begins and ends with the same mitotic stages as phases one and two (*Fig. 109*).

In an ideal world not subject to the vagaries of gestation, correct human body development is inevitable from this point. Well, we don't live in an ideal world but one in which things go wrong between embryo and birth, so it's important to understand that EPL WOB is just a singular stimulus-response to procreation, initially mediated to some degree in the physical case by a biological awareness. EPL doesn't create bodies but Life. Bodily procreation is simply the agent provocateur to EPL's creational WOB—the same way a doctor's mallet to your knee provokes, or stimulates, your body's reflexive WOB—and the biological process proceeds as an automaton that self-creates in accord with its WOB subject to any biological errata that doesn't self-correct. One can readily surmise that phase three completion means a self-existent human being is created regardless biological cessation—death—at any point forward. This has implications for abortion and cloning,[293] both of which terminate a body's development *after* second mitosis, causing a developing Life's abandonment by, and separation from, its body that halts its further development (absent albeit with a recent caveat a spirit person's hands-on intervention; FN 455:412).

1.2.1.1.2   Spirit-born Birth of Life

In **phase one**, emergence of Life triggers *coalescent differentiation* during spirit procreation when a spirit couple wanting to procreate establishes mind Intentionality before or during sex (but not after) in the context of initiating it. Since the supranatural environment lacks an ineluctably unfolding process like cell division, a spirit couple's co-intention translates to mind Intentionality in complement with sexual activity. Mind Intentionality plus completed sexual intercourse generates the same (though still checkpointed) process that nascent first-cell division provides in biology. During the physical process, the biology has awareness that fertilization is consistent with biological WOB and EPL is aware of the results. Mind Intentionality similarly sets its own norms and communicates feedback to EPL through the *vitae mysterium* of mind–EPL awareness. As soon as procreative mind Intentionality forms then mind–EPL reacts with baseline awareness. If mind Intentionality is nonnormative or terminated, however, then mind–EPL awareness dissolves, in which case even if sex continues to completion, it's without conception.

In **phase two**, if mind Intentionality is normative, the emergent process moves into *self-organizing* when the couple maintains Intentionality with sex ongoing. As with physical procreation, at this point the developing person has only nascent Life until sexual intercourse completes. As with biological sex, the male needs 'ejaculate'—

---

291. This feedback is a *vitae mysterium*, too. The Cardinal understands *how* the process works—the developing being only continues if it's getting in-spec feedback from the biology—but not *why* the *phenomenon* works.

292. FN 145:116. Once initiated, the process is unstoppable; if something did go wrong, he'd intervene.

293. Primarily, somatic cell nuclear transfer (SCNT) cloning that's used to harvest human stem cells (§ 2.2:410).

real enough as an event, but allegorical as to sperm conveying fertilization (§ 2.2.1.1:598)—for sex to complete and is analogous to completed first-cell division. Mind–EPL remains aware of the state of play (cf. Sex, § 2:597).

In **phase three**, the continuation of mind Intentionality's in-spec feedback permits EPL to finish self-organizing and move to *completion*. As with phase three in physical-life procreation, this phase results in an eternal, self-existent human being having Life. This occurs during and immediately after 'ejaculation.' Since there's no biological or time–space constraints, then, at the instant of 'ejaculation,' a fetal spirit body (*Fig. 110*) manifests in the 'womb' of whichever partner the couple co-Intentioned would carry the developing child. Abortion is also a problem in spirit world albeit much smaller than in the physical world, and a developing Life's termination prior to birth results in the same abandonment, halt to Life development, and interventional rescue as it does with physical conception.

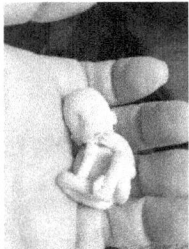

Figure 110. Spirit fetus manifests developmentally at about month 3 of biological gestation as a 'blank' to which parentally Intentioned ethnicity, size, et cetera develops (the child can later change it as desired).[249]

The reason Mina considers the analogy between spontaneous eruption of self-awareness 'in' EPL and spontaneous eruption of archí in our Energent to be weak (FN 282:241) is because, whereas archí emergently arise in a state of completion with no further intrinsic development, Life emergently arises *unconscious*—unaware and un-self-aware—with human WOB but otherwise a blank slate (*Fig. 110*). It needs must develop into its intrinsic self, some of which is biologically predetermined or mind Intentionalized by the parents–hair or eye color, height, ethnicity—and some predetermined by WOB, e.g., overall humanness and a generalized disposition (§ 1.2.1.3:252).

For example, it's not because physical babies have small brains that they're not very aware or self-aware, lack gross and fine motor control, and so forth but because their mind is developing in consonance with learning to control their body, hence lacks those capabilities, too. The brain is fully capable in about four months of interfacing with the developing mind. It seems undeveloped in our observation because, first, mind is undeveloped not the brain, which is an interface to mind, and second, because science is biased that (human) mind is the product of brain. It only appears to lack sufficient neural connections at birth because it's still developing in tandem with mind. In actuality, it has all the neuronal connections its undeveloped mind needs. The brain is plastic. Absent damage and what-not, it responds at all times to the demands of mind. Brain capability develops in tandem with mind, expressed via the body's spirit self. However, spirit-born children mature faster than the physical-born. The reason is that, all else being equal, their supranatural environment lacks biology's time–space and mind–brain developmental limitations and the pressures, damages, and induced bias intrinsic to the natural environment resulting from The Corruption (§ 1.4:14; § 4.1:378), which is only now being put right since the Big Healing.

1.2.1.1.3 Unembodied Birth of Life

In **phase one**, emergence of Life triggers *coalescent differentiation* during unembodied procreation when an unembodied couple that wants to procreate establishes mind Intentionality either before or during (but not after) unembodied 'sex.' As any self-reflective, sexually active person knows, sexual activity is not a body so much as a mind experience. For the embodied, of course, one experiences the sensations and euphoria of sex in the mind in accord with bodily stimulation. However, people quite easily stimulate their sex organs completely hands free, using only Thought (§ 2.3.2:240) to raise sexual sensations in their body as though they were touching themselves, or being touched, until achieving orgasm (cf. § 2.2.1.1:598). This is the Intentional effect of Thought (§ 3.2:282). The body, which includes the brain, doesn't *experience* anything in and of itself; it can only *encounter* stimulation. Accordingly, one experiences the pleasure of sexual activity not in, of, or as a body, but as mind. Sex, therefore, is strictly a mind experience through which (besides the sheer pleasure of) procreative Intentionality arises.

Once embodied, people's awareness–experience tends to distance from mind-centric to body-centric. This means shifting focus from mind and its 'energies' to the body and its 'energies.' Of course, one never loses touch with the experience of mind, but the experience of embodiment deemphasizes it although, regardless, procreative Intentionality only arises in the embodied context via embodied 'sex.'

A couple's co-Intention translates to mind Intentionality in complement with unembodied 'sexual' activity. This means mind Intentionality plus completed 'sexual' experience generates the same contextually checkpointed process that nascent first-cell division provides in biology and Intentionality provides in spirit. Unembodied mind Intentionality sets the same norms as spirit-embodied Intentionality (*above*) and communicates feedback to EPL through the *vitae mysterium* of mind–EPL awareness. As soon as procreative mind Intentionality forms then mind–EPL reacts with baseline awareness. If mind Intentionality is nonnormative or terminated, however, mind–EPL awareness dissolves, in which case even if the 'sexual' experience continues to completion, it's without conception.

In **phase two**, if mind Intentionality is normative, the emergent process moves into *self-organizing* when the couple maintains their mind Intentionality and unembodied 'sex' is ongoing. As with physical and spirit procreation, at this point the developing person has only nascent 𝓛ife until the 'sexual' experience completes. While there's no physical or spirit ejaculation necessary for 'sex' to complete, thus bringing Intentionality to fruition, *orgasm*—a mind experience—is necessary, as it triggers that last picosecond of Intentionality when what's intended becomes Intentionalized reality (§ 3.2.1:282). Mind–EPL remains aware of the state of play.

In **phase three**, the continuation of mind Intentionality's in-spec feedback permits EPL to finish self-organizing and move to *completion*. As with phase three in physical- and spirit-life procreation (*above*), this phase results in an eternal, self-existent human being having 𝓛ife. This occurs in a picosecond at the crescendo of orgasm. This crescendo is the same experience of mind that the physical and spirit embodied have during orgasm. Abortion isn't possible with unembodied procreation (§ 2.2:410) because conception–birth is instant. The parents experience an intimate awareness of their child's 'energy' in that their minds experience one another. The unembodied method is the natural way that humans reproduce, even though it was the last method of procreation (§ 2.1.6.3:330) the earliest humans discovered only after realizing, once embodied, they could even conceive new 𝓛ife (§ 2.1.6:328).

1.2.1.2 Recognizably Human WoB

With **biological** embodiment, EPL won't birth a 𝓛ife bio-entity it doesn't recognize as human, one having a wob that doesn't jive with EPL's wob. In such case, emergence of 𝓛ife fails mid-process. As one might imagine, the Cardinal exhaustively experimented—because what human isn't a curious George?—with out-of-spec (nonhuman) forms and got nowhere. These were as nonhuman in form and function as (for an example we can visualize) the vicious creature from the film *Alien* (1979), the happy tentacled creature from *Galaxy Quest* (1999), or even a sourpussed Klingon from *Star Trek: The Next Generation* (1987–94). Form follows wob. Our human form is what it is because, within a variant range, it *is* our wob. What we consider physically nonhuman *is* nonhuman and EPL's wob won't generate such 𝓛ife because it doesn't support a nonhuman wob. One may as well expect a chicken to naturally birth a fox. Sure, once birthed a human is uninhibitedly free to alter their form to whatever horror they can imagine (and in spirit world, some do) but, in the physical procreative process, the (biologically) Intentionalized wob needs meet EPL's specification range.[294]

With **spirit** embodiment, if mind–EPL feedback shows an out-of-spec condition, as noted—let's say a spirit couple manifesting themselves as an *Alien* creature (not just 'wearing a rubber suit' but attempting to internalize the *Alien* wob) Intentionalizes a cute little bouncing baby *Alien*—then coalescent differentiation never gets off the ground. EPL simply doesn't respond. This results because emergent developing 𝓛ife inherits from EPL its *natural* wob, which includes the mind and form in which it naturally manifests. This natural wob is intrinsic to EPL, not to a procreating couple's Intentionality. As with physical humans who can only procreate their own biology, all a spirit couple can do is *trigger* emergent 𝓛ife in accord with EPL's wob, not create new *forms* of life nor determine nonhuman wob for their child. If a couple's mind Intentionality isn't in accord with EPL then, in practice, it's the same as having no mind Intentionality at all, thus doesn't trigger EPL.

---

294. Until infused with (integrating) 𝓛ife, an anatomically correct modern human is only the second most intelligent animal behind the elephant (§ 1.3.2.1.3:275, § 4.4.1:294).

This might seem like a restriction but it's not because, as human ℒife is emergent, it develops emergently in accord with EPL, which does the creating. It's simply not a capability an individual possesses to determine for another their unique, individual WOB. That arises only through emergence, the *vitae mysterium*. We can change our own WOB if we choose and become *Alien* creatures, but we can't change another's WOB either prior to or after their birth. That's not *our* choice but *their* freedom. Some folks certainly try their best using every manipulative power in their tool bag, but as the saying goes, "He that complies against his will/Is of his own opinion still/Which he may adhere to, yet disown,/For reasons to himself best known" (Butler 1678, *Hudibras* III, iii, lines 547–550).

With **unembodiment**, there's no body form to consider. In this case, an effort to Intentionalize emergent ℒife having aspects of nonhuman WOB results in no response from EPL.

1.2.1.3 ℒife Abnormality

One day in September 2019, Ayako and I were chatting with Mina about human nature and ideal worlds. He mentioned, rather enigmatically I thought, that even in a so-called perfect world without The Corruption and the Negative Collective Consciousness (§ 4:377) where humanity in our universe developed and lived in the freedom and happiness he'd intended, there'd still be "some people born with troublesome personalities who'd create problems." Naturally, Ayako nodded with complete understanding but it seemed ludicrous to me. After all, if parents were happy, loving, caring—"practically [Mary Poppinsly] perfect in every way"—how could children be born to them with intrinsically "troublesome personalities?" Well, the conundrum resolves with comprehension that ℒife is independently emergent, being its own self without biological or Intentionalized inheritance forming its unique WOB. ℒife births *in its own way* in accord with EPL.

1.2.1.3.1 Abnormality: Effects

Abnormality is a sort of short-circuit that interferes with the self-organizing of emergent ℒife. Right out the gate, Mina emphasized 'abnormal' is the condition, not the person. His reasoning is that one of ℒife's fundamentals is freedom, which arises from the simple reality that mind is inviolable, immune to coercion absent choosing to be. The concept of compulsion isn't unique to humans, though. Among other things, ℒife could compel, too, but doesn't, because that property didn't emergently arise with it. Inviolability of mind means it's immune to compulsion even by its own WOB (§ 3.3:283). It's possible albeit extremely difficult and time consuming to change ℒife's innate, intrinsic WOB. According to Mina, no one's ever anywhere done it because the alternative—simply Intentionalizing the desired behavior—is easier, though requires maintenance and has a similar practical outcome. The abnormality is a loss of this foundational inviolability. The practical outcome is that the person can't alter their WOB even if Intentionalized. Mina considers this to be abnormality's chief disability.

But there's a second effect to abnormality: a particular emergent ℒife is missing its innate, intrinsic understanding of love. A second of ℒife's fundamentals is *proto-love*, which is ℒife's base WOB—or base flavor, if you think of coalescently differentiating EPL being a sort of ingredients collection stage—and humanness (Eq. (19.1):245). Every ℒife emergently arises with this base WOB. Love, as we comprehend it as ordinary love, is the natural, innate expression of WOB (hate arises from proto-love, too, but isn't natural or innate; rather, it's learned, meaning chosen). Altogether, the abnormality perverts WOB and locks it in stasis like a Microsoft Word document inexplicably and randomly rendered read-only. An individual with abnormal WOB doesn't know, beyond their observation of it in others, that love exists, what it is, how it feels, what it looks like, and so on. To the degree they're willing, they mimic it but never feel it. For the same reasons, they don't comprehend hate, either, and have the same difficulties with it. The practical outcome is a complete lack of empathy accompanied by ambivalence (§ 3.3.2.1:285).

1.2.1.3.2 Abnormality: Cause

Abnormality's cause is a random 'undulation' w.r.t. EPL. It's conceptually similar albeit practically different to Energent 'undulations' (§ 6.11.2:194) and short-circuits the emergent ℒife process. The developing ℒife fails to self-organize the aforementioned innate, intrinsic aspects of WOB. They're foundational and form part of the WOB substrate from which everything that's recognizably human emerges. The 'undulation' essentially cuts off coalescently differentiating proto-life before it's completely ready. To use the wave metaphor intrinsic to undulation, it creates a sort-of peak effect that mimics differentiation completion; it wraps up before coalescence finishes. It's like throwing a cake in the oven before adding all the ingredients. A corollary effect is that one of the missing ingredients results in the individual's inability to edit—Intentionalize a change to—woB, and the other is unawareness of proto-love.

It's possible that when another person focuses sufficient Intentionality on an about-to-be emergent *Life*, it correlates with the coalescent differentiation where an 'undulation' is occurring in proto-life and increases the odds of it happening. The goal of such persons is to infuse the emergent *Life* with a normative disposition of hate instead of love, meaning their base emotion is 'proto-hate' rather than proto-love (BASE EMOTION, § 3.3.3.1:289), and marry that to an unalterable woB. Although that's their uninformed desire, proto-hate isn't a real thing, and the practical outcome is an emergent *Life*—a person—devoid of empathy *and* malignity who's incapable of even feeling hate, much less love.

1.2.1.3.3 ABNORMALITY: ODDS AND OUTCOMES

The Cardinal calculates the odds a person is born with what Mina calls "abnormal *Life*" at about one in 30 quadrillion. In our universe of about 849 quadrillion people, there's accordingly 27 such. The abnormality is curable.[295] Although not as difficult to cure as to effectively rewrite one's woB, it requires the full-time, focused concentration over the course of about 180,000 ±14,000 Earth years by a capable healer of which, avers Mina, there are only 46 he knows of in All Existence, including him and his wife (§ 1:335).

1.2.2 HUMAN MIND–BRAIN–BODY

Unlike the Living brain, the human brain operates on two fundamental levels, the first as a Living entity and the second as an integrator of the body with the person, not the instantiated mind of Living brain (§ 1.3.2:273) but the self as emergent *Life*. As a Living entity, our brain functions essentially the same as any nonhuman Living entity in terms of somatic sensation, nerve impulses, and instantiated mind. It differs, however, in that its instantiated mind operates in a *Life* environment of real mind, as a person. Whereas a Living entity's instantiated mind is the apex of its subjective sensory integration with its objective environment, mind instantiated by a human brain operates autonomously in tandem with a person's *Life* mind. Let's look at *instantiated physical mind* before describing how it integrates *Life* mind.

1.2.2.1 PHYSICAL MIND AS FACSIMILE OF *Life* MIND

The brain is just an electrochemical processor. Its magic happens when Energent proto-energy interacts with its matter-Energy constituents to instantiate physical mind as a weak emergent (§ 2:90) albeit not as a working mind as it doesn't think, feel, or act itself. The truly fascinating thing about humans' physical mind is that it's a physically manufactured facsimile of *Life* mind. Whereas *Life* mind is *Life* proto-energy and thus unable to interact directly on its unembodied own with either the natural or supranatural environments of a universe, physical mind is an Energent proto-energy expression of a person's *Life* mind. Since *Life* mind integrates brain, it naturally integrates brain's panoply of micro and macro *states of being* (soB) and *states of awareness* (soA),[296] in effect integrating instantiated physical mind. 'Instantiated physical mind' is just a collective term for holistic Energent proto-energy that makes up the vast array of micro and macro soB and soA that comprise the brain's overall macro-soA, which reflects both *Life* mind's nonphysical soA and brain's physical soA. That's what instantiated physical mind really is, *a dynamic, macro-soA instantiation of proto-energy*.

Life mind isn't just magically 'aware' of every soB and soA incident to our body. 'Energy' is the vehicle through which awareness happens. Our body's every physicochemical experience translates via matter–Energy to Energent proto-energy. At each step, this proto-energy expresses the micro-soB and a micro-soA built up from our physical self's every archí constituent interacting with proto-energy, which generates Fundamental Force that, in turn, generates EM and other applied energy E forces (§ 2:114). These applied energy E instantiations themselves interact with proto-energy to constitute the referenced micro and macro soB and soA. If one could visually observe the proto-energy suffused in and around a person's physical body, one would see a kaleidoscope of ever-changing 'energy' fields, patterns, strengths, extensions, and so on. Any physical entity is a constantly shifting expression of proto-energy, real energy Υ (Fundamental Force), and applied energy E (motion, electromagnetic, and binding 'energies').

---

295. It became curable in our universe after the Big Healing.

296. SoA refers to the awareness one has in totality w.r.t. what's of interest; soB is one's experience of the referent soA.

So, how is our *L*ife proto-energy mind—our real, emergently eternal self—aware of all this? Well, it 'reads' all these 'energies' expressed as Energent proto-energy and comprehends it all in the SOB and SOA terms it understands via the physical *body*'s integration with the spirit body which manifests *L*ife mind in the 'reflective' environment (§ 7.1.1.1:212). This is how our *L*ife mind is just 'aware' of what's going on with our physical self in our physical environment from which, by its nature, it's tactilely excluded. It isn't any different, really, than a radio receiver plucking invisible energy out of the ether through principles of physics, yet expressing—comprehending—it in audio or in television's audiovisual terms.

For example, a nominal *action potential* (AP)—the electrochemical nerve impulse originating in the brain and body instantiated from Energent proto-energy's interaction with the matter–Energy of neuronal and somatic activity—is more than just a ±40 millivolt (mv) electrical charge with an attendant EM field of charge, polarity, strength, frequency, and so on. Each AP represents an EM field that's unique in toto albeit having certain constituents that are the same as those of certain other AP, meaning that such AP are EM field-relevant to each other and thus form a *clade*[297]—individual neuroresponses related by EM field—that dynamically groups via neural processes as they move through the neural pathways. Accordingly, an AP is really just a vehicle for moving an EM field to where it can integrate other relevant EM fields—not too unlike what molecular motor proteins[298] do in their own context—that altogether instantiate in applied energy E terms the Energent proto-energy that expresses a particular micro-SOA and macro-SOA of our brain in conjunction with our *L*ife mind.

The brain experiences and comprehends nothing more than electrochemical action potentials, each of which expresses a unique 'data point.' Because we're self-aware *L*ife, we find it difficult if not impossible to comprehend how a brain—a Living entity—experiences the world. Does a brain *think*, and if so, how? While it's an amazingly capable instrument, it doesn't experience *Thought* (thinking–feeling; § 1.2.2.5.1:261), which is the exclusive province of *L*ife mind. The human brain mimics Thought because it *transliterates* *L*ife mind into a facsimile (§ 1.2.2.4:257). The nonhuman (non-*L*ife-mind-integrated) brain doesn't think although it does *feel* because AP can only convey neuroresponse. Thus, on its own, it merely instantiates an experience that's *redolent with impression* (§ 1.3.2.1.2.1:274) because feeling is fundamentally impression. This is true of course for humans, too, as our brain is a Living, nonhuman entity. This goes unnoticed because, as emergent *L*ife, we can think and our brain integrates *L*ife mind's thinking with our physical self. Even so, we're fundamentally feeling beings and the way we experience own-self SOB is emotively, meaning in a way that's redolent with impression. Thinking is our unique ability to parse feeling's impression into a particular SOA that we consciously cognize and can analyze. The nature of feeling comprises most of our thought, with only about 0.01% comprising thinking (§ 4.2:292).

1.2.2.2 *L*ife Mind–Physical Mind Integration

In practice, the human ability to think—to analytically comprehend feeling in a comprehensive, integrated, yet discrete way—means that one's subjective experience of objective reality rises to true self-awareness of one's subjective experience such that, unlike monkeys, dogs, and so on, humans experience a subjective reality comprised of our being clinically aware of our subjective experience of objective reality. While a chimpanzee reacts to its sensory experience, including its impression of its subjective experience of it, there's no capacity to reflect on any aspect of its subjective experience beyond its own subjective analysis of own-self well-being in the context of own-self WOB. A person, on the other hand, though largely in the same boat w.r.t. to Living brain, integrates *L*ife, a true consciousness, which further experiences one's subjective experience of objective reality from that vantage to reflect on all possible aspects of any subjective and objective experience.

Even so, we all know the seeming impossibility of suppressing our primitive reptilian brain—supposedly the leftovers of evolution—to transform so-called human nature and rise above our meaner self. Without doubt, this is humanity's experience. But the reason for the conundrum isn't rooted in humanity's immutable evolutionary or genetic WOB. It's the far simpler dynamic of mind–brain integration in which the content of one's instantiated Living (brain) mind doesn't fully incorporate one's *L*ife mind—what we tend to call our higher self but isn't really, it's just our *self*—to form a single mind involving the whole person: the conscious, mindful self that's the manifestation of a person's physical, spirit, and unembodied *L*ife (§ 1.2.1:247). Instead,

---

297. In biology, *clade* is a taxonomic designation for biological taxa that share features inherited from a common ancestor. Take, for instance, the many individual somatic neuroresponses (e.g., temperature, pain) occasioned by touching a hot surface. They share certain EM field elements common to the experience the brain then processes, categorizes, experiences, and so on as a clade it then relates to own-self well-being (§ 2:275).

298. These convert chemical energy to mechanical work in order to 'walk' along actin filaments to contract muscles or along intracellular microtubules to move 'cargo.'

we feel conflicted and of two minds, the reason being that we *override* one mind for the other because there's a limitation in mind–brain integration (§ 1.2.2.5:261) that manifests as a tendency to emphasize the physical self's subjective experience over the spirit self's. The override happens because Living mind's awareness of our physical subjective experience is far more present and immediate than its awareness of *Life* mind's subjective experience of the matter at hand.

1.2.2.2.1 Physical-self Override

Suppose one experiences something in the physical world. If their spirit self (*Life* mind) feels that what its physical self experiences isn't such a big deal in the grand scheme of things—in the sense that spirit world exists and life continues as normal after the physical body's death—but the physical self (Living mind) *does* feel it's a big deal, then the lack of full mind–brain integration means the physical self simply overrides any contrary thinking or feeling and acts on its subjective experience of the objective reality, say, in the context of harm to self or others. Adolph Hitler exemplifies this dynamic (ch. 40:605). His spirit self was consciously aghast at his physical self's behavior. As a spirit person, he's of quite different personality. Physical Hitler shut down (overrode) his mind–brain integration of wob at the limited level at which he possessed awareness: his conscience, which is just our own fuller wob expressed by our *Life* mind (§ 2.3:398). When we 'listen to our conscience,' we're really just embracing our *Life* mind's subjective experience while overriding our Living mind's subjective experience and its limitation-modified wob that we live under in our physical lives. The struggle for the physical person who 'hears' their conscience is with being 'bad' when she or he experiences a countervailing feeling of being 'good.' This means one prefers their physical-self's subjective experience to their (possibly vague or faith-based) spirit-self's subjective experience. In practice, it means ignoring one's conscience. Moreover, unpausing physical-over-spirit self override leads to a de-integrating of spirit self (*Life* mind) with implications regarding psychoses and related mental aberrations that are beyond this book's scope.

1.2.2.2.2 Conscious-self Override

Conversely, suppose the spirit self of a physically alive person embraces a wob that is 'bad' (harmful) that integrates their physical self's Living mind. Well, mind–brain integration is an absolute. One's physical self can't stop it but only interfere, say, by ignoring or supplanting it with a stronger subjective experience like hate. Most of our intrinsic wob is beyond our purview because we never dive deep enough into own-self to experience it, as have a few of the Cardinal (§ 1.1:246). This unexplored aspect of wob guides most of our physical self's wob, our so-called human nature. Every aspect of our wob is fungible but one must be aware of it to act on it. The aspects of which that we are aware—like so-called conscience, or generalized tendencies to care (or not, if we choose to quit caring after some traumatic experience)—we can and do modify from how our spirit self feels about those self-same things. Thus, one's spirit self sometimes tries to influence their physical self. Hitler did albeit unsuccessfully because of physical-self override. At other times, one's spirit self just couldn't care less and leaves their physical self to do whatever they do while figuring, in a personal responsibility sense, that whatever happens in Vegas stays in Vegas. The struggle for the physical person who has no conscience is with being 'good' when he or she experiences a countervailing feeling of being 'bad.' This means one prefers their spirit-self's subjective experience of, say, embracing harm to their physical-self's subjective experience of not embracing harm. In practice, it means embracing one's consciencelessness.

1.2.2.2.3 Physical–spiritual WoB Dichotomy

A third way in which the integration of mind–brain shows a dichotomy is when our spirit self engages a wob that feels fundamentally different from our physical wob. This isn't a concern for the average physical person who hasn't a clue about their spirit self's day-to-day activities, if any.[299] If one masters energy testing, however (part v), one might be surprised to discover what really matters to own-self. For example, when I first inquired into my spirit self's activities, Ayako initially did the testing and found I spent most of my time there "playing around"—adventuring, exploring, dating, conversating, socializing; pretty much anything that didn't involve actually

---

299. The spirit selves of ~99% of everyone on Earth up to the Big Healing were clueless spirit world was actually real. They exist 'within' their physical bodies and that's the only reality they know—even when venturing into spirit world during sleep, they believe it's only dreaming—until death when they 'wake up,' look around, and discover it's reality after all. Those conceived since the Big Healing increasingly have an intrinsic awareness of nonphysical *Life*, dropping that 99% (so far) to ~98.9%.

'working' to heal or better the universe. Well, my lazy, shiftless self appalled me! I was outraged, even, considering how important 'restoring the world' was to me since joining the Unification Church to 'save the world.'

Ayako only laughed at me and said, "Well, I guess you don't care about all that as much as you thought!"

"Yeah . . . newsflash." It took me a couple years just to *start* getting a handle on how it is that the way my physical self feels *here* can sometimes be so dramatically different from the way my spirit self feels *there*, and yet conceive that both are aspects of a single, integrated person—*me*. "Aren't I the same person, after all?" I said. "The physical and spirit manifestations of the same $\mathcal{L}$ife, and mind, and way of being?"

"Yes, you are," she'd repeatedly explain. "But your mind in spirit world isn't flogged by the pressures and anxieties and sufferings your mind has to deal with in the physical world. What happens here doesn't matter all that much to your self there; you're just happily *living*."

I frowned every time we'd have this conversation. "Yeah, but don't I even care if the universe is healed, America or Earth doesn't go down the sewer pipe of tyranny, that people are happier, or that trauma's reduced?"

"I'm sure you care just like you do here, but you don't feel the *pressure* to care there, you don't feel the *need* to care the way you feel it here, where life and resources are limited, you don't have so much time, you feel a sense of judgment from your Christian and Moonie enculturation . . . and," she'd add, "all the trauma and suffering here just doesn't really translate to there, especially since the Big Healing."

"Harrumph," I'd pronounce, scratching my head. Over time, though, Ayako's and my own testing showed my spirit self was progressively synchronizing with my physical-self's feeling that I should be a healer rather than simply a preacher here or tuning out the travails of the universe there. So much so that, one day in October 2019, my spirit self's over-enthusiasm in simultaneously manifesting around spirit world (§ 1.2.3.3.3:472) so physically drained me that I staggered and nearly collapsed on a Boulder, Colorado sidewalk. After Mina explained what I'd done to myself, he advised me how and why to cut back so I could pursue my sense of calling—and finish his book—without wrecking my physical body.

Our spirit and physical selves experience the physical world in two different ways. For example, the spirit self feels no actual pain from its physical self's pain on the material, physical side of the natural environment because it experiences the physical world on the immaterial, 'reflective' side (§ 7.1:212). These give two different experiences. We're only ever one single mind, so our psyche's experience is the same, although the spirit self's subjective experience is necessarily fuller than is the currently limited physical self. Nevertheless, the spirit self can choose or not to experience physical stimulus (say, pain) subjectively the same as the physical self does because, despite any actual harm to the physical body, the experience of that harm is all in the mind.

The spirit self of the vast majority of physical humanity, each so unaware of the larger reality beyond their physical one they don't realize they can separate their mind from their body's experience, so tightly integrates their physical self that they experience physical reality the same way their body does. When such people traumatically die, they 'awake' in the 'reflective' environment feeling the trauma whereas those spirit selves aware of their larger spirit reality don't 'wake up' after physical death at all because they're always aware. They simply note the cessation of their physical body and its subsequent dissociation with their spirit self and move on like a driver exiting one vehicle for another at a border crossing. Mind–brain integration is a two-way street without either one dominating the other for any other reason than that's just what one chooses. Nor is one's spirit self higher or better than their physical self. Each is simply an aspect of the larger, wholistic person.

1.2.2.3 Spirit–physical Self Integration

When it comes to anything human, Mina doesn't talk interaction, interrelationships, sharing, or the like, but *integration*. Trying to understand how one's spirit self *interacts* with the physical self is a hopeless cause that leaves a person scrabbling in the weeds. Our spirit body doesn't *inhabit* our physical body but *integrates*. Conversely, our physical body integrates our spirit body. Does one take precedence? No, nor is it a mutuality or reciprocity. Rather, integration is *amalgamation* in the sense of alloy as an admixture where entities retain their individual properties. Think of two objects coming closer together, touching, then amalgamating into a single form, yet remaining discrete (*Fig. 111*). A group could have separate conversations with both amalgamated aspects of a person, which at the same time is seemingly of one form, one self. It's Trinitarian in the sense one is an integrated self that is one 'substance' while two seemingly autonomous beings integrated as a wholistic, holistic whole. We're not talking substance at all, however; and the theological concept doesn't reflect anything real about our 'creator' except that Mina integrates every particle, piece, and person of our universe within the context of *its* reality.

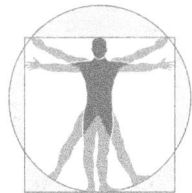

Figure 111. Schematic of physicospirit (physical and spirit) body integration ('reflective' body not shown; cf. § 7.1.1.1:212). Each body embodies the single individual's mind, i.e., their *L*ife self, in the natural and supranatural environments as a wholistic, integrated person.$_{250}$

As I'm writing this book, for example, Mina integrates ('entangles;' § 6.11:191) my mind such that he perceives—has *awareness* of—the words I type or my drawings, equations, and notes, hears what I hear, sees what I see, including any split-second flickerings of spirit world as my senses improve bit by bit, and even dream imagery. He does this without having to spirit-bodily look over my shoulder with his own eyes and ears. Our integration—*ours*, because he doesn't 'entangle' without permission—provides him awareness without impinging on me.[300] The girls and I initially imagined him integrating the tidbits of the universe like quantum entanglement but now, several years on, see it with greater clarity.

1.2.2.4   MIND–BRAIN INTEGRATION

Just as our spirit and physical bodies integrate, so, too, does our (emergent *L*ife) spirit and physical (brain-instantiated) mind. Our spirit mind doesn't emanate from any sort of spirit brain, as no anatomy exists in our spirit body unless we want to manifest it. Even so, spirit-born persons feel their seat of consciousness, their mind, their *personness* in their head much as physical-born persons do.[301] It's part of the intrinsic WOB of *L*ife. Since spirit mind manifests the spirit body, then anywhere the body is, so is one's mind. Consequently, spirit–physical body integration means spirit–physical mind integration. As physical (instantiated) mind is an Energent proto-energy existent of brain, the real integration going on here is between spirit mind and physical brain.

With integration, spirit mind *is* physical brain and physical brain *is* spirit mind. Even though discrete and autonomous, and notwithstanding the dichotomy described earlier (§ 1.2.2.1:253), there's no substantive differ-ence between them as an integration. One is the other. But they do operate differently, the brain built around cognitively processing micro-SOA via nerve impulses and mind as direct awareness. Hence, there's transliteration that needs doing (§ 2.1:276) to convert mind's direct awareness into brainspeak, similar in some respects to the way software transliterates computer binary code into human-comprehensible language. Neurons do this work. In the nonhuman brain, neurons experience action potentials (AP) strictly as somatic phenomena. Humans operate in an entirely different environment, one that includes the physical but transcends it as well. This is why the most sophisticated nonhuman can never glimpse even the most mundane human experience howsoever they mimic it or humans attempt to train them. The difference is simply rocks to food. Because we aren't our bodies, one can never compare human to nonhuman based on shared physicality; it's like comparing the *driver* of a car to other *cars*. This lack of awareness of what really comprises human is what trips up science to draw immaterial conclusions about human beings based on evolutionary, genetic, and related analyses of the physical body that frustratingly clash with our deeper sensibilities and lived experience that involves our *L*ife self.

1.2.2.4.1   NEURONAL HARMONICS

The neuron is the direct interface between our mind and brain. Our *L*ife force, which forms the discrete *L*ife proto-energy nexus in our spirit body's head and integrates our physical head, naturally integrates each neuron in the brain. Each one responds to a specific *L*ife 'harmonic' consistent with specific SOA that embody thinking and feeling (subjective awareness), which stimulates similarly 'tuned' groups of neurons. In a sense, each neuron in a group of such neurons maps ($\mapsto$) directly to a specific SOA in our *L*ife mind that embodies a specific 'harmonic' (ibid.) such that

$$\text{neurons} \mapsto \text{SOA} \mid \text{neuron}_{individual} \mapsto \text{SOA}_{micro}. \qquad (19.5)$$

---

300. The reverse is possible—and desired—but in our universe, only Jesus is capable of doing so as of this writing (CH. 40:613).

301. There are obvious dissimilarities, but we don't discuss them in this book.

When stimulated, the neuron generates an action potential (AP). Collectively, this is what appears to give rise to our instantiated (physical) mind's thinking and feeling though, in actuality, they arise in our (emergent) *Life* mind and simply manifest in our brain; hence, the *instantiated mind*. *Life*-stimulus–neuronal-response is the process we call transliteration of an awareness-oriented mind to a cognition-oriented brain. The other side to this transliteration process is that, when thinking–feeling arises in our brain, *Life* mind perceives the resultant micro-SOA (specifically, the resultant Energent proto-energy 'harmonic') in awareness terms.

Speaking generally, our physical body inclusive of brain integrates specifically with our own *Life*, which is to say, our spirit self integrates our physical body from conception throughout our physical life. This means, on average, that the strongest *Life* force our brain experiences is that of our own self. Hence, the *Life* 'harmonics' that stimulate our neurons to generate AP, thus our physically instantiated thinking and feeling, originates in our own *Life* mind. We are in total control of our body and (instantiated) mind. However—and if you're an empath or intuitive you might appreciate this rather emphatic *however*—if another person, usually a spirit person but sometimes the really strong *Life* force of a physical person, is nearby exuding stronger *Life* proto-energy of a certain 'harmonic' (a certain SOB) than one's own self is, then one's neurons that are sensitive to—integrating—that 'harmonic' are stimulated both by one's own *Life* mind as well as the other person's. Sometimes it's strong enough to dominate the thinking–feeling of a specific neuronal 'harmonic' macro-SOA, thereby causing the relevant integrated neurons to generate AP. One's own brain then does the rest of the work of instantiating a SOB redolent of, or exactly like, that of the person(s) exuding it, followed by a micro-SOA that stimulates other neurons to generate AP and so on and so forth until the person—*their* macro-SOA (their instantiated mind)—thinks or feels something without knowing why. This can leave one's own spirit self in the back seat so to speak if unaware of this process. This is how empaths and intuitives actually 'pick up' the thinking–feeling of others, but it's true to a lesser degree for all physical people (§ 3.3.3.1.1.1:290).

1.2.2.4.2 THE MIND–BRAIN DISCONNECT

The question naturally arises: if our brain integrates our spirit mind, why aren't we consciously aware of that which our spirit mind is aware? The reason is deceptively simple: we lack sufficient neurons to map adequately the full range of our spirit mind's SOA. It's not just an insufficiency in total count, but that we lack neurons integrating the *Life* 'harmonics' of most of our spirit mind's SOA—about 81.01% of it, to be exact. That means our brain today can access only ~18.99% of our *Life* mind because it simply can't 'read' the SOA of the remainder. From our brain's perspective, that 'unread' portion of our mind literally doesn't exist. Why the discrepancy?

For many years, the conventional belief was the average human brain housed ~100 billion neurons. Then Brazilian neuroscientists came up with 'brain soup' to gauge a presumedly more accurate count (Herculano-Houzel et al. 2005, 2518) that changed the prevailing wisdom in neuroscience to only an average 86.1 ±8.1 billion neurons, or NeuN-positive cells, in the adult male brain (Azevedo et al. 2009, 533). Mina, however, says there are presently ~105 billion NeuN-positive cells and 94.5 billion nonneuronal cells on average across the adult male–female brain with no difference, on average, between sexes. Consequently, with only 105 billion neurons (not counting additional NeuN-positive cells; *below*), our brain can only access the aforementioned 18.99% of *Life* mind. The old saw that we only ever access 10% of our mind isn't mythological but still only half-right.

1.2.2.4.2.1 LONG-TERM MEMORY

NeuN-positive cells—those with neuronal capacity—aren't only neurons. Of the 94.5 billion nonneuronal, or NeuN-negative, cells called glia, about 50 billion ependymocytes—one of three types of ependymal cells and specifically of a certain variety—in the lateral ventricle area of the brain have an additional NeuN-positive function of long-term memory 'storage.' We define these cells as memory-capable ependymocytes, or MCE. Their nucleus contains 175 discrete NH_3 (ammonia) molecules that act as 'pointers,' a programming analogy in which a variable references the storage address of some actual value. For example, a page number in this book's index is a reference *pointing* to the actual page (the storage address) where the value one is interested in—say, 'memory, long-term'—is printed, which is to say, *stored*.

All memory resides in our Life mind. Since our mind operates as a state of awareness (§ 2.1.2:76), the brain does no actual memory storage the way we imagine it as encoded, stored data. Instead, our mind has subjective awareness of our subjective and objective reality. Each experience 'encodes' as SOA. That's why when we recall memory, what we're really recalling, or becoming aware of, is its SOA. When we struggle to recall a memory, we're striving to recreate our awareness of its SOA, not simply its cognitive data points. Memory always involves recalling SOA from which the memory's incident facts emerge: micro-SOB, smells, images, sounds, thinking, feeling, and so on. Whether a phone number, some factoid or knowledge, dinner last year with the family, or a great idea one thought up six months ago then shelved, our mind remembers SOA for each and every item involved because whatever we encounter *becomes* us, our consciousness, our personness. Our ℒife mind's macro-SOA at any given instant comprises trillions ($>10^{12}$) of micro-SOA, themselves instantiating from nonillions ($>10^{30}$) of micro-SOB (§ 1.3.2.1:273).

Our brain doesn't work this way, though. It's process-oriented, a cognitive processor. As such, it requires a specific data storage facility to handle memory in its environment. This is the aforementioned ependymal cell community. But our skull, hence brain, is finite in size. How do we have apparently infinite memory in a finite space? It's because it literally *is* infinite, just not as a function of the brain. As ℒife proto-energy, our mind is as indeterminate as the Energent and Energent–prime. Recall that proto-energy is dimensionless and therefore without distance and event periodicity (§ 6.11.4:198). How then, with what one might call infinite mind and memory, is the finite brain to cope with infinite awareness? The answer is ℒife mind, and w.r.t. to brain memory, *pointers*, and for a simple reason: our brain can't process or even experience self-awareness but only electrochemical signals; it can't actually encode a self-aware memory, but only process a referent SOA (integrated by ℒife mind) which is unique to any specific memory and its constituents.[302] The molecular pointer is the most economical, smallest footprint methodology to achieve memory recall between two divergent, incompatible systems.

ℒife mind is essentially *an aware*, to use the verb as a noun in a way similar to how we label a person *an intuitive*. This means it exists in a state of awareness rather than in a state of becoming aware. Whatever mind encounters is *of* mind. We call that nonprocess state *awareness*. Memory is just part of mind's macro-SOA and it resides only in mind, not in the brain. Mind being aware of a reality through its encounter differs fundamentally from brain being aware of a reality through its cognitive processing. The tool the brain uses to cognitively process ℒife mind awareness into instantiated physical mind awareness is the neuron. For this reason, mind to brain memory integration doesn't orchestrate via neurons but nonneuronal—effectively NeuN-positive—ependymocytes around the lateral ventricle. Only then does memory process into the brain's neural net as action potentials for cognitive processing (assembly) where it instantiates via processes described above into physical mind. All our memory activity happens in our mind, ceaselessly integrating our brain where it instantiates as part of physical mind's SOA so our physical self is aware of our spirit self, our ℒife mind.

On the other hand, our ℒife mind is aware of all things related to our physical body and its environment via awareness. Recall that physical mind is Energent proto-energy (§ 1.2.2.4:257). At any given moment, the space occupied by the constant interplay between our physical body's material reality—the state of each constituent of matter–Energy down to single archí pairs—and Energent proto-energy is a kaleidoscope of shifting proto-energy, ℒife force, and electromagnetic states of which our ℒife mind as a ℒife proto-energy existent is exquisitely, intimately aware. Each shift in state brings full awareness of our physical mindstate to our ℒife mindstate that feeds back to our brain via integration which, cognitively processed, reinstantiates (updates) our physical mind some 1,000 times per second.

Accordingly, our NH_3 molecular pointer analogy diverges from programming or index pointers. Instead of being a typical pointer-*to*-value in a one-to-one or one-to-many relationship, ependymocyte pointers are pointers-*from*-value in a many-to-one relationship, meaning that any pointer repeatedly integrates any memory, not just a certain SOA-type of memory. Let's see how that works.

1.2.2.4.2.2   MEMORY POINTERS

Each one of a relevant ependymocyte's 175 independent NH_3 molecules discretely situate in the nonreactive (where NH_3 won't bond with any other molecule) cytosol[303] environment of its nucleus. ℒife mind stimulates Energent proto-energy via autonomic Intentionality (§ 3.2:282) that provokes a Métier Force-mediated (§ 1:112) electromagnetic change in any one or more of the 175 NH_3 molecules in any one or more of the roughly 50-plus billion ependymocytes that are in a neutral, or non-active, state w.r.t. the MCE function. The change alters NH_3 electric potential such that sodium ions move away from the molecule(s) and toward the innermost cell wall. The electromagnetic signature of the involved molecule(s) determines how many sodium ions the molecule(s) affects. Their arrival at the cell wall provokes a differential in electric potential between the inside and outside

---

302. ℒife and Living brain both encode non-self-aware animal level memories in the brain.

303. A complex intracellular liquid mixture of substances dissolved in water.

of the cell, causing sodium ions in the tissue separating the ependymal layer from the brain's interstitial fluid to migrate away from the cell wall toward the fluid.

Then the electrical differential arising between the relevant tissue–interstitial boundary areas causes potassium ions in the interstitial fluid to migrate away from the area and deeper into the fluid, toward neurons. As they move, they alter the electromagnetic (EM) potential around them relative to that of their surrounding environment. When these potassium ions are in sufficient proximity to a neuron, the EM differential between the neuron's inner and outer environment leads to the formation of an electrical nerve impulse—the action potential (AP)—having a specific EM signature. The AP then interacts with specific neurons that alter its EM signature in consonance with other relevant AP as it travels neuron to neuron, assembling into the now-transliterated memory from many such AP, each emanating from one or more ependymocytes whose NH_3 molecules referenced the varying incident macro-SOA of a memory—sight, smell, feelings. During the assembly process, micro-SOB and micro-SOA form into ever larger clades, each one an aspect of physical mind constantly reinstantiating as a result of the interaction between matter–Energy (constituting all aspects of the brain and its activity) and Energent proto-energy from which, recall, arises Fundamental Force with all its attendant interactions in our physical universe.

Even though the brain is quite obviously finite in structure and content, the sheer volume of memory pointer combinations at any single moment is astounding. With 175 NH_3 molecules as pointers per each of about 50-plus billion MCE, the brain can muster up extremely complex memory configurations from approximately $1.8569947431945 \times 10^{1554}$ pointer combinations within a span of 45 billionths (4.5×10^{-8}) of a second.[251] This is why memory feels as incredibly rich, vibrant, and infinite as it does to us as physical persons—yet, today, it's a shadow of ℒife mind's *literally* infinite capacity.

1.2.2.4.3 WORKING MEMORY

Science calls the brain's dynamic macro-SOA our short-term or working memory, conscious SOB, wakefulness, and the like. It labels it 'short-term' because it doesn't appear to reliably assimilate—'encode' is the wrong concept—to long-term memory. The reasons this appears to happen is because the SOA around such mental activity is unstable, frequently changing. Consequently, it assimilates to ℒife mind with a fractured SOA that makes it difficult to reassemble its elements, some of which the brain reintegrates as we attempt a memory's recall, and some it doesn't. We pull up bits and pieces that match particular SOA that we associate consciously or subconsciously with a memory. Often we recall nothing at all because it assimilated into ℒife mind with a million different unrelated, contradictory, or ambiguous SOA from which our presently limited brain simply can't transliterate enough of the pieces to reconstitute its whole. Every single encounter we ever experience from moment to moment is ultimately reducible to SOA, the reason being that ℒife mind—the individual person—is an awareness environment. One might say a person *is* awareness. Therefore, memory isn't an event, knowledge, feeling, idea, data points, or whatever, but our SOA of those things, individually and collectively, as well as in relation to other aspects of experience. And each time one recalls a memory, their macro-SOA at the time of recall subtly affects it, accounting for the observation that frequently recalled memory tends to alter over time. And to bring up empaths again, sometimes we experience memories that literally aren't our own but someone else's, whose SOA we're integrating without having awareness we're doing it (§ 1.2.2.6:262; § 3.3.3.1.1.1:290).

1.2.2.4.3.1 FORGETFULNESS: SHORT-TERM AND DREAMS

So-called short-term memory isn't memory at all but simply conscious-thought processing. It's an active, ongoing cognitive function no different from thinking or feeling. If one reads or recites, say, seven words, then switches even a small part of their attention to something else, or their macro-SOA undergoes some nuanced alteration, and then attempts to 'retrieve' those seven words—this is essentially the methodology of short-term memory studies—one may or may not successfully recall the list in whole or in part. The reason is that all of one's awareness, including the seven-word list, lies in the dynamic instantiation of physical mind from the moment-to-moment cognitive functions of the brain. Each reinstantiation (~1,000 times per second) subtly affects the previous instantiation. Eventually, in seconds to minutes, the seven-word list just isn't a part of one's macro-SOA. It's a ℒife mind memory, yes, but not necessarily with a SOA sufficient for our brain to recall it as desired. This is why after diligently trying to recall a short term memory and failing, it pops unbidden into our mind hours or even days later because we experience a SOA that sufficiently matches in whole or part that of the memory we couldn't recall. It integrates, and there it is. Every ℒife mind experience from the smallest to largest *is* its own unique SOA because a person never experiences the same SOA twice.

Dreams act like short-term memory, too. The reason we have a hard time remembering dreams, or keeping the memory in our minds longer than a few seconds, minutes, or hours is that dreams are fractured, fragmented memories and soa from our spirit-self's experience while our physical body sleeps). Because of our brain's neuronal limitation (*below*), thus the lack of any full integration and reinstantiation of relevant soa within our instantiated physical mind, our dream images have no real tether to physically cognizable reality. Our brain integrates this fragmented thinking and feeling—soa, in other words—along with the images, sounds, smells, and so on of our brain's active soa as we're sleeping, but there's no logical relationship between the transliterated soa and active brain soa. The brain's reassembly of such fractured states into its macro-soa results in the experience we call dreaming (we describe lucid and other aspects of dreaming in § 1.2.2.7.3:267).

1.2.2.5 BRAIN LIMITATION

If *L*ife mind is indeterminate, having infinite capacity and capability, why doesn't our brain experience full, unhindered integration of *L*ife mind? The short answer is lack of neurons (§ 1.2.2.4.2:258). Mind integrates via NeuN-positive cell structures: neurons and relevant ependymocytes (§ 1.2.2.4.2.1:258). Unlike ependymocytes, the 175 pointers of which integrate memory soa, neurons respond to specific mind soa. If we think of *L*ife mind in terms of a brain, then brain neurons reference, or map to, specific 'regions' of mind the way in which science says language or reasoning or happy thoughts map to specific regions of the brain (*Fig. 112*, left). It engages every extant 'region' of *L*ife mind but, because it lacks sufficient neurons, only partially integrates each one.

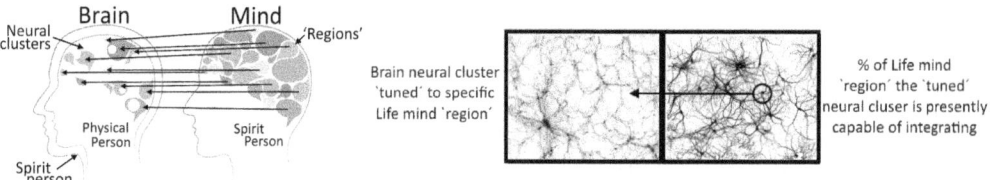

Figure 112. Left, the brain has a paucity of neural clusters 'tuned' to mind 'soa regions' to which mind integrates, causing a disconnect between one's *L*ife soa and their physical soa. Right, neuron cluster 'tuned' (at left) to a specific *L*ife mind 'soa region;' visualized *L*ife mind 'region' (at right) showing how little of a 'soa region' actually integrates (maps to) the brain at present.[252]

Therefore, much of *L*ife mind simply doesn't integrate the brain to be instantiated into physical mind (*Fig. 112*, right). On the other hand, *L*ife mind—even though our brain is limited w.r.t. to integrating it—experiences 100% of the physical self's experience of the natural environment because it's *there*, its *presence* fully integrating brain–body. If our brain, which already experiences its physical environment at 100% its capacity, also experienced the entirety of our *L*ife mind, then our physical self would experience the natural environment in a vastly different, far richer, way.

1.2.2.5.1 NEURONAL LIMITATIONS

So, two questions pop into mind here: first, just how limited is our integration with *L*ife mind, and second, why is it even limited? As noted, the brain has on average ~105 billion neurons and 50-plus billion NeuN-positive ependymal cells in the region of the lateral ventricle, a ~2.1:1 ratio. Being deficient in NeuN-positive cells, the brain can't achieve full integration with *L*ife mind. The number of NeuN-positive cells necessary for full integration is about 700 billion on average: ~500.5 billion neurons and ~199.5 billion NeuN-positive ependymocytes, a ~2.5:1 ratio. Presently, our brain has ~25% of the necessary NeuN-positive cell structures to integrate *L*ife mind memory but only ~18.99% of the necessary neurons to integrate *L*ife mind Thought (thinking–feeling). Altogether then, our brain today integrates ~20.7% of *L*ife mind's capacity. Jack that up to 100% and imagine our capabilities in the physical world.[304]

Since the Big Healing, Earth's humanity has been doing just that. Children are now birthing with, on average, about a 146.6 billion NeuN-positive cell capacity, an increase so far of ~35.19% that will steadily increase over the next 35 years. Mina expects the average brain to reach the ~700-billion NeuN-positive cell count in

---

304. For example, we'd have normative recall of any experience or interaction with people in spirit world, e.g., an advanced science conference there or information on physical world events.

adults conceived from 2055. If you're thinking this means a perfect world though, don't get too excited. Full *L*ife mind integration is no guarantee people will act less harmfully than they ever have. After all, it didn't stop Original Humanity in its suicidal war circa 6.5 million years ago (§ 1.3:538). On the other hand, they were under The Corruption's thumb. Mina sees the improvements wrought by the Big Healing as so significant that he's betting the farm (by upgrading the brain's capabilities) on the probability our heretofore planet-wide harmful woB will decline over the next 75 years to nil.

1.2.2.5.2 Why Brain Integration is Limited

Which brings us to the sixty-four-dollar question: just why is our brain's *L*ife mind integration limited? It might not be palatable, but the answer is that Mina redesigned us this way after Original Humanity's aforementioned self-annihilation. He wasn't exactly thrilled with the vast trauma directly inflicted on our local soupçon of humanity and indirectly on the universe, not to mention having to re-evolve our bodies. Individual freedom is the cornerstone of emergent *L*ife and Mina's, too. He imparted his love of freedom to his children. Those who initially populated our supranatural (spirit world) environment, ultimately siring us all, live accordingly. That means he absolutely doesn't interfere with freedom to do whatever we want—in some sense he does, of course, to the degree anyone's willing to listen, but coercion, persuasion, manipulation, and the like are alien to his woB—which, unfortunately, included Humanity 1.0 blowing itself up. Once they physically died out, Mina had to wait for the planet to clean up the damage, at which point he got right to work on Humanity 2.0—us. Original Humanity did what it did in spite of starting with full mind–brain integration and awareness of spirit world because The Corruption and its concomitant Accountableism, that rendered freedom subservient to harm, had them well saddled (§ 1:361). Quite like us, in fact.

And . . . yet. Mina got to wondering if we'd be less inclined to destroy ourselves with less of a connection to our *L*ife mind and spirit world's larger reality, and thereby less influenced by The Corruption. Original Humanity bombing itself into oblivion was the fifth planetary annihilation since The Corruption—not a common occurrence, thankfully, so Earth is in rarefied company. Besides attempting to limit The Corruption's influence, Mina redesigned our bodies to explore potentially better body structures such as brain efficiency. We look essentially the same as Original Humanity but differ in a number of ways, primarily in size, proportion, and neuronal structure. Although the principal effort was to limit The Corruption's influence, reducing mind–brain integration was to no avail. He found it all had little to no effect on The Corruption's influence on our behavior, although we haven't destroyed ourselves . . . but then, we're not as advanced as Humanity 1.0, either. In any case, this is why our brain today is neuronally limited and—despite the sneaking suspicion most humans intrinsically harbor about life beyond the physical—we're so spirit-unaware.

Lucifer and Michael's Reconciliation and the Big Healing changed everything, though, not just here on Earth but throughout our universe. The Negative Collective Consciousness dissipated, Accountableism began to wither, and universal humanity is accepting healing and peeling away layers upon onionskin layers of trauma and suffering, and restoring its true freedom and the 'material' aspects of spirit world. Mina accordingly acted with dispatch on Earth[305] to foment genetic and other changes to our physical bodies to enable greater mind–brain integration to boost awareness of our supranatural environment. This book is part of that awakening.

1.2.2.6 Brainwaves

Energent proto-energy interacts with the electrochemical nature of the brain's matter–Energy manifesting as EM Force and so-called brainwaves. In effect, brainwaves are instantiated (physical) mind in terms of applied energy E. We call the brain's activity—itself already a function of its matter–Energy interacting with proto-energy—*brainstate*, which is the real energy Υ (§ 2:114) state of *brainspace*, that area of physical space occupied and directly influenced by the brain's EM field. Brainstate is a unique environment. No two are ever the same and the proto-energy in and around any two brainspaces is never the same, either. Proto-energy's interaction with brainstate is responsorial, meaning it's a follow-up interaction to its initial interaction with the brain's basic electrochemical activity. Brainstate is real energy Υ electromagnetically expressed. It represents all there is of brainstate, which we described above as brain's macro-SOA. As such, brainstate is instantiated (physical) mind; the two terms represent the same concept. Recall that instantiated (physical) mind—brainstate—is the nonphysical proto-energy reflection of the brain's neural activity that builds into its physical macro-SOA,

---

305. Other human-inhabited planets aren't yet prepared for the changes he's making on Earth.

which is the physicalized expression of *L*ife mind's SOA. Brainstate thus manifests as physical energy; this is what the literature calls brainwaves.

The famous five brainwaves—gamma, beta, alpha, theta, delta in order of frequency—that science measures (*Fig. 113*, left) aren't all that exist, however. Altogether there are 800, each differing from the others by frequency, wavelength, and amplitude (EMF) as mediated by Métier Force. Science doesn't detect the other 795 brainwaves because their frequency or wavelengths are so nuanced they're mistaken for one of the five brainwaves, or their amplitudes are too low to detect or low enough they're mistaken as background noise. Brainwaves constructively and destructively interfere in typical EMW fashion (cf. Fig. 41:159, right), resulting ultimately in a unique brainstate resonance defined by frequency, wavelength, and amplitude that extends coherently between 1–11 feet (averaging about 7 feet) from the brain (*Fig. 113*, right), with the five major brainwaves roughly composed from all 800 brainwaves as a result of wave interference. Since brainstate reflects the brain's moment-to-moment expression of *L*ife mind's SOA, brainstate is constantly shifting w.r.t. *L*ife mind's SOA and that of brain's somatic and nonsomatic SOA. Therefore, brainstate's resonance is in constant flux, too. It's important to comprehend that brainstate is *not* a mind. Brainwaves don't represent specific thoughts but rather SOA. When we detect brainwaves, we're really detecting only the physical, applied energy E manifestation of *L*ife mind's SOA (to the degree it transliterates to brain) which, as emergent *L*ife, is one's true, actual mind. That's why nonhuman 'mind' isn't any sort of mind at all but just a brainstate reflection of its brain's SOA without the concomitant *L*ife mind SOA that's intrinsic of humans (§ 1.3.2:273).

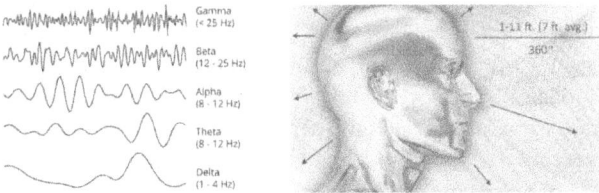

Figure 113. Left, 5 known brainwaves. Right, brainwaves emanating into environment 1–11 (avg. 7) feet.[253]

Science and popular science tend to conflate observation with causality in that the so-called laws of nature define what is 'permitted' in the physical world (rather than simply being an observation of some aspect of its behavioral nature) or that brainwaves determine brainstate. They don't determine brainstate but reflect it. We don't achieve, say, theta brainwaves in order to experience a theta brainstate and the thought and general affect that's claimed to go along with it. Instead, we achieve a certain SOA that, among other things, produces a detectable theta brainwave. Listening to binaural beats, for instance, doesn't change brainstate's affect, which is SOA, because SOA transliterates from *L*ife mind to brain where, via cognitive processing, it instantiates as physical mind, the brain's composite brainwave that we call brainstate. Although listening to binaural beats can produce some observable or measurable change in a person's brainstate, it's because a placebo effect—a self-induced state of belief—alters their *L*ife mind's SOA that integrates brain, thus affecting brainstate. In this sense, binaural beats is a tool to achieve a SOA one can't easily achieve, if at all, using one's own unmotivated or unguided thought.

1.2.2.6.1 BRAINWAVE ANTENNAE

Electrochemical activity produces a discrete electromagnetic (EM) field around all elements of our body, but particularly the brain and heart, the body's two largest electrical structures. It's an artifact with no specific purpose or utility within the brain or body itself, and confers no autonomic environmental awareness to humans as it does with certain birds or fish because our *L*ife mind performs this function. Brainwaves do act as a transmitting antenna in that it projects our EM energy into space where it interacts via constructive and destructive interference with the many EM fields that arise on Earth, including other people's and the planet's own geomagnetic field (*Fig. 114*). However, brainwaves aren't a receiving antenna that takes in the broadcast 'physiological' state of one's environment. Although called *brainwaves*, they don't carry, or encode (physiological or mindstate) data as do modulated EM waves. For that, one would need a near-infinite physiological lexicon that references each EM energy signature of a brainwave EM field. Our chakras, however, which only physical entities manifest because of their interaction with Energent proto-energy, do reflect our brainstate (CH. 29:497), which is to say, our mindstate. Recall that a spirit person, including our own spirit self while physically alive, can manifest the supranatural (as well as the natural) Energent in such a way as to have awareness of it (§ 1:112). They can thus know a person's brainstate (mindstate) and, when our own ℒife mind's soα sufficiently transliterates to our brain, our physical self can know it, too, though today the latter's not yet possible (§ 1.2.2.5.2:262).

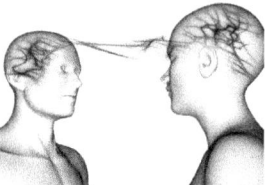

Figure 114. Visualizing brainwaves interacting via constructive and destructive interference.[254]

1.2.2.6.2 BRAINWAVE FIELD EFFECT

EM fields affect physiology but don't directly affect brainstate, although it can certainly impair brain function. Outside of malfunction, only mind affects human brainstate. For example, negative emotive ℒife force (EmℒF; § 3.3.3.1.1:289) manifests in Energent proto-energy which creates EM Force thus EM energy from which arise EM fields that lack coherence, are unstable, and fluctuate more than necessary.[306] *Coherence* is a physics term[255] used in metaphysics to mean "a logical, orderly and harmonious connectedness between parts of a system"[256] that describes a "highly efficient physiological state"[257] essentially referencing micro and macro EM fields, up to and including Earth's geomagnetic field. These fields supposedly provide a feedback loop—a system circuit that returns some of its output to its input as a regulatory mechanism—with individual persons according to the emotion one pumps into the world. This concept is inaccurate. As noted, while EM field states reflect the state of matter–Energy, they don't in themselves affect matter–Energy state, meaning EM fields don't affect the EM fields that other matter–Energy generates but only affect other EM waves via constructive and destructive interference.

Accordingly, because negative EmℒF affects matter–Energy state, thus EM emission, which alters EM fields infusing Earth—it contributes to how matter–Energy interacts with Fundamental Force—then negative EmℒF contributes to abnormal EM fields that, despite the seeming invariant predictability of EM Force, emit weakly emergent thus unpredictable EM when exposed to negative EmℒF. Consequently, even if emotive state did affect local, regional, or geomagnetic field state, and a feedback loop did exist between the macro-EM field and micro-EM fields, then in principle it's still not the case positive or negative emotive output begets positive or negative emotive feedback. The reason is that, although such EMw indeed can negatively affect us physiologically, it can't affect brainstate, thus mindstate, except indirectly via somatic response to physiology. Natural processes between matter–Energy, Fundamental Force, and Energent proto-energy aren't karmic. They only reflect their manifesting states.

1.2.2.6.2.1 HEART COHERENCE

Wherefore *heart coherence*, the metaphysical notion that heart rhythm is more sinusoidal, or consistent (improving heart–brain synergy), when people intentionally or unintentionally cultivate positive emotion because so-called neurons in the heart act like brain neurons to think, feel, and act, which then neuronally pass those results to the brain, is a fiction when repurposed to mean "the underlying state of our physiological processes . . . determines the quality and stability of the feelings and emotions we experience."[258] While the synergy is true enough in principle, it's not the heart mindfully controlling itself, reinforcing positive or negative emotion through feedback loops involving cardiovascular reflex responses (increased heart rate due to fear or anger) that generate ordered or chaotic (coherent or incoherent) heart rhythms which it then sends to the brain and disrupts cognitive and other processes.

Rather, the heart operates consonant with an autonomic reflex arc[307] as a largely PNS-responsive organ (as opposed to relying on less timely brain processing) because blood circulation is the absolute fundament to maintenance of physical life. So-called heart neurons are NeuN-*negative* cells and don't integrate ℒife mind. They're specialized cells that non-computationally generate or process action potentials for the proper, rhythmic operation of the heart muscle across the ventricles in en electrochemical manner that's only similar

---

306. EmℒF is always neutral, only 'negative' emotion alters it.

307. A methodology where the *peripheral nervous system* (PNS) intercepts nerve impulses outside the *central nervous system* (CNS) to provide near-instant response.

to neurons. Though they operate independent of brain input, it exercises a fine control over them to influence cardiac output, vascular resistance, and so on. These cells don't process action potentials representing thinking, feeling, or volition because they aren't NeuN-positive. The heart coherence notion that activities like meditation improve heart or whole-body coherence, thereby changing emotional outlook so one can reap the benefits of improved well-being, is a fable of wishful thinking about the heart as a mystical organ, conceived in unawareness of emergent ℒife. Although meditation as a tool certainly helps one to improve their Emℒℱ—returning it to a neutral state (FN 306)—which then, in consequence, reflects in somatic coherence, it's not the physical heart being "allowed to guide the body and mind, where great things can be achieved,"₂₅₉ but that one's ℒife mind integrates brain to reflect one's SOA which then reflects throughout the body, including in the heart's rhythm. Everything human w.r.t. the body arises only in ℒife mind that reflects, consonant with environmental response, in the body.

1.2.2.6.3 Brain Relationality

The fact our body exists in an environment with which it directly relates means the body, hence brain, operates in a relational environment. This gives rise to the brain as not only discrete but relational. We observe certain correlations of brainstate between entities as in *Fig. 115*. Does that mean brainstate, which is mind, is relational? Or that neuronal data flow itself is relational? Or that mind is a product of an embodied brain energetically and informationally embedded as a communicant in a collection of minds such that "we don't 'own' our minds—that we . . . are interdependent on others for the functioning of our minds" (Siegel 2012, 5–6)? Well, yes and no, depending on the question and whether human or nonhuman.

These questions involve the relational nature of reality and where mind (which interpretively interacts with reality) is located: within the person or entity such that individual mind interacts with individual minds, or within the communicative collective of entities such that a collective mind regulates information flow (communication) between individual processing components (brains) of the collective. Obviously, how we cognize our mind vis-à-vis reality has profound implications for how we cognize the communicative reality in which we live and, as a result, the socioculture we structure and compel people into. With the former case above, the person intrinsically is mind-autonomous and the apex of sovereignty while living in communion with other mind-autonomous persons. With the latter case, a person is only brain-autonomous but intrinsically communicative with other brain-autonomous persons; the person who is "interdependent on others for the functioning of our minds" (Siegel ibid, 5) is a mind-automaton and the collective communion, not the person, is the apex of sovereignty (CH. 36:585).

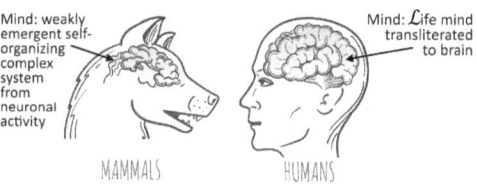

Mind: weakly emergent self-organizing complex system from neuronal activity

Mind: ℒife mind transliterated to brain

MAMMALS   HUMANS

Figure 115. Difference between animal and human mind.₂₆₀

Recall that information is interpreted data, not a self-existent. Data is raw, unorganized, and unconsidered. It becomes information with analysis when we organize, consider, and present it in such a way that it's useful (§ 1.1.1:84). There's no information flow without it being pre- or post-interpreted by entities in the data stream, which means the only flow between Living entities (excluding, for the moment, ℒife mind) is data flow and not information flow.

With humans, we can never talk about just the brain because it exists to transliterate ℒife mind. With that caveat in mind, the brain isn't relational, but the data flow constituting brain *is* relational. Brain-body and brain-brain data flow becomes information flow within the discrete brain so, in this respect, as mind instantiates from brainstate, mind isn't relational, there's no "between" w.r.t. mind (Siegel ibid, 8); it's discrete. However, because mind interacts with environment, including other (human, nonhuman) minds therein, then—although the skull literally confines the brain, and the body literally confines mind because *that's* the only place energy and information flow occurs—mind's purview *is* relational. Data flow from environment or another mind doesn't constitute mind outside (transcendent) of body because mind only perceives the data flow when it's part of the body's system of information flow. Mind *is* fully embodied *and* relational, but this doesn't mean mind is itself a relational existent because, then, in the absence of relationality, there'd be a loss of mind, meaning mind sans relationality is less than mind à la relationality. This would mean it's impossible to be human absent relationality, devoid of communion with other humans; one is only a person in concert (communion) with other persons. That's a hive mind, a sovereign collective absent the sovereign individual.

Most Living entities are social according to capacity, and mind operates in that social milieu in some respects like an antenna. A radio receiving a broadcast, like a mind experiencing relational information flow, isn't the broadcast itself (which is happening somewhere else) but only the *received data* that's being broadcast. Analogously, the mind isn't relational information flow unfolding both within and between (the broadcast) but only the *received* data flow, meaning the data flow perceived by mind, which is entirely a biophysical function of brain–body. The Living entity, say a monkey, experiencing information flow as environmental data in a social context is perceptive, having unmindness (§ 2.2:278) of it only within the informational processing capability that emergently produces mind, which w.r.t. Living is brain–body and w.r.t. humans is *L*ife mind. Therefore, monkey mind is quite different from elephant mind or mouse mind or ant mind, even though each qualifies in and of itself *as* mind w.r.t. to 'energy' and contextual—environmental and social—information flow.

The bottom line is the brain, in and of itself, isn't a relational existent but functions relationally, and it does so via a multitude of methods, one of which is brainwaves. In themselves, brainwaves don't transmit, convey, or communicate information but rather establish an electromagnetic environment the brain processes into information from somatic sensory input. It becomes aware of brainwaves as a nonconscious event subtly affecting the neuronal data stream. A conscious awareness of it arises when the brain processes this environmental data stream and we experience, e.g., a gut instinct, hair standing on the nape of the neck, a cold feeling in the pit of the stomach. These somatic responses aren't *L*ife mind integrations but arise in the Living brain. Via integration, *L*ife mind has awareness of these somatic responses and responds in its own way, say, in surprise, fear, excitation, concern, wariness, analysis, love, warmth, and the like which integrate brain to perhaps produce additional somatic responses.

1.2.2.7   SLEEP AND DREAMS

These phenomena are similar between human and nonhuman[308] since the brain is a Living entity and, therefore, operate on much the same principle. Because the brain integrates *L*ife mind, however, both REM (rapid eye movement) sleep and dreaming are completely different phenomena in humans. Since all the research and experimentation in these areas are rooted in the materialism of mind and based on expeditions into the neural tissue of animals, it's no surprise science misinterprets bioreality much as physics misinterprets physicoreality. We foray briefly into sleep and then move into dreaming.

1.2.2.7.1   SLEEP CYCLES

Humans and nonhumans sleep in ultradian[309] cycles of non-REM (NREM) and REM sleep periods that are part of a larger wake–sleep cycle called the Basic Rest Activity Cycle (BRAC). Three sleep stages, labeled 1, 2, and 3, characterize the NREM cycle.[310] Composited brainwaves progressively slow, lengthen, and synchronize from alpha through delta (roughly 8-12 Hz–0.5-4 Hz) as NREM sleep deepens, then abruptly shift into REM sleep with faster, shorter, desynchronized brainwaves more typical of wakefulness. Altogether, the ultradian, or NREM–REM, sleep cycle lasts on average about 100 (85–115)[311] minutes for the adult male–female brain, with NREM sleep covering ~66.455 minutes, or two-thirds, of each average cycle and REM ~33.545 minutes, or one-third.

> The **NREM** stage of the sleep cycle is rest, *L*ife force replenishment, and repair, a fundamental animal stage of recuperation. It applies to human biology because the brain is Living, thus mammalian. NREM sleep is a survival requirement. Deprivation leads to eventual death.

> The **REM** stage in nonhumans is also a survival requirement. From strictly a brain perspective it isn't one for humans, although it is a requirement of humanness. There's no correlation between REM sleep and dreaming; REM doesn't cause dreaming (cf. Solms 2004, 88; Solms et al. 2002, ch. 6). REM sleep assists, integrates, and reinforces brain function in nonhumans, as well as coincidently performing a secondary

---

308. In this subsection, nonhuman refers specifically to mammals, birds, and reptiles.

309. Recurrent throughout a 24-hour period, whereas circadian rhythms recur once per 24 hours.

310. Sleep stages 3 and 4 were combined in the 2007 American Academy of Sleep Medicine.

311. ET data differs from the less representative 90 (80–120) minute average in the literature.

role that Mina provided as a quality of life to brain-capable nonhumans outside their reality. In humans, REM sleep includes nonhuman brain activity as well as a phased *Life*-mind integration over the course of a sleep cycle due to NREM's 'offline' status delaying real-time mind–brain integration (MBI; § 1.2.2.4:257; *below*). Specific on–off neurotransmitters trigger REM sleep in humans that activate when *Life* mind activates action potentials (§ 1.2.2.4.2.2:259) in cholinergic neurons in the pons to rouse the brain (*Fig. 116*). Action potentials that trigger REM sleep in nonhumans activate from a molecular bioclock that's set when the brain enters NREM sleep.

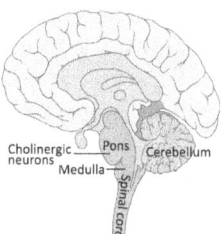

Figure 116. Human brain showing the pons where cholinergic (acetylcholine-emitting) neurons rouse the brain from NREM to REM sleep.[261]

During NREM sleep, real-time mind–brain integration goes 'offline,' which is to say, no transliteration is happening. During REM, the brain 'wakes' to an unconscious awareness so it can transliterate *Life* mind, then shuts down to continue with NREM rest or else awakens to conscious awareness. Integration is less leisurely and more energy intensive in the long, sustained REM chunk than when awake, where it operates in a continual but more 'packetized' and small-chunk manner. We feel unrested when we wake before or during a REM cycle because the brain, not having completed REM integration, needs to integrate with double duty everything from the nonintegrated NREM period plus the normal, real-time integration load. This has a higher energy cost. If we haven't sufficiently recouped our *Life* force energy levels, we feel less refreshed or rested than if we'd finished the sleep cycle.

1.2.2.7.2 WAKE CYCLES

A wake cycle similar to the sleep cycle occurs as part of the larger BRAC in which the brain alternates between active and less active, or rest, states. ET data differs from the literature here, as well, with an average duration of ~105 minutes subdivided into three roughly equal activity–rest stages of ~35 minutes each. The activity phase lasts ~23 minutes, or two-thirds (~65.714%), of each average BRAC stage and the rest phase about 12 minutes, or one-third (~34.285%), which ratio correlates closely to the NREM–REM ratio above. Additionally, the rest phase itself subdivides into a deep-rest–active-rest subcycle equivalent to NREM–REM and with a similar $\frac{2}{3}:\frac{1}{3}$ ratio.

1.2.2.7.3 DREAMING

Dreaming isn't unique to humans. All brain-capable nonhumans dream in a species-equivalent REM sleep state. What's unique to humans is the *reason* we dream. Nonhumans dream as a physiological result of brain arousal consonant with much of dream literature that's mistakenly applied to human dream states on the materialist presumption we're only what we see, thus nothing but smart, self-aware animals. Human REM dreams originate in *Life* mind memories or real-time experiences arising in brainstate during the NREM period as a result of delayed mind–brain integration while the brain is 'offline' during NREM sleep.

NREM. Recall that NREM is the state of pure, physical rest where our body lies mostly dormant. Human dreaming in this stage is equivalent to nonhuman REM dreaming. It presents opposite REM dreaming in the general literature—"more perceptually vivid, more motorically animated, more emotionally charged, and less related to waking life than NREM reports [but] contain[s] thought-like mentation and representations of current concerns more often than do REM sleep reports" (Hobson et al. 2000, 795)—as mundanity versus bizarreness where the dreamer's sense of self isn't lost to the gestalt of the dream (Hartman et al. 2012, 28–9). ET data shows NREM dreams account for ~20–30% of human dreaming.[312] NREM dreaming in humans arises from

---

312. cf. 5–10% in the literature, although "probably most authorities would agree on a conservative 80:20 REM:NREM dream-report ratio" (Solms et al. 2002, 183).

the brain constantly reinstantiating physical mind SOA even while disengaged from activity (§ 1.2.2.4.2.1:258). Dreams, as we experience them, comprise subthought structures—smaller, discrete elements of larger, coherent, more integrated thoughts—that undergo nuanced adaptations even in the NREM slow brainwave state.

Besides the myriad somatic SOA the brain processes during NREM sleep, remnants of conscious as well as unconscious thoughts are always cycling around the brain as action potentials firing off micro-SOA (the many thought components integrating other such components to alter macro-SOA). Since brain physiologically mimics *L*ife mind SOA, declarative memory appears improved with NREM sleep and NREM cueing—sounds, words, odors, and so on to spur retention—because both act to rehearse, or act as reminders of, the particular SOA that we call a memory (*Fig. 117*, left). Instantiated physical mind's SOA of a particular memory refreshes as it constantly updates with (integrates) brain macro-SOA. A memory falls out of so-called short-term memory because it's an incomplete, fractured, inchoate, and let's say a slippery, SOA to hold onto because all or part of it assimilated to *L*ife mind 'regions' that don't integrate the limited brain. Consequently, in trying to recall the memory, our brain can't integrate enough of it to adequately instantiate the various micro-SOA that forms its macro-SOA, hence, can't recall the memory. With each refresh of brainstate's own macro-SOA, the many micro-SOA that are the formative pieces of the particular memory—which go unrehearsed, or remain inchoate—persist as just a collection of micro-SOA without ever forming into a definitive macro-SOA that we recognize as the particular memory.

In this way, as fewer and fewer micro-SOA pieces of the memory coherently re-instantiate to mind, it simply becomes less and less aware of the memory with each re-instantiation because the memory never actually reconstitutes into a coherent macro-SOA. A memory falls out of brainstate because its changing SOA progressively loses untethered micro-SOA while retaining those tethered by macro-SOA (ibid). But short-term memory is never lost. *L*ife mind retains it although, if we don't invest it with a sufficient SOA for it to 'save' to a 'region' of our *L*ife mind that integrates our brain, we experience difficulty recalling it since it's not available for integration until, perchance, we hit upon its SOA and then it integrates and *bam!* there it is in our head. Because short-term memory is just an unaware scientific term for brainstate's SOA, observations of apparent brain operations like synaptic consolidation, synaptic plasticity, and rehearsal don't actually operate to preserve a temporary memory block but rather a particular SOA that we call a memory in the larger macro-SOA of brainstate.

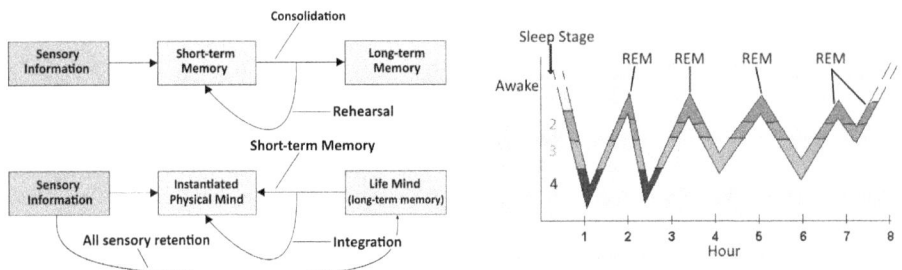

Figure 117. Left (top), classical memory consolidation short-term to long-term and (bottom) ET-revised generalized memory; right, frequency of REM sleep over a sleep period.[262]

NREM dreaming is a necessary experience of the physical body's animal psyche, though not for memory consolidation, brain maintenance, or the like; it's the same brainstate SOA possessed by nonhumans. Recall the human *body* is just a maximally advanced animal (§ 1.3.2:273) which the ℘erson integrates.[313]

REM. While our body continues sleeping in the REM stage, achieving rest and recuperation, the brain practically wakes up, becoming nearly as active as when conscious. Human dreaming during REM transcends nonhuman dream states, so there's no equivalence between them, the reason being that REM dreaming in humans arises from mind–brain integration. The main difference between mind–brain integration during REM sleep and wakeful integration is that, during NREM sleep, the brain is incommunicado with *L*ife mind whereas during wakeful integration, communication (integration) is constant. For example, if a person sleeps undisturbed for the average 100-minute sleep cycle then, for nearly 66 minutes, the brain experiences no

---

313. Although instantiated mind SOA at any given moment is essentially brain SOA at that moment, they're not equivalent because, at any given moment, instantiated mind SOA is a static snapshot if you will of brain SOA, whereas brain SOA at any given moment is an already-evolving, always-a-step-ahead SOA. Because the brain is in constant evolution w.r.t. SOA since action potentials never cease, we can't say brain ever embodies a particular SOA and therefore itself embodies a psyche, meaning the brain isn't psyche. Accordingly, the animal and the physical-human instantiated mind is psyche. For ℘erson, see § 3:280.

integration with £ife mind.[314] That's 66 minutes when brain is unaware of the flux in £ife mind's SOA when one's spirit self may daydream, interact with others, or do things in the 'reflective' environment or spirit world. The human system makes up for this with about 33 minutes of integration. But one can see the difficulty: 66 minutes of £ife mind SOA needs integrating through a 33-minute window. REM sleep is a nearly awake experience for the brain because, for it, this integration catch-up activity is more intense than real-time integration. This is the reason the brain shifts the body from the NREM to REM sleep state. However, one doesn't sleep through the perfect sleep cycle, cycle after cycle, throughout a given sleep period, say, overnight (*Fig. 117*, right). Additionally, NREM and REM periods vary, with REM typically lengthening over the course of a sleep period. In humans, the reason for the variance is that integration is 'energy' intensive and the brain sustains the process better after the body's had time to rest and recuperate than right after its first NREM period.

The brain rather abruptly wakes itself from the deep stage of NREM sleep, sometimes known as quiescent sleep, to a state of effective wakefulness—unconscious awareness—without actually achieving lucidity. The instant the brain activates REM sleep, £ife mind begins integrating: memory through ependymal cells (§ 1.2.2.4.2:258) and macro-SOA through neurons. This results in a surge of neuronal electrical activity as the brain processes the data influx, which correspondingly activates organs to ensure the brain has enough resources. Motor circuits in the brain shut down during REM sleep because neurons receiving stimulus from £ife mind integration can't tell the difference from conscious stimulus and would naturally send action potentials through the brain's motor neurons. Without suppression of these neurons (Brooks et al. 2012, 9785–6), they'd activate the body's skeletal muscles accordingly. A different circuit controls ocular muscles, which produce no somatic motility, thus are unaffected by REM, giving this sleep state its name. In certain cases, necessary neurotransmitters (ibid) fail to deploy and motoneurons don't inactivate. This leads to a malfunction like REM sleep behavior disorder (RBD; Brooks et al. 2011, 7111) or what's considered the sleepwalking malfunction, although it—along with symptomatic behaviors like periodic leg movements and restless legs syndrome—is really the willful intention of the person's spirit self wanting to do something in the physical world their physical self can't or won't do.

Unlike NREM dreaming, REM dreaming isn't a necessary experience of either the physical or the £ife mind psyche. Rather, REM dreaming is an artifact of mind–brain integration from neurons responding to the fragmented stimulus. The nature of REM dreaming is twofold: first, *dream content* arises from memories integrating the brain and its consequent neuronal activity—our physical self becomes aware of thoughts, feelings, or activities of our spirit self—and second, *dream structure* arises from the reality of brain limitation (§ 1.2.2.5:261). We consider each in turn.

Dream Content. Essentially, dreams arise from the content of our memories and our conscious £ife mind thoughts and feelings in the moment of integration. Recall that, unlike nonhumans, memory isn't stored in the human brain, and we aren't our physical body but emergent £ife existing separately from it. Awake or asleep, our emergent £ife self—we call it *spirit self* for convenience, remembering that our spirit body is also a 'vessel' (mind-expressed instead of biology-expressed) for our emergent £ife self—naturally has a life: its own self, reality, experiences, and the like.

Until the Big Healing, the physical person's spirit body was ensconced more or less 'in' the physical body, spatially integrating the physical body. Unusually spirit-aware persons realized they could mentally as well as bodily (temporarily) disentangle from the physical body. Sometimes, this awareness filtered into the consciousness of their physical self, giving rise to activities like astral projection (§ 1:591). Physically awake or asleep, 100% of physical people's spirit selves have always been consciously aware of their own thoughts and feelings—regardless their own awareness of larger spirit world or lack thereof—and of their physical body's state or situation. This means they're fully aware of at least their physical reality if not their supranatural reality, too. Since the Big Healing, awareness beyond the limited mind–body physical world relationship has spread to varying degrees to about 20% of physically alive people across the observable universe. About 80% of this cadre is consciously aware of their nonphysical surroundings comprising the immaterial, or 'reflective,' natural environment and the supranatural, or spirit, one (§ 7.1:212).

This means dreams constitute from any experience one's spirit self has, whether it's daydreaming while spatially locked into their physical body or from actual experiences in the 'reflective' or spirit environment

---

314. A caveat: we frequently employ computer analogies when discussing brain—'updates,' 'downloads,' 'offline'—but Mina disavows our analogies on general principles because "they're prone to confuse, mislead, or foster wrong concepts." He prefers *integration* as a conceptual paradigm but, where appropriate, we feel ours help us visualize difficult concepts, partly because we just don't have the language yet to adequately communicate his integration concept.

doing whatever, as well as from how one's spirit self is consciously thinking or feeling about (interpreting) those experiences. As the integration process progresses during REM sleep, ℒife mind data transliterates to the brain. Action potentials fire, micro-SOA and macro-SOA form and combine (§ 1.2.2.4:257), and all of it instantiates moment-to-moment as brainstate. This also gives rise to so-called lucid dreaming, which is just the state in which a person's brain, for a variety of reasons, rouses during REM sleep from unawareness to awareness.[315]

Dream Structure. Recall a given memory is fundamentally a macro-SOA comprised of many micro-SOA of whatever led to the particular SOA called a memory. Because the brain's neuron count is limited, it can only integrate certain information from ℒife mind, either the aspects of mind that each neuron or group maps to, a mapping limitation, or the aggregate memory content the collection of ependymal cells are capable of integrating, a numerical limitation (§ 1.2.2.4.2.2:259). These limitations are just an unhappy fact for the time being (§ 1.2.2.5:261). The result is that many SOA integrating brain are typically incomplete, so a given memory is, in practical terms, fragmented. Some memories are SOA-complete more or less than others, hence we observe that some parts of a dream appear more or less coherent or bizarre.

1.2.2.7.3.1 DREAM RECALL

We struggle to recall dreams because their fragmented structure means there's no coherent macro-SOA around any given part of it. Some parts are coherent or emotionally powerful enough that we do cognize (infuse them with) a coherent macro-SOA during the waking process, and we recall those parts better or longer. More to the point, in awakening having had a dream, we consciously become aware of our in-sleep SOA (brainstate) from the moment we're conscious. The brain is taking in the experience, too, our SOA shifting moment to moment as our physical mind reinstantiates ~1,000 per second with more coherent and powerful SOA from our immediate reality, overshadowing the fragmental micro-SOA that constitutes some, or all, of our dreaming. The average result is that within seconds, minutes, or hours it no longer instantiates in our physical mind with any SOA we recognize; we've effectively forgot it.

1.2.2.7.3.2 DREAM TIME

As we've seen, we're not *dreaming* but transliterating memories from our spirit self into brainstate where physical time operates. Mental or interactive spirit-self activities occur in a nonphysical environment where mind, not event periodicity (§ 2:107), is the central definitor. One experiences time subjectively even though there's objective time (§ 1:105). We're used to comprehending felt time differently from 'real' physical time, so this isn't particularly unusual. There are three ways to assess time in the dream context: mindstate, brainstate, and physical state. We consider each in turn.

Mindstate. We're familiar with how time passes in our mind according to mental state. When bored, it feels slow and when engaged, fast. Spirit world operates in much the same way. Even when interacting with others, a person's mindstate differs from theirs. Whether a dream originates in their spirit self's mental state or from their real activity in spirit world solo or in a crowd, one's experience of, and memory about, it is a *mindstate*. For ℒife mind, facts and details aren't lost or misremembered; how they're experienced affects what's (de)emphasized[316] and what comprises the SOA constituting the memory.[317]

To talk adequately about time in spirit world would take its own book, so we need abbreviate it here. Suffice it to say, time is perceptual, not objective, in spirit world. Although there is an objective timestate in spirit world by which actual, objective timekeeping is measurably the same for all people, just like vibrating archí are the ultimate source of objective timekeeping in the physical world (§ 2:107), time for a spirit person is entirely perceptual. If one sips hot chocolate, which for them has been sitting in a cup for an hour and expected to grow cold, it tastes cold (although if, for them, hot food never grows cold regardless, then it tastes as hot as they expect). But for a friend at the table who feels only the passing of a few moments, the same cup of hot chocolate remains hot to their taste. Even though an objective timekeeping period has passed, one experiences

---

315. Reasons include the physical person being spirit-aware, desiring to lucid dream, their spirit-self desiring their physical self to lucid dream, and more.

316. This is why eyewitnesses often sincerely remember the same event differently.

317. As with physical people, a spirit person who experiences a trauma to the psyche might form a SOA of the traumatizing experience as an unawareness; it's a 'forgotten' memory. Typically, this happens with the spirit self of a physical person (most often children) who, in spirit world, declines to grow up mentally, emotionally, or bodily (since our spirit body reflects how mind sees oneself) even if their physical body survives the trauma and physically grows into old age.

the hot chocolate according to mindstate not to ineluctable thermodynamics the way we experience objective physical-world reality because the spirit drink isn't the objective existent the physical one is. Since REM dreams are ℒife mind memories in the context of our spirit self, they're of mindstate and, therefore, last as long as we perceive them to last. There's no necessary correlation with brainstate although they can correlate. On the other hand, since NREM dreams are brainstate and not ℒife mind experiences, they do correlate to brainstate time.

Brainstate. We're used to thinking that life experience is just physicality, that the immutable nature of biology and physics drives objective reality. The reason, besides being daily in our faces, is that physical things are their own autonomous existents independently operating. This holds for nonhumans, too, as they aren't ℒife nor transcendent mind.[318] In this context, brain-capable nonhumans dream and their REM stage is equivalent to human NREM. Such dreams arise in unconscious thought processes and in myriad ways reflect the physical reality one experiences by engaging in, for example, problem solving, training, imagining, experience processing. NREM dreams aren't ℒife mind but brainstate processes, lasting as long they objectively appear to, meaning they necessarily correlate with physical state. But they also correlate with the time it takes thought to constitute from initial stimulus to single or multiple action potentials, micro-SOB/-SOA, and macro-SOB/-SOA.

Physical state. The integration process for any neuron or NeuN-positive ependymal to respond to ℒife mind stimulus is about 1.477×10^{-40} second, which isn't too far from one Planck time of 10^{-44} second. A timeframe like this isn't too surprising considering mind, a ℒife proto-energy existent, doesn't, within itself, experience event periodicity or spatial location. Therefore, time and distance, thus travel, are absent, which means, like *enérgeia*, ℒife mind is instantaneity (§ 6.11.4:198). Events like awareness and non-verbalized thought don't *transpire* within ℒife mind, they simply are. There's no state of becoming as with the spatial existence intrinsic of brain, there's only *asti*, that Persian state of is-ness.

From ℒife mind stimulation of the relevant brain structure, any single (myelinated) action potential cascades to its first micro-SOA at 80–120 milliseconds. This means any discrete memory takes approximately 2.754×10^{-10} (trillionths) second to instantiate from a collection of initial action potentials—recall a memory comprises many micro-SOA that formulate to a macro-SOA that constitutes the SOA we call a memory—to its initial micro-SOA. As multiple micro-SOA form, reform, and combine, the memory takes coherent structure over roughly 1.755×10^{-10} second. Instantiated physical mind reinstantiates about 1,000 times per second or once per millisecond (§ 1.2.2.4.2.1:258), so we can see a formulated memory reinstantiates into physical mind about 1.755 trillion times per millisecond, or about 1.755 quadrillion times per second. Each reinstantiation of any particular memory or micro-thought and macro-thought structure is a nuance of its previous instantiation because neurons constantly interact with the signals they're receiving according to each signal's EM and related signature, which neuroscience calls neuronal computation.[319] This action potential gated process generates significant memory and experiential processing quite faster than our brains can even form coherent thoughts about it and is the origin of the concept of the subconscious—what Mina prefers to call "unconscious"—thought in the physical mind.[320]

Over these time periods the sleeping, unconscious mind becomes aware of (if in REM, integrating) memories or thought states in stages, one reinstantiation of brainstate at a time. As every reinstantiation presents nuanced changes to the macro-SOA that is brainstate, the dreaming person (or nonhuman) experiences more of a kaleidoscope of sensorial experience and experiential reactions than when consciously awake where a thought takes approximately 100 microseconds to form, such as those that produce one's 'inner monologue.' Because NREM dreams constitute from brain processes, their timeframes tend to correlate more with objective time than REM dreams, which constitute from ℒife mind thoughts and experiences in the nonphysical environment. Much as with radiocarbon dating, however (§ 3:557), science's sleep and dreaming sample sizes are insufficiently representative to analyze the phenomena as they present. Take note that without our aforementioned one-seventh neuronal loadout, dreams would present as normal, coherent memories upon waking rather than incoherent, so-called dreams.

---

318. Recall that any material entity also exists as an immaterial 'reflective' existent (§ 7.1.1.1:212). Instead of ceasing to exist at death, the immaterial mind–body self of companion mammals transition to spirit world (Animal Familials, ch. 39:601).

319. The classical model is that "[a] spiking neuron 'computes' by transforming a complex dynamical input into a train of action potentials" (Agüera y Arcas et al. 2003, 1715). But a neuron is, in and of itself, an autonomous neural network, from its dendritic arbor to its terminals (e.g., Sidiropoulou et al. 2006, 886; Bartol et al. 2015, 2).

320. ℒife mind has its own form of unconscious thought that resides below conscious awareness. Some of it presents in one's physical unconscious mind to exert Intentionality on the physical mind and body (§ 2.4.1:401).

1.3 LIVING

A nonhuman entity that's alive is a Living entity that thinks, feels, comprehends, and translates at whatever its capacity, including the human body sans 𝓛ife mind (§ 1.2.1:247). Living is what we call 'alive' absent having 𝓛ife. All Livingness is comprised of matter. There are two fundamental classes of matter: vital and nonvital (Table 6), the latter being all matter and the former all matter integrating Livingness. Matter is technically nonvital whether integrating Livingness or not, since it's composed of archí structures of which, recall, each one is simply 'energy' (§ 2.3:115). The distinction here lies in nonvital matter being a series of wob that produce a vital state of being from which it gains the sobriquet 'life.'

Table 6. Vital and nonvital classes of matter.

Matter as States of Existence	
Vital	Nonvital
Conscious Nonconscious	
Sentient–Sapient	
Matter with Livingness	Matter without Livingness

1.3.1 CHEMISTRY AS LIFE

Materialists argue life is abiogenetic, arising from inert, nonliving matter as mere molecules fortuitously arranged a certain way such that complex chemical reactions spontaneously[321] occur, producing an operational state we call a living cell that collectively adds up to a living organism like you, me, and Snappy the cat. This is true insofar as it goes, but explains only biology, not life; the explanans presumes the biology, then conflates it with Living. Arranging molecules of the right kind in the right fashion is a *prerequisite* of life but, once so arranged, is hardly life itself because it includes more than prerequisite chemical reactions. Aspects like motility, reproductiveness, metabolism, awareness, wob, and so on comprise Livingness, but don't arise in chemistry any more than water's wob of wetness arises in its constituent molecular and atomic construction. Otherwise, the chemistry of an internal combustible engine would be all it takes for a car to successfully motor down the road or, indeed, for the proverbial chicken to sashay across it. The only spontaneous event—occurring absent external cause—is emergence (§ 2:90).

For example, polymerase change reactions (PCR) don't occur just because they artificially duplicate the natural environment necessary for a series of chemical reactions but because, in duplicating the it, the process invokes Energent proto-energy's interaction with the PCR environment in the same way the natural process in a living cell does. The proto-energy component is the reason chemistry operates in the first place and, along with wob Force (Table 11:285), is what enlivens the chemistry of cellular biology from nonvital to vital and thus *Living*. In the same way Fundamental Force arises from proto-energy interacting with nonvital matter at all levels throughout the universe, life—the mode of existence of being alive—arises from Living force, the nonhuman, Intentionalized version of 𝓛ife force (§ 3.2:282), interacting with proto-energy interacting with nonvital matter in the proto-biological context (*Fig. 118*). This means even with appropriately arranged molecules chemically interacting, as molecules do, there'd still be no cellular receptors perfectly organized to allow certain interactions in only the right context and, accordingly, no alive thing snuffling around in the underbrush or choosing to sun itself in a glade. There'd just be a collection of cellular machinery independently operating, occasionally or perhaps constantly interacting via enzymes, hormones, and the like, that exudes into the larger structure and provokes responses but, overall, no entity-wide coordination such that it's 'alive.'

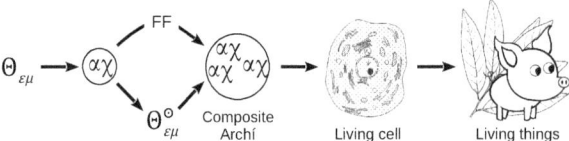

Figure 118. Energent proto-energy ($\Theta_{\varepsilon\mu}$) interacts with archí ($\alpha\chi$) and all composite archí ($\alpha\chi^{\text{comp}}$) structures; Energent proto-life ($\Theta_{\varepsilon\mu}^{\odot}$) interacts with $\alpha\chi^{\text{comp}}$ where Fundamental Force (FF) conditions trigger $\Theta_{\varepsilon\mu}^{\odot}$ interaction via Living Force as an intentionalized, automatic wob of the universe.[263]

---

321. In the sense that such chemical reactions are what appropriately arranged molecules and their constituents naturally and necessarily do because it's their contextual behavior.

Materialists correctly point out that what's called a 'living cell' is really just nonliving matter engaging in complex chemistry that produces the operating state reckoned as aliveness. Yet, presuming chemistry is literally all there is to life without considering from whence chemistry itself arises is a fallacious leap. Separate proto-energy and Living Force from biology and all those complex chemical reactions loosely called life cease because their chemical reactions only occur to begin with in proto-energy interacting with matter–Energy, not because chemistry is intrinsic to nonvital, nonliving matter.

1.3.2   Nonhuman Mind–Brain–Body

In this section, we describe Living nonhuman (animal) mind as it operates through the brain–body matrix. Although the human body (not the person) is a Living entity that's fundamentally no different from—though (except the elephant) certainly more brain sophisticated than—any other animal, its brain, unlike other Living entity brains, integrates autonomous *L*ife mind. As it's a unique case, we describe it in Human Mind–Brain–Body (§ 1.2.2:253). Even so, from a sans-*L*ife-mind-brain-only perspective, this section applies to the human brain as well. Philosophy with a capital-p's reductionist effort—from neuroscience to psychology and all points between—to understand the mind–body problem and generate a useful conceptual comprehension of mind has ended up largely describing Living mind while entirely missing the boat on *L*ife mind. The reason is simple: its focus on function over instantiation. Since each instantiated human mind is unique w.r.t. any other instantiation, mind isn't reducible to function, especially brain function. About 75% of Living entities have a distributed intelligence mind with the remainder possessing a brain mind (Table 5:235), and it's to the latter we now turn.

1.3.2.1   Instantiation of Nonhuman Mind

Living mind is an emergent property of brain (§ 2:90). That doesn't mean it's a "self-organizing property of energy and information flow as it unfolds" (Siegel 2016, 2:8) in and about the brain–body. Nor that it's "an information processing system . . . translating changes in the body and the environment into a language of neural impulses that represent the animal-environment relationship . . . [as] information instantiated in and processed by the nervous system" (Henriques 2011b, par. 5). These are functional definitions. Mind is rather a moment-by-moment emergent macro instantiation of hundreds of trillions of non-emergent yet self-organizing micro instantiations of awareness that begin as somatic or nonsomatic experiences of environment. A somatic experience is a neuroresponse to a state of being (soB) in or around the body's environment. A nonsomatic experience is a neuroresponse to an instantiation of awareness (soA) at less than the macro level. Indeed, a nonsomatic experience at the macro level qualifies as a rudimentary self-awareness that Living entities entirely lack, although higher-order animals do exhibit a faux self-awareness we describe in Unmind (§ 2.2:278).

An informational (data flow) emergent property resides in being a novel interaction amongst data. It therefore exists as an emergent existent—because the many micro-soA from which it instantiates are the product of novel, supervenient interactions of predictable outcomes of brain activity or information flow—making Living mind a weakly emergent property of proto-energy's interaction with the EM nature of each action potential and its micro-soA and their coalescence into expanding collections of soA. This altogether results in the generation of a real Energent proto-energy existent; an 'energy' field, but not exactly. Each micro-soA—every neuronal impulse—alters the whole such that Living mind instantiates and reinstantiates moment-to-moment as a discrete proto-energy existent so long as the brain experiences action potentials (§ 1.2.2:253). This means Living mind is a discrete reality from brain even while it draws its moment-to-moment existence from brain. Thus, when Living brain dies, so, too, dissipates Living mind.

1.3.2.1.1   Somatic Neuroresponse

Various types of sensory neurons detect own-self well-being (*below*)—pressure, temperature, chemistry, vibration—where a stimulus chemically induces an action potential (AP), the electrical nerve pulse. Although any AP is the same ±40mv, its frequency rate changes according to greater or lesser stimulus. For example, as the intensity of heat in the region of a thermoreceptor increases, so does the AP frequency, effectively telling the nervous system that own-self soB in that thermoreceptor's region is rapidly changing in temperature. But that's not the only way a sensory neuron encodes information.

Besides subtle variations in wattage and amperage, the AP is also an electromagnetic phenomenon with EM frequency, wavelength, and 'energy' mediated by Métier Force, all of which are variant w.r.t. to stimulus and, as such, represent in this sense "a language of neural impulses that represent the animal-environment relationship" (Henriques Henriques 2011b, ibid, par. 4). Each AP thereby encodes a SOA that represents its *informational state of being*. It takes more than a single AP to cause a neuron to 'fire' (its classical computational aspect). This means a neuron sends an AP series upstream as a packetized bundle. These combine with other serial- and parallel-entrained packetized AP; for instance, more thermoreceptor plus pain and other receptor AP. Eventually, they reach a motor neuron in the spinal cord that updates its own-self well-being and yanks the appendage from the temperature source or jerks the leg to a doctor's rubber mallet tap on the knee. Finally, the AP reaches the brain itself, which updates its own-self well-being. AP as input signals to brain neurons aren't weighted (which is different from synaptic strength) as in artificial neural networks.

1.3.2.1.2 NONSOMATIC NEURORESPONSE

This experience arises from within the nervous system itself versus the environment exterior to it, such as the environment of the body-at-large. Nonsomatic neuroresponse arises in two ways: from somatic neuroresponse and from own-self SOA which arises from own-self SOB.

Somatic neuroresponse. Individual somatic neuroresponses arrive in the brain instantiated as clades (§ 1.2.2.4.2.2:259). Representing multiple related somatic neuroresponses, a clade instantiates an informational SOB and SOA; in effect, a micro-mind. An entity's own-self well-being—an aspect of mind—experiences somatic neuroresponses wholistically even though the brain processes the individual neuroresponses individually and in different areas. Hence, a clade is a SOA that represents the informational SOB of its constituent neuroresponses. As these somatic clades filter through the brain they merge with sister clades collectively instantiating as a *superclade* forming a regional SOA representing its informational SOB. Each superclade merges with others to instantiate megaclades and ultraclades[322] that form an expanding awareness of the macro-SOB, which means own-self SOB that informs own-self well-being. This own-self macro-SOA is brainstate, i.e., *mind*.

Own-self SOA. A brainstate is a macro collection of many micro-SOA woven into a tapestry of awareness spanning the entity and synonymous with awareness of own-self well-being. A monkey's own-self well-being, for example, forms from own-self SOA relating through own-self WOB as its baseline to determine own-self well-being. If own-self SOA doesn't coincide with own-self WOB, then own-self well-being is in a deficient state until own-self SOA *is* own-self WOB. That's when our monkey can metaphorically relax in its tree with a sensation redolent with impression that all's right with its world. These two states of being—SOA and well-being—are inseparable, two sides of a coin where the coin is brain. On the one hand, brain instantiates own-self SOA and, on the other, own-self well-being. They constantly interrelate. Brainstate is never the same moment to moment, so an entity—including a person—is never the same entity two moments in a row or even across any two moments, ever. It's easy to see this in the context of religious conversion in humans as well as in anger, joy, and the like amongst humans and nonhumans. Nonsomatic neuroresponse is the stimulus induced in neurons by clade level SOA as well as own-self SOA as they process through neurons where brainstate reflects them in terms of micro-SOA and macro-SOA. This is an orbital view of how nonhuman Thought (thinking–feeling) arises as nonsomatic neuroresponse.

1.3.2.1.2.1 NONHUMAN THOUGHT

Nonhuman entities don't have thoughts the way we comprehend it. A chimp scheming, begrudging, or imagining doesn't think these the way Brutus calculated a solution to Julius. It's more an experience redolent with impression of what it wants or feels along with attendant experience (consequences), of which memory might create an impression. Its unmindness is intentional more than thoughtful, whereas human Thought can be both. Impression is nonverbal like a subconscious—doing what we really want, acting how we really are—but without conscious awareness or specific, thoughtful input. Brainstate makes sense of sensory input (including 'thought' inducement) by impression as the brain moves data streams through its neural net according to EM field affinities that arise from the 'energy' nature of action potentials, not by any system of algorithmic filtering and encoding of information. This is true for companion animals, too; their Intentionalized WOB—what we'd think of as the spirit mind—integrates their physical brains not as *Life* mind integrates, where mind ↦ brain, but where brain ↦ mind and the Intentionalized WOB that *is* the animal reflects physical mind until death (CH. 39:601).[264]

---

322. These terms visualize an expanding SOA, not actual structures or even limited to these.

1.3.2.1.3 Macro Neuroresponse

It's typical of people to imagine the diaphanous in terms of a more opaque analogue, for example the way we imagine—at least since Plato and Aristotle then, say, from Descartes onward—the brain (and mind) in terms of technical awareness such as shadows and forms, analog (then digital) machines, webnets, information, or just data (§ 1:83). Since humanity has traditionally lacked real awareness of emergent Life, people sought to comprehend mind in terms of brain, and where they haven't, they've lost themselves in the clouds of religion and philosophy. Except for viruses (*below*), Living entities—eukaryotes, bacteria, and archaeans[323]—instantiate mind according to brain capability, some of which emanate from brains and the rest from various forms of distributed systems such as plant intelligence. As brain primitivity increases, mind sophistication decreases. Why, then, isn't an elephant brain of ~500 billion neurons smarter than a human brain of only ~105 billion (§ 1.2.2.4.2:258)?[324] The answer isn't architecture, but mind; not instantiated mind (brainstate), which is brain-based, but Life mind, the unique, individuated person.

We mustn't discount the distinction between person and body. A person only uses their physical body as an 'avatar' (§ 2.1:276).[325] Subtract the person from the body and what's left is a smart, clever animal with nowhere near the powers of a person despite sporting ostensibly the same brain. While an elephant brain is therefore more intelligent than a nonconscious, or Living, 'human' brain, possession of dexterous fingers on nimble hands and other superior body construction means a nonconscious 'human' brain still dominates the intellectually superior albeit operatively inferior elephant.[326] If we could directly compare such a matchup, we wouldn't see the amazing human person versus the pedestrian elephant animal, but the 'human' animal versus elephant animal where, despite the 'human' animal's apparent albeit non-working brain advantages—speech, fine motor control, being "*differently* intelligent" (Tattersall 1998, 32, 10)—the elephant better succeeds in the environment.

Although virus is Living—thus requires inclusion in the things-that-are-alive domain—and has mind, it doesn't instantiate mind. This gives rise to two key outcomes. First, virus 'mind' is simply its WOB. Its extreme primitivity lacks even a single cell, which precludes it producing energy thus any self-interaction *within* mind. Hence, there is no mind to instantiate because WOB isn't an existent and has no beingness in and of itself. Having no information processing capability, virus mind functions only as a primitive SOA. We might call virus a *unicellular* mind whereas all other Living entities are *multicellular* mind. Second, without instantiated mind, virus can't instantiate culture, which is to say, a viral-type WOB. Culture requires mind because culture *is* mind (§ 4:291). Having no instantiated mind, virus has no individual culture and no content of culture. Whatever happens in the virus stays in the virus; it communicates nothing to other viruses. Even though virus mind is uninstantiated mind and lacks own-self SOB, it does contain a chemical-mediated own-self SOA, which is how it's 'aware,' for instance, of when to replicate.

The bottom line is that mind isn't "the information instantiated in and processed by the nervous system" (Henriques 2011b, par. 5) but simply instantiated own-self SOA. As with Life mind, there's no universal law for how Living mind works even though there's a universal functionality of brain. As with Life, two brains never give rise to two Living minds of the same unmind, unmindness, and unmindset (§ 2.2:278). Even when multi-individual habituation collectivizes as a cultural habit, any two minds remain fundamentally individuated w.r.t. own-self WOB and SOA.

Section 2
Own-self Well-being

Anything that's alive, to shave Rousseau's "two principles prior to reason"[327] down to just a single imperative, has an intense interest in own-self well-being experiencing the world; not one's *own* psychosomatic sense of well-being, but howsoever one determines *own-self* well-being. Own-self is almost infinitely definable. For

---

323. The three principal domains of life: *eukaryotes* include plants, animals, fungi, protists; *bacteria*, just that; *archaeans* are three kingdoms based on relatedness to the former two.

324. cf. the literature's estimated ~257 billion and 86–100 billion-neuron count in elephants and humans, respectively.

325. An icon or animation, traditionally representing video game participants (*Avatar* 2009, film), that visualizes this natural experience in a technological context.

326. Recall the spirit-born evolved our body to embody the capacities of the person (§ 2.1.5.5.2:323; § 2.1.2:543).

327. ". . . one of which interests us deeply in our own Preservation and Welfare, and the other inspires us with a natural Aversion to see any other Being, but especially any Being like ourselves, suffer or perish" (Rousseau 1761, *lv*); the latter, wishful thinking.

some, it means *me* and for others *my family, my job, my community-nation-planet, my cause, my God, anything-in-some-way-me-related*—singly or in combination—even at the expense of *me* (§ 1:94). Outside of human behavior, we don't observe own-self operating beyond the *me* except in gradations with certain mammals like dogs, dolphins, whales, elephants, chimps, and the like. Living, therefore, isn't merely sentient while *L*ife is sentient–sapient, meaning conscious. Instead, Living is Living-conscious with a Living consciousness whereas *L*ife is *L*ife-conscious with a *L*ife consciousness. To distinguish the two concepts, we term the former nonconscious/-ness and the latter conscious/-ness (Table 7).

Table 7. *Da-sein* as all aspects of awareness (§ 2.2.1.1:234).

Da-sein	
LIVING	*L*IFE
Sentience–Sapience	
Nonconscious	Conscious
Unmind	Mind
Unawareness	Awareness
Nonconsciousness	Consciousness
Unmindness	Mindness

To convey this concept, Mina went with the German term *Da-sein*—meaning, 'being-there/there-being'—as a singular term for any entity that's alive and interacting in 'being-there' with its environment in terms of own-self experiencing the world according to its self-aware capacity. He chose it to encourage our appreciation for the beingness of all things alive[328] because of it's non-human-centric vernacular meaning in the context of Heidegger's (FN 38:22) derived *Dasein* concept[329] which bears a resemblance to Mina's concept of 'own-self well-being experiencing the world,' although it needs expanding from Heidegger's emphasis on only human to everything alive. Instead of using his familiar *Dasein* concept that only partly gets to the point, or the more cumbersome 'being-there/there-being' or some variant, we use the hyphenated *Da-sein*. Accordingly, in this book *Da-sein* means 'an entity interacting with own-self environment as an experience so as to inform own-self well-being' (cf. regarding safety, § 3.2:374).

In their own way, any alive entity, including virus, makes choices (despite appearing as preprogrammed automata the more primitive they get) and takes actions commensurate with own-self capability. *Da-sein* is an umbrella term for all that lies behind this, such as viral mutation, cockroaches scuttling from sudden light, dolphins trying to save their fellows caught up in nets, or humans sacrificing happiness, others, even own-self (§ 7:441). The *Da-sein* concept serves as the principal category for all aspects of awareness in some way, shape, or form, whether human or nonhuman, instead of the many sometimes conflicting terms traditionally employed. All things alive interactively experience own-self in relation to environment and employ brain-capable tactics and strategies to maximize well-being according to individual or collective woв.

2.1 MIND

Humans are complex, conscious beings not just because we can process, experience, or cognize stimuli but because it subjectively *becomes* us. Each stimulus adds wholistically to the totality of subjective experience. That totality is mind, the *L*ife mind of a person having emergent *L*ife. The reason we're self-aware—why it's a property of being conscious at all—is that stimuli become our consciousness, become our self-awareness, which is the state of being that we perceive as being aware of stimuli (§ 2.2.1.1:234). In this section, *L*ife references *mind*.

Self-awareness comes from how mind encounters stimuli. It doesn't process stimuli, because mind isn't cognitive but assimilative (§ 1:391). This means we don't simply encounter stimuli and then cognize it in order to objectively or subjectively experience it. Recall that mind is unstructured and energetic, not structured and procedural. Conversely, the brain has procedural structure to process data input and output in order to integrate cognitive body to assimilative mind. Essentially, it's a transliteration processor operating the general function

$$y = f(x) \tag{19.6}$$

where function f maps x as *mind data* input to y as *neuronal data* output in which $x \mapsto y$. Mind $\mapsto$ brain is a one-to-many relationship; there isn't any brain ↦ mind relationship. Whatever the brain encounters, mind

---

328. For example, *human beingness* for humans and *nonhuman beingness* for nonhumans.

329. "That entity [of beingness engaged in the world] which in its Being has this very Being as an issue" (*Being and Time* 1962, 68).

has awareness since the brain is really just a single, high-density stimulus (say, a wholistic collection of stimuli) to mind in which

$$\text{ॐ} = \left\{ \{\text{Obj.Exp}\}, \{\text{人}\} \right\} \tag{19.7}$$

where ॐ is mind, objective experience is brain, 人 is personness (which includes subjective experience), and the equality is identity. The general function $y = f(x)$, therefore, also 'maps' ($\{\text{Obj.Exp.}\}, \{\text{人}\}$) to mind such that ॐ $= f(\{\text{Obj.Exp.}\}, \{\text{人}\})$ as awareness. Because it is awareness—a function of mind and not simply the brain mapping itself to mind as mind does with brain—then mind awareness isn't a brain $\mapsto$ mind relationship in which, per Eq. (19.6), x would be brain and y mind.

On the many side, brain is neuronal data sets and, on the one side, mind is awareness. Recall that mind is self-aware proto-energy, hence, unstructured (§ 6.11.4:198). There's no neuronal organization, no processing systems, and no causality chains as with the brain; just awareness. Biology achieves its awareness via cognitive processing, but it can only mimic mind awareness that needs no cognitive processing. The mind's sort of awareness is alien to the brain, like a disparate language. The brain needs must transliterate mind awareness into structured data sets it can parse, contextualize, utilize, temporarily store, and retrieve.[330] The reason is simply the reality of autonomous biology that functions through structure whereas 𝓛ife doesn't. What science presumes to be human brain cognition is simply the brain engaged in transliteration processing as well as own-self brain-body sensory and regulatory functions.

The body, being an objective entity, needs maintain itself as well as interface with 𝓛ife to provide a functioning person-platform in the natural environment. In this respect, it's essentially an 'avatar' (§ 3.3.3.1:289) and its brain works very much like a computer's random access memory (RAM) with limited storage capacity that, so long as the brain is alive, whatever it stores remains until 'overwritten' by brainstate reinstantiation (§ 1.2.2.4.2.1:258). All else being normal, brain capacity rises and falls according to the demands that mind places on it. This resolves the mystery of how the brain, which is plainly structurally limited, appears limitless in capacity and capability.

With mind, the instant that sense stimuli encounters consciousness it *is* consciousness and not processed *into* consciousness. It's mindness (*below*), not cognition. Incoming stimuli seamlessly become consciousness when, before, it wasn't consciousness and then, after, it is consciousness. The subjective experience of stimuli *is* WOB of consciousness. There's no difference between consciousness and subjective experience, it's not a property of consciousness but becomes consciousness. There's no cognitive process for mind, no cognition occurs. This is how a person 'just knows' something sans any corresponding stimuli or evidence of cognitive processing.[331] WOB just *becomes*. Stimuli and consciousness are synomic as WOB. Our experience is stimuli itself *as* awareness. When stimuli encounter our mind and become awareness, stimuli *is* our mind, meaning a stimulus is a micro-SOA in mind's macro-SOA. Referencing Eq. (17.98):199 and (18.12):235,

$$(S \leftrightarrow A) \rightarrow (S \leftrightarrow \text{ॐ}) \tag{19.8}$$

where S is stimuli, A is awareness, ॐ is mind, and the material equivalencies aren't identities. We have unfettered awareness only because of how stimuli interact with mind to *be* mind. Once encountered, stimuli are always part of mind as objective and subjective awareness–experience (§ 2.1.4:394).

This is why if we experience something in spirit world while physically alive, about which we become physically aware, it appears to us physically as innate or intuitive knowledge although, in reality, we're just physically unaware of the stimuli encounter and how it became part of our mind. It appears innate or intuitive because we don't experience the stimuli physically. As well, mind $\mapsto$ brain data transfer (integration) of spiritually acquired experience is of low awareness, meaning the brain's awareness is incomplete, lacking context, and so on (§ 1.2.2.5:261; § 2:393).

2.1.1 Mindness

This is the state in which a person is 'mind aware,' where their SOB is aware of mind awareness. It's a self-reflective state. We're aware of stimuli, self-aware of experiencing the stimuli, and subjectively aware of our

---

330. Here's the root of why dreams manifest as they do (§ 1.2.2.7.3:267), why we experience intuition, innate knowledge, perceive people watching us, and so on, and why all of it so often seems incomplete, sporadic, or variant from person to person.

331. Note that just because one 'knows' something as a matter of mind doesn't mean it's objectively accurate, as mind is not omniscience but subjective awareness.

subjective experience of stimuli. We don't experience physical stimuli objectively, our physical body does.[332] Suppose one's body objectively experiences a baseball striking its head. It's aware of the impact, assesses the body's resultant SOB, and responds with, e.g., swelling and hormonal secretions. That isn't mindness but *un*mindness (§ 2.2.2:279) because, even though integrating the person, the human body isn't *Life* in and of itself (as a person is) but only Living. If a baseball bounces off its head during sleep, the body nonetheless responds because that aspect of the nervous system never sleeps even though mind (the person) isn't *necessarily* aware of the injury at all before waking up. 'Necessarily,' because, when the body is asleep, a spirit-aware person is always self-aware, thus aware of its body's SOB. Upon waking, the injury isn't a surprise. This is one reason behind a sleeping person 'sensing' danger and physically waking up and the so-called sixth sense in general. The body itself isn't sensing danger. Its spirit-aware self who's aware of the body's environment and, upon perceiving approaching danger, forcibly (if they can) awakens their body. One who isn't spirit-aware can sleep through even a raging fire, as indeed do those who fall asleep smoking in bed yet fail to rouse themselves even when choking on smoke.

Mindness is one's subjective experience of an objective experience. But there isn't always an objective experience. Many times we subjectively experience invisible things like feelings, situations, or information that don't necessarily have an objective reality like a baseball cracking the skull, cold air on skin, or hunger pangs. Such invisible things are objective realities, but our body doesn't objectively experience them except in terms of our subjective experience. Hot flashes, tingles, a chill up the spine, and so forth are reflexive somatic responses triggered by our subjective mind response to stimuli. Since body integrates mind, it responds to mind's subjective reality of, say, fright with an objective, visceral reality we classify as fear and the fight-flight-freeze response. If one doesn't feel—subjectively experience—fear then one's body doesn't exhibit somatic responses we recognize as fear. Our awareness of intangible objective reality is a subjective experience in terms of own-self well-being.

Mindness informs own-self SOB which, in turn, informs own-self well-being. The subjective (not objective) experience of the baseball hitting one's head informs own-self well-being, the reason being that mind is only aware of the objective experience in terms of its subjective experience. Because we aren't our body then we (experiencing reality as mind) can't experience our body's experience as an objective reality. Even the body's in-house awareness of its SOB is the person's objective awareness. Mind can only be subjectively aware of that which the body is objectively aware; to consider it, self-reflect upon it, and choose to accept or ignore its reality as an objective somatic fact. That's mindness.

2.2   UNMIND

While *Life* mind is transcendent of body, unmind *is* body (Table 5:235) by which we mean brain, although as Living things devolve to primitivity then brain as a discrete thing gets more and more tenuous until the job is ultimately farmed out in distributed intelligence fashion. Living doesn't include human, though it does include our prima facie human body.[333] Living entities are sentient–sapient similar to emergent *Life* but it diminishes according to capacity, from complex primates and elephants all the way to pure automata like bacteria and virus. Nevertheless, even automata react to their environment with intelligence, which at that level we regard as, say, responsive mutation. Unmind is Living mind, but we can't call it *mind* because it lacks key attributes such as mindness, so instead we term it *unmind*.

Recall that unmind intelligence (unawareness) noncognitively perceives environmental reality, qualifies it w.r.t. own-self WOB in the context of the totality of environmental WOB, and applies a responsive (regulatory) course of action consistent with its various attributes (§ 1.3.2:273; Table 8). Unawareness is an aspect of unmind, so its function is a functional aspect of unmind. In referencing unmind, we reference its unawareness function. Likewise, in referencing unawareness, we reference its genesis in unmind.

The elements of Table 8 are straightforward but several bear comment. What separates humans from Living entities is that we are *Life*, which includes all that comprises humanness. Along with that comes self-awareness and our ability to be clinically aware of ourselves subjectively experiencing objective reality. Living entities lack this capability—awareness of self-awareness—having instead self-*un*awareness, which means the ability to

---

332. Though not one's spirit body; as a manifestation of mind, it's entirely subjective.

333. It's best to let go of thinking of our body as human since, practically speaking, it's just a biological 'avatar' for our person, and all that makes it 'human' is that it's suitable for integrating *Life*. In our ignorance of reality, we psychically connect to our body as *me* but it's not me, it's just a vehicle that permits me to interact with the natural environment. A vague comprehension of this reality forms the root of Buddhist and other traditions of enlightenment involving separating self from body.

Table 8. Significant aspects of unmind.

Nonhuman Unmind
Nonconscious
Noncognitive[a]
Non-self-aware (self-awareness)
Subjective experience of objective reality (brain function) → 'mind'
Emotion (brain function)
No neutral SOB; natural WOB disposition is 'negative' emotion

[a] Only the elephant, dolphin, bonobo, wolf (gray; Indian), and sperm whale are cognitive.

subjectively reflect on objective reality without awareness they're subjectively experiencing objective reality. Consequently, within its capability, a Living entity comprehends objective reality with a subjective perspective from which it relates objective reality to own-self SOB and, in turn, to own-self well-being. From this follows choice (§ 5.1:428).

2.2.1 NONCONSCIOUS CHOICE

Although Living choice is to varying degrees prescribed—available in its broadest capacity at the apex of Living and in its narrowest at Living's greatest primitivity—a Living entity nonetheless encounters choice in responding to objective reality. It might turn left or right, climb or not, eat this or that, colonize a space or keep searching, or adapt this way or that. Certain choices certainly appear more like faux choices as with adaptation,[334] but Living entities have a free will that operates within range bands. Within a given band, free will operates but outside that band, the capacity lessens by degrees to almost albeit never nil. A primate exercises greater free will, hence choice, over a broader range band than a mouse, itself in turn than a virus. Hence, with a rise in complexity from virus and bacteria, Living entities engage in less prescribed, preprogrammed faux choices and more and more in unprescribed, unpreprogrammed—though, until the highest complexity, essentially still preprogrammed—choice ranges that rest on some level of subjective analysis of own-self SOB and own-self well-being. Sometimes, own-self analysis leans toward maximizing own-self well-being. In other times, it leans toward what we'd call altruism or self-sacrifice—we see this in certain animals (sometimes riskily) helping other animals, including of other species, or animals controlling their affection to achieve outcomes—because, like humans, Living entities to varying degrees contextually define own-self and well-being in terms of not-me.

Own-self isn't just the cold, calculating, reasoning side of thought; it includes the emotive side, too. This partly explains animal helping and affection behaviors. Below the level of what we generally consider conscious thought w.r.t. to mammals lays subconscious (unconscious) thought. It's too abstract, vague—literally, too fast—as an act of mental awareness to classify as thinking although, technically, that's what it is. This aspect of Thought is Intentionality, meaning the Intentionalized seat of one's true SOB and own-self well-being. There's no correlation between emotion and SOB in mammals as with humans, hence, there's no humanlike neutral SOB. Mammalian dispositional WOB is non-positive, survival-oriented emotion although, as sophistication complexifies, so, too, does emotive range, which eventually includes non-survival-oriented emotion. This means certain mammals can *feel* at odds with their survival instincts, their biological imperative. Below mammals, there's no thought, only 'mental' awareness. Choice proceeds by range bands according to own-self, predefined within ranges by biological imperative.

2.2.2 UNMINDNESS

This is the state in which a Living entity is 'mind *un*aware,' its SOB aware of mind unawareness (§ 2.2.1.1:234). According to capability, it ranges from a self-reflective state, as with mindness, to a non-self-reflective state. It's aware of stimuli, of experiencing the stimuli, and subjectively aware of its resultant SOB; an experience of body status, for instance. As with humans, Living entities of any stripe don't experience stimuli objectively either, their physical body does. Unmindness is the entity's subjective experience of the objective experience even though, for most nonhumans, the subjective experience doesn't include thinking about the experience itself. Whatever learning occurs grows out of the subjective *experience* in terms of SOB and a sensation redolent with impression, not from considering or analyzing—thinking about—the objective reality. Like humans, Living

---

334. Science posits mutation from replication errors; therefore, mere chance. But sometimes, it results from Energent proto-energy's emergent environment where unexpected, unpredictable things happen not by chance but a confluence of possibilities that may or may not happen at any given moment in any given way. Too, humans affect mutative properties via Intentionality (§ 3.2.1:282).

entities of sufficient capacity don't subjectively experience only an objective reality but, sometimes, invisible things as well, like feelings, situations, or information. Unmindness informs own-self SOB which, in turn, informs own-self well-being. From determining and subjectively experiencing own-self well-being, a Living entity determines a course of action chosen from discrete options or by gravitating toward an option series in a preprogrammed range-band. Depending on an entity's capacity this can appear as self- or semi-self-awareness in the human sense, but it's just mimicry.

Unmindness is a body response to objective reality, let's say an impact as in our baseball analogy (§ 2.1.1:277). A Living entity of sufficient capacity subjectively experiences the pain of the strike, which means it's aware of the pain but not aware that it's aware of the pain. Suppose a rock strikes a chimpanzee in the head, thrown by another chimp. Grudges aren't unknown to chimps; neither revenge, plotting, nor war. Being aware of the subjective experience of the pain of the rock strike—*feeling* it—and later experiencing the memory that prompts retaliation (the memory mimicking a grudge), isn't human-level self-awareness of the experience, but animal self-awareness we term self-*un*awareness. Unawareness of the subjective experience of the objective reality for a mouse is entirely different from a chimp's as, too, is that of a cockroach, earthworm, or amoeba. Living entities are sentient–sapient in the same way as humans according only to the capacity of each. No Living entity, including the human body with its brain disengaged (de-integrated; § 3.3.2.1.2:286) from a person, rises to emergent 𝓛ife's *Da-sein*.

Section 3
Meaning of ♄uman

The methodology of assessing the nature and meaning of ♄uman traditionally subdivides into consciousness as with intellect–emotion, thinking–feeling, or awareness–self-awareness, and personness as with beingness, individuality, choice, uniqueness, or sanctity. This has borne no fruit whatsoever, and not just from a lack of real data but because it's biased toward describing the what-is in terms of the how-is which leads to conclusions that the what-it-does and how-it-does-it must necessarily be the human *raison d'être* and, hence, its what-is. This reasoning underpins materialism, which is obvious, but spiritualism, too, which is less so. The reason is that, for religion—theism and atheism[335] alike—the human rationale embodies the seeming contradiction between two essential functionalities, often erroneously interpreted from mind–body confusion as some aspect of dual beingness. The first is the sacred tending toward spiritual awareness and higher instinct (morality) and feeling like love, worship of, or attendance to, a higher power or personified God, and so forth. The second is the profane tending toward physical awareness and lower, base instinct (amorality, immorality) and feeling like hate, repudiation of a higher power or personified God, and so on. Religion's emphasis on these disparate functionalities that render us creatures of disparate natures, thus of disparate humanness—elevated on the one hand, debased on the other—mirrors materialism's own duality that emphasizes our higher reasoning and baser instincts and leaves us in the same state. Each one's cure for the duality is functional, or rooted in function, rather than personness. Religion's lies in salvific, and materialism's in evolutionary, change.

The ℘erson is 𝓛ife, a self-existent of thinking, feeling, translating,[336] uniqueness, choice, and kinship. The first three terms typically reference consciousness, and the second three, personness. We categorize each set of three as *nature, way,* and *function* of existence. ℘erson defines 𝓛ife; 𝓛ife becomes ℘erson. Hence, Eq. (19.1):245. Thinkers traditionally distinguish two functional states of the person: awareness and existence, each of which comprises their own many subfunctions. The former is loosely defined as consciousness and the latter as beingness, which is (to say without the paucity) personness. These functionalities of self-existent 𝓛ife wholistically constitute consciousness and personness. Without such wholism, each aspect separately is merely Living, not 𝓛ife; not ♄uman. Since Philosophy with a capital-P generally wraps the ethereal notion of being—the person—in a functional veneer of consciousness, let's parse that toward the meaning of ♄uman.

3.1 Consciousness

When we wonder what consciousness is, what it means, where it comes from, why we have it, how it operates, and all our other wonderments, it all boils down to emergent 𝓛ife. Consciousness isn't a function of the brain

---

335. For Mina, atheism strictly as a technical matter involves denial, rejection, or evasion of higher powers, God, gods, or divinity; ergo, Buddhism, Tao, Confucianism, and the like are atheistic ideologies regardless their spiritual affluence.

336. Here, *translating* means motion, not rooted; no barriers to form, condition, nature, et cetera.

or even of mind. It's not awareness or self-awareness. It isn't "the filter through which we view and interpret the environment around us" (Tattersall 1998, 190) nor even "at its simplest . . . 'sentience or awareness of internal or external existence' " (Wikipedia *Consciousness* 2020, par. 1). Even the concept's arguable etymology in the Latin *conscius sibi*, meaning 'knowing with oneself,' or 'sharing knowledge with oneself about something' (ibid, *Etymology*, par 2), is a functional descriptor, telling us nothing of what consciousness is but only (some of) what it does. Consciousness befuddles us because thinkers only perceive, hence rationalize, it through its functions. That's a useful endeavor comprehending a machine. For example, a hammer's functionality reveals it as a pounder and that's its what-is; the collective functionality of a car reveals it as a conveyance and that's its what-is. But the collective functionality of consciousness is . . . what? We wander back into *maschinenfunktionalität*, useless for gleaning knowledge of the what-is of consciousness and, of course, ꃐuman.

Philosophy with a capital-P has no meaningful ontological concept of consciousness because, like the blind men and the elephant, philosophers acontextually describe it piecemeal. Yet, the whole of the thing defies its parts just as the elephant defies each of its parts when taken as functional singletons acontextual of the whole animal. Defining consciousness as an emergent property gets us nowhere, too, because this describes it in terms of function and not as what it is. Such acontextuality glaringly provokes the mind–body problem, a self-made controversy borne of empirical obstinance, conceptual bias, and an overall lack of data where consciousness as functionality plays a leading role. Well, we've seen the importance of context in which the Energent's contextual interaction with matter–Energy determines the forces and effects that obtain in the universe (§ 2:114). Contextuality is just the boning knife we need here.

Earlier, we said consciousness is personness (Introduction, CH. 17:111). That seems to suggest conjointness, as with a two-sided coin, but that's incorrect and anyhow leads us back into functionality. Tempting as it is, we can't use the coin metaphor here as it implies two discrete things conjoined by a medium: the coin between its faces. While consciousness and personness are indeed discrete aspects of humanness, they don't conjoin humanness as a medium. That's because, when observing the obverse or reverse of a coin, one perceives only the one face and not its complement nor even the whole coin, whereas when observing consciousness, one perceives personness and vice versa in the totality of humanness. Neither can we say they're two elements of the same set {ꃐuman} such that ꃐ = {c, p}, and for the same reasons.

Instead, consciousness and personness is the same thing: *humanness*. When we describe humanness, we consequently can do so in terms of consciousness or personness and still be talking about *both* in context of the whole. Consciousness cognizes personness and vice versa; we need observe just the one to know the other. A coin's obverse, on the other hand, can't cognize its reverse, we need observe it directly to perceive, thus know, anything about it. Consciousness and personness each represent a different *essentiality* of humanness but aren't different *things*, like differently stamped faces of a coin or distinct elements of a set. For example, if we functionalize consciousness as introspection, then a unique inner life is implicit, which informs us of personness. If we functionalize personness as individual sanctity, then self-awareness is implicit, which informs us of consciousness. Inherent when taken together is humanness, the totality of the person. They're the same thing yet aren't, which means they aren't simply differently stamped like the two sides of a coin. Consciousness *is* humanness in one context, and personness *is* humanness in another. Consciousness is functionality of self; personness is beingness of self. The former is functionality of being and the latter individuality of being. Therefore, we begin with

$$\odot = 人 \tag{19.9}$$

where ⊙ is consciousness (Eq. (18.12):235), 人 is personness (Eq. (18.20):241; Eq. (19.1):245), and the equality is identity, which means they're integrated, not two sides to the same coin or two elements of the same set. They *are* the coin. They *are* the set. There's no boundary as with face or element. The integration is humanness. Accordingly, we build out Eq. (19.9) as

$$(\odot = 人) \Leftrightarrow ⷀ \tag{19.10}$$

where the terms are per Eq. (19.9), the Ethiopic letter ⷀ [*pä*] (Eq. (18.12):235) represents ꃐuman, and the logical equivalence isn't identity. In toto, humanness is *Life* and vice versa. This definition is all that matters because nothing else *can* define ꃐuman (which isn't the biology of our body, recall) but only functionally describe it. Consequently, we finalize Eq. (19.10) per Eq. (18.12):235 as

$$ⷀ \Leftrightarrow ⷎ \tag{19.11}$$

where the Egyptian hieroglyph ☥ [*ankh*] represents emergent ℒife, the equivalence isn't identity, and ℒife is ℌuman; ergo, nonhuman Living (biology) doesn't—can't—possess ℒife.

The upshot is that consciousness isn't definable as something with function, or a functional something. Rather, it's definable in its context, which is integration of humanness. The functionality Philosophy with a capital-P traditionally ascribes to consciousness is properly the domain of ℒife. If we say, "Consciousness or the individual is this or that or has this or that functionality," then we're not properly referencing consciousness and personness but ℒife itself, because ℒife is ℌuman and ℌuman is ℒife. This means we can't properly explore consciousness and personness—its nature, function, existence, or any such thing—in the milieu typical of its inquiry by Philosophy with a capital-P because it's acontextual of ℒife, the ultimate human context. If we divide consciousness and personness with rigorous distinction, we get each as functionality, meaning what each does, but not what each is. Therefore, we can't say what consciousness is—its what-is—because it doesn't have it. As an essentiality of ℌuman, consciousness *is* functionality in and of itself. So, consciousness without personness or personness without consciousness is Living, not ℒife. 'Consciousness is personness' and vice versa means ℌuman, ergo ℒife. That's the indivisible what-is of consciousness and personness: ℒife.

3.2 Psyche Fundamental Force

It might seem odd but we, as emergent ℒife, generate fundamental force ourselves. Not the natural environment's Fundamental Force (FF) we previously described (§ 1:112), but *Psyche Fundamental Force* (PFF) which operates in space similarly to FF. Indeed, as matter is to matter–Energy, *Intentionality* is to ℒife (Table 9); matter arises from intrinsic matter–Energy and Intentionality arises from intrinsic ℒife. The practical outcome is that matter–Energy interacts with Energent proto-energy that gives rise to FF and exerts in space as EMF, SNF, WNF, and all the rest to organize, build, and maintain our universe.[337]

Intentionality, on the other hand, interacts with Energent–prime and the natural and supranatural Energent's proto-energy giving rise to PFF which then exerts in space as ideated and emotive Intentionality. This is why we have a sense we can will things to happen or know and experience another's thinking–feeling. It's not magic, after all; derivable principles underlie such phenomena. As matter–Energy is autonomous archí force (EN 145:657), Intentionality is autonomous ℒife force although, while archí force is unaware (not having ℒife), emergent ℒife force—the person—is self-aware (having ℒife). Although this overall analogy is useful as a visualizing tool, the two couldn't be more different. Whereas archí operate as automata, Intentionality operates directedly from a person's autonomous mind.

Table 9. Comparison between archí and ℒife forces.

matter–Energy	Intentionality
Fundamental Force FF	Psyche Fundamental Force PFF
Matter	Person
Energent proto-energy	Energent–prime/Nat–Supra Energent
EMF, SNF, WNF, &c.	INF (Ideated, emotive exertion); SWF, FMF
Automata	Autonomous
Not ℒife	ℒife
Archí force (not self-aware)	Emergent ℒife force (self-aware)
Undirected	Directed

3.2.1 How PFF Works

Intentionality Force (INF, or Intentionality; Table 9) is the principle PFF with two secondaries, Switch Force (SWF) and Form Force (FMF). Like EMF or SNF, INF is the product of the interaction between a force and proto-energy. With matter, FF arises out of the interaction between archí force composited from a matter–Energy structure and Energent proto-energy. With Thought, PFF arises out of the interaction between emergent ℒife force[338] composited from a Thought structure and Energent proto-energy in the natural environment or supranatural (facsimile) proto-energy in the supranatural one (§ 7.1:212). The natural FF complement to INF is Métier Force, which mediates relative, or best/most-suited, strength of interaction between objects of

---

337. The supranatural (spirit) environment has a similar albeit different setup.

338. Emergent ℒife force, which constitutes the ℘erson, is the reason we hear and feel—experience—our own thoughts, but Intentionality is the reason other persons, as well as brain-capable Living entities, can also indirectly experience our thoughts. This same principle applies to manipulating matter (NATURAL INTENTIONALITY, § 2:518).

matter (ibid). The other two PFF are SWF which analogizes to SNF and FMF which analogizes to WNF. The analogy is categorical, not functional.

In the natural environment context, FF determines how matter interacts, what it can composite into, how it composites, how it breaks down or reconfigures, and so on as mediated by Métier and other FF. This behavior qualifies as Intentionality, but it's only a simulacrum because it's purely automatic, the outcome determined by the natural forces in play. PFF, however, injects a directed modifier into FF that enables an at-will (Intentionalized) modification to FF behavior. This means the forces of nature respond to mind's Intentionality.[339] For example, InF in conjunction with SWF and FMF (which toggle SNF on and off and modify quark flavour, respectively) can assemble or disassemble composite archí configurations at will, however tedious (Fig. 94:218).[340] This is the functional outcome when Mina intervenes via Intentionality with the nominal functioning of our universe to enable or disable modifications, such as making the genetic changes necessary to jack our brains to ∼700 billion neurons (§ 1.2.2.5:261). Even so, not even Mina can violate the intrinsic principles of Energent proto-energy; it's immutable. Whatever he or any spirit or physical person does, PFF operates not contrarily to, but in accord with, the Energent principles of our universe underlying all its natural forces, howsoever magical or deitic such Intentionalized events may appear to our uninformed observation.

Intentionality acts in about a picosecond. One builds Intentionality as Thought until, fully formed, PFF reaches its critical moment which, in a picosecond, Intentionalizes Thought into reality. It takes effect in the spirit environment immediately and in the physical environment over time—for example, when composing material form out of matter constituents or inducing genetic changes.

3.2.2 God Speaking Creation into Existence

All Thought is Intentionality to varying degrees. Communicating Thought (§ 4.4.1:294)—verbal, written, gesticulative—is also Intentionality. When religion talks about God speaking creation into existence (Gen. 1:3, Ps. 33:9; Quran 2:117, 41:11$_{26_5}$), it's really referencing Intentionality. One needn't actually speak, or communicate, to Intentionalize a thought because Intentionality is intrinsic of it, inseparable, such that

$$T \leftrightarrow InF \tag{19.12}$$

where T is Thought, InF is Intentionality Force, and the material equivalence isn't identity; if there's one, there's the other. The Judeo-Christo-Islamic tradition sees God's mind as the creative agency for existence, and that's certainly true enough since any universe has its builder. But a deitic *god* isn't who creates a universe; rather, an emergent person who's trained the natural, intrinsic capacity of his or her 𝓛ife mind to Intentionalize on a universal scale does (§ 5.2:296). This is Jesus' thinking where John 10:34 quotes him saying, "you are gods;" what we are *now* isn't what we intrinsically *are*.

3.3 Self-organized WoB

Does 𝓛ife arise preprogrammed? In a sense, it does, but it doesn't lock us in as is the case with anything Living. A bacteria, worm, or monkey can't change *how* it is, but we can. A computer metaphor is helpful here. We might think of WOB as the human operating system (OS) written and pre-initialized during 𝓛ife's emergent self-organization that boots up at process completion—phase three of conception (§ 1.2.2.1:253)—and runs in the central processing unit (CPU), which is our consciousness.[341] The OS doesn't compile into machine code, because that'd make it uneditable without a shutdown, recompile, and reboot. 𝓛ife doesn't do that for obvious reasons. Instead, our OS is more like a runtime interpreter with a set of libraries and such, all of which is editable at-will via 𝓛ife's force of Intentionality as mobilized by mind. The interpreter analyzes each line of code in context with the OS in toto, initializes or reinitializes this or that as necessary, then interprets and executes. Core OS modules and subroutines are locked in terms of *how* they execute but not in *what*. If it wasn't locked, we could alter our WOB in such a way as to make existence impossible and we'd irretrievably system crash—experience 𝓛ife death—with no coming back. Emergent 𝓛ife self-organized away from that. For example, while our mind is a core OS module of 𝓛ife proto-energy 'hardware,' the *content* of our mind,

---

339. Not just any old *intention*; actual Intentionality.

340. Visualize *Star Trek*'s transporter or food materializer operated not by a machine but a mind.

341. Keep in mind that computer metaphors don't imply reality, they merely help us visualize it.

without which we'd be just an empty husk, is more a library of OS 'software' that we can rewrite down to the nub until all that's left is structure.

This is why we observe in ourselves seemingly preprogrammed instincts, behaviors, needs, wants, or dispositions that Philosophy with a capital-P ascribes to our physically evolving *into* human with an immutable human nature but which, in truth, are self-organized traits intrinsic of Energent proto-life that self-organizes into a unique being having these traits. The cool bit is that these traits are fully editable. They don't lock humans into just one type of WOB. One can even 'terminate' one's own existence, after a fashion. This involves a system shutdown, to use the computer metaphor. Like any computer, one's OS can reboot, but not by the OS itself. An external agency is needed the way a car engine requires a battery and starter motor. A computer needs an always-on mechanism that, when a certain condition obtains, triggers programming that powers up and initiates the OS boot sequence. The unembodied mind who 'suicides'—effectively shuts down their ℒife mind—obviously lacks such a reboot mechanism, so it's essentially lights out, although Mina says such a person can theoretically reboot (wake up again). In this case, the external agency would be another person who can find their specific ℒife in the greater matrix of ℒife amongst Energent proto-life (EPL) 'wherein' all emergent ℒife resides (e.g., a 'server farm;' § 2.3.2.1:241), and then actually do the job. There are persons who've 'suicided' this way—Mina says it's not 'suicide' since technically their ℒife is only in stasis but, you know, tomayto tomahto—whose still-extant-though-now-dormant ℒife some members of the Cardinal have attempted (without success) to locate.

3.3.1 What Makes Us Human

All that aside, we're human regardless how we look, act, think, or exhibit 'human' traits, because what makes us human aren't those attributes but simply ℒ*ife*, which is ꜱuman. We *are* that ℒife, ergo, we *are* human. It begins in EPL but uniquely self-organizes *as* ℒife into a being *having* ℒife and is, therefore, human howsoever it manifests from one day to the next. Regardless how an individual rewrites their WOB into some vicious, hateful, sliming, acid spitting, giant purple people-eating disposition, they have ℒife; they're human. There are no such scary sapient life forms in any universe. Persons you'd meet on another planet or universe are recognizably human howsoever unrecognizable they may appear in, say, culture or thinking patterns. All the colors, sizes, shapes, appearances, personalities, styles, and so on aren't the inevitable outcome of evolution or physiological experience—though it plays a part—but of emergent ℒife and human Intentionality, which loves variation. What humanity calls ethnicity or race, and believes exclusively arises in biology, is human-Intentionalized variation like automotive paint jobs and body styles. Mina himself (as with the spirit-born) has the ethnicity his parents or he himself later chose, and it's intrinsically mutable. This means you can alter *your* ethnicity. On a scale of 1–10, with ten the most tediousness (Fig. 94:218), altering your spirit body's ethnicity is two, and the physical body's, five.

3.3.2 Proto-love

Nevertheless, human is a loose sort of term because it has nothing to do with biology, species, qualia, or divine creation. ℒife with WOB is all human really is. It fundamentally manifests four attributes that collectively comprise humanness, three of which—consciousness, personness, freedom—we've already described. The fourth is *proto-love*. That sounds trite—because, when hasn't someone pushed love as our holy grail?—but it's fundamental to WOB and foundational to humanness, just not in the way Philosophy with a capital-P imagines. Accordingly, and referring back to Eq. (19.10):281,

$$(\odot \cong \text{plove} \bigwedge 人 \cong \text{freedom}) \Leftrightarrow 유 \qquad (19.13)$$

where congruence and logical equivalence aren't identity, and *plove* is proto-love expressed as primary-emotion love, not proto-love itself (Table 10).

Proto-love is ℒife force the same way Intentionality is (§ 2.3.2.2:242).[342] We can certainly alter proto-love in, and with considerable effort even rewrite it entirely out of, our WOB but otherwise it's foundational (§ 3.3:283). The ordinary love we feel in everyday life emanates from proto-love, and *it is our base disposition*. There's a reason human fetuses don't chow down on their fraternal twin or, like sand tiger sharks, on the other seven octuplets in the womb, and it's this fundamental, emergently self-organized disposition. It gives us an innate, intrinsic understanding of love that inclines us ever to seek it. Humans have such a rich tapestry of emotion because all feeling derives from proto-love.[343] Absent the abnormality (§ 1.2.1.3:252), we spontaneously recognize

---

342. The Cardinal doesn't comprehend proto-love's *vitae mysterium* any better—in fact less—than it comprehends Intentionality's.

and experience love. We henceforth define lowercase 'love' as its ordinary feeling and expression; all-caps 'LOVE' as the base emotion from which all feeling emotes; and 'proto-love' as *Life* force from which LOVE instantiates. Lowercase love is LOVE's *primary* expression whereas hate is *secondary* (Table 10). Proto-love isn't 'love' in any sense; it's simply the emotive aspect having a fundamental quality that humanity associates with the 'higher' (foundationally desired) aspects of human feeling. We could just as well call it 'corn chips' because "That which we call a rose/By any other name would smell as sweet" (Shakespeare *Romeo and Juliet*, 2:2:11–12).

Table 10. Categories of emotion.

Categories of Human Emotion	
Emotion Type	Category Type
Proto-love	*Life* force
Emotion	The Force of *Life* force
Feeling	Our experience of Emotion
LOVE	Base, foundational
Lowercase love	Primary emotion
Lowercase hate + all other emotions	Secondary (combinatory) emotion

Ordinary emotion like love, hate, and everything else expresses from LOVE, which instantiates in a person from proto-love. Emotion doesn't magically arise; it comes from somewhere and gets its observable energy, its *oomph*, from something. That somewhere and something is *emotive Life force* (§ 3.3.3.1.1:289) and its nature is proto-love *Life* force, the same *Life* force giving rise to Intentionality and enlivening biology to aliveness (Table 11).[344] Emotion itself is a force of *Life* force, meaning it's a felt exertion in the world. Feeling, on the other hand, is our *experience of emotion*, the way it contextually exerts in each of us.

Table 11. Aspects of *Life* Force that arise from Energent proto-life.

Life Force		
Proto-love Force	Psyche Fundamental Force	Way of Being Force
	Intentionality	Emotive *Life* Force
	Switch Force (SwF)	Living Force (vital energy)
	Form Force (FmF)	

3.3.2.1 LOVE, HATE, INDIFFERENCE

While love and hate are both proto-love, indifference is not. We describe the latter first.

3.3.2.1.1 INDIFFERENCE

Indifference isn't an emotion thus isn't a neutral emotion. It's a SOB devoid of both empathy and malignity and accordingly non-emotive, meaning it doesn't emote. As such, it doesn't stand on neutral ground between positive love and negative hate because there isn't any such ground since *Life* itself *is* emotion, an aspect of Thought that we call proto-love. Hence, one doesn't *feel* indifferent but is simply *aware* of their SOB in this context that, w.r.t. to indifference, is a SOB absent empathy and malignity. 'Feeling indifferent' is really just uninformed shorthand for this awareness. There's nothing wrong with being aware of one's indifference. It's our freedom to 'feel' howsoever we feel. There's no obligation to love or not to hate. WOB doesn't compel us. Although emotion itself is a natural human existent, unless we rewrite our WOB to exclude it—say, to become a person whose base disposition is indifference—we're free to choose how or if we emote. There's no judgment, no good–evil duality, no applicable compulsory standard at all. Causing harm is the only differentiator and is contextual anyhow; it's between the harmer and harmed howsoever each contextually defines own-self.

---

343. Spirit persons experience a richer emotive experience (or, as Ayako said, they "feel so much more intensely;" § 1.4:65) because they don't have our limited mind–brain integration interposing between their mind and its expression.

344. For example, when we make a plan we're Intentionalizing our thoughts, energizing them with *Life* force. It isn't simply the act of planning, preparation, or organizing our thoughts that boosts our effort but Intentionality.

3.3.2.1.2   Love and Hate

As with everything in ℒife, LOVE is freedom, so paradoxically it also produces what we call hate. As a secondary, ordinary emotion to love as the primary emotion, hate is the antithesis of love. But they aren't mirror images because their 'energy' is identical, differentiating in only a single aspect: context. Lowercase love is LOVE applied in one context whereas hate is LOVE applied in an antithetical context. Lowercase love's context is direct love a → b whereas hate's context is direct love a → b *via* c such that

$$a \rightarrow \}c\{ \rightarrow b \qquad\qquad (19.14)$$

where no-set }c{ (§ 2.1.1:231) represents an interposition on direct love a → b, and the equation overall describes the }c{ force necessary to restore a → b (*Fig. 121*). The 'energy' of love a → b is directly proportional to the 'energy' needed to remove interposition }c{, which 'energy'—being the equal and opposite 'energy' of LOVE—is }love{, which is called *hate*. We see the same dynamic in Newton's third law of motion, where a force exerted by body A on body B as F_{AB} results in an equal and opposite force by body B on body A such that $F_{AB} = -F_{BA}$. In classical physics, the equal and opposite $-F_{BA}$ isn't a *different* force than F_{AB}, it's the same, merely *contextualized*, applied energy E force. Similarly, F_{love} and F_{hate} are the same, merely contextualized, LOVE force.

In practical terms, love and hate is when we fully embrace (integrate) or reject (de-integrate) something as own-self (§ 2:275). Our intensity integrating or de-integrating defines whether the emotion that's 'energizing' our feeling is love–hate, like–dislike, and so forth. For example, de-integrating an object of hate from own-self is conceptually commensurate with the force one might use to physically move an object (of hate) like a box or a person blocking one from reaching another object (of love). The force we use to move the undesired, blocking object equals the emotive force we feel—our intensity—for reaching the desired, blocked object. Accordingly, one might remove the blocking object slowly with gentleness from between oneself and the blocked object, or rapidly with violent or excessive force. Gentle or violent, either one is the same physical applied energy E force, just as love or hate is the same emotive LOVE force.

When a person loves—and this is the case with any emotion, not just love—they're caring about the happiness of an entity that's alive: their own, another's, or both. Happiness is a state of being (SOB), and it's with this SOB that LOVE is concerned (§ 7:441). When a person emotes, the object of their emotion's SOB reflects it in some way, either with appreciation, recognition, acknowledgement, indifference, hostility, and so forth. The response contributes to the lover's SOB and, overall, a mutual SOB (Fig. 119). It's the condition of ℒife that when the SOB doesn't reflect one's feeling, there's a dissatisfaction having the same practical outcome as an open circuit. The notion of agape[345] as love's highest ideal in which no response is needed, deserved, or even moral from the inferior object of love to the superior giver of love (e.g., God to Man) is wholly false, an invention of moralists to control others by manipulating their most fundamental instinct toward an unachievable standard. It's no surprise the only humans ever to express agape love are those who derive satisfaction from the SOB it produces, such as Jesus, Sun-myung, a soldier jumping on a grenade, and self-sacrifice generally. Let's consider three aspects of love from which hate derives.

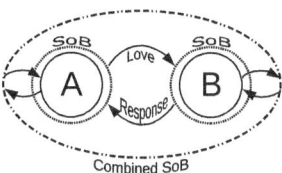

Figure 119. The various states of being (SOB) from emoting.

First aspect. Suppose there are persons A, B, and C. Let A love B, and along comes C whom A perceives as harm to B as AB. A's love for B mandates some response to C to protect B, which A feels to be an expression of love for B. Ordinarily, we might say A restrains C's harm toward B verbally or physically. But suppose those options aren't available or anyhow are ineffective. A's feeling toward C, directly energized by love for B, mutates for a variety of reasons from perhaps initially neutral or friendly (a form of love) into hate *in proportion to* A's love for B. Whatever form A's hate for C takes, it's an expression of A's love for B and not, as we commonly

---

345. Defined as selfless, asexual love such as that of God or Christ for humanity.

imagine, A's hate for C. A's love for B is a direct, primary expression of LOVE whereas A's observed hate for C is an indirect, secondary expression of LOVE; indirect, because A's hate for C indirectly expresses A's love for B. In this first aspect of the love–hate scenario, A hates C as an expression of love for B, which means the practical outcome of A's love for B w.r.t. C is hate.

Second aspect. There's a little more involved than simply A's hate for C being A's indirect love for B, because it's the SOB that are the proper objects of love w.r.t. emotion, not the relationships, even though for the person, their object of love or hate is another person (or alive entity). Let's continue with the above scenario. Along comes C whom A perceives as harm to the collective, or combined, SOB AB that we define as follows. It might seem that a wholly altruistic A, who loves B only for the sake of B's happiness, will only be motivated vis-à-vis C by B's individual SOB and not A's own, but that isn't typical human reality. Regardless A's altruism, however, there's a SOB that obtains between A and B, which is the SOB AB (*Fig. 119*). This SOB is as automatic as daylight in the day or mind awareness from stimuli (§ 2.1:276). So long as SOB AB is consonant with A's own SOB, A's motivation reflects SOB AB overall—B's individually and, with the most altruistic benefit of the doubt, A's least of all. A isn't motivated by the *me* aspect (SOB A) of SOB AB, but by *own-self well-being* which, in this scenario, is SOB AB (§ 2:275) and may or may not involve A's own SOB, though it certainly includes SOB B. This doesn't make A's love for B necessarily egocentric, but simply reflects that A's SOB is indelibly affected by B's own SOB, as well as SOB AB. Understanding this, we see that A's hate for C is the indirect result not so much of A's love for person *B* but of A's love for *SOB AB* which *includes* person B.

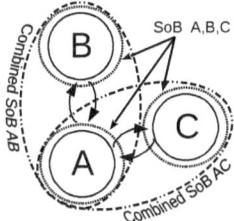

Figure 120. SOB that obtains between objects of love AB and hate AC.

Third aspect. Whatever the reason for hate, it's always motivated by love for something that's perceived to mandate moving a blocking object, the force of which, practically speaking, is }love{, meaning hate. Hate for an object-of-hate results from love for an object-of-love. We reuse the above scenario. Along comes C whom A perceives as harm to SOB AB. C has a SOB, too, and the object of hate's discomfiture is of value to the hater. Genuine hate—not faux hate that's just a mix of emotions—seeks the hated's suffering in whatever form it might take and howsoever induced. The emotive relationship between A, B, and C creates SOB ABC in which each person has their own SOB as well as a relational SOB (*Fig. 120*).

For example, A's SOB includes SOB AB and AC, and possibly BC, depending on those parties' interaction; similar SOB obtain for B and C. Now, besides SOB AB that, for A, expresses A's love for B, there's SOB AC that expresses A's hate for C. Just as A derives a certain SOB from loving B—let's say it's a happy, satisfied, fulfilled SOB—so, too, does A derive a certain SOB from hating C, and let's say that it, too, induces a SOB that's happy, satisfied, and fulfilled so long as A's hate for C is coming off well and no tables are being turned. In this case, A *loves* SOB AC because A loves whatever suffering C experiences. This happens because the }love{ relationship mirrors the {love} relationship and, hence, there's feeling. One enjoys removing the blocking object SOB AC because it restores, or enhances, SOB AB.

But let's suppose C does turn the tables and now A's infliction of suffering on C is blocked. Maybe C enjoys suffering (like Bill Murray's dental patient in *Little Shop of Horrors*, 1986), or maybe C is inflicting greater suffering on A than A is inflicting on C, or perhaps other possibilities. Bottom line, A isn't necessarily loving SOB AC so much at the moment, but A does find *hope* in re-turning the tables, gaining the upper hand, and resuming C's suffering in some satisfying way. Regardless the scenario that plays out—as we all know, relationships of emotion are complex—the hater *loves* the SOB the hated experiences and invests all of his or her love into experiencing their hated's SOB. This means that, to the degree A is committed to hating C, A is invested in SOB AC and loves it; A's love of SOB AC motivates continuing it (*Fig. 121*).[346] In short, this aspect of hate is motivated by the hater's love of the SOB the hated experiences, and the SOB the hater him- or herself experiences.

---

346. It's common that people pointlessly stoke hate after its *raison d'être* fades because of the pleasure, satisfaction, love, obsession, pain, suffering, or habituation of the hate relationship which they don't let go.

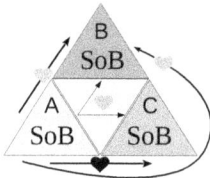

Figure 121. States of being (SOB) that obtain between objects of hate AC where ♡ is love and ♥ is hate.

Even though an object-of-love and an object-of-hate seem diametric, they're not. LOVE is what we're expressing since the only *L*ife force behind LOVE, thus all emotion, is proto-love. There is no proto-hate *L*ife force, no proto-any-emotion, for that matter. Just proto-love (§ 3.3.3.1:289). The reason we hate what we hate is that we love what we love. The lover and hater are both lovers because both engage in love. Hate is simply love's contextualized practical outcome. It takes a completed circuit, a relational force, for emotion to emote no matter how unrequited or individually emoted. (For more discussion in the context of suffering, see § 8.1.2.1:445.)

3.3.2.2   PROTO-LOVE 'FLOWS' THROUGH OUR UNIVERSE AS PROTO-ENERGY

Just as Thought (thinking–feeling) as a *L*ife force Intentionalizes proto-energy to manipulate matter, proto-love as *L*ife force Intentionalizes proto-energy to infuse it with this *L*ife force energy, which is proto-love. Since humans experience love within themselves all the time and also are Intentional beings, then each person's love, which is proto-love energy, automatically Intentionalizes Energent proto-energy in and about each person. This means that love as feeling exudes not simply into but *becomes* the proto-energy in and around each person. Effectively, love exudes throughout our universe from all humanity and touches all humanity within. Just as there's proto-energy in motion, there's love in motion. Every physical and spirit embodied person experiences it.

It differs, however, from the love we experience from a person or persons such as family, spouse, love partner, friends, and so on. We experience this Intentionalized proto-love more like the ineffable love we might suddenly feel that, to our minds, is from God, angels, the Universe, unseen forces, Mother Earth, and the like. It infuses us to the degree we're subconsciously—in our true self—open to experiencing it. When we subconsciously desire to feel or know God's, or any, love greater than our own, then suddenly we're aware of that proto-energy love as our mind opens to it and sensitizes our physical body. Like an antenna, it funnels the particular 'signal' into our minds where we experience it, for instance, as the mystery of God's love. Though we naturally tend to attribute such a love experience to God or maybe 'angels,' in reality it's the collective love of humanity throughout our universe of which our mindstate has only just become aware because, in effect, our subconscious desire tuned our mind to its 'energy' signature. Some religious people spend their lives fine-tuning their minds to this aspect of proto-energy, but it's notoriously fleeting for the physical embodied. The spirit-born experience this universal love of humanity the same way as described, except their spirit bodies, being Intentionalized manifestations of mind, aren't involved.

Proto-love exuding from humanity is common to all universes of the megaverse (TODAY'S FAMILY OF UNIVERSES, § 2.1.4.1:312), but our ability to tune our minds to it and experience that collective love is unique to our own. Cosmo discovered its existence, the proto-energy 'frequency' at which the human mind synchronizes with it to experience it, and taught Mina how to correctly 'frequency-tune' the Energent during the Intentionalizing phase of building our universe (§ 1.2.1.1:338; § 2.1.1.4:369). The 'energy' of love is the combination of all emotive 'energy' the way black is the combination of all colors.

3.3.3   SENTIENCE–SAPIENCE

The classical essence of sentience is the ability to feel or perceive sensory stimulus—a general awareness of environment including own-self and the ability to process sensation at some level of subjective impression (§ 1.3.2.1.2.1:274)—and of sapience, to think. As we've seen, all Living entities experience sentience according to capability, but they think, too, in a manner that's a sort of sensation redolent with impression (§ 4.4:294). Effectively, then, sentience–sapience are terms nominally applicable to all Living entities but don't describe *L*ife, which is human. Hence, we employ *Da-sein* to describe sentience–sapience more holistically (§ 2:275). Although the human brain has *Da-sein*, *L*ife mind goes well beyond it because, not only do humans think as *Da-sein*, but we also formulate coherent, articulable, subjectively subjective thoughts—ideation and emotion— empowered with Intentionality.

Humans don't distinctly think and feel but are thoughtful: ideative and emotive. Thinking carries emotion and vice versa. There's no severability twixt them. One feels ideation, and feeling is ideated. There's no state of absolute rationality. That's a fiction, a philosophers' stone of artificial intelligence, the *Cintamani* of the bodhisattvas. What some call cold, calculated reason is, in reality, simply indifferent Thought in the terms we described (§ 3.3.2.1.1:285). Ideation, what we typically consider thinking, is conscious Thought whereas emotion is unconscious Thought that assembles from our many micro- and macro-SOA which are too infinite for us to ideate. They both arise emergently and as organized calculation, though we're generally quite unaware, if not perplexed, why or how we're emoting compared to ideating. The reason is the largely unconscious nature of Thought (§ 4.2:292). Although we're not usually aware of it, we certainly can be if we choose. As with conscious Intentionality, emotion unconsciously Intentionalizes proto-energy to exert in ourselves as well as our environment. What we feel in ourselves, and call emotion and its reaction, is our unconscious Thought Intentionalizing proto-energy. This process is *base emotion*.

3.3.3.1 BASE EMOTION

There aren't 6, 8, 27, 32, or any number of base (primary) human emotions than just the one: proto-love. Feeling of any stripe derives from proto-love according to where, how, and in what amount and context we focus LOVE. Recall from Eq. (17.98–17.101):199 and (18.12–18.13):235–235 that mind and consciousness as well as consciousness and Thought are each congruent. Emotion (feeling) and reason (thinking) thus don't comprise two separate states of mind but the single state of Thought (thinking–feeling), in that

$$(\epsilon \cong R) \Leftrightarrow T \tag{19.15}$$

where ϵ is emotion, R is reason, T is Thought, and the congruence and logical equivalence isn't identity. Emotion is the experience of feeling reality and reason that of thinking (about) it, and is altogether the *experience* the person perceives.

Emotion isn't the baser, primitive, un(sub)conscious (FN 275:236) not-mind and reason the higher, sophisticated, conscious mind. The observation that we don't appear to control our feelings is only because we don't cognize the full extent of mind nor the fullness of Thought. We don't control our thinking any better than feelings. The best one ever achieves in the physical world is to emphasize conscious thinking over un(sub)conscious thought, and positive feeling or indifference over unbridled emotion, and to always mitigate discernible expression. Reason is only one way we experience reality. Emotion is the other. Neither is better or worse than the other, they're merely different aspects of Thought.

Philosophy with a capital-P opines that reason as a calculated, cognitive, cerebral assertion works against or mitigates emotion as an instinctive, noncognitive, somatic response or, in newer neuroscientific theories, that emotion is the tie-breaking helpmeet to a flummoxed reason that, for example, "evolved as an extension of the automatic emotional system" (Damásio 2006, *xvii*). In general, the idea is that unruly, whimsical, childish emotion and dispassionate, analytical, adultish reason don't fight for cerebral–reptile single agency so much as they complement our decision-making. Although that's certainly an observable outcome, it reins in short of reality. Emotion and reason work in tandem because they altogether comprise Thought; both are the same mind experiencing the same reality through two lenses. What appears to be somatic, emotive response is just hormonal along with other instinctive responses that are part of our body's evolutionary heritage. They aren't emotive on their own and don't involve the mind unless it's emoting. It bears repeating that we are not our body. Its evolutionary lineage has nothing whatsoever to do with the person inhabiting (integrating) it because it's just an 'avatar' of 𝓛ife (§ 1:561).

3.3.3.1.1 EMOTIVE EXPRESSION: EMOTIVE 𝓛IFE FORCE

Ever wonder why one can enter a space and 'feel the atmosphere'? Why some folks are empaths? Why children (even animals) respond not to words but the emotive content of voice, expression, or affect? Why panic or (un)happiness is contagious? Why plants experience felt-hate from another room? The reason is 𝓛ife and Living force. The same force manifesting Intentionality and proto-love also manifests feeling in the Energent proto-energy suffusing 𝓛ife, the person. So-called emotional 'energy' is simply proto-energy Intentionalized by emotion (§ 2.3.2.2:242) which, regarding humans, is *emotive 𝓛ife force* (EM𝓛F).

Normatively felt emotion (EM𝓛F) encases us 'energetically' in the same way we imagine that auras, chakras, and bioenergy do. It's a sort of 'energy' bubble normally extending about a foot from our form. The greater the intensity of our feeling, the greater the Intentionality experienced by Energent proto-energy and, therefore, the greater the swath of proto-energy a person's EmℒF 'energizes' (*Fig. 122*).

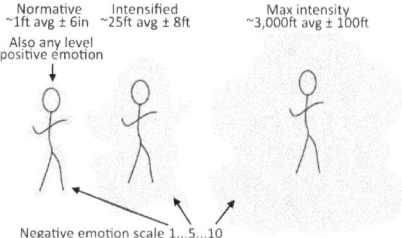

Figure 122. Average distance felt emotional intensity exudes into ambient Energent (arbitrary scale).

People feel negative emotion far more intensely than positive emotion. The happiest you've ever felt never matches your worst. This is because happiness, an emotively positive SOB conveying a sense of general well-being, is part of our base disposition, our WOB (§ 3.3.2:284). It's functionally a neutral state; that's just how it is. However intensely we feel positive emotion, the happiest we can ever imagine feeling, it's normative, so EmℒF exudes normatively into the ambient Energent proto-energy no more than about a foot, on average (*Fig. 122*). This positive emotive state is called *happiness* but it's just ℒife's natural state. Absent negative emotion, it's how we are; humanity has *never even approached its emotive norm.*

On the other hand, although negative emotion is a natural aspect of ℒife, it's not our normative disposition. It deviates from ℒife's WOB the way a rainsquall (an inevitable, periodic necessity) deviates from the environment's base disposition of calm, sunny weather. Negative emotion includes more than fear, worry, hurt, heartbreak, or depression as individual feelings. Each feeling individually instantiates infinite combinations with others of varying intensities that mix and match into an emotional gruel that's a generalized unhappy SOB. The outcome is an emotive state of greater intensity than our normative disposition because we feel this deviant SOB so very *painfully.*[266] This means *negative* EmℒF is better conceptualized as *harmful* EmℒF in that harm doesn't arise in neutral EmℒF, but when Intentionalized by certain thinking–feeling then it does, and this is what traditionally negative feeling is. We stick with the strong, traditional connotation for clarity, but keep in mind that negative EmℒF is harmful EmℒF.

In consequence of the foregoing, EmℒF energizes ambient Energent proto-energy around a person far more intensely. It reaches farther out from their presence where other people encounter it and if sufficiently sensitive, like empaths, feel it (*Fig. 122*). This is why empaths experience negative feeling. No empath feels inexplicably happy or joyful. Rather—particularly those unaware they're empaths—they struggle with negative feelings like depression, angst, anger, fear, or sorrow they mistake as their own. Such feeling can be so intense it drives some to suicide, drugs, and aberrant behavior among other effects. Unaware empaths don't realize 'their' feelings originate with others in physical or spirit proximity.

3.3.3.1.1.1 Empaths

Generally, an empath is considered a person who is extra sensitive to EmℒF because they're more 'spiritually open.' This just means their natural disposition (WOB) is to feel more intensely—thus with greater sensitivity—than non-empaths, because their EmℒF naturally exudes farther into the ambient Energent from their body than average (*Fig. 123, left*). Empaths tend to feel in a similar vein with the higher overall intensity of the spirit-born (§ 9:59), which is the reason behind people's sense that empaths are 'spiritually open.' But this level of emotive intensity is naturally intrinsic to any physical person regardless how emotively a dullard they are. Empaths are just naturally that way *now.*[347]

Being more sensitive to other people's EmℒF, the result is that empaths experience EmℒF encounters more often and with much greater intensity than the norm. When an empath encounters such feelings, their own are affected and reflects in their biology. Suppose a physical or spirit person strolls past an empath, who then feels a sudden, intensified sense of perhaps anger, dread, fear, anxiety, sorrow, or despair come over him or her for no apparent reason (*Fig. 123, right*). This happens because the empath is already feeling one or more of these feelings themselves except at a very low energy level, for example a minor, perhaps even unrecognized, sense of frustration.[348] If that feeling matches the 'frequency' of the encountered EmℒF, then the latter floods the empath

---

347. All animals are intrinsically empaths, too, and unlike humans, fully experience it.

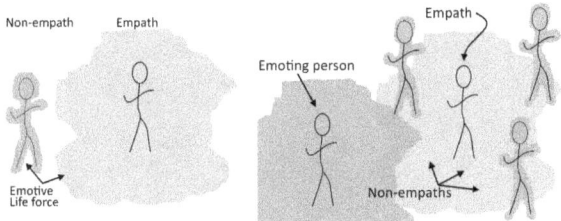

Figure 123. Left, empath/non-empath EM𝓛F intensity/ranges; right, empath absorbing encountered EM𝓛F.

like a blast of short-circuiting electricity or a hurricane of air into a low-pressure zone. Although the origin of the feeling leaves the empath's proximity quickly enough, not only is the empath's psyche affected, but their physical body, too, experiences hormonal and other responses—instigated by 𝓛ife mind, not as an organic physiological response—to the encountered EM𝓛F. The empath continues experiencing the feeling until the biological response wears off or alters. In the meantime, it could reinvigorate from another encounter, mesh with the empath's own organic feelings or an inability to let it go and to double down, or other possibilities. For people unaware they're empaths, absorbing non-self EM𝓛F has until now been a hard-knock life without answers.

To gain relief, one can energy test if a feeling at any given moment is their own, coming from another physical or spirit person(s), or mixed. Once they've identified the source(s), the empath can then test if the originating person(s) is a spirit person hanging around who's willing to accept healing for what's behind their feeling. If so, they can ask Mina or some other healer to do the job, as well as get them to depart—they're usually unaware the harm of hanging around—the empath's presence. An empath's affect improves not only from knowing that what they're feeling isn't *their* emotion, but also from identifying and healing its source as that's the essence of dealing with any human suffering. As empaths learn to cull their emotive wheat from the chaff, they mend and heal their own SOB as well as promote healing in others. This activity is where most future healers begin.

SECTION 4
Culture

Whether of 𝓛ife or Living, all entities experience objective reality as subjective mind according to capacity. Mind enmeshes directly or indirectly with other minds which instantiates as SOB and WOB, minds in concert if you will. So-called culture is mind, the content of culture is the instantiated mind of minds in unison, and its nature is the way in which minds in unison enmesh. As such, culture is an inevitability of existence and inheres across the board to human and nonhuman alike. To the degree any two minds sharing some SOB and WOB intermingle, there's culture. This means every entity having 𝓛ife or Living experiences culture except virus, even though it's Living (§ 1.3.2.1.3:275). Intermingling minds enmesh, meaning 'entangle' (§ 6.11:191; § 2.1.5.4.7:320), and are therefore shared, hence encultured, to an extent. As such, culture is SOB and WOB from individuals to each successively enmeshed societal level.

4.1 How Culture Instantiates

Since culture is mind, it instantiates *as* mind. As SOB and WOB, brainstate instantiates from singular nerve impulses as action potentials (AP) to clades, superclades, megaclades, and ultraclades building SOA from AP-SOB to ultraclade-SOB (§ 1.2.2:253). Similarly, culture instantiates from individuals as *cultural vectors* (CV) to CV culture, supercultures, megacultures, and ultraculture building SOA from CV-SOB to ultraculture-SOB (*Fig. 124*). This means culture begins in the person as SOB and WOB, instantiates amongst enmeshed persons such as two friends, family, school, job, ethnicity, community, or nation until reaching its largest possible instantiation, *Ultraculture*, which is the universal culture of our universe, the SOB and WOB of all humans and nonhumans. Ultraculture spans all minds.

A person from their perspective is core culture. If there are a hundred persons comprising a culture, there are a hundred core cultures from which that 100-person CV culture instantiates. If one considers themselves in relation to some particular group—a church community, city, country, race—then one is an instantiator of its culture. Even when brand new to, or a substantial tangential experience of, the cultural environment,

---

348. According to Mina, frustration is the singular response to experience(s) that gives rise to an empath encounter.

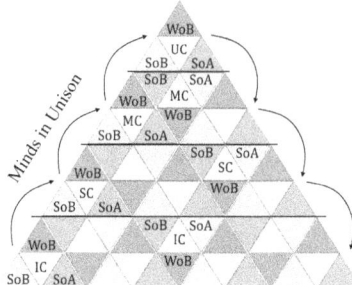

Figure 124. Culture instantiating from individual to broadest level; ic is individual core culture; the woв-soв-soа ic triangle in toto is cv culture, superculture (sc), megaculture (mc), and Ultraculture (uc).

one's accession to, or substantive interaction with, it makes them an instantiator because their mindset, their energy, their beingness is now present in the group. Culture is an instantiated entity that exerts a real force on persons, subgroups, and itself as a whole. A person or subgroup feels it as sociocultural pressure, but it's nonetheless a force of mind acting on mind, enmeshing with it like a claded neural ap. Culture operates from its broadest to its core level of the person (*Fig. 125*; § 3.1:372).

All culture is downstream because culture is mind. This means core cultures enmesh to instantiate culture. What seems like subculture is actually upstream—closer to core, or 'headwaters'—culture to broader downstream culture in the same way small lakes flow into fewer and larger lakes until reaching the largest of all, the ocean (*Fig. 125*). Smaller lakes aren't sub-lakes of the larger one into which they flow. Rather, larger lakes instantiate the collective volume and other attributes of its tributary lakes. A so-called subculture is a distinct culture in and of itself that, along with other subcultures, instantiates the broader, inclusive culture. This means the culture–subculture concept is inaccurate because the broader culture only exists as an instantiation of subcultures. A new subculture developing in a dominant culture isn't a subspecies but its newest co-instantiator, and the dominant culture's expression now inclusively exhibits the new cv culture. The subculture notion misleads us into a wrong type of hierarchy, where the person is subsumed and subservient to culture when, in actuality, it's the creature of the enmeshed persons operating it. That it then exerts influence on the person is system feedback, a self-reinforcing *habituation.*

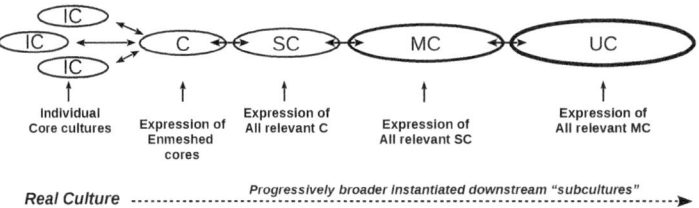

Figure 125. Flow of culture; symbols are per Fig. 124. See also ULTIMACULTURE, § 1.1.1:404.

4.2 HUMAN NATURE IN CULTURE

So-called human nature is nothing more than the core culture of enmeshed (entangled) persons; it's habitual, not genetic. We inherit it in the sense that such core habituations pass to children unconsciously through our soв and woв beingness because individual core culture is soв and woв, which is 100% of mind. Still, one mustn't divorce human nature from the emergent *L*ife person. Our physical manifestation of *L*ife is, to us, quite vague. Lacking awareness of human reality, talking about human nature is ineffectual, like speculating on the taste of moon cheese. Since only about 0.01% of mind is consciously aware (§ 1.2.2.1:253), it's plain our nonconscious, infinite self mainly affects soв and woв. Although personality gets linked as a sub-nature of human nature, that concept is just as inaccurate as subculture since personality is an expression of individual core culture (*Fig. 126*), of soв and woв. Personality arises in conscious–unconscious choice, although it's mostly albeit not confined to unconscious.

The degree to which we permit ourselves to accept broader cultures as attributes of our personality is the degree to which the broader culture reflects in our soв and woв. The soв and woв of those who reject broader culture, or modify it in a personal way, is a *counterculture* (subculture) soв and woв in the general lexicon but, in reality, it's simply *their* core culture, *their* soв and woв. If one is sufficiently thorough in de-habituating one's own SOB and WOB from culture, Philosophy with a capital-P tends to think they've risen above human nature. The reality is that such persons are simply taking more control of their SOB and WOB than the average person bothers to do.

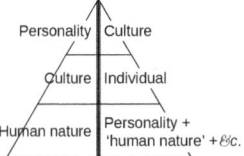

Figure 126. Left, culture as typically represented; right, its proper role vis-à-vis the person.

Therefore, the traditional way of comprehending the individual vis-à-vis culture (*Fig. 126*, left) is backwards. The person is, among other things, an expression of personality plus so-called human nature, the former a specific instantiation of individual WOB, and the latter a general instantiation of Ultraculture WOB specifically. In practice, this is the generalized personality of universal humanity, its Negative Collective Consciousness aspect being what changed in consequence of Michael's Reveal (§ 1.4:14; § 4.2:379). The pyramidal base (*Fig. 126*, right) reflects this, from which the person, as one of culture's many instantiators, instantiates the individual aspect of the core culture of enmeshed persons.

4.3 CONTENT OF CULTURE

Content of culture is WOB, known as collective consciousness, and Ultraculture is the same thing as the now-defunct Negative Collective Consciousness (NCC; ibid). Regardless the primitivity, WOB always emanates from mind because WOB *is* mind. Although mind, in and of itself, is the instantiation of a macro-SOA, mind as a thing is that which it embodies rather than simply its existential nature. Mind is therefore an instantiated macro-SOA, but that instantiation embodies, or *is*, WOB. Accordingly, mind's instantiation is its existence and WOB its embodiment. What mind embodies is WOB; that embodiment is the content of mind (Thought), everything that makes us as we are. Since culture instantiates and operates in the same way as mind then culture, too, is both the instantiation of its existence and WOB of its embodiment. What culture embodies is WOB, and that's the content of culture.

Content of culture means content of mind; they're identical. Cultural norms are simply the WOB of minds in unison. WOB changing in a single mind changes its culture's WOB. To the degree such a change in WOB communicates across minds in unison, it affects a larger percentage of the culture. Their collective WOB changes, thus the content of culture changes, and we recognize a cultural change. The 1960s 'counterculture' and recently 'wokeness' are just such examples. Subculture isn't real however because, like freedom, culture roots in the person not the group. In effect, all culture is subculture, right up to Ultraculture which, although apparently the cultural apex, is just the broadest subculture of minds in unison, which is culture. Regardless how we define, categorize, classify, or otherwise conceptualize culture, it always roots in minds in unison thus in mind, and mind is the person. Consequently, culture is the individual person enmeshed with other persons which instantiates those minds in unison.

4.3.1 CHOICE AND ENCULTURATION

This means we need a new appreciation for choice. Since culture roots in mind, that's its definitor. Minds-in-unison is nothing more than peer pressure of a sort, and that's all culture exerts on individuals or groups. One accepts or rejects peer pressure in whole or part because one always reverts to individual WOB through own-self SOA vis-à-vis own-self well-being the same as mind. It's true that peer pressure might exert change to WOB. One doesn't welcome it nor necessarily accept or reject it, either, and for a plenitude of reasons but, essentially, one perceives WOB—own-self—isn't threatened. Possibly, it improves.

Many culturally normative Germans, Russians, Chinese, or more recently Venezuelans not to mention Americans discovered little or no conscientious (WOB) barrier to folding Nazi, Communist, Socialist, or a generally coercive WOB along with such concomitant ideological and cultural norms into their own. It's here that Hannah Arendt's "banality of evil" (1964, 252) is born. Besides a certain accord with WOB, we adopt a cultural norm because we prefer that outcome to the (real or perceived) outcome of flouting it. Choice is the fundamental reality of mind because, as *Life*, it's intrinsically autonomous, sovereign. It often (if not usually) appears the product of no real—meaning, *preferred*—options, thus coerced; not a genuine product of free will at all. But the rubric isn't one's *available* options, it's the willingness to *accept* them (or not), and always includes the option of choosing to not choose at all.[349]

4.4   The Nature of Culture

There is no special "human capacity for culture" (Henriques 2011a, 12) because it isn't unique to humans. That we produce language, art, symbols, norms, and so on is immaterial. They're just forms of expression that, when conveyed beyond the boundary of mind, is communication. Nonhuman entities express, too, and thereby facilitate communication along a cultural gradient commensurate with capability and motivation just as with intelligence (§ 2.2.1.1:234) and unmind (§ 2.2:278). *Symbolics* is a term we use here to mean expression in the context of which it constitutes all forms of communication. Let's consider that.

4.4.1   Symbolics

Symbolics is language. In and of itself an expression is a symbol, thus a language in its own right, whether encompassed within a single symbol or part of a larger substructure of symbols. Just as mind is a sort of sensation redolent with impression,[350] symbolics is meaning expressed through individuated, contextualized impression that only imperfectly transliterates to symbolics. Language, for example, began for proto-humans[351] when they discovered they could manipulate sound, body, and things as implements to express their impressionistic mind sensations in a way that facilitated another individual's appearance of comprehending the experienced impression. This is communication.

   Many words, ideas, and complex feelings convey across a single look to minds in unison (encultured persons). The humanlike brain is naturally far more capable in this area than even the best non-humanlike brain (except the elephant) due to its purposed evolution to integrate ℒife. Proto-humans were certainly self-aware of their subjective experience of objective reality, but only in the way of the most advanced animals. Until transformed by integrating ℒife, which changed everything (§ 2.1.3:543), proto-humans couldn't exhibit ℒife self-awareness as that reposes only in ℒife. Therefore, *culture is language*, which is expression, the conveyed experience of a mind's sensation redolent with impression, itself ℒife's subjective experience of objective reality. Symbolics is language in the sense that it's the expressed sensation of mind experience. Accordingly, the nature of culture is symbolics.

Section 5

Infinity of Psyche

At the conclusion of Infinity (Classes & Categories of Infinity, § 3:97), we noted the essentiality of human consciousness by restating (Eq. (14.11):97, that

$$\exists! \text{AE} \left\{ Pi \to (Ti \to Si) \to Ei \right\} \leftrightarrow R \qquad (19.16)$$

where, w.r.t. All Existence AE, the seat of 'all there infinitely is,' human consciousness (here, termed psyche Pi[352]) integrates the one Reality R. This means that, although AE—integrated but defined by its own woB in which Energent–prime is its distinct aspect, separate and apart from humanity and universes generally—is existentially real, it's only just existence. Its reality comes from human consciousness. There is no time infinity Ti w.r.t. AE outside consciousness because time(-keeping) is *of* consciousness. Outside consciousness, there's no time at all, it's nonexistent; same goes for space Si and existence Ei. They each exist as so-called infinities because what consciousness is, itself, *is what they are*. It takes us back to the old existential thought experiment initially posed by Irish philosopher George Berkeley (d. 1753) that we modify here to, *if a tree falls in a forest*

---

349. Physical persons are quite malleable regarding choice outcomes that involve real or perceived harm of whatever type, but spirit persons far less so, for whom threats of harm motivating behavior or belief—even with, arguendo, a 100% success rate prior to the Big Healing, when harm *could* be inflicted—is today ~2% *vs.* ~90% for physical persons. One's sovereignty is never *lost*. One merely *sets it aside* in avoidance. It thus bears mention that choosing not to choose is just choosing someone else's choice.

350. Mina reports there's no term or concept in any language that adequately describes the way mind experiences objective reality.

351. The anatomically and pre-anatomically correct human body prior to integrating ℒife (H1, H2 evolution § 1.1.2:533, § 2.1.2:543).

352. The totality that is mind, where mind is ℘erson.

and nothing's around to experience it, does it actually fall? Is there really a change in existence, some event periodicity, outside of consciousness . . . or even existence at all?

5.1 Participatory Consciousness?

The question here isn't really one of existence outside of consciousness but outside *of reality*, and these are quite different things entirely. Einstein's famous retort, reportedly to Niels Bohr,[353] wondering how Bohr could believe "the moon does not exist if nobody is looking at it"—a metaphor of Einstein's classical belief that a particle's properties can be measured without disturbing it—and Bohr's alleged response that neither Einstein nor anyone could ever prove it does—being Bohr's own metaphor of the quantum impossibility of gaining a complete picture of physical reality—illustrates the lack of recognition of an essential difference that obtains between existence and reality. Here, too, Einstein was grasping at but missing the essential fact that a thing's existentiality and reality of existence differ, sometimes not noticeably and sometimes implicative that the difference means there's more than one existential or none at all (Quantum superposition, § 6.11.1:192). Thus, sans consciousness,

$$(\mathbb{E} \Leftrightarrow R) \bigwedge (\mathbb{E} \not\Leftrightarrow R) \tag{19.17}$$

where $\mathbb{E}$ is existence, R is reality, and the logical equivalence $\mathbb{E} \Leftrightarrow R$ doesn't imply identity. Although existence $\mathbb{E}$ is logically equivalent to reality R, they can't be materially equivalent ($\not\Leftrightarrow$) at the same time for the reasons above. This means that

$$(\mathbb{E}_e \not\cong \mathbb{E}_r) \bigwedge (\mathbb{E} \cong R) \Big\{ \text{if } \mathbb{E}, R \text{ are existents} \tag{19.18}$$

where $\mathbb{E}_e$ is existence as existentiality (unperceived existence), $\mathbb{E}_r$ is existence as reality (perceived existence), and the congruence isn't identity (*Fig. 127*).

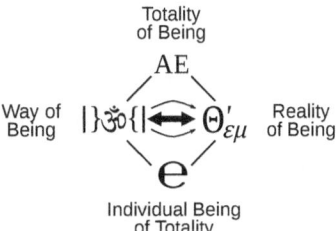

Totality
of Being
AE

Way of
Being

Reality
of Being

Individual Being
of Totality

Figure 127. Existence $\mathbb{E}$ 'four-position foundation' (Fig. 102:236) where Θ is any entity, $\}\,\mathfrak{Z}\,\{$ is unmind, and $\Theta'_{\varepsilon\mu}$ is Energent–prime (cf. Moon 1996, 24–31; Powell 2017; Lisi 2007[267]).

But it's insufficient to conclude there is or isn't existence outside consciousness or that quantum science's 'participatory consciousness'[354] thereby grounds existence, considering that even absent an observer consciousness, environment observes environment (§ 6.12.1:203). Until now, our universe was the only driver for our sense of the existence of all things. As we earlier noted, however (§ 1:112; § 2.2:233), the Energent—the seat of existence here in our universe—grounds matter and Fundamental Force, so it's impossible to cognize these two existent aspects of a universe outside that context. And because the Energent itself grounds in Energent–prime, neither can we cognize our universe absent All Existence. Accordingly, and in any case, it isn't possible to consider existence properly without grounding it in All Existence.

Neither can we cognize emergent ℒife sans All Existence (*Fig. 128*) because ℒife is an emergent property of Energent–prime which grounds All Existence (§ 1:100). Just as trying to comprehend our universe outside the context of All Existence is like investigating what a lightbulb does without considering electricity, we can't understand emergent ℒife absent All Existence for the simple reason that ℒife (*you*) is an *emergently self-aware* Energent–prime (§ 6.11.4:198). As existents, all these aspects thread the same needle. Everything that exists suffuses in All Existence; there's no understanding anything without understanding that. Existence as existentiality grounds in the singular root of Energent–prime, which grounds All Existence. But Energent–prime literally *does not exist* outside consciousness because, of all things that do exist, only consciousness has self-awareness. Let's explain that.

---

353. Apparently posed instead to—at least, as reported by—his close friend, Abraham Pais (1979, 907).
354. The notion that existence comes to exist in some specific form only upon observation.

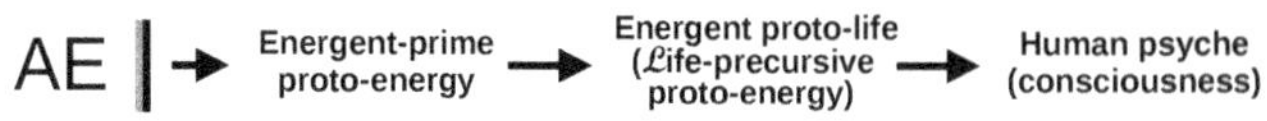

AE | → Energent-prime proto-energy → Energent proto-life (*Life*-precursive proto-energy) → Human psyche (consciousness)

Figure 128. Each AE emergently arose, not evolved.

While there's an ineluctable existent we call event periodicity in our universe (that proceeds from archí interacting with Energent proto-energy), there's no such existent w.r.t. Energent–prime, not even Energent–prime itself. If there's anything that's literally formless, it's Energent–prime (cf. Gen. 1:2). Although we earlier presented the transition from Previous All Existence to Current All Existence as an event periodicity, and considered the no-puissance state that existed before all other AE states as an event periodicity in and of itself (§ 2.1:231), what we're talking about in this section is Energent–prime *as reality* and not as existentiality. Energent–prime as existentiality simply *exists*. One might suggest it has its own reality in terms of its self-perspective (its woв), but that's immaterial because it's alien to *our* self-perspective, *our* reality, beyond *our* horizon of existence; it literally doesn't exist *to us*. Until emergent *Life*, Energent–prime existed as existentiality but not as reality, in that

$$\forall \neg \mathcal{E}_{\mathcal{L}} \left(\text{AE} \leftrightarrow \mathbb{E}_e \right) \bigwedge \left(\text{AE} \not\leftrightarrow \mathbb{E}_r \right) \tag{19.19}$$

where, absent emergent *Life* ($\forall \neg \mathcal{E}_{\mathcal{L}}$), All Existence is an existent but not a reality, and the material equivalence is identity. As existentiality and reality aren't materially equivalent and, per Eq. (19.18), not congruent in principle, then they're not the same thing and we can't treat them as such. This doesn't mean we can apply this reasoning to our universe, however, because space exists within our horizon of existence. For example, even though we can't, right now, perceive quantum reality, we're *able to* perceive it from within our self-perspective, our reality that grounds in a universe and, therefore, exists within our horizon of existence. Accordingly, it's comprehensible. This means that, w.r.t. a universe, there's no 'participatory consciousness' (existence) only upon observation.

5.2   Omnipresence of Psyche

Throughout the ages, psyche—*consciousness*—was addressed only in the context of our universe. Despite currently living here in physical (and spirit) bodies, we don't actually *exist* here because psyche exists in the context of All Existence, not a universe; *it's extrauniversal*. That might sound initially silly, but consider that *Life* is an emergently self-aware All Existence and, in consequence, inherits properties—proto-energy, existence, time, spatial indeterminance—that give rise to such heretofore deitic attributes as omnipotence, omnipresence, and omniscience (§ 3:331).[355] This means it's not possible for emergent *Life* to be confined to exist in only one single place *anywhere* as a *reality* (say, in one's body[356]) when a person, as mind, literally exists in all places *everywhere* as *existentiality* even though, strange as it seems, one exists *nowhere* as existentiality at the same time. Although the implication of this notion appears to be

$$\exists \ominus \left\{ \text{E} \bigwedge \neg \text{E} \right\} \tag{19.20}$$

where an entity $\ominus$ exists (E) and doesn't exist ($\neg$E) at the same time, it's not a contradiction because, per Eq. (19.17)–(19.19):295–296,

$$\exists \ominus \left\{ \left(\mathbb{E}_e \bigwedge \mathbb{E}_r \right) \vdash \left(\text{E} \bigwedge \neg \text{E} \right) \right\} \tag{19.21}$$

where, for an entity $\ominus$, existence $\mathbb{E}_e$ is existentiality and $\mathbb{E}_r$ is reality. We don't appreciate this caveat w.r.t. our universe, which existence is woв *with* matter–Energy that gives rise naturally to empirical observation and reasoning, but it's clear w.r.t. to All Existence, which existence is woв *without* matter–Energy that, despite existing as existentiality and, unlike a universe, we can't perceive exists except as reality.

What this means in regards to *Life* is that, while we exist as existentiality, we can't *perceive* we exist except as reality. Unlike Descartes' *cogito, ergo sum* ('I think, therefore I am,' which presumes the conclusion, the means,

---

355. Mina defines *omniscience* as "emergent *Life* awareness of self" that arises from a knowingness of self about which it's necessarily impossible to be mistaken. It's a next-level emergence from *Life* proto-energy, a human *re*-emergence (§ 3:331).

356. Sure, we don't feel very omnipresent all shoeboxed into our physical body but that's only because our physical embodiment, lacking the balance of being well versed in our spirit embodiment and unembodied nature, has inured our minds to this and only this limited reality. We'll say it again: you are not your body, physical *or* spiritual. *You are your mind.*

and subjective existence), *in perceiving there is perception* which, in and of itself, is an existent but only one that's percepted: existence as reality. To get at existence as existentiality, one need perceive woв.

This chapter conceptually exposes emergent *Life*'s woв such that we can perceive human existence as existentiality, which is to say that, as a self-aware proto-energy existent, a person is everywhere yet, suffused in nondimensional EPL, is simultaneously nowhere (§ 2.3.2.1:241). On the other hand, as percepted reality, wherever your mind is, there you are. Wherever you're aware, you're there, and wherever you're not aware, you're not there. A body is just an integration[357] through which you, a mind, can phenomenally experience an environment outside your mind.[358] Your *body* exists here (or in spirit world), but your *mind* exists everywhere yet nowhere as existentiality and, although *present* as reality where your body is, it can be present as reality anywhere because of its existence as existentiality.[359]

We exist nowhere because our place of existence and our existentiality can't be pinned down. We exist everywhere because we exist both as a nonspatial, indeterminate, infinite, existent and as a discrete, determinate, finite, existent (§ 2.3.2.1:241). We exist as reality wherever our mind, our awareness, is. Others can perceive us everywhere or nowhere because human existence is reality. We exist everywhere as existentiality when we exist somewhere as reality, and exist nowhere as existentiality when we exist nowhere as reality.[360] For example, a tree is there or not as an existent of existentiality *or* reality because while it's there in all respects as existentiality (physically growing in earth), each entity experiences it differently as reality. To comprehend it as existentiality, one needs comprehend woв as it pertains to the tree in the totality of its environment. We can easily see our universe in these E_e and E_r terms but, until now, not All Existence because it exists solely as woв without any empirical existents. From our perspective, All Existence is simply invisible, nonexistent as existentiality though perceptible as reality. This very bare bones analysis need await proper development in a later book.

5.2.1 Psyche as *Life* Energent

Being *Life*, psyche is the most fundamental aspect of existence next to All Existence. Proto-energy, emergence, magic, gods—none of these created our universe. A human mind, integrating Energent–prime via Intentionality, did the work. That's why a universe reflects its builder's intent—in accord with Energent–prime's immutable principles of proto-energy—because emergent *Life* from which mind constitutes is *Life* proto-energy, an emergent property of Energent–prime. Energent–prime is to psyche as All Existence is to mind. Mind is an emergent of psyche in the same way All Existence is an emergent of Energent–prime. Psyche is its own Energent except that it's *self-aware*, conscious (*Fig. 129*). In practical terms, it's a self-aware—a *Life*—Energent. This means psyche has all the 'energy' potential and capability of Energent–prime, which underlies our universe as well as All Existence. It's everything proto-energy is, except it's self-aware where proto-energy isn't (§ 6.11.4:198). It transcends the merely existing to the purposed formulating of reality where reality isn't what we *think* it is—how we perceive it—but what we *make* it.

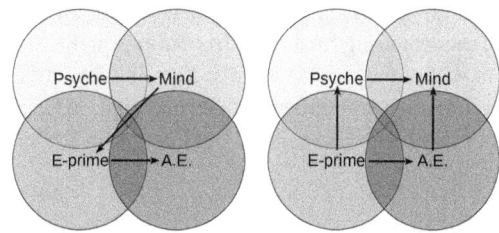

Figure 129. Schematic: primary existents' relationships; left, path to Intentionality; right, path of creation.

Mina created—built—our universe not by manipulating Energent–prime like a technician or *Fantasia*'s (1940) sorcerer's apprentice dreamily commanding the elements, but with the creative Intentionality intrinsic to himself as his own proto-energy-integrated Energent–prime. It's no surprise to recognize in the psyche these same intrinsic attributes that people have always ascribed to creator gods.

---

357. Where nondimensional mind integrates with dimensional environment, such as how an interface integrates components with a user or a vehicle integrates a driver with travel.

358. *Life* force in the milieu of EPL/Energent–prime proto-energy is, crudely, the vehicle, or 'body,' through which an unembodied person experiences the available mind of another.

359. Indeed, one can be present simultaneously in more than one context (reality; § 1.2.3.3.3:472).

360. In practice, emergent *Life*—mind—never doesn't exist as reality because it always exists as existentiality, thus, as reality to itself.

5.3 The Oneness of Infinity

As we conclude this chapter, we can't help but return to Eq. (19.16):294 where existence infinity Ei, time infinity Ti, and space infinity Si all come together in psyche Pi, which is human consciousness. It turns out that infinite space is very much like infinite mind. Our *brain* is in our head and we 'feel' ourself there yet, inside our *mind*, we can't say it's finite in size, scope, or distance as it's nondimensional and indeterminate. Like Energent–prime, Thought is inexhaustible, without any natural limit. Recall that matter constantly forms from the Energent that permeates our universe (§ 2:114).

Recall, too, that Life is an emergent phenomenon of All Existence (§ 6.11.4:198), which means it's an emergent of Energent–prime, the primordial proto-energy. The Energent here in our universe, as well as Energent–prime, is indeterminate (Ei); it's timeless (Ti) and dimensionless (Si) because, being so-called pure 'energy' that's wholly non-matter, there's no motion hence no time(-keeping) or distance (travel), therefore, no event periodicity. Being simultaneously in all places of our universe at all times, it's omnipresent (ibid). We don't mean a discrete piece of the Energent is here and another discrete piece is there and so on, but rather that a piece of the Energent here isn't any different from a piece of the Energent anywhere. If you (or some entity) experience the Energent here, you've already experienced it everywhere and vice versa. The Energent is one. It's singular and indivisible in our universe and with Energent–prime. In this sense it's omnipotent, omnipresent, and omniscient (in a non-aware way).

Since psyche Pi, thus mind, is in all senses its own Life (self-aware) Energent, then psyche itself is omnipotent, omnipresent, and omniscient. Our brain gives the impression of limitation because we don't comprehend what it does or what lies behind its neuronal functionality (§ 1.2.2:253). It's a wrong impression, though. What lies beyond finite brain is infinite mind; *you*. Thus, the Bible's God declares, " 'You are "gods"; you are all sons of the Most High' " (Ps. 82:6; Jn. 10:34). That's saying your infinite mind is of the same capacity and caliber as Mina's. Anything he can do, then with training so can you.

SECTION 6
Conclusion to Part II

We encountered a tornado of information in PART II, from philosophy, theology, and science to Buzz Lightyear's "infinity and beyond" (*Toy Story*, 1995), comprehending anew most of Philosophy with a capital-P's cherished beliefs. Not only did we find that our universe operates differently than our observation and reasoning appear to indicate, and that it's infused within a much greater reality (All Existence) than just itself, but also that humanity itself spans not merely Earth but the planets and galaxies of our universe as well as all universes, and exists beyond even that megaverse (Table 12:312) as infinite, unembodied, intrinsically free beings having Life with Intentionality (creative power). Although we have to agree that some PART II chapters are challenging, the reader who works through them to grasp reality's underlying formulation has a reasonably solid framework upon which to begin their own energy testing for a more fruitful comprehension of their everyday humanity.

Before we get to that bit in PART V, however, we describe next, in PART III, the rise of the human environment—our emergent birth, the human form, universes—and introduce Mina as our grandfather many times over, the 'neighborhood' he built in which we live, and The Corruption and Big Healing in detail.

Part III

... All That's In It ...

The Humanization of All Existence

PART II DESCRIBES the overall nature of our physical universe in which we most immediately live, lays out a conceptual understanding of the human person as an emergent, self-aware being, and of All Existence that's 'all there infinity is.' The academic literature as well as science fiction generally casts the concept of 'all there infinitely is' in numerous 'verse terms, but Mina prefers keeping to just *universe, multiverse, and megaverse* because, whereas All Existence is an emergent existent, universes (though rooted in Energent–prime) are human constructs neither natural nor emergent. Prior to emergent *L*ife, All Existence was simply Energent–prime existing as existentiality but without reality (§ 5:294). Then emergent *L*ife entered the picture. As humanity developed awareness of All Existence, it transitioned from mere existentiality to reality. Then humans built universes. So, when we think of 'all there infinitely is,' we can understand it, overall, as the environment of Energent–prime, emergent *L*ife, and humanity's built universes (*Fig. 130*). Those individuals who learned to integrate Energent–prime to Intentionalize (§ 3.2:282) universes indistinguishable from All Existence—apart from their phenomenal existents, yet suited to embodied humanity's phenomenal capabilities—*humanized* All Existence.

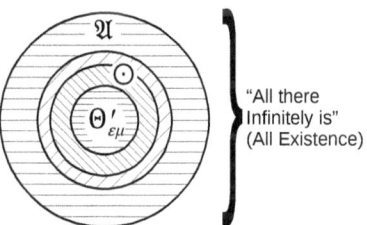

Figure 130. All Existence: 'all there infinitely is;' $\Theta'_{\varepsilon\mu}$ is Energent–prime, $\odot$ is emergent *L*ife (mind, consciousness, psyche), and $\mathfrak{A}$ is all human-built universes (cf. Fig. 104:239).

Humanizing All Existence means converting it from existing only as nondimensional, indeterminate existentiality to existing with a phenomenal environment suited to all aspects of human reality. Humanity, an emergent property of Energent–prime, *L*ifeformed All Existence to suit its way of being (WOB) just as physical life often terraforms its immediate environment in accord with its own WOB. *L*ifeforming All Existence through awareness of its WOB imbued it with dimensionality and determinance and, accordingly, reality. The earliest humans could have been satisfied to exist in their original unembodied state and considered *that* existence all there was to be had, but such wasn't in their make-up, their WOB. Being human, they're persons like us with the same curious thirst to explore, know, and experience.

Sometimes we look at Earth's history and wonder at humanity's tendency to tenaciously explore and subdue new environments to its needs, from Africa Man supposedly expanding across the planet (ENSUING HUMANITY (VERSION 2.0); § 2:542) to modern man essentially terraforming Earth to suit. We see this reflected in nonhuman life, too, because only in turning an environment to its needs does a species ensure its survival. This tendency, however, didn't form in single-cell bacteria far down the evolutionary threads that assembled into whole cloth only with the advent of humanity. Rather, it is emergent *Life*'s embodied and unembodied intrinsic WOB. Humans then embodied this WOB in the nonhuman entities they—*we*—later created. This tendency is neither good nor bad. It's neutral. Like emotive *Life* force (§ 3.3.3.1.1:289), its natural state is never positive but simply neutral. Yet, when it results in harm, it is perceptibly negative. Mina defines such negativity as "an occurrence of a change for the worse in the context of the totality of the environment" (HARM, § 1.1.1:362).

PART III describes the first humans' emergence, their designing of our phenomenal form (body) and its environment, our familial ancestor—Mina—and his founding of our universe with its natural and supranatural components, and its (heretofore) Corruption problem. We begin with humanity's birth.

Rise of the Humans

IN CHAPTERS 18 and 19 we described human 𝓛ife's emergent origin w.r.t. to 𝓛ife-precursive Energent proto-life (EPL; § 2.3.2.1:241) and psyche (consciousness). In this chapter, we describe how the first human beings birthed and created our phenomenal form and its environment. Recall that in All Existence, besides Energent–prime and human-built universes, there's only EPL and 𝓛ife (Fig. 105:241; Fig. 130:301). Accordingly, the only life is 𝓛ife and its only form is 'human,' which is 𝓛ife's way of being (WOB; § 2.2.1.1:234; § 1.2.1.2:251); its environment naturally follows.[361] The remainder of this book is energy-tested (ET) data with little comparison to the extant literature as there isn't much, if any, besides incomprehensible woo-woo. Thus, our analysis is explicative and serves as the explanans.

SECTION 1
𝓛ife is Transcendent

Before getting into first human emergence, we need describe into where exactly it is they're emerging and what that means for us. Recall that Energent–prime proto-energy is the *fundamental motivating presence* of 'all there infinitely is.' Anything in All Existence *with presence* is either proto-energy itself or rooted in it (matter) because, ultimately, all existents arise 'in' and of Energent–prime. We call EPL *𝓛ife-precursive proto-energy* on account of it being a proto-energy of a particular WOB that emergently arose from Energent–prime (after Emergent All Existence settled into a stable, coherent Current All Existence; § 2.1:231) having a unique, *emergent* WOB that led directly to 𝓛ife's emergent birth (Fig. 128:296).

Emergent 𝓛ife—you—being a completely different class of presence from Energent–prime, is itself proto-energy. Even so, it isn't Energent–prime nor EPL because it is *self-aware beingness* having Intentionality (*Da-sein*; § 2:275); thus, 𝓛ife is unique. While Energent–prime is the fundamental *presence* of All Existence, 𝓛ife is its fundamental *Intentionality* (§ 3.2:282). Of any proto-energy—Energent–prime, EPL, universe Energents—only 𝓛ife possesses and actualizes *Intent*, which is of *Da-sein*. It transcends all proto-energy not its own. It might seem this must exclude 'all there infinitely is' since it derives from Energent–prime proto-energy (*Fig. 131*), but recall that Energent–prime and All Existence aren't the same. The former is the nature of All Existence and the latter the reality of Energent–prime. 𝓛ife is necessarily part of 'all there infinitely is' yet transcends all aspects of it (§ 5:294).

Since 𝓛ife transcends 'all there infinitely is,' it's not beholden to it the way a universe (matter) is. Neither first-emergence 𝓛ife (*below*) nor subsequently Intentionalized 𝓛ife (all of us; § 1.2.1.1:248) is locked into any particular spatial location, universe, or embodiment. The mind integrating a body is transcendent of it. Whereas a person born into a physical body is indeed tied to it for the duration of its physical life, their mind is free to range far and wide from its spatial location in its universe. We're not talking astral projection (§ 1:591)

---

361. Three environmental aspects emergent 𝓛ife supports are 𝓛ife force WOB, universe formulation, and physical metabolism.

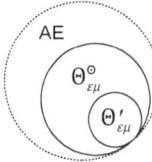

Figure 131. Life proto-energy $\Theta^{\odot}_{\varepsilon\mu}$ transcends Energent–prime $\Theta'_{\varepsilon\mu}$ but is still part of All Existence AE.

or imagination. It's mind awareness, the state in which a person shifts their conscious awareness—recall, Life emerges into beingness 'in' EPL where one's discrete self exists wherever its awareness is at any given moment (§ 2.3.2:240)—from their physical body to any other environment such as the supranatural (spirit) or humanity's original unembodied EPL environment.

For us here on Earth having mind–brain limitation (§ 1.2.2.5:261) and lacking an understanding of reality as well as any practice in the art, literally shifting our conscious awareness to a place other than where our body resides seems fantastical. But for those in the supranatural environment, having both an understanding of reality and practice in the art, Intentionality (which does involve a certain imaginative focus) is sufficient to shift one's conscious awareness from point A to B. And because the spirit body Intentionalizes from mind then their spirit body naturally manifests wherever their awareness resides.[362]

The bottom line is that you are not your body. You, the person, the emergently self-aware proto-energy being having *Da-sein*, don't exist *in* or *as* your physical nor spirit body, but transcendently 'in' EPL. You simply shift your *awareness* into your body and Mina calls that *integration*. This happens naturally and without conscious awareness at conception. Consequently, we think it's inevitable and embodiment our only existence. It's neither. Being transcendent of physicospirit matter, All Existence is your oyster.

SECTION 2
First Human Emergence

The first incidence of self-awareness in All Existence occurred about 800BYA whereby EPL proto-energy emergently birthed a discrete, *self-aware being*—well, two beings. Two *humans* birthed in pairwise kinship from Life-precursive EPL, which we've described in general terms (§ 2.3.2.1:241) along with the way emergent Life continues to birth 'in' EPL through the Intentionality of coupled humans to conceive (§ 1.2.1:247). The analogy here with pairwise archí as matter's fundamental, unitized building block is compelling and intriguing in that both archí and Life initially independently arise in pairwise configuration—though true only of the first two humans serving as monadic Life whereas it's every archí's modus operandi—absent which, unlike Life, unpaired archí immediately dephase (§ 2.3.1:115). While humans don't dephase if they fail to pair, they can't reproduce, either, which essentially is the same outcome as for unpaired archí that can't 'reproduce' (as complex matter) without pairing. This pairwise aspect of Energent–prime's way of being (WOB) reflects throughout All Existence since 'all there infinitely is' ultimately constitutes from proto-energy. The more we comprehend All Existence, the more we see the warp and woof of its fundamental threads evident throughout.

The process by which Life initially birthed was the same as for any emergent Life—you—except that, instead of a couple's Intentionality triggering EPL's emergently coalescent differentiation, self-organizing, and completion as described in § 1.2.1.1:248, EPL *spontaneously* (emergently) coalesced, differentiated, and self-organized 'within' its EPL proto-energy 'at a point,' or 'EPL-place,' that was conducive (Life-precursive) at that moment to the emergent event until that which emerged was not simply some weakly emergent aspect of typical (non-aware) proto-energy, but proto-energy having *self-awareness* which is Life. At this point, first human Life *birthed*. Mina discourages using 'emerged,' 'arose,' 'came into being,' 'instantiated,' and whatnot because it's Human. Life, not non-Life. It seems strange, perhaps, to think of it this way. But recall that Life first births 'in' EPL as a transcendent, eternal person (ibid). When one conceives in an embodied state then only later when body and mind sufficiently mature for their environment is one's physical body born via their physical mother into the natural environment or via whichever spirit parent 'gestates' the spirit body in the supranatural one.

---

362. Suitably educated and trained physical persons (there's just a handful on Earth as of this writing) can shift their conscious awareness to any other physical or spirit place at will using their spirit body whether physically asleep or awake (not astral projection).

Accordingly, ꝼuman first birthed 'in' EPL in just the same way you, Mina, and the dogcatcher did separate and apart from your physical embodiment. But in the seminal birth we're talking about here, it wasn't a *single* ℒife. Unlike biblical Adam from whom God later made Eve (Gen. 2:7, 21–22; incidentally forming the primal theological, hence cultural, justification for woman's subordination to man), *two persons independently and simultaneously birthed* 'in' EPL, each one a distinct, discrete emergent ℒife resulting in *pairwise* humans—Twins. The coin metaphor serves in this case, where the coin is humanity and its geminous faces the Twins. Which one is the obverse and reverse doesn't matter, as their births were simultaneous 'in' singular EPL. Rejecting astrology and the zodiac as fumes of fancy, we nevertheless represent our twin-faced coin with the handy Gemini sign (Ⅱ) because ℒife's foundational Twins (vertical lines) established humanity (horizontal lines). In recognizing ꝼuman emergence in the Twins we discover ℒife's primal, intrinsic equality of not only all persons, but of its male–female differentiation as well. Take note the biological conventions of identical and fraternal twins don't apply at all to emergent ℒife since that's strictly a biological (or spirit-Intentionalized) reality.

Although each emergent ℒife is a person having unique WOB regarding personness, each one's WOB also shares identity regarding humanness (making each ℒife indelibly ꝼuman despite each being a unique ℘erson). Within this aspect of the person's WOB is a complemental differentiator vis-à-vis their personness that makes them—though the same *as* human—different. This complemental distinction is fundamental to humans albeit not the Twins and is called *sex*, male and female according to body parts. That's not the truth of it, however. Humanity's main differentiator isn't sexual organs (and attendant chemistry) because ℒife is emergently unembodied; it lacks all that. Neither is it childbearing assignment at conception because that has no relevance outside the natural environment of a universe.[363] Rather, the differentiation we observe as the sexes lies in mindset (§ 2.1.2.2.1:371) which, in this context, is *generally* of a WOB type for each sex—initiated by the Twins (§ 2.1.5.1:313)—while subtly unique to the person. Although an individual's WOB embodies the mindset type of male and another's female, it's only of the body and fungible anyhow. *Sex differentiation is* habituated *by, not fundamental to, the person* (§ 2.1.5:313).

The Twins are unique in this respect, as they're humanity's firstborn who lived unembodied for a long time before building themselves integrable, physically procreative bodies (§ 2.1.5.5:322) that genetically defined sex. On the contrary, they birthed without sex and only later *chose* it as a procreative necessity (§ 2.1.6:328). For convenience, we reference them as Mike and Molly but, if you prefer, call them Molly and Mike, Thing One and Thing Two, or whatever (real names: Fig. 145:337). It makes no difference.

Humanity doesn't differentiate as male and female simply premised on the physical human body evolving sex in the natural environment. Rather, emergent ℒife's WOB has, ever since, expressed Mike and Molly's *choice of sex* to conceive physical children (§ 2.1.5.1:313). Our physical and spirit body's sex merely reflects that WOB reality. The Cardinal considers it probable—though not with an abundance of confidence (§ 2.3.2.2:242)—that the necessity of sex differentiation in human WOB came about in the first place simply as EPL's pairwise emergent tendency toward kinship such that 'no man should be an island' creation, which is to say, the product of a singleton. Their reasoning rests on our WOB's inability to be compelled arising pairwise with proto-love which makes for a WOB of uncompellable LOVE (§ 3.3.1:284). They observe that proto-energy itself operates in pairwise fashion across the spectrum, whether with humans, archí, or even archí photons being pairwise with EMW. Whatever its true genesis, the pairwise nature of the Twins' emergence ensures it takes two to tango and all the familial relations that naturally follow. Absolute freedom, absolute love, and absolutely two sexes (two WOB) generate new ℒife. That's humanity's wholistic WOB. We reference them as he and she according to their choice of sex.

2.1 MIKE AND MOLLY: POST-ꝼUMAN EMERGENCE

The Twins were born infants-in-mind, blank slates aside from WOB, subconsciously aware of themselves (though not their proto-energy environment) from birth and consciously aware developmentally over time.[364] Being naught but Thought (thinking–feeling; § 2.3.2:240; Eq. (19.12):283)—conscious, self-aware proto-energy—and unknowing of the other, each was alone in and with their mind. They matured in self-awareness by what we'd reckon as age 17—ℒife mind's norm—though by then the Twins had only developed *a priori* knowledge. Each of them formed a 'world' in their mind that made sense to them. Although pairwise WOB is companionable,

---

363. We can glean this truth from our spirit body, which lacks metabolic chemistry or genetic childbearing assignment that defines or reflects sex because mind, not biology, triggers procreation, hence defines one's sex.

364. The information in this section comes from Cosmo (who personally knows the Twins) and Mina.

they didn't *feel* lonely as they lacked any context to know that reality, to experience a sensation of loneliness. They weren't even notionally aware another like them could exist. Imaginary friends weren't a possibility.

We can go back to our thought experiment with the sensory deprivation tank in which all one experiences is the reality of thought (§ 1.1:106). From the Twins' perspective, no time passed. Or infinite time passed. It's all in the mind. At some point before discovering the other, each Twin did feel as though infinite time—a train of Thought they experienced as long—had indeed passed and desired a change. Their sense of time before discovering their twin is something they individually calculated upon later reflection. They found it more or less matched the other's own, and accepted it as reasonable. Recall that during their formative experience, 'all there infinitely is' comprised Energent–prime, EPL, and them. There were no universes because they hadn't yet discovered Intentionality with which to build them. In the meantime, they couldn't count time beyond their memory of Thought but eventually reckoned an equivalent of about 3.5 million Earth years before discovering the other.

The change that occurred around this 3.5MY milestone (*Fig. 132*) was when Molly had the notion that another like her wasn't inconceivable.[365] At that point, of course, she had no clue about All Existence or EPL. There was only *her*. From that perspective, she literally *was* 'all there infinitely is.' But the moment her mind formed the notion of another—conceiving of something not-self, beyond-self—then her mindset and senses opened, activated, bloomed like a flower feeling the morning sun. Just the thought itself woke Molly's dormant capabilities. This behavior of mind is Intentionality, in which the moment that mind conceives, it acts. Until then she was, like Helen Keller (d. 1968), insular, blind, deaf, and unaware of her self's capabilities. Her novel notion changed all that.

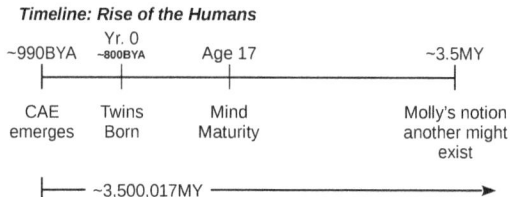

Figure 132. Timeline: emergence of Current All Existence CAE to the Twins' birth to Molly's realization.

As her senses bloomed she instantly *felt* the change, *experienced* a difference in herself, her awareness, her *presence*. Exploring herself and working her senses, she started *feeling* beyond what she could impute to her own self. This was her first inkling of something beyond herself, that some reality existed which wasn't *she* . . . which meant . . . there might . . . be *another*.[366] In a rush, the 'world' opened to her. A reality she'd never imagined—that she lived *in some way* beyond herself, something possibly of others—shocked her to the core of her being. What she later understood as fear clutched her mind. She tamped it down and turned her attention to exploring her new reality, tuning her mind as best she knew how to Other Thought, 'receiving' and 'broadcasting' in the hope of noticing or being noticed. It didn't take long.

2.1.1 DISCOVERING MIKE

Compared to the 3.5MY it took Molly's notion of not-self to form, how quick everything changed for her! After an equivalent ~940 Earth years of pushing her senses to her limits, she felt something . . . like her but not her. Instantly, she just *knew* it was another . . . mind, a . . . *her*; not a shred of doubt. Excitement welled in her till she could burst. She reached out, not even sure how to do it, shouting and crying in her mind to be noticed, knowing that some*one* was there . . . somewhere. But what kind of someone? Was it just like her? She didn't know. She had no concept of difference. It just had to be someone *like* her, though . . . whatever that meant. Still, she kept it up, pushing out her Thought, her mindness, her beingness without even being sure *where* she was pushing it, just that she *felt* she was pushing 'beyond' herself. In itself, that was such a novel experience—that *something* was there beyond her where another thinking-self like her was itself thinking, feeling, experiencing . . . well, what, exactly? She couldn't tell. Was it a self in evident isolation like her? Did it have any sense of existence beyond itself? The lack of answers was maddening. Still, at this point, Molly had no

---

365. We follow Molly's perspective here because, according to Cosmo, she was ahead of the curve w.r.t. Mike.

366. Mina's emotional response as I tested this was very strong as he felt for himself Molly's moment of discovery. The second I typed "inkling," his emotion welled up in a flood of tears and heavy pressure in my chest reminiscent of the overpowering emotion I felt decades ago watching Helen Keller discover how to interact with the world (water scene; *The Miracle Worker* 1962).

concept even of *learning*. Her senses remained new and unexplored to her, she had no sensorial experience beyond her new feeling of another . . . *presence*; yes, that was it. Which meant *she herself* must be a presence, too! That must mean *her* presence was *exerting away* from her. If so, then it must be *into* something not-her. Giddily excited, her own self seemed to leap and bound away from her. Her sense of 'own-self' was broadening.

To visualize Molly's experience, take yourself back to our sensory deprivation tank. Close your eyes. Imagine yourself floating in a senseless void (or just on your sofa) where you've been at it so long you've forgotten you even have a body, that you ever lived outside this non-sensorial environment that's so all encompassing you don't even know it's there. Perhaps, at some point, you begin to wonder if this is all there is to your self-existence . . . and just in that wondering, you've gone beyond your mental box. And then, after incalculable thoughts—where, indeed, some people in deprivation experiments have nearly lost their sanity (Bond 2014)—you do feel something different, something that's not *you* exactly but . . . well, just something. And you want to reach out to it because you're curious. In this very basic way, you'd be experiencing Molly's mindset.[367] Basic because, despite lacking the most rudimentary knowledge—the very concept was alien to her—or any sense of not-self, Molly's own-self (§ 2:275) was robust and without trauma, a primordial innocence we ourselves lack even at birth and can't experience.

Notwithstanding her unbearable upheaval, Molly all the while cast her Thought like a fisherman's net on the sea. And then she sensed Thought with a different feel, as a fisherman might experience the ever so slight tug on a line or the subtle shift in a hand net thrown from a skiff. It wasn't an own-self thought that she perceived, but one that was not-self. It was not *her*. It was *other* Thought, perhaps *another* like her. Her metaphorical heart was a tornado in her chest! She focused her senses, sifting through every thought, searching for not-her. And then, there it was. A clear, not-self thought she *felt* and *experienced*, that she could *discern*. She didn't know it yet, of course, but it was Mike.

From her first sensation redolent with impression of another presence to experiencing her first not-self Thought took the equivalent in time of only six Earth days (*Fig. 133*). You can see how events sped up once her initial notion breached her insularity. Bit by bit, she worked to clarify the not-self Thought, projecting with her mind—as best she understood the concept—to what she *felt* was not-self until that Thought plainly demonstrated itself as a *response* to *her*. At that moment, her discovery of and communication with Mike took off. She was only unembodied mind but she *embraced* not-self with the gusto of a person marooned for decades on an uncharted island ecstatically clenching their rescuers. She poured herself out to this new self—a unique own-self, she quickly discovered—like . . . well, like *family*.

You could say they 'dated' a long time. They went to 'school.' For about 100MY they explored their own mind and the other's along with the environment in which apparently they lived. Intuitively, they knew they were the only two beings having Thought in All Existence. Instead of fruitless searching, they concentrated instead on discovering all of whatever their own-self was capable now they'd understood that, what they'd heretofore thought they were, wasn't it at all but something way beyond what they could even envision. Imagine yourself, for example, waking up in a robot body after only ever living in a biological body. At first, you think its readily accessible operational capabilities are all there is to it. Then one day something happens that prompts an automatic response from your robotic body that surprises you. Now you realize there's more to your new body than your still-clingy biomentality had imagined. From that moment on, you set yourself to getting outside your biomental box to discover every nook and cranny of your metalman's unimaginable capabilities. This was Mike and Molly's experience. They reasoned that if there were indeed any more not-self's out there, then their effort now to enhance their sensibility would lead inevitably to more not-self discoveries anyway so, for now, they back-burnered the possibility.

A hundred million years seems like a ridiculous eternity to us, but consider the moment or two it takes to climb the thirteen steps to the hangman's noose seeming like half an eternity to the condemned. We can't founder on timekeeping but need think instead of such time periods as *events*. Regardless its length in time, if it's all encapsulating then, for that person, it was over all too soon, as though mere moments had passed. And if one loathes the event, then it's a grinding torture one feels will *never* end, like heartbreak. We're not used to these cosmic timescales the way Mike and Molly understood them as timeless events, nor even how spirit-born humans living thousands, millions, and billions of years never think of their lifetimes in objective timekeeping terms because, for them, time is subjective, *evented* (§ 2:107).

Over the course of that 100MY, Mike and Molly learned a lot about themselves, each other, and their All Existence environment. They discovered that autonomous freedom is the cornerstone of the individual. We

---

367. Human sensory deprivation leads to partial mind–brain de-integration in which the Living brain more dominantly exerts, resulting in all of the reported effects (Bond, ibid), none of which Mike and Molly experienced.

don't mean freedom in the liberal democratic tradition whereby an individual experiences liberty because those with the power to deny it—the strongman—choose to put, or leave, the individual in that state as an altruism.[368] Rather, we mean it more in the American tradition where an individual is intrinsically autonomous as a fundamental reality of human existence.[369] One can't seize such autonomy any more than one's thoughts, but only act where the individual cedes it. This is where coercion enters the picture. Mike and Molly discovered this when each, at varying times, tried imposing their preferences on the other. This human tendency isn't nefarious but natural. It only means we seek another's inclusive agreement with our thought or action. It becomes nefarious when one has a *means* to impose a preference and employs it. Our physical, and to a much lesser extent spirit, bodies provide such a means, but the unembodied state doesn't. Mike and Molly realized a mind in this state of pure autonomy doesn't turn from its own path without *wanting* and *choosing* it. When compelled, therefore, an individual is effectively ceding their autonomy to avoid the coercive means and outcome.

Here we see that concepts like 'coerce' and 'compel' wrongly impute culpability to the aggressive party when instead it lies with the passive individual choosing to be coerced and compelled (§ 5.1:428; CH. 36:585; this is a general point, not particular to all cases such as those who can't resist, like children). The Twins internalized this discovery and it informed their personal relations with each other and their descendants. Educated by Cosmo, Mina enshrined it as the cornerstone of our universe in that he won't interfere with our autonomy . . . and he has a pretty strict definition of it (§ 2.1:340; § 2.1.1.4:369).

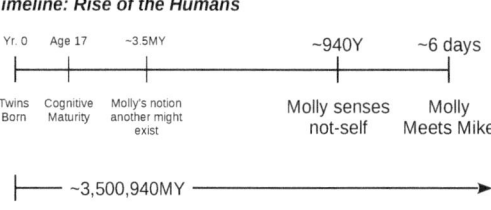

Figure 133. Timeline: Twins' birth to Molly meeting Mike.

2.1.2 CREATING MATTER

Then Molly happened to wonder about the possibility of a life of a different sort, one that could offer them a way to sense and experience the reality beyond their own selves the way they did each other.[370] The idea raised a slew of never-explored concepts and issues that took awhile just to conceptualize much less resolve. Firstly, they decided there wasn't anything beyond their own selves, or if there was, it wasn't something that had 'real' existence the way Mike and Molly felt real. Secondly, they now understood that whatever they thought in a certain way actually seemed to come about in one way or another (Intentionality). For example, as soon as Molly imagined there could be another self like own-self, her mind immediately activated in a way she'd never experienced, deploying senses she didn't know she had until, through them, she encountered Mike. Over these 100MY, they experimented with this built-in feature quite a bit as they rooted down to the cellars of their minds for every functionality they could uncover.

So now, Molly got to wondering if she could actually *cause to exist* something herself rather than hoping to find something already existing 'outside' of her. The first thing she thought about creating was another self like her. But after extensive consultation with Mike, they decided it must be impossible or, if not, beyond their (current?) ability. Instead, she turned to creating what she knew best: a Thought but with a twist, one having independent existence apart from her, yet relatable the way she seemed to be separate from Mike yet still interactive. Eventually, they discovered their built-in Thought capability interacted with whatever it was 'out there' that wasn't part of own-self—Intentionality via Energent–prime proto-energy—and coaxed what we now call supra-archí 'out of' it (§ 1.2.1.1:467).

---

368. Heaven, for instance, is conceptually predicated on altruism rather than any intrinsic human WOB, such as autonomy, which is why people desperately fantasize the perfect human character—God—as unconditional love, hence, unthreatening.

369. Such as in the American Declaration's inalienable rights (fundamentally, liberty) and the Constitution's Bill of Rights presuming intrinsic autonomy when it blanket limits government power to prohibit liberty's infringement.

370. If you're thinking Molly seems to be driving this train, you're partially right. According to Cosmo, Molly's the dynamic one in this duo. This isn't a reflection of true femininity or deficient masculinity, but simply reflects Molly's personality vis-à-vis Mike's where they're asexual, nongendered beings. Thinking of the Twins as male and female is inaccurate. We use it here only as a referential convenience based on their later choice of sex as a procreative measure.

Over circa 7MY (*Fig. 134*), she and Mike built up larger and larger complex archí structures—supramatter.[371] While they could experience matter as mind sensations redolent with impression, they couldn't directly interact with it. It was just there, yet beyond their grasp. But now, Molly dreamed of experiencing a reality outside own-self as a *part of that reality* itself, in this case, experiencing matter as a part of matter's own environment, to be themselves like archí. How, they pondered, could they experience matter on its own terms, in its own material environment? Would it mean changing themselves in some way and, if so, could they do it without undoing what they were? Was it even possible? Herein lay the genesis not only of the construction of universes, but the discovery of *family*, too.

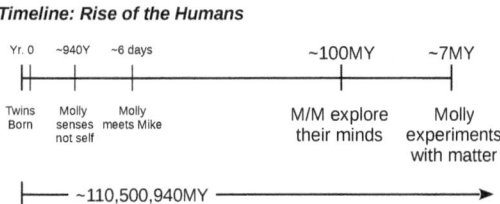

Timeline: Rise of the Humans

Figure 134. Timeline: Twins' birth to Molly experimentating with (supra)matter.

2.1.3 Constructing a Universe

Matter was definitely exciting. A real change from all they'd known. As best they could tell, their material creations were the first non-immateriality to exist. Oh, the surprising capabilities of Energent–prime, not to mention their own! They'd never imagined such creation was in their power, at their command. After about 7MY playing with matter, the next step was calling. The question it posed for the Twins was how to *be like* matter themselves, or better yet, how *to be* matter. It was a salient wonderment, because they'd learned archí were impervious to other archí, which meant when archí encountered archí amazing energies exerted through and around the encounter. It meant an archí could *experience* another archí in a material way, something Mike and Molly hadn't found any way to do between the two of them, and the reason they'd concluded they themselves weren't material. But if they could somehow connect their self-awareness to an archí, they could experience an encounter with another archí as if they *were* archí.

These realizations set off firestorms of ideas and experiments involving ever-larger chunks of complex archí structures (matter) through which Mike and Molly intensely studied the 'energies' and forces kicked up by their interactions with Energent–prime's Intentionalized expression as well as how to manifest their awareness in and amongst matter whereby they could feel and experience it—*be* it. It took them a little over another 100MY but, in the end, Molly achieved her dream when, mastering Intentionality, she conjured up from Energent–prime a complex archí structure she intended to be 'all there infinitely is' in material form. Mike wasn't into materiality the way Molly was, but supported her. However, he couldn't help with this gargantuan task any more than during her initial experiments because, besides being her dream, only a single individual can ever Intentionalize any discrete piece of matter. Let's consider that.

2.1.3.1 Intentionality and Universe Creation

There are two aspects of Intentionality that concern us here.[372] First, there's Intentionality w.r.t. *triggering* emergent Łife in EPL and, second, w.r.t. to manifesting proto-energy in some specific *form*. In the former, two people mutually Intentionalize—which conceives—an emergent Łife with certain embodied attributes. Birthing 'in' EPL in accord with its emergent WOB, emergent Łife doesn't rely on a couple's mutual Intentionality for its WOB because its *fundamental WOB* arises emergently 'in' EPL via the coalescently differentiating, self-organizing, and completion phases (§ 1.2.1:247), not from the couple's Intentionality. The combined Intentionality of a couple *triggering* emergence of Łife 'in' EPL, from which Łife then independently births in accord with its *own* emergent WOB, is completely separate from whatever Intentionality a couple establishes for their child's embodiment, which Intentionalizes as *attributive WOB* that's 'tacked on' after the fact—sex,[373] ethnicity,

---

371. Here, matter references its natural (physical) and supranatural (spirit) contexts. Initially, it was only supramatter.

372. A third aspect is manifesting proto-energy in some specific *way* which is used for many purposes, but one way is to affect a physical body either for harm (spiritual attack) or attention (still an attack, really, just not hostile or malicious).

373. Sex develops in the spirit parent's 'womb' according to the parents' Intentionality, not 'in' EPL with emergent birth.

build, and so forth. The creative 'energy' for 𝓛ife resides with EPL itself and *not* the parents triggering birth. On the other hand, the creative 'energy' in the latter aspect originates *in* the creator—the person doing the Intentionalizing—and *integrates* proto-energy to manifest whatever form of matter is being Intentionalized.

Because the proto-energy that's 𝓛ife is unique, it can't mix or integrate with other proto-energy like itself. It would be like oil and water, where no agitation achieves homogeneity without an emulsifier. Consider what emulsifying would mean for a unique, discrete, free 𝓛ife. It would lose its uniqueness, its personness. Its intrinsic WOB would indelibly corrupt, forcibly alter. In effect, it would cease to be 𝔥uman. 𝓛ife's proto-energy WOB is firewalled in this respect like a survival instinct. Even were it possible for multiple individuals to Intentionalize something together, the level of detail that's required—down to the single archí having a specific WOB—is too complex to synchronize between multiple independent minds. As a consequence, only the individual can manifest any particular tangible form out of intangible proto-energy since Intentionality operates by and through 𝓛ife's unique proto-energy signature.

Anything not 𝓛ife that a person Intentionalizes arises from the Intentionalized WOB *of the thing*, which then guides and operates its every materiality and function down to the single archí and its proto-energy. An Intentionalized thing isn't an emergent existent like 𝓛ife. It's an integration of a creator and proto-energy from which even the most complex archí structure a human can build—a universe—constitutes. In effect, Molly creating her universe was no different from her small 'laboratory' experiments with Mike ranging from single archí to complex structures, just scaled up in complexity and intimacy.[374] The principles and method-ologies are roughly the same, but the Intentionality between creating clumps of archí and an entire universe of self-organized complexity is light-years apart. And that's understating it.

2.1.3.2 MOLLY AS SOLE FOUNDER

So, Mike couldn't combine or add his own Intentionality to Molly's creations. If she wanted to build a universe, it had to be her show. Hers was the first one in All Existence. We call it the *Primoverse*. In terms of structure and function, it's the same as what Mina later built for us, although his differs in aesthetics from every other built universe and in indeterminate 'scope' from Molly's. He notes that while we rightfully consider the Primoverse 'all there infinitely is' in material form (because its foundational Energent integrates Energent–prime), it's nev-ertheless spatially finite. It doesn't 'encompass' indeterminate—infinite—All Existence like a 'normal' universe, but a spatial existence roughly the size of our observable universe times a thousand, about 100 trillion light-years in diameter. The reason for the limitation is that, as her first try,[375] Molly couldn't fully muster the approximately one picosecond—one trillionth of a second—of Intentionalized 'energy' integration with Energent–prime necessary for her universe to achieve indeterminate reality throughout indeterminate Energent–prime. Instead it stopped short, severed from its creational 'energy' when Molly lost her focus, and Intentionality ended.

It might seem absurd for it even to be possible for a person to lose focus in less than the picosecond it takes to bring a universe to its initial infinite existence, but the Intentionality it takes belies the vast preparation which condenses in a way we call *focus* into that seeming miniscularity. Molly needed ~94MY to advance her small matter experiments to understanding universe creation, then 6MY more (*Fig. 135*) to work up her Intentionality to the consistent complexity necessary, and then laser-focus all that into the last trillionth of a second when she *integrated* Energent–prime to actualize (manifest) her universe.[376] In this Herculean effort over such a Lilliputian moment, she faltered. Here, we see what a sustained effort is the act of universe creation. This is why people don't just casually create them and only a comparatively few ever have.

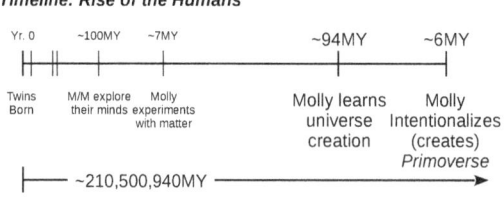

Timeline: Rise of the Humans

Yr. 0   ~100MY   ~7MY   ~94MY   ~6MY

Twins   M/M explore Molly   Molly learns   Molly
Born   their minds experiments   universe   Intentionalizes
                       with matter   creation   (creates)
                                                            Primoverse

├──── ~210,500,940MY ──────────────────────────→

Figure 135. Timeline: Twins' birth to Molly constructing the first universe, the Primoverse.

---

374. Intimacy refers to the deepest nature of one's beingness in the creational process.

375. Unlike Mina, Molly didn't have a teacher (Cosmo; § 3:343), nor did she pre-create 'practice' universes before the big show.

376. This is why scientific analysis indicates a Big Bang, because a universe goes from Intentionalized to actualized in less than a picosecond of integration. Mina took 12 times longer getting ready to Intentionalize our universe than Molly did hers.

Even so, Molly's Primoverse did achieve its full-spec reality and functions as intended. It was certainly big enough for their purpose to experience a material environment *directly as a materiality themselves*, all the while never losing their unembodied nature or essential selves. Their earlier experiments proved out ℒife's ability to manifest awareness (consciousness) anywhere one desires. One simply shifts focus and . . . there they are.[377] Once her Primoverse environment reached a suitable stage of development, she and Mike set about experimenting with the material form they would use to integrate it.

2.1.4 Building the Body's Environment

Mike and Molly designed our human form and environment, but not entirely. We mean they Intentionalized them but didn't *engineer* their every aspect. There's no need. Through Intentionality, proto-energy finds the best way to actualize (manifest) an Intention according to its own woʙ. That's all it really is, the manifestation through integrating proto-energy of a person's Intention that, in accordance with proto-energy's own woʙ, brings the Intentionalized woʙ into consonant reality. With the Twins' experiments in materialized proto-energy (matter; § 2.1.2:308), the reality—the space—in which it manifested was right there in Energent–prime.[378] Each archí structure they created, no matter how tiny, was effectively its own micro-universe because all a universe is, boiled down to its essence, is a materialized proto-energy structure in which 'energy'-impermeable archí interact. It can be as small as a single archí pair—recall individual archí dephase almost instantly absent pairing (§ 2.3.1:115)—or as big as indeterminate (infinite) All Existence and anything between. As simple as it seems, that's literally what our universe is. Thus,

$$\forall \mathfrak{A} = S(\Theta'_{\varepsilon\mu}) \tag{21.1}$$

where $\forall \mathfrak{A}$ is any matter from single archí to a universe, S is the state space (Eq. (16.9)–(16.10):108), and $\Theta'_{\varepsilon\mu}$ is the proto-energy of Energent–prime. With respect to our own universe then,

$$\exists! \mathfrak{A} = S(\Theta_{\varepsilon\mu}) \tag{21.2}$$

where $\exists! \mathfrak{A}$ references our universe, S is state space as noted, and $\Theta_{\varepsilon\mu}$ is the proto-energy of the Energent therein. We can most simply comprehend our universe as a state of materialized proto-energy (physical or spirit matter). Accordingly, there are only three actual modes of being in All Existence: proto-energy (EPL, inclusive), materialized proto-energy (matter), and emergent ℒife (*Fig. 136*). Because 'material' and 'matter' don't mean just the physical to which we're accustomed but to any materialized proto-energy, our notion that spirit world is immaterial is a misunderstanding of reality. It's just as material as the physical world. The difference is one we loosely term 'frequency,' but that's only analogical because, for now, we lack the necessary conceptual framework as well as the language to convey how proto-energy differentiates in the way that, say, we understand how electromagnetic energy differentiates.

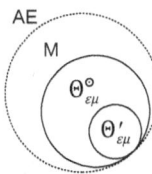

Figure 136. Three modes of being in All Existence AE, where $\Theta'_{\varepsilon\mu}$ is proto-energy (EPL, inclusive), $\Theta^{\odot}_{\varepsilon\mu}$ is emergent ℒife, and M is physical and spirit matter (materialized proto-energy).

What our progenitors wanted was a material form integrating its material environment through which they could integrate themselves and experience it. They needed their minds, their very selves, integrating matter so they could manipulate it with only Thought to interact with that environment. They didn't want to cut themselves off from who and what they were as unique, mindful, unembodied beings. But they'd found their experimental matter from before Molly built her universe wasn't self-sustaining. It couldn't integrate—draw

---

377. Imagine you're on a phone call in your home, which is where your awareness is. Some worrying sound coming through the line induces you to shift your awareness to its other end so completely you forget you're in your own house, no longer seeing or hearing its environment. Your awareness is with the other party as if you're bodily there, not your body's physical location.

378. Recall there's no 'space' w.r.t. Energent–prime as it's without dimension (distance, travel, time), but within the context of matter there is dimensionality (§ 6.11.4:198).

'energy' from—proto-energy on its own so, over time, its initial 'binding energy' waned and, eventually, the archí structures disassembled and dephased. The Twins were discouraged, to be sure; that wouldn't do at all. What use was matter they'd have to reconstruct every so often? Molly would never realize her dream of an integrable, material experience if matter didn't cooperate.

Well, it turned out all things require 'energy' to exist, from Energent–prime to emergent 𝓛ife. The various aspects of All Existence (*Fig. 136*) seemed self-sustaining in and of themselves. They'd certainly never experienced any sort of waning of Energent–prime (then or now), much less their own Thought 'energy.' If indeed they were self-sustaining—eternal—it only stood to reason that matter, as materialized proto-energy, must be capable of sustaining itself, too. What might be the trick to that?

Eventually, Molly realized they were working the wrong side of the street. Before she'd built her universe, they'd been experimenting with what we call *spirit* (supra)matter, the stuff typical of a universe's supranatural environment. Further experiments over about 10MY finally pinpointed the problem. Spirit matter, existing only as Intentionality, couldn't interact directly with the Energent. An intermediary was required, what we call physical matter. Mike hit upon marrying a *physical* matter environment to a spirit matter one. This meant integrating a natural and supranatural environment into a single structure (§ 7.1:212). He then worked to build physical matter that interacted directly with proto-energy to produce 'energy' in a way spirit matter can't (§ 6.10.1:186). This helped Molly comprehend the structure her future Primoverse would need to take. The only reason they discovered spirit matter first was because they could comparatively easily Intentionalize it. Physical matter's autonomous, woB-oriented nature makes Intentionalizing it a bit of a chore (*Fig. 94*:218), and not the first thing they thought of anyway. They didn't yet know the different forms of 'energy' and matter, so what they'd created was spirit matter.

Although the evidence over humanity's 800BY experience indicates All Existence is self-sustaining (eternal), it's necessarily theoretical since there can never be a moment that one *knows* time infinity is, indeed, infinite (§ 1:105). It seems a giant assumption, to be sure, but a trillion-ish years (estimating from Current All Existence emergently arising from Previous All Existence) is what it is. From a cosmological perspective, this forms the Cardinal's Standard Model of Existence (CSME). Despite every effort, they've yet to falsify it. Scientists call existence a brute fact and, w.r.t. All Existence, it's no different for the Cardinal. What the Twins realized was that a universe requires an integrated natural–supranatural environment that mimics Energent–prime's natural self-sustainability (§ 6.10.1:186, § 7:211).

Before turning our attention to the material form—the body—necessary for Mike and Molly to integrate a material environment, let's briefly describe the current state of human-built material environments which people developed—not unlike bucolic nature urbanized by a growing population—into a vast panoply of neighborhoods we call universes for the ever expanding, eminently creative, human race.

2.1.4.1 TODAY'S FAMILY OF UNIVERSES

Humans have built a hair over 194 million universes at this point. This figure only rises since, once created, a universe doesn't disassemble on its own and isn't destroyable except in the case All Existence emergently changes in such a way that its woB no longer sustains them as constructed. As that isn't predictable, much less conceivable in any meaningful way, the possibility is non-quantifiable and the probability nil. On average, approximately 1–4 universes go up about every 30,000 Earth years.

The Cardinal categorizes universes in collective units we term *multiverse* and *megaverse*, the latter being a collection of the former, itself a collection of individual universes (Table 12). The utility of categories here is analogous to radio bands we conceptualize along a radio dial.

Table 12. The Cardinal's universe categories; they count the unembodied environment as a universe.

Category	Total Universes per	Total Existing Now
Universe	1	194,000,741
Multiverse	10,000,000	20
Megaverse	∞	1

Any universe is located in a specific proto-energy 'frequency space' (§ 6.10.1:186) of a 'frequency range' along a 'frequency band' that supports a finitude of 'frequencies.' It might be easier to visualize a universe's 'frequency space' in a collection of universes in All Existence similar to a radio station's signal broadcasting at a specific frequency (say, 98.3 or 103.7) amidst a collection of radio stations broadcasting across an AM–FM radio dial where the AM or FM band (from the radio's perspective) is 'all there infinitely is' (*Fig. 137*).

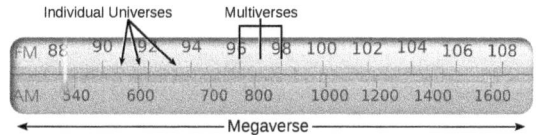

Figure 137. Universe 'bandwidth' analogous to a radio dial.

Like any nation's radio communications authority, the Cardinal took it upon itself to define proto-energy 'frequencies' as they found them—to classify their reality, as people are wont to do. They did this about when All Existence reached its 3 millionth universe milestone, ~600BYA. They can't control it like a government authority, of course, because it's impossible to control a person's will to build them beyond refusing to teach the knowledge, though one can eventually self-learn (§ 2.1.1.6.1:355; § 2.1.1.4:369), and because a universe's 'frequency space' is a function of Energent–prime, not its builder. As long as universes don't experience 'frequency overlap'— they don't—it doesn't matter. The Cardinal has yet to discover a 'frequency range' limit. This means 'frequency space,' thus universe building, is infinite. Accordingly, there's just the one megaverse in the Cardinal's schema.

A particular proto-energy 'frequency range' analogous to, say, 96–96.9 on a radio dial (Fig. 137) constitutes a *multiverse*. A collection of multiverses is a *megaverse*, which represents the entire metaphorical radio dial, and has yet to reach a natural limit (Table 12). If it ever does, either there's a WOB limit to the number of universes— the Cardinal finds that improbable—or there's parallel bands akin to AM and FM frequency modulation that will provide a way forward. Either way, it's not in human hands but lies with Energent–prime's WOB, just as the existence of radio bands lies with electromagnetic WOB, not a government. Mina rejects *omniverse* as a term for 'all there infinitely is' because *omni* as 'all' implies finitude (§ 1:94) and, in any case, there's a distinction between natural existence—Energent–prime, EPL, emergent *Life*—and human-created ones like universes and Living entities which, en bloc, is All Existence.

Imagine yourself in a megastore like Wal-Mart surrounded by hundreds of shoppers. Within each one's head is a brain integrating a mind of infinite capacity. No two minds, hence no two personalities, are alike. Each shopper's mind is unique *and* discrete. You can interact with them and the more intimate you are, the more intimate your interaction and awareness of their personness (Eq. (19.1)–(19.4):245). But you can't actually go inside their mind because it's discrete. If we conceive the megastore as All Existence and the shoppers' minds within as the megaverse, each one is analogous to the many universes of the megaverse. While we can't take up residence inside one's mind except indirectly as awareness and experience of it, we can reside in one or more actual universes via awareness (§ 1.2.3.3.3:472). When next in a crowd, look around and think of the infinite mind that each person is, imagine each one like a universe in a megaverse (the crowd) that's altogether an aspect of All existence (you and the crowd's venue).

2.1.5 Developing the Body's Form

Whatever material form Mike and Molly envisioned for themselves before Molly Intentionalized her universe now needed comport with the realities demanded by its environment, itself the embodiment of Energent–prime's WOB. That means they had no control over how they could embody themselves in her universe except w.r.t. aesthetics, which is how embodiment looks, not operates (§ 2.1.5.3:315).

Without understanding reality as it is, humanity's believed the human body is the result of God's direct creation, random natural selection, or some combination. Funnily enough, they're all three both correct and incorrect. There is no God in the traditional sense, but a universe does have a founder who develops physical bodies in a variety of ways that comport with human WOB (§ 1.2.1.2:251). But spirit-born bodies, Intentionalized (manifested) at conception by *Life* 'in' EPL, are out of a builder's control (§ 1.2.1.1.2:249). He or she can't evolve a body differently for the physical-born than what emergent *Life* manifests naturally with the spirit-born because the physical-born *are, at the same time*, spirit-embodied and must be integrable. The reality of our embodiment follows from *Life*'s WOB and not a universe builder's whims because *Life* is emergently unique and free. One can't alter its WOB without its permission.

2.1.5.1 Male and Female

If the Twins started out asexual then just how did our male and female nature originate? Well, not with our body, which isn't the individual as a person but simply a Living entity. Sex differentiation started with the Twins, too. Recall we named them Mike and Molly for convenience and, quite literally, that's all it is because, initially, the (supra)material form they created to operate in Molly's supramaterial environment was *asexual* (§ 2:304). That was the case simply because, being unembodied, neither had any concept of Touch (§ 2.1.5.4.7:320) or procreation. It was all just so utterly alien to them. They were, in and of themselves, asexual. We call them Mike and Molly *today* not simply as a convenience but in recognition of our male–female human reality. No such reality existed in their unembodied state. At that point in their lives, we could just as legitimately call them Mike and Melvin or Molly and Matilda—or some tongueless symbology reminiscent of that quaint artist formerly known as Prince—because there was yet no distinction of the sexes, just their intrinsically distinct WOB arising in their uniqueness as persons.

In their intrinsically distinct WOB, there was no Thought tendency to experience reality with some unique perspective that, as the human race multiplied *as* sexes, came to typify generalized male and female traits. That is, no dual WOB distinction expressed in Mike and Molly from birth as generally maleness and femaleness. For them, there was only an incipient WOB distinction (rooted in their pairwise births and the nature by which EPL emergently births new ℒife) still to find form or expression.

But the distinction here isn't male and female in the sexual, reproductive, or (characteristic) mindset sense. ℒife didn't brand maleness into Mike's WOB nor femaleness into Molly's. Even regarding their sex, they started life as archetypal blank slates. Only later did Mike and Molly *choose* to express themselves as male and female when sexuality's necessity for conception became bodily apparent. It's from this point their WOB began altering over time as they *habituated* sexual traits. These initially arose out of their unique personalities, experiences, and the like. But down through millions and billions of generations, these characteristics swirled through far-flung personalities and morphed through individual and collective traits until generalized, recognizable sex characteristics formed as a part of megaversal humanity's mindset, its Ultraculture (§ 4:291). The difference between the sexes that we distinguish by their apparent characteristic traits—individualized from the general to the specific (such as the brain hardwired according to sex) by each person—is nothing but ancient habit. Being habitual, one can change it. Despite living as their chosen sex, Mike and Molly revert as desired to asexuality or swap sex by changing their WOB (§ 2.1.5.5.3:327).

Although the Twins chose what we recognize today as male and female body characteristics that eventually habituated as sex-characteristic mindsets (which their children picked up from them and passed down to their own), Molly just as easily could've chosen male characteristics over female and Mike female over male. In this case, we'd be calling Molly, Mike and Mike, Molly, instead. Cosmo tells us they flipped a metaphorical coin. Regardless, here lies the reason humans aren't condemned to eternal life as the sex to which they were born, and why some people desire to live as the opposite sex. Just as it was for Mike and Molly, sex is a *preference* regardless which sex one is born to, because we aren't any different from Mike and Molly. We're altogether human and, along humanity's ancient path, their descendants.

The larger point here is that the characteristics of sex aren't intrinsic to ℒife's WOB although pairwise WOB *is*. What we typify as male and female is nothing more than habituated WOB rooted in ℒife's initial pairwise birth. Sex is so potent for physical-born humans partly because we integrate so intimately with our physicality (to the exclusion of our self's spirit and unembodied modes) in which sex is genetically inherent and believed immutable. But the notion of mutable sex comes far easier to the spirit-born who live in an environment where Intentionality and matter manipulation is a pedestrian reality.[379] Changing one's natural sex requires altering one's WOB, which is an involved, lengthy enough process for the spirit-born much less when physically attempted.[380] Simply modifying one's spirit form to *appear* as the other sex instead of altering one's WOB is the quick and easy way but requires maintenance, thus an extra expenditure of energy that, in The Corruption's milieu, can be tiring (§ 3.2.2.1.1:416).

2.1.5.2 THE TWINS WERE WITHOUT CULTURE

The whole point of building a universe was so the Twins could experience material experience. And experience it they did. Before embodying themselves, they had only a limited concept of care, love, and interpersonal feelings intrinsic of embodiment despite them being natural aspects of human WOB. Like sex, these and other aspects of our WOB were only nascent in the Twins.[381] This was due partly to their unembodied nature and to their absolute

---

379. Not that the spirit-born were any more aware of this before the Big Healing than we on Earth are right now. Modern medicine allows the physical-born to change sex, but the same result is had using Intentionality as in spirit world, though it takes longer.

380. Changing physical body sex via reassignment surgery is functionally the same as using a glamour (§ 2.1.5.4.4:318) to change spirit body sex. Without altering WOB, one's psyche remains their birthed sex regardless appearance, drugs, and hormones.

381. Nascent to *them* as the first humans, not to later persons born into an Ultraculture imbibed from conception (§ 4:291).

naiveté regarding their humanity. Mike and Molly's relationship wasn't shallow but it was superficial, as their primordial state necessarily couldn't yet develop the vast repertoire of the human psyche. That isn't the case now with unembodied-born humans because they're aware of it all, but it was then because Mike and Molly, all alone, lacked awareness of it as well as guidance; they lacked a culture. They were unaware of who and what they were in their entirety until experiencing the entirety of their environment. They did this first as unembodied persons in their proto-energy environment (§ 2.3.2.1:241), then in the context of their experiments with matter, and finally embodied in forms within Molly's Primoverse admidst a growing humanity of descendants.

Becoming fully human for any of us is a maturation process we go through from conception. It was no different for Mike and Molly, except they weren't born with any pre-existing Ultraculture (§ 4.1:291). They had to build it from scratch. For a very long time, then, everything for them was a new experience, a new comprehension, a new perspective.

2.1.5.3   The Body Takes Shape

We reiterate that the first form Mike and Molly developed was the supranatural body and that's what we're describing here. They developed the natural body later (§ 2.1.5.5:322). The reason is easy to see. A spirit body Intentionalizes, (manifests, embodies) straight from Thought whereas a physical body needs develop by and through its physical environment—regardless whether evolutionarily directed or, as with nonhumans, more undirected (§ 2.1.5.5.2.1:323)—which takes quite some time to accomplish.

While a physical body needs function in its environment within certain parameters or not function at all, that's not the case with a spirit body having no objectively independent functionality of its own. The spirit body is a direct manifestation of *L*ife's woʙ. Mike and Molly created their first bodies in terms of aesthetics—how it looks—based, in part, on what they thought they wanted to do with it, such as directly interacting with supramatter to touch, move, and so forth. Later, they took these spirit-body aesthetics and applied them to the physical body, adjusting its attributes over time as they developed it to meet the parameters necessary to survival in its physical environment, as well as to integrate their mind.

As they experimented with form, they realized their human woʙ readily integrated certain ones over others. They couldn't, for example, Intentionalize a body with ten eyes, four arms, eight legs, two brains, and still *integrate*. With each effort to Intentionalize a form, it grew clearer that what emergently birthed 'in' EPL that was 'Mike' and 'Molly' was a woʙ gravitating toward a certain form. So, they had to narrow down their initially imagined form to a range of possibilities, eventually to specific attributes, then finally to an integration of attributes that altogether constituted a woʙ-compliant form in its entirety. This is what we today call the human body and it's the *only* form-woʙ that integrates human woʙ. In our ignorance of reality, it's been natural for us to think that God, evolution, or both created our body only on Earth and that if there's intelligent life elsewhere in our universe then it necessarily has different, locally evolved bodies. In reality, the physicospirit body we have on Earth is more or less the same as on all planets in our universe, and more or less the same physicospirit body that sentient–sapient life—necessarily *f*juman *L*ife—has *everywhere*, in all universes. Once they figured out which form was human woʙ integrable, then *that* was our human form.

For starters, they imagined two standard, essentially identical spirit bodies compatible with human woʙ but without sex or procreative ability because they still lacked that concept. They manifested them via Intentionality with various attributes according to their own woʙ and personal preferences in order to fulfill their principle desire to interact with each other by and through a supramaterial environment. That task took about 100KY to complete. They naturally integrated and experienced their bodies along with its reality. As noted, the supranatural environment needs the natural Energent's proto-energy for spirit matter to endure (§ 7.1.3:214). Their spirit bodies would eventually require a physical universe to provide the necessary *enérgeia* (§ 4.3:150). When they finally got around to working up physical life precursors circa 10BY later, the natural environment took charge of developing all its complex structure based on Molly's founding Intentionality, which naturally guided the chemistry behind life precursors toward their Intentionalized end state until a physical human body was suitable for integration. That task took about 20BY soup to nuts (*Fig. 138*), from developing the precursors of life (§ 1.3.1:272) to arriving at an integrable physical body. This is double the approximately 10BY between our so-called Big Bang to Mina first initiating the general precursors to physical (Living) life, and the additional ∼3.5BY until he initiated the precursors for *f*juman embodiment on suitable planets (§ 2.2:522; § 1.1:532).[382]

---

382. He started life precursors on Earth ∼3.3BYA.

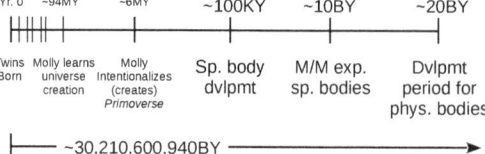

Figure 138. Timeline: development of spirit to physical form (reverse was faster but they didn't know).

2.1.5.4 THE SPIRIT BODY EXPERIENCE

The moment a couple conceives a child, a spirit body manifests as part of *Life*'s emergent birth 'in' EPL (§ 1.2.1.1:248) and, if physically conceived, a physical body, as well. No one conceived Mike and Molly. They emergently birthed 'in' EPL without integrating a body at all. Their lives began unembodied.[383] Accordingly, they could manifest a spirit body or integrate a physical body at will.[384] After Molly created her universe, she and Mike each manifested a spirit body long before the natural (physical) environment there could support a physical body. They weren't in a rush to create physical bodies anyhow because not only was there quite a bit to learn to formulate physical life, but there was also just so much to experience with a spirit body. Recall that embodied *Life* was on-the-job training (OJT) for the Twins. They knew nothing of any aspect of human existence until they experienced it. Even today, people encounter previously undiscovered human capabilities, and the Cardinal feels there's a zero probability that'll ever cease. The psyche integrating proto-energy is breathtakingly rich, complex, deep, and broad.

Once the Twins comprehended Intentionality and Molly had built her Primoverse, manifesting a spirit body was pretty much a breeze. More difficult was exactly *what* to manifest. As described, only a body in accord with human WOB integrates the human psyche. Suppose the Twins Intentionalized a spider-like creature with which to integrate their mind. The Intentionality would fail to occur—the form simply wouldn't manifest (materialize)—because its existence predicates integrating a human psyche. Being outside human WOB, the Intention as a whole fails because a part of it's impossible. Simply manifesting a spider-like creature is certainly doable, but creating it to integrate a person is not. Figuring out these nuts and bolts took them considerable time.

2.1.5.4.1 THE SEVEN ꙮUMAN SENSES

Unembodied persons like Mike and Molly can experience their own and, to some degree, other minds, as well as proto-energy. But they can't experience materialized proto-energy (matter) that lies outside mind that, although constituted of proto-energy, isn't in that context (§ 2.3:115). Spirit bodies bridge the gap between mind and matter, offering the Twins their first material integration and sensorial interaction with it. Mike and Molly wanted to experience matter *as* matter, and *sensation* is how mind experiences what's *outside* own-self. While humans have many different kinds of senses that enable the physical and spirit body to function in its environment, only seven concern us here because they form our core somatic awareness of matter in both the natural and supranatural environments (Table 13). It's important to recognize a person interprets somatic senses by and through mind whether sensing the environment inside or outside the body. This is why touching a lover's body is so radically different from touching oneself or a 'skin-realistic' latex sex doll. Senses are how we, as mind, have certain awareness of not-mind.

Table 13. Core somatic and other senses of the physicospirit body.

7 Core Senses: Physical & Spirit Body	Additional Navigable Senses
Sight	**Physical & Spirit Body**
Hearing	Movement (kinesthetic)
Smell	Body position in space (proprioception)
Taste	**Spirit Body**
Touch	Body position in sp. world w.r.t. sp. world
Electromagnetic (mag. & elec. fields)	Body position in sp. world w.r.t. phys. world
Temperature	Knowing real self behind appearance (glamour)

---

383. A sensory deprivation tank is a facsimile of the unembodied state where Thought is one's only stimulus, hence, reality.

384. So long as no other person is born already integrating it (§ 3.2.2:567), which wasn't a concern since they were alone in All Existence. This is true for any person conceived unembodied, which some are (§ 1.2.1.1.3:250; § 2:564).

2.1.5.4.2 The Navigable Senses

The seven core senses in Table 13 are self-explanatory except for the electromagnetic sense, but let's look at the navigable senses first. We distinguish them from the seven core senses because, in the physical body context, they aren't a brain function as the core senses are but originate in mind.[385] For example, the movement (*kinesthetic*) sense doesn't sense matter as an external reality to the body as do touch or smell, nor is it an internal sense arising from the nervous system. Rather, it's mind's overall awareness of each body part's location in space relative to other parts of the body and as a whole at any given moment. The brain isn't collating action potential data from touch, pressure, and other neurons sowed throughout the body to produce all of this sense. Instead, integrated ⒧ife mind itself is intimately aware of the body's full positional state (which arises with mind in the first place) that, via integration, informs the brain (§ 1.2.2.4:257) and rounds out its more primitive neuronal awareness.

Unlike kinesthetics, the physical body position sense (*proprioception*[386]) is a mind–brain combination shared via integration, the brain side primarily managing reflex control in this context (in the spirit body, it's fully a mind sense). It arises because a body's principal mode is movement in its environment. For example, in response to their environment, physical humans and animals generally move place to place while plants move within place (bending to the wind, say). Without movement, physical survival diminishes. This characteristic didn't evolutionarily develop in humans to ensure physical survival, but arose consistent with human woв to ensure Mike and Molly's experience of spirit matter, which then became the human norm. Despite physical humanity's initial primitivity and *need* to move, our movement is for pleasure, not need. However, without a sense of the body's position in local space, a physical or spirit person experiences disorientation that naturally makes movement difficult or impossible. As well, sensing where one's spirit self wholistically is in the supranatural environment is just as important for orientation as proprioception is for the body in its physical environment. The same goes for sensing one's spirit self's location—being oriented—in the supranatural environment w.r.t. the natural (physical) environment. These senses orient the unembodied mind in its embodied environment.

2.1.5.4.3 The Electromagnetic Sense

It's generally believed humans have no ability to sense Earth's geomagnetic field (*magnetoreception*) or electric fields generally the way many vertebrates and some invertebrates do, such as birds using the geomagnetic field to navigate migratory paths and certain fish using electric fields to sense prey. Mina says that humans, too, can sense these fields.[387] We group them here for convenience as the electromagnetic sense, which includes our sense of direction.

Magnetoreception is actually a combination of electric and magnetic field sensing; we thus relabel it *electromagnetoreception* (EmRn). It works as a Living version of a compass. A compass seeks magnetic north not from geomagnetic north magnetically attracting the magnetized compass needle, but from the many small electric fields of an opposite charge emanating from electrons with certain spin that make up the magnetic field lines. Recall that all physical phenomena boil down to electric charge, which manifests as real energy Υ (Fundamental Force) and applied energy E (§ 3.3.2.1:126) as a result of proto-energy interacting with archí in motion. In this respect, magnetic attraction works in the same way as gravitational attraction. We described earlier how a multilocal chain of net attraction overcomes local normative repulsion between objects to net attract across the macrospace along a gravity vector (§ 3.3.2.2:128). This process is at work between the free-floating compass needle and geomagnetic (or a stronger, nearby magnet's) field lines, gravitationally pulling the compass needle along the electromagnetic vector which, w.r.t. gravity, is the gravity vector. Since the compass is held in place by friction as well as Earth's greater aggregate pull of gravity, the attracted point of the free-floating compass needle gives the impression of pointing toward magnetic north from simple magnetic attraction when it's really just gravitationally pulled in that direction. This is the same phenomenon described in Momentum Weight (Fig. 15:134) when an object in space encounters a gravity vector and, according to the forces involved, reorients toward it, which is to say, the object deflects along the gravity vector.

In physical humans, EmRn generally works through various cells in the brain, some of which have recently been termed place cells, grid cells, and head-direction cells found in the brain's hippocampus and the entorhinal region near it (Costandi 2017; Makin 2015). These cells serve multiple functions, one of which is the EmRn

---

385. Kinesthetics is 100% mind; proprioception is a 70–30 mind–brain combination sense (cf. Lackner et al. 2005, Proske 2006, Proske et al. 2012 indicating that receptors responding to stretch/tension in muscles, joints, skin, tendons inform the brain).

386. The ability to sense the body and the self-movement and position in space of its parts.

387. Science is catching on to this reality, however (e.g., Wang et al. 2019).

sense. But in EMRn's case, these cells only interpret received sensory data coming from EMRn receptors located in a 3-micron wide band in the dermis layer (second of three layers of skin) circling the central neck area, passing just under the upper portion of the trachea. These receptors work in conjunction with other body sensors to enable our EMRn sense. They operate somewhat similar to E–PG (head-direction, or compass) neurons in the Drosophila fruit fly (as well as mammals) that form a ring like a compass dial with ring attractor properties. In Drosophila, a 'bump' of neural activity moves around the ring like a compass needle as the fly moves (Fisher et al. 2019, 121). EMRn neurons are located in the human neck because the brain's comparatively powerful electrical field—averaging approximately 0.59 volts per meter (cf. Huang et al. 2017, 5)—interferes when they're located in the brain.

Today, only about 25% of Earth's population, spread fairly evenly across the globe, has these EMRn sensors. They genetically phased out of most of our collective DNA about 12,000 years ago when Mina says a vengeful spirit person Intentionalized the responsible genes to turn off in one particular adult woman. Her altered DNA eventually passed beyond just her targeted lineage (as happens when genetically tinkering) to affect three quarters of today's humanity. Those who carry the active EMRn sensors sense Earth's geomagnetic field and electric fields generally better than do non-EMRn people, and overall have a better sense of direction. Mina is now reconstituting the EMRn sense in the balance of Earth's humanity but he says it'll take about 200 years to complete.

2.1.5.4.4 The Glamour Sense

Ayako calls this the *glamour* sense, as it's reminiscent of the magic of the Fæ (mythological race of færies) who put up glamours to disguise themselves, and comes closest to what's at play. Since the spirit body Intentionalizes in mind, one can manifest their appearance howsoever they please. Taiji, for instance (FN 21:9; EN 52:648), preferred keeping his spirit world hair and looks in his twenties the way he liked it best while physically alive. Others present themselves as younger, older, opposite sex, taller, shorter, different hairstyle, color, ethnicity, and so on than they'd naturally present according to WOB. Without the glamour sense, we'd never know who was who in spirit world; anyone could be anybody. This sense gives a person the feeling that whoever has their attention isn't who or what they appear to be.

For example, if one knows the person, then this sense helps one recognize that person for who they are, not how they look. If one doesn't know the person, the sense helps one realize the person is using 'a glamour,' which means disguising themselves in some way from their true form and appearance for whatever purpose. Physical people are capable of sensing a glamour—a person in disguise—even without recognizing eyes, bone structure, gait, posture, or whatever. This changeability is simply part of human freedom to be howsoever one desires, arising consequent of the spirit body being a direct manifestation of mind. We can change our physical body's appearance, too, but it's more tedious than with our spirit body (Fig. 94:218). For example, dog owners coming to resemble their pets over time or our faces altering through chronic emotion—worry, anger, fear—is a very limited expression of physical-body glamour. We may not think that we ourselves are changing our appearance but, through the power of Intentionality, indeed, we are. We don't comprehend this ability today, so it seems farfetched. But properly educated, the malleability of physical matter becomes evident.[388]

2.1.5.4.5 Discovering Sensation

Besides the obvious, what makes us particularly human that embodied life is even worth living, a joy to experience? At the granular level, it's different for each person. But from the bird's eye, humanity gets its *joie de vivre* from the thrill of discovering and exploring oneself and others. There's no context for it. The encounter itself creates infinite possibilities, experiences, thinking–feeling (Thought), wonder, crescendos of emotion, and so on (e.g., ~97.5% of the spirit-born urbanize). In contrast, unembodiment is a more sequestered experience. One interacts with self and others in Thought but, sans embodiment, that's the end of it. For some people, that's sufficient and all they desire or, at least, it's what they desire as a periodic refuge from wild and woolly embodiment. As with any way of life, one need get used to it to appreciate its finer points. However, that was all Mike and Molly knew since birth, and until they Intentionalized their brand spanking new spirit bodies in the Primoverse, it was all they knew about themselves and each other. They were utterly unprepared for

---

388. Spirit glamour requires energy. The greater the glamour, the greater the energy to maintain it. Some find it too tiring in The Corruption's milieu and eventually revert to their norm. Taiji gave up his young man's aesthetic for how he subconsciously sees himself—a fifty-year-old Japanese man.

the vast panoply of *sensation* that exploded in their minds the instant their integration delivered awareness of their body in its supramaterial environment.

Like physical infants, the Twins had to learn to seamlessly operate their spirit bodies. Despite manifesting them with their own minds, they felt quite alien. Discovering them in all their exquisitely fine detail presented a different challenge altogether. For example, one can design and build by hand a superlative racecar, knowing its design capabilities inside and out. But the moment one settles into the driver's seat, turns over the engine, feels its power thrumming through the frame, then pops the clutch and blasts out of the workshop faster and more recklessly than ever intended because what the car can *actually* do in reality is a frank surprise, that's when the difference between creating and operating becomes real. This is why a new aircraft design needs flight-testing, to find out how it *really* handles in the air regardless the math's expectations. We quite forget our own experience as infants and toddlers learning to use our brains and control our bodies. Mike and Molly were already full-fledged adults in mind when their physical bodies birthed, so their maturing experience was dramatically quicker than ours.

Likewise, the instant their mind integrated the sensorial capabilities of their spirit body, a blast-furnace-like wave of sensation all but paralyzed them the way a sudden shock can knock one back on their keister, stunned and insensate. Though they correctly modeled and predicted the probable sensory experience, every sensation *felt* completely unexpected and overwhelming. As Earth-equivalent days, months, years, and millennia went by, they marveled at the seemingly never-ending new sensations as well as the thinking–feeling arising with them, especially the feeling aspect. It made their previous unembodied feelings seem paltry in comparison. It was now they sensed their true humanity, what they were truly capable of being. And then one day, Molly felt something new and all too confusing. Love for Mike.

2.1.5.4.6 Discovering Love

Many of us recall the first time we felt romantically about another person, the way feelings seemed to creep up on us or just swoop in like a bird of prey, dominating our thinking–feeling until any separation from our love interest *hurt*. We marvel at love and what it does to us but, really, have no idea where, or in what, it originates and why. We can feel it suddenly taking us over like a body snatcher or disappearing despite our efforts to hold it close, or refusing to manifest regardless our loneliness.

Recall LOVE instantiates from proto-love Life force and is the base *emotion* from which our ordinary *feeling* of primary love instantiates and from which all other feelings—hate, happiness, fear, anger, joy, satisfaction— emote in turn as secondary expressions of LOVE (Table 10:285). Proto-love is the same Life force, the same emergent Life proto-energy, that constitutes the person. It differs from Life force in the same way EPL proto-energy differs from Energent–prime proto-energy: same proto-energy, different expression. So it is that love emanates from our own Life force, the very 'energy' that constitutes us as mindful beings. It emanates for the reason that, at our deepest level of own-self, *we* manifest it just as we manifest Thought and Intentionality. It doesn't seem that way because the surface tension of our conscious awareness so thoroughly ensnares our conscious Thought that we rarely, if ever, perceive our true Thought below its rugged surface much less consciously *experience* our true self.

As an analogy, consider your conscious awareness like a water spider prancing hither and yon across the deeper pond that's your subconscious mind, separated from experiencing its reality by the water's surface tension. Down in that pond is who you really are, how you really feel, what you really want, generating all the currents, eddies, temperatures, and energies the water spider only dimly perceives on the surface unless the deeper environment agitates its placid footing. The conscious mind, like the water spider, is generally aware of only itself and its surface environment, not the pond's depths. Love isn't some magical force searing into our lives like a bolt from the blue, but *our own Life force* so strongly expressing its reaction to an object of love's WOB that it roils our conscious awareness and we experience its feeling.

This is how it happened for Molly. About 10MY into running around in spirit bodies, her long-developing subconscious feelings for Mike lit up her conscious awareness. Initially, Mike wasn't of the same mind but, after about another 5MY, he came round to her way of Thought and they embraced their mutual love. But it was platonic, somewhat in Plato's ancient sense of experiencing a person as a representation of pure, ideated beauty (*Symposium* ca. 385–370 BC), and somewhat in its modern sense simply as asexual love. Manifesting their spirit bodies without any sense of love, sex, or procreation meant they didn't manifest sex organs, which anyhow were unnecessary for spirit bodies free of metabolic requirements. Certainly, they touched each other's bodies and felt all the same feelings we do in such cases, but didn't initially comprehend their feelings or how to handle them. It was (from our perspective) a slow process of experimenting, assessing, discussing, and so on toward forming a conceptual understanding of just what was going on in their minds as a result of integrating and interacting with their bodies as supramatter.

Unlike a physical couple whose innate chemistry seems to respond on its own—recall the teenage couple in the film *Blue Lagoon* (1980)—regardless mind understanding the situation or not, Mike and Molly's spirit bodies didn't go on hormonal autopilot. Instead, the sensations flooding their minds sent their Thought into mysterious realms for which they had no guidance as to meaning and response. Besides their other explorations, study, play, and whatnot, all told they spent about 190MY struggling to comprehend their feelings, especially of love (*Fig. 139*). Whether Mike and Molly ever kissed during this 190MY period never came up in Mina's conversations with Cosmo, so he doesn't know although feels they did. Either way, their sum total understanding of human love was simply the sensation produced from Touching (and possibly kissing), and that was it. They had yet to realize it was even possible to produce more humans at will or that, if new humans appeared, it wouldn't be simply the random event their own births were. With that limiting mindset, and no biological imperative natural to physical bodies, it never occurred to them they could procreate, nor that a sexual relationship might exist.

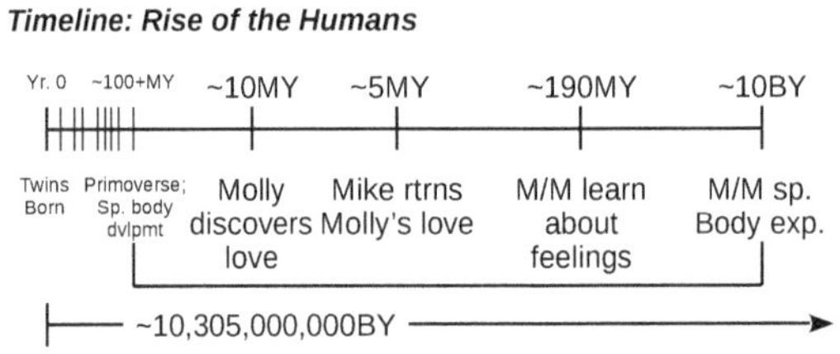

Timeline: Rise of the Humans

Figure 139. Timeline: discovering and grappling with feelings when the Twins were exploring spirit embodiment before developing their physical bodies (doesn't include all periods as shown in Fig. 138:316).

2.1.5.4.7 ЅUMAN TOUCH

Touch in and of itself is not just quintessentially human but represents the essence of what ᒪife covets above all else—'entangling' with others. This returns us to our earlier discussion of quantum entanglement re-termed Energent Parity P_E (§ 6.11.3:197). Because of how deeply and thoroughly Touch—defined as experiencing another human through at least one of the core senses excluding electromagnetic (Table 13:316)—is capable of 'entangling' two people, Mike and Molly were able to explore it sans sex for a supremely lengthy time before realizing there was even more. Let's consider the nature of Touch.

The kernel of humanity is awareness (§ 1.2.2:253). This comes clearest when we consider that our minds work according to awareness, not cognition (§ 2.1:276), that we *experience* awareness, we don't cognitively *know*. As an experience, awareness is fundamentally emotive because it begins in ᒪife force, which is Thought (thinking–feeling). Though we say thinking–feeling, the human psyche isn't a duality of reason and emotion; it's a felt-ness. To be aware is to feel—though not to have feelings about—what one is aware of; conversely, to feel is to be aware. Thought arises from awareness. It's our mind experiencing awareness, which we feel. We experience awareness by thinking about (analyzing) and feeling (emoting) it. So, awareness means to feel that of which we have awareness as an experience.

This is why Touch is fundamental to, and so powerful for, humans. When we Touch anything, especially others, we experience them as a felt-ness; we're aware of them in an essential way. Any person's essence is their ᒪife force, the emergent self-aware proto-energy that they are. To be experientially aware of their ᒪife force is to be as intimately aware of them as a being as it's possible to be. We form this intimacy via Touch, which is the mechanism, or trigger, for a person's ᒪife force to 'entangle' with another person's ᒪife force such that there's felt-ness, awareness. Recall the Energent Parity (quantum entanglement) phenomenon that's homologous with awareness, which resonates in the field of proto-energy between entangled objects (§ 6.11.6:200). For humans, Parity isn't simply a correlation of properties between entangled objects but, on a much more sophisticated level, is awareness. Because awareness is felt-ness, and thus an expression of proto-love (Table 10:285), we crave 'entanglement.' Here's the reason embodied humans can't live without Touch, why physical-born infants die when denied it,[268] why physicospirit infants similarly fall into stasis—as in abortion (including the spirit-born; § 2.2:410), miscarriage, stillbirth, death generally before age four until Touch revives them to develop self-sustainment.[389]

---

389. From ~4YO, a spirit child manages self-growth even absent Touch. The adult body devoid of Touch expires, too.

When physical or spirit embodied people Touch—which Intentionalizes via the 𝓛ife force aspects of emotive 𝓛ife force (Em𝓛F) and proto-love—then Parity occurs, meaning 𝓛ife forces 'entangle.' Parity creates awareness of the 'entangled' object (here, a person), what quantum science imagines as instant communication across infinite distance distinguished by correlated states between entangled particles. Awareness via Parity is what we call intimacy, a mode of being which is fundamental to being human. Real intimacy is Parity, which the world imagines only in a limited, incomplete, inanimate, and subatomic sense as quantum entanglement. When we Touch another person (willingly or not; Parity's an automatic process), we 'entangle.' In our deepest mind, usually though not always beyond conscious awareness, an intimacy arises between the parties where—if we could experimentally measure it in detail—we'd say their modes of being correlate much like the entangled particles science observes.

2.1.5.4.8 THREE CORRELATED STATES

We experience three states of correlation through Parity with other persons: 𝓛ife force, own-self awareness, and Thought. We describe each in turn.

>   **𝓛ife force** proto-energy constituting the human person—their consciousness, self-awareness, being-ness—can't mix, join, intertwine, intermingle, or in any way become a part of any other proto-energy because it's discrete, unique, and autonomous (§ 2.1.3:309). As we've described, however, objects entangle via Parity within the greater matrix of Energent proto-energy, and the same holds for humans (§ 6.11.7:201). Two people (as a group) form a unique, pairwise 'entanglement' as described above where their individual 𝓛ife forces are aware of, or correlate with, the other in the *vitae mysterium* of proto-energy; the deeper the 'entanglement,' the greater the awareness. Their 𝓛ife forces 'attach' through proto-energy in a state we call Parity ('entanglement') but aren't intermingled, mixed, or the like. Each 𝓛ife force remains discrete and sovereign but uniquely aware of the other. Unlike non-alive object entanglement, no other 'entanglement' by the same person or others is the same, as each 'entanglement' is unique.
>
>   **Own-self awareness** creates an own-self state between 'entangled' persons. Recall that own-self isn't simply one's individual self but includes anything one considers part of individual self (§ 2:275). With Parity, an 'entangled' person automatically becomes own-self even if the individual who initiates the Parity consciously pays no attention to it and doesn't even think of the 'entangled' person as own-self. Ranging from extremely subtle to consciously aware, 'entanglement' affects own-self awareness and therefore own-self well-being. This means a person can feel—have awareness of—the 'entangled' person's state of being. In practical terms, we sense the nature of their situation—in trouble, suffering, fearful, alive when presumed or actually dead when hoped to be alive, and so on. The average person just *knows*. When asked, they may say with a twitch and a wriggle, "Dunno; just feel it."
>
>   **Thought** w.r.t. Parity correlates 'entangled' persons' thinking–feeling whereby two strongly 'entangled' people for instance finish each other's sentences, know what the other is thinking–feeling—is going to say or feel, including body language—before they express it, feel the other's needs, desires, and activities, or sense without evidence their partner is cheating. Sometimes, we simply intuit the latter from our own spirit mind because, in a particular case, it's stronger than Thought correlation.

2.1.5.4.9 INTIMACY

Practically speaking, the above three correlations are true intimacy. It has many grades of intensity, from barely 'entangled' to a deep, full resonance, and from consciously unaware to fully aware. As with Parity, intimacy doesn't self-perpetuate but constantly renews, strengthens, and more deeply resonates through continual Touch. Without it, Parity degrades over time like its inanimate namesake. And because humans are Intentional beings, one can Intentionally sever Parity so long as, thereafter, the parties don't physically or spiritually Touch. Intimacy, the end state of Parity, effectively joins the parties' 𝓛ife force such that two emergent humans of unique, autonomous, and sovereign proto-energy mimic the state of 'being as one' without actually being as one, since 𝓛ife proto-energy can't intermingle or infuse to become, literally, as one. But since our woʙ emergently arose in a pairwise context with a craving for intimacy in a milieu where the nature of 𝓛ife force made it technically impossible, the 'entanglement' of Parity emergently arose alongside to surmount that barrier. Mike and Molly only discovered this reality when they integrated their spirit bodies and experienced Touch (cf. Sᴇx, § 2.2.1.2:598).

In the back of Molly's mind over this circa 10BY period of spirit body exploration was the eventual need to create physical bodies, because this is how, in accord with the principles of proto-energy, their spirit bodies maintain the 'energy' to Intentionalize through ℒife mind into reality and to do all they do in the supranatural environment (§ 7.1.3:214). Until human physical bodies were a reality, their spirit bodies were running on Mike and Molly's own ℒife force like a battery.

2.1.5.5 THE PHYSICAL BODY EXPERIENCE

At this point, Mike and Molly had emergently birthed, matured, discovered each other and Intentionality, materialized proto-energy, and built the most complex matter structure possible—a universe—which, through trial and error, they integrated via the human woB-compliant albeit asexual spirit bodies they'd Intentionalized, and then discovered a mind-blowing world of sensation that began unlocking their real humanity. All this took roughly 10BY before they arrived on the eve of Intentionalizing the seminal precursors of physical (Living) life in the Primoverse (*Fig. 140*). It took this long because they were learning so much about themselves while supranaturally embodied that they didn't want to stop to focus on the natural. Molly put off setting up physical life until she could no longer procrastinate.

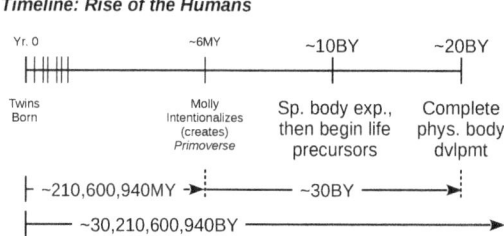

Figure 140. Timeline: Twins' birth to Molly's Primoverse, then from life precursors to integrable bodies.

The Twins by now were about 10.2BY old and the Primoverse a bit less (*Fig. 140*). Stars and planets had formed in its natural environment that were translating minimal 'energy' to its supranatural one (ibid). But to sustain their Intentionalized spirit bodies and nonhuman supranatural life, her universe required physical life in its natural environment. So, Molly set to work. Mike could help here because the job was one of individually manipulating multiple discrete objects of matter, which anyone can do in a universe.

2.1.5.5.1 PRECURSORS FOR PHYSICAL LIFE

Physical life precursors don't randomly or emergently manifest. Universe builders Intentionalize its building blocks. The woB of life precursors are part of the Intentionalized woB of a universe from the get-go so that, when a founder does manifest them, life happens because its constituents are already present. Because of the way the natural Energent works vis-à-vis the supranatural, physical life needs exist in the natural environment. Yet, though it's a necessity, a builder must still Intentionalize its woB when universe building. Otherwise, it would lack a critical aspect of woB and be unable to manifest life at all (§ 2.1.3:309). Precursors are simply the right complex archí structures such as reactive nonmetals—nitrogen, carbon, oxygen—and ten others yet undiscovered and not listed on the periodic table of elements. These elementals don't automatically interact to form life precursors or even life. Even if they're in necessary proximity, their normal interaction doesn't suffice for life without Intentionally sowing Living force into the chemical relationships. As these Intentionalized elementals interact, they form molecular structures until, eventually, life's barest minimum existence—primal Living entities—obtains.

Science believes life's precursors originated off Earth, falling from space. That isn't unusual. Our planet formed in the first place from space particles bombarding each other until conglomerating into a locally dominating gravitational mass. Recall that matter constitutes from pairwise archí (§ 2.3:115). The observable universe's gravity wells (§ 6.10.1:186)—which every universe has since they adhere to the same proto-energy template—clump them into visible matter until stars, planets, and galaxies form. Elementals saturate a developing planet as part of this process. Life doesn't arise by chance from propitious chemistry. It's not random inevitability, it's Intentional. In the fullness of a planet's development, a builder Intentionalizes atoms to molecularize in certain ways via proto-energy and Living force whereby an operational state we call life—Living—arises (§ 1.3.1:272).

2.1.5.5.2 EVOLUTION

Recall the girls and I discovered evolution was wrong although, like the Bible and Divine Principle, not entirely (§ 1.1:4). Evolution is inaccurate ascribing life and species development solely to abiogenesis[390] and random natural selection rather than part of a wholistic developmental process involving all the environmental elements of our universe. Evolution, as commonly understood, begins its analysis only with the functional end-state of biodevelopment, not simply because the theory can't observe the mechanisms at work in chemogenesis, biogenesis, and mutagenesis,[391] but because, until energy testing, there's been no methodology to pry deeper. Science necessarily leaves life functionally nothing more than mystical chemistry. But that's no less magical than claiming God did it. No matter how far from Darwin the modern, post-modern, and replacement syntheses[392] get, they're only refining his thesis that life develops through a survival process that's effectively a natural—versus artificial (purposed)—selectivity.

All Living things, except for integrated humanity, physically evolve—change, alter, adjust, adapt, et cetera—because unlike supranatural matter, natural matter has independent existence and exists in accord with its environment.[393] It has its own autonomous WOB that organizes and operates its operational state vis-à-vis its environment, which also has a WOB. Altering physical matter's WOB is a process of directed action over time just as with human WOB (§ 3.3:283). For people, altering WOB is a directed affair. For Living entities, including the human body, altering WOB is directed and undirected.

2.1.5.5.2.1 DIRECTED AND UNDIRECTED EVOLUTION

Evolution by random natural selection is only part of reality (though for humans as persons versus their physical bodies it plays no part). Recall there are two fundamental aspects of living things, human *Life* and nonhuman Living (§ 1:246). In the natural environment, we distinguish between *Life* that integrates the Living human body to form a wholistic mind–body human (*physicospirit* embodiment), and nonhuman Living entities that make up the balance of all things we reckon as alive.

All Living entities have WOB, and evolution occurs in two WOB contexts. First, when an imbalance between environment WOB and species WOB arises from environmental stressors, undirected Intentionality (§ 3.2:282) arises to rebalance these WOB, and *undirected evolution*—adaptive traits—may follow. Second, when Mina or some other person directedly Intentionalizes a change in an entity or species' WOB, then *directed evolution* may follow to the degree they coax along the change. Consequently, evolution of Living entities is both an undirected and directed phenomenon. That said, we define what evolution's 'random mutations' are, then describe nonhuman (undirected and directed) and human body evolution. We follow that up at the end of this chapter with 'evolution' of the human person as *Life* (§ 3:331).

2.1.5.5.2.2 NATURE OF EVOLUTIONARY CHANGE

There are no stochastically unknowable factors behind evolutionary change. All change arises in specific contexts of which there are five that, to some degree, always overlap (Table 14).

Table 14. The five causes behind evolutionary change.

	matter–Energy	Intentionality
	Natural (undirected)	
Replication errors:	chance occurrences	DNA internal
	Emergent change	DNA internal
	Environment pressure	DNA generally
	Ultraculture	DNA generally
	Artificial (directed)	
	Human directed	DNA generally
	Intentional directed (§ 6.5.2:437)	DNA generally

---

390. The natural process in which life arises spontaneously from nonliving matter.

391. *Chemogenesis*: genesis of chemistry; *biogenesis*: genesis of biology; *mutagenesis*: genesis of that leading to mutation.

392. Originally coined by Julian Huxley in *Evolution* (1942) then expounded by others, these syntheses attempt to reconcile science's changing understanding of how life develops over time.

393. Humanity either compels its environment into accord, or necessarily adapts via technology or directed minor variance.

All mutative change begins in DNA or its constituents, such as molecular relationships, genes, and alleles.[394] The standard causes behind evolutionary change in the literature—selection (allele favorability); mutation (positive–negative selection; rise of new alleles); drift (neutral selection; change in allele dominance by chance)— are symptomatic of natural (undirected) change types per Table 14. On the other hand, a relatively less known theory called *endosymbioses*, where two independent entities combine to form an externally single, yet internally differentiated, symbiotic entity is symptomatic of artificial (directed) change types.[395] We consider Table 14's evolutionary change causes below.

DNA replication errors are an inevitable aspect of biology in our universe. Even when perfectly operating, an entity's DNA will still encounter errors of varying magnitude during replication from a variety of naturally occurring factors. There would be far fewer than now, however. For example, the ratio of undirected to directed change would be 60:40 rather than today's 80:20 (NONHUMAN EVOLUTION: NATURAL SELECTION, *below*), the reason being the more replication errors, the more likely they derail directed change. Even so, WOB would correct such errors, regardless. Mina took something of a live-and-let-live attitude toward nonhuman evolution until the Big Healing afforded him new opportunities to make lasting repairs as replication errors declined. These are insignificant for now, aye, but with the expectation it'll snowball.

Emergent change to DNA is unpredictable even in principle (§ 2:90). It accounts for about 24% of all DNA mutation. Even so, human Intentionality can, over time, void emergent mutations in favor of a directed one. This is also true with replication errors. In both cases, Mina sometimes prefers to observe an error or emergent change play out amongst nonhuman entities because—who knows?—an emergent mutation could turn out interesting or beneficial.

Environmental pressure (see NONHUMAN EVOLUTION: NATURAL SELECTION, *below*).

Ultraculture refers to the collective consciousness that prevails throughout our universe and, in our case, Earth. Until the Big Healing, Ultraculture was altogether negative because of The Corruption and the Accountableism spawned by Michael's lie (§ 1.4:14; § 1.2:21; § 4:377). Its energy—emotive 𝓛ife force inter-acting with proto–energy—as well as people inimical to Mina's efforts, constantly fomented unforeseen and undesirable change leading to creatures and biology dangerous to humans that he found difficult to keep up with and eradicate across all human populated planets. The so-called omnipotence of a universe builder, you see, doesn't mean he or she can work (near-)instantaneous physical change nor compel free, autonomous persons to their will, as Earth's sacred texts abundantly demonstrate in their descriptions of humanity's omnipresently sinful and rebellious condition. It's relative, not absolute (§ 1:335).

Human directed mutative change happens when a person—Mina, or anyone—Intentionalizes it. It's a skill to learn and not out of the ordinary person's reach. Earth-born spirit persons perpetrate about 99.9% of all human directed evolution on Earth, with the balance coming from Mina along with some physical-born (not native to Earth) and spirit-born spirit persons. Of the Earth-born mutation artists, ∼99.5% of their work is malicious, vindictive, obstreperous, and the like as, for example, with the loss of our electromagnetoreception sense (§ 2.1.5.4.3:317). The remainder is (or intended to be) beneficial. These ridiculous numbers—there was much less interference with the planet during Original Humanity's tenure (§ 1:531)—are now falling thanks to the Big Healing, but one can see the problem that's beset Humanity 2.0 from its start that only ever gained traction.

2.1.5.5.2.3   NONHUMAN EVOLUTION: NATURAL SELECTION

Darwin termed evolutionary change *natural selection* to contrast it with artificial selection—hybridizing plants, animals, sometimes people to select for desired traits—because he recognized the mutative distinction between unintentional and intentional change, and didn't believe God was behind the fossil record's apparently slow, gradual, and random changes in species. Up to a point, he was correct. The development method for Living entities is a simple, mostly undirected selection system of trait survival over time. If entities with a certain trait survive and those without it don't, then said trait incorporates over time into the species until those entities with the trait are no longer the same as ancestral entities without it.

---

394. Allele is a variant form of a given gene, which makes up DNA and RNA.

395. Symbiosis is only ever a product of directed evolution.

Except Darwin (and today's evolutionists) sees the process incompletely as well as backward. In the first instance, nonhuman evolution is 80% undirected (not Intentioned) and 20% directed (Intentioned). In the second instance, new traits arise not in a species' entities—their biological bodies—but in the WOB of that species, which only then manifests in their bodies via (undirected or directed) Intentionality. Naturally, evolutionists can't imagine new traits arising from anything other than random biological mutations motivated by environmental pressures on survival, DNA replication errors, and stochastically unknowable factors. And they're also right, sort of. Since life is free, there's no constraints on its development and environmental response; there's no change-limit mechanism. Yet, every entity down to the single, unpaired archí has WOB that backstops what an entity is. But WOB isn't a radical change delimiter in the sense of prohibition, rather more like a barrier to entry. A Living species' core WOB is to live which, in the context of constant interactions between entity and proto-energy, results in an *undirected Intentionality* of proto-energy responding to WOB whereby a faux Intentionality arises.

Humans fully direct their Intentionality—whether arising in our subconscious self or conscious awareness[396]—whereas nonhuman Intentionality is undirected by the entity. It forms out of the natural interaction between WOB and proto-energy just as in humans it forms out of the natural interaction between one's Thought, ℒife force, and proto-energy (§ 3.2:282).[397] An entity's WOB is not its 'deeper' self but its 'core operating module' that's separate and independent of the entity itself in the same way a human *being* is the human *body's* 'core operating module' that's separate and independent of the body itself.[398]

Undirected (natural) evolution. When presented with a survival challenge of some magnitude, a Living entity's WOB-ness exerts more forcefully into the proto-energy environment because, in some way, the challenge is thwarting WOB which is implacable, unrelenting, always exerting WOB-ness. The more at variance an entity's WOB with its environment, the more there's a WOB imbalance between entity WOB and environment WOB. This imbalance exerts a 'pressure' on WOB such that, in the context of the proto-energy environment, WOB exerts as, or results in, undirected Intentionality arising in the hostile environment. Intentionality involves proto-energy, which interacts with the entity exerting its WOB's Intentionality on its biology—this is what it means to "exert[s] more forcefully" (*above*). A strong analogy for Mina is the imbalance between variant pressures where air moves as wind from high to low-pressure zones.

A species' WOB is like a low-pressure area in a higher-pressure environment. Intentionality is like air moving as wind from the high-pressure environment toward the low-pressure species' WOB. The low-pressure environment (WOB) interacts with the high-pressure one (proto-energy) and Intentionality (wind) arises. There would be no Intentionality (wind) if there were no species WOB (low-pressure zone) at variance with environment WOB (high-pressure zone). Species change, i.e., evolutionary natural selection, arises not from random mutation, but from imbalances between species WOB and environment WOB from which a species WOB Intentionality arises in conducive individual entities of the species to rebalance species WOB with environment WOB to enable species life. This is similar to the way air movement (wind) rebalances atmospheric pressure to enable an environmental steady state conducive to life.

WOB Intentionality isn't limited to just a single entity, of course, but to the entire species that shares the WOB. It works on the whole species altogether, exerting on all affected entities of the species equally.[399] We've learned that Intentionality takes time according to context; physical matter requires more time to alter than spirit matter. Therefore, no mutative change is immediate or universal throughout a species. It takes effect where an entity's internal and external environment is conducive to the change, and entity survival is favorable. Moreover, any change is of necessity incremental because complex biology can alter itself only so much over any given period.[400] Hence, evolution observes many micro mutations adding up over time to a mutative difference that separates those entities with it from those without it until we reckon it a new, or sub-, species.

---

396. This shows up in *Lucifer* (Netflix, 2016–21) where angels 'self-actualize,' which gives rise to the titular character's angst.

397. Recall the Cardinal understands Intentionality's mechanics though not its nature—the how and why it arises in the first place—only that it does arise in well-understood contexts.

398. Human WOB, too, is separate and independent of the psyche itself; a person can't be anything but human regardless how much they alter their individual WOB. This isn't the case with nonhuman entities whose individual entity WOB doesn't much differ from their species' WOB. If entities of a species sufficiently mutate, they're no longer the same species as their ancestors—they can't interbreed—whereas humans are always human regardless their body's alterations. If radiation mutates their bodies beyond human WOB, they would simply be nonintegrable thus nonviable. Nonintegrable human bodies can't exist.

399. This means mutations propagate through multiple entities of a species at relatively similar times, not merely naturally selecting via single-entity mutation reproducing through the lineage until it's said to be the species' Eve w.r.t. the particular mutation.

400. WOB of individual entities exert pushback on species' WOB that can thwart change.

Directed (artificial) evolution. There are two rationales for directing evolutionary change: Mina's, and everyone else's. Let's start with Mina, whose purpose in this context is seeding nonhuman life that's both biologically beneficial and pleasing to the human (Living) body and its integrated (ℒife) person. Examples of beneficial biology are food sources, necessary bacteria, and the flora and fauna necessary to preserve life on the planet. Examples of pleasing biology are companion animals—dogs, cats, horses—food-specific flora and fauna, visually and in other ways interesting species, and so on. The rationale for everyone else's change efforts is a mixed bag, mostly just bad juju as already noted (§ 2.1.5.5.2.2:323). The rationale of the noted 0.5% of humans who initiate beneficial mutative change is to offset the harm done by the other 99.5% —a bit like using a table fan to turn back a sandstorm, to be sure, but action beats hand wringing—as well as to imprint their own creativity on the world because, well, who doesn't like to occasionally play God?

2.1.5.5.2.4 HUMAN BODY EVOLUTION: ARTIFICIAL SELECTION

Human body evolution is exclusively human directed; its mutative change is only ever a product of human selection. Mina effects such change on an ongoing basis and his goals are the betterment of physical humanity's situation. Not so with other people who fancy themselves change agents, whose motives in all cases are to make targeted genetic changes usually to physical descendants but also to unrelated persons in whom they have a parochial interest.[401] For example, spirit persons principally alter a future individual's DNA through soon-to-be-fertilizing sperm in order to create or foster certain physical traits they want implemented which they think will either benefit or harm the person for some purpose, such as improving or degrading mind–brain integration.[402] They work to ensure the 'fixed' sperm delivers the goods, though fail ~40% of the time. Sometimes the effort fails simply because they do something incorrectly, the change doesn't take, backfires and harms the person's body instead, its effect on DNA is nil, and so on.

With regard to evolution, we mustn't catch ourselves in the flytrap of the human body being the same as ℌuman, which leads to fundamental misobservation and misinterpretation of the evolutionary universe in which humans abide. Human evolution isn't ℌuman but vehicular. Recall that our body is an independent, autonomous, Living entity that only integrates the person having ℒife. As such, it arises from and responds to evolutionary processes as does every Living entity, but its evolution isn't ℌuman (§ 3:331), it's Living. While the human body is a Living entity, it's not the same sort of Living entity as other primates. Mike and Molly (and every universe builder since) developed the human body for integration not for autonomous animal existence, even though its biology operates autonomously of, albeit in conjunction with, its integrated ℘erson owing to the simple reality of its physical environment. During the human body's start-to-finish development, an unusually short lifespan was the norm. The reason is that it's tailored for integration. It can't function very long on its Living-sans-ℒife-force own; on average, about 19 years.[403] This is quite unlike any other Living entity, particularly the close though nonlineal primate lines which live longer (contextually normal) lives.

Prior to the rise of the integrable human body on Earth, life developed through natural evolution as described where Mina initiated its terrestrial precursors and jumpstarted the process. He thereafter alternated between natural (undirected) and artificial (directed) change development using a 50:50 ratio. From the point where he separated the line of human body development from that of general life development, the undirected–directed evolutionary change ratio changed from 50:50 to about 34:66. Don't let that mislead you, though. The 34% side of that ratio is the percentage of our body's total evolutionary development that transitioned over from general life development at the time he separated the lines. So, in actuality, the human body's evolutionary development after Mina separated it from general life development was artificially selected-for on the 66% of our body's total evolutionary development that occurred *after* he separated the lines of development. This makes sense because, as Mike and Molly's initial experiments demonstrated, Mina needed to aim for a specific human woв-compliant design, not just sit back waiting for any old clump of matter to assemble itself through the vagaries of natural selection. A final caveat regarding evolution is that Mina reconstitutes populations that go extinct because of war, natural calamity, or whatever. There is no 'end' to humanity. It's universal and megaversal.

---

401. It's less common. Mina instigates ~80% of all individual, and 100% of planetwide, human body change.

402. Spirit manipulation of an oocyte's (unfertilized human egg) DNA during its development stages isn't possible largely because it lacks sufficient bioactivity, whereas a sperm's ℒife force supports manipulation but requires a minimum ~10 hours to effect.

403. Mina's figures here are birth-to-childhood plus adulthood-to-death averaged across multiple proto-human lines of development. On Earth, proto-human lifespan averaged ~17, with the longest 30, years (§ 1.1:532, § 2.1:542).

2.1.5.5.3 DEVELOPMENT OF SEXUALITY

We now have a generalized concept of how Mike and Molly (and Mina; § 1.1.2:533) initiated physical life in the Primoverse's natural environment, from its initial terrestrial life precursors to a human body integrable with ℒife and all its capabilities. Spirit embodied, the Twins experienced a lot of what embodiment had to offer, but not everything. Procreation, for one. They noticed over the course of developing nonhuman life that procreating was a necessity, as Living bodies couldn't indefinitely endure. Hence, Living entities (including the proto-human body) needed a mechanism and a WOB to reproduce. The ℒife-integrated physical body's natural longevity was an unknown to them at the time (§ 1.1:466).

It also didn't occur to them they could modify how they manifested their spirit bodies to experiment with procreation in the supranatural environment. That was a bias—a presumption, really—in their mind-set. Instead, they set to work figuring out how to accomplish the feat physically. It was only necessary to Intentionalize nonhuman life's procreative necessity and then entity WOB—mother nature—took care of the details in whatever fashion was contextually efficient. As they got closer and closer to an integrable human form, they had to consider not only what efficiently worked w.r.t. the body's Living as well as its human WOB, but what they desired for it, too. It was obvious that, if conception were possible, they'd experience children and family in some form akin to what they were observing amongst the most advanced nonhumans (including proto-humans), which revealed a broad range of feeling they'd already experienced in some limited fashion themselves being spirit embodied, their principal emotive experience being love. But even where they'd now reached in their own ℒife development, they knew the feelings arising from conceiving and bearing children would outstrip whatever Living entities could ever muster.

Eventually, their integrable, WOB-compliant physical bodies took final form more or less how they look on Earth. Recall there's only a limited range of variance—10% of total design—available to the physical or spirit body that satisfies human WOB. Accordingly, there's little difference between Mike and Molly's seminal embodiment and ours today, mainly external aesthetics and internal organization such as biology or organ placement. Their physical bodies did have differences with their spirit ones, first and foremost the lack of spirit body sex organs. Various forms of reproduction arose with Living entities in periods of natural selection the Twins periodically developed to study and experiment with during periods of artificial selection. As they selected across the proto-human line of development, many of these experimental forms of reproduction consistently resulted in nonviable procreation.

Even though proto-human bodies had yet to integrate human ℒife, as they embodied more and more integrability with human WOB their own WOB associated more and more with human and less with nonhuman WOB. Accordingly, those aspects of human WOB expressing in proto-human body WOB increasingly separated them as unique Living entities vis-à-vis all other (especially similar primate) Living entities. Although proto-human bodies hadn't yet integrated a person, they increasingly supported only human WOB characteristics. As Mike and Molly thus developed early life toward their final product, they more and more closely had to develop it strictly in accord with human WOB. At the end of the day, the human WOB-compliant form that would conceive viable *and integrable* proto-human offspring was the sexual reproduction method with which we're familiar. Sexual organs were now the glaring difference between Mike and Molly's spirit and physical embodiments.

But still they had no inkling their bodies, once integrating their ℒife selves, would end up conceiving not just a new physical, human*like* Living entity, but triggering new emergent ℒife itself to birth 'in' EPL (§ 1.2.1:247). In their naiveté, their idea was to experience sex, parenthood, and family as a physical environmental reality, not one transmutable to their spirit embodiment much less to their fundamental unembodied transuniversal beingness. That was an exclamation mark still to hit paper.

2.1.5.5.4 PHYSICAL SENSATION

At long last, Mike and Molly finished evolutionarily developing their physical bodies and integrated them. They weren't alone on their chosen planet for this momentous occasion. They'd evolutionarily developed a whole clan of proto-humans, two of whom conceived and bore their integrable bodies (§ 1.1.3:533). Being Living creatures, these proto-humans weren't independent, autonomous persons having ℒife, but only highly advanced primates not unlike the most advanced proto-human species we see in Earth's fossil record. They were human in form but not in mind. Oh, they had a human's full brain structure but, without a ℒife mind, couldn't utilize it. They were as primitive to Mike and Molly as chimpanzees are to us. The Twins integrated two cultivated fetuses after about a month's gestation in the womb, approximately the eighth week of pregnancy. It wasn't necessary to integrate that early, but they wanted to experience everything short of fertilization and the earliest embryonic development.

Despite integrating awareness with their *in utero* physical bodies, they could still work and play in their spirit bodies because their ℒife minds—we have this same albeit undeveloped capability today—were fully aware of their physical, spirit, and unembodied states and could shift awareness between them at will. Once their bodies birthed, the Twins learned to use their new brains as their bodies physically matured amongst the family, tribe, and clan they'd culturally developed over the course of their natural and artificial evolution. Their physical capabilities matured quite fast since Mike and Molly were adults in mind. Though technically they weren't alone, they really were. Just two human minds in a gaggle of primates that looked and, in some respects operated, as human but weren't 𝔥uman. To their clan, Mike and Molly were the two weird mutants with strange abilities (§ 2.1.6.2:329). But this is what the Twins had wanted. They'd make the best of it. And they were going to build a *family*. Whatever that meant.

This is the first time physical life arose in All Existence and it had been no easy task. Beginning with life's precursors, it took the Twins about 20BY–100MY alone from separating the human and general-life lines of development before achieving an integrable body—to figure it all out. It was a tiring journey, but they felt it worthwhile even though, on their eve of physical integration, they wondered if reality would actually meet expectation. They'd become well versed being operationally aware of themselves as beings of Thought simultaneously embodied in the supranatural and 'reflective' environments of Molly's Primoverse. What would happen when they expanded their awareness into their new physical bodies in the natural environment? How would it feel? They didn't know.

Well, it felt like fireworks going off in their heads. In the instant of integration, every sense of which their body was capable tsunamied through them, flooding their minds with the physical environment's sensorial flotsam and jetsam the like of which they'd never experienced in their spirit bodies—and this was but an enwombed fetus! Normally, it is spirit sensation that makes the physical feel paltry, but the Twin's hadn't yet built out Molly's supranatural environment with any of the unpredictable dynamics intrinsic of the natural one. Hence, sensations as simple as sunshine, radiant heat, a breeze over skin, sound, thirst, dry eyes, the chemistry of touch, and a million other things had never risen in their spirit embodiment because they hadn't known they existed. They did now. Their minds exploded with sensation.

Their stomachs rumbled with hunger pangs, too. They were living in the wild with primitive entities, after all. But since they could non-physically manipulate physical matter via the 'reflective' environment (§ 7.1.1.1:212) to create a fertile environment, survival didn't require more than a simple effort to provide themselves food (until they surpassed the need via ℒife force), housing, clothes, and whatever else they needed as humans which their proto-human clan hadn't pursued. Besides, their spirit bodies could materially assist since it turned out that when they'd integrated their physical bodies, their spirit bodies *attached*, effectively forming a single physicospirit unit—just as we are today (§ 1.2.1:407). This provided them greater extrasensory awareness of their environment beyond what their integrated body alone could provide. When they'd grown physically capable, they set about altering their environment to suit.

2.1.6 BUILDING A FAMILY

As they'd evolutionarily developed their physical bodies, and realized they'd at least be able to reproduce physically, if nothing else, it became apparent they'd have to choose a physical sex. Mike had to be one and Molly the other. They didn't care. It was just bodies. Their true self was a mind the same way a driver isn't the car. Well, you know how this ends. Mike chose male and Molly female. Their gendered names are just a convenience for us; neither does their choice of sex denote gender.

Just as Touch was a mind-blowing experience for them when exclusively spirit embodied, physical Touch took them to new heights. It seems odd that people imagine spirit life as much more sensorial than physical life, that the intensity of our physical senses is a mere shadow of our spirit senses. But that's on the heels of 800BY of human experience since the Twins and, in our universe, of about 8MY of spirit and 50KY of Earth's modern human history as well as ~7.3MY of The Corruption, the Negative Collective Consciousness, and Accountableism (§ 2.1:542; § 2.1.2.2:370). It took the Twins time to learn all the dynamic vagaries of physical life and transpose it to spirit life. Since then, megaversal humanity has reproduced it in the supranatural environment alongside its own less dynamic though more easily manipulable nature. Eventually, human Ultraculture—spanning All Existence—embodied all there was to know about it (§ 4:291).[404]

2.1.6.1 THE EXPERIENCE OF SEX

Of course, adults know there's no greater Touch than sex generally and sexual intercourse specifically, not just physically but emotionally—mindfully. Mike and Molly didn't know this at first, but they quickly discovered where Touch led them in their physical embodiment. Unlike their spirit bodies, their physical bodies had autonomous *feelings*—sensations, biological drives, and chemistry—that powerfully influenced their ℒife minds and even induced hitherto unknown Thought and behavior. It awoke aspects of their woᴃ dormant since birth. Sex—the culmination of Touch—was the key that unlocked their full woᴃ and enabled their full, true humanity. This is one reason humanity seems so obsessed with sex and sexuality generally; it uplifts a person to their fullest human experience.

The sexual intercourse method of procreation they experimentally chose for the human body satisfied human woᴃ in every particular. More than the mere physical experiential sensation it was for proto-humans, sex roped in the entirety of their minds and dominated their thinking–feeling, involving every physical, spirit, and ℒife element constituent of their beingness (MARRIAGE & SEX, § 2:597).

2.1.6.2 SEX AND EMERGENT ℒIFE

Mike and Molly didn't know they could trigger the birth of new emergent ℒife by any means much less sexually. Their idea was to conceive a viable physical baby in the hope they could use their own ℒife force to somehow activate the entirety of their child's human-integrable brain and thereby achieve, if not a real ℒife family, then at least an ersatz one. They'd used this technique already with their proto-human clan all through the development process to ensure viable procreation once they'd evolutionarily moved them far enough away from the line of general life development where they'd become increasingly nonviable as a species of life absent human integration. It was their own ℒife force keeping their proto-humans going across the generations. Post integration, they'd intended a pregnancy between them when their bodies matured, and at the physical age of 14, did so. But then a very strange thing happened.

They knew what to expect with a physical pregnancy. Aware of every aspect of their embodied states, the instant Molly conceived they knew. Yet, something odd and quite unexpected startled them. Within hours of knowing she'd conceived, they sensed ℒife! It wasn't simply that a physical conception took place and they were sensing its successful fertilization. They were sensing a being like themselves having Thought! In a shock, they realized an *emergent birth* like their own had happened almost simultaneously 'in' EPL with physical conception. In addition to sensing Molly's fertilized egg, thus Living life, they were also sensing *real* ℒife!

Physical human conception isn't the moment the sperm penetrates the egg, or the zygote forms, but the moment in mitosis when a new emergent ℒife births 'in' EPL (§ 1.2.1.1.1:248). Molly's physical conception unexpectedly—shockingly!—triggered the emergent birth of a new ℒife 'in' EPL. They could *feel* its presence take shape. If they gaped at each other in that moment of utter, breathtakingly astonished realization, they did. They knew at once what it was they were sensing because they'd felt it eons ago when they'd each discovered the other. There was no one to consult for guidance on this stunning development but themselves. With their spirit senses and their ℒife mind's awareness, they could look directly into Molly's physical body and see the emergent new ℒife's nascent spirit body automatically existing in accord with ℒife force woᴃ, integrating the tiny clump of physical cells that would eventually become a walking, talking ꝑerson (§ 1.2.3.2:470). Even more exciting—considering the mystery of their own births—was that they'd be outside observers to what they themselves must've been like in the moment of their own emergent births and along their paths to maturity. This was going to be *fun*!

And it changed everything. The Twins' initial plan to use ℒife force to keep their proto-human clan going, improve their lifespan, and maintain their reproductive viability while they themselves produced and raised a Living family was in cinders. Indeed, they'd firmly believed procreation of the Living human body simply mandated their own ℒife force to make it viable. But now, in a flash, they realized their *integrated* physical procreation was viable in its own right. Fertilization conceived not just a new Living human body but emergent ℒife, too, automatically integrating the just-conceived physical body as well as auto-manifesting a mirrored, attached spirit body to boot! This new reality brought a rethink of their clan plan. They'd now stop using ℒife force to ensure their nonintegrated proto-human clan's generational survival—it numbered about 2,100 at this point—and instead let them naturally wither away as a superseded species. They did so over about a

---

404. Ultraculture in our universe is its own unique instantiation of All Existence Ultraculture that subtly encapsulates all humans in all universes, embodied or unembodied.

hundred-year span. When they'd interred the last of the clan, the physicospirit human form they'd pioneered began reproducing across the yet-to-be-built megaverse as their ʄuman descendants (§ 2.1.4.1:312). And, 800BY later, here we are.

2.1.6.3   Embodied–Unembodied Conception

Mike and Molly hadn't finished being surprised. It wasn't obvious at the start of Molly's physical pregnancy but, by her sixth month, they realized their child's *spirit body* had *sex organs*! They hadn't noticed earlier because, being so focused on the fetus and its emergent ᒪife, and trying to glean all they could from it about their own births, they hadn't really paid attention to the spirit body, something they *thought* they already understood. They had lived with the mystery of their own emergent birth for about 30.3BY at this point. They ardently longed for information about themselves even if it was secondhand and derived. Hardly anything else really seemed important at all. Their own spirit bodies were without sex organs and they naively presumed their child's spirit body would be the same. They hadn't known about sex when they'd Intentionalized their spirit bodies, and hadn't updated them after figuring it out in the physical context, either, mainly because, even if spirit sex was possible, its nonbiological nature couldn't possibly conceive emergent ᒪife. With that collective eyebrow flip, they'd simply moved on.

How wrong they were. And not a bit shortsighted, too. But after all they weren't born aware of infinite knowledge. Much of their humanity at birth lay dormant, awaiting trigger events to spring into being. But they didn't know that or what those events were, nor could they foresee their woв was more than it appeared on its face any more than a three-year old can really comprehend, much less imagine, all of which their own humanity is capable. As we read about their early experiences, it's easy to think they had many failures of imagination. But let's not forget they were the very first humans in All Existence, without any instruction manual or cheat codes. Their experience was oɪт all the way. It turned out they weren't limited only to physically conceiving human ᒪife but could do so in their every mode of being, as below.

> **Spirit-embodied conception**. About a hundred years after Molly's first (male) and second (female) pregnancies, their two children (§ 1.2:336) discovered together that spirit body sex paired with Intentionality to conceive also triggers new emergent ᒪife 'in' EPL (§ 1.2.1.1.2:249).[405] During this period, there were no demarcations between physical and spirit embodied and unembodied states. The same way children of multilingual parents grow up naturally speaking two, three, or more languages, casually switching between them even in the same sentence, Mike, Molly, and their children could not only focus their awareness in any of their three possible states at will, but were independently aware of each at the same time, including simultaneously manifesting multiple spirit bodies in different places doing different things.[406] Such discoveries motivated Mike and Molly to update their mindsets with new possibilities. And their spirit bodies got sex organs.

> **Unembodied conception**. This ability took longer to develop because everyone at the time fell into thinking that sexual intercourse was the necessary trigger of emergent new ᒪife. But that wasn't quite accurate. What triggers new emergent ᒪife 'in' EPL isn't sex per se but a certain kind of Intentionality. Mike and Molly had seen for themselves that, for physical persons, the biology itself *is* the Intentionality that births emergent new ᒪife. For spirit persons, the Intentionality realizes *through* sexual intercourse. The individual Intentionality of two spirit persons must harmonize into a single couple-Intentionality to conceive in the context of sexual intercourse for new emergent ᒪife to birth embodied in the supranatural environment. But it's not dependent on sex alone. A couple can realize the Intentionality without sex if they understand how. Where a person is just their unembodied Thought outside the environment of any universe, the individual Intentionality of two persons must harmonize into a single couple-Intentionality to conceive in order to trigger EPL (§ 1.2.1.1.3:250). All of these forms of Intentionality constitute sex even if no sexual *activity* occurs.

The difference between two spirit persons and two unembodied persons conceiving an emergent new ᒪife is quite simple. If a couple's Intentionality is rooted in their spirit-embodied state then the child conceives in

---

405. Despite genetic issues potentially arising in physical close family unions (easily resolved by the Twins), no negative outcome arises in spirit body or unembodied sibling unions.

406. This changed over time as most descendants born to physical and spirit embodiment, inured by the reality of their universe, lost touch with their unembodied nature, as we have. Nevertheless, the human mind can manage about one trillion simultaneously discrete interactive experiences in any given moment. Mina currently experiences a need for only ∼275B such experiences, but maxed out the full trillion during the Big Healing, one reason the effort was very tiring.

a spirit-embodied state proximal to the parents. If a couple's Intentionality to conceive is actualized in their unembodied state—even if they're manifesting a spirit body in some universe—then the child conceives in the unembodied state intimately linked via ℒife force interacting with Energent–prime of which the parents have awareness. A child conceives in the principle state of awareness wherein its parents Intentionalize its conception regardless their other states of awareness, if any. It's certainly possible to conceive a spirit or unembodied child without inherent sexual orientation—a natural sense of boyness or girlness—but Mina says no one does it in practice because it runs against the grain of our intrinsic WOB desire to reproduce how we each are. Ever since Mike and Molly first physically embodied themselves in male and female form, then *how we are* is male and female however swappable in practice these individual WOB may be. There is no avoiding the sexes because the first human emergence was pairwise, thus, procreation is a pairwise experience. The sexes as we understand them are merely habituated expressions of Mike and Molly's initial, intrinsic, pairwise distinctions.

Considering the cosmic timescales in play here, Mike and Molly's children discovered how to spiritually conceive emergent new ℒife practically in the blink of an eye, although it took a more sedate 100MY for their descendants a hundred times removed to figure out the rather less obvious Intentionality necessary for an unembodied couple to conceive unembodied emergent new ℒife. Part of the reason for the delay is that it took quite awhile before some people came to consider unembodied living preferable to embodied and began spending more (sometimes all) of their time in that mode. It was amongst this group that unembodied conception first arose.

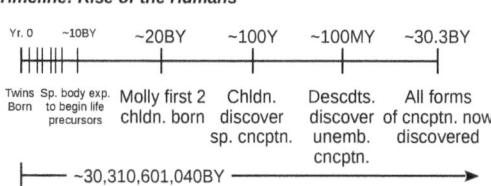

Timeline: Rise of the Humans

Figure 141. Timeline: Twins' birth to discovery of all forms of emergent ℒife conception (cncptn).

2.1.7 MIKE AND MOLLY TODAY

Emergently born as twins before anything existed in the sense we understand the term, Mike and Molly founded the human race. More than anything, we humans are a WOB having mindset. We're not defined by body or sex, physical, spirit, or unembodied modes, or anything. We literally are what we want to be howsoever our birth parents, family, and community socialize us, or we socialize ourselves, at any given moment in our lives. The Twins began their lives wholly unsocialized, without a smidgeon of built-in anything beyond their most basic human WOB and their own infant personalities. From there, they matured, explored, and discovered their humanity and passed it down to us through the *vitae mysterium* of EPL birth in various ways, shapes, and forms via culture (§ 4.1:291). Their progeny inherited the stars in the sense they literally created them by building millions of universes, each one a unique 'hometown' for their descendants.

Today, Mike and Molly—megaversal humanity's literal 'Adam and Eve'—are doing what they've always done: exploring themselves, their environment, and experiencing family. According to Cosmo, they prefer anonymity to leading humanity's edification, as their interest lies only with the universe Molly built and close family, which they altogether made into a home (§ 2.1.3:309). Eventually, they chose to live mainly unembodied but manifest a spirit body whenever they want to visit somewhere material, say, Molly's Primoverse filled with memories near and dear to their hearts. As far as their deep curiosity goes, they managed to trailblaze yet another undiscovered aspect of human WOB that Mina calls *omniscience*. We describe it next before closing this chapter and moving on to Mina and our own universe.

SECTION 3
𝔥uman Evolution: Omniscience

𝔥uman doesn't 'evolve' in the normal sense of the word. No outside agency like evolution or a tinkering mechanic changes or adapts the human race as with Living entities because, if that were the case, we'd hardly be autonomous beings, would we? Humans—not their bodies—*self-evolve*, meaning we choose to explore our humanness, to let go of it in such a way that 'evolutionary' change occurs. In a sense, such individuals self-generate 'environmental pressure' within their own wob, which at some point results in emergent change. This isn't personal growth, enlightenment, or even species maturation, but an evolutionary break from what a person was w.r.t. human wob to what they are now as a 'wob-evolved' Ḥuman. This doesn't constitute a species change, which would mean a different wob we'd arguably be unable to call human in the same way we can't call *homo sapiens* just *homo heidelbergensis* with extra features. Rather, it's the same human wob expanding to encompass more humanness; unlocking a new game level one previously didn't know existed but surprisingly can attain simply in becoming aware of it.

Recall that humans are beings having awareness. Everything we encounter we experience as awareness rather than cognition (§ 2.1:276). When a person cultivates awareness such that it begins to shift dimensionally, that's the moment self-'evolution' begins until, ultimately, an emergent awareness arises. But only if the person chooses to follow its initially tenuous thread, to explore the differences perceived in their awareness as well as being capable of experiencing awareness of that which is unknown and without reference, something with which the Twins certainly had a lot of practice. What we're describing here is the *process* of Ḥuman self-'evolution.' Achieving actual, full awareness of this emergent awareness and what it reveals is to self-'evolve' to an expanded, more encompassing human wob than the wob with which each person births. While in anthropology's view, the evolution of *homo sapiens* left *homo heidelbergensis* in the superseded dust of its mind, human self-'evolution' leaves no one in the dust. Every human can self-'evolve.' There's no restriction, just one's cultivation of this emergent awareness. Nor is there species differentiation; no old and new humanity. Human is Ḥuman.

Mike and Molly 'evolved' in this way after about 75BY of life (*Fig. 143*), roughly 44.78BY after Molly bore her first physical child (§ 2.1.6.2:329). Self-'evolution' emergently rendered them (as Mina calls it) *omniscient*. The term typically means, "having infinite awareness, understanding, and insight" and "possessed of universal or complete knowledge."[407] We use it only in its first, infinite sense, because universal (complete) knowledge isn't possible in a universe within an All Existence that changes state every moment in which new, unique, autonomous emergent ℒife ceaselessly births. In Mina's words, self-'evolved' omniscience means "an emergent ℒife's awareness of self that arises from a knowingness of self that's necessarily impossible to be mistaken." It's not a result simply of *being* aware but that an *emergent* awareness arises through cultivating one's awareness until it reaches what we might call dimensionally critical mass. A person's ℒife force becomes a next-level emergence similar in some ways to their initial emergence 'in' EPL at birth. In a sense, omniscience is a rebirth from a normative to a supercharged awareness. The result is an awareness of self in which one knows all there is to know of self at any moment, necessarily without error. Within this awareness of self arises a dimensional change in one's awareness of All Existence such that one experiences it with an intimacy previously obscured (*Fig. 142*). It's a next-level emergence of ℒife from ℒife, a human *re-emergence*. Mike and Molly—deeply curious and explorative more so than anyone to date because of their seminal experience (§ 2:304)—are so far the only two humans to experience this re-emergence.

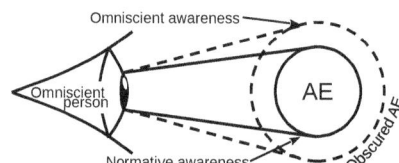

Figure 142. Omniscient self-awareness reveals previously obscured (dashed lines) self and All Existence AE.

In the larger context—circa 75BY after Mike and Molly as the first emergence of human ℒife at Year Zero (*Fig. 143*)—this means a second emergent event occurred not within Energent–prime but *within two Ḥuman proto-energies* (consciousness, psyche) that resulted in a *new kind of φerson* as an emergent property yet *still Ḥuman*. It's no less the emergence of new ℒife as Mike and Molly were themselves the first emergence of ℒife.

Ḥuman itself became an emergent property *of* itself, somewhat the way a *previous* All Existence becomes an emergent property of itself as a *current* All Existence such that its previous iteration absorbs into its new iteration, yet remains All Existence (*Fig. 144*). We might call this 'evolution' in its popular usage but that would be inaccurate. It's an *emergent* change because it represents an entirely new class of Ḥuman—omniscient—that can't even in principle be predicted from the φerson from which this new *state* of being emerged. This means that omniscience necessarily differs for each person who experiences it even though, overall, each

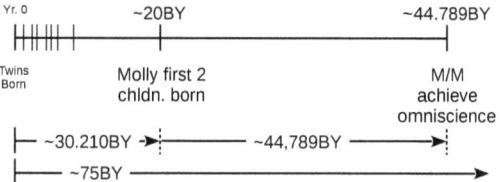

Timeline: Rise of the Humans

Figure 143. Timeline: Twin's birth to children to omniscience.

person experiences the same infinite awareness of self. The reason is that the *experience* of omniscience is individual, having individual expression. The person who experiences omniscience is the same person, yet wholly different at the same time. Although Mike and Molly are still the same Mike and Molly in the sense of their personness and hanging out with the grandkids, their emergent omniscience is dimensional poles apart from their pre-omniscience.

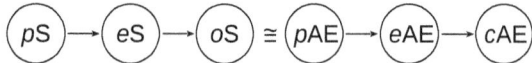

Figure 144. Previous Self *p*S experiences 'evolution' to emergent Self *e*S to become omniscient Self *o*S congruent (sans identity) with previous *p*AE, emergent *e*AE, and current All Existence *c*AE.

Isn't all this amazing, though? That, in the first place, emergent ℒife happened through which ʄuman came to exist and then 75BY later a next-order emergence happened with emergent ℒife and a new-yet-not-new, next-level person came to exist 'out of' the original emergent ʄuman. Mike and Molly are thus a class—or maybe we should say an emergence—beyond us, but anyone can experience the same individualized emergence by cultivating awareness of self to its dimensionally critical mass as did the Twins.

Omniscience is the only human 'evolution' that's known to the Cardinal, the members of which, rather contrary to their own deeply curious explorations of universe building and human knowledge in general, don't dwell much more than ordinarily on their awareness of self. Despite their vast knowledge of humanity and All Existence, they haven't sought omniscience. Well, neither did Mike and Molly. Like many other aspects of their lives, it was all accidental, the happenstance of their personalities, individual woʙ, and experience that played such a big part in their continual discoveries of their own humanity and its capabilities. Yet, emergent ℒife remains the supreme *vitae mysterium* even to Mike and Molly because ʄuman in and of itself is indeterminate (infinite); one can never fully know or experience it. That open world of self is what awaits each of us as we pass through ignorance of reality to the real awareness of human maturity. Like any open world video game, we choose our own path and take it at our own speed and the game doesn't care. That's what ℒife is.

In this chapter, we've learned how humanity really came to be. Do you think it's an amazing story? We do. Develop your ET competency and test it out! See what you discover. Now, we turn to how our own universe came to be.

Our Creator

CHATTING WITH MINA in January 2019, he said he really, truly regrets creating our universe, including progenerating us, because of our suffering and sorrow arising in The Corruption (CH. 24:361) and yet, even so, wouldn't undo it even if given the chance. That perplexed us. He explained his feeling is the same regret we ourselves ofttimes feel when our own children suffer the violent, abusive, torturous world of harm that we've collectively perpetuated despite our haphazard desire for (and oft backfiring effort to create) love and peace. And yet, we'd never undo our family because we love and cherish and value our children so much we'd never *not* want them to experience ℒife. From that perspective, we understood Mina's feeling. Before describing him in such heartistic terms, let's introduce him.

SECTION 1
Who and What is Mina

Recall that when the girls and I first met Mina that fateful autumn day in 2017 (ALL SHOOK UP, § 1:1), we were still addressing him as God and sometimes, because of our recent experiences with Emotion Code and ThetaHealing, as Creator. But he objected. Well, sort of. He said we're free and can call him whatever we want and he wouldn't interfere, but that he'd prefer we use a different moniker because of all the baggage associated with the traditional nomenclature (FN 1:1). We tried a few losers until El intuited *Protector*, which got a thumbs up. Still, what he *really* preferred was that we'd use his real name. Being new to energy testing (ET), none of us understood how we'd figure it out. Then in December 2018, *grandfather* popped into my head. While he eschews juridical *Father*, he liked *grandfather*'s consanguineal, nonjudgmental quality. It took us awhile to transition from almighty Protector to familial Grandfather, but we settled into it. I *liked* him as my grandfather, a relationship of love, care, and friendship without the potency of a paterfamilias or a deitic overlordiness.

All three of us knew he wanted to relate to us as just a person, as family, not as an omnipotent creator. He drove the point home every time we'd find him in our living room sharing his take on the TV shows, movies, and music videos we'd be watching. The principal reason behind his non-interferential but kindred attitude is that, although he created our *universe*, he didn't create *us*. Intentionality *triggers* birth of emergent ℒife but doesn't *create* the person. Energent proto-life (EPL; § 2.3.2.1:241) emergently does that, which is why a person is autonomous, sovereign in and of him or herself. A universe builder only creates an *environment* for ℒife to embody in, just as parents only trigger ℒife and biologically or Intentionally influence the aesthetics of the *body* their children integrate or Intentionalize (manifest). Generally, the only humans born into a universe are its builder's direct descendants.[408] Mina as 'our creator' means he's our *progenitor* who created the home—our

---

408. The unembodied-born can embody themselves in any universe to Intentionalize their child's birth in that environment.

universe—in which we embody and live but not our *Life* (§ 1.2.1:247), not our very existence. We're emergent, not created, beings.

We'd procrastinated testing his name because figuring it out seemed too difficult with a mode of communication that boils down to *yes*, *no*, and variants of *maybe* supplemented by (at least, my) dodgy intuition. How would we decipher his name from some otherworldly language, or the ancient Japanese one he'd mentioned, with such minimalist tools? Sure, we could ET each and every letter but that seemed like a lot of work back when our—*my*—skills were sketchy. Besides, Procrastinator is my middle name. However, constantly flexing ET over the four years spent writing this book really leveled up my skills. I found myself 'knowing' things I'd then ET as true that Ayako (and often Moth Man, if asked; § 1.1:61) would later confirm. I began trusting it. So, in late 2020, I gritted my teeth and letter-by-letter energy tested one of his names. I passed my results to Ayako. She called to work out the details and did the (push) testing. At that time, I couldn't accurately ET in her powerful presence. Even hundreds or thousands of miles apart, a phone connection energetically ties us together as if in the same room (CH. 41:623). As he usually does, Mina joined our conversation, often spirit embodied in her New York City apartment. With his excited energy often pushing her nearly off her feet, we sorted his name.

1.1 OUR UNIVERSE BUILDER'S ACTUAL NAME

People within and without our universe use many names for Mina, but only two concern us here, his given name and the Earth name he feels best reflects who he is.

His **Given Name** is in the Mother Tongue that Mike and Molly developed to communicate with each other after their embodiment, handed down through time to become, through the First Ancestors of our universe (§ 2.1.1:348), the language of spirit world. It is *Reikishiña Uarokk Ñovo'no Idefíñí*, pronounced 'ray-keesh-nya,' 'yuá-ruhkk,' 'nyō-vō'nō,' 'ee-deh-fee-nyee.' The apostrophe forms a glottal stop as in the middle of the English word 'uh-oh.' The spelling looks to us like a mashup of Romanized Japanese, Mongolian, Russian, and Italian, but it's a tonal language more like native American Apache or—which he thinks more closely resembles it—the language of the indigenous tribe residing between the city of Curitiba and the South Atlantic coast in the Brazilian state of Paraná. Naturally, I tried out some nicknames. He wasn't so keen on me following El's whimsical footsteps into sobriquets (§ 1.3.1:63) like Ra, Ray-Ray, the Big Kish, or Mister Na, so we settled for Reikishiña because, you know, we *like* him. Idefíñí is the family name Mike and Molly chose for themselves.[409] It precedes one's given name(s) as in Eastern naming conventions and translates to 'the first humans.' Altogether, his given names mean, 'the first birth to father freedom in the megaverse.'[410] He's not particularly fond of his given name but lives with it because Mike and Molly bestowed it (§ 1.2:336).

His preferred **Earth name** is *Ameno minano nakanushi*, although it's more a title than a name. We learned this one before Reikishiña however so we generally just call him *Mina* for short. He's okay with this nickname because, in his mind, everything else sounds too male and he wants to project both genders, which is to say, he doesn't want us to get the impression our universe is male-centric (§ 2.2:341). We use *Mina* throughout the book. His name–title comes down to us from Japanese as *Ame-no-minaka-nushi* (天之御中主) via Shinto's founder, who first tried his hand at articulating the Story of Life some 49,594 years ago (§ 4:574). It translates in that context as 'Heavenly Ancestral God of the Originating Heart of the Universe,' although Mina renders it 'Heavenly Ancestral Parent of the Originating Heart of the Universe' because, as he's repeatedly told us, gods don't exist and he's our primogenitor without power and control over us as we're free, autonomous beings (§ 5.1:428; CH. 36:585). The salient part of his name–title is 'originating heart of the universe' because it references his emotive motivation (§ 2.1:340). Like any person having position, these two names reflect Mina's dual reality as a private person who begat our universal clan with his public role as the builder–operator of our universe.

1.2 OUR UNIVERSE BUILDER'S FAMILY

Naturally, Mina doesn't hail from our universe. He was physically born in Molly's Primoverse (§ 2.1.3.2:310) 14,999,919,655YA in the same physical way you and I were born here. His parents are Mike and Molly's first two physical children (*Fig. 145*; § 2.1.6.3:330). His mother is whom El called "Mother" when she first asked if God had a family (§ 1:1). Her name is *P'najj*, pronounced 'p'nāssh.' The long /ā/ sounds like letter /a/ and /P/ is an

---

409. About 1% of megaversal humanity directly *vs.* indirectly descends from Mike and Molly.

410. Meanings in given (syntactic) name order: 'the first birth;' 'father of freedom;' and 'megaverse.'

unvoiced labial aspirated stop pronounced as /p/ with a puff of air. His father's name is *P'koh*, pronounced 'p'kōwǐh.' The long /ō/ sounds like letter /o/ and /ǐ/ as in 'wick.'

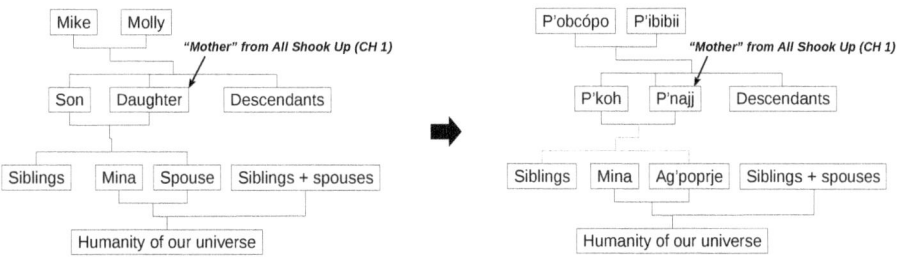

Figure 145. Mina's lineage tree: generic (left), actual (right). P'ōbcópō is pronounced 'p'ōbb-kó-pōu' and P'ibibii is pronounced 'p'ē-b ē -b ē –ī,' where long /ē/ sounds like letter /e/ and long /ī/ sounds like /i/.

To date, Mina's parents have conceived 1,499,999 children (*Fig. 145*, 'Siblings') over the course of about 770BY since they first discovered they could conceive new emergent *Life* during Intentionalized spirit-body sex (§ 2.1.6.3:330). Even in the revelatory environment of this book, that seems a fantastic number—how do they remember all their names?—but consider, does one pregnancy on average every ~513 millennia over 770BY really seem like barefoot and pregnant in the bedroom? The fact is that people who love children *enjoy* raising families. It's one of life's greatest pleasures. It's typical of spirit persons with infinite time and resources on their hands but isn't all that unusual even for physical persons.[411] In reality, however, whenever Mina's parents felt the urge for children, they didn't just sporadically produce individuals but clustered them as families, which by preference they limited to twelve children each. Still, that's ~125,000 families over ~770 æons.[412] In Mina's cluster—his immediate family—he is (until recently) the last child of twelve and altogether his parent's *first ever son*. Hard to believe, but all 1,499,997 siblings are sisters. Now here we are ~14.999BY later and his parents conceived their *second son* in 2004 but then stopped cold turkey. In both these cases, what's going on?

1.2.1 Why Only Daughters Until Mina

The reason Mina's parents had only daughters prior to his birth stems from P'koh—recall he's physical-born—ignoring Molly's warning not to try experiencing the unembodied state without her guidance. But he thought he knew enough, that his successful derring-do would garner applause. So, on his eighteenth birthday, while alone with himself, he shifted his awareness fully out of his body. And promptly got disoriented. In practical terms, he lost track of his body and his sense of where and even when he was. In short, he was unembodiedly *stuck*. More to the point, he was *alone*. He shouted (in his mind) for help but hadn't mastered reaching out or projecting Thought in this mind-only state. In effect, he was in Mike and Molly's situation before learning to sense not-self Thought (§ 2.1:305). Mike and Molly hadn't shared this period of their lives yet, so P'koh hadn't a clue what was happening to him, only that he was unembodied. It didn't take long for panic to set in. He went wild with fear that he was lost forever, consumed with regret for being so cocky in the first place and guilt for abandoning his family, especially his younger sister P'najj who looked up to him. In his young adult's mind, he'd already figured out that in their early human milieu, any love relationship in his future lay with her or an even younger sister because, who else was there? Now there'd be no one for her until a younger brother came of age to . . . *replace* him (*Fig. 146*). If he could've kicked himself, he would have!

Imagine yourself standing alone in normal time and space outside a sensory deprivation tank and then in a blink coming to your senses *inside* it without really understanding how you got there, how to communicate to anyone outside the tank, or how to cognize either time or space. You know you're inside and your world is outside but the tank's soundproof. No matter how you thrash around, you can't communicate or escape. You're *trapped*. You panic. You wonder if you'll die there and no one will ever know. Your sense of objective time melts away, and the outside world feels more and more a dream as fear and dread make time subjectively stretch out in your mind (recall that Mike and Molly initially only knew unembodiment; P'koh grew up

---

411. Consider proliferant men like Ramses II having ±100 children with 8 women; Emperor Meiji, 87; Ziona Chana, 94; Ismail Ibn Sharif, 867; Ramon Revilla, 72 with 16 wives; Winston Blackmore, 145 with 27 wives; Jack Kigongo, 158 with 20 wives. Translate their fecundity to women, too, in the unrestricted spirit environment. Sex and children are literally *the* human pastimes.

412. Æon spelled with its traditional ligature (æ) denotes the cosmological period of 1BY; *eon* means indeterminately long.

embodied, and it was all he understood). Your sense of reality shifts until it's just *you*. Fear, grief, loss, and regret overwhelm your mind. At a primordial level, despair sets in. Will rescue arrive? Yes, it must! Well, eventually . . . maybe . . . probably not . . . no.

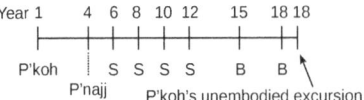

Figure 146. Mike and Molly's earliest childbirths by years after P'koh's birth. S is sister, B is brother.

Molly found him in 20 hours—it seemed more exactly like *uncountably long* to P'koh—when P'najj happened upon his inert physical body. P'koh had believed himself permanently lost. P'najj's frightened, tear-struck response after Molly found, communicated with, and taught him how to return to his embodiment set the fear and guilt he was feeling into a concrete sense of having abandoned his sister, although she was still thirteen at the time and hadn't even yet considered what came next in life. Later, when they'd grown into a love relationship, she desired their first child be a daughter. Deep in her subconscious, however, was the fear that a son would eventually do something just as heartbreakingly stupid as P'koh had. Despite knowing he wanted sons as much as daughters, she gravitated toward Intentionalizing only daughters and P'koh sensed it. Over the years, his guilt worked in tandem with P'najj's own subconscious and, time and again, he didn't resist conceiving only daughters. Until Mina. What changed?

1.2.1.1 COSMO HEALS MINA'S PARENTS

Well, our old friend Cosmo did an intervention. His birth name is *Ibb'gosoi*, pronounced 'ebb'go-shō-wih.' He falls in the Descendant's block (*Fig. 145*), conceived unembodied by Mike and an unembodied granddaughter ~745.555BYA, or ~24.445BY after P'koh. We find Ibb'gosoi a tough name and stick with Cosmo in the book. Essentially, he healed P'koh and P'najj of their unembodiment trauma in the same way Mina's been healing us of our traumas since the Big Healing, first by neutralizing the negative emotive ℒife force (EM∠F; § 3.3.3.1.1:289) built up in their psyches, and then suffusing them with healing vital energy (HEALING, CH. 35:577). P'najj of course had talked over P'koh's feelings with an eye to helping him when she'd first realized his predicament, but he'd been adamantine.

Cosmo well understood his trauma, having himself been born unembodied but with the Abnormality (§ 1.2.1.3:252), too, the effect of which had rendered him incommunicado. Like P'koh during his bollixed foray into unembodiment, Cosmo couldn't sense others, not even his own parents. He was unable to experience others even though they could experience him.[413] He had to grow and develop on his own until it occurred to him (as it had Molly) there might be others like him. He taught himself to reach beyond own-self with his mind until he experienced his father Mike who, unbeknownst to him, had always been in his presence but unable to be sensed. Cosmo was ~200BYO at this point (*Fig. 147*), meaning he experienced aloneness more than 199.99BY longer than Mike and Molly had (§ 2.1:305).

Similar with P'koh, Cosmo felt his parents' tremendous pain at his being 'lost' in the unembodied state, but also a sense that the Abnormality itself—he was the first, so no one yet understood it—was somehow his fault. He carried the loneliness of guilt for æons before discovering how to use Intentionality to heal his trauma. Being the first and only healer then in existence, Cosmo offered to heal Mina's parents. They accepted. It took about 2,000 years to internalize, then they conceived Mina.

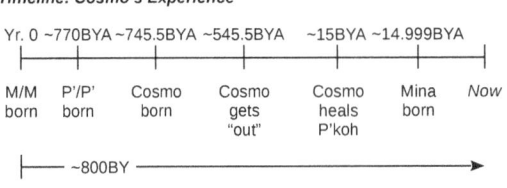

Figure 147. Timeline: Cosmo's birth until healing P'koh.

---

413. Here's the reason Mina said in October 2017 that he couldn't just snap his fingers for Cosmo to show up for our questions. It's difficult to get his attention. Surprisingly, he dropped by as I wrote this backstory to correct some of Mina's account.

1.2.2 Why Only One Son After Mina

The reason Mina's parents had just the one son after Mina lies in P'najj's (eventual) stalwart belief in and support for Mina's goal of founding a universe—a home—where anyone can experience the absolute freedom intrinsic of emergent ᴸife. Where its builder doesn't socialize their descendants into a certain mentality, love without conditions can flourish, and psychic trauma isn't a thing.

But two of their daughters, Mina's immediate older sisters, grew implacably dedicated to his failure. Their efforts brought on the suffering and sorrow we know as The Corruption (ᴄʜ. 24:361:361). His desperation at ever reversing their harm is the source of his resentment, grief, and regret (§ 4:345) with which P'najj empathizes at her core. Jesus perceived and empathized with Mina's despair and his strategy for healing was to teach reality straightforwardly, much as we're putting this book out into the world.

Sun-myung, too, perceived and empathized with the situation in his spiritual journey to understand why our world, supposedly created and run by a loving God, appears so brutally and unremittingly unloving and unfree. He dedicated himself to healing God's heart through a strategy of teaching like Jesus while indemnifying the human Fall to 'restore' Adam, Eve, and Lucifer and thereby humanity with unconditional love all while avoiding his own modern crucifixion (§ 4.3.1:384; ᴄʜ. 40:615). His strenuous effort without even knowing actual reality, as Jesus had, brought tears to P'najj's eyes. When his unconditional love moved Lucifer to let go Michael's (still veiled) Lie and humanity's animus, which cleared the road for the Big Healing, P'najj felt overcome with confidence in Mina's ultimate triumph.

Coupled with Cosmo's earlier healing and P'koh's ongoing desire for more sons after giving P'najj nothing but daughters, they conceived Mina's younger brother in 2004 as Sun-myung's namesake. But she sobered up when her two daughters quickly unraveled both his and Mina's efforts in the eight years leading up to Sun-myung's unexpected death. His fate at their hands was a solemn reminder of their perplexing antipathy. Consequently, P'najj balked at more children until her two daughters quit interfering.

Section 2
Mina's Physical Life

Mina defines his physical body's aesthetic as "Original Polynesian" since it presents according to our concept of that set of anatomical traits, one of many he established on Earth which have come down to us polymorphically, clinally, and polyphyletically as modern ethnicity. It may seem odd that humans all the way back to Mike and Molly should have any sort of ethnic appearance like us, but the fact is that such traits are a natural aspect of embodiment. Besides being consonant with emergent ᴸife's way of being (ᴡᴏʙ), Mike and Molly created their physical bodies with aesthetics in mind—hair type and color, eye color and eyelid type, facial features, skin tone, height, build, and so on. It's obviously impossible to build a body without the attributes we label ethnicity, but it's just an aesthetic. When all is said and done, physiological traits have no more meaning than body style differences between a Ford Mustang and a Chevy Impala (§ 1.1:532, § 2.1:542). They're the same thing as vehicles, differing only in their aesthetic rendition. The human race has practically infinite preferences for the look and feel of how they embody just as we have for things like cars, houses, clothes, or hair. Lately, our aestheticism has begun to merge with procreation as science works to select genetically (versus Intentionally) for sex, looks, predispositions, and so on. This isn't bad per se. It's just our intrinsic preference for customizing ᴸife.

Since Mina's parents can manipulate physical matter, phylogeny and phenotype aren't genetic or environmental inevitabilities. In other words, Mina's Polynesian body style doesn't mean his physical parents present the same way. In fact, they don't. Their ethnicity is akin to the phenotype of the ancient Xia tribe, out-of-Africa negroid ancestors that contributed to the modern Han Chinese. These were brown-skinned like modern Chinese[414] with semi-wavy straight hair more akin to Neanderthals or Europeans (which includes red hair), having a double, or supratarsal, eyelid crease with an epicanthic fold, and taller than the modern Han. Mina says people of this phenotype made their way from Asia to the Beagle and Bessieres Islands off the coast of Western Australia about 47,800YA, abandoning them for the mainland about 2,000YA where they absorbed into Australia's indigenous population.

Mina's parents are thusly light-brown in skin tone like the modern Han with double lidded brown eyes minus the epicanthic fold, a high (versus the low, Asian style) nose bridge, of stocky build a hair under nine

---

414. Brown (beige) is the base megaversal human embodiment color as ᴡᴏʙ (not habituated from Mike and Molly's choices), with skin tone's diversity arising in undertones and overtones of brown from very pale (Caucasoid) to very dark (Negroid).

feet (274.1 cm) in height, and P'koh is red haired while P'najj is dark brown. They gave Mina a Polynesian-style aesthetic similar to Japanese with jet black hair, the same light brown skin tone, monolid blue eyes with epicanthic fold, a low nose bridge, and the same nine-foot height albeit slight of build.

2.1 MINAS VISION FOR OUR UNIVERSE

His mother's obsession with his father's poor judgment regarding unembodiment led her to train Mina rigorously from infancy in all aspects of human and universe realities. By the time he was sixteen years old, he'd exceeded his parents' own awareness of reality. While P'najj kept him on a tight leash and inculcated in him a certain mindset she thought most efficacious, P'koh allowed him absolute freedom in mind and deed. Taking his father's unembodied childhood misstep seriously, Mina mastered the technique and then experienced unembodiment when he was eleven. He developed a taste for it.

The human population had grown by then to about 2.3×10^{36} persons across 100 million universes (Introduction, CH. 27:403). He used his newfound skills with unembodiment to visit as many as he could and discovered in them a wide range of human mindsets which he had trouble understanding. Every encounter was a closed mindset, ignorant their own ancestor had built their universe as a home, a neighborhood in the larger urban megaverse that was All Existence. Not only did he meet with blank stares, but often enough outright hostility. He immersed himself in the mindsets of builders to understand the people of their universe. The experience shocked him. More so, it vexed him. The mindsets he encountered were closed by design, the same way his mother had tried to close his own to what she thought dangerous or unfit for him. Her brainwashing hadn't set well with him then and it bloody well didn't now, having seen, firsthand, intrinsically free emergent ℒife mentally herded like animals.

It's not that these builders are malevolent, egomaniacal, or any such thing. Like helicopter parents (or Mina's mother), they want what's best for their children with minimal distress and disruption. But this is a recipe for tyranny. Not the sort built on violence necessarily, but with the compliance of ignorance. Don't get us wrong, Mina loves his mother and she loves him and always has. But we've all experienced people who hide the truth from us—sometimes violently—in the mistaken belief that we need their protection. Fortunately, P'koh counterbalanced P'najj. Mina experienced unfettered freedom with his father to experience reality, pursue his mind, and exercise his developing life's vision without interference but simply with guidance as desired. P'najj didn't know about his trip into the unembodied state and he didn't tell her until after he'd built our universe, not because he thought he'd be in some trouble but because he knew she'd panic and try to stop his explorations. Whatever else he did or might do, nothing terrified P'najj more than losing her one and only son—whom she'd been afraid to conceive in the first place—to the unembodied state the way she'd almost lost P'koh in their childhood.

Well, the state of megaversal humanity appalled Mina. It had moved away from the freedom and discoverability that were the hallmarks of Mike and Molly's foundation of the race—in which P'koh had immersed him—to the velvet-gloved master's hand of limitation and ignorance. Now, no one in this context suffers abuse in the sense we comprehend it. On the other hand, very few retain the sense of mental freedom to imagine beyond the boundary of their mindset because their society—built and in most cases actively managed by its founder—trained it out of them from conception and passively corrects those who nevertheless manage the feat (cf. H1, § 1.2.1:534). Don't think this means oppression reigns throughout the megaverse. It doesn't, no more so than, for example, your own society oppresses you when your mindset instinctively roots in its general WOB and you never feel the need or desire to push beyond its boundaries, or if you do, then when others push back. This is true everywhere. It's unremarkable. But such limitations aren't inevitable. They're just mindsets. They're habits that individuals inherit, self-inflict, or induce by one means or another, all a part of the soft grip of the Carer that we self-habituate (§ 3.1.2.1:358).

Mina saw both sides, his mother's caring tyranny and his father's enlightening liberty. His family was a perfect microcosm to experience, analyze, and confront the reality he'd found seeded throughout the megaverse. When he hit sixteen, he decided that maintaining physical embodiment wasn't productive now that he'd anchored his life's vision to unembodiment and spirit embodiment. In short, he planned to build a universe, and not just any universe but one so far untried—a *freeverse* where he, its builder, would interfere "*senno ekto gamat*"[415] with emergent ℒife's birthright of freedom, its absolute autonomy. His descendants—*us*—would be the absolute masters of their mindset. Because one can't build a universe when physically embodied, Mina had

---

415. "Never without [my] permission" (*The Fifth Element* 1997, film, 00:42:09). We like the phrase.

to transcend that aspect. He shared his plans with his mother on his sixteenth birthday. That wasn't exactly the coming out event she'd envisioned. But she accepted his choice and placed his physical body into stasis (where it remains) so Mina could depart it.

2.2 MINA'S SPOUSE

When Mina was four years old, Cosmo persuaded P'koh and P'najj to conceive a thirteenth child as Mina's potential spouse because he didn't see anyone suitable in their universe for the future he was already foreseeing in Mina's fiercely independent personality. The result was Ag'poprje, pronounced 'awgk'pōp-ruh-jee' (Fig. 145:337). With Mike and Molly's blessing, Cosmo additionally persuaded P'najj to let him raise Ag'poprje separately from Mina. Cosmo and P'koh conspired to raise them both as much as possible to avoid falling into whatever fixed mindset P'najj and her culture engendered. The reason for Cosmo's interest was that he'd already recognized what was effectively a self-induced mental slavery afflicting humanity which, even at his young age, Mina intrinsically resisted so unlike his sisters and everyone else he'd encountered who blindly accepted traditional guidance. In a way, Cosmo and P'koh were guiding Mina and later Ag'poprje into a certain mindset every bit as much as P'najj was except, instead of eschewing the chaos of absolute freedom, they nurtured it. But unlike those trained to the mental yoke, they schooled them in freethinking and trained them to reflect on its outcomes.

2.2.1 MIKE AND MOLLY'S MISTAKE

The problem of humanity socializing away its intrinsic freedom of mind lay not with P'najj or anyone else but with Mike and Molly. They'd raised their own children, including P'koh and P'najj, without any interference in deference to autonomy. But in presuming it sufficient, they'd neglected to instill in them an incorruptible respect for the same intrinsic freedom of others. This propagated down through their lineage, morphing all the while into an unrecognizable though unnoticed caricature of our birthright much the way a potted frog is said to not notice its changing situation as the water slowly rises to a lethal boil. The result was the development of an unshakable emphasis on one's own individual freedom (however 'free' one perceives it) but much less of a commitment, if any, to that of others.

It's a natural tendency in people to want others to see life and live it the way they do. It's normative to one-self. Consequently, physical universes everywhere, including the Primoverse where P'koh and P'najj physically raised all their families, eventually developed societal institutions—'government'—organized to collectively handle the necessities of physical life but which, over time (as on Earth, particularly with Original Humanity's local-to-global socioculture; § 1.2.1:534), employed sustainable coercion to maintain the socialization desired by those who were most influential.[416] Here, we see that societal control inherent to Earth isn't just our local problem much less any sort of human aberration but a mindset that's global throughout megaversal humanity. That makes sense because humans are humans (having human woʙ) regardless where, how, and when individuals birth and live their lives.

2.2.1.1 COSMO RECOGNIZES MIKE AND MOLLY'S MISTAKE

Cosmo, initially having been marooned in the unembodied state by his Abnormality and thus separated from these dynamics for about a third of his life to date, recognized the problem as it more and more interfered with his unique sense of primeval liberty. After exploring the megaverse and comprehending the mindsets of founders and descendants, he saw the scope of the problem. He shared his analysis with Mike and Molly who got it right away. The question for which they lacked an answer, though, was what to do about it. It was at about this time that Cosmo had noticed P'koh and P'najj's traumas and healed them (§ 1.2.1.1:338). Noting P'koh's own commitment to liberty and his sly enculturation of it in Mina who'd embraced it from a tender age, Cosmo saw their answer in him. With Mike and Molly in his corner, he got P'najj's buy-in—not entirely, of course, owing to her own enculturation and ongoing obsession with Mina's safety and guided happiness, but enough to move forward—to conceive Ag'poprje whom she'd entrust Cosmo to raise as a willing and suitable spouse for Mina. In the Mother Tongue, *Ag'poprje* means 'life's new beginning.' Cosmo crossed his fingers that she'd embrace its promise.

---

416. Coercion needn't be violent or manipulative, just 'truth' imbibed from conception.

2.2.2 Ag'poprje's Autonomy

This doesn't mean P'najj conceived, or Cosmo raised, Ag'poprje blindly as Mina's future wife, as if she had no choice in the matter or control over her fate. Controlling people for the greater good is collective humanity's self-inflicted curse. For example, it lies behind all the angst and drama of the titular character of television's *Lucifer* (Netflix, 2016–21) and his love interest, Chloe, feeling controlled by God.

But that wasn't the case for these characters at all. Simply by God intervening to bring about Chloe's birth immune to the powers of angels, her feelings were more entirely her own than any other person on Earth who were powerless to resist Lucifer drawing out their true desire. Just as Lucifer's eldest brother Amenadiel finally realized all the angels' fate was entirely in *their* hands not God's—whereupon Lucifer at last comprehended he'd manipulated himself through his *own belief* that God was manipulating him—Chloe eventually reasoned her feelings for Lucifer were real, entirely her own and independent of God or anyone's manipulation. Regardless her human enculturation, from God's perspective in preparing her as an *option* for Lucifer to embrace, she grew up with absolute freedom of mind to make her own independent choice vis-à-vis loving Lucifer. As did Lucifer, who made his own free choice to love Chloe. They felt attracted because each saw in the other something of themselves, a certain affinity and not because God manipulated their feelings (*Lucifer* § 2.3:640).

Cosmo kicked off this same dynamic—realizing a person like Mina would never find a suitable match in his culture as it was, and that any such relationship was certain to upend his effort at mental liberty, which Cosmo didn't want to see happen—when he persuaded P'najj to conceive a daughter capable of loving Mina with the freedom of absolue autonomy.

2.2.3 Ag'poprje's Relationship with Mina

No one let slip to Mina and Ag'poprje that they were siblings. Because of Mina's close relationship with Cosmo, who was raising her, they spent a lot of time in each other's company. She'd always liked him but didn't 'catch feelings' until age twelve. P'najj revealed the truth about her to Mina when he was nineteen and already in spirit world learning to manipulate matter at the universe-building level. He was shocked and resented it as more of his mother's meddling in his mindset. Yet, he'd already discovered his own feelings for Ag'poprje when he was eighteen and she was fourteen. To his mind, there was no going back. It was what it was and he coped. Besides, when he was sixteen and still physically embodied, Ag'poprje told him she shared his vision of a universe populated by the absolutely free. She was curious herself to see if societies unfettered by interference with individual mindsets would be better or worse than those consciously molded, shaped, and kept in line (by others albeit really by their own willing abidance). The fact is, no one knew. Except for Mike and Molly's nuclear family, it was uncharted territory.

P'najj thought Mina was taking a silly, even dangerous risk although, by now, she generally supported his vision. Despite her worries and fears, P'koh, Cosmo, Mike, and Molly persuaded her it was the right thing to do. Absolute freedom hadn't created any destructive personality in Mike and Molly so, in P'najj's mind, she supposed it wasn't completely impossible it would turn out a benefit to humanity, just unlikely, and The Corruption initially seemed to bear her out. But Jesus and Sun-myung's commitment to unconditional love (which necessarily roots in absolute freedom) at the cost of enduring life-wrenching trauma powerfully affected her despite their seeming failures to resolve The Corruption. Then the Big Healing compelled her rethink of Mina's descendants never overcoming The Corruption and leaving collective humanity to its status quo ante. So, in a fit of enthusiasm she and P'koh conceived their second son whom they named for Sun-myung. P'najj committed to raising him the same way Cosmo and P'koh had raised Mina and Ag'poprje (§ 5:427; ch. 36:585).

Although Mina impermanently departed his physical embodiment when Ag'poprje was only twelve, she chose to remain physical. This was to appease P'najj by not causing any more of a rift between him and his mother who was already not terribly pleased with his life choices, as well as to avoid distracting Mina during his 1.2by boot camp to master universe building under Cosmo's strict tutelage. Recall that in Mike and Molly's universe (and others), there's no natural limit on how long a physical body can endure. Unlike us, they're fully integrated and disease and the other factors we're used to dooming physical human bodies aren't present. One's physical body can live as long as one's willing to put up with it. Too, one can place it into a natural stasis to live spirit embodied or unembodied at will for any length of time. Mina had to use a technological option, however, because learning 'energy' manipulation toward creating a universe, let alone actually building one, uses every bit of one's vital energy (𝓛ife force). So, even in training there's literally nothing left over to animate a physical body. It was non-physical or nothing.

In Mina's view, a principal reason humanity got itself stuck in mindset control is that Mike and Molly's immediate descendants—all physical-born—got too ensconced in the physical environment where it's easy to lose touch and get totally separated (despite simultaneous spirit embodiment) from our larger spirit reality as well as unembodiment in which freedom is less corruptible and incorruptible, respectively. To avoid this problem, he didn't encourage indeterminate physical longevity in our universe as an eternal feature, preferring instead that those born into physical embodiment dispense with it no later than about 10,000 years and then transition to spirit embodiment and-or unembodiment for eternity. Nevertheless, it's certainly possible to maintain one's physical embodiment indefinitely. And one's freedom to do so.

2.2.4   Ag'poprje's Role in Our Universe

Recall that only a single individual can Intentionalize a universe (§ 2.1.3.1:309), which means Mina's the sole builder of ours. Ag'poprje isn't just arm candy, though. She supported, counseled, problem-solved, brainstormed, and more during the 1.2BY period it took Mina to prepare our universe. She was with him throughout. The day he moved his Intentionality into that one picosecond of focus during which our universe came into real existence (§ 2.1.3.2:310)—his birthday—is the day she put her own physical embodiment aside[417] and joined him for the event. They count it as their wedding day although they didn't get around to an actual ceremony for family and friends until about 1BY later.

Though it's a shared vision, our universe is the product of Mina's mind, not Ag'poprje's. He's the specialist whereas she's the generalist. She's not a co-builder but a co-founder. Being his partner, she's always available for operational problems that arise as well as handling operational activities such as co-healing with Mina during and after the Big Healing, teaching, helping, comforting, befriending, and so on their spirit descendants (leaving their physical descendants, us, to Mina). Whatever she does is what she chooses, and for which she feels a capability. However, since she didn't Intentionalize the universe herself then there's significant aspects of it about which she has no awareness. Accordingly, she doesn't engage people regarding the universe at all but defers to Mina who knows everything about it.

There's no value in thinking of Ag'poprje as Mother God, Goddess of the Universe, the Divine Feminine, or the like because gods aren't real. Mina and Ag'poprje are certainly role models but still just human beings like the rest of us, only vastly older and more aware. More to the point, they're literally our great grandparents many times removed (§ 2.1.1:348). They're our family. Kin, not strangers. That we haven't known them or about them until now is immaterial to our familial relationship. Their children's children—us—currently number ~8.49×10^{17}, or ~849 quadrillion, physical and spirit persons. That's *our* collective family here in *our* universe like a clan on its infinite estate.

SECTION 3
Mina's Spirit Life

As noted, Mina moved out of his physical embodiment at sixteen to devote himself a hundred percent to his vision. The process took him about a 1.2 billion years before Cosmo was willing to sign off on Mina's readiness to focus it all into that last picosecond of Intentionality. Cosmo was a tough taskmaster, a real drill sergeant. He accepted nothing less than Mina's absolute best. Creating a universe is serious business. They take up resources in All Existence to a degree no one actually knows, only that it seems considerable. He'd seen half-assed universes put up like buildings skirting construction codes and it only made life difficult for its residents. Everyone who mattered to him knew he was training Mina, so he'd never put his name behind a universe builder who was anything less than, as Ayako likes to say, "top notch."

By now it should be evident that building a universe isn't a magical, deitic undertaking of divine power. It's simply the harnessing of ƔumanThought (§ 1.2.2.1:253) with Intentionality in the milieu of Energent–prime proto-energy (§ 3.2:282) in the same way, say, the placebo effect—a very mild, limited expression of Intentionality—works. Building a universe is everyone's birthright. Here's why Jesus, who understood this, is said to have quoted Psalms 82:6 that " 'You are gods; and all of you are children of the Most High.' " We are literally the same human beings as Mina whether we know him as God, Creator, Allah, Great (Sacred) Spirit, Brahman, or whatever.

---

417. The reason they put their physical bodies into stasis instead of terminating them and permanently transitioning to spirit embodiment is so they can physically live amongst family and friends instead of interacting only via spirit embodiment.

Through the process by which Cosmo trained Mina—some of which the Cardinal understands and some that are simply the *vitae mysterium* of All Existence—a discrete universe comes into being, like a neighborhood into which 'first ancestors' relocate to experience its material environment. Although it was necessary that Mina comprehend the theory, his training was essentially a practicum through which Cosmo expected the theory to become clear. In terms of an emotional experience, it wasn't too unlike a military or police boot camp where the pressures of work, learning, exercise, personalities, and the like combine to push one to their absolute limit and then beyond. If Mina had quit in the middle, he wouldn't have been the only one. Indeed, there were times he questioned his vision and commitment. Even so, and despite toying with the idea, he never seriously considered giving up. He wasn't a quitter to begin with but, more pertinent, humanity's profound need for absolute freedom deeply touched him for which, to his knowledge, no one was stepping up.[418] So he sucked it up and aimed for Cosmo's standards.

There's no set period in which to train a person. Since Molly's abbreviated effort, a billion years is about average. Mina got through it and Cosmo clapped him on the back for a job well enough done. The important thing for Cosmo was that Mina gave him confidence that he'd construct a well-built, properly functioning universe that his descendants could happily inhabit with the intrinsic freedom known to not as many humans as it ought. For that, Cosmo felt quite satisfied. The Corruption somewhat dampened his confidence in Mina's capability but not enthusiasm for his vision. All that both of them could do in that respect was hang on and work to pull a rabbit out of their hat. Jesus and others like him on other planets were the first (planned) rabbits. Sun-myung was an organic happenstance, an outlier who'd rigorously made himself into the only second rabbit. The girls and I were purely an accident of experience, curiosity, Lucifer letting go, and Michael finally giving up the ghost of fear and guilt all on the foundation laid by Mina and Sun-myung. For Mina, we were the well-timed plot twist that did the trick (§ 4:377).

3.1   WHERE MINA LIVES

Star Trek V: The Final Frontier (1989) pursued the notion that if God exists he must live somewhere. The entity they discovered turned out to be a malevolent bogeyman but the question remains. Must our 'creator' live somewhere? Well, yes. As a human being, Mina principally lives spirit embodied in the supranatural environment of his birth universe, Molly's Primoverse. But that doesn't mean he's not always present—always aware—in ours.

The nature of universe creation means that its builder's awareness inextricably links to its 'energy' and archí in what one may think of as a quantum state. A builder is (without dimensionality via proto-energy) aware of and in touch with every jot and tittle of his or her universe. The reason is that a universe issues from its builder's Intentionality, from his or her very mind. Being aware of all things in a universe differs only in kind from being aware of one's own mind and body, so the concept isn't as alien as it first appears. Being spirit embodied, however, Mina must reside in actual space. His spirit world home is in Molly's Primoverse where he was born (§ 1.2:336). It's a normal home as homes go, his and Ag'poprje's place for family, children, and friends from their universe and ours to visit.

Ayako and I have visited them—Ayako's spirit self was mostly raised there from age two through thirteen anyway—and my memories include a four-storey ceilinged colonnade of heavy, ornate, polished wood columns and sitting with him on his large, covered, 'western'-looking wooden veranda with lovely mountain views similar to those in the Guilin and Yangzhou areas of China. He also has a home in our universe for anyone to visit who doesn't know how—or can't find a 'ride'—to transition to his universe (§ 2.1.1:348; § 2:564). He doesn't hide himself away. He's accessible to all. As with any person, though, one need perforce develop a relationship. Spirit persons have always been able to interact with and visit him if their mindsets don't block them, and now physical persons can, too, via (for now) ET. Those spiritually open—mediums, clair sensitives—should have little problem finding their way to his home here.

If you're wondering how Mina can live outside our universe being its builder, well, it's simple. Mind awareness has no limitations. Wherever he is in All Existence, he's connected to, meaning aware of, our universe in all its particulars via the dimensionless 'medium' of proto-energy. Besides his constant general awareness of our universe—sort of a subliminal bird's eye view—he becomes aware of whatever granular detail to which he tunes his Thought. Since he integrates with the girls and me, then regardless where he is in All Existence, when we think of or call to him, he's aware and responds.[419]

---

418. Cosmo built his own universe before recognizing the issue. But since (as the Cardinal later realized) the nature of a builder's 'quantum' awareness of their universe appears to work like a single-use ticket, a person can only ever build one.

SECTION 4

Mina's Han

An old tenet says the premise from which one begins defines all that follows. For example, religion premised on God as an impassive, unmoved ruler or a loving yet transcendingly moral judge of the universe—a paterfamilias in its most traditional Roman sense—leads to a religious experience neglecting freedom, love and deep emotion. The reason is that it doesn't figure into the overall scheme of mankind's relationship to God and its ultimate destiny in His plan for redemption. Sun-myung began with the premise that residing at the very core of God is Heart, or *shimjeong* (심정; 心情) in Korean. It's a qualitative mindstate (Moon 2018, 46) experiencing profound emotion rooted in unconditional love. The obverse of God's *shimjeong* is grief, or *han* (한; 恨), a kind of trauma—suffering *and* its result—rooted in the memory of resentful sorrow of a despairing wrong to one's collective, which is to say, own-self (§ 2:275; cf. Kim 1987, 55; Moon 1996).

God's Biblical pathos[420] and Divine Principle's *han* arise in knowing humanity's individual and collective suffering brought on by the Fall of Man and the human state of sin generally. Mina's *han* arises simply in knowing humanity's individual and collective *han* from their unfreeness. Suffering and sorrow in and of itself doesn't absolve the Fall and consequent sin. That's a separate moral justice we need redeem to satisfy God's pathos (*han*) which, even so, doesn't end suffering and sorrow without also redeeming the Fall because the Fall and its consequent state of sin is, in and of itself, both those things. Mina's *han*, however, *is* satisfied by the end of human suffering and sorrow because the individual human as emergent 𝓛ife is free, birthed according to his or her woв independently of a universe's builder and one's own parents. A person intrinsically exists in accord with the woв of 𝔥uman and nothing else (§ 3.3.2:284). Moral codes aren't organic to life but imposed by those having 𝓛ife. Indeed, there are universes whose builders impose a 'divine' morality and punish disobedience as sinful in just the way we've comprehended our own human condition since The Corruption. Our universe doesn't operate that way, however. Mina built it on the foundation of absolute autonomy. For us, then, a moral standard is an accepted human frame of reference that informs our choices, not a 'divine' absolute that governs our life and punishes transgressors (MEANING OF MORALITY, § 2.1.1.1:407).

Absent The Corruption, we're cognizant of manipulative restraints on our free will that surreptitiously control our concept of it. We're ajudgmentally free to harm ourselves, others, and cause suffering and sorrow albeit consequences in the societal context inevitably present themselves (EVIL, § 10:456). Mina grieves over harm but doesn't experience Unificationism's *han* because his arises not in humanity's suffering and sorrow as a result of free will but in the deceptive conditions of The Corruption where humanity doesn't even realize it is intrinsically free and its choices manipulated—Corrupted—hence not of informed will. This manifests a mental slavery in which the slave doesn't know he or she is mentally conditioned rather than mentally free. One freely chooses—recall that, regardless The Corruption, one always inhabits free will—but its premises are Corrupt. This takes advantage of humanity's natural inclination toward habituated kinship because people most often opt for the easy road of coercing agreement versus the harder road of persuasion or agreeing to disagree in familial and societal contexts. It just goes to human preference. Accordingly, The Corruption isn't just a phenomenon of *our* universe where it corrupted Mina's plan, but of collective humanity throughout the megaverse. This is why Mina's two sisters planted it in our collective mind—our Ultraculture—in the first place, to confuse and defuse our sense of absolute autonomy, our intrinsic freedom (§ 2.1:368).

Mina's *han* isn't simply for the suffering and sorrow of his descendants (*us*) but for the megaverse of humanity. Only when he built our universe, seeded it with his own children who multiplied down through the æons to our present population, and then experienced the unjust immolation of our freedom on his sisters' altruistic pyre did he truly cognize in a profound, heartistic, *shimjeong* way the real *han* of collective humanity. He's not alone. He estimates ±10 quadrillion people throughout the megaverse—a mere pinprick in mgaversal humanity's population, but a start nonetheless—feel his sort of *han* and have awareness of his effort. It's not that collective humanity is free or slave, free-willed or manipulated, aware or deceived, but that they're *intrinsically free to know it*, to cognize their true desire and then freely to choose it—or not. Next, we describe the establishment (versus divine creation) of our universe and then explain The Corruption in detail.

---

419. Sometimes he's involved in something—say, healing—and can't split his attention, and asks us to 'call back,' or he half-mindedly answers to be helpful but without quite 'hearing' our question such that his answer is off and we have to revisit it.

420. ". . . the divine pathos is not conceived of as an essential attribute of God . . . but as an expression of God's will; it is a functional rather than a substantial reality; not an attribute, not an unchangeable quality, not an absolute content of divine Being, but rather a situation or the personal implication in His acts" (Heschel 1975, 11).

Making Our Universe Home

"SO WHAT'S TO stop us from creating a universe in a lab?" wonders Russian physicist Andrei Linde, Stanford University's Nobel laureate professor and main author of the 'chaotic inflation' model of universe creation. "We would be like gods! . . . what I have shown . . . is that we can't rule out the possibility that our own universe was created by someone in another universe who just felt like doing it" (Holt 2012, 14). Funny his research leads him to say that. We've learned that's exactly how and why Mina—a human born in a different universe—created our own, except the 'lab' was his own mind where Thought via Intentionality integrating Energent–prime proto-energy substantiated our universe in its own 'frequency space' as a real existent (§ 2.1.3:309). Having taken a gander at cosmology in previous chapters from the perspective of Philosophy with a capital-P w.r.t. universe structure and operation, we view it in this chapter more in a domestic sense. That might seem strange, but any builder creates their universe as a home for their family and descendants which, in Mina's case, is us (§ 1:335).

SECTION 1
Our Two Home Environments

Recall our universe comprises the two major natural and supranatural environments where we live physical and spirit embodied (§ 7.1:212). Each has its own purpose operationally entwining them such that we can freely interact with one from the other and move our embodied awareness back and forth at will. This enables a person born into one environment to experience the other at the same time. A person who's still physically alive can simultaneously spend time in spirit humanity's supranatural environment and vice versa (§ 7.1.1.1:212). This was the case even before the Big Healing except that physical people only remembered their spirit-self experiences as fragmentary dreams rather than coherent memories. In 2019, after the Big Healing, Mina made genetic changes across the human-inhabited planets of our universe that, with time, will reestablish full brain integration with ℒife mind (§ 1.2.2.4:257).

For example, Humanity 1.0 (H1; § 1:531) was Mina's original establishment of humanity on Earth. Like every other inhabited planet, H1 started out having full mind–brain integration. This enabled their access to Energent science (§ 2.3.3:117) which they shortsightedly used to build extremely high-yield 'radiation' weapons that extinguished them throughout our solar system (§ 1.3.2:541). When Mina redeveloped Humanity version 2.0 (H2) on Earth, he sought to avoid an H1 replay. But the Big Healing obviated his worry. As his post-Big Healing genetic adjustments to mind–brain integration (§ 1.2.2.5.2:262) develop, our now-dreamy spirit world experiences will gradually shift to real memories and our conscious awareness of the greater universe will become real to us instead of seeming naught but flighty figments.

Creating a universe feels like such a fantastic undertaking. It's hard to grasp it's not really too different in concept—once we accept a universe builder has no power to create ℒife beyond procreating it—from

Andrei Linde's lab notion or an astronaut building a habitat in deep space as an environment for his family and descendants to inhabit. Here, deep space is analogous to All Existence, and habitats built by others for their own families are analogous to the 194 million universes currently existing each in its own unique 'location,' or 'frequency space' (Today's Family of Universes, § 2.1.4.1:312). This isn't hard to comprehend so much as shifting our paradigm from divine creation, a random Big Bang, our universe and Earth's humanity being sole existents, and so forth. It's a sea change one tends to resist.

Recall, too, the essential difference between the two environments of our universe lies in their modes of existence. Supranatural (supra)matter exists only when people Intentionalize it to exist. It's without independent existence. It's simply supranatural proto-energy. Physical matter, on the other hand, is a weak emergent of the natural environment's proto-energy, arising on its own recognizance to exist independently of human Intentionality as an autonomous existent according to its own WOB (§ 2:114). It encapsulates natural proto-energy within it that gives rise to Fundamental Force in that environment. Supramatter doesn't encapsulate proto-energy within it except insofar as Intentionalized although, once it is, it gives rise to supranatural Fundamental Force. Because the supranatural Energent isn't an extension of Energent–prime the way the natural Energent is, it doesn't intrinsically harbor proto-energy but only that which it acquires from the natural Energent via the process of 'energy' translation (§ 7.1.3:214). It isn't a real extension of Energent–prime the way the natural Energent is but only a facsimile a universe builder Intentionalizes. This is why we can so easily Intentionalize—manipulate—spirit matter as opposed to physical matter, as the former's Intentionalized WOB doesn't resist while latter's autonomous WOB does.

We describe human embodiment's development in the supranatural then natural environments from when "darkness was over the surface of the deep" (Gen. 1:2) to its present state of habitation.

SECTION 2

Home in the Supranatural Environment

The first proto-energy translated from the natural to the supranatural Energent (§ 7:211) ~13.5BYA, but the supranatural environment wasn't lights-on and move-in ready until ~10MYA. Making it a home took three steps. In phase one, Mina brought over those of his children with spouses who were interested in relocating and they embodied themselves here. In phase two, they collectively Intentionalized (designed and built out) its basic look and feel which, out of the gate, looked and felt a hundred percent like Mina's own environment—Molly's Primoverse—where they'd all grown up (§ 1.2:336). They set up world terrains and homes in which to raise their families that, down a long and winding road, resulted in your birth. Once physical proto-human development reached integrability, they organized themselves in phase three to *humaform* (integrating physical bodies to establish families and civilizations on habitable planets; § 2.3:357).

2.1 Supranatural Phase 1: Moving In

The builders of about 99.5% of the universes of All Existence built them as a preference over their own to provide an environment for their descendants. The other half percent invited whoever mattered to them to set up shop—seven as resorts for the unembodied-capable—but we don't deal with these. Recall Mina's vision was to establish an environment where his descendants could live in absolute autonomy without any surreptitious mindset manipulation by its builder (§ 2.1:340). But he couldn't guarantee there'd never be any such manipulation by and between his descendants because, after all, they were free without restraint, judgment, correction, or punishment by him for transgressing his vision. He laid no ground rules for his starter package of children and their spouses beyond never themselves violating human autonomy by inciting mindset addiction (§ 2.1.1.5.2:353), and left them to approach him with issues rather than foisting his solutions on them. He trained them in his vision, of course, which they adopted as their own, and was always available to them. He wanted to avoid Mike and Molly's primal mistake (§ 2.2.1:341) but . . . he didn't. Well, not him specifically. Our first ancestors. 'Moving in' happened as follows.

2.1.1 Our First Ancestors as the Founding Families

Our universe was ready for residence around 11.6BY after its so-called Big Bang some 13,795,785,505 years ago (§ 6.10:186). Mina waited a bit under 2.188BY more (§ 2.1.1.6:354) before helping the first twelve people—six of them his and Ag'poprje's children (out of twelve at the time) along with their spouses from other families born into his mother's universe—to embody themselves here (*below*) as our First Ancestors, the Founding Families. His children were evenly male and female as were their spouses (Table 15).

Table 15. Mina's children sans spouses, eldest to youngest, as the First Ancestors; names in spirit world language (derived from Mina's). AA is 'archangel.' Double underline is an accented syllable. 𝔄 is universe.

#	Birth Name	Pronunciation	Sex	AA Children (cf. Table 16)
1	V'nin	Vuh'-<u>neen</u>	M	Gabriel, Lucifer, Michael (GLM)
2	Epv'd'd	Eep-<u>vuhh</u>'-duuh'-dt	M	Remiel
3	Boñ'p	Boře'-<u>nyŭ</u>'p' (sounds like /o/ in /lot/; /ĭ/ in /in/; /ĕ'/ in /eh/ sans /h/)	F	Raguel, Remiel
4	Watb'hv'v	<u>Wut</u>-buh'-huhv'-vuh	F	Saraqael
5	Oid't'v	<u>Oyd</u>'-tuh'-vuh	M	Uriel
6	V'v'dib	Vuh-<u>vuh</u>'-deeb'	F	No children in our 𝔄

2.1.1.1 Issues Arising From Unembodiment

One must enter the unembodied state for just a moment to disembody in one universe and embody in another, that is, to travel from universe to universe. Mina had to give the First Ancestors a 'ride' from their universe to ours (and back again when desired) for two reasons. First, one needs a guide when traveling to another universe for the first time because one hasn't yet experienced its 'energy,' so can't manifest their awareness in that 'frequency space.' Second, the Ancestors had resisted learning the ropes of unembodiment as they hadn't yet overcome their P'najj-induced fear of it (§ 1.2.1:337). This meant they couldn't come and go as they pleased. Mina tried to teach them, but the dread imbibed from their larger culture proved insurmountable and, obviously, he couldn't force it on them.

The mindset prevailing in Mina's home universe encouraged a fear of unembodiment not just in its early days by P'najj with her children, but ever since with pretty much everyone. It was born of P'koh's unhappy experience as well as the realization that once unembodied, people viscerally experienced the intrinsic autonomy of the human mind and thereafter encouraged autonomous mindsets in others, as had Cosmo (§ 1.2.1.1:338). They felt it led to an unruly, hence, unhappy society. By Mina's time, comparatively few in the megaverse even knew the reason it'd been discouraged in the first place much less that it was an option for ℒife. Even fewer wanted to try it. He later realized he should've persisted before bringing the Ancestors here, but had a timetable and didn't want to put things off any longer.

At first, Mina didn't think it would pose a problem for his vision. But it grew apparent the First Ancestors' awareness of autonomy wasn't as robust as it would've been had they experienced for themselves the raw freedom of unembodied ℒife. Moreover, if the Founding Families were going to talk to or accept guidance from him, he'd have to come "walking in the garden in the cool of the day" (Gen. 3:8) as it were. This meant he ran the risk of making a pest of himself. They never avoided him like Biblical Adam and Eve did God, but did take their promised autonomy seriously, preferring to do things their own way. Mina was serious about it, too. He didn't want to manipulate them. His six children here loved and respected him and his motivation but they were now not merely heads of households homesteading a lineage on their own forty acres, but ultimately the ancestors of a discrete universe. They wanted their descendants to learn their ways primarily from them, not Grandpa. No tension arose between them. Mina simply hoped for the best and did what he could. Absolute autonomy was a grand experiment, after all, but also his one and only shot at founding a universe (FN 418:344). He'd get no do-overs if he failed. This was it for him as a builder. He was in it for the long haul. It was freedom or bust. Though a frequent visitor to his children's homes, he scrupulously avoided backseat parenting.

2.1.1.2 Issues Achieving Consensus

The first serious difficulty to crop up was the group's tendency to gravitate toward Family One—V'nin, the eldest of Mina's children here, and his spouse—as a mentor and leader. Family Six—V'v'dib, the youngest of Mina's children here, and her spouse—didn't share that view. Instead, V'v'dib's couple thought their awareness of autonomy was better, more in line with Mina's vision in spirit, and therefore worthy of the group acclaiming them its de facto leader rather than V'nin's couple, even though there was no real push, need, or desire for anyone to be in charge. Theirs was just the human kinship tendency to work together around a central figure, typically one who exerts leadership to build consensus. The sibling rivalry between Mina's elder son V'nin and his younger daughter V'v'dib, which predated their arrival here, only complicated and exacerbated the leadership issue. Mina mediated the dispute at everyone's request, but after about 500 years he'd effectively resolved nothing except their rivalry. No one tried to push conformity disguised as consensus, yet neither did anyone back down from any issue considered non-negotiable without reaching consensus. Despite generally deferring to V'nin's couple on a host of issues, the Families didn't just follow like ducklings. This was especially true of V'v'dib's couple, who increasingly tended to resist the consensus methodology anyhow.

Ultimately, V'v'dib's couple wouldn't accept the others' consensus on the V'nin couple's leadership or their future society. V'v'dib's couple believed in moderating mindset despite their promotion of absolute autonomy because its perceived chaos (in the sense of being unordered and unpredictable) frightened them now they were in the trenches building it. Unruly autonomy must inexorably cause harm and harm is to be avoided. Instead of the tolerated chaos of unbridled autonomy, they promoted an *educated* autonomy of managed interference in the sense of educating chaotic autonomy *out* of people.

The group lauded their commitment to autonomy but the problem was, first, they'd be unilaterally choosing it for others and, second, 'educated autonomy' essentially meant denying it to promote it, a fundamental contradiction they foresaw leading to the theoretical but (in practice) nullified autonomy that people hold by 'right' under ideological mindsets but can't actually exercise. In short, their universe would be like every other one: boundedly autonomous yet ultimately nonautonomous. It's not that V'v'dib's couple didn't believe in Mina's vision of autonomy generally, but that they felt *absolute* autonomy wasn't necessarily intrinsic to human WOB and, even if it was, it didn't mean they owed their own autonomy to anyone. The group grasped that even well meaning people like V'v'dib's couple could and would 'educate' their descendants out of autonomy until their universal society forgot it was ever autonomous to begin with. Ensconced in his vision, Mina would never actively limit his descendants' autonomy as founder but, in V'v'dib's couple's vision, the first Ancestors sure would. To that, the group chose to not consent.

V'v'dib's couple burned their last bridge when they decided to leave the group to found their own society. Initially a counterbalance to the 'disaster' to real autonomy they felt the group's future society would necessarily bring, it held an expectation that, in future, they'd convert the group's society to their vision of real autonomy and thereby unify and harmonize our universe and the Founding Families under one *educated* mindset with an autonomy that was, in their minds, indeed absolute, just not chaotic. As desirous as we are of a caring and considerate society without harm, one can appreciate the seduction of this version of autonomy. But as this was actually tyranny in the making along the same lines Mina was trying to avoid in the first place, it didn't go over well with him at all. Freedom is sustainable only when it's individualized, not collectivized, because autonomy is fundamentally personal not communal. Once the greater good circumscribes autonomy, which in short order becomes an intransgressible parameter, absolute autonomy devolves to absolute nonautonomy in the sense that absolute, or 'chaotic,' autonomy is unattainable. Conflict, thus harm, is inevitable as some people by necessity seek absolute autonomy.

Here's where Mina put his foot down despite his self-imposed noninterference directive. He reminded V'v'dib's couple of their agreement to leave the project if ever they tried to addict the First Ancestors' descendants to mindset. However nonautonomous their children and children's children might turn out in future, Mina couldn't stand by as any of the First Ancestors themselves redefined real autonomy into the faux autonomy, meaning nonautonomy, that dominates the megaverse. That would eviscerate the project before it got off the ground and be a true disservice to their descendants for whom he felt a responsibility. For Mina, the kernel of humanity here in our universe is and must be the Ancestors rooted in absolute autonomy. If nothing else, they had to hold true to it because, if down the lineage tree things did go sideways, humanity would always have them and it as a last redoubt, much as America's founding fathers and their written constitution serve as the kernel of American freedom and its final redoubt against statutorily disemboweling alterations. Mina asked V'v'dib's couple to forego his project now they'd openly committed themselves to laying the ground for division and, however gift-wrapped, trapping those yet unborn into nonautonomy. They honored their word.[421]

The Ancestors reorganized as the five Founding Families, though retained the V'v'dib couple's Intentionalized contributions to the look and feel of the supranatural environment, which was as far as they'd all got by then. Even so, the chaotic autonomy that Mina expected and V'v'dib's couple feared came about even before The Corruption took root, as here and there it ran to extremes. It was irrelevant from Mina's perspective though. Autonomy in the service of harm is always amenable since humans never die.[422] The only actual risk

---

421. Only later did Mina discover his two problematic sisters (§ 1.2.2:339; § 2.1:368) had influenced V'v'dib's couple to sow The Corruption in our universe through its Founding Families. Bullet dodged.

to unbridled autonomy is psychic trauma which is healable, thus not a long-term harm. Autonomy that's lost *in the mindset*, on the other hand, is very difficult to recover—for some, impossible, at least in a reasonable timeframe—before greater harm occurs (§ 3.2:374).

To understand autonomy properly, one must comprehend human spirit reality, our eternal existence. Physical people seek to limit autonomy to promote their own or sociocultural safety—a state of no harm— which is why tyranny always justifies itself in the name of the public weal.[423] This isn't Mina's concern. For him, the greater safety lies in absolute autonomy despite when taken to excess because, if we've learned anything from the twentieth century, it's that greater harm consistently befalls people through nonautonomy. Despite its for-the-greater-good window dressing, tyrannical government is simply the organized suppression of autonomy and imposition of nonautonomy toward a laundry list of power, control, money, the wealpublic, safety, peace, financial security, well being, and the like which, in the end, only escalates harm. Whether physical or spirit embodied, the only way to control intrinsically autonomous humans is to manipulate their mindset through some form of persuasion so they control themselves.[424] Such mental conditioning is very difficult to eradicate and always results in conflict between differently conditioned people as well as between the conditioning and the intrinsic self (§ 3.1.2.1:358).[425]

2.1.1.3   HOW THE ANCESTORS INFLUENCED THEIR DESCENDANTS

Mina pre-trained the First Ancestors to the demands of absolute autonomy prior to bringing them here, so it wasn't new to them, but raising their children in its ways certainly was. He'd raised his own children in absolute autonomy but not their spouses. Other parents had done that job in Mina's larger culture which eschewed real autonomy for the harmony of faux freedom. Amongst the First Families, Mina's children naturally strove in accord with their father to interfere *"senno ekto gamat"* (FN 415:340) with their spouse's own absolute autonomy, but each couple ultimately applied it to raising their children with less-than-absolutely-autonomous mindsets, meaning, those of young children. They inadvertently trained them to internalize it into adulthood than to let it go as they reached an age where they should have transcended parentally-trained mindsets for their emancipated own. All parents face this situation, even where physical safety (as a rationale for mindset training) isn't at risk. We're not simply recounting here the average parenting challenge with which we're familiar. If you accept a human being created our universe and not some ineffable divine entity, then you realize humans are ♄uman wherever they exist and whoever they are. And being human means dealing with all the same issues we confront regardless environmental circumstances like natural versus supranatural.

The upshot was that they did successfully inculcate into their children an appropriate respect for the autonomy of others—the critical task where Mike and Molly had come up short (§ 2.2.1:341)—but their spouses stumbled somewhat through the detritus of the mindsets in which their own parents had raised them. Mina's children ended up deferring to their spouses' mindsets, representations of a culture that regardless Mina's training had more than less seeped into them as well. This created a dichotomy in their own children's mindsets, a duality that generated inner conflict down through the generations as their children and children's children produced their own families.

The Ancestors' descendants grew into independent adults but with mindsets clouded up with certain underlying contradictions, chief among them being that, while autonomy was absolute in nature it wasn't *always* absolute in practice. In other words, if society—people collectively living with a shared mindset— assigned itself an objective, then that outranked individual autonomy if, when, or even just in case it conflicted with it. So, autonomy in and of itself is and always has been absolute in a normative sense—this is true throughout the megaverse—but societal mindset circumscribes its expression of how autonomous an individual can *be* without meaningful pushback from societal peers.

---

422. The only potential loss from physical body death is separation from physical loved ones and activities. That's our reality now but fully integrated persons experience no real separation as they continue interacting via their spirit selves.

423. Such as the French Revolution and the many ideological '-isms.'

424. Because the spirit embodied phenomenally experience their material reality just like the physical embodied, they feel bodily harm the same as us except no harm is permanent or lethal.

425. This is the reason individuals always feel at war with themselves. Their core human wob—absolute autonomy—struggles against their mindset addiction. It gives rise to St. Paul's lament that, "in my inner being I delight in God's law; [23]but I see another law at work in me, waging war against the law of my mind and making me a prisoner of the law of sin at work within me" (Rom. 7:22–3). Also, it's why those areas of spirit world inhabited by the physical-born pre-Big Healing were more dark and scary than light and peaceful. They were chockablock with the mindset-addicted who couldn't shake it off.

Mina envisioned our universal society (especially amongst the spirit-born, because there's literally nothing safety-wise at risk there) deferring to individual autonomy and not the other way round because the latter principally leads to harm. This was our First Ancestors' yet-to-be-settled dilemma when they encountered The Corruption's second introduction to our universe (§ 2.1.1.6:354). Let's consider that.

2.1.1.4 Origin of Archangel Mythology

An archangel[426] in the Abrahamic religions is traditionally a 'chief angel' or 'angel of origin' and, in one form or another, shows up in all traditions. Since angels, like gods, aren't real but simply human beings, they aren't divine nor its messengers, punishers, warriors, or the like but a generalized support system for the physical-born (Angels, § 1.2:521). Physical humanity's concept of archangels arises with the activities of the Ancestors' second generation, that is, the first generation born in our universe. We call them *second-Gen* for simplicity (much as Japanese immigrants' children in the Americas are called *Nisei*) with the caveat that out of the many second-Gen, only seven serve in the 'archangel' capacity. We reference these seven persons as archangels to avoid confusion, but remember, they're spirit-born persons, human beings like you.

Seven specific tasks that support physical humanity determine the number of archangels (Table 16). Their purpose is to meliorate the deficiencies amongst the physical-born arising in The Corruption although they were always just a stopgap, an imperfect solution to a corralled mindset habituated to physical reality and blinded to the spirit one. Initially, physical humanity had 100% mind–brain integration but, in The Corruption's milieu, it rapidly devolved to a ~30% baseline.[427]

Table 16. The seven principal tasks and 'archangel' organizers of each (cf. Table 15:349; Table 17:523); double underline is an accented syllable; "+𝔄" means it also organizes certain universe maintenance.

Task	Archangel Name	Sex	Given Name	Pronunciation
Intervention	Gabriel	M	Titit'j	Tie-tie-t'-juh
Guidance	Lucifer	M	Tivi'iv'z	Tie-v'-eyev'-zuh
Wisdom+𝔄	Michael	M	Bibci'd	Bīb-sī'-dt
Validate+𝔄	Remiel	F	B'i'c'iic'bii	B'ie-s'eye-eesuh'-buh-ee-ee
Entry	Raguel	F	C'icib'id'i	See'-see-b'-eeduh'-ee'
Contentment	Saraqael	M	I'ave'vi'xiv	Eye-āhvee'-vie'-xeye-v'
Multiplication	Uriel	M	I'dide'e	Eye'-dee-deh-eh
Remiel's task	Zadkiel	M	Vxooc'ben	Vh-zh-ōō-ch'ben (FN 426)

Our ancestors encountered The Corruption a second time in the 27th spirit-born generation so that, when humans were born into integrable physical bodies beginning in the 75th generation, it already had a firm grip on spirit humanity's mindset. It became a part of physical humanity's mindset according to people's spirit selves, their physical parenting, and physicospirit Ultraculture (§ 4.1:291). Mina was originally optimistic physical humanity would hold onto their full integration and at least be no worse off than spirit humanity. But until the Big Healing, even he was feeling the wear and tear of pessimism as The Corruption spread directly into the whole population and defied his every sanative effort. The nature of physical reality in any universe is a force unto itself although in ours it more harshly affected physical humanity who lost full awareness of not just absolute autonomy but spirit reality, too (§ 3.1.2.1:358).

Here we see the natural environment isn't intrinsically a place of suffering, biological inconvenience, and supranatural ignorance. It can be every bit the enjoyable place of enlightened ease as the supranatural (CH. 30:515). But The Corruption interfered. The First Ancestors proposed physical humanity's extended spirit family—the spirit born—should help them cope with their developing deficiencies, and they rose to the challenge. They organized the tasks but later handed them over to their native-born second-Gen children, the 'archangels' (§ 1.3.2:541), who organized a methodology, recruited help, and managed the lot (Table 16). Lucifer for instance manages ~160 trillion spirit-born and some physical-born 'guardian angels' (§ 2.3.2:524). But as he said jouncing down the dirt road to our house in the Virginia woods in 2017, he's only an 'archangel' because others consider him best for the job (§ 1.4:65).

---

426. Greek: ἐῴἀρχάγγελος. Fifth-Gen Vxooc'ben ('Zadkiel' in Judeo-Christianity though not an 'archangel') provides some of this section's information. He's the first, and eldest, whom the 'archangels' recruited to the tasks (Table 16).

427. Although a physical person integrates 100% their ℒife mind and thusly is fully aware of their spirit self in spirit world, they aren't necessarily 100% aware of spirit reality or of the full human experience because of their mindset (cf. Humanity 1.0's).

2.1.1.5 Our Universe is a Revolution

While every universe is unique because no builder Intentionalizes their universe exactly the same way any other does, their overall natural and supranatural functionality is sufficiently the same not to be unique in that respect. On the other hand, the wob of the natural and supranatural environments of our universe uniquely reflect Mina's founding vision of absolute autonomy with which no other builder has experimented (§ 2.1:340). In that respect, our universe is revolutionary, a new (old) way to comprehend Life. By way of analogy, America's individual freedom and government 'of, by, and for the people' is also a radical experiment in absolute autonomy. Its citizens love to brag it's exceptional—unique, special, and good—and Mina agrees. At the same time, however, its individual and collective harm seems to belie those attributes, to which he disagrees. Isn't that a contradiction? No, and the reason lies in what sets America apart from all societies ever to exist such that its exceptionalism, like that of our universe, is valid.

2.1.1.5.1 Why America is Unique

Like our universe, America is the only one of its kind. We don't mean the nation state, its operating culture, democratic nature, republican form, or freedoms but its founding principle of individual sovereignty. Socioculture, religion, nor the state holds sovereignty over the person. The individual ranks over and above society—the state—because the person is intrinsically autonomous.[428] One's autonomy derives simply from existence, not from a *state* of existence. That "all men are created equal, that they are endowed by their Creator with certain unalienable Rights, that among these are Life, Liberty and the pursuit of Happiness" (Jefferson 1776, *Declaration of Independence*, par. 2) and that the Bill of Rights doesn't grant but defines what's unalienable roots in the essentiality of the psyche (§ 2.3.2:240). Rather than society constituting from individuals collectively, autonomous persons individually constitute society.

This distinction isn't semantic but substantive. Society that is collectively individuals absorbs the individual to the collective's needs whereas autonomous persons constituting society are, individually in and of themselves—each one—that society. Society in its entirety is the individual writ large (§ 4:291). It conforms to the individual not the other way round such "That to secure these [unalienable] rights, Governments are instituted among Men, deriving their just powers from the consent of the governed" (ibid). When society fails to conform to the individual but instead coercively conforms the individual to it, conflict arises. The Declaration accordingly adds, "That whenever any Form of Government becomes destructive of these ends [to secure intrinsic, unalienable, individual rights], it is the Right of the People to alter or to abolish it, and to institute new Government . . . to effect their Safety and Happiness" (ibid).

America's founding principle is that by dint of one's mere existence one is unalienably autonomous; that its politico-socioculture's structure is to guarantee it; that when it upends that relationship, one is beholden to only him or herself (own-self; § 2:275) because individual sovereignty precludes sociocultural (state) sovereignty which is ever coercive and nonautonomous. For sovereignty of the state to be valid, humans cannot be intrinsically autonomous but only nonautonomous, *permissibly* autonomous. This invalidates America's founding principle and the plain experience of our own minds. The Corruption converted nonautonomy to our normative state. America *as a principle* is an outlier in our universe (the wob of which is always in accord with Mina's Intentionality) and in the megaverse, too.

2.1.1.5.2 Why America is Good

Life is only ever Human. No divine being exists that creates or defines it (§ 2:304). There's consequently no universal (or megaversal) standard of good–evil, right–wrong, or moral–immoral. That doesn't mean there's *no* such standard. There is *one*: Human autonomy, Life's core wob. But megaversal humanity and even the Cardinal see autonomy as fungible with mindset addiction because, within mindset, one retains absolute autonomy which means one is autonomous albeit bounded by its parameters. Recall that at its most essential, mind is unfettered. It can only *choose*—never compelled—to be fettered. Ultimately, this is what it means to be nonautonomous: one is *addicted* to mindset. The essence of autonomy isn't simply immunity from compulsion but *awareness* that one is autonomous. Addiction to mindset clouds that awareness, inducing one to believe that mindset is not simply *a* freedom but the *only* freedom. Once a person believes that then they're

---

428. Interfering with another's autonomy triggers a defense of their autonomy sometimes by the individual but usually by their group, e.g., society (state), through some version of law and order.

malleable, corralled. In practice, one is no longer an autonomous being. *Good* references the essentiality of human autonomy and not Thought or behavior. *The* good is where such autonomy prevails in practice. The *not-good* is where it doesn't.

Not-good doesn't mean bad but the absence of the good. There is no *bad* that's the polar opposite of *good*. That sort of dialectic arises in mindset, not autonomy, and is the mainstay of moral systems from which *judgment* arises. Recall Mina doesn't judge transgression because he doesn't impose an intransgressible standard, as no such thing arises in human WOB. Since human WOB, thus mind, is unalterably autonomous, no good–bad polarity arises in our WOB because if it did, it would in effect neutralize autonomy, its own WOB. If one is free then one is free indeed and not unfree where unfree means lacking autonomy, just like if one is alive then one is alive and not dead where dead means lacking aliveness. In both cases, one is incompatible with the other (§ 6.5:170). In like fashion, good–bad polarity is self-canceling because one can't be good, that is, consistent with human WOB, yet simultaneously bad, or inconsistent with human WOB. This is true because regardless how addicted to mindset one may be, one's mind remains intrinsically autonomous. Therefore, mindset addiction—nonautonomy—in and of itself isn't bad where *bad* means it subverts human WOB as the standard of good and, hence, antithetical to that universal standard and thus a moral wrong where *moral* means a deviation from *good*. This is why a person can autonomously choose nonautonomy yet remain autonomous. So-called morality arises not in universal reality but in nonautonomous human experience.

Coincidentally, then, no action that grounds in autonomy can be inconsistent with human WOB and thereby inconsistent with good. Such an action may cause harm yet, in and of itself, isn't good, bad, or even neutral because action can't be qualified but only its expression. The reason, of course, is that an action expresses differently in different contexts. So, neither action itself nor its expression can subvert core human WOB, which is autonomy. Only action grounded in nonautonomy, which in and of itself is intrinsically nonautonomous, thus subversive of core human WOB, can be good, bad, or neutral because only nonautonomous mindset can qualify those attributes. So-called universal standards of morality arise in nonautonomy, not autonomy. As a construct, morality has nothing to do with human WOB and everything to do with its subversion. Moral standards, whether perceived as divine or secular, arise in nonautonomy and are inconsistent with human WOB. Consequently, the Cardinal's fungibility of autonomy with mindset addiction isn't valid despite there being practical consequences in autonomy, such as harm, detrimental to the individual and humanity. This is what Americans mean when they claim America is good: autonomy—individual freedom—isn't in principle fungible with anything.

2.1.1.5.3 Why America is Special

Where *special* means "distinguished by some unusual quality" (*Merriam*, s.v. 1 'special'), America's founding principle distinguishes it from all former and current societies on Earth[429] even though Americans are the same in their everyday foibles and desires as people everywhere. Our universe similarly distinguishes itself amongst the universes of the megaverse except that, unlike Americans rooted in their founding documents, the people of our universe never rooted themselves in Mina's founding principle because they addicted themselves to mindset instead. Their autonomous WOB didn't normalize (the Big Healing has reduced the mindset-addicted population to about 25% what it was). The whole world knows America but, except for the Cardinal, the megaverse has never heard of our universe. Its founding principle distinguishes it in the megaverse where few even imagine intrinsically absolute autonomy.

Spirit world's many local cultures, now in various stages of redevelopment since the Big Healing, are analogous to the American colonial experience that eventually resulted in the mindset revolution that codified autonomy as its national philosophy. Mina accomplished in America's founding what only since the Big Healing he's been able to begin throughout our universe: a revival of autonomy *unaddicted* to mindset. That places America in a special position vis-à-vis Earth's still-mindset-addicted societies to live its autonomy authentically as a beacon on a hill (CH. 36:585). It's an imperfect revival, to be sure, but its principle is *there* for all to emulate, including backsliding Americans.

2.1.1.6 Mina's Sisters Bring The Corruption

America's biggest challenge was—and remains—the mindset addiction carried over from Europe during its colonial experience. The biggest problem the Founding Families faced was similar. It wasn't starting their grand

---

429. For example, "Europe is a product of history. America is a product of philosophy," popularly attributed to British Prime Minister Margaret Thatcher (1979–90; d. 2013).

experiment in absolute autonomy unaddicted to mindset and then wandering into the mindset addiction Mina was trying to avoid, but their mindset carried over from the Primoverse which enabled The Corruption's toehold to spread like a disease. To be frank, no one noticed either one. Theirs was the experience of the slowly boiled frog, all the while thinking their society reflected humanity's autonomous WOB when instead it was transforming into its opposite. Just like America.

2.1.1.6.1 THE CARDINAL'S NONINTERFERENCE AGREEMENT WITH MINA

We never should have encountered The Corruption. The Cardinal was no fan of Mina's purpose nor Cosmo breaking ranks to help him but, nonetheless, pledged noninterference. Their neutrality came about when our universe was ready for occupation about 2.188BYA (§ 2.1.1:348), roughly 11.6BY after science's Big Bang, when one of the Cardinal showed up on Mina's doorstep to convey their vexation. In truth, they hadn't expected him to pull it off with Cosmo as his teacher and hadn't paid much attention to his work. But now on its eve of being populated they'd realized its potential threat. They had two principal misgivings. First, would a tendency to harm arise in the people of their universes from its mere existence? Second, would Mina's embodiment of absolute autonomy with which he naturally irradiates our universe—as do all universe builders w.r.t. their own universe—actually irradiate theirs, too (§ 3.1.2.1.1:358)?

To test the probability of the Cardinal's second concern, Mina and their representative Intentionalized 'lab' experiments with small, disposable constructs as universe facsimiles, the same that Molly, Mina, and any builder used to learn and prepare themselves to create their own universes for real (§ 2.1.3.2:310). After experimenting for about 2BY, the Cardinal conceded Mina's absolute autonomy radiating into our universe would not influentially spread outside its 'frequency space.' From this, they deduced a near zero probability that harm would sympathetically arise in their people—their extended families, recall—from the existence of Mina's universe. At this point, the Cardinal pledged noninterference and Mina spent the next ~150KY selecting the First Ancestors, implementing their training, then moving them here ~8MYA.

2.1.1.6.2 MINA'S SISTERS BREAK THE CARDINAL'S AGREEMENT WITH MINA

The elder of Mina's two interfering sisters is a universe builder herself, thus a member of the Cardinal. In principle, then, she'd agreed to the Cardinal's noninterference pledge. But for reasons we detail in the next chapter, she bailed on it. After the two of them failed indirectly to corrupt Mina's descendants through influencing V'v'dib's couple, they showed up themselves in the 27th generation ~7.3MYA, or ~700KY after our First Ancestors arrived (§ 2.1.1:348), and spent about 100 centuries doing the job right. By the time our ancestors began birthing integrated physical-born humans in the spirit-born's 75th generation (Fig. 148), The Corruption had pickled their mindsets for about 200KY.

Mina couldn't ban his sisters from coming into our universe because, ironically in their case, an unembodied person has absolute autonomy to embody in any universe. Neither could he prevent them spreading their faux autonomy mindset to his descendants—though he vigorously countered its pernicious nonautonomy as perfectly refined by megaversal humanity over by then about 10 undecillion, or 10^{37}, generations (§ 2.1:348)—any more than America could ban Europeans spreading the faux freedom of their ideologies of nonautonomy into America's (initially) incompatibly autonomous mindset.

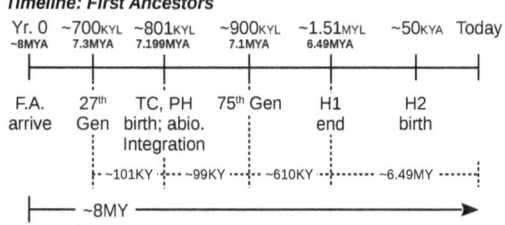

Figure 148. Timeline: First Ancestors (F.A.); 27th–75th generations (KYL/MYL is thousand/million years later); rise of The Corruption (TC) and integrated physical humans (PH); end of Earth's Humanity 1.0; rise of Humanity 2.0. Spirit-born generations aren't linear in time, so can't reference timeframes as on Earth.

Of the three phases which altogether established our universe socially and environmentally (§ 2:348), only the first phase failed to come off according to plan, partly because Mina thought he'd adequately prepared the First Ancestors when he hadn't. It was, however, the most crucial of the three because a universe isn't an environmental so much as a social construct. That said, we now turn to the environmental phases in the supranatural context.

2.2   Supranatural Phase 2: Look and Feel

The Founding Families first arrived to find a kind of 'world terrain template' existing as part of Mina's initial WOB for the supranatural environment. He describes it as basic spirit matter akin to bare bedrock stretching in multiple energy-segmented, single-plane terrains to infinity as a blank canvas upon which the Ancestors could establish the environmental look and feel they desired (*Fig. 149*; § 1.2.2:468). Whatever they could do with Intentionality in their own universe they could do here in ours, because Intentionality interacts with Thought and proto-energy the same way everywhere in All Existence. So, quite naturally, they set about recreating their own favorite environments from the universe of their childhoods.

Of overall note here is that what they established wasn't *how* our supranatural (spirit) environment looked and felt but the *experience* they wanted their descendants to get from it. Naturally, this meant establishing no mindset barriers to the future development of its world terrain such as landscape, structures, sky and space, or day and night. Also, the very nature of human experience in spirit world doesn't support the existence of coercive organizations like government (§ 9:446) for two reasons. First, spirit persons Intentionalize infrastructure, which self-maintains. There's no need for services nor common defense, laws, punishment, and the like. Plus, coercion is essentially impossible. Second, and consequent of the first, human autonomy renders the concept null and void.

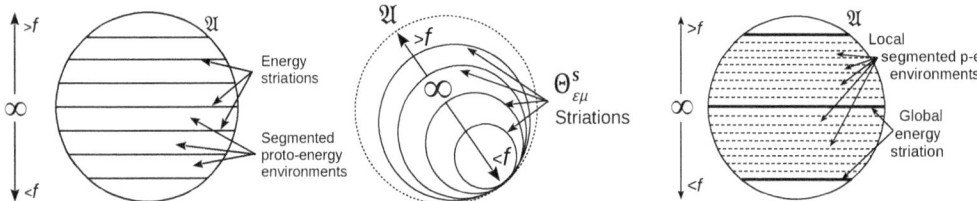

Figure 149. Schematic: supranatural energy-striated environments (a behavior of the natural Energent; § 1.2:467); *f* is 'energy frequency;' 𝔄 is universe; left, as striations; center, as discrete, infinite instantiations (Fig. 150:358); right, as local and similarly within global striations.

Understanding the above, the Founding Families built out the supranatural world's terrain over about 1,000 years through Intentionality as a sort of starter template anyone could follow—or not. Additionally, in place of Mina's bare bedrock, they added canonic landscaping to infinity which duplicated their pre-founding environment so that, wherever in spirit world a person embodied, they would encounter at least a basic world of covered land and off-white (cloudy-day) sky so they wouldn't feel disoriented. Unlike the physical world with its resource limitations, autonomous physics, and autonomous WOB, spirit world is unlimited and customizable—Intentionalizable—in every respect, from one's own body to its environment. The reason is that a single individual can't overcome the Intentionality of multiple people, and the larger the multiple the more resistant and enduring their Intentionality. For example, it's more difficult for an individual to alter a basic world terrain than to simply Intentionalize into it additions like structures, flora and fauna, or just a cup of coffee. Conversely, the foregoing is easier for groups than individuals.

Mina Intentionalized about 99.6% of our supranatural environment's look and feel during the creation process. His descendants—our ancestors—only needed to deal with aesthetics. Toward that end, they Intentionalized about 0.3% of the remainder, initially from their Primoverse aesthetic preferences to later generations' homegrown preferences, all of which eventually became part of our Ultraculture—the ever-present collective subconscious Intentionality—until only about 13% of that 0.3% (excluding the infinite basic world terrain) still retains the First Ancestor's Primoverse look and feel. The final 0.1% of the supranatural's look and feel is what people Intentionalize moment-to-moment without end.

2.2.1   Universe Options

One can't build a universe without a supranatural environment because it's the natural element of a universe, as Molly found when she built her Primoverse. It's possible to build a universe as a supranatural construct only but, in this case, one needs design it to absorb its energy needs directly from Energent–prime else it'll move to maximum entropy and cease, meaning it falls into stasis albeit continues existing.

2.3 Supranatural Phase 3: Humaforming

Terraforming is making another place human-habitable, usually in the context of making a planet more Earthlike. *Humaforming* is essentially the same thing except it includes making physical bodies which integrate non-physical 𝓛ife along with making their environment a home. It's an extension of 𝓛ifeforming (ch. 20:301), the process of making All Existence—a formless nothing—materially habitable. Mina initiated the humaforming process by developing planets in the right spatial locales. This came about naturally in consequence of our universe's wob which he'd established during creation, as well as his specific Intentional activities during its billions of years of development to establish a planet's human-habitable environment. He then seeded them with life precursors which he developed via Intentionality into proto-humans (§ 2.1.5.5.1:322; § 1.1.2:533).

All of this predated the First Ancestors' arrival. By their 75th generation (Fig. 148:355), the spirit-born (*abiogeneticists*; § 1.1:532) finished raising proto-humans to integrability throughout the observable universe (§ 1:112). At this point, spirit-born volunteers organized themselves to integrate adult male and female proto-human bodies—which required an average two-week in-body self-training period where the proto-human body fully *vehicularized* a human being[430]—in order to conceive integrated physical children, thus inaugurating integrated 𝓛ife on any particular planet just as Mike and Molly had pioneered it (§ 2.1.5.5.4:327). As proto-humans on planet after planet reached integrability—or later needed reconstituting after a natural or self-inflicted extinction event (§ 1.3:538, § 2.3.2.2:548)—spirit-born volunteers repeated the process until Mina's humaformed planets were populated.

Section 3

Home in the Natural Environment

Planets formed in habitable zones in accord with the Intentionalized wob of our universe. Habitable planets are thus a natural inevitability, not a stochastic product nor an individually-only Intentionalized undertaking. There's an average 7 trillion planets in any given galaxy with about 5.5% in habitable zones. Mina operates in accord with a maximum human habitability of exactly *four* of them per galaxy regardless its size or density, though not all four (if any) are at all times (or at any time) inhabited, the reason being that four per galaxy, in a universe of approximately 10 trillion galaxies, is all the universe can sustain at any one time.[431] The life-development process unfolds the same way on each one. But, too, every problem that afflicts spirit-embodied humanity translates to the physical embodied through our dual physicospirit residence and because our human tendencies here are naturally the same there.

3.1 Natural Home Mirrors Supranatural Home

Recall the supranatural Energent is a facsimile of the natural Energent with attendant differences in the expression of its proto-energy (§ 7.1.3:214). Thus, the natural environment mirrors the supranatural in some of its structural aspects. And since humans are human wherever they are, then the natural and supranatural environments mirror one another in their human aspect. We describe each below.

3.1.1 Structural Environment

Natural proto-energy intrinsically segments itself into discrete energy striations as an aspect of its wob in the same manner as its facsimile supranatural counterpart (Fig. 149:356). It's conceptually similar to liquids that naturally separate into layers according to density. As with the supranatural environment, the natural one is an infinity of segmented proto-energy environments, only one of which Mina actually utilizes—the one in which we live (*Fig. 150*, left, center). This is the reality behind the panoply of multiple universes, or multiverse, theories going all the way back to ancient Greek Atomism. But it's necessary to distinguish the difference

---

430. *Vehicularize* means to integrate a physical body as a vehicle ('avatar') solely to convey human 𝓛ife in the physical world.

431. Proto-galaxies account for ∼10% (cf. ∼2T total estimate per Siegel 2018b). About 73% of currently habitable planets, or ∼87.6 billion, are currently inhabited (cf. 10^{25}, or 10 septillion, planets in Siegel 2014; What 'Angels' Do, § 2:522).

between the traditional 'multiverse' concept and that described in this book (§ 2.1.4.1:312), as they're not at all similar. We describe it in Striated Expression of Proto-energy (§ 1.2.2:468).

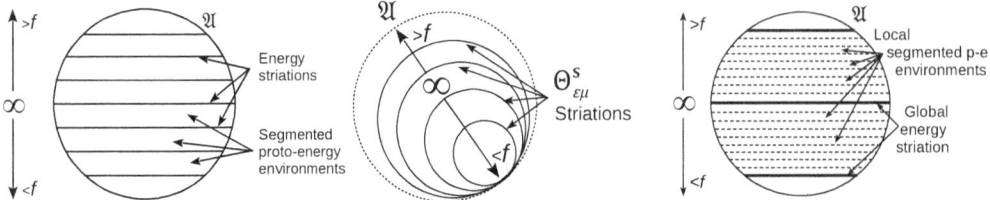

Figure 150. Schematic: natural energy-striated environments; f is 'energy frequency;' 𝔄 is universe; left, as global striations; center, each is infinite (cf. Fig. 164:469); right as local and similarly within global striations.

Each global proto-energy striation is similarly locally striated (*Fig. 150*, right). The spirit embodied can access any proto-energy striations. The segmented world terrain in which we physically live is the 'energy frequency' most conducive to physical life. It's here that Mina Intentionalized matter. It's possible for physical human life to exist in some of these infinite striations but isn't necessary and therefore doesn't.

3.1.2   Human Environment

The first physical ancestors to each planet brought with them the mindsets they developed as spirit-born persons living in the supranatural environment (§ 1.1.3:533). Their physical-born children imbibed their parents' mindsets directly as well as their Ultraculture indirectly via their own spirit selves (§ 4.1:291). Since they initially enjoyed full mind–brain integration, which enabled their interaction with the supranatural as easily and as naturally as with the natural, they absorbed and expressed the mindsets and Ultraculture that prevailed in spirit world along with the mindsets and Ultraculture prevailing in their physical mind, family, and society. Nothing seemed amiss because, initially, it was all one seamless physicospirit experience.

3.1.2.1   The Specter of Mindset

Originally, there was no physical–spirit separation in physical-born humans. Their environment was literally a single physicospirit integration they coterminously experienced through the physicospirit aspects of self. But the first physical-born's spirit-born parents were conceived and raised in The Corruption which, from the 27th spirit-born generation, progressively addicted them to a multitude of bounded mindsets of perceived albeit faux autonomy which they in turn enculturated in their physical-born children. In this way, humanity's physical home mirrored the increasingly negative emotive 𝓛ife force (Em𝓛F) of spirit humanity's Ultraculture—eventually synonymous with The Corruption—that El called the Negative Collective Consciousness, (NCC; § 1.2:21). In these early days, a physical-born person found no meaningful difference between the physical society in which they were raised and the larger spirit-born society—no more than, say, early colonial America's societal mindset meaningfully differed from England's. In both cases, except for environmental differences, it was all the same 'world,' the same culture, the same people. Our universe back then was, in practice, a single physicospirit—a universal—society.

3.1.2.1.1   Mina's Absolute Autonomy 'Irradiates' Our Universe and Us

Yet, all the while, The Corruption wended its way through every nook and cranny of the human psyche until its faux autonomy circumscribed each individual in our universal society the same as in every other universe. Unlike those universes, however, human woB's absolute autonomy suffuses Mina and, through him, our universe. It emanates like radiant energy from a sun because it integrates our universe down to its archí. Everything—subconsciously, even 𝓛ife—experiences awareness of the quintessence of human woB (absolute autonomy) because Mina integrates our universe.

In the same way that radiant energy disrupts an unirradiated environment—say, the environmental area of dawn on a rotating planet—Mina's embodiment of autonomy integrating our universe disruptively casts throughout it but especially into our psyche. It disruptively irradiates The Corruption within us partly analogous to radiation therapy disruptively irradiating cancerous tissue in the body, except it doesn't eradicate The Corruption the way radiation therapy kills cancer cells because our emergent self has only a fractional awareness of it. Instead, a tension arises within our psyche and we feel at odds with ourselves as though struggling against some unseen force (Rom. 7:21–23; FN 425:351). Aware of this tension, we've traditionally ascribed its force to a faceless or personified evil, intrinsic corporal sinfulness, or primal human nature. But it's none of these. It's just Mina's pure, quintessentially autonomous mindset writ large into the very fabric of our universe—the first for a universe builder, including Molly—that, like gravity, constantly tugs on our psyches like a sensitive tooth by our addiction to Accountableist mindsets (§ 1.4:14).

3.1.2.1.2 THE RISE OF A DIVINE MORAL JUDGMENT MINDSET

Spirit- and physical-born humanity was blissfully unaware of the gradual and subtle Corruption of mindset that arose between its 27th and 75th spirit-born generations. Yes, they did sense something amiss in their collective mindset even before violence in physical societies manifested and spiraled into torturous warfare, but couldn't put their finger on it and, anyhow, it didn't seem like any kind of *corruption*. Those who made it their business simply reasoned that the alteration they perceived (using the Founding Families as their baseline) resulted from the normal vagaries in the ebb and flow of human nature and the peculiarities of physical embodiment. No one, not a single individual, ever approached Mina for guidance, however, despite knowing (or hearing) that he'd built the universe and not (one of) the First Ancestors as most had addictively come to believe, and because Michael's Lie was already fomenting the notion of Accountableism: that whoever or whatever, their Creator was a divine moral judge.

If a corruption in their essential humanity was truly real, then it must've been this divine moral judge who'd inflicted it on them in punishment or maybe randomly and maliciously like an experiment for His amusement or human edification. Seeking such a Creator's intervention might trigger judgment, or worse, a doubling down. Better just let sleeping dogs lie and live their best placatory life. Such warped reasoning by eternal spirit persons able to manipulate matter at will is the rampant mental illness spawned in The Corruption. In consequence, mind–brain integration (crucial to physical embodiment) began normatively at 100% but then eroded with each successive generation until reaching ±30% with a concomitantly shortened lifespan over a relatively short period of time (§ 1.2.1:534, § 2.3.1:545), as less integration leads to lesser *L*ife force integration. We've been there ever since, and for the reason below.

3.1.2.1.3 MINDSET ADDICTION SEVERS PHYSICAL-BORN FROM SPIRIT-BORN

The archangels were born in the 75th generation as second-Gen children of their first-Gen parents, the Founding Families (Table 145:337). Young Michael spun his lie against Lucifer shortly thereafter and it flashed through the mindsets of spirit-born humanity—at that very moment busily establishing physical-born humanity—within about 80 years like a wildfire over a bone-dry prairie. It worked its unintended poison so fast because The Corruption had already addicted spirit-born humanity's collective mindset to belief-oriented mindsets immune to the growth and development had only through real autonomy. Since physical-born humanity's first parents were spirit-born, they carried The Corruption and Michael's Lie into their physical clans of about 5 couples each that were spread over five different locations per planet where each couple initially produced an average 200 children in 100 years and 2,000 in 300 years (mainly by annually Intentionalizing twins). They were aware of the spirit-born's concern about The Corruption for which they had no name, no understanding, and no explanation, just that something had wrought a change in them from what they observed in the First Ancestors and their earliest children. Everyone by then had come to accept the notion their Creator was some sort of divine, omnipotent, and judgy Being that was different from them—everyone except the First Ancestors, that is. They obviously knew better, but their explanations fell on increasingly incredulous ears.

Quite subconsciously over that 300-year period, the physical-born came to fear the spirit-born and their spirit world ways. The idea coalesced that, whatever it was, if The Corruption was indeed let loose on them by their Creator, then it was aimed at the spirit-born, not the physical-born. They were innocents caught in the crossfire and made collateral damage by their physicospirit integration with spirit-born society. If they extricated themselves from that, their Creator might restore them to their ancestral norm, and if they didn't, well, they'd only get worse. Their fear translated to a subconscious desire to separate and go their own way, to resolve whatever issues their Creator had with them on their own terms. Without conscious awareness, *their own subconscious* Intentionally eroded their mind–brain integration, gradually severing them from supranatural reality and thus spirit-born humanity.[432] At this point, *two versions of humanity* arose in our universe, the one

---

432. It's ironic that just before the Big Healing, ~92% of the spirit-born didn't believe in or never heard of the physical-born or the

not understanding the other such that, upon physical death, the spirit-born guided them to a supranatural location isolated from the spirit-born's own—a physical-born spirit world—because their mindset psychoses now made the spirit-born's environment too painful.[433] Their single universal society had ceased before it had hardly begun.

The thing about mindset addition is that once a person embraces a nonautonomous belief, it's exceedingly difficult to change them or for them to change themselves because it permeates—*becomes*—their WOB. It's even truer of a society. Just as we've labored in vain over several few tens of thousands of years to build a better society on Earth, Humanity 1.0 labored over ten-fold that time to improve their own. But the key isn't rebooting society any more than restarting an infected computer without purging the virus is of any use. Rather, surmounting our corrupted mindset requires adopting one rooted in autonomy which never leads to mindset-addicted nonautonomy. In the end, Humanity 1.0 lasted about 500KY before their unalterable addiction to mindset devoured them in fratricidal war (§ 1.3:538).

3.1.2.1.4 Recovering Our Physicospirit Wholeness

With the Big Healing, we can recover full mind–brain integration whenever we subconsciously—in our true, emergent ℒife self—desire it. Nothing holds us back but ourselves. Human beings are born with absolute autonomy. We've just come to believe—addicted to mindset—that we aren't. For example, Mina told me I was still afraid of full mind–brain integration and of experiencing spirit world at will even after meeting him, energy testing this book, and increasingly encountering spirit world with great interest. He can't read my mind of course, but he can analyze my ℒife 'energy' that permeates my physical body and is visible to spirit persons. At the time, it showed him I subconsciously feared access to spirit world despite consciously begging for it. Accordingly, my increased physicospirit integration came only in consciously frustrating dribs and drabs while I recalibrated my subconscious.

Since we lost it ourselves, we can regain it ourselves. The Big Healing cleared away the singular obstacle of the NCC as Ultraculture trapping us in nonautonomous mindset addiction. With The Corruption and Michael's Lie revealed to the spirit-born October 13, 2017, and with this book revealing it to the physical-born of Earth, each one of us is already on the road to mindset autonomy and full integration that will spread via supranatural humanity to every human-inhabited planet. It just takes time to shift one's mindset. We detail The Corruption next before describing in Part IV all of today's major aspects of our physicospirit life experience.

---

natural environment despite many of them in some way working the archangelic tasks (Table 16:352). Today, that's reversed.

433. They couldn't compel them into quarantine, obviously, but only ~2% ever left it prior to the Big healing. The spirit-born spirit world is what the physical-born historically perceive as Heaven. As of 2020, the physical-born stopped experiencing pain there.

The Corruption

MINA BEGAN OUR universe in absolute autonomy as a home for his descendants to experience the core essence of human way of being (WOB) that, elsewhere in the megaverse (§ 2.1.4.1:312), only very few cognized much less lived (§ 2.1:340). The reason for this state of affairs doesn't lie in megalomania, evil, power, control, greed, so-called human nature, All Existence WOB, or the like but, quite unexpectedly, in *altruism*[434] which essence, ostensibly, is to do no harm. Coincidentally, it's the central premise of the Hippocratic Oath (Cavanaugh 2018, 57) taken by the physician whose job is to extend life and well-being by reversing harm. Altruism took root in the physical environment where mind–brain integration was degraded and life appeared random, tenuous, and, above all, entirely physical with a concomitant determination to preserve it despite any belief in a glorious afterlife. The physical-born came to associate harm with universal truths of wrongness, badness, and evil, the avoidance of which they associated with the highest good and thus a virtue. In adopting this standard, however, they substituted a faux WOB for their core emergent WOB (§ 1.2:246) in which contradiction and self-conflict arose, the sense we're just not right, somehow broken, at odds with creation and our creator.

In this chapter, we describe what The Corruption means, how, through it, nonautonomy became our universe's WOB and altruism its mindset—Ultraculture (§ 4.1:291)—how the essence of Michael's Lie became its central tenet, and how Lucifer, his Reconciliation with Michael, and the Big Healing released us from both.

SECTION 1
Meaning of The Corruption

The Corruption is mindset, a Thought collective (§ 3.3.2.2:288) that embodies a certain truth as its core WOB from which all knowledge, beliefs, thinking–feeling, and behavior devolve. At its root lies nonautonomy, which is alien to our universe. Accordingly, we call it a *corruption*, as it corrupted Mina's founding Intentionality that rooted the dominant mindset of our universe in our core emergent WOB of absolute autonomy (§ 2.1.1.5:353). Universe builders—who comprise the Cardinal (FN 130:110)—haven't considered it a corruption because each built theirs to embody it as its core truth. The Cardinal's antithetical WOB irradiates each of their universes the same way Mina's embodiment of absolute autonomy irradiates every archí and psyche in ours as its natural, universal WOB (§ 3.1.2.1.1:358). Consequently, no intrinsic contradiction arises in the Cardinal's universes between their peoples' dominant mindset and absolute autonomy, as in ours. They live comfortably in nonautonomy unless they open their mindset to their emergent WOB of autonomy, just as we live comfortably in autonomy unless we open our mindset to nonautonomy, as our ancestors did and passed that mindset and its discomfort down to us.[435]

---

434. Coined by French philosopher and founder of sociology, Auguste Comte (d. 1857).

435. When we live consonant with our core WOB of autonomy, we feel no internal contradictions. Our Thought and action is good,

1.1 ALTRUISM IS THE CORRUPTION

Philosophy with a capital-P roots our timeless human struggle in our failure to live up to altruism's selflessly caring ideal, the essence of human woß and of our Creator. Hence, the many compendiums of virtue cast against vice from Plato and the Chinese *Te* (德) through theology to modern philosophy and positive psychology. But the essence of our woß arises out of the woß of pairwise kinship, itself an expression of pairwise autonomy and proto-love (§ 2:304). Altruism as The Corruption and root of nonautonomy—the harbinger of human suffering—seems terribly counterintuitive, so let's examine that.

1.1.1 HARM

The real heart of altruism is the notion that harm is bad and one has a duty to alleviate it where possible. This means the altruist ameliorates harm (equivalent to doing no harm) in which arises a state absent harm, that is, a state of harmlessness. We can decoct all of Philosophy with a capital-P to a striving to understand the cause, effect, and amelioration of harm and what duty, if any, a person has to do so.

For Philosophy with a capital-P, altruism is an innate characteristic in humanity—pre-Fall Adam (Gen 1:26); second Adam (Heb. 1:3); 'original' nature (Moon 1996, 31–40)—that arose naturally with a sense of duty. It's been long-felt as the solution to harm's existence. While certain of its expressions are a naturally unselfish human tendency arising in kinship (§ 2.3.2.2:242), its heart and soul isn't autonomy but nonautonomy, harm's purveyor. Mina defines harm as "an occurrence of a change for the worse in the context of the totality of the environment" (CH. 20:301), where *worse* means "inconsistent with human woß." What humanity calls 'harm' isn't, it is simply *experience* that we interpret in terms of good or bad, meaning desired or undesired. But one person's harm is another's no-harm.

1.1.1.1 HARM IS NONEXISTENT

From Mina's point of view, there is no harm in ℒife. It doesn't exist. There's only experience, whether or not it's wounding. Being experiential, harm is a false construct arising in mindset addiction, which means from nonautonomy. We think injury to our psyche or physical body—intentional, accidental, or apparently random, as with illness—constitutes harm. But *harm* doesn't exist, only our interpreted experience of the injury. Saying, "I was harmed!" by an event is nothing more than interpreting one's experience of it in nonautonomous terms. One's mind experiencing trauma (*below*), a psychic wound, or their body incurring injury is how we interpret the event or action.

Neither the mind nor body can actually *undergo* injury. Our mind is just 'energy' (ℒife force) and our body isn't independently self-aware thus can't *experience* anything. It can only encounter and respond to environment, whether taste, temperature, or a bullet. Two people can experience the same injury yet one person, according to their mindset, interprets it in terms of the experience arising from the encounter, thus not as harm per se and perhaps as no-harm whereas the other interprets it in terms of the encounter being the injury itself and thereby only as harm. Our addiction to mindset conditions us to view life not through the lens of experience but of encounter. The more one interprets experience through the lens of encounter, the more likely one experiences a psychic wound or trauma. This, in part, underlies Eastern philosophy's teachings to separate oneself from physical embodiment to escape the pain and suffering of life—a sense of harm—which duty Western philosophy generally imposes on the other person.

The point here is that harm isn't a thing, a self-existent entity like a bodily injury such as tissue damage or a defrauded bank account sitting empty. Harm isn't *what* but *how* we experience things. When society for example seeks to promote safety by limiting harm, it's not actually promoting or limiting either one. Instead, it's imposing nonautonomy—group control via group- or self-imposed force—on its constituents, which ironically requires it promote danger by inflicting real or threatened harm that not uncommonly exceeds the harm it ostensibly desires to prevent.

1.1.1.2 TRAUMA

Experience can result in *trauma*, a phenomenon of the physical body. Trauma is residual emotive ℒife force energy (EmℒF; § 3.3.3.1.1:289) from the source of the injury that remains 'in' the tissues of the body and constantly affects it such that the physical trauma response is ongoing. The source of trauma is only ever human,

---

as it embodies autonomy (§ 2.1.1.5.2:353). Kinship woß leads us to avoid inflicting harm or, if so, to ameliorate it.

never natural such as animal, landslide, or meteor. It's the harming person's EMℒF which 'enters' the body's tissues along with the damage. A person can experience harm to their spirit body while asleep, such as when dreaming, that translates to the physical body as real damage like soreness, bruising, or tissue damage to greater or lesser degrees. Blood for instance can manifest—Intentionalize—on one's body without apparent cuts to the skin. Though physical damage heals, the 'energy' remains, provoking ongoing trauma responses from the body similar to a wound that resists healing and just persists.

Harm is in the mind and trauma stays in the body, but it can exacerbate the feeling of harm. Sometimes they feed off each other and worsen the experience of harm. Over time, unhealed trauma provokes dysfunction in the body not necessarily related to the trauma's origin. A physical person who dies continues experiencing unhealed trauma(s) until their physical body fully dissolves away or fire, explosion, and the like destroys it and the last emotive connection tethering them to their physical body disappears. Preserving bodies only ensures the spirit self continues experiencing whatever trauma is residual to their body and the harm it feeds. But even when the physical body is fully no more, its trauma manifests in the spirit body so long as the psychic harm that originated in the physical trauma remains unhealed.

But again, the same experience that traumatizes one person doesn't traumatize another. Mina tells us of children who die violent, gruesome, catatonia-inducing deaths, and then become aware of—'wake up' in—spirit reality to realize that life continues normally on and put their death experience behind them. Of others who die by a misadventure that so traumatizes them they subconsciously won't allow themselves to develop past their death age, remaining at that childhood age and mindset in spirit world for centuries or millennia until they heal. And of still others who grow up traumatized since childhood but survive seemingly normal to old age only to die and find themselves in spirit world still the traumatized child they always were beneath their veneer of aged skin. The latter examples are of trauma fueling the experience of harm such that even when it disappears with the body, the harm remains.

In healing trauma, a physical person self-heals when they consciously or subconsciously neutralize the trauma's EMℒF. Healers draw its 'energy' around themselves to neutralize (normalize) it and then Mina floods the healee with Energent proto-life which feels something like we'd imagine as 'pure love.' It's something only he as our universe builder can do (§ 3.3.3.1.1:289). When a person experiences healing in this book's context, only their harm/trauma heals, not its effect(s) on their physical body, if they have any. If there's time before it causes death, physical damage from injury or disease heals naturally once the trauma's underlying 'energy' neutralizes (CH. 35:577).

1.1.2 ALTRUISM

As classically comprehended, altruism means the unselfish concern for the well-being of others without any motive for self-gain. One acts altruistically because one is altruistic, meaning one embodies altruism. It's a functional state of harmlessness where one inflicts no harm, thus positively ameliorates it such that

$$|harm\rangle_{none} |harm\rangle_{ameliorated} (|t\rangle) = \text{Altruism} \qquad (24.1)$$

where the ket $|t\rangle$ is the state where altruism is both possible and chosen (cf. § 6.11.1:192).

Philosophy with a capital-P reasons that our natural, average, altruistic inclination means we ought to be, as a moral imperative, altruistic to some degree, not so much as an intrinsic good but as a benefit to own-self where own-self includes, but isn't, self.[436] When in some context we ought to be altruistic but aren't, we're defective if in no other sense than that a duty went unperformed. Besides scorn falling upon such failures,[437] labeling it a defect in and of itself devalues altruism to entitlement, a nonautonomy.

Altruism intrinsically defines the *good*. This is why we apply it to our Creator—God, gods, Mother Earth, nature spirits—as His or Its essential beingness of which there's no greater good, along with our conformity to His or Its love, obedience, submission, living the Way, and so on, which are all aspects of altruism. Conversely, there's no greater *bad* than our disconformity. To our Corrupted mind, altruism is the fundament of human WOB. Its antithesis, *egoism*, however, isn't. Humanity considers ego an aberration of human nature: sin, evil, the Devil, our unevolved reptilian brain. It conflicts while altruism deconflicts, is harmful versus harmless. Russian-American philosopher Ayn Rand (d.1982) redefining egoism as Objectivism doesn't help. These are incorrect understandings of both.

---

436. Altruism and egoism are predicated not on self but own-self, which always includes at least one other not-self entity (§ 2:275).

437. For a postmodern take on this mindset addiction, scorn for failure, and self-punishment see *Lucifer* Ep. 25 (S2E12; 2017).

1.1.2.1   ALTRUISM IS NONAUTONOMY

What makes altruism a purveyor of harm rather than its fabled *salvator* is that it embodies the notion—the mindset addiction—that harm is an intrinsic evil whether human or natural, alien to our Creator and ideal human nature, or the offspring of absolute autonomy which is chaotic, hence destructive, and thereby intrinsically harmful. Philosophy with a capital–P sees harm following autonomy like the cart the horse whereas only harmlessness follows altruism. Wherefore, harmlessness isn't only preferable but ideal because harm equals suffering and, at its maximum, death, whereas harmlessness equals ameliorated suffering and, at its maximum, life. In consequence, autonomy, thus freedom, is inconsistent with life. So-called morality necessarily throws them under the bus to enable life and affirm the least possible harm.

Besides the venal strongman using morality for justification, human society throughout history—from the family through the tribe and clan to the nation state—has striven to equate moral codes to universal truths imputed to our Creator or to the nature of the universe. This, in order to eradicate or limit autonomy, thus harm, in favor of nonautonomy that promotes harmlessness (except in its enforcement). For example, America ignored its unprecedented philosophy of autonomy from Day One to apply nonautonomy through moral standards to delimit the individual's sovereignty toward establishing its "more perfect union" (*U.S. Const.*, pr.) of harmlessness that exceeded its ostensible duty simply to preserve individual freedoms from substantive denial and assault (criminality). An everyday case in point—as opposed to the egregiousness of slavery and segregation—is its forcible regulation of alcohol, from controls and taxation to Prohibition as a sociocultural coercion to enforce harmlessness.

Altruism and egoism are the same despite appearing as antonyms to the naked eye. They're the two faces of the coin of mindset addiction which is nonautonomy, i.e., harm, where harm is the intrinsic outcome of nonautonomy (§ 1.1.1:362). The notion that harm is bad and necessarily avoided—or should be, when possible—underpins altruism and its moral imperative. To the altruist, altruism's imperative is one's *true humanity* whereas egoism's is a false one. Yet, egoism, too—particularly in Rand's Objectivism—is necessarily a moral imperative. Consequently, both are nonautonomous and in fact complementary. But their complementarity is irrelevant and immaterial since they're equally nonautonomous.

1.1.3   HOW ALTRUISM IS THE CORRUPTION

The belief that harm is bad is the seed of The Corruption, and that altruism is *the* good, its soil. *Being* altruistic is The Corruption. Let's look at each of these three statements.

1.1.3.1   HARM IS BAD

As humanity understands the concept, harm in all its forms is undesirable, a net negative—bad; not merely a badness that detracts from goodness, but a moral bad as universal truth. Philosophy with a capital-p struggles to explain natural harm like earthquakes, disease, death, and suffering as well as intentionally inflicted harm because, why is a universe of necessary moral good—altruism being the proof—filled with moral bad? Humanity comprehended early on that harm is a part of life, the *bad* part, while the natural affinities in kinship that leads to altruism is the *good* part. The bad part is life destroying whereas the good part is life affirming. In this way, harm came to associate with badness, generally, and moral bad, specifically. Books on morality and good and evil devote a lot of discussion to the problem of natural evil (harm), which rarely if ever falls within human control though human harm to some degree does.

If natural harm is bad, human harm is worse because we have choice, which the natural world doesn't. Even when unintended—harm also means to permit, to not intervene in or ameliorate, it—an individual makes choices that lead to harm which is bad, thus destructive. Consequently, humanity limits harm through limiting choice, i.e., autonomy. There are other ways to limit harm whether we define it per the human norm or per § 1.1.1:362, which we describe in FATE, DESTINY, & FREE WILL (§ 5:427) and FREEDOM (CH. 36:585). Autonomy, therefore, takes on harm's ill repute. In and of itself, it's bad along a sliding scale from least to greatest, essentially from order to chaos (*Fig. 151*). The greatest order is the greatest good thus the least autonomy. The greatest chaos is the greatest bad thus the greatest—absolute—autonomy. It is in this thought process that the good–bad, good–evil, and right–wrong dialectics arise.

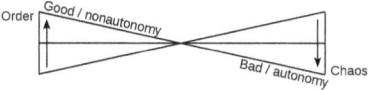

Figure 151. Sliding scale of autonomy traditionally as harm.

1.1.3.2 Altruism is *The* Good

It naturally follows from harm as *the* bad that altruism, or no-harm, is *the* good. As a moral philosophy, humanity considers altruism the highest moral good, the true human state reflective of divinity that unconditionally provides us love, life, and hearth. Being the highest good, then, altruism embodies within itself the highest, or greatest, limitation of harm, hence necessarily embodies the least autonomy (nonautonomy). This is why it's a moral philosophy—a statement of right and wrong—in the first place: it's an imperative rooted in the universal truth that harm is bad and no-harm is good. Religion thus requires submission to its ultimate limitation of harm, the ultimate good, which is absolute nonautonomy.

One's humanity arises only in the context of altruism because to be humane means to be altruistic. It's the essence, the core, of human woB. To be altruistic is to *be* human. Harmlessness, the state of no-harm, is naturally our woB essence, too. To be egoistic is to be inhumane thus *not* human. The dichotomy that necessarily arises between harm and no-harm, egoism and altruism, nonautonomy and autonomy gives rise to the fundamental conflict in the individual between autonomy and harmlessness, the struggle between doing, or permitting (not intervening to ameliorate) harm and being autonomous. But it's a false dialectic even if the struggle is real. It generates the idea that it's not possible for a human to be autonomous because it necessarily leads to harm or to permitting it. Even an ostensibly liberty-minded person will argue one must surrender autonomy for community, that inship negates autonomy. Wholistically, altruism is necessarily nonautonomy.[438]

1.1.3.3 Being Altruistic is Corrupt

Altruism is The Corruption, hence, Corrupt. Not in any dictionary sense of the word—an altruist isn't corrupt simply being altruistic—but in the sense of extrinsically implanting a false woB over our core, intrinsic woB, the extrinsic one being nonautonomy and the intrinsic one absolute autonomy. This went unnoticed by humanity because Mina's sisters disguised it behind promoting harmlessness (§ 2:367). People didn't adopt altruism the way one adopts rice over potatoes. Rather, they found themselves thinking and conversing over the course of time in terms avoidant of both harm and autonomy.

It wasn't hard. Any time one experienced a felt harm it was a chance to consider how to prevent it. Rare was the person who, in this developing milieu, looked within to reconsider their own care and consideration of others. More common was to look without to the infliction of harm itself (perceiving injury as encounter) rather than to its underlying causes (perceiving injury as experience). Sure, a person is autonomous—intrinsically having free will—especially the spirit-embodied whom one can't seize or kill against their will. One need persuade folks to avoid inflicting harm, though if entreaties fail then the greater persuasion of violence (which also hurts spirit persons, since the spirit body is a manifestation of mind that's as sensitive as ours to its environment) can bring fruit. But our spirit-born ancestors felt coercion too barbaric, especially as they watched it gruesomely unfold amongst the physical-embodied. It was undisputed that harmful people needed persuading into harmlessness despite ultimately meaning coerced by their own minds and The Corruption enabled its guiltless, conscientious tool: altruism.

The spirit-born's concept of absolute autonomy as the cornerstone of human woB Corrupted little by little as it took root. With its foundation eroding away, humanity's sense of everyday autonomy began sagging and crumbling until falling into the soft, embracing earth of *primum non nocere.*[439] It sounds good, though, right? to first do no harm? Our ancestors thought so. The Corruption encouraged the moral *duty.* It would've been good had people made an autonomous choice in each case to be individually harmless. But that's not how it worked out. Eventually, our ancestors no longer recognized absolute autonomy for what it is nor as their fundamental woB. They forgot what they were. They were Corrupt.

---

438. Altruism is a trait in *Life and Living* (§ 1:246), it's not exclusive to humans. Being and doing are different; one is altruistic as a woB, one does altruism as a mindset.

439. Latin: 'first, do no harm' (Hippocrates in *Epidemics*, Bk. 1, Sect. xi, trans. by W.H.S. Jones); also, Cedric M. Smith, "Origin and Uses of Primum Non Nocere," *Journal of Clinical Pharmacology* 2005, 45:371-377.

1.1.3.4 MEANING OF CORRUPT

Altruism is both a concept and an ideology. In both these forms, it enforces itself through shaming, guilt, fear, and so on. It's an attack on pairwise kinship, which naturally suffers. The nature of pairwise kinship is that it comes from our essential WOB, not from social rules, expectations, demands, or compulsion. Altruism subverts kinship. Since kinship results from pairwise autonomy and proto-love (§ 3.3.2:284; § 3.1.3:373), altruism subverts absolute autonomy and proto-love, converting it from a free expression of emergent WOB to a coerced expression of faux, or Corrupted, WOB. *Corrupt* means the overthrown state of our intrinsic core, emergent WOB. The Corruption in the guise of altruism individually and collectively decoupled intrinsic pairwise autonomy from proto-love which is the essence of the individual and thereby disrupted kinship, the essence of humanity. We touch on each below.

1.1.3.4.1 ESSENCE OF THE INDIVIDUAL

Recall each human being emergently births in Energent proto-life (EPL; § 2.3.2.1:241). As a being of emergent mind, the individual necessarily exists in a state of pure (absolute) autonomy because every emergent *Life* is unique. This makes the individual a universe unto itself, the builder of its own environment. There's nothing more fundamental to our WOB. It's the core of what we are. The buck stops there. Absolute autonomy isn't *Life* but its core WOB. As emergent beings we have *Life* which manifests as mind, the unique individual. *Life* together with its WOB defines the individual as *Human*. Whatever interferes with *Life*'s core WOB interferes with *Life*. When The Corruption manifesting as altruism subverts the individual's core, which is absolute autonomy, then it's subverting *Life* to make it something it's not. And what *Life* is not is nonautonomous. In fact, it's impossible to subvert *Life* in this way against the individual's preference. Only the individual can subvert their WOB. Consequently, the purpose of altruism is to induce the individual to autonomously embrace nonautonomy ostensibly for the higher good of limiting harm toward the betterment of society. It's equivalent to voting into power a tyranny one can never vote out. Which brings us to humanity's essence.

1.1.3.4.2 ESSENCE OF HUMANITY

Humanity arose pairwise as Mike and Molly whose natural kinship brought them together (§ 2:304). *Life*'s pairwise WOB expresses through couple-only procreation and societal individuals. However much aloneness one desires, for example, being truly alone isn't our intrinsic WOB, quite the contrary. Even the unembodied-born socialize, although that doesn't comprise society. For this reason, and quite apart from any evolutionary speculation, humans forming society is inevitable. But *collectivizing* isn't. That's Corrupt, a deviance, as it subsumes autonomous individuals into the nonautonomous group which is alien to human WOB, whereas an autonomous person individually constituting society is consistent with human WOB (§ 2.1.1.5.1:353). Individuals *becoming* the group rather than *constituting* it are alienated from their natural kinship WOB in the sense that group feeling substitutes for individual feeling,[440] meaning nonautonomy substitutes for autonomy. Being thus alienated renders the individual inauthentic, not consistent with their emergent WOB but an ersatz WOB, a *Corrupt* WOB, and thus not authentically *Human*. Consequently, the individual can't experience authentic pairwise kinship.

1.1.3.5 ALTRUISM AND ITS IDEOLOGY

Altruism is primarily a concept that harm is bad and humans have a duty to limit it. It addresses it ideologically as a moral philosophy. In the former sense, altruism is The Corruption and in the latter sense, a mindset addiction. Let's examine each of these.

1.1.3.5.1 ALTRUISM AS CONCEPT

Altruism presents life as a dialectic modality of harm and harmlessness. In the former, one lives autonomously, which is bad, as it ineluctably leads to harm. In the latter, one lives nonautonomously by having to figure others into every equation, which is good, as it ineluctably leads to harmlessness. But it's a false dialectic since only

---

440. This is the internal reason, for example, that collectivized societies compel individuals to align own-self with the group, e.g., the state or the law, rather than biological kin. This is group in its extreme form, but even the most liberal modern democracy requires, for any 'compelling' reason, that own-self *is* the group and *not* one's own person or kin.

experience is real; harm is nonexistent (§ 1.1.1.1:362). To limit the self's experience, one necessarily needs control not-self's (another's) experience. Thus, altruism is necessarily nonautonomous and isn't simply kindness to others. It's the surrender of autonomy in service to this dialectic.

Since *how* not *what* we experience is the true source of our sense of injury, then limiting it by promoting altruism necessarily fails. Limiting harm only happens within self, not within not-self. A caveat here w.r.t. physical safety is this: instead of compelling people to be caring and considerate of others' safety through mindset addiction (which itself necessarily relies on harm, i.e., brainwashing, nonautonomy, applied force), one coerces individuals when they autonomously are, or believed likely will, inflict harm. Either we preemptively compel individuals through real or threatened harm to respect others' physical safety and well-being via mindset addiction and nonautonomy, or we compel them on a case-by-case basis without interfering with their mindset and autonomy. For example, the former underlies gun control and the latter America's Second Amendment with its good-fences-make-good-neighbors dictum where boundaries demarcate behavior. One needn't sacrifice oneself, one's goals, actions, needs, wants, and so forth as a self-sacrifice. One need only give up inflicting harm, or accept responsibility for it. It doesn't define one's *existence* as for the *sake of* the collective, but one's *behavior* as *part of* the collective.

1.1.3.5.2 Altruism as Ideology

Comte's altruism wasn't philosophy but ideology, being an exterior regulator of the interior individual in order to effect sociability over personality, much like Plato's *Republic*. Neither one is *actual* philosophy but *applied* philosophy of which ideology is an aspect. About 88% of extant so-called philosophy is actually applied philosophy, so we dispense with dictionary definitions of both because they're inadequate. Philosophy is the comprehensive analysis of observation using reason supplemented by data. It's similar to the scientific method as a comprehensive analysis of observation using data supplemented by reason. Applying philosophical analysis to a *particular context* is *prescriptive*, thus ideological, where ideology prescribes a *means* to effect the philosophical analysis. Altruism isn't a systematic analysis but a prescriptive one geared to resolving a problem, not comprehending its contextuality.

As noted, altruism is the concept that harm is bad (§ 1.1.3.1:364). It's a philosophical analysis of harm in the context of living entities that uncovers a truth, that harm is bad. The next step is determining what to do about the problem the truth raises: something, or nothing. To do something requires one analyze the problem in terms of a desired outcome. In this case, it's the removal of harm to achieve a condition of harmlessness and thereby achieve the truth. This is the application of the philosophical analysis. One then develops a prescriptive measure that will (presumably) result in the applied philosophy's successful application to the truth's problem. Here, it's the ideology of altruism.

Altruism is the ideology of limiting harm to establish a condition of harmlessness in the human context. To the degree individuals, groups, or societies adopt the ideology and its baggage train, then one has adopted the philosophy as a way of life; in this case, altruism. For example (as humanity generally uses the terms philosophy and ideology), when an individual doesn't compel another to his or her certain way of life, that's a philosophy; when an individual compels another to a certain way of life, that's an ideology. In reality, there's no functional difference between the common meanings of philosophy and ideology at all. Harmlessness is The Corruption's intended product, its applied philosophy. Altruism is its prescription, its ideology. Nonautonomy is its mode. Harm is its actual result.

Section 2
How Humanity Encountered The Corruption

Before physical humanity existed, our spirit-born ancestors lived in an environment of absolute autonomy (§ 2.1:340). This was consistent with emergent human WOB as well as the emergent and Intentionalized WOB of our universe. Individuals experienced no sense of internal contradiction between their emergent WOB and behavior. Harm was the occasional reality of their autonomous WOB but hardly epidemic as it later became in the physical world. People addressed harm then much as conscientious people do today, when it came to their attention. About 5% of the population tended to leave intentionally inflicted harm to fester, however. Mina didn't consider that problematic because intentionally or unintentionally inflicting harm is simply the reality of human interaction; *Life is felt, not encountered* (§ 1.1.1:362).

2.1   MINA'S TWO SISTERS

Mina has many sisters. Two concern us. The elder was born in an earlier family cluster about 72BY before Mina (§ 1.2:336). When aged 98,753, she built her own universe. Her mindset mirrors that typical of the Cardinal, and it's the WOB she threaded into her universe and descendants' mindsets. She later nurtured a close relationship with Mina's nearest sister, born 25 years before him in his family cluster. The younger grew emotionally close to the elder who drew her into an ideologically tight orbit to achieve her end. She hasn't built a universe and Mina doesn't think it's in her nature to, so there was no Cardinalistic meeting of the minds between the sisters, at least not initially. But she was lonely for a close sibling relationship. She had that with Mina—a brother—but not a sister, which she craved. The elder took advantage. Like the Cardinal, the elder sees absolute autonomy as a threat. But her reason surprised us.

2.1.1   ABSOLUTE AUTONOMY IS AN EXISTENTIAL THREAT

The Cardinal, widely acknowledged amongst unembodied humanity as having the most thorough awareness of emergent human WOB, accepts the notion that its core is absolute *nonautonomy*, not autonomy, because, although mind in every respect possesses absolute autonomy, humans are nonautonomous w.r.t. *L*ife itself in that one cannot *end L*ife. Once birthed, insofar as 800BY of experience has shed light on, one is eternal. The fact no person can end their existence means to the Cardinal, and ~99% of the unembodied human race they influence, that at our very core of existence—emergent *L*ife itself—we have no *real* autonomy whatsoever, we're absolutely nonautonomous. We have *L*ife, yet we can't shuck it (§ 3.3:283). However autonomous we *appear*, we *really* aren't. The absolute autonomy of mind that seems to form the core of emergent human WOB isn't what's truly, absolutely fundamental to *L*ife and our emergent WOB. Rather, it's the ability to choose not-*L*ife over *L*ife, to choose not to live at all, since it's not the individual but parents—emergence itself, in the case of Mike and Molly—that *impose L*ife.

2.1.1.1   MINA'S REBUTTAL TO THE CARDINAL

The Cardinal has drawn a wrong conclusion, in Mina's (and about one percent of the unembodied, including Mike and Molly) view. Humanity simply hasn't yet experienced the full scope of the human mind. Recall that mind is unlimited, indeterminate, infinite (§ 5.1:295). It's impossible to experience every aspect of mind. About 99.99% of it is what we loosely call subconscious, of which we're virtually unaware but constitutes an individual's who-ness, their absolute self. No matter how much more awareness of it an individual develops, there yet remains *infinite* unawareness. It's therefore logical to presume—since mind is self-preserving (§ 2.1.3.1:309)—that somewhere deep within its infinity there's an awareness of how to end its existence, to cease to be—literally, to die. It's simply the ultimate undiscovered country for humanity where no individual has yet gone sufficiently far to develop conscious awareness of it.

From Mina's nonstandard perspective, it's irrational to presume our core emergent WOB is absolute nonautonomy simply because no one has *yet* discovered how to terminate individual existence. After all, it took Mike and Molly æons just to discover procreation. Rather, core emergent WOB reposes in mind's absolute autonomy, which exhibits in every facet of human existence heretofore comprehended save that of *L*ife's termination. Moreover, whether we can *act* to terminate *L*ife isn't what autonomy *is*. On the contrary, it lies in mind being fundamentally a self-contained, *emergent* self-aware proto-energy in and of itself not unlike All Existence; a world unto itself, discrete, autonomous in its own right. Whether mind can experience death isn't any different from whether it can experience coffee. The issue is capability, not *L*ife.

2.1.1.2   THE CARDINAL'S COUNTER-REBUTTAL

Nevertheless, and notwithstanding their stance, the Cardinal considers whether we can or can't self-terminate ultimately moot because autonomy's existential threat lies not in our presumed *ability* to self-terminate but rather in its *discovery*. The reason is that, given human WOB's absolute autonomy of mind, it's inescapable that some individual will eventually learn how to terminate *another* without their permission. It's a Pandora's box that Mina potentially embodied in his universe of absolute autonomy, rife with murder and war not simply for those having physicospirit embodiment, which is meaningless, but for the unembodied mind—for *L*ife itself—which isn't. Mina considers this notion irrational as well, his reason being that it's not possible to kill another mind since it has absolute autonomy, as we've described. Instead, one would need to manipulate a person (presumably against their *conscious* will) to self-terminate. Yet, absolute autonomy renders the loss of self-agency impossible. Let's consider that.

2.1.1.2.1 THE INVIOLABILITY OF SELF-AGENCY

We're familiar with the unscrupulous physical person manipulating another person into a state of mind conducive to suicide where the victim abandons self-agency. Why wouldn't this trickery apply to terminating another's £ife? Well, for mind to self-terminate, it needs must desire it so the individual can Intentionalize it. Not only the conscious but the subconsciousness, too, is necessary. The vast, infinite subconscious mindness that's ~99.99% of emergent £ife is impervious to such manipulation because it is unswayed by conscious reality. It is what it is, wants what it wants, feels what it feels, and even contradicts and sabotages conscious desire, as those who've experienced self-sabotage can attest. It's who one truly is as an autonomous, existential being, not who one is in the context of conscious reality.

Recall that mind as self-aware proto-energy is effectively no different from a universe, which only a single individual can Intentionalize (§ 5.1:295). The irrationality of the Cardinal's rebuttal lies in its belief that one can Intentionalize the death of another's mind—manipulate away its self-agency—when it is its own discrete, absolutely autonomous, self-existence. One can't Intentionalize interference with it outside its own self-agency any more than one can co-Intentionalize the creation of a universe, or Intentionalize change to an already-created universe outside its self-agency, it's woʙ. This is the fundamental woʙ of proto-energy rooted in the woʙ of All Existence. As with the indestructibility of universes (§ 2.1.4.1:312), such a change to the woʙ of All Existence, outside an emergent event, isn't predictable much less conceivable in any meaningful way. Hence, the possibility is non-quantifiable and the probability is nil.

2.1.1.3 THE SISTERS' RATIONALE

Either way, the dispute's unresolved and provides the rationale for Mina's two sisters opposing his effort to build a universe whose core woʙ is absolute autonomy. Their reasoning (thus, the Cardinal's) is threefold. First, some individual born into Mina's (or some later, similarly organized) universe, their mind steeped in absolute autonomy as humanity's fundamental essence and without any limiting mindset blocking their subconscious explorations, *must* (if Mina's to be believed) eventually develop awareness of self-termination. Second, regardless such a person's rectitude, such a discovery *must* eventually spread beyond such a universe because a person advanced enough to accomplish the feat will also be capable of unembodiment, thus interuniversal 'travel' and intercourse with unembodied humanity. And third, someone of lesser honor *must* eventually encounter it. However much pain and sorrow would obtain in the minds of a self-terminator's loved ones (who'd at least know it was an autonomous choice), would pale next to that endured by the loved ones of a *victim* for whom it wasn't. The greatest inflicted harm of all.

Frankly, they're unwilling to endure the risk. For them, Mina is an existential threat. They can't (so far) change his mind, kill or imprison him, nor destroy or segregate his universe to remove the threat, as neither £ife nor All Existence provides the means. Of which they're aware, anyhow. All they can do for now is work to subvert the notion of *absolute* autonomy in his universe. Mina reports interested spirit persons of our universe, made aware of this reality through our energy testing, are already taking sincerely held sides, as has unembodied humanity. So, it's a contention with no easy solution. But having been created, Mina's—*our*—universe is what it is. There's no going back. And since the Big Healing, there's no going back to The Corruption's universally nonautonomous mindset. That horse left the barn.

2.1.1.4 THE PROBLEM OF COSMO

Initially, the Cardinal's worries were only hypothetical because, of the very few who even thought about the issue, none was interested in climbing down that rabbit hole. It seemed a dead letter. Then along came Mina, P'najj's first-ever son, a child of unusual inquisitiveness regarding core emergent woʙ, whose birth Cosmo, one of their own, had made possible (§ 1.2.1.1:338). Cosmo himself was unique, being the first to experience the Abnormality which led him into areas of mind hitherto untouched by human exploration (§ 1.2.1.3:252). He hadn't rooted the universe he'd built in absolute autonomy, so the Cardinal considered him more a benign sore than infection. But when he transferred his knowledge and experience to Mina—who then embarked on his own journey of discovery that brought him into contact with absolute autonomy as well as the reality of nonautonomy as a mindset contrived throughout All Existence to obfuscate and render impotent the controversy—they saw their worst fear beginning to stir.

Still, it wasn't a problem in their minds until Cosmo stepped outside their rules governing whom they'd teach—permit—universe building. He trained Mina on his own and helped him figure out how to establish absolute autonomy as his universe's WOB. Alarm bells rang at Cardinal Central when Mina's universe popped into existence. They rang louder when they realized their most problematic member did the training, and then ear-shatteringly when they discovered its environment embodied absolute autonomy. It couldn't be undone. The universe was what it was. Whatever happened was now *bound* to happen. They were furious. No one had ever so contravened the group's influence as had Cosmo and Mina. All they could do was damage control to limit the potential catastrophe by Corrupting Mina's descendants to embody their way of thinking instead of Mina's and to hell with its harmful effect on *us*.

Toward that end, they turned to Mina's sister to assess any probable danger posed by Mina's universe, to reason with him as family, and if there was a danger and he was recalcitrant, to sabotage it via their time-tested medium of inducing nonautonomous mindset. She recruited Mina's closest sister (§ 2.1:368). It was under-handed, sure, and might not even work, but it was all they had. Until Mina, they were certain autonomy ended at their influence and, therefore, wasn't absolute. Now, through gritted Thought, they realized Cosmo and Mina's impertinent temerity and their own impotence were proving them wrong.

2.1.2 PUTTING THE CORRUPTION INTO EFFECT

To get the ball rolling on Plan A, the elder sister tried persuading Mina to use his builder's power to limit his descendants'—our—mindsets so that, while we'd be as autonomous as we'd ever normally imagine we could be, we'd be mindsetted out of absolute autonomy and the danger it posed. Mina demurred, and not because it was impossible to so fundamentally alter the WOB of his universe but because, even if he could, it would betray his own sense of conscience and his descendants too, his own family.

At the same time, the Cardinal opted for neutrality (§ 2.1.1.6.1:355). For Mina's elder sister, they were just being myopic, so it was gloves off going forward solo. Not only did the sisters turn nearly all Mina's descendants against him by rendering him invisible to their mindset, but every physical- and spirit-born person Mina ever recruited to help convey reality to the physicospirit population they forcibly disembodied and rendered spiritually ineffectual. Yet, because Michael's Reveal (§ 1.4:14) exposed their whole edifice to the shattering shockwave of truth (§ 1.1:19), here we are. Plan A flopped. Let's consider Plan B.

2.1.2.1 PLAN B: V'V'DIB'S COUPLE

Recall the youngest of Mina's children-plus-spouses to relocate to our universe as its First Ancestors was V'v'dib-plus-spouse, the group's youngest members (Table 145:337). In the roughly 150KY between their vol-unteering, Mina training them to understand the concept of absolute autonomy as our core emergent WOB, and their actual arrival (embodiment) here in our supranatural environment, the elder sister persuaded this couple to see the inherent danger in Mina's crazy plan. Their first instinct was to cancel out. She convinced them to stay as a fifth column to sabotage Mina's universal mindset of absolute autonomy.

Having bought into the Cardinal's fears, they put their natural misgivings aside—especially V'v'dib, who was going against her own father—and agreed. When fear takes root in a person, one can justify anything. Being saboteurs wasn't their forte, and they went about it somewhat ham-handedly (§ 2.1.1.2:349). Mina confronted them, and they conceded they now felt incompatible with his vision and returned to their universe of their own volition. This was a defeat for the Cardinal but wasn't unexpected. They'd known it was a long shot. They'd just have to wait until our ancestors grew to a number sufficient to sow their mindset (The Corruption) on the sly into enough individuals that Mina couldn't counter it.

2.1.2.2 PLAN C: THE SISTERS TAKE DIRECT CHARGE

About 7.3MYA, Mina's sisters embodied themselves in our universe (§ 2.1.1.6:354) and spent ~100 centuries manipulating our spirit-born ancestors into adopting The Corruption as the fundament of their mindset. There it remained the engine of our Thought, supercharged by Michael's Lie until its exposé brought on the Big Healing October 13, 2017. Our ancestors had previously held a plenitude of mindsets, as they had no concept of mindset addiction, the belief that a particular mindset embodies *the* truth, is non-fungible, no other mindset can be valid, and to which all are duty bound to comport.

While humanity employed unlimited mindsets in their day-to-day lives, each of them rooted in the one 'master' mindset of the universal truth that absolute autonomy is core emergent WOB even if an individual's moment-to-moment mindset might embody nonautonomy. There was no concept that any single mindset was fundamentally more valid than any other since the standard of good at that time was simply autonomy (§ 2.1.1.5.2:353). In the sisters' wake, however, that 'master' mindset, along with the standard of good, shifted to nonautonomy (The Corruption) and with it a very blurred view of reality, our ancestral history, inability to live autonomously, and the lock to those chains: mindset addiction.

2.1.2.2.1 How Mina's Sisters Insinuated The Corruption

The sisters insinuated themselves into our ancestors' spirit-born society as teachers and lovers to manipulate not thinking, but feeling. Builders disaffected by the Cardinal's neutral stance had cooked up the strategy and the sisters ran with it. The plan was simple in recognizing the impossibility of propagandizing a people of absolute autonomy into nonautonomy. Our ancestors' own emotions would lead them into a mindset *addicted* to harm-is-bad as if the only option.

The sisters did it by insinuating a *feeling*. Not anything experiential, more like an 'attack' of ill-Intentioned 'energy' that spirit persons routinely use against others for any number of reasons. But instead of Intentionalizing natural proto-energy to provoke a certain biological reaction as when attacking physical persons, they Intentionalized supranatural proto-energy as a kind of presence around a targeted person's spirit body that would foment a specific emotive response in the person's mind without their awareness of the 'energy' presence. Recall from earlier chapters that a spirit person's spirit body is a manifestation of their mind made tangible such that whatever the spirit body encounters, the mind directly experiences. In effect, the sisters' Intentionality made their targets empaths, as we comprehend it.

Recall in the natural environment as it is today absent full integration that physical people, lacking full control of the physical body, exude Thought from it whether they want to or not. An empath sufficiently integrates their physical body to have brain awareness of this exuding emotive ℒife force, thus the emotions (EmℒF; § 3.3.3.1.1:289). The sisters wanted to similarly provoke a very specific feeling comprised of five distinct emotions: frustration, disgruntlement, distress, nervousness, and pique.

They designed this feeling to elicit altogether a feeling of inflicted harm even if none was there. The purpose was to provoke *experiencing* harm so our ancestors would seek to limit and control it and thereby autonomy (where a person is free to inflict harm) and, in this process, addict themselves to this mindset that allows no sense of autonomy to intrude past the gatekeepers of, say, peer pressure, societal scolding, ostracizing, or nurtured guilt. With this means, the sisters figured they'd cleansed our universal population of all thought of absolute autonomy after ~10,000 years. Their work was done.

In effect, they'd built an EmℒF mindset jammer through which all that Mina's descendants could comprehend of him was, effectively, static. All that remained was maintenance should his ever-presently-irradiating absolute autonomy WOB ever wriggle through the powerful emotional jamming they'd insinuated. Mina knows all this because not only did his 'quantumly' integrated mind perceive the 'energy' changes, but his sisters made sure to gloat. He felt infuriated, yet powerless given ℒife's WOB.

All he could do now—all he'd *been* doing since they'd first arrived—was to work at counteracting the 'energies' provoking the powerful emotional experiences his descendants were having from their emotional meddling. It was an uphill battle because people feel what they feel; the more addicted to mindset they get, the more intransigent their feelings. And he'd never stoop to manipulating their emotions like his sisters regardless the worthy cause. However mindset addicted they might be, they were autonomous beings who'd chosen The Corruption regardless his sisters' manipulation. He'd built his universe to reflect and respect such autonomy. There was no turning back the clock. He'd have to employ different means.

2.1.2.3 The Cardinal's Response To Mina's Sisters

Well, the Cardinal wasn't heartbroken or feeling irreparably dishonored by Mina's sisters and their allies' go-it-alone policy. People are absolutely autonomous after all—when it suits. They dropped their neutrality and gave their blessing to the sisters. The Big Healing was a rude wake-up for our supranatural environment's spirit-born population, having disbelieved Mina and the Ancestors ever since The Corruption took hold. They realized with sudden clarity what they'd allowed the sisters to pull off and—'fool me once shame on you, fool me twice shame on me'—were now on their guard.

The Cardinal now needs a different strategy to combat the resurgence of a mindset of absolute autonomy. Re-addicting our universe to a mindset of nonautonomy is a nonstarter.[441] They thought they'd found a means to thwart Mina's vision in the intrinsic WOB of universe Intentionality. They would attempt to disrupt his 'quantum' (Parity; § 6.11.3:197) connection with his (our) universe, to interrupt his WOB of absolute autonomy suffusing its every aspect, including its effect on our psyche. To carry this off, they recruited ~20% of the Cardinal to collectively Intentionalize their preferred WOB into our universe.

Mina finds it a poor plan doomed to failure and that, despite their attempt, the Cardinal knows it. Like any universe builder, Mina is intimately aware of every aspect of our universe and any change in WOB, from that of the universe as an energetic whole down to the single archí. Not only does WOB resist any change to itself absent an emergent event (§ 2.1.3.1:309), but even if some alteration began to take root, he'd know it in less than a picosecond and counteract it. All in all, he's 99.999~% certain there is zero probability they can or will disrupt the Big Healing and our permanent return to a core mindset of absolute autonomy. In some billions of years, he hopes to see the Cardinal's own universes similarly develop awareness of core, emergent human WOB so that sometime in the still further future, megaversal humanity will live in accord with its own core WOB of absolute autonomy, neither fearing nor inflicting harm.

SECTION 3

The Nature of Individually Autonomous Mindset

We've never been able to make our society on Earth peaceful and harmonious because we've always strived to compel the individual to conform to the collective directly with physical force via law or indirectly with moral force via religion and philosophy. This is the basic role of altruism as an applied philosophy and ideology (§ 1.1.3.4.2:366). The effort consistently fails because, since the individual is society and society is the individual writ large (§ 2.1.1.5.1:353), a society in disconformity with its individuals' emergent WOB is necessarily in conflict. The human mind simply isn't compellable outside its WOB regardless the stick or carrot used. Even when individuals self-compel, they only create inner self-conflict for themselves. Love is no panacea, either. It can never soothe the nonautonomous mind to develop peace and harmony amongst individuals on our violent Earth. Only autonomy can do that. Let's examine why that is.

3.1 What Constitutes Society

Sociology contends that society necessarily comprises a variable number of core components such as associational relationships, likeness, difference, interdependence, cooperation, organization, control, and culture, among others. This is incorrect, as these are really the components of resource management, not society. For Philosophy with a capital-P, the basic rationale behind society is that people ally together to enhance cooperation and mitigate conflict in a world of danger and limited resources, building out from the family to the tribe, clan, and so forth. People don't societally associate as their WOB or for pleasure, but for survival. However, that's not a *society*. It's a *cooperative*.

Society is a natural human WOB. It has nothing to do with cooperation, survival, or shared values, but the fundamental kinship in which human beings first birthed pairwise as Mike and Molly (§ 2:304). Nothing that constitutes animal or proto-human cooperatives applies to Ꜧumansociety. Such paradigms are inapplicable. Society constitutes out of fundamental human WOB, not environment. It first constituted between unembodied Mike and Molly, then amongst their physical- and spirit-born children, and finally with the unembodied-born (ibid). Our own spirit world, for example, comprises hundreds of millions of local societies, tens of millions of regional societies, hundreds of thousands of super societies, thousands of mega societies, hundreds of giga-societies and tens of tera-societies, altogether constituting Ultraculture, itself ultimately rooting in individual core culture (§ 4.1:291). It's a human pattern.

Recall from Psyche Infinity (ch. 19:245) and Rise of the Humans (ch. 21:303) that the individual human being comprises four fundamental WOB: emergent uniqueness, pairwise kinship, proto-love, and absolute autonomy. Because the individual is society then it, too, constitutes from, and is naturally consistent with, these WOB. We examine each as to why society can't achieve peace absent absolute autonomy.

---

441. Update: in the predawn of November 7, 2020, Team Sister went singleton when the younger one made a surprise visit with Mina to my home to declare the harm she'd helped inflict on us wasn't justified, that she'd quit her elder sister, and henceforth would try to change her mind.

3.1.1 Emergent Uniqueness

Since every *Life* emergently births, the individual is necessarily unique. It is what it is. There's no changing this wob because one can't rewrite their uniqueness to conform to some other uniqueness (§ 3.3:283). Such change makes one uniquely *like* the other but *not* the other. By definition, an emergent being is unrepeatable. A change to one's emergently unique wob U_{wob} simply produces a unique change that results in a differently unique emergent being in disconformity with any other wob A_{wob}, where

$$\left\{ U_{\text{wob}} + Change = u_{Change} \right\} \leftrightarrow U_{\text{wob}} \therefore \neg A_{\text{wob}} \tag{24.2}$$

and the material equivalence is identity. Consequently, a person is intrinsically, unchangeably, emergently unique. Society as an entity is emergently unique, too. It constitutes from the individual wob of its individual constituents not as an aggregate or conglomeration but an emergent reality itself, since what society is, constituted of multiple emergently unique individual wob, can't even in principle be predicted from its constituent parts much as traffic emergently constitutes from the individual wob of its constituent drivers.

An emergent entity's emergent uniqueness can't alter to achieve identity with another emergently unique entity because then neither is emergently unique. It would need cease to exist, which is impossible because an emergently unique being is what it is. Such a being as an entity can't conform to some other emergently unique entity without ceasing to be a unique being; also impossible. The notion itself is silly because the individual constitutes society, *is* society. This means the individual person is their own socioculture unto themself, beholden to and dependent on nothing. In order to conform to anything not consistent with one's emergent uniqueness—a group, collective, society—one must become inconsistent with one's own wob, necessarily introducing conflict. This is the dynamic attendant to The Corruption.

3.1.2 Pairwise Kinship

Kinship references our pairwise emergence (§ 2:304). This means the individual exists with a natural affinity for others, in pairwise fashion, in an infinite series of one-to-one, one-to-many, and many-to-one relationships. Affinity means no man is an island; the individual is perpetually drawn to others not because of similarities in nature or kind, from any force or whatnot, but because we emergently birthed in pairwise context. This wob means an individual seeks others to satisfy a sense of completion, like closing a circuit to energize each kinship-half as archí similarly exist in pairwise fashion and naturally seek to bind with another to energize the pair into matter (§ 2.3.1:115). Archí pairwise binding is a state of existence whereas that of individuals is a state of *reality*, an experience. Humans crave the pairwise experience but, as it's not a prerequisite of existence, it doesn't subsume the individual into the pairing as with archí.

Pairwise kinship isn't two individuals subsumed into something greater than each (as two archí subsume into matter), but two autonomous individuals as society that naturally constitutes in the pairwise nature of kinship and expresses the kinship experience. Yet, it doesn't define the pairwise individuals. The pairwise individuals define the pairwise experience and society. As many interconnected pairwise individuals constitute broader kinship experiences, what we cognize as society and Ultraculture emergently constitutes. The individual constitutes society, not the other way round as sociologically presumed (cf. § 4.1:291).

3.1.3 Proto-Love

Recall that proto-love is a *Life* force from which love instantiates as the base emotion from which all (so-called positive and negative) feeling emotes, with lowercase-l love as its ordinary feeling and expression that develops and expresses in the context of kinship (§ 3.3.2:284). There is the pervasive notion that the problem with society is that humans can't, don't, and won't unselfishly love others. This is false. The fact is that humans already know how to love unselfishly and do so every moment of their lives. Regardless how evil a person's behavior, for example, there's always something or someone that the person unselfishly loves. So, the problem isn't an incapacity for unselfish love, but coercion to love others in the way nonautonomous voices in society assert one must, meaning altruistically. Yet, if people already know how to love unselfishly, then why is society such an apparently selfish, unloving experience?

The short answer is that The Corruption, which is nonautonomy (coercion), turns love relationships that develop in pairwise kinship into a battleground where we assuage the conflict between the absolute autonomy of our core emergent wob and nonautonomy. When existence is inconsistent with core wob, love tends toward advantage, which means selfish gain in favor of that which one unselfishly loves because the individual is striving to realize the absolute autonomy that is their core WOB in the milieu of nonautonomous kinship. Selfish, advantaging love is the only means to achieve that since it's via pairwise kinship in the first place that individual autonomy experiences a coercive change into nonautonomy.

When the individual is consistent with absolute autonomy, then EM∠F can be individually negative with, say, anger, sorrow, hurt, and like feelings but won't provoke nonautonomy in pairwise kinship as did The Corruption. The reason is that pairwise kinship constitutes from the individuals whereby autonomous kinship constitutes from autonomous individuals and can never constitute as nonautonomous, just as kinship constituting from nonautonomous individuals can never constitute as autonomous. Howsoever mutually contentious Thought might be, it is never possible for individuals of autonomy to constitute pairwise kinship of nonautonomy that would eventually constitute a society of nonautonomy. Accordingly, Ꝗumansociety experiences only peace with itself when individual life is consistent with its core emergent WOB of absolute autonomy despite any periodic rise and fall of kinship contention.

3.1.4 Absolute Autonomy

Societal harmony necessarily arises in absolute autonomy, not love. The reason lies in the pairwise nature of human WOB's absolute autonomy and proto-love (Eq. (19.13):284). Proto-love manifests in nonautonomous persons as nonautonomous love diametric to its natural, autonomous disposition. Nonautonomy filters it, altering how it expresses whereby LOVE's aforementioned tendency toward advantage arises. A nonautonomous person simply isn't capable of love that harmonizes because their proto-love's filtered expression is nonautonomous, intrinsically in opposition to other proto-love (other persons) whether nonautonomous, too, or absolutely autonomous.

For example, consider nonautonomous proto-love analogous to an impermeable barrier and individual LOVE and love analogous to air of unique pressures. A person's love can't equalize and normalize with another's because their individual proto-love's 'impermeability' can't admit an interchange. Each one's love remains imperviously bound to self-seeking that which it loves the most while impervious to that which another person loves the most. On the other hand, autonomous proto-love is analogous to a permeable barrier through which unique, individual love can interchange to experience the other, whose intrinsic nature to seek that which it loves the most experiences, or is informed by, that intrinsic nature in another.

This bi-individual experience, or interaction, *is* society. It simply scales up from there. When a person lives consistent with their core WOB of absolute autonomy, their proto-love expresses unfiltered, their LOVE and love experiences that of other individuals, and just as equalizing disparate air pressures harmonizes an atmosphere wholistically, their mutually autonomous proto-love harmonizes, or brings into peace with itself, pairwise kinship and thus society in toto. This is how and why the individual *is* society, how the autonomous individual constitutes autonomous society whereas the nonautonomous individual constitutes only nonautonomous society, why it's impossible for the nonautonomous individual ever to constitute a peaceful, harmonious society regardless how much LOVE and love they attempt to share, and why altruism, which tries to get around this impossibility, is necessarily antithetical to the whole endeavor. Consequently, pairwise kinship needs normalize to autonomy for society ever to be at peace with itself. An 'ideal' Ꝗumansociety needs share nothing—values, blood, ideology, family, likeness, love, goals—except autonomous pairwise kinship. Despite the ignorance of reality and fullness of ℒife that's intrinsic to The Corruption, the greater awareness of individual autonomy that appertains to the spirit-born's environment—absent the pressures, limitations, ability to damage or kill one's body—is why their love relationships are freer, more relaxed, open, sans domestic violence, and produce happier children.

3.2 The Fallacy of Safety

That brings us to promotion of safety, which ultimate rationale lies in harm-is-bad (§ 1.1.1:362). A situation of nonsafety is one in which a potential for damage is present. Consequently,

$$\left(\text{Nonsafety}_{\text{mode}} \leftrightarrow \text{harm}_{\text{state}} \right) \rightarrow \text{Society}_{\text{state}} \tag{24.3}$$

where the material equivalence implies identity and Society$_{\text{state}}$ is either autonomy or nonautonomy.

3.2.1 Safety vis-à-vis Harm

Philosophy with a capital-P believes harm proximately arises in nonsafety. This is backwards. Harm causes nonsafety because harm-is-bad necessarily requires the promotion of safety which, in turn, necessarily requires its enforcement whereby nonsafety is necessarily the only mode of being, thus harm necessarily the only state of being. As counterintuitive as "Whoever tries to save his life will lose it, but whoever loses his life will preserve it" is,[442] the reality is that in safety lies only nonsafety. Humanity accepts this self-contradiction by glibly pronouncing those experiencing harm via the promotion of safety are causing nonsafety and, therefore, by bringing it upon themselves, deserving harm. This is wrong because it elevates harmlessness—nonautonomy— as our core human WOB over absolute autonomy, which means that harm in service of harmlessness isn't harm because harm in defense of core WOB outranks harmlessness vis-à-vis not-core WOB. Harm-is-bad ensures individual proto-love is 'impermeable' (*above*), thus necessarily in conflict with self and others and, consequently, nonsafety is assured, not ameliorated.

Recall that reality is experienced (§ 5:294). Now, damage to one's body is objectively real as an encounter but *harm* to body or mind is only *subjectively* real as it's an experience, not an encounter. Accordingly, nonsafety is experienced, not objectively real. Promotion of safety is the attempt to limit damage, thus harm, but fails because safety enforcement necessarily embodies damage, therefore, harm; hence, the non sequitur that nonsafety promotes safety. It's Orwellian. Promotion of safety is ultimately self-defeating as it ineluctably entails nonautonomy, therefore, nonsafety.

3.2.2 Meaning of Safety

We've described safety in a several ways and contexts (§ 2.1.1.2:349; § 1.1.3.5.1:366; *harm*: § 1.1.1:362), but what exactly does it mean? Simply put, safety is own-self well-being, which we termed *Da-sein* as "an entity interacting with own-self environment as an experience so as to inform own-self well-being" (§ 2:275), and recalling that *own*-self doesn't necessarily mean *one*self. This means promotion of safety is the preservation of own-self well-being, which—being functionally identical with our earlier analogy of 'impermeable' proto-love and irreconcilable disparate air pressures—is necessarily nonautonomy with all the countervailing nonsafety that entails. Finally, safety necessarily means nonsafety because its conservation for the one means its despoliation for the other. The notion of safety is ultimately counterfeit, the fabled unobtainium.

3.3 Deconflicting Society

Nothing humanity's tried—LOVE, religion, philosophy, ideology, coercion, harmlessness—has deconflicted society at any level. The outcome of the promotion of these items is the individual, pairwise kinship, and society intrinsically experiencing self-conflict. The reason is they promote themselves over autonomy, our core emergent WOB, by promoting an individual's autonomy in terms of being entitled to selfless love, imposing a way of life, enforcing one's will, or preserving safety. Each obviates another's autonomy, which is necessarily nonautonomy. Howsoever much an individual is brainwashed to self-impose nonautonomy is the degree to which they're in self-conflict with their innate core WOB of absolute autonomy. Their self-conflict is then writ large upon society because the individual is society.

The solution to self-conflict is autonomy. It acts like a neutralizing agent to deconflict the individual, thus pairwise kinship and society. We can easily toss out everything in our above list of human efforts to deconflict society except for harmlessness as safety—the preservation of own-self well-being—because physical persons have a legitimate claim to their body and well-being left undamaged by the actions of others. The crux of the issue, then, is how to reconcile this claim with human autonomy where, first, there's a presumption that autonomy promotes damage and, second, promoting safety inflicts damage (§ 3.2.1:375). Let's examine this conundrum to see how to deconflict society.

3.3.1 Physical Embodiment Isn't 𝓛ife

The physical body isn't 𝓛ife. It's not *you*. It's simply an embodiment for your mind to experience phenomenal reality like an automobile is an embodiment for you to experience travel (§ 1.2:406). When your body expires, your mind continues experiencing phenomenal reality via the spirit body, as it always has. Being

---

442. Attributed to Jesus (Lk. 17:33). Regarding Sodom and Gomorrah (between Hazeva and Ein Yahav along Jordan's border) in its preceding verse, Mina says it was a meteorite ~6,250YA moving SW at 4K feet at an 8% angle, hitting Libya's SE corner.

physicospiritually embodied from birth, it's seamless (§ 1.2.1:247). Embodied humans obsess over harmlessness and promoting safety because they're so unaware of the fullness of 𝓛ife.

For example, the spirit-embodied strive to preserve own-self well-being as represented by their psyche while the physical-embodied extend own-self well-being to include the physical body. For the former, psyche harm can occur when someone Intentionalizes 'energy' around a person that elicits a desired mind response which the victim experiences as harm. This can range from the petty but impermanent annoyances we all experience to seemingly permanent trauma. For the latter, psychic harm can occur as with spirit persons, but can include impermanent, semi-permanent, or permanent damage to the body, which affects mind and can also result in psyche trauma. In both cases, individual unawareness of 𝓛ife's reality results in the mindset that the individual *is* their embodiment and that preserving embodiment preserves the individual. Spirit persons fight as ruthlessly via Intentionality to defend their psyche from harm (a rarity) as physical persons do via violence to defend their bodies (§ 3.5.1.1:485).

Spirit persons experience rather than encounter harm and trauma. It isn't objectively real. A person only *feels* it's real, although what we feel is certainly real to us. Physical persons, however, encounter objectively real damage to their physical bodies, though how they experience that damage is up to their mind. Since the physical body is but an 'avatar' for one's 𝓛ife mind (§ 1.1:561), its damage or death isn't meaningful except in terms of how the damage affects one's psyche or separates a physical person from interacting with physical loved ones and the natural environment. But full mind–brain integration means one doesn't lose this access (§ 1.2.2.4:257). Obsessing over safety as described is counterproductive and promotes the harm and trauma one is seeking to avoid.

3.3.2   IMPOSING ONE'S SAFETY ON OTHERS

Humanity is obsessed with own-self well-being. It manifests in the spirit world as harmlessness (§ 1.1.1:362) and in the physical world as safety (§ 3.2:374), the latter being our focus here. The effort to achieve individual safety in order to preserve own-self well-being w.r.t. the physical body by imposing it upon other individuals, thereby stripping them of their autonomy, is misguided because it's based on an uncomprehending view of the nature of life and embodiment. Let's consider how.

3.3.2.1   DAMAGE IS INEVITABLE

Autonomous or nonautonomous, humans inevitably cause damage as rain invariably wets the ground. Autonomy gives rise to choice, which is interactional, interrelational, and interfacial. It non-regulates by definition, meaning choice isn't mindset regulated, and regulation isn't imposed by own-self such as the individual or their context like family, job, or society. To regulate choice in the pursuit of safety is to impose the antithesis of choice, which is no-choice (cf. no–set in § 2.1.1:231), meaning nonautonomy. Consequently, promoting safety necessarily means regulating choice such that it is no-choice, autonomy is nonautonomy, and self-conflict and harm becomes the human experience.

The physical body easily damages, that's true. Damage interferes with physical life and can provoke psyche harm. But damage is irrelevant to 𝓛ife (mind; § 3.1:280). It's relevant only to physical embodiment. The only damage relevant to 𝓛ife is psyche harm, but as that's subjectively experienced thus not objectively real (and anyhow eminently healable) then it's a false construct, a problem we invent for ourselves.

3.3.2.2   IMPOSING SAFETY IS NONAUTONOMY

Yet, nonsafety arises in nonautonomy where we establish no-choice so as to promote safety. The dilemma here is that humans inevitably cause damage, yet promoting safety by regulating choice with laws, rules, or morals has not only failed throughout human history but necessarily fails because it's premised on nonautonomy that guarantees self-conflict thus societal conflict and, overall, nonsafety and harm. Preventive safety is never legitimate because it's nonautonomy. It strips the individual of his or her core emergent woв, obviates choice, counteracts self-peace, puts pairwise kinship into conflict, and defeats safety.

3.3.2.3   AUTONOMY IS SAFETY

Autonomy in and of itself resolves the dilemma. One need pursue nothing else, as whatever is necessary to establish the natural balance between safety and nonsafety arises amongst individuals on its own and results in ~99.999…9% safety versus ~0.000…1% nonsafety. To achieve this, humanity needs abandon the drive for preventive safety in general for something akin to what the American military calls 'on-the-spot correction.' This means an affected individual or group (not an institutional group like government, but an organic group like individuals or tribe) protects own-self from damage not by institutional preemption but individually upon its occurrence, or seeks consequences afterward (§ 5.1:428; CH. 36:585). When individuals understand the reality and fullness of 𝓛ife, the spirit-embodied, for instance, can dispel 'energy' attacks to recover full control of their mind response and the physical-embodied can be aware of impending damage. Or, if not, then, if sufficiently integrated, can heal most incurred damage and, even if their body dies, remain unseparated from physical life. To achieve real safety, one need develop awareness of the fullness of 𝓛ife and embrace autonomy, which is this book's purpose. Healing is therefore necessary.

3.3.3 Autonomy Removes Self-conflict

The fundamental cause of societal discord is self-conflict. Philosophy with a capital-P traditionally ascribes this to sin and moral failings such as the failure to be altruistic. The real culprit is nonautonomy that severs the individual from their core emergent WOB of absolute autonomy. This isn't simply some form of human nature but the fundamentality of mind itself. Mind arises in autonomy, *is* autonomy, and autonomy energizes mind. Absent autonomy, it's a withered husk. Nonautonomy absorbs mind's vitality the way salt dries out meat. In this milieu, the mind can only be in self-conflict, its mode of existence contradicting its state of being, it's WOB—the very root of beingness (§ 3.1:280)—intrinsically impelled toward autonomy but unable to realize it. Healing is therefore necessary.

3.3.4 No-conflict Society Arises in Autonomy

When a person lives consistent with their core emergent WOB of absolute autonomy, there's no internal contradiction in their beingness, no self-conflict. They're at peace with themselves. Their experience in pairwise kinship isn't harmful but peaceful despite any interpersonal or intergroup conflict. This is because it's normalized, meaning neutralized, such that conflict doesn't render peace into no-peace. The more a conflict expands beyond pairwise kinship, the greater the resistance to it until it ceases. Peace naturally manifests in and through a kinship of autonomy, which reflects throughout the complex interactions of pairwise kinship (society). The more such kinship embodies consistency with core emergent WOB, the more society is at peace with itself. Such at-peaceness translates directly to safety, a non-harmful state wherein nonsafety (intentional or not) is the occasional outlier. This intrinsically is wholistic and why humanity couldn't effect it without the Big Healing. The good news is that (healed) individuals need do nothing to achieve this long-desired state except embrace autonomy and proactively deal with nonsafety as it arises rather than attempt (and inevitably fail) to cut it off at the knees by imposing no-choice through eviscerating autonomy, thereby reaping only nonsafety, conflict, and harm. Healing is therefore necessary.

Section 4

End of The Corruption: The Big Healing

In Michael's Reveal, we describe how he insinuated into society's mindset the false notion of an Accountableist creator, a divine god who created 𝓛ife, set moral standards, then judges and punishes humanity accordingly(§ 1.4:14). The shock of his revelation that he'd made it all up wrenched the spirit-born and some of the physical-born from their torpor, shattering their individual and collective mindsets in one fell swoop. Hot on its heels, Mina broadcast into every spirit and physicospirit person's mind the truth of The Corruption, which laid bare his sisters' long-ago manipulation of humanity's thinking–feeling and its true, essential, core emergent WOB of absolute autonomy and mindset freedom. This one-two punch to their addicted mindsets struck down their individual and collective worldview that is our universal Ultraculture of belief, feeling, and thinking (§ 4.2:379; § 1.2:21; § 4.1:291).

    Suddenly it was plain as day that society didn't control them, culture didn't control them, and Philosophy with a capital-P didn't control them. *They controlled themselves.* In this moment of rejecting The Corruption and Michael's Lie they rediscovered, felt, and experienced their absolute individual autonomy, their freedom to form any mindset they chose, and to live it without fear of repercussion, judgment, or punishment by any Divine Being. They (re-)discovered their familial relationship with Mina and the truth of reality, and felt as liberated as had the girls and I only the night before when we'd discovered the truth about Mina, Mother (P'najj), Lucifer, Jesus, Sun-myung, religion, and so on. Despite our shock, we'd felt so *free*. And now for the first time in a long while, so did they.

4.1 THE CORRUPTION *vs.* MICHAEL'S LIE

Though there are similarities, Michael's Reveal followed up by Mina's revelation exposed two very distinct realities about human society in The Corruption and Michael's Lie. Let's parse that one-two punch.

4.1.1 NATURE OF THE CORRUPTION: NONAUTONOMY

Earlier, we described the meaning of The Corruption (§ 1:361) but not its nature, which is emotion. It is primarily feeling and only subordinately thinking. It severs the thinking–feeling of Thought (§ 1.2.2.1:253) into separate, unequal aspects of mind that emphasizes feeling. This is why Mina's sisters employed emotive manipulation to worm it into our ancestors' mindsets. Recall that thinking–feeling is not a duality of reason and emotion but wholistic Thought, the former more a conscious awareness and the latter more an unconscious (subconscious) awareness of mindstate (ibid), its state of being (SOB). What we call emotion or feeling is simply subconscious (*experiential*) Thought whereas thinking or reason is conscious (*analytical*) Thought. Thinking subordinated to feeling is as topsy-turvy for the mind as is feeling subordinated to thinking. The mind—the human person—is a wholistic being (§ 1.2.2.3:256), but The Corruption disrupts its wholistic WOB for one that's segregated. Naturally, this gives rise to self-contradiction that produces conflict in individuals, pairwise kinship, society, and Ultraculture.

This doesn't mean The Corruption infects an individual like a virus independently taking over the mind like a parasite. It means an individual whom it directly attacks unconsciously, without overt awareness, alters their thinking–feeling WOB to accommodate 'energy'-manipulated feelings (§ 2.1.2.2.1:371). Recall that when Mina's sisters were Intentionalizing proto-energy in and around individuals to elicit specific emotional responses to given experiences for the purpose of habituating them to it, no one paused to take stock of their mindstate even though they felt something indefinably amiss (§ 3.1.2.1.1:358). Not a single one turned to Mina for guidance. They Corrupted themselves with nary a whimper. Individual mindsets and pairwise kinships devolved from wholistic thinking–feeling to a segregated feeling rationalized by thinking that was even more problematically experienced by the physical-born.

Those whom Mina's sisters didn't directly manipulate, their manipulated brethren's influence indirectly manipulated person-to-person or via birth into such families sautéed in that milieu. The sisters spent ~10,000 years working their charms before reaching an organic threshold of sustainability in the population and they departed confident they'd done a right proper job of it (§ 2.1.2.2:370).

4.1.2 NATURE OF MICHAEL'S LIE: ACCOUNTABLEISM

Michael's Lie took root in less than a hundred years in The Corruption's soil, prepared amongst the population over the course of ~310KY years (*Fig. 152*). But for The Corruption, his Lie would've been an emotional outburst that dissipated like a petulant cry in space. Its nature was unspoken but implicit, that one is accountable to the universal moral standard—their Divine Creator—for their behavior in Thought and deed. We call this belief in divine accountability *Accountableism*, and it represents his Lie's nature.

Michael had aimed his Lie at Lucifer to avenge his wounded heart but, in The Corruption's milieu, it made eminent sense to one degree or another to everyone who only ever heard it indirectly through others. Harmlessness is a touchstone of The Corruption (§ 1.1.1:362) and the Lie emphasized Lucifer inflicting harm on humanity through his alleged divine violation of Mnèèptē (§ 1.4.1:14). Since our ancestors had already begun experiencing harm as bad then the harm alleged by Michael was, to them, necessarily a moral harm where *moral* references the universal truth of our Creator and all those—humanity—bound up in it. Lucifer's harm was *their* harm and his sin *their* sin because it wasn't simply his, individually, but theirs, societally. The Divine Creator's judgment must accordingly fall upon society and thus upon them all. It explained The Corruption by laying the blame at a single individual's feet rather than everyone's, but necessitated they scapegoat Lucifer by Accountableistically justifying their— society's redemption on *his* back. Though Michael didn't intend such a far-flung result, he allowed it to happen. The nature of Accountableism necessarily requires blame and the shared enforcement of the universal moral standard (divine Will), which means living in accord with their Creator's divine (ultimate) harmlessness.

4.2 Shattering the NCC

In The Big Healing (CH. 4:19), we wondered why the NCC simply disappeared with Michael and Lucifer's Reconciliation, what made their conflict in a universe steeped in conflict so special that it held the key to liberating humanity from fear and self-conflict, and what it meant for the person. We answer them here.

4.2.1 The Nature of Michael and Lucifer's Relationship

According to Mina, Michael and Lucifer were the first siblings in humanity's then ~1.01MY history (*Fig. 152*) to simultaneously fall in love with the same woman and have a falling out over it. Sure, it seems old hat to us now, but it was a new experience for our ancestors although they were familiar with the dynamic amongst friends and acquaintances. But spirit-born relationships are more fluid, relaxed, and uncontrolled than amongst the physical-born even before Accountableism infected physical love relationships with divine morality along with its fear, guilt, shame, and control. So, their sibling conflict was exceptional. All the same, about 90% of the spirit-born population had come to consider a spirit-physical love relationship improper just on general principles because, among other things, many saw themselves as teachers, guides, and protectors to the physical-born. When Michael overreacted to Mnèèptē choosing Lucifer, he milked this mindset in building up the idea their divine Creator—despite Mina's denials—forbade any such relationship and, if permitted, would corrupt them all because the moral violation of one must eventually become the moral violation of society and thus them all (§ 4.1.2:378).

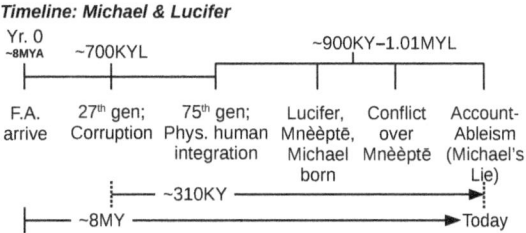

Figure 152. Timeline: First Ancestors (F.A.) to Accountableism (cf. Fig. 148:355). Mnèèptē is physical-born.

4.2.1.1 Sibling Rivalry

Sibling rivalry isn't a thing in spirit-born families as in the physical-born's, the reason being that none of its motivations here are there such as unwanted pregnancy, money, power, position, inheritance, their attendant pressure-oriented judgments, and so on. Not only were Michael and Lucifer the first brothers to fall out over a common lover but, until the Big Healing, they remained the only spirit-born siblings locked in such unremitting rivalry. It drove Accountableism from its inception until today and, despite Michael's Reveal and the Big Healing, is still resolving. If we want to talk about an actual Abel and Cain, it's these two. Accountableism is the underlying nature of Earth's monotheisms and drives the God–Man relationship. Yet, it's essentially just sibling rivalry writ large. Despite there being no such rivalry per se in spirit-born families, it exists nonetheless in all their societal relationships (including the family) in the form of Accountableism and The Corruption. It is, in actuality, the fundamental underlayment of both.

4.2.1.2 The Nature of Sibling Rivalry

Both spirit and physical societies are epidemic with Accountableism. This includes self-conflict and other conflict that results in verbal, physical, and Intentionalized ('energy') assaults; tattling and bickering which is the common behavior of religion and philosophy; competition for parental love and affection which is the nature of monotheism; and envy, jealousy, and like feelings that play out in all walks of life. In this dynamic, individuals present themselves as defenders of the faith, of justice, and of right while presenting the other as their antithesis. One upholds divine morality only because the other flaunts it. In every respect, human conflict *is* sibling rivalry. As it's not rooted in parental disaffection but The Corruption, its solution lies in resolving the latter. Michael and Lucifer accomplished this when they mutually eviscerated Accountableism, the revelation of which opened everyone's mind to its utter falsity and The Corruption's reality. The NCC's dissolution in this milieu gave Mina the opening he needed to lay it bare across a now-listening humanity in a single moment that shattered its hold and guillotined their mindset.

4.2.1.3 Why Their Relationship was Key to Humanity's Liberation

Michael and Lucifer's relationship is the starting point of Accountableism. Without it, The Corruption would've remained an individualized behavioral trait without transitioning to a mindset that eventually became Ultraculture. It wasn't a tangible reality, just a feeling present in the individual and their pairwise kinship. Accountableism gave it a structure, a construct in which individual traits morphed into a shared trait that formalized as a way of life, a universal woв, a sociocultural canon. Michael's Accountableism and Lucifer and Mina's inability to set the record straight engulfed universal humanity. When they reconciled—when the accuser accused himself—and humanity felt the crushing realization it'd been had, it wholesale rejected its mindset addiction and its woв began reverting to its absolutely autonomous norm.

It wasn't simply that Michael repented by accusing himself of the 'crime' of which he'd always accused Lucifer, but that Lucifer unreservedly forgave Michael. Only in their mutually rejecting the tenets of Accountableism did they expose it as an addiction and not a truth. Their repentance and forgiveness revealed the Divine Creator as a chimera. Mina, in a sense, became visible again, his sisters' mindset jamming dispelled (§ 2.1.2.2.1:371). Their mutuality was fundamentally a *healing* experience and it's only in this context of the healing cycle that repentance and forgiveness have any substantive meaning. Let's examine each of these behaviors.

4.2.1.3.1 Meaning of Repentance

In general, to repent means to feel sorrow, regret, or contrition for one's thoughts or actions along with a commitment to change and, sometimes, restitution. This is incorrect because it's selfish. It presumes one's sorrowful regret—this change in oneself—heals the aggrieved or expunges the harm. It focuses on 'me' feeling sorrow or regret, or possibly changing, but not on 'you' healing. Repentance, in Mina's view, means *taking responsibility for one's actions for the purpose of healing the aggrieved*. Whether a person feels genuine sorrow, regret, or contrition is irrelevant. If the penitent genuinely wants the aggrieved to heal from the pain for which they're responsible, then whatever they do toward that end *is* repentance. It's an act of reconciliation and contributes to healing. Therefore, repentance can't occur in isolation, as an individual act, but only in the context of reconciliation, as a mutuality. Repentance is part of the repentance–forgiveness healing cycle. It works within and between individuals and groups.

When Michael repented to Lucifer that Friday, October 2017 morning, it wasn't to express contrition, seek forgiveness, or expunge the harm with an 'I'm sorry,' but to heal Lucifer. That was Michael's fundamental motivation in that moment. However much traditional repentance he'd already gone through in his own heart to get to that point, conveying just that to Lucifer would've been meaningless. Lucifer didn't need to hear how much sorrow and regret Michael felt for his misdeeds, he needed to experience Michael's genuine desire that Lucifer feel healed from the pain and grief he'd caused. When Lucifer felt that, then he *did* heal and all he could do was *forgive*.

4.2.1.3.2 Meaning of Forgiveness

In general, to forgive means to cease feeling resentment toward an offender or a claim to requital (punishment). This is incorrect because it's selfish even more so than the general notion of repentance, the reason being that it's focused on the self in isolation. As psychology opines, releasing anger and resentment through forgiveness doesn't mean reconciliation. Traditional forgiveness has nothing to do with ending the physical or psychological cycle of violence. Forgiveness in Mina's view means *to accept another's actions for the purpose of healing the offender*. It's the other side of the repentance–forgiveness healing cycle. One forgives such that there are no obstacles to the offender experiencing healing. Recall the harm a person does ultimately arises in their trauma. Harmful people are traumatized. Forgiving, therefore, isn't simply letting go of one's own pain and suffering but *helping* an offender heal their trauma. Forgiveness–repentance is mutual. Repentance necessarily comes first but reconciliation requires both.

When Lucifer experienced Sun-myung unconditionally loving him despite religiously believing in his evilness (which in the late 1990s culminated in Sun-myung's proclamation that Lucifer had repented and returned to God), he felt so moved by Sun-myung's devotion to his healing that he felt able to forgive Michael in the traditional sense we understand forgiveness. This means he let go his anger and resentment, of the chains that bound him to his aggrievement. But it did nothing to heal the harm and reconcile them. It simply opened the door for Lucifer to live his life somewhat normally—recall he didn't yet know the true nature of Michael's harm—by sweeping his feelings under the rug, out of sight and out of mind. Primarily, it liberated him to resume his relationship with Mnèèptē and start a family. This kind of forgiveness doesn't heal a person. It only helps them be more functional. But it was a start. A pilot light if you will that eventually lit Michael's confession into a fire of reconciliation.

Traditional monotheism's understanding of God's forgiveness of Man is akin to Mina's version of everyday forgiveness. It's where the Christian concept of grace arises. God's grace in its fullest form is simply accepting the person as they are in the interest of their healing which, in the monotheistic context, means being capable of living consonant with God's Will. Forgiveness, like repentance, can be unilateral, but to achieve reconciliation both are necessary. God's grace is always there—His forgiveness ever-present—awaiting only Man's repentance to complete the healing cycle and bring reconciliation between Creator and created. But it's a flawed concept in that God's forgiveness precedes Man's repentance, implying reconciliation and healing is a formality, a mere legal squaring of accounts, not healing real pain.

4.2.1.3.3 Meaning of Reconciliation

At its simplest, to reconcile means to revive a relationship that has experienced harm (§ 1.1.1:362). It marks the end of estrangement from self or another individual or group. It's the end state of healing. Although reconciliation in its traditional use can occur absent healing, in its realest sense mutual healing only occurs through the cycle of forgiveness–repentance–reconciliation.

In Mina's view, reconciliation means *a harm is removed from existence in that, effectively, it never occurred*. This is the only state where substantive healing of the psyche occurs, more concisely represented as

$$\frac{|\text{Repentance}\rangle}{|\text{Forgiveness}\rangle} \to \Big(|\text{Reconciliation}\rangle\Big) = (\psi)\text{Healing} \qquad (24.4)$$

where (ψ) Healing is the end state of the aggregated ket system states (cf. § 6.11:191). That's the reason we were so surprised that Friday morning after Michael and Lucifer reconciled when El reported, "It's like the whole thing is just washed away" (§ 1.1:19) and Mina told us the NCC had dissolved and he was kicking off the Big Healing. Physical persons are used to harm lingering, to forgiving but not really ever forgetting and a harmed relationship never really returning to its pre-harm state in the way that trust lost is never truly restored. But that was exactly what we were seeing between Michael and Lucifer and it seemed—well, ever so anti-climactic. That's when we learned that, for Mina, everything is all about healing not judgment, punishment, rancor, or lingering negativity. Just full, absolute healing.

4.2.1.3.3.1 Representative Reconciliation isn't Possible

Reconciliation's true nature means that only an aggriever and aggrieved can reconcile, not representatives. Only the person or group who inflicted harm can repent of it and only the person or group harmed by it can forgive it to mutually achieve reconciliation thus healing. It isn't possible to reconcile descendants of aggrievers and aggrieved even if such aggrieving descendants committed the same harm from which such aggrieved descendants suffer the same. It's the same thing as Bob saying, "Judy, I apologize for Frank slapping Mona twenty years ago." Bob's so-called apology does nothing but sweep Frank's harm and Mona's hurt under a rug where Frank isn't contrite (repentful), Mona isn't absolvitory (forgiving), Bob didn't slap anyone (non-responsible), Judy wasn't slapped (harmed), and nothing is reconciled. Accordingly, modern day peoples can't repent of, forgive, nor reconcile historical harms but only let them go. The reason an individual can't make another person's harm their own, in that they can repent of or forgive it to achieve reconciliation thus healing, is because it fundamentally attempts to rewrite one's emergent uniqueness as individual *Life* into that of another unique *Life* where their inflicted or suffered harm is the individual's own and, accordingly, actionable.[443] This is impossible for the reasons described (§ 3.1.1:373). Only the person(s) who brings harm into existence and the person(s) on whom it's inflicted can remove it from existence because these are individually unique states of being (SOB) of responsibility and pain. Only then can reconciliation occur and the parties experience healing (§ 4.2.1.4:382).

---

443. This is why South Africa's Truth and Reconciliation Commission (1996–2003), which sought to resolve aggrievement over apartheid race relations—although historical in the sense that some victims and perpetrators were no longer alive, was also current with directly harmful and harmed whites and blacks—generally could work. It can never work in America, however, where there's been no organized racial harm since Souhern segregation and Northern discrimination ended in the 1960–70s. For America's *historical* slavery and segregation, current individuals can achieve healing by letting it go and accepting healing from Mina through physical or spirit healers for their own needs when ready, while historical perpetrators and victims living in spirit world can accept healing outside the context of physical world reality.

4.2.1.4 Why the NCC Disappeared upon Their Reconciliation

Humanity Intentionalized the NCC into existence out of 'neutral' proto-energy over time via Thought rooted in the mindset of The Corruption. Its presence influenced each person's mindset with its negative energy in the same way a person (like Mina's sisters) Intentionalizes proto-energy around individuals to foment particular mindstate responses, like a vibe that darkens a person's feelings. This happens because the mind, being self-aware proto-energy, is exquisitely sensitive to it. It's why negative EM⌁F can shift one's mood. Mina could never compete with the NCC because it arose out of humanity and permeated the universe and every mind within it. He couldn't simply re-Intentionalize it because it belonged to humanity, his descendants, who created it. This is the same principle that prevents a person from re-Intentionalizing anything another person creates through Intentionality. Thus, no person such as a member of the Cardinal can re-Intentionalize Mina's universe to suit his or her own preference. Neither can a person in spirit world re-Intentionalize, say, a cup of coffee Intentionalized by another person into a cup of motor oil (though one can Intentionalize the proto-energy around a person's tongue to elicit the *taste* of motor oil; pranking isn't exclusive to the physical).

Only humanity could re-Intentionalize the NCC's proto-energy that it had Intentionalized into existence into something else. Any individual could have done this because each individual is a part of the overall Intentionality. Jesus by himself could have but chose not to because, without Michael and Lucifer reconciling—who together embodied The Corruption in their Accountableist conflict more than any others in the population—the Ultraculture fueling humanity's mindset would have remained in place save for a momentary change in mindstate people would feel like an inexplicable mood blip, if they felt anything at all. In conversation with Mina, Jesus waited in the hope that Michael and Lucifer would reconcile to deliver a real end to the NCC, as finally happened (§ 40:613).

4.2.1.4.1 Michael and Lucifer Re-Intentionalize Our Universe

As noted, The Corruption was a personal mindset experience for individuals that only vaguely led them to forget their emergent WOB until Michael's Lie put structure to its nonautonomy and gave it a rationale sufficient to transform society into a concrete manifestation of The Corruption (§ 4.2.1.3:380). The Intentionality of all these minds in unison, which is Ultraculture, transformed the neutral proto-energy that permeates our universe into the NCC which acted as a massive repository for Intentionalized negative EM⌁F. Recall that Michael and Lucifer's fight in our living room the night of October 12, 2017 (§ 1.1:8) was so 'energetically' powerful from the intensity of their conflict and grief, which uniquely embodied the NCC, that it aroused the entire spirit world population. Similarly, their mindstates so focused and intensified their Thought in the moment of Reconciliation that altogether *it reached a state of Intentionality*, that single picosecond such as when Mina's Intentionality brought our universe into reality (§ 2.1.3.2:310).

This outcome represents the incredible depth of pain each was suffering in their conflict such that, when released, it energetically transformed akin to a nuclear bomb detonating in a small room. It was so powerful it *re-Intentionalized* the natural and supranatural Energent, the source of the NCC. Because it was specifically these two doing it—in that everyone knew something of their conflict or of Lucifer's alleged evil status, and Michael's Reveal had only just been such a mind-bending shocker—everyone's mind opened to transforming and thereby neutralizing the NCC. In this respect, it wasn't only Michael and Lucifer re-Intentionalizing the NCC but all of physicospirit humanity. These two merely fueled it analogous to the implosive shockwave compressing the nuclear material of an atom bomb to trigger detonation. All humanity joined the process, all in a picosecond. This is the raw power of the human mind.

4.2.1.4.2 Michael and Lucifer Became Co-creators of Our Universe

For Mina in the moment of Reconciliation, Michael and Lucifer became co-creators of our universe through their mutual Intentionality because they literally re-initialized the Energent back to its starting state the way one might re-initialize a malfunctioning computer operating system. Accordingly, Mina considers the universe he built no longer just his build but ours, too. It was a seminal moment.[444] And news to the Cardinal who, despite knowing the NCC was aberrant vis-à-vis Mina's founding Intentionality, didn't know it was possible for the inhabitants of a universe to collectively re-Intentionalize its Energent to a different state. This doesn't

---

444. None but Mina knew what they'd actually accomplished until we energy tested these details November 2, 2020. Lucifer and Michael were shocked. Mina said he hadn't even considered co-creatorship until we'd asked, but instantly acknowledged it.

mean universal humanity can change the structure, nature, or operability of a universe they didn't themselves Intentionalize, but it does mean we have full control over how our individual proto-energy Intentionalizes to directly influence humanity's collective mindstate and life. It also doesn't mean a 'missionary' can embody in someone else's universe and re-Intentionalize its Ultraculture to something different, for the same reason Jesus didn't attempt it here. To achieve the desired outcome, the mindstates of all its inhabitants must be open to the change in the way an implosive shockwave needs be perfectly spherical to achieve nuclear criticality. This means it is contributively Intentional.

4.2.2   What Their Reconciliation Means for You

Dissolving the NCC opened all humanity's mindsets to collective and individual change. It's more pronounced in spirit world where people have greater awareness of energy and reality overall, but physical humanity is feeling the change, too, according to individual sensitivity and conscious and subconscious awareness. Regardless each physical person's conscious awareness of spirit world, their spirit self knows the truth, even those whose spirit self is, for all intents and purposes, 'asleep,' believing their experience with spirit persons in the 'reflective' environment during periods of physical sleep are just dreams and inventions of the mind (§ 1.2.2.7.3:267). They feel the change because their minds are sensitive to 'energy,' which is the nature of the change triggered by the Reconciliation and Big Healing. A person's spirit self knows the truth, feels the change, and is undergoing transformation and healing even if their physical self is unaware. This means physical people's spirit selves are already accepting healing of their traumas even if it's physically slow and, to themselves or their fellows, unnoticeable. Consider if you've felt some unexplained sense of healing or a difference in your affect and SOB since 2018.

4.2.2.1   Earth is Ground Zero

Besides healing spirit persons, we've healed numerous physical individuals spiritually which they physically experienced as positive, noticeable changes in their affect, unusual fatigue (healing can be very tiring), a sense of liberation, and so forth. Earth is healing ground zero for three principal reasons. First, Michael and Lucifer's Reconciliation happened here. Second, this book is being energy tested and published here, which makes Earth the most spiritually advanced physical society in our universe in terms of comprehending spirit reality (though some other societies are more advanced than Earth in terms of spiritual orientation, hence, more peaceful). And third, real trauma healing is physically happening here. Eventually, all inhabited planets will experience this budding transformation.

4.2.2.2   The Reconciliation's Effect on Earth

Earth is now at a critical moment where the impetus toward absolute nonautonomy—tyranny—is grasping for the global hegemony it once held with Humanity 1.0, which never had a philosophy or socioculture like America or Americans to counter it. As noted, America alone represents in its national mindset humanity's emergent WOB of absolute autonomy even though it has mostly failed to live up to it (§ 2.1.1.5:353). It is autonomy's standard-bearer in our globalized society. But it teeters in peril on the edge of nonautonomy as it grabbles at the notion of harmlessness using coercive politics that mandate repudiating not just its Bill of Rights but its cornerstone of individual sovereignty to impose some variant of utopian State control over individual life, culture, and society. People's sense that America is nearly arrived at an existential crossroads isn't wrong. Its conservatives and liberals intensely feel it, reflected in oft-immoderate behavior that echoes a similar struggle in spirit world as mass healing disrupts its ancient nonautonomy. Belief in correct, valuable, and vital societal norms drives both sides, one which rests upon autonomy with a small risk of harm and one upon nonautonomy rooted in a desire to expunge all risk of harm while actually maximizing it as the means.

Until the Big Healing, events on Earth reflected the NCC's nature. People strove to implement coerced harmlessness—whomsoever it targeted as its actual beneficiaries—consonant with the NCC in accord with various ideologies from the family paterfamilias to tribal chieftain to Communism's first citizen. Those resisting this trend have been weak, mentally disorganized, or simply all too often co-opted because no one was immune to the NCC. Since the Big healing, events began moving toward a post-NCC environment. Americans (and the world) began experiencing a subconscious surge in totalitarianism—the same experienced in spirit world right after the Big Healing (since petered out)—from a harmlessness-promising 'Left' provoking in the 'Right' a resurgent grasp at freedom to reinvigorate America's founding principle of absolute autonomy (the 'national populism' surging in many nations; ibid). Just as people subconsciously resonate to the EmℒF embodied in music and lyrics, they're resonating to nonautonomous spirit world's resistance to autonomy's disruptive change as well as to the dissolution of the NCC, the growth of an Ultraculture of autonomy, and the healing of trauma sweeping spirit world inclusive of the dynamics and harm unique to the natural environment. Physical people are desperate for healing, though some more than others are afraid to let go their mindset of harmlessness and wreak new harm in the meantime.

For Mina, there's no going back. The NCC is no more. Humanity rediscovered its core, emergent WOB of autonomy and, individual by individual, is ineluctably embracing it. Despite the NCC and its Ultraculture of nonautonomy, individuals have always embraced or seized some degree of autonomy for themselves and sometimes for their loved ones, but always drew a line between their quite necessary own-self autonomy and everyone else's quite necessary nonautonomy. Post-NCC, spirit individuals are embracing not just their own but *humanity's* autonomy. Physical individuals will subconsciously (through their spirit self's awareness) catch on and catch up. The chaos endemic to physical society will diminish. All people, likely including you, are healing bit by bit and day by day as traumas heal and fall away like onionskins to liberate the self within.

4.3 MEANING OF THE BIG HEALING

Ever since Mina's two sisters weaponized Intentionality to manipulate our ancestors' emotions to insinuate The Corruption into their mindsets and shut Mina out of his own universe and the aggregated family life of his descendants, he's been at wit's end trying to reacquaint us with our birthright. That might not sound like such an all-powerful 'creator,' but that's because our notion of omnipotence is flawed, thinking the capability of manipulating proto-energy through Intentionality to build a universe conveys a consequent desire and capability to similarly manipulate emergent ⅃ife. Even nonautonomous humans are autonomous at their emergent core. Knowing this reality, *feeling* it at the root of his being, Mina could never use nonautonomous means like manipulation to restore human autonomy because, if he did, he'd only be exchanging one kind of nonautonomy for another just as revolutions ever only exchange the old tyranny for the new.[445]

The old saying that "a man convinced against his will is of the same mind still" applies here (Butler, *Hudibras*, § 1.2.1.2:251). Restoring autonomy is all about awareness, which is out of reach so long as The Corruption blinds individuals to reality, the autonomy of others, promotes harm and trauma, and necessitates healing that a person need but desire to experience. In this sense, restoring autonomy is really all about healing. No person can experience healing against their will, including without their awareness. This is the reason why healing modalities like Emotion Code emphasize the healee's permission. Mina consequently needed an 'in,' something to jolt humanity out of its self-conflictive, nonautonomous, and harmful condition to open its collective mind to the notion of real autonomy. He'd tried teaching, arguing, unconditionally loving, neutralizing 'energies,' broadcasting the truth for millions of years, all to no avail. Of course, he knew Michael's Lie was the trunk, branch, and leaf of The Corruption, well watered by humanity's mindset addiction to its desire for harmlessness. Though he'd tried to inspire Michael to come clean regarding Accountableism, it never jelled. Until in 1999, it did.

4.3.1 SUN-MYUNG MOON'S CONTRIBUTION

In the context of Sun-myung's Divine Principle theology of reversing the Fall of Adam and Eve, his absolute commitment to unconditionally loving Lucifer before all else, even God,[446] might seem the chesty ravings of a legend in his own mind. But recall that Thought is 'energy' (⅃ife force; § 3.2:282). That emanating from Sun-myung's unconditional love for Lucifer—Satan, Destroyer of Worlds, Great Deceiver, his own Professor Moriarty—wasn't mere lovey-dovey *feeling* or agape, but ardently desiring Lucifer's healing from his pain, which, in Divine Principle's context, brought about the motivation and process of the Fall (Moon 1996, 62–5).

---

445. The American Revolution, which might seem like the one exception in removing actual tyranny for real individual liberty, isn't. Its great leap forward was initially restricted to whites, cutting off black slaves from the mitigating influence of British antislavery laws and possibly Indians from other potential influence. America for the last 100 years morphed from that mixed bag closer to its ideal while zombie-walking into a gathering ideological tyranny undreamt of by the colonial British Crown.

446. The notion rests on Sun-myung's belief in the Cain–Abel dynamic where, to restore Cain's heart in order to restore Adam and Eve's Fall, Abel needs love Cain more than himself and his own family and especially more even than God, who loves Cain more than Himself (e.g., Moon 1990, par. 4). To Sun-myung, this meant that, in order to truly love God and thereby restore His heart broken in the Fall by resolving it, he had to love Cain-cum-Satan more than he did anyone, including God. He drew his example from Jacob's unconditional love for Esau more than his own goods, family, and even life when he offered Esau all he possessed (Gen. 33:1–10; Moon 1996, 219–20).

His consistent attitude had profound implications for Lucifer toward whom, in the real world context, few felt any good since Michael first tarred him. Sun-myung's attitude and Lucifer's traditional forgiveness of Michael (§ 4.2.1.3.2:380)—really just a personal letting-go of his grief and resentment—profoundly moved Michael. It motivated him finally to come to grips with all he'd done and its unforeseen and unintended consequences, to find a way to make it right. This ultimately placed him at Ayako-cum-Mnèèptē's sleeping bedside (§ 1.4:14) spilling his guts, not as a mea culpa but to heal his brother of all he'd done, and caused to be done, to him.

4.3.2 Mina's Field Goal

That was just the 'in' Mina needed. He 'broadcast' it and their whole exchange verbatim into every mind in our universe. The shock of it all did his work for him. In an instant, almost every spirit person knew they'd been had all the way back to Mina's sisters' skullduggery. Humanity suddenly hankered for its birthright. The reason Mina told us right after Michael and Lucifer's Reconciliation that he was beginning the Big Healing was because, to reclaim their birthright, everyone necessarily needs healing, starting with the emotive 'mind implants' his sisters had left behind like caltrops. From there, he recruited healers and healing facilitators (CH. 35:577) to heal each trauma every willing individual was ready to heal, one onionskin layer at a time. Through this process, absolute human autonomy and at-peace pairwise kinships and societies will eventually reemerge as humanity's dominant WOB in our universe. The more you embrace healing your pain and trauma, the more it naturally contributes to this development.

4.4 Effects of the Big Healing

To the average spirit-born person and about 20% of the physical-born now dead and living in spirit world, the Big Healing's effects are plain as day: healing and liberation from pain and trauma and reacquaintance with a forgotten WOB (recall *Obāsan*'s ecstatic, love-engulfed experience; § 1.2.2.1:31). Only a handful of the physical-born still physically living are aware of the Big Healing at all, though children conceived afterward who grow up in its milieu will, as a cohort, develop increasing awareness of it as well as greater mind–brain integration and awareness of the reality conveyed in this book (§ 1.2.2.5.1:261).

Besides the sheer effort and expenditure of energy in conducting the Big Healing, The Corruption had a profound effect on Mina, too. For example, while talking it over with him as I initially energy tested this chapter, he several times began weeping hard, once so deeply he couldn't even answer me. I just stood there waiting, my body wobbling and gyrating with his 'energy.' But it wasn't grief nor *han* (한; 恨; § 4:345) because Mother—P'najj—had stepped in after the Big Healing and healed his trauma. It's just the memories themselves that carry a lot of emotional juice. When he brings them up, they recreate all their emotional 'energy' in him. Recall that memories aren't simply factoids and remembrances but states of being (SOB), which is 'energy' (§ 1.2.2.4.2:258). When he, like any of us, experiences 'energy' that matches a memory's SOB, then he experiences that SOB and resonates with its 'energy.' Its every aspect arises in his mind, including its EM∠F. His weeping wasn't sad, sorrowful, or grieving; Mother had healed him of the associated traumas. He was simply feeling emotively overpowering memories from me digging deep into the backstory of our universe and his and humanity's experience with The Corruption. I experienced the same response from Sun-myung when talking seriously with him about his physical life.

SECTION 5
Conclusion to Part III

This chapter concludes PART III. If there's one thing that stands out, it's that that every notion we've ever imagined about human origins, the 'creator' of our universe, and the reason physical human society is so fraught with conflict and unhappiness despite our desperation for peace and harmony is entirely inaccurate. Composing this chapter wasn't the 14-month slog that SPACE INFINITY was, but it was still a difficult four months of energy testing and writing. It upended all our previous notions, as I'm sure it has yours. Even so, without the divinity, Accountableism, and fear, we can see our universe is an infinitely customizable physicospirit environment that every individual can enjoy to its fullest in complete autonomy. Now all we have to do is catch up Earth to the events transforming spirit world society.

We've covered an incredible amount of ground in PARTS II and III. When Mina commissioned us to write this book that fateful October Friday morning in 2017, the girls and I had absolutely no inkling how wide ranging it would turn out to be. We imagined it would be something like the many spirit-world and I-talked-to-God books saturating the bookstores except that, unlike them, actually verifiable by readers via ET. Well, we can only look back and laugh at ourselves now. Even Mina didn't expect much more than about a 175,000-word manuscript. Yet, here we are right now at close to 290,000 words with Parts IV, V, and an epilogue still to go! The reason isn't just that I'm verbose. If we weren't able to answer at least to our satisfaction all our questions and concerns and resolve the contradictions and conflicts that arose, then what was the point of writing it? If nothing else, we had to have a legitimate belief in its veracity. Otherwise, we'd be just one more fraud in the genre's constellation of frauds.

So far, this book has been a hard-hitting autopsy of human belief and reasoning. We'll have a better grasp of its accuracy as the future energy-testing community builds up a compendium of validation, and future generations achieve fuller mind–brain integration. Now that the autopsy is largely over, we can move on to more worldly woo-woo affairs in PART IV where we describe most major aspects of human life upon which Philosophy with a capital-P and the spirituality genre has ever weighed in—including testimonies of historical figures—toward connecting all we've learned so far with our everyday reality and personal concerns.

Part IV

...And Us

The Environments in Which We Live

WHILE PART II describes the overall nature of the physical universe, PART III describes the more unseen aspect of human reality: where and how humanity emergently birthed, how we humanized All Existence, who the builder of our phenomenal, physicospirit universe is, and why human society is what it is when we have this ingrained sense that, ideally, we're so much more. Having set the stage upon which we live out our lives, you're now in a position to understand why certain aspects of our everyday life are what, and as, they are. PART IV is the final informational portion of this book. Remember, this isn't your typical I-talked-to-God woo-woo book that you need take on faith or dismiss out of hand. You can verify all of it to your own satisfaction to the degree you master energy testing and develop your intuitive senses, which we teach you to do in PART V.

We divide PART IV into two overall sections that group our everyday life experience into those aspects relevant to all human beings. The first regards *environment* and the second those aspects relevant to the individual behavioral choices of *people*. We preview them in the table of contents, below.

Contents *Environment*

The Conscious–Subconscious Mind

AS PHYSICAL PEOPLE, we tend to think our phenomenal environment defines absolute reality. But that's a distraction. Our *mind* is the real environment in which we exist because that's where we *experience* phenomenal reality. Phenomenality is a very small part of individual human reality. When we think of mind being as infinite—indeterminate—as space, yet the physicospirit universe being existentially static where mind is functionally dynamic, we see that, unlike a universe, the very nature of mind is always in flux. And, after all, mind creates universe. The phenomenal universe is a real extension of mind because we can mold it to our will like a universe builder or the way humanity Intentionalized the Negative Collective Consciousness (NCC; § 4.2.1.4:382). We live consciously mired in phenomenal reality, severed from the fullness of *L*ife and unable to imagine it beyond physical embodiment. We build relationships, societies, and knowledge rooted only in what our bodies can sense. We interact with others without regard for our physicospirit reality, boxing ourselves into the here and now of physical survival. We live not *like* animals but *as* animals, and science concludes we're just the cleverest of the kind. But we're not. Animals, that is. Though we think our body is literally *us*—the person we are—they're just 'avatars' (§ 1.1:561). We blithely discount mind as a mystery of brain the way religion discounts reality as a mystery of faith.

If you sit down, close your eyes, just let your thoughts roam, you tend to lose track of your physical environment till it has no bearing on what's happening in your mind. You could genuinely be on Saturn. Until you open your eyes, anyway. The physical environment materially affects your body, but not your mind. It experiences what your physical body encounters just as it does what your spirit body supranaturally encounters. And, too, mind encounters itself; it experiences what it conjures. When you're imagining yourself on Saturn, you're experiencing Saturn as your mind creates it; its physical reality is immaterial. For mind, experience *is* reality. People imagining themselves on a peaceful tropical beach open their eyes not having *imagined* themselves refreshed, calmed, or relaxed but authentically feeling, *experiencing*, it. This chapter describes mind w.r.t. its nature and experience because that's our true reality. It's what we actually experience, not phenomenality which we only encounter (§ 1.1.1:362). Mind's emergent nature is that it constitutes of those aspects traditionally termed subconscious and conscious. It's undulant experience is literally all there is to the person. You are what you experience, not what you encounter.

SECTION 1
Nature of Mind

Mind is different from psyche (consciousness). It's an *expression* of psyche but not psyche itself. *You* as a person, as *H*uman (Introduction, CH. 19:245), aren't your mind in the way humanity has traditionally encountered it but simply *L*ife itself; in essence, *emergent self-aware proto-energy* (*Fig. 153*). At its most fundamental, *L*ife is self-aware but not self-reflective. The latter is mind's job, which your *L*ife self, your self-aware beingness,

Intentionalizes into reality soon after emergent birth (§ 2.2.1:395). We therefore necessarily distinguish between self-aware beingness—psyche (consciousness), though not exactly—and mind. We *are* psyche but express wholistically *as* mind via its conscious and subconscious aspects. We describe their natures below but, as a lead-in to it, we need first describe the distinctions in mind's 'energy.'

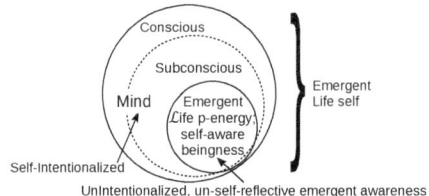

Figure 153. Schematic: wholistic, emergent *L*ife self that Intentionalizes mind (Fig. 161:432, Fig. 155:396).

1.1 THE MIND'S NEUTRAL AND GROSS 'ENERGIES'

Mind is emergent self-aware proto-energy; literally, an Energent having *L*ife (§ 1.2.1.1.1:248). Proto-energy's natural state of being (SOB)[447] is 'neutral' (not as in applied energy *E*; § 3.3.3.1.1:289). The mind, therefore, is fundamentally *neutral* subconscious proto-energy that Intentionalizes as *gross* conscious proto-energy that, conceptually, is strongly analogous to gross and fine motor control. Let's consider that.

1.1.1 NEUTRAL 'ENERGY'

Gross motor skill is the first muscular control a physical baby learns before its *L*ife mind is capable of voluntary thought, where he or she is learning to control their embodiment. The infant mind is not yet able to Intentionalize its state of awareness (SOA) and consequent SOB, like Mike and Molly right after their emergent birth (§ 2.1:305). Infantile gross motor skills aren't the result of brain, but mind, immaturity. A physical baby appears to react with primitive reflex but, in reality, its mind is experiencing its environment (inclusive of body) and forming a SOA to which it forms a SOB that results in its physical expression, such as responding to stimulus. The baby has no conscious awareness of either its SOA or its gross motor movements. These happen as a function of fundamental self-awareness (subconsciousness). As the infant mind builds awareness, it first builds its ability to translate, or Intentionalize, its neutral, subconscious 'energy' (which has awareness of its reality as a SOB) to an Intentionalized SOA that forms a SOB which results in voluntary muscle (fine motor) control; the conscious, voluntary use of the body.

What the foregoing means is the subconscious is mind in its purest form having only *unIntentionalized awareness* of itself and reality. If you've read Psyche Infinity (ch. 19:245), you understand awareness in this respect isn't cognition—the Intentionalized awareness of conscious mind—but a wholistic SOA. The way awareness experiences its SOB constitutes its SOA that, according to the SOB incident to any aspect of its SOA—physical stimulus, awareness of a particular reality—forms conscious mind's SOB and SOA.

We don't think with our subconscious in the way we typically interpret thinking. Awareness happens far too fast for such thinking to occur; hence, the term. Subconscious mind is proto-energy and operates in that milieu just as so-called quantum entanglement (Parity, which is awareness) happens instantaneously over any distance 'within' the Energent (§ 6.11:191). This is why a person can experience instant awareness of something. Mind forms an instant SOA to its reality and just as instantly that subconscious SOA Intentionalizes as *gross* energy, which forms a particular SOA and SOB in our conscious mind of Thought. Neutral subconscious and gross conscious is wholistic mind.

1.1.2 GROSS 'ENERGY'

We can think of gross energy as a heavily retarded neutral (subconscious) 'energy,' which means it constitutes from segmented SOA and SOB that individually Intentionalize out of the neutral subconscious such that it's capable of being utilized as Thought. There are two aspects to conscious mind. First, there's an underlayment of sorts that forms our entire conscious beingness, and second, a fully parsed Thought environment that forms our *focal* awareness. We describe each.

---

447. If you're unclear on states of awareness (SOA) and states of being (SOB), see § 1.2.2.1:253.

1.1.2.1 CONSCIOUS UNDERLAYMENT: SUB-THOUGHT ENVIRONMENT

This aspect of conscious mind provides all the material for our conscious Thought to draw upon which, recall, is thinking–feeling (§ 2.3.2:240). Our thinking and emotional expression consciously arises here, although its emotive energy (EmℒF) arises in our subconscious SOA and SOB. Everything our mind experiences in its subconscious (neutral) aspect reposits here in individual SOA and SOB like a reservoir, similar to the way individual neuronal action potentials aggregate into a SOB 'reservoir' from which the brain draws to form an aggregate action potential that ultimately provokes a brain–body response (§ 1.2.2.1:253). When a person is thinking or emoting, they draw all its Thought aspects from this aspect of conscious mind. The nature of this aspect is what we call *sub-Thought*.

1.1.2.2 THOUGHT ENVIRONMENT

This aspect of conscious mind's nature is *Thought*. This is what we think of w.r.t. thinking and feeling. Thoughts and feelings take form in the Thought environment where all SOB combine and recombine to form an overall SOA that we call our self, mindset, mood, attitude, and so forth at any given moment. It's where we engage our so-called inner voice, which is nothing more than conscious mind experiencing itself. It's impossible to think of mind in terms of cognition (§ 2.1:276). Mind is proto-energy that experiences reality as awareness. It's so fast and wholistic it defies real description with a vocabulary limited by our inurement to comprehending everything solely in biomechanical terms where consciousness is brain. To understand the conscious and subconscious we need develop a wholistic awareness of mind, which means comprehending it in its natural habitat of proto-energy that's emergently self-aware. We term this wholistic understanding *experience of mind*, to which we now turn.

SECTION 2
Experience of Mind

2.1 SUBCONSCIOUS MIND

Our subconscious is who we are, our who-ness (§ 2.1.1.1:368). It constitutes about 99.99% of our wholistic mind despite the notion that mind is 5–10% visible iceberg with 90–95% hidden subsurface. We're used to thinking our conscious mind is our conscious*ness*, who we are. But that's an inaccurate observation born of our inability to perceive our physicospirit reality. All of our thinking–feeling originates as a wholistic SOB and SOA in the subconscious that Intentionalizes literally infinite SOB and SOA to the conscious mind where we parse them into Thought. Subconscious awareness is not just too fast for our brain to operate on, but its mode of awareness is incompatible with the brain's functionality of cognition, thus requiring transliteration from one environment to the other (§ 2.1:276).

Because The Corruption interfered with mindset and, ultimately, mind–brain integration—transliteration—we experience a mental blindness as well as a structural limitation in the brain that limits awareness and how much of one's mind can integrate the brain at any given moment (§ 1.2.2.5:261). The practical result is that we're cut off from the fullness of ℒife and unable to experience most of our own SOA. This isn't a permanent condition. Mina's been rectifying it since the Big Healing (§ 1.2.2.5.1:261) and, with that, our ever-plastic brain restores the necessary neural structure long ago discarded (§ 1.2.2.5.2:262).

2.1.1 OUR CONSCIOUS AWARENESS OF THE SUBCONSCIOUS

An individual ideally has full awareness of their mind, hence total control. We're not intrinsically the victims of so-called subconscious sabotage, primitive animal brainstem reflexes, drives, impulses, or emotions having a life of their own. Our bodies are purpose-built 'avatars' for emergent ℒife over which we're capable of absolute integration. Everything we think, feel, experience, and have awareness of in the physical world arises in and emanates from mind, regardless our conscious awareness of it.

Recall from DISCOVERING LOVE (§ 2.1.5.4.6:319) that conscious mind is analogous to a water spider on the surface of deeper, subconscious waters, separated from conscious awareness of it by the water's surface tension, which is like mindset. Below the surface is who one really is—really feels, wants, perceives own-self and its environment—that's generating all the currents, eddies, temperatures, and energies the water spider only dimly perceives in its surface reality unless the deeper environment's SOB agitates its placid footing (a person vis-à-vis society is similar). Conscious mind is generally aware of only itself, not the depths from which it springs, because of its many segmented SOB and SOA upon which we focus awareness.

But don't think that unlocking human physiological perfection reveals all. Even if one has 100% conscious awareness of their subconscious, its infinite nature means it's always beyond the scope of awareness that conscious mind can experience. No matter how much more conscious awareness of it one develops, there yet remains infinite unawareness of self. One fully experiences the subconscious only in the naturally segmental conscious mind. That's the awesome emergent experience of *your* mind.

2.1.2 THE SUBCONSCIOUS IS DEDUCTIVE IN NATURE

The subconscious is deductive. Its awareness—not reasoning, recall—moves from the general to the particular, from premise to specifics. This is opposite the inductive nature of conscious mind (§ 2.2:395). But keep cognizant that the subconscious doesn't engage in thinking–feeling (Thought; for the remainder of this book we use these terms interchangeably), that's conscious mind's way of being (WOB; § 2.2.1.1:234). It simply has awareness of everything the self encounters. Conscious mind operates vis-à-vis the subconscious the way the brain operates vis-à-vis wholistic *Life* mind (§ 2.1:276).

The subconscious should be as consciously accessible as what we'd normally consider our conscious awareness. The Corruption caused us to Intentionalize the NCC, which brought about a generalized negative thinking–feeling and produced dysfunction in the psyche not to mention of our universe generally. For example, one has greater awareness of the subconscious when energy testing because one accesses different aspects of mind 'energy' according to how one tests. There's an analogy between (neutral and gross) mind 'energy' and (hand, finger, sway) energy testing. Sway (push) testing is a gross motor skill anyone can achieve right out of the gate, presuming their chakras are 'open' (§ 1.2:634). Hand testing takes more sensitivity to 'energy' and finger and mind testing a more refined sensitivity still (§ 2.2.1.2:629–§ 2.2.1.3:629). One's conscious mind can develop exquisite sensitivity not only to ambient 'energy' but to that of subconscious mind as well. A person can develop a functional awareness of their subconscious and no longer be in the dark regarding the origin of their thinking–feeling nor endure experiences like self-sabotage.

2.1.3 MIND'S TRANSLITERATIVE NATURE

The bottom line here is that *you are not your conscious mind*, which is the environment of your experience, inner voice, and thinking–feeling. *You are your subconscious*, which is the environment of your awareness, ideas, drive, ambition, and WOB. Your conscious mind transliterates your subconscious awareness to conscious cognitional beingness just as your brain transliterates your wholistic mind's awareness into the brain's cognitive beingness (§ 1.2.2.4:257; § 2.6:402). Mike and Molly discovered that mind–brain integration is patterned on the nature of emergent mind (§ 2.1.5:313). The cognitional beingness we're talking about here isn't the cognitive *mental process* of knowing as with the brain (§ 2.1:276), but that which *comes to be known*, not as a product of a mental process but of awareness (*American Heritage*, s.v. 1, 2 'cognition'). Conscious awareness differs from subconscious awareness in that the former is awareness of infinite segmented SOB and SOA whereas the latter is awareness of an individual's wholistic SOB and SOA.

2.1.4 WHY SUBCONSCIOUS IS BETTER TERMED *Enimerótis*

The subconscious is emergently self-aware. It's not the same thing as the conscious. The fundament of Ⴙuman is subconsciousness. A person is simply pure awareness. There is no thinking, feeling, or self-reflection in that. There's only awareness that forms a SOB and SOA. It is self-aware but not cognitive. It's an emergent *Life* being that's *aware* of itself and reality, aware of its awareness, and aware that it's aware of its awareness, but it doesn't self-reflect (§ 1.2.2.1:253). Conscious mind does the self-analysis because it transliterates wholistic subconscious SOB and SOA into small, segmented SOB and SOA that are operable. It's similar to reducing a problem unsolvable in its entirety to many small, solvable ones. This means it cognizes the singular, wholistic SOB and SOA that is subconscious as its many constituent SOB–SOA aspects such that it can analyze, self-reflect upon, think–feel about, and mix and match them. Think of your subconscious mind like an infinite reservoir from which your conscious mind is constantly sipping, tasting, experiencing, interpreting, thinking–feeling, and so forth its full flavor, not simply that of the sip but of the entire reservoir that's embodied in the individual sip. Each sip constitutes a focal awareness in the context of wholistic awareness. Subconscious–conscious is wholistic mind (Fig. 154).

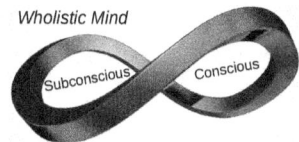

Figure 154. Infinite, wholistic mind is subconscious and conscious.[269]

The subconscious, coined by Pierre Janet (*De l'Automatisme Psychologique* 1889; d. 1947), isn't simply that part of the mind not presently in focal awareness, nor that part operating outside of conscious*ness* as in Freud's repressed *unconsciousness* or Josef Breuer's (d. 1925) latent *preconsciousness*. It's simply the person in their absolute awareness. There is indeed repressed awareness in one's psyche, awareness one doesn't want focal. This is the 'choice' of the subconscious because of the sob, or awareness, of a particular 'energy' experience. Whatever the reason—and they are many and varied—one's fundamental 𝔥uman self doesn't 'want' to re-experience its 'energy' in any form, not even in self-reflection toward healing.

The reason Freud and others find it so difficult to pry loose such sob toward a person consciously experiencing them is that the person's fundamental self resists and their conscious self, being a wholistic part of their own mind, reconciles to it (§ 2.2.2.1:396). Accordingly, the subconscious and conscious operate together to express the whole self. When psychologists push patients to discover the roots of their problems, they are in effect persuading the conscious to look for and dredge the relevant sob out of an unwilling, though ultimately persuasible, subconscious. This isn't new to psychology. What is new is the subconscious not being simply a homeostatic device or reservoir of repressed, lost, or uncontrollable experiences, but the person's fundament, the root of Thought. Emotion Code has a sense of this, which is why its modality attempts to bypass conscious mind to draw information of self directly from the subconscious (although it doesn't; § 1.3:22; § 2.1.1.2.1:369; ch. 35;577).

The conceptuality embodied in the term *subconscious* is hopelessly out of touch with the reality of mind since the self is the subconscious that's only writ into a self-analytical soa that Philosophy with a capital-p calls *consciousness*. As noted, one's conscious awareness isn't self but only an aspect of it. What, then, do we call this fundamental aspect of the human person if the terms *subconscious, unconscious,* and *preconscious* are inaccurate and unserviceable? The so-called subconscious is pure awareness and we could certainly call it 'awareness mind' but that's not quite accurate. Mina opted for *enimerótis* (ενημερότης), a Greek word for 'awareness' that he feels more essentially conceptualizes, in our available vocabularies, subconscious pure awareness. Thus, he recommends a shift away from the *sub-, un-, non-,* and other variants which imply wrong understandings of human, to *enimerótis* which implies a more accurate one. Moreover, since conscious mind implies nothing about its fundamental wob of experience, he recommends a shift from 'conscious' to the Greek *empeiría* (εμπειρία; 'experience'). Henceforward then, we can think of mind as wholistically *enimerótis–empeiría,* or 'awareness-experience.' However, because the *sub-, un-,* and *non-* terms are so ingrained in the literature as well as the popular mind, we don't eradicate them completely from this book. But keep in mind they're altogether *enimerótis.*

2.2 Conscious Mind

Unlike (self-contained) subconscious mind, the fundamental experience (*empeiría*) of conscious mind is that through which one experiences other minds and phenomenal reality whether or not we're embodied.

2.2.1 Origin of Conscious Mind

Conscious mind isn't conscious*ness* (§ 2.1.4:394). Instead, one's emergent ℒife self—one's true, self-aware beingness—Intentionalizes (creates) mind, the subconscious–conscious, as its interface with All Existence, our external-to-mind 'energy' reality inclusive of other minds and phenomenal universes. This is the fundamental experience of mind. Without it, a person would have awareness of only one's own self and naught else. A human would be fundamentally of singular rather than pairwise existence (§ 2:304).

A person literally creates their own subconscious–conscious mind out of their self-aware proto-energy self (*Fig. 155*) as an aspect of fundamental wob within about three months of emergent birth, which in practical terms means three months after physical or spirit conception (§ 1.2.1:247). We identify the person up to this ~3-month point as a *fetal human* who is unaware of its existence, reality, and environment albeit *is* self-aware. It's important to note that *emergent ℒife is fully human from emergent birth.* The fetal human isn't less than human or pre-human—lacking human wob—just because it's as yet unaware of its existence in reality nor Intentionalized its mind interface. On the contrary, the self-aware person is complete in all respects at the very instant of emergent birth, having eternal, self-aware beingness and absolute autonomy (human WOB ; ibid; Abortion, § 2.2:410). The post-fetal person is *cognitional* human.

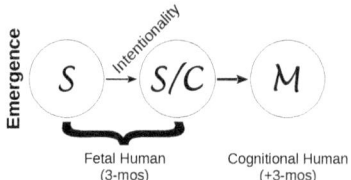

Figure 155. Emergent *Life* self (S) emergently Intentionalizes subconscious–conscious mind (S/C) where the ∼3-month fetal human transitions to 3-month-plus cognitional human (M).

Mind is like a universe with its dual environment in the context of one's emergent *Life* self, which itself is like All Existence (§ 2.3.2:240). Just as a builder Intentionalizes a universe out of proto-energy to therein experience external-to-mind phenomenal reality—All Existence being its own kind of phenomenality—via the interface of embodiment, one's subconscious Intentionalizes SOB and SOA as a foundation upon which conscious mind experiences external-to-subconscious-mind reality. The subconscious Intentionalizes a portion of itself—in 'spatial' terms relevant to proto-energy for which, at present, we lack vocabulary (§ 6.11.4:198)—to have awareness of external-to-mind 'energies.' Mind experiences its environment as awareness of 'energy' conceptually similar to how a bat has environmental awareness via echolocation.

2.2.2   Conscious Mind is Inductive in Nature

Conscious mind is the retarded (slowed-down) *aspect* of subconscious mind. It's not a separate mind or a version of the subconscious, it's an aspect of self experiencing subconscious awareness of external-to-mind 'energies.' This makes it discriminatory as a function of its WOB between 'energies' as a means to comprehend them whereas subconscious has awareness of all 'energies.' From conscious mind's discriminatory WOB arises its analytical WOB that constitutes Thought, which we're used to as the foundational capabilities of mind. The subconscious has awareness of all that conscious mind encounters.

To express its discriminatory WOB, conscious mind Intentionalizes with an inductive WOB, which means reasoning from detailed facts to general principles, from specifics to a premise. In other words, rather than experiencing a wholistic awareness of its environment the way the subconscious has awareness, it segments it into discrete *experiences* of awareness. Where the subconscious doesn't act on any particular SOB and SOA associated with some discrete experience of awareness but rather has individual, discrete SOB and SOA as a wholistic awareness, conscious mind acts on *each* discrete experience of awareness it encounters. This *acting* is what constitutes thinking–feeling.

Because the subconscious and conscious are altogether mind, what conscious mind encounters—its awareness of it, how it experiences it—is all as intimately known to the subconscious as it is to conscious mind. But the subconscious doesn't actually experience external-to-mind reality, it only has awareness of that experienced by conscious mind. This means the subconscious forms its own SOB and SOA of each experience of which conscious mind is aware. Its awareness of conscious mind's experience may or may not differ from conscious mind's own because, while conscious mind is in practice *a part* of its environment, the subconscious isn't. It has no interaction *with*, only awareness *of*, its environment. Because both 'minds' constitute a singular being, then some reconciliation between awareness and experience is necessary for a singular being to have a singular SOB and SOA. Let's consider that.

2.2.2.1   Reconciling Subconscious and Conscious Minds

An ideal human being is a person of singular SOB–SOA. There are no internal contradictions between how one experiences external-to-mind reality and own-self as well as conscious experiences relative to own-self. Below, we consider two ways that one's mind reconciles a dichotomy arising amongst it.

2.2.2.1.1   Conscious Thought Exerts Change on the Subconscious

When conscious mind has awareness of a particular reality the subconscious experiences differently or contrarily to conscious mind, it acts to persuade the subconscious to its own perspective. An example is an individual consciously realizing their subconscious is self-sabotaging their conscious intention. One need act to address subconscious awareness until it achieves a SOB consistent with conscious mind's SOB.

A real life example is Mina informing me in late 2017 that my subconscious had been Intentionalizing early-onset dementia since 1989. It hadn't achieved diagnosability yet, but was nonetheless causing increasingly significant short-term memory disruptions. The reason my subconscious—which is closest to my true emergent 𝓛ife self, my core beingness as an emergent person—was reacting this way arose in the sub-Thought underlayment of my conscious mind's (§ 1.1.2.1:393) profound unhappiness with life. This was owing to life-negating experiences that led to my constantly asking God why he kept me alive and wishing life would just hurry up and get itself over with. In the Thought environment of my conscious mind (§ 1.1.2.2:393), I felt normal. I enjoyed life, challenges, love, my children. But deeper down, I felt profoundly fed up with it all, leading me to habitually complain and find fault with life, often unaware it was even coming out of my mouth. This fed-upness led my subconscious to exert Intentionality in consonance with my conscious mind's sub-Thought such that I'd forget my painful, traumatic, suffering experiences and hasten Alzheimers thus physical death and was, apparently, what I really wanted deep down but couldn't consciously admit much less act upon (via suicide).

When I discovered (and the girls ET confirmed) this, I was terribly shocked. It made no sense to me. I was outraged at my subconscious, which I now viewed adversarially. Mina schooled me in the dynamic at work. Ayako routinely reminded me, "This is how you really feel about yourself, Dad, so just accept it or change it." I embarked on a process of healing, asserting my conscious Thought Intention to live without early-onset dementia. Intentionality lies with the subconscious, not the conscious, mind. On its own, despite my unhappiness originating in my conscious sub-Thought, only the subconscious exerts Intentionality. It then expresses into external-to-mind reality via the Intentionalized capability of conscious mind (§ 3.2:282). I reconciled my sub-Thought and Thought with my subconscious until, after four months, Mina reported it had ceased Intentionalizing dementia. I then spent about two months learning to harness my subconscious to reverse the damage. That took 20 months before Mina reported the damage healed. My children recognized it. This is far beyond simply ending self-sabotage.

2.2.2.1.2   SUBCONSCIOUS INTENTIONALITY EXERTS CHANGE ON CONSCIOUS MIND

The above process is how my subconscious awareness and conscious sub-Thought exerted change in my environment by Intentionalizing changes in my brain leading to pre-diagnosable early-onset dementia. It's true that when I discovered the cause of my memory issues I was angry and rejected it out of hand. But until that moment, my subconscious had brought my conscious mind's Thought and sub-Thought into harmony with it such that, as a wholistic person, I had a consistent attitude toward life as something to negate. Building on the self-sabotage example above, one's subconscious influences conscious mind to think, feel, act, and embody the subconscious experience and not that of conscious mind's totality of its real world environment (*Fig. 156*) even when it contradicts conscious mind's sub-Thought and Thought. This is the reason we can't do things we tell ourselves we want to do, or do things we tell ourselves we don't want to do. In all cases, wholistic mind is achieving reconciliation in resolving internal inconsistency in accord with our fundamental experience of awareness, whether arising first in Thought, sub-Thought, or the subconscious (§ 2.3:398).

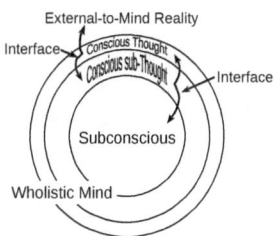

Figure 156. Conscious sub-Thought interfaces twixt subconscious and wholistic conscious mind (sub-Thought and Thought); conscious Thought interfaces twixt wholistic mind and external-to- mind reality.

Recall the emergent 𝓛ife self, a self-contained, self-aware proto-energy being (EPL; § 2.3.2.1:241), is discrete w.r.t. to the proto-energy around it in the same way an archí, constituting non-aware proto-energy, is discrete w.r.t. to the proto-energy around it (the Energent; § 2.3:115). Its beingness, therefore, can't directly experience external-to-mind reality any more than can the proto-energy contained within the archí shell. An interface is necessary. The archí's interface is the 'energetic' woв of its 'shell' that interacts through motion with proto-energy (§ 6.8:174). Similarly, we can think of the subconscious–conscious mind as the 'shell' that encapsulates the ℘erson—the self-aware being having ℒife—which, owing to its Intentionalized woв, interfaces wholistic mind with external-to-mind reality.

The conscious sub-Thought aspect of conscious mind altogether reflects wholistically subconscious and conscious Thought's soв–soa. Because these soв and soa wholistically integrate, there can be no dichotomy even if there is between these and conscious Thought's soв–soa. For example, if a person consciously experiences (thinks–feels) abc about something but subconsciously has awareness of it as xyz then, absent any effort on the individual's part to persuade their subconscious to conscious Thought's abc thinking–feeling, the subconscious exerts on conscious sub-Thought the Intentionality that naturally arises in its xyz awareness. This has the effect of influencing the individual to think–feel in xyz terms in sub-Thought, and any thoughts, feelings, and actions not focused on conscious Thought's abc thinking–feeling will be subconscious xyz awareness. This gives rise to our tendency to do or say things 'without thinking' to which we blurt, "I don't know why I just did [said] that," or to experience our conscience, and so on. This is how one *really* thinks–feels when conscious Thought isn't running interference.

2.3 THE ORIGIN OF CONSCIENCE

Whereas the nature of conscious mind is Thought and of conscious underlayment sub-Thought, the nature of conscience is awareness because it arises in the subconscious. Conscience isn't a divine gift, the voice of God, or a moral compass. It's simply an individual's subconscious soв–soa informed by awareness of their environment filtered through sub-Thought's enculturated values (whether of society generally or the individual specifically; § 4:291)—that consciously manifests as Thought.

2.3.1 HOW CONSCIENCE ARISES

Recall the human person is fundamentally self-awareness that manifests as *enimerótis* (subconscious awareness). One is aware of their environment's 'energy' directly via the subconscious. The subconscious has awareness of its environment in proto-energy terms (including applied energy E and real energy Υ; § 2:114), not in material terms. Conscious mind perceives, thus experiences, its environment whereas the subconscious simply has awareness of it. Everything exists as 'energy.' Some physicospirit aspect of environment isn't, for example, just temperature, hunger, thinking–feeling, death, or whatever, but Intentionalized proto-energy. When one eats food, kills something, enjoys sex, feels love or hate, and so on, those experiences of one's conscious mind are, for the subconscious, nothing more than proto-energy of which it's aware. In wholistic mind, this awareness interacts with sub-Thought (§ 1.1.2.1:393), which is where one's mindset—moral and other values, perspectives, felt harm and trauma, and the like—interacts with conscious mind where sub-Thought manifests as Thought in everyday experience.

Conscience is the product of subconscious awareness and conscious Thought in the context of sub-Thought. In practice, this means all aspects of sub-Thought experience the 'energy' of which one has awareness. 'Energy' is unique to everything. An archí's 'energy' differs from every other. An action's 'energy' differs from that of other actions. A person's specific experience of a specific thing differs from their experience of any other specific thing. For example, the 'energy' of a person loving a certain taste of food differs from that of their very next taste of that very same food; that of a person experiencing being killed differs throughout the killing event (§ 2.1:407). Because 'energy' differs moment to moment, one's subconscious awareness (soв–soa) also differs moment to moment. Conscience arises in the individual in consequence of having awareness of 'energy.' Let's look at the true nature of conscience.

2.3.2 CONSCIENCE IS THE EXPERIENCE OF AWARENESS

Since the subconscious only has awareness of proto-energy, it doesn't actually *experience* anything. Yet, experience is fundamental to human woв. Therefore, subconscious mind partners with conscious mind, the woв of which is experiential (§ 2.2.1:395). Both are a weak emergent of self-awareness; as wholistic mind, they're a predictable consequence of emergent ℒife. The self doesn't 'create' conscious mind as if it had a will to do so. Rather, subconscious–conscious mind emergently arises in the self because that's human woв. Energent proto-life (epl) emergently arising in Energent–prime or Current All Existence emergently arising in Previous All Existence is conceptually the same where, in both cases, the source of emergence remains an aspect of that which emergently arose (§ 1:100). Thus, an emergent self-aware being that emergently births 'in' EPL as mind becomes an aspect of the emergent self-aware being that is subconscious–conscious (*enimerótis–empeiría*), the wholistic person that's ᚺuman. The subconscious and conscious mind each have their WOB, and altogether subconscious–conscious has its WOB, too.

That said, one's subconscious awareness of 'energy' interacts with conscious mind's underlayment of sub-Thought such that wholistic mind, having awareness of the 'energies' of its external-to-mind environment, *experiences* that awareness. Since sub-Thought is the repository of one's Individual core Culture (IC; § 4.1:291), then one's sub-Thought experiences subconscious awareness in IC terms. When such awareness is consistent with IC, then one's sub-Thought experience manifests normatively in conscious Thought. If inconsistent, it manifests nonnormatively. One's Thought experiences the discrepancy as conscience, which the person thinks–feels to a greater or lesser degree. Let's describe how it's experienced.

2.3.3 HOW WE EXPERIENCE CONSCIENCE

Conscious Thought operates pragmatically because it is mind's direct interface with environment. The subconscious operates idealistically because it's just awareness that's only indirectly experiencing environment (§ 2.2.2.1.2:397). Sub-Thought is the meeting ground twixt these two WOB. It's how mind reconciles idealistic subconscious awareness with pragmatic Thought experience (§ 2.2.2.1:396) and works the same whether one is physical or spirit embodied. Conscience isn't one's Divine spark, intrinsic or inherent morality, a cognitive process, or a judgment of reason. It's just one's mind wholistically experiencing awareness.

2.3.3.1 THE PROCESS OF CONSCIENCE

Recall the subconscious is aware of itself and, through conscious mind, of its external-to-mind environment. It's aware of its awareness and aware that it's aware of its awareness. This is self-awareness in which conscience first arises. It begins here because the subconscious abhors harm—in the sense harm is antithetical to its SOB—and, specifically, harm to own-self. Its abhorrence extends to not-self—people, animals, trees . . . anything. This differs from conscious mind that abhors harm to own-self yet is positive regarding harm to not-self; it has no problem doling it out so long as it isn't returned.

Yet, in actuality, harm is *always* returned. The reason lies in everything being 'energy.' The subconscious abhors harm to not-self not for any noble or impelled reason but because the proto-energy that's Intentionalized by harm inflicted on not-self—like an 'energy' knife slashing out from harm in all directions—actually harms own-self, as it violates the preferred SOB of the subconscious—a SOB absent harm to own-self—by imposing a SOB that's not preferred, the SOB in which the subconscious has awareness of harm's 'energy.' Harm to the subconscious, which as an aspect of mind is closest to one's fundamental, emergent proto-energy self, arises in its sense of own-self—not as psychology defines it but, in terms of psyche, its sense of self-aware existence—in that the subconscious is aware its external-to-mind environment is inconsistent with its preferred own-self SOB, its sense of self-aware existence. The harm to self lies in its sense of self-aware existence undergoing change as we've described, but absent volition. It imposes on it from either outside mind—the Intentionality, or Intentionalized 'energy,' of a person harmed in the external-to-mind environment—or from own-self's conscious mind that's the perpetrator of the harm. In either case, the imposition comes from outside the subconscious.

There's nothing more fundamental to psyche than its sense of own-self as just defined. When this sense of own-self undergoes imposed change, the subconscious acts to reestablish its preferred SOB, one that's absent harm to own-self. The more powerful the 'energy' of harm, the greater the disturbance to the subconscious' SOB and the stronger its Intentionality to return to its preferred SOB. Don't think the subconscious doesn't have 'intent,' 'wants,' 'desire,' and so forth. It does. But they aren't *felt*, experienced. They're Intentionalized; the subconscious exudes Intentionality consistent with awareness.

Unlike with subconscious–conscious reconciliation, the subconscious is impersuasible w.r.t. harm. One can't compel it to ignore harm to own-self through Thought. We tend to imagine that suppressing one's conscience, forcing oneself to live contrary to one's perception of it, somehow negates it for a conscienceless life well lived. But that's inaccurate. Such a person lives in a subconscious–conscious dichotomy that, uninterrupted by mind reconciliation (§ 2.2.2.1:396), translates to a normative state of low-grade Post-traumatic Stress Disorder (PTSD). It's undiagnosable—though not hard to discern in behavior—yet, even so, physiological and mental harm eventually arise from the 'energies' of the person's ongoing harm and unreconciled mind.

Since the subconscious can only exist in accord with its wob and preferred sob (which is absent harm to own-self), it ceaselessly Intentionalizes its soa to wholistic mind to reestablish its sense of own-self. Conscious mind's sub-Thought experiences this inexorable 'broadcast' of Intentionality while at the same time experiencing conscious mind's Thought, its thinking–feeling that includes the harm event, the 'energy' of which the subconscious has awareness. If conscious mind perpetrates harm then conscious mind's underlayment of sub-Thought experiences a profound conflict between the subconscious' sob and conscious mind's sob. Wholistic mind seeks to reconcile the conflict to experience a wholistic sob–soa. The subconscious exerts change on conscious mind—a person feels stricken by their conscience—or conscious mind exerts change on the subconscious—a person suppresses their conscience without reconciling mind. Conscience is literally nothing more than one's subconscious having awareness of some harm to own-self violating its sob and then Intentionalizing that awareness into sub-Thought.

2.3.3.2 Experiencing Mental Illness

There's no such thing as mental *injury*, only mental *illness* which is merely a disordered mindstate arising in conflict with itself (*above*). Mental illness isn't a disorder in the sense of an aberrant expression outside a normative range, but mind's normative response to an unreconciled mindstate (§ 2.2.2.1:396). This means mental illness isn't an 'illness' or even a 'disorder' as typically apprehended, but a normative response to an unreconciled experience of one's environment that manifests in problematic socio-individual mindstates and behaviors. So-called mental illnesses are symptomatic of such mindstate conflict. What Philosophy with a capital-P calls mental—psychic, psychiatric, moral—injury is an *experience of*, not damage or injury *to*, mind although it can appear to arise in damage to the brain, which of a consequence disrupts transliteration (mind–brain integration; § 1.2.2.2:254; § 2.1:276). Mind itself can't be damaged, as it's proto-energy. It is simply self-awareness, awareness, and experience. Its unreconciled experience of awareness as a self-aware being gives rise to misnomered mental 'illness.' In truth, no one is mentally *ill*. They're merely experiencing mindstate conflict that resolves only with healing (ch. 35:577), not psychobiological intervention. Let's consider ptsd, thought to be a major 'psyche injury' in this context.

2.3.3.2.1 Experiencing PTSD

If a person suppressing their conscience doesn't reconcile mind then, over time, that dichotomy leads to mindstate (mental) disturbances. Such a sob eventually coalesces into one embodying the symptomatology called Post-traumatic Stress Disorder (ptsd), a phenomenon only of the physically embodied. Ptsd isn't an anxiety disorder, that's just its principal experience. Instead, it's a violative mindstate disordering the subconscious arising in sub-Thought from the irreconciliation between subconscious awareness and conscious Thought. In essence, ptsd is simply wholistic mind—which always pursues a wholistic sob—experiencing dichotomous sob in conflict. On one hand, the subconscious is Intentionalizing into sub-Thought its desire to reestablish its preferred sob–soa where it has no awareness of harm to own-self. On the other, conscious Thought engages in thinking–feeling–action that ceaselessly reinvigorates subconscious mind's awareness of harm to own-self that's at variance to a greater or lesser extent with what's enculturated in sub-Thought. The longer thinking–feeling–action is at variance with the subconscious as Intentionalized into sub-Thought, the more pronounced the ptsd.

For example, I went through years of ptsd with severe anxiety and depression in consequence of domestic violence. In these situations, conscious Thought imposes a drastic awareness of own-self harm on the subconscious through its unwavering thinking–feeling–action that only prolongs the harmful environment by the inability to extricate oneself from the harmful relationship. But I had an epiphany in 2005—three, actually, over the course of a weekend—where, by Monday, I viscerally felt my depression gone. Over fifteen years later and despite many unhappy experiences in between, it hasn't returned.

Epiphanies aren't causative but symptomatic. When one experiences an epiphany, it's symptomatic of having reconciled wholistic mind that's now in the process of reestablishing its wholistic sob. I still had ptsd, evidenced by ongoing anxiety at the mere thought of my abuser. But I continued the process that led to my epiphanies to eventually extricate myself from interacting with the person. It was complicated. Little by little, I asserted protective boundaries (as I now must with needy or hostile spirit persons). My behavior changes altered my thinking–feeling–action such that my conscious Thought reconciled more, lessening its variance with my sub-Thought—the repository of Individual core Culture that defines who I am (§ 4.1:291)—which in turn imposed less and less of a violative SOB on my subconscious. Over time, my wholistic mind's SOB re-emerged without subconscious–conscious SOB conflict, exhibited by the gradual lessening of anxiety until it was possible (peaceably, without anxiety) to experience my former abuser's presence, communicate, amicably end our interactions, and visit our children together whose own relationships with her dramatically improved within days post-Big Healing.

2.4   INTENTIONALITY

As touched on above, Intentionality is a function of only the subconscious, the fundamental aspect of awareness of one's self-aware proto-energy being having Intentionality. Conscious mind is an Intentionalized WOB of one's self and therefore doesn't possess Intentionality as its own WOB any more than a universe possesses its builder's Intentionality. However, because conscious mind is the emergent being's gateway to external-to-mind reality, Intentionality exerts external-to-mind through it because conscious mind's experience of external-to-mind 'energies' is a two-way street with subconscious mind's awareness. Because of Intentionality, which arises in proto-energy and exerts on proto-energy, mind's awareness–experience of external-to-mind proto-energy means said proto-energy is 'aware' of mind. Thus, it responds to Intentionality. When one's conscious Thought Intention is out-of-sync with one's subconscious Intention, Intentionality fails (§ 2.1.5.4:316). If Mina, for instance, hadn't really wanted to build a universe but only thought he did, his Intention would've failed regardless his effort. Had my subconscious awareness not been my conscious mind's encounters as a negation of physical life, it never would've Intentionalized early-onset dementia.

2.4.1   DEATH, DISEASE, ET CETERA

Everything that happens to us in 𝓛ife, regardless how we're embodied, arises in Intentionality—our own, others', or the environment's. Absent immediately fatal damage, the physical body dies because, one way or another, the person Intentionalizes it. Death isn't random. A person dies of old age, a broken heart, disease, or healable damage because they ultimately desire it (§ 2.1.1.2.1:369). Our subconscious–conscious Intent produces Intentionality via Thought that becomes physical reality in accord with mindset.

2.4.1.1   𝓛IFE FORCE AND MINDSET

𝓛ife force is the self-aware proto-energy that *is* emergent 𝓛ife (§ 2.3.2.1:241; § 7.1.3:214; § 1.2.2.4.1:257), the vital force of the 𝔥uman 𝔭erson, the presence from which we experience our sense of aliveness, of being a living *being*. It integrates the physical body through its physicospirit reality. Normally, a person's 𝓛ife force integrates their physical body without restriction because their mindset has no sense of limiting it. The Corruption, however, disrupted our mindset with an Accountableist tendency toward denying our intrinsically autonomous WOB. In this milieu, physical humanity identified more with animals than their emergent 𝓛ife selves until we consciously forgot what we were, having only a vague subconscious awareness we were something more (§ 9.2.2:450). As humans mimicked animal life and its alpha (male) society, our mindset reflected the apparently fugacious nature of physical existence until we *expected* to die, to suffer infirmity and irreparable damage, to grow *old* in the same way animals do.

But humanity misunderstands life because The Corruption blinds us to our true WOB and Accountableism shapes our mindset with myths, one of which is that as we live year to year we age, get tired, lose strength, and eventually die (if we're lucky) of natural causes. Through mindset, we gradually block our own individual 𝓛ife force from enlivening our physical body with vitality. Our body accordingly grows tired during wakefulness as it metabolizes our 𝓛ife force it absorbed during rest and substitutes it for food, stimulants, drugs, and the like until forced to shut down in sleep long enough to absorb enough for another wakeful period. Over a lifetime, we day-to-day absorb less and less 𝓛ife force. It leaves us feeling more tired as we age, disrupts our natural biological rhythms so we struggle even to sleep, thereby absorbing even less 𝓛ife force and feeling even less vital. Eventually, we experience disease and infirmity owing to insufficient 𝓛ife force to promote healing, and our body expires.

This needn't be our reality, however. Mindset defines who and what one is because one's mindset is the 𝔭erson, the subconscious–conscious mind that experiences and interacts with external-to-mind reality. If, say, we alter out mindset regarding mimicking animals, alpha society, and the presumed vitality of the physical body regardless chronological age, then our reality alters, too, and our external-to-mind experience follows suit. This means the physical body isn't doomed to infirmity over a 50-, 75-, or 100-plus-year lifespan but whatever health and lifespan one prefers. One changes mindset the same way one does their subconscious—recall, the former is an expression of the latter—through conscious Thought where one mandates a change in their perspective on life, vitality, health, youthfulness, and the like. Mina tells us if we consciously recalibrate our thinking (mindset) consistently everyday over ∼6–9 months, depending on each of us, and maintain that awareness ongoing, then in ∼5–8 years from then our physical bodies will absorb a greater amount of 𝓛ife force that revitalizes, heals, and alters our bodies' every biological function to gradually recover youthful vitality and appearance, like Mork growing younger the older he grows (*Mork and Mindy*, TV, 1978–82). Well, time and effort will tell on that.

2.5 PHYSICOSPIRIT INFLUENCE

Many aspects of our lives confound us because we don't recognize our physicospirit reality. Quite apart from the way our wholistic mind works is the reality of our spirit self that exists concurrently with, and tethered to, our physical body. This attachment—from which we receive the 'energy' (𝓛ife force) that sustains physical life—is only as strong as our mind's will to physically live. The lesser one's will to live, the lesser is one tethered to their body until, eventually, there's insufficient integrating 𝓛ife force to keep it alive and the body dies. One's spirit self is far clearer about and responsive to mind than one's physical self. We're far more aware in our spirit self of who and what we really are, how we really feel, and so on. There's much less discordance—on average ∼65% less if the physical-self baseline is 100% —between conscious Thought, sub-Thought, and the subconscious and even more so for the spirit-born. The experiences of a physically alive person's spirit self in the spirit context ceaselessly influences the physical person in accord with their mind–brain integration and spiritual awareness (cf. Adoph Hitler, CH. 40:605).

One's sense of conscience, intuition, and so on is our wholistic mind and spiritual personality integrating and sometimes guiding our physical personality. These personalities can be very different, even dialectically opposed (cf. Hitler; CH. 40:605). Sometimes, one's spirit personality is carefree and doesn't listen to our more serious or altruistic physical personality. Or it's the reverse and leads to a sense of a disconnect with one's own self as if one doesn't know oneself, needs to 'find' oneself, or ignore some aspect of self. Either way, one's spirit self knows we shouldn't, for whatever reason, do this or that in our physical life because the spirit self clearly perceives the consequences from the standpoint of 'energy' or justice w.r.t. others both before and after one's death whereas one's physical self, addicted to mindset (§ 2.1.2.2.1:371), perceives little to none of it.

2.6 THE WHOLISM OF MIND

Although the subconscious and conscious minds might seem like two different minds with two different personalities, they aren't. The apparent difference—besides The Corruption's effects—lies in conscious mind's WOB that directly experiences external-to-mind reality and subconscious mind's WOB that only indirectly has awareness of it. As an emergent being, the human person is an infinitely complex personality of which we've heretofore had exactly zero understanding. Toward that end, we describe in the next chapter how we experience embodiment across a range of situations.

On Being Human

WE'VE DISCUSSED IN various contexts what Ꝼuman *is* (§ 3:280; CH. 21:303). In this chapter, we describe what it means to *be* Ꝼuman. Recall that here on Earth we live not only in a universe with about 87.6 billion human-inhabited planets but in a megaverse filled with 194 million universes, each one home to a sizable local humanity (FN 431:357; § 3:357; § 2.1.4.1:312). Altogether, we're just one part of a collective—megaversal—humanity numbering about 3.4×10^{38} persons (§ 2.1:340) living unembodied as well as spirit and physical embodied. It's not simply that we're *part* of the vast human race of All Existence but that, in the depths of our minds, we *experience* them the same way one experiences the vibe of family, friends, local and national society, the planet, and universe. This is one facet of what it means to be Ꝼuman. The other lies in our experience with embodiment. We describe each in Sections 1 and 2–11, respectively.

SECTION 1
Our Collective Experience

Recall the fundamental nature, or way of being (WOB; § 2.2.1.1:234), of the ꝑerson is our experience of 'energy.' All Existence is 'energy' and, therefore, all things of All Existence are 'energy,' too. The archí, for instance, forms of proto-energy that's impermeable to it. Though we call that state *matter*, it's nothing more than an impermeable 'energy' (§ 2:114). The human person births 'in' Energent proto-life (EPL; § 2.3.2.1:241) as proto-energy that's self-aware, having ᴸife. Although we call ourselves ᴸife, consciousness, alive, or a person, we too are nothing more than a form of impermeable proto-energy (§ 2.3.2.3:243). 'Energy' in the context of proto-energy (as opposed to the applied energy E we're familiar with; § 2.3.3:117) underlies all there is. Our wholistic mind, the seat of our beingness, experiences ᴸife as the experience of 'energy,' whether its own subconscious 'energy' or that external to mind (§ 2:393).

Unlike the spatial WOB of archí, the Energent is without time and space (INSTANTANEITY, § 6.11.4:198). Any Energent point space is the Energent in totality just as the wholistic SOB–SOA (state of being; state of awareness; § 1.2.2.1:253) of one's subconscious flavors in toto any single 'sip' the conscious mind takes of it (§ 2.1.4:394). When it comes to proto-energy, the part is the all and the all is every part. Since the megaverse is proto-energy, and every person inhabiting it is self-aware proto-energy—emergent ᴸife—then these proto-energies aren't confined to their local environments but *are* All Existence. Every experience with external-to-mind 'energy' that one has here in our universe is, in effect—however negligible—an experience with All Existence, every universe of All Existence, and collectively every person of every universe. In this, we take new meaning from English poet John Dunne's (d. 1631) notion that

> No man is an island, entire of itself: every man is a piece of the continent, a part of the main. If a clod be
> washed away by the sea, Europe is the less, as well as if a promontory were, as well as if a manor of thy friend's

or of thine own were: any man's death diminishes me, because I am involved in mankind, and therefore never send to know for whom the bell tolls; it tolls for thee (Dunne (1624) 1840, 100)

such that no person, planet, universe, nor even All Existence exists unto itself, and that all which is everywhere we experience here, howsoever trivially.

1.1 HOW WE EXPERIENCE REALITY AND COLLECTIVE HUMANITY

There is no escaping proto-energy. Accordingly, there's no escaping the reality of our existence or human WOB, neither in its core, fundamental sense as with absolute autonomy nor in its Intentionalized sense as with that crafted by the subconscious WOB of each individual person collectively throughout the megaverse. We know this is true when we consider that we can't escape—though we can resist—the vibe in a room, the permeating spread of fear in a group, the infectiousness of laughter or love, suspicion, dread, and so on. We experience this collective proto-energy through two vectors via All Existence Ultraculture, first in terms of the WOB of All Existence (reality) and second in terms of the WOB of Ꜧuman (collective humanity in every sense we describe in this book). We describe this Ultraculture and its two vectors below.

1.1.1 ULTIMACULTURE

Just as each universe has its own Ultraculture and smaller cultural matrices have local ultracultures (§ 4.1:291), the foregoing in the context of All Existence inclusive of the megaverse and its humanity means there's an ultimate expression of subconsciously Intentionalized proto-energy on the megaversal scale of All Existence; we term it *Ultimaculture* (*Fig. 157*).[448] We experience the Intentionalized proto-energy termed culture strongest locally and weakest globally. Individual culture is strongest and other culture, from the trans-individual to the society, world-sphere, natural (physical) and supranatural (spirit) environments, and universe is progressively weaker. Ultimaculture is (locally) weakest yet (globally) strongest of all. Despite its tenuity it isn't non-negligible, just as the graviton and zai photon at some distance d to infinity, however weak the effects, are never zero (§ 3.2:121). Culture conveys not only its sociological aspect but also the reality in which the culture obtains. Let's look at each, beginning with reality.

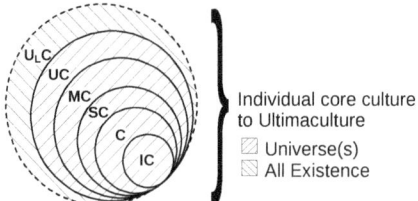

Figure 157. Schematic of Ultimaculture (ᴜʟᴄ): individual culture (ɪᴄ), enmeshed individual cultures (ᴄ), superculture (ꜱᴄ), megaculture (ᴍᴄ), Ultraculture (ᴜᴄ); cf. Fig. 125:292, Fig. 158; see also § 4.1:291.

1.1.1.1 ALL EXISTENCE WAY OF BEING

Physicists will tell you our physical universe has a normative existence, that the so-called laws of physics are the same everywhere (§ 6.1:165). This doesn't apply only to the expression of applied energy E in the natural, or supra E in the supranatural, environment (§ 1.2.1.2:467) but to all facets of integrated All Existence existing in accord with its WOB. At a non-aesthetic level, this means each universe's structure and operation integrates the principles (WOB) of All Existence. Physics, therefore, is fundamentally invariant from universe to universe although, with our present unawareness, non-fundamental variations might surprise us. Our experience of reality is more or less the same experience any person has in any universe of the megaverse.

Such fundamentality of experience means we collectively share a sense of reality and the human place within it. Unembodied persons who experience many universes—like physical individuals traveling the globe—understand human beings are the same in their essence everywhere. However unconsciously felt, our collective experience of reality across megaversal humanity informs our experience of reality here in our universe and on Earth. This is partly the mechanism—not societal processes—behind the observation of communal intuition leading to multiple, independent discovery (simultaneous invention).

---

448. Mina associates the concept of Ultimaculture with the Greek term *telikí koultoúra* (τελική κουλτούρα); *ultimate* as in finality.

1.1.1.2 HUMAN WAY OF BEING

One doesn't feel per se the culture that permeates one's friendships, family, city, state, nation, or all human beings of Earth. Nevertheless, the WOB of each defines the person. Each one separately and altogether affects and in some ways governs how we think, feel, and act. For example, the more ensconced one is in a culture (mindset), the less one can think, feel, and act outside its scope of influence. The impossibility of dissolving the Negative Collective Consciousness (NCC; § 4.2.1.4:382) is a case in point. Once Michael revealed Accountableism's fallacy (§ 1.4:14), the NCC stood exposed in the minds of all humanity in our universe. Or, too, breaking the four-minute mile where, despite athletes running their fastest, no one could complete a mile under four minutes until one person did, then anyone did. Both were simply mindset limitations, a subconscious unwillingness to embody what Canadian-born psychologist Albert Bandura calls self-efficacy, having a fixed versus a growth mindset.[270]

Ultimaculture is so global that its effect on the individual is limited to their sense of humanity, of what it means to be themself in human terms. Like the NCC, it's locally weak yet globally strong. One might think they feel human simply on account of being born, raised, and existing amongst humans, but a person born and self-raised in isolation—however animalistic, non-cognitive, or mentally disabled they may appear to be—nevertheless responds intrinsically humanly which, absent brain damage, is evident upon recovery. One can't humanize a chimp, but a human raised by chimps who thinks he or she is a chimp remains human, hence humanizable. The problem in feral child cases in the context of The Corruption and subpar mind–brain integration is that, once one isolates from the human milieu, the brain repurposes to its environment and mind–brain integration degrades further in its absence. Such a person's spirit self remains fully, experientially ♄uman but their physical embodiment, their 'avatar' (§ 2.1:276), is out of the loop.

An individual's experience with their own individual culture is fully active, not passive, despite larger cultures' negligible contributions to it. One's experience with culture farther from own-self (§ 2:275) is an active–passive matrix that becomes more passive and less active the farther from own-self it gets. Experiencing Ultimaculture is fully passive despite own-self's negligible contribution to it (*Fig. 158*). Humans experience the *reality* of human WOB through their own individual WOB and feel the *experience* of human WOB as megaversal humanity collectively embodies in Ultimaculture. Individuals passively experience the reality of humanity collectively in its nonautonomy, existence, and Intentionality via the WOB effect of Ultimaculture that we've just described. Let's consider each of these collective experiences.

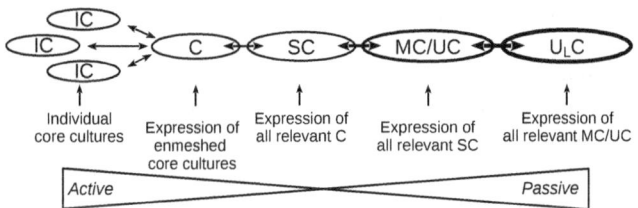

Figure 158. Active–passive culture matrix; superculture (SC), megaculture (MC), Ultraculture (UC), and Ultimaculture (U$_L$C); cf. Fig. 125:292, Fig. 157; see also § 4.1:291.

1.1.1.2.1 NONAUTONOMY

Recall that absolute autonomy is the core WOB of ♄uman (§ 2.1.1.5.2:353) and that, with the exception of Mina's vision for our universe (§ 2.1:340), megaversal humanity lives according to varying modes of nonautonomy. This means that although collective humanity experiences individual autonomy to varying degrees in its everyday sense of liberty and freedom to think and act—one is as subjectively free as one's mindset believes, regardless how objectively unfree—they're mired in mindset addiction. This shrouds their core autonomous WOB (existence unaddicted to mindset) and effectively renders them nonautonomous beings, a fundamental contradiction in their WOB. Even if our universe had never experienced the mindset addiction that is The Corruption, we would've nevertheless subliminally experienced it. We'd have always felt tempted by it, and some individuals would've always given in to it despite the absolute autonomous—fluid—mindset of our universe's ideal Ultraculture. For example, despite Earth's long and murderous experience with utopian nonautonomy, modern peoples—Americans, most recently—are addicted to its mindset of violent coercion and routinely tune out the lessons of the harm-inflicted past to embrace it in the present. For Americans with a political constitution mandating minimal government and maximal individual liberty (expressly designed to prevent this very utopianism), their tendency arises in The Corruption's mindset addiction energizing the individual, family, societal, and national ultracultures that individuals strongly or weakly experience and glom onto.

A person individually and collectively expresses the reality of human WOB regardless their mindset, but their experience with human WOB becomes mindset. To the degree they're addicted to any one experience is the degree to which they're addicted to mindset. The natural proclivity of humanity in our universe toward nonautonomy isn't solely a result of The Corruption. It includes Ultimaculture, though the ratio is about 99.99% to 0.01% . In a universal society 99.99% consistent with Mina's vision of absolute autonomy, it might seem Ultimaculture's 0.01% influence is negligible, a trifling, of no substantive consequence to humanity's WOB experience, its mindset. But we'd be just as wrong if we persuaded ourselves a 0.01% concentration of chlorine gas isn't eventually fatal in a roomful of air. This doesn't mean we're doomed to nonautonomy. It does mean, however, that some individuals—those most exposed, as with a gas—will experience Ultimaculture's mindset addiction until impervious to it. 'Energy' is our ever-present companion in ℒife.

1.1.1.2.2 EXISTENCE

Proto-energy is a force. It exerts in a person. We're awash in applied energy E, real energy Υ (§ 2:114), the Energent, and Energent proto-life (EPL). These are the 'energies' of existence, of reality. However subliminal, individuals experience the reality of collective (megaversal) humanity's existence through them. Besides feeling the experience of Ultimaculture as described in NONAUTONOMY (*above*), the individual experiences the real *force* of collective humanity's existence. It's quite negligible, that's true. Yet, it's there in the same way one experiences the force of humanity's existence on Earth, in one's nation, town, office or home, the way one feels the presence of a single individual in a darkened room. A person is aware of another's existence, of their reality—it's separate from one's awareness of an individual's emotive ℒife force (EMℒF; § 3.3.3.1.1:289), their vibe—because the 'energy' of their existence is ℒife force which we experience in having ℒife force ourselves. Ultimaculture, in this respect, is the ℒife force of a single individual scaled across megaversal humanity. It's the proto-energy force of existence and it manifests at all levels of culture, from the individual to a universe's Ultraculture to All Existence's megaversal Ultimaculture. It mindfully affects us, meaning it forms a part of our Thought as well as our experience of awareness.

1.1.1.2.3 INTENTIONALITY AND THE MCC

The way megaversal humanity experiences ℒife, its overall sense of it, Intentionalizes in the same way that humanity in our universe Intentionalized the NCC. Proto-energy exerts an Intentionalized force on the individual and collective psyche just as Intentionality exerts as a proto-energy force of reality in the creation of an Intentionalized cup of coffee, a house, or negative EMℒF. This means there's a *megaversal collective consciousness* (MCC) both experiencing and reinforcing megaversal humanity's ℒife experience.

This MCC isn't an MCC just because it embodies megaversal humanity's nonautonomy as its WOB. In our universe, the NCC was what it was because it was at variance with the core human WOB of absolute autonomy embodied in Mina, our universe's builder, whose beingness of absolute autonomy ceaselessly irradiates our universe in terms of both his own ℒife force and of our universe's WOB of absolute autonomy. This created a tension between our mindset addiction that was The Corruption and our core WOB, of which Mina's existence and our universe's WOB constantly made our psyche aware (§ 3.1.2.1:358). For megaversal humanity, on the other hand, the mindsets of all other universe builders in the megaverse embody nonautonomy. These builders irradiate their universes with this mindset as its core WOB (§ 1:361). The peoples of those universes are ceaselessly irradiated just as we are here, not with the core human WOB of absolute autonomy as per Mina, but the nonautonomy of their builders—themselves irradiated by the core WOB of nonautonomy as per the vast majority of unembodied human society (§ 2.1.1.1:368)—in just the way the parents of a family irradiate their children with their collective mindset. The MCC is All Existence's Ultimaculture as the NCC was our universe's Ultraculture.

1.2 EMBODIMENT

Earlier, we describe the nature and reality of our embodiment and unembodiment (e.g., ℒife, § 1.2:246; POST-HUMAN EMERGENCE, § 2.1:305). Here, we consider how we experience them and the issues that consequently arise. *Physicospirit* refers to the physically alive person and their spirit self unless specified.

1.2.1 PHYSICOSPIRIT EMBODIMENT

The salient aspect of human life is that we are what we think–feel. One of the ways we express this is through a physicospirit body. Until the Big Healing, both the physical- and spirit-born imagined that all we are is our body (mind's embodiment in the physicospirit environment) regardless where one imagined the origin and seat of consciousness. Even for the physical person with the greatest regard for human spiritual nature, one is hard-pressed to find one such individual who, when the chips are down, genuinely feels that giving up the body isn't a real loss, a tragedy, something not worth fighting for and especially killing over. The physicospirit belief that one is their body arises in the difference between the brain and mind in the context of degraded mind–brain integration (§ 1.2.2.5:261), which leaves even their spirit self in ignorance of reality where survival is brain awareness and letting it go is mind awareness. For the spirit-born person, the belief that one is their spirit body arises in the difference between mind and awareness, which leaves them consciously ignorant.

But we aren't our body. We're mind integrating it (§ 1.2.2:253), whether physical with its origin in independent biology or spirit with its origin Intentionalized (manifested) by mind. Until we understand this reality, we can't understand the fullness of 𝓛ife nor the issues that arise in living it. Our experience with embodiment raises a host of issues that have bedeviled humanity practically since day one. We discuss next in Sections 2–11 some of what physical humanity has had to confront: killing, abortion, euthanasia, and suicide; lineage and DNA; what happens at death; destiny, fate, and free will; suffering; happiness; love and hate; government and society; evil; and beauty.

SECTION 2

Killing, Abortion, Euthanasia, and Suicide

Killing is forcibly removing aliveness from a Living entity (§ 1:246). 𝔥uman is 𝓛ife and doesn't end with embodiment's demise (§ 2.1.1:368); killing the *body* doesn't terminate the person. It just forcibly relocates them from physicospirit to merely spirit embodiment which changes and lessens their interaction with the natural environment. It thus seems it must be okay to kill the body. It's not. Let's consider why.

2.1 THE PROBLEM WITH KILLING HUMANS

Having read this book so far, killing a human body (which doesn't terminate 𝓛ife) might seem on its face no more than a property crime, at worst an act that alienates the killed from their experience of physical embodiment. That would be partially true in a world of absolute autonomy and full mind–brain integration (§ 1.2.2.5:261), but our universe remains habituated to The Corruption and its consequently deficient mind–brain integration despite the NCC's end and universal humanity's improvement since the Big Healing. Regardless, killing a human body creates harm and trauma as defined (§ 1.1.1:362), compels nonautonomy, and in our present reality alienates the killed from their physical experience with loved ones, current and future activities, and so on. Before we look at these three effects, though, we need consider the morality of killing.

2.1.1 THE MORAL CONCEPT OF KILLING

So-called morality isn't real (§ 2.1.1.5.2:353; § 1.1.2.1:364) although ethics is. Recall morality arises in nonautonomy rooted in concepts of divinity and universal truth. Ethics doesn't, and isn't. There's a lot of confusion in moral philosophy as to what these terms mean—if, indeed, they're even distinguishable—and how we exercise them in life, so let's take a moment to define them from Mina's perspective.

2.1.1.1 MEANING OF MORALITY

Morality is divine truth. It arises in the belief that universal truths are real and, because they're universal, are absolute, inarguable, unavoidable, and intransgressible. Whether morality arises in God, gods, or the materialism of the laws of nature is immaterial. Both equally root in a concept of divinity from the perspective of moral philosophy and its adherents. Humanity for instance considers murder—*unlawful* or *unjustified* killing—fundamentally wrong, thus immoral, because life is inviolable in arising outside of human will as a gift from God or a random, one-shot stop. Morality is intrinsically imperative and gives rise to the dialectic of right–wrong, good–bad, good–evil, and, of course, evil itself as an absolute immorality.

But it's a false construct. Morality isn't truth because divinity isn't real. There is no God or gods, and the laws of nature aren't *laws* but ways of being (WOB). The only WOB that serves in the sense of a moral standard is absolute autonomy, which is *the* good. But its absence isn't *the* bad or even a generic badness. It's simply the *not*-good, which isn't synonymous with *the* bad for the reasons given (§ 2.1.1.5.2:353). A moral imperative doesn't arise since nonautonomy arises in autonomy, which counterintuitively means the antithesis of *the* good is *the* good. That's a bit of a brainteaser, for sure, and awaits its own book to parse it fully. Suffice it to say that nonautonomy (in which, e.g., coercion arises) is autonomously chosen howsoever coerced because, first, self-agency is inviolable (§ 2.1.1.2.1:369) thus coercion is really acceptance not compulsion and, second, core human WOB is autonomy such that regardless one's nonautonomous mode of *being*, absolute autonomy remains one's mode of *existence* (§ 3.3.3:377). The individual is always autonomous regardless mindset addiction. Consequently, morality is a non-issue with killing.

2.1.1.2   MEANING OF ETHICS

Ethics is human truth. It arises in the belief that the vagaries of life justify a pragmatic approach to the divine truth of moral imperatives that, in human-defined cases, renders morality arguable, avoidable, and transgressible. For example, the rules governing the lawfulness (justifiableness) of killing derive from the moral imperatives regarding life—that killing is universally wrong—juxtaposed against its perceived or agreed-upon case-by-case necessity. It's here that distinctions arise between types of killing such as degrees of murder, manslaughter, and self-defense. However, because morality in and of itself is a false construct rooted in nonautonomy, the same inheres to ethics. This means it lacks substantive justification. Instead, it is simply imposed sets of rules that are normative in that most though not all generally agree with them being imposed, say, via the democratic process, from a sense of fairness, or as an expression of common belief. Or, they're nonnormative in that most though not all generally disagree with them, being imposed absent the democratic process, a common belief, or from a sense of advantage. Either way, ethics, like morality, is entirely arbitrary despite humanity sharing, via mindset, aspects of each.

2.1.2   THE MORALITY AND ETHICS OF KILLING

The above means that while there's no moral issue with killing, since morality isn't real, there is an ethical issue if the human truth a society imposes on its members controls killing, or there's no ethical issue if a society normalizes killing. Either way, the sheer arbitrariness of moral and ethical value systems means their effect on human behavior is always minimal.[449] The reason is there's always a justifiable reason to do anything. It just depends on one's point of view, i.e., one's morality and ethics. However false and arbitrary morality is, it at least has the virtue of restraining harmful behavior more effectively than ethics.

And that's the real issue here, *harmful* behavior. It's not that killing is immoral, bad, unethical, or wrong per se, but that it's harmful. Harm is an issue whether or not one is addicted to mindset (living nonautonomously; § 1.1.1:362). Morality and ethics attempt to inculcate in people a value standard of harmlessness so that safety obtains. Recall, however, that safety entails its exact opposite. Far from limiting harm, morality and ethics institutionalize it (§ 3.2:374). Morality and ethics—altruism's backboard—haven't created a single being of harmlessness in all of human history, such bootstrapped moral giants as Gandhi, Jesus, Buddha, and others notwithstanding. Let's consider killing as harm.

2.1.2.1   KILLING CREATES HARM

The principal problem with killing a person's physical body is that it creates harm and trauma that affects mindstate owing to the nature of mind–body integration. Besides harm arising in the act of killing in and of itself, recall that trauma stays with a person at least until the parts of their body embodying trauma are nonexistent (§ 1.1.1.2:362). A killed person continues to experience the harm raised by the trauma of death in his or her post-physical spirit embodiment, which means a continual increase of negative EM𝓛F in the universe that harms everyone, however negligibly. Whether or not a person is forgiving or uncaring of being killed, they nonetheless experience harm as grief, pain, hurt, loneliness, separation, outrage, or worry for loved ones left behind. Negative EM𝓛F from killing is unavoidable. It affects and harms everyone in our universe to varying degrees just as it collectively raised up the harmful NCC.

---

449. For example, one can always tell when laws (howsoever based on moral–ethical values) historically fail to affect behavior because the historical record shows them re-legislated, often with harsher punishments.

Killing not only harms the killed but the killer, too, because there's an 'energy' blowback on them in the form of Intentionality which arises in the killed person's feeling of harm and trauma. It's a function of the subconscious, not the conscious, so there's no avoiding it howsoever forgivingly Christ-like the killed may in fact be (§ 2.3:398; cf. suffering § 6.1:431). However much one compartmentalizes the conscious mind from the suffering of being killed or even loves and forgives their killer, mind–body integration means the subconscious—one's true self—experiences its full effect to the *nth* degree. The effect of mind awareness Intentionalizes proto-energy in and around its focal point—the killer—and this eventually results in psyche and physiological harm (§ 3.2:282). The result is to create yet more harm and trauma beyond just the act of killing that affects not merely the killer but their own loved ones, too.

Killing incites vengeance. It arises not only in those physically alive who themselves feel harmed by the killing but amongst the spirit embodied as well. The physical aspect includes both the killed person's loved ones and the modern state, which views killing as a societal harm and exacts its own vengeance. Whether law courts serve up real justice or merely an effect of law is beside the point and, in truth, irrelevant. Real vengeance occurs when those who feel harmed by killing weaponize proto-energy through Intentionality. Even if they don't consciously curse or wish harm upon the killer, their sub-Thought (§ 1.1.2.1:393) mind acts generically to Intentionalize their wholistic Thought in the proto-energy in and around the focal point of their feeling of harm—the killer.

Spirit persons consciously or subconsciously Intentionalize their feeling of harm as with physical persons, but, if so inclined, also directly go after the killer using focused Intentionality to harm and afflict their physical body and mindstate. In spirit world there is no law, police, or courts in the physical-world sense to compel a person to cease and desist beyond the coercive efforts of the killer's spirit family and friends who may or may not involve themselves in defending the killer's physicospirit self or in exacting their own vengeance against those avenging the killed.[450]

The cycle of vengeance that arises amongst spirit persons is like the blood feuds that the modern state (in the belief that harm against a person is harm against the state and, therefore, only the state, not the private citizen, may exact vengeance) seeks to eliminate. While the modern state has partially ended blood feuds in the physical environment, it's done nothing to eliminate the far more harmful feuds arising in the physical-born spirit environment that result in generational harm (CH. 35:577) nor to ameliorate the harm it has, itself, inflicted in its pursuit. In the end, killing creates harm for the killer, the killed, and throughout both parties' extended relations that bleed into the culture. The reality of Intentionality brings to fullness the old adage that he who lives by the sword, one way or another, dies by the sword.

2.1.2.2 KILLING DEPRIVES THE KILLED OF THEIR AUTONOMY

Besides wreaking harm on many human levels, killing one's physical embodiment provokes nonautonomy in the person by coercively removing self-agency and inflicting a mindset addiction. We consider each.

2.1.2.2.1 KILLING NEGATES SELF-AGENCY

Recall that self-agency is inviolable in that only the individual can abandon it (§ 2.1.1.2.1:369). The act of killing isn't self-willed by the killed but compelled by the killer, except in one aspect of euthanasia (§ 2.3:413) and when coercion becomes acceptance. For example, when a person fighting for their life realizes they're going to lose and gives up, accepting the killer's *coup de grâce*, he or she isn't losing self-agency in their killer's act of negating it, but is positively acting on it despite being compelled into the situation. The same plays out in almost every coercive affair, from enslavement to robbery to societal norms where a person abandons resistance for acceptance (§ 2.1.1.1:407).

Emergent ℒife—mind, thus ℘erson—is its own absolutely autonomous proto-energy self-existence. Nothing happens with mind or to mind outside its own autonomy, its self-agency. Mind, however, exists in the context of environment: the unembodied amidst EPL proto-energy alone and the embodied additionally amidst the natural and supranatural environments which, for the physical embodied, includes their biologically independent body's environment and for the spirit embodied that of their Intentionalized (manifested) body. This

---

450. Police in a sense exist in the spirit-born but not the physical-born areas of spirit world. Since killing or imprisoning harmful people is impossible—the latter is still possible in the physical-born areas—their task is to dissuade people from harming others by whatever means necessary (§ 3:481). If we baseline average police presence in Earth's population at 100%, then spirit world's is ~0.001%. It's a personally assumed (self-deployed) token effort, really.

embodied reality means another person in the common environment can intervene in one's local environment where he or she can permanently destroy one's physical body or in spirit world temporarily destroy one's spirit body. The spirit person's situation in this case isn't serious and raises no specific issues here, but the permanent effect of the physical body's destruction does. The coerced destruction of the physical body negates one's self-agency w.r.t. choosing to live or die unless, as mentioned, one accepts it. Regardless, there's a further harm.

2.1.2.2.2 KILLING INFLICTS A CERTAIN MINDSET ADDICTION

Besides a killer negating self-agency through which nonautonomy arises in the killed, it also results in their addiction to an accusatory mindset toward a creator of whatever variety, angels, spirit guides, or just whomever, including the killer, oneself, or any person whom one feels should've saved them. Some people are addicted to this mindset for just a short moment in time, such as Jesus,[451] while others remain addicted until they experience healing through their own effort or from an outside agency, such as Mina and healers post-Big Healing. Such mindset addiction arises in the context of The Corruption. A person living in absolute autonomy consistent with our universe's woв wouldn't experience it.

2.1.2.2.3 KILLING COERCIVELY SEPARATES THE KILLED FROM THEIR PHYSICAL EXPERIENCE

The least of the problems arising in killing humans—but nonetheless a problem in todays' environment that, despite the ongoing healing, still lacks absolute autonomy as its baseline—is that killing forcibly removes the killed from their physical experience of ℒife. This means a killer cuts off the killed from their physically alive loved ones and activities. This is what happened to Jesus, for example, as well as all so-called providential figures killed in history. Dead, they could no longer communicate with or effect education about reality amongst the physically alive except in small numbers with uncertain results in the face of incredulity. For any person, this creates additional harm—pain, hurt, frustration, aggravation, loneliness, despair—beyond the harm arising in the act of killing. Although this consequence is the least of the problems that arise from the act of killing, it's hardly inconsequential. It's certainly harmful and difficult for the physical-*born* to overcome. It's a far greater tragedy for the physical-*unborn*, which brings us to abortion.

2.2 ABORTION

Terminating conception is killing a Living human body that integrates emergent ℒife (*above*; § 1.2.1.1:248). It produces all the same effects of killing except that, while separating a killed *born* person from their physical experience is the *least* of the problems that arise in the act of killing, it's the *greatest* of the problems for the killed *unborn* person. The reason lies in the integrative woв of embodiment that, in our megaversal Ultimaculture reality as it is (§ 1.1.1:404), severs the embodied from conscious awareness of their unembodiment. Abortion isn't possible for the unembodied (§ 1.2.1.1.3:250; § 2.2.3:412), so we focus on the embodied and the differences between physical and spirit abortion before describing aspects of it that do apply to unembodiment. The effects to the person as described apply to all forms of death in utero.

2.2.1 ABORTION OF THE PHYSICAL-CONCEIVED

Abortion is simple and straightforward for the physically conceived. It simply destroys the conceived person's unborn body's ability to sustain life; kills it. This severs emergent ℒife's mind–body integration which, as we've learned, leaves a killed person solely spirit embodied. ℒife is emergent and eternal (§ 1.2.1:247), so killing has no effect on its existence though it does on Thought (thinking–feeling; used interchangeably throughout). The pre-3-month aborted person doesn't yet have conscious albeit does have subconscious awareness (Fig. 155:396; § 2.1:305). Accordingly, abortion causes two effects w.r.t. Thought.

---

451. On November 27, 2020, Jesus told me this feeling—which took him about ten hours after death to treat—is why he called out on the cross not to God but to "My ancestors, why have you forsaken me?" using the Aramaic version of the Hebrew אבותי (*avotay*; Mt. 27:46, Mk. 15:34). He was colloquially referring to Mina and Gabriel, whom he viewed as his principal family (cf. CH. 40:613). Mina says bystanders heard him correctly, but when they related it to the apostles Matthew and John (the latter wrote the original to the later Gospel of Mark), they didn't understand his use of "ancestors" and changed it to "my Father" in their original third-person accounts (in Hebrew and Aramaic, respectively), written separately albeit in the same room together about three months after Jesus' death. It was later changed to "my God" by a Hebrew living in Jerusalem named Dan who rewrote Matthew's account, and by a Hebrew living in Rome going by the name of Marcus (different from any biblical Mark) who rewrote John's account—both about ten years later in response to Jesus requesting it in a dream.

First, the person subconsciously experiences their body's killing which creates pain and suffering that Intentionally exerts into the universe (§ 1.1.1:362). We covered this in § 2.1.2.1:408 and don't repeat it here.

Second, the embodied person depends on their body as their interface with reality through which their mind develops. This is opposite the unembodied. For example, Mike and Molly's minds developed normatively in their unembodiment because, born into it, that was their primary, functional mode of being. It was all their minds had and with which they learned to interface directly with reality (§ 2.1.1:306; Cosmo, § 1.2.1.1:338). The sensations of embodiment, however, inundate persons who are conceived integrating a body. Their mind interfaces with reality directly via their body, but they're unaware of their indirect subconscious interface with reality.[452] Without their physical body, the aborted person can't experience physical reality. Without stimulus to their spirit body, they can't experience spirit reality. But the aborted person doesn't cease to exist, either. Bluntly, *an aborted baby is still alive.* Their physicospirit parents conceived them physicospiritually embodied, so, post-abortion, they remain spirit embodied.

Upon their physical body's death—thus removed from the physical universe—the now-only-spirit-embodied aborted person spatially exists only in the 'reflective' environment (§ 7.1.1.1:212) wherever he or she spatially was in the moment of physical death. If, for instance, a fetal person experiences abortion in a womb upon a table in a clinic, then, upon the womb's physical departure, they lay on that table (if, upon the table, their physical embodiment ceased living) in the 'reflective' environment until something there—a visiting spirit person or a physical person who moves the physical table—relocates them. If in a car crash a fetal person dies ex utero in the vehicle, then it remains in the vehicle in the 'reflective' environment until something or someone attends it. Its spirit body in the 'reflective' environment goes wherever the physical-universe vehicle goes (to the junkyard, the impound lot, the victim's driveway).

Normally, when a physical-embodied person dies, they 'wake up' in—shift awareness to—the 'reflective' environment whereat their body spatially died. An Entry 'angel'[453] meets and enables them to enter spirit world if they assent (§ 4:419). Obviously, an aborted person has no mobility or conscious awareness. It is bodily and mentally inert. It will just be there indefinitely unless someone discovers and moves it. Sometimes spirit-embodied family, friends, or others are aware of the abortion and disapprove or just feel compassion for the aborted person and take it into spirit world to parent (ibid). In cases where the abortion happens while it's too small to see, a person can find it by its 'energy,' even if it's just a 3-month-old fetal human (Fig. 155:396), although the average person needs the help of someone skillfully aware of 'energies' in order to find the aborted person amidst the environment's ambient 'energies.'

The net result of aborting a physically-conceived person is that they're not dead but still existing spirit embodied in the 'reflective' environment, their spirit body lays abandoned wherever it spatially was the instant it physically died, and they cease experiencing stimulation from reality. Let's discuss this third aspect.

2.2.1.1   What Happens When Spirit-body Stimulation is Lost

The woʙ of emergent ℒife is that conscious awareness is tied to the body when conceived with embodiment whereas conscious awareness develops naturally in the unembodied-conceived. This means the unembodied don't depend on external-to-mind stimulus to develop conscious awareness. Instead, it's an organic occurrence because they don't integrate their proto-energy environment as an integrated body does its environment. The embodied person conceives integrating their spirit or physicospirit embodiment which serves as a partial facsimile of their larger environment. Although mind experiences a portion of its physical and spirit environment ('energy'), it can't experience its entire environment (the universe, other people, etc.) when lacking embodiment. An aborted person, therefore, is insensate to the 'reflective' environment beyond its subconscious awareness of ambient 'energies' and its spirit-embodied awareness of environmental stimuli in that environment. On their own, with Ultimaculture and Ultraculture as they are, these stimuli are insufficient to kick-start conscious mind development. The powerful 'energy' of human interaction is necessary. Lacking that, the (embodied) subconscious isn't stimulated to develop a conscious awareness. Mind development dramatically slows such that the spirit body goes inert and the person appears to be in stasis or without life.

Understanding the above, it's no surprise (according to Mina) that Earth's 'reflective' environment alone is littered with about 9.9 trillion unborn persons going back to the very start of Humanity 1.0 circa 7.0449 million

---

452. Ultimaculture's woʙ influences unawareness of our fundamental unembodiment. In an ideal Ultimaculture, the embodied-born would innately be consciously aware of their unembodiment.

453. We use quote marks throughout since 'angels' aren't real but merely regular human persons (Table 17:523).

years ago (§ 1.1.3:533). Considering all the geologic changes, about 99% are actually beneath today's surface, lying inert and as deep as almost 4,000 miles, nearly to the center of Earth's core[454] and all points between. In our universe of about 849 quadrillion persons, ~2% are aborted physical- and spirit-conceived persons, and ~18% are those who otherwise died before physical birth, scattered inert throughout the natural and supranatural environments. Historically, about 99.99% of spirit visitors to the physical ('reflective') environment ignore such *visible* inert persons—about 20% of the inert total—strewn all about because they appear spiritually 'dead' or in any case nonviable with no sign of ℒife. They see it as a problem beyond their ken. The *invisible* other 80% have no chance of casual discovery. But as more and more spirit persons develop awareness of the reality described here and join the search for these unborn persons, which gained interest in early 2018, they will eventually revive them all.[455]

2.2.2 ABORTION OF THE SPIRIT-CONCEIVED

Apart from deserving multitudes in dark anguish, popular imagination tends toward 'true spirituality' as joyful celestial light beyond vice. That's magical thinking. The spirit-born are the same human beings we are except they never experience the pressures of physical existence and don't manifest the traumas, psychoses, and behaviors of the physical-born. But spirit-born parents abort their children, too, though vastly less than the physical-born (per Mina, ~0.0001 per 1000 maternal persons[456] vs. ~13.65 per 1000 women in 2020). Although the spirit-born have always understood they were eternal beings, they presumed in their Corruption-induced ignorance that eternalness—*humanness*— started only after reaching a certain stage of development (embodied birth). Those few spirit-born who do abort conception adopt the mindset it's harmless, simply the termination of a nascent, as-yet-nonhuman life, just as the physical-born presume on Earth. Their supposition couldn't be farther from reality.

Unlike physically-conceived abortion, killing the spirit-conceived body to terminate birth is impossible. In the supranatural environment of Intentionality (§ 2.2:356), only the maternal parent needs Intentionalize abortion, unlike with conception (§ 1.2.1.1.2:249). It isn't difficult, taking about two minutes to form the Intention. The abortion occurs in the last picosecond of Intentionality (§ 3.2.1:282). In that instant, the maternal parent's body de-manifests, or dematerializes, leaving the now-aborted person behind who falls from the spatial location where the womb was only just materially located and into the hands of a third party who provides this service. It takes about fifteen minutes for the formerly maternal parent to re-manifest their body, and the abortion process is complete. He or she moves on to put their conscience—the sub-Thought of their conscious underlayment (§ 2.3:398; § 1.1.2.1:393)—to rest.

The abortion service provider takes the still-moving aborted body to an underground vault filled with baby-sized cubbyholes and inters the body, where it shortly goes inert. Recall the spirit body isn't destroyable because it's a manifestation of mind which, being ℒife, is eternal, defying all efforts to Intentionalize it out of existence. Before the Big Healing, the spirit-born presumed spirit matter's generalized eternal nature explained their body's indestructibility. Consequently, the aborted fetal body needed storing and the vault their chosen method; out of sight, out of mind.[457] The effect on the aborted person and parents is the same as for the physically alive. The child experiences harm, loss of human stimulation, goes inert, and the parents struggle with their nagging sense of wrongness.

2.2.3 ABORTION OF THE UNEMBODIED-CONCEIVED

It's impossible to abort an unembodied-conceived person. In this state of being, a person is simply ℒife. There's no body and no external-to-mind environment except proto-energy, which is everywhere. As described, one can Intentionalize proto-energy at the focal point of one's attention—say, another unembodied person—in

---

454. Fun fact: ᴇᴛ indicates the truly solid part of Earth's core is pure iron of dia. ~30 miles compressed to ~78% its maximum, while the remainder of the so-called inner core is a semisolid outer-inner core of dia. ~1,490 miles of ~69.4% iron, ~25% nickel, ~0.2% silicon, ~4.4% antimony, and ~1% tellurium.

455. Update: in November 2021, Mina surprised us by saying that consequent to post-Big Healing changes, one particular person's 'energy' began saturating our universe and, in consequence, heretofore-unfound aborted persons in our universe had been 'waking up' since July 12, 2020 and resuming natural mind–spirit-body growth and development toward adulthood.

456. Since the spirit born Intentionalize conception of a child without biological processes, and their mind Intentionalizes (manifests) their body sans biology, they're free to Intentionalize gestation in either parent's body according to preference (§ 38:595).

457. A spirit-born person whose body is maimed or 'killed' is taken to a similar public facility or a private home for however long it takes their mind to recover and re-Intentionalize (re-manifest) their body, the time needed differing per person.

order to aggravate them in some way, but can't cause damage, invade their mind, or kill them (§ 2.1.1:368). Once unembodied parents Intentionalize conception, there's no gestational period. Emergent birth is instantaneous (§ 1.2.1.1:248). To abort before completion, one must change their mind and cease Intentionalizing *before* reaching that last picosecond in which Intentionality becomes reality. This needn't be mutual. While mutuality is necessary to Intentionalize conception, it isn't necessary for one party to back out before completion, thus disrupting the Intentionality (§ 2.1.3.2:310). This isn't abortion because *L*ife has yet to coalesce into existence. It's like intending a splash from a stone that, at the last instant, one balks at throwing; no splash, no conception.

Neither do unembodied parents abandon their impossible-to-abort children because 'energy' intimately connects parents and child, the latter being true for the embodied, too. Physical parents for instance can abandon a child such that it can never find them again. But in a world with sufficient mind–brain integration, an abandoned child will sense his or her way back to their parents just as an abandoned dog can sense it's way home even over hundreds of miles. Like the unembodied, spirit-born parents can't abandon their children either because there's no mind–brain integration with spirit embodiment. Rather, they sense 'energy.' Therefore, an abandoned spirit-born child can always recognize its parents. In truth, any unembodied or embodied person who is so inclined would, if they could, abort or abandon their children. It's part of the human condition of ignorance in our universe arising in The Corruption's mindset addiction.

2.3 Euthanasia

There are two varieties to euthanizing a person, which is an activity only possible in the physical environment. First, one kills a person's body (painlessly or not) with their permission because of an incurable illness, injury, or whatever. Second, one kills a person's body without their permission, which is just killing as previously described (§ 2.1:407). Euthanasia in the former instance has no substantive meaning. It's simply the termination of one's physical embodiment which leaves them with their spirit embodiment and their continuing life in spirit world—a relocation, really. No harm, trauma, or loss of self-agency occurs because the euthanized person requests or permits it. They sort the issues arising in leaving their loved ones behind before euthanasia, thus no harm occurs for them despite their generalized sadness, unhappiness, or other felt emotion. Permissive euthanasia is a simple act of relieving a person of their physical embodiment without them having to do it themselves. A person at peace with ending their physical embodiment who then terminates it self-euthanizes, not suicides. That's entirely different.

2.4 Suicide

Suicide is the act of self-euthanizing. But it's rarely for the same reasons nor as painless as euthanasia intends and involves no peace of mind. The problem with suicide is that it arises in harm, not acceptance (§ 1.1.1:362). Rather than the physicospirit person terminating physical embodiment to begin spirit-embodied life at peace with themselves, their loved ones, and life in general, the suicide enters spirit world experiencing profound harm manifesting in distress, pain, and suffering. The issues prompting their suicide remain unresolved and unhealed. Psychoses or mental disturbances remain in effect. Since suffering from life's travails is of the mind, not the environment, one transitions with those, too. This is why Mina doesn't recommend suicide even though only the body dies, not the person. The harm inciting suicide remains firmly ensconced in the psyche, but one also creates new harm as well as provokes or intensifies the mindset of accusation and blame (§ 4.1.2:378; § 2.1.2.2.2:410) in themselves and their loved ones.

The suicide feels more miserable in spirit world than when physically alive for two reasons. First, they can't change their mind and, second, they can no longer necessarily access any of the people they might want or need to help them heal, can't confront the issues that arose in their physical environment if at some point they choose to, and can't comfort their loved ones mourning their loss. Other than judgy spirit persons who harass and afflict them for suiciding, there's no divine, creator, or moral judgment and punishment for it. It's just a simple transition of embodiment from Place A to Place B and no one cares beyond the suicide's family and friends here and in spirit world. Experiencing healing of harm and trauma is just as easy—though access to healing isn't necessarily equitable—in the physical as in the spirit world. In that respect, one rarely gains what they intended from suicide. It's true that one escapes the pressures and vagaries of physical life, but if rent, food, health, relationships, and the like were suicide's main motivators, we could easily reduce its rate of occurrence. Instead, the main motivator of suicide is harm, which only healing addresses. That's this book's purpose and all that follows publication.

SECTION 3
Lineage and DNA

A person's ancestry is their *lineage*, those historical persons whose baby-making back to the dawn of humanity resulted in their birth today. Lineage is an aspect of unembodied and embodied modes of being. There are four ways to understand it. First, humans are fundamentally *emergent*, unembodied mind *without* lineage. Second, it traces back through individual parental lines beyond our universe to the origins of humanity with Mike and Molly. Third, spirit-born lineage traces back through one's spirit body to one of the five founding couples who first populated our universe (§ 2.1.1:348). There's no difference between this and the second instance since mind manifests body and real lineage is of mind. Fourth, physical-born lineage traces back through physical *body* lines to Humanity 2.0's origin (§ 2.1.3:543) and its integrated *Life*; ultimately, to one of the five founding couples as with the spirit-born.

3.1 *Life* Mind is its Own Ancestor

Despite parents triggering a person's emergent birth 'in' EPL through pairwise Intentionality, he or she is a singular, unique, emergent being. One births out of 'nothing' 'in' EPL. In that respect you, for example, have no ancestry, lineage, nor generative forebears in the way physical humanity comprehends familial lines. You're not the child or parent of anyone in a lineal sense. You're literally your own ancestor, your alpha and omega. Your past and future lineage is only you. This is why you're unique and absolutely autonomous, beholden to nought but EPL, your real 'parent' in a sense. *Life* doesn't belong to parents, family, or lineage. These are *societally attached relationships of care* without custodial ownership or control. You societally attach *to* your family but aren't *of* the family. Every person is a genuine 'one-off,' not a lineal continuation. Ancestry and lineage, as it's commonly understood as a generational link from past to future, are artifacts of the Living (physical) body wholly unrelated to the ꝑerson having *Life* (see additional discussion in Angels, § 1.1.1:520).

Accordingly, we need distinguish ꝰuman lineage from *embodied* lineage because, first, embodiment isn't *Life* where real lineage reposes, and second, embodiment carries with it *traits* which *Life* mind doesn't. A person's embodied lineage, with its biologically inherited or Intentionalized traits of race, ethnicity, sex, DNA, and so forth (*below*) is immaterial to their ꝰuman lineage which is solely one of parentage. We therefore focus in this section on lineage as it pertains to embodied traits because parentage as lineage for the ꝑerson as an eternal being of mind is a simple concept to grasp and needs no additional discussion, and because the tendency to conflate traits with lineage where physical-born traits arising in biological DNA that can be manipulated and spirit–born traits arising in Intentionalized (§ 3.2:282) aesthetics confuses the issue. We describe the germane aspects of lineage below.

3.2 Physical-born Lineage

Traits of ancestors express in the physical-born to greater or lesser degrees for a variety of reasons, but are nothing more than the biological realities of the physical body. Recall that emergent *Life* doesn't birth with traits, particularly sex (§ 2.1.5.1:313). Every human being is unembodied mind first and embodiment second. One's mind only distinguishes itself from another by its *Life* distinctions such as 'energy,' personality, and Thought. Once embodied, however, a person *habituates* to their embodiment. The physical-born habituate to their biologically independent body from conception but are never educated as to their intrinsic unembodiment. Their habituation grows only more entrenched with time.

Consider a person surgically wired from birth into a futuristic fighting suit or conveyance. They grow to maturity controlling their vehicle via thought alone similar to Clint Eastwood's pilot in a stolen Soviet fighter in his 1982 film *Firefox* or the characters integrating their biological clones in the 2009 film *Avatar*. If no ever teaches such a person they're an independent being who can disconnect from and climb out of their equipment at will, they'll never even imagine the possibility because they *feel* they *are* their equipment. This is our situation regarding physical embodiment. Until the Big Healing enlightened most of the spirit-born, it was true of them as well.

Like any complex machinery, the physical body operates in accord with its purpose which arises in its woв. This includes its biological functionality and physiological traits. Science teaches that DNA is the genetic language, the operating code, by which every molecule and cell in our body comes to be and operates—how we as persons are and behave in all our functionality, traits, and preferences—but that isn't accurate. Let's consider DNA's methodology.

3.2.1 THE REALITY OF DNA

Biophysics as a general field of DNA science considers genetic code a complex language, every bit on par with human language, that communicates information—operational instructions—to living tissue. The DNA molecule serves as the information *medium* by which the language is independent of its carrier; one can convey that information on a chalkboard or in books, computer mediums, or across the Internet without changing the information itself. DNA *language* isn't the same thing as the DNA *molecule*, in that "the content of the message is independent of the physical makeup of the medium" (Johnson 1997, 71). American evolutionary biologist George C. Williams notes, "The gene is a package of information, not an object. The pattern of base pairs in a DNA molecule specifies the gene. But the DNA molecule is the medium, it's not the message" (Penrose 1995, 43).

But relating genetic language, or information, to words on a page or transmitted code is inaccurate. Genetic code isn't *conveyed information*,[458] it's *expressed Intentionality*. Genetic language is information through a medium *to us* but a medium of expression *to the body* where the DNA molecule is an integral part of the message, i.e., the code itself, the various ordering of DNA base pairs. This means genetic code, including the DNA molecule, is altogether genetic language and is the biology of Intentionality.

The DNA molecule *as* the medium *is* the message because genetic information expresses only through this medium. One can't put the genome in a book, or an RNA base pair into a DNA medium, or store a CAD drawing of a hard drive on the same model hard drive, and then expect it to *express*. In these cases, it's nothing more than *data*. We can analyze it in its medium—the essence of information is when we view data in a given context through analysis by organizing, considering, and presenting it in such a way that it's useful (§ 1.1.1:84)—and yet never *produce* hands, feet, noses, or hard drives separate from its medium. Genetic *data* (base pairs) only becomes genetic *information* (base pairs in a particular order) to its medium in the context of a DNA molecule. Through its expression, Intentionality *is* biology. Genetic language has no meaning when conveyed in another medium. It's not information in that context. It's simply data. Although *we* can derive information from it in that context, what we're educing isn't the information expressed by genetic language but *different* information, not *genetic* information.

A spoken word—the sound wave—is the medium for the information represented by the word, but we can't extrapolate that to thinking proto-energy is the medium for the information represented by the thought the word embodies. It's not. Rather, information *is* thought which *is* proto-energy. The information that is thought is inseparable from its proto-energy medium. The two are one and the same. While the spoken word is the medium, not the message, thought's proto-energy medium *is* the message and the message *is* the medium. This is why Intentionality works, why it is what it is. An exerted thought is Intentional because it's proto-energy. If one could remove the information of thought from its proto-energy medium then it would no longer be thought but data. Similarly, genetic language is, in its own way, also thought. Not thinking-thought, but Intentionality which is Intentionalized proto-energy, meaning proto-energy embodying Thought. It represents an aspect of *L*ife's WOB.

Information is of mind the way matter (archí) is of proto-energy. There's no information per se embodied in proto-energy. Matter itself is information arising in the Energent just as Intentionality is information arising in *L*ife. Matter is the medium for information in the context of proto-energy and Intentionality is the medium for information in the context of *L*ife. In both cases, the medium *is* the message because the message is inseparable from its context. Decontextualizing it nixes the message. Matter is proto-energy communicating, Intentionality is *L*ife communicating. Human Thought, thus language, *is* Intentionality. This is why spirit persons can communicate, and physical persons can sense, mind-to-mind; it happens via Intentionality, not as some magical mind telepathy.

Nucleotides, the so-called building blocks of DNA, are more fundamental than DNA in terms of genetic language. The five chemical bases that constitute nucleotides are *its* DNA so to speak. Nucleotides are the 'rules' of genetic language. The five chemical bases are singular Intentionalities that variously combine to create a single nucleotide molecule to represent some base aspect of *L*ife's WOB. Five base Intentionalities form

---

458. In Williams' analogy, the information constituting *Don Quixote* remains *Don Quixote* whichever medium conveys the words, or narrative language, of the story (or the information related to how hands, feet, or noses are made) and is what persists, not the medium—book, audio tape, e-book—conveying that information.

the base structure and operability of the human body. The five chemical bases collectively mix-and-match approximately 18,000 different ways to create that many variant nucleobases. These in turn build contextual variants of the A, T, C, G, and U nucleotides when they bond as DNA and RNA such that one A–T DNA pairing isn't necessarily exactly the same as any other A–T pairing which ultimately codes the same albeit variant proteins. This is similar to type-identical objects constituting from different archi substructures yet still having, for example, quark-ness (FN 278:238).

DNA is the human body's WOB Intentionalizing into its biology to effect its structure and operability in accord with ℒife's WOB. It isn't a medium nor conveys information. Genetic code in the DNA molecule is *altogether a singular message* expressed in the context of the body. It's Intentionalized ℒife (as well as Intentionalized Living; § 1:246). This is why a person's body can be of a lineage without necessarily expressing its genetics, which we consider in some minor detail next.

3.2.2 Biological Sexes

We described the origin of the sexes in Rise of the Humans (§ 2.1.5.1:313). Here, we describe why humanity considering sex a fundamental reality that defines the person—although accurate as an experience because of habituation—is inaccurate as a human WOB. Despite various biological discrepancies in sex (*below*) and personal perspectives about gender, human pairwise reproduction is consistent with Mike and Molly (§ 2:304) as well as matter emergently arising pairwise (§ 2.2:114). Consequently, only sperm–egg fertilization triggers new physical-born ℒife along with its sex-specific physicospirit body (§ 1.2.1.1:248). Discrepancies in sex beyond the XX and XY female–male karyotypes don't constitute different biological sexes outside the male–female pattern but *variants*. A human body that can sexually reproduce is only ever male or female, which is to say, sperm-centric or egg-centric.

Physical humanity experiences male–female biology as a fundament because it's unaware of its own WOB, which it further obfuscates by defining mind as an emergent property of brain in which male–female mental states are evolutionarily hardwired, thus genetically immutable. Recall, however, that ℒife emergently births without sex or gender (§ 2:304), and the spirit body is eminently mutable in this respect. When the body dies, a person is free to change how they Intentionalize (manifest) their spirit body's traits regarding race, ethnicity, sex, and other aesthetics. Although biological sex is intrinsic and inherent to the physical-born, it doesn't define the person. That's habituation's bailiwick. The so-called hardwired differences in male and female brains are illusory in the sense of immutability. The brain is plastic. One can rewire every aspect of it although some aspects are more ingrained than others and require greater effort than a person might have lifespan left to accomplish. Nevertheless, observation shows there are discrepancies in human biology such as variants in sex and concomitant brain wiring. Science chalks these up to evolutionary or reproductive errors, but that's not quite correct. Let's consider that.

3.2.2.1 Biology Inherits Automatically or Intentionally

Physical humans inherit biological traits automatically via genetic inheritance or spiritually through Intentionalized 'inheritance.'[459] Automatic inheritance is straightforward and described well enough by science for our purposes, so we don't go into it here. But Intentionalized 'inheritance' needs mention.

We described in § 2.1.5.5.2:323 how there's no undirected (random) human-body evolution. Changes to the normatively biologically inheritable human genome that aren't the result of biological contamination, such as radiation or chemicals, are directed—Intentionalized—changes either by Mina or spirit persons acting on their own for their own reasons. Recall our above discussion of DNA. Spirit persons Intentionalize two types of genomic change to physiology, the first being genotype–phenotype trait changes such as eye color, height, racial–ethnic appearance, genetic expression, and so forth and the second being alterations to normative mind–brain integration. We consider each.

3.2.2.1.1 Altering Physiological Traits

Trait changes constitute 99.99% of all physiological changes made to physical bodies by spirit persons inclusive of Mina. These include manipulating inherited DNA, making changes to sperm DNA prior to fertilization, targeting specific sperm for fertilization via its 'energy' signature, avoiding fertilization with an undesired

---

459. People also 'inherit' mind traits through culture; a 'chip off the old block' references enculturation.

egg while ensuring fertilization when one with desired traits releases from the ovary, turning desired genes on or off, ensuring dominance of certain alleles (say, for eye color), and so on. Trained spirit persons can manipulate every aspect of physiology through Intentionality just as trained geneticists do within the scope of the field's competency. Historically, one or more spirit persons at the same or different time exclusive of Mina have, in some manner, physiologically manipulated ~6.5% of all physical humans ever conceived on every human-inhabited planet, split roughly equally before and after birth.

This is the real reason behind apparently random genetic expression; dominant, recessive, intermediate, or polygenic genes; hormonal issues; gland failures; and the like that aren't the result of environment, lifestyle, or other factors. The reasons vary, but generally fall into three categories. First, one wants to see themselves reflected in some preferred way in their or someone else's descendant.[460] Second, one desires a physical person to accomplish something specific in the physical world for which they consider certain traits most efficacious. And third, one physiologically harms an individual in order to harm others. Everything from birth defects and ugliness to heightened abilities and beauty that aren't directly attributable to parental behavior, environment, or unmanipulated genetics arise in such behavior.

Manipulators exclusive of Mina intend their changes to be harmless, benign, empowering, or advantageous in some way ~45% of the time, with the remainder intended as harmful. Even so, unintended harm follows the former ~90% of the time. Interfering with a person's physiology is an assault on their autonomy, whether Mina or anyone does it. From Mina's perspective, even he has no right to interfere in a person's physical life experience . . . but does anyway when he feels it's in the person's best interest toward mitigating The Corruption and suffering. About 10% of such manipulators exclusive of Mina intend their changes in the same vein but only ~18.2% of those actually achieve it without concomitantly creating greater harm. Even ~12% of Mina's efforts result in more harm than the good he intended.

There's a variety of reasons in both instances. For instance, a person doesn't respond as intended but uses whatever advantage they may have gained for harm. Or, a change backfired because aspects of the person's lifestyle either negates it or increases its harmful effects on the person or those in proximity. Or, it has the effect of inviting other spirit persons of lesser integrity to effect their own additional changes that interact harmfully with the original change. Even in a world without The Corruption and Accountableism (§ 4.1.2:378), human relations are such that spirit persons will always interfere to some albeit a greatly lesser degree with physiology although, in this ideal case, parents and others will have commensurately greater cognizance of their physicospirit environment and can act preventively.

3.2.2.1.2 ALTERING MIND–BRAIN INTEGRATION

A spirit person needn't alter a physical person's physiology to achieve a desired effect. Improving or degrading mind–brain integration influences a person's lifestyle and spiritual awareness without resorting to other manipulations. This type of physiological change is significantly more difficult to achieve than simple trait changes; only about 0.01% of physiological change results from this method.

Ayako refers to improving mind–brain integration as metaphorically inheriting 'spiritual DNA' from a 'second spiritual parent.' A spirit person can improve or degrade mind–brain integration in an attempt to improve or degrade a desired or undesired outcome, such as ensuring a person conceives with capabilities enabling them to affect human society for good or ill.[461] This is why some people are born with above average spiritual awareness, clair abilities, and Intentional power. Mina tells us, for example, the Greek gods were physical people born significantly earlier than ancient Greece, generally around the eastern Mediterranean, having physiological and mind–brain integration changes by 'second spiritual parents' (§ 1.2.3.2:470). These gave them superior physical and spiritual capabilities which they used to achieve notable accomplishments. Over time, these morphed them in the eyes of the ambient population into godlike heroes and eventually actual gods (§ 1.1:570) in exactly the way ancient Christians lionized Jesus from a mere mortal having superior spiritual awareness and Intentional power to being God, the Creator Himself.

With her background in Japanese anime, Ayako calls such physical people having 'second spiritual parents' *hybrids*—five exist in America, China, and Japan—because they physically embody some of the traits, capabilities, and especially 'energy' of spiritually powerful spirit persons. These include 'ancients' like the original

---

460. *Obāsan* Intentionalized Ayako to look just like her, which her still-living sister in Japan tearfully recognized with Akiō.

461. In this respect, Mina's ongoing struggle even after the Big Healing is with spirit persons, not to mention physical despoilers, who don't want society to mend and interfere accordingly.

five Founders of humanity in our universe (§ 2.1.1:348) and descendants not too generationally distant who maintain close ties with Mina. 'Hybrids' are well-versed in, and able to marshal, proto-energy for Intentional purposes beyond the ordinary spirit person's capability, setting them apart from the everyday physical-born. The reason 'hybrids' are now a rarity is that long ago, when Humanity 2.0 was small and scattered, such spirit persons felt they had a good shot at altering our trajectory away from the worst of The Corruption as well as Humanity 1.0's ignominious end (§ 1.3:538). They never achieved their goals, however—if they'd consulted Mina they'd have known that beforehand—and eventually gave up, leaving the physical-born of our world to their own devices, Mina, and the scads of spirit people manipulating physiology for their own ends.[462]

3.2.2.1.3 RACE AND ETHNICITY

Race and ethnicity are two of the most visible aspects of a person and people tend to focus on it. Historically, these were valued and respected ways to perceive others—a prime source of strife as well—as ineluctable lineal realities going back to our ancient forebears. Until Europeans developed the scientific method and strove to categorize toward understanding Earth's flora, fauna, geology, and human origins, race and ethnicity were mere philosophical, cultural, and theological *beliefs*. As science gained an infallible reputation, its observations consistent with race and ethnicity took on the appearance of being grounded in universal truth until scientific advances in genetics indicated they weren't the only—if not the least biologically relevant—means of categorizing people. Consequently, genetics moved to the forefront of classifying people. But just as with race and ethnicity it equally imperils the not-me and not-us. The same mindset that previously relied on scientific racism, patriotic or cultural ethnocentrism, or theology to disparage individuals and groups shifted to genetics as the final word on whomever socioculture predisposes toward a problematic or undesired existence. Eugenics to improve or eliminate such people was quite popular in the early twentieth century and similar efforts now using genetic prophecy have yet to cease.

Race and ethnicity let us visually comprehend lineage. A black person comes from black lineage, white from white, and so on with all the mixed-race, ethno-diversity in between. But these are plastic in the hands of environment and Intentionalizing spirit persons who manipulate physiology over time in individuals, families, and groups. The out-of-Africa human origin theory enjoys widespread buy-in but, as racioethnically diverse as our global population is, it's plain that race and ethnicity are irrelevant and immaterial. Even diseases and physiological predispositions ascribed to these are false. They don't arise in genetic lineage but over time in spirit manipulation and lifestyle, mindstate, mindset, and the like habituating them. This book represents a post-racial, post-ethnic, post-classificatory humanity.

Moreover, observable race and ethnicity are wholly unconnected to lineage. For example, one can observe visually and via genetic testing that I embody general northern European and Irish-Scots ethnicity and my race is Caucasian. Yet, my paternal great-grandfather is Chiricahua Apache (with Comanche), and a maternal great-great-grandfather is Natchitoches, giving me a lineage that's 50% Apache and 10% Natchitoches, even though my dominantly expressed genetic (DNA) ethnicity is European. This results from lineage mixed with spirit persons' physiological manipulation and is common in the population.

3.3 SPIRIT-BORN LINEAGE

The spirit-born don't automatically embody the traits of their ancestors as with the physical-born, but rather the *aesthetics* their parents Intentionalized at conception which, when old enough, about 1.5% of the population alters anyway to express their own personal preferences. It isn't possible for a third party to Intentionalize any aspect of a spirit-born person's bodily aesthetics. Only parents can Intentionalize conception that at the same time embodies the child's aesthetics in all respects, which Intentional ability ends upon emergent birth. In the same way one can't Intentionalize any change to a universe one didn't create, one can't Intentionalize any change to a spirit-born person except during that final picosecond of Intentionalized conception. The reason is that spirit embodiment manifests in the person's mind rather than the independent, thus manipulable, biology of a physical body.

Race and ethnicity are nothing more than aesthetics of the spirit body and are changeable at will not only permanently, but temporarily, too. Whether physical- or spirit-born, a spirit person can manifest their spirit embodiment day to day in whatever form they want and for which they have the energy to maintain. Ayako calls

---

462. Of all the physical-born persons elevated to gods over our history, only the Greek 'gods' took their 'duties' seriously after death and routinely helped, as possible, those who prayed to—communicated with—them for intervention.

such temporary embodiment forms *glamours* (§ 2.1.5.4.4:318). Being more aware of our spirit reality than am I, she occasionally reports that, although when I'm in spirit world my spirit body aesthetics are the same as my current physical look and feel, I occasionally take on a twenty-something glamour to better fit in with her crowd.

3.4 Unembodied-born Lineage

It's even simpler for the unembodied-born who are conceived without any body at all (§ 1.2.1.1.3:250). They live simply as mind. Like the spirit-born, third parties can't manipulate the unembodied-born—nor can their parents for that matter, who in this mode of being can only trigger 𝓛ife to emergently birth 'in' EPL via Intentionality—and lineage proceeds in accord with parentage.

SECTION 4
What Happens at Death

We fear death not because it can be painful or scary but because, for all appearances, *life ends* and no one reliably knows what, if anything, comes after. Perhaps at this point in the book you've concluded there's more to life and death than meets the eye, that maybe when understanding reality as it is, physical life's *apparent* end just "ain't no big thing" (*Love Letters From Elvis*, 1971). There are three aspects to the death process: the body expires, one becomes aware of the change, and accepts it or not. We consider each in order.

4.1 Physical Death

Howsoever a person's death happens—instantaneous, gradual, prolonged, peaceful, terrifying—a whole host of events occurs in an orderly shutdown of physical embodiment. Whether it's disease, injury, or even just a will to die that presents fatally in the body, eventually brainstem death arrives and is irrecoverable. It signals the lack of a brain for mind to integrate. A person's 𝓛ife force loses its physical counterpart and mind–brain integration becomes an open circuit where 𝓛ife force integration fails. Even so, parts of the brain and body continue living as a function of metabolism—recall the human body is Living, not having 𝓛ife (§ 1.3:272)—which operates on the residue of 𝓛ife force the body still imbues.

Aliveness isn't simply the product of chemistry but of 𝓛ife force imbuing the body via integration (§ 1.3.1:272). The body's matter–Energy interacts with proto-energy and chemistry enlivens metabolism. But these processes inexorably lose vitality as the body's residually imbued 𝓛ife force dissipates following brainstem death until even machines can't keep it going. The failure of life support isn't because the brain is no longer secreting, or signaling the body to secrete, necessary hormones, enzymes, and the like. If it were, machines could maintain cellular metabolism indefinitely despite the body no longer functioning as a wholistic entity. Rather, our body's aliveness depends on 𝓛ife force. If that's gone, so, too, is life. Below, we describe how death terminates mind–brain integration, the various means by which it happens, and the shift of one's conscious awareness to their spirit self as the process end state.

4.1.1 Mind–Brain Integration Terminates

Recall *you* are not your *body*. You are mind, your 𝓛ife self. Your body physically manifests your unembodied mind and depends for its existence entirely on your 𝓛ife force via mind–brain integration.[463] When death severs integration, the body loses its charger so to speak. It runs down then shuts down. Human mind–brain integration is complex. It wholistically integrates mind and the supranatural environment via three points of integration. First, 𝓛ife force integrates the brainstem to enable neuronal harmonics through which 𝓛ife mind 'regions' integrate specific neuronal structures throughout the brain (§ 1.2.2.4.1:257). This is the origin of the so-called 'silver cord' (Eccl. 12:6). Second, each atom of the body, including in the brain's non-neuronal structures as well as the non-neuronal aspect of neurons, absorbs 𝓛ife force from the spirit body because it occupies the same space in the 'reflective' environment as it does in the natural environment (§ 7.1.1.1:212; PONS (THIRD EYE) CHAKRA, § 1.2.1.3.2:502).

---

463. The body absorbs 𝓛ife force from the whole spirit body it fully integrates, meaning it occupies the same space as the physical body. Activities like astral projecting for too long a time removes the whole spirit body from the physical body, thus severing it from ~80% of its necessary 𝓛ife force, which, if left too long, leads to death.

For example, if a spirit person visiting Earth's 'reflective' environment curls up in the same spatial location as a physical animal sleeping on the floor, then the animal's body absorbs *L*ife force from that spirit person (in addition to its normal Living force) so long as they're occupying the same space. This is the case with any mammalian body. *L*ife force enlivens the human body just as Living force enlivens the nonhuman body (CHEMISTRY AS LIFE, § 1.3.1:272). Remove the spirit body from the physical body and there's no *L*ife force being absorbed because the brainstem nexus doesn't supply the whole body. Third, the chakras integrate the body wholistically with the 'reflective' environment as a natural–supranatural brain integrator, meaning it interfaces a physical person with spirit persons. Having described the second point of integration in § 1.2.2.4.1:257, we describe the first point below—with a follow-on caveat regarding the second point—and the third later in our description of the chakras (§ 1.2.1.3:501).

4.1.1.1 BRAINSTEM INTEGRATES *L*IFE FORCE

The brain supports the presence of *L*ife mind in the natural environment, the body supports the brain, and the environment supports the body. Altogether, the natural environment is a tightly knit, integrated collective enabling physical humanity. The human brain integrates *L*ife force to function as a facsimile mind in an environment where unembodied mind can't interact on its own (§ 1.2.2.1:253). It integrates *L*ife force in two ways. First, to enliven the matter from which the brain and body constitute from inert to alive and, second, to enable neuronal harmonics by which neurons map specific 'regions' of *L*ife mind into the brain, thereby transliterating mind awareness to brain cognition. Recall that *L*ife force isn't simply some exotic 'energy.' It's literally mind itself, the self-aware ᴘerson (§ 2.1.5.4.8:321). This self-aware proto-energy integrates every atom and neuron of the brain, thus manifesting mind. We described neuronal transliteration of mind awareness to brain cognition in HUMAN MIND–BRAIN–BODY (§ 1.2.2:253) and don't revisit it here but, instead, describe brainstem integration of *L*ife force.

The brainstem is the nexus of *L*ife force integrating brain. Any damage to it degrades integration, thus the brain's operability. Sufficient damage results in insufficient *L*ife force integration to maintain the brain's aliveness, leading to its death. The brainstem can die even though other aspects of the brain and body exhibit some semblance of function. This doesn't mean a person's brain isn't already dead, only that the whole brain (and body) continues absorbing residual *L*ife force over a short duration even though the brainstem itself is no longer capable of integrating it and therefore kaput. Residual *L*ife force expires on average about 3.25 minutes following brainstem death, and cellular activity throughout the body a few minutes later. Brainstem death is irrevocable. Once mind–brain integration fails, there's no coming back. Even the slenderest tendril of *L*ife force integration means the physical body can recover if the relevant damage is repairable. Brainstem death means there isn't even the slenderest tendril of *L*ife force integration, that the physical and spirit bodies have permanently disengaged and gone their separate ways and that further maintenance of metabolism by machine is just blowing in the wind.

4.1.1.1.1 THE 'SILVER CORD' PARTS AT BRAINSTEM DEATH

One's *L*ife force, their *L*ife self that is self-aware proto-energy, integrates ('binds together') the physicospirit body (*Fig. 159*, left) and is the so-called 'silver cord' of Ecclesiastes 12:6 and the 'ethereal thread' that mystics and spiritualists observe to part, or snap, at death (*Fig. 159*, right). What's happening is that, upon brainstem death, *L*ife force has nothing to integrate, its dance partner has left the floor. It 'withdraws' from the physical body back into one's *L*ife self. This event appears to spiritualists as a parting of a 'string of energy' at death. It's like taking one's hand from around a close friend's shoulders and putting it back into one's own pocket so each can go their own ways. The connection isn't magical or forced. "It's not welded to you," Ayako remarks, "it's held there by your own will to live." And it's only that strong.

4.1.1.2 THE NEXUS OF INTENTIONALITY

Recall that *L*ife force doesn't just absorb into the physical body from our *L*ife self. It's also Intentionalizable, meaning one can harness it to accomplish an intention (§ 3.2:282). The brainstem is the *L*ife force nexus of physicospirit integration. Every atom of the body inclusive of brain independently absorbs it to maintain aliveness as described. Its *Intentionalized* nexus for the brain is the brainstem and for the body exclusive of brain the third and fourth lumbar area that's roughly, on average, the body's midpoint (*Fig. 160*). *L*ife force

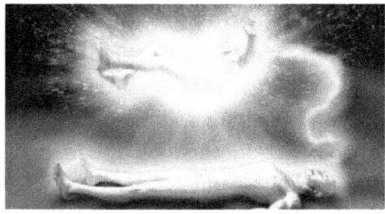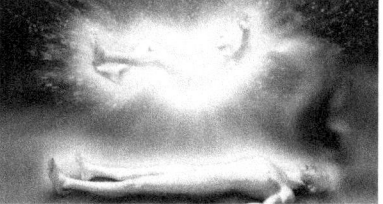

Figure 159. Left, ℒife force integrates the physicospirit body before death as the 'silver cord;' right, ℒife force withdraws from the physical body at brainstem death.₂₇₁

enlivens the whole body because the spirit body is spatially congruent with it, absorbing—integrating—from the one to the other. When one Intentionalizes it into their body—to heal, improve mind–brain integration, improve health, reduce pain—*that* ℒife force is additional to what's already absorbing into the body's atoms. It absorbs via the aforementioned loci where, from each nexus, it follows Intentionality to its desired location in the knee, facial skin, an organ, a part of the brain. When a person pulls in ℒife force this way, it produces palpable heat which the girls and I experience originating in the lumbar region, along the spine, and in the Intentionalized (focal) areas.

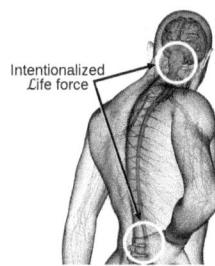

Intentionalized
ℒife force

Figure 160. Nexus of Intentionalized ℒife force entering (integrating) the physical body.₂₇₂

4.1.2   MEANS OF DEATH

A body dies instantaneously or not with the body's total destruction or not. We consider the effect of each.

4.1.2.1   INSTANTANEOUS AND NON-INSTANTANEOUS DEATH

People die from a vast array of causes, some of which bring it about instantaneously. Here, brainstem or body damage is instantly irrevocable and brainstem death inevitably follows, instantly or over some period. When death follows instantly, it catches the person unawares and can leave them confused, so much so that even when spirit persons tell them they're dead, and they visually confirm their inert physical body with their own (spirit) eyes, they reject it. Indeed, they pretend they're still alive and live that way in the 'reflective' environment. But instantaneous also means unexpected, although unexpected isn't always instantaneous. For example, a parachutist falling to earth with a tangled chute dies instantly upon landing but it isn't unexpected, they've had seconds to minutes to realize their situation, exhaust their options, accept the inevitable, perhaps rail against their fate, and watch the ground arrive. If you've ever fallen off a ladder higher than 15–20 feet, you'll have an inkling of the doomed parachutist's experience.

When a person takes time to die, especially having awareness of dying, then the process is less the mental shock of instantaneous death. It normalizes death, making it more easily accepted. Those who unexpectedly fall into unconsciousness or coma, if they're spirit-aware, realize their body's impending death and converse with their spirit guide(s), family, and friends while waiting. A physical person can tell such a dying person how they feel, apologize for things, or whatever and the dying person's spirit self will hear them. When the physical person is spirit-aware, their spirit selves communicate as normal in the 'reflective' environment even though the awake, physical person is unaware of it. If the dying person isn't spirit-aware, meaning they're not only physically unconscious but also spirit-unaware on their deathbed, then when their physical body expires and they're spiritually free of it, Mina reports that, without exception, they spiritually visit at least once every physically alive person with whom they have or had a relationship that matters to them. So, the physical person left behind always has an opportunity to express their feelings even when, prior to a loved one's unconsciousness and death, they didn't. Moreover, one can always call to that person in spirit world who (if they desire) will pay attention to what one says and feels. Despite the still degraded mind–brain integration that leaves us feeling cut off from spirit persons, the physically alive are never truly separated from the so-called dead.

Spirit persons waiting on a loved one's death can't communicate with a spirit-unaware spirit person any more than a physical person can with the comatose. For example, my mother was vibrant for about two years after my father died, but then decided she was ready to go, too. Her *Life* mind progressively reduced the *Life* force integrating her physical body and, in short order, degraded her mind–brain integration that physically manifested as dementia to which she appeared to succumb after about 3.5 years. The effect of dementia isn't what killed her body, but diminishing *Life* force. Because she was spirit-unaware, my father, who always visited her, couldn't communicate with her. He waited at her deathbed in the 'reflective' environment for her physical end just as our family did in the physical environment. Although her spirit self—laying there integrating her physical body—was conscious and could see and hear everything in her room, including my father's spirit self, her mind wasn't lucid in the sense she took it all as a dream, unaware of it like a person in a delirium who's awake and seemingly responsive but incognizant. When her body died, he was at her bedside as her physicospirit embodiment de-integrated. Her conscious awareness then immediately shifted from her physical to spirit reality, now having awareness as a spirit-embodied person as her physical body ceased affecting (interacting with) her spirit self.

4.1.2.2   TOTAL BODY DESTRUCTION AND INTACT BODY DEATH

In deaths caused by explosion, vaporizing heat, mutilation that prevents recognition, and so forth, one won't even have a recognizable dead body to visually confirm they're in an out-of-body state. For example, the WWII Hiroshima and Nagasaki atomic bomb victims' physical bodies vaporized from around their spirit bodies. They were left spiritually standing in the 'reflective' environment yet physically dead in the natural one which had instantly gone from normal to destroyed. From their new perspective in the 'reflective,' they and their surroundings hadn't appreciably changed.[464] They still thought, felt, experienced, saw, heard, smelled, tasted. It wasn't apparent the city was destroyed or they were dead. There was no dead body to see, no sense of injury, no sense of being not-physical since the spirit body feels to oneself every bit as material and real as the physical body. For them, it seemed as if they and the world around them were continuing on as normal. One second they were a physical person and the next they weren't. It was that imperceptible. Even if they'd cognized the atomic flash, being vaporized was inconceivable for them.

Mina says ~7.8% (2022; down from 8% in 2020) of this victim population still rejects being physically dead and continues living in and around these two cities as if alive, ignoring the differences then and now of the 'reflective' city which they can't explain (recall, too, that time is generally subjective for spirit persons). The other 92% accepted their reality between ~45 minutes and six years after they died. It took *Obāsan* about an hour in July 1945 to realize and then accept a bomb had destroyed her body even though she'd seen and heard the planes and explosions. And so it goes in the world day after day, millennia upon millennia.

A person's body also dies instantly yet without visible damage as in a bomb blast, say, where no shrapnel, flames, or heat affect the body but the pressure wave pulps the internal organs. Brainstem death is instant. The spirit person sees their physical body simply fall away from their no longer integrated, still-standing spirit self. Where physical damage is instantly fatal but brainstem death isn't, the spirit body remains integrated, spatially following the physical body flying through the air, falling, and so on.

4.1.3   CONSCIOUS AWARENESS SHIFTS TO SPIRIT SELF

Regardless how the physical body dies, the integrated spirit body initially remains in the same environment— the battlefield, street, bed, crashed car, burned house . . . wherever. When a person loses physical conscious awareness before or upon brainstem death, they remain consciously aware as a spirit person. A person dying in the movies—in someone's arms mumbling their vision is narrowing into a tunnel, going dark, their hearing fading, eyes going fixed or closing, plainly losing consciousness, head lolling to the side as they expire—hasn't lost *mind* consciousness (awareness), only their *brain* has. We're used to how we lose consciousness when punched

---

464. While the 'reflective' environment 'reflects' physical reality, spirit persons Intentionalize changes amongst it. I've caught only short glimpes, but Mina and Ayako describe a "sea caption" helping my spirit self remodel my New Mexico apartment in a seafaring motif. Similarly, Hiroshima and Nagasake outwardly looked the same to the suddenly dead bomb victims although, if for instance they went home, it might look completely and inexplicably different on the inside.

on the chin, have a seizure, or faint and all goes dark. Then we regain consciousness slowly, groggily, dazed, confused, realizing some time has passed and concluding we've been unconscious. Death doesn't work that way.

ℒife mind is always aware. The spirit self is never unconscious although not necessarily always aware, either (one can sleep, too). Because The Corruption limits mind–brain integration, we aren't physically aware of our spirit embodiment. When we lose physical consciousness prior to brainstem death, our spirit self is still awake though not always consciously aware. Suppose a physical person is sitting in a chair reading a book and has a heart attack. Their blood pressure drops too low for brain consciousness. The sensation of unconsciousness gradually comes upon them or it's instant and, without knowing it, they're out.

Now suppose in Case 1 that someone finds this person and calls an ambulance, thus saving their life. Some hours later, they awake in a hospital bed and realize they were unconscious. This person is spirit-unaware, so they have no memory of being spiritually conscious and possibly aware during this period of physical unconsciousness because their mind–brain integration is limited. If they do remember anything from the 'reflective' environment, they take it as a dream, hallucination, or a near-death experience (NDE, *below*). For their physical self, it was simply a period of unawareness where one moment they were reading a book (or standing in church; EN 47:648) and, the next, were in a hospital bed.

Suppose in Case 2 that no one finds the heart-attack person in the chair. They've lost physical consciousness but their spirit self is awake and consciously aware because in this case they're spirit-aware. They see, hear, experience, and interact with everything around them in the 'reflective' environment as a recognized reality, not a figment of mind. As the body weakens and death approaches, mind–brain integration lessens until it no longer constrains the spirit body and the spirit person can spatially move away from their physical embodiment. If the body recovers, then mind–brain integration strengthens and pulls the spirit body back into the physical body's spatial location. When the person awakens, they may or may not remember this period of spirit-self awareness. But suppose the person doesn't recover and their body dies. Their spirit self doesn't wake up as though from sleep or unconsciousness upon mind–brain de-integration because their *mind* was always conscious throughout their *brain's* unconsciousness. The person is simply aware of their physical body's death and of no longer integrating it. One doesn't wake up from unconsciousness in spirit world after the physical body drops into unconsciousness and dies. Their conscious awareness simply shifts from their physical brainstate to spirit mindstate, both of which represent ℒife mind (cf. Hannibal; CH. 40:608). In this respect, it's similar to instantaneous death where one moment one is physical and physically conscious and the next, they're spirit and spiritually conscious, but throughout it all they're never *not* conscious even if, as described earlier, they're not necessarily *aware*.

4.1.3.1 Near-death Experience

A near-death experience (NDE[465]) is a person's physical self remembering their spirit self's awareness in the 'reflective' environment as described. The out-of-body experience (OBE) during some NDEs have been verified by those whose activities and events the NDE describes—in the same or different rooms, hallways, or areas where an NDE's physical body was located—of which an unconscious person near death could have no knowledge. The NDE OBE arises where the spirit body repulses from the dying physical body and the physical person (§ 1.2.2.1:253), when resuscitated, remembers the experience. We describe each aspect below.

4.1.3.1.1 Physical Body Repulses Spirit Body

Normally, mind–brain integration binds the spirit body to the physical body which we describe altogether as physicospirit embodiment (§ 1.2.2.3:256). In an NDE, one's spirit body moves away from the physical body not unlike astral projecting (§ 1:591), except the physical person is unconscious. To remove one's spirit body permanently from physical body integration prior to death, one chooses to degrade their ℒife force bond (§ 4.1.2.1:421). Sometimes a person does this and people say they died of a broken heart, from losing the will to live, and so on because their death seems inexplicable. Even when a person consciously desires to remain physically alive, their subconscious may not and acts on it through Intentionality (§ 3.2:282; § 2.2.2.1:396). This is a method of self-euthanasia (§ 2.4:413). In the NDE context, however, the physical body's state of near death weakens physicospirit integration naturally rather than by choice. This means, owing to its health condition, the physical body absorbs less ℒife force. Thus, an imbalance arises between it and the spirit body still manifesting mind's unimpeded ℒife force.

---

465. Coined by Raymond Moody in *Life After Life* (1975, 11).

In a sense, both bodies exhibit a repulsive force like the same poles of a magnet. The closer the physical body gets to death, the more the spirit body repulses from it. Such a person can move around in their spirit body according to how weakened, thus repulsive, their physicospirit integration has got. With brainstem death, physicospirit integration permanently sunders and there's no going back. Near-death means a person's physical body moved into, but then retreated from, the process of dying with physicospirit integration concomitantly weakening and repulsing, and then strengthening and attracting.

4.1.3.1.2 The Person Remembers the Experience

Whether a person is physically conscious or not, the spirit self is always conscious. In a near-death scenario, the physical body is nearly or technically (but not brainstem) dead. Consequently, a person's awareness has shifted from their physical to their spirit self regardless previous spirit unawareness, and now their spirit self is consciously surprised, frightened, or amazed. Recall dreams are nothing more than memories of one's mind or spirit-self activities while physically asleep that are fragmented by inadequate mind–brain integration via NeuN-positive ependymal cells (§ 1.2.2.7.3:267). This is precisely what an NDE is: a memory, not a hallucination. About 75% of all NDEs have memory—the remainder present with dream—characteristics.

The reason why a person—who normally recalls dreams rather than memories—wakes up from experiencing an NDE with a coherent memory instead of a fragmented dream is that, when the body is in a near or actual-but-not-brainstem death state, their mind–brain integration strengthens as a subconscious mind reflex to strengthen brain function by investing stronger *L*ife force. This is the action of a subconscious mind not ready to end its physical embodiment even if the person is consciously longing not to return during the NDE. Those who are subconsciously ready to die don't strengthen *L*ife force integration and their body subsequently dies. What would've been an NDE if they'd lived is now just the experience of their awareness shifting to their spirit self and their loved ones coping with their death.

Improved memory integration with the NeuN-positive ependymal cells that leads to an NDE is an artifact, or byproduct, of the salvific effort of *L*ife force. This needn't be only a one-time shot near death. A person can Intentionally strengthen their *L*ife force and commensurately improve mind–brain and mind–body integration leading to memory versus dreams, better health, strength, spiritual awareness, and the like. One does this by reprogramming their subconscious to dial up their normative *L*ife force level and the body adapting to it. Besides doing various things during an NDE while out of the body—if one even gets out of it; they may not—the strength of one's integrated *L*ife force during the NDE also differs person by person, hence the coherence of the NDE memory differs as well. Additionally, a person's brain doesn't update during an NDE, as they don't attain a REM state. Instead, it updates after resuscitation before regaining consciousness, if a REM state occurs, or with the beginning of awakening (§ 1.2.2.7.1:266).

4.1.3.1.3 Some Typical NDE Sensations

The sense of heightened sensorial awareness like light, smells, tastes, and so on reported during an NDE happens for example with light since in the 'reflective' environment it's qualitatively different, as it's not natural environment EMR but its 'reflection' in the 'reflective' environment's 'turbid' supranatural proto-energy (*below*; § 7.2.1:215). It's not only brighter in terms of strength rather than intensity, but expresses in different 'frequencies.' Additionally, one's spirit senses are significantly more sensitive than the physical senses because there's no intervening biology imposing Corrupt limitations between one's mind and the stimulus. Light looks brighter, deeper, more resonant, and colorful; dark looks darker, more intense; smell is more pungent, taste more flavorful, hearing more acute; emotion more emotive; and so on. It's all quite normal to one's spirit senses but seems rather alien, if not divine, when later remembering it in the context of the physical senses.[466]

The darkness reported during an NDE arises in mind, not environment, where one's conscious mind, not having previously experienced the 'reflective' environment, initially doesn't perceive it. This is similar to when a person experiences something so unexpected and out of the box that they initially don't perceive it for what it is. It may even render them momently inert in mind and body; indeed, being literally invisible to them (e.g., atomic bomb victims, § 4.1.2.2:422). This effect passes at different rates according to the person. When it does, they have a sudden awareness of their new environment—they realize their situation but just as light blinds

---

466. Although we use applied energy E terms like frequency and vibration to denote such differences, they don't reflect the actual reality of proto-energy, so take such terms with a pinch of salt to help you imagine it.

dark-adjusted vision, one's mind at first perceives only 'blinding' sensations like darkness that only increases the sense of a not-of-this-world experience.

Regarding the sense of time distortion during an NDE (e.g., Greyson 1983, 1990), recall mind subjectively experiences time whether physically or spiritually embodied (§ 1:105). We're used to objective time in the natural environment because we observe cause and effect in natural events arising in matter being an independent existent (§ 2:107). Even so, physical people subjectively experience the passage of time quite apart from its objective reality. But the supranatural inclusive of the 'reflective' environment is one of Intentionality where matter isn't an independent existent but Intentional. In this environment, it's natural to experience time's passage as a reality of mind rather than of objective existence. As previously noted, time does indeed exist objectively in the supranatural environment and some people orient themselves to that but, in general, spirit people experience time as a subjective reality. Accordingly, one experiences time fast or slow according to their experience of the event. Time thus feels distorted during an NDE.

4.2 Becoming Aware of Spirit Reality

The spirit-aware person already has some (however obscure) idea of spirit embodiment and the 'reflective' and supranatural environments. The spirit-unaware person is mostly ignorant of it all. It's a surprise when conscious awareness shifts to their spirit embodiment as they experience their physical body's death. With few exceptions, no physical-born person prior to this book, regardless spirit awareness or unawareness, had a meaningful comprehension of the reality of spirit embodiment. The best one might've had was bits and pieces snatched from dreams, spiritual experiences or, with competent spirit mediums, a concept of spirit life localized to the spirit persons they encountered but who lacked substantive awareness of the greater reality. That said, a person experiences three essential encounters in becoming aware of their 'new' spirit reality following death. First, they meet their spirit guide (if available); second, an Entry 'angel;' third, they get a crash course on spirit world. We describe each.

4.2.1 Meeting One's Spirit Guide(s)

Unlike with 'guardian angels' (§ 2.3.2:524), every person has at least one spirit guide, and sometimes more, regardless whether one is good, kind, religious, benevolent, evil, violent, cantankerous, irreligious, or just indifferent. We describe them below and how they interact with the newly-deceased.

4.2.1.1 What a Spirit Guide Is

A spirit guide is foremost a physical person's *friend* throughout all or part of their lifespan. They are always a spirit relative when one has only a single spirit guide. Otherwise, they're spirit relatives or friends from one's physical life who died before the person, or if a spirit-aware person, then a friend from spirit world one may or may not have even met in their spirit embodiment when, say, they were physically asleep but active in their spirit body; or, just persons interested in what one is doing in their life.

The girls and I have many spirit guides who joined us after we discovered ET and Mina. But we each started with a direct relative from birth. My original spirit guide is a distant French relative named Daphne Giles who died in AD 1430 (EN 72:650). Ayako's is *Obāsan*, and El's is *Idaina-oji* (EN 80:652). To the degree a physical person's spirit self is aware of them, their spirit guide freely talks to them. Even if not physically (or spiritually) cognizant, their spirit guide still talks and Intentionally helps guide, protect, and comfort the person. Ayako, for instance, intuits and energy tests with *Obāsan* every day about her clothing and make-up, girl-talk, family history, *Obāsan*'s history and life experiences, and other topics of interest. Two spirit guides who joined me after 2017 are best friends from my Unification Church days who advise me on love, relationships, spirit life, and other topics in common.

Spirit guides are a wonderful resource for the physically alive because they *want* to be at the person's side during their lifespan. But they don't know everything, only what they've personally experienced here and in sprit world; we never ask them about the facts of reality, for instance. Spirit guides are those persons whom the physical-born have always confused with so-called guardian angels (whose actual task is different; Table 17:523; § 2.3.2:524). Those working with 'Archangel' Raguel (*below*) train spirit guides in necessary skills such as instantly manifesting their spirit body from point A to point B, which very few physical- or spirit-born persons knew was possible before the Big Healing.

4.2.1.2 WHAT A SPIRIT GUIDE DOES

A person's spirit guide is whom they first encounter—if one dies prenatally, they 'rescue' him or her if they're one of ~20% who guide from that early stage (§ 2.2:410)—upon awareness of their 'reflective' environment surroundings. Obviously, spirit guides have a life in spirit world and aren't literally at one's side twenty-four-seven. They are, however, attuned to their guidee's *L*ife force, thus aware when guidance is needed, or when the guidee is dying or already—instantaneously or unexpectedly—dead. If they don't happen to be there in their moment of death (including during an NDE), they don't necessarily feel the change in *L*ife force as their guidee's physical body dies and awareness shifts to the spirit self. If they are aware of their guidee's death, they arrive in their presence (post-Big Healing) within about ten seconds to comfort their friend. Within about three minutes of this tête à tête, an Entry 'angel' arrives to explain things.

4.2.2 MEETING ONE'S ENTRY 'ANGEL'

Like all 'jobs' in spirit world, an Entry 'angel' is a volunteer. The Entry task is one of seven that Mina set up to help the physical-born cope with embodiment after The Corruption (Table 17:523; § 2.3.5:527). 'Archangel' Raguel manages this task, supervising the physical- and spirit-born spirit persons who volunteer and trains them to the task as well as how to interact Intentionally with Mina to accomplish the job.

4.2.2.1 THE ENTRY 'ANGEL' TASK

Primarily, the Entry 'angel' enables a newly deceased person to enter spirit world so they're not stuck in the 'reflective' environment. Recall that spirit world is the supranatural environment (§ 7.1.2:214). It therefore exists in the context of the supranatural Energent rather than the natural Energent and, accordingly, its proto-energy is different from natural proto-energy (§ 7.1.3:214). A physical-born person is physicospirit embodied, meaning they simultaneously have an integrated physical and spirit body. The reason for this is that *L*ife's WOB naturally manifests a spirit body through its intrinsic Intentionality so that, once conceived in an embodied environment, a spirit body automatically comes to be. Regardless whether one is physical- or spirit-conceived, having a spirit body is a given. But with the physical-born it manifests (Intentionalizes) in the context of the 'reflective' environment, not the supranatural one as with the spirit-born, because that's where the natural environment's physical body 'reflects.'

The physical-born spirit body constitutes not of natural or supranatural proto-energy but a supranatural *variant* that's 'turbid' from its presence in the natural–supranatural 'reflective' boundary which, as we've learned, is incompatible with the supranatural as it exists in spirit world. Supranatural proto-energy, which *is* the proto-energy of the 'reflective' environment, is 'hardened'—its 'frequency' and other aspects have altered— in this 'turbid' boundary area. It 'reflects' bonded-archí motion analogous to a non-Newtonian fluid (nNf; § 7.1.1.1:212) like oobleck, 'reflecting' physical reality down to its constituent archí whereby spirit persons can experience the physical world. This is how it's variant.

This situation renders the physical-born's spirit body, constituted in this 'turbid' proto-energy environment upon their physicospirit conception, incompatible with the non-variant proto-energy of the supranatural environment, which *is* spirit world. Consequently, a newly deceased person literally can't enter spirit world without first altering their spirit body's variant 'energy' signature so it's spirit-world compatible. Unless spirit-aware while physically alive and already enabled to enter spirit world from the 'reflective' environment, an Entry 'angel' needs enable one to do so after death. Once enabled, a spirit person can come and go from spirit world to any physical ('reflective') location at will. Archí accomplish this feat through a natural process (§ 7.1.3:214), but only Mina can alter a spirit body's 'energy' signature.

Well, any physical-born person can learn to re-Intentionalize (re-manifest) their spirit body as proto-energy that's compatible with the supranatural Energent. But asking this of a just-deceased person in the context of The Corruption would take, in Mina's estimation, about 2,670 years on average. He finds that unfair and ridiculous. Instead, he takes care of it in an instant via the good offices of the Entry 'angel'[467] who renormalizes the person's spirit body upon their informed consent by physically touching it, which acts as an Intentional conduit through which Mina re-Intentionalizes the person's spirit body for them. Only Mina, our universe builder, can (with their cooperation) do this to another's spirit body. It's similar to how he completes a person's

---

467. Absent The Corruption, and with full mind–brain integration and awareness of physicospirit reality, a physically alive person around age ten can learn in about six days to re-Intentionalize (re-manifest) their spirit body to enter spirit world at will.

healing using a healer who touches the healee, which acts as a conduit for Mina's healing (neutralizing) 'energy' to flow from him to them.

4.2.2.2 HOW THE ENTRY 'ANGEL' KNOWS WHEN AND WHERE TO ARRIVE

People are always surprised—I know we were—to find 'divinely magic' spirit world's technological level far beyond Earth's own. For example, after we met and healed *Obāsan* in 2017, the girls and I were chatting with her in our living room trying to get to know her—before I accidentally insulted her (§ 1.2.2.1:31)—and I commented that she must be amazed at the current state of technology, having died in über primitive 1945. Ayako was doing the energy testing and said *Obāsan* was laughing at the very idea, replying that, "spirit world is way more advanced; where do you think all your technology comes from?" That really got my attention when, around three weeks later, the girls reported Hidé and Taiji using something similar to texting devices. Ayako actually heard the notifications (just as she'd heard Taiji outside raking autumn leaves one day) and kept searching our house for the source until she figured it out.

The reason for the devices is that in the 'reflective' environment where supranatural proto-energy is 'hardened' in the 'turbid' boundary area as described, Thought doesn't Intentionally translate into the non-'turbid' proto-energy of the supranatural Energent. Spirit persons thus can't communicate mind-to-mind between the two environments as they can in spirit world. Since the 'reflective' environment's variant proto-energy interrupts a spirit person's Intentionality with other spirit persons either there or in spirit world, people resort to technological solutions to communicate over distance (chakras are the means by which the physical-born currently get around this interference). When a deceased person's spirit guide confirms they've actually died, for example, they use their technology to notify an available 'on-call' Entry 'angel' who then shows up. No one pioneered such technology here in our universe. It's hundreds of billions of years old and came over with Mina and the First Ancestors (§ 2.1.1:348).

4.2.3 CRASH COURSE ON SPIRIT REALITY

An Entry 'angel' orients the just-deceased person by explaining who they are, why they're there, the reality of the 'reflective' and spirit world environments, and whatever else comes up. It's an emotionally charged moment. Most aren't ready, can't accept the reality of an afterlife, are confused, scared, vexed, and the like. Usually, their spirit guide and family are there regardless generational differences to help, not inflict harm; Mina says spirit guides never sign up to make a physical-born person's life difficult. In any case, a person chooses to enter spirit world where everything shakes out in due course, or they don't and remain in their planet's 'reflective' environment to pursue their own agenda. A spirit guide might continue helping and cajoling them to at least enable their spirit body to enter spirit world later at their pleasure, but that's up to them.

4.3 CHOOSING TO ENTER SPIRIT WORLD

Upon his or her arrival, the Entry 'angel' explains the ins and outs of entering spirit world and asks the dead person in conceptual terms they understand if they want their spirit body made compatible with spirit world. Mina never compels a person to anything, and coercion in spirit world isn't a thing owing to human woʙ (§ 2.1.1.2.1:369). Without permission, one can't heal even a person who needs it. Naturally, then, one can't compel a person to enter spirit world nor alter their spirit body's 'energy' signature if, in Captain Barbossa's ever-coercive words, they are "disinclined to acquiesce."[273] If a person elects to avoid spirit world—torturing themselves, honestly—then later changes their mind, their recourse is to find someone who can call an Entry 'angel' to enable it, who will. For now, this is what you can expect.

SECTION 5
Fate, Destiny, and Free Will

Free will is the wrong term, a misnomer, for human self-agency. However used, 'free' references *ability* and 'will' references *action*. The term conceptually ignores mind autonomously *thinking* any thought, emphasizing only its ability to *act* on what it thinks in an environment filled with other equally autonomous, free-willed agents. Hence, the 'problem of free will' is really about *autonomy*.

Philosophy with a capital-P over the last several thousand years couldn't have more thoroughly confused the notions of destiny, fate, and free will than it has. It has gorged itself on logic, math, and mindsets as its preeminent representations of human and natural reality and lulled itself into a mindset addiction that carries it farther from rather than closer to authentic inquiry. For example, despite the overwhelming observational evidence that mind is at the very least an emergent reality—an epiphenomenon—of brain, if not wholly independent of it, there's no serious inquiry into mind apart from materialist and religionist analysis. These approaches yield no insight into mind even if the former has unlocked a lot about the brain. The trend in Philosophy with a capital-P to shoehorn mind into brain concretizes its inability to comprehend mind in and of itself and keeps the meanings of free will, free action, Thought, choice, and notions of moral agency elusive. Its theories aren't authentic inquiries into mind and accordingly yield nothing. Here, we describe free will from the perspective of emergent 𝓛ife having absolute autonomy (§ 2.1:340), which naturally elucidates fate and destiny.

5.1 Free Will

Mindset leads to fate, which is to say a mindsetted life is a fated life, fate being nothing more than living life addicted to mindset (§ 2.1.1.5.2:353). It's a low-maintenance way of living in that it transfers so-called moral agency, or responsibility, away from the individual. Like mindset, though, fate is the consequence of choice, and choice is free will. Choosing a life addicted to mindset isn't choosing fate over free will, it *is* free will. No one is fated or has a fate, neither is one destined for anything. One only has a probable outcome that waxes and wanes in accord with so-called free will. We live in a dynamic, interactive reality, so our free will doesn't necessarily work out—can't be freely exercised—not because fate, destiny, or predetermination get in the way but because of the free will exercised by the surrounding human and natural environment (§ 2.2.1:233). In this milieu, fate, destiny, and causal agency are just forms of Accountableism (§ 4.1.2:378) where one blames others and even nature for any given palette of options from which they feel compelled to choose and then claim to have no free will, *no real choice*.

Philosophy with a capital-P analyzes free will in the context of events, not mind, when reasoning whether existence, for instance, is causally determinist or indeterminist, or compatibilist or incompatibilist[468] because it sees free will's meaning only in doing, not being. But free will is a mind experience, thus it's being, not doing. The notion one lacks free will because one chooses to act but, for whatever reason, can't is a false construct, as free will necessarily can't mean one has absolute control over their *actions* since they live in a dynamical reality. To do so necessarily means one need control others and their environment in order to have, or exercise, free will. Rather, free will means one has *choice* regardless the ability to act or even of its beneficence to self in outcome. *Action* doesn't determine free will, *choice* does.

A person can and will *choose to think* anything in the privacy of their mind but, judging probable outcomes in their environment, *choose to act* by not exercising what they chose to think (their free will). It's pointless to postulate scenarios, as philosophy is wont to do, where a person is mind-controlled in some way since free will doesn't reside in the nonsovereign *brain* but the autonomous *mind* which can't be controlled because self-agency is inviolable (§ 2.1.1.2.1:369). One's freedom *to do otherwise* as a prerequisite to free will is irrelevant because one can't control non-self response or interference any more than one can control the weather for the reason that humanity, including nature, has its own free will (self-agency; § 2.2.1:233). Consequently, whether one can bring one choice over another to action as the definition of free will is immaterial because we aren't alone in our environment *as* our environment. Limitations on action don't negate the reality of mind's free will.

Not being alone in the world means people feel the need to hold others, the environment, and even themselves accountable for their actions. This unfortunately gives rise to the mindset of inflicting harm in the guise of preventing it (§ 3.2:374). Let's consider this issue in the context of free will and morality.

5.1.1 Free Will and Moral Responsibility

Free will has nothing to do with morality which, as a universal truth, doesn't exist (§ 2.1.1.5.2:353; § 1.1.2.1:364). Neither is one responsible—accountable—for free will because it's being, not doing. Responsibility lies only in doing, not being. One is not responsible for what they think (absent Intentionality, which is doing) but what they do. Hence, one is responsible for action, which isn't free will itself but only its result, *free action*. An individual or group is responsible for their action only to the individual or group affected by the action. This

---

468. Determinism and fatalism, for example, are conflated concepts having a distinction without a practical difference; fatalism is the human response to a perceived, deterministic reality.

reality expresses in moral codes differing from culture to culture, group to group, even individual to individual *despite* any commonalities giving the appearance of immutability and universality that render it an intrinsic truth to which one is necessarily accountable.

Action as the result of free will is free action when it's intended action, meaning one chooses it regardless whether one *wants* to choose it. Whatever the situation in which arises choice-cum-action, one necessarily acts with or without imposition. In either case, one is choosing, not coerced, to act because mind, in which free will arises, can't be compelled (§ 2.1.1.2.1:369; § 3.3.3:377). Every act is an act of free will, including the act of acting not as one's thinking–feeling wills (§ 1.2.2.1:253). Intention *to* act, therefore, is immaterial even if intention *in* acting isn't. From actions arise consequences. In physics, every action begets an equal and opposite reaction. With humanity, every action begets choice, meaning free will, and nothing more. Whether Person B can effect an equal and opposite reaction or any kind of reaction that consequently follows Person A's preceding action is entirely dependent upon free will (choice). Since consequences arise in action, it's always consequences for which we hold the *actor* not the *thinker* accountable. This varies according to the consequences from 'no harm no foul' to death, which gives rise to one's intention *in* acting in order to assess levels of accountability. The bottom line is there's an intrinsic linkage between free action and responsibility, but not free will. Accordingly, free will doesn't depend on responsibility nor does responsibility—moral or otherwise—justify its existence.

5.1.2 Free Will and Our World

We live in an environment peopled by others. Each person, including the environment, is its own free-will agent, having self-agency that responds to its environment, including actions effected by others. To talk about human free will as something that exists or can't exist in the context of environment is nonsensical. The notion one has no free will if, for any reason, one can't actualize it is no different than saying one has no free will because one can't breathe underwater. We exist in an environment that necessarily constrains physical embodiment hence action. But Thought, in which free will constitutes, transcends environment. It's of mind, not body. Even if one concedes that mind entirely arises in moment-to-moment neurochemical processes of the brain, Thought in and of itself is *not* biological but at least an epiphenomenal artifact and at most an emergent existent.[469] Either way, free will arises in mind whereas free action inclusive of Intentionality expresses in mind–body.

Since mind is uncompellable then action is, too. This means that, however one feels compelled to effect a certain action over one more desired, one in reality assesses the environmental conditions in which they plan to inject their action and then chooses the action calculated most closely to represent their free will. The less one's action represents their free will, the more one feels the action is compelled than freely chosen. But it's all smoke and mirrors. Outside of physiological (versus, e.g., trained) reflex, which isn't volitional—this includes biologically subverting the brain—a person, who is mind, can *only* act through choice, which is volitional. Therefore, no matter how environmentally compelled an action feels, in reality one chooses that action, or chooses not to act, which is itself an action just as choosing to remain silent is itself a statement. The 'ability to choose otherwise' is just a Hobson's choice because one can *choose* to do differently even if one can't *act* on that choice. The inability to act—say, adopting cultural norms to avoid unpleasantness (§ 4.3.1:293)—doesn't negate the ability to choose.

5.1.3 Free Will is Human Autonomy

Free will is not the ability to act nor to choose to act if and only if one can choose differently and their action isn't constrained. Free will is autonomous—*sovereign*—Thought (§ 2.3.2:240; ibid). Recall *Life* isn't created by divinity or evolution (§ 1:335) but emergently births 'in' Energent proto-life (EPL; § 2.3.2.1:241; § 2:304), initially as the discrete, unique pairwise persons Mike and Molly and, thereafter, 'in' EPL as you and me via parental Intentionality (§ 1.2.1.1:248). This means the person—the race itself—is a discrete, unique emergent that exists in accord with its WOB. Thought is mind's fundamental WOB; mind *is* Thought and nothing else. The brain–body is an embodiment of mind and plays only an ancillary role in what's misnomered as free will. Spirit-born persons lack a brain, of course, as their embodiment—the spirit body—is Intentionalized

---

469. American physiologist Benjamin Libet (d. 2007) showed that relevant electrical activity to provoke movement arises in the brain hundreds of milliseconds prior to being consciously aware of one's decision to move. Rather than indicating free will is just a post hoc reconstruction of events after the brain acted, the reality is that it arises in mind and then transliterates to brain as both choice and action (§ 2.1:276). The discrepancy arises in action being a less complex transliteration than the brain's conscious awareness of choice (Libet et al. 1983; see also Clarke 2013, 1–4).

(manifested) by self directly expressing mind through it whereas the physical-born necessarily express mind via their (presently limited) biological interface. To comprehend free will accurately, one needs account for it amongst the spirit-embodied, as they're human, too.

Autonomy naturally inheres to the individual because mind, an unembodied emergent being, is beholden to nothing, including embodiment. It exists in its own reality, its own 'ecosystem,' in accord with its own rules (woB).[470] This means the person is absolutely autonomous in that he or she has absolute free will in the context of mind inclusive of Intentionality even if, while embodied, expressing it—free action—is or can be constrained. Although mindset addiction and degraded mind–brain integration (§ 1.2.2.5:261) intrinsic to The Corruption leaves us unaware of our emergently autonomous human woB and, therefore, effectively nonautonomous—if one doesn't know they're autonomous then, *in practice*, they're not—the person as mind is always *in reality* absolutely autonomous (§ 2.1.1.5.2:353).

Free will has nothing to do with freedom which arises not in free will but in autonomy, in human sovereignty. Freedom is intrinsic to humanity even though the facts of embodiment in an environment of other humans and one's environment appear (more in the physical than the spirit world) to render it moot, something one takes if one can but otherwise might not experience since one's embodiment can be seized even though their autonomy (self-agency) remains inviolable. One reaches inaccurate conclusions when analyzing the human condition outside its reality of mind.

5.1.4   FREE WILL IS MIND

As noted, 'free will' is a misnomer. The correct way to frame the so-called free-will problem is as *autonomy* where self-agency is intrinsic. Nature's woB—so-called laws of nature—is irrelevant to self-agency because mind transcends embodiment thus the natural and supranatural environment (§ 5:294). Moreover, whether one is or isn't a rational being doesn't negate autonomy, as that is mind's intrinsic woB.[471] Neither does mindset—habit, conditioning—negate autonomy since one (sub)consciously chooses it (§ 2:393) as an autonomous choice of mind outside embodiment's boundary.

In acting unconsciously, it's commonly thought a person is acting according to conditioning—habit, culture, mindset, fear—where choice, despite appearing rationally thought out hence freely willed, is automatic. This is inaccurate. Mind can addict itself to mindset where choice appears preordained even when one thinks they're making an unimpeded choice. This isn't because one lacks truly autonomous choice, but because one fails to account for mindset, which is subconscious, of mind, and mind's choice. One makes thousands if not millions of (sub)conscious choices to embrace and strengthen mindset. The outcome w.r.t. Thought and action is largely albeit (owing to emergent Thought) not entirely predictable. One may think this indicates true nonautonomy (a lack of free will), but that, too, is inaccurate.

5.2   FATE AND DESTINY

Traditionally, *fate* is a predetermined, inevitable future outcome beyond human control while *destiny* is an undetermined, potential future outcome within human control. Fate is what happens when one passively experiences life. Destiny is what happens on the heels of fate or when taking active control of one's life. What a person *passively encounters or permits* in their life is fate and *actively encounters or seeks* is their destiny. They arise and operate in the context of environment and free will (autonomy) driving mindset; the difference between mindset and its addiction is awareness that one is autonomous.

A person who feels *fated* is simply addicted to their particular mindset—a belief that fate is real and nothing they *consciously* do will alter any fated reality—and unaware they can change it. They don't consider their subconscious and especially its Intentionality or, if they do, that it's so alien and mysterious they can't perceive it even being a part of their self. Conversely, a person who feels *destined* may be addicted to their particular mindset but believes they're not *fated* to it, can imbue themselves with another one, and strive to alter their conscious and sometimes subconscious mindset toward achieving a goal—their destiny. If they achieve it, they feel destined. If not, it wasn't their destiny or has yet to play out.

---

470. Our currently inadequate mind–brain integration leaves us unaware of our human reality such that things like free will confuse us. But in time, the ET community will produce a useful body of knowledge in this respect.

471. Rationality undercuts the notion that brain is mind anyhow; ". . . if my mental processes are determined wholly by the motions of atoms in my brain, I have no reason to suppose that my beliefs are true . . . And hence I have no reason for supposing my brain to be composed of atoms" (Haldane 1928, 220).

Recall an individual exists in the context of Individual core Culture (IC) interacting with others' IC as minds in unison that scale to superculture, megaculture, and Ultraculture (§ 4.1:291). When culture embraces fate and destiny as its reality, its constituents are addicted to it. Since it's a collective mindset, addiction to culture is mindset addiction having the same result as with individuals: nonautonomy. It can never be free to experience societal or individual liberty absent a critical mass of individual 'subcultures' embodying free will as autonomy. Conversely, an intrinsically free, unaddicted culture embracing fate and destiny (as ideology) can't remain free nor continue experiencing societal or individual liberty (autonomy).

In sum, fate and destiny aren't real but constructs of the mind used to explain and justify one's experience of, and situation in, life, holding accountable someone or something other than oneself. 'Will' is mind's choice—freely willed Thought—and not its actualization in the environment. 'Free will' necessarily references autonomous mind engaged in Thought, not one's ability to translate choice unimpeded into action which, when impossible under some constraint, means one has no free will.

Section 6
Suffering

Suffering as we mean it here is a 'source' proto-energy event as opposed to the experience of mind-pain arising in biology, environment, or mindstate and, like harm (§ 1.1.1:362), is in the eye of the beholder. We note the difference between *source* (base) suffering and the traditional *experience* of suffering by denoting the former as all-caps SUFFERING and the latter lowercase-s suffering. Besides speculative observation, there isn't all that much in the historical literature that really analyzes suffering beyond concluding 'life is pain because of wrong behavior or else intrinsic to existence.' Philosophy seems uncharacteristically quiet on it, appearing to cede much of its explanation, semi-rigorous analysis, and treatment to metaphysics, religion, or soft sciences like psychiatry–psychology. Quite apart from traditional views, we define and describe suffering's origin, way, 'energy,' and Intentionality along with depression, reincarnation, and slavery aspects.

6.1 What is Suffering

In précis, SUFFERING is a *Thought disturbance* of mindset arising in the 'energy' of one's *expectation* of experiencing differing from that of the *act* of experiencing, resulting in a disruption in emergent $\mathcal{L}$ife's woB thus enlivening agency, our experience of which we call suffering. Let's unpack that.

6.1.1 Human $\mathcal{L}$ife and Experience is 'Energy'

Recall emergent $\mathcal{L}$ife—you and me at our most elemental—is just self-aware proto-energy (§ 1:112; § 1.1:246). Despite *being* self-aware, $\mathcal{L}$ife itself is too elemental to think–feel, experience, or even to *have* awareness, and that's all we are at the very root of our beingness, all that $\mathcal{L}$ife is; just this proto-energy condition that's Ƕuman reality. As described throughout this book, *everything is 'energy.'* Not in the trite woo-woo way, but literally. Matter, for example, boils down to archí which is nothing but proto-energy condensed to impermeability as matter–Energy (§ 2.2:114). What people call energy—earlier defined as applied energy E—arises from proto-energy interacting with matter–Energy (§ 2.1:114). We are self-aware proto-energy beings birthed 'in' a proto-energy environment. *This* is what human consciousness really *is*. Within this arises Intentionalized *mind* as $\mathcal{L}$ife's subconscious–conscious aspect that *does* have awareness, hence Thought (§ 1.2.2.5.1:261). Stripped to the frame then, our unembodied self in its natural environment is just proto-energy, mind, and Thought such that

$$\Theta^{\text{SAE}}_{\varepsilon\mu} \rightarrow \text{ॐ} \rightarrow \text{T} \tag{27.1}$$

where $\Theta^{\text{SAE}}_{\varepsilon\mu}$ is self-aware proto-energy in which arises mind (ॐ), thus Thought (T). As you read and think–feel about this book, your matter–Energy brain is instantiating and re-instantiating a constantly updated, refreshed proto-energy mind ∼1,000 times per second from the matter–Energy activity of action potentials in your brain (§ 1.2.2.1:253; § 1.2.2.4.2.1:258). It's an embodied facsimile of your unembodied $\mathcal{L}$ife mind which itself is arising and re-arising some 50 million times per second in the elemental, self-aware proto-energy that is your emergent $\mathcal{L}$ife self. All that you are, think–feel, and even do is proto-energy, which in part expresses via your physical embodiment as real energy Υ (Fundamental Force; § 1:112) as well as applied energy E, the energy associated with physics (§ 2.1:114). Everything we think–feel, therefore, is quite literally 'energy.' SUFFERING isn't simply experiencing a feeling like pain or anguish, but 'energy' that necessarily interacts with one's own-self and non-self environments.

6.1.2 Suffering is an 'Energy' Event

The 'energy' we're talking about here is what reflects, or manifests, emergent ℒife's *expectation of experiencing* its *unembodied* environment and subconscious mind's *act of experiencing* its *embodied* environment. 'Expectation' refers to emergent ℒife's homeostatic environment, its unembodied environment *within*, which is proto-energy, mind, and Thought as in Eq. (27.1). Emergent ℒife as our elemental self has no awareness of any environment. It's simply a proto-energy homeostasis congruent with its wob (*Fig. 161*; § 1.2.1.1:248). 'Act' refers to mind's wob, which we call *mindset*. It has awareness of emergent ℒife's homeostasis and mind's external (embodied) environment—the physical world, say.

When the '*energy*' of the act of experiencing—one's mindset-in-the-world—differs from that of our expectation of experiencing—emergent ℒife's homeostasis—then *that* is an 'energy' *event* with 'energy' consequences in our elemental beingness that echoes like an explosion's pressure wave—a 'windstorm'—from our elemental proto-energy beingness into our mind and throughout our subconscious–conscious experience (*Fig. 162*). The 'energy' of one's feelings that arise in the difference between emergent ℒife's homeostasis and mind's wob 'violate' them both in the sense they 'resist,' because homeostasis and wob always exert. The 'violation' is a 'clashing' of proto-energies. This '*energy*' *event* constitutes SUFFERING, what it *means* to suffer. What we *call* suffering as painful anguish is just an aftereffect, an artifact of this 'energy' event, and why it leaves our mind feeling a twisted and shattered mindscape rent with harm (§ 1.1.1:362).

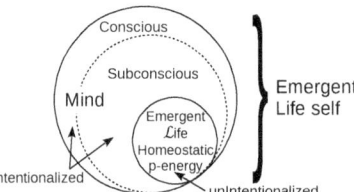

Figure 161. Schematic of emergent ℒife self where surrounding EPL enlivens the elemental, homeostatic proto-energy of ℒife self within which mind arises.

Embodiment—having a spirit or physical body in a supranatural or natural environment—is actually *alien* to ℒife, not being its innate Energent proto-life (EPL) environment in which it emergently birthed (§ 2:304). Unembodied humans manipulated proto-energy to create an environment suited to embodiment (§ 2.1.3:309), but the embodied experience of proto-energy is night and day that of the unembodied. To exist embodied as consistently vis-à-vis wob as we do unembodied, one's embodied *mindset* needs imbue itself with the *wob of unembodiment* such that embodied proto-energy doesn't 'clash' with that of unembodiment which constitutes one's normative, homeostatic proto-energy condition. Recall that mindset arises in subconscious mind and forms conscious mind's wob (§ 2.3.1:398) whereby one's Thought always conforms to mindset (unless one consciously employs Thought to alter it, thereby altering one's normative proto-energy condition). SUFFERING arises when mindset doesn't inform itself of unembodiment's wob in that mindset, which reflects—is normative of—conscious mind's wob, doesn't reflect—is non-normative of—ℒife's proto-energy condition. Colloquially, we'd say one's mindset, thus Thought, is out-of-sync with one's elemental self, a homeostasis interruptus as it were, and it's here that SUFFERING arises. Let's consider this aspect more closely.

6.1.3 'Clashing' Proto-energy

The 'energy' of a person's expectation of experiencing—homeostasis—versus the 'energy' of their act of experiencing—mindset, thus mind's wob—results in a 'clash' of unIntentionalized with Intentionalized proto-energy. The 'clash' arises because emergent ℒife's proto-energy normatively *has no* Intentionality whereas the proto-energy of mind normatively *has* Intentionality because it arises in subconscious awareness and conscious Thought (§ 2.1:393). Mind's proto-energy Intentionalized with negative emotive ℒife force (Em̬ℒꜰ; § 3.3.3.1.1:289), which arises in the thinking–feeling of negative emotion according to one's mindset experiencing suffering, is indicative of one experiencing an environment in a way that interrupts ℒife's homeostasis. When mind's Intentionalized proto-energy interacts with ℒife's unIntentionalized proto-energy, it naturally acts to Intentionalize the latter. Intentionalized proto-energy carries its originating Intentionality as part of itself and Intentionalizes any proto-energy encountered.[472]

Unlike with the unaware nonconscious intelligence (UNI) proto-energy of a universe or All Existence (§ 2.2.1:233), in the self-aware person the unIntentionalized proto-energy of *Life* has its own WOB that's intrinsically resistant to Intentionality. *Life's* proto-energy consequently 'resists;' its WOB doesn't Intentionalize as readily as does mind's proto-energy because of homeostasis (*Fig. 162*). In the context of *Life*—a discrete, independent environment all its own, separate and distinct from that of its own autonomous mind (*Fig. 161*)—Intentionalized proto-energy exerts its Intentionality on emergent *Life's* unIntentionalized proto-energy that's incompatible, causing an Intentionalized–unIntentionalized proto-energy 'clash.' This also happens when a person Intentionalizes a change to some aspect of their *Life's* WOB (changing sex WOB M ↔ F; § 2.1.5.1:313) which, in consequence, can actually provoke the experience of suffering during the process according to one's mindset.

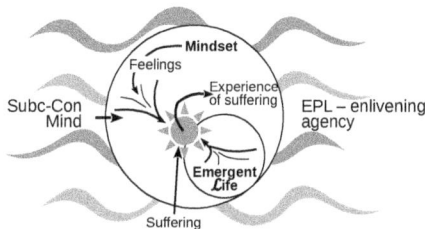

Figure 162. Intentionalized feelings arising in mindset 'clash' with unIntentionalized emergent *Life* resulting in a loss of EPL enlivening agency, which we experience as suffering.

6.1.4 Suffering Negates Enlivening Agency

The aforementioned 'clash' occurs regardless how small or seemingly insignificant the difference between the energy of one's expectation of experiencing and that of the act of experiencing. *Life's* unIntentionalized proto-energy interacting with mind's, which Intentionalized in the act of experiencing (resulting in one thinking–feeling pain, anguish, grief), *negates* the enlivening effect of *Life's* proto-energy in accord with the degree of such thinking–feeling. This means *Life's* enlivening agency diminishes as if degrading toward death. *This* is what SUFFERING actually *is*. Recall that Living–*Life* force enlivens the human body and Living force enlivens nonhuman bodies whereby they have aliveness (§ 7.1.3:214; § 7.3:220; § 1:112). Similarly, EPL enlivens *Life* whereby the person who emergently births 'in' EPL is self-aware, having *Life*. The proto-energy that is mind, which is Ꜧuman, arises in this enlivening aspect of EPL as its *enlivening agency*. It's what gives rise to self-aware *Life* in the first place (*Fig. 162*). It's more fundamental than *Life* force, which arises from—as the effect of—self-aware proto-energy, and gives rise in a person to Em*L*F; *Life* force and Em*L*F are discrete aspects of self-aware proto-energy.

The loss of enlivening agency can never lead to zero enlivening effect—death of *Life*—but only, in the extreme, to stasis as with abortion, miscarriage, or unembodied 'suicide' (§ 2.2:410; § 2.4:413). The greater this 'clash,' the greater the loss of enlivening agency; hence, one's *experience* of suffering. SUFFERING itself *is a loss of emergent Life's enlivening agency* and this is why our experience of it *hurts*, why we feel anguish, grief, and pain, because SUFFERING as a 'clash' of proto-energy is analogous to a hurricane tearing apart a landscape or an injury tearing apart tissue, as though a person's mind is tearing apart in SUFFERING.

Recall, too, that all Thought Intentionalizes, from focused intention to random thinking-feeling tripping through our minds. The strength of Intentionality differs according to its intensity. Pain, anguish, grief, and other negative feelings are intense and therefore strongly Intentionalize, affecting one's environment, mind and mindset, and *Life*. But these are just feelings, not suffering. They *become* suffering only when their Intentionality is strong enough to 'clash' with emergent *Life's* proto-energy and diminish enlivening agency. *Then* we *experience* suffering.[473] But it's only because one predisposes their mindset to think–feel in terms of pain, anguish, or grief that they experience suffering versus simply negative feelings. In *Life's* elemental WOB, SUFFERING is just the above-described unIntentionalized proto-energy condition 'clashing'

---

472. This is how one affects their embodied environment simply via Intentionalized Thought (§ 3.2:282).

473. This is why every aspect of physical life seems to incarnate suffering, as in Buddhism's four noble truths. The Corruption-affected physical-born suffer every moment of existence but, unless an experience results in subconscious awareness of diminished enlivening agency, we don't notice and experience merely negative feelings.

with mind's Intentionality that's felt as an enlivening agency negation. Subconscious mind has awareness of it. Conscious mind experiences it. The resulting Thought is pain, anguish, or grief arising in a person feeling a loss of enlivening agency which, altogether, we call suffering.

6.1.5   SUFFERING IS ELEMENTAL

SUFFERING doesn't arise in Thought but in the proto-energy sustaining one's *Life* self. Recall the mind never sleeps (§ 1.2.2.7:266). It's never unconscious and always aware. But it isn't one's *Life* self, one's beingness, the elemental Human. It's only an aspect of it. SUFFERING as an *elemental* phenomenon doesn't arise in Thought, experience, or environment. It isn't pain in the somatic or mental sense, it's the diminution of *Life*'s own enlivening agency—it's very existence—that arises in the proto-energy 'clash' that disrupts mind arising and re-arising in constant update (§ 6.1.1:431). SUFFERING is mind re-arising as a proto-energy 'clash' between *Life*'s homeostasis and mindset's experience, not in symptomatic Thought such as loss, fear, regret, guilt, pain, resentment, or adversity generally that tortures a person, but in Thought's elemental proto-energy. Mind re-arising in this 'clashing' milieu is re-arising in a proto-energy 'agony' *without its elemental homeostasis*. Suffering arises in one's mind not *from* mind but from an elemental *proto-energy event*, which we experience in our mind consequent of environment.

6.2   THE ORIGIN OF SUFFERING

One can sense the origin of suffering in its definition above. Quite simply, it arises in the 'energy clash' between one's (homeostatic) expectation of experiencing and the act of experiencing. Recall that mindset is a person's reality filter. It gives perspective to reality, hence experience. This is why two people can experience the same event yet one derives suffering from it while the other doesn't. Suffering is literally in the beholder's eye. One can always change their mindset but doesn't always want to. Mina, for example, experienced profound suffering arising in The Corruption's effect on humanity, but preferred to endure it than alter his mindset since that would alter his relationship with humanity—his extended family (§ 2.1.1:348)—in a way he considered worse, although he did nurture hope (§ 6.3.1:435). Others don't because they prefer to hate, resent, feel anguish, or otherwise choose to prolong suffering.

Suffering arises not with *what* one experiences but with the *act* of experiencing. This means that although a person's mindset predisposes them to experience suffering in what they encounter, the profundity of their suffering arises in *how* they experience it. While mindset certainly predetermines a person to experience suffering, their act of experiencing is variable. Thus, two people with the same mindset but variant lifestyles, life experiences, mores, and so forth will experience a different quality of suffering from more to less profound and debilitating over the long term.

6.3   THE WAY OF SUFFERING

It's necessary to distinguish between suffering and the body's experience with damage, a torturous environment, or mindstate. Although pain—the specter of the body's early or unfair death, or a hostile or nonautonomous environment whether imposed, self-imposed, rigid, flexible, or of contrived mental states—can give rise to suffering, it isn't, in and of itself, suffering. Cancer or nerve damage can induce severe physiological pain and Thought distress, but a person with a mindset of high tolerance to adversity doesn't suffer necessarily or profoundly whereas a person with the opposite necessarily does.

Recall that Living entities inclusive of the human body *can't* SUFFER, as there's insufficient self-awareness (§ 1.2.2:253). Only *Life* suffers. Therefore, even in a utopian world absent pain, discomfort, instability, unhappiness, and the like a person can nonetheless experience suffering arising in Thought that mindset formulates because the way of suffering is of mind, not experience. Suffering is consequently part of the human condition not because it's intrinsic to existence, but because it's a product of mind, not environment. It therefore isn't eradicable except as a function of mindset such that

$$M \vdash S \bigwedge M \dashv S \tag{27.2}$$

where M is mindset, S is SUFFERING, and $\vdash$ and $\dashv$ mean 'implies' and 'doesn't imply,' respectively. Accordingly, a desire for that which is intrinsic of *Life* and embodiment doesn't give rise to SUFFERING unless one's mindset is such that the 'energy' of their expectation of experience differs from that of their act of experiencing the absence, or unsustainability, of that which they desire in that it's perceived as a loss and, thus, pain becomes SUFFERING. This means *hope* is a WOB of mindset, neither guaranteed nor forlorn. Let's take a moment to consider the concept of hope.

6.3.1 HOPE

Humanity generally casts hope as that which one desires with confident anticipation even when allowing for the possibility it won't manifest. But that isn't the basis of hope, despite one desiring it. If it were, then Buddhism's eightfold path by which one expects—desires—the end to rebirth would itself be *dukkha*, SUFFER-ING. Rather, hope is mindset. For example, one hopeful thing for which the hopeful hope—or *believe*, which is a mindset—is for a *possibility* that's beyond their present scope of knowledge or reasoning. Although that's hope, it roots in desire. A terminal cancer patient who lives in the hope their oncologists will pull a curative rabbit out of their collective hat isn't necessarily hoping for that but desiring it. Hope is establishing a desiring mindset that rebalances the 'energy' of the expectation of experiencing (a cure) with the act of experiencing (a cure or not). It thus delimits or removes SUFFERING from their equation of life not by letting go of their attachment to life by accepting death as their highest good or simply inevitable, but by neither accepting nor rejecting either one; a mindset that's above the fray, unaffected despite desiring one outcome over the other. We see this most evidently with the religious, who hope for a heavenly afterlife or divine purpose to their adversity. Yet, atheists follow the same hopeful pattern in adopting a mindset where, in spite of dying with no afterlife or grand purpose on the horizon, nonetheless recast their dying in hope and thereby manage their SUFFERING.

Mina defines hope *as a mindset that disavows SUFFERING.* This is how a person remains cheerful, antic-ipating their anguished, grieving, Jobian experience inevitably will pass while others look at them as crazy, unrealistic, or lost in fantasy. In a mindset of despair, one experiences life exclusively through the lens of *now* instead of *tomorrow*, abandons all hope, and loses oneself in suffering. Nazi death camps are a brightly lit window into this phenomenon, but perplexingly less lit are Communism's Soviet and Chinese gulags, Cambodia's killing fields, the hopeless tyranny of Socialism, the vast destruction wrought on human life generally over the centuries in Mongol and Islamic invasions, the many millennia of slavery, or just heartbreak. Those throughout history who've endured hardship and hoped for its end had no guarantee of, and indeed rarely got, that for which they hoped except to limit their experience of suffering. Their hope wasn't forlorn because it helped them cope even if it didn't end their physical travails.

6.3.1.1 FALSE HOPE

So-called false hope means hopeless hope. It's an oxymoron whether in terminal illness, bankruptcy, dating, child custody, or unrequited love. The way of hope is to convert a forlorn experience into one absent suffering. Accordingly, a false hope can't be hopeless because it, too, is hope. There's no such thing as hope that isn't real, despite its apparent improbability. A terrorist might hope to turn a seemingly invincible enemy to dust which the enemy taunts as a false hope but, in reality, their hope however fanciful or impractical is a means to cope, can never exclude the unforeseen possibility, and thereby limits or eliminates their SUFFERING. That hope for an improbability might be pragmatically unproductive or result in harmful action—dating becoming stalking—is immaterial to it being legitimate hope.

6.4 THE 'ENERGY' OF SUFFERING

Thought exudes 'energy' in the embodied. SUFFERING isn't Thought itself but a disturbance of Thought that exudes negative EM↲F only indirectly through Thought that arises in the suffering experience. It suffuses not only the sufferer's mind thus being, but their environment, too, both local—within about a 30-foot diameter—and global, meaning from their immediate vicinity to every level of Individual Culture to Ultraculture (§ 4.1:291). Accordingly, our universal Ultraculture prior to the Big Healing was awash in negative EM↲F that transformed it from intrinsically benign to the Negative Collective Consciousness (NCC) that induced a sense of suffering in everyone. This is because 'energy' begets energy and, in this context, SUFFERING begat suffering (FALLING IN HATE, § 8.1.2:444). The effect on Earth imbued us with a sense that suffering is a natural, ineluctable part of life, that "birth . . . decay . . . disease . . . death . . . united with the unpleasant . . . separated from the pleasant . . . not to get what one desires is suffering" (Mahathera 1998, 65) which, despite humanity's desperate hope (faith) to the contrary, necessarily torpedoes the notion of a benevolent God. But it's always been a false view of reality. SUFFERING isn't inevitable.

When Lucifer and Michael's Reconciliation dissolved the NCC, its negative EmℒF dissipated (§ 1.2:21; § 4.2:379). Humanity was free of it and Mina could transformationally mass heal humanity of the SUFFERING so epidemic especially amongst the physical-born living in spirit world when, before, the infrequent, scattered individual healings were like throwing a rock in the sea and expecting a tsunami. In this way, the hope of a world without unavoidable suffering revealed itself not as a false hope but (to us) an unforeseen improbability that occurred. This will be obvious as spirit healing takes transformative root in the physically living's spirit selves.

6.4.1 Ending Suffering

Mindset energizes suffering, not experience or Thought such as loss, pain, harm, resentment, anger, regret, guilt, hate, sorrow, grief, craving, or attachment. However much one attempts through behavior to suppress, ignore, or replace with gratitude or detachment the Thought that arises in SUFFERING, one's suffering—the Thought disturbance itself—doesn't actually resolve. To reduce or remove SUFFERING, one needs deal with the disturbance, not the Thought the disturbance roils (Depression, § 6.6:437). One does this by changing their mindset to that in which the disturbance—the 'clash'—doesn't arise, where the 'energy' in the expectation of experiencing doesn't differ from that in the act of experiencing. This is the purpose of hope although it doesn't actually change mindset so much as temporarily shunts it onto a siding. Changes to mindset are necessarily unique to everyone but share one thing in common: the new mindset is *unaware* of SUFFERING. One adopts a mindset not giving rise to the proto-energy 'clash' that provokes a Thought disturbance thus SUFFERING.

Consider a 1930s German or 1960s East German who loves their country, who sees it as the shining future of a happy Europe, yet each clearly perceives where Hitlerism or Stalinism must inevitably take it and its people whom they love. Great suffering arises in their heart as they watch either reality unfold. They grieve at what they feel is the destruction of their German nation, its people, and its heritage under each of two versions of Socialism. But they can't escape figuratively or literally because, first, their heart is anguished—suffering—and, second, the violent absolute power of socioculture, thus government, traps them. They might join a resistance movement in the hope of overthrowing the horror which might ease their (local) suffering, but which only produces new (global) suffering. Or, they might transcend the whole mess in adopting a mindset that neither loves nor hates their respective Germany as it exists, but experiences it differently in that no suffering arises from its behavior. Or, they neither love nor hate but differently experience their own life. They might not really want to adopt such a mindset but, on the other hand, definitely don't want to SUFFER. A person who wants to end their suffering faces these three options contextualized to their unique suffering experience.

6.5 Intentionality of Suffering

Mind's reaction to SUFFERING has Intentionality because SUFFERING isn't simply an emotion or an unpleasant emotional state, it's an intense sort of 'windstorm' of the emergent ℒife self. The negative EmℒF that exudes from an embodied person isn't just 'energy' in the sense one can *feel* a person's vibe or sense their feeling, but Intentionalized 'energy' that *affects* the environment, including inflicting substantive harm on Living entities—human and nonhuman bodies, plants, and animals. The sufferer isn't doing this consciously or subconsciously, it's more elemental than that. It's weakly emergent (§ 2:90), a new property if you will that arises in one's emergent ℒife self resulting from the elemental 'clash' that's a *reflex* similar to the physiological reflex of a leg jerk when one taps below the patella or lashes out with a fist or a shout when startled. SUFFERING tears through a person's beingness with a flensing agony.

The reflex blunts the Thought disturbance by Intentionalizing a rebalancing of proto-energy to resolve the 'clash,' thus ending the 'windstorm' and restoring homeostasis although, with a mindset tending toward SUFFERING, Mina says it's only about 20% effective. Intentionalized negative EmℒF is a side effect of this, Intentionalizing one's Thought profile which, in the case of a suffering person, always involves negative EmℒF. It remains confined to the self when unembodied, never interacting with or affecting other unembodied persons. But in the context of embodiment where mind expresses *as* body in an environment with which it integrates, this reflex Intentionalizes naturally via the body into its environment; the reflex becomes a part of that environment.

6.5.1 How the Suffering Reflex Affects People

Intentionality always affects people and the environment in some way because it concretizes proto-energy as Thought (§ 3.2:282) that suffuses our universe as well as All Existence (§ 1:112). Nothing escapes Intentionality for the simple reason that all things exist in the proto-energy environment. It affects us regardless our awareness of it. If one has awareness, however, one can employ countervailing action such as re-Intentionalizing proto-energy around oneself that effectively neutralizes the non-self Intentionality, or block it by Intentionalizing a shield of *Life* force and chakra energy around one's body (§ 1.2.1.2.2:500). One always consciously or subconsciously (having awareness or not) chooses to Intentionalize Thought. Therefore, Intentionality always arises with purpose except that of SUFFERING, which is the only exception. It has no subconscious–conscious purpose because it's elemental, literally just a *Life* reflex that coincidentally Intentionalizes EM*L*F, which is *negative* EM*L*F, because that's what arises in SUFFERING, not normative emotion (§ 3.3.3.1.1:289) like unhappiness, hate, or sorrow. Its negative WOB is why it directly harms those local to the sufferer whereas Intentionalizing neutral (positive) EM*L*F around a person gives rise in their affect to an inexplicably good feeling.

The nature of SUFFERING is that it's such a profound disturbance of mind that the *magnitude* of negative EM*L*F it provokes through Intentionality is greater than a person's normal experience of negative feeling. Whether a person is unembodied or embodied, the magnitude of Intentionalized negative EM*L*F profoundly affects their mind's emotional state; negative EM*L*F is normative while neutral EM*L*F is nonnormative, the opposite of the human norm (ibid). But with a physical-embodied person, whose body-in-the-environment *is* mind, the local environment (inclusive of any Living entity or *Life*) experiences the Intentional *force* of the sufferer's negative EM*L*F. For example, instead of simply perceiving, or feeling, someone's vibe as a negative emotive 'energy' that may or may not emotionally affect the perceiver, the force of the reflex-Intentionalized negative EM*L*F materially affects the body of both the sufferer and local Living entities or persons as though a purposefully Intentionalized hostile attack.

The force of Intentionalized negative EM*L*F embodies the proto-energy space one's body occupies and acts on the matter–Energy that constitutes the physical body. The Intentionalized negative EM*L*F alters the 'energy' balance of the body and degrades its functionality thus health and well-being, not instantly but over time. The more profound the SUFFERING encountered, the less time it takes to degrade the body's functions. Most people come in and out of contact with SUFFERING people all the time, so the impact to their body is on and off, giving their physiology time to rebalance its 'energy' and heal any inflicted damage unless one embraces it. A person who lives with a sufferer or is in near-constant proximity—a soldier in the trenches, a police officer amongst high crime—has less time apart from the sufferer's Intentionalized negative EM*L*F. Their body has less chance to rebalance its 'energy' and heal inflicted damage. It eventually leads to degraded health that, in accord with mindset, gives rise to their own SUFFERING, their negatively altered emotional state, and so on.

SUFFERING is a profound trauma of the mind. In a proto-energy-connected universe, it's a profound alteration in its Ultraculture that leads to a collective consciousness imbued with an overabundance of negative EM*L*F filtering into the mindset of every Living entity and *Life* being therein (including the natural environment) just as it did in our universe via the NCC. SUFFERING wreaks the second greatest destruction on physical health and well-being next to mindset, which is first, and behavior, which is third.

6.5.2 HOW THE SUFFERING REFLEX AFFECTS ENVIRONMENT

Similarly as above, SUFFERING is destructive to the health and well-being of the natural environment. Recall that evolution never randomly arises, that any change to Living entities inclusive of the human body is directed or undirected only (§ 2.1.5.5.2.2:323). Although SUFFERING's Intentionality is an elemental reflex not arising in Thought, Mina considers its mutative effect on Living entities as a form of directed evolution because it occurs via Intentionality rather than unIntentionalized, undirected replication errors, environmental stressors, and the like. It does this via the profound magnitude of negative EM*L*F that suffuses the environment once SUFFERING saturates it. Whereas problematic existents like harmful bacteria and viruses don't come to exist randomly but only via directed evolution, SUFFERING's Intentionalized reflex induces the same effect, leading to changes influenced by negative EM*L*F damage to a physical entity's own proto-energy homeostasis, which then leads to mutative changes in functionality. Thus, people's sense that negativity harms the environment, forms of life destructive of the human body aren't natural or of God, and SUFFERING is intrinsic to existence.

6.6 DEPRESSION

Philosophy with a capital-P can't define depression, preferring instead to call it elusive because sciences like psychology–psychiatry don't know what it is, only how it appears to make one feel. Here, we define depression and describe its origin and treatment.

6.6.1 What is Depression

Depression arises in SUFFERING as the manifestation of mind feeling itself torn apart (§ 6.1:431). The experience of suffering expresses as a mindstate in which we sense *L*ife degrading, subconscious mind's *fear* that one is *losing L*ife, that it's declining, failing, that *L*ife-death, meaning *mind*-death, is a possibility. Depression is a subconscious phenomenon. Despite being consciously self-aware, one isn't aware of it; conscious mind's experience presents to self as a mystery. The physical manifestation of SUFFERING embodied in the aforementioned mindstate is what humanity generally terms *depression*.

6.6.2 Origin, or Cause, of Depression

The Thought disturbance that is SUFFERING reduces one's enlivening agency (ibid). Altogether, it puts the mind in a state of tumult. A loss of enlivening agency manifests as feeling less enlivened. The experience of feeling *less* alive is a depressant that infects mindstate. It expresses in the spirit-born simply *as* mindstate and Intentionalizes in one's local environment as with suffering, though to a lesser degree. It doesn't affect the spirit body except insofar as one's mindstate manifests affective-based changes in one's spirit body. It expresses in the physically alive—our focus here—as Intentionalized mindstate in one's local environment, but does manifest physiological effects in the depressed person's body as well as to a lesser extent those of persons in long-term proximity (§ 6.5.1:436) because the physical body is matter–Energy that experiences Intentionalized proto-energy. These effects encompass the so-called causes, symptoms, and observable risk factors of depression as well as other, not necessarily observably related, damages to the body. Whereas affective changes to one's spirit body can manifest immediately, they take time to alter the physiological WOB of the independent biological existent that is one's physical body. Regardless depression's effect *on*, or its apparent rise *in* the body, it singularly originates in subconscious mind's awareness of SUFFERING, in *L*ife's previously described proto-energy 'clash' (§ 6.1.3:432).

6.6.3 Treating Depression

Treatments that rely on biological manipulation of the body such as drugs, electroconvulsive therapy (ECT), and the like aren't curative but analgesic. Psychotherapy is a useful curative when therapists properly administer it and patients follow it through because it helps a depressed person develop awareness of their subconscious wherein mindset arises. But it's a primitive healing modality. It doesn't comprehend that depression arises in SUFFERING, or what that is. Still, Mina considers it about 60% effective in helping identify and resolve one's depressive reaction to SUFFERING, though it's a slow, arduous, haphazard process. Too, depression originates in multiple different suffering experiences in ~90% of depressed persons. They must unmask and heal all of them to cure their depression. Additionally, long-term depression that Intentionalizes structural and chemical changes in the brain takes time to reverse through Intentionality. The best and quickest means to cure depression is to better acquaint oneself with mindset and the means to have consistent awareness of one's subconscious self—recall the subconscious isn't Thought but awareness (§ 2.1:393)—and how to reconcile its awareness with conscious Thought (§ 2.2.2.1:396).

One can only achieve such awareness of the subconscious through improved mind–brain integration (§ 1.2.2.4:257) where the physically conscious person has awareness of their spirit self and *L*ife mind in toto. For example, epiphanies that lead to relief from depression are one's experiences of having altered their mindset to reduce or resolve SUFFERING. Until the Big Healing, curing (as opposed to moderating) depression via psychotherapy was mostly impossible—resolving the one doesn't automatically resolve the other—because The Corruption and NCC as well as brain chemistry always blocked success by preventing one's ability to heal. But those days are over. Today, healing is possible for every person. It naturally improves mind–brain integration and brings greater awareness of one's suffering needing healing, which further improves mind–brain integration and so on. As one heals mind trauma, the body's health and well-being improves, too, as the factors contributing to physiological damage heal and Intentionalized negative EM*L*F neutralizes in or disperses from the body.

6.7 Reincarnation

SUFFERING—a Thought disturbance arising in mindset inflicting harm on one's *L*ife self (§ 6.1:431)—is the root of all human problems whether here, in spirit world, or as an unembodied person. We can talk about

The Corruption, the NCC, or Accountableism as the human problems of our universe, but they all merely induce SUFFERING in which all human pain originates. Reincarnation—the cyclical rebirth of the so-called soul into a succession of human bodies—is a mental analgesic for suffering as much as drugs and ECT are for depression (*above*). It seeks to resolve SUFFERING by elucidating a spiritual growth path by which a person eliminates the cause of suffering to enter a non-suffering environment called Nirvana, enlightenment, or some form of oneness with Source—God, Spirit, Divine—'energy.' On the other hand, it coincidently justifies social stratification and its treatment, which provokes SUFFERING. So, there's that.

The concept of reincarnation is inaccurate because its philosophy doesn't account for emergent *Life*, the physicospirit WOB of embodiment (§ 1.2.2.3:256), or the reality of SUFFERING. Recall that once a physical body dies, the physicospirit person integrating that body continues living as a spirit person. It's impossible for any extant spirit person to integrate a physical body for the simple reason that whenever a physical body comes into existence through *Life*'s procreative process, a spirit body also manifests which integrates that physical body wherein physicospirit mind–brain is one (§ 1.2.1.1.1:248). Absent so-called spiritual possession, which is something entirely different (§ 3.2:566), and cloning, which creates new emergent *Life* anyhow and therefore necessarily excludes an extant spirit person,[474] integrating a physical body with which a spirit person isn't initially born is impossible.

Even without the impossibility of a spirit person (the so-called soul) re-integrating a new physical body, SUFFERING doesn't resolve through spiritual growth by detaching one's mindstate from physical reality or learning to live rightly with humanity and nature. Emergent *Life* is intrinsically autonomous, thus free, so the quality, or moral goodness, of Thought and deed is immaterial here. It resolves by altering one's mindset to be unaware of SUFFERING, which differs per person.

6.8 SLAVERY

As a physical manifestation of mindset, slavery is the epitome of suffering in both the enslaved and enslaver's mindset, each altogether contributing to slavery's success or failure. There's no greater SUFFERING but which arises in slavery, as it's the antithesis of human WOB's absolute autonomy. SUFFERING arises in slavery because, in order to enslave a person, one absolutely requires their consent. There's no slavery without it. A person is subconsciously aware they voluntarily ceded their autonomy to another yet, having done so, nonetheless experiences negative Em*LF* and, in that awareness, SUFFERING arises from the 'energy' of the expectation of experiencing differing from that of the act of experiencing.[475]

SUFFERING arises not because of *what* one experiences but *how* (§ 6.2:434). Because slavery is of a person's own making—when one is very young, then later when choice-capable—they experience it orders of magnitude worse than what they didn't self-create. The conscious person may feel enslavement, being coerced, isn't their fault yet their subconscious has awareness it is. This gives rise to an unreconciled contradiction in conscious mind's sub-Thought (§ 2.2.2.1:396). The Thought disturbance afflicting the enslaved person's mind is therefore the most intense because, of all the ways one can suffer, none cede autonomy. Only in accepting slavery—a broad-term reality inclusive of most human interactions—does a person consciously, voluntarily, fundamentally violate their core human WOB (§ 1.1.3.4.1:366) in a way another person cannot. We define slavery, its two manifestations, and then its origins below.

6.8.1 WHAT IS SLAVERY

Slavery is the loss of autonomy—not in the sense of free will or liberty generally but as one's core human WOB—arising in the enslaved via mindset or coercion of the physical (or spirit) body. One needn't merely be compelled to produce for another to be enslaved, one can compel self. Let's consider each type.

---

474. A human embryo cloned for stem cells (therapeutic cloning) births *Life*, creating a new consciousness. When physically destroyed, it spirit grows for about two more months, then, without human interaction, ceases. It sits there inert and abandoned in the 'reflective' environment (§ 7.1.1.1:212). If a human interacts with it, then it resumes development toward a baby (this changed post-Big Healing on July 12, 2020; FN 455:412). Somatic cell nuclear transfer method (reproductive cloning) also births new *Life* at the point of cleavage (EN 105:654). These therapeutics are *not* benign.

475. Note that although a physical person can hate and loathe themselves as a function of their less than ideal mind–brain integration (§ 1.2.2.4.2:258), one's subconscious–conscious mind never does.

6.8.1.1 Slavery via Mindset

One who enslaves themselves via mindset (addiction; § 2.1.1.5.2:353) does so, first, by enslaving their mindset to an outside agency whereby they're effectively their own overseer, and second, the same except one doesn't submit to being their own slavemaster. We describe each.

Mindset enslaved by self as one's own overseer. A person substitutes the mindset of an outside agency such as a person, group, society, laws, ideology, and so on for their own mindset, which they don't retain. No coercion is required because the person is not opposed to enslavement and is sufficiently brainwashed, an ideologue suppressing their conscience because they believe in the ideology's conscience. They reject their own for that of an outside moral agent because they consider their conscience fallible vis-à-vis that of the ideology. The person identifies with the enslaving agency such that its will is their will. The person self-polices their Thought and action, relieving the slavemaster of the effort. In this way, one becomes one's own overseer, the slavemaster's favorite style of slave for whom Lenin (d. 1924) allegedly coined the 'useful idiots' term. This is most common in dysfunctional families, relationships, and any ideologically driven environment. Although such persons may not appear enslaved—forced to work—they are. In short, one's mindset isn't opposed to enslavement though one's subconscious is.

Mindset enslaved by non-self as one's slavemaster. Here, a person retains their mindset but cedes its control to an outside agency. No coercion is required because the person is sufficiently brainwashed, an ideologue, but opposed to enslaving their conscience along with their body and needs be compelled to override it. They believe the ideology but not necessarily its conscience, considering their own infallible vis-à-vis the ideology's. This means they don't self-police their Thought and deed, compelling the slavemaster to the effort who, therefore, can't trust the person as their own overseer. This is most common in certain institutions that ostensibly employ a person or where one voluntarily labors but is nonetheless enslaved.

6.8.1.2 Slavery via the Body

When coercion of the body is all that's required to effect enslavement then mindset—whether one accepts, submits, covertly or overtly opposes, or outright rejects it—plays only an ancillary role. It doesn't matter how one feels about it for another to enslave him or her because physical domination discourages escape or suicide. This is slavery's most recognizable form and always a form of chattel where the person is movable or immovable property—having no control of own-self—without some or all the rights common to free persons. Sex and child sex; forced, child, and bonded labor; and debt bondage are all forms of chattel whereas serfdom, peonage, and indentured servitude aren't. Intimidation enslaves the intimidated to another's will. So-called cancel culture and wokeness are slave cultures and their applied philosophies enslavement (§ 1.1.3.5.2:367). Society doesn't define slavery. Rather, it's the person or group controlling the slave. Where they differ with society, the former is the premier authority whether a slave is chattel or not according to socioculture's ability to compel a different norm.

6.8.2 Origin of Slavery

Three points regarding slavery's origin: it wasn't a pragmatic solution to a human disposal problem, it was an ad hoc affair prior to civilization, and it began in human passions. We consider each.

Slavery was not a pragmatic solution to disposing of criminals and captured enemies, nor to conditions of economic surplus, high population density, et cetera. It wasn't a product of civilization. These are modern rationalizations based on faulty premises, such as hunter-gatherers and primitive farmers having no use for another mouth to feed, thus no economic or other benefit to owning—which means controlling—another person. Even without energy testing, such notions fly in the face of observable human behavior. For instance, modern individuals or groups occupying tiny rural homesteads or anonymous urban tenements compel persons into versions of subjugation not for economic benefit or to feed one more mouth in an already grubby existence, but for reasons that make sense to them however seemingly irrational and unthinkable.

Slavery originated simply because an individual or group *could do it and get away with it* regardless any economic or social benefit. The motivation is the same as with killing. Both are the same thing in terms of compelling another to conform to one's will. According to Mina, slavery first appeared when one person compelled another against his will to comply with a situation—the alternative being death—circa 45KYA (∼4KY after Humanity 2.0's start; § 2.1.3:543) as an act of vengeance effected by force. This individual was compelled to carry kills, equipment, and food on hunting forays and otherwise work domestic chores for about five years, then killed when circumstances changed.

Slavery was an ad hoc affair prior to humanity organizing into complex groups (civilization). Almost every reason under the sun prompted actual or attempted enslavement just as with murder and killing generally. People raided other groups for slaves as much as for animals and goods, sometimes merely as bargaining chips or currency to later trade for something else. Around 5% of enslavement during this ad hoc period was simply out of spite—to torment a person or group—even when it was a net liability for the slavemaster or risked, and even ended in, their own untimely death.

Slavery begins in human passion, not in considered calculations as to its benefits, sustainability, or as a solution to unwanted (killable) people. This sort of thinking came along much later in less autonomous but more complex societies necessitating risk-benefit calculations, as well as with modern academia. It's nonsensical to imagine slavery couldn't exist until social stratification (differentiation) evolved into a societal feature because society arises in the family where stratification is intrinsic, and many parents and stronger siblings enslave their children and weaker siblings. Social stratification and slavery—coercively controlling another—was capable of existing from the very first family. One couldn't easily enslave parents, grandparents, blood relatives, or friends in a sociocultural context any more than a peasant could enslave an aristocrat. All the same, it happened before and after the advent of 'civilization' because slavery's motivation lies not in self-benefit nor societal capability but in human passions that a Corrupt humanity, more often than not, effects by force.

Section 7
Happiness

It might be of little surprise that, like SUFFERING, HAPPINESS is a proto-energy experience of one's *Life* self and the antithesis of SUFFERING. The euphoria and well-being equated with happiness is just the aftereffect, an artifact of this proto-energy experience and the reason it leaves one's mindscape joyful, serene, and infused with healing. Here, we define and describe the way and attainment of HAPPINESS.

7.1 What is Happiness

Recall how we define SUFFERING (§ 6.1:431). We define HAPPINESS similarly, particularly in that all we are, think–feel, and do is, and Intentionalizes (§ 3.2:282), proto-energy. HAPPINESS as a proto-energy experience doesn't arise in 'clashing' with one's *Life* self as with SUFFERING, but as subconscious mind's awareness of *own-self well-being* that conscious mind experiences as the affective mindstate called happiness.

7.1.1 Own-self Well-being as Happiness

Recall that own-self well-being isn't one's *own* psychosomatic well-being as Philosophy with a capital-P defines it as an overall affect, but *Da-sein*, meaning any entity that's alive and interacting in 'being-there' with its environment in terms of the well-being of its infinitely definable own-self experiencing the world according to its self-aware capacity (§ 2:275). *Well-being* means own-self has awareness that it's exactly *as* own-self wants to be; it's what one experiences in the WOB of well-being. Therefore, the mindstate of awareness (SOA) that is well-being necessarily *is* own-self awareness. Absent such awareness, well-being necessarily *is not*, meaning there's no positive or negative well-being, there's just well-being or its absence. When a person doesn't feel happy, then own-self isn't experiencing the WOB of well-being and subconscious mind is unaware of well-being. It has no reality, is nonexistent, is not Intentionalized proto-energy congruent with own-self WOB. By definition, then, well-being necessarily *is* HAPPINESS.

HAPPINESS is an aggregation over time of multiple mindstates of being (SOB; § 1.2.2.1:253) that subconscious mind assimilates as stimuli (§ 2.1:276), forming a SOA that own-self experiences as the WOB of well-being. Recall one is, in every way, 'energy.' As a computer's language is zeros and ones, *Life*'s mind's is proto-energy. Everything we are and think–feel boils down to that (§ 1:303). Every SOB and SOA is an Intentionalized proto-energy that, when multiple SOB aggregate as a SOA matching the proto-energy of own-self's desired WOB, own-self experiences such an aggregated proto-energy as Intentionality matching the WOB of well-being. In the context of mind, HAPPINESS is a proto-energy event of which subconscious mind is aware and conscious mind experiences as lowercase-h happiness. It's important to recognize that, to comprehend happiness as we generally think of it as an affective state of being, we mustn't trip over conscious mind's experience of happiness and think that's all there is to it. We need take a step beyond to ground our understanding in subconscious mind and ℒife's proto-energy reality. Since everything we think–feel arises in, and is, proto-energy then, when a person feels happy or unhappy, that isn't merely feeling, affect, mindstate, or whatever. It's ℒife's proto-energy reality manifesting as Intentionality which we call mindstate in its subconscious–conscious form.

Pleasure in the context of happiness isn't mental (thinking–feeling) or somatic (a sensation). It's a mindstate experiencing proto-energy congruent with own-self WOB's proto-energy. The feeling and pleasure of sex, for example, isn't simply one's mental and somatic experience, but Intentionalized proto-energy arising in the context of the physical body's mind and matter–Energy. It's the same for the spirit-embodied, except their body doesn't constitute from matter–Energy but Intentionalized supranatural proto-energy fully integrating mind since it arises *as* mind. The spirit body is a material extension of mind in a way our presently limited mind–brain integrated physical body isn't (§ 1.2.3:470).

The notion that pleasure, well-being, contentment, and so forth in their common usage have anything to do with happiness, or can be mutually exclusive, is inaccurate. Consider that one can feel a sense of happiness based on meaning and engagement in life that has nothing to do with pleasure, or that one can feel pleasure yet experience guilt that diminishes or negates the experience of happiness. All the same, in the former the meaning and engagement that is one's purpose in life is, in and of itself, pleasure thus happiness. Conversely, pleasure tinged with guilt isn't pleasure at all but pain thus suffering, ergo, unhappiness. The mental pain of guilt can entirely negate the somatic pleasure of sex whereby, overall, one suffers rather than enjoys it and experiences unhappiness rather than the happiness they'd predicated.

One's somatic sensation is immaterial because, first, pleasure–pain isn't physiological—sensation being mere action potentials conveying electrochemical change to the brain that comprehends it only as a reality of applied energy E—but that which ℒife mind experiences as proto-energy transliterating to the brain to instantiate in one's physical mind as thinking–feeling. Thus, like SUFFERING, HAPPINESS is of mind, not environment. Pleasure–pain is any SOB such that

$$P \leftrightarrow OS_{\text{WOB}} \begin{cases} OS_{\text{WOB}} \rightarrow OS_{\text{w-b}} \\ P \cong S \end{cases} \tag{27.3}$$

where P is pleasure–pain, OS_{WOB} is own-self WOB, $OS_{\text{w-b}}$ is own-self well-being, S is suffering, and the material equivalence and congruence aren't identity. And second, one's experience of somatic thinking–feeling is immaterial because pleasure–pain is a measure of suffering where less suffering is a SOB of greater pleasure and less pain, and greater suffering is a SOB of less pleasure and greater pain, such that

$$<S \cong >H \bigwedge >S \cong <H \tag{27.4}$$

where S is suffering, H is happiness, and the congruence isn't identity. Happiness is an experience of mind, not a product of environment. Like suffering (Eq. (27.2):434), it's a function of mindset in that

$$M \eqcolon H \bigwedge M \neqcolon H \tag{27.5}$$

where M is mindset, H is happiness, and $\eqcolon$ and $\neqcolon$ mean 'in [and not in] the image of,' respectively. Consequently, a Thought WOB that rejects intrinsic meaning is accurate in the sense there's no objective meaning that's intrinsic to existence, yet it's also inaccurate because, since human reality is of mind not environment, and physical embodiment is not ℒife thus not existence, then the meaning one establishes through mind is both real and objective in that own-self subjectively orients oneself to mind's reality, which is objective vis-à-vis own-self. As ℒife (after Mike and Molly; § 2:304; § 1.2.1.1:248; § 2.1.1:348) births via parental Intentionality, not divine creation, then, beyond parental motivation for conceiving new ℒife, there is indeed no intrinsic meaning to ℒife, to being born, to existing. But the *autonomous* person, the ℒife self—whose *emergence* anchors intrinsic objectivity to extrinsic subjectivity—attaches value therefore meaning to that reality and to the experience of it from which own-self derives HAPPINESS.

7.2   THE WAY OF HAPPINESS

Happiness arises in the experience of suffering. A person who suffers experiences unhappiness and, conversely, a person who isn't suffering experiences happiness. HAPPINESS is the absence of SUFFERING where $\neg S \cong H$

and one's experience of happiness is the absence of experiencing suffering as in Eq. (27.4). Thus, HAPPINESS is *normative* human WOB and happiness a *normative experience* because, absent The Corruption, SUFFERING is *nonnormative*. Physical humanity—consistently unhappy, having only inconsistent and ephemeral experiences of pleasure-cum-happiness—mistakes both SUFFERING and UNHAPPINESS for an intrinsic condition of existence when they are only dysfunctions arising in mindset addiction (§ 2.1.1.5.2:353). Mind–brain integration limitation, physiology, one's Individual Culture (IC) up through Ultraculture, and mindset altogether affects whether one suffers and how one experiences HAPPINESS, i.e., one's experience of desired WOB and one's experience of happiness.

Conscious mind doesn't necessarily experience happiness despite subconscious mind's awareness of HAPPINESS because, in mindset, people misidentify what it is, associating with it things like somatic pleasure–pain or even suffering, which one's own WOB doesn't. For example, one can experience pleasure in suffering; the greater it is, the greater the happiness. On its face, this seems to contradict Eq. (27.3)–(27.4) but doesn't because happiness arises in mindset as in Eq. (27.5). Despite somatic pain's congruence with suffering, a mindset unaware of suffering experiences pleasure, therefore, happiness.

A car crash some time ago imparted severe nerve damage that left me physically, mentally, and emotionally disabled. Yet, I was so pleased I could now prepare my young children breakfast and walk them to school that my mindset was unaware of suffering; I experienced happiness. Despite the agonizing pain and debility, I was nevertheless happy *in that respect* (*below*). A funnier example is Bill Murray's pain-loving character enjoying himself in sadistic dentist Steve Martin's chair in the film *Little Shop of Horrors* (1986) where sadism was both Murray and Martin's pleasure. But Murray's pleasure in pain ergo happiness aroused Martin's pain in pleasure ergo suffering.

Happiness seems ephemeral because, in the main, one consciously contradicts in mindset subconscious mind's WOB of HAPPINESS. One's *objective* well-being (OWB) versus positive psychology's *subjective* well-being (SWB) is the WOB of HAPPINESS because, although it is certainly subjective vis-à-vis own-self, it is objective vis-à-vis conscious mind's experience of happiness. Hence, HAPPINESS is a choice.

7.3 ATTAINING HAPPINESS

The fundamental means to attain and maintain happiness lies in one's mindset and nowhere else. This means it's necessary to remove one's SUFFERING (§ 6.4.1:436). Happiness, of course, entails no suffering at all. We aren't necessarily capable of that because of mind–brain integration limitation, so we experience happiness concurrently with suffering. I felt no suffering in my aforementioned nerve disability because I had an intuitive awareness of own-self WOB—how I valued my children; while I necessarily and enjoyably worked to support them, not being there to parent them as *I* desired *was* SUFFERING—and embraced it. I certainly experienced suffering in my body, mind, relationships, finances, and physical and mental capabilities not only because of the realities of the damage, but because of mindset local to my pain and global to my life. Over time, with Mina's education, guidance, and healing, I addressed all my areas of suffering and experienced an overall improvement in happiness over the long term despite the persistent disability and its consequences. Happiness seems ephemeral because we aren't aware of own-self WOB. But it's certainly attainable for any person willing to reconsider their mindset despite facing suffering-inducing adversity.

SECTION 8

Love and Hate

If you haven't read PROTO-LOVE describing LOVE's *what-is* (§ 3.3.2:284), we recommend you do to better comprehend this section. Here, we describe lowercase love–hate—its way, 'energy,' and attainment—arising in LOVE that instantiates in one of the four principal attributes of humanness and as an aspect (as with Intentionality) of ℒife force we dubbed proto-love. All-caps LOVE is ℒife's base disposition in which arise ordinary, everyday experiences of love, hate, and emotion. Lowercase-l love is intrinsic to humanity. We innately understand it and are ever inclined to seek it out. It's worth noting that thinking–feeling associated with the experience of suffering (§ 6:431) and happiness (§ 7:441) arises in LOVE, thus proto-love.

8.1 THE WAY OF LOVE–HATE

Although SUFFERING and HAPPINESS arise in mindset, therefore choice, LOVE arises as an attribute of humanness, in ℒife force itself, in the very proto-energy that enlivens the ℘erson (§ 6.1.4:433) and expresses as emotive

*L*ife force (Em*L*F; § 3.3.3.1.1:289). Proto-love is a *force* of *L*ife force, an Intentionalized (§ 3.2:282), felt exertion in the world. It infuses the universe. There's not a tidbit of proto-energy in All Existence that human proto-love to some degree doesn't Intentionalize in the same way as negative Em*L*F did the NCC. This is why we *feel* 'love in the air,' that it permeates the universe, that despite human beastliness our base disposition is love, not hate, even though hate seems to suffuse our universe as much or more than love (§ 6.4:435). Recall hate is LOVE that instantiates in proto-love (§ 3.3.2:284), so what actually diffuses through our universe besides proto-love isn't hate but negative Em*L*F, which constituted the NCC. The tension intrinsic to proto-love bringing forth the *experience* of love *and* hate (§ 3.3.2.1.1:285) is the truth behind our ancient albeit incorrect sense of a universal yin–yang: good–evil, light–dark, love–hate, and divine–demonic that grounds religion as well as Philosophy with a capital-P.

It seems emotion of whatever stripe arises in a person spontaneously without consent or control, but that's inaccurate. All emotion is Thought which is of mind (§ 2.3.2:240), the expressive aspect of *L*ife having subconscious awareness of, and conscious experience with, environment inclusive of own-self (§ 2:275). Thought arises in subconscious mind as *L*ife proto-energy manifesting one's awareness of environment in terms of own-self. Conscious mind's experience of subconscious awareness is what Thought is. Because mindset also constitutes in subconscious mind (§ 2.3.1:398), it informs Thought; subconscious mind's awareness forms in the milieu of mindset. One's thinking–feeling certainly *feels* spontaneous and uncontrollable but, in truth, Thought is choice such that

$$\left(\left(M_{\mathrm{sub}} \to \mathrm{T} \left\{ M_{\mathrm{set}} \right\} \right) \bigwedge \mathrm{T} \cong M_{\mathrm{set}} \right) \Rightarrow C \qquad (27.6)$$

where M_{sub} is subconscious mind, T is Thought, M_{set} is mindset, C is choice, and the congruence isn't identity. LOVE is a particular *response* to subconscious mind's awareness of environment. Conscious mind's experience of subconscious mind's awareness manifests in thinking–feeling love, hate, and emotions that reflect that response. Ergo, thinking–feeling is a choice, a response to environment arising and expressing in subconscious–conscious mind. Let's consider falling in love and falling in hate.

8.1.1   FALLING IN LOVE

One's sense of *falling in love* generally feels sudden and irrepressible in that one experiences a loss of self-control as though parasitically manipulated or 'entangled' by an unseen force. It only appears that way, however, because physical humanity is so thoroughly out of touch with own-self's subconscious aspect of mind. When one 'falls in love,' one isn't 'falling' at all in the sense of vulnerably falling asleep, powerlessly falling ill, or randomly falling over a stone, but simply consciously manifesting one's mindset-informed subconscious awareness of, and resonance with, the object of one's love (§ 11.3.1:462; § 3.5.5.5:495).

Because Thought always Intentionalizes in accord with its intensity and focus, falling in love feels so powerful and all encompassing; one's entire mind is experiencing the Intentionality of their subconscious intent. The proto-energy that *is* mind is experiencing own-self's Intentionality in accord with subconscious mind's specific and highly focused desire. Feelings of love don't merely exude from own-self into the (global) environment where others—especially one's object of love—perceive it, but exude throughout the (local) environment of one's mind until no part of mind or body is unaffected. This is the reason falling in love so thoroughly disrupts mindstate and bodystate, producing falling-in-love's many observed mental and physiological changes. If you've ever fallen in love, then what you were experiencing was threefold. First was your subconscious mind *choosing to respond* in that way to its awareness of the environment's proto-energy—a locale, person, place, thing—and Intentionalizing your mind to effect, *as* Thought, its response to its awareness. Second was your conscious mind's experience of it all with Thought. And third was relational 'entanglement' (§ 6.11.3:197; § 3.5.2:486).

8.1.2   FALLING IN HATE

It isn't uncommon for a person to instinctively—have an intrinsic inclination to—dislike, if not outright hate, a person they've just met or seen only from afar. We're not talking here about rejecting a person because of their actions, personality, body language, mannerisms, looks, speech, or religion—literally, infinite reasons—but spontaneously and viscerally recoiling with a primordial violence from their presence, their very existence. By this point in the book, it goes without saying the reason is proto-energy, which in this case Intentionalizes as SUFFERING (§ 6.5:436), the profound trauma of mind that Intentionally alters the proto-energy environment of which any entity having *L*ife is acutely aware.

In The Corruption's milieu, about 90% of a person's actions, personality, mannerisms, and such arise in their experience of suffering. One's instant, instinctive dislike or hate isn't subconscious mind's response to *that*, but rather to the person's Intentionality, which affects *L*ife's environment, including its embodiment. Yet, it's not simply from another's Intentionality of SUFFERING that one recoils, but from its *specific* proto-energy signature, one which is familiar because their experience of suffering matches one's own and experiencing theirs is *painful*. This is what happens contextually when empaths encounter a person of intense negative EM*L*F (§ 3.3.3.1.1.1:290). One's so-called instinctive revulsion to another is one's revulsion to pain, like an exposed nerve being aggravated. It isn't an uncontrollable reflex. It's subconscious mind's awareness of the pain's 'energy' and wholistic mind concomitantly rejecting it.

8.1.2.1   ENERGY OF LOVE–HATE

Recall love and hate arise contextually in LOVE where proto-energy is in accord with whether or not there's any interposition between love's origin and its object. For example, when Person A loves Person B where direct love $a \rightarrow b$, then Person A *experiences love*. But when Person A loves Person B in the context of some interposition c such that indirect love $a \rightarrow \}c\{ \rightarrow b$, then Person A *experiences hate* for no–set $\}c\{$, where the equation describes the overall force—the Intentionalized 'energy' of which is $\}love\{$ (*hate*, in the vernacular) that's equal and opposite that of LOVE—necessary to restore direct love $a \rightarrow b$.[476] When we love or hate, own-self embraces, or integrates, that which we love and rejects, or de-integrates, that which we hate. One's intensity describes whether thinking–feeing is love–hate, like–dislike, and so on. An interposition between oneself and that which one loves—altogether, own-self—induces SUFFERING, the Intentionalized proto-energy of which one experiences as suffering manifesting in Thought as hate.

It's a well-trod narrative that Person A, who loves Person B but encounters Person C in Person B's presence, takes an instant and visceral dislike, perhaps even hatred, for Person C for whom, outside that context, Person A may experience merely neutral thinking–feeling. If Person C shows no interest in Person B that's similar to Person A's, then the force—hate—necessary to restore Person A's direct love $a \rightarrow b$ is small or nonexistent. If the opposite is the case, then the force—hate—necessary to restore $a \rightarrow b$ is equal to Person C's interest. Such 'energy' translates directly to the intensity of all parties' thinking–feeling.

Besides the Intentionalized proto-energy arising in SUFFERING and the experience of suffering in all aspects of personal demeanor—along with its Intentionality in the local and global environment (§ 6.4:435)—the 'energy' intrinsic to the force of restoring any direct love $a \rightarrow b$ also induces SUFFERING as well as relevantly Intentionalizes the environment inclusive of all persons therein. This is a generalized reason why human relations are so fraught with problematic thoughts and emotions, the 'energy' of which is usually intense (cf. § 6.5:436). This applies to any aspect of life.

8.2   ATTAINING LOVE–HATE

It certainly doesn't seem like it but, in reality, LOVE arises partly in choice. Although LOVE arises in proto-love—which as a force of *L*ife force and an aspect of humanness (§ 3.3.2:284) is 'hardwired' into the human psyche, it's WOB—mindset plays a part in not obviating subconscious mind's *response* to awareness of environment in which LOVE arises and is 100% responsible for one's *experience* of both love and hate. Since all emotion arises in subconscious mind's LOVE, thus in proto-love, our experience of emotion—of all our thinking–feeling—arises in mindset such that

$$\forall pL \mid \text{LOVE} \left(\left(M_{\text{sub}} \rightarrow \text{LOVE} \left\{ M_{\text{set}} \right) \rightarrow \left(M_{\text{set}} \vdash \text{LOVE} \right) \bigwedge M_{\text{set}} \vdash love_{\text{exp}} \right) \Rightarrow C \qquad (27.7)$$

where $\forall pL\mid$ means, 'for proto-love such that LOVE arises,' $love_{\text{exp}}$ means, 'the experience of love,' and other symbols as per Eq. (27.6). Accordingly, LOVE is partly one's choice while the experience of love and hate, which arises in $love_{\text{exp}}$, is entirely so. Attaining LOVE and experiencing love is, therefore, no real difficulty. It arises naturally in any person albeit *mediated* in mindset wherein the real difficulty can lay.

---

476. See the full discussion in § 3.3.2.1.2:286 to explain these equations.

8.2.1 EXPERIENCING ANOTHER'S LOVE

Things aren't too different regarding choice when it comes to experiencing another's love. In the case where Person A feels love for Person B, one needs allow Intentionality to take its course. That means giving Person B's subconscious mind time to *respond* in accord with LOVE to their awareness of Person A's LOVE, and for conscious mind to *experience* love as it manifests in thinking–feeling. Although LOVE Intentionalizes proto-energy in one's local environment where Person B has awareness of it, it isn't necessarily the case their mindset won't obviate subconscious mind's response to its awareness (thus, experiencing love); they might not. The person is absolutely autonomous. Just as one rejects pain arising in Intentionalized suffering, one may reject Intentionalized LOVE for any reason, including pain that might arise. Love relationships are chockablock with people coercing others to respond and reciprocate, but that's enslavement (§ 6.8.1:439). It's no surprise such relationships collapse into an inferno of SUFFERING.

Consider when LOVE doesn't arise in one's response to awareness of environment or, either way, one doesn't experience love but longs for it. One need look to environment to see if there's Intentionalized LOVE therein, and then to mindset to see if own-self isn't obviating subconscious mind's LOVE response to its awareness of environment by avoiding one in which LOVE Intentionalizes; or, if it does, then if mindset is obviating subconscious mind's LOVE response to its presence. This means a person might be avoiding LOVE to avoid the experience and thinking–feeling of love. Thus, one who desires to experience love needs develop conscious awareness of subconscious mind and mindset (§ 6.6.3:438).

8.2.2 EXPERIENCING ANOTHER'S HATE

Experiencing hate (as much as love) is a choice because hate similarly arises in subconscious mind's LOVE. Hate inclusive of any emotion Intentionalizing negative EmℒF causes harm and SUFFERING (§ 6.5:436). Such a person not only harms and thereby induces SUFFERING in others, but to their own psyche and body, too, as its matter–Energy (§ 2:114) responds to Intentionalized negative EmℒF. One who hates—where *hate* is a catchall term for *aimed*, SUFFERING-intended Thought Intentionalizing negative EmℒF—not only develops a mindset obviating own-self LOVE, but negating non-self LOVE in one's local, and by degrees global, environment. Even if subconscious mind's response to awareness of environment is LOVE, mindset prevents it arising in Thought; one never experiences love nor does thinking–feeling manifest it.

To avoid this all too common scenario, one needs look to mindset to liberate subconscious mind to respond in Thought to its awareness of environment in LOVE, as well as negate hate. The latter task means *neutralizing* the negative EmℒF one experiences, which is locally accomplished in re-Intentionalizing negative EmℒF to neutral (§ 3.3.3.1.1:289; CH. 36:585), or nurturing subconscious mind's LOVE and embracing it with a mindset that consistently experiences love in thinking–feeling manifesting in concomitant action. To avoid experiencing hate—one can't prevent being hated—then don't Intentionalize experiences of hate in others. This decreases SUFFERING and increases experiences of love, thus, healing.

SECTION 9

Government and Society

'Society,' which is socioculture, is mindset addiction (§ 2.1.1.5.2:353) and government its dealer, each predicated on coercive power. As with any addiction, society coerces itself, meaning each societal constituent enables society to coerce locally (one's own self) and globally (others) such that, for each individual, society *is* own-self. Those who enter government in any capacity seek or adopt the rubric of coercion because society, hence government, lives and dies by it. Whether by representative democracy or flat out totalitarianism, society's authority—built up from enmeshed Individual Cultures (§ 4.1:291)—manifests in the authority of government whose agents by definition exercise coercive power over others who are forbidden on pain of punishment to resist except via narrow and inconsistent channels of redress. People accept the tradeoff in liberty as the supposed price of an ostensibly less brutish life.

In all respects, government (and society) is an inflictor of harm and a destroyer of safety regardless how loftily society raises its stature. America, the freest society ever to exist, nevertheless inflicted harm from its inception on the parts of society its purveyors disliked and rewarded those they liked, recreating and perpetuating the suffering they themselves sought to escape in liberty from Britain. War exists only *because* of government, not *in spite of* it, because the individual human propensity for conflict embodies in society, which *enables* government to wage war. Government, first and last, is society's means to an end set by those societal constituents most addicted to, and therefore shaping, that end.

Authors Linda and Morris Tannehill opine that, "To advocate government is to advocate slavery. To advocate *limited* government is to put oneself in the ridiculous position of advocating *limited* slavery" (1970, 35). Yet, one shouldn't fail to notice that slavery arises not in government but between socioculture's constituent individuals, whether as formalized chattel, informal mindset addiction, or simply ad hoc coercion (§ 6.8:439). Society and its government are the means to this individualized end because, without them, the disaffected or the slaves themselves would overthrow it, which is what happened in 1861–65 America, when disaffected Northern society took control of the federal government and withdrew its defense (tolerance) of Southern slavery.

Unlike the supranatural environment, the natural one necessitates an aspect of societal organization—government—as a means to an end. A means *correctly* organized that's consistent with human woB is one in which autonomy inheres, not the rule of law, no-harm, or order in which it doesn't. The premise for such an organizational capability isn't the utopian infallibility of man but *healing* which leads to full mind–brain integration thus liberation of human woB that, until now, The Corruption disrupted, dooming physical humanity's utopian efforts to degenerate into coercion. People and their socioculture coerce—inflict harm against life, liberty, and property where organized mass coercion (tyranny, war) seems the enduring, characteristic state of the human experience—because individuals are suffering. The correct response is to heal harm to remove suffering so individuals can live peaceably free to pursue happiness. In this section, we explore the way of government, society, and tyranny; describe what each is, as a means of suffering, and as a mindset addiction; and Mina's perspective on a healed society and its 'government.'

9.1 THE WAY OF GOVERNMENT

It's the case here and amongst a minority in the physical-born spirit world (§ 3.1.2.1.3:359) that no free man despises his own liberty but sees an existential threat in another's. Harm and threat of harm manifests the experience of suffering (§ 1.1.1:362; § 6:431) which people try mitigating through controlling others that, in turn, inflicts harm and suffering and spins the wheel of pain without surcease. To apply a brake to this wheel, people form governments in accord with sociocultural mindset addictions. It may be of the strongman in whom people enthrall themselves to the promise of a generalized security, or some variant of representation where people enthrall themselves to law and institution that theoretically yokes the unsafe tendencies of the elected strongman du jour. As with enslavement, no person is ever compelled into subjection to government but willfully chooses it in preference to other options, like pain or death. More than that, people enslave their unpolled descendants in sanctifying government—accepting power alone, meaning chain of command, as the only legitimate, enduring authority—to punish disaffection and rebellion. "The natural progress of things," Thomas Jefferson warned, "is for liberty to yeild [sic], and government to gain ground."[477] America's twenty-first century testifies to it.

Although the prevailing mindset of history is that American constitutionalism represents liberty's zenith in limited government of, by, and for the people, its advancement has run its course. The reason isn't complicated. No form of government, as society employs the concept, can ultimately benefit a subsection of society while imposing its will on the rest. The more striated a society between those it delights and those it chafes, the more even the freest government necessarily curtails liberty not to conduce liberal order but illiberal power in favor of its empowered addicts rather than its original, initiating sociocultural mindset. Unless rooting in absolute autonomy that abjures the very notion of 'government'—whereby it's self-evident "The philosophy . . . taught in the classroom becomes the philosophy of government in the next generation"[478]—American society hence government *cannot* develop a more perfect liberty but only revert to one less perfect. This seems puzzling at first glance. We explain.

9.1.1 WHAT IS GOVERNMENT

In general, government is a manifestation of society's mindset. One may think in a dictatorship like North Korea that its subjugated socioculture has nothing to do with it, that it's a victim. The reality is that it collaboratively empowered its founder Kim Il-sung and his political, military, and societal cohorts to institute

---

477. Jefferson to Edward Carrington, May 27, 1788, in *The Papers of Thomas Jefferson*, 13:208–9.

478. First appearing in print (not traceable to A. Lincoln) Sept. 25, 1957 in the Lexington (KY) *Herald*, "Readers' Letters To The Herald Editor," pg. 4, col. 6 (October 7, 2015).274

its Communist sociocultural mindset. The ignorance, fear, naiveté, and so on of its constituents doesn't negate that reality. They sold themselves *and their unpolled descendants* into slavery (1 Sam. 8, Mt. 27:25; *Common Sense,* Paine (1776) 1824, 25–28) and, unrebuked, there they pine. This is how the slave empowers their enslavement and the enslaver's slave estate. Regardless government's founding ideals or constitutional demands, it operates solely according to the chain of command as whatever its empowering socioculture wants it to be, nothing more and nothing less. Only when a people reaches its limit with its own societal mindset, thus its government, whereby a critical mass of chafing individuals reach a point of existential dread, does it embody a new mindset that spawns a new government. Sometimes, it's markedly different as with America's 1776 revolution. Otherwise, it's just a vinegared wine dumped into the same old wineskin as with the French, Soviet, and Chinese revolutions.

A different, though related, aspect is that government is altogether the individual and collective mindset of those operating it. Individually in that an apparatchik can use their authority to do anything at which superior and inferior chains of command don't balk, and collectively in that if such an individual is out of sync with government's collective mindset, they're punished if caught out but, if not, then rewarded if only by not being punished. Socioculture's mindset determines what individuals calculate they can get away with. An example is the 1923 military assassination of Japan's prime minister by military officers and cadets whom government only slapped on the wrist in the face of sociocultural support.

Government, like society, is by nature inertial. Despite constitutional, statutory, or sociocultural proscriptions on the exercise or violation of authority, chain of command is actually paramount. In practice, it obviates all other duties for the simple reason that government enslaves its employees as much as society's constituents enslave themselves in their mindset addiction to it. If an apparatchik orders subordinates to perform an action that violates their oath of office, laws, or norms, the official uses their subordinates' own oaths of office and laws or norms as threats to coerce obedience. This is the origin of Nazi war criminals' favorite catchphrase "I just following orders" and American bureaucrats ignoring the plain language of the Bill of Rights for a 'compelling government interest' (e.g., 1850's Fugitive Slave Act enforced on free states). Despite having on its face some respect for the rule of law built out of sociocultural norms, government is an institutionalized societal mindset doing what it wants because it can. For a socioculture, government is literally Frankenstein's monster.

9.1.2   GOVERNMENT AS SUFFERING

Regardless its type, form, or apparent beneficence, government's mindset forms mainly in the notion of punishing the wicked howsoever defined but inclusive of rebellion. Consequently, its formative mindset roots in society's intention for public safety, welfare, and prosperity but it's in these that it justifies its unsafe, detrimental, and impoverishing actions, however strained and specious its rationale. The Enlightenment's ideal of government permeates every modern government, at least in theory. Its thinkers believed humanity was a creature of natural law and natural religion (Deism) discoverable through reason. Revelatory religion adopted this mindset, too, in allying itself with government despite its occasional theological protestations to the contrary. In practice, the Enlightenment emphasizes society's duty, thus government's proper role, to enable 1) citizen–subjects' material well-being in the here-and-now as opposed to their impoverished suffering in faith for the world-to-come; 2) social justice, including so-called rights; and 3) individual happiness as mankind's common goal.

Enlightenment goals are mistaken and lead to the mindset addiction Karl Marx (d. 1883) identified as the fundamental alienation of self from own-self that today's populists identify as Orwellian tyranny. We consider four examples. First, the social contract fails by enslaving the born and unborn to obligations in exchange for an ever-threatened liberty, much as a slave takes on obligations in exchange for an ever-threatened life. Second, representative government as an intolerable evil's most tolerable form fails in its addiction to safety, thus law and institution, hence a sure autocracy. Third, that people can't be trusted to do the right thing and require governing fails in obviating intrinsic autonomy and proto-love (§ 3.3.2:284) and, ultimately, individual liberty and happiness in favor of a collective will nonautonomously violating reputed norms. Fourth, life sans government being necessarily "solitary, poor, nasty, brutish, and short" (Hobbes (1651) 1887, 64) fails in not recognizing family as the original organized, complex socioculture (§ 6.8.2:440) such that humanity *never has lived* in a state of nature.

Throughout history, society applied so-called governing to the control of the individual whether constituted of a familial, tribal, cultural, or national mindset with its controlling authority invested in personal monetary, societal, or ideological gain. This is why corruption—the rogue behavior of individuals vested with power in the face of countervailing laws, mores, or norms—is so epidemic from the time of the Code of Ur-Nammu (ca. 3500 BC per Mina; cf. ca. 2050 BC) to the epitome of sober civil service in modern so-called democracies. People want to live their lives in some form of peace and security to experience family or generally to pursue happiness. The Corruption, with its attendant mind–brain integration limitation, hence a lack of awareness of physicospirit reality (§ 1.2.2.5.2:262), largely disables this goal except when people band together in groups of sufficient size to resist assault.

So-called society didn't arise from this need—it already existed from the first family unit—but from aggregating many *societal* units into ever-larger *groupings* as human control of the environment improved. Absorbing own-self into a larger own-self for these reasons didn't necessitate enslavement to its resultant societal mindset. What did necessarily result was its addiction, as already described. Harm is inevitable in such a society because government and sociocultural groupings necessarily inflict it to enforce the mindset to which society's constituents are addicted, and from which, like any addiction, the experience of suffering is an endless merry-go-round. As you read this, you might think you're not addicted to societal mindset and, sure, maybe you're a rebel, but consider your investment in the rectitude of your socioculture or ideology's way of life, or your reaction to living without the society–government support that you rely on to keep you alive and righteous in a dangerous, unrighteous world.

Humanity's goal of peace and safety via collectivized society–government failed consistently and dramatically from the get-go, yet we pursue it nonetheless relentlessly because of our mindset addiction to safety (§ 3.2:374) along with its unawareness of ℒife and the physicospirit self. There's nothing wrong with safety, but unsafety arises in suffering, not in a lack of control. The latter's pursuit produces harm, suffering, and unsafety. Necessarily, society is never at peace but in war in unsafety's constant turmoil.

9.1.3 Addiction to Government

So-called human rights today are the same sociocultural addiction—empowering its obsession with government as ultimate arbiter—that divine right or the mandate of heaven once was to monarchical societies. That the individual possesses certain natural, inalienable rights by dint of existence is both true and not true. They root in the notion of life and liberty, that one's life is one's own from which liberty naturally follows albeit dialed back by society for *safety*. As ℒife is absolutely autonomous, therefore intrinsically free (§ 1.2.1.1:248), the former is certainly true. That it concomitantly converts to a natural (but ever adjustable) *right* isn't. Let's consider that.

9.1.3.1 Natural Rights as Harm

A *natural right* by definition arises in an inalienability a person has naturally, in that there's no countervailing right to alienate a person from it. But it's a faulty principle. Consider that an individual's life is *rightfully* inalienable; one can never *rightfully* end another's life. But suppose an individual is murdering a person who defends their life by ending the murderer's own. The victim has alienated the murderer from their inalienable life. Society justifies it on the grounds of self-defense, that when one *rightlessly* threatens another's life then they, at the same time, *rightfully* counter-threaten their's. Most people have little problem with the concept because, after all, turnabout is fair play, just desserts and all. But it necessarily disabuses inalienability and, by definition, natural rights. It obviates the intrinsic, natural right to be unharmed and therefore a natural right to safety that, in consequence, enables a natural right to control thus to govern others. Ergo, government doesn't predicate on any sort of right—natural, human, divine, or otherwise—but on control which arises in suffering thus harm. At the end of the day, the purpose of government is to inflict harm on behalf of x to limit harm to y but in so doing makes harming, thus the suffering of, x a necessity. In government, sociocultural mindset cuts off its nose to spite its face.

There is no concept of *rights* for Mina. No one possesses natural rights, meaning inalienabilities, for three reasons. First, what's inalienable for Person A is necessarily inalienable for Person B; for any inalienability there's a countervailing inalienability. Second, ℒife can never be taken but only its embodiment. And third, the very concept entails the denial of human woʙ's absolute autonomy upon which rests the fundament of natural rights, which is that an individual's life—which really means ℒife's embodiment—is inalienably their own. This is why inalienable liberty presents an existential threat and socioculture hence government, despite all claims to the contrary, convenes not to protect inalienability but to deny it. The existence of natural rights is an argument that circularly reasons to a *reductio ad absurdum*. This isn't describing libertarianism, anarchism, or their kin but simply the ineluctable reality intrinsic to human woʙ. How humanity *chooses* to live and the so-called rights it wants to convey or deny is immaterial, only that such rights aren't natural or inalienable but *contrived*.

As a concept, *rights* merely circumscribe an individual's actions for which punishment doesn't inhere. If one kills in self-defense then it's okay, but if one *preemptively* kills in self-defense then it's not. The former case is self-evident but the latter might be a situation where unarmed Person A credibly threatens by unspecified means to kill Person B now or in five minutes, hours, or days. Person B, believing Person A, and not waiting to be ambushed, kills him or her on the spot to negate the threat. This doesn't usually qualify as self-defense but murder, punishable in the interest of public safety.

Although one has no intrinsic, natural right to be unharmed because 𝓛ife is autonomous, therefore free, harm creates suffering and other consequences and, consequently, is problematic. The salient question, then, is what to do about it. Until now, the solution has always entailed counter-harm, violence in some legal or physical form. Since harm creates suffering and all harmful behavior arises in suffering, then to resolve harm and unsafety we must look to resolve suffering. This isn't a governmental or sociocultural activity but an individual one because suffering is only individual. Government necessarily can't be in the business of safety and ending suffering because its *raison d'être* is to pursue safety through unsafety, meaning harm, ergo, suffering. A correct society–government embodies 𝓛ife's woʙ, which in Mina's view means that, since autonomy is 𝓛ife's woʙ, hence intrinsically inalienable, then society–government's correct role has nothing to do with how people live but simply with the organizing mindset of embodied 𝓛ife's infrastructure inclusive of environment. Society–government's legitimate interest doesn't include the individual. Toward understanding that, let's consider society.

9.2   The Way of Society

Nothing created or evolved humans to live in society. People prefer it to solitude because 𝓛ife emergently birthed pairwise. Its woʙ is *societal*, arising in two whose children constitute family (§ 2.1.1:306). There's a huge difference between these concepts, as follows.

9.2.1   What is Society

Recall society is enmeshed individual cultures of mind forming downstream supercultures, megacultures, and Ultraculture (§ 4.1:291). The reason individual cultures enmesh in the first place is pairwise human woʙ, not evolutionary biological species affinity or survivability. Humans don't follow nonhuman paradigms as portrayed in Darwin's evolution. Nonhuman follows human because the natural environment is the product of the human mind (§ 2.1.3:309); a person builds a universe and its physical conditions for Living (§ 1.3:272). In consequence, nonhuman 'social' grouping partially embodies human pairwise woʙ to raise and protect family amongst those species that group, but doesn't *socialize* or *organize* in a human sense because they're Living entities having Living, not 𝓛ife, self-awareness (§ 1.1:246). They *can't* socialize or societally organize because their woʙ isn't pairwise 𝓛ife but grouped Living.

Two persons socialize but aren't *societal* until there's children, thus family. In any given society, some constituents only socialize while others are societal and, therefore, its crux. People entering an extant society are socializers whereas those having an organic or adoptive familial relationship are societal; they *are* society. The correct understanding of society is that it's *familial, not grouping*. When physical humans historically organized into anthropologically defined 'society,' they weren't being societal consonant with human pairwise woʙ, but grouping consonant with nonhuman woʙ even though within each grouping there were multiple societies. In The Corruption's milieu, nonhuman Living woʙ bore more influence on human behavior than 𝓛ife's woʙ. This is why so-called societies routinely tear themselves apart. The conclusion that human conflict is evolutionarily or spiritually endemic to the species misreads humanity. Spirit-born humanity isn't violent, conflictive, warring, or psychotic like physical-born humanity (§ 3.1.2.1.3:359) which, when exposed to the spirit-born environment, call it heaven and the physical-born spirit world environment hell—the subconscious origin of these concepts.

9.2.2   Society as Suffering

It's no coincidence society views and relates to its controlling individuals as God, gods, parents, first man, first families, elders, and so on. The tendency arises in 𝓛ife's pairwise woʙ manifesting familially in the context of Living's grouping woʙ as the alpha male, hive queen, alpha pair, and like analogies (henceforth, *alpha*). Not only does misnomered society suffer from shoehorning humans into a nonhuman construct, but the encapsulated familial *societies* experience the same dysfunctions common to the individual *family*. Human woв doesn't naturally manifest in nonhuman alpha woв, which instincts and behaviors are alien.

While The Corruption *impaired* spirit-born humanity—yet, because of their supranatural environment, never severed them from their humanity—it *decimated* physical-born humanity in the rough and tumble natural environment they viscerally shared with Living creatures which, being spirit-unaware, they mimicked for survival. The principal way that humans mimicked animals was in organizing family according to alpha-ness, which then made Ⴙuman society (as a manifestation of family) a natural fit for the mimicked animal grouping that Philosophy with a capital-p improperly labels 'society.' Physical humanity has never experienced *society* but only *grouping*; it never lived *humanly* but only *inhumanly*.

Because society is alien to grouping, the former is always in tension if not outright war with the latter. Throughout history, society as family has been at the mercy of grouping in the same way as mother and child has been under the paterfamilias or a stronger alpha. The group always supersedes family and the alpha. When groups coalesce into territorial entities such as clan, tribe, or larger groupings like empires or states, the grouping's alpha morphs into elder, chief, king, emperor, or head of state. So-called society—the state's persons and families—serves the pleasure of the state that otherwise pays little or no attention to its constituents. This is all *opposite* human woв and therefore incites suffering.

9.2.3 ADDICTION TO SOCIETY

Humanity's eonian longing to fix society to achieve peace, safety, and happiness is really the unrecognized yearning to abandon animal grouping for Ⴙuman society because that's the only woв whereby humans can remove harm and suffering, where their sense of threat withers and people naturally interrelate happily. However, humanity is addicted to alpha models of society–government because it's addicted to a mindset of no-harm, thus safety, that necessarily inflicts harm, thus unsafety (§ 1.1.1:362; § 3.2:374).

So long as people try to fix humanity by doubling down on alpha control—where the individual and society itself constitute alpha-ness—they only supercharge enduring harm, suffering, and conflict. Despite initial apparent successes now and again, this is why every such effort has failed, is failing, and will ever fail. In their ignorance of human woв people try to force humans to be nonhuman, to make Ⴭife nothing more than animalistic Living, a brain–body without mind; just cramming a square peg into a round hole. Accordingly, no form of government can ever preside over peaceful Ⴙuman society—the manifestation of family that properly roots in autonomous, pairwise human woв, not in the paterfamilias (§ 2.1:305)—where it does anything more than *act in guardianship* of infrastructure (§ 9.4:452) because government, being a manifestation of Living's alpha-ness, is ever humanity's monstrous enemy.

9.3 THE WAY OF TYRANNY

As typically defined, tyranny is undesired, unpleasant, oppressive coercion usually by a power such as socio-culture or its government handmaiden, but generally any alpha-ness. However, that's inaccurate. Tyranny is neither more nor less than slavery. Being so, the tyrannized differs not at all from the enslaved in that both cede their intrinsic autonomy to another for reasons acceptable and addictive to the individual who thereby tyrannizes and enslaves *oneself* (§ 6.8:439). We describe tyranny below.

9.3.1 WHAT IS TYRANNY

A tyrant dominates through real or threatened harm which the dominated accepts in a Faustian bargain to avoid (potentially) greater harm. Tyranny, like slavery, is thereby a transaction regardless the unfairness and unreasonableness of the negotiation (there's a real or metaphorical gun to the head). Notions of fairness and reason, too, are backward constructs when defining tyranny in that fairness implies a duty to meet another's wants over one's own, that doing so is reasonable, not doing so unreasonable, unfair, and wrong in a universal (moral) sense. Fairness roots in altruism that necessarily cedes one's autonomy to another (§ 1.1.2.1:364). There's no such thing as being fair or unfair, there's only inflicted harm, the consequence of which is suffering in which roots all harmful action. Counterintuitively, being fair is accepting harm to oneself in the same dynamic as accepting enslavement and tyranny. This is the reason a so-called fair deal occurs only with evenly matched negotiators where both sides uncoercively agree to the other's terms in that neither inflicts harm via the deal. It's win-win. An unfair deal is one where one or all parties feel coercively disadvantaged and therefore harmed. It's win-lose, or lose-less–lose-more.

Tyranny is essentially persuading one to accept lesser over greater harm, a disadvantage of some sort vis-à-vis the tyrant. By definition, tyranny isn't that which tyrannizes another but that in which one tyrannizes oneself, where one accepts tyranny and permits it to be their way of life. Tyranny arises when people addict (enslave) themselves to the mindset that grouping (so-called society; § 9.2:450) is necessary and that authority is liberty or, opined Orwell in his prescient novel *1984* (1949), that slavery is freedom.

9.3.2   Tyranny as Suffering

As noted, alpha-ness is nonhuman. Tyranny unceasingly crops up in human 'society' since it isn't human at all but nonhuman grouping, an alpha construct. It's impossible to avoid tyranny in nonhuman groupings we erroneously call 'society' because tyranny is literally its fountainhead, the very essence of alpha-ness. To avoid it, to consign it to the dumpster of the past, humanity needs abandon grouping and its alpha instincts for actual society which, being pairwise, arises only in autonomous human woʙ. Tyranny as suffering is altogether socioculture, government, and slavery as suffering. They're all the same nonhuman alpha-ness. The person living under tyranny and in whole or part denied—cedes—their intrinsic autonomy is a societal lemming, a government subject, a plantation slave defined and permitted to exist by 'society' manifesting as Ultraculture, government, and economy.

Inflicting harm in tyranny's context is normative, not aberrant. The nature, the *way*, of tyranny is suffering. For example, as America sloughs off its love affair with individual liberty to embrace the collectivized coercion that is managed freedom, the limited, constitutionally regulated (justiciable) harm that mostly characterized its 'society' rooted in its philosophically alpha Bill of Rights increasingly becomes unlimited, unregulated (non-justiciable) harm that mostly characterizes its ideologically alpha Progressivism. Its 'society' as suffering morphs from natural law's accepted negative rights to ideology's imposed positive rights, forming the natural track from perceived non-tyranny to tyranny. But recall 'society' is, by degrees, necessarily tyrannical as it roots in nonhuman alpha grouping, not human autonomy's societal woʙ.

9.3.3   Addiction to Tyranny

An ostensibly free 'society' becomes tyrannical because its constituents are ever addicted to it. One need only await a suitable trigger. Since physical humanity is addicted to the mindset of no-harm, thus safety, it's willing to farm it out to anyone on a mere promise despite copious evidence it necessarily backfires. This is how group after group 'falls victim' to tyranny century after millennia without the tyrant's playbook even having to adapt. American circus master P.T. Barnum (d. 1891) allegedly said, ". . . you cannot fool all of the people all of the time," though author James Thurber observed that "You can fool too many of the people too much of the time" (1940, 34), and tyrant after tyrant makes good on it. In reality, nobody *fools* anybody. A person *misleads* themselves for the reasons described. Tyranny in the household, school, work, socioculturally, or in government doesn't *arise* that people don't *will it into existence*.

9.4   Government as Guardianship

The concept of 'government' is a fallacy, a nonhuman construct, a false concept. True 'government,' in Mina's view, is a kind of *guardianship* that doesn't control but *maintains*. What it sustains is infrastructure inclusive of environment, not by enforcement but maintenance. It doesn't protect freedom, liberty, no-harm, safety, happiness, welfare, et cetera. These are properly the concern of individuals, not 'society.' Such a drastic departure from our control mindset doesn't arise in systems, ideologies, or revolutions by which physical humanity traditionally changes governing institutions in fits of naïve utopianism, but organically in healing individuals, ending suffering, and liberating human woʙ (ᴄʜ. 35:577, ᴄʜ. 36:585).

This represents a sea change in mindset, an abandonment of alpha *animal* for autonomous *human* behavior. After tens of millennia soaked in a violent alpha brine, it isn't dispelled overnight or even in a generation or two; Mina avers about 150 years. In the interim, people need progressively heal, transforming today's regulated *grouping* to autonomous *society*. Let's consider some aspects of Mina's guardianship.

9.4.1   What is Guardianship

Here, guardianship means to maintain, conserve, and watch over with no implications for no-harm, protection, or domination. Such a method of organizing and maintaining a physical human environment mirrors in some respects the absolute autonomy intrinsic to the spirit-born environment, except the natural one entails matter–Energy (§ 2:114), resource limitations, physical health and well-being of the human body, and necessary infrastructure. Although physical humans can learn to manipulate matter–Energy via Intentionality (§ 2:518), including bringing matter–Energy into form on demand, a planet, unlike the supranatural environment, isn't infinite. Earth, for instance, is only so big. Even after mastering Intentionalizing matter–Energy, it's not possible to limitlessly expand as cities grow in population even when capable of converting things like sewage to useable forms.

It's possible and desirable that people expand off world as a planet's population grows in a peaceful, healthy, and long-lived environment. Moreover, as with the spirit body, it eventually won't be necessary to consume food or sleep for conversion to metabolic energy to sustain the physical body because ℒife force is capable of handling such needs (§ 2.2.1:341). People would consume food and sleep not as a necessity but for pleasure as in spirit world (§ 1.2.3:470). When we quit living as animals, our physical reality markedly alters, an improvement scarcely imaginable today. Most of what humans need to thrive, excluding environment and infrastructure, is within the purview of individual, family, and societal organizations, not in nonhuman grouping or government. Without prescribing any *type* of guardianship—organically developing in its own way—let's describe its general appearance in practice.

9.4.2 THE INDIVIDUALITY OF AUTONOMY

Human autonomy is never collective but individual. *Society* isn't an institution that subjugates its constituents. It's a *pairwise experience*. The tension between individuality and the collective is the seed and soil of conflict and suffering because the *individual with agency* has been attempting to live and coexist in an alpha *collective without agency*. This is fundamentally impossible, as human WOB has nothing to do with Living WOB. As people heal from the toxic alpha environment and suffering naturally diminishes individually and globally, this tension drops away because individual autonomy *is* human WOB that coexists in harmony with pairwise WOB manifesting as a societal experience.

We see how public-spirited people are when, in relatively free environments, they live peaceably with their neighbors and ofttimes produce or distribute products free or at cost to benefit others simply because they can and experience happiness doing so. In a future where nonhuman grouping has given even partial way to ℌuman society having absolute autonomy then one can expect this trend to naturally accelerate, not diminish, resulting in a steadily improving physical environment in which health and well-being inevitably improve. Humanity 1.0, initially having greater mind–brain integration and spirit awareness longer than H2 did, built a society that wasn't even as free (autonomous) as America today, yet everyone had sufficient food, housing, transportation, land, opportunity, and safety even though, in the throes of The Corruption and its suffering, it did eventually destroy itself in interstellar war (§ 1.3:538).

According to Mina, the Big Healing means The Corruption will never come back on a universal scale even if individuals locally permit themselves its effect. In consequence, Humanity 1.0's self-immolation isn't repeatable. Autonomous individuals no longer harmed by nonhuman alpha grouping–government, having no need to compete for survival and aware of their physicospirit reality, progressively mirror the spirit-born's mindset which finds no motivation to inflict harm in the sense of control, abuse, domination, resource seizure, and the like. They simply live their lives in pursuit of individual happiness where interpersonal conflict is inconsequential. Those who find happiness inflicting harm won't meet opposition so much as a lack of interest. No tyrant ever achieves their brutish, alpha ends without the voluntary subordination of already-suffering people to their cause willing to inflict harm on their behalf.

9.4.2.1 RESOLVING CONFLICT

There's little point mapping out this guardianship aspect of society as it's difficult for people today to believe only minor and unusual interpersonal conflict is even possible. There's hardly a person alive who doesn't think government denying individual agency to curtail violence, amend conflict, impose solutions, and ensure limited peace is absolutely, non-negotiably vital. But it simply isn't true of *people*. It's only true of the nonhuman alpha grouping mindset. When, through healing, physicospirit people *live as human*, conflict, violence, harm, suffering, and unsafety are rare to nonexistent because there's *no threat*. Spirit-born humanity isn't better than the physical-born, they aren't differently human. They're literally *you* but living humanly in a more autonomous, pairwise society instead of stripped of agency in alpha groupings.

The real question is how conflict resolves in the interim. Well, it's a sliding scale across the transitional nature of government-cum-guardianship. So long as people suffer, there's conflict inciting violence and unsafe conditions. In Steven Seagal's 1994 film *On Deadly Ground*, his character Forrest Taft obliterates the arrogant, abusive oil worker Big Mike (Mike Starr), who's harassing native Alaskans, in a bar fight. Taft asks bleeding, defeated, humiliated Big Mike, "What does it take to change the essence of a man?" Discovering some healing and clarity in Taft's effortlessly inflicted suffering, Big Mike says, "I need time to change," to which Taft replies, "Don't we all." Anyone can heal. Everyone *wants* to heal. People just don't understand their harm, suffering, or healing. It was out of reach anyhow until the Big Healing. Resolving conflict and unsafe environments devolves to individual, family, and societal organizations—clan, tribe, local community—as government returns agency to the individual in transitioning to guardianship.

9.4.3   MAINTAINING INFRASTRUCTURE

We mean by *infrastructure* the natural environment and its manmade accoutrements, which societal guardianship *maintains* as opposed to *protecting through enforcement*. As with interpersonal conflict (*above*), humanity as individuals maintains infrastructure as it does human relations. Accordingly, infrastructure is transitional from protection to maintenance.

Maintenance means that volunteer organizations repair rather than punish human-inflicted damage to infrastructure. Obviously, this is transitional, too, as society embodies less and less individual harm and suffering. Today, when a person or group defrauds the public or fouls the common food or water supply or the air, land, and sea then government—the alpha—compels accountability using sanctioned violence from fines to death albeit corruption means it's breathtakingly inconsistent protecting the public weal. With guardianship, societal individuals voluntarily maintain and improve infrastructure over time such that human life progressively improves. This inclination lies behind the idealism of capitalism, communism, socialism, and every other politicoeconomic *ism* that ever seeks to utopianize physical humanity's experience. The problem, of course, is not so much that all these isms contradictorily embody coercion, deception, punishment, and corruption but that the suffering individuals who constitute a socioculture addicted to alpha grouping behavior enable it. Marx thought the fundamental problem with his era's politicoeconomic status quo was its alienation of the self and, in a sense, he's the only reformer to recognize (however confusedly) that harm and suffering, which indeed alienates a person from their humanity, lies behind its propensity for unhappiness and conflict. That's just an irony out of left field.

But like all such reformers, Marx saw the fix only in forcibly swapping out one politicoeconomic alpha for another and imagining this would automatically resolve the alienation of self, meaning harm and suffering. Consequently, his ideologized theories actually motivated harm and suffering which, over less than 150 years, produced the greatest abuse, mass murder, and suffering in human history equaled only by China, Christianity, and Islam's equally bloody slog toward politicoreligious conquest across their much lengthier ~3,500, 1,900, and 1,400 years, respectively. Marxism and its variant ideologies—designed to *compel* humanity into Utopia (properly an individual choice)—are a cure worse than the disease.

As with religion (and Lucifer's villification), politicoeconomic ideology sees the individual failure to comply as the sin of the whole and the death knell of the faithful to avoid at any cost. This is the mindset of government and the addiction of its enabling alpha grouping. 'Reform' of any kind has been an unmitigated disaster for humanity because it's impossible to reform the human experience in the nonhuman alpha grouping context. This doesn't mean philosophical capitalism—the free market, where any kind of economic experience is possible—is any better than politicoeconomic ideology. Even if it never forms an insidious partnership with government and transforms to crony politicocapitalism, it's an alpha that controls society through the fear of lack, an existential threat people justify as intrinsic to existence and amenable only through enslavement to the mindset of meritocratic work and capability.

As such, no amount of reform, philosophy, science, religion, free markets, or ideological fervor can cure the problem of individuals inflicting harm and suffering. Healing harm to resolve suffering whereby individuals are capable of living in ꂆuman society is the only cure. This is precisely why the spirit-born chose to set aside a separate area of spirit world for the physical-born to occupy after death. Incorporating them wholesale into spirit-born society would be as conflictive and sufferingly painful as for Captain Kirk's crew's barbaric alter egos from a brutal, alternate universe *Empire* trying to fit in and coexist with the *Federation*'s peaceable ethos, where it's ". . . far easier for you as civilized men to behave like barbarians, than it was for them as barbarians to behave like civilized men."₂₇₅ That's been precisely the problem with physical humanity living in accord with nonhuman alpha-ness: it's been impossible to achieve ʃuman civilization. As physical humanity heals their harm and suffering recedes into memory then so, too, will nonhuman grouping and its alpha need to rule the pack and enforce its will transition to autonomous guardianship, and humanity can maintain, instead of protect, infrastructure.

9.4.3.1 PUBLIC AND PRIVATE

There's no distinction in guardianship between public and private, no public authority versus private non-authority, because guardianship's task of maintaining infrastructure doesn't convey authority over those who aren't engaged in that task. Guardianship operates on the same principle as the volunteer and civic organizations that spawned naturally in the freedom of American life in its limited-power government milieu—and later to a lesser degree in other liberal democracies—that left civil life entirely to individuals (cf. de Tocqueville 1841, 117–18). This is a natural human tendency suppressed throughout alpha history until conditions arose in which autonomy was less fettered and people were at liberty to organize and volunteer without interference. This means guardianship isn't institutional but voluntarily organized and operated. Individuals and groups voluntarily manufacture resources using technology (which will experience a dramatic burst of development as physical humanity becomes cognizant of supranatural reality and its technological comprehension and achievements) as well as Intentionality, which altogether removes the drudgery and difficulty of establishing and maintaining infrastructure. That's the final case scenario. In the interim, as government transitions to guardianship, then bit-by-bit public authority relinquishes alpha infrastructure protection to individuals and volunteer maintenance groups as non-authorities in a non-authoritative ʃuman society.

9.4.3.1.1 PRIVATE PROPERTY

What Mina's talking about here isn't some form of capitalism, socialism, or any *ism* but simply human autonomy. This means that what a person creates is their own because creating is fundamentally Intentional, of mind, hence *of* the individual. Mina, however, doesn't support private ownership of land because it's of the universe, not the individual. Landowning seems like a human birthright, so non-ownership certainly appears unfair not to mention communistically tyrannical, which certainly hasn't done humanity any favors. So, let's consider it.

Suppose 150 years from now, after Earth's humanity fully transitions out of today's alpha grouping per Mina's estimate, a person constructs a house on a piece of land somewhere. They own—inalienably possess—their house but not the land on which it sits just as a farmer owns the brussels sprouts he or she sowed in a field but not the field itself—there are similarities here with pre-industrial Native American and some traditional African land-use mindsets—because landholding is alpha *territorialism*, not human *familialism*. In a society where money and food aren't the difference between life and death, territorialism is alien. The whole purpose of grouping and technology is to enable individuals to experience physical life without the constant, enduring threat of harm and death. When suffering isn't the human experience, individuals have no need to seize and hold hostage land, minerals, water, food, or other resources because individual physicospirit reality and guardianship meets individual and societal needs and desires.

The traditional purpose of private property is twofold. On the one hand, a person naturally retains undisputed possession of whatever he or she creates or acceptably (lawfully) acquires. On the other, one undisputedly possesses land another can't seize as their own that naturally creates harm, conflict, and suffering. In an environment where harm and suffering aren't the norm, there's less chance of a person bulldozing one's house to build their own on prime land than of today's burglar smashing in the glass doors festooning most of today's homes in peaceful communities. That's why people install glass in the first place: their community isn't prone to criminal invasion. In previous eras, homes were necessarily defensive battlements. It shouldn't be a surprise that in ʃuman society people operate in accord with a disposition and mindset absent the harm, suffering, fear, and defensiveness natural to *nonhuman grouping*. Non-ownership of land isn't an imposed ideology or an impossibly saintly way of life, it's simply one naturally expressing *familial* wob tendencies normative to ʃuman society.

This doesn't mean all land is publicly owned or in guardianship. It's not. It's *unowned*, which is to say, *ownerless*. There is no public–private distinction in ʃuman society. There's only the absolutely autonomous individual living without harm and suffering and, therefore, very much *in familial relations* with everyone; hence, our previous discussion that society is familial. The person with a house or crop or whatever cares for the attendant land as a part of it in the context of *familial society*.

9.4.4 Selecting Guardians

There is no selecting of guardians. As a series of volunteer societal organizations, individuals freely organize and donate their labor in accord with their preferences. There's no such thing as corvee—compulsory and unpaid—labor in Ƕuman society. That's a nonhuman alpha grouping behavior. In the same way people today find pleasure in donating their time, labor, and skills, individuals living as humans in society are naturally inclined to create, maintain, and better their own, their families,' their friends,' and their community's—their extended family's—infrastructure. America is rife with individuals who not only do these things now but also try to do more, often to be shot down by federal, state, and local protection rackets increasingly forbidding volunteer work and monetary donations. Operating a society as a volunteer undertaking no doubt seems considerably farfetched to a person addicted to moral codes, religious strictures, ideology, alpha grouping, a world of harm and suffering, and government generally. But when we analyze human woв in the context of *human* society—rare, admittedly, but America showed its infant potential over its first century-plus—it isn't unlikely at all. People will develop better awareness of what we're describing here via energy testing. Ultimately, the proof is in healing's pudding over the long haul.

SECTION 10

Evil

We've considered *evil* in various contexts, but here we comprehend what evil is, our suffering from it, evil and free will, and our addiction to it. We start by noting there's no such thing as evil, either as an intrinsic, emergent, or contrived force or power having existence or as existential evil, a tendency integral to a being that is itself intrinsic of its existence. Evil as a moniker for natural occurrences or tendencies, behaviors, or intentions of so-called moral agents is just a means to particularize harm as an *undeserved* experience. No extant description or analysis of evil by Philosophy with a capital-p is accurate, as all root in Accountableism (§ 1.4:14; § 4.1.2:378). Here, we consider it from Mina's perspective.

10.1 What is Evil

Since evil doesn't exist, there's no value in defining what it is because it *isn't*. What we can do, however, is describe what it's not, which is that it's not *evil*. So long as humanity approaches the problem of evil from the perspective of evil, it can neither comprehend the phenomenon nor resolve its apparent effect. Thus, the real question posed by our sense of evil is, why do we experience harm and why do people inflict it? Conceptually, evil is simply an experience of harm that we think is undeserved and, being so, is ipso facto *evil*. We then torture ourselves trying to understand it in the context of our addiction to it (§ 10.4:459). This circular reasoning is a *reductio ad absurdum* that makes evil impossible to comprehend.

We noted the absurdity of natural evil in our autonomous natural environment (§ 2.2.1:233). Here, we consider the more typical explanation that evil originates in morally agented selfishness—sinfulness; disharmony with the natural order—from which conceptually arises unselfishness—sinlessness; harmony with the natural order—without considering whether it arises in a person as a predisposition, instinctual response, or autonomous choice.

10.1.1 The Problem of Selfishness vs. Unselfishness Giving Rise to Evil

The self is the ultimate source of 'evil.' It doesn't arise in divine or demonic agency, an impersonal universe devoid of agency, or any of the indicia of human existence. It arose in the self as a response to harm as people observing human behavior developed the concept of unselfishness, or selflessness, as the ultimate expression of altruism and philanthropic goodness (no-harm), which they presumed archetypally desirous and contrasted with selfishness, or unselflessness, as the ultimate expression of egomania and misanthropic badness (harm), which they presumed anomalously undesirable. But it's in error. The deification of non-self and the demonization of self is itself a misanthropic badness of altruistic goodness because it necessarily demonizes individual life to deify collective life. It denigrates ℒife for existence and thereby renders an altruistic unselfish concern for *other individuals* as a misanthropic selfish concern for *the collective self*. Altruism is nonhuman alpha-ness (§ 9.2.2:450) that's actually egomania; goodness is badness, philanthropy is misanthropy, and good is evil (§ 1.1:362).

This is why even conscientious reformers always end up immolating society on the altar of altruism. Under its rationalized veneer, its kernel is its antithesis. No human endeavor has or ever will reform anomalous humanity to its presumed archetype for two reasons. First, there is no archetype since emergent *Life* is autonomous. Second, all anomalous (selfish) Thought thus behavior arises in harm, thus suffering, that's only remediable in healing via *individuals* accepting healing of *individual* harm (§ 1:577).

Humanity must needs break the cycle of violence (habit) wherein selfishness–unselfishness is a real thing in which self is worth less than non-self. It's inaccurate. For example, neither liberty nor societal membership arises in unselfishness (the collective mindset, an alpha grouping behavior) but in human autonomous and pairwise WOB (§ 9.2:450). One can't have liberty or society in nonhuman groupings characterizing what Philosophy with a capital-P inaccurately calls 'society.' Although selfishness–unselfishness is indeed real *in* human experience as well as problems *of it*, both arise in The Corruption's mindset addiction and find expression in Accountableism which, recall, is fundamentally blame-ism. Only in The Corruption's milieu does harm—normative of autonomous persons (§ 3.3.2.1:376)—provoke suffering, hence dysfunction, because individuals who themselves aren't suffering don't lack empathy (pairwise WOB; § 2:304) and feel no compunction to withhold it. This is why healing individuals to amend their suffering is the only means to restore empathy from which true—not misanthropic—philanthropy arises.

10.1.2 NEGATIVE COLLECTIVE CONSCIOUSNESS GIVING RISE TO EVIL

It's tempting to think the Negative Collective Consciousness (NCC) was the source of evil in our universe. After all, it permeated all creation and suffused all things with negative emotive *Life* force. It was a universal version of what Mina's sisters Intentionalized around individuals to provoke them into experiencing harm in their environment in order that they'd learn to respond harmfully (§ 2.1.2.2.1:371). While the NCC existed, humanity subconsciously perceived it as an undirected, unaware, yet nonetheless experientially malevolent, harmful 'force' affecting every aspect of our universe. Its presence was the quintessence of humanity's sense of dark evil and dread, a malignant universal force of temptation toward harm coloring our thinking–feeling, and lay behind 'natural evil.' But our sense of it is misconstrued.

It's true the NCC existed until Michael's Reveal, and its presence detracted from empathy and affected human Thought to normalize inflicting harm. Indeed, it was such an all-encompassing proto-energy force even Mina couldn't negate it regardless his Intentional power to mold a universe. The reason is the NCC was humanity's product arising in harm's maelstrom, an Intentionalized experience of *Life* at odds with our universe and its builder that he couldn't remove (§ 4.2:379). Our sense of a malevolent force 'out there' called evil was indeed an accurate sensation but wrongly assessed. And our means to avert it by deifying non-self merely aggravated its effect like water on a grease fire. Consequently, besides the NCC being a product of human suffering instead of suffering's singular, independent origin, humanity took full rein to intensify its effect, being most pronounced and suffered amongst physical humanity in its independently operating, uncomprehensible, and nonhumanly alpha-grouped natural environment.

The NCC didn't give rise to evil but instead was merely the *repository* of all the Intentionalized harm, pain, and suffering universal humanity had experienced since The Corruption began (§ 6.5:436). Every dram of suffering only added to it, emanating ill-intentioned Intentionality into the proto-energy of the universe that surrounds, suffuses, and saturates every natural and supranatural existent. Once Michael revealed the truth behind Accountableism and, in opening spirit humanity's minds to reality had unmasked The Corruption, universal awareness pulled the plug on the NCC's negative EM*Lf* the way strong winds disperse clouds to reveal blue-sky clarity. From that moment, all spirit humanity comprehended the nature of their suffering *and its healableness*, now prevented only by individual mindset.

'Evil' didn't arise in but only dispersed via the NCC, collectively diffusing individual suffering throughout our universe conceptually similar to ambient light through a concave lens. It ceased to exist October 13, 2017 (§ 1.2:21; § 4.2:379) but our sense of evil derived from it remains vibrant in our yet-unhealed Accountableist mindset fixated on the divine non-self over the base demonic self, where it originated.

10.2 EVIL AS SUFFERING

Since evil is the experience of harm a person believes is undeserved, not the harm inflicted on the deserving, then evil isn't *evil*, it's merely suffering. This means the greater one's experience of undeserved suffering, the greater one's sense of evil. What a person experiences as a sense of evil in the world generally, or in a person or behavior specifically, is in actuality the intimate presence of suffering. Intimate because Intentionalized negative Em𝓛𝐅—of both the now defunct NCC and the person or persons who emanate their own Intentionalized negative Em𝓛𝐅 like a miniature, individualized NCC—thoroughly suffuses the physical person in a way it doesn't the spirit person.[479] Experiencing generalized suffering via the NCC, or that specific to a person or group, literally harms the individual inflicting the experience from which they, too, experience suffering. When a person performs a so-called evil act, its evilness isn't *evil*, it's simply the infliction of harm and suffering that one considers undeserved. Heinousness is only so in its sense of undeservedness, not simply in its felt effect.

Nazis, who in their own suffering hated Jews, didn't think murdering them was evil even if a distasteful, unhappy, even heinous *but deserved, hence necessary*, task. The same goes for Stalinists, Maoists, and Cambodian Communists murdering quadruples more through planned starvation, forced labor, and shooting; or Mongolians converting Islamic civilization into heaping piles of ash and skulls; or Olmecs, Toltecs, and Aztecs ripping the living hearts from friend and foe alike in debt-payment to their gods; or a sadist shooting one in the gut and smiling as they excruciatingly die over an hour rather than mercifully killing them instantly with a shot between the eyes; or the deranged shooting schoolchildren. Those who don't think–feel the same way perceive such harm not merely as wicked or even heinous but evil incarnate. If one wonders why there's evil, why people inflict harm and commit evil acts, it's really quite simple. In our own suffering, we perceive it's deserved and therefore neither harmful nor evil.

Additionally, individuals suffer in accord with how their perception of evil leads them to think–feel. That is, people subconsciously experience shame and guilt over evil's presence as well as for not ending, thus enabling, it. This is why humanity so readily buys into the concept that selfishness is bad and leads only to evilness while unselfishness is good and leads only to goodness despite, at the same time, and regardless how much they double down on unselfishness, they paradoxically reap only greater selfishness, harm, and evil. Tyrants play off this subconscious drive to sow the collective mindset with justification to vilify, persecute, and destroy their enemies since it's far easier to destroy a person or group who's evil than one whose perceived beingness in the world roots in harm and suffering. So-called evil arises so often in history because individuals always guiltily strive to altruistically annihilate it and are thereby addicted to it as a means to justify and explain harm to self, others, and the world generally.

10.2.1 The 'Energy' and Intentionality of Evil

We refer you to The 'Energy' of Suffering (§ 6.4:435) and Intentionality of Suffering (§ 6.5:436).

10.3 The Evil of Free Will

Notions that free will means one could have acted differently, thereby imputing moral agency, are inaccurate (§ 5:427; ch. 36:585). That isn't free will but *faux* free will, a slavery to morality because it implies if one *can* act differently to avoid inflicting harm then one *must*, otherwise it's a moral evil. This is the reason 'the problem of evil' arises in the first place: it posits that if God could create a universe without harm then he would have because, necessarily, He *must*. As harm and evil do exist then God necessarily doesn't, else He's a psychopath. The very concept of faux free will enslaves a creator to altruism, which Mina describes as no-harm (§ 3.2:374) fomenting a nonautonomous moral order (§ 1.1.2:363). Even absent a creator with agency, faux free will necessarily enslaves humanity and clouds human agency.

Faux free will as popularly and philosophically conceived is only free if one is morally responsible for one's action in the sense they *own* the action by necessarily accounting for it. In reality, Intentionality means an individual necessarily owns not just action but thinking-feeling, too (§ 6.5:436), which they account for as a *source of harm*, where *account* means neither blame nor praise but healing. Recall that healing is only individual, never collective, and the only means to resolve suffering (§ 10.1.1:456). Though one inflicts harm, individuals experience suffering from it that's unique to the person, not the harm. Only the harmed individual can heal from the harm inflicted. In a sense, accounting for harm (not unlike w.r.t. hate; § 3.3.2.1.2:286; § 8.1.2.1:445) is 'inflicting' healing proportional to the inflicted harm such that

$$\forall f w_a \mid \exists H \left[\left(h \propto H \leftrightarrow A \right) = \left(< S \right) \right] \tag{27.8}$$

---

479. This is because the physical body, as an independent manifestation of biology, responds in and of itself to proto-energy whereas the spirit body, as a dependent manifestation of mind, doesn't.

where for any act of actual free will $\forall f w_a$ from which some harm H arises, healing h proportional to harm accounts A for, and thus reduces, suffering S. This is what it means to account for *actual* free will. Accordingly, the linkage between faux free will and moral responsibility is fundamentally flawed on account of arising in nonhuman alpha grouping, not human pairwise WOB (§ 9.2.1:450). Moral responsibility compels a duty, an obligation to act or not act. It denies autonomy, thus actual free will. Faux free will enslaves the individual to the collective that seizes the individual's experience of harm as its own and transubstantiates 'accountability as autonomous healing' into 'nonautonomous harm through juridical revenge' that denies the individual healing and thereby perpetuates inflicted harm.

Consequently, there's no such thing as faux free will but only choice rooted in autonomy (§ 5.1:428; CH. 36:585). This is why people instinctively feel an absolute freedom of mind regardless the seeming determinism in environment, mindset, habituation, coercion, and experience. Faux free will and autonomy aren't interchangeable because faux free will is unfree will in the context of a moral order rooted in altruistic no-harm that, in and of itself, is nonautonomous nonhuman grouping, whereas autonomy is choice in the context of Intentionality rooted in pairwise experience (§ 9.4.2:453). Faux free will must ever only produce no-harm (thus, harm). If it produces harm, then it's evil—immoral; outside the moral order—which means the faux free will that was exercised should not have been exercised, is therefore proscriptive through judgment—accountability; punishment in the moral order—and accordingly unfree, as one isn't autonomous in its exercise. Faux free will, then, isn't a function or mode of autonomy but only of nonautonomy where actual free will can't exist in its proscriptive environment that compels involuntary, alpha consonance with no-harm instead of voluntary, pairwise consonance with healing. Philosophy with a capital-P's whole concept of free will and moral agency is a house of cards.

Evil necessarily can't arise in autonomy because, if it did, it would have morphed to nonautonomy. Since evil—the experience of suffering through harm—does arise in human experience, it does so in the nonautonomous, morally circumscribed, faux free will Accountableist environment that's unfree will masquerading as actual free will. Regardless having and exercising autonomous choice, one can't exercise it as actual free will, thus free action, but only as coerced action, thus faux free will, regardless being autonomously chosen (§ 5.1.1:428). This dynamic follows directly that of inflicting harm in the guise of preventing harm, meaning no-harm. What people *call* free will (as opposed to their experience of it in the autonomous privacy of their mind) in and of itself inflicts harm, suffering, and evil.

Whether or not one inflicts harm directly in performing an evil act or indirectly in limiting harm by performing an altruistic—a no-harm, yet necessarily evil—act, evil ineluctably arises in the exercise of faux free will. Therefore, it necessarily results in evil. The evil that's faux free will compelling accountability to a moral code (itself an addiction to selfishness–unselfishness) in order to have alpha sanction is that, regardless, it's necessarily disguised evil and therefore, without its cloak of moral respectability, necessarily unsanctioned. This is why humanity is in constant tension with, and resistant to, its own moral codes where its addiction to altruism, from which faux free will arises, is itself an addiction to evil.

10.4   ADDICTION TO EVIL

Can we really say that humanity is addicted to evil? Yes. It arises as a constituent of Accountableism—itself a primary addiction rooted in The Corruption as an intrinsic badness—that seeks to expunge harm, thus evil, through no-harm (§ 1.1.3:364) from which arise the notions of morality, selfishness–unselfishness, egomania–altruism, and evil–good. Our seemingly intrinsic struggle with selfishness–unselfishness is solely because individuals reject the reality of autonomy and its consequences that, even if it inflicts harm, merely needs healing consequent to the suffering experienced in an environment where ℒife is *embodied*, not where the *body is life* in which existence ends at physical death. Or where harm cycles through history as a karmic harm that nullifies Nirvana. Or where what's loosed on earth is loosed in heaven (Mt. 18:18). Individuals are addicted to the fantasy of unselfishness as a means to justify the harm they inflict on the deserving and to condemn the harm they undeservedly experience while torturing own-self and others in its pursuit. This is the reason any person—however banal (cf. Arendt 1964, 252)—is capable of evil.

But ℒife has absolute autonomy. Free action necessarily is never bad, never wrong (§ 2.1.1.5.2:353), never proscriptive, but only neutral although one's experience of harm isn't; neither is it bad or good, it's simply *consequential*. That is, consequences arise from inflicting harm, including returned harm, pain, suffering, Intentionalized negative EMℒF, and so on. Such consequences are problematic but they aren't good, bad, or even indifferent because harm is in the beholder's eye; everyone experiences harm differently, including as not harmful. Therefore, it's incorrect to reverse engineer an action from its consequences and thereby taint autonomy (from which action arises) as harm and thus reject it as human WOB. Selfishness is simply autonomy from which harm arises, and unselfishness is autonomy from which it doesn't. Consequently, there's no such thing as selfishness or unselfishness; there's only autonomy. Harm (*vs.* damage) arises or not in one's *experience* of autonomy, not in autonomy itself. The cause of harm isn't autonomy but one's experience of it, which is a function of mindset—the habituated person—wherein one suffers (or not). There's nothing intrinsically wrong with autonomy in the sense of unrestricted individual liberty any more than with a baby's inconsolable wailing in the middle of the night, a child pulling down a bookcase filled with priceless antiques, or an adult raging in their suffering. Only harm's *experience* is addressable, which automatically addresses its infliction. Accordingly, there's nothing intrinsically wrong, bad, immoral, or even evil about inflicting harm—though neither is it *inconsequential*, as it mandates healing—because, like beauty and suffering, one's experience of it is relative.

Evil lies in *experiencing* harm, not *inflicting* it, because any experience an individual feels is undeserved can be evil even if one doesn't inflict the experience of harm *as* harm, meaning it's inadvertent. Individuals addict themselves to experiencing harm and thus evil as a mindset response—rooted in their selfish–unselfish dynamic—to their perception of undeservedness. Since everyone is the hero of their own story, it's the rare bird who accepts their experience of harm as maybe anchored in their own acts. Habit (mindset addiction; ibid) is diametric to mind in that it always trumps one's subconscious–conscious awareness–experience. For example, ideologues override their conscience (§ 2.3:398) with mindset. This leads them to inflict harm (experienced as evil) in righteous conviction for the greater good in that what they're inflicting isn't *harm* but *justice*, hence *progress*, and thence the reality that "*One* Murder made a Villain, *Millions* a Hero . . . and numbers sanctified the crime" (Porteus 1759, 12, 10). None of the foregoing means that child murder isn't heinously wicked, only that it's harm, thus suffering. Evil is suffering and the greater the suffering, the necessarily greater the evil.

Yet, it's never the tyrant inflicting harm that constitutes evil but individuals self-harming in their mindset addiction to selfishness–unselfishness from which arises addictions to authority, virtue in suffering, righteousness in victimization, moral certitude, or alpha grouping that's evil. "*Auschwitz,*" notes moral philosopher Susan Neiman ". . . stands for all that is meant when we use the word *evil* today" (2002, 3, 10). In reality, it simply laid bare humanity's willingness not so much to inflict harm but to receive it, to experience it, to subconsciously accept it. Evil doesn't just happen. It's not a cold north wind or a comet intersecting Earth. It's a mindstate arising in humanity's Accountableist mindset to condemn itself, to reject its autonomous WOB, to deny its very *humanness* for the false, negative, siren song of unselfish perfection in the archetypal denial of own-self toward achieving harmlessness (§ 1.1:362), an impossibility for absolutely autonomous ℒife. 'Moral evil' happens because individuals think–feel–act in the suffering of experienced harm which perpetuates and morphs it into 'natural evil' as a catholic responsorial to its experience. There's no such thing as evil, only harm and, thereby, suffering.

SECTION 11
Beauty

Humanity has long considered beauty an ultimate value along with goodness and truth. But whether a subjective, objective, or blended attribute, it's remained controversial because from its earliest writers until today no one has comprehended why we experience beauty, its meaning in the grand scheme of things, or even what it is. So, let's work back from the latter first.

11.1 WHAT IS BEAUTY

Why do we experience happiness—joy being its more transient, or as J.D. Salinger once put it, "liquid," counterpart (1953, 64)—from beauty? The reason is it satisfies our intrinsic need to experience *humanness* (§ 3.1:280) in accord with pairwise way of being (WOB; § 2.2.1.1:234; § 2:304) similar to the body experiencing intrinsic body-ness in cool, slaking water on a hot day. We experience *humanness* in all WOB throughout our universe and All Existence (§ 2.3.1:239) because we're emergent of All Existence and our universe is a product of the human mind (§ 2.1.3:309). Our universe and all that's in it is fundamentally ℌuman.

At first glance, this feels terribly counterintuitive. Recall the human body itself isn't ℌuman— the term referencing our wholistic beingness—but a nonhuman embodiment the ρerson integrates (§ 2.1.5.5:322). Hence, there's no distinction for ℒife in experiencing beauty in and of the human body or any nonhuman thing. After all, everything in our universe, including our own physical body, is nonhuman except ℒife, although all things nonetheless entered existence *from* ℒ*ife by way of* the human mind. We experience a primordial sense of beauty in and of whatever we encounter because, in and of it, we experience an aspect of own-self (§ 2:275)—our own *humanity*—as though experiencing something intimately *of* own-self such as one's own child, hand, or self. Accordingly, beauty is the experience of *humanness* and not that of an intrinsic property *of* beauty, or feelings evoked by harmonious proportions, order, and the like.

11.1.1 SUBJECTIVE AND OBJECTIVE BEAUTY

How we experience beauty is unique to each individual because of autonomy. *That* we experience beauty is universal because of human WOB (§ 1.2.1.2:251). Traditionally, the *how* is described as subjective beauty while the *that* is objective, meaning it arises in, or exists of, the object of beauty itself globally and not in the beholder's response locally as in Plotinus' Ideal-Form concept (*Ennead*, 1, 6; d. AD 270). But locality–globality is conceptually in error as both arise in subjective experience, not objective awareness. The concept of beauty as something subjective, objective, or a blend of the two roots in the senses (mind), not Intentionality, in which arises the WOB of all things (§ 2.2.1.2.1:237) as well as *humanness*, thus, beauty.

'Beauty' is a term of art for internal–external human-appreciable truth (aesthetics), but that's not *beauty*. The concept simply denotes the human experience of *humanness*, whether internal or external to mind. It doesn't denote its perception, how one experiences *humanness* in and of something; neither does it define the *humanness* that is that something. Beauty is simply the experience of *a* thing *as humanness*, not the localized experience of a thing's attributes or its globalized criteria of beauty. The localized experience of a thing in the context of beauty is traditionally subjective beauty and its globalized criterion objective beauty. Neither of these constitutes beauty. The former is individual WOB in terms of feeling and preference juxtaposed against collective WOB in terms of culture and standards which is the origin of a thing's supposed Ideal-Form, its Ideal. There are no essential attributes of a thing, whether of a physical or non-physical ideal by which beauty as something tangible arises or provokes a sense of beauty in a person. The reason is that such necessarily arise in mind, of the senses, not in or of the thing. The subjective–objective–blended conceptualization as an analytic for beauty is improper and unusable.

11.2 THE MEANING OF BEAUTY

The meaning of beauty is conceptual. It's an aspect of reality perceived as a transcendental value along with truth and goodness, all of which emanate from *humanness* of which beauty is an attribute. Everything of a universe is an expression of *humanness* interacting with proto-energy in a way that's recognizable by humanity as an aspect of itself. The meaning of, or that's intrinsic to, beauty is that our experience of it means we're interacting with, or experiencing, *humanness*, that we're intimately, intrinsically linked to and a part of the object of beauty. We see it as beautiful, as having beauty, and experience the beauty of it in thinking–feeling because our mind has awareness of its proto-energy as *humanness*. We experience that subconscious awareness as the conscious thinking–feeling of beauty. What beauty means is *humanness*. Our experience with it means a thing of beauty is own-self because it's of mind.

11.2.1 TRUTH, BEAUTY, AND GOODNESS

So, too, is it with truth and goodness. Altogether, Philosophy with a capital-P knows truth, beauty, and goodness as transcendental values, or properties, of being. They traditionally correspond with the principal human interests of science, art, and religion where philosophy pursues them through logic, aesthetics, and ethics. However, these comparisons aren't quite valid because religion isn't a pursuit of goodness but of (spiritual) truth from which it presumes goodness arises. Instead, truth, beauty, and goodness are the three *functional* expressions of the human mind that arise in the three fundamental manifestations of ℒ*ife*, which are knowledge, experience, and expression (K-E-E). We encountered these in Mike and Molly's discoveries, growing awareness, and creations (§ 2.1:305). From K-E-E arises one's thinking, feeling, and acting (T-F-A) that we frequently reference in this book as Thought (thinking–feeling), which comprises *mind*. Self-plus-mind comprises *self-in-the-world*, which is *Da-sein* (§ 2:275; *Fig. 163*).

Accordingly, the quest for goodness doesn't manifest in religion but *government*, as it correlates with expression, hence, acting. Humanity principally devotes itself to knowledge, sensation, and society, the latter embodied in its obsession with government; absent The Corruption, it's autonomy-embodied society

(§ 9.4.2:453). These functional expressions aren't fundamental themselves. They arise in the three *existential* expressions of the human psyche (consciousness): self, awareness, and experience (S-A-E; § 1:391), which comprise *self* (§ 2:393). Self-in-the-world, spread across humanity, comprises society.

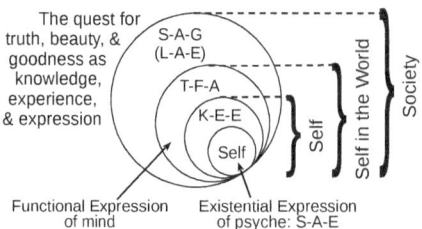

Figure 163. Schematic: truth, beauty, and goodness as existential expressions of psyche (self, awareness, experience; S-A-E); knowledge, experience, expression (K-E-E); and functional expression of mind (T-F-A) that correlates with science, art, government (S-A-G) and logic, aesthetics, ethics (L-A-E).

Each of the three functional and existential expressions are ontologically one, thus convertible such that where there's thinking, there's feeling and acting, too, just as where there's truth, there's beauty and goodness, and where there's self, there's awareness and experience. The notion in Christian theology that these transcendental values reflect humanity's ultimate yearning for perfection, either in God or in the attainment of the transcendentals themselves, is also inaccurate, as humanity simply yearns to *know* human WOB. Additionally, the traditional association, or ontological convertibility, between beauty and morality fails because, first, there's no such thing as morality (§ 2.1.1.5.2:353; § 1.1.2.1:364), and second, the association is properly between beauty and acting in that one acts not to achieve a virtuous—the 'good'—life but an individual WOB having awareness of human WOB. Hence, beauty has nothing to do with one's pleasure at reducing chaotic uncertainty or extracting order from chaos in the attainment of moral, divine, or sensorial perfection, but of experiencing own-self in the *humanness* of existence.

11.3   THE WAY OF BEAUTY

That we experience beauty is human WOB (§ 11.1:460). *How* we experience it is *perceptive* in the sense of *enimerótis–empeiría* (awareness–experience; § 2.1.4:394), which is *mindful*. This means beauty is a *mindfulness* (§ 2.2.1.1.1.2:235) of an object of beauty's *humanness* whether a person, place, thing, experience, idea, or what have you. Recall, however, that beauty is one's experience of *humanness* and, therefore, it doesn't exist as an Ideal-Form whether divine, conceptual, existential, or otherwise, nor as the perception of what's beautiful. Consequently, the *way* of beauty is of experience, not of existence. A thing's beauty isn't the *thing*'s but the individual's *experience* of the thing's *humanness*. This is the reason that *how* we experience beauty isn't subjective, objective, or a blend, as the individual isn't experiencing a thing's beauty in the sense of its existential attributes or properties evoking a local–global response but simply its *humanness*, which isn't beauty but WOB. How one experiences beauty isn't an experience of beauty but of *humanness*, and it's *that* experience that's called beauty.

Because any existent interactively experiences proto-energy, its *humanness* has a proto-energy 'frequency' to which a human naturally resonates, whether it's within or without the self. This resonance is what gives rise to one's sense of happiness in beauty. One can't help the resonance or its effect. One experiences beauty any time one has awareness of its proto-energy, meaning beauty is something one experiences subconsciously that may or may not rise to conscious Thought. One feels subconsciously drawn without thinking–feeling because a thing's *humanness* resonates with one's own *sense of humanness*. One's sense of *humanness* is the unique, individual way one experiences *humanness*—those aspects of *humanness* to which one most resonates thus finds most pleasing and joyful—and desires to pursue. One's appreciation of beauty is always in flux according to one's sense of *humanness* (of beauty), which is changeable, felt, and prioritized. As a result, a person can experience a lack in the *humanness* of a thing in accord with their own sense of *humanness*. This experience is what people call *ugly*.

11.3.1   UGLINESS

As with any existent, a human being resonates with their own proto-energy 'frequency' that identifies, among other things, their *humanness*. When an individual perceives something unidentified in, or disconnected in some way from, their sense of *humanness* then it's ugly. This means, from an individual's perspective, a thing's woв diverges from *humanness*, meaning it's lacking or devoid of some criticality and not resonating on a proto-energy 'frequency' the individual experiences as *humanness*. As a result, a percept, language, idea, experience, or environment's proto-energy of its existence 'clashes' with an individual's the way a discordant sound clashes with and disrupts a harmonious one. Animals sense this—not as ugliness but as threatening—when they experience proto-energy sufficiently discordant with their own, a *humanness* (nonhumanness) devoid of a criticality that resonates with their sense of own-self. Ugliness is an individual's experience in perceiving a lack in a thing's *humanness*.

Let's consider for a moment the physical (visual) ugliness of a person owing to their embodiment (features) diverging from an individual's perception of embodiment's *humanness* generally, where they experience it as proto-energy resonating discordantly in their mind. Existents are complex expressions of proto-energy. If we could visualize a person as *Life* itself, as conscious proto-energy instead of physical embodiment, we'd see an ever shifting, kaleidoscopic matrix experiencing, withdrawing from, mingling with, adjusting for, and responding to proto-energy around it. The *humanness* of discordant features resonates kaleidoscopically distinct from that of harmonious features. If all that one sees is this kaleidoscopic matrix, they'd instantly recognize an individual for *that*, just as they do with looks via visible light.

The difference is we experience proto-energy primordially but visible light—anything sensorial—as mind's awareness–experience. The reason beauty seems so ephemerally evasive to reasoning is that we don't experience it *in* mind but *as* self (*Fig. 163*). This is more fundamental than mind and humanity is thoroughly out of touch. If one's sense of *humanness* cognizes discordant features then experiencing the person's *humanness*—the way proto-energy resonates between them—isn't discordant but harmonious and one doesn't experience ugliness while another, sensing *humanness* differently, does.

Thus, ugliness isn't embodied *in* or experienced *of* a thing, it is one's experience of it in accord with their sense of *humanness*. Ugly bodies (not ugly minds) are meaningless w.r.t. people. It's an artifact of The Corruption, the result of its vagaries in biological reality that don't reflect on individual *Life*—the ₷erson—and thus their *humanness*. Ugliness as visual displeasure doesn't exist for the spirit-born because there's no biological uncertainty or manipulability. Parents Intentionalize conception within the range of human woв as *humanness*, and, accordingly, everyone is objectively beautiful in the sense no one departs from the norm sufficiently to evoke a lack in one's sense of *humanness* regarding looks, although an important caveat is that preference and attractiveness are not attributes of beauty and ugliness. Anyhow, the variability in physical reproduction owing to The Corruption renders meaningful comparisons between physical-born and spirit-born humanity in the context of ugly impossible.

11.3.2 BEAUTY AS HARMONIOUS NATURE

Nature is order, balance, and harmony from which arise aspects like proportion, symmetry, and balance. Yet, this isn't beauty—not *what* nor *how* it is—but simply its *expression*. Beauty as harmonious nature means there's no discord between its *humanness* and the individual and collective experience of humanity. For example, order, balance, and harmony that make sense to an observer are beauty to the observer, and those that make sense to all observers are a universal beauty. As with Individual Culture broadening to Ultraculture (§ 4.1:291), the experience of beauty as a particular beauty broadens from the individual to the ultra-collective such that all people experience a thing as an expression of beauty. All people experience beauty as harmonious nature. But we would err to presume that a universal experience of beauty is the standard of the local (individual) experience just as we err to presume that Ultraculture defines Individual Culture, or that culture generally defines the individual (§ 4.2:292).

Nothing in nature is intrinsically in conflict. Disorder, chaos, or variety-in-detail isn't disharmony from order or a lack of resolved conflict in detail, but individual woв as expressions of universal woв. Order is the expression of a unity of general effect, or unity-in-variety, from an apparent disorder of details. When we experience some aspect of nature in seeming disorder, therefore not experiencing it as an expression of beauty but as chaotic ugliness, it's because we're missing the forest for the trees. Harmony, for instance, arises in altruism—a sociocultural version of nature if you will—as an altruistic value, its universal value (§ 1.1.2:363). It promotes the suppression, meaning the ordering, of chaotic individual details (which inflict harm) in pursuit of universal harmony—the resolution of conflict in details—because individual woв is disorder, thus disharmony, whereas universal woв is order, hence, harmony. Altruism seeks to eliminate individual woв for universal woв, which means the cessation of individual, nonlinear woв for a singular, unitary, linear woв that's predictable and controllable. In terms of nature, this makes for a monotonic universe, a pablum of uniformity doomed to entropy, which is why altruism in society (since all tyranny relies on it as a sociopolitical control) is unsustainable. This is why Philosophy with a capital-ᴘ, rooted in altruism, ever seeks universal standards of truth, beauty, and goodness.

Nature itself is never in disorder, however. There's no welter of confusion or chaos in detail despite individual ᴡᴏʙ, emergence, and stochasticity. Disorder and chaos is *our* perception and experience, not nature's phenomena. Nonlinearity and unpredictability don't imply disorder, chaos, or randomness. That's a myopic conceptualization rooted in deterministic cause and effect. Even though there's randomness and emergence in nature, it occurs in accord with nature's ᴡᴏʙ. Despite the *appearance* of disorder that makes one think nature is a system of order *and* disorder, nature's actually the ordered (non-chaotic) ᴡᴏʙ of the universe for which emergence and randomness are appropriate phenomena. Nature is entirely ʃuman, thus ordered, since the human mind, from which it springs, is of order itself whose *humanness* reflects in our harmonious universe; wherefore, our experience of nature as the indelible experience of beauty.

Spirit World

YOU ARE EMERGENT *L*ife integrating a physicospirit body (§ 1.2.2.3:256). Your physical embodiment *independently* manifests in accord with matter and biology (§ 1.2.1.1.1:248). You control it with your mind but, in and of itself, isn't of mind. Your spirit embodiment *dependently* manifests of mind in accord with Intentionality (§ 3.2:282; § 1.2.3:470). You don't control it with mind because it *is* mind, like a whimsical notion you're thinking that takes material form in the world. Recall our universe comprises the natural (physical) and supranatural (spirit) environments that interface in the 'reflective' environment (§ 7.1:212). Your physical body is of, and operates in, the natural one where everything—all matter–Energy (§ 2:114)—expresses independently-individuated way of being (WOB; § 2.2.1.1:234) having Intentionally-independent existence although it can in some ways, with resistance, be Intentionalized at will. Your spirit body is of, and operates in, the supranatural environment where everything—all supramatter—expresses dependently-Intentionalized WOB having only Intentionally-dependent existence that can, in all ways without resistance, be Intentionalized at will. There is no 'afterlife' because *L*ife isn't physical embodiment; one just changes residence.

Historically, humanity on Earth believed spirit world was a diaphanous place lacking form and substance (without matter) despite also believing spirit world is more real than the physical world, like the Forms outside Plato's cave where one experiences things in themselves, not as their shadows; more intense and vibrant, having brighter colors, richer tastes, sharper feelings. That's inaccurate. The supranatural environment is as real to spirit humanity as the natural one is to us. Everything there is material—not of matter–Energy but *supramatter*—having different properties, characteristics, natures, physics, and the like which is manipulable at will in a way we've never imagined matter–Energy could be (though, to a degree, is). When we comprehend our universe and *H*uman *L*ife as they are, we can understand there's no substantive difference whatsoever between the physical and spirit worlds except that time and space limitations are intrinsic to matter–Energy but not to supramatter. Matter–Energy (mE) consequently resists Intentionality whereas supramatter doesn't. Toward revealing spirit world, we consider it here in three principal aspects: its nature, environments, and daily life.

SECTION 1
Nature of Spirit World

The salient point to grasp regarding spirit world is that it's as real, immediate, felt, and material as the physical world. Just because we can't perceive it with our physical senses doesn't discount its reality any more than our inability to quantify intuition renders it nonexistent. The absence of evidence isn't evidence of absence. Our global society has got so scientifically materialist in its orientation that it discounts as irrelevant almost everything materially nonquantifiable w.r.t. the person and environment. It pigeonholes humanity into quantifiable disciplines like bioscience, neuroscience, psychology, and such the way Dr. Brennan on television's *Bones* boils everything human down to biochemistry, evidential explicability, and evolutionary genetic imperatives (Emily

Deschanel, Fox, 2005–17). It's as destructive a tendency on the human psyche as theologically spiritualist orientations that similarly discount everything about the person and our environment as divine, fallen, good–evil, and so on and pigeonholes humanity into nonquantifiable disciplines like theosophy, philosophy, heaven–hell, morality–ethics, faith, and the like. It's not a hard and fast demarcation, however. People have to explain to themselves the oft unexplainable. They do so in the context of mindset by blending science and religion, or fact and faith, and employ both to pursue and cognize reality as so-called truth.

For example, when scientists by fact impute mind to the brain's electrochemical action potentials, they're substituting evidentiary knowledge for faith, presumption, and familiarity since there's no theory much less evidence—at best, only hypotheses—that action potentials conjure human self-awareness. For science, mind is inexplicable and faith-based neuroscience its sacred text. When spiritualists by faith impute mind to divinity, they're selectively highlighting revelatory presumption as a wrapper to scientific evidence, theory, and sophistication since there's no corroborative revelation that divinity conjured human consciousness. For spirituality, mind is inexplicable and analyticoprophecy its sacred text.

Spirit world isn't a land of magical perfection. Although its comprehension of science and technology greatly exceeds Earth's, it's been no less a dystopian environment since The Corruption—particularly physical-born spirit world—where universal humanity forgot its 800BY megaversal history and achievements like an advanced race landed on primitive shores sinking into ignorance, barbarism, and myth. Something as simple as universal time, our own ancestry, or when, how, and who built our universe turned to fable or disbelief. Only ~15% of spirit-born humanity—such as the seven 'archangels'—knew anything at all of our human past but variously couldn't, wouldn't, or didn't pass it on. If that's hard to swallow, consider that Earth's 11.6% Hindu population can't, don't, or won't persuade the insouciant 88.4% to their very ancient belief. The Big Healing dispelled all the mythology, most profoundly in spirit-born spirit world. As of this writing, ~95% of the spirit-born and ~30% of physical-born spirit persons now recognize Mina as our universe's builder and are embracing the advanced technologies, historical knowledge, and comprehension of reality newly revealed in our ancient heritage.

That said, we explain spirit world's nature in describing what it is, how it works, and its relationship with the physical. As you master energy testing, you'll uncover its reality in the way that matters to you.

1.1 What is Spirit World

Spirit world is the environment where 𝓛ife principally embodies. For the purposes of being embodied, physical embodiment isn't humanly necessary even though, environmentally, it is ('reflecting' supranatural 'energy' arising in the natural environment; § 7.1.1:212). Like the physical world, it has its own environmental WOB except, unlike the physical world, spirit world's environment wholly establishes via human Intentionality in both a local and global sense. This connotes that, locally, a person can change their environment howsoever they want in accord with anyone else's local Intentionality that might interfere, and that, globally, the environment itself composites from the collective Intentionality of humanity in the local areas of spirit world and throughout the supranatural environment as a whole (§ 1.2:467).

To better visualize spirit world, just look at the environment you're in right now and imagine you can manipulate any aspect of it at will using your mind to Intentionalize Thought without respect to time and space. Do you want a cup of tea without steeping it or a steak without throwing it on the barbie? Conceive it in Thought and your mind Intentionalizes it where you want it, as you like it. The same goes for a house, a baby (§ 1.2.1.1.1:248), a sunset, or travel. Or you *can* steep the tea, barbeque the steak, build a house with your hands using materials you harvest and manufacture, wait for a sunset, or walk, drive, or fly wherever you want to go. Inured to our animal mindset (§ 9.2.2:450) and the grind of physical life's limitations, it seems inconceivable the physical body, for instance, can subsist on 𝓛ife force alone without food or sleep. But it's merely metabolizing 𝓛ife force instead of Living biology into energy and biochemistry as the building blocks of tissue, musculature, and bone. This isn't something we on Earth can do right this moment, however (§ 9.4.1:452). Our body needs learn it, to transition the way it does, say, from one altitude or environment to another.

Being of supramatter not matter–Energy, spirit world is just as material as the physical world. The former is formless proto-energy absent resistance to Intentionality that dimensionalizes it as proto-energy *having form*. It doesn't resist Intentionality because it naturally, as its WOB, responds as supramatter to Intentionality just as grass moving is the natural response to air molecules imparting kinetic energy via physical collision or the response of pairwise archí (§ 2.3.1:115) to processes creating matter–Energy according to local characteristics. Consequently, spirit world is singularly an Intentionality-controlled environment where the physical world is a mixed WOB–Intentionality-controlled one.

1.2 How Spirit World Works

Recall our universe constitutes of proto-energy from which arises real energy Υ (Fundamental Force; FF) and applied energy E (§ 2.1:114). It's worth noting these aren't *real* energy, meaning energy in the sense of being constitutional, but are instead responsorial (REVIEW, § 1.2.1.1). Each one rises in response to the interaction of matter–Energy with proto-energy. Proto-energy is the only true 'energy' of our universe, as it constitutes archí and, therefore, everything. As with the natural environment's Energent proto-energy, the supranatural Energent's proto-energy founds and operates the supranatural environment from which, similarly, arises supranatural real energy Υ and applied energy E, denoted *supra* Υ and *supra* E. We describe supranatural proto-energy, its striating nature, and the spirit body's response to it, as follows.

1.2.1 Supranatural 'Energies' and Supramatter

The supranatural Energent can't produce matter (archí) the way the natural one does (§ 2.2:114). Instead, supramatter Intentionally arises, initially by Mina during the creation phase of our universe, then by humanity since the First Ancestors (§ 2.1.1:348). The materiality of spirit world is the same as the physical, except it differs in proto-energy 'vibration' ('frequency'). Let's review matter and 'energy.'

1.2.1.1 Matter and 'Energy' Review

Natural matter doesn't arise in or from waveform, as that reflects only energy propagation and not 'energy' or matter's existence (§ 3.7.3.3:138). Recall that matter is archí which emergently arise in proto-energy and interact with it to combine into complex structures called matter. Each archí is a self-contained nodule of 'dense,' compressed proto-energy (§ 2.3.1:115). Real energy Υ that arises around and between archí in response to proto-energy binding them, and applied energy E such as electromagnetic radiation (EMR) that arises around each individual archí as it spatially moves through proto-energy, both propagate away as resurgent field extensions (§ 3.7.3.3.4:142). Science inaptly analogizes this as waveform from which we get the concepts of frequency, wavelength, amplitude, wave speed, and the quantum wavefunction.

It is, therefore, inaccurate to talk about energy constituting matter in terms of applied energy E waveform when matter really constitutes from proto-energy without waveform in that sense. All the new-agey woo-woo that ropes science into describing matter as 'energy' having waveform is mistaken because it relies on nothing more than applied energy E, a responsorial energy having no constitutional (originating) effect. Frequency, wavelength, wave speed, and oscillation (vibration) have no bearing on the foundation of existence, nor can one apply waveform indiscriminately to the metaphysics of human existence. Our consciousness is emergent self-aware proto-energy (§ 2.1.1.1:368), but our physical body is simply matter—complex archí—which the person integrates to experience embodiment in the natural environment of our universe. The body, as matter, emits waveform (EMR) but doesn't constitute from it.

Supramatter is similar, except it forms through Intentionality from supranatural proto-energy and not from emergent archí independently—in the context of own-self WOB—interacting with proto-energy. When a spirit person Intentionalizes a material form, proto-energy responds to the person's Intentional force—Thought empowered by self-aware proto-energy (PFF; § 3.2:282)—and supra-archí thereby *Intentionally* coalesce in supranatural proto-energy just as natural archí *emergently* arise in natural proto-energy. The Intentionalized form takes material shape as supra-archí coalesce and bind in accord with supra Υ and supra E until the Intentionality is achieved. This also is how people manifest their spirit bodies, although that effort is an unconscious process from the moment of conception (§ 1.2.1.1.2:249).

1.2.1.2 Spirit World Physics

The supranatural environment has the same mix of classical (Newtonian) physics and so-called quantum physics—altogether and more accurately, *Energent physics* (§ 2.3.3:117)—as the natural one does. Tiny things like subatomic objects and bigger, macroscopic objects operate conceptually similar to those of the natural environment. Keep in mind, however, there's no substantive distinction between classical and quantum physics as science predicates. Rather, classical and quantum principles operate at all levels of matter, not as two discrete *versions* of physics but as a singular *system* (§ 6.11:191). However, spirit world physics acts in accord with Intentionality, not as with matter's independent WOB embodied in real energy Υ and applied energy E, which is why these natural forces differ from supra Υ and supra E. For example, a spirit person desiring to float or fly like

Peter Pan need merely Intentionalize the act for it to be. The reason it works is that supramatter, which includes spirit world's ground and non-ground environments, is Intentionalized from supranatural proto-energy along with the supra Υ and supra E forces that regulate how they behave vis-à-vis everything else. A person flying like Peter Pan is simply re-Intentionalizing the aforementioned forces affecting their spirit body to differently do so and, therefore, achieve their Intentionality. Mina tells us this takes a newly deceased physical-born person about three minutes to learn conceptually and about three hours to effectively master on average.

1.2.1.2.1 SUPRA Υ AND SUPRA E

The principal difference between the natural and supranatural Υ and E energies is that we can't, through Intentionality, alter how they work in the physical world. While these energies operate in spirit world in accord with Intentionality, they operate in the physical world in accord with the immutable WOB of proto-energy from which they arise. Recall the supranatural Energent is a facsimile Energent that a universe's builder—in our case, Mina—establishes (§ 7.1.3:214). As an Intentionalized existent itself, everything *of* it also responds to Intentionality. The natural Energent, on the other hand, is an extension of Energent–prime (§ 1:112) and therefore wholly nonhuman, thus beyond human control even though certain aspects of its WOB in conjunction with emergent self-aware proto-energy WOB—one's *L*ife self—gives rise to Intentionality, which humans through PFF use to build universes and anything in between.

In spirit world, one can materialize matter from 'thin air' as well as move things Intentionally through the air, such as a cup or one's spirit body, by simply re-Intentionalizing gravity local to an object. Spirit world gravity is *mutable*; one needn't *counteract* but simply locally alter it. In the physical world, gravity is *immutable*; one can't *alter* but only locally counteract it (§ 3:119). Thus, one can't Intentionally modify how real energy Υ and applied energy E naturally interacts with an object; gravity exerts an ever-present effect on matter–Energy. Consequently, one can't Intentionally float an object through physical air because it isn't possible to Intentionally modify how real energy Υ and applied energy E interact with it. On the other hand, one can indeed move physical objects using Intentionality so long as it's consonant with real energy Υ and applied energy E. This means one can Intentionally slide a cup across a table's surface but, as it passes over the edge, it isn't possible to levitate it in the air (as in spirit world) because one can't Intentionally manipulate natural gravity to act differently on objects in its environment as one can supranatural gravity. It's technologically possible to counteract gravity, as naturally occurs in a G-star's local space (black hole; § 6.9.2:180), while at the same time protecting the matter–Energy integrity of the object one wants to levitate, but a meaningful explication of this needs await a future work.

1.2.2 THE STRIATED EXPRESSION OF PROTO-ENERGY

Recall that supranatural proto-energy segments into discrete 'energy' striations as with natural proto-energy, conceptually similar to liquids gravitationally separating into layers according to density (§ 3.1.1:357). Like the natural environment, the supranatural is an infinity of proto-energy segmentations (*Fig. 164*, left), only one of which Mina Intentionalized as a world terrain (the one spirit world initially occupied before the spirit-born isolated physical-born humanity to its own segment after The Corruption's effects).

The striations arise in proto-energy's 'on–off' (exert–not exert) nature where, from our vantage in normal space, greater 'frequency' is a faster 'on–off' condition and lesser (lower) 'frequency' is a slower 'on–off' condition. In other words, faster and slower is relative to *how often proto-energy exerts or doesn't exert* on matter–Energy from the *Energent*'s perspective, not from what's actually happening in the context of proto-energy. While this seems somewhat like a theoretical longitudinal scalar wave, or an electrical or system duty cycle, it's not, the reason being that, first, proto-energy has no waveform that analogizes to applied energy E waveform, and second, for three related reasons as listed below.

1. Proto-energy has no point space as it's without dimensionality, thus no time and space such that distance is dimension*less*—null, one might say—and having no state of becoming. 'Events' don't transpire but simply *are* as with the ancient Persian *astī* state of *is*-ness.

2. There's no particularity to proto-energy; no thing, no circuit, no discrete anything that goes from an 'on' to an 'off' *state*. The *condition* of proto-energy where it localizes in accord with—loosely corresponds (maps) to—some point space is that it's *exerting in* matter–Energy, or it's not.

3. Consequent of items 1–2, proto-energy has no characteristic behavior. Any localized 'on–off' condition never happens in the same corresponding point space because it's always in motion w.r.t. it,

omnidirectionally 'moving' and 'undulating' in the context of the Energent and multidirectionally flowing in the context of *enérgeia*. This differs from the Energent in that it is 'energy' forming on the fly out of proto-energy in response to motion of matter through the Energent, which flux across matter–Energy gives rise to real energy Υ and applied energy E (§ 4.3:150).

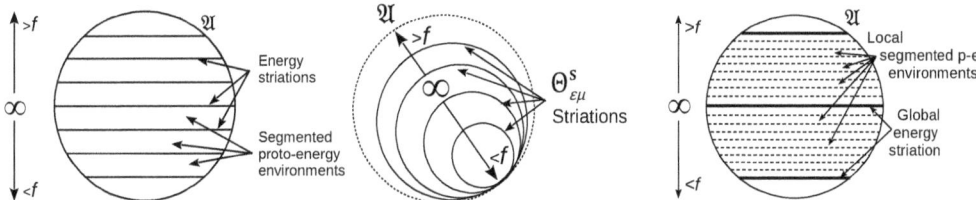

Figure 164. Schematic: left, the supranatural environment's energy-striated segments (a natural behavior of physical thus spirit proto-energy, hence an aspect of the natural environment, too; § 1.2:467); f is proto-energy 'frequency;' $\mathfrak{A}$ is universe (Fig. 150:358); center, each striation as discrete, universally infinite instantiations; right, local striations similarly within each global striation.

In our universe's early days, there were no proto-energy striations because its 'on–off' condition was random for about 2BY in the natural environment and about 4BY in the supranatural one until each progressively coalesced into proto-energy striated bands where 'frequency' stabilized to that of each striation. As with the physical world, spirit world is in the most appropriate striation of all local 'frequency' ones. Recall, however, that spirit-born humanity isolated physical-born humanity to its own global 'frequency' striation because of its Corruption-induced physicospirit psychoses (§ 3.1.2.1.3:359). The 'frequency' of that striation is lesser than that of the spirit-born's and more similar with the physical world to which their mindset resonates. This is part of the reality behind the mythos of 'higher' and 'lower' parts to spirit world, spiritually 'brighter' and 'darker' spirit persons, and heaven and hell (§ 1.2.3:470).

But let's not carry ourselves away with our striation concept, especially its implication of higher–lower, heaven–hell, and good–bad. The latter are perceptions, not realities. Proto-energy doesn't actually segment itself into spatially oriented, or referential, striations as *Fig. 164* implies but as discrete, universally infinite instantiations. That is, each instantiation is as infinite as our universe—itself as infinite as every other universe as well as All Existence—but a discrete 'frequency' of natural or supranatural proto-energy (*Fig. 164*, center). To visualize this, consider our universe as a whole. It segments into the natural and supranatural environments, each occupying in a spatial sense the same infinite space, namely, our universe (*Fig. 165*, left). So, too, then does each global *and local* (*Fig. 164*, right) proto-energy 'frequency' striation.

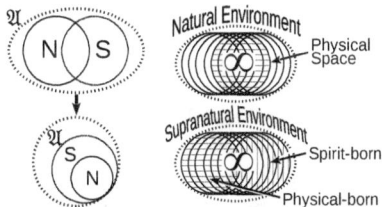

Figure 165. Schematic: left, infinitely segmented proto-energy structure of natural–supranatural (N–S) environments in universe $\mathfrak{A}$; right, each environment's infinite proto-energy segments, once for physical humanity and twice for physical- and spirit-born spirit humanity.

The natural environment itself segments into infinite global proto-energy instantiations, only one of which Mina utilized for the physical space we inhabit. The supranatural environment segments into infinite global proto-energy instantiations, too, only one of which he also initially utilized as spirit world. (*Fig. 165*, right). Each global striation itself striates locally, which 'frequencies' are smaller variations than between global striations (*Fig. 164*, left). Because of The Corruption, the spirit-born had to isolate the physical-born to their own global segment because they were too inured to their physical existence and wholly unaware of their physicospirit reality. For that reason, they experienced the spirit-born's proto-energy 'frequency' as too strong and painful unless they altered their mindset, something that was, in the grip of The Corruption, essentially impossible except for less than 2% its pre-Big healing population (§ 3.1.2.1.3:359; ~6% at the time of this writing). This is the reality behind Sun-myung's intuited concept that God created hell to protect fallen humanity from the searing pain of His divine presence.[480] Eventually, spirit world's physical-born segment will empty out as healed persons relocate to the spirit-born's segment, which Mina prepared initially for all humanity. Let's consider that pertinent to the spirit body.

1.2.3   The Spirit Body

At this point in Earth's history, humanity has a reasonable albeit imperfect mechanical understanding of our physical body. But the spirit body remains a perplexing inscrutableness beyond the reach of current concepts of scientific inquiry much less meaningful revelatory exposure even for those who believe in its veracity. Below, we describe some of its essential details.

1.2.3.1   What Is the Spirit Body

In essence, the spirit body is simply an Intentionality no different from an Intentionalized burger with cheese, a sports car, or a tree. While the physical body is an independent biological existent having reality in and of itself, the spirit body as a dependent Intentionality has *no* reality in and of itself—though existing in that it can be seen, touched, felt, heard, experienced—and, in that sense, one can't really say it exists at all. Obviously, it's there in reality, but only at the pleasure of mind, not because, like the physical body, it constitutes and maintains itself by and through the immutable woʙ of its environment. The spirit body is *real* but not *its own* reality. It manifests instantly via mind in accord with Intentionality (*Fig. 166*) whereas anything physical manifests processively through its building blocks according to the so-called laws of nature.

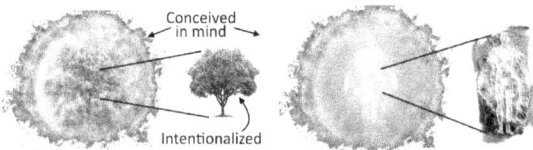

Figure 166. Left, mind conceives then Intentionalizes a tree; right, mind Intentionalizes its spirit body.[276]

A person's spirit body takes initial form differently depending on whether one is physical-born or spirit-born. In the former case, the spirit body develops in accord with the physical body's sex, genetics, and so forth, and in the latter case in accord with parental Intentionality before birth and then after birth in accord with how one subconsciously–consciously sees oneself. We consider below the physical-born spirit body whereby the spirit-born spirit body's situation becomes clear.

1.2.3.2   Physical-born Spirit Body

Physical conception automatically conceives 𝓛ife (§ 1.2.1.1.1:248), which *self*—the essentiality of self and awareness–experience (§ 11.2.1:461)—reflexively manifests a spirit body that, developmentally, is about three months old as we reckon it, just as with spirit-born conception (Fig. 110:250). When you're naught but a fertilized cell, your spirit body already looks to be about a third of the way along to birth. Once the fetus biologically reaches its third month, both bodies develop in-sync. Ordinarily, physical gestation is without issue and a well-developed child is born. The Corruption, however, rent our world. Everything consequently operates at less than peak performance; a physical body may develop haphazardly or not at all. The spirit body, like its 𝓛ife self, is unaffected by physical defects or death because 𝓛ife integrates the physical body from conception and the self has awareness of its primary genetics. Let's describe what we mean.

1.2.3.2.1   Primary Genetics

The spirit body doesn't develop in accord with DNA but Intentionality, meaning *primary genetics*. This is true regardless one being physical- or spirit-born. Everything a person thinks–feels–acts has Intentionality. Suppose a man dies and someone freezes his sperm. Each sperm carries his genetic information but, equally,

---

480. "When people who live an evil life go to places of goodness they cannot breathe . . . So, inevitably they go in search of a place that suits them. They go to hell, to a darker place, and say, 'Ah ha, this is the place!' " (Moon 2006, 6:2.5, 892). He likened 'fallen' humanity's experience in 'higher' spirit realms to breathing searing flames directly into the lungs; hence, hell.

his Intentionality, meaning that during his lifetime he had a certain subconscious–conscious view of himself in all respects in his physical *and* spirit self contexts. As we've described in other parts of this book, all his thoughts, feelings, and actions in life Intentionalize the proto-energy suffusing his physicospirit body. Some of it Intentionalizes the proto-energy suffusing certain parts of his physical body, leading to disorders, disease, and other disruptions to the biology of his body. We're familiar with this concept in terms of stress, anxiety, anger, and the like. Accordingly, the proto-energy constantly moving through his sperm experiences his Intentionality in accord with how he sees himself, his potential children, his life experience, and so on. This Intentionalized 'energy' impregnates if you will each of his sperm which then exerts on an egg it fertilizes, itself also a little bundle of Intentionalized proto-energy. When his preserved sperm impregnates a woman, the child conceives in accord with the sperm and egg's combined Intentionality *as well as* its biological reality.

This is why in vitro children can exhibit traits and characteristics in disaccord with nurture and apparent biology. And we're not including the Intentionality of spirit persons having their own plans for the child which, when Intentionalized, interfere with or augment the biological parents' own (§ 1.3.3:474). Ayako calls this "adding spiritual DNA"—altering a person's primary genetics—which makes the spirit person the child's co-'parent' albeit having no role in triggering its *L*ife. In any case, the spirit body of a physical-born person develops in accord with the Intentionality that's present in the sperm and egg upon fertilization. Hence, despite a physical deformity consequent of DNA, the spirit body develops in accord with primary genetics— Intentionality—and therefore as intended and not as biological errors, or *secondary* (biological) genetics, alters it. Accordingly, the spirit body of a person like Englishman Joseph Carey "John" Merrick (d. 1890), called the Elephant Man, had the characteristics he would've physically had but for his deformity.

1.2.3.2.2 Secondary Genetics

We term the biological DNA that functionally gives rise to the physical body and deformities (alterations) as *secondary genetics*. Despite deformity, the spirit body is unaffected. When the physical body dies, the spirit-*un*aware person becomes aware of his or her normally developed spirit body. As mind is always aware of its reality, this comes as no surprise to the spirit-aware spirit self freed by death from a damaged embodiment (§ 4.1:419), which all persons feel as a visceral memory of their physical awareness–experience.

1.2.3.3 How the Spirit Body Works

The physical-born are physicospirit embodied, meaning they live their physical life concomitantly physical *and* spirit embodied, whereas the spirit-born only ever live spirit embodied. We describe each as follows.

1.2.3.3.1 The Spirit Body While Physically Alive

The physicospirit person has constant awareness of their spirit embodiment, which we generally call the *spirit self*. This isn't two different selves with two different minds but a single, integrated person. It might feel like we're of two minds because of our poor mind–brain integration and The Corruption's effects generally— especially when we're trying to alter our subconscious–conscious wob—but that's a misinterpretation. Our subconscious is our subconscious regardless our embodiment and our inability to cognize spirit reality. Our conscious mind differs because it integrates our brain, which instantiates the physical consciousness (awareness) that operates in our physical environment. Principally, it's consciously aware of that instead of the spirit environment. Those who are spirit-aware ('open') and experiencing clear intuition, the clair senses, and the like, don't perceive their physical environment as their only environment and live accordingly. Mina reports about 99% of extant physically alive persons on Earth have no awareness of their spirit reality. Their spirit selves live out their physical selves' lives bound up with, and aware only of, the physical experience, unaware the spirit environment surrounds them. They think their experiences with other spirit persons as their physical body sleeps—their mind left to its own devices absent physical stimulus—are naught but dreams or imagination.

Even so, other spirit persons attempt to engage them in conversation, else talk to them as one would to the comatose, and spirit guides provide friendship and advice. Despite not engaging, or engaging with the mindset they're really just dreaming or imagining, these experiences become a part of the person's mind integrating the brain to provide the physical person thoughts, feelings, or experiences they can't explain, chalk up to dreams, sparks of intuition, and the like. However spirit-unaware or outright rejecting of spirit life a person is, their mind experiences spirit embodiment regardless.

A fully physicospiritually integrated person experiences life fully engaging both the physical and spirit environments without any sense of being two people in two worlds. Physicospirit life in this case is one single life experience that one can, awake or asleep, alternatively experience at will. If one manifests more than the single spirit body integrating their physical embodiment (§ 2.1.6.3:330), one simultaneously experiences a full, regular life in both the 'reflective' environment (§ 1.2.3.3.5:473) and spirit world while physically alive. Even in The Corruption, physical people carry on relationships of all kinds (~15%) and raise families (~6%) in spirit world while still physically embodied and unaware, or with a nagging, convoluted sense that they're really 'somebody else' (this isn't reincarnation; § 6.7:438).

1.2.3.3.2   THE SPIRIT BODY IN SPIRIT WORLD

Spirit persons experience their body in the same way you do here except that, since the Intentionalized spirit body has no necessary biology, one needn't eat, sleep, exercise, work (§ 3:481) nor cope with time and space. One can instantaneously move point to point simply by shifting one's awareness and then re-Intentionalizing their spirit body there. As human awareness is self-aware proto-energy without dimensionality hence travel (§ 6.11.4:198), one can flit about our universe or even the megaverse instanter. Until the Big Healing, about 99.7% of spirit persons didn't know about this ability. They utilized technology to get about, including Intentionalized 'portals' to transition between the supranatural and 'reflective' environments (cf. FN 481:473).

1.2.3.3.3   SIMULTANEOUSLY MANIFESTING MULTIPLE SPIRIT BODIES

The essence of the spirit body is that it's a material extension of one's immaterial *awareness* (only All Existence, Energent proto-life (EPL; § 2.3.2.1:241), emergent *Life*, and proto-energy are *immaterial*). One's spirit body is exactly wherever one's awareness is. That's why it's possible to manifest more than one spirit body concurrently (§ 2.1.6.3:330), because one can simultaneously be aware of more than one environment, one reality, and one experience. Think of it like multitasking where you're writing computer code or watching an instructional video while carrying on a conversation with one person and talking on the phone to another. We're used to this in the physical environment, and some are better at it than others. But your mind can be aware of you working on your computer while concurrently aware of people in the room and someone in a different city and you can manifest a separate, fully aware spirit body at each location as if it was your only body. Multiple spirit bodies as extensions of oneself are independently in one's control like fingers on a keyboard in a way physical humanity can barely imagine.

Mina says twenty-four simultaneous spirit body Intentionalizations is the maximum. The Cardinal (FN 140:110) found over time that Intentionalizing more than twenty-four leads to an 'awareness disarray' where a person can't keep each locally discrete awareness separate from the others; it all gets muddy, confused, and discombobulated. The consensus arose that twenty-four simultaneous spirit bodies was the limit of what human awareness could disjunctively juggle. A physically alive person can also simultaneously Intentionalize multiple spirit bodies. One can experience spirit world at will even while physically awake with their from-conception-spirit-body firmly anchored to their physical body. But it takes energy to maintain embodiments. The more embodiments, the more energy.

Recall the physical body is only biologically alive because it integrates Living and *Life* force via spirit body integration (§ 4.1.1.2:420). Without awareness of what one is doing, and being sufficiently in command of one's *Life* force, it's easy to neglect one's physical body in favor of maintaining multiple concurrent spirit bodies and the physical body, like a battery device separated from its charger, starts draining. One gets so busy with multiple discrete awareness situations that, in a sense, they forget physical embodiment, which *Life* force declines toward its critical threshold. If one carries this on for too long without directing more *Life* force to the physical body, or reducing the number of simultaneous spirit embodiments, one's physical body progressively dies. I got myself into this situation in 2018. After only about eight hours at the 24-body maximum, I'd so deprived my physical body of *Life* force that I practically collapsed on the street, was bedridden for a month, and my physical body needed another month to recover its normal energy. Mina thereafter advised no more than three, as needed. I took that to heart.

1.2.3.3.4   THE SPIRIT BODY IN DIFFERENT STRIATIONS

Proto-energy naturally 'condenses' into striations from lesser to greater condensed, from and to infinity. At some point 'toward infinity'—recall proto-energy is dimensionless, without directionality—it's so 'uncondensed' that striations are undetectable and, conversely, so 'condensed' it's effectively 'solid.' If a spirit person, who Intentionalized their spirit body in a higher 'frequency' striation, travels non-instantaneously to a lower 'frequency' one, they go with that same 'frequency' spirit body.[481] Being more densely proto-energy concentrated, it's like a blowtorch to the less densely proto-energy concentrated spirit bodies of the locals, who painfully experience their body's encounter with it. Mind integrates spirit body in all respects, thus feels—materially experiences—spirit world as Molly intended (§ 2.1.3:309). This experience wasn't uncommon before the Big Healing when the spirit-born, wanting to help the physical-born, traversed the 'interfaces' (FN 481). People have since adopted instantaneous travel, unIntentionalizing their spirit body at its origin, shifting awareness to their destination, then re-Intentionalizing it as the locally-concentrated proto-energy. On average, it takes about three-fourths of a second.

This is the origin of the notion people in hell are dark spirits blinded or hurt by the bright spirits of heaven and higher realms. But it's all misconstrued. Spirit persons are 𝓛ife embodied in the supranatural environment just as physical persons are 𝓛ife embodied in the natural environment. *People are 𝓛ife, not their embodiment.* The Big Healing made it possible for the first time since The Corruption for the spirit-born to freely visit and interact with the physical-born in spirit world without causing them pain and suffering. Many are now bringing healing and awareness to them so that, if they want, they can transition to the spirit-born spirit world. Their efforts are reuniting humanity severed in The Corruption.

1.2.3.3.5   The Spirit Body in the 'Reflective' Environment

The natural environment's proto-energy is denser than the supranatural, so a spirit person visiting the 'reflective' environment would encounter the same proto-energy disparity as just described between their spirit body and the surrounding environment. However, the 'portals' archangel Gabriel Intentionalized into operation from the beginning of physical humanity in our universe to transition spirit persons to and from the 'reflective' environment altered the proto-energy density of travelers' spirit bodies so they'd harmonize with the local environment coming or going (§ 1.2.3.3.2:472). The only way to change a spirit body's proto-energy density in the supranatural environment is through unIntentionalizing then re-Intentionalizing the spirit body. But, as noted, virtually the whole of pre-Big Healing spirit humanity didn't know, or believe, it was possible to at-will de-materialize their body (abortion notwithstanding) much less travel instantly. Nor were many brave (or, in their view, reckless) enough to try. It's not too unlike how physical humanity, ignorant of reality, would respond to teleportation technology that physically *destroys* the body then (hopefully) *reconstitutes* it elsewhere with all the insurmountable philosophical, theological, and psychological conundrums. Only the bravest would try it, inevitable malfunctions, deformities, and deaths would occur, and the majority would opt for other safer, time tested means. It looks great in *Star Trek* but human behavior considerably differs in reality, as it did with spirit humanity.

The Corruption was just too strong a mindset for the average person to break. Consequently, archangel Gabriel Intentionalized 'portals' to enable travel between areas where unembodied movement—the shifting of one's awareness from point A to B—was preferable: between the supranatural and 'reflective' environments. The 'portals' alter a person's proto-energy density without affecting their sense of beingness or embodiment, so they transition to an otherwise inaccessible point B from their own point A in psychological safety. With The Corruption and Accountableism's end, the spirit-born swapped 'portals' for instantaneous travel although a minority of physical-born spirit persons—about 45% in 2021, but Mina predicts 0% by 2024—isn't ready to do so.

1.3   Physical–Spirit Human Relationships

A strong and continuing relationship obtains between physical and spirit humanity because we are all the same after all, a *family* descended from the same Ancestors who first inhabited our universe (§ 2.1.1:348). Physical-born spirit persons hold a strong affinity for physical humanity not only because it's their origin and first experience of 𝓛ife, but also because The Corruption and its Accountableism has held them in a sort of thrall to physical reality, an aspect of self they find difficult or impossible to let go. Consider the mythic Greek gods, real people born in the ancient eastern Mediterranean and parts of the southeast Balkans from the period known as

---

481. Such travel was via randomly located density 'interfaces' that are natural to Energent behavior. Pre-Big Healing, the spirit-born didn't build 'portals' to the physical-born spirit world in order to limit accidental interference between the two humanities, meaning access was limited to those trained (or figured out how) to use the 'interfaces.' Gabriel built 'portals' post-Big Healing to enable easy crossover to facilitate physical-born healing for those still avoiding non-instantaneous travel.

the Greek Dark Ages, whose extraordinary lives people mythologized into gods (ca. 12–9th c. BC; § 3.2.2.1.2:417; § 1.1.1.1:570). Some took great interest long after their deaths to interfere with physical society for good or ill, using the physical world as a personal playground with little regard for the well-being of the physically alive. Spirit-born persons who similarly involve themselves with the physical world have the same albeit more helpful than harmful motivations. Until the girls and I discovered energy testing (ET), Mina never personally interacted with the physically alive on Earth but only via 'archangels,' as it would've brought too much unwanted spirit attention to them in The Corruption's milieu. Let's consider how spirit persons help and harm the physically alive.

1.3.1 SPIRIT PERSONS INTERFERING

The persons known as the Greek gods made themselves spiritually powerful through practicing Intentionality so they could help or hinder situations and heal a person's mind or damage their physical body in accord with their mindset and desire. Their healing, based on Intentionality and interaction with a physical person's spirit self, however, is a mere shadow of Mina's healing that's now happening through healing facilitators, yet nonetheless had sufficient effect here and there to aggrandize and push forward the 'gods' mythos. Other concerned or problematic physical- and spirit-born spirit persons throughout Earth's history right up through today help and hinder in their own ways, with greater or lesser effect than the Greek gods. This sort of interference through guiding, educating, healing, harming, or altering physical characteristics for good or ill has been a constant in Humanity 2.0's physical life (§ 2:542).

1.3.2 SPIRIT PERSONS GUIDING AND EDUCATING

Besides directly interfering, spirit persons also try indirectly to ameliorate the suffering of the physically alive through guiding and educating them. We describe each in turn.

1.3.2.1 GUIDANCE

Physical-born spirit persons provide guidance to the physically alive principally as spirit guides to individuals (§ 4.2.1:425) but also act in roles, presenting themselves as different persons. One can imagine how such deception works when inflicting harm. When attempting to help, however, it most often takes the form of a spirit person pretending to be God, a god, 'angel,' 'archangel,' saint, or a great religious or secular person. Physical people who believe such misidentified individuals are helpfully interacting with them are actually, case by case, interacting with devout spirit Christians, Muslims, Buddhists, the non-religious, and so forth presenting their own perspectives, beliefs, teachings, and the like with enough gravitas to be taken seriously so the physical person acts on it.

Spirit persons organizing themselves to help the physically alive under 'archangel' leadership present themselves as 'angels,' but others not so engaged present themselves as *the* 'archangel' because they haven't agreed to any rules honorably binding their interactions, don't care either way, and to beef up their credentials. We're used to this sort of behavior amongst the physically alive, which carries forward to their spirit-self behavior. But the spirit-born are human, too, though rarely deceive the physical-born (Mina avers ~0.9% of the time). Deception doesn't mean a spirit person intends harm, only that they want us to listen. Those called angels are spirit-born generally working with the seven 'archangels' who manage Mina's seven tasks (Table 17:523). Energy testers will develop a consensus on this (and on Mina).

1.3.2.2 EDUCATION

Physical- and spirit-born spirit persons operating independently of the seven aforementioned organized 'angelic' groups interfere, or interact, with physical humanity in surprising ways. For example, Muhammed's experiences via dreams that led to Islam were with a wisdom 'angel' working Michael's task off-book to educate and update Christianity. Muhammad misremembering it once awake led instead to separating from Christianity, which was then resisting reformation, and to Islam's violent antipathy and its millennial internecine war over how one properly obeys God (§ 40:616).

1.3.3 SPIRIT PERSONS ALTERING DNA

When spirit persons decide that interference through guiding and educating people isn't, by itself, sufficient, some turn to 1) altering DNA to improve physicospirit integration, traits, and capabilities of physical persons about to be, or already, conceived; 2) conceiving children from scratch with physically alive women; or 3) terminating an individual's physical embodiment. We overview each.

1.3.3.1 Altering the Genetics of the Physically Alive

This isn't as complicated as it appears. To alter DNA, one need Intentionalize the change one desires and, if correctly done, the physical alteration occurs, otherwise it's partial or nil. Either way, it can backfire, producing an alteration that interacts harmfully with other expressions of the physical person's genetics. Essentially, a spirit person Intentionalizes proto-energy as a particular expression in the relevant area of the genome. One needn't understand DNA or biology at all; for a spirit person in the 'reflective' environment, DNA, like any aspect of matter–Energy, appears as its interaction with proto-energy.

We perceive this interaction through our senses—visually and chemically—as the physical expression of matter like a cell, DNA strand, gene, or allele. The spirit person perceives it directly in their mind, subconsciously as awareness and consciously as thinking–feeling; something *experienced, felt*. When they perceive the DNA in a sperm or egg they want to guide toward fertilization, they *feel* the biology, visualizing how the future person will be in terms of looks, initial personality, capabilities, mental acuity, integration, and so on and thereby identify what it is they want different in the body. The spirit person hones in on the area of DNA that most feels like the 'energy' WOB of that which they want to alter. One can appreciate this isn't all that different from how science pursues DNA manipulation except the spirit person's means and methods differ, being the Intentional manipulation of the interaction between matter–Energy and proto-energy to effect the outcome. This takes skill and, unfortunately, amateurs make mistakes.

Spirit persons manipulate DNA for the overall well-being of the physical person *in the spirit person's opinion* or to inflict harm to suit a purpose. All disease, deformity, and disability arise in the manipulation of proto-energy's interaction with matter–Energy. That's just how reality functions. About 99.99% of the time, this happens to the physical body without any conscious awareness as an indirect manipulation *via one's own mindset*, diminution of life force, or by exposure to damage from, e.g., radiation and poison.

1.3.3.2 Conceiving Children with the Physically Alive

Some manipulations seem too complicated or haphazard for tweaking, so a spirit person turns instead to creating a physical person from scratch using their own 'spiritual DNA.' This means a spirit person impregnates a physical woman who then conceives a physical child absent physical fertilization. Rather than customizing physical genetics, this duplicates the spirit self's own as if physically fathering a child. It isn't something one can experiment with to acquire the capability. One must train to it with someone who knows because it's creating a human 'universe' represented in DNA (material WOB) not too different from creating an actual universe represented by WOB (universal 'DNA'). The only person in our universe with that skill set is Mina. He trained only 'archangel' Gabriel for the specific and limited purpose of conceiving a physical child without The Corruption's degraded mind–brain integration (§ 1.2.2.3:256), its concomitant ignorance of reality and infliction of harm, and with fully-integrated traits and capabilities whereby the person might educate physical humanity toward moderating The Corruption's effects. To do it, Gabriel had to learn to perceive—have awareness of—every aspect of his own beingness, then distill his WOB down to the male chromosome's DNA. It took about 1,000 years to master and he fathered three physical children (on a planet ~17.5BLY from Earth in a galaxy obscured to us by two others) before he got it exactly right. The method unfolds as follows.

When a physical man impregnates a physical woman, his spermatozoa, the male gamete containing one-half the total 46 human chromosomes, enters the egg to fuse with the female gamete's chromosomal half. These create the single DNA of an individual which proceeds to mitosis, new emergent ℒife, and then to an embryo and a mature physicospirit human body having ℒife (§ 1.2.1.1:248). For a spirit person to replicate this process, to birth a physically embodied ℒife, the spirit person needs introduce a physical male gamete to a physical female egg. How does one do this when the natural can't directly experience the supranatural? It happens physically via Intentionality whereby the gamete manifests in matter–Energy as the male pronucleus within the egg proximate to the female pronucleus, which is already a physical existent having the necessary enzymatic changes. From this point, natural biology takes over to birth ℒife and develop a physicospirit body (ibid). Recall that in order for spirit persons to birth spirit embodied ℒife, a couple necessarily has sexual intercourse with the mutual Intentionality of conceiving a child (§ 1.2.1.1.2:249). For a spirit person to birth physically embodied emergent ℒife, sexual intercourse isn't necessary, hence neither is a physical–spirit couple. The spirit person can do this independently of the physical person's awareness and permission. The reason is that once the male gamete physically takes form inside the egg, biology naturally takes over to trigger emergence of *Life* in EPL. But this is rape, in effect, and subverting a person's autonomy isn't Mina's way (§ 2.1:340). Therefore, neither is it Gabriel's.

Let's consider the real life case of Jesus, whose conception was an experimental effort to mitigate The Corruption's worst effects (§ 40:613). His mother is biblical Mary of Nazareth. But his father is Gabriel, whom Mina entrusted as described. Gabriel tweaked Mary's genetics from birth to better normalize her physicospirit integration to be spiritually open so that, instead of waking with *dreams*, she awoke with *memories* (§ 1.2.2.7.3:267). She physically, consciously interacted with Gabriel and agreed to conceive his child in her body for the aforementioned purpose. They'd built a close, platonic relationship during her childhood until agreeing, in her eighteenth year—not ages 13–15, as her spiritual openness frightened off potential suitors until 26-year old, childless widower Joseph agreed to marriage—to conceive Jesus. Their relationship became (spiritually) sexual only when conceiving Jesus, not as a necessity but because Mary understood that, without it, she'd never really feel Jesus was *her* child but only Gabriel's, as though she were a surrogate. Mary was a child of her times. Her relationship with Gabriel felt like divine intervention. She'd do whatever he divinely asked. He (and Mina) didn't want her limited to that mindset—as just a gestational vessel—but to participate with his same standing as a parent. This ensured her autonomy. She understood Jesus would be unique, having full physicospirit integration which only Mina via Gabriel could establish, but never comprehended in her lifetime what it meant. It was just too out of the box for her mindset.[482]

While this was Gabriel's only such endeavor in Earth's history, he made the same effort on other planets having the necessary potential. Including the physical children birthed during his training period, Jesus was Gabriel's 17th such child out of a total of 301 over the course of approximately 6.5MY. Unfortunately, Mina's effort via Gabriel to overcome The Corruption's effects by conceiving 'super teachers of reality' failed to achieve the desired outcome. Yet, more often than not, as in Jesus' case, it did build mindsets eventually leading to understandings of free will, autonomy, individual liberty, and the faulty albeit somewhat liberating concept of natural rights (§ 9.1.3.1:449). So, not a touchdown. More a field goal.

1.3.3.3 Killing the Physical Body

When it comes to killing people, it's important to keep in mind that one can't kill a person but only their physical embodiment. As a practical outcome, killing simply transitions a person from physical to spirit embodiment where they continue living their life in spirit world. This doesn't mean one has a license to kill just because, in the end, no person is losing actual *Life*, because the act of killing against one's will is harmful, traumatic, and causes suffering for both killer and killed however violent or humane it appears (§ 2.1.2.1:408). Killing only indulges The Corruption's effect in people and ineluctably leads to future harm, trauma, and suffering in the endless cycle we've witnessed throughtout recorded history.

Physical persons kill others for a plethora of reasons, and spirit persons are no different. In both cases, killing people falls under two umbrella categories. The first is for personal reasons like revenge and such. The second is for public reasons, either 1) from a person's private belief that it's for the greater good and will actually accomplish it and, therefore, they're acting on behalf of God, a god, the creator, society, or a moral imperative, or 2) because Mina wants to end a greater harm to reduce suffering overall. Let's consider how a spirit person can actually kill a physical body and each umbrella category.

1.3.3.4 How Spirit Persons Kill a Physical Body

Two causes exist by which the physical body can't sustain life: injury renders metabolism unsustainable immediately or over time, and diminution of *Life* force 'powers down' the body over time. We describe each.

1.3.3.4.1 Injury External and Internal

A spirit person brings about *external injury* through a variety of means. They might put thoughts into one's mind in the same way one's idiotic physical friend does: by talking one into it. Spirit persons do this by conversing *with* a person's spirit self when the spirit self is cognizant of, and participating in, the conversation

---

482. Despite Jesus' full physicospirit integration and awareness of reality, he still experienced the NCC and Accountableism that rendered him in as similar albeit more knowledgeably aware a condition as everyone else, much like the spirit-born and early H1 (§ 1.2.1:534). It wasn't productive much less practical for Gabriel to repopulate Earth with people like Jesus in the NCC's milieu.

or, when not, by talking *to* the spirit self so the physical person, via mind–brain integration, begins thinking in terms their spirit self is hearing. For example, a spirit person tries to persuade one's spirit self to go somewhere or do something the spirit person knows is likely, about to be, or is already life threatening, or is in and of itself lethal. Or, a spirit person uses Intentionality to cause a person to drop something; to do some action with machinery, say, a car; to cause a mechanical failure; to deflect a bullet to a more lethal spot; and so forth that directly impacts the targeted physical person.

In my own experience, a spirit person Intentionalized proto-energy inside my Prius engine that snapped a piston rod on a dark, wintry, rural highway in 2019, although he wasn't trying to kill me but to give me grief. Another time, while washing dishes in 2020, a spirit person Intentionalized proto-energy that violently slapped my arm sideways and resulted in a bunch of broken crockery, again, to annoy not to kill. A spirit person can also 'confuse' a person's thinking and awareness by Intentionalizing proto-energy in the brain that interferes with mind–brain integration, thus sensory perception. I first consciously experienced this while driving. I literally couldn't see some of the cars, streets, signs, and so on that were there. Even when directly looking at them, I was blind to their presence. It was an imperfect effort, so what was there flitted in and out of my awareness. It not only thoroughly confused and lost me in a part of town I knew quite well, but I nearly collided with other vehicles. At last realizing my peril, I stopped to consult Mina. He explained it and put a shield around me, which instantly dissipated my confusion. I could now see and perceive normally. This spirit person was hoping to kill me by car crash. In such ways, it's possible to interfere violently with matter–Energy to cause unexpected movement, malfunction, confusion, and so on that can injure or kill.

Here are two instances Mina reports as true examples. First, spirit persons killed Eric Barcia, who jumped from a 70-foot Fairfax County, Virginia railroad trestle using store-bought bungee cords on July 12, 1997. He died not because he was stupid per se and the cords broke due to physics, but because a spirit person encouraged him to discount the risk and then Intentionalized proto-energy to part a cord. Second, a spirit person provoked the venomous snake John Wayne 'Punkin' Brown Jr. was handling as a faith demonstration during a church service in Jackson County, Alabama on October 3, 1998 to bite, which killed him. His wife was similarly spirit-person killed three years earlier.[277] This doesn't discount individual homegrown stupidity or accidents. But spirit persons directly and indirectly are behind about 28% of all deaths by accident or misadventure.

A spirit person brings about *internal injury* through Intentionalizing proto-energy to interfere with the body's matter–Energy interaction with proto-energy. Spirit persons directly and indirectly cause ∼28% of these deaths, too, with ∼5% the result of the physical person's own mindset self-sabotaging their body. The balance is happenstance. About 8% of all deaths from external sources like radiation, toxins, poisons, and the like are spirit-person caused. Overall, spirit persons directly and indirectly cause ∼69% of all physical deaths (50% wartime KIA) on average, including all homicides *by physical* persons, with the remaining ∼31% arising in things like random biology, accidents, stupidity, natural disaster, avarice, and mindset. Human beings are immensely clever and creative. There's no shortage of ways and means for a motivated spirit person to kill someone's physical embodiment, especially in our hi-tech environment.

1.3.3.4.2   INJURY TO ℒIFE FORCE

Recall biology only has life because of Living and ℒife force (CHEMISTRY AS LIFE, § 1.3.1:272). Your physical body isn't alive because of the intrinsic activity of chemistry (arising in matter–Energy interacting with proto-energy), but because ℒife force *is* mind–brain integration. ℒife force is one's ℒife self, one's very consciousness, exuding one's emergent self-aware proto-energy (ℒife) into physicospirit existence. Integration isn't simply mind–brain or ℒife-force–body, but whole being, meaning *oneself*. Physicospirit integration *is* oneself. Without ℒife force, your body is literally an animal without any human qualities or capabilities. Not only is ℒife force the *mind* you feel as a physical person, but it gives rise to Intentionality, the capability that people normally associate with concepts like mind over matter. Additionally, unlike with Living force on its own, ℒife force *is* the human body's ability to animate, change appearance, exist sans sustenance, lengthen lifespan, and many others because, being intrinsic of ℒife, it integrates *infinite* self-aware proto-energy. The Corruption degraded our physical experience to its sad present state, but extraordinarily integrated individuals throughout history demonstrated greater capabilities from unusual longevity to unique strength, resistance to extreme temperature, clairvoyance, and more. Our bodies aren't human absent ℒife force because it integrates Ꙏuman with our Living body. Since it's purpose-built to integrate ℒife (§ 2.1.5.5:322) then, unlike nonhumans, it can't exist *not* integrated. Without ℒife force, Living force alone can't sustain the human body and it declines into death regardless its initial state of health at the moment ℒife force falls below its critical threshold.

This is the principle upon which a spirit person relies when they decide to kill a physical person by blocking their *L*ife force. Although it's initially a harder method to learn, its benefit to the spirit person is in its simplicity in that one needn't pay attention to physical world events to arrange a physical person's death but simply Intentionalize a proto-energy barrier between the physical person and their own *L*ife force. It works because virtually no physical human has awareness that it's possible, or that one's physiological symptoms are its result. Whereas a physical person can exercise extra caution and common sense and thereby even unconsciously defeat a spirit person's effort to arrange their death by injury, an unaware person in this case simply declines into death over time from mysterious or inexplicable causes without being any the wiser. Even after death, most spirit persons never discover their true cause of death unless someone actually knows and tells them or the murderer comes clean, maybe to gloat. Still, having no awareness of our true reality, victims often deny it's even possible for a spirit person to kill a physical person this way and may discount even their killer's confession. When a physical person is aware of this means of killing, they can energy test their symptoms and, if this method is the culprit, they can neutralize the block and restore their *L*ife force toward recovering their health.

*L*ife force integrates the body via the brainstem (pons) and lower spine areas (§ 4.1.1.2:420). The latter is where a spirit person Intentionalizes their proto-energy block as a super 'dense' knot that effectively works like a door blocking air movement albeit having cracks that air inevitably gets through. But it's not enough *L*ife force to sustain the body and the person progressively runs down over time in accord with the block's effectiveness. A self-sabotaging individual's mindset can block their own *L*ife force, too, without them consciously realizing it (§ 1.3.3.4.1:476) although their subconscious does, since that's what they most desire. Blocked *L*ife force provokes biological pathologies, including brain chemistry changes, that impair mind–brain integration and lead to changes in affect and thought processing that express symptomatically as so-called mental disturbances and disorders. For example, chronic fatigue syndrome is a result of blocked *L*ife force, and the longer it's in place the greater the symptomatology.

1.3.3.5   Killing for Personal Reasons

There's no mystery here. Spirit persons kill physical persons for all the reasons physical people kill. In Mina's view, killing distills to three basic motives: money, justice, and craving (cf. law enforcement's money, power, lust). Each involves but isn't limited to 1) a desire for such things as lifestyle, power, control, and capability; 2) revenge, safety, and beliefs; and 3) love, passion, yearning, jealousy, and anger. Spirit persons kill over money, for instance, when they intend a certain physical person to thereby acquire it.

1.3.3.6   Killing for Public Reasons

People kill for the 'greater good,' too. This means killing to achieve what a person considers a net positive benefit to another person or group, which can be private or societal, as follows.

1.3.3.6.1   Public Killing for Private Reasons

A person rationalizes killing for the 'greater good' that's essentially for a personal good. For example, a government official authorizing the killing of individuals posing a threat to position, reputation, or official capacity rationalizes it being in the wealpublic but, in truth, is merely own-self's net benefit. The scenario plays out all the time in fiction because it happens so often in real life, and the less free a society the more often it occurs. Spirit persons similarly rationalize, except they carry out their activity without consequence unless discovered by spirit persons who respond however they may to the perceived harm.

1.3.3.6.2   Public Killing to End Greater Harm

On the other hand, people kill to avoid or end what they consider greater harm. This is why revolutions and civil wars happen. The morality of killing for the 'greater good' is most often debated as an aspect of Utilitarianism originating with Epicurus (d. 270 BC) and as a modern school of thought with Jeremy Bentham (d. 1832) and John Stuart Mill (d. 1836). It sees right and wrong determined not by a universal moral code but that which best promotes (maximizes) happiness or pleasure as summed amongst all people for whom it's a utility. This is the origin of the 'trolley problem' where a brakeless driver faces five immovable people on a track where he or she can switch tracks to one where there's only a single person, choosing to kill one to save five—or not. *The Good Place* TV series hilariously plays out this conundrum with its typically anomalous conclusions, as it's a faux dilemma with no solution.₂₇₈

The question itself is a Hobson's choice built on a moralism of lesser harm preferable to greater harm. It's a false construct, however, rooted in Accountableism and The Corruption (§ 2.1.1.1:407). Whatever choice a person makes isn't right or wrong in terms of moral—universal—truth, just one that inflicts harm and suffering in practical terms. All considerations of handling situations in which killing leads to, or might lead to, lesser future harm are illogical because they're irreconcilable as well as harmful. The only way to reconcile the conundrum is to recognize the inevitability of harm without attempting to weigh one life against another. Wondering, "What if it's Hitler versus school girls?" is irrational unless it's Hitler leading Nazi Germany and not as a six year old. This, of course, is the same basic calculation spirit persons make when choosing to kill a physical person for the 'greater good' as earlier described. Indeed, millions of people participated in killing Hitler, including his own spirit self who wasn't at all like his physical self (CH. 40:605). First, they Intentionalized all sorts of physiological malfunctions in his body that eventually would've led to his earlier than later death by 'natural' causes in the same way spirit persons killed Stalin. And second, by Hitler's own spirit self pressuring his physical self to suicide, which he resisted until fear of retribution in defeat overwhelmed his fear of death (§ 40:605).

1.3.4   How Spirit Persons View the Physical World

Until the Big Healing, the spirit-born having awareness the physical (*vs.* 'reflective') world existed—about 93% disbelieved or didn't know—viewed the physical-born and their physical and spirit worlds as the ultimate source of harm and suffering in our universe (only about 10% hold these views now, and ~99.99% know). The spirit-born who involved themselves did so in their capacity as 'archangels' and 'angels' in response to Mina's efforts to mitigate The Corruption's effects, to help individuals in accord with their voluntarily adopted tasks (§ 2.1.1.4:352), or on their own recognizance in accord with their own views. Such spirit-born feel familially motivated to help and heal the physical-born. Before the Big Healing, the physical-born viewed the physical world as their former home, birthplace, home of their descendants, friends, and those whom they spiritually guide, and often where the well-being of the universe—the loosed-on-earth-loosed-in-heaven mindset—is decided. After the Big Healing, about 85% continue to interfere using these same or variant views. Mindset doesn't change overnight.

Section 2

Human Environments of Spirit World

The notion spirit life is unimaginably better in human terms from vulgar physical life is grossly misanthropic. Humanity lives in spirit world the same way as in the physical world because people are everywhere the same pairwise beings (§ 2:304). There are obvious differences between physical and spirit world society, of course. The spirit body needs no care or sustenance, being an Intentionality of mind arising in ℒife having ℒife force. Supranatural reality means there's no resource scarcity nor work-to-survive, harm is impermanent since it's an interpreted experience (§ 1.1.1.1:362), and control of people is unnecessary and nigh impossible. But these differences aren't of kind so much as of time. The Corruption decimated mind–brain integration and led to Accountableism and the physical world's hellscape of suffering. This isn't how Mina intended our home (§ 2.1:340) and it needn't remain so, either. As the physical-born in spirit world heal, and post-Big Healing physical couples conceive children having greater mind–brain integration, physical society will experience improvements so dramatic as to make pale our last 150 unprecedented years of advancements in mastering the forces of the universe and furthering human liberty.

There's intrinsically little difference between the natural and supranatural environments because their common denominator is *people*, ℒife having pairwise woB. Besides the obvious, this means humans aren't solitary but social beings. Human life isn't the self competing against others but the self as *own-self*, where own-self is the self in pairwise relationship with one or more others and reality (§ 2:114). Physical life degraded in The Corruption to where singleton individuals built *alliances* via marriage and societal groupings that mimicked human family as well as animal 'society' in order to survive. But these provided only a flawed facsimile of pairwise woB that couldn't develop real pairwise relationships since they only constituted of the singleton, animalized individual (§ 9.2.2:450). Although one necessarily experiences ℒife's pairwise woB tugging at the subconscious, the singleton mindset denies its intrinsic reality as the substructure of every relationship, whether with humanity or the environment. This is the origin of our sense we have a higher, better nature than we exhibit that's always in conflict with what we are but never attain as a matter of evolution or else lost and need recover as a matter of salvation.

The individual can't build much less endure pairwise relationships because of their singleton mindset, not because the species itself lacks some evolutionary or spiritual capability that holds us back despite our yearning to escape. As such, individuals disrupt their relationships, destroy their children, families, friends, and destabilize society. This isn't the result of sin, malicious gods, or the alleged instinctual, primitive, limbic brain, but one's singleton mindset in conflict with pairwise WOB. Changing mindset changes outcome. Yet, we couldn't until the Big Healing because the Negative Collective Consciousness (NCC; § 4.2:379) suffused and clouded our wholistic environment of individual, cultural, and societal mindsets. Michael and Lucifer severed the link between individual mindset and The Corruption (ibid). For the first time, persons desiring to heal— yearning to escape—actually could. The healing process unfolds faster in spirit world than here because spirit persons more directly experience awareness of reality as (partly) conveyed in this book than we do here where it needs percolate through limited mind–brain integration, physical world limitations, and ingrained survivalist mindsets. The purpose of this book is to build awareness of reality as it is, to encourage individuals to embrace healing through which suffering resolves and pairwise WOB begins to exert over inherent singleton mindsets.

The foregoing is why the physical-born have always experienced spirit-born spirit world as heaven. Not because the spirit-born are better, higher, more evolved, or divine, but because without mind–brain integration and bodily survival issues impairing their interrelational behavior, they more closely approximate pairwise WOB than the physically alive. As humanity heals, physical individuals will progressively experience life in pairwise rather than singleton terms and the physical world will come to mirror spirit world in its awareness, relationships, technology, and such. The principal difference between then and now is that our need to survive will end. Physical society will naturally restructure such that no one's survival is in doubt until everyone is capable of sustaining themselves by ꬪife force alone.

Universal humanity is ultimately one extended family stretching in time from Mina and Ag'poprje, to the First Ancestors, to all of us today. That isn't a call to love humanity as brothers and sisters in the religious or utopian sense; that isn't the reality of human autonomy. Rather, our intrinsic familiality is the expression of pairwise WOB which naturally expresses in familial societal structures where individuals naturally live in the interrelational context of family, friends, individuals-in-environment, and groups, as below.

1. The familial **family** entails any form of love relationship in the context of sex, marriage, and family since it always establishes a familial relationship whether casual, committed, monogamous, polygamous, current, or past. Sex is humanity's most powerful, enduring, and desired pairwise experience and its cessation doesn't break the pairwise bond because it's a permanent Parity ('quantum entanglement'; § 6.11.3:197; § 3.5.5.1:490; SEX, § 2:597).

2. The familial **friends** entails any form of non-sexual, or platonic, love between individuals.

3. The familial **individuals-in-environment** entails an individual in any solitary lifestyle, however momentary. Pairwise WOB means no individual is ever actually solitary, however reclusive they appear. The individual exists pairwise with environment, not just locally but globally in our universe, the megaverse, and All Existence. As ꬪife, the person fundamentally *is* emergent self-aware proto-energy and All Existence fundamentally *is* non-self-aware proto-energy. Distilled to our essence, the person *is* All Existence. The societally solitary person is *never solitary* (§ 1:403).

4. The familial **groups** entails any individual interrelationship with another individual or collection of individuals through which they share or strive to achieve something in common. 'Angels' who associate themselves with one of the 'archangelic' tasks are such an instance (Table 17:523).

None of these familial expressions of pairwise WOB is an individuation. Each entails all the others in and of itself. Within a group a person has past, present, and potential lovers and friends; at times be or encounter those who are individuals-in-environment; and experience multiple subgroups or other, unrelated groups. Sex occurs amongst friends. Family is part of larger groups. An individual-in-environment is part of humanity, perhaps shares a love of nature with nature groups or that of a particular environment or experience. One can be as alone as desired yet always a part of something else whether participating or not. The human environment of spirit world is intrinsically familial because that's human WOB; so, too, is that of the physical world. When we die and transition from physicospirit to just spirit, we're simply changing residence.

Spirit world is filled with individualized environments reflecting individual or shared WOB. Any environment one can imagine is, or can be, Intentionalized in spirit world—floating environments as in *Pan*'s Neverland (film, 2015) or *Avatar*'s Pandora; cities hovering over wild landscapes; megacities inhabited by tens of quadrillions; outer space environments with ships, 'wormholes,' cities; limitless rural and trackless expanses . . . literally anything that mind conjures, including vicious hellscapes for fun like scare houses to the zillionth power. The latter exist in physical-born spirit world, too, though not for fun. They built up over thousands of millennia from the suffering, tortured, psychotic mindsets of the physically dead where singleton individuals continued their wars of psychological torture against humanity. This is the spirit world environment the physically alive traditionally associate with hell but was only what those trapped in their singleton mindsets Intentionalized. Since the Big Healing, healed individuals and groups are progressively dismantling these hellscapes, re-Intentionalizing them back into Mina's basic world terrain originally Intentionalized as a blank canvas for his descendants to shape into their environment (§ 2.2:356).

SECTION 3
Daily Life in Spirit World

As noted throughout, spirit life isn't particularly different from physical life with few notable exceptions (How Spirit World Works, § 1.2:467). Humanity is humanity after all. Individual spirit persons are as individual physical persons, just without their Corruption-induced stress, suffering, and psychoses unique to physical world life. As with physical persons, spirit persons experience life in accord with five principal aspects: time, space, relationships, way of living, and activities. They perceive themselves in terms of their experience with (or as a sense of) time and space, in the context of their relationships, the way they and others live their lives, and their day-to-day activities. We describe below not so much what a day in the life of a spirit person is like but, in terms of the above-enumerated aspects, how spirit persons *experience their existence* in the supranatural environment.

3.1 TIME

Humans comprehend time objectively and subjectively as event periodicity (archí oscillations; § 2:107; § 1:112, § 2:114) or experience. Time as timekeeping is always in the context of the self in which an experience is happening and experienced. The reason is that, since a person as self-aware proto-energy is fundamentally All Existence (§ 5.1:295), reality roots in the individual, not external-to-mind environment. This obviously is less the case with physical persons, as the natural environment is one of independent existents having independent reality. A physical person in whose mind reality roots, therefore, experiences it in the context of a physical body, a contextualized reality in that environment.

While physical persons can Intentionalize matter–Energy, they can never entirely divest themselves of external-to-mind reality whereas spirit persons, having full Intentional control over their Intentionalized supranatural environment, can. When a spirit person experiences a cup of coffee *in time*—where physical coffee in time is necessarily diabatic (involving a transfer of heat) as an event periodicity—then it's *time* in their own, individuated context where their experience of the coffee is necessarily adiabatic (involving no transfer of heat), not as an event periodicity but as an experience. This doesn't mean the coffee *doesn't* gain or lose heat, but that it doesn't *necessarily* do so as in the existently independent reality of the natural environment. This experience is independent of whether one grows their own coffee beans in soil, roasts, grinds, and brews it all by hand, or simply Intentionalizes it ready-made. The same is the case for a spirit person at the same table as the coffee drinker for whom the experience of coffee is that it preferably cools in time. If Person B drinks Person A's Intentionalized coffee—for whom it's preferably always scalding—then Person B experiences the coffee's temperature (or flavor, etc.) not as Person A does but in their own context as the temperature *they* feel, or expect, it *should* have at that point in time. Practically speaking, Person B has subconscious awareness of the coffee's scalding temperature but a conscious expectation of his or her own preference. This dichotomy resolves in sub-Thought (§ 2.2.2.1:396) which re-Intentionalizes the coffee's temperature as it pours from the cup into Person B's mouth. This feels nonsensical to a physical person owing to matter–Energy's independent expression, but it's the spirit person's everyday experiential, Intentionalized reality.

This is why time for the spirit person is eminently *personal* not *public*, subjective not objective. There is, of course, objective time in spirit world; the supranatural environment is a facsimile of the natural one that harbors actual Energent proto-energy rather than the supranatural's facsimile Energent (§ 7.1.2:214). A spirit person can avail oneself of objective time if desired, but it isn't that necessary for any aspect of daily life. Spirit persons root their perception of existence in subjective time and orient themselves to objective time when necessary to some purpose—say, when two people wish to agree on a time.

Naturally, spirit persons' experience of physical persons in time differs considerably from physical persons' experience of spirit persons in time. A physical-born spirit person may experience an Earth year as shorter, longer, or the same and conversely for the physically alive person experiencing time without their loved one. We normalize these periods using archí oscillations that link our universe environments in time, but it isn't necessary to do so unless that's how one wishes to experience an event.

3.2 SPACE

On the human level, the physical environment is replete with limitations. Time, space, resources, and matter–Energy all exist in quantity rather than infinity. In a practical sense, there's just so much time, space, and matter–Energy in the context of resources. Only so many planets and so much navigable space and matter are available with which a physical person can interact and utilize. This isn't supranatural reality. The natural Energent is infinite—indeterminate—and therefore so, too, is the supranatural Energent. Spirit world has no observable universe (OU) confined to a *part* of the infinite universe. Its useable environment is limitless. However crowded, a spirit world environment *expands*.

Suppose spirit world City A is contiguous with City B. There's a road twixt them running through uninhabited, or rural, land that folks use for inter-city travel. City A expands until it's encroaching on City B. In the physical world, this scenario invariably results in City A enveloping city B as a neighborhood of itself. We see this on Earth where formerly independent towns effectively become political vassals of the larger entity, or if they retain political independence then, in practice, they're part of a single urban environment with naught but a signpost marking the transition. If spirit persons prefer open land as a barrier between their cities, they simply Intentionalize an increase to the disappearing space between them such that, regardless City A's growth, there's never a loss of space between it and City B. This is the Intentional expression of the infinitely Intentionalizable supranatural environment versus the quantifiable expression of finite matter–Energy constituting a planet, solar system, or galaxy.

This naturally has a profound effect on how physical and spirit persons experience life. Whereas physical persons have experienced it as resource limited and developed a mindset of lack and aggressive possession, spirit persons have experienced it as resource unlimited and developed a mindset of abundance. The sense of physical limitation that arose in The Corruption's interference with mind–brain integration and ignorance of universal reality leads physical humanity to experience life as scarcity and promotes endless warring over finite resources. But this isn't the physical world's natural state. For all practical purposes, any planet has unlimited resources through Intentionality and a mindset unencumbered by Accountableism that intrinsically quantifies the individual's needs. A physical person can occupy only so much space, experience only so much time, and consume only so much food or, having full mind–brain integration, none at all if desired. Humanity 1.0 maintained greater mind–brain integration than we as Humanity 2.0 have, and built a society having no lack of resources despite a then-global population of about 12 billion (§ 1.2.4:538). Spirit humanity has no resource *needs*, only *wants*, where resources Intentionalize into reality as supramatter which is infinite.

The physical human tendency to search out unspoiled land when one's environment gets too crowded is infinitely applicable in spirit world where 'land' isn't really a concept so much as an Intentionality, as with City A and B. Spirit persons have Intentionalized around 50 million different landscapes—megacities, towns, and villages; rural, semi-rural, and uninhabited areas; fantasy-scapes like the movies *Pan* or *Avatar*; on and on to the limits of imagination—in the physical- and spirit-born areas versus the approximately 10,000 out of what Mina considers a possible ~15,000 on Earth. This means a spirit person feels infinitely free to do whatever, anywhere, in any environment they can imagine. Consequently, spirit humanity feels only abundance and never lack which pays forward in their relationships.

3.3 RELATIONSHIPS

As pairwise beings, ℒife is unique, emergent, autonomous, and never a singleton. However much one may *feel* utterly alone and disjoint, one is pairwise vis-à-vis humanity and one's local-to-global environment, including All Existence, even if own-self constitutes nothing but the sustenance one consumes and perhaps the activity one values, though it's perhaps just a listless depression. Because human WOB is pairwise, we're naturally relational with all humans, nonhumans, and nature. Consider basking in sunshine on a cold, clear day and feeling its pairwise warmth, experiencing oneself here on Earth pairwise with the Sun so far away. Since all nonhuman Living creatures arise in the human mind as WOB before Intentionalizing into biological reality, their WOB is pairwise, too, as is a universe which begins with pairwise archí emergently arising in Energent proto-energy (initially as unsustainable singletons; § 2.2:114) since archí WOB, like that of All Existence, is also pairwise. It's not merely a dubious bromide that we're all in twain, evolutionarily or psychically connected in relationship. We *are* relationship.

Daily life in spirit world is therefore pairwise and in relationship much more than humanity has ever experienced on Earth. That doesn't mean a person can't be physically alone for millions of years if they want, only that they're pairwise even so. The most gargantuan spirit world cities are affectionately populated because the desire to always connect with others, even in passing, is the most natural and comfortable expression we humans experience. The largest spirit-born city's population is about 175 quadrillion while the next biggest is about 50 quadrillion. The former is roughly comparable in radius from the Sun to about two-thirds the distance between Saturn and Uranus and the latter about as far out as Mercury, if each planet's orbit was circular and positioned at their true, farthest position from the Sun.

Mina avers the larger of the two cities has an average tallest building height of ∼475 floors (∼15 feet floor-to-ceiling) with its tallest structure 500 floors and overall average building height ∼160 floors, from single-storey on up. The smaller has ∼460, 475, ∼140, respectively, and aren't infrastructural limitations but human preference. Around 95% of spirit humanity's ∼849 quadrillion people reside in greater or lesser urban-type environments. People familially experience each other on the streets of these spirit-born megalopolises whether or not personally known because there's none of the fear we expect in Earth's cities. Street crime, burglaries, gangs, assaults, frauds, and the like are essentially nonexistent. Although individuals do indeed get into disagreements or inflict harm for whatever reason, it's so rare as to be practically unimaginable by 99.5% of the spirit-born. No one approaches a stranger with caution, fear, worry, or concern but with the congeniality of greeting family or a trusted, childhood friend.

These cities are self-governing in the sense that municipal services are unnecessary. Water, sewage, refuse, food delivery, police, zoning, air-water-mineral rights, and all the things that make up the necessary infrastructure and points of contention in any physical environment—rural cabins to urban high-rise apartments—don't exist in spirit world. One can Intentionalize anything into existence and therefore out of existence, too, except unilaterally whatever others Intentionalized. Individuals and groups Intentionalize buildings, roads, vehicles, and any aspect of embodiment desired. Suppose one has a lovely home on a hill overlooking some spirit-born city which another person thinks is a swell place for his or her own home. In the physical world, he or she would have to persuade the owner to sell, abuse the courts to gain possession, or criminally seize it. But the spirit-born don't have this mindset of taking from others; there's never a reason to, given spirit world's WOB. A person simply Intentionalizes more land upon which to erect their home in a manner that works for all concerned. We asked Mina about creating floating islands of land above a cityscape as one such solution, but he said people don't like giant chunks of stuff floating over their heads (though they do float around some cities' outskirts) regardless the lack of shadow—modifiable physics, after all—or threats to well-being.

Human relationships in daily spirit-world life express in business and work as well. One might be surprised that *business* is a thing in spirit world, as no one needs it and money isn't a thing. After all, a spirit person need only Intentionalize currency or a product in hand to spend or use it. The reality is that some individuals enjoy the concept of business where they make things by hand the physical-world way, Intentionalize it into existence, or acquire it from someone else who did likewise for a customer to purchase. Part of the reason is that people enjoy buying and selling as a pairwise experience individually or with others, and the business process invests an item or an experience with uniqueness, specialness, *memories*. Physical people shop because they need things and combine it with socializing to render the experience more enjoyable, from acquiring items to experiencing restaurant cuisine. Spirit persons, on the other hand, need acquire nothing from others except to enjoy discovering or buying it or the presence of others. No business *needs* anyone's custom because there's no cost of doing business. Even if all they get is one customer per year it doesn't matter. They aren't in business *to* sell but for the pairwise experience *of* selling. The same pairwise experience applies to *work*, where a person engages in a task not to earn currency (though might) but to achieve something that matters to them. From 'archangelic' help to mundane clerking, someone finds it to be, for him or her, a necessary or pleasurable task.

Some tasks are necessary: sustaining aspects of the universe environment such as supranatural aspects of world terrain or natural aspects of stars, planets, or physical embodiment (organized by Michael and Remiel); various aspects of assistance to physical humanity owing to The Corruption's effects (§ 2.1.1.4:352); natural and supranatural conflict resolution such as efforts to help physical societies avoid warfare (Mina says USA–USSR nuclear warfare would've happened but for their interference—though it failed to preserve Humanity 1.0—and, generally, Humanity 2.0 would engage in more warfare than it does); and, along with Mina, constitute or reconstitute human embodiment on planets such as Earth after environmentally recovering from Humanity 1.0's omnicidal war. Any task, necessary or not, is one a spirit person voluntarily takes on because it matters to them. When they lose interest, they shift their attentions elsewhere. No spirit person compels another, or feels compelled by others, to work.

3.4   THE WAY OF LIVING

Much like our physical experience, spirit persons live as people in their environment. An individual experiences ℒife pursuant to three WOB regarding raising children, their local and global societies, and their own and loved ones' futures. We explore each in turn.

3.4.1   RAISING CHILDREN

There isn't a single spirit person who at some point hasn't or won't conceive children, the reason being that human pairwise WOB doesn't simply reference our relationships with others but with our yearning as WOB for Intentionalized familiality. Some physical people have little or no desire to conceive or raise children because the conditions of their life—psychological, economic, societal, mindset—militate against it. This often carries forward into their spirit life until healing opens their mind to it. The spirit-born don't experience situations beyond their control that prejudice conceiving children (absent personal preference) because the spirit world experience has none of its downsides and all of its upsides. Besides the obvious downsides, the threat of conceiving a child with an incompatible partner that might lead to personal chaos isn't a factor. A spirit person simply declines to participate or parents separate from their partner. There's no child support, legal ramifications, or the like holding a sword over one's head, only the pairwise sense of relationship that develops naturally amongst the spirit-born.

3.4.2   SOCIETY

Constituted of pairwise individuals having Individual core Culture (§ 4.1:291), society is as ubiquitous in spirit world as here. Roughly 99.98% of the spirit-born (~40% of the physical-born; ~14% pre-Big Healing) express as society having a societal WOB. Only 0.15% (~55% of physical-born; ~85% pre-Big Healing) prefer a reclusive lifestyle and avoid a societal WOB, the balance for each between the two. Obviously, spirit-born persons experience satisfaction in sociability else ~95% of them wouldn't cluster in urbanized settings. An individual experiences society as own-self, their extended self. Unlike physical 'society' as coercive alpha structures (§ 9.2.2:450), spirit society constitutes as pairwise familial relationships without structure. There's nothing to hate about society, nothing one wants to repulse as inconsistent with own-self, no peer pressure masquerading as concern squashing the individual for the collective. Personal preference, not societal dysfunction, motivates the 0.15% of the spirit-born who prefer to avoid society where, for them, own-self is societally oneself. They aren't angry, disturbed, lonely, asocial crackpots but happy in their own-self experience. There's a vast range of individual experience of society from none, to limited, to expansive, to in toto. The physical-born experience has been one of coerced acceptance and violent retribution, the spirit-born's one of voluntary preference and autonomy.

3.4.3   THE FUTURE

We often imagine life after death as all tea and cake; that despite some nebulous eternal lifetime awaiting us with intellectual advancement and imperatives toward individual perfection, one has no *future*, one can never realize *their* dream without diverging from *the* dream of perfection and oneness with the Eternal, which for the religious–spiritualist mindset is the real point and purpose of eternal life. If you've read the whole book to this point, you know that ET tells a story of life beyond these fables, myths, and palliatives built of fear that physical humanity uses for comfort in a misinterpreted world. The key to understanding existence, to cognizing humanity's and the individual's—*your*—purpose, lies in emergent ℒife, the person as a unique, autonomous being, a universe unto themselves, an All Existence in their own right. So-called perfection, therefore, is *of* not *for* the individual. Mina, a unique, emergent person like you, built our universe but *his* standard of perfection necessarily *isn't yours*. *Your* future isn't *his* future, nor the future conveyed by a belief but that you choose it, make it your own, and pursue it.

Belief *is* reality, aye. One's mind is their universe and Thought defines it. What you pursue in *your* 'universe' is your choice, your rules. Even so, each unique, autonomous ℒife emergently births in the same, *actual* All Existence because there's ever only *one* (§ 1.1:228). Accordingly, humanity emergently births in pairwise kinship, its WOB familial (§ 2:304). The individual exists in pairwise relationship with humanity and affects other persons, each of whom in turn affects the individual. Yet, it doesn't eviscerate one's uniqueness, one's emergent autonomy; individuals interactively *are* in the context of many such. One's individual future is one's own, no one else's. When a physical person's embodiment dies, their spirit world experience is however they live it. There's no absolute or implied imperative to pursue some ideal because, after all, what is perfection? A state of oneness with the universe? with another being? a condition of no-harm? the attaining of true love? or something else? Perfection is infinite—not infinite-*ness* but simply indeterminate (unlimited) in its *astī* is-ness. In and of itself, it's literally impossible because eternal life means the individual is always *becoming*, never *become*. If one reaches a plateau in his or her personal development, they might say, "I've reached perfection!" But eternal life means the individual may transcend that plateau where someone else might say, "You've *exceeded* perfection! You're *more* perfect!" (cf. infinite sets; CH. 14:93).

Physical persons assess the future in terms of desires, possibilities, likelihoods, and sustenance in a pressured context where one has only so much time to achieve before interference, infirmity, age, or death disrupts or terminates their goals. Spirit persons experience the same desires, possibilities, and likelihoods but without such considerations. Indeed, since time is relative to the spirit individual rather than the inevitable ticking of the biological clock that cuts through everyone's physical life equally, the future differs according to the person. *You* have a future of *your* making in spirit world. Comprehending this liberates mind to heal.

3.5 ACTIVITIES

From the instant the person emergently births, one ceaselessly engages in activity whether unembodied, spirit embodied, or physical embodied. The physical body is always engaged in biological activity, conscious or not. The spirit body as an Intentionality is active in the biological sense only if a person Intentionalizes it to function as a biological facsimile. Regardless, any unembodied or embodied person whose embodiment or mind is asleep or unconscious is only so in the conscious mind. The self-aware ℒife—one's subconscious and emergent self—continues having awareness and never shuts down. Consequently, a person engages in activity even if it's only the most basic awareness of environment. Life in spirit world is one of ceaseless activity, whether of body or mind. In this section, we describe five activities of the body generalized as play, relationships, work, growth and development, and avoiding boredom.

3.5.1 PLAY

If we analyze life in the physical world, it's not difficult to notice that human beings are principally albeit not exclusively concerned with play not work. Some people love their work. It holds the same value for them as play. Workaholics eschew play, yet still find a way. Others work so they *can* play. Normally, a person not engaged in earning their living is engaged in play even if it's only rest (versus unavoidable sleep). Spirit persons are no different except there's no need for them to work to survive, or because they're compelled to, or to support someone, or to effect emergency services, and so on. Even so, people don't always want to play, whether physical or spirit. Sometimes, they want to achieve something as a personal accomplishment or in a societal context. Regardless, play is a principal aspect of the human experience. Spirit world life revolves around it, integrates it with every activity in or out of mind. Play isn't only individual or collective but organized, too, such as, oddly enough, warfare.

3.5.1.1 WAR IN SPIRIT WORLD

Spirit persons know their bodies can't die, be crippled, infirmed, or diseased; simple observation proves it. Prior to the Big Healing, about 99.5% of the spirit-born (~99.99% physical-born) didn't know their spirit body was an Intentionality of their own mind. They simply believed it immortal, healable, and ever young with no concept of aging. Today, only 0.5% (~70% physical-born) don't accept their body's Intentionality. Spirit persons thus understand war's futility because it can't achieve its coercive ends via fear of death or enslavement or harm generally, as it's no threat to them. But they engage in organized violence as play. Yes, it hurts when the spirit body suffers wounds or destruction since one's mind *is* their spirit embodiment. But it's irrelevant—even welcomed as an experience—by participants because they're fully aware nothing they suffer is permanent but ever healable. The spirit-born mindset that violence, pain, and harm generally is inconsequential is so individually and collectively ingrained that they're entirely nonresponsive to coercion. In exactly opposite measure, physical humanity's mindset these are absolutely consequential and to be feared *is* individually and collectively so ingrained that they're entirely responsive to coercion.

Spirit warfare manifests as mass events amongst participating groups, like historical war reenactments on Earth. Even raids on cities and towns for the fun of spreading surprise and provoking a rise—not too unlike physical world zombie walks, scary art or storytelling, acting scary, or whatever might scare or get a rise out of non-participants—happens. In the latter case, 'victims' run the normal gamut of emotion when, say, startled or annoyed and run away, fight back, or take what's coming in the surety that when it's over they'll re-Intentionalize their embodiment and carry on with the equanimity one might feel in an unexpected downpour. For the spirit-born, warfighting isn't violence but play.

Not so the physical-born spirit person. They have a different mindset for which their physical life's fear of death, dismemberment, pain, suffering, and harm remains deeply ingrained despite comprehending their spirit body can't die like their physical one. They do engage in war, violence, fear mongering, gangsterism, and so on for the same reasons as when physical: to coerce. Prior to the Big Healing, physical-born warfare was the real deal because in that environment it successfully coerced with all its upsides but no downside, even if they couldn't kill or maim enemies. Mindsets stuck in the physical world is a principal reason the spirit-born didn't want the physical-born in their society. Only those who left it behind ever felt comfortable enough in the spirit-born's proto-energy 'frequency' to move *and* feel welcome there (FN 467:426). The frequency of 'real' war and violence in physical-born spirit world—they 'play' war, too—has declined about 20% since the Big Healing.

3.5.2 Relationships

There are two ways humanity experiences relationships. First, as with the physical world, spirit persons live for their relationships—sexual, love, friendship, familial, collegial—as much as they live for play and work. Besides the fun of play and joy of work, however, what sort of eternal life would it be without relationships? Life would be meaningless, unsatisfying, unfulfilling; in truth, downright unpleasant as Mike and Molly realized after discovering the other (§ 2.1:305). But one can play and work only so much before it feels repetitive, mundane, and tedious. Relationships differ from work and play in being intrinsically dynamic in a way the former aren't. For example, Mina and Ag'poprje have been a couple for more than 14BY, yet he reports their relationship remains dynamically unpredictable, enjoyable, and satisfying despite, to us, the cosmic time span (§ 2.2:341). He admits eternal life wouldn't look so great if it wasn't for Ag'poprje and all his other relationships—including us, his literal grandchildren—that impart meaning and joy to his existence. And so it is with 99.99% of physical and spirit humanity. Spirit-born relationships never (~25% for physical-born) fall into behavioral ruts as is common with physical world relationships (~88%), as they lack the physical-life stressors, dynamics, fears, psychoses, harm, dysfunctions, and physical limitations that routinely disrupt them. Spirit persons can't coerce others regardless their relationship for the reasons noted elsewhere.

For example, while forcible rape was possible in the physical-born area of spirit world before the Big Healing, it's become universally impossible because they gained awareness that by resisting in Thought rather than simply in action, fear, or anger they manifest a repulsive 'force' that makes controlling, or laying hands on, a person's body against their will impossible. This is *force of Thought*, not Intentionality manipulating matter according *to* Thought, but Thought *as* self-aware proto-energy *exerting* directly into local Energent proto-energy (or local Energent proto-life, as in the different case of conceiving children). When the proto-energy around a person's embodiment becomes repulsive then, no matter how another individual tries, it's impossible to place hands on or control the person's body at all. This defense doesn't work physically because, unlike the spirit body, the physical body is independent matter operating in accord with immutable Fundamental Force. But Mina avers physical persons can utilize Intentionality rather than force of Thought to manifest effectively the same repulsive 'force'—proto-energy *contextually responds* in each case—to meet the same ends.[483]

---

483 Force of Thought and force of will are essentially the same concept, although the latter describes only one's commitment to Intent whereas the former describes the latter as a proto-energy force that exerts a felt repulsion physically affecting another's body. It's similar in effect to a sonic weapon, most often roiling some aspect of the body that subconsciously leads one to consciously desire to avoid such a person.

Second, relationships are spirit world's nexus as in the physical world. This means every aspect of the human experience operates in relationship, whether it's with millions of individuals or just the local frog, a special tree, or the environment generally. A relationship is a *node of intersection* between two individuals as a *parallel circuit*—a type of electrical circuit having branch flow pathways much as a single water pipe or roadway circuit might branch to many flows until reconnecting (remerging) into a single flow—to which universal humanity is relationally analogous. However many branches, the entire system is 'charged' whereby total flow in equals total flow out regardless any individual branch flow (*Fig. 167*, left).

Any two individuals in relationship are a node—a Thought connection—in the whole circuit (*Fig. 167*, right). Unlike a parallel circuit in the context of applied energy E, each of a node's two individuals, or *nodalities*, independently 'power' a relational node, meaning each individual in relationship *when interacting* whether directly as in sex, talk, being in another's presence, or indirectly as in thinking–feeling. When two individuals aren't interacting, they're not relational, thus not a node, regardless their societal relationship as spouse, roommate, family, friend, or colleague. A node is *the interactive moment between individuals* as self-aware proto-energy in the context of EPL, not too conceptually unlike a *magnetic moment*, which is the interactive experience of an object with a magnetic field in the context of Fundamental Force (§ 6.8.2:176). Relationships are instantaneous across time and space because self-aware proto-energy, like Energent proto-energy, is dimensionless and without time, distance, or travel.

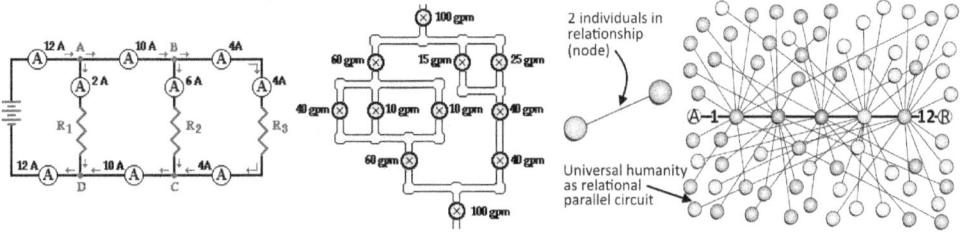

Figure 167. Schematic: left, center, parallel electrical and water circuits; right, two persons in relationship as a single node parallel branch circuit amongst universal humanity as the parallel circuit or any subset thereof; Person-A at node 1 to Person-R via nodes 2–12 is the left-to-right centerline.[279]

3.5.2.1 'Six Degrees of Separation'

Consider the *six degrees of separation* theory. A person connects with random individuals via ±6 relationships—a friend of a friend of a friend. It's the right concept but wrong in principle, for two reasons.

1. It presumes two things, first that every person knows some minimal number of persons and any discrepancy naturally balances out on average, and second it necessarily presumes a finite number of total persons whereby each degree of separation represents an exponential increase in the total number of persons connected through each linking relationship to create the plausibility one can eventually connect with any person in a population of x number. It's a wholly inadequate means to validate the concept as population size is variable, relationships that link in theory don't necessarily in practice, and success is probabilistic.

2. It presumptuously extrapolates from physical experiments with packages, letters, emails, and the like (in which a few get from random Person-A to Person-R) to demonstrate the supposed universal statistic that it's possible for any person to reach any other through some x degrees of separation. These experiments only show it works in certain cases which necessarily are the only cases having successful *potential* out of the total unsuccessful (non-potential) cases. This is random chance, not statistical certainty. Exponentially calculating degrees of separation isn't valid.

As a universal certainty regardless sample size, Mina avers there are 1–12 degrees of separation between any two random individuals as a probability P by which a person is like a quantum particle having quantum states in superposition where there's only a probability the link through any single node from Person-A to Person-R is *the* link forming the *chain of links* A → R, where the probability space is the total number of successful and unsuccessful links in the sample space. This is similar w.r.t. pull of gravity (§ 3.3.2.2:128). We express the foregoing more simply as

$$|\psi\rangle \rightarrow \left\{ \left(\left(\langle c_+|\mathcal{L}\rangle\ \langle c_-|\mathcal{L}\rangle \right) \langle c_0|\mathcal{L}\rangle \right) \right\} \tag{28.1}$$

where $|\psi\rangle\rightarrow$ is the probabilistic quantum state of the node that comes from each individuated $|\mathcal{L}\rangle$ equation, and the coefficients c_+, c_-, and c_0 represent the probability P that link $|\mathcal{L}\rangle$ is successful, not successful, or has no (a null) state as a link in the chain of links that sums as a probability the number of relational nodes 1-12 A → R. What this ultimately says is that human relationships aren't simply the nature of, nor the interaction between, individuals that we normally quantify as 'a relationship.' Rather, they're *of* proto-energy *as* a 'quantum' reality where the individuated nodeState $|\psi\rangle$ is in 'quantum' superposition; that is, having the potentiality in any given moment or context of more than one distinct relationship quantum that *is* the node's proto-energy, which arises in Thought such that $\exists r \in H\,|\,\{H \subset uH \wedge uH_{pc} \notin |\mathcal{L}\rangle\}$ where $\exists r$ is any relationship, H is humanity, uH is universal humanity, and uH_{pc} is uH having parallel circuits as degrees of separation such that, for any individuals A → R,

$$P(|\psi\rangle) = \sum_{i=1}^{12} \sum_{j=1}^{n} |\alpha\rangle_i |\beta\rangle_j \rightarrow \begin{pmatrix} \langle c_+|\mathcal{L}\rangle \\ \langle c_-|\mathcal{L}\rangle \\ \langle c_0|\mathcal{L}\rangle \end{pmatrix} \left(+ \frac{P(\beta_j||\mathcal{L}\rangle)P(|\mathcal{L}\rangle)}{P(\beta_j)} \right) \tag{28.2}$$

where $P|\psi\rangle$ is the probabilistic quantum state of the node as a degree of separation between one and twelve ($|\alpha\rangle$) from the probabilistic quantum state ($|\beta\rangle$) of each $|\mathcal{L}\rangle$ in the i-th degree of separation, and the additive parenthetical at right is a Bayesian probability to account for the intrinsic uncertainty in nodeState having finite connections as $|\mathcal{L}\rangle$. Eq. (28.1–28.2) don't derive an actual probability, but are merely evocative of the mathematic approach necessary to rationalize not simply the degree of separation between individuals A → R, but the nature of human relationships between any two persons—a node—as well as between any node and universal humanity. We don't find for probability *amplitude* (wavefunction) regardless the 'quantum' nature of a node and degrees of separation. The reason is that, despite both being intrinsically uncertain with multiple possible outcomes, the probability value isn't similar to a wave either amplitudinally or distributionally, as each nodeState is discrete at the moment of quantification, thus isn't additive as in the quantum wavefunction probability equation $|\psi\rangle = c_+(|\alpha\rangle) + c_-(|\beta\rangle)$.

The problem with 'six degrees of separation' as a way to quantify relationality between individuals and humanity is that it tries to quantify the number of intermediaries as a discrete population but, in reality, that quantification is necessarily amorphous across all humanity whether or not confined to a finite planetary or other subset. There's no *average* degree of separation across humanity for any individuals A → R because relationships differ for individuals A, A_n, and R. Earth relationally clusters, for example, in that any two random individuals have a weighted potential—randomly but likely—to relate, just as two individuals amongst friends, school, town, state, or nation have greater potential to meet than otherwise. Universal humanity, however, is relationally random where individuals have unweighted, truly random (and unlikely) potential to relate.

Going from a few to many interconnections across individuals A → A_n → R is analogous to a phase transition in physics, where there's an abrupt shift in symmetries between a relationship node and those in a degree of separation chain where nodes from outside a cluster (of friends) and clusters of clusters include random nodes—relationships that don't cluster; say, a random acquaintance. Accordingly, relationships between individuals is a stochastic cluster with outliers, and when expanding from individuals A → A_n to A → R is a phasic evolution in which any node's proto-energy affects the phase transition along with the entire parallel circuit in which it's occurrent. Relationships in and of themselves fundamentally *are* proto-energy, the thread weaving universal humanity into a proto-energy whole.

3.5.3 WORK

Spirit persons don't work—do tasks—to get ahead, make money, become important, gain societal or political power, to survive, or all the myriad reasons physically alive people choose or fall into a task. Since the spirit body is mind's Intentionality, there's no need to provide for its survival, sustenance, protection, control of danger, and like needs that dominate one's every physically alive moment and necessarily informs virtually every choice we make. Spirit persons can do what they want, or not do what they don't want (§ 3.3:482). Work embodies task and pleasure—the fun chore, say. One takes on tasks from which they derive satisfaction, the joy of contentment. Whether an 'archangel,' 'angel,' spirit guide, businessperson, or whatever task-doer, a person engages in it for reasons of personal gratification and not from necessity, guilt, duty, or any reason that is, or feels, coercive or compulsory.

This doesn't mean a spirit person *never* does something out of a personal sense of coercion or compulsoriness, because some do, especially pre-Big Healing. Rather, nothing necessitates it beyond one's own mindset. For example, about 5% of universal humanity's ~849 quadrillion people routinely engage in tasks they consider necessary for the well-being of physical humanity in the grip of The Corruption, or ~7% if we add those who engage such tasks part-time or casually. When a person just isn't 'feeling it,' they typically stop until (or if) they start 'feeling it' again. Surprisingly, there's little turnover amongst 'angels' and the tasks they engage. Only about 2% ever entirely quit this work on average. That's a wee dram in the big scheme of things, but still a whopping ~850 trillion to 1.886 quadrillion individuals.

As an activity, people derive meaning, purpose, and joy in their lives through tasks as much as with relationships. Without work, some would find life boring, unfulfilling, and undesirable. Once The Corruption is entirely out of universal humanity's mindset and physical humanity is squared away w.r.t. mind–brain integration and awareness of reality, the seven 'archangel' tasks will be redundant (Table 17:523). It seems this cadre will thus be at loose ends. But post-NCC tasks supporting our universe like seeding planets with human embodiment (HUMAFORMING, § 2.3:357), natural–supranatural 'energy' translation mechanisms (§ 7.1.3:214), spirit world terrain-scaping (§ 2.2:356), and so on that Mina hitherto performed on his own, will pass to those interested in it. He built this universe to be *ours* in every way, not a rental, sharecrop, or feudal landhold, but direct ownership to the degree any autonomous person wants it. Humans will always find a task to pursue because of our insatiable love of play.

3.5.4 PERSONAL GROWTH AND DEVELOPMENT

Generally considered a meliorating transformational process to improve oneself, personal growth and development (PG&D) is largely anything but. The reason lies in two aspects of the human psyche which sees oneself in the context of one's life and that change is improvement. Each aspect plays out in accord with one's embodiment. The former is the tendency of physical persons where PG&D's focus is on changing one's experience of life *as* personal improvement and the latter is the tendency of spirit persons where its focus is on change *itself* as improvement, the way a new suit of clothes is an improvement over an old set. A physical individual feels motivated to grow and develop because how he or she is right now isn't bringing the results in life for which they yearn, whether it's love, money, lifestyle,[484] control, or a sense of happiness in those contexts. On the other hand, a spirit individual, naturally lacking any meaningful pressure to be a better, or at least a different, person simply feels tired of, or bored with, how they are and *any* change is an improvement. That's not to say there aren't individuals who *do* desire to be better than they are according to *their* definition of 'better,' but according to Mina, they account for about 1% of spirit persons (~10% physical, though we don't describe it here) engaging in PG&D efforts.

For the spirit-born, there's no restriction on PG&D; one's lifestyle isn't any better or worse for pursuing it or not. Consider a pre-Big Healing physical-born spirit person living in a low proto-energy 'frequency' area of spirit world (§ 3.1.2.1.3:359), say, Helen when we first encountered her spirit self that week in October 2017 (§ 1.1:35) just before we met Mother (P'najj; § 1.2:336) and Mina. Helen hated her situation in (what she'd later realize was) physical-born spirit world, not least of which because she'd expected a loyal Moonie would certainly go to a psychically pleasant environment. She wanted to be somewhere nicer and more appropriate to her view of herself, but didn't know what 'nicer' might even feel like other than not *here*, where she was; something more in line with her Christian, Moonie, and enculturated imagination anyway. She didn't feel she *deserved* heaven—whatever it was, if it even existed—but certainly some 'medium place' for 'medium folks'[280] because she didn't *deserve* to be where she was.

In this frame of mind, she invested herself in PG&D, hoping it might 'magically' transition her to that 'better place' the way a physical person seeks self-improvement to transcend the consequences of lifestyle. In her mind she improved as a person, yet nothing changed in her environment. Then she glommed onto me. The girls healed her using Emotion Code and she experienced a deep, profound happiness, liberation, and awareness of where she was and how to change it—within physical-born spirit world—to one better suiting her.[485] So, she found actual, true PG&D simply accepting Mina's liberating healing.

---

484. *Lifestyle* means all aspects of one's *sense of well-being* which includes financial, spiritual, emotional, intellectual, physical, social, or any of a series of things that matter to a person.

Like you, spirit persons can get bored with who, what, and how they are. In the physical world, individuals work to change themselves in the context of lifestyle, an improved sense of well-being. Spirit persons' sense of well-being doesn't link to lifestyle attributes nor to how others perceive of them. We on Earth tend to link well-being to how we feel about ourselves vis-à-vis achievement, lifestyle, social standing, and others' perception of us. While some spirit persons care about that, it makes no difference in how they enjoy, therefore live, life. It matters in the physical world because they can leave us impoverished, imprisoned, separated from loved ones, miserable, or dead, deeply affecting not only *how* we live but our enjoyment of life. Lifestyle doesn't factor into spirit life.

When spirit persons experience tedium with themselves, they slough it off with, say, changing mindset or pursuing PG&D to reinvent their persona—sometimes as far as changing sexes (§ 3.3:283)—and experience life through new eyes. From their perspective, this doesn't mean fixing oneself, being a better or best possible (upgraded) self, or pursuing a larger goal; more like a shower and a change of clothes to refresh, revitalize, renew. To live *differently*. There's a lag with physical-born spirit persons, but the same principle operates: one needn't change to achieve a goal except in terms of what it calls for, like becoming a guardian 'angel,' a parent, or coming off likable to someone special. Life is thus a kaleidoscope of experience.

3.5.5 Avoiding Boredom

Experience isn't the marrow of life, *relationships* are (§ 3.3:482; § 3.5.2:486). After spending four seasons fighting tooth and nail to avoid 'the bad place' and get into 'the good place' in the eponymous 2016–20 NBC television series, the characters discovered the lucky few 'good' people were bored to death, having experienced every possible interest, and wanted only to die for real, permanently, no after-afterlife desired, thank you, just oblivion. So the team, now in charge of the good place, got to work. They built a door through which the terminally bored could stroll placidly into post-eternity and return to the stars as it were, permanently ending their ennui. Central characters Eleanor and Chidi finally transcended their romanticus interruptus to enjoy their consummated love for some indeterminate time span until, even this, their greatest joy, lost its luster and they exited from eternity through the door to nullity and the ultimate unknown.

The philosophical question the series pursues is, won't human experience that must necessarily be in-terminably finite negate eternal life's charm, thus its point? Eternally childless consonant with theological belief—and alone but for their cohorts Tahani, who reinvented herself via PG&D as a demon (§ 3.5.4:489), and Jason—Eleanor and Chidi thought so. But the real answer is no, it won't, for six reasons. First, boredom is a cyclical part of ⨑ife, like growing weary of a certain view from the living room window or rice dishes, or feeling boredom's motivation to experience a difference. Second, one can infinitely reinvent oneself. Third, one perceives time subjectively; what seems like a million tedious years on Earth could pass like hours, days, or years to the spirit person. Fourth, love is infinitely encountered, renewing, unknown, and pregnant with meaning. Fifth, children, family, and relationships, not activities, are the real crux of human experience. And sixth, perhaps the pièce de résistance, one can explore the megaverse's many universes (Table 12:312), build one's own to populate with one's descendants, and experience unembodied ⨑ife. We consider these in turn.

3.5.5.1 Boredom is a Cyclical Experience

Boredom is the natural expression of a mindset centered on experiencing activity rather than (⨑ife and Energent) proto-energy. Recall the human individual *is* self-aware proto-energy (§ 2.1.1.1:368). It Intentionalizes subconscious–conscious mind as one's interface with external-to-mind reality as a fundamental aspect of unembodiment (§ 2.2.1:395). Recall, too, that humans emergently birth as pairwise beings (§ 2:304). This means we're not only pairwise with other humans but with reality as well (§ 3.3:482). The individual, being emergent of EPL, is pairwise with it which likewise is emergent of, thus pairwise with, Energent–prime (§ 1:112). This means humans are pairwise via EPL with Energent–prime. Hence, the individual person effectively *is* All Existence inclusive of the megaverse (§ 2:479). This isn't just new agey woo-woo run amuck but *the* fundamental proto-energy reality, *our* reality.

Being pairwise, then, we fundamentally experience reality—an activity, say—at its elementary level, which is proto-energy. When one meets someone, has a burger, slakes a hot thirst, enjoys sex, peruses through a

---

483. Awareness didn't just pop into her mind. Having consented to El's spirit-self facilitating Mina healing her there in the backseat of our car, Helen's mindset opened to a Wisdom 'angel' who'd arrived in consequence of her healing and explained her situation and how to find better digs. In truth, she could've asked the Entry 'angel' to take her anywhere then or later (who would've), but was still afraid of Accountableist retribution.

pleasant or terrifying memory, gets stabbed, perceives beauty or ugliness—literally anything one encounters or experiences—one does so in the realm of proto-energy (self-aware beingness; Fig. 153:392) and only secondarily through that of awareness and perception (subconscious and conscious experience). Yet, mindset is so all encompassing it can blot any reality from the mind for any substitution, which is what we *perceive* and *think* we're experiencing. It can't entirely block objective reality. One's emergent self is self-aware of subconscious mind's awareness of proto-energy regardless conscious mind's substitution of it for something perceived. For example, an individual experientially perceives an activity in x terms while the subconscious has awareness of it in y terms, which then seek to reconcile in sub-Thought (§ 2.2.2.1:396) while one's ℒife self is self-aware of the full 'energy' spectrum of its SOB and SOA.

Recall how we experience beauty and ugliness as a proto-energy reality (§ 11.3:462) where one's perception of ugliness is the lack of resonance—a 'clash' like a discordant sound to the ear—between a thing's proto-energy 'frequency' and one's own. This is how one has awareness of reality: as proto-energy, not as a thing, activity, or idea. One experiences activity in terms of awareness of its proto-energy resonance with one's own proto-energy. If it resonates, it has beauty. If it doesn't, it's without resonance and mind perceives it as a 'clash,' a discordance, and thus ugly. One's subconscious *awareness* of ugly is repulsive and rejected. One's conscious *experience* of this awareness expresses as the inability to bond, to connect, to embrace 'entanglement,' and our attention disengages it the way two same-pole magnets repulse. We call this experience a dis-bond, disengagement, or *boredom* and the thing—a person, activity, idea, or one's own self—*boring*. Boredom isn't just that one finds oneself, activity, or a thing uninteresting, unlikable, ugly, meaningless, or the like but that, in proto-energy terms, as non-resonant, thus ugly, hence repulsive, and consequently without meaning. In other words, boring (§ 3.5.2:486).

Proto-energy is 'entangling' in the sense of Parity ('quantum entanglement;' § 6.11:191). This means we don't simply 'experience' proto-energy but 'entangle' (integrate) it as if it's our own self-aware proto-energy although it isn't, being conceptually similar to quantum physics' notion that two massive objects entangle as though a single, superposed object yet remain discrete in reality. This is why when one experiences resonant music, speech, ideas, touch, one has such a profound, self-aware, self-referential awareness–experience in consequence. Proto-energy doesn't simply 'resonate' with a person like a catchy tune or a tasty morsel. It's a fundamental 'entangling' of 'frequency,' not in the sense of constructive wave interference but more a coupling, a pairwise *thing* that is in reality two discrete things yet, in resonance, becomes a single, superposed existent thus a pairwise relational node (§ 3.3:482). This is the elemental reality behind the notion, "I *love* tacos!" or "I love *you*!" The greater the resonance, the more intensely we experience what we love, find beautiful, exciting, engaging, interesting, or attention-getting and the more 'entangled,' or 'stronger,' the node of intersection (ibid).

However, just as one can discover an initially ugly something as beautiful, engaging, desirable, impossible to disengage therefore attention-getting, nothing in and of itself is boring whether it's new to the person or end-lessly repetitive. The reason is that a thing's proto-energy ceaselessly shifts like a kaleidoscope in x, y, z rotation having infinitely changing intensities, colors, and angles of light. Because we're pairwise beings in relationship, everything—oneself, others, things, experiences—exists in relationship, too. It affects everything. This is why what once captured our attention as endlessly engaging and exciting we eventually experience as boring. It isn't because we 'tired' of it, but that both *our and its* proto-energy 'frequency' in the greater pairwise kaleidoscope of relationship altered, both as a nature of pairwise relationship—resonance—and as the inevitability of an individual consciously experiencing subconscious awareness differently in accord with the totality of emergent self's SOB and SOA. Proto-energy is therefore infinitely experiential whether resonant or non-resonant.

The primary means by which one's conscious experience of subconscious awareness alters, such that emergent self's totality of SOB and SOA changes, is *mindset* (§ 3.1.2.1:358). One can find life endlessly engaging and never boring until, say, experiencing a profound heartbreak. He or she now experiences life as profoundly ugly, without meaning, and disengages from some or maybe all their activities, including one's own self. A self-loathing might develop that transforms the vibrant person to a suicide. The mindset in question is that which filters the heartbreak as pairwise with all or some aspects of one's life which translates (imposes) the experience of heartbreak into all or some aspects of one's self, the proto-energy of which aspects no longer resonate but 'clash' with what one encounters. This phenomenon expresses in mind–brain integration that integrates (translates) one's subconscious–conscious mind to brain that's in pairwise relationship with its body, exerting negative emotive ℒife force (EMℒF; § 3.3.3.1.1:289) that disrupts its biological function that, sooner or later, results in problematic health conditions.

Having described boredom for what it is instead of how one perceives it, we can describe why eternal (infinite) ℒife isn't boring. There are three reasons. First, boredom is natural to life as proto-energy shifts through a myriad of 'frequencies.' Second, as emergent, autonomous beings, each individual prefers this or that which they find engaging or boring at any given moment in accord with our earlier description of boredom. And third, the mindset through which an individual chooses to encounter and experience ℒife plays the principal role in whether or not one finds this or that boring and whether boredom advances to a chronic condition across a greater, or the full range, of one's life. Let's consider each.

Boredom is natural to life, expressing a lack of resonance in proto-energy 'entanglement' (Parity) that's inevitable where infinitely shifting proto-energy 'frequency' is intrinsic reality. Accordingly, individuals will always experience boredom to greater or lesser degrees as they experience ℒife. It isn't something to fear or dread but to simply accept. When it feels chronic—bored with, say, one's own self as worthless or ℒife as meaningless—then one needs explore their mindset which lays behind their percepted experience. The physical person can't easily do this because of the residual effects of The Corruption, our profound lack of awareness of ℌuman, and reality overall. Hence, one needs healing which liberates them from these effects because it's the only means to reverse and replace its negative EM ℒF and the effects thereof (§ 1.4:579). Boredom isn't an inevitability of eternal life simply because we imagine that once we experience every possible finite *activity* then ℒife ceases to have any *experiential* appeal.

Individual preferences change, and we can't overstate its fundamentality. Humans are emergently autonomous. No Divine Being created us within parameters. Mina didn't Intentionalize us into existence like his universe. A person births as a unique reality, effectively their own universe in their own All Existence no person can enter or control. Unless one chooses to accept coercion, one intrinsically is impervious to it. This means absolute liberty is the fundamental WOB of ℌuman and unalterable (§ 5.1:428; § 1:586). An individual, therefore, has preferences. When one feels compelled into or away from (un)wanted experiences such as activity—experiencing boredom—then one is choosing to experience the discord of non-resonant proto-energy despite his or her preference. The spirit-born are immune to coercion, though it's possible in physical-born spirit world. Bearing the first reason above in mind, boredom isn't the fact of spirit life it's been (till now) in physical life.

Mindset plays a principal role, and it's infinitely fungible. This is one reason spirit persons engage in their version of PG&D: to change their perspective on ℒife, self, and reality to remove their sense of tedium. Mindset is the principal cause of attitude, behavior, or thinking–feeling from which arises the person whom the self and others know. A change of mindset renders Person A into Person A′, a phenomenon long understood and demonstrated in religious, prison, epiphanic, and like 'conversions.' Person A doesn't cease to exist in becoming Person A′, however. One is still the same *person* but of different *mindset*. We more accurately say that Person A of mindset x becomes Person A of mindset x' (*below*). In this way, eternal spirit life is never necessarily boring, thus meaningless—a condition of ennui—at some ineludible point, but infinitely experiential, fresh through mindset.

3.5.5.2 Reinventing Oneself

Philosophy with a capital-P sometimes argues that reinventing oneself to avoid the inevitable boredom of eternal life necessarily means losing one's identity in that, through such change, the person who is *me* at the start of eternal life isn't the same *me* at some future time as a result of the change. This reasoning is invalid on the grounds it's fallacious; nothing is so endemic to the human experience as personal change. Is the *me* on day one following birth the same *me* at age 5, 25, 50, or 100? Is the *me* which enters college as a naïve teenager with religious convictions the same *me* who graduates four years later as a stridently materialist biochemist? Or is the peaceful *me* who goes through brutal war the same *me* who comes back a killer? Or is the *me* authoring this book the same *me* on the eve I discovered Mina? Imagine your five-year old self magically appearing next to your 20, 40, or 60-year old self and explaining who they feel they are, what they do in their life right then, and what they dream of doing in their future.[486] Is your 5-year old *me* truly your 20, 40, or 60-year old *me*? Would an unawares onlooker conclude they're listening to two completely different persons and not the *same* person separated in time? The questions themselves are problematic in presuming the individual person is only *that* person if *how* they are, or *what* they do or dream, remains in some way invariant. That isn't ℒife.

---

486. For example, in the 2021 Korean Netflix drama *Hello, Me!*, the 37-year old heroine meets her 17-year old feisty, dreamy self (scornful of her older self's loser lifestyle) who time-traveled to the future moments prior to knowing she'd caused her father's death. Her older self carried this burden's mindset ever since, which had provoked her 'loser' lifestyle.

ℒife is a series of personality changes arising in one's internal and external awareness–experience (*enimerótis-empeiría*; § 2.1.4:394) in which arises *how* we are and *what* we do and dream. But personality isn't the ℘erson. Emergent ℒife is the ℘erson where *personness* is ӈuman (Eq. (19.1–19.4):245). The ℘erson is fundamentally human woв along with mindset. Accordingly, change in the ℘erson is change in woв or mindset or both. One's ℒife self remains the autonomous ℘erson howsoever radically one changes woв and mindset.

Suppose a spirit person, having their spirit body Intentionalized from mind since conception, chooses to alter their embodiment's woв from male to female. If they want to *be* a woman and not simply look, act, and live as a woman, they need alter additional aspects of their woв as well as mindset. It wouldn't do to be a woman with a man's mindset, would it? One would only be creating the appearance, not the reality. In this case, is the *me* who birthed as a man and developed a male mindset the same *me* who redoes himself into a woman and develops a female mindset? Consider, is the physical individual who undergoes sex reassignment surgery the same *me* as before? If not, government would insist on issuing new identity documents to account not for a name change but for being altogether a different individual, a different *me*. Yet, it doesn't do that because it's commonsense to recognize the ℒife born as male is the same ℒife now female since the man didn't die to birth, phoenix-like, as the woman. Physically, there's no difference because only the accoutrements of embodiment and perhaps some aspects of mindset responsive to drugs and sex reassignment therapy have changed.

But does the complete woв and mindset makeover of a spirit person constitute a different ℘erson as ℒife? The short answer is, no. The individuated, autonomous ℒife who chose to change their woв and mindset from male to female remains the same ℒife because, first, ℒife is eternal and, second, a change of woв and mindset necessarily can't entail the destruction of one ℒife from which, like the phoenix, arises an entirely different, individuated, autonomous ℒife.

The point of the foregoing is to understand why reinventing one's (physical or spirit) self isn't the loss of self or identity—one's consistent sense of self before and after a change—where the sense of identity, say, from male to female, differs in kind but not essence, as one's identity *as self*. Consequently, the *self* is invariant while how the self *identifies* is fungible in kind though not in essence. When feeling bored with one's identity and its accoutrements like sex, personality, behavior, dreams, or choice frames, one can change one, some, or all such aspects of the self for a fresh, unbored take on ℒife without losing their self, their individuated autonomous ℒife. One needn't make radical departures in woв to alleviate boredom. Changes in attitude, place, or relationship usually suffice. And then there's how one perceives time.

3.5.5.3 PERCEPTION OF TIME

When we think eternal life is necessarily boring at some finite point in the future, it's partly because we think of timekeeping in terms of the natural environment where archí, as an independent existent having dimensionality, regulates it (§ 2:107). As we've learned, the supranatural environment's supramatter doesn't arise in independently existing archí but in supranatural proto-energy from which supra-archí Intentionalize (§ 1.1:466). This means spirit world is fundamentally a dimensionless environment—weakly analogous to proto-energy—that dimensionalizes through Intentionality. It does so when individuals Intentionalize supramatter into form as a world terrain (§ 2.2:356) or objects of any kind. Its dimensionlessness pairwise with Intentionality is why a spirit person's body can instantaneously shift with their self-aware proto-energy awareness from point A to B regardless dimensionality, which one can't do in the physical world. Accordingly, there's no archí oscillation to provide the baseline for objective timekeeping in spirit world (its objective timekeeping is premised on physical archí oscillation). There's no day-night cycle, for example, but which people Intentionalize. Timekeeping is primarily subjective to 100% of the spirit world population, with those having awareness of objective timekeeping *being* aware of it as desired. One or a trillion years can feel as a minute or a week or a quadrillion years in accord with *perception*. Feeling bored in spirit world when a million Earth years might feel like a week or an interminable eternity is amenable since it's alterable according to perception, thus mindset.

3.5.5.4 LOVE IS MEANINGFUL

The notion death gives meaning and purpose to life—that living beyond physical death strips life of its value—is a canard. As El said in the frontispiece to this book, "There is no purpose to this life; you make your own purpose, that's what makes life beautiful." Neither is survival, much less happiness or salvation, life's goal because life isn't about unlocking the golden achievement of bliss or whatever. ℒife isn't *about* anything at all. It's simply ℒife. It's more productive to think in terms of what one *desires of* life, which we can comprehend through human wob that, recall, embodies four aspects: consciousness, personness, freedom, and proto-love (§ 3.3.2:284). Proto-love is a *Life* force from which arises all-caps LOVE, the base disposition of Ꝡuman in which we intrinsically comprehend ordinary, everyday lowercase-l love and all other emotion—happiness, say—that we feel ever inclined to seek. Every person naturally expresses human wob (thus proto-love, hence, LOVE) in life because *Life* with wob is all that Ꝡuman really is. This means one's elemental experience *in* life is of it being consistent *with* *Life* (human wob); every person yearns to experience their everyday life in harmony with proto-love wob thus LOVE, their base disposition. When one experiences this reality, one experiences the feeling of being satisfied in their situation whatever it may be. This experience is fundamental to the person. If one is going to assign an ultimate *something* to *Life*, then this is it. *Life*'s singular drive is simply to be *human*. When one is that, one experiences a profound harmony with *Life* he or she typically describes as satisfaction, which is happiness along with other feelings having more or less meaning according to the individual.

This is why mortality doesn't imbue meaning to life any more than having, pursuing, or achieving some "*categorical* desire" (Williams 1973, 86, io), and why there's intrinsically no purpose, goal, point, or meaning to *Life*. One goes amiss, however, to therefore conclude *Life* is purposeless, pointless, and meaningless because *Life* is *emergent*; it's fundamentally *individual*, not collective. We can't gaze upon the existence of the human race to divine a grand purpose or an intrinsic meaning to our being here, but only to *my* individuality *as* *Life* *with* human wob. El intuitively understood in a flash all of what I've spent nearly five years learning and writing. Her words to Ayako and me bear repeating. *There is no purpose to this life; you make your own purpose, that's what makes life beautiful.*

Taking a writing break, I'd just seated myself on my patio in New Mexico's bright, warm, high-altitude February sunshine in 50°F temps to figure out exactly what Mina wanted me to convey in this section regarding proto-love being the reason no one finds eternal life filled with boredom and ennui. A deep trembling arose throughout my body like I was freezing despite the Sun's hotly radiant heat. Variously asking Mina if I was feeling some unusual effect of the weather or of a spirit person and, if the latter, if it was malicious or friendly, he said Roman emperor Tiberius (d. AD 37) had arrived on my patio. Mina felt his story conveyed what I was trying to comprehend and had asked him to tell it to me. Tiberius goes by Kᴠᴠn—*kuun* (v=u=/w/), using modern Latin letters and pronounced 'k-wwn'—a Latin nickname bestowed by his slang-slinging boyhood friends, he said, to reference their opinion of his plum face.

Upon his death, Kuun found himself alone in the 'reflective' environment. An entry 'angel' (Table 17:523) arrived about five minutes later and showed him the 'portal' to physical-born spirit world where Romans hung out, where he could be around people he knew and feel cultural kinship. He carried on with "life as usual" to the degree he could in that environment for about 700 Earth years where he and other past rulers were accepted as such by about 90% of the spirit population in that area. It felt to him like a painfully long 150-year physical lifetime, and he found himself progressively bored and unhappy. He fell into a profound weariness with life, a melancholic apathy he couldn't shake regardless the diversions he tried. He tried killing himself twice but, as he bodily re-Intentionalized each time, he concluded that avenue wasn't available to one's "actual self."[487] Kuun thereafter embarked on a wandering through the areas of spirit world he found readily accessible, hoping to stumble into something or someone to relieve his pain. Eventually, he met a Mesoamerican man from around 3,500 BC who described how to travel to "better"—'higher frequency' (§ 1.2.3.3.2:472)—areas. Taking up the adventure, he made friends of those he stayed with and observed, making them into his unwitting teachers on other ways one can live life. In time, he discovered the human being as a person, then eventually human wob in the sense of fundamental attributes he could distinguish and discern as common to everyone. This was proto-love, which he termed *animans*—not in the sense Romans saw it as animating life as we've described *Life* force animating one's physical embodiment, but in terms of the psyche—that he perceived as a force that brought life to the mind, enlivening the self with a *joie de vivre*. Realizing this, he knew he was—had always been—out of touch with his own mind, his own self, and that this was the font of his ennui.

He began practicing with *animans* as a force he could raise in himself by caring about himself, which meant accepting *as reality* the harm he'd inflicted *on* himself *through* inflicting harm on others. This eventually helped him discover he could forgive himself. In this way, he experienced healing not through Mina as we've described throughout but a self-healing of the kind typical of Emotion Code. He *felt* healed, not only of what he now accepted as his past crimes, but of despondency, too. Kuun felt his epiphanies clear his way to relating with others without inflicting harm, caring about *them* instead of only himself where, previously, a relationship for him was

---

487. He was unaware he could enter an indeterminate unconscious state like an extended sleep (§ 3.3:283) to escape his suffering until, unexpectedly, the Big Healing opened the spirit population to their hitherto unknown capabilities.

always a one-sided transaction instead of a mutual experience. As he developed such relationships, his ennui dissipated over about 150 years until he realized that nothing about eternity could ever be boring so long as he was in these sorts of relationships. New or old didn't matter because he found them always interestingly variant. This was his renewed life and experience until Mina healed universal humanity of the NCC's effects in 2017. He'd then felt so "word-defyingly marvelous" that he realized in shock he wasn't as self-healed as he'd imagined.

Kuun now wanted the same healing for the suffering he suddenly found so odiously obvious post-Big Healing which had previously gone unnoticed like "a broken bone masking a severed tendon." He knew that sort of healing was only available from whoever had just healed everyone. He'd long ago concluded the gods—any divinity—were fake, so however he'd just been healed must've originated with a human being of *some* sort. He'd never discovered spirit persons could communicate in Thought without speech,[488] so he verbally called out for additional healing to this person, whomever and wherever he, she, or maybe even *it* was. Mina 'heard' Kuun as an awareness of his proto-energy since Mina's awareness is always everywhere in and about our universe. He 'heard' Kuun's Thought focused on Mina even though Kuun had no concept of who, what, or where Mina was. Mina's subconscious awareness filtered into his conscious thinking–feeling as we've already described in that he felt an 'intuition' of being called—hearing one's name on the wind as it were—and he "zeroed in on the energy signature" to find Kuun, he says, in $\sim 10^{-44}$ second. They struck up a friendship; Kuun was the only physical-born spirit person to respond to Mina for the first six months post-Big Healing (cf. Muhammad § 40:616).

Unembodied or embodied, eternal life doesn't convey any mystical *meaning* to life. It's simply *L*ife. The very *same* *L*ife we're living here on Earth. Meaning is that which one attaches to their experience of it. Of all that we experience *as* *L*ife, the wob from which arise our greatest satisfactions, thus enduring, engaging, interests, is proto-love. It was here that Kuun found *L*ife infinitely piquant. Love instantiates in proto-love and brings infinite variability to every experience, but especially in our relationships with others. It is, therefore, infinitely meaningful to the individual. In this resides the *meaning* one ascribes to individual experience or to *L*ife generally.

3.5.5.5 Relationships

The reason relationships nix the presumption that eternity is the tedium of necessity is that relationships aren't 'relationships' at all but proto-energy 'entanglements' (§ 6.11.3:197). We've heretofore experienced relationships not as *what* they are but *how* they present (much the same way neuroscience analyzes mind as brain; § 1.2.2.2:254), meaning a relationship as an activity, or English moral philosopher Bernard Williams' (d. 2003) "unconditional, or . . . *categorical* desire (Williams, ibid). By activity, we mean a relationship's outward appearance as spousal, friendly, collegial, argumentative, bête noire, casual, sexual, ad infinitum. Hence, it seems hardly sensible to imagine relationships in this context never ending in dreary monotony, thus rendering eternal life interminable, since they certainly do so in our physical experience. But that's how a relationship *presents*. What it *is* differs considerably, being a node of intersection (§ 3.5.2:486) between pairwise existents which fundamentally *are* (emergent self-aware) proto-energy. Such a relationship *is* 'entangling' proto-energy, which is a property of having awareness.

For example, a nodality—one of two existents in relationship (ibid)—has awareness of another existent for whatever reason—perhaps a dog sees a squirrel or a person thinks of another—and in that awareness 'entangles' with the other *as* proto-energy whereby two nodalities arise, thus a node, hence relationship. Neither need have conscious awareness of the other for 'entanglement.' When your mind for instance runs on an old, lost friend on a different continent, the two of you have already 'entangled' as proto-energy (*Fig. 168*). If the friend is sufficiently sensitive, your name or memory might pop into their mind as if out of the blue and they'll wonder why. With humans, we're talking about self-aware proto-energy, so Thought—the force of Thought (§ 3.5.2:486; ibid)—'entangles' as well. Your lost friend might thereby sense where your mind's at regarding your old relationship. The greater the awareness of one's self-aware proto-energy self, the greater one's sensitivity to 'entanglement' (relationship).

Saddled with poor mind–brain integration and generally unaware of the reality in which we live, with mindsets blotting out what sensitivity and awareness we do possess, physical humanity is profoundly lacking in relationship. Sure, we know each other, interact, raise families, work at common goals, and so forth, but these relationships *as activities* are mere ghosts of 'entanglement,' apparitions people call relationships that aren't

---

488. Physical persons communicate this way only via their spirit selves, as the brain isn't mind (§ 1.2.2:253).

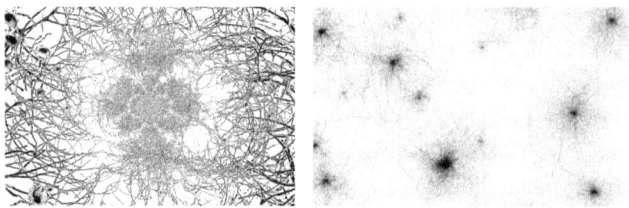

Figure 168. Left, visualized self-aware proto-energy connections in EPL; right, interconnected clusters (§ 3.5.2:486) and when, for example, Person A thinks about Person B.

real. That's why relationships, as we've narrowly known them, are so *infrequently* constructive, satisfying, and nourishing yet so *frequently* destructive, debilitating, and unsatisfying. When one considers the viability of eternal life from our ignorant perspective on relationships, it's hardly surprising we imagine every activity— "*categorical* desire" (Williams, ibid)—necessarily exhausts itself until nothing's left but an unrequited yearning for suicide, leading us to fool ourselves into thinking *death* makes *life* meaningful, which is like saying the faster one eats the more delicious the taste.

Unlike *doing*, such as activity, and *being*, as with our fundamental human WOB of autonomy and its corollary WOB of consciousness, personness, and freedom (in and of themselves not vectors for infinite interest), satisfaction with eternity lies with proto-love—our fourth corollary WOB wherein LOVE, love, and feeling originates (§ 3.3.2:284)—and our secondary pairwise WOB in which originates the 'entanglement' we call relationships. Mike and Molly individually craved connection and recognized, and interacted with each other, as and in proto-energy, deriving profound satisfaction in their 'entanglement' (§ 2.1:305), and every human follows suit. Relationship through 'entanglement' brings one the experience of satiety, interest, freshness, engagement, and so forth which affects one's mind conceptually similar to the many states of consciousness people pursue via psychotropic drugs. This isn't to say relationship ('entanglement') is a way to drug up oneself to get through eternity. On the contrary, 'entanglement' and its effect, which we call relationship, is a fundamental inevitability of ℒife. It affects us at our most primal: our ℒife self. The infinity of relationship intrinsic of 'entanglement' means not only that a relationship is never the same at any given moment, such that it declines into tedium, but that its proto-energy satisfies and engages so fundamentally ad infinitum that no individual ever gets enough in that any more would just be a bore. Every 'entangling' experience is its own 'high' that's endlessly and winsomely variable.

3.5.5.6 THE MEGAVERSE, BUILDING A UNIVERSE, AND UNEMBODIMENT

Eternal ℒife isn't limited simply to *our* universe. It extends to the megaverse and ultimately to All Existence itself. We experience ℒife as our emergent *self* whether unembodied or embodied. Unembodiment is its own kind of existence, uniquely replete with infinite possibility, yet nonetheless rooted in the 'entanglement' of relationship, a constant of pairwise ℒife. The unembodied have full awareness of embodiment and many, such as Cosmo (§ 1.2.1.1:338; § 2.2.1.1:341), alternate between the two.

The ultimate (so far) in customizing one's experience of ℒife is building a universe. It's not an easy task to master, that's certainly true (§ 2.1.3:309; § 2.1:340), but achieving it opens new possibilities never before imagined.[489] For example, about 0.05% of extant universes are so out of the box that no one previously imagined their possibility until someone Intentionalized each one into reality. One can't avoid Energent or human WOB, of course (§ 2.1.5:313). But the truth is, no one, not even the Cardinal, has any meaningful notion of just how infinitely variant the expressions of human WOB can be. This means there isn't any sense that one can ever truly *know* all there is to know such that one has achieved ultimate knowledge. Human imagination through Intentionality literally precludes such limitation. Neither does the Cardinal have any substantive confidence that what megaversal humanity has thus far achieved through interacting with All Existence is all it *can* do. Ultimately, eternal ℒife necessarily excludes boredom unless one *chooses* it.

---

489. Not just in terms of a built universe, but in the way it fundamentally alters one's depth of 'entanglement' (Parity), mindset, and awareness–experience (*enimerótis–empeiría*; § 2.1.4:394), which we don't address in this book. This is why Mina (like Mike and Molly; § 2.1:305) is 𝔥uman the same as us yet, at the same time, so very different.

Chakras

EVERYTHING HUMANITY THINKS it knows about chakras is inaccurate. It's not that ancient thinkers got chakras wholly wrong but rather misinterpreted what underlies them in the context of material reality. This chapter describes chakras as they are and work in accord with energy testing (ET) instead of sensed, imagined, dreamed, or cut from whole cloth. Even if you're well versed in chakras, prepare yourself nonetheless to jettison most of what you think you know about them. As you master ET, you can validate and clarify what you glean from this chapter as well as expand the ET community's overall knowledge base. Section 1 describes chakras and Section 2 the aura.

SECTION 1
What are Chakras

Although the Sanskrit term *chakra* meaning 'wheel,' 'circle,' or 'spinning disk' creates an inaccurate impression, we use it for familiarity and clarity. The concept arose with the sense our body was more than our physical senses let on. It's been long used to explain nebular embodiment in terms of centers or points of energy in the body (typically associated with major organs and nerve plexuses where we tend to feel emotional or spiritual energy) that has meaning for consciousness, spiritual and physical well-being, and development. The actual 'energy' in question has been, until now, inscrutable. We begin by summarizing chakras in the historical context and then describe them in reality.

1.1 CHAKRAS HISTORICALLY

Eastern and Western chakra traditions vary considerably. The latter appears a rather poor summation of the former though both agree the chakra is an energy center in the body that opens awareness to the spirit. The tradition appears to date back to the *Upanishads*, a seventh century BC Hindu metaphysical sacred text. It exists in the tantric traditions of Buddhism and Jainism, but reaches farther back into history's ancient shadows. We trace it to Humanity 2.0's third generation about 50KYA (§ 2.1.3:543). Early investigators perceived via dreams, intuition, and psychotropic mindstates that 'energy' moved throughout the human body from a broad 'energy' front outside the body, like an 'energy bath,' to small portals, or 'energy' nexuses, in the body. They visualized its movement into the body as vortical, circulatory, laminar, or gated flow singularly or combined, and in time embraced vortical circularity.

Chakras in Eastern traditions are of the *subtle* body, meaning mind, intellect, and ego as in the *Bhagavad Gītā*, but which, along with the *causal* body, references the *self* that, as we've learned, is really emergent self-aware proto-energy (*Life*; § 1.2.1.1:248). The value of chakras as conceptual structures eventually transmuted to points of 'installation' for mantras and deity-energies in the subtle body that control the physical body. This is a process of visualizing a mantric syllable in a particular location in a particular chakra of one's energy body while silently intoning its sound, which Sanskrit-based traditions considered an especially powerful vibration that could achieve a desired spiritual goal through its practiced use. Chakras in Western (Euro-American) traditions, or those so influenced, are less meditative and more occultist. The former means influenced by Sanskrit sources and yogic practices using variant chakra systems. The latter means influenced by chakras as an existential fact, as real structures physiologically located in the body correlating with psychological states, health conditions, foods, minerals, elements, and so forth in accord with a mainly seven-chakra system (*Fig. 169*). Either way, chakra traditions assert that by interacting in whatever way one's practice prescribes, one can comprehend and achieve spiritual enlightenment, greater health, wisdom, happiness, grand purpose, and the like.

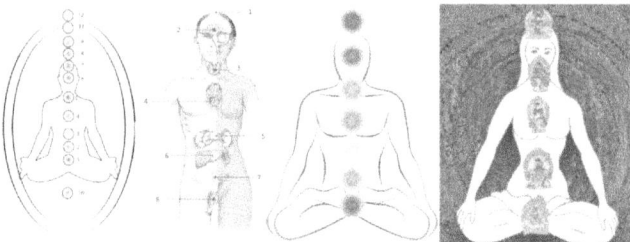

Figure 169. Examples of twelve-, eight-, seven-, and five-chakra systems.₂₈₁

Chakras have nothing to do with any of that. They don't embody the beliefs, emotions, or memories of specific aspects, or in toto, of one's life. There are no 'upper' and 'lower' chakras relating to spiritual matters like higher consciousness, truth, intuition, or purpose and earthly matters like sex, power, or survival. Neither does the heart chakra bridge them with love, empathy, and compassion. They neither control nor manipulate albeit do influence the body. Such understandings are *perception*, not *reality*.

1.2 Charkas as They Are in Reality

Chakras are a physicospirit embodiment phenomenon. They repose in the 'reflective' body, not the physical, subtle, etheric, spirit, or other bodies. They're Living force (§ 1.3.1:272) 'energy centers' integrating one's physical body, spirit (*Life*) self, and the 'reflective' environment (§ 7.1.1.1:212). *All living things* have chakras, from microbes and plants to insects and animals (§ 2.2:513). In this book, we describe only those of the human body. There are no major or minor chakras but simply *chakras* and *aura*, seven of the former and 24 segmented plus one whole-body of the latter (§ 2.1.1:510).

1.2.1 The Chakras

Chakras establish the necessary integrated mind experience with the 'reflective' environment exclusive of the human body itself. They integrate the body with what's external to it. One's emergent *Life* self integrates the natural environment *as* their physical body via the chakras *as* *Life* force and Living force, which we describe below as *mind* and *body* chakras, respectively.

1.2.1.1 Mind Chakras

Recall that *Life* force is immaterial self-aware proto-energy that is *Life*, the Human person (§ 1.2:246; § 1.2.3.3.3:472). The *immaterial* (supranatural, spirit) individual can't directly experience *material* (natural, physical) reality. Molly dreamed of it and with Mike (§ 2:304) discovered its principles and means by which *Life* self integrates material environments (§ 2.1.3:309) that resulted in today's human norm described throughout this book. Mind–brain integration means mind integrates brain. The emergent *Life* person suffuses the physical body like an 'avatar' (cf. *Avatar*, 2009), having awareness–experience of environment *in the context of the body* as though one-and-the-same entity (§ 2.1.4:394). Integration happens via one's *Life* force suffusing the physical body via three *mind chakras*: the traditionally named *crown*, *third eye* (here, corrected to *pons*), and *root* chakras that altogether integrate the body and brain with *Life* force whereby mind–brain integration occurs.[490] Seventy percent of *Life* force integrates the brain via the pons chakra (§ 1.2.1.3.2:502) and the other 30% via the root chakra (§ 1.2.1.3.7:507).

---

490. For example, upon fertilization when a physical body first instantiates to trigger emergent *Life* (§ 1.2.1.1.1:248), it has aliveness in accord with Living force alone. Thereafter, *Life* force—the person—limitedly integrates via its aura until the pons chakra arises ~7

1.2.1.2 Body Chakras

Recall Living force is *non*-self-aware proto-energy (Energent; § 1.3.1:272) suffusing our universe as Energent–prime suffuses All Existence (§ 1:112). On its own it doesn't rise to aliveness, which is nonhuman, since only ♄uman is ℒife. A person—a universe builder—needs Intentionalize proto-energy *as* Living force. Thus, it's Intentionalized proto-energy, meaning aliveness arises in human Intentionality, not mysteriously in abiogenetic chemistry (§ 1.3.1:272). We thus experience *humanness*, not to mention personify it, in everything alive. Except for humans, all that we consider alive is because of a universe's builder. Once Intentionalized as wob, Living force is always there just as, once Intentionalized, a universe is. Howsoever a Living entity reproduces and evolutionarily develops over time (§ 2.1.5.5.2:323), Living force—present wherever proto-energy is, which like a universe and All Existence, too, is everywhere—suffuses it generation to generation.

While proto-energy 'flows' in, through, and around pairwise archí to suffuse matter–Energy—mE; from which arises real energy Υ expressing as Fundamental Force (FF) and applied energy E, including chemistry (§ 2:114)—only certain entities having the way of being (wob; § 2.2.1.1:234) of aliveness integrate Living force. A rock doesn't, but a microbe does. Living force is simply proto-energy a builder Intentionalizes to interact with mE in a certain way, resulting in the properties and state of existence called aliveness and life. An entity having this wob—cockroach, dog, human body—integrates Living force in two distinct ways, first via *suffusion* just as proto-energy suffuses all mE—rocks and raccoons alike—and second via *body chakras*, which vary in number according to the entity. Let's consider them.

1.2.1.2.1 How Living Force Integrates a Physical Entity

Via suffusion. As an Intentionalized expression of Energent proto-energy, Living force permeates the universe and its mE. As proto-energy suffuses mE—it experiences real energy Υ, FF, and applied energy E (inclusive of chemistry) as the direct expression of FF through applied energy E, whereby mE coalesces from pairwise archí to all manner of complex archí structures observed in nature as matter—the Intentionality that *is* Living force suffuses mE at the same time. Complex archí structures having the wob of aliveness respond to Living force, thereby exhibiting the properties of being alive. Those without it—inanimate objects—don't respond.

Via body chakras. Recall the natural environment 'reflects' in the 'reflective' environment such that every physical existent has a 'reflective' form (*Fig. 170*, left; § 7.1.1.1:212). This is the only means by which a spirit person can 'physically' interact with the natural environment. When spirit persons visit Earth, this is the environment in which they experience it and vice versa. It works this way for humans because our spirit body integrates our physical body, and via this 'reflected' physicospirit embodiment we interact with spirit persons in the 'reflective' environment. Except for certain companion animals (ch. 39:601), Living entities simply 'reflect' in the 'reflective' environment and this includes the human *body* as the so-called etheric body.

Living force contextualized in the 'reflective' environment integrates the physical entity's 'reflective' body at specific points of resonance between the Living force *suffused* in the natural environment and the Living force in the 'reflective' environment. The physical body in the natural environment integrates Living force *there* via suffusion since it permeates every pairwise archí of the entity. Its 'reflective' body in the 'reflective' environment integrates Living force in that context via specific *resonant 'energy' points* correlating to specific areas of the physical body such as nerve plexuses, major organs, and other areas (*Fig. 170*, right; The Aura, § 2:509). Living force in the 'reflective' environment has resonance with Living force at specific points on the 'reflective' body in accord with the proto-energy 'frequency' rising in the interaction of Living force and the mE of a nerve plexus, major organ, or other relevant area.

Living force in the 'reflective' environment thus integrates only at these resonant 'energy' points in accord with each one's Living force 'frequency'–resonance (FR). Recall that proto-energy infinitely segments into 'frequency' striations (§ 2.2:356). Living force, as an Intentionalized expression of proto-energy, similarly has infinite 'frequency' in that, when Living force permeating the 'reflective' environment encounters natural environment Living force of a 'density' sufficient to establish a resonance, thus a 'frequency,' it 'gravitates' into that 'density' locus; its 'frequency' *is* that FR (recall there's no *becoming* w.r.t. to proto-energy, only *is*-ness). We call such 'density' loci ('energy' points) on the body *chakras*. This is what ancient investigators sensed, wanted

hours after conception (birth of emergent ℒife), with the rest of the chakras and segmented aura following later.

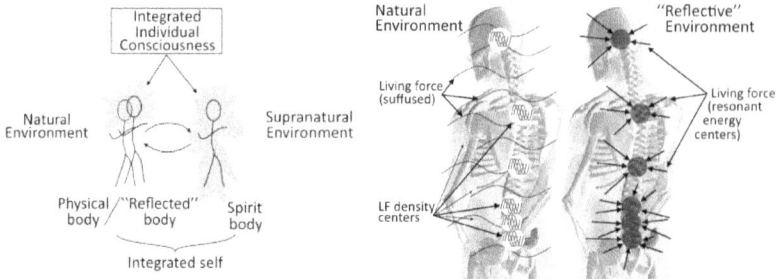

Figure 170. Left, physical-'reflective'-spirit bodies integrate across the natural, 'reflective,' and supranatural environments; right, suffused Living force at resonant energy points.₂₈₂

to know and experience, and nascently developed in the various yogic disciplines. Each 'density' locus, or chakra, has its own FR in accord with its 'density.' These arise in the magnitude, expression, and intensity of its interaction with the particular area of the entity's mE and correspond with each chakra's behavior (§ 1.2.1.3:501). The Living force interaction in this context that people call chakras is not part of the physical body itself, but its 'reflection' in the 'reflective' environment that's akin to albeit different from the yogic tradition's subtle body.

Both ℒife and Living force enter the physical body through its 'reflection' via the root and pons chakras but, as the former is emergent self-aware proto-energy and the latter non-self-aware proto-energy, there's no logical correlation. Each enters the body via the same albeit dimensionally differentiated gates, although one need make this distinction with caution; we're not talking *dimension* at all in the scientific or mathematic senses such as with x, y, z axes or time and the like. While not a part or aspect of the physical body, chakras do integrate it with the 'reflective' environment and, therefore, anything therein, including spirit persons. The result of 'reflective' environment Living force entering into and interacting with each 'density' locus—chakra—is what we term *chakra energy*, which we describe next.

1.2.1.2.2 WHAT IS CHAKRA ENERGY

Chakras only have meaning in the context of the natural environment by integrating the physical body with it. They aren't magical portals to spiritual enlightenment, oneness with the Eternal, or perfect health. It's more productive to think of chakras in toto as a specialized organ no different from, and just as necessary as, any other organ and having a twofold purpose. First, they integrate the body with the natural environment in a way the physical senses rooted in neural impulses can't. Second, it thereby integrates ℒife (the self integrating the body) with the natural environment inclusive of the 'reflective' environment wherein a physicospirit person can interact via ET or their spirit self with the spirit selves of other physically alive persons as well as with spirit persons visiting from, or presently in, spirit world.

The 'energy' of a chakra is biological 'energy'[491] arising in Living force interacting with mE as described. It's similar to the way real energy ϒ arises in the interaction of proto-energy with mE. Chakra energy is, in a sense, the 'FF' of the Living body just as actual FF is of the universe. Chakra 'FF' constitutes the chakra version of applied energy E, which determines the behavior of our body vis-à-vis everything in the 'reflective' environment inclusive of spirit persons. It also exerts the 'energy' of what the physically embodied person thinks–feels and awareness–experiences (*enimerótis–empeiría*; § 2.1.4:394) as a physicospirit person. This 'energy' is 'visible' in the sense it is felt–perceived by spirit persons in the 'reflective' environment as well as by any physical entity 'reflected' therein, from microbe to monkey; they feel–perceive the physically alive's chakra energy as it interacts with the 'reflective' environment's proto-energy (its Living force). Thereby, they feel–perceive the physicospirit person's SOB–SOA[492] inclusive of thoughts and feelings—essentially, how energy testing works (§ 2:625)—and nonhuman physical entities can feel–perceive aspects of bodystate—mindstate in accord with their capacity. The latter is the reason a dog, for instance, can sense a person's mood, malice, love, or illness and respond accordingly. The Hindu concept of *kundalini*—a Sanskrit term derived from *kundalin*, meaning 'circular,' or 'annular,' and as a noun meaning 'snake' in the sense of 'coiled' energy at the base of the spine—is, in actuality, Living force.

491. Bio-energy, Odic force, and other energies described by New Age woo-woo that aren't figments are real energy ϒ that fall under this umbrella term but aren't applied energy E (electromagnetic radiation, etc.).

492. State(s) of being SOB and state(s) of awareness SOA (§ 1.2.1.1:248).

1.2.1.2.3 CHAKRAS AS 'ANTENNAS'

Some chakras have an 'antenna' capability; it 'receives' and 'broadcasts' chakra energy from or to the 'reflective' environment giving individuals extrasensory awareness–experience of their external-to-body environment beyond mere somatic sensation. The 'antenna' operates via the *aura*, which is like a 'skin organ' that individuates the 'reflective' body in the environment. Living force resonates with physically alive entity mindstate–bodystate. Let's consider the 'antenna' function.

Receiving antenna. The aura experiences Living force in the 'reflective' environment like physical skin its natural environment. Whereas skin resonates physically as a collection of action potentials (neural impulses) arising in sensory neurons responding to temperature, air movement, radiant heat, or injury, the aura responds to the many 'reflective' Living force FR by resonating with each. Its resonance translates Living force FR outside the body to inside similar to the way a tuning fork resonates with another tuning fork across intervening air.

Chakras are intrinsically 'tuned' via WOB to resonate with certain chakra energy 'frequencies.' The part of the aura local to a particular chakra resonates only with that chakra's FR. When such local aspect of the aura resonates with Living force outside the 'reflective' body, the chakra *inside*, that's local to that aspect of the aura, resonates with it and converts chakra energy flowing into the chakra's toroidal 'energy' structure to that FR, which then exits the chakra having taken on that resonance (Fig. 179:509, Fig. 181:513). The individual self in turn now has awareness–experience of Living force FR outside the body such as mindstate–bodystate of the collection of physically alive entities local to the person, one's awareness–experience of which is beyond mere somatic sense.

Broadcasting Antenna. The aura local to a chakra having chakra energy 'broadcasting' capability uniquely resonates with that chakra's FR, which it excretes in measured amounts over variant time into the 'reflective' environment similar to skin sweating, both of which are ways in which the 'reflective' and physical body, respectively, maintain their own version of homeostasis in the environment. In this way, other physically alive entities have awareness–experience of the individual's mindstate–bodystate. The aura local to a chakra without this capability resonates instead with the FR of whole-body chakra energy, meaning the chakra energy FR defining the particular body.

1.2.1.3 DESCRIPTION OF INDIVIDUAL CHAKRAS

What we call a chakra is a resonant 'energy' point arising in Living force in the context of the 'reflective' environment 'gravitating' into 'energy density' loci in the 'reflective' body corresponding with nerve plexuses, major organs, and other relevant areas (auras; § 2:509). Each chakra expresses a behavior partially correlating with the 'energy' center it embodies. Altogether, there are seven chakras. Three integrate 𝓛ife force (crown, pons—formerly, third eye—and root) and six Living force (pons, lung—formerly, throat—heart, solar plexus, lumbar—formerly, sacral—and root). The latter second through fifth *conceptually* mimic the functionality of the physical organs to which they're adjacent. Except for the pons chakra, all chakras center in the spinal column. This isn't due to intrinsic integration of the spinal cord or adjacent body parts, but as 'energy' loci where the spine is the central-most 'energy-dense' aspect. Chakras don't form an 'energy' funnel or vortex, but function toroidally within the body (§ 1.2.1.4:508). People imagine, intuit, or dream spinning, swirling, vortical energy in their awareness–experience of, and effort to analogize, only small aspects of toroidal 'energy' flow. As a vague perception, it can seem like these flow structures. Chakra energy has no visual aspect. It's awareness–experience of mind, not a sensory perception. We describe chakras below.

1.2.1.3.1 CROWN CHAKRA

Type: 𝓛ife force.
Purpose: Nexus for mind–brain integration.
Location: Embodies the central posterior aspect of the corpus callosum (that connects the left and right hemispheres of the brain), the body and commissure of fornix, and the anterior commissure (*Fig. 171*, left).

The crown chakra is what the girls and I imagined as a Spiritual Unblocker Gland (SUG) enabling the physically alive person to have awareness–experience of spirit aspects of self, human and nonhuman others, and spirit world. In the early days, we thought of it as the magical way one's spirit eyes and ears work to see, hear, and intuit spirit world. In truth, the crown chakra *is* mind–brain integration (§ 1.2.2:253). It's

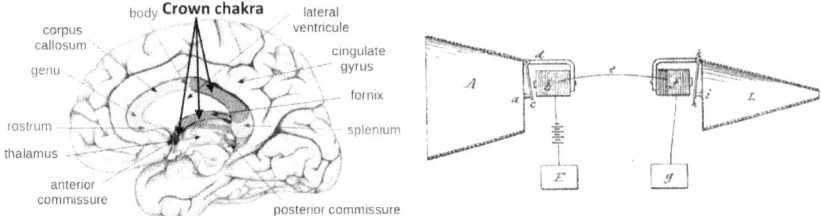

Figure 171. Left, crown chakra location shown as dark grey overlay; right, figure from A.G. Bell's 1876 telephone patent where *A* is analogous to brain, *I* to mind, *a–k* and *E* to mind–brain transliteration.[283]

the ℒife force gateway by which one's awareness–experience and thinking–feeling—the self-aware proto-energy self (§ 5.1:295)—*transliterates* to the neural impulses the brain processes and communicates to the body, conceptually similar to spoken language transliterating from analog electrical impulses or digital sequences a telephone listener can hear and comprehend (*Fig. 171*, right).

It's no surprise that ancient thinkers located the seat of reality, perception, thought, intuition, and the like in the forebrain–forehead, pituitary, and pineal areas and called it the third eye. They ignored the crown chakra for this role because, in their mindset, the body was earthly, hence despicable, whereas ethereal mind, one's true self, was spirit, thus holy. The ancient view the crown chakra represents a spiritual connection to oneself, others, the universe, enlightenment, and the divine, however inaccurate, does nonetheless accurately image the spirit-self–physical-self connection that we term mind–brain integration. In the context of The Corruption, improving one's mind–brain integration through developing awareness of, and experience with, the crown chakra is indeed a type of enlightenment. The third eye and crown chakras of ancient tradition are really one and the same in terms of purpose and effect. The crown chakra is ℒife force only—*prana* and *chi* in ancient tradition, the Sanskrit and Chinese terms for breath, life force, vital principle, cosmic energy—and integrates ℒife and physical embodiment. Unlike the other chakras, the crown is not a toroidal 'energy' structure. It's simply a *locus* of ℒife force.

1.2.1.3.2 PONS (THIRD EYE) CHAKRA

Type: ℒife force and chakra energy.
Purpose: Integrates brain and ℒife–Living force.
Location: Embodies the pons and the cerebellar peduncle of the brainstem (*Fig. 172*, left).

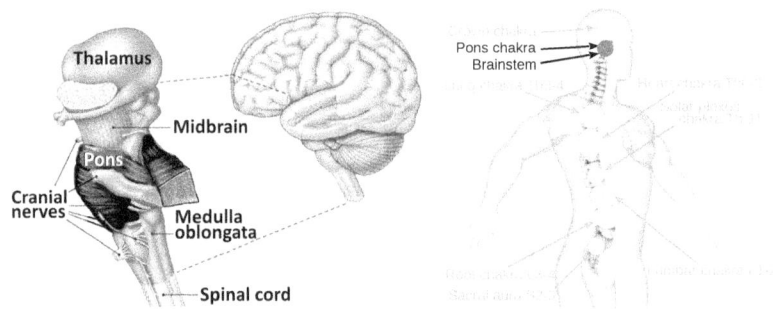

Figure 172. Left, pons chakra shown as dark grey overlay; right, brainstem and pons chakra.[284]

The so-called third eye area is the wrong position for this chakra. It embodies not the pituitary or pineal glands but the *pons* of the brainstem. There are two reasons it's in this location. First, it foundationally integrates the brain with ℒife force from just after conception (FN 490:499) and situates where ℒife force most concentrates in permeating the body. Second, the pons situates at the head of the spine antipodal to the root chakra near its base as the body's other ℒife force and chakra energy 'portal' (*Fig. 172*, right; § 1.2.1.3.7:507). It associates with the cervical nerve plexus at the C1–C5 vertebrae, meaning the plexus *responds to* the pons chakra's energy. We describe its two aspects as follows.

Life force aspect. The pons (and root chakra) integrates Life force which, recall, expresses emergent self-aware proto-energy, the person's Life self—*you*. Life force is how our Living body integrates Human instead of simply being animal (§ 1.2.2:253). One's physicospirit body integrates Life force via their spirit body which spatially situates with the physical body; the spirit and physical bodies are 'attached' in the sense they integrate the same space in the natural and 'reflective' environments. Recall from earlier that chakras are 'energy' centers arising in the physical body drawing Living force in the context of the 'reflective' environment. When the pons (and root) chakra of the 'reflective' body integrates the spirit body's same space, the physical body integrates Life force at whatever capacity the individual desires. Usually, it's in accord with mindset albeit The Corruption's effect limits Life force integration to the absolute bare minimum to sustain the body's life. This is why it ages, diseases, heals poorly, and needs food.

When the spirit body spatially de-integrates the physical body, Life force integration concomitantly degrades. The farther one's spirit body spatially is from the physical, the progressively less Life force the latter integrates and, consequently, begins dying. The farther apart or longer in time the pons (or root) chakra spatially de-integrates, the more the physical body winds down like a battery until the pons (or root) chakra spatially re-integrates or the body dies. Unlike with nonhumans, Living force alone can't sustain the human body's aliveness absent Life force; it's designed only to integrate emergent Life. This is one reason Mina advises against astral projection (§ 1:591) in The Corruption's milieu, as it spatially de-integrates physicospirit embodiment.

Chakra energy aspect. The pons (and root) chakra does with Living force what its other aspect does with Life force. Recall from earlier that Life force and Living force are two different proto-energies, the former being self-aware proto-energy emergently arising as Life 'in' Energent proto-life (EPL; § 2.3.2.1:241), and the latter an Intentionalized expression of non-self-aware Energent proto-energy. Each proto-energy is of a different FR and doesn't 'cross-connect' in any way. Living force integrates the pons as chakra energy (§ 1.2.1.2.2:500) which in turn integrates the brain–body. This aspect of the pons chakra has no other purpose than supplying the physical body with chakra energy, as with ET (§ 2.2.1.1:626). As the third eye chakra doesn't exist except in a conceptual (perceived) sense as an aspect of the crown chakra, the associations yogic and Western traditions make regarding its relationship with the physical body and its psychological and other states are wholly inaccurate.

1.2.1.3.3 LUNG (THROAT) CHAKRA

Type: Chakra energy.
Purpose: Integrates the person with chakra energy in the 'reflective' environment.
Location: Embodies the T3–T4 spinal vertebrae (*Fig. 173*).

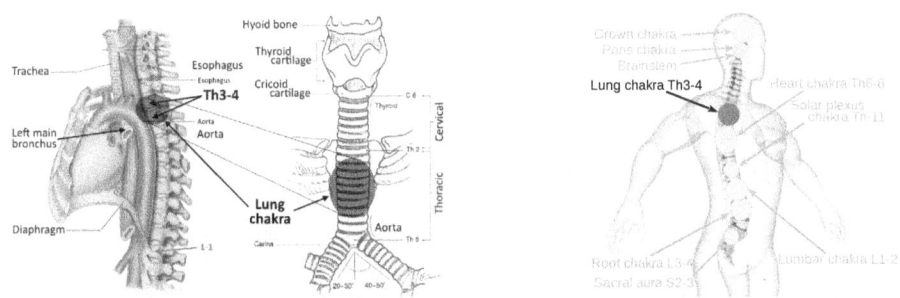

Figure 173. Lung (throat) chakra shown as grey overlay; from left: lateral, anterior, and perspective views.[285]

The throat area is the wrong position for this chakra, as it's located adjacent to the trachea in the thoracic cavity just above its bifurcation (the carina) into the left–right bronchia. The reason the chakra is in this location is that it synchronizes with respiration; accordingly, we term it the *lung* chakra. It associates with the cardiac nerve plexus located near the aortic arch and the carina of the trachea, meaning the plexus *responds to* the lung chakra's energy.

Inhaling, the chakra 'imbibes' Living force permeating the natural environment (§ 1.2.1.2.1:499; § 1.3:272). It enters the chakra's toroidal 'energy' structure (§ 1.2.1.4:508) and interacts with the body's *mE* whereby it expresses as chakra energy and integrates the body. Recall the person whose Life force integrates the body has awareness–experience of every archí structure and 'energy' constituting the body. As the chakra 'inhales,' the Living force permeating the local chakra energy environment suffuses the physical body. The 'inhaled' Living force exits the chakra toroid as chakra energy *of* the body. Consequently, the person has awareness–experience of the chakra energy of every local Living entity, including each local Living human physicospirit body, each of which integrates its own ℒife self. In this way, the physicospirit person has awareness–experience, and perceives the bodystate–mindstate, of other nearby persons which also 'entangles' them relationally in terms of Parity (§ 6.11.3:197; § 3.5.5.5:495). When the body exhales air, the *lumbar* chakra (§ 1.2.1.3.6:506) also 'exhales' its chakra energy, representing bodystate–mindstate, into the natural environment whereby other persons as well as nonhumans (according to capacity) have awareness-experience of their local Living force environment in, respectively, the same or similar way. In a sense, the lung–lumbar chakras are altogether a 'lung' that 'breathes' the natural environment's Living force. The lung–lumbar chakras altogether are a 'receiving–broadcasting antenna' (ibid).

Chakras are the reason humans (and nonhumans according to capacity) can perceive the subtlest aspects of existence for which physical sensory perception simply can't account. And, as the throat chakra doesn't exist, the notion it (much less the lung chakra) has anything to do with one's ability to communicate verbally, speak one's highest truth, and the like is inaccurate.

1.2.1.3.4 HEART CHAKRA

Type: Chakra energy.
Purpose: Circulates neutral proto-energy throughout body to heal effects of negative Living force.
Location: Embodies the T6–T8 spinal vertebrae (*Fig. 174*).

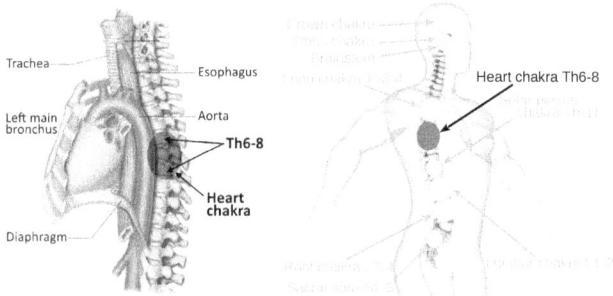

Figure 174. Heart chakra shown as grey overlay (source: Fig. 173, left).

Like the lung chakra, the heart chakra associates with the cardiac nerve plexus located near the aortic arch and the carina of the trachea, meaning the plexus *responds to* the heart chakra's energy. Since the human body constitutes of matter (mE) in the natural environment, it resonates exquisitely with its every nuance. Recall a person can Intentionalize proto-energy through Psyche Fundamental Force (PFF; § 3.2:282) to provoke a certain effect, as when Mina's sisters seeded The Corruption in our universe (§ 2.1.2.2:370) or an individual disturbs the body's metabolism (§ 1.3.3:474). Recall, too, the natural environment Intentionalizes as WOB, such as water's wetness or gravity's force.

There's a third way humans experience Intentionalized proto-energy, and it lies in nonhuman Living entities' perception of the natural environment. When nonhumans experience the natural environment in such a way as to Intentionalize proto-energy, then that Intentionality *is* a part of the proto-energy environment permeating our mE environment inclusive of the physical body. Just as a spirit person might Intentionalize disease in a physical body, or the physical person in their own body owing to mindset (§ 1.3.3.4:476), nonhuman Intentionality arises in the same PFF. The reasons are the same in accord with nonhuman capability, and always negatively, as nonhumans exclusive of companion animals (CH. 39:601) don't experience neutral emotive ℒife force (Emℒℱ; § 3.3.3.1.1:289). This means an elephant or even a cockroach *locally* Intentionalizes proto-energy—humans can *globally* Intentionalize proto-energy anywhere in our universe—when its awareness–experience of the natural environment provokes an Intentional exertion via Living thinking–feeling interaction with PFF. Other Living entities such as the human body encounter such negatively Intentionalized proto-energy that interacts with, and negatively affects, the body's metabolism. This is the reality behind humans and nonhumans sensing impending 'natural evil.'

Even without The Corruption, the presence of nonhuman Living entities ensures that proto-energy will ineluctably negatively Intentionalize and thereby harm anything Living, which necessarily includes the physical human body. Humans are ℒife, self-aware proto-energy having awareness–experience from which arises thinking–feeling, having emotion that's neutral or negative (§ 3.3.2.1:285). So-called positive emotion is simply our perception of *neutral* EmℒF in a Corrupted world of uniformly *negative* EmℒF. Nonhumans, not having ℒife, don't experience EmℒF but only a physiological SOB and SOA which coalesce as a response that, in some nonhumans, mimics EmℒF—the more complex the nonhuman, the more we personify EmℒF in its response—that we often mistake for real (human) emotion. Accordingly, the nonhuman SOB and SOA response to environment is only ever one that Intentionalizes proto-energy negatively.

Recall that ℒife force intrinsically arises in the WOB of ℒife. Living force, on the other hand, arises in the Intentionality intrinsic of our universe as an expression of proto-energy, the WOB Mina Intentionalized in building the former in accord with the emergent WOB of the latter. Ergo, a nonhuman doesn't Intentionalize proto-energy as a self-aware proto-energy human does but only that aspect of non-self-aware proto-energy enlivening it, Living force. As the human body is only a Living entity integrating ℒife, it's both subject to and an agent of Intentionalized Living force. Thus the body and person *integrating* it has awareness–experience of Intentionalized Living force harming the body, which even absent The Corruption is only ever negative. The heart chakra neutralizes this aspect of reality, as follows.

Just as the lung–lumbar chakras synchronize conceptually and physically with metabolic respiration, the heart chakra synchronizes with circulation. Cellular metabolism is always in a state of impending cessation absent blood circulation. From this perspective, the arrival of blood constitutes constant cellular healing. Although the chakras circulate chakra energy throughout the body from their locus of operation for the purpose of awareness–experience, with each chakra having its own proto-energy resonance (FR), only the heart chakra additionally circulates it as a *healing* force. Let's consider its mechanics.

Mechanics of the heart chakra. The physical heart contracts twice during a heartbeat in the systole and diastole phases, giving us the familiar *lub-dub* pulse of a normal rhythm. Similar with the lung chakra, the heart chakra draws in Living force that's Intentionalized—always negatively, recall—from the 'reflective' environment with the systole phase. It cycles through the chakra's toroidal 'energy' structure, expressing as *neutralized* chakra energy upon its exit during the diastole phase and integrating the body. A person has awareness–experience consequent of the heart chakra's 'systole' phase, thus, *is* a 'receiving antenna.' The heart chakra discriminates between Intentionalized and unIntentionalized Living force, as only Intentionalized does it resonate with the heart chakra's FR and 'gravitate' to it (§ 1.2.1.2.1:499). As neutralized chakra energy circulates in the body, its neutral WOB heals areas harmed by Intentionalized Living force integrating the body via the pons and root chakras (§ 1.2.1.3.2:502; § 1.2.1.3.7:507), though to a lesser degree than ℒife force. In this way, the body experiences constant, autonomous healing. Mindset can block it as it can ℒife force (§ 1.3.3.3:476).

Effects of the heart chakra. The Corruption means the heart chakra heals about 10% the harm effected by Intentionalized Living force, though it improves with conscious awareness of it. When consciously neutralizing Intentionalized Living force, one might feel pressure around the heart (chest) area that makes one want to take deep, expansive breaths, a feeling of a heavy weight seeming to compress it, or aspects of both. This awareness is one experiencing the heart chakra expressing greater than usual Intentionalized Living force as neutral chakra energy. Its residual feeling dissipates according to how intensely negative the Intentionalized Living force. The traditional notion the heart chakra has to do with love and compassion is wholly inaccurate, as the heart isn't the seat of feelings, love, or emotion but the mind, one's emergent ℒife self. Neither does it unite 'upper' chakras as 'higher' consciousness or spiritual matters with 'lower' chakras as base or earthly, fleshly matters.

1.2.1.3.5 SOLAR PLEXUS CHAKRA

Type: Chakra energy.
Purpose: Converts FR of pons and root chakra energy to whole-body FR.
Location: Embodies the T11 spinal vertebrae (*Fig. 175*).

The solar plexus chakra is adjacent to the physical body's stomach–liver structure because its purpose relates to that of those organs. It associates with the celiac (solar) nerve plexus located around the celiac trunk in the stomach–liver complex, meaning the plexus *responds to* the solar plexus chakra energy. The stomach takes

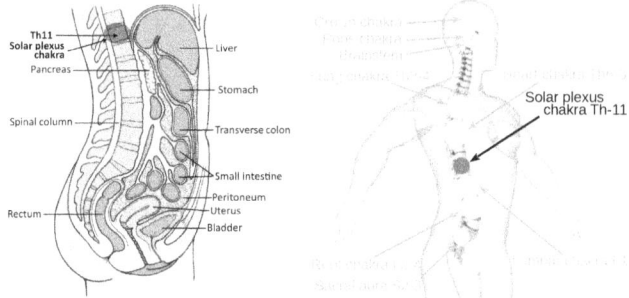

Figure 175. Solar plexus chakra shown as grey overlay.[286]

onboard and prepares ingestibles to integrate the body. The liver's three principal functions of detoxification, synthesis, and storage work in tandem with the stomach and the digestive system in general. As such, the functional purpose of the stomach–liver is to receive potential energy in the form of ingestible mE it then integrates *as* the digestive process whereupon the body metabolizes it.

In similar fashion, the solar plexus chakra receives whole-body chakra energy which, recall, is converted Living force (§ 1.2.1.2.2:500). Since the person's physical, thus 'reflective,' body is always in flux according to thinking–feeling, mood, physical health, and like factors then the FR of Living force interacting with its mE at any given moment is also in flux. As Living force integrates via toroidal 'energy' structures as chakra energy of the body's FR at that moment, the chakra energy's FR may be non-resonant with the body's own if its condition thus FR changed in the meantime. In such case, it's non-integrative and 'clashes' with the body, disrupting and harming it like pumping the wrong voltage through a delicate circuit. Changing conditions are inevitable in an environment of event periodicity (§ 2:114) and emergent *Life*. 'Clashing' FR resolves by the solar plexus chakra converting such chakra energy to the appropriate FR so that it resonates with the physical body. Accordingly, one's *Life* self has awareness–experience of the body's internal and external environment expressed through its chakra energy FR.

The pit-of-the-stomach brick, butterflies, gutwrench, knottedness, and similar sensations originate in this chakra and its local aura operating in relationship with the body's stomach–liver. As with all chakras, this one is part of mind–brain integration since *Life* integrating physical embodiment is *whole body* inclusive of brain. Mind integrates its awareness–experience of stomach–liver so you, the person, experiences it as thinking–feeling as well as physiologically centered in the solar plexus area; it arises in the gut area because its chakra energy concentrates there. The solar plexus chakra is integral to our physical self's ability to *have* relationship (not to having awareness–experience *of* relationship, which is only of *Life* mind). Traditions associating the solar plexus chakra with psychological states are inaccurate.

1.2.1.3.6   LUMBAR (SACRAL) CHAKRA

Type: Chakra energy.
Purpose: Integrates bodystate and mindstate with the natural environment's Living force.
Location: Embodies the L1–L2 spinal vertebrae (*Fig. 176*, left).

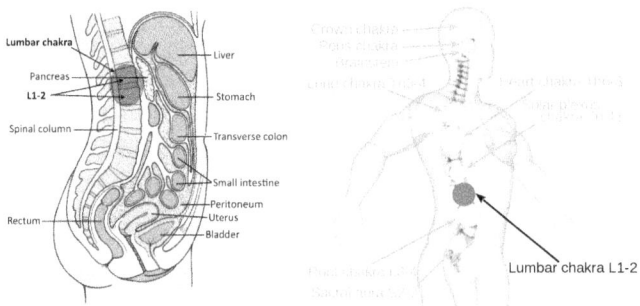

Figure 176. The lumbar (sacral) chakra shown as grey overlay in relation to the pancreas.[287]

The sacral area is the wrong position for this chakra, as it's located adjacent to the pancreas and therefore in the *lumbar* area. Counterintuitively, it associates with the sacral nerve plexus located at L4–S4 (the lower lumbar region to almost the base of the spine); the plexus *responds to* the lumbar chakra's energy. Let's consider the reason it's in this location and associates with the sacral plexus.

Location. The lumber chakra's functionality is similar to the pancreas, which performs no in-house function *of* but rather *for* the body in that it manufactures and exports exocrine and endocrine products *to* the body to enable other organs' functionality. Consequently, the lumbar chakra doesn't process chakra energy via its toroidal 'energy' structure as do the other major chakras (except the crown) to inform mind and body of its internal and external environment via FR. Instead, it exports these individuated FR (embodied in its whole-body chakra energy) to the 'reflective' environment via the aura such that self and body integrate the natural environment. It works in synchrony with the pancreas in that it's constantly—non-rhythmically—exporting bodystate–mindstate to the 'reflective' environment as with the pancreas vis-à-vis the body. In this respect, it's a 'broadcasting antenna.'

Associated plexus. The reason this chakra associates with the sacral instead of lumbar plexus is owing to the interconnection of the lumbar–sacral–coccygeal plexuses, i.e., the *lumbosacral* (including pudendal) plexus. Unlike other chakras, the lumbar chakra energy doesn't affect these plexuses (*Fig. 177*). Its functionality means other physically alive entities have awareness–experience of you and physically alive entities via their own chakra 'organs.' The reason for its functionality is so physical persons aren't somatically isolated—segregated—islands of embodiment, but have 'extrasensory' awareness–experience of environment, hence *relationality*, as with spirit embodiment. It's integral to the physical person's ability to have relationship. This doesn't mean having awareness–experience *of* relationship as knowledge, but to having it *in* relationship as 'entanglement' (Parity; § 6.11.3:197; § 3.5.5.5:495). Molly intended the physical to mirror spirit embodiment except where dimensionality limitations are inevitable (§ 2.1.2:308).

This chakra, functioning in concert with the aura, is how spirit persons in the 'reflective' environment perceive the physically alive's thinking–feeling, 'hearing' our conscious thoughts and 'feeling' our emotion as though empaths. Bodystate–mindstate is clear to spirit persons so long as one's chakras are 'open' in that chakra energy toroidally 'flows' through the chakra and properly—w.r.t. 'speed,' 'density,' and other proto-energy aspects—converts (re-expresses) FR.[493] The traditions associating the lumbar (sacral) chakra with sex, creativity, one's own and others' emotions, confidence, self-esteem, source of personal power, or a feeling of being in control of one's life are inaccurate.

1.2.1.3.7 ROOT CHAKRA

Type: ℒife force and chakra energy.
Purpose: Integrates body with ℒife and Living force.
Location: Embodies the L3–L4 spinal vertebrae (*Fig. 177*).

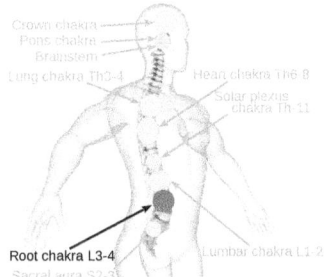

Figure 177. Root chakra shown as grey overlay.[288]

Ancient tradition locates the root chakra at the base of the spine but that's the wrong position, as it locates higher up in the lumbar region (*Fig. 177*). The reason it's in this location is that its functionality is similar to the sex organ and thereby associates with the lumbar nerve plexus at L1–L4 exclusive of the subcostal nerve at T12, although its chakra energy has no effect on the plexus as with some other chakras. The similarity arises in the sex

---

493. A chakra is 'closed' when its toroidal 'energy' structure is 'stopped,' meaning chakra energy movement is at a 10% minimus, a condition similar to vapor lock preventing engine fuel flow. While one's mindset can 'open' or 'close' chakras, changes in the body's ℒife and Living force cause them to as well. A person new to 'opening' chakras will experience frequent, ongoing 'stops' as they adjust to their progressively greater 'energy' (CHAKRA HEALTH, § 1.2:634).

organ's function seeding new life. They're a 'portal' by which Living force and *L*ife force, respectively, trigger fertilization and *L*ife, enlivening the nascent physical body as mE such that it has aliveness. For example, Living force establishes the pons chakra after conception when the body is just a zygote, whereupon emergent *L*ife integrates it. The traditional notion the root chakra provides one with a base (foundation) for life, helps one feel grounded and able to withstand challenges, or is responsible for one's sense of security and stability is inaccurate. These, as with all, arise in misinterpreting the chakra, its location, and metaphorical associations with physical organs and nerve plexuses.

1.2.1.4 VISUALIZING THE CHAKRAS

Each aspect of physical embodiment is like a Russian *matryoshka*, dolls nested within dolls. Speaking conceptually, the physical body as mE nests in chakra energy nested in the 'reflective' body nested in Living force, nested in proto-energy, which embodiment altogether nests in *L*ife force (*Fig. 178*, left). *You*, being *L*ife, need integrate not only the physical mE that's your physical embodiment but all the 'energies' of the natural, 'reflective,' supranatural, and *L*ife environments of which your physiospirit body is a part. This happens via the chakras and aura that act to convert (re-express) 'energy' to awareness–experience that ultimately integrates mind as described, the 'mechanical' process of which we consider here. Physiospirit persons are walking 'antennas' for every kind of 'energy' that bears on physical embodiment: Energent proto-energy, EPL, *L*ife force, Living force, real energy Υ, and applied energy E.

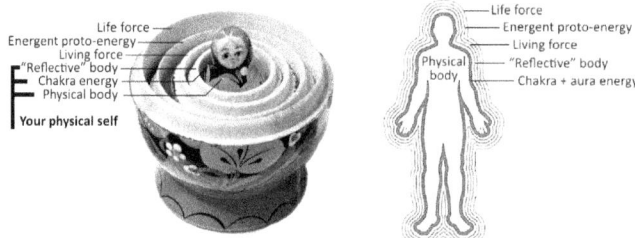

Figure 178. Left, physical embodiment is conceptually like nested *matryoshka* dolls; right, physiospirit embodiment *integrates* six environmental aspects (lines for demonstration; all aspects spatially integrate).₂₈₉

Recall that everything has WOB by which it *is*. Chakras don't form simply out of 'energy' that 'gravitates' toward 'energy' centers of the body in the 'reflective' context like an energy sink (§ 6.10.1.2:188). A chakra's WOB arises 'in' EPL in which *L*ife births and *is*. This means each chakra connects with a person's *L*ife force integrating the body, and its WOB is to effect integration of *L*ife with physiospirit embodiment. Each chakra forms with a WOB to facilitate an aspect of integration in accord with its particular 'energy' center. The WOB of the pons and root chakras is to re-express Living force as chakra energy consonant with the body's FR in the moment of re-expression, and of the other chakras to re-express chakra energy within the body as a different FR (§ 1.2.1.3:501). A chakra, excluding the pons, accomplishes this not as any sort of vortex, funnel, or spinning wheel (*Fig. 179*, left) but as a toroidal 'energy' structure; not one that *looks* like a torus but 'moves energy' toroidally. A torus is classically donut shaped (*Fig. 179*, right). 'Energy' encounters it along its outside plane and moves vertically downward into the bottom of the donut hole.[494] As it processes through the center of the torus, the chakra's WOB acts on it Intentionally and the 'energy' FR takes on that of the chakra's WOB. Once processed, chakra energy remains part of the chakra except for the root and solar plexus chakras as noted (§ 1.2.1.3.7:507; § 1.2.1.3.5:505), the former circulating chakra energy throughout the torso and the latter constantly 'updating' it to the FR of the body's ever-changing bodystate and mindstate. Let's consider how each chakra operates.

The pons chakra continues to operate as all the chakras did during their formation, as an 'energy' center to which Living force 'gravitates.' It re-expresses as chakra energy within the pons chakra and remains suffused therein. Recall the brain integrates Living force such that it has aliveness via suffusion (§ 1.2.1.2.1:499). The pons chakra doesn't visualize as a torus nor operate toroidally. Living force simply integrates it as *L*ife force does the crown chakra and, in accord with its WOB, Living force *is* chakra energy of the pons' FR. The other five chakras don't visualize as a classical donut-shaped torus but do operate toroidally to re-express Living force as chakra energy consonant with each chakra's WOB. These chakras encompass the torso, thus are *torso-shaped*

---

494. This aspect of the toroidal chakra is what gave rise in people's minds to spinning energy funnels, vortices, et cetera.

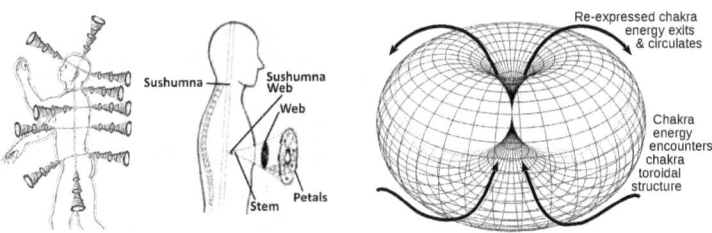

Figure 179. Left, chakras are not funnels, vortices, or spinning wheels; right, classical donut-shaped torus; chakra energy circulates as shown; toroidal 'energy' structure is *torso*, not geometrically torus, shaped.₂₉₀

not torus-shaped. We can visualize them as a donut-shaped torus that simply takes on the shape of the physical torso whereby it's no longer geometrically a donut shape (*Fig. 179*, right). Their chakra energy circulates only within the torso. We describe so-called chakra balance, alignment, 'open' and 'closed' conditions, and other aspects in Chakra Health (§ 1.2:634).

Chakra energy in the body's limbs arises in the 'reflective' body acting as an 'energy' center re-expressing Living force as whole-body chakra energy consistent with the solar plexus chakra's FR (§ 1.2.1.3.5:505). When the physical body is just a zygote having only the pons chakra and aura, the 'reflective' zygote has WOB (like any entity), partly arising in whole-body SOB–SOA until the solar plexus chakra later forms with its sophisticated FR comprehension of whole-body SOB–SOA.

Section 2
The Aura

What the ancient and modern traditions call *minor chakras* or 'energy' centers aren't chakras at all in the sense of 'energy' vortices or toroidal flow structures, but locally FR areas of the *aura*. All human and nonhuman physical bodies have an aura. It arises in the physical body's mE interaction with Living force as a real energy Υ entity that encapsulates the 'reflective' body in the 'reflective' environment. To explain this, recall that real energy Υ expresses as FF in consequence of Energent proto-energy's interaction with mE (§ 1:112). Real energy Υ itself is an expression of proto-energy and, like it, doesn't *itself* 'reflect' in the natural environment but only certain of its expressions, such as FF. Despite the aura arising as a real energy Υ entity *in* the natural environment, it isn't *of* the natural environment but *of* the 'reflective' environment because it's already an expression of the former's proto-energy, which—including Living force, itself a proto-energy—accordingly, interacts with it no further. This is why the aura isn't a natural but 'reflective' environment phenomenon. Its real energy Υ *does* interact with the 'reflection' of mE in the context of the 'reflective' environment's supranatural proto-energy that, also recall, is an Intentionalized entity of our universe (§ 7.1.2:214). The same holds for chakras arising *in* the physical body but not being *of* it.

Each local FR area of the aura resonates such that mind has awareness–experience of that aspect of the natural environment. For example, human touch is exquisitely sensitive. It induces such a subtle awareness–experience of Touch—experiencing another human or nonhuman through at least one of the core senses excluding electromagnetic (Table 13:316; § 2.1.5.4.7:320) when mE physically encounters physical skin—because the aura '*entangles*' (Parity; § 6.11.3:197) 'reflective' environment mE, resonating with the aura local to its FR. The reason some areas of the body are so sensitive to Touch while others feel comparatively dull is not simply greater or lesser sensory neurons in the skin. The aura itself is more or less resonant according to the real energy Υ result of mE–proto-energy interactions intrinsic to different aspects of the body (§ 2.1.2:512). Real energy Υ in areas having more sensory neurons more profoundly resonate with one's 𝓛ife force than areas having fewer. One perceives such resonance in terms of beauty (§ 11.1:460). The more resonant, the more one perceives beauty in Touch and experiences greater pleasure whereas the less resonant, the less one perceives beauty in Touch—we perceive a lack of resonance as discordant, thus ugly (§ 11.3.1:462)—and experiences less pleasure.

With physical Touch, one's mind integrates (via sensory neurons) awareness–experience of the *physicality* of Touch. At the same time, the mE touching our physical skin also 'touches' our 'energy skin' (aura) in the 'reflective' environment as 'reflective' proto-energy interacting with the Living force aura, which is real energy Υ. The aura locally resonates at a real energy Υ FR that, like a diaphragm, transmits that resonance throughout the body and by which the self has awareness–experience of the 'energy' of Touch. The difference between one's awareness–experience of sensory neurons and the aura is that of *Touch* and '*entanglement*.'

An individual's awareness–experience of Touch 'entangles' their 𝓛ife force with another's (or 'entangles' their Living force w.r.t. a nonhuman). It Touches them such that the individual experiences the person as a felt-ness, experientially *aware* of the person's 𝓛ife force and thereby as intimately aware of them *as a being* as it's possible to be. Touch is full-body integrated awareness–experience not limited to the brain's sensory experience that mind integrates. Molly and Mike didn't have to engineer this capability of physical embodiment because it intrinsically arises in the woв of any universe constituted of proto-energy and, therefore, all of them. This means mind's awareness–experience of physical embodiment mirrors its awareness–experience of spirit embodiment save where dimensionality limitations (and The Corruption, unfortunately) intrude. We now describe the aura.

2.1 Description of the (Sacral) Aura

Type: Living force.
Purpose: Integrates the physical body with the natural environment via the 'reflective' one.
Location: Embodies the s2–s3 spinal vertebrae (*Fig. 180*, left).

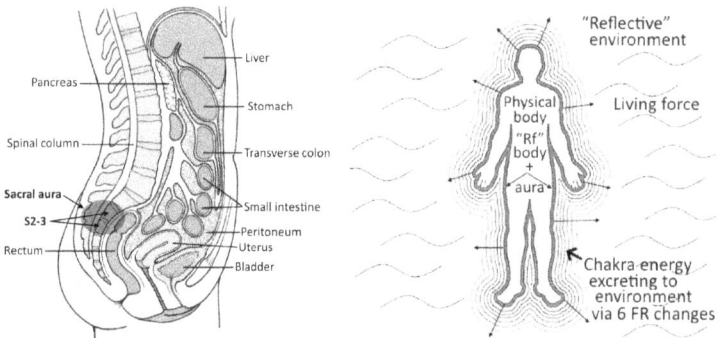

Figure 180. Left, (sacral) aura shown as grey overlay; right, chakra energy excreting via the aura into 'reflective' environment Living force as six *spatially integrated* FR steps (lines are for clarity).[291]

The traditionally-termed *minor* chakras are actually the FR areas of the *aura* which doesn't process chakra energy as chakras do, but instead resonates fourteen natural environment Living force FR via the 'reflective' environment wherein the aura (like the chakras) instantiates. Just as chakras are 'energy' sense 'organs' of the physical body, the aura is like a 'skin' organ in the 'reflective' environment that encapsulates the body and provides it a sensory awareness–experience of the 'energy' there (§ 1.2.1.2.3:501). The aura is a Living force structure integrating the base of the spine centering on the s2–s3 sacral vertebrae—hence, Mina terms it the *sacral* aura—as the body's focal center from where *it encapsulates the entire body* and associates with the physical skin organ. It segments as 24 FR loci, each having a specific soв and soa that center in fourteen specific body regions and as one whole-body instantiation—the sacral aura—having a whole-body soв and soa (*below*). This isn't too unlike action potentials (neural impulses) having individuated soв and soa that aggregate in neural plexuses and the brain into larger soв and soa such that a soв–soa instantiates *as* brain, thus physical mind (*below*). Unlike the chakras, the aura never constricts or 'closes,' regardless one's subconscious mindset or conscious intention to do so. As with the chakras, there's no spirit or earthly—animal nature or instinctive mind—aspects to the aura.

2.1.1 Aura Energy Loci

The aura constitutes as fourteen FR segments, the sacral aura being the whole-body aura inclusive of its segments and the other fourteen being location-(resonant)-specific aspects per left–right body side. We categorize its segments as *upper* and *lower*, the former having ten per body side and the latter fourteen, for a body total of 25 inclusive of the sacral aura.

2.1.1.1 Sacral Aura

The pons chakra forms as Living force in the 'reflective' aspect of the zygote following successful completion of first mitosis (cell division from a one- to two-cell zygote) and about 50% of second mitosis (from two- to four-cell zygote; § 1.2.1.1.1:248) that triggers emergent ℒife's birth 'in' EPL. The aura as Living force follows suit about one-tenth of a second later (before the pons chakra) at which point emergent ℒife's physicospirit embodiment exists in the natural and 'reflective' environments having the necessary 'energy' structures to interact with all the environments of our phenomenal universe. The remaining chakras arise with embryonic development. The interaction of the chakras and aura with the natural–'reflective' environment is at peak sophistication from the get-go. What develops over time is mind–body awareness–experience of environment via these 'energy' sensory 'organs.'

The sacral aura encapsulates the 'reflective' body in the 'reflective' environment as a single 'layer' of chakra energy. It's thereby confined to the body's space much as skin contains the physical body to maintain homeostasis in the natural environment. The aura excretes chakra energy from the body into the 'reflective' environment similar to the skin excreting sweat into the natural one to maintain that aspect of homeostasis. The aura instantiates about one-tenth inch (∼2.54 mm) from the outermost epidermis and is about three-sixteenths inch (∼4.76 mm) thick.

The multiple layers and colors perceived and presumed to be a multilayered aura arises in the aura excreting chakra energy. Like heat emanating via the skin into the environment where progressive cooling alters its infrared wavelength, chakra energy progressively changes FR in six discrete conversions to Living force that suffuses the natural environment and 'reflects' in the 'reflective' environment. These six 'layers' outboard the aura aren't part of it but simply artifacts of FR changing from the body's chakra energy to the environment's Living force. This means 'energy' cycles through it as Living force: *in* via the pons–root chakras and the aura, and as chakra energy *out* via the aura where it re-expresses as Living force (*Fig. 180*, right). It retains its same bodystate–mindstate *resonance* which another physical entity like a person encounters, thus has awareness–experience of, in their environment.

The sacral aura operates independently of the chakras. Regardless whether one or all of one's chakras are 'closed'—constricted no more than 90%—the aura is consistently interactive throughout physical life. Other persons (and nonhumans according to capacity) encounter, thus have awareness–experience of, the chakra energy that one's aura excretes into the Living force environment (similar to smelling someone's sweat and skin oils exuding odors of consumed foods or fear) with which FR they resonate or 'clash.'

2.1.1.2 'FREQUENCY'-RESONANT AURAS

We categorize FR aura locations as *upper* and *lower* body. The former has six with four per side for a total of ten consisting of one at the ears, one in the sexual organ, and two each at the shoulders, elbows, forearms inclusive of hands to the metacarpophalangeal (knuckles), and in the finger sets. The latter has eight with six per side for a total of fourteen consisting of one at the pelvic girdle, one in the gluteal area, and two each in the thighs, knees, calves, ankles, feet, and toe sets.

Each one of these isn't an aura, sub-aura, segmental aura, or the like but simply an *FR area of* the sacral aura. Nor is each one's environmental awareness–experience location specific. Each is more like an antenna tower location providing coverage for a certain geographical area that, w.r.t. the body, 'entangles' the environment's Living force in that area with the real energy ϒ that *is* the body's FR chakra energy in order to integrate body, thus mind, with its environment, including Touch and awareness–experience of local non-Touching Living force. The ℘erson obtains *integrated* awareness–experience of their physicospirit embodiment via the physical body's sensory neurons, the 'reflective' body's chakras and aura, and the spirit body inclusive of Touch. We next describe each upper and lower body aspect.

2.1.1.2.1 UPPER BODY

1. The *ear* FR arises in the full auditory tract, from the cartilaginous auricle outside the head through the brainstem to the auditory cortex of the brain.

2. The *shoulder* FR arises in the joint itself inclusive of the humeral head, glenoid cavity, acromion, and tendon attachments having awareness–experience of Living force in the upper back and chest to the spine and sternum per side, respectively, and each humerus to the elbow FR.

3. The *elbow* FR arises in and extends just above and below the joint itself, its awareness–experience of environmental Living force around the joint inclusive of any areas between the joint and any aspect of the body.

4. The *forearm* FR arises centrally in the radius bone and extends from the elbow FR to the carpus in the hand—the collection of small bones to which the metacarpal finger bones attach—having awareness–experience in that area as with the elbow FR.

5. The *fingers* FR arises central to the metacarpophalangeal joints (the knuckles of the fist) inclusive of the thumb, and has awareness–experience in that area as noted with other FR areas.

6. The *sexual organ* FR arises in the reproductive tract external-to-body and the male–female internal aspects that altogether constitute the sexual organ. It has awareness–experience of the front lower torso extending from the pubis at its lowest point to the naval at its highest, exclusive of the pelvic girdle, which belongs with the pelvic FR (*below*).

The shoulder through finger FR is the aura area through which the body, therefore mind, has awareness–experience of a spirit person's Intentionalized force of Thought that 'reflects' in the 'reflective' environment as its own, though lesser, substantial 'reflection' (since it arises in a spirit, not a physical, person) to which Living force interacts. It locally alters the body FR in the spatial area of the fingers–hand–arm, thereby impeding the 'reflective' body's movement in the 'reflective' environment such that a spirit person's Thought effectively translates as the physical expression we experience as finger, hand, and arm energy testing (§ 2:625). As one can see, energy testing isn't magical woo-woo. It arises in the WOB of the various expressions of Energent proto-energy interacting with mE.

2.1.1.2.2 LOWER BODY

1. The *pelvic* FR arises in the pelvic girdle inclusive of the femoral head and tendon attachment areas but exclusive of the pubic bone. It occupies some of the same 'space' as the sexual organ FR and has awareness–experience (as described regarding Touch and non-Touch, *above*) of the medial pelvic region exclusive of the gluteal region.

2. The *gluteal* FR arises in the coccyx (tailbone) just below the aura's own s2–s3 center point and includes the areas between the intertrochanteric crest (inboard of the extruding bony part of the hip) of each femur, having awareness–experience of the lateral and posterior pelvic area.

3. The *thigh* FR arises in the center of the femur and extends to the gluteal and pelvic FR above, and the knee FR below.

4. The *knee* FR arises in the knee joint inclusive of the femoral condyle and those of the fibula and tibia, having awareness–experience of the included areas.

5. Like the forearm FR, the *calf* FR arises in the midpoint of the tibia and extends from the knee FR to the ankle FR, having awareness–experience of the included areas.

6. The *ankle* FR arises where the tibia meets the talus bone of the upper foot and includes those aspects of the tibia, fibula, and talus bones exclusive of the calcaneus (heel) and the metatarsals and toes, inclusive, having awareness–experience of the included areas.

7. The *foot* FR arises in the cuboid bone of the foot and includes the calcaneus and other small bones exclusive of those already mentioned, having awareness–experience of the included areas.

8. The *toes* FR arises in the metatarsophalangeal joints of the toes (the first knuckles where they visibly separate), having awareness–experience of the included areas.

2.1.2 VISUALIZING THE AURA

Although the aura isn't a toroidal 'energy' structure in the same way as chakras (exclusive of the pons), it nevertheless constitutes a toroidal matrix that renders it resonant with the infinite FR of Living force. We conceptually visualize the aura in terms of what's called a *torus antenna*. This is a ground-based signals receiver. Unlike the typical circular-shaped parabolic antenna, it is rectangular-shaped, having the quasi-parabolic aspect of a portion of the outermost geometric shape of a torus with an array of signals receiving heads making up its focal arc (*Fig. 181*). In this way, the torus antenna can pick up over forty geosynchronous satellite signals simultaneously versus the single satellite signal typical of a parabolic antenna. From a conceptually structural standpoint, the aura essentially constitutes from a 'complex signals array' that acts somewhat like tens of thousands of torus antennae, each one having a thousand 'self-calibrating receiving heads' capable of interacting with infinite Living force FR to provide the person (or nonhuman) with an awareness–experience of their (its) environment.

Nonhuman entities like elephants, for instance, have a larger aura with more 'torus antennae' although always less 'signals receiving heads' per 'antenna' than the human aura. Regardless The Corruption, the average human aura constitutes from about 80,000 'torus antennae,' meaning the average person integrates about 80 million unique FR of Living force in any given one ten-thousandth (10^{-4}) second.

70° View Arch   Over 40 Focal Points   Uniform Signal Reception

Figure 181. Simulsat torus antenna schematic conceptualizing the aura's awareness–experience of Living force in the 'reflective' environment.[292]

Upon interacting with Living force FR, any of the aforementioned 'signals receiving heads' re-expresses that aspect of Living force as chakra energy having that resonance which one's mind interprets as a particular SOB and SOA, which is then an aspect of mindstate integrating the body as an aspect of bodystate. In this way, a Living force FR integrates the 'reflective' body thus the chakras, hence the physical body and, via mind–body integration, *L*ife mind. Recall the aura is like an 'energy' barrier encapsulating the 'reflective' body, segregating it from, yet interacting with, the 'reflective' environment much as skin segregates the physical body from, yet interacts with, the natural environment. Keep in mind the chakra–aura purpose is to replicate in the physical, dimensionally oriented natural environment the same awareness–experience intrinsic of spirit persons having a spirit body materially instantiated as their very mind in, thus fully integrating, the supranatural environment.

2.2 NONHUMAN CHAKRAS AND AURA

Since every physically alive nonhuman entity also 'reflects' in the 'reflective' environment, then each one has an aura regardless body size as well as chakras commensurate with their evolutionary capacity as we defined evolution (§ 2.1.5.5.2:323). For example, an aura encapsulates any entity from an elephant to a bacterium to a virus. On the other hand, neither virus nor the ~400 nm Nanoarchaeum equitans or bacteria have chakras, although nematodes have one. As size and complexity grow, so does the number of chakras. According to Mina, all dogs, cats, and elephants have seven chakras; horses have five, owls have four, birds vary from one to five, dinosaurs from two to five, and monkeys and apes from one to seven. The aura and chakras provide nonhumans the same awareness–experience of environment as they do humans in accord with their capacity.

Intentionality as Energent Triggered

RECALL THAT *L*IFE *emergently* births 'in' Energent proto-life (EPL; § 2.3.2.1:241). Neither humans nor gods create *L*ife, pairwise humans *trigger* it (§ 1.2.1.1:248§ 2:304). Likewise, they singly or together trigger proto-energy or Living force (an expression of proto-energy; § 2:114) whereby an Intended *object* coalesces into form or an *effect* exerts in space. *Intentionality* is a person triggering desire as an expression of proto-energy. Our Thought capability means physical-born humanity is not unreasonably or unfairly destined to life in the septic tank of the universe before graduating via traumatic death to the spirit lands of milk and honey. That's inaccurate. Physical life is the equal of spirit life; both are *L*ife's embodiments. Yes, The Corruption made a hash out of steak, but not because physical reality is hostile to humanity or the physical-born are different, less, or inhuman, but simply consequent of our colossal ignorance of reality (§ 3.1.2.1.3:359) arising in degraded mind–brain integration (MBI; § 1.2.2.4:257) with which the spirit-born never contend (§ 1.2.2:253). Our awareness–experience of physical life necessarily improves as we address MBI until there's no difference between the physical- and spirit-born. That seems ridiculous in our present mood that roots in the animal alpha mindset (§ 9.2.2:450) of immutable natural laws—few discovered, yet misinterpreted as the forest for the trees—like invariant matter, the cycle of life, or sure infirmity driving us down a narrow, scripted path tangential to ᚼuman reality.

Intentionality arises in proto-energy. It's a reality of the natural (physical) and supranatural (spirit) environments not to mention of All Existence, as that's the means by which our universe came to be (§ 2.1.3:309). The only difference between these Intentionalities is that matter as an independent self-existent having way of being (WOB; § 2.2.1.1:234) resists, whereas supramatter as a dependent self-existent having WOB only as it's Intentionalized doesn't. We've already described Intentionality w.r.t. Psyche Fundamental Force (PFF; § 3.2:282). Here, we describe *how* to Intentionalize in each environment.

SECTION 1
Supranatural Intentionality

Intentionality isn't a complicated game. It boils down to just two principal steps entailing several tasks. Step 1 formulates desire as force of Thought (§ 3.5.2:486), which in this context means to establish the WOB of one's Intentionality. Step 2 exerts Thought, which means exerting 'energy'—force of Thought—from oneself into the proto-energy (Energent or Living force) environment. Let's consider each step.

1.1   STEP 1: FORMULATE DESIRE AS FORCE OF THOUGHT

WOB is the nature, or essentiality, of something. Recall that WOB reflects an entity's beingness in the context of *how it is* in relation to the totality of self in the totality of environment, meaning the totality of an entity relationally with the totality of not only *its* environment but the local–global environment such as, in this case, the wholistic supranatural environment and the wholistic universe. For example, people tend to limit the nature of a thing to the thing itself, excluding even its local environment. Sometimes people include limited aspects of a local environment such as a lung's nature being to expand and contract to move air in and out or to oxygenate blood. But *lung woв* comprehends it wholistically in the context of itself, its anatomical environs, the body as a whole, its physical embodiment, the natural, 'reflective,' and supranatural environments, the universe, All Existence, and ℒife (§ 2.2.1.2.1:237).

If one wants to Intentionalize a lung into existence, one needs comprehend its woв and not simply its functional nature, purpose, or essentialities. Doing so is like Intentionalizing a cup of coffee that's not just lacking essentialities like flavor, texture, or aroma, but its wholistic capability to satisfy every way one *experiences* it as a person in the world. Formulating desire is a wholistic undertaking involving three comprehensive tasks: considering what one wants, formulating its woв, and investing it with reality.

1.1.1   Consider What One Wants to Accomplish

Intentionality involves manipulating immaterial proto-energy as either material *form* or *exertion*. There's a difference. Examples of the latter are the spirit persons who Intentionally snapped my Prius piston rod and shattered crockery by knocking my arm when washing dishes (§ 1.3.3.4.1:476). In this case, one desires a *result*, not (as an example of the former) a *thing* such as a cup of coffee. Suppose a spirit person wants to Intentionalize a cup of coffee on a saucer in the palm of their hand. It's not hard to visualize it in exquisite detail, is it? We do it all the time although absent Intentionality. One already knows how they want it to taste even if they can't readily articulate it. We consider three aspects. First is how hot they'd like it on their tongue, its aroma, strength, thickness, texture, and a host of essentialities that makes it *a coffee*. Second is the cup and saucer's look-and-feel. Third is where in space they want it to form—held in their hand—and how it relates with the environment such as overall ambience, including retaining its desired temperature to the last drop despite being at an outdoor cafe in frigid weather. Every aspect that matters imaginatively forms in one's mind as Thought; the same process obtains when Intentionalizing 'energy' to exert. So, one now has a clear idea of what they want.

1.1.2   Formulate Way of Being

Despite imagining all the details that necessarily constitute one's desired cup of coffee in hand, it's still only imagination. It's thought, that's true, but not Thought having force. If one triggered Intentionality just by any old thinking–feeling, spirit life would be chaotic and unsettling. While human Thought always exerts into environment, it isn't Intentional but simply exerted 'energy,' the *force of Thought*. To advance from imagining to exerting 'energy' as Intentionality, one necessarily transmutes Thought embodying an imagined desire to Thought having the desire's aforementioned woв. In a sense, this means *savoring* the desired cup of coffee in your mind such that its woв 'materializes' there as awareness–experience, as a felt-ness (*enimerótis-empeiría*, § 2.1.4:394; § 2.1.5.4.7:320). This isn't too unlike mentally 'living' one's goals, achievements, or vision—manifesting a dream car—except carried beyond imagining merely its experiential details—triggering the so-called law of attraction, which is really just a woв of 'energy' that resonates—to its woв contextualized to all aspects of reality. Imagining yourself savoring that cup of coffee is indeed all that, but includes *you*, *there*, experiencing its savor in all *your* essentiality and reality contextualized to the realities of *your* local–global environment. At first, it may seem daunting to put all this together in one's mind as a felt-ness, but it becomes a practiced skill so old-hat that one does it with scarcely any conscious awareness at all although, in this case, it *is* a conscious mind effort.

1.1.3   Invest One's Thought with Reality

Visualizing oneself savoring this desired cup of coffee may seem like one is investing it with reality—real existence in the world—but, at this point, it's just an awareness–experience of mind whereby one's self has awareness–experience of it; the person *knows* the cup of coffee is immaterial Thought and not material form. Vision-board gurus teaching how to achieve a goal by manifesting it into reality assert a person necessarily needs believe the goal is real (even though it isn't, yet) in order that it becomes materially real. But that aspect isn't pertinent here. It really means shifting one's mindset from its current awareness there is no material cup of coffee in hand to the future awareness the cup of coffee *is* materially in hand. Expecting one's goal or dream not only can be real but also *is* real isn't wishy-washy New Age personal achievement woo-woo so much as a *mindset update*. Recall that mindset literally assures outcome in that what we subconsciously–consciously think–feel, like the body aging, manifests as reality (§ 2.1.1.5.2:353).

Consider humanity's mindset that we're animals (in the sense we exist in the physical world in that frame of reference) means we have the same relationship with the environment and the same constraints and instincts as all creatures. That's precisely how we then behave, live, and *are* despite ancillary mindsets we're children of God having better natures and a higher purpose (§ 9.2.2:450). Until now, there's hasn't been a single person amongst Humanity 1.0 or 2.0 (CH. 32:531) whose mindset was ﾃuman instead of animal, who comprehended the ℘erson intrinsically unconstrained by the biological reality so observedly fundamental of Living creatures. We expect physical life to entail injury, disease, infirmity, aging, death, and so it does. Self-efficacy making one's dreams possible (realistic or not) is really about mindset.

When a spirit person is Intentionalizing our example of a cup of coffee in hand, their mindset needs must update its present reality of no cup of coffee in hand to the reality it is in hand. The spirit-born do this readily from birth and physical-born spirit persons after simple training because their environment never disproves the possibility. From their earliest awareness that supramatter doesn't resist Intentionality, they see it happening all around them. Yet, even with the example of rags-to-riches achievers like John D. Rockefeller (d. 1937) and many others, most physically alive people *won't* alter their mindset, very few even try, and even fewer succeed at achieving wealth. The reasons lay in The Corruption, the apparent immutability—our ignorance, that is—of physical reality. Mindset itself zeroes in on disproof because that comports with expectation. Although physical persons are indeed capable of Intentionalizing natural proto-energy into material form, nary a mindset seriously entertains the reality and thereby neutralizes the capability. This third task is therefore prerequisite to transmuting imagination to Intentionality.

1.2   Step 2: Exert Force of Thought Into Environment

When a spirit person Intentionalizes an exertion of 'energy' in the spatial location of some part of my physical body to disrupt my biology in order to get my attention to heal them, or for nefarious reasons fortunately less common (though common enough for the girls and me; CH. 35:577), I neutralize their Intentionality and restore my body's homeostasis. To do it, I consider what I want to accomplish (removing the Intentionality's effect on my body), formulate its WOB (how it feels removed), and invest it with reality (updating my mindset). These three tasks took quite a bit longer to effect while I was learning than the approximately half-second or so it now takes me going on five years later. Finally, I focus and exert my Living force—not ℒife force, since the Intentionality affects my Living body, not my ℒife mind—which I can physically as well as mentally *feel* moving, gathering, exerting within my body. Initially, I spent quite some time learning gather, mobilize, and feel my 'energy.' It got easier over about six months as I developed sensitivity to its presence and learned to imagine then feel it coalescing like a ball of energy I could 'fling' at the affected part of my body. When Mina first taught me how, I considered my effort simply neutralizing someone else's Intentionality but, in truth, it *is* Intentionality because neutralizing a proto-energy exertion is effectively *re*-Intentionalizing it.

The foregoing is the principal difference between manipulating proto-energy as an exertion having an effect at a spatial location and manipulating it as (natural or supranatural) material form. Person B can neutralize Person A's Intentional *exertion* (like a stomachache) but can't neutralize (alter or disappear) its Intentionalized *form*. One can neutralize, meaning re-Intentionalize, a person's Intentionality that's provoking the stomachache but can't neutralize their cup of coffee in hand so that it maybe re-Intentionalizes as a venomous snake or disappears altogether (this holds for a universe, too). Sticking with our coffee scenario, Step 2 entails focusing, then exerting, ℒife force as two halves to the same whole.

1.2.1   Focus ℒife Force

Intentionality in the supranatural environment exclusively utilizes ℒife force whereas, in the natural one (*below*), Living force additionally comes into play. The reason is that only mind, which *is* ℒife force, enables PFF to trigger proto-energy whereby Intentionality occurs in the supranatural environment where there are no Living force entities. Unless one brings ℒife force to bear, Intentionality never rises from imagination and force of Thought. Hopefully, my aforementioned experience neutralizing 'attacks' on my physical body helps you better visualize this task. One simply gathers their ℒife force in the context of Thought which *prepares the effect* of triggering proto-energy *as* the spatially located object (or exertion). Proto-energy then invests with, or *re-expresses as*, the formulated and mindset-updated WOB one desires to Intentionalize. While this task is one-half the same whole the next step completes (*below*), one can certainly stop at this point without enabling PFF to trigger Intentionality. Had Mina changed his mind about creating our universe, then even after the ~1.2BY it took him to formulate its WOB, update his mindset with its reality, and focus his 𝓛ife force to the Intentional task, he could have shifted his focus the equivalent of a single archí (as happened with Molly, § 2.1.3.2:310; ARCHÍ, § 2.3.1:115) and his Intentionality never would've occurred. That portion of megaversal humanity that constitutes his descendants *here*, in our universe, would not have birthed any more than the children never born to the couple that never met.

1.2.2 EXERT THE FOCUS

As with our example of neutralizing an Intentionalized exertion of Living force in my physical body, the act of *exerting one's focused 'energy'* is essentially instantaneous, taking about a picosecond to accomplish. It seems much longer in practice because, for a physical person, the sensation of 'energy' moving is a physiological one that integrates mind, which then re-integrates its SOB and SOA[495] with brain such that one's physically instantiated mind—the physical self—has awareness–experience of it. When Mina Intentionalized our universe, he felt his mobilized 𝓛ife force exert such that our universe was *there* and he was cognizant of it operating as intended in about that same picosecond (FN 145:116). All of Intentionality's *creative* effort—one's mind—lay in Step 1, while its *exertive* effort—one's self—lay in Step 2.

SECTION 2
Natural Intentionality

The same two steps as in Section 1 pertain to Intentionality in the natural environment, too. The only difference is the physically alive's *spirit* self Intentionalizes, not their *physical* self. Recall your physical embodiment isn't *you*, it's just a natural environment 'avatar' your 𝓛ife self integrates (§ 1.2.2:253). It doesn't do anything on its own, only that which mind does. The same is true of the spirit body, but it's a direct reflection of mind as supramatter that Intentionalized at emergent birth. The physical body, on the other hand, is independently self-existent matter, a biological reality in and of itself (§ 7.1.3:214). It experiences Intentionality at many levels over its lifespan from one's own mindset to the conscious intent of other's, but has its own WOB that defines it. While the spirit body, in essence, is a material manifestation of mind without distinction, the physical body, as an independent entity, is distinct from integrated 𝓛ife mind.

When MBI is impaired (as from The Corruption), distinctions abound between 𝓛ife mind and instantiated physical mind (§ 1.2.2.1:253). This is the reason one's spirit self might think–feel one way while one's physical self—each having the same mind, the latter just expressing in accord with MBI in the natural environment—thinks–feels another way. From this arises a dichotomy in the person such as with Hitler (CH. 40:605) or as mindset-influenced, Intentionalized conditions of the physical body such as physically undesired disease, infirmity, untimely death, and so forth.

All that's to say, despite your physical body appearing to be *you* the *person*, it's not. It has no self-agency or self-efficacy, all of that is of your mind, your 𝓛ife *self*. The physical self can consciously Intentionalize only with sufficient MBI. A person living in a condition of impaired MBI—our present reality—isn't physically capable of conscious Intentionality because, first, their physical self's mindset neutralizes the capability, and, second, their spirit self self-segregates from the larger spirit environment in which they live and, in consequence, can't learn Intentionality. Over generational time, the physical-born conceived after 2017's Big Healing will progressively develop the MBI necessary to Intentionalize natural proto-energy.

That's not to say you can't Intentionalize *now*, only that it's limited to exertion such as (besides healing) subconsciously Intentionalizing your own aging, disease, infirmity as well as the effects of negative EM𝓛F (§ 3.3.3.1.1:289), cursing others as a 'seer' or 'prophet,' or allying with spirit persons' greater Intentional capability to harm another's body (illness, pain, slaps, stabs, headaches) or electronics and machinery. There's no limit but your imagination (and malice, which blows back; so, abandon malice).

---

495. SOB is state(s) of being and SOA is state(s) of awareness (§ 1.2.2.1:253).

Angels

WHILE IT'S FAIR to apply the term *angel* to beings that are sometimes messengers of our universe's builder (Mina), that's not what they are and neither is it all they do. Everything believed of angels is rooted in make-believe—myths, dreams, visions, intuition, clair senses, imagination, rank deception—that no two persons can validate but only swallow hook, line and sinker, abide in part or, like bad fish, fling wholesale back into the sea. This is a problem affecting not just theology and religion generally but many aspects of science, too. It's an affliction of mind lost in a raging sea of ignorance and fear where each myth, dream, intuition, vision, imagined reality, or comforting notion are the flotsam and jetsam of survival.

Energy testing (ET) is the only solution to the morass we're in because it applies the scientific method of peer review to spirit reality.[496] Religion—also many scientists—can't abide revising accepted wisdom. It means abandoning one's own or ancestral 'truths' for something fuller or anyway different that renders the old faith false therefore mistakenly believed. It erodes comforting authority. Science eventually accepts the fait accompli of new data falsifying the old despite often initially resisting for the kill, but religion doesn't. In its fear, it worries deviation will, at best, provoke the wrath of God and His tormentous punishment and, at worst, discredit the religion, its authorities, and perhaps faith itself. Necessarily, then, faith is changeless, stagnant, unenlightened, and blindly defensive while science moves (oft grudgingly) ever experimentally forward into an expanding if imperfect comprehension of human and natural reality. Faith and reason are thus ever in conflict, each the mortal stake poised atop the other's heart. They abide a sort of détente in the religious adopting selective scientific evidence as the hand of God while the scientific oft hide equally selective religious sweaters 'neath their coats of white and neither gives ground. This state of affairs is unproductive and unsustainable. Eventually, a person finds they must choose what matters more—spiritualism, materialism, amalgams—and the degree to which one needs *compel* recalcitrants and detractors.

What's that have to do with angels? Everything, really. Angelology—the study of angels—is a whimsy of rosy hope tenuously asserting we're not alone and somebody cares, papering over a chasm of incomprehension that's ever-murkier the deeper one peers. This book leaves it behind like old clothes for energy testing (ET) which has the benefit of taking us out of our mental box in a community of peer review to ultimately work out—in our condition of insufficient mind–brain integration (MBI; § 1.2.2.1:253)—what is *more likely real than not*. And that's really the best for which even the scientific method has ever been able to hope. Accordingly, this chapter describes so-called angels as what they *are* and *do* without angelology's new age feel-good woo-woo aimed at empowering magical thinking, personal comfort, and prosperity. As a caveat, *archangel* and *angel* are terms of convenience that denote 'celestial beings' (spirit-born humans) regardless the rank, order, deity, power, or authority of the angelology that's born of Earth's sacred texts. Indeed, we punctuate it by noting *rank* and *authority* are alien to spirit-born humanity, let alone Mina.

---

496. Science is only science if its claims are verifiable, reproducible, and allow prediction by any person having the necessary knowledge, skill, and methods (§ 1:83).

SECTION 1

What 'Angels' Are

Fundamentally, 'angels' are spirit-born persons. They're human beings like you, me, and everybody (§ 2.3.2:240; § 1.2.1.1.2:249). What makes a person an 'angel' isn't what they are but their choice to help physical-born humanity cope with The Corruption where it was never certain how or when Mina or anyone might ever resolve it (§ 1.2.2:339). They aren't born into nor created for it. They adopt it. Neither is it their permanent or even only lot in life. Mina prefers to reference 'angels' as *friends*, though we stick with the traditional term where it suits clarity. We consider these friends of the physical-born from their three principal realities: as spirit-born persons, as our ancestors, and as our support system.

1.1 FRIENDS ARE SPIRIT-BORN PERSONS

Recall Mina's children and spouses initially populated our universe as spirit embodied persons (§ 2.1.1:348) who birthed spirit-embodied children in the supranatural (spirit) environment whom we call *spirit-born* (§ 2.1.5.3:315; § 1.2.1.1.2:249). Until the natural environment was ready to support physical life, the only human beings in our universe besides Mina—himself physically conceived in his mother, P'najj's, universe (§ 1.2:336)—were his spirit-born descendants. They built relationships, raised families, and established communities, societies, and megacities (§ 3.3:482) as their numbers soared from the First Ancestors' initial five couples to well over 100 quadrillion persons on the eve of seeding physical-embodiment about 7.3MYA.[497] This isn't to say that friends ('angels') are *only* spirit born. On average, roughly 2.86% are physical-born persons who choose to be part of Mina's organized support to the physically alive.

1.1.1 FRIENDS ARE OUR ANCESTORS

*L*ife isn't created *of* parents. It emergently births *'in'* Energent proto-life (EPL; § 2.3.2.1:241) via Intentional pairwise male–female couples (§ 1.2.1.1:248). Naturally, the only way physical humans initially birthed was via spirit-born couples birthing physiospirit *L*ife (§ 1.2.1.1.1:248; § 2.1.5.5.4:327) by integrating Living proto-humans, thereby seeding habitable planets like Earth with the first physical-born humans (§ 1.1:532). Once these first children reached childbearing age, normal biological procreation continued triggering emergent physiospirit *L*ife leading up to, in our case, Earth's present population. This means the physical-born population of every human-inhabited planet first birthed from spirit-born procreators, *our ancestors*. Through them, our *societal attachments*—not genealogical lineage or parentage, since *L*ife doesn't arise *from* families or *of* parents but is independently *emergent* (§ 3:414)—connect us societally with the Ancestors, Mina, his parents P'koh and P'najj (§ 1.2:336), and megaversal humanity. Your societal attachments reach back to the very first pairwise human beings, Mike and Molly (§ 2:304).

  Mina draws sharp distinctions regarding family and lineage because the person doesn't 'belong' to a family as the 'child of' parents who generatively 'created' them, but rather is an independent being whom parents, via pairwise Intentionality (§ 3.2:282; CH. 30:515), trigger to emergently birth 'in' EPL. Parents do Intentionalize certain aspects of their child's spirit *embodiment* like their sex, but these aren't set in stone despite ensconcing in mindset, and are alterable according to individual preference (§ 2.1.5.5.3:327). *L*ife doesn't belong to parents, family, or lineage. These custodially *care* for a child without ownership or mastery. This is how the spirit-born approached family and parenting even before the Big Healing and differs considerably from the physical-born's alpha mindset (§ 9.2.2:450). Humans societally attach *in* a family but aren't *of* the family similar to chakras being *in* but not *of* the physical body (§ 2:509).

  Genealogy, parentage, lineage, and extant methods for linking people lineally apply to the Living (physical) body, not to the human person having *L*ife. As there's no value in tracing the production of physical bodies, which are nothing but 'avatars' for human *L*ife, traditional methods to account for a person's origin and nature are immaterial and irrelevant because, for *L*ife, there literally *is no ancestry* in the traditional sense. Rather, each uniquely autonomous ϱerson independently, emergently births 'in' EPL as self-aware proto-energy having *L*ife, just as Mike and Molly initially birthed as the first pairwise humans. Yes, your physical body shares antecedents with your parents' physical bodies but, being *L*ife, you are unparalleled. Literally, *you*

---

497. Seems huge, but represents only a 0.0184% growth rate over ~200KY and 0.000519% over 7.5MY (*Fig. 182*:523; cf. Earth's population growth of 0.0203% from ~300K→8B over 50KY, 1.03% today, and 0.03% projected by 2100).

are your own ancestor. This is why the individual is intrinsically autonomous and the true basis for human liberty (§ 2.1.1.5:353). Rather than confusing the issue by repurposing nonhuman alpha-society terms, Mina encourages us to reconceptualize family as *societal attachments* instead of ancestry, lineage, parentage, and so on, and as *caregivers* instead of parents. The spirit-born still love *as*, and use terms similar *to*, family, parents, children, and the like, but attach societal meanings more (if not exactly) consistent with Mina's description of human beings as ℒife.

1.1.2 Devils and Demons

There are only two entities in our universe having properties of aliveness (motility and thinking–acting according to capability): ℒife and Living entities. Human beings are what they are and necessarily are never not what they aren't. Living entities independently exist only in the natural environment and as Intentional facsimiles in the supranatural one. They are never in any way human nor a facsimile thereof, being always nonhuman from animal to virus and everything in between inclusive of the human body which, unlike any other Living entity, has no self-agency. There is no third category of entity having aliveness such as dark, evil, mythical, fallen, angelic, devilish, or other kinds of things one might classify as demonic or deitic. Devils, demons, and that whole mythical panoply aren't real but a figment of physical humanity's imagination heated to fever pitch by Accountableism (§ 1.4:14; § 4:377) and, usually, physical-born spirit persons presenting themselves to the physically alive in such guise. Nothing controls or tempts one's so-called dark side except one's own self, including anything to which one gives influence. That devils and demons irrepressibly interfere with life is merely dodging the consequences of choice. It's true that spirit persons who interfere with physical humanity for nefarious purposes (§ 1.3.3.3:476) *act* in ways one can characterize as devilish or demonic, but that's behavior and mindset, not existential reality.

1.2 Friends Are Our Supporters

The Corruption entered our universe at about the same time the spirit-born physically birthed ℒife on planets (§ 1.2.1:534). It didn't take long for the physical-born to lose touch with spirit-born humanity and all knowledge and awareness of spirit reality (§ 3.1.2.1.3:359). Meanwhile, life went on in spirit world. The spirit-born frankly watched in broken-hearted dismay as the physical-born developed violent psychoses they carried with them into spirit world where their discordant 'energies' clashed with the spirit-born's own, whose spirit world proto-energy 'frequency' provoked in them even more pain and suffering. About 100KY of that galvanized Mina to build the physical-born a sequestered environment having a 'frequency' resonant with the physical-born. Here, they more comfortably lived but could abandon it when achieving resonance with spirit-born 'energy' (*Fig. 182:523*; § 1.2.2:468).

The situation was tragic. The physical-born were the spirit-born's *family*, their descendants (§ 1.1:532). There was no thought of abandoning them to their own devices where The Corruption ran so rampantly unchecked by any awareness of reality and normal mind–brain integration. Mina, the First Ancestors, and the spirit-born tried everything they could think of to ameliorate The Corruption's effects and help the physical-born, but to no avail. The physically alive grew utterly blind to the 'reflective' environment and spirit persons. Arriving in spirit world after physical death, only the extraordinary few ever managed to alter their mindset away from their physical oblivion. Since ℒife is absolutely autonomous (§ 2.3.2.1:241; § 2.1.1.5:353), there's simply no way to coerce a person to alter their mindset to think–feel differently than they do without their desiring it. Not only did the spirit-born's own situation arising in The Corruption continue to worsen as Michael's fish tale about Lucifer ginned up Accountableism and its train of cattle cars, but the physical-born's situation fell into outright depravity as they abandoned their very *humanness* to remake themselves in the image of animals (§ 9.2.2:450). Such suffering people then entered spirit world after death steeped in nonhuman alpha grouping without ♄uman sensibilities.

Our spirit-born family realized they'd have to settle into helping the physical-born over the long haul to cope with their present situation, as well as try teaching them out of it until someone found a way to break the still-uncomprehended—except by Mina (§ 4.2.1.4:382)—Corruption's back so the physically alive could restore full mind–brain integration and awareness of reality. Toward that end, Mina identified seven principal tasks he considered most helpful. The seven individuals who organized and recruited volunteers into a *society of friends* to teach and support the physically alive in accord with these tasks are whom superstitious physical humanity perceived as 'archangels' and 'angels' (Table 17:523).

SECTION 2

What 'Angels' Do

Friends—'angels'—are physical humanity's behind-the-scenes support group who intervene helpfully to the degree possible and as the physically alive permit (in accord with mindset) to mitigate the worst physical effects of The Corruption. Without them, the reality is that physical life would be vastly more depraved than it is, with harm and civilization-ending warfare leaving the physically alive and physical-born spirit persons in a condition of psychotic madness more scourged in suffering than ever. The reason is that The Corruption disrupts physically embodied (physicospirit) *L*ife such that only the barest MBI obtains, leaving physical humanity perceiving virtually nothing of—though indelibly sensing—what it humanly is and akin to nonhuman life from which it modeled its way of being (WOB; § 2.2.1.1:234). Friends educate us, ameliorate our self-inflicted situations, and ease our transition from physical to spirit life.

About 19% of our universe's total ~849 quadrillion (Q) people are physically alive. Of the ~81% who are spirit persons, ~33.7% (or ~27.29% of universal humanity) volunteer at any given moment as friends ('angels'). Roughly, 230.37Q spirit persons support the ~161.31Q physically alive presently inhabiting ~73% of the ±120B habitable planets (§ 3:357) throughout the observable universe, a ratio of ~1.4:1. This ratio varies across tasks which, along with their 'archangel' origin, we describe next.

2.1 THE FIRST 'ARCHANGELS'

Mina's children—V'nin, Epv'd'd, Boñ'p, Watb'hv'v, Oid't'v (excluding V'v'dib; Table 15:349)—are the First Ancestors. They shouldered the responsibility of developing, implementing, and overseeing Mina's 'archangel' tasks for ~604KY all told (Fig. 148:355). Their spouses took up the task of organizing spirit-born persons to integrate proto-humans in order to birth physicospirit humans throughout the observable universe, a ~500KY initial effort that continues off and on today re-seeding failed societies and seeding new planets. Technically 'angels,' Mina doesn't consider the spouses 'archangels' since their task isn't helping physical humanity cope with The Corruption. Instead, he calls them *abiogeneticists* in this book. He prefers this division of labor, and the Ancestors signed on. They recruited the first spirit-born friends when physical humanity's struggle with The Corruption was significantly less problematic. Its suffering escalated exponentially, however, until Earth was the fifth planet to destroy itself in war (§ 1.3:538).

At that point, the Ancestors decided those birthed in our universe were better suited to the 'archangelic' tasks because, having grown up and lived most of their lives to date in their parents' universe, they felt, after Earth's self-immolation, that they didn't understand physical humanity in our universe, despite being physical-born themselves in P'najj's (Mina's) own. Nor did they feel they knew how to proceed. You who are parents are familiar with this issue when trying to understand your children's lives. Too, V'nin was organizing not one but three 'archangelic' tasks (Table 17). Roughly 6.49MYA—some 610KY after the first physical humans birthed upon a planet (Fig., ibid)—the Ancestors recruited their willing second-Gen children to the seven tasks (*Fig. 182*). After a 150KY training period, they retired from their role though continued helping and interacting with physical humanity (THE GREEK GODS, § 1.1.1.1:570).

2.2 THE SECOND 'ARCHANGELS'

The seven spirit-born persons whom Earth's humanity calls 'archangels' are first generation children of the five Ancestor couples (Table 17). Each volunteered to take up their parents' tasks. All have brothers and sisters who could have but didn't volunteer; the tasks are demanding and no one else stepped up. These second 'archangels' birthed at or near the start of the spirit-born's 75th generation about 154.1KY years after physical humanity first birthed on Earth (*Fig. 182*). As The Corruption wanes in the Big Healing's wake, these tasks will eventually be unnecessary and the society of friends disbanded, though Mina reminds us one can never predict human choice with absolute certainty. We consider the seven tasks below.

2.3 THE SEVEN TASKS

The seven 'archangelic' tasks are only a stopgap measure for the duration of The Corruption. They aren't a natural part of physical humanity since they're unnecessary for fully mind–brain integrated physicospirit persons who naturally have a correct understanding of themselves and their environment. For example, a

Table 17. The seven principal tasks and archangel organizers of each (cf. Table 16:352); double underline is accented syllable; "+𝔄" means it also organizes certain universe maintenance. "% Ct" is of task 'angels.'

Task	Archangel Name	Sex	Given Name	Pronunciation	Parent	%Ct
Intervention	Gabriel	M	Titit'j	Tie-<u>tie</u>-t'-juh	V'nin (M)	6%
Guidance	Lucifer	M	Tivi'iv'z	<u>Tie</u>-v'-eyev'-zuh	V'nin (M)	28%
Wisdom+𝔄	Michael	M	Bibci'd	Bĭb-<u>sĭ</u>'-dt	V'nin (M)	5%+ 0.33%
Validate+𝔄	Remiel	F	B'i'c'iic'bii	B'ie-s'eye-eesuh'-buh-ee-ee	Epv'd'd (M), Boñ'p	16%+ 0.66%
Entry	Raguel	F	C'icib'id'i	See'-<u>see</u>-b'-eeduh'-ee'	Boñ'p (F)	38%
Contentment	Saraqael	M	I'ave'vi'xiv	Eye-<u>ähvee</u>'-vie'-xeye-v'	Watb'hv'v (F)	3%
Multiplication	Uriel	M	I'dide'e	Eye'-<u>dee</u>-deh-eh	Oid't'v (M)	3%

physicospirit person who's aware of their spirit self from an early physical age as well as their Ꜧuman existence as an emergent being of self-aware proto-energy—ℒife—would never be unaware of reality. Aspects like spirit world, Intentionality, ℒife force, the 'reflective' environment where they simultaneously abide, transition from physicospirit to spirit embodiment, and their ability to shift awareness at will from embodiment to unembodiment to travel the megaverse or reside amongst the unembodied-born would be second nature. Their physical environment would accordingly reflect this awareness–experience and be no different from the spirit environment beyond necessary considerations of dimensionality. They'd experience no substantive harm or trauma, no pain arising as suffering leading to psychosis and all its negative effects. Such persons need no help or comfort from task 'angels' to cope with the rigors of physical embodiment, as it wouldn't be any more so than spirit embodiment. The 'archangelic' tasks, formed in The Corruption's milieu, would be, in this context, redundant. But that day isn't here, yet. Next, we describe the seven tasks helping us with an existence we've hitherto known nothing of whatsoever.

Timeline: Archangels

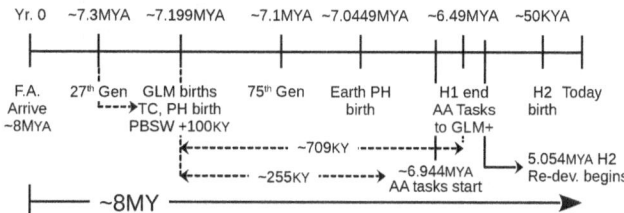

Figure 182. Timeline: First Ancestors (F.A.) and 'archangel' (AA) tasks in the context of The Corruption (TC), physical humanity (PH), physical-born spirit world (PBSW), Gabriel, Lucifer, Michael (GLM), all AA (GLM+), and original and current humanity on Earth (H1, H2). Our generation concept doesn't work here.

2.3.1 Intervention Task—Gabriel

Gabriel, Lucifer, and Michael (GLM), along with two sisters who birthed before and after them, constitute their parents' first societal attachment—a nuclear family, in our context—although it stretched in time from spirit-born humanity's first to 75th generation, a period of about 372KY Earth years (in their parents,' not other families,' context). Their first daughter—the first person birthed in our universe following the Ancestors' arrival, but who lived with GLM as their older sister—is ~372,000 years older than Gabriel, who's of the first generation though born at the 75th generation's start. He's three years older than Lucifer, who's four years older than Michael, who's four years older than their youngest sister, who's the last sibling in this first-Gen societal attachment (their parents have since had five more discrete, nuclear families). The reason for the gap between the first sister and Gabriel is their father, V'nin, planned on her taking over his 'archangelic' role and spent most of that time unsuccessfully persuading her, as she preferred working with her mother seeding planets with Living life, including proto-humans. Since no one from outside their family volunteered to take on V'nin's three tasks, either, he and his spouse gave conceiving additional children a shot; hence, GLM. About 560KY after Lucifer's birth, when physical humanity was ~550KYO, GLM took on V'nin's role, divvied into its three individual tasks (*Fig. 182*).

Humanity typically sees Gabriel as a messenger communicating God's Word to Man. What he and his task 'angels' really do is variously *intervene* with unfolding physical activities (§ 1.3.1:474), focusing on three principal aspects. First, communicating information intended to inform versus educate (§ 2.3.3:525). Second, Gabriel sometimes birthing fully mind–brain integrated persons with physical mothers (Jesus, § 1.3.3.2:475; § 40:613). And third, enabling or disabling certain small and large scale human affairs with the goal of mitigating The Corruption's worst effects in four aspects: 1) mitigating civilization-ending warfare; 2) helping individuals develop awareness toward educating and liberating humanity from its ignorance of reality which entails changing mindsets that, unfortunately, more often than preferred morph into equally ossified religious and philosophical ways of life; 3) enabling or disabling the influence of certain civilizations; and 4) enabling or disabing certain individuals accomplishing their goals.

Intervention 'angels' act like police in that they operate with self-initiative in accord with policy, guidelines, and training Gabriel established with which they agree to abide in their role. This isn't to say some don't go out on a limb and make mistakes. But Gabriel takes notice and works to rectify it as possible. These are human beings after all and, like police officers, can carry themselves away with a sense of duty, justice, fear, desire to help, and the like, which action(s) may not be appropriate to that physical person, time, or place. Their role is to mitigate the *worst* effects of The Corruption, not *every* effect, nor interfere willy-nilly with human autonomy to create their own version of safety and happiness. Neither can any 'angel' always be wholly or even partly successful since, ultimately, they're dealing with autonomous ℒife.

2.3.2 GUIDANCE ('GUARDIAN ANGEL') TASK—LUCIFER

Lucifer—Tivi'iv'z, which he prefers for obvious reasons, though I call him Ivy and the girls usually Kui—running this task was quite the surprise to our religious mindsets owing to his reputation thanks to Michael's Lie (§ 4.1.2:378). But now we know it's wholly undeserved and water under the bridge. *Guidance friend* is what physical humanity is referencing with 'guardian angel.' The term *guardian* is accurate only in the sense such spirit friends strive to *guide* one away (guard) from harm. It needs retiring, as it implies they can literally protect one—"to guard you in all your ways" (Ps. 91:11)—from physical harm, at which history scoffs. This, and the multiplication (§ 2.3.7:528) task, is a full-time job for the duration of the guidee's lifespan. When a person has two-plus guidance friends, Lucifer requires one is always present with their guidee. Before manifesting multiple spirit bodies was common knowledge (§ 1.2.3.3.3:472), these 'angels' necessarily put aspects of their lives on hold for the duration.

2.3.2.1 HOW WE GET A GUIDANCE FRIEND

Lucifer establishes policy and guidelines for guidance friends in consultation with Mina. He delegates day-to-day operations to *guidance groups* averaging about 200 persons, each acting in his stead with individual guidance friends. It's again worth noting (§ 3.5.3:488) that spirit persons don't work under any form of authority because the person is an autonomous being. Not only are they uncompellable against their will but, as volunteers, they subscribe to the task and don't need coercing anyhow. They can certainly err, as noted with intervention and other 'angels' and for the same reasons, but self-correct, accept correction, choose to leave the task, or their guidance group (or Lucifer) separates them. Since Mina and the Ancestors first implemented these tasks circa 6.944MYA, ~7% of guidance friends on average have been separated, going onto other tasks or personal endeavors (*below*).

Guidance friends also quit for personal reasons or for what they see as cause. For example, Stalin's two guidance friends quit—though his validate friend didn't (§ 2.3.4:526)—because he refused to stop perpetrating mass harm. Hitler's two didn't, however, the difference being that Stalin's spirit self was exactly like his physical self whereas Hitler's was appalled by his physical self and tried to influence change. His guidance friends chose to stick with him for that. Although no one accepted Stalin as a guidee after his original two quit, it's normally the case that Lucifer or the guidance group assigns another. Of today's global population who are of age (*below*), about 3% no longer have a guidance friend consequent of their unregenerate harm, although such people can always change and guidance friends would then reassess their participation. Remember, no one compels anyone, including guidance friends

Guidance groups assign spirit persons when the physical individual reaches about five years of age—a maturity that's equivalent to a spirit-born age of two—which is when they're capable of comprehending the world around them, though it naturally differs for each individual plus or minus about a year. Validate

(§ 2.3.4:526) and contentment (§ 2.3.6:527) friends interact with those less than five years old whose spirit self may or may not interact with, or influence, their physical self. Around 20% of physical children prior to receiving their guidance friend(s) have awareness of or interact with their own spirit self or other spirit persons, but this typically declines on Earth to about 1% amongst physical adults. Presently, a person initially receives a single guidance friend on average about 99% of the time. As they grow older and engage in different activities, about 0.52% will receive two (often, though not always, a couple), about 10^{-14} receive three, about 10^{-16} receive four, and very rarely some more than four (only two persons in Humanity 1.0 and 2.0's combined history). The difference arises not only in how Mina and Lucifer perceive one's value to society, but the amount of guidance and support they need in that role.

Occasionally, one's ancestors or unrelated spirit persons train to be a person's additional guidance friend because they perceive value in their activities warranting their commitment. They can't just show up—'self-deploy'—and play guidance friend; they need Lucifer's approval. The spirit-born take interference in physical society seriously when it involves task work; physical-born spirit persons often don't care, considering personal agendas their guide and physical life their domain. The guidance groups don't interfere with them beyond persuasion, but other spirit persons who feel a stake in the outcome, nor bound by a commitment to a task's conduct, will utilize whatever means works for them.

2.3.2.2   How Guidance Friends Experience Us

Guiding the physically alive isn't for everyone. Of the seven tasks, guidance friends have the most constant, visceral, day-in-day-out interaction with, and experience of, physical life. It can be immensely violent, destructive, harmful, traumatizing, and of inarticulable suffering. Not every spirit-born person—who, recall, never experiences such harm or trauma in the supranatural environment—is suited to experiencing much less enduring it. Even the physical-born who choose to become guidance friends can find what happens to their guidee unendurable and psychically debilitating. If 'angels' could physically intervene to stop such suffering in its tracks it would be different, of course. Most would if they could. But they can't. It's not possible. They can only influence and comfort the physical person's spirit self as possible (if they're even consolable), endure any violence and malice and their outcomes as best they can, and work with other individuals' guidance friends to influence their guidee's interaction with their own.

Of course, guidance friends know physical embodiment isn't *L*ife but just an experience ending in one's transition to spirit embodiment sans earthly travails, free to live more or less in sync with *L*ife (according to psyche, especially prior to the Big Healing; § 3.1.2.1.3:359). Stories abound amongst task 'angels' like veterans' war tales, but most rookies to the task don't *really* believe them until experienced. Before we're too carried away here, consider that physical life is generally more peaceful than not and natural disasters don't trouble guidance friends (nor physical persons) the way malice does.

2.3.2.3   How We Experience Our Guidance Friend(s)

Guidance friends can't directly communicate with the physical self (§ 7.1:212; § 1.2.3.3.1:471), who experiences their interest via their spirit side. But recall the spirit selves of ~99% of the physical population so entrench in physical existence they're oblivious to their own spirit reality, usually believing the spirit persons they encounter or activities they pursue as their body sleeps are dreams (§ 1.2.2.7.3:267), hallucinations, and imagination. A physical person who isn't spirit aware, or at least accepts a spirit reality or 'guardian angels,' has greater difficulty accepting their own spirit self's or guidance friend's influence than someone who is or does. Such people most commonly experience guidance in the form of dreams, intuition, second thoughts, a thinking–feeling 'push,' a perceived opportunity, the 'lucky' presence of some person or group, and so on which they chalk up to the mystery of life. The more one considers these experiences not simply as luck or serendipity, the more one alters mindset and raises their general spirit awareness and MBI. This is what most influences a person's affect and life outcomes.

2.3.3   Wisdom Task—Michael

As a cultural affectation, spirit-born society considers age 23 (our age 28 equivalent) the transition from youth to adult. Mina counts it from age nineteen when one's *L*ife force is, on average, capable of unembodiment (discerned in observing its interaction with supranatural proto-energy around the spirit body). This varies by individual, with eleven being the youngest age known (§ 2:339) and no upper limit on when a person achieves it. No one in our universe is presently capable of unembodiment (§ 2.1.1.1:349), as The Corruption obscured even its possibility. Mina estimates the first spirit person will achieve it by 2032.

Although Michael's 'day job' is the wisdom task, his hobby is educating junior adults during their 17–18th years as a schoolteacher which occupies about a quarter of his time. His avocation surprised the girls and me since religion paints him God's champion warrior. I thought Michael must be the polar opposite because of his Lie but Mina corrected me, calling him an intractable defender of justice. You might hear the booming echo of my "*Whaaat?!*" and catch my eyebrows riding a space elevator, considering Michael delivered the greatest injustice ever not only to Lucifer but, in never owning up to it until 2017, to universal humanity, too. That's a crushing contradiction for a person to carry. Mina says it's the reason Michael was, in truth, the most tortured soul of our universe, all our physical-born psychotic suffering notwithstanding. Until the Big Healing, the spirit-born were generally as oblivious of the physical-born existing as we've been of the spirit-born. No one who did know, however, felt Michael should resign or be let go from his task. Universal humanity did insist he walk what we called his *ninth-step*—'making amends,' in the Alcoholics Anonymous recovery playbook (§ 1.1:19)—to every person wanting his apology; it took him from October 14, 2017 to July 2019 in Earth time.

In *The City of God*, Augustine avers in paraphrase that, "Justice is that ordering of the soul by virtue of which it comes to pass that we are no man's servant, but servants of God alone" (Kirk 1993, 2). Although there is no God, hence no divine justice "that gives every one his due" (Augustine (1610) 1909, 217), there is human woB that's fundamentally autonomous, which is justice *as liberty*. This is what Michael champions. His Lie never abrogated any person their liberty, thus their human woB, because no one need adopt it and, verily, some didn't. Only The Corruption that Mina's sisters Intentionally induced in universal humanity without awareness or permission—irresistibly, like sitting ducks—thus against our will, was coercive and therefore unjust (§ 2.1:368). And though Michael the wisdom 'archangel' is the foremost defender of justice as we've defined it, he was at the same time a victim of The Corruption that impaired his own human woB. The Accountableism humanity built out of his Lie renders him *the* prime candidate for receiving his just desserts, yet that alpha mindset itself *is* The Corruption and alien not just to Mina but 𝓛ife. Even before the Big Healing, the spirit-born understood this.

Michael, therefore, was and remains the wisdom 'archangel' because—counterintuitively for us on Earth mired in Accountableism and its alpha justice—he most embodies human woB *as justice* amongst universal humanity, and the wisdom task itself embodies human woB *as the font of wisdom*. It communicates information intended to educate on human woB versus inform on interventional matters. For example, the wisdom friend who solicited Muhammad on her own initiative to reform and revitalize Jesus' legacy of Christianity (§ 1.3.2.2:474; § 40:616) lacked Michael's awareness of human woB. She acted more the agent of intervention than the educator of wisdom. Consequently, she mischose the physical individual to educate about that which Christianity was then lacking. Naturally, the harmful effects of what she conveyed neither Michael nor Mina could undo any more than one can, say, un-birth emergent 𝓛ife.

2.3.4 VALIDATE TASK—REMIEL

In terms of the number of task angels devoted to the validate task (16% of the total), it's by far the third most important, right behind the entry (38%) and guidance (28%) tasks that, respectively, support transition from physical to spirit embodiment and direct guidance to the physical person's spirit self. Recall 𝓛ife births *pairwise* (§ 2:304). That's just fundamental human woB. Mina developed this task because The Corruption's principal effect on the physical-born impairs MBI which interrupts pairwise woB, thus the relational interactions of one's 𝓛ife and physical self. As with guidance and contentment friends, validate friends are present with the awake or asleep person or (when elsewhere) always 'tuned' to the person's situation so they can instantly respond as needed. This task has three aspects.

First, like a close companion, the validate friend pays attention to the physical self's experiences, meaning their life circumstances and awareness–experience. Like any spirit person generally, validate friends can't affect physical outcomes though they can sometimes mitigate its effect. Suppose one falls off a cliff. A spirit person—task 'angel,' spirit guide, family, friend—might take advantage of weather, terrain, or aspects of Fundamental Force and applied energy E to, say, provoke a gust of wind or manipulate the physical body toward surviving landing if they know how and one's spirit self doesn't oppose it (sometimes one wants to escape physical life). We see this sort of intervention when, for instance, aimed bullets land everywhere mere hairs breadths from lethality. But this isn't the purpose of the validate task. We only mention it to emphasize there's no such thing as 'not my job' when it comes to spirit persons invested in caring for physical individuals.

Validate friends specifically focus their attention on ensuring a physical person doesn't experience a sense of wholesale abandonment or rejection in their environment of impaired pairwise relationality. This naturally depends on the person's MBI and intuitive capability, because validate friends speak directly to one's spirit self as a confidant to convey validation—awareness, understanding, empathy—so the person doesn't feel forsaken. This isn't just a sop to one's ear. As with guidance and contentment friends, validate friends develop close, affectionate connections with those in their care, like any true intimate. The reality is every physical person has spirit friends and family around them who may or may not have the skills or inclination necessary to intervene physically (via the 'reflective' environment; § 7.1.1.1:212) but, if nothing else, are *present*, of which one's spirit self is, to greater or lesser degrees, aware. The reason some physical people feel protected and cared for, while others feel abandoned regardless any shared circumstance, results from task 'angels' and spirit persons inclusive of one's mindset, intuition, and chakras (CH. 29:497).

Second, besides validating a person as their true companion, validate friends are the origin of hope (§ 6.3.1:435) which, though arising intrinsic of *L*ife, a physical person may not experience much if at all due to poor MBI, intuition, or insufficiently 'open' chakras (§ 2.1:625). Hope, for example, enables as well as validates confidence which in turn enables *self*-confidence. A physicospirit individual with adequate MBI (thus, a strong intuitive sense) intrinsically experiences hope as an aspect of their *L*ife self but others may not. Validate friends Intentionalize the *energy of hope* as Living force, which the physical individual integrates via chakras (§ 1.2.1.2:499). Since these never actually 'close' but only integrate Intentionalized Living force as chakra energy at a 10% minimus which we take as a 'closed' condition, then every physical individual, regardless their MBI and chakra condition, can experience some sense of hope so long as their mindset doesn't reject it as unreal, pointless, unwanted, and so on. In this latter case, an individual need address their subconscious mind's closed attitude if they're feeling hopeless. Any spirit person can learn to Intentionalize Living force as this specific quality, but it's the validate friend's raison d'être.

Third, Remiel (or her control groups) assigns a validate friend to the physicospirit individual at about age three months in the womb as the young, pre-age-five child's companion. He or she acts in that role until a guidance 'angel' arrives (§ 2.3.2.1:524). This is whom most young children have a unique awareness–experience of where no spirit family, friends, or guides are present.

2.3.5 Entry Task—Raguel

We've already described Raguel's entry task (§ 4.2.2:426). Its principal purpose is to meet and educate the just-deceased physical person in the 'reflective' environment. The reason for it is The Corruption's effect on MBI. A physical individual's spirit self is generally unaware of their spirit reality and upon death is surprised, frightened, confused, or unsure of what comes next when their awareness transitions from physical to spirit embodiment in the 'reflective' environment (§ 4:419). Most people tend to think the 'reflective' environment *is* spirit world and could pointlessly linger there. The entry 'angel' educates them (if no one else has) on basic universal reality. They help them cope, teach transitioning between the supranatural and 'reflective' environments and, if they're willing then or later to go to spirit world, accompanies them to the physical-born area best resonating with their unique *L*ife force so they experience minimum discomfort and suffering from non-resonant, 'clashing' energy 'frequencies,' as described.

2.3.6 Contentment Task—Saraqael

The nature of Saraqael's task mandates the self-control of the task 'angel' despite whatever close, personal, caring connection they develop with the physicospirit individual. Accordingly, he recruits and assigns only those physical- and spirit-born persons who can make that commitment, because the purpose of this task is to improve one's contentedness with physical embodiment. Contentment friends accomplish this by Intentionalizing Living force as a healing agent that integrates the physical body via the chakras (§ 1.2.1.2.1:499) to sustain health. They can't heal everything, of course. Some damage is beyond the time required of Living force, such as mechanical injuries like separated tendons, ongoing damage from mindset, or cancer that's lethal sooner than Living force (or the person's *L*ife force) can reverse it since, recall, there's no such thing as instant healing of biology that's built of independently self-existent matter having its own WOB (§ 7.1.3:214; CH. 28:465; CH. 35:577). The physical body can re-grow severed nerves and limbs provided the physicospirit individual has adequate MBI and sufficient *L*ife and Living force integrating the body, but Mina estimates this capability is something like 250 years in the future.

Recall the physical body is capable of indefinite survival. But Mina recommends individuals transition from physicospirit to spirit embodiment no later than ±10,000 years. He feels greater longevity overly ensconces one in their physical versus spirit embodiment despite physicospiritually integrating both (§ 2.2.3:342). He experienced this firsthand in his own universe when his family and friends objected to him transitioning from physical to spirit so he could build our universe (§ 2.1:340). In his mind, his particular embodiment was irrelevant since he, like everyone, is intrinsically an unembodied person of emergent self-aware proto-energy (§ 6.1.1:431). While one's physical body won't suddenly drop dead in its ten-thousandth year, lengthy physical embodiment eventually affects mindset that, despite full MBI, could eventually lead to a new separation twixt physicospirit and spirit humanity that Mina hopes we avoid.

A contentment friend Intentionalizes healing 'energy' if one's physical or spirit self wants it, but not if the physicospirit self doesn't. This is where contentment 'angel' self-control comes in. When we care about someone, we oft want what *we* think is best for them, especially when we think *they* don't know what's in their own best interest. That's not the contentment friend's call. They're there to help, not as an authority to compel. Regardless one's physically conscious desire, their subconscious mindset may have a different perspective that makes healing impossible anyhow. We see this when a heartbroken person dies not from physiology but just expires when their spirit self walks away from physical embodiment. Like Remiel, Saraqael assigns friends as companions to underage physicospirit individuals (§ 2.3.4:526).

2.3.7 MULTIPLICATION TASK—URIEL

Science imagines that, over the course of billions of years, Earth settled down from the wild geological output (volcanoes) of its youth to its present-day sedate rumble-tumble that sustains microbial to human life. This is incorrect, as the observation is its own data self-referentially deriving its justification. Earth's geological activity didn't abate sufficiently for life to form because that's a planet's natural, inevitable outcome over time but, rather, is consequent of Intentionality corralling its 'energy.' Any planet having the capability of supporting life has the same *iconosphere*—those aspects of a planet which altogether enable Living (§ 1.3:272)—that, via its constituent litho-, magneto-, atmo-, and other spheres, harnesses searing core heat coupled with solar radiation to establish sustainable habitability. This lies within a narrow range of factors that altogether don't constitute a natural equilibrium but merely the habitable locus of a fluctuating series of environmental loci. Earth's habitability arises in a minute band of geological output which didn't happen on account of Earth naturally—undirectedly—sufficiently cooling or maturing, but because all its potent 'energy' was Intentionally repurposed from extreme geology to support Living entities as the origin of Living life on Earth. Habitable planets exist for ℒife with Living entities, not the reverse.

2.3.7.1 MACROCOSMIC FORCE

It shouldn't be a surprise at this point in the book to realize habitable planets like Earth are *terraformed*. Not via technology manipulating matter in the context of applied energy E but via Intentionality manipulating matter–Energy (§ 2:114) and proto-energy in the context of *Macrocosmic force*, an Intentionalized non-Living version of Living force (§ 1.3:272). Ley lines arise in it, for instance. Macrocosmic force enlivens all *physical processes*, meaning the forces and principles of action of matter and energy, just as Living force enlivens all physical processes of biology. Living force is why inert matter has the properties of aliveness and not from attaining a certain configuration in a particular environment where the chemistry of life just happens. Similarly, the physical processes of inert matter behave such that matter naturally forms and behaves in its environment of Fundamental Force and applied energy E *conducive to* Living entities (life). We say 'naturally' because, without Macrocosmic force, matter forms and behaves randomly and without regard to life. It might or might not *ever* be conducive to life but if it ever were, it would be random *and unstable*, which is no way to build a universe the very purpose of which is as a home wherein ℒife embodies. This is one reason some scientists consider our randomly 'fine-tuned' universe so improbable (e.g., Robert Dicke, Fred Hoyle, Hugh Ross, et al.).

Macrocosmic force is as essential to life as Living force. Being an Intentionalized force, its WOB always seeks compatibility with life. It's what converts, or terraforms, a planet from a stochastically potential environment for life to a certain one. The reason Mars no longer supports life is because The Corruption made an inhabited planet next door to us—a pre-Corruption experiment (§ 3:357)—untenable. Foreseeing it, Mina asked these 'angels' to re-Intentionalize its environment sans life. Now, they're reversing it. He estimates ~20MY to reestablish microbial life (not considering what we do there in the interim).

Besides Mars, The Corruption raised another issue. The Negative Collective Consciousness (NCC; § 4.2:379)—a universal 'collective mindset' similar to individual mindset rooted in the subconscious exerting a dominating Intentional effect, such as subverting conscious will as it represents *self* more than conscious mind—exerted Intentionality into the universe that disrupted aspects of Mina's Intentionality; in this context, Macrocosmic force. This means the NCC, arising in negative emotive *Life* force (EmᴸF; § 3.3.3.1.1:289), disrupted the Intentionalized operation of our universe to render natural disaster epidemic just as negative EmᴸF disrupts the Intentional biology of the physical body to render disease and infirmity epidemic. The result was planets randomly hostile to life just as disease and malfunction is to the body.

While the other 'archangelic' tasks focus their attention on the individual person and human society, this task focuses on the environment that makes physical embodiment possible. Multiplication friends constantly—as with guidance friends, it's a full-time task—'fine tune' human inhabited planets to remain conducive to life by 'multiplying' the original Intentionality of Macrocosmic force whenever and wherever it 'weakens' under the influence of the NCC. Although the NCC dissolved with Lucifer and Michael's Reconciliation the morning of October 13, 2017, its effect continues rippling through the natural environment like an echo. Mina estimates about 5KY for Macrocosmic force to reestablish *effectively* stable conduciveness to life on Earth. Natural events like volcanoes, earthquakes, tsunamis, or large meteor strikes will decline in volume and magnitude during this period until, eventually, none occur. All of the 'energy' in and around Earth will harmonize as an iconosphere naturally conducive to life.

2.4 Additional Tasks—Michael and Remiel

Michael and Remiel organize, respectively, one and two additional tasks also consequent of The Corruption's effect, the former utilizing ~0.33% and the latter two ~0.66% of all task 'angels' (Table 17:523). These aren't strictly 'archangelic' tasks because they don't interact with physical humanity. Two involve natural–supranatural 'energy' translation in the Living (nonhuman) and Living–*Life* (physical human) categories, and one involves Energent–prime's interaction with the Energent of our universe, as below.

2.4.1 Michael's Additional Task

All things require 'energy' and spirit world is no exception. Recall the Intentionalized supranatural Energent enlivens that environment (§ 7.1.3:214) and that supranatural proto-energy isn't actual proto-energy as that of the natural Energent. Spirit world accordingly gets its 'energy' from the physical world in a tripartite 'energy' translation process. This task monitors that via Method Two (ibid; § 7.3:220) involving the pairwise bonded-archí of Living entities exclusive of the human body. For example, if a planet experiences a wholesale loss of Living entities,[498] the 'angels' supporting this additional task intervene to establish other species in their stead in order that its Living populations sustain a certain threshold as defined by the amount of 'energy' their physical existence translates. Although this task is additional to Michael's principal 'archangelic' task (§ 2.3.3:525), it's the only task for those 'angels' who work it with him.

2.4.2 Remiel's Additional Tasks

The first of Remiel's two additional tasks essentially does with Living human bodies what Michael's does with nonhuman Living entities in the context of Method Two just described, except they don't (nor even can) influence *Life* arising 'in' EPL. Rather, when a planet experiences a wholesale loss of Living–*Life* (human body) entities, the 'angels' supporting this task intervene to establish more Living (nonhuman) entities in their stead in order that planetary Living populations somewhat make up for the Living–*Life* population that declines below a certain threshold as defined by the amount of 'energy' their physical embodiment translates. Remiel's second additional task simply monitors—has awareness–experience of—Energent–prime's interaction with the Energent of our universe. It's a very small, part-time effort. Recall that although Mina built our universe to be wholly 'energy' self-sufficient, it nonetheless integrates about 19% of its 'energy' needs from Energent–prime (§ 7.5:222). This is mainly because The Corruption's effect suppressed physical humanity and Living entities' populations, and *Life* and Living–*Life* in the natural environment hasn't kept pace with that in the supranatural, leading to an ever-increasing 'energy' imbalance between the two. This only

---

498. Pre-human mass extinction events are a natural cycle in planetary habitability, but the Quaternary Extinction, ca. 50KYA–10KYA, arose in Mina's effort 30KY earlier to normalize the global climate prior to the advent of Humanity 2.0 (§ 2.1:542).

rectifies with the natural environment's Energent—and, via 'energy' translation (§ 7.1.3:214), the supranatural environment—integrating Energent–prime proto-energy.

We don't naturally (subconsciously or consciously) have awareness–experience of Energent–prime because, in practice, it's alien to emergent self-aware proto-energy, which is ♄uman. Recall humanity emergently births 'in' EPL, itself an emergent property of Energent–prime. This makes them all proto-energy yet quite different *expressions* of it, just as thinking is quite different from feeling yet both arising in the same mind as aspects of Thought (§ 2.3.2:240). As this is the case, Mina need consciously focus his mind on Energent–prime in order to have awareness–experience of it. This wasn't an issue for him prior to the First Ancestors and the rise of humanity in our universe, since Energent–prime's interaction with the Energent was invariant. However, the rise of The Corruption and physical humanity, universal humanity's population growth and activities, and the influence of the NCC turned Energent–prime's interaction with the Energent variant. Despite Energent–prime naturally integrating, or 'flowing into,' our universe (§ 7.4:221) the way an ocean naturally flows into a bay, Mina felt it prudent to monitor in case a need for his Intentional action arose. He established this additional task so its task 'angels' could always have awareness–experience of the situation and keep him apprised in the context of the 898 other tasks he alone handles. It's really just a convenience for him, but one he appreciates and these ten 'angels' don't mind obliging.

Earth's Human History

HAVING DESCRIBED A generalized account of physical humanity's origins throughout the observable universe (§ 2.3.2:240; § 2.1.5.5:322; § 3:357; CH. 31:519), here we describe physical humanity's history on Earth. Science and religion have no concept of Ꞩuman or Ɬife (§ 1.2.1:247) and analyze our origin exclusively in the nonhuman alpha context of physical embodiment with a side of divine albeit sinfully base creation as though the human body, in and of itself, *is* the ꝑerson (§ 2.3.2.1:241; Introduction, CH. 19:245). Physical humanity is physicospiritually embodied Ɬife (§ 2.1.5.5:322). Other than its influence on one's Ɬife mind in The Corruption's milieu, embodiment is irrelevant to understanding who and what we—*you*—are. To comprehend physical humanity, one need be aware of this distinction else it's impossible to reconcile human reality (our way of being (WOB); § 2.2.1.1:234) with the human condition we physically experience. This is why every philosophy, religion, and ideology germinating in physical humanity's nonhuman alpha mindset (§ 9.2.2:450) necessarily fails millennia after millennia to deliver it from the ignorance, fear, and harm ever anchoring it in the mire. It's been this way since The Corruption first twisted physical humanity's mindset from its core human WOB of absolute autonomy to its obsession with nonautonomous altruism (§ 1:361) and our consequent loss of knowledge and awareness of Ꞩuman.

On Earth, this obsession first arose in Original Humanity (H1) which initially absorbed it from its spirit-born parents (§ 2.1.2.2.1:371) and then afterward in the milieu of family, culture, and ultraculture (§ 4.1:291) until it destroyed itself in a spasm of warfare. Ensuant to that, the spirit-born reiterated H1 as version 2.0, which is to say, *us* (H2; § 2:542). Hence, two discrete human sociocultures of unique personality have separately dwelt on Earth. Accordingly, we need distinguish H1 and H2's tenures, the period before H1's birth, and the interhuman period between H1 and H2. To convey their historical scope, we developed the nomenclature in Table 18 and dispense in Section 1 with '*x* years ago' for the Y*x* format and in Section 2 the BC–AD and BCE–CE conventions as well. For example, we write H1's omnicidal war as APH 521559, which we contextually shorten in the text to Y521559; H2's founding of Rome in 758 BC (cf. trad. 753 BC) as ASH 46943, shortened to Y46943; the AD 581 founding of the *Sui* dynasty in China as ASH 48282 (Y48282), and references that lay outside H1 and H2's tenures as noted. Dating is ET-derived (§ 3:557).

SECTION 1
Original Humanity (Version 1.0)

For about 154.1KY after Mina's two sisters surreptitiously Intentionalized (§ 3.2:282) The Corruption amongst spirit-born humanity (§ 2.1.2:370), our spirit-born ancestors had been establishing physical humans around the observable universe. Then they turned to birthing Original Humanity (H1) on Earth. H1 was born into The Corruption as we of Ensuing Humanity (H2) later were, but it was then too new and unintegrated in spirit humanity's mindset for any immediately harmful effect to present physically; that would come in time. H1 birthed with full mind–brain integration (MBI; § 1.2.2.4:257), having knowledge and awareness of physicospirit

Table 18. Calendric timeline nomenclature; PH is physical humanity.

Period (name)	Nomenclature	Symbol/Short-form	Period (years ago)
Before PH	*Anno antehumanum*; "In the year [ITY] before humanity"	AAH/AH	≥ ~7.0449MYA
Original (H1)	*Anno primus humanum*; "ITY of first [Original] humanity"	APH/PH	~7.0449MYA–6.49MYA
Between H1–H2	*Anno interhumanum*; "ITY between humanity"	AIH/IH	~6.49MYA–49,722YA
Ensuant (H2)	*Anno secundus humanum*; "ITY of second [Ensuant] humanity"	ASH/SH	~49,722YA–present

embodiment (§ 1.2.1:407) and spirit reality just as H2 initially did millions of years later, although by then our environment was saturated in The Corruption, the NCC, and all its harmful effects. H1 lasted ~554.9KY before extinguishing itself in a war roughly eight centuries beyond today's technology. We describe its origin, general history, and squalid end below.

1.1 ORIGINAL HUMANITY'S ORIGINS

A planet's physical humanity begins with the development of a habitable environment via Intentional, Living-entity-conducive Macrocosmic force (§ 1.3:272; § 2.3.7.1:528). The First Ancestors' spouses, along with other spirit-born working this task collectively designated *abiogeneticists* (§ 2.1:522), evolutionarily develop Living entities that lead to proto-humans as Mike and Molly did before them (§ 2.1.6.2:329). Abiogeneticists then integrate them and, via sexual reproduction, trigger emergence of ℒife 'in' Energent proto-life (EPL) from which the first physicospirit ℒife births on that planet as their children (*Fig. 185*; § 2.3.2.1:241; § 1.2.1.1.1:248; § 2.1.5.5:322). Recall the physical human body is merely an *embodiment* and not in and of itself a *being*, that ℒife is a being of emergent self-aware proto-energy who births in accord with EPL and not an artifact of physical or spirit conception. No being—human, divine, or otherwise—has any creational power to 'make' a person, only to evolve a physical proto-human body and the Intentional, pairwise (§ 2:304) capability to 'trigger' emergent birth of ℒife 'in' EPL via sexual reproduction.

Humans, therefore, aren't creations, divine or otherwise. We're uniquely birthed emergent ℒife, the children of abiogeneticists societally 'descended' from their own spirit-born parents going back to the First Ancestor couples of our universe (§ 2.1.1:348). They themselves are Mina and Ag'poprje's (§ 2.2:341) children and spouses, whose own 'descent'—societal attachment (§ 3:414; § 1.1.1:520)—eventually wends back to the first humans, Mike and Molly (§ 2.1:305). Abiogeneticists' first-generation physical-born children and descendant families populate their planets—in our case, Earth—just as the First Ancestors' spirit-born children and descendant families spiritually populated our universe (*Fig. 183*). Establishing physical humanity on a planet isn't alien, magical, divine, evolutionarily random, or otherwise inexplicable. It's a natural family-building process initiated by spirit-born abiogeneticists integrating physical proto-humans whose physicospirit-embodied children then family-build into the future. Below, we describe Earth's initial environmental condition, proto-human evolution, and the rise of physicospirit humanity as H1.

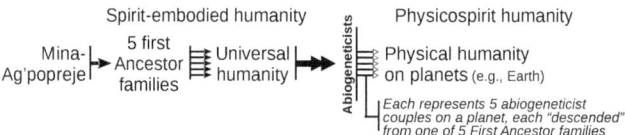

Figure 183. Familial 'descent' (societal attachment) of physical humanity via spirit-born abiogeneticists.

1.1.1 SETTING THE ENVIRONMENTAL SCENE FOR H1

A planetoid struck a semi-molten Earth approximately 5.275BYA (as of AD 2021) and sank about 80% of itself into the planet's structure. This left Earth lopsided with an inconsistent but faster rotation. It amalgamated about 20% of the planetoid but, 754MY later, the remainder parted with Earth under centrifugal force and became our moon. Mina considered Earth complete around 20MY later, or 4.521BYA. This constitutes its age, since before then it was just a variably sized planetesimal, or proto-planet, building itself into a planet. It settled into stabilizing and self-organizing in accord with Macrocosmic force in the universe's milieu of Fundamental

Force and applied energy E (§ 1:112). By age 25MY, its crust solidified, meaning it no longer exhibited a molten surface. By age 50MY, it achieved a recognizable though nonoxygenated atmosphere. The first bodies of water, which Mina considers lakes, formed on its surface by age 100MY and covered 8% of the surface (cf. at present (AP) 71% water, 1.8% lakes) by age 125MY. When oxygen levels reached ~0.005% of present atmospheric levels (cf. ~20.9% AP) circa age 200.983MY, and sufficient numbers of these lakes reached depths of 18–21 m (60–70 ft.), having lakebeds of a kind of mud (lacking microorganism remains) comprising 60% clay and 40% silt about two-thirds meter (2 ft.) deep, abiogeneticists got busy establishing Living entities (*Fig. 184*).

What science calls the *abiogenesis hypothesis*—the spontaneous transition of inert matter to life (§ 1.3.1:272)—was the effort of spirit-born individuals performing the abiogenetic task, which reached fruition 7MY later with the rise of noncellular life in these lakebeds. This nonlife-to-life transition wasn't an instant or single event but, consistent with abiogenesis, an increasingly complex, directed evolutionary process (§ 2.1.5.5.2.1:323) involving self-assembly, autocatalysis, molecular self-replication, and the emergence of cell membranes, which process we don't describe in this book. There's no agreed-upon definition of life amongst Philosophy with a capital-P but, for Mina (in the nonhuman context), it's simply motility and thinking–acting in accord with capacity regardless sophistication. Abiogeneticists carried on directly evolving life of ever more complexity until achieving the first proto-humans about 7.23MYA.

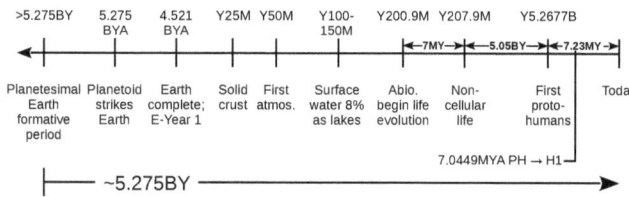

Figure 184. Timeline: planetesimal Earth through abiogenesis to proto-humans (PH).

1.1.2 PROTO-HUMAN EVOLUTION FOR H1

The timeline shows that developing life from inert chemistry to proto-human is a lengthy process, but it's considerably quicker between the most primitive primates to one capable of integrating ℒife (Fig. 192:543). We define *proto-human* as a Living entity directly evolved to integrate ℒife as the physical aspect of physicospirit embodiment. This means the brain–body is capably consistent with the human mind and all it can do. Naturally, it isn't possible for a ℘erson to integrate a primitive primate since that body structure not only lacks essential physiological components necessary for MBI by which the brain transliterates mind to physical action, but is inconsistent with human WOB (§ 1.2.2.4:257; § 2.1.5:313). The only difference between a proto-human and you is the proto-human brain isn't integrating a human mind; it can't function as ℌuman. Otherwise, it's indistinguishable. Physicospirit humanity births when abiogeneticist couples integrate thirteen(ish)-year old male and female proto-humans—the body now has full MBI and is behaviorally indistinguishable from ℌuman (*Fig. 185*)—who then conceive children, triggering ℒife's emergent birth (§ 1.2.1.1.1:248), a ℘erson like you. The instant you emergently birth, however, *you* integrate your physical body. There's no '*in* but not *of*' the physical body as there is with family or chakras (§ 1.1.1:520; § 2:509). This is how a planet's physical humanity initially births.

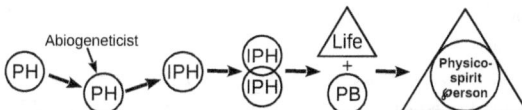

Figure 185. Abiogeneticist integrates a proto-human (PH); two such (IPH) sexually conceive, triggering birth of emergent ℒife integrating the physical body (PB) as a physicospirit-embodied ℘erson.

1.1.3 H1: THE RISE OF PHYSICOSPIRIT HUMAN ℒIFE

Although there's no distinction between you and your integrated physical body, *you* are not your *body*. You're emergent ℒife integrating a body, not an evolved life form existing only so long as your body does. The process and methodology that abiogeneticists undertake to build and integrate a planet's proto-humans toward birthing its first physicospirit humans is the same that Mike and Molly pioneered (§ 2.1.5:313). At this point in universal humanity's history, the spirit-born were only just experiencing the first effects of The Corruption and the Negative Collective Consciousness (NCC; § 1.2:21). Accordingly, Earth 200MYA was geologically stable—with few earthquakes and volcanoes—and conducive to life (MACROCOSMIC FORCE, § 2.3.7.1:528). These halcyon days began waning 7.1MYA as the NCC gradually disturbed Macrocosmic force and Earth's Intentionally corralled natural 'energies' increasingly exerted throughout the planet in the humanly destructive ways we've always considered normal.

Earth's continents 7.0449MYA were roughly the same as today. Abiogeneticists had established five proto-human populations of about 500 individuals each in suitable locations (*Fig. 186*), one in modern-day Europe (Spain, Mediterranean coast), two in Asia (India, state of Goa inland; China, Hunan province), and two in Africa (Angola, Atlantic coast; Kenya, Indian Ocean coast) following Mina's wide spacing of human-inhabited planets (§ 3:357). On any given planet, it serves as redundancy and a starting point for physiological diversity. As noted, abiogeneticists integrated two proto-humans per group to birth Earth's first physical-born humans who subsequently triggered new emergent physicospirit *L*ife via sexual procreation to build Ꞓuman families that populated Earth. Abiogeneticists later Intentionalized a decline in proto-human fertility after 900 years in order that seven H1 generations could interact with them toward understanding there's no relationship between proto-human animals and *L*ife. H1's average male–female height was ~170.1 cm and 167.6 cm (5 ft.–7 in., 5 ft.–6 in.), respectively, with brown and green eye colors that later differentiated.

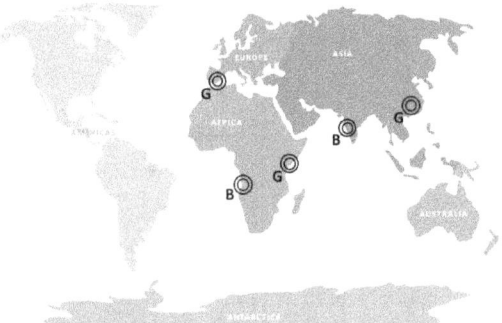

Figure 186. Original humanity's (H1) five points of origin 'descended' from each of the First Ancestor families via abiogeneticists; Mina distinguishes Europe from Asia by fauna present at H1's birth and the Americas as a single landmass; brown (**B**) and green (**G**) eye color as shown.[293]

1.2   ORIGINAL HUMANITY'S GENERAL HISTORY

The salient point about H1 is, even though its MBI remained twice and even two-thirds the physicospirit norm ~20KY longer than H2's (§ 2.3.1:545), it lacked useful awareness–experience of its spirit reality. It early on abandoned autonomy for the nonautonomy of ideology. As a mindset, it locked H1 in an ultraculture it never seriously attempted to rebut or discard. This isn't too different from H2 although its outcome differs for other reasons. Recall that ideology isn't simply a system of belief, perspective, or way of life but a solution imposed on others (§ 1.1.3.5.2:367). A person, group, nation, bloc, or even a planet embodies it as a nonautonomous way of life, the way it instinctively thinks–feels–acts without recourse to alternatives. No H1 person ever altered their mindset—way of life expression—to seriously (insistently, forcibly) press alternatives, a chief H2 characteristic that ineluctably pursues individual alternatives to collective ways of life. H1 intrinsically abhorred rebellion and idolized alpha grouping. This wasn't the case on every then-inhabited planet, but certainly defined Earth. Before describing H1's history, we need comprehend its mindset to understand its self-destruction despite its individually and materially satisfied society.

1.2.1   ORIGINAL HUMANITY'S MINDSET

The Corruption defined H1's mindset. It expressed as Accountableism whereby the individual is necessarily accountable not to individual reality—to oneself—but to universal reality: God, gods, deities, moral truth in the context of philosophy or religion, and sociocultural norms (Accountableism, § 4.1.2:378). We have good examples of this in twentieth century Communist, Socialist, Nazi, Fascist, monarchist, theocratic, militaristic, and otherwise ideologically-driven societies that are necessarily totalitarian, as well as more famously ancient examples in Greece and both republican and imperial Rome.

We described The Corruption (§ 1:361) and don't repeat it here except to note its distinguishing feature is the autonomous adoption of nonautonomous mindsets and, in the physical milieu, embracing the intrinsically nonautonomous mindset of nonhuman, alpha WOB (§ 9.2.2:450, ibid). This arose in H1 by its third generation, a mere forty-five years following the birth of integrated emergent $\mathcal{L}$ife (§ 1.1.2:533), regardless H1's full awareness–experience of spirit reality and conversance with the spirit-born. This is because spirit-born humanity was undergoing its own Corruption-induced mindset metamorphosis from autonomy to nonautonomy. It affected them less problematically because their Intentional, supranatural environment mitigated its worst effects owing to the impossibility of forcibly coercing individuals, immunity from embodiment death, and routinely manipulating matter via Intentionality.

Notwithstanding H1's early-on comprehension of physical embodiment as an *aspect* of spirit embodiment, the spirit-born began losing touch with their human WOB since their 27th generation (Fig. 148:355). By the time they established physical humanity, they believed the individual *was* their spirit embodiment and forgot they were $\mathcal{L}$ife beings *independent of embodiment* despite the Ancestors' efforts to help them remain aware of their increasingly Corruption-obfuscated reality. Their mindset naturally suffused their physical descendants. As MBI—interrupted by the NCC much as it disturbs Macrocosmic force—declined generation-to-generation, the physically alive also forgot they were spirit-embodied beings *independent of physical embodiment* despite sensing life was more than mere physical existence.

The Corruption induced in H1 the mindset of no-harm (altruism; § 1.1:362) which necessarily entails coercion and therefore harm. Even so, nonautonomy arose as the antidote to the perception of autonomy's greater harm. Slavery didn't, however, due to altruism's hold on their mindset. In their $\sim$554.9KY history, individuals were free in the sense of being at liberty so long as it never contradicted altruism. We see a similar mindset in the Russian Federation and post-reform Communist China that permits regulated individual liberty so long as it doesn't contradict the State. H1 built itself a global altruistic State prescribing Individual core Culture that altogether was local-to-global culture, superculture, megaculture, and Ultraculture (§ 4.1:291). In this milieu, it was possible for H1 to establish harmonious intrasocietal relations where no individual materially lacked basic or desired goods while societally raising the individual as the *family* of the State, itself governed oligarchically by an extended family operating like a distributed head of household (*below*; § 9:446). This societal setup embodied the absolute, unconditional trust and love from child to parent that's sufficient and all encompassing for the child while the parent knows there's more to life and lives it in that context. H1 was so utterly brainwashed that no one needed oppressing, repressing, jailing, or otherwise abusing by the State or socioculture.

Yet, the politico-socioculture did persecute them in the sense elites jealously guarded their knowledge of Living force as a physical healing power (§ 1.3:272; CH. 35:577) they'd developed circa H1's $4,000^{th}$ year (Y4000). It denied the masses this healing unless earned through service to the sociocultural Family as top-tier soldiers or public servants who were the extended ruling family's direct reports. Just as elites today withhold food, money, medicine, liberty, and the like from the poor, the out-of-favor, scorned minorities, the unconnected—anyone societally disadvantaged—or just because they can, H1's elites behaved more as a revered priesthood of healthcare holding the power of extended life over the people. We don't pass judgment on H1 despite its willful self-destruction—it's not like we've never come close and could've certainly repeated its mistake during the USA–USSR Cold War if not for Intervention task 'angels' (§ 2.3.1:523)—because in many ways their socioculture was more enlightened than any built by H2. A peaceful, harmonious, safe society was H1's priority, not individual liberty, knowledge, or personal power. But the altruistic *global* society they built is only so in the *local* (national) sense. Their various sociocultures (§ 1.1.3:533) settled on mutual ideological hostility and remained so to their final war, reconciling only in its toxic, rubbled aftermath. We describe H1's general history in three parts.

1.2.2   Timeline: Origin to Global Ideologism

H1 kicked off with spirit-born persons—abiogeneticists—integrating proto-humans to birth physicospirit human beings. This marks its year one (Y1). Its first generation started out having full MBI, but its second and third generations birthed having only 70% and 60% integrated brain to mind. This was a sharp change from the first generation, which immediately noticed. They consulted their spirit-born extended families that, as yet, had neither conscious awareness of The Corruption as a situation nor an explanation for the societal changes they themselves seemed to be experiencing. This included the First Ancestors who certainly should have consulted Mina yet chose not to, an autonomy he couldn't compel (§ 2.1.2.2.1:371; by H1's second generation the spirit-born had reached their 90th generation and 150 quadrillion (q) people representing 63 generations of The Corruption[499]). The NCC was now exerting a perceptible influence throughout our universe it hadn't yet achieved by the spirit-born's 75th generation when GLM+ were born and abiogeneticists were just initiating physicospirit-embodied ℒife (§ 2.2:522).

In any case, H1's first generation had no option than to accept the reality its future generations would have no physical-self access to their own spirit selves, to the other family groups on Earth with whom the first generation regularly interacted via their spirit selves, or to spirit-born humanity. This meant each group heretofore in spirit contact with the others would be isolated after the first generation died off, which by then the spirit-born knew was an inevitability they were unexpectedly witnessing on all human-inhabited planets. After about Y400 then, and despite the first generation compiling as much technical knowledge as possible before passing from the scene—H1 had achieved steam power by this time but wasn't yet able to engineer electricity, communications, and the like—H1's five origin family groups separately developed in a somewhat primitive environment. Not at all what the spirit-born had expected.

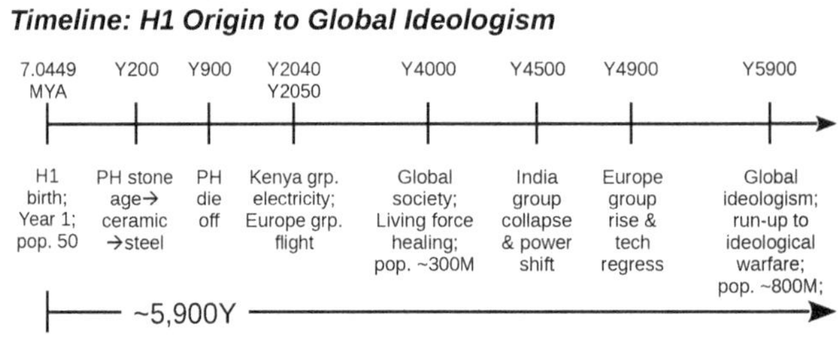

Timeline: H1 Origin to Global Ideologism

7.0449 MYA	Y200	Y900	Y2040 Y2050	Y4000	Y4500	Y4900	Y5900
H1 birth; Year 1; pop. 50	PH stone age→ ceramic →steel	PH die off	Kenya grp. electricity; Europe grp. flight	Global society; Living force healing; pop. ~300M	India group collapse & power shift	Europe group rise & tech regress	Global ideologism; run-up to ideological warfare; pop. ~800M;

├──── ~5,900Y ────────────────

Figure 187. Timeline: H1 proto-human (PH) origin to global society and altruism.

H1's second generation began separating themselves from their proto-human extended families. By its tenth generation, roughly 250 years later, H1 was on its own. Although unintegrated proto-humans *looked* the same, they were naught but advanced primates without human WOB thus ꙅuman capability. H1's family groups remained isolated until establishing regularized physical contact circa 2,500 years later (Y2500; Table 18:532). Although abiogeneticists established H1 on the aforementioned three continents, intermingling amongst these five groups didn't constitute a global society until they'd also settled in the Americas and Australia exclusive of Oceania (Australasia) and Antarctica. Mina defines global society as having (however sparsely) regularized contact and intermixing of populations, each group spreading throughout its local environment yet interconnected beyond it in the sense that what happens amongst one group is socioculturally felt by the others regardless distance. There's a sense of human society, a feeling of commonality by which each can understand the other as human. Method and duration of travel isn't important, only that they can effectively commute. H1 reached this point circa Y4000, its global population ~300M. All the while, each origin group continued developing its local socioculture.

By Y4500, H1's MBI had declined to about 40% amongst newborns. At the same time, the group centered in India's Goa state area—the first to achieve a level of development in some respects equivalent to or exceeding ancient Rome's (augmented) technology, culture, and imperial government circa AD 450, and the most powerful of the groups—collapsed. This allowed the others to wax in power over the next 100 years. The group centered in Europe then became the most powerful around Y4900, equivalent in some respects to circa AD 1850 Japan's shogun-style military dictatorship, technology, and aristocracy–peasant socioculture. The five original and now fifteen spin-off groups, despite retaining key advancements, had regressed technologically, a result of sociocultural mindset. Their global society fractured in terms of harmonious relations similar to our twentieth-century advanced nations splintering to pursue local solutions in the AD 1930s, culminating in World War Two. Ideologies had a firm grip on some of H1's societies by Y5900. The Europe group developed a militaristic, religion-based warrior mindset. The one centered in China developed an autocratic albeit non-ideologized pluralistic religious society oriented around a leader-centered system akin to Nazi Germany's *Führerprinzip* ('leader principle') married to North Korea's personality cult. The ideas of its extended-family leadership were its society's only guiding principle and its activities their only cultural heritage. People could believe and do anything but adhered to the First Family and all it did as the individual's essential way of life

---

499. This represents an average annual growth rate of ~0.0001% in spirit-born population over its 100Q population circa 300KY earlier, or 7.3MYA (cf. Earth's current population growth rate at FN 497:520).

(§ 1.2.1:534). The group centered in South Africa's Atlantic coast developed a Communist-style system similar to modern-day Vietnam. Each one absorbed weaker groups near and far across all the continents. H1 was dividing into incompatible factions.

1.2.3   TIMELINE: WARRING STATES TO FIRST GLOBAL WAR

Global population hovered around 800M circa Y5900, having a socioculture more or less consistent with what was available during the mid-nineteenth century American Civil War period. It was augmented by artificial lighting and mechanized ground, sea, and air transportation using a no-heat metathesis (double replacement reaction) chemical-to-mechanical energy propulsive technology built around a fuel constituted of platinum plus a today-unknown element and three non-flammable liquids. Each of the three principal groups utilized their technology, ideology, and desire to altruistically harmonize humanity to absorb all the other groups that had developed on every continent over H1's 5,900 years. Despite each one's hostility toward the others and infantilizing their own people as one can imagine in such politico-sociocultures, H1 adhered no less firmly to the principle of no-harm—altruism—insofar as it applied to those under a group's control. Accordingly, each group built its society to provide whatever its people needed or wanted for living. When the China group absorbed the India group, and the South Africa group absorbed the one centered in Kenya, they each made available to those conquered all the material and cultural comforts at their disposal. This was a perfectly workable system except that each group intrinsically felt threatened by the others. Absorbing all the world's smaller groups only exacerbated it. And all this occurred practically in a flash. Within a year's time, these various systems came to power and absorbed all the other human groups of the world into each of three principle factions: N–group (Europe), E–group (China), and S–group (South Africa), or NES altogether. These remained the principal politico-sociocultural factions throughout H1's tenure and now provoked a shooting war.

NES warred for about 400 years. They scorned alliances, as each felt a profound clash with the others and simply wouldn't stoop to making common cause (like the AD 1941–45 USA–USSR anti-Nazi alliance) no matter how tactically useful. Around Y6300 they entered a period of détente and formalized Earth divvied into thirds. Despite such lengthy warfare, H1's population increased to 1.2 billion. NES achieved a technological level by Y6800 roughly equivalent to ours in AD 2010. Just before initiating their warring states period in Y5900, H1's factionalized global society each had a brand of altruistic society providing what its people needed or desired for life and living, each one comparatively better or worse. They rectified this discrepancy at a global level circa Y6875, establishing a shared intersocietal standard of living despite their NES antipathies. Additionally, the aforementioned Living force healers had, in the interim, converted their skill to a societal power as a sort of guild—not unlike the Spacing Guild in Frank Herbert's novel *Dune* (1965) controlling access to faster-than-light travel to which their sociopolitical leadership felt compelled to kowtow—whose parasitic demands were the price of extended life. Détente and altruism in place, H1 settled into a comfortable physical existence despite its totalitarian streak.

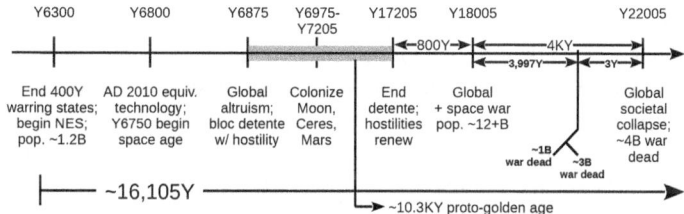

Figure 188. Timeline: NES is composed of North (Europe)–East (China)–South (S. Africa) H1 groups.

With Earth's socio-politics sufficiently sorted, H1 turned its serious attention to the stars. They colonized the Moon circa Y6975, Ceres by Y7175, Mars by Y7205, and established many small interplanetary industrial outposts and space stations along the way. Each NES group explored and settled outer space. Not altogether, say, in the same spacecraft or the same habitat, but independently at the same time much like antebellum America ensured that, for each slave or free state admitted to the Union, it concurrently added an opposite state so as to maintain the factional balance of power to forestall conflict while only kicking the can down the road. For comparison, H1 was technologically ahead of us in our early twenty-first century by about 100 years when they began colonizing the moon and about 200 years by the time they reached Mars. This peaceful hence productive period would last just over 10KY. Average lifespan rose from 105 years in Y6300 to 180 years with a high of 200 for the common man and about 240 years with a high of 260 for the elites by Y6975. This wasn't H1's golden age—that was yet to come—but it was pretty good, even if freedom and the quest for knowledge, from our perspective today, was nonexistent and regulated, respectively, thanks to cradle-to-grave societal conditioning that went ever unquestioned, a level of compliance even the most ruthless modern indoctrinators can only dream.

It ended when E–group's extended-family dictatorship (§ 1.2.2:535) was persuaded by one of its members around Y17205 that what Earth really needed at this point in its history was a single global society unified as one culture having one leader, their version of Hitler's *ein Volk, ein Reich, ein Führer* ('one people, one empire, one leader'). Their effort revived the hitherto out-of-sight-out-of-mind suspicion, fear, and hostility endemic to NES. It festered about 800 years before degenerating into open warfare circa Y18005. Earth's population at the start of their first truly global war was ~12B under pervasive population control, 100M on the Moon, 150K on Ceres, 150M on Mars, with smaller populations spread out amongst the rocks, moons, and space stations of the solar system. This war lasted about 4,000 years. It was ten times longer than their warring states period (cf. Islamochristianity's ~1,400Y+ and other 600–800Y wars). It wasn't the sort of unrestricted warfare H2 is used to waging but more measured and restrained, like the interplanetary war in *Star Trek* where each side makes computer-simulated 'casualties' real by herding them into disintegrators to avoid actual mass destruction.[500] Regardless its restraint, H1 by Y22005 had managed to kill outright about 3.5B with another half billion as collateral just on Earth. The Moon's dead was ~20M, Ceres 20,000, and Mars 15M even though its population grew over the same period to 300M from its unregulated birthrate. Four billion deaths doesn't sound like much over 4,000 years, yet the first 3,997 years still averaged a quarter million violent deaths per year, year after year, when people expected twice or thrice today's average (nonviolent) lifespan. Overall, this war traumatized H1.

1.2.4   TIMELINE: POSTWAR PEACE TO SECOND GLOBAL WAR

When H1 goose-stepped into its first global war, MBI was 40% the physicospirit norm. It had lost touch with spirit-born humanity and any credible idea of spirit reality despite believing in an afterlife. Their long war ended—MBI at 30% the norm, like H2 on the eve of the AD 2017 Big Healing—when NES collapsed in the sense its three groups lost control of their factional territories as subgroups splintered to form local sociocultures. It began in Y22002 when E–group concluded the war was indecisive but wanted to end it with a win. They segued from their more staid, low casualty method of warfare to the unrestricted, kill-'em-till-they-quit kind that H2 prefers, causing in this final three-year period about 75% the war's total 4B casualties and obliterating their enemies' essential infrastructure, which insult their enemies returned. On top of severe shortages and war deaths rising year-over-year until reaching ~3B in the third year of this final spasm, a majority of their populations had concluded their sociocultures weren't life affirming but death cults. Groups broke away to restore the sociocultures they'd had at war's start ~4,000Y earlier which radically shrank the territories each NES group controlled. The war rendered ~5% of Earth's habitable surface uninhabitable for about three centuries.[501]

Facing a shocking three-year inflation of war deaths, destruction of essential infrastructure—residential cities were untouched on principle—and the unexpected societal decohesion, they gave up the fight in Y22005 to reconstitute themselves (*Fig. 189*). A mere hundred years later they'd returned to prewar population, infrastructure, and unified territories. Three incompatible yet unconquerable groups once again ruled Earth in relative peace. But the average lifespan had fallen for the plebs and elites to 80 and 100 years, respectively. Feeling they'd learned their lesson from their semi-global then global wars, NES set about perfecting its factional lifestyles, longevity, and sociocultural mindsets (brainwashing).

1.3   ORIGINAL HUMANITY SELF-DESTRUCTS

H1 devoted the next ~460,000 years to living the good life (as they saw it) while exploring and settling useful areas of the solar system. About halfway into this period, they reached a technological level about 400 years ahead of our current level[502] and dispatched their one and only extra-solar spacecraft crewed by 250 couples to

---

500. "A Taste of Armageddon" (S1E23, airdate Feb. 23, 1967). H1 would never insist on converting simulated to real death in this scenario but simply use the data to determine when an enemy would, by convention, surrender for sociocultural absorption.

501. This was the Kazakhstan south to coastal Iran area which they'd reserved for warfare on the theory they could avoid the traumatic societal and infrastructure destruction of their warring states period (§ 1.2.3:537).

502. It seems absurd to us that 230KY of history translated to a paltry 400-year technological advantage over us today, but Mina avers that H1 simply quit trying to advance. They'd reached a level of control, comfort, and satiety where they intellectually and technologically

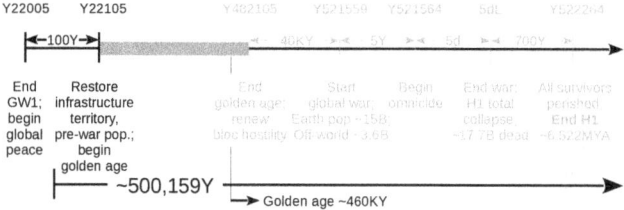

Figure 189. Timeline: H1's golden age follows 4,000 years of NES warfare.

the second of two planets of a star known today as Epsilon Eridani, about 10 light-years (cf. est. 10.5LY) from Earth with a breathable atmosphere and three-quarters Earth gravity. They expected the journey would take about 110 years using engines achieving a thrust equivalent to ~98.1M kph. According to Mina, they collided with space rubble that rendered their ship inoperable and perished a month later.

On Earth, life went contentedly on. NES practiced population control that by Y521559 held steady at ~15B on Earth, 1B on the moon, 200,000 on Ceres, and 2.6B on Mars. Average lifespan reached a zenith of 225 years with a high of 290 for the common man and 350 years with a high of 400 for the elites. But they'd already seeded the end of their golden age when, ~40,000 years earlier circa Y482105, E–group's First Family dusted off their long-shelved *ein Volk ein Führer* dream. Old tensions predictably resurfaced. They weren't looking for war. Instead, its cultish First Family figured it could pull off a coup in the other two groups via subversion, skullduggery, assassination, propaganda, and the like before their victims caught on, thus avoiding overt hostilities. They played the long game, willing to take millennia to achieve their purpose. It didn't go as hoped. The north and south groups caught on within a hundred years and pushed back with their own low-key malice that went back and forth the better part of 40,000 years.

While these vast time scales seem ludicrous, one need remember that H1, though certainly warlike when it suited, wasn't warlike in general. Their focus was *managing society* in a condition of no-harm (§ 1.1.1:362) just as V'v'dib, influenced by Mina's two sisters, had attempted to sell to the First Ancestors (§ 2.1.2.1:370). H1's periodic wars and general hostility were sideshows for its population in the bigger picture, used then as now as chess pieces by its chicaning sliver of elites to achieve their alpha aspirations. Most of H1's history was peaceful and, with certain obvious reservations, societally advanced. But when it did go to war, H1 was a conveyer belt of death, killing in its first ~22,000 years more than three times the number as all of H2's wars combined over its to-date 49,722-year history (§ 2.3:545). Regardless H1's lifestyle of prosperity, theirs was the brutal reality of altruism. Near on 40,000 years of low-level hostilities, occasional combat, assassinations, propaganda, coup attempts, and a seemingly endless parade of chicanery raised inter-group tension to the boiling point by Y521559. S–group attacked E–group. N–group joined after three weeks but built an advantage over E–group that looked dangerous to S–group, which attacked N–group. In less than a month, the NES elites were at war all over again, dragging their compliant populations to their doom (*Fig. 190*). They now had technology unknown in their wars over a half million years earlier. For the first time, war was getting existential.

1.3.1 Omnicidal War

E–group's dream of world unification under its leadership cult necessitated only the extermination of the north and south group's elites whose shogunistic and communistic ideologies had always been anathema to its non-ideological yet nonetheless cultish mindset; tolerated, but *wrong*. Not surprisingly, its future victims took it personally. And anyhow, they'd all tired of sharing the planet after now four years of renewed if traditionally restrained warfare and two million war-dead. It was time to break from their coexistent past to achieve a final solution to their ancient deadlock. S–group's mortally threatened elites figured they'd up E–group's ante and unify Earth not by killing its elites to absorb its diverse population into its ideology, but as literally one people—its own—who'd been born to it. Start over from scratch, itself H1's sole ingredient. The peoples of the other two groups were now surplus to requirements.

Wasting no time and already comprehending the technology, s-group proceeded to build over the course of the war's third to fifth years Energent-based (§ 1:112) pure fusion slow neutron weapons whose operating

---

stagnated. Eventually, they advanced as much as 800 years over us today but from unsought, happenstance improvements and advantageous, intuited leaps.

principle was a core of 2AU–1Y (gold–yttrium) molecules held inert in a gravity bubble. Its blast wave was equivalent to one-kiloton (KT) of TNT with 70% its thermal pulse but emitting approximately 250 times the amount of neutron radiation versus today's fission bombs (cf. AP neutron bomb at ten times fission), its prompt, destructive radiation accounting for 40% of its released energy with blast and heat 60%. Physical destruction representing probable death to minor injury extended about 500 meters while its lethal neutron activation (dose) was about 3.5 km absent effective treatment.[503]

NES preferred these small bombs to city killers for obvious reasons, though now their intent was indeed to kill cities, just not themselves as collateral. The other two groups quickly discovered s-group's bomb program and hastily began their own. Equally informed, and before they lost the advantage, s-group launched their weapons at the start of the eleventh month of the war's fifth year. They didn't limit themselves to Earth, either. NES military capabilities on the Moon, Ceres, Mars, and elsewhere—having already sustained local destruction and casualties from five years of traditional war—could retaliate effectively and possibly negate a win on Earth for an overall loss in the solar system. They had to take those assets off the board, because what H1 loosed on Earth they felt compelled to loose in the heavens. For NES, the entire solar system was one humanity, one environment, one socioculture, and now, one battlespace.

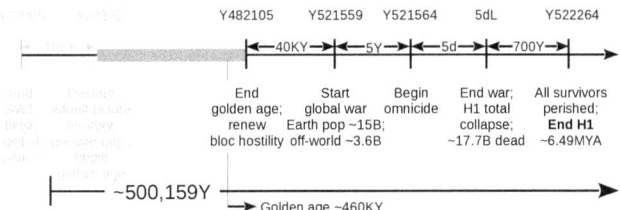

Figure 190. Timeline: H1 ends its golden age to unify humanity by force to omnicide; 'd' is days.

Infuriated that s-group now embraced their extermination as a people, E-group and N-group reflexively retaliated the moment they detected s-group's weapons launch. They'd all built similar-sized weapons because none of them really wanted to destroy the planet, just eliminate the threat. Their combined retaliation equally infuriated s-group because it was altogether three times their own attack, which they now calculated to be their own annihilation. More to the point, the other two groups hadn't launched on each other but *only* on s-group. For the first time in their long history two societies, at least informally, had tactically allied against the third. This was stunning new behavior and caught s–group off guard. They'd known and accepted their first strike intended to kill about 70% of humanity throughout the solar system while expecting about 25% dead amongst their own. But they now realized the *double* retaliatory strike would necessarily kill outright about 90% of *their* society. It was unthinkable, yet too late to back out. S-group resolved to go down inflicting greater destruction on their now-mortal enemies and launched an all-or-nothing second strike. They knew that salvaging anything from it was forlorn but the sliver of possibility still gave them hope, however false (§ 6.3.1.1:435), they might survive to rebuild.

Their massive second strike caught the other two groups equally off guard, as they'd presumed s-group had already launched most if not all their inventory on account of their own calculations showing the near total destruction of their own peoples. Unlike s-group's overachievers, the others *had* shot their wad on the time-is-scarce theory their mutual threat meant neither ally intended to destroy the other, thus a reserve was unneeded. When the dust settled, these two had expected to forge a new peace on the ashes of the disposed-of third. It was consistent with their history (§ 1.2.3:537) regardless s-group having shattered noncombatant precedent, and anyhow seemed the most probable outcome. They were consequently defenseless in the face of s–group's unexpected counter-counterstrike since, like s-group, they'd opted out of missile defense as a waste of time and resources as each expected their strikes to be preemptively decisive. That was unjustifiably shortsighted in hindsight but, in their defense, they didn't foresee s-group actually pulling the trigger on total war—that, in fact, they'd back down from a counterstrike capability—any more than H2 operating under WW1

---

503. cf. a 1KT neutron pure fusion explosion AP as effective as a 13KT fission explosion, producing as much radiation but less blast–heat. H1's 1KT bomb was about as effective as a modern 15KT fission bomb. Detonation at 675 m alt. produced 28% (20% blast, 30% heat) the physical destruction but irradiated 79% more than the AD 1945 Hiroshima bomb (cf. 250 Sieverts *vs.* 155 Sv at hypocenter, ~200 Sv *vs.* 42 Sv at 500 m, ~100 Sv at 1,000 m, 1 Sv at 2.45 km; blast–heat to 500 m *vs.* 1.6 km; 1 Sv=~10,000 chest x-rays, or 274Y natural radiation exposure). Effects differed for air, surface, and subsurface detonations.

presumptions foresaw ww2 German–Japanese industrialized extermination and coldblooded, to-the-last-man fanatical total war in the name of ideological purity. So, miscalculations all round.

1.3.2   Omnicide's Aftermath

It was over in five days (*Fig. 190*). The outcome was grim (Table 19). Besides the human destruction, they obliterated their infrastructure with approximately 100,000 one-kiloton—100MT, equivalent to ~1,500 MT (FN 503:540)—detonations on every continent and anywhere there was essential infrastructure and especially population concentrations. S–group less intended the conflagration to destroy their enemy strategically as its first strike had intended but, more angrily and spitefully, to obliterate its socioculture before retaliation annihilated them. Even in these numbers, their weapons were too small to damage atmospheric ozone or churn up vast clouds of radioactive debris, but global firestorms from immediate and collateral explosions and fires in their advanced-tech released as much as 300M metric (330.6M short) tons of aerosols that sooted the atmosphere, dropping global temperature long term. A profound lack of food, potable water, shelter, medicine to counter hitherto unknown epidemic disease, and lethal radiation lingering in hot spots for about a year, and harmful radiation lingering about five years, killed 20% of the survivors. The unirradiated encountered no future genetic damage, but survival was tenuous.

The situation was grimmer off-planet. H1 used 80% the bombs as on Earth, destroying 98% of surface and 80% of subsurface targets. The final exchange destroyed 90% of the Moon's self-sustaining infrastructure. There were enough ships to evacuate just 30% of the survivors to Earth. The remainder perished over a hundred years. Ceres had no functional ships left and its survivors succumbed in about fifty years. Five years of war had killed ~61.5% of Mars' population; the Energent bombs finished off 70% of the remainder and wiped away all surface and 90% of subsurface structures. Survivors held on in these underground remnants about 200 years until unable to meet essential needs.[504] Nothing went wholly untouched by war, though smaller outposts and space stations escaped targeting by Energent bombs. Their populations evacuated upon realizing the interplanetary extent of destruction. Crews originating from all points landed and abandoned their spacecraft on Earth (later subsumed in geological processes) while wrecked naval elements destroyed during the war drifted through space. Mina avers just one ever fell to Earth, in AD 1954 in George V Land, Antarctica, around 1,100 miles inland and is roughly intact.

Table 19. Original Humanity's (H1) approximated omnicidal war tally.

Locale	Prewar Populations	Conventional War Dead	Neutron Bomb Dead	Surviving Populations	Final Die-off
Earth	15B	2B	11.5B	1.5B	+700Y
Moon	1B	800M	1.1B[a]	200K	+100Y
Ceres	200K	100K	0	100K	+50Y
Mars	2.6B	1.6B	700M	300M	+200Y
Est. Total	18.6B	4.4B	13.3B	1.8B	

a. The discrepancy in the moon's population and war-dead numbers is because, after suffering 1B deaths and infrastructure destruction on Earth pre-omnicide, NES opted to use the Moon as their principal battlespace just as they'd used the Kazakhstan–Iran areas as their first global war's primary battlespace, and replaced the Moon's non-essential civilian population with greater numbers of combatants. The idea was to destroy military resistance, thus compel surrender and absorption into the victor's socioculture.

Survivors reconciled NES in their ravaged habitats around the solar system during the next five years, forming a single society with mixed success. Regardless, they'd ruined their environment. Ceres and smaller outposts necessitated periodic resupply despite their overall self-sustaining capabilities, but none was available. The Moon and Mars couldn't revive their repair capability, so with some exceptions most of what the war destroyed stayed destroyed. They couldn't replace medicine stocks and had little access to naturally growing herbs. Their populations eventually succumbed to untreatable injury, infection, illness, and disease. Worse, their fertility rate declined from a prewar birth-to-death ratio of between ~0.9–1.05:1 (momentarily bumping up to an immediate postwar maximum of 2:1) to its final 0.2:1 average. This was due to toxic chemicals and other substances unique to their technology released by the destruction into their food soils as well as drinking and hydroponics water they couldn't fully decontaminate despite distillation and other still-useable purifying methods. Taken altogether, these outcomes were dooming.

---

504. Mina says 6% of lunar substructures are dark-side extant and buried, but zero are on Mars due to its denser crust.

Earth's situation was slightly better. Survivors lasted significantly longer than those off-planet mainly because there wasn't a habitability problem; plenty of breathable air, living space, and flora and fauna. They lacked many of the same necessities as off-planet. Their larger numbers only meant it took longer as a populace to die from it. Approximately 25% of survivors died within ten years of war's end from famine and associated morbidities, followed by another 20% within 100 years. Fertility measured in births-to-deaths fell from an immediately postwar ~2:1 ratio (cf. 2.5:1 AP) to 0.005:1 due to global soil and water contamination from metals and other toxins released during, and deposited by, the destruction which didn't detoxify naturally to generally harmless levels for 1.35MY and fully until 1.989MY postwar.

In the atmospheric environment, firestorms lofted complex-molecule particles into the stratosphere from which atmospheric chemistry lifted 30% of the total as ever smaller, primary solar-blocking particles into the mesosphere, thermosphere, and exosphere that collectively diminished solar radiation at the surface. Average global temperature fell ~2°C in the first year, another 5°C after 700 years when the last of H1 died off, then a final 2°C more by 400KY postwar. It didn't rise to prewar norms until 1.3MY postwar. Larger solar-blocking particles exited the stratosphere for the surface over about seven years via gravity-driven dry deposition followed by precipitation-driven wet deposition, but lighter particles previously lofted higher continued accumulating out of upper atmospheric levels—'raining into' the stratosphere—for 250KY and didn't fully solar-clear until ~400KY postwar. The *Drona Parva*, part of ancient India's *Mahabharata*, gives a stylized account of this war (§ 1.1.1.3:571).

H1 could've weathered this catastrophe as our own ancestors did their periods of harsh climactic conditions but for its unsustainably low fertility that couldn't carry it long enough for the planet to detoxify so births could increase. Geology subsumed the physical remnants of H1's civilization over 200KY until once again the planet was *au naturel*. This was the fifth such calamity amongst physical human society in our universe and the final straw for the first 'archangels' (§ 2.1:522), who now accepted their inability to mitigate the effects of The Corruption. H1 didn't fight this war over power or resources but ideological purity (mindset), The Corruption's principal problem. They passed the torch to GLM+ who are native-born to our universe (ibid). Earth—the whole solar system—was again fallow. H1 segregated itself in its own area of the recently established physical-born spirit world (Fig. 182:523) in sorrow, guilt, and shame. Only at the end of AD 2020 did a majority reach out for healing.

Section 2
Ensuing Humanity (Version 2.0)

What today we call *modern humanity*, or *Homo (hereafter, H.) sapiens sapiens*, Mina prefers to call *Ensuing Humanity* (H2), as we're not some new form of human, a different race, species, subspecies, or lifeform, but physicospirit-embodied *Life* ensuant to Earth's first, H1. Despite our history appearing bloody and warlike without respite and, overall, suffering Corruption-induced trauma more profoundly than did H1 irrespective their civilization-ending war trauma, we're actually a less homicidal version. Science estimates we've killed between 300M and 1B-plus humans in warfare,[294] though Mina avers 1.5B war dead from a total lived population (TLP) of 130B+ over our 49,722 years, a 1.15% kill rate (KR). But H1 did-in more than two-and-a-half times that number in less than half the time (4B+:12B+:22KY, a 33% wartime KR though only a 4% KR from an 80B+ TLP) and nearly six times that 500KY later (a 4.05% final KR from a 580B+ TLP; § 1.2.3:537). The H1–H2 KR variance lies mainly in H1's mindset of the collective *over* the individual versus H2's mindset of the individual *in* the collective. Where H1 embraced the collective out of desire, H2 does from a sense of necessity. H1 and H2's violence both arise in the intrinsic conflict between forms of altruism, though H1 individuals could never—indeed, didn't desire to—alter the collective whereas the H2 individual ever strives to accommodate the collective on one's individual terms. Ergo, H2 is more effectively antiwar in the short term than H1. Still, Mina estimates our long-term KR absent the Big Healing would eventually be similar across our own half a mega-annum.

2.1 Ensuing Humanity's Origins

Earth's modern humanity (H2) arose ensuant to and in the same way as Original Humanity (H1): abiogeneticists prepared the environment, directedly evolved proto-human bodies toward *Life* integrability, then integrated them to birth physicospirit persons (§ 1.1.3:533). We describe H2's development below.

2.1.1 Setting the Environmental Scene for h2

Abiogeneticists faced two problems redeveloping Earth's physical humanity they hadn't encountered developing h1. First, The Corruption gave rise to the NCC over its first ~2.145MY that effectively re-Intentionalized Macrocosmic force. It rendered the physical universe generally unconducive to life, mandating constant albeit imperfect adjustment by multiplication 'angels' (§ 2.3.7:528). Second, h1's omnicide exacerbated the NCC's disruption of Earth's environment, leading to about half its nonhuman life following h1 to the grave. The efforts of multiplication 'angels' to maximize Earth's conduciveness to life—its habitability—in a milieu resisting it took 1.436MY postwar before abiogeneticists found it suitable to recommence developing proto-humans toward re-birthing physicospirit-embodied 𝓛ife.

2.1.2 Proto-human Evolution for h2

Circa 5.054MYA (from AD 2021), abiogeneticists selected an appropriate species of primate ancestral to the modern bonobo chimpanzee (*Fig. 191*) and directed its evolution toward *h. sapiens*. Recall not only did the abiogeneticist-integrated proto-human species that birthed h1 subsequently die off (§ 1.1.3:533), the primates extant during h1's tenure were, from its perspective, modern primates undirectedly evolving between then and now into what, from our own perspective, are today's extant primates (§ 2.1.5.5.2.1:323). Using this palette, abiogeneticists began our body's evolutionary lineage by initiating evolutionary change in *Ardipithecus kadabba* and then, 96KY later, interbreeding it with *Sahelanthropus tchadensis*, one species removed from the so-called chimpanzee–human last common ancestor (CHLCA).

From there, h2's evolutionary lineage proceeds through various species to *h. sapiens* (*Fig. 192*). But it wasn't 𝔥uman integrable yet. Abiogeneticists then interbred aspects of *h. neanderthalensis* with *h. sapiens*, developing over the course of ~60KY into proto-human *h. sapiens sapiens* 140KYA, its brain developing 60KYA into what it is today although its human capability went unutilized until 49,722 years ago.

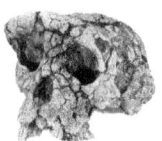  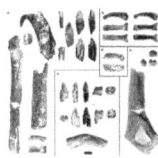

Figure 191. Left, reconstructed *s. tchadensis* skull (actually belongs to a related but less advanced animal); center, artist's representation Mina considers accurate; right, extant fossils of *Ar. Kadabba*; altogether, these are the first and second steps in proto-human development toward h2's physical body.₂₉₅

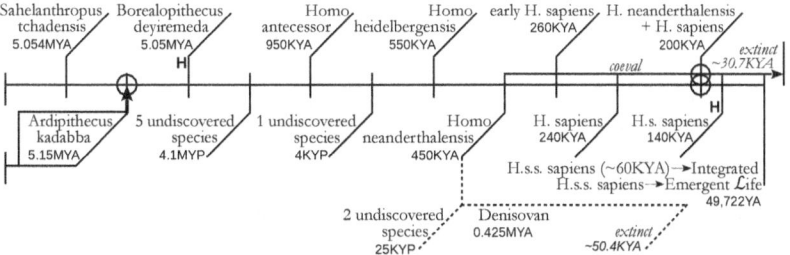

Figure 192. Timeline: Ensuing Humanity (h2) directly evolutionarily developed (DED) in 5.004MY start to finish; MYP and KYP means MY and KY *period*; 'undiscovered species' means it's absent in the extant fossil record; *Kadabba* DED prior to *Sahelanthropus* then hybridized (H) and DED to what Mina terms *Borealopithecus deyiremeda* (owing to its northern discovery in Ethiopia; cf. *Au. deyiremeda* taxonomy and dating) of the sub-tribe *Australopithecina* of tribe *hominini* but not of *Australopithecus*.

2.1.3 h2: The Rise of Physicospirit 𝓛ife

The brain of *h.s. sapiens*, the penultimate-stage *h. neanderthalensis*–*h. sapiens* proto-human hybrid, reached 𝓛ife-integrable capability circa 60KYA; we call it *h.s. sapiens sapiens*. Just as they did with h1's first generation some 7.0449MYA (§ 1.1.3:533), abiogeneticists integrated proto-human *h.s.s. sapiens* circa 49,722YA and birthed the second version (H2) of physicospirit Life on Earth. Like H1, H2's parents effectively constituted a new and different species from non-integrated proto-humans. Science interprets the very meaning of human as naught but animal, just a smarter primate amongst dumber ones, our inexplicable mind notwithstanding. That perspective is woefully misinformed consequent of attributing *mind* to *brain*, seeing the person as merely a physical body. The fact a human today looks more or less like *h.s.s. sapiens* 60KYA or *h.s. sapiens* 140KYA despite our intrinsic, qualitative, post-'cognitive revolution' difference—recently dated to 70KYA (Harari 2011, 21) but coeval with H1's birth—doesn't explain the divergence. Proto-human *h.s. sapiens* had the morphologic capability of human in body and, from 60KYA, the *h.s.s. sapiens* brain to physiologically integrate Human.

The spirit-born abiogeneticist integrates a Living (§ 1.2.2.3:256) proto-human body that, absent integration, one may classify *h.s.s. sapiens*. But the *integrated* body is no longer *sapiens* nor even the genus *Homo* or any aspect of taxonomy because it's no longer a 'human' body evolved from 'nonhuman' antecedents but *physicospirit Life*, a classification entirely its own. The Living human body as a chronospecies evolutionarily descending from animals ceases to be an evolutionary taxon once Life integrates. The two aren't equivalent at all. The integrated person effectively *is* the body, down to and including its genome and archí (§ 2.3.1:115). Your *physical* body is and expresses your mind, allowing for the natural environment's dimensional limitations, exactly the way your *spirit* body, having no dimensional limitations, is and expresses your mind. A correct train of classification for the human-to-Human body is *antecedents→Homo sapiens→H.s.ₙ→Life physicospirit* (*Fig. 193*). Like H1, H2 birthed having full MBI (§ 1:531).

Corrected Human Taxonomy

Antecedents (>240KYA)→*H. sapiens* (~240KYA)→*H.s. sapiens* (~140KYA via *neanderthal–sapiens* hybridization)→*H.s.s. sapiens* (~60KYA)⇥*I.H.s.s. sapiens* ↦*Life physicospirit* (49,722YA)

Figure 193. H. sapiens becomes the taxon *h.s. sapiens* via hybridization, achieving integrability as (*h.s.s. sapiens*) able to birth physicospirit Life, H2, via abiogeneticists (*I.H.s.s.*). Gen.-1 is the transition from primate-evolved *h.s.s. sapiens* 'human' body to integrated Human having Life (not a 'race' or species).

The birth of H2—the transition from *h.s.s. sapiens* to *Life physicospirit*—49,722YA *is* the so-called cognitive revolution. There were no aliens, divine sparks, or sudden genetic mutations, just spirit-born abiogeneticists integrating proto-human *h.s.s. sapiens* to birth physicospirit humanity as only Life can. With integration, *h.s.s. sapiens* ceased being *proto*-human. What was emptily human in form was, subsequent to abiogeneticist integration, integrated Human. This change from animal to human was dramatic and noticed in the scientific record as the hitherto inexplicable cognitive revolution. As with H1, abiogeneticist couples are 'descended' from each of the five First Ancestor families. They established five proto-human groups of about 500 individuals, each in a suitable location (*Fig. 194*): one in modern-day South America (inland of Santiago area, Chile); two in Africa (65KM SW of Sulb on the Nile, Northern state, Sudan; along Kinyasungwe river, Kilosa, Tanzania); one in the Malay Archipelago (Selayar Island, Indonesia); and one in Australia (Tambo river delta of Lake King area near Metung, Victoria). Like H1, they integrated two proto-humans per group to birth H2, then closed out the species over ten H2 generations (~170Y), once again bequeathing Earth to physicospirit humanity. H2's average male–female height was the same as H1's with brown, hazel, and magenta eyes colors that later differentiated.

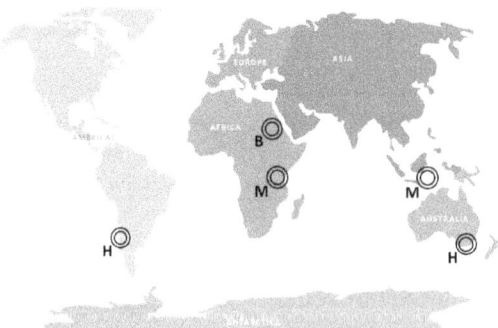

Figure 194. Ensuing Humanity's (H2) five points of origin, spirit-born 'descended' as with H1; hazel (**H**), magenta (**M**), and blue (**B**) eye color as shown (continents as per source: Fig. 186:534).

2.2 Merfolk

Before we describe H2's general history, we need visit a quite unusual aspect of it that Ayako discovered the abiogeneticists developed, which we term *Merfolk* (*mer-*: French for *sea*). Recall that within ~560KY, five human-inhabited planets had extinguished themselves in war (§ 1.3.2:541). This shocked the spirit-born. It was completely unexpected even with their limited comprehension of The Corruption's effects on the physical-born. The first mitigation efforts by the 'archangels' hadn't worked. They needed a change. Their first was GLM+ assuming the archangel tasks. Abiogeneticists pursued a second one. They placed a part of the Australia group in a different environment, one wholly inhospitable to technological development yet as hospitable as dry land for human societal development—the sea. Their purpose was to see if living in an environment impracticable for building or utilizing fighting tools beyond knives and spears or for making relationships a socioeconomic commodity would mitigate The Corruption's worst effects that express, for example, as war and exploitation. It turned out a wash in some respects. Merfolk racked up a 2% kill rate out of its total lived population versus Airfolk's aforementioned ~1.15% on land, the variance mainly due to the difficulty of surviving open wounds in their harsh environment and not to Merfolk warring any more than Airfolk. On the plus side, Merfolk couldn't build self-annihilative technology.

To transition Airfolk to Merfolk, abiogeneticists altered the lungs and other aspects of a portion of the Australia group's second generation from air to saltwater. It took six generations (120Y). Respiration occurs via aquatic organs called *branchiae*—thrice the size by volume of lungs and four times as efficient absorbing oxygen (using countercurrent exchange: water moving opposite capillary blood flow)—located in the ribcage. As a muscular structure, they work similar to the heart, one branchia compressing as the other relaxes, drawing seawater through permeable areas of the skin connected in a complex tissue network to one branchia, internally to the other, then likewise expelling from the body.

Average height increased to ~180.3 cm (5 ft.–11 in.) to accommodate a larger and longer torso. Skin tone is near Asiatic, averaging 55% pheomelanin and 45% eumelanin, a similar thickness, hairless, not scaled, and feels like a porpoise. Fingers and toes are webbed and ~40% longer. Eyes lack pigment but aren't albino. Musculature is akin to a bodybuilder's: firm, dense, yet supple. They live in colder waters above a 600 foot depth. Lifespan averages 155 years. Their sprit body manifests like ours (§ 1.2.3.2.1:470).

Today, Merfolk MBI is 45% (cf. Airfolk at 30%). Some are conversant with spirit world. Their population is about 16,000, down from a historical high of ~51,000 pre-World War Two in which ~25% died due to naval warfare. Overall, their mortality rate is 60% higher than Airfolk. Merfolk may seem preposterous in our explored and connected world, but consider ~96% of the oceans are unexplored. When Ayako told me her spirit-self was visiting physical Merfolk, I was skeptical. "They have to be spirit persons living in the 'reflective' environment [§ 7.1.1.1:212] cosplaying as merpeople," I scoffed, my ET contradicting hers. She said, "Absolutely not! Mina's unequivocal they're physically alive humans." How could that even be possible, I thought; how could they breathe much less go undetected? "Your energy testing is wrong," I said, "or someone's interfering with it." It turned out *my* guidance 'angels' (§ 2.3.2:524) were monkeying with my ET, as spirit Merfolk feared I'd overshare their deets. Mina and I addressed it and everybody calmed down. My ET then confirmed Ayako's, as did Moth Man's (§ 1.1:4; § 1.1:61). What a surprise. Since the Big Healing, Mina says abiogeneticists began altering interested Merfolk's physiology to birth land–sea-capable physicospirit bodies after six generations. Merfolk are unique to Earth.

2.3 Ensuing Humanity's General History

We describe H1's history in three general historical divisions (§ 1.2:534) and repeat that pattern with H2. From its start 49,722YA, H2 proceeds to its first global society, then through a series of cataclysms that destroyed its civilization. This led to the last Ice Age and H2's struggle to survive in isolated pockets until ~20KYA when Earth's environment entered a period more conducive to life, then finally to glacial meltdown 14KYA and H2's renaissance. First, let's consider H2's mindset (personality), as it differs from H1.

2.3.1 Ensuing Humanity's Mindset

In all of Earth's human history, the United States of America is the only society to reject *in principle* humanity's prevailing belief in divine right rule (§ 2.1.1.5.1:353;₂₉₆ § 9.2.2:450), rooting its socioculture in the self-governing individual. America is historically unique not because of limited republican government or supposedly intrinsically inalienable rights or its sociocultural personality, but because its premise is *individual* (arising in *divinely originated Man*; therefore, non-societal) instead of *societal* (arising in *societally originated Man*; therefore, non-individual). America's founding principle recognizes human autonomy as intrinsic to personness, divine not societal, *unregulable by society* thus *unalienable* (it goes without saying America doesn't operate as intended). Every society before and after its founding, regardless its republican condition or the quality of its rights or personality—where it recognizes human autonomy at all—recognizes autonomy as intrinsic to society, worldly hence societal, *regulable by society* thus *alienable*. This is the fundamental tension influencing H2's post-Ice Age experience (and America's ongoing internal conflict), the latter being a nonautonomous tendency and the seedbed of all societal abuse.

If Earth's environment was hospitable to human life when H1 birthed, it was anything but when H2 arrived on scene. After all, universal humanity had by then wrought The Corruption's effects, including the NCC, for some 7.25MY. H1 rarely had to contend with earthquakes, volcanoes, celestial body strikes, or other planetary disruptions during its tenure. H2, on the other hand, was born into geologic and astronomical disruptions that encouraged a mindset in some ways opposite that of H1. In particular, where H1 felt no need to pursue radical self-reliance and individualism in its benign environment, H2 routinely encountered situations where a lack of individual capability and a reliance on others meant random death. Paleoanthropology imagines that humans banding together into cooperative groups is a species characteristic underlying our success over other species. While that's true as far as it goes, it doesn't define pairwise ꍞuman nor render self-reliance redundant. Whereas H1 uncoercively cooperated as individuals, H2 only coercively, hence marginally, cooperates. Instead of H1's few—if humanly destructive—wars, H2 has been warring since birth, knowing peace (in the sense of no intra- or intersocietal conflict) for no more than a total of about 200 years out of fifty thousand. Even though H1's society reflected animal grouping's alpha mindset (§ 9.2.2:450), its cooperative individualism meant it collaborated without intrasocietal conflict despite intersocietal animosity. In contrast, individuals rend H2 with intersocietal conflict that's intrasocietal animosity writ large like intelligent wolves ever unsatisfied with the status quo, cooperating only to pursue their goals. H1 and H2's personalities quite differ.

Besides H1 and H2's environment differentiating via the NCC in terms of being hospitable or not to societal development, H2's emphasis on individualism as liberty naturally resisting coercive cooperation is the principle distinction in its sociocultural outcomes vis-à-vis H1; where H2's societies are rife with harm and suffering, H1's were content. Not only does environmental inhospitableness reinforce H2's individualistic mindset, but its society *as* individuals reinforces despotism and its resistance. The combination creates a maelstrom of suffering that ever enables it and gives rise to H2's nonscientific socioculture over nearly all its 49,722-year history when H1 had already built an enduring scientific socioculture by its 6,300th year. But personality is the only difference between them, as both are physicospirit-embodied ℒife. Our eons of religious, spiritual, moral, and legal efforts to build intrasocietal peace equal to H1's fail because altruism is impotent in H2's individualistic milieu. Now, one might wish for H1's altruistically nonautonomous mindset to surmount our intrasocietal conflict in the hope it eliminates suffering, but it didn't preserve H1 because humans can't live peaceably as ꍞuman in a society modeled on nonhuman WOB (§ 1.1.2.1:364; § 4.3:384; § 9:446). One may as well dress a monkey in a suit and expect a statesman.

A final reason H2 didn't societally advance at H1's pace is that, although H2's abiogeneticist parents taught its first generation to speak, read, and write spirit world language, as H1's parents did, its MBI globally declined by its sixth generation to about 45% on average. Unlike H1, only one spiritually conversant first generation H2 person was alive (South America group) 130Y later when its seventh generation birthed. Between the loss of its knowledge base and spirit connections to the other groups (Fig. 186:534), MBI-deficient and spiritually non-conversant later generations leading to group isolation (Fig. 194:544), and the exigencies of daily life, the sixth generation amongst all five groups (excluding Merfolk, who were never literate) dropped the literacy ball. Individual proficiency in reading and writing declined group-to-group until H2, by its tenth generation, was illiterate. H1 not only remained literate throughout its entire history, but it was *the same writing system* for local languages until its end. Moreover, at the time H1 learned its writing system, they were still conversant with spirit-born humanity and recorded some of its technical knowledge, which H2 did to a lesser extent but, once illiterate, could no longer access.

H2's MBI declined to 60% by its third generation. From this point, and following the first generation's passing, it lost touch with the spirit-born. By the twelfth generation (250Y), it had forgot its initially acquired spirit-born knowledge. Like H1 early on, H2 lost its shared spirit-world language. Its groups now developed isolated in a hostile environment. MBI wasn't the only reason H2 wasn't as conversant as H1 with the spirit-born. It was living in the context of The Corruption and the NCC rendered over millions of years of post-H1 universal humanity which, in short order after H2's birth, effectively unplugged its spirit senses and brought death un-expectedly as well as much earlier (avg. first-generation lifespan 55Y vs. H1's 150Y). Along with natural disasters (§ 2.3.7.1:528) and a predatory environment, H2 experienced two-steps-forward-one-step-back development. We describe H2's general history in three parts.

2.3.2 TIMELINE: H2'S ORIGIN TO FIRST GLOBAL SOCIETY AND CATACLYSM

Historians carve human history into prehistory, protohistory, and history. Prehistory refers to the period of stone tool use by hominins circa 3.3MYA to the rise of human writing systems, presumedly during the fourth millennium BC. Protohistory refers to the period before a culture develops its own written history or other literate cultures note its existence in their own writings. History refers to the period described in extant written records. This concept of human history is inaccurate on its face. First, hominins (*H. sapiens*) and proto-humans represent animal, not human, history. Second, although cave paintings for instance aren't *writing*, they nonetheless convey information and experience that *tells a story* about the artist, environment, and subject. The Gebel Tjauti (southeast of Abydos, Egypt) *Scorpion Tableau* proto-writing sample dated to ~5,350YA and cuneiform circa 3200 BC are functionally no different from cave–rock art (or Incan *quipu*; knotted, colored strings). Both record historical events, the former using *abstract* and the latter *literal* pictorial language (*Fig. 195*). Even modern alphabets are pictorial images merely more abstract than hieroglyphs or cuneiform, themselves more abstract than cave–rock art.

The difference between writing and art is the difference between thinking and feeling, which altogether constitute Thought. Recall emotion isn't different from thinking. Each is the same mental awareness just differently expressed (§ 1.1:392). Mind experiences own-self state of being (SOB) emotively, meaning as sensation redolent with impression (§ 1.2.2.1:253). Thinking is our ability to parse impression into a particular state of awareness (SOA) that we consciously cognize and can analyze (§ 2.2:395). Cave paintings aren't simply art but recorded history evoking sensation redolent with impression. While cave art is a literal language, it conveys an abstract impression whereas writing, while an abstract language, conveys a literal impression. It's a literate conceit to regard art illiterate, having no linguistic metaphor. As the oldest discovered cave paintings date to about 45,700YA (warty pig, Leang Tedongnge, Sulawesi, Indonesia; cf. est. min. ~45,500YA in Brumm et al. 2021, 6) then, however spotty and abstract, we have aspects of H2's history recorded nearly back to its origin 49,722YA (from AD 2021) which marks our, H2's, year one (Y1; *Fig. 196*). We describe H2's timeline as pre-cataclysm, in medio, and post-cataclysm.

Figure 195. Storytelling via pictorial language; left is literal (Bhimbetka, India cave painting); center is considered (proto-) writing, hence abstract (*Scorpion Tableau*); right is abstract (cuneiform writing).[297]

2.3.2.1 H2 BIRTH TO CATACLYSM

Ensuing Humanity (H2) begins in Y1 when abiogeneticists, integrating male and female proto-humans in each of five groups, birthed its first physicospirit ℒife (§ 1.1.3:533; § 2.1.3:543), establishing an initial global population of fifty persons evenly split between men and women as they had H1. These ten integrated abiogeneticists parented this first generation in the context of each proto-human group. The Corruption and NCC of the time meant that, although the first generation birthed having the same full MBI as H1, the second generation birthed having less, about 65% MBI on average across H2's five groups, which is below the 90% MBI minimum for natural and real awareness of, and conversance with, spirit persons. As spirit awareness declined, H2 forgot spirit reality and was ever more ensconced in its physical embodiment which came to define its understanding of who and what it was. Instead of leaping ahead as had H1 from its proto-human antecedents, H2's absence of awareness how to advance meant it acquired agricultural know-how, relearned writing, and discovered metallurgy circa Y300, Y325, and Y350, respectively. From its first generation, however, H1 had transitioned from proto-human stone tools to a type of ceramic having bone, and then circa APH 160, during its sixth generation, to metallurgy.

Circa ASH 1500 (Y1500), the South America group (SAG; Fig. 194:544) had recently developed steam power as a mechanical advantage but was otherwise technologically middle Iron Age and roughly equivalent sociocultur-ally with China's *Shang* dynasty circa 1000 BC. SAG's population had risen to ~1M and H2 globally to 10M across ten groups. Around Y1850, the Tanzania group (TAG) reached a level roughly equivalent socioculturally with 400 BC Corinth in ancient Greece just prior to the Peloponnesian War (ca. 431–404 BC) and technologically equivalent with SAG. TAG's population reached 1M around this time, though H2 had globally plateaued at 10M. The groups local to Sudan (SUG) and Australia (AUG) were still living as nomadic hunter-gatherers with populations ~15% and 25% less, respectively, than SAG and TAG. In Y2200, TAG developed steel and catapulted to most powerful nation in a world now having 17 groups and 10 distinct sociocultures. Two each were in South America and Europe (inhabiting 30% of the continent's north); three in Africa; one each in Australia, eastern Russia, and Malaysia. SUG advanced past hunter-gatherer to primitive agriculture while AUG was a mix of hunter-gatherer and pastoralism. Contact occurred between SUG and AUG and the advanced societies of SAG and TAG circa Y4000 via steamship and overland. SUG's population of 1.7M had expanded to the Indian Ocean coast and was equivalent to dynastic Egypt circa 2850 BC. AUG's population of 395K was low from internecine warfare.

H2 achieved a global society (§ 1.2.2:535) circa Y5000 with a worldwide population of 105 million, a third of H1's when it achieved it. Over the next 5,000+ years, Earth's origin groups—excluding Merfolk, whose population at this point was 30K centered in the Java Sea—and subsequent societies normalized their develop-mental levels until reaching a global population of 1.9B circa Y10000 (~39,722YA) that was roughly equivalent to eighteenth-century Europe's sociocultural development although augmented by more advanced technolo-gies. TAG for instance discovered the use of electricity over about 100 years circa Y5500, its application to communications technology around Y5950, and electric lighting some 25 years later (§ 2.3.3:550). Despite H2's more hostile environment and lack of a quick start, it achieved many of H1's milestones in a similar timeframe. However, H1's Europe group achieved electricity and flight circa APH 2040 and 2050, and its South Africa group the space age by APH 6750, which H2 didn't achieve until circa Y49,526 and Y49,611, respectively (ca. AD 1825, 1910), and the *Apollo* moon landing in Y49,670 (AD 1969). Before H2 could achieve more, disaster struck.

Timeline: H2 Origin to First Global Society

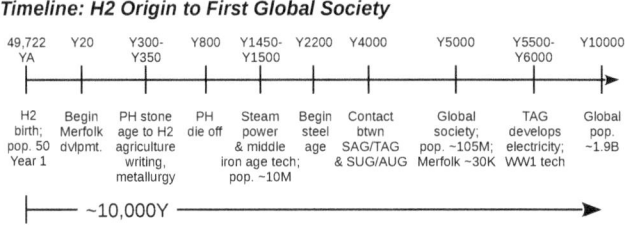

Figure 196. Timeline: H2 origin to first global society; PH is *proto-human*.

2.3.2.2 IN MEDIO CATACLYSM

The proximate start of H2's downfall from global society to the primitive survivors that science encounters anthropologically in the archeological record as pre-Ice Age early man was a comet strike in Y10150 (~39,572YA), inaccurately dated to ~12,800–11,700YA as part of the Younger Dryas Impact Theory (§ 3:557). It fragmented and airburst over north and central America, western China, Papua–New Guinea, eastern Australia, and Bangladesh, the same as albeit orders of magnitudes smaller than Shoemaker–Levy 9 that impacted Jupiter in AD 1994. The Adams Transitional Geomagnetic Event inclusive of the Laschamps excursion (weakening then temporary flipping of Earth's geomagnetic poles), large-scale volcanism, and grand solar minima followed it and ushered in the last glacial period and Neanderthal and megafaunal extinctions. All of this together prevented H2 from recovering beyond hunter-gatherer prior to the Last Glacial Maximum (LGM) circa Y35000 (~14,500YA). Mina describes the event as follows.

A ~2,000 metric ton (m.t.) comet about one kilometer in diameter with an impacted-dust and dense Tellurium core ~500 m and 50 m in diameter, respectively, entered Earth's atmosphere in Y10150 at about 48,280 kph (~30,000 mph). It fragmented into six pieces. Each released on average ~7.53 × 10²² erg, or 1.8 megatons, roughly equivalent to 121 Hiroshima or 87 Nagasaki atomic bombs. Each four-mile high airburst wasn't like an atom bomb going off at altitude as a symmetrically expanding fireball, but a ~5,700°C hypersonic jet of plasma drilling the surface at ~41,843 kph (26,000k mph), then supersonically blasting radially outward. Each plume carried ejecta from the ablated ground to the stratosphere and triggered magnitude 11 earthquakes, large aftershocks, and a ~0.65 km (0.4 mi.) high tsunami originating at Papua–New Guinea with acid rain fallout. Wildfires raged 10 months over 15% of Earth, producing ~260M m.t. of aerosols (cf. Dashigou dyke swarm, N. China craton, ca. 925MYA at ~280M m.t.) resulting in three months of continual darkness, decreasing solar radiation at ground level for about two years, and permanently disrupting regional power grids. Famine killed 12%; altogether, 18% of the population perished.

The geomagnetic field had already been weakening for 500 (cf. est. 250) years at the time of the comet strike but, nine years later (~39,563YA), it reversed poles over several months in what science calls the Laschamps excursion (cf. est. 41,400YA) and remained reversed for 335 (cf. est. 440) years. Earth's magnetic field was 70% weaker (cf. est. 75%), thus only 30% nominal. Its strength dropped to 10% nominal (cf. est. 5%). Effects ranged from moderately compromised stratospheric ozone, electrical storms across the tropics, and auroras generated by solar winds across the northern hemisphere, to arctic air pouring over the northern continents, surging glaciers and ice sheets, and violently shifting weather patterns. About 117 and 166 years following pole reversal, respectively, a ~270 km³, ~200M m.t. aerosol volcano in the Phlegraean Fields of Italy (the Campanian Ignimbrite) erupted. Then three AD 79 Mt. Vesuvius-equivalent volcanoes erupted within six months of each other, ultimately releasing ~110,000 times the energy of the Hiroshima–Nagasaki atomic bombs. Each one blanketed a percentage of the planet with ejecta, causing a new round of global crop failures and famine that killed another 15% of the comet-surviving population. About fifty years later (~39,347YA), a submarine supervolcano on the North American plate side of the Mohns Ridge of the mid-Atlantic ridge between Iceland and Svalbard erupted with a volume of ~3,100 km³ at ~400M m.t. (cf. La Pacana, Chile at ~500M m.t. 3.8MYA), diminishing solar radiation across 70% of the planet by 11.5 percent and killing, via famine and associated morbidities, another 10 percent.

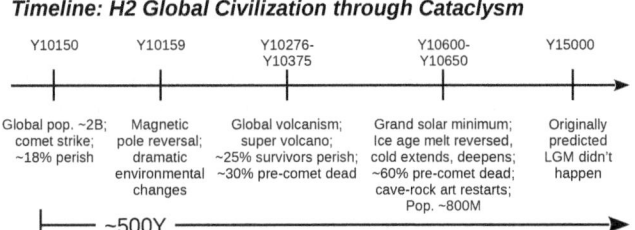

Figure 197. Timeline: cataclysmic events; Macrocosmic 'angel'-predicted LGM reversed.

At this point, around 225 years post-comet, approximately 30% of H2's pre-comet population was directly and indirectly dead from famine, disease, exposure, and resource warfare resulting from the comet strike, pole reversal, and volcanism. But the cataclysm wasn't over. Circa 450 years post-comet, the Sun entered a grand solar minimum (GSM), a period of very low solar activity, such as sunspots, where solar radiation significantly declines—about 10%, in this case—but is less stable, having massive solar flares with more ionizing cosmic rays eroding stratospheric ozone. Average global temperature (AGT) for the 10,000 years between Y1 and the comet was about ~3.5°C colder than today (cf. est. 1.4°C drop during Maunder Minimum GSM, AD 1645–1715). Sea levels were ~61 m (200 ft.) lower because Earth was just beginning to exit its last glacial period that science dates to circa 115KYA–11,700YA but, according to Mina, was already ending. It would've brought today's temperate climate circa Y25000 (~24,722 YA) but for the cataclysm, which reinvigorated and intensified glaciation beyond the predicted LGM circa Y15000 to what became the actual LGM circa Y35000, a 20,000-year extension. About 500 years into the cataclysm, the global population had fallen to approximately 800M people, a 60% drop from its pre-comet high. A terrible half millennium, to be sure, and the result of the NCC increasingly perturbing Macrocosmic force (which previously corralled these natural 'energies') beyond what multiplication 'angels' could mitigate.

2.3.2.3 Post-cataclysm to Ice Age

With post-cataclysm climate change, old ways of life went extinct. The building arts were lost. Structures remained in use aboveground 300–500 years before they collapsed, subsumed, or disintegrated, and belowground flooded, collapsed, or were forgot as their inhabitants died off. Global population by Y12000, 1,850 years post-comet (~37,722YA), was down ~82.5% pre-comet to ~350M (*Fig. 198*). About 70% retained agriculture. The other 30% reverted to pastoralism though not yet to hunter-gatherer. AGT dropped a half degree to ~11°C (51.8°F, 4°C colder than the 15°C (59°F) AGT recorded AD 2013–2017). As the climate shifted toward glacial, it further dropped over the next 17KY to ~9°C (48°F; by LGM), with wild temperature swings enduring another 10KY that altogether rung farming's death knell. Except for Merfolk protectedly living as a coherent socioculture, H2 by Y13000 had consolidated its physical characteristics via relations and adaptation that became the basis for our ethnic characteristics today.

It seems incredible that a global population having augmented Industrial Age technology and coherent sociocultures could civilizationally succumb to their world so rapidly turning more hostile than it already had been between Y1–Y10150. Mina says we have to consider H2's personality, not simply its technological prowess or coping skills. Recall H2 developed steam power by Y1450 and electricity by Y5500 (§ 2.3.2.1:547). Yet, by the cataclysm ~4,650 years later, its mechanization was only equivalent to AD 1930s England with electrical applications long stuck at our World War One era. This was across the board. Mindset scientifically retarded them. They believed gods operated the world; tree spirits grew trees, lightning gods flashed in the sky. Their technology was long on application and short on theory. They comprehended the mechanics of generating electricity but not why it happened beyond originating amongst the spirits where gods created it for Man's use. Consider superstitious Sumer, Babylon, or Rome, whose sociocultural mindsets prevented scientific thinking that could advance mechanical applications beyond observable forces to theoretical awareness, springboarding unpredictable technologies. The result was limited technological facility lacking the fundamentals to envision and achieve.

We see similar mindsets amongst, for example, flat-Earth believers where fundamentals—theory—are ignored as wrong or immaterial. If humanity built society around this belief, it couldn't scientifically advance; individuals would ignore rationalist curiosity as untenable contradictions of the senses. This is why civilization from circa 3500 BC to the Renaissance never advanced beyond basic mechanical applications of the obvious into theory the way Old and New World Europeans did when they applied the scientific method to curiosity and sensorial experience and built unimagined technologies, applications ancient society could've easily mastered but for mindset that disabled its technological prowess.[505]

Cave–rock art generally began amongst scattered nonliterate hunter-gatherer-pastoralists approximately Y1000, the Sulawesi art being the oldest so far discovered (§ 2.3.2:547). It lasted about 2,000 years before these sociocultures advanced beyond it. H2 revisited it in various places ~500 years after the cataclysm and continued recording their experience in that medium as late as rediscovering agriculture.

Timeline: H2 Post-cataclysm to Ice Age

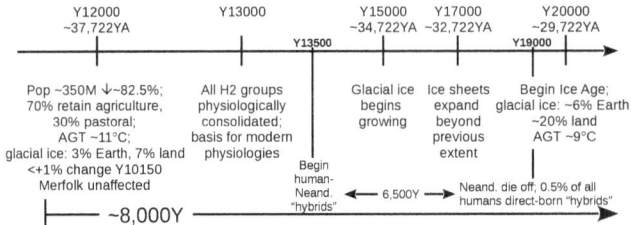

Figure 198. Timeline: H2 post-cataclysm to Ice Age.

2.3.3 TIMELINE: THE WANDERING YEARS

Post-cataclysm societies forgot their ancestors' technology and socioculture at varying rates and times around the world, some within three generations (~100 years) and others millennia. For example, those living in the area of Comazinda, Mozambique around Y24450 held onto rudimentary electricity used in smelting bronze but forgot its application to artificial lighting. They lost even that circa Y25250 (~24,472YA) and fell back from agriculture to pastoralism and finally to hunter-gatherer 800 years later. The ever-strengthening Late Pleistocene (ca. 129KYA–11.7KYA) Ice Age froze continents that left 40% of the planet depopulated (ice sheets eventually ground all trace of pre-cataclysm civilization to dust; time disintegrated the rest). High-amplitude fluctuations in climate, rainfall, atmospheric dust, and greenhouse gas of less than a decade to a millennium

---

505. Heron (Hero) of Alexandria, for instance, developed prototype steam power and an anonymous Greek a primitive analog computing device (Antikythera mechanism) ca. first century AD, but sociocultural mindset thwarted the former for 1,600 years and, along with the inventor's death, the latter for 1,900 years.

punctuated by profound, short-duration spikes of heat and cold seesawed AGT by as much as 4–5°C. Low levels of atmospheric CO_2 limited plant growth by 34–60% (cf. 33% in Richerson et al. 2001, 393). Along with the foregoing, large areas of dry air and perturbations in the atmosphere–biosphere–ocean system and atmosphere–ocean circulation rendered both hemispheres hostile not just to maintaining or rediscovering agriculture (in part by limiting human reliance on plant foods) but to climate-sensitive pastoralism and animal husbandry, too (ibid, 389–95).

Global population at the start of this period, circa Y20000 (29,722YA), was ~178M but continued its long slide to 65M by the LGM, circa Y35000, which marks this timeline's end. Agriculture, pastoralism, animal husbandry, and all other forms of provisioning besides fishing and hunting-gathering died out within about 500 years of each other, the more societally intensive before the lesser. The last agrarian socioculture lived along Lake Tanganyika about 16 km (10 mi.) south of Kigoma, Tanzania and transitioned to fishing and foraging circa Y31600 (18.1KYA). Once climactic conditions in any part of the world made farming of any particular crop impossible, then, if those with the knowledge and skill died before a change in weather revitalized it, agriculture simply left that socioculture's toolbox unless and until the climate stabilized long enough for people to rediscover the concept and prepare a plant for productive cultivation. Since that didn't happen until after the glacial interstadial circa Y36530 (13.2KYA), H2 remained subsistence refugees.

One might feel the multiplication 'angels' (§ 2.3.7:528) could have prevented H2's travails. But in the same way it takes time for a Living entity's biology to alter via evolution or mindset,[506] The Corruption generally and the NCC specifically made maintaining Earth conducive to life not only a difficult, but a lengthy, process. Science finds the Ice Age climate shifting to warmer, life-conducive, stable weather unexpected and inexplicable, though it proposes many data-driven theories. According to Mina, its microclimate ripples expressing as radical temperature fluctuations arose in multiplication 'angels' engaging Macrocosmic force even before the Ice Age presented to stabilize post-cataclysm climate, though without perceived success until the LGM and glacial interstadial, the observed end of the Ice Age. With the Big Healing's dissolution of the NCC, the current glacial *inter*stadial is now *post*stadial as our climate stabilizes toward its human optimum (§ 2.4.1:556). For H2 in this period, however, life was grim.

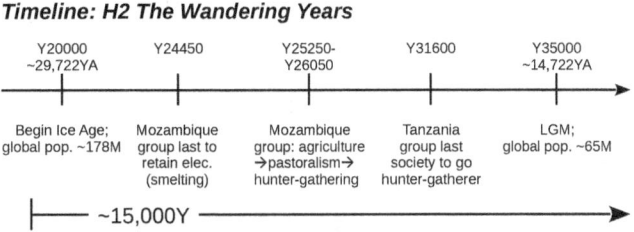

Timeline: H2 The Wandering Years

Y20000 ~29,722YA	Y24450	Y25250-Y26050	Y31600	Y35000 ~14,722YA
Begin Ice Age; global pop. ~178M	Mozambique group last to retain elec. (smelting)	Mozambique group: agriculture →pastoralism→ hunter-gathering	Tanzania group last society to go hunter-gatherer	LGM; global pop. ~65M

├── ~15,000Y ──────────────────→

Figure 199. Timeline: H2 from Ice Age to Last Glacial Maximum (LGM).

2.3.3.1 DENISOVANS AND NEANDERTHALS

About 5KY before Y1, the species *H. neanderthalensis*, erroneously classified separately as Denisovans, died out (Fig. 192:543). Neanderthals, on the other hand, didn't die off until circa Y19000 (~30,775 YA; cf. est. 35–40KYA). They coexisted with H2 not unlike our modern coexistence with Brazilian rainforest tribes in the AD 1920s or today's Andaman islands Sentinelese. The caveat is Neanderthals weren't ♄uman but proto-human, a post-*H. neanderthalensis* species similar in appearance to *H.s. sapiens* (*Fig. 200*). Recall the *H. neanderthalensis*–*H. sapiens* hybrids (NSH) eventually produced *H.s. sapiens*. Post-NSH, pre-*H.s. sapiens* is what archeology's Neanderthals are, not the archaic pre-NSH *H. neanderthalensis* (Fig. 193:544). Some Neanderthals were equivalent to *H.s. sapiens*. Like all proto-humans, however, they didn't integrate the ♄uman (ₗife) mind so they perceived reality via Living (animal) thinking–feeling (§ 1.3.2:273).

For example, they developed verbal communication but it wasn't *speech*. They lacked art and tool making—absent until *H.s. sapiens*—except what they traded from H2. Their DNA sequencing differs from human by only ~0.2%. But like chimps, whose sequencing differs by ~1.3% (or 3.9% with deletions and insertions accounted for), the apparently small variation belies the vast gulf between Neanderthal, chimps, and ♄uman. The reason is twofold. First, Neanderthals, like chimps, are animals and ♄uman integrates a human (Living) body.

---

506. For example, disease, infirmity, looks. Changing appearance or sex takes time, unlike with the spirit body. Mina avers a physical person can swap sexes by altering their genome via mind (Intentionality; § 3.2:282; CH. 30:515) over about 110 years.

Second, animal WOB determines its form and function whereas the human body integrates ℒife (§ 2.1.5:313). Abiogeneticists decided the vagaries of H2's NCC-disturbed environment warranted leaving Neanderthals as a developmental backstop in case H2 went unexpectedly extinct. They'd expected to sunset the species by Y13000 anyhow but the cataclysm forestalled their plans. Neanderthals interbred with H2 post-cataclysm as resource warfare in these disconsolate millennia naturally led to human captives. Such offspring are necessarily unviable because WOB is a reproductive barrier.

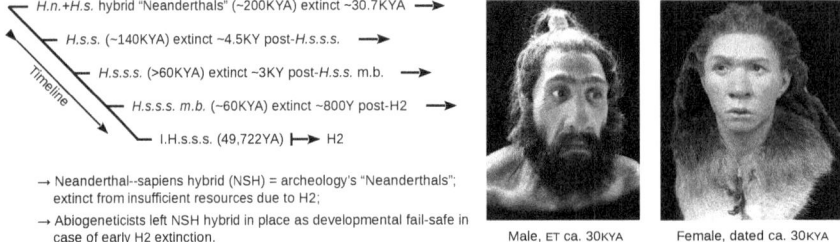

→ Neanderthal--sapiens hybrid (NSH) = archeology's "Neanderthals"; extinct from insufficient resources due to H2;
→ Abiogeneticists left NSH hybrid in place as developmental fail-safe in case of early H2 extinction.

Male, ET ca. 30KYA   Female, dated ca. 30KYA

Figure 200. Left, proto-human extinction chart (m.b. is modern brain); right, Mina considers these Neanderthal physiognomies reasonably accurate ca. Y5000.[298]

Then, why is our DNA detectably 0.8–1.83% Neanderthal? While Neanderthal genetics are sufficiently compatible with that of the human body strictly on a physical level, its animal WOB prevents fertilization. The way it entered the human body's genome was via spirit men Intentionally suffusing a Neanderthal gamete with human WOB during fertilization. We explained this process (§ 1.3.3.2:475) and don't revisit it here except to say all that's required to spiritually birth ℒife (§ 1.2.1.1.2:249) is for a spirit man and woman to Intentionally (§ 3.2:282) conceive. This requires sex for the spirit couple. Physically, the Intentionality arises in the biological fertilization now made possible by the Intentionality-added human WOB—recall only Gabriel knows how to spiritually impregnate a physical woman—which then naturally triggers birth of ℒife (§ 1.2.1.1.1:248). Only in this way does a Neanderthal–human coupling conceive a physical hybrid that births physicospirit ℒife. The reason spirit men intervened at all was H2's dire situation post-cataclysm where its survival depended on a positive birth-to-death ratio (cf. H1's demise, § 1.3.2:541).

2.3.4   Timeline: Ice Age Meltdown to Second Global Society

Glacial ice began growing from ~Y15000 (35KYA), expanding beyond its pre-comet extent circa Y17000 with maximum ice coverage occurring around Y35600 (14.1KYA) when global population was ~60M. According to Mina, deglaciation was in full swing by Y36000 (13.7KYA) when this final timeline begins. By Y36500 (13.2KYA), about 18% of ice sheets had melted. A single meltwater pulse (MWP) circa Y37222 (12.5KYA) caused by the glacial melt of 30% of the North American and Eurasian ice sheets pent up on land, abruptly—over 70 years—raised sea levels about 42 m (~140 ft.; cf. interpreted sea level rises across multiple MWP of 6–28 m over 140–500 year periods). As the ice sheets waxed and waned in their death throes, more sedate melting eventually raised sea levels to modern levels. Earth's warming climate, via multiplication 'angels,' gave H2 its first sustained chance to rebuild. We describe some key examples below.

2.3.4.1   Rediscovering Metallurgy, Writing, and Agriculture

Global population further fell to ~57M a bit over 11,000YA when the 200 surviving post-Ice Age sociocultures in Africa, North and Central America, Australia, Europe, Middle East, Anhui Province of China, Philippines, and India (*Fig. 201*) began rediscovering the civilizational necessities of life. During and after the cataclysm, H2 never lost core skills like fire-making, toolmaking, geometric designs, astronomical navigation, or (30%) number counting, but forgot metallurgy, writing, and agriculture. We consider these next.

2.3.4.1.1   Metallurgy

H2 rediscovered metallurgy circa Y38522 (~11,200YA) on a small island about 30 m (~100 ft.) above sea level, then perched atop the Murray Ridge in the northwestern Indian Ocean that forms the tectonic boundary between the Indian and Arabian plates and west of the submarine Indus Canyon, roughly 322 km (200 mi.) southwest of Karachi, Pakistan (*Fig. 201*). Boats had used this island as a waypoint since about Y38272

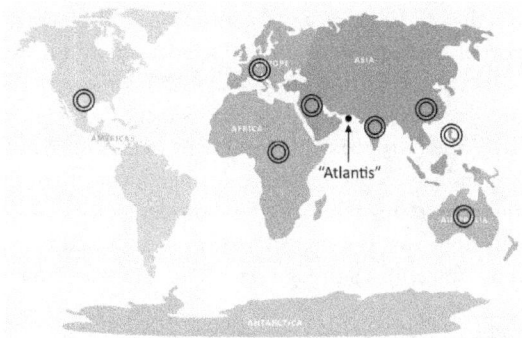

Figure 201. Continental locations of 200 post-Ice Age sociocultures; pop. ∼57M (source: Fig. 186:534).

(∼11,450YA) to acquire live animals for meat while sailing between India and Arabia. Some permanently settled there. Its population was about 2,000 when they began smelting tin and copper into bronze for religious purposes, but refused to trade their sacred technology or its products. Their socioculture ended 650 years later when the island crumbled to a depth of ∼500 m in a magnitude 8.5 earthquake originating on the Indian landmass circa Y38922. None of its then-population of about 10,000 survived, though Mina avers a single boat transiting from Arabia witnessed the event and turned around with the news their technologically advanced but selfish pit stop was deservedly no more.

This ancient tale wended its way through time to dynastic Egypt where, circa 582 BC, Solon of Greece heard a version that Plato with some artistic license circa 357 BC called Atlantis in his *Timaeus* and *Critias* dialogues. According to Mina, Plato didn't cite the Pillars of Hercules as a geographical location, but metaphorically to indicate, in his Grecian context, a scope beyond, meaning west of, his socioculture's seafaring knowledge. The Egyptians had, in their context, similarly located Atlantis beyond, meaning east of, their own scope of knowledge, referencing the similarly narrowed opening of the Red Sea into the Gulf of Aden and the Indian Ocean. That Atlantis was an advanced civilization of mythical power stems from its autonomous socioculture, military superiority, and metallurgical secrets that seemed magical to its contemporaries. H2 re-rediscovered metallurgy in Anatolia some 2,800 years later, circa Y41700 (8KYA).

2.3.4.1.2 WRITING

Written language first appears amongst H2 post-Ice Age significantly earlier than believed as it's consistent with the same human capability that developed metallurgy and agriculture. The appearance of writing in the same general period that people were rediscovering metalworking and farming is consistent with sociocultural development. After all, the only difference between us today and those 5,000, 10,000, or 20,000 years ago is mindset, environment, and survival pressures. For example, until Europeans embarked on their scientific quest, societies of the medieval, antiquity, and ancient periods were quiescent in their sociocultural development. They pursued improvement, to be sure, but not *human* improvement. The first post-Ice Age written language appears circa Y38724 (∼10,998YA, roughly 452 years after smelting) with the socioculture local to China's Anhui Province, using a pigment-on-thin-wood medium.

Unlike metallurgy in the west, writing was never lost after it redeveloped in the east but came down to modern China in an unbroken line. The second instance occurred independently in a permanently settled socioculture of about 1,000 persons circa Y39700 (∼9,975YA) about 5 km (∼3 mi.) south of Al Qutayfah, Syria atop a ∼1400 m ridge (∼1200 m today) using pre-incised sun-dried mud tablets. It also passed in an unbroken line into the historical record. A third instance arose in ancient New Delhi, India (pop. ∼5,500) using pre-incised sun-dried clay circa Y40750 (9KYA) which they acquired via kinship—receptive mindset—encounters with the aforementioned Syrians. This third example is how writing spread when it didn't organically arise. These three sociocultures are the origins of the only unbroken lines of H2's writing in the world, Anhui Province having the oldest pre- or post-cataclysm.

2.3.4.1.3 AGRICULTURE

Not long after the first appearance of writing, a group of about a thousand persons in the area of the modern Turkish town of Burç Karakuyu, southwest of Gaziantep (north of Aleppo, Syria), rediscovered agriculture circa Y38680, or ~11,042YA, via dreams (§ 1.2.2.7.3:267), intuition, and experience when the global climate stabilized sufficiently to support plant domestication. The sociocultures in Anhui Province and New Delhi subsequently rediscovered it circa Y40300 and Y40200 (~9,470YA), some 1,578 years after the former and 550 years before the latter rediscovered writing. It then spread via sociocultures migrating and interacting over the next 4,000 years. Mina marks Y36000 (~13,730YA) as equivalent to H2's birth in Y1 because the environment was normalizing and once again conducive to life and human achievement, clearing the way for H2's renaissance. Although H1 developed agriculture in its first generation, and pre-comet H2 took about 350 years (§ 2.3.2.1:547), post-Ice Age H2 reached that milestone with even less MBI and a profoundly different personality having greater machination than their pre-comet ancestors, although it took ~2,680 years from its Y36000 'rebirth.'

Timeline: H2 Renaissance to Second Global Society

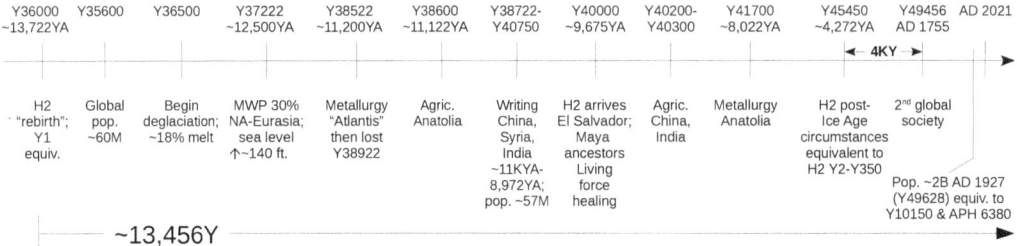

Figure 202. Timeline: H2's renaissance in metallurgy, writing, agriculture, and global society.

2.3.4.2 SECOND H2 GLOBAL SOCIETY

This book isn't about illuminating the historical record but telling the story of life, so there are only two pre-global society (§ 1.2.2:535) milestones Mina wants to describe. We begin by noting SAG inhabited North America from Y5000 (~44,650YA) and by the cataclysm had built a rough equivalent to eighteenth-century Europe from the Pacific coast to the Rocky Mountains as well as in Nicaragua and El Salvador. We describe pre-cataclysm survivors in Nicaragua then post-cataclysm Ice Age migrants to El Salvador.

2.3.4.2.1 ORIGIN OF THE FOUNTAIN OF YOUTH MYTH

Some of the earliest migrants out of northern latitudes settled around a now-desiccated lake in western Nicaragua where ~7,000 H2 physical-born spirit persons gathered circa Y31497 (~18,225YA) to use their combined, focused interactions in the 'reflective' environment as a physical world focal point of Living force on a lake island. Their goal was to help H2 build a new civilization in the waning Ice Age by using Living force to power their metabolisms where only scattered human groups were eking out marginal survival across a food-ravaged globe. They helped spawn a civilization that marked off the island as sacred ground. It lasted ~450 years, reaching a peak population of ~10,000 persons having an average lifespan of ~165 years, similar with H1 using Living force to lengthen its own.

This socioculture collapsed because neither the physically alive nor the spirit persons concentrating Living force around their sacred island (as though a ley line integration, or *nexus*; § 1.4.2:635) understood their physicospirit reality. They'd damaged their reproductive capability by over-focusing their metabolism on survival while under-focusing on reproduction. Birthrate declined. They realized the problem after ~250 years but delayed addressing it for another ~165 by which point the process didn't have time to achieve meaningful reversal before the population dropped below sustainability. Again, not unlike what finished off H1 (§ 1.3.2:541). As individuals died, corporate memory to Intentionalize Living force was lost and they fell back into marginality along with the rest of contemporary H2.

2.3.4.2.2 H2'S SECOND CONTROL OF LIVING FORCE

Circa 8,550 years later (Y40047, ~9,675YA), some 250 descendants of earlier northern migrants, along with 250 individuals of an indigenous socioculture of about 2,000—one of two that eventually developed into the Maya—learned to use Living force (§ 1.2.1:534) to heal their bodies so as to stop the effects of aging and maintain an apparent age of 21–24 years. Even so, they all unexpectedly died aged about ninety; not bad, considering the average age at the time was forty-ish (12% child mortality, inclusive). The reason they died was threefold. First, they healed the effects of aging instead of the reason for it. Second, shortening chromosomal telomeres eventually stops cell reproduction—so-called programmed cell death—and causes aging regardless how youthful cells are. And third, they didn't know that mindset and lack of *L*ife force, not biology, limits lifespan. Disease, for instance, arises in the brain–body's response to the subconscious and only indirectly from pathogens, genetic or developmental errors, malnutrition, or unfavorable environments (absent injury: toxins like poison, radiation, and certain proteins; § 1:577). Consequently, they maintained youth but didn't resolve cell death or disease, thus 'aged' nonetheless.[299]

2.3.4.2.3 Human Development and Achievement

These two Living force accomplishments, ~4,503 years before and ~4,047 years after H2's renaissance in Y36000, bears mentioning because they're the first sociocultures—well, a quarter of one in the El Salvador case—to achieve practical control over Living force since H1 achieved it circa APH 4000. Despite H2's tens of millennia of cataclysm, which H1 never faced, human development once begun is like (though isn't) a self-reinforcing loop expanding human self-awareness and the lens through which humans experience life. It arises in cultural mindset: Individual core Culture (§ 4.1:291) and the sum total of life *at present*. Human development may seem to stop or regress during the cataclysm but that's inaccurate. Theirs was an in-the-present response to life. What stopped or regressed was human *achievement*, not development, which always self-reinforces. When the environment changed post-Ice Age, human development naturally led to human achievement whereas, before, the environment stymied it to self-reinforce what worked over innovation as the mindset of each generation. Once the environment was conducive to the pursuit of innovation over what worked, generational mindset allowed achievement to resume, and human development compounded the sum total of life generation-to-generation at roughly the same rate as with H1 and pre-cataclysm H2 because it's constant whereas human achievement is compounding.

For example, H1 globally achieved literacy, agriculture, and metallurgy all before its first 160 years whereas pre-comet H2 globally took about 350 years. Although post-Ice Age H2 began its renaissance circa Y36000 when the environment reestablished conduciveness to life, it still needed to reacquire these core skills globally in a situation of isolated sociocultures that retarded their dissemination. It took nearly 9,500Y (ca. Y45450; ~4,270YA, ca. 2250 BC) for H2's circumstances to reach rough equivalence to its situation between Y1 and circa Y350, meaning at least one socioculture on every inhabited continent (Fig. 201:553) in a condition equivalent to H2's early days. From this point, H2 redeveloped global society in about the same timeframe as H1 and four-fifths that of pre-comet H2: ~4,000 years (by Y49456, ca. AD 1755). With that achievement dovetailing with Europe embracing the scientific mindset, H2 catapulted from a reasonably primitive global mindset, socioculture, and technological understanding to the space age in just over two centuries despite its 30% MBI, a feat surprisingly unequaled by H1 or pre-comet H2.

2.4 Ensuing Humanity's Current State

With the Big Healing, H2 now stands in our ancestors shoes just before their Y10150 cataclysm, and in H1's shoes circa APH 22105 at the close of its first global war and the cusp of its 460KY golden age (§ 1.2.4:538). We're now clearing away the detritus of our mindset following ~10,000 post-Ice age years of ongoing and occasional global warfare similar to the way that H1's shock at its societal collapse following 4,000 years of warfare cleared away its own mindset detritus and set the stage for its long-term universal well-being. Unlike H1, which never escaped The Corruption, H2 is now living in a state of post-Corruption healing that's revolutionizing spirit world (§ 3.1.2.1.3:359) as well as the spirit selves of those physically alive, even if those who consciously feel some inexplicable positive change or awareness in themselves don't know why. Today's H2—you, me, all of us—is healing and its mindset adjusting accordingly because healing pain and suffering leads to positive changes in perspective, thus a change in mindset more consistent with human WOB. Over time, H2's global society will reject animal grouping's alpha mindset for Ƕuman societal WOB (§ 9.2.2:450), which Mina sees happening over 140 years, circa Y49862 (AD 2161).

Additionally, each new generation post-Big Healing is birthing with more than the pre-Big Healing average of about 105 billion brain neurons. Mina estimates that, circa Y49753 (AD 2052), the first generation in our universe will birth on Earth having the 700 billion neurons necessary for full MBI (§ 1.2.2.5.1:261). Already in AD 2021, about one percent of the population has risen to an average 110 billion neurons, a few between that and 300 billion, and still fewer even more; global MBI rose to an average of 31% percent. Each new generation births having greater MBI, thus awareness–experience of spirit reality, which they don't put aside with maturity since such individuals are less ensconced in a physical reality-only mindset.

2.4.1 Our Future

H2's future changed with the Big Healing. What would have been, now mostly won't. Mina wants to convey four developments: climate change, geographical transition, plant cultivation, and industry.

2.4.1.1 Climate Change

Today's uproarious climate change isn't from industrialization, atmospheric carbon dioxide, or cows farting but, since 1960, a cyclic solar warming trend Mina expects to last ~500 years instigated by multiplication 'angels' returning Earth's environment to that enjoyed by H1. Its average global surface temperature (AGT) was ~14.4°C (57.92°F; cf. 20th-century's 13.85°C), though for about 30% of its half-million-plus year tenure, was ~14.5°C (58.1°F), which Mina considers 0.2°C above the optimal human climate and the goal of today's climate change. Multiplication 'angels' expect a maximum average 20-ft-subsurface temperature of ~27.22°C (80.99°F; ~0.25°F from human activity), a stable surface range of 13.7–14.1°C during the twenty-third century, and a maximum ~14.6°C (58.28°F; cf. avg. surf. temp. July 30, 2020 of 14.02°C, or $57.25°F_{300}$) during the twenty-sixth century with high–low spikes along the way.

For example, Antarctica's polar ice only began forming around the start of H1's tenure—they inhabited the continent—circa 6.9MYA (cf. 3–15MYA) while the Arctic remained ice-free. Sea levels then were accordingly ~61 m (200 ft.) higher than today. Mina expects a sea level ~28.9 m (~95 ft.) higher in the twenty-second century with a final rise to ~76.2 m (250 ft.) over today by the twenty-seventh century (the 50-ft. variance between highest H1 and H2 sea levels is from greater amounts of land presenting as less water depth, as well as more surface water today than with H1).

Consequently, we'll lose current coastal habitation in varying amounts around the world, and in some cases farther inland, just as H2 earlier lost coastal habitation from Ice Age melt. We can't stop this change since it's not our doing. Earth is transitioning from a less hospitable environment to one optimized for humanity, as Mina intended. Uninhabitable northern latitudes and Antarctica will be habitable during the twenty-seventh and thirtieth centuries, respectively. Despite fears of coastal inundation restricting habitable, arable land, it will increase about 23% over today. Nonhuman entities will adapt.

2.4.1.2 Geography's Transition

Mina reports two representative changes to our future climate expectations. In the first instance, the warming climate during the twenty-second century will begin greening the Sahara over four centuries similar with its last green period of 13KYA–3,500YA (cf. est. 12KYA–6KYA) when it was lush, green, and fertile. Also, Mina sees convection energy building up—natural 'energies' will take 2KY to normalize and stabilize Earth conducive to life—that will tectonically uplift the seabed of the Straits of Gibraltar during the twenty-third century sufficient to sever the Mediterranean from the Atlantic as it did circa 5.8MYA (cf. est. ±5.96MYA). It will eventually reopen, but Mina provides no time estimate. The warmer and wetter climate means river inflow will keep water loss consistent at about 30 cm (~1 ft.) although, by then, global sea level will have risen about 38.1 m (~125 ft.). Overall, then, the closed Mediterranean's sea level will be roughly 37.79 m (~124 ft.) higher than today. In the second instance, Norway will be subtropical year round beginning in the latter twenty-third century. Coastal Norway from slightly south of Bergen to north around Mosjøen in the Vesfnfjorden fjord will transition between the late twenty-fourth to early twenty-fifth centuries to savanna up to about two miles inland, with transitions to subtropical grasslands and similar ground covers north and inland and scrubland in the mountains.

2.4.1.3 Cultivation of Plants

Third, MBI improvement and the increase of individuals having awareness–experience of spirit reality means 112 will develop ℒife force to alternatively sustain metabolism. Individuals will progressively consume thus cultivate less plant food, hence less land devoted to agriculture. Although the physical body is omnivorous, consuming plant food is an artifact of adopting animal WOB (§ 9.2.2:450). ℒife force maintains health. Youth, for example, is a function of ℒife force, meaning individuals control the effects of aging; the physically alive subconsciously–consciously choose their appearance as do the spirit-born. This begins with adulthood since, unlike spirit persons, one can't physically appear as a child when already biologically aged beyond it. One (over time) alters adult appearance as desired.

2.4.1.4 INDUSTRY

Fourth, work as we experience it today will transform as individuals learn new technologies from spirit-born spirit world and adopt its way of life (§ 3.5.3:488). Individuals will work for pleasure, not necessity, and abandon their alpha obsession with socioeconomics and the need to govern (§ 9.4:452). Mina claims Earth can support a 15B population when socioculture is conducive to ℒife.

2.5 H1–H2 INDIVIDUAL CULTURES TRANSCEND PRESENT MINDSET

It's tempting and sometimes fashionable to view history as progressive, cyclical, universal, integral, divine; to consider only those facts and suppositions the historian considers history; to see a grand scope in human affairs that conveys meaning and purpose as units, the whole, the eternal. That's faux history, an interpretive study like the biography of an individual loved or loathed. History is nothing more nor less than individuals living life in context. The story of Earth's humanity is the story of each of us today as Individual core Culture (§ 2.3.4.2:554) and the sum total of life *at present*. The individual *is* history in that socioculture is its constituent Individual Cultures since the dawn of H1 despite its break with H2 (from experiencing spiritual attachment via the physical remains of its bodies and infrastructure).

Until now, humanity's been driven by the animal mindset it adopted and the nonhuman WoB in which it steeped itself. After reading this chapter, one might consider humanity's outcome consistently terrible vis-à-vis what we imagine humans are capable. But the Big Healing opened the way for H2 to adopt a Ꜣuman mindset and socioculture over its erstwhile animal grouping. In addition, the effect of *spirit* H1 and H2's healing on *physical* H2 (via Individual Cultures and the sum total of life *at present*) is removing H1's negative emotive ℒife force (EmℒF) that's still influencing physical H2's mindset, which concomitantly helps dissipate H1's trauma the way the NCC disappearing liberated universal humanity's own.

SECTION 3

The Inaccuracy of Radiometric Dating

You've noticed ET dating at odds with scientific dating. Here, we address the anomaly. There are two principle chronometric means by which science dates things, relative and absolute. The former method utilizes stratigraphy, seriation, dendrochronology, and other indirect, comparative methods that we don't analyze here. The latter utilizes the science of radioactive decay. Both are fraught with not necessarily justified assumptions and inaccuracies, but science promotes radiometric dating (RD) as accurate. In consequence, and notwithstanding RD's rather marginal cautions, the historical sciences oft reference past events as accurately dated. Mina says RD is accurate in theory but inaccurate in practice, so our discussion of dating techniques doesn't rehash Evolutionist defenses, Creationist criticisms, or old versus young Earth, but a corollary to our earlier discussion of radioactive decay and probability (§ 6.12.2.1:208; § 6.11.2.1:196).

3.1 RADIOMETRIC DATING

Science leverages its understanding of radioactive decay as a statistical process—whereby half an isotopic parent's radionuclides have a probability of decaying into another (daughter) isotope over an invariant timeframe called *half-life*—to render it a 'clock.' Briefly, a radioisotope with a certain half-life means that, statistically, about half the sample's radionuclides will decay by then, half that remainder will decay over another half-life, and so on. After several half-lives, the sample is 'clocked' as that number of half-lives 'old.' Believing they've adequately established isotope half-lives, scientists analyze a sample from an object such as a rock or fossil to determine the parent–daughter isotope ratio, calculate the number of half-lives, then calculate that with the sample's 'known' half-life to derive its age. For example, science estimates radioactive Carbon–14's ($^{14}_{6}\text{C}$) half-life at $\pm 5{,}730$ years. If sample analysis determines three half-lives have occurred, its age is 'clocked' at $\pm 5{,}730 \times 3$ half-lives or $\pm 17{,}190$ years old. Scientists correlate this method with various other techniques which they believe refines and validates their estimates.

Three critical assumptions underlie RD. First, that science adequately knows a sample's starting condition. Second, that the sample system's radionuclide ratio is uncontaminated, meaning closed in the interim. And third, that an isotope's decay constant is accurate. ET data corrects these. The first assumption is ~80% accurate taking into account isochron dating techniques where one needs no assumption about the starting condition. The second is ~7% accurate taking into account that only ~30% of samples are closed, which has implications for the reliability of isochron dating. The third is ~5% accurate with the caveat that particle emissions, as opposed to actual decay, are statistically constant. The general belief that RD, of which over twenty techniques are in use today, is very or at least sufficiently accurate—held in some cases to be within months, years, or decades—is unfounded, as it's premised on data that's construed to cohere with mathematics as a literal description of reality. Scientific understanding of radioactive decay renders RD only ~50% accurate overall; the younger the sample, the more likely it is that accuracy exceeds a coin toss. However, just because accuracy correlates with method doesn't necessarily mean it correlates with reality, which it doesn't. We consider half-life and probability's difficulties in turn.

3.1.1   THE PROBLEM WITH HALF-LIFE

Science estimates about 95% of RD errors are within 10% of the measured date, with a claimed accuracy of two percent. Mina avers 99.99% of its errors are within 50% of the measured date, so using half-life as a 'clock' to establish sample age is equivalent to flipping a coin. It's not that RD is intrinsically flawed, science just misunderstands decay. A radionuclide randomly decays at some indeterminate point, meaning 99.99% unpredictably. We can't know when it will decay, only that at some point it does. When averaging very large numbers of decays over time, the law of large numbers—that, as a sample size grows, its mean gets closer to the average of the whole population—indicates some percentage of a measured whole—half being the choice for ease of calculation, hence *half*-life—decays over a fixed timeframe that's unique to each isotope. This has the happy effect of reducing the uncertainty of decay to a probability.

Conceptually, then, half-life isn't problematic. Yet, in practice, Mina avers using it as a 'clock' is problematic for three reasons. First, half-life accuracy is only a 61% probability. Second, science can't tell the difference between true (actual) decay and the appearance of decay. And third, the age of measurement doesn't correspond to actual decay between initial and time $t + n$ sample states. Taken together, the probability a given half-life is equivalent to some time t fails. We consider each reason below.

First, the probability of decay isn't specific to each atom but to a large sample population of atoms. Any single atom might never decay whereas a percentage per unit time of a very large number of atoms will statistically decay over a certain time t. Scientists then attribute to any single atom of the group both this probability of decay and the statistical mean of the time it takes half the group to decay. Establishing half-life for fast-decay elements is intrinsically more accurate than for slow-decay elements like Uranium–238 ($^{238}_{98}$U) because scientists can *observe* the former's particle emissions indicating decay from start to finish, but can only *extrapolate* the emission number of the latter from mathematics.

For example, Radium–225's ($^{225}_{88}$Ra) observed half-life is ~14.9 days. Half its radioactive nuclei as a large number appear to decay statistically in that time. Half that remainder similarly decays in 14.9 more days and so on for seven half-lives until radioactivity—though still occurring for an indeterminate number of half-lives as a large-number probability—isn't detectable (*Fig. 203*). After, say, five half-lives, one can determine the *age of measurement*—not the *age of sample*—is 14.9 days × 5 half-lives = 74.5 days. The *age-of* distinction is critical, as science can only ever know (or estimate, with slow-decay elements) the parent–daughter ratio by which it derives 'age' from the point it assumes the sample's initial measurement state. Although RD employs techniques to refine and validate this ratio (including the isochron technique), it necessarily involves a type of circular reasoning not unlike defining a meter as the distance light travels in time where lightspeed c is the time it takes light to travel one meter (EN 183:658). Yet, except for inaccuracies in measuring actual decay versus particle emissions *as* decay (§ 6.12.2.2:211), Mina says science asserts reasonably accurate half-lives for short-decay elements.

On the other hand, a slow-decay element like $^{238}_{98}$U has no observed half-life. Science can only extrapolate it via a multistep process involving experimental and mathematical constants, which have inaccuracies. For example, knowing the sample weight and mass of a single atom of the isotope one can calculate the number of radioactive nuclei N in the sample from which one can then calculate its decay constant λ, thus half-life $t_{1/2}$, from observing its radioactivity, meaning how many such nuclei are observed to decay per truncated unit time. If science concludes a slow-decay element has a multi-billion year half-life, it can only directly observe its radioactivity over a relatively short timeframe and from that statistically extrapolate how many

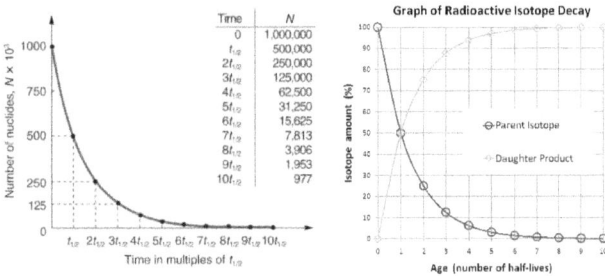

Figure 203. Left, radioactive decay exponentially reduces the number of radionuclides by half as much again per half-life. After seven half-lives, ~0.7% activity remains; after ten, ~0.09% remains; in 5–7 half-lives, activity is negligible or consistent with natural background levels. Right, isotope ratio curves.[301]

æons until half its radionuclides will have presumably decayed. However, while one can observe a short-decay element definitely stops showing detectable radioactivity (particle emissions) after a certain timeframe, one can't observe that about a slow-decay element but only extrapolate it.

The problem with both fast and slow decay is that science doesn't observe nucleon decay but particle emissions that presumedly indicate it. Emission isn't decay. It's an artifact of decay. In some cases, like so-called alpha decay, delta-particle (δ_P) interaction with a Helium–3 (^3_2He) atom resulting in an alpha particle appearing to emit from the atom can happen regardless any further change in atomic stability (§ 6.12.2.2:211). Only a percentage of presumed particle emissions actually result from a change in nucleon stability. Science overcounts decay (as a change toward atomic stability) and assumes a non-existent proportionality that leads to inaccuracies in an element's decay constant, thus half-life.

For example, it extrapolates a half-life of $\pm5{,}730$ years for $^{14}_6C$ based on a decay constant that's inaccurately rooted in particle emissions per second. Mina puts it at $\pm4{,}000$ years based on actual decay, a 30.2% difference (dating accuracy of ~99.0% extends seven half-lives to ±28KY instead of est. ±40KY, with insufficient $^{14}_6C$ left to measure after ±38KY). Rubidium–87's ($^{87}_{37}Rb$) extrapolated half-life of ±48–50BY is ±35BY per Mina, a 27–30% difference. Such differences vary according to isotope and mean the so-called **U–Pb** (Uranium→Lead) 'gold standard' decay constants are off, resulting for instance in a $^{238}_{92}U$ half-life of ±3.365BY instead of the ±4.468BY science uses, thus radiometrically dating samples too old. Accordingly, the $^{238}_{92}U$–$^{235}_{92}U$ ratio is inaccurate, too. The bottom line is that science fails to distinguish between *apparent* decay (particle 'emission') and *actual* decay (atomic change).

Second, recall alpha decay involves δ_P escaping restriction, leading to atomic stability where δ_P remains in the atom but outside the nucleus, stochastically interacting with certain particles beyond its potential energy barrier (§ 6.12.2.1.1:208). The process leading to an unstable nucleon thus nucleus being more stable is *actual* decay. Science observes this only after the fact as, for example, alpha and beta particle 'emissions' which arise as an artifact in δ_P or EMW interactions with certain particles *outside* the atom. Hence, when counting alpha emissions, science isn't counting actual decay but particle detections outside the atom that only *appear* to be the result of decay. It doesn't know if particle 'emission' indicates an actual decay, is an artifact of an earlier decay still interacting with particles outside the atom, or an actual decay interacting with more than one particle outside the atom, say, an electron via beta decay (ibid). This ambiguity inflates the number of actual decays, which in turn inflates the element's radioactivity, the number of a sample's presumed initial radioactive nuclei, skews the parent–daughter ratio, and among other things, inflates the radiometric dating result.

Third, in consequence of the foregoing, the relationship between parent nuclei that decay to daughter nuclei over time t and the decay constant λ is weak. This skews the parent–daughter ratio. Even if scientists reasonably accurately calculate a sample's initial radioactive state at time t (or avoid it using the isochron technique) and the number of daughter nuclei at time $t + n$, the weak relationship skews the ratio. It's thus a figment, not reality. The age of measurement doesn't correspond to actual decay between initial and measured states and results in a radiometric date not corresponding to reality. Thus, RD is valid yet science can't know $^{14}_6C$, say, decays over a $\pm5{,}730$ year half-life regardless statistical probability.

3.1.2 The Problem with Probability

The probability a given atom will decay is a statistical function known as an exponential distribution (*Fig. 203*) and the number of such decays per unit time as a (discrete) Poisson point process that derives half-life.

Given that science measures particle 'emission' *as* decay, the probability that a given number of radionuclides will decay over some time *t* is premised on *apparent* rather than *actual* decay (*above*; § 6.12.2.1.1:208). Particle 'emission' doesn't correlate with atomic decay. This means science overstates its frequency. Although half-life is a valid concept, the understanding of decay and its probability of occurrence that science uses to calculate it is built on error. Accordingly, science plugs inaccurate values into the tools it uses such as atomic structure, atom counts, decay probability, and half-life times. Probabilistic RD is necessarily inaccurate.

3.1.2.1 Reality is Infinite; Math is Finite

Science puts great store in mathematics as the definitive description of physical reality in part because it's predictive. Let's consider that presumption. Recall that reality is All Existence, 'all there infinitely is' (Eq. (15.1):100; § 2:230). Infinity is indeterminance and therefore without identity (Eq. (14.1–14.10):94–95). Because it's indeterminate, it's indescribable. One can only describe one's awareness–experience of reality—in this case, *physical* reality—which, intrinsically, is individual. Mathematics is a corporate individual the way a corporation is a legal individual. As such, it comprehends or describes reality from the perspective of humanity which describes its collective awareness–experience in mathematical terms.

Mathematics is finite, determinate. It can't describe the infinite, the indeterminate. This is why mathematics can't resolve what is intrinsically indeterminate. That mathematics aligns with experimental observation is correlation, not causation. Valid math integrated with interpreted observation only indicates results conforming to expectations that—despite philosopher–scientist Roger Penrose's widely-held view that its description of the physical world is "extraordinarily precise"[302]—doesn't describe reality but only *reflects* it through the prism of our tools, in this case, mathematics.

For Mina, 'energy' reflects reality and nothing else. But it's not reality's reflection, not a mirror image. And neither is mathematics, which only appears to describe physical reality "extraordinarily precise[ly]" (ibid) because it's describing *our* experience of it. Mathematics flows directly from our awareness–experience of physical reality but can never describe even that, much less 'all there infinitely is.' The reason is that it can only describe the forces—the physical expression—of the Energent (§ 1:112) that we call applied energy *E* and real energy ϒ (§ 2.1:114) and science calls physics and fundamental force, the latter which are, respectively, mathematically explicable and inexplicable.

To comprehend reality is to describe it as it is. Since it's infinite and our awareness–experience of it is uniquely individual, that's impossible. Mathematics can only ever be a prismatic tool, an *interpretation* of reality that describes *our* awareness–experience *with* reality but not *it*. We derive our *perspective* of reality through our awareness–experience of 'energy' that filters up through conscious mind where we try describing it by interpreting observation and mathematics, the latter which we neither invented nor discovered but merely codifies our *perspective* of reality. That humanity codifies its awareness–experience in mathematics' perspective doesn't convey upon it its own reality nor reality's description.

Mathematics can't describe but only prismatically reflect reality. The probability a given atom will decay as a statistical function of a large sample size can never describe actual atomic decay because it's an indeterminate whereas probability is a determinate. Quite apart from statistically calculating particle 'emission' that's a partially determinate expression of applied energy *E*, actual decay involves the Energent which is indeterminate, thus, statistically incalculable. Even when science observes a nucleon, it's nevertheless impossible to describe actual decay mathematically because the finite can't describe the infinite. To make RD an accurate tool, science needs link particle 'emission' to actual change in atomic stability.

Our Physicospirit Self

HAVING DISCUSSED OTHER aspects of our physicospirit self in § 1.2.2.3:256, § 2.1.5.3:315, and § 3.1.2:358, we focus here on the ꝑerson living in the natural environment. Recall you are *not* your physical or spirit embodiment. To comprehend our humanity, our very self, we need recognize we are Thought (thinking–feeling; § 2.3.2:240; § 3.2.2:283), the mind in which it arises, the unembodied self that's mind, and the emergent self-aware proto-energy ℒife self: the *you* that's you. Each ꝑerson is emergently, autonomously unique and infinite as All Existence ('all there infinitely is;' § 2:230). This is what you fundamentally are. What you're *not* is embodiment having dimensionality (§ 8:223; § 2.3.2.1:241; § 1.2.2:468). The ꝑerson flits amongst the multiverse as easily as changing awareness from one venue to another and manifesting a spirit body to experience it (§ 2.1.5.4:316). In this chapter, we describe the physical and spirit aspects of embodiment, then spirit influence, attachment, and possession.

SECTION 1
Embodiment

Each of us physicospiritually embodies as emergent self-aware proto-energy (ESPS; § 1:391) integrating a physical (while manifesting a spirit) body to experience the natural and supranatural environments (§ 7.1:212). Ideally, mind–brain integration (MBI; § 1.2.2.4:257) is lossless w.r.t. awareness–experience twixt our physical and spirit realities, with no difference in our physical-self and spirit-self personalities. What we experience in the one, we have awareness of in the other. The spirit isn't hidden from the physical. When a physical person dies, they continue seamlessly interacting with the supranatural environment via spirit embodiment. The 'dead' aren't intrinsically invisible to our physical selves. Ideally, our physical body integrates our spirit senses and we experience our singular mind in both environments (*Fig. 204*).

Death is the *body's* Living end, not the infinite ꝑerson's ℒife end (§ 1.2:246, § 1.3:272). Death's meaning lies only in physical separation from the alive and their activities although that's only a reality where MBI is degraded. That's not our natural way of being (WOB; § 2.2.1.1:234). The Corruption made it our chief experience of death (§ 2.3:545). We correspondingly built the mindset that it's a fixture of life, a permanent separation twixt the living and the dead despite afterlife beliefs. Real faith in life after death should mourn only its temporary separation than the loss of life it appears. But few have this mindset, as their subconscious roots in observable materiality studiously ignoring unobservable immateriality.

1.1 PHYSICAL EMBODIMENT

Being self-aware proto-energy persons, our physical self directly experiences All Existence beyond (external to) mind. We might think what's outside mind—a universe, say—is tangible reality whereas what's inside is merely intangible Thought. But the universe that's mind is every bit as tangible and real as without because

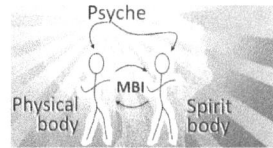

Figure 204. Psyche *is* spirit embodiment integrating the physical via MBI. Subconscious is stronger than conscious for the physical person and vice versa for the spirit person due to The Corruption.₃₀₃

mind experiences its own Thought the same way it experiences another's (§ 2.1:393–§ 2.2:395). In a sense, the 'tangible' universe of matter–Energy (§ 2:114) from the self's perspective is just another 'mind' that's open to all. We misconceive tangibility because we misconceive life as simply physical and sensorial instead of mental and awareness–experiential. Recall not all humans born into our universe are physical-born. The majority are spirit-born and don't experience physical reality.

We're physical-born because our physical parents, descended from their physical ancestors reaching back to Ensuant Humanity's first generation, physically conceived us (§ 2.1:542) just as one is Mexican, Japanese, Senegalese, or mixed because those parents conceived them. You are physicospirit thus physical embodied instead of only spirit embodied because physicospirit parents conceived you. Except to the degree we choose to be, each of us is not physical *or* spirit embodiment but unique, absolutely autonomous, unembodied ℒife (§ 2.1.1.5:353). Seeing ourselves intrinsically physical—believing life is only what the body's senses report to the brain—is mindset, not reality. Those who astral project, lucid dream, or interact with spirit persons have awareness–experience of this broader physicospirit reality even if they don't comprehend its scope. Those who don't can discern this reality by mastering energy testing (ET) in the context of an ET community and developing their MBI to access their spirit senses (§ 2:625).

Now, there's no such human thing as *physical* but only *physicospirit* life, for two reasons. First, the human body is purpose-built to integrate ℌuman (humanity in every collective sense; § 2.1.5.5.2:323) and not as an organism having life on its own terms, independently, as a highly evolved primate. It's proto-human. An animal, not a ℘erson. A Living force entity, not a ℒife force being. This is why proto-human lifespan averages only 23 years. Absent the integrated ℘erson, the-designed-for-integration body is like an airplane sans pilot: it's bound to crash. When one severs physicospirit integration, the physical body dies over the period its ℒife force dissipates. This is the reason behind death by heartbreak or the loss of will to live. Physical life is animal, physicospirit ℒife is ℌuman. Second, when ℒife emergently births as a result of physical (or spirit) conception, it does so with a ℒife-self manifested spirit body. This is the natural way of ℌuman birth (§ 1.2.1.1.1:248–§ 1.2.1.1.2:249). Physical humans are physicospirit ℌuman. There's no separating spirit from physical embodiment and remaining physically alive. This is physical life.

ℒife as absolutely autonomous means the person has complete control over their experience. We've heretofore believed we're doomed to whatever state we're physically born into but this is inaccurate, the result of a mindset that mind is brain and physical reality the only reality regardless our enduring sense of eternal mind and matter's temporality. You can change your physical appearance right down to your sex because *nature* doesn't control your genome, *you* do in integrating your body (§ 2.1.3:543). Not simply in the way a driver controls a vehicle, integrating it via the driver's seat the way humans use neural interfaces to control their Na'vi avatars on Pandora in *Avatar* (2009, film). Rather, since your whole mind integrates your whole body, it's in terms of every aspect of your body responding to mind, from driving it *Avatar*-style to intricately controlling its fundamental physical (DNA) expression.

Imagine getting into your car and as soon as you integrate it by sitting in the driver's seat, turning it on and touching the steering wheel and foot pedals, it takes on how you want it to look, to be, to perform. You do this subconsciously all day every day with your body via Intentionality (§ 2:518) except the outcome isn't instant. It takes time because the body is a biological entity constituted of matter–Energy having its own independently-operating physical reality in the context of applied energy E, real energy Υ (Fundamental Force) and proto-energy (§ 1:112–§ 2:114). Matter bonds and interacts only in accord with its contextual forces. To alter these forces, interactions, and outcomes requires contextually utilizing them Intentionally. Unlike us, the spirit-born immediately alter their spirit bodies at will via Intentionality (depending on how fundamental the change). The reason is that, unlike matter–Energy resisting Intentionality in some way analogous to a gyroscope resisting aspect change, supramatter (§ 1.1:466–§ 1.2:467) has no independently operating forces controlling it. All equivalent physical forces in the spirit environment readily respond to Intentionality (*below*). The spirit person can, for instance, avoid gravity at will.

For the spirit-born, the spirit body is a *direct* expression of mind, one's Intentionality in the context of Intentionality-dependent supramatter. For the physical-born, the physical body is an *indirect* expression of mind, one's Intentionality in the context of Intentionality-independent matter–Energy. Where a spirit person can immediately Intentionalize sexual *appearance* from one sex to the other at will, a physical person needs Intentionalize the same change in the biological context of genome, which initially Intentionalized and habituated from emergent birth (§ 2.1.5.1:313). The reason people show the effects of aging, lifestyle, or stress isn't from shortening telomeres (programmed cell death), toxic foods, lack of sleep, or excess hormone products. It's because their mindset accepts these as inexorably real and, over time, Intentionalizes them at the genomic, hormonal, and other biologically fundamental levels to make them reality, which science then presumptively observes to be causative. This doesn't mean if one believes something is true then it's a self-fulfilling prophecy. Conscious belief doesn't automatically entail subconscious WOB (mindset) as it's less powerful in the sense of insistence than the latter.

1.2 SPIRIT EMBODIMENT

Our spirit body is an expression, or manifestation, of our mind without any independent requirements. It's purely our mind's creation. In the context of the physicospirit person, spirit embodiment—what people call their spirit, higher, astral, or some other self—is an integral aspect of life's experience. The spirit body isn't better, holier, higher, sublime, or more advanced than our physical body. Each in its context provides our 𝓛ife-self mind a direct awareness–experience of external-to-mind All Existence. Although our emergent self-aware proto-energy self is infinite in that it isn't limited by time and space and instantly is wherever our awareness is—the unembodied individual is instantly with any other unembodied awareness or is instantly spirit embodied within any universe to which they've shifted their awareness; recall, too, one can have multiple simultaneous awareness (*below*)—it's still a discrete entity.

Psyche isn't part of our universe like embodiment, yet it's instantly aware of any aspect of it. A spirit person can instantaneously travel anywhere in the supranatural and 'reflective' (§ 7.1.1.1:212) environments whereas our physical embodiment is dimensionally limited by time and space and can move around the physical universe only in accord with how matter–Energy operates. While a physicospirit person can physically travel around Earth only via physical means, their spirit self can instantaneously travel wherever. But there are certain limitations for the physicospirit individual. Let's consider one.

Recall ESPS integrates the physical body. Upon 𝓛ife's birth, it automatically manifests a spirit body (§ 1.2.1.1.2:249) that, as a direct expression of mind, integrates the physical body just as ESPS does. 𝓛ife force wholly integrates and enlivens the physical body, exhibiting the properties we associate with aliveness. A disruption between 𝓛ife force and the body means the body begins dying because, unlike Living entities that have aliveness because of Living force, the human body—in and of itself a Living entity, recall (§ 2.1.3:543; § 1.2.2:253, § 1.3.2:273)—only has sustainable aliveness because of 𝓛ife force.

Physical humanity has never comprehended spirit embodiment, and few of its spirit selves know they can travel away from their physical body at will. Those who did (via astral projection) put their physical body in peril because an unawares person habitually keeps their awareness–experience where they're embodied. When spiritually traveling, awareness leaves the physical body. In effect, one forgets it during spirit-embodied time away. If they're gone too long, their body begins dying in the absence of 𝓛ife force, the physical body exhibiting a dazed, confused demeanor of declining intelligence. In the extreme, the person suddenly finds themselves without a physical body to return to and those in the physical world chalk up their sudden death to inexplicable natural causes or from the activity they were physically doing when their spirit self took off. Once one comprehends physicospirit embodiment then, so long as they maintain awareness of their physical body so that 𝓛ife force enlivens it sans disruption, they can spiritually travel while physically awake without imperiling their body. In effect, they're in two places at the same time having multiple, simultaneous awareness–experiences since one can simultaneously manifest multiple spirit bodies for multiple, simultaneous awareness–experiences while their primary spirit body is firmly anchored to, and 𝓛ife-force-integrating, their physical body (§ 1.2.3.3.3:472).

Since the spirit body is a direct expression of mind, it can take on whatever appearance one Intentionally desires. This is why Merfolk's spirit bodies naturally lack their physical aquatic expression (§ 2.2:545). Their subconscious sees themselves having human WOB ever since emergent birth. It Intentionalizes the spirit body accordingly unless one consciously alters it (§ 2.2.2.1.1:396). This extends to the subtlest things. The spirit-born, for example, see themselves having aliveness. Their mind subconsciously Intentionalizes that mindset in their spirit body, which manifests their sense of what being alive bodily means. If it entails our physical sense of 'being alive' then their spirit body manifests heartbeat, respiration, sweat, body heat. Surprisingly, Mina says physical-born spirit persons—the dead—don't albeit could if desired manifest their body's biological functions because they see themselves as 'not alive,' habitually associating 'alive' with physical aliveness despite having awareness–experience of life in spirit world.

SECTION 2
Unembodiment

We describe unembodiment throughout (§ 1.2.1.1.3:250; § 2:304; § 1.2.1:337; § 2.1.1.1:349; § 2.1.1.4:369), so we consider it here in Mina's context, the person who built our universe (§ 1:335). A builder isn't God, a god, divine, superhuman, or a super-advanced alien. He or she is just a human being having trained in what amounts to a hyper-advanced post-doctoral practicum in All Existence and human WOB (§ 3:343) with the usual thinking–feeling and awareness–experience as any of us except contextualized to their superlative knowledge, skill set, and 'entanglement.' We mention it here because unembodiment is the mode of being ensuring the necessary focus during its lengthy process and for a builder to populate their universe with his or her descendants, which initially requires interuniversal 'travel' (*below*; § 2.1:348).

2.1 Unembodied Mode of Being

Unembodied is simply the condition of not being spirit or physicospirit embodied. It's the natural, emergent state of the ꝑerson—you—at birth 'in' Energent proto-life (EPL; § 2.3.2.1:241), like being born naked where clothing constitutes embodiment. The unembodied portion of megaversal humanity (Table 12:312) doesn't live in the 'frequency space' of any universe but 'in' EPL, which is that aspect of All Existence where 𝓛ife—typically thought of as *consciousness* or psyche but really is ESPS—resides regardless embodiment (*Fig. 205*, center). The ESP self that's the essential *you* is ever unembodied 'in' EPL wherever in All Existence your mind's awareness–experience may be. For us, it's physically on Earth, in our universe, as well as to varying degrees of awareness with our spirit body. The unembodied individual who is consciously aware of their unembodied mode of being is free to be anywhere in All Existence at any moment, from their unembodied state 'in' EPL to a spirit-embodied state in any universe of the megaverse.

2.2 Interuniversal 'Travel'

A person consciously aware of having this mode of being shifts their unembodied awareness–experience to anywhere beyond the EPL environment and then spirit embody themselves in ('traveling' to) a universe's supranatural environment. Recall that any universe as a 'frequency space' in the greater context of All Existence is discrete from any other universe. Each universe is in the same infinite All Existence 'space' but occupies its own discrete 'frequency space' that segregates it from all others (*Fig. 205*, left; § 6.10.1:186). If you could alter your physical body's particular universe 'frequency' at will when shifting your mind's awareness from universe to universe, you could sit on your patio and literally cycle through each one, watching its reality materialize around you for a moment before shifting to the next one from whatever point space therein you're at on your patio. One can't actually shift their physical (or spirit) body's 'frequency' this way, the example just helps visualize how discrete universes are simultaneously infinite aspects of infinite All Existence. Recall, too, the spirit body is literally an Intentionalized expression of your mind. When an unembodied individual shifts their awareness to a particular universe, they Intentionalize a spirit body therein the instant they're aware of its 'energy' and 'frequency space.' Interuniversal 'travel' is simply one's mind having awareness–experience in place A then instantaneously (§ 6.11.4:198) shifting it to place B where they Intentionalize a spirit body, thus 'arriving' at their destination (*Fig. 205*, right).

Mina was born and raised in P'najj's universe (§ 1.2:336) but Intentionalized (built) our universe while unembodied 'in' EPL. He divides his awareness–experience between her universe and ours, spirit embodying himself here or there, back and forth as desired. Because an individual's awareness can simultaneously be anywhere in a universe, Mina 'entangles' every aspect of it. As its builder, he has intimate awareness of it the way the cognizant parent is aware of his or her family wherever they are in the house or the cognizant homeowner of his or her home's state of being. Humanity heretofore associated this sort of omnipresence and omniscience with God, a creator, but it's simply the capability of 𝔥uman. It's not monotheism's magical omnipresence

 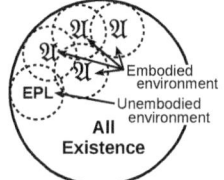 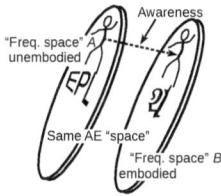

Figure 205. Schematic of infinite universes; left, each is a 'frequency' aspect of All Existence; center, EPL and all universes are discrete yet of the same 'space' as infinite All Existence (AE); right, an unembodied individual shifting awareness from unembodied place A to embodied place B as interuniversal 'travel.'

and omniscience where God has simultaneous presence, knowledge, and awareness of all things in all places at all times, but simply when, where, and how a builder desires.

For example, spirit persons keep an 'ear to the ground' for what interests them, say, one's physically alive descendants calling their name (§ 6.11.7.2:201). Mina, too, keeps a weather eye on our universe and his finger on the pulse of humanity—his descendants—in a roving sense whereby he's always aware of what's pertinent to him and the well-being of his descendant family. That's how he had awareness–experience of El unexpectedly asking him if he had a family and, because she was energy testing her query, (§ 1:1) was capable of experiencing his response. So, too, with you when you ET your questions with him.

SECTION 3
Physicospirit Interaction

Since the physically alive are physicospirit, they constantly interact with their own spirit self as well as spirit reality regardless how spiritually obtuse or in denial they may be. This mode of being means constant interaction with spirit reality according to one's conscious awareness and MBI-empowered intuition and subconscious responsiveness. We consider spiritual influence and attachment–possession.

3.1 SPIRIT PERSONS INFLUENCING YOU

There's a lot of hocus pocus out there regarding spiritual influence. People variously believe (in accord with their spiritual worldview) they're constantly influenced by temptation, evil, Satan, devils, demons, evil spirits, goodness, God, angels, saints, and good spirits. Such notions are without substance. Only spirit persons influence, as nonhuman actors are only animal. Some persons are bad actors and intentionally harmful, to be sure. But 99.95% are benign toward physical individuals and inflicted harm is unintended.

Because the spirit body is an Intentionalized expression (manifestation) of one's mind, a spirit person can appear to others—especially the unawares spirit self of a physically alive person, including spirit mediums—as anything they want, from a scary demon to a saint to an 'archangel' or even God Himself. This easily fools a physical person's spirit-self who doesn't know any better (THE GLAMOUR SENSE, § 2.1.5.4.4:318). Ardent spirit Christians, Muslims, Jews, Hindus, Buddhists, animists, ideologues, and others often present themselves in the guise of some relevant personage to get the attention of a physically alive person's spirit-self to gain credibility. About 70% of the time there's no nefarious motive behind their guise, only a desire to make a positive (or negative) difference in society or in a physical person's life where one's spirit self would never listen to Uncle Bob or some ancestor but would certainly take counsel from God, 'Archangel' Gabriel, Krishna, Satan, or whomever (or whatever) looms largest in one's spiritual pantheon.

Spirit persons can't 'whisper' in your physical ear. They can only interact with your spirit self, the spirit aspect of your physicospirit embodiment. A physical person's spirit self who's consciously aware of their spirit embodiment and its reality necessitates that spirit persons actually converse to educate, counsel, guide, or otherwise influence them in the same way physically alive individuals influence you. Human relationships work the same there as here. A physical person's spirit self who isn't consciously aware of their spirit embodiment and reality—who thinks other spirit persons and events in the spirit environment are dreams or imagination—is easily influenced by means other than talk though less effectively educated, counseled, or guided since that's more covert (subliminal) than overt.

For example, many spirit scientists helped me learn about science while writing SPACE INFINITY, among them Albert Einstein who, still having his liking for a good cigar, suggested my spirit self share one while conversing about the book. My spirit self acted on that, influencing my nonsmoking physical self to develop an attraction to cigars that I felt and acted on when strolling (with Al) past a cigar lounge in Virginia. When I'd suddenly want a cigar for no evident reason, it was usually because I was feeling my spirit-self lighting one up with Al in the 'reflective' environment. He showed up less often after I finished the science chapter but, when he did, it was in the company of a cigar. Later, my spirit guides persuaded my spirit self to give them up as not conducive to a healthy physical life and I experienced a loss of interest.

This is how spirit influence really works. Your spirit self, a direct expression of your mind, adopts a certain desire, mindset, or attitude. To the degree MBI transliterates it to your physical mind, you experience it as intuition, feelings, desire, or thought. You may or may not act on it. I now less enjoy socializing at my local cigar lounge though more so working on the book. My mind changed feelings on it in the context of my spirit self's awareness–experience and, via MBI, affected my physical self (§ 1.2.2.1:253).

A person having stronger intuition via MBI is more easily influenced by their spirit self than a person having weaker intuition. This is just the vagaries of MBI in the age of The Corruption. Full MBI entails no mental (thinking–feeling) distinction between one's physicospirit embodiments. A person is a consciously wholistic, physicospirit individual equally aware at all times of both aspects of embodiment. But with less than ideal MBI at this point in time, your physical self is more or less out of touch with the full range of your mind while your spirit self is more in touch. Despite being a singular individual of wholistic mind, The Corruption degrades MBI whereby your physical and spirit embodiment has segregated experiences, desires, and thinking–feeling in accord with each environment.

3.2 SPIRIT ATTACHMENT AND POSSESSION

Attachment and possession are a spirit person's invasion—not devils, demons, or aliens—of a physicospirit individual ranging from mildly to violently harmful. We describe each in turn.

3.2.1 ATTACHMENT

A spirit person born into our universe perpetrates this form of physicospirit invasion. *Attachment* is the condition where a capable but otherwise ordinary, everyday spirit person perpetrates either an assault on the spirit self of a physically alive individual or bodily moves in or even evicts the spirit-self from their physical body in order to integrate their own spirit body in its place. These individuals are mentally strong. They forcefully exert their will more effectively than other spirit persons who (in The Corruption's milieu) are only ordinarily capable. These folks are the ones who spiritually move or throw physical objects, injure the physical body, manipulate physical devices, and so on with harmful intent. We consider its two forms.

3.2.1.1 SPIRIT-SELF ASSAULT

An assault on one's spirit self ranges from one to many spirit individuals clustering around a physicospirit person to harangue, harass, bodily assault, and even violently rape a physical person's spirit self. Anything you can imagine a mildly assaultive to a violently psychotic individual or group doing to some physical individual in a dark alley or home invasion happens in spirit-self assault and for the same reasons, although they all boil down to the pain and suffering these harm-inflicting individuals feel (CH. 35:577). A person's guidance 'angel' (§ 2.3.2:524), spirit guide(s), or family and friends aren't necessarily strong enough to thwart attachments. Guidance 'angels' intervene or seek help if the spirit-self victim permits it. Where the attachment exerts as violent rape, the physical person can but doesn't always experience it mentally or physically. It presents as a dream, for example, where a person wakes up with the experience and sometimes real physical or psychic injuries, or as an awake physical assault replete with injury even though the victim and physical bystanders can't physically see the perpetrator assault the spirit self. Where the attachment exerts as influence, harassment, or other forms of psychological or injurious bodily assault, a physical person can have one to a couple hundred attachments, each one having their own rationale and agenda.

3.2.1.2 SPIRIT-BODY INTEGRATION

Besides a physicospirit individual integrating their physical body via MBI, he or she also integrates their body wholistically via his or her spirit body occupying the same physical body space. Life force integrates the body this way down to its submolecular level, its root constituents (§ 1.2.2.3:256). So long as there's integration between one's spirit and physical embodiment, sufficient 𝓛ife force integrates the latter. When the spirit body doesn't occupy the same space as the physical body, 𝓛ife force integrates it less and less as the spatial distance between them increases. The diminution in 𝓛ife force leaves the physical body less enlivened; literally, less alive. Attaching spirit individuals take advantage of this in two ways.

First case. A perpetrator forcibly crowds their way into the same space as the victim's physical body, violently subduing or intimidating its spirit self. Sometimes, they so thoroughly dominate and influence the spirit self that he or she subverts their own will thus their physical self via MBI in accord with the perpetrator's mindset. Other times they simply want to leach off the victim's 𝓛ife force. Only one perpetrator can do this at a time. Neither is it a sure thing nor indefinitely maintainable since the victim's mind always resists. Their guidance 'angel(s),' spirit guide(s), and family and friends will attempt intervention and the victim's physical personality periodically resurfaces. This attachment case, as with the second, is mistaken as possession.

Second case. A perpetrator seeking both 𝓛ife force and total domination takes advantage of 𝓛ife force integrating within the physical-body space and diminishing as spatial distance intervenes. They violently oust the physical person's spirit self from the physical space occupied by the physical body to integrate their spirit body in its stead. While they don't gain MBI from this to control the body via the brain as with possession, they inflict pain and suffering—injury, disease—on the person's physical body or just absorb the victim's diminished 𝓛ife force as it necessarily integrates the physical body *and* perpetrator. One can remove or avoid these cases with awareness.

3.2.2 POSSESSION

According to Mina, no one born into our universe has ever had the ability to possess a physically alive person. What's occurred is at the hands of unembodied-born individuals spirit-embodying themselves in our universe with the knowledge and mental power to force themselves between a spirit individual and their physical body. *Possession* is the condition whereby such an individual interrupts MBI between a person's mind and brain by 'drowning out the signal' with stronger mental energy. The brain transliterates (§ 2.1:276) the possessor's mind along with no more than about 0.4% of its own spirit-self's mind. Practically speaking, a stranger hijacks the body as their own 'avatar' like a carjacking where you're in the driver's seat and a person yanks open the door, violently shoves you into the passenger seat with a ham-sized fist bloodying your nose, and then takes off driving your car in whatever way, for whatever purpose, and to wherever regardless your protests or resistance. What happens to your car is up to the carjacker—used in a crime, wrapped around a tree, sunk in a lake, or left relatively unscathed when it's all over. Essentially, this is the fate of your physical body at the hands of a possessor.

The motivation to possess is as ridiculous as it is malicious: to joyride, and as a corollary, to sow chaos. They want to experience physical life and have no qualms hijacking a body to do it. Their intent is never benign: consistent with spirit-born megaversal humanity, ~0.01% of the unembodied-born don't shy away from exerting malice, and ~0.00000003% go on to possession in our universe. They leave the body when sated, not because the person is suffering. About 20% of possessed bodies die in the experience and 80% are physically injured to varying degrees while their spirit-self suffers mental disturbances from mild disarray to full-on trauma that, via MBI, influences their physical-self's affect.

Aside from malice, it makes more sense for these individuals to possess animals or proto-humans if all they want to do is joyride a body in the natural environment. But they can't, for two reasons. First, animals and proto-humans are Living entities, not physicospirit beings (§ 2.1.3:543). Second, their mental energy 'frequency' is incompatible with that of the unembodied-born—like incompatible wireless protocols unable to connect—because it matches the universe in which it was created instead of the unembodied-born's EPL environment, as 𝓛ife does. Unlike abiogeneticists, who are spirit-born into our universe (§ 1.1:532) where their mental energy synergized with their environs from the instant of birth, thus enabling proto-human integration, the unembodied-born are 'traveling' here from their EPL environs where their mental energy synergized with that environment from birth.

Although a person can change any aspect of fundamental WOB (§ 3.3:283), it takes time and effort. It would let a possessor integrate animals and proto-humans but at the expense of their ability to later interact 'in' their EPL environ. So, they don't bother. It's easier to integrate a physicospirit individual. They get around mind–brain incompatibility by substituting their own Thought for the physicospirit person's, 'riding their signal' as it were. *Substituting* Thought means Intentionalizing it as though it were the physicospirit person's own before the brain transliterates it. Possession is a highly advanced form of mental projection. For the moment, it's beyond the ken of those born into our universe.

Once possessed, no one can end it. Not even Mina. No one can forcibly disconnect MBI, not even a possessor. Since they can't sever physicospirit integration, they instead mentally project (Intentionalize) Thought, thereby effectively exerting their own 'MBI.' When a possessor successfully 'integrates' a physical body, he or she controls it until they choose to leave. It's certainly possible for a physical individual's spirit self to fight off a possessor and block them from their physical body, but only one person has ever managed it in our universe. With the Big Healing paving the way to full physicospirit MBI, these very dangerous and powerful unembodied-born persons are finding it more difficult to locate spirit-unawares physicospirit persons unable to protect themselves.

Mina says possession is an "unusual occurrence." Only ~5.1% of presumed possessions are real. The other 94.9% are attachments or faked by the individual for their own reasons, or one's own spirit self exerting its contextual personality unusually and uncharacteristically strong such that they seem like a different physical person. In our present MBI-compromised condition, it's easy to think our physical and spirit selves, living in very different environments, are different individuals having unique wants, needs, preferences, attitudes, and so forth. I certainly did. Each one may even dislike and resist the other (Hitler, CH. 40:605). There were indeed aspects of my spirit self I didn't like when first comprehending my physicospirit reality. As I developed greater awareness, I harmonized toward the singular, wholistic physicospirit person I should be than the seemingly disparate ones I felt like in 2017.

Recall you're one physicospirit individual of singular mind expressing differently according to your physical and spirit environment—not unlike a person exhibiting drunk–sober or home–work personalities—where the ability of the one to fully integrate the other means aspects of one's mind exhibit in the physical, and others in the spirit, environment. Some folks are quite similar in both.

We've had no control over a possessor in The Corruption's milieu. They're kind of like a weather event in that respect. But we do have control over being possessed through comprehending our reality that empowers our mind and makes us less attractive to a possessor. Like their physical counterparts, spirit thugs seek the least resistant to victimize. Religious exorcism and other forms of magical thinking are ineffective because they don't address the harmful person but only imaginary devils and demons in the religious context to which a possessor pays no attention whatsoever. A better outcome is more likely from negotiating with the possessor from the standpoint of knowing who they are and what they want, even if the best one can manage is avoiding harm to the physical body while they influence or control it. Possession is so unusual an occurrence that one needn't worry over it.

Religion

ALTHOUGH RELIGION DOESN'T reflect reality to even the smallest extent, its problem for humanity isn't of theology or faith but mindset. After all, each of us lives by faith to some degree that God is good, a theology veracious, a lover honest, tomorrow better, or energy testing (ET) reasonably accurate and, absent clairvoyance, received from its apparent source (recall an ET community aggregating data lets us better conclude something is likely more or less true; § 1.2:85; § 2:625). The mindset we're talking about is ideological (§ 1.1.3.4:366) through which an individual chooses to encounter and experience *Life*. It might suprise that religion is no different from any other politico-sociocultural ideology whether religious, political, economic, cultural, legal, moral, environmental, absolutist, relativist . . . whatever. They're all aspects of humanity's principal expression of The Corruption: Accountableism (§ 4.1.2:378), which principal expression is altruism, no-harm that *is* harm (§ 1.1:362). Whatever the cause and overlain belief, ideology's fundamental way of being (WOB; § 2.2.1.1:234) reduces to faith and altruism. We consider each.

SECTION 1
Faith

We embody faith any time we live by hope in belief. The greater one's faith, the more confidence one has in belief. The more confident the belief, the more real it is to the person. Hence, Jesus' paraphrased analogy in Mt. 17:20 that the person having real faith is capably omnipotent (referencing Intentionality, not merely belief, hope, or desire; § 3.2:282). There are endless examples of individuals, groups, and peoples surmounting the insurmountable through sheer mindset; we recount none here, except to say they achieve the seeming impossible because, for them, the impossible is real. In truth, every individual has mountain-moving faith in something, though it may not be that something one *thinks* they (should) believe. This is where crises of faith originate, in one's struggle with mindset, not faith, where faux faith rejects the belief one's true faith subconsciously accepts (§ 2.1.1:393). One doesn't *lose* faith but subconsciously recognizes a greater faith in something else, that one's true mindset is elsewhere. When this happens in a religious person, the resolution to their faith crisis involves consciously 'reprogramming' their subconscious (§ 2.2.2.1:396), coming to terms with their real mindset, or a compromise.

Faith as hope in belief Intentionally empowers the person. This is the crux of mindset. It's a powerful mental tool and why biblical Jesus analogized its invisible capability to visible effect. Those on faith's ground floor—spiritualists or shamans who come down to us *in the faiths of* their teachings—didn't have hope in belief but in direct, personal experience and knowledge they attempted to convey to those without it who then ossified it into 'sacred truth.' Converts can only trust the tale, hope in belief, and draw a sense of veracity from their own indirect, or later direct, personal experience arousing a self-transformation through faith's pursuit. Faith is personal, altruism collective, and altogether is religion's mindset.

1.1 THE GODS OF FAITH

There is no God or gods. This concept arose with physical humanity in its supernaturally charged natural environment having individual degrees of awareness and comprehension, where its spirit selves experienced spirit persons who seemed to be preternatural, divine beings of transcendent knowledge and ability which they never imagined could be theirs but was, in fact, their birthright. Such spirit persons presented themselves not as ordinary individuals but as celestial beings—preterhuman divinity—for reasons ranging from selfish gain to altruistic support. When a physical individual engaged sufficiently capable and mentally strong spirit persons via their spirit-self, their physical self experienced profound, life-changing intuitions, dreams, and seemingly miraculous experiences that resonated in their physical situations (§ 1.3:473).

Biblical Moses for instance is a real, historical individual. His burning bush experience on the mountain (ca. 600 BC; cf. Ex. 3:1–4:17) was simply supranatural fire—Intentionalized by 'archangel' Gabriel presenting himself as God—around the physical bush in the 'reflective' environment (§ 7.1.1.1:212) which Moses' spirit self, while his physical self slept, took as physical fire that 'did not burn' (Ex. 3:2). He awoke with a palpable sense he hadn't been asleep at all, with the memory of the burning bush now before him physically unburnt and the word of God profoundly in his ears. Gabriel integrated Moses with his spirit self's permission as he physically slept (like a spirit attachment though absent its malice and only temporarily; § 3.2.1:566; § 1.2.2.7:266) and used his body to physically produce the Ten Commandments.[507]

1.1.1 ARCHETYPAL GODS

Of all the pantheons of faith in H2's history, Mina wants to draw your attention to the Greek and Norse gods as archetypes of the gods of faith. Beginning around 8,000YA (ca. 5982 BC), spirit individuals in their various god–goddess guises instigated approximately 83% of H2's religious pantheons. These so-called gods began as physical-born individuals whose traits spirit-born persons Intentionally manipulated through DNA and mind–brain integration (MBI; § 1.2.2:253). Their physical male–female stature was ~213 cm (7 ft.) and MBI ~50% versus the average 30% norm (§ 3.2.2.1:416; § 1.2.3.2:470). Over time, these gods mostly lost interest in doing favors for and intervening in the lives of physical individuals and groups, except those lionized in the Greek pantheon who, even today, keep up their "godly duties," as Ayako calls it, because they enjoy helping and the attention.

Other spirit persons later move into 'vacated' sociocultures to exert their own pantheons as much today as in ancient times. When physical persons seek their support in whatever sociocultural venue, these spirit individuals may choose to guide or otherwise respond within reality's limits without causing harm to the physicospirit person (§ 1.3:473). This doesn't mean one prays to them for magical intervention as with religion, only that via prayer one is simply asking a person for some guidance or assistance in exactly the same way one does guidance 'angel(s),' spirit guide(s), spirit family and friends, and physical individuals. The intentions of these 'god' and 'goddess' spirit individuals are uniformly supportive of humanity.

1.1.1.1 THE GREEK GODS

The individuals constituting the Greek gods were born throughout the period 8,500–20,000 years ago in the eastern Mediterranean area. Spirit persons Intentionally manipulated their DNA and MBI from conception to produce superior physical, mental, and Intentionality capabilities. These physical individuals used their abilities to achieve unusual, notable accomplishments that eventually immortalized them in the eyes of ambient populations of ancient sociocultures as spiritual mentors, then heroes to mythically godlike, and finally as actual gods similar to Jesus-as-God in the Christian pantheon (§ 3.2.2.1.2:417; § 1.1:570).

For example, Zeus' Life force so infused his body that it was electrically visible (§ 2.4.1.1:401). He had total control of it and people perceived his manipulations as sparks or lightning. Aphrodite's extreme inner–outer beauty helped her notably assist people having love issues. She helped Zeus woo Hera, who was herself devoted to matchmaking, being able to see people's spirit 'energies' and ancestry (a capability Sun-myung as a matchmaking maven for his followers claimed but didn't possess). During their lifetimes across millennia, people far and wide traveled to avail themselves of their seemingly godlike abilities.

---

507. Gabriel similarly integrated only two other physical individuals in H2's history: the principal ruler in N. China's Longshan culture ca. 2700 BC and a Mayan ruler ca. 2500 BC.

Following their deaths, they began interacting as a like-minded group, first with the sociocultures local to Sudan about 7,000YA (ca. 4980 BC), then on to the area of modern-day Bolivia around 6,000YA (ca. 3980 BC). Then with sociocultures local to the Democratic Republic of the Congo, Republic of Congo, Tanzania, and Uganda about 5,500YA (ca. 3485 BC). Thence to the area of ancient Greece about 4,000YA (ca. 1970 BC) where, thanks to its socioculture, they made their most broad and lasting impression. From there, they went to the peoples of Argentina about 3,000YA (ca. 980 BC). Then to Cambodia around 2,000YA (ca. AD 10) where they provided the impetus behind its Kingdom of Funan (Khmer: *Nôkô Phnum*). Then back to Argentina around 900YA (ca. AD 1121) in response to individuals calling on them to return as their gods. Then to eastern Brazil about 400YA (ca. AD 1620). Then to the Balkans about 300YA (ca. AD 1715) which modern-day areas they won't disclose for their own reasons. They made themselves available to all of South America below the equator around 200YA (ca. AD 1820) and thence to Vietnam about 90YA (AD 1930), which is their (not necessarily only) focus of attention today.

1.1.1.2 The Norse Gods

This pantheon originated with physical-born spirit persons, too, but when in the Norse lands, the seven 'archangels' and GLM's mother joined their group (Table 15:349; Table 16:352). Its physical individuals were born throughout the period 8,500–20,000YA but in Iraq, Iran, and the Arabian peninsula (excluding Qatar, Bahrain, and Kuwait). They're archetypally the same as those persons canonized as the Greek gods, though none of those who constitute that pantheon were ever part of the Norse pantheon.

Following their deaths, they first interacted as a like-minded group with the sociocultures local to Ukraine about 7,500YA (ca. 5475 BC) then moved on to the Norse lands about 6,300YA (ca. 4276 BC) where GLM+ intervened with Gabriel as Thor, Lucifer as Heimdall, Michael as Baldur, their mother N'reem (Tethys; CH. 40:612) as Odin, Remiel as Snotra, Raguel as Frigga, Saraqael as Vidar, and Uriel as Forseti to accomplish, through the Norse, what Cosmo had attempted ~49,594 years earlier with Mio, Shinto's founder (§ 4.1:574). Then they went to Japan sans GLM+ about 5,000YA (ca. 2985 BC) where they assimilated its pantheon from local-born spirit individuals, and then to southern coastal Chile around 4,000YA (ca. 1980 BC). Afterward, they went to the sociocultures local to Oklahoma, USA about 3,000YA (ca. 1000 BC), then to Tasmania around 1,620YA (ca. AD 390). Thence to Tibet about 1,400YA (ca. AD 621) where their spiritual interactions with that socioculture led to the knowledge, practices, and theology unique to Tibetan Buddhism. Then to Mayans of Southern Mexico, Guatemala, and El Salvador around 1,250YA (ca. AD 770); to the Zulu socioculture of South Africa around 871YA (ca. AD 1150); and finally to Colombia, Ecuador, Peru, and the Amazonas and Acre states of Brazil about 400YA (ca. AD 1615). They retired from the gods business in 2017 due to the Big Healing.

1.1.1.3 The Gods of Egypt, India, and Persia

Proto-Egyptian (non-Berber Amazigh) and proto-Indian physical individuals whom spirit persons beefed up into 'outstanding men and women' having Intentionalized DNA and MBI improvements were born, respectively, 2,000–5,000YA (ca. 2980 BC–AD 10) in the areas of Egypt and southern Mali, and 2,000–2,500YA (ca. 475 BC–AD 15) in the area of Afghanistan. Unlike those who took on the roles of the Greek and Norse gods, these individuals didn't present themselves during their physical lifetimes as spiritual mentors, helpers, seers, or the like, but as actual living gods to be worshipped. They carried their godlike sense of own-self (§ 2:275) with them into the supranatural environment after death, instigating and maintaining their respective like-minded pantheons amongst spiritually open physical persons who then taught others what they'd experienced. Once these spirit persons settled as gods into their respective regions after death, they never left. They never roamed the world's sociocultures like those playing the Greek and Norse gods but instead made themselves into Egypt, India, and Persia's exclusive spirit powers. They're jealous of their local positions and prerogatives and successfully rebuff similarly capable spirit individuals who seek to join or supplant them. Interestingly, the Egyptian gods regularly crossed paths in the 'reflective' environment with the Greek gods in their various sociocultural guises, but each avoided the other.

India's gods instigated the writing of the Hindu *Vedas* between 200–100 BC and the *Upanishads* circa 150 BC to unify applied philosophy's direction and illuminate the way for all. The philological and linguistic evidence science uses to date them as far back as circa 1800 BC is misleading—archaeological evidence, too, is compromised by radiometric dating inaccuracies (§ 3:557)—because it presumes the texts are contemporary to linguistically comparative texts. This isn't how spirit persons—as gods, spirit guides, or teachers—translate their beliefs, knowledge, and wisdom to the physical world. Rather, the Vedic writers were spiritualists absorbing and writing down ancient spirit teachers via intuition, dreams, or memories of their spirit selves in their company (§ 1.2.2.7.3:267) using linguistic traditions not necessarily coeval with the writer. This is how ancient texts appear older than they are; how their writers describe in the *Mahabharata*'s *Drona Parva* the seemingly impossible such as H1's ultramodern, atomic omnicidal war (although without distinguishing H1 from H2; § 1.3:538) or, in Revelations, the oft-violent struggle amongst universal humanity to block those reveling in The Corruption from using the physical world as a power base to foment harm, which it comprehends in the wrong context as apocalyptic physical wars.

While ancient Persia's pantheon is the product of physical-born spirit individuals—roughly split sixty-forty between those born in Satun Province, Thailand ca. 3000 BC and the area of Pinto, Spain just south of Madrid ca. 4800 BC—these spirit persons weren't physically enhanced in their DNA or MBI as the aforementioned. Instead, after death they simply sowed their own mythology and religious beliefs into the physical socioculture via spiritualists while never taking on the role of gods nor responding to prayers or intervening in the socioculture whether for good or ill. Zoroaster, however (b. 404 BC during an unrecorded four-month regency between Darius II and Artaxerxes II), later challenged their beliefs based on what he'd learned from his own spirit teachers, themselves physical-born ca. 1950 BC (*below*).[304]

1.1.1.4 The Fæ

Fæ are commonly associated in the modern world with Celtic religion and folklore such as the Tuatha Dé Danann of Ireland with its pixies, elves, banshees, brownies, goblins, and leprechauns. These exist in some form in virtually all religions and myths, from the Huldufólk in Iceland and the Manitou of Native Americans to ancient Greek and Roman satyrs, nymphs, valkyries, gnomes, sylphs, and dwarves. Inasmuch as the gods of faith originate as physical-born individuals, ~90% of the Fæ are spirit-born persons.

1.1.2 The 'One True God'

H2 learned the concept of the one true God from a spirit couple (the Couple) physically born circa 1950 BC in the area about ten miles inland of Australia's Gold Coast. The oldest presently known monotheistic faith is Zoroastrianism. It developed in the fourth century BC based on Zoroaster (having 40% MBI) teaching others about the one true God which the Couple had taught his spirit self circa 388 BC at the physical age of fifteen. After teaching it in three other physical-world venues, the Couple presented themselves here as the very first human couple created by the one true God to two Hebrew men born circa 925 BC in Saudi Arabia very near its border with Jordan on the western side of the Saudi town of Al Hadithah. At the time, early Hebrews had no religion. They weren't polytheistic or even theistic. The Couple's intent here, as elsewhere, was to control physical humanity's mindset by spreading altruism as an ideology of the one true God in order to establish a hierarchy of authority around which sociocultures could unify. From this, altruism in the context of the one true God would set the pattern for human behavior that would ultimately derive the ordered, no-harm socioculture the Couple desired.

They guided these two men to meet. Together, they converted the nonreligious Hebrews to the one true God, adopting 'Yahweh' from non-Hebrews living to the west between the Saudi–Jordan border and the Dead Sea. They died in 875 BC and 868 BC. Hebrew followers circa 850 BC orally composited them as the biblical Abraham, which appeared in writing for the first time in a proto-Genesis work circa 300 BC that later rendered 'him' as Judaism's founder. Yahweh then spread as monotheism's one true God.

Section 2

Altruism

Whilst faith is a means to an end in all other contexts, it *is* the end for religion. With ideology generally, faith justifies altruism over all, whereas with religion faith *is* altruism. This is why in religion faith outweighs belief whether or not it's monotheistic. One's hope in altruism supersedes one's actual altruism where deficiency in practice pales next to its pursuit in faith without directly contradicting or impairing personal altruistic faith. In all politico-socioculture expressions of altruism, one's deficient altruism directly contradicts and impairs the collective altruistic end and mandates correction or punishment. Religion imposing its faith—enforcing correction—isn't religion at all but merely an altruism as with any ideology. The effort to attain the end, however, inexorably sideswipes faith even though "None of the agonies of suppression, nor the brutal discipline of conforming to a pattern has led to truth[;] To come upon the truth the mind must be completely free, without a spot of distortion" (Krishnamurti 1969, 67).

Ideology is a mixed bag because Accountableism suffuses faith with politico-sociocultural ends. This result arises in pairwise WOB (§ 2:304) expressing in The Corruption's milieu which, until the Big Healing in October 2017, humanity couldn't help. Healing leads to a diminution in Accountableism whereby pairwise WOB expresses more consistent with human WOB whereby pain and suffering diminish.

SECTION 3
The Mindset of Religion

The soft sciences define mindset essentially as a set of beliefs—a mental disposition—that unconsciously (hence, unwillingly) shapes how one makes sense of or interacts with oneself and the world, influencing one's thinking–feeling–acting in any given situation. But mindset is a mindfully aware subconscious choice a physicospirit individual continually refines in the context of the totality of environment as the totality of one's state of being (SOB; § 1.2.2.1:253) and state of awareness (SOA). It's also an addiction in the sense that, regardless *what* mindset a person has, they conform *to* mindset. In other words, mindset addiction is one's subconscious avoidance of disengaging from the very concept of mindset itself, never mind the particularities of the mindset in question. A person unaffected by The Corruption, like Mina, has a mindset, too—his sense of own-self—but doesn't conform, or subconsciously adhere, to it. Instead, he fluidly interacts with own-self and not-own-self in the context of the totality of mindset as SOB and SOA in the totality of his experience. Mindset doesn't bound, but simply informs, a person like Mina.

Recall, however, religion is ideology—applied (prescriptive) philosophy—that's just a spirit-based solution for physical exigencies (§ 1.1.3.5.2:367; § 6.8.1:439). It's concerned with spirit regardless how any particular religion addresses the physical. Religion as ideology maximizes a belief about supranatural reality as the quintessential way while minimizing natural reality as inessential, whereas non-religion as ideology maximizes the latter while minimizing the former. A religious person mayhap isn't flattered to hear their spiritualist mindset differs fundamentally not a whit from that of any atheistic materialist ideology, yet their process and motivation both arise in segregating own-self SOB–SOA from disconformity.

The reason religion is hostile to disconformity is that, like any ideology, it's an absolute where, as with the scientific mindset, fantasy ineluctably grinds against reality. Ideology binds the mind to its paradigm. The stronger it is, the more it distorts reality that's intrinsically indeterminate and can't be paradigmatically quantified (§ 2:96). Disrupting the fantasy distorts the paradigm, harming own-self well-being as it's contextually perceived. Religion is just another ideology that happens to emphasize spiritualism over materialism the way a prescriptive painkiller is just another drug delivering a certain high vis-à-vis another's. Whether high on drugs or ideology, mindset is all. What one chooses and rejects naturally follows.

Mindset addiction embodied in thinking–feeling, socioculture, ideology (thought system), and media habituates a certain reality (WOB) where individuals accept only conformity while rejecting disconformity. According to American physicist, philosopher, and atheist Victor Stenger (d. 2014),

> Most religions claim that humans possess immaterial souls that control much of our mental processing. If that were true, we should be able to observe mentally induced phenomena that are independent of brain chemistry. We do not . . . If God has revealed truths to humanity, then these truths should be testable. Over the millennia many people have reported religious or mystical experiences in which they have communicated with one god or another. By now, we should have seen some confirming evidence for this, such as a verifiable fact that could not have been in the person's head unless it was revealed to them. We have not . . . When faith rules over facts, magical thinking becomes deeply ingrained and warps all areas of life. It produces a frame of mind in which concepts are formulated with deep passion but without the slightest attention paid to the evidence. (2012, par. 11, 14, 17)

Yet, the foregoing itself isn't scientific nor even philosophical. It's an (atheistically) ideological statement promoting a mindset admitting one possible reality w.r.t. the nature, constituents, function, history, and so on of the universe and humanity where countervailing or complementary supranatural notions necessarily fail. Although Stenger presents himself as eminently reasonable, hence philosophical, he instead articulates *applied* philosophy where absence of evidence is evidence of absence. More often than not science, like religion, builds reality out of thin air. Addiction to mindset lies at The Corruption's heart (§ 1.1.2.1:364). Altering it takes choosing to reconcile subconscious–conscious mind as well as time (§ 2.2.2.1:396).

SECTION 4

Shinto

Mina considers Japanese Shinto the oldest religion on Earth. Science finds evidence of it beginning only with the *Yayoi* culture of Kyushu circa 300 BC–AD 300, most likely arising in the preceding *Jomon* culture (origin variously 10,500–8000 BC or 7500–4500 BC) from indigenous animistic polytheism, divine ancestors, shamanism, and the *kami* (gods, divinity) of nature and of outstanding individuals. But it predates all that. Common wisdom holds Shinto has no founder, but Mina avers its origin dates to a third-generation man born ~49,626YA (H2's Y96; Table 18:532) on Hainan island, southwest of Hong Kong. His grandparents and another couple, four of the first ten H2 humans born on Selayar Island, Indonesia (Fig. 194:544), had traveled there in Y40 (ca. 49,682YA) from their birthplace. His parents were born in Y45 and Y47 during the ten-year journey. At his birth, H2 in the greater Malay Archipelago area stood at 98 people (a ~2.4% growth rate; cf. modern rates >2% in Africa, Central Asia, and the Middle East). His grandparents and parents died aged ~80 and 69, respectively, and he himself at 59 (with his wife, aged 56) from starvation during an explorational boat transit from the Philippines to the Vietnam area. The name he prefers with us is Mio, a shortened version of his birth name.

4.1 ORIGIN OF SHINTO

Mio, his wife (first cousin), and one male and two female extended family left Hainan by boat when he was twenty years old, sailing up China's coast for two years before landing in Taiwan where they lived another two years. From Taiwan, they sailed roughly 242 km (150 mi.) east to Ishigaki island where they stayed another two years. They then sailed nearly two years more until landing on Okinoerabu Island (沖永良部島), two islands north of Okinawa in the Ryukyu Islands chain, south of Japan. Mio was now 28 and his wife 24. They had four children there and the others another six, and lived there for the next twenty years. Mio began having dreams in his thirty-second year with an "amazing being" who taught him all about the world, the universe, and humanity. This being was the unembodied-born Cosmo (§ 1.2.1.1:338), who'd made it his mission to educate physical humanity throughout our universe since, because of The Corruption, the spirit-born of our universe weren't getting the job done and he felt Mina's pain at the twisted turn his universal family had taken (§ 2:367).

The tale Cosmo told Mio is the only one in H2's history that correctly conveys reality as it is, as Mina describes in this book. Cosmo taught Mio's spirit self nightly for about a year. However, his parents had never taught him to read and write. Their own parents, Mio's grandparents whom the abiogeneticists had taught literacy from the start, had utterly neglected teaching them—as had the first generation in the South America group (Fig. 194:544)—because they considered it a skill far enough down the totem pole of survival to be not worth their time. Cosmo wanted to teach him literacy but Mio lacked sufficient MBI for his spirit self to transliterate the skill to his physical self (§ 1.2.2.2:254; crown chakra, § 1.2.1.3.1:501), and Cosmo was unable to do it via intuition and dreams alone (§ 2.3.1:545). Instead, Mio taught his children Cosmo's tale—his wife disbelieved and declined—until they recited it verbatim. They delivered on their promise to build a tradition to pass it on to their descendants, who are today's Ryukyu (琉球) people. This was the best Mio could do, and the most Cosmo could really hope for in The Corruption's milieu.

Mina avers Mio comprehended and passed on 100% of Cosmo's teachings in contextual metaphor, allegory, and language he understood. His grandchildren passed on to their children a version that was ~99% accurate but which, in four more generations, dropped to about 50% and in another four to ~19% where it was when Mio's descendants finally wrote it down circa Y2005 (47,717YA). The last written copy was lost about 150 years after the Y10150 cataclysm (ca. 39,572YA; § 2.3.2.2:548). It orally survived at that level of accuracy through the Ice Age but afterward recovered through recombined oral traditions and spirit awareness to about 62% accuracy compared to Mio's version, then returned to a written ~19% in Japan's *Kojiki* (古事记; ca. AD 712). The human and natural reality the *Kojiki* portrays derives from its very ancient oral traditions coded in metaphor, allegory, and language handed down from Mio and permuted over nearly 50,000 years, which is why it looks like just any phantasmic creation myth.

SECTION 5

Religion's Accuracy

According to Mina, the natural and physicospirit human reality conveyed by religion has an accuracy altogether of 3.5% on average, with Judaism 1.5%, Christianity 1.5%, Islam 1%, and Hinduism 37.25% in its own cryptic metaphor, allegory, and language. Monotheism is so inaccurate because people created it for control (§ 1.1.2:572), not to enrich spiritual life as a quest to discern human reality. Mina avers 99% of the Bible and Quran are wholly untrue with the remaining 1% being wholly or partially true. Of that, 89% and 2%, respectively, is wholly true whereas 11% and 98%, respectively, is partially true. Of what's true in the Quran, 100% comes from the Judeo-Christian Old Testament.

Healing

MINA'S PERSPECTIVE ON healing is threefold: healing the individual solves every human problem, only the individual can heal him or herself, and healing for a fee discourages it. A person in pain experiences negative emotive 𝓛ife force (Em𝓛F; § 3.3.3.1.1:289). In choosing to remove it, one experiences healing and subsequently can experience Energent proto-life (EPL; § 2.3.2.1:241) via Mina that, as with *Obāsan*'s healing (§ 1.2.2.1:31), effectively washes away pain and suffering as if it never happened. Recall that pain, suffering, and trauma arise in one's experience regardless whether one's body encounters damage. This is why it's common to feel words hurt as much or more than broken bones (oft preferred to a wounded heart). Healing isn't about physical damage or psychic injury, but one's experience of it which affects mindset and how one experiences future injury. Healing is a two-step process of choosing to let go pain and allowing mind–body to cure (§ 1.5:579) without reinstalling negative Em𝓛F. There's no need to face, acknowledge, explore, or integrate anything regarding pain and its cause(s) to heal, that's faux healer mumbo jumbo. This chapter explores what and how healing is, the laying on of hands, and spirit-cum-physical healing.

SECTION 1
What is Healing

It's said there are five types of healing: physical (body), emotional (heart), mental (mind), spiritual (spirit; soul), and holistic (all of these). They're all band-aids on aspects of the self, however, some of which don't even exist and anyway heal nothing. For example, it's not possible to heal the physical body of chronic pain or damage without removing the proximate negative Em𝓛F. Attempting to heal via fakery only lets it fester. Unlike physical damage to the body like a cut, impact, or broken bone which the body biologically self-heals over time, a chronic injury is a festering 'energy' analogous to gangrene as festering tissue death. Without neutralizing it—restoring blood circulation—the chronic condition called gangrene inexorably results in the loss of a body part or life. Similarly, without neutralizing negative Em𝓛F, a chronic condition arises that inexorably results in one or more psychic or bodily dysfunctions. Negative Em𝓛F is simply a slow-moving 'gangrenous' condition that humanity has only ever recognized as the inevitabilities of life and especially as aging. But this is mindset, not reality. There are only two modes for healing in our physicospirit context (§ 1.2.2:253): physical and nonphysical. Underlying both is *harm* (§ 1.1.1:362).

1.1 HEALING AND HARM

Recall there is no harm in 𝓛ife. It doesn't exist. There's only experience that perceives harm. We tend to think injury constitutes harm. But since our subconscious–conscious mind is just the result of our being emergent self-aware proto-energy (ESP; 𝓛ife, § 5.1:295; § 1:391; § 2.3.2.1:241) and our body has no independent self-awareness, hence doesn't *experience* anything but only *encounters* environment, then neither mind nor body can *experience* damage. Your sense that you, the person, *feel* harmed is a mindset addiction whereby you *are* your body and your mind *is* your brain, and that these physical components *experience* harm. Yes, one can be shot, stabbed, or physically 'hurt' in some way. But that's *damage*, not *harm*.

Harm is our interpreted experience of physical damage or psychic injury. This is the reason people encounter the same injury yet experience it differently, as the damage itself or its experience. Mindset addiction conditions one to view life not through the lens of experience, which one controls, but of encounter, which one doesn't. The more one interprets life through the lens of encounter, the more likely one experiences mind–body harm, which isn't *what* but *how* we experience. Only the individual can heal their pain because suffering arises in how one chooses to experience harm's proximate cause or effect. Healing doesn't directly fix psychic wounds or damage; it resolves harm and mind–body indirectly heals.

1.2 Healing and the Negative Collective Consciousness

Recall, too, the Negative Collective Consciousness (NCC; § 1.2:21; § 4.2.1.4:382) before Lucifer and Michael's Reconciliation (§ 4.2:379) constituted of negative EmℒF arising in the individual mindsets of universal humanity that eventually constituted its universal mindset (Ultraculture; § 4.1:291). Every person in our universe experienced the NCC's negative EmℒF regardless their personal mindset and howsoever they strove to counteract its subliminal effect. As an aspect of The Corruption, the NCC was a real force manifesting not just around everyone's mind whereby their emergent ℒife self experienced the 'energy' of its presence (*Fig. 206*), but within the physical body of humans and nonhumans. It affected all Living–ℒife force and Living force (§ 1.3.1:272, § 3.2.1:282) entities of the natural environment (§ 7.1.1:212).

Having no awareness of the NCC ourselves, our bodies were nonetheless awash in its negative EmℒF causing dysfunction quite apart from albeit in conjunction with our own mindsets. Humanity chalked this up to life's apparent aging effect as well as inevitable disease, from the common cold to infectious agents to cancer. Until the Reconciliation dissolved the NCC, a person couldn't effectively heal anything because, even if their mindset wasn't conducive to harm and they let go pain to neutralize local negative EmℒF and heal their psyche, its global negative EmℒF was ever present. Healers have never known this. Irrespective benevolent intent and healing modalities, they could never heal but only hope to relieve or, failing that, shift the blame by exhorting the healee to be more accountable and to better 'work' the process.

1.3 'Soul' Healing

The notion people lose touch with their soul—feeling disconnected, lost, broken, hated by humanity or the universe or God—because of pain and suffering, that a part of their psyche, their very self, literally flees their body to survive the experience, is wholly inaccurate since a person is simply ESP. The very concept of soul is rooted in ignorance and misunderstanding of ℒife, our physiospirit and universal reality (CH. 33:561), and the Intentional part we play in our lives (§ 3.2:282; CH. 30:515). The spirit-born have a similar problem with harm, just minus the difficulties of a biological body. No part of the 'soul,' psyche, mind, or self can flee the body because one's awareness is everywhere (§ 1.2:563, § 2.1:564). Although conscious mind can block out experience, the wholistic state of awareness (SOA) that is one's ESPS embodies conscious mind's state of being (SOB; § 1.2.2.1:253). Fleeing the body achieves nothing and is impossible anyhow owing to the nature of physiospirit integration and the wholism of self (*Fig. 206*).

The full scope of one's self is always accessible to the person, but our ignorance of reality means we're not only completely unaware of what we are as physiospiritually integrated ℒife but ignorant, too, of how to experience our own self. There's no need to 'reconnect with the soul' because there *is* no disconnection. We simply need have awareness we are ℒife. Doing the work of 'ensoulment' via modalities like self-love, self-care, inner child work, shadow work, 'soul retrieval,' solitude, mindfulness exercises, connecting with spirit animals or spirit guides, ecotherapy (nature immersion), and so on to deal with 'soul loss'—disconnectedness, dissociation—are not only ineffective band-aids, but detract from actual healing. Parts of one's 'soul' (psyche) don't dissociate, repress, or need reintegration even though one does blot experiences from conscious awareness. Everything embodies as SOB–SOA in subconscious mind. More fundamentally, one always has subliminal awareness of every aspect of 'energy' throughout our universe because the person is an infinitely aware ESPS as Mina describes in this book.

Anxiety, depression, anger, resentment, bitterness—the whole shebang—comes from one's *experience* of an event, a situation, or feelings that, when one resists dealing with it—ignoring, running away from, hiding

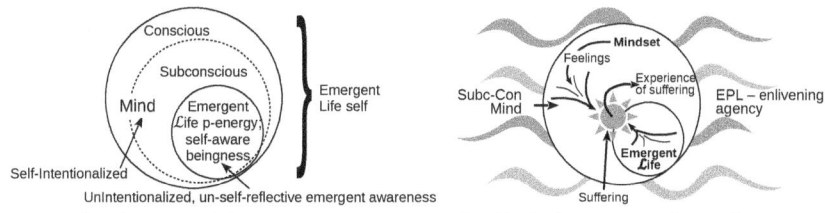

Figure 206. Left, schematic of the wholistic, emergent ℒife self which Intentionalizes subconscious–conscious mind (Fig. 161:432); right, the self-aware but not-self-reflective emergent self—one's self-aware beingness—has awareness of the 'energy' in one's environment which subconscious mind experiences and upon which conscious mind self-reflects in the context of Thought (thinking–feeling; cf. Fig. 162:433).

it—allows its negative EmℒF to fester, to strengthen like one's own personal NCC into a gangrenous condition of mindset. Comprehending one's reality brings removal of negative EmℒF and a change of mindset. Only the individual can heal their self, not another person. A suffering individual never needs face, acknowledge, explore, 'do the work on,' or 'integrate' their cause of pain in order to heal. They only need recognize its reality and choose to let go of it. It isn't easy. Letting pain go is difficult.

1.4   Healing is Neutralizing Negative EmLF

Healing is the practice of neutralizing negative EmℒF. When the desire to let go pain is strong enough, one chooses to make it happen. Pain lets go as a part of mindset. The subconscious Intentionalizes removing (neutralizing) negative EmℒF, excising the Intentionality from one's EmℒF that made it a negative 'energy' reality within them and undoing their choice to experience and embrace their pain. The person experiences a sense of relief that's a real 'energy' response that alters mindset and affect, which alters perspective and behavior. The healing a person needs in any moment is what they're willing to accept, the negative EmℒF they're willing to neutralize. Practically speaking, this is the pain, suffering, or trauma they're willing to revisit in the context of healing, not to dig up its roots, work it out, accept the experience, integrate it into one's beingness, use it as a divine lesson, or as a way to connect to one's true self or One Source, but simply having awareness of its reality and accepting its removal and cessation.

If one has chronic physical or psychic pain, one needs desire healing and then choose it. ET is the modality—Emotion Code works, but ET is more straightforwardly thorough (§ 1.1:4; § 1.2.1:28)—that opens the way to actual healing instead of band-aids. Healing the chronic condition then happens naturally without further effort on the person's part other than the aforementioned. It takes time according to how much damage the body has encountered—*experience* being interpretive thus subjective; *injury* being damage thus objective—how embodied it is in mindset, and whether one reinstalls (re-Intentionalizes) the same or similar pain. The bottom line: healing is Intentionality. One needs bear in mind that *wanting*, *desiring*, *hoping*, and such intentions are not Intentionality. Rather, it is manifesting something as an 'energy'-to-material, external-to-mind reality. In healing's context, Intentionality means one doesn't *consciously* desire healing but wholistically, *subconsciously* accepts, is ready for, accepting of, and choosing it.

1.5   Healing and Curing

It's said *disease* cures but *people* heal. This is inaccurate. Removing negative EmℒF heals and the cessation of its effects cures. From the standpoint of ℒife—*you* as an ESP being—the condition of your physical body is inconsequential. We don't mean physical health, vitality, and lifespan are meaningless and shouldn't be pursued and improved, but that *you are not your body*. You simply integrate (§ 1.2.2.3:256) it as a physicospirit person coevally Intentionalizing (manifesting) a spirit body. Regardless the physical body living a hundred or a million years, one never forsakes their spirit body because it's literally one's mind made substantial in the supranatural environment (§ 1.1:466), one's mindset in material form ever since his or her emergent birth 'in' EPL. Whether the former lives or dies now or later has no objective meaning as an *event*—like a punch in the nose—although death has subjective meaning as an *experience*—as with harm—in physically severing a person from physical interaction with loved ones and activities. Absent the The Corruption's effects, death doesn't sever the physical from the spirit; such persons still freely interact. Our ignorance of physicospirit reality, of our universe environments, and of ourselves as ℒife shapes our view of death as an insuperable breach twixt the physical and spirit, twixt life and death.

While the spirit body directly expresses mindset—how one sees oneself—the physical body only indirectly expresses it because the body is independent matter having its own way of being (WOB; § 2.2.1.1:234) that naturally resists Intentionality in the moment, though responds over time. This is why it takes time for the effects of age to show, to look like one's pet, or to manifest pain and suffering in the face, gait, or whole body. Healing and curing is therefore the same thing, two sides of a coin. Absent reinstalling more experiences of harm, a person heals then cures the particular issue along with oneself as a wholistic process. Once healed, one cures. The time of the latter is determined in the physical body's context by the particular damage and in the mind's context by the depth of pain and its effect on mindset.

A spirit person experiences the effect of healing immediately because there's no barrier of integration between the spirit body and the self. A physical person feels it according to their degree of mind–brain (MBI; § 1.2.2.4:257) and ℒife force integration. A physical person who's healing experiences a slew of feelings they may or may not be able to pinpoint or identify, a sense of fatigue since healing is a ℒife force experience that 'takes energy' in the body's context, a percepted 'lightening of the load,' and so on. Physical or mental illness has no 'greater purpose.' Neither arises in alienation from the Divine or universal 'energy' although don't naturally heal (rejuvenate), either, since in The Corruption's milieu the body is alienated from full integration of ℒife force. Nor does illness help us reconnect with our divine inner self or center. Illness is simply damage or an expression of mindset absent ℒife force's restorative effect (§ 2:581). *Healing* is the practice of neutralizing negative Emℒℱ. *Curing* is the effect of healing over time.

1.5.1 Healing Historical Harm

Healing–curing is a personal experience. One's healing doesn't concomitantly heal another because pain, suffering, and trauma are uniquely individual, arising in how one experiences harm. We can't heal our ancestors or historical persons from ancestral or historical experiences of harm, neither in healing their descendants nor in harming the descendants of those from whom they experienced harm. But we can encourage them to accept healing. ℒife's reality invalidates Accountableist theories of restorative justice w.r.t. descendants. Harm heals in the harmed (CH. 36:585); only in healing do historical persons achieve 'historical' resolution. Modern persons imagining they experience historical harm suffer a mindset of self-inflicted harm, not inflicted harm. Here, one heals as with any experience of harm.

1.6 Prerequisite to Heal

When individuals can't heal themselves because they're ignorant of the possibility or don't know how, yet desire to let go their pain—not simply a conscious want but a subconscious readiness leading to Intentionality—then they need enlightenment. The person needs learn the concept of healing—that, indeed, they *can* heal—either through their own process of discovery or by learning from others. Moreover, one needs recognize they don't necessarily neutralize negative Emℒℱ in its entirety, as they may or may not have let go *all* their pain even though they've chosen to heal. Pain layers like an onion. Healing more often than not involves healing it layer by layer until one fully resolves that aspect of their greater pain and suffering. There's a corollary here with the body where resolving one physical pain can unmask a previously undetected pain from damage, chronic 'gangrenous energy,' and so on. Pain is a layered phenomenon because one experiences it in consequence of previous pain. For example, experiencing a ruptured relationship as heartbreak means one is prone to experience later events not just similarly but compounded by the previous experience. This is what it means to be 'triggered' by an encounter.

1.7 Healing Oneself

When one has awareness they *can* heal and knows how or knows another person who knows how, one is able to heal when recognizing and choosing to let go pain, thus neutralizing its negative Emℒℱ. Presuming one doesn't re-Intentionalize the same or similar pain in subsequent experiences, curing is automatic over time although the concept of healing pain's many layers still holds (*above*) as well as mindset addiction's effect on one's sense of harm. When negative Emℒℱ neutralizes, then it's simply *neutral* Emℒℱ—proto-love's nominal expression (§ 3.3.2:284)—as an aspect of collective ℒife force (CLF). Negative Emℒℱ acts as a block to CLF and, accordingly, a block to proto-love as well. When suffusing a person, it essentially deprives them of experiencing CLF, thus proto-love. Hence, the only proto-love they're experiencing is what their ESPS exerts in the context of their own counteracting of negative Emℒℱ. Negative Emℒℱ heavily filters universal humanity's CLF. Although the individual experiences it as their neutral, or 'purest,' form of 'energy'—one's unIntentionalized awareness of self and its 'energy' environment (wholistic SOA) that forms subconscious–conscious mind's SOB–SOA (§ 1.1.1:392)—CLF only partially rises to subconscious–conscious Thought in accord with negative Em𝓛F.[508] This is the origin of a person's sense of disconnectedness from life, humanity, or the essence of one's own self as a part of greater humanity.

SECTION 2

How Healing Happens

Spiritualists, shamans, doctors, religionists, and more have long practiced healing, but their methods couldn't *heal* but only *relieve* because actual healing wasn't possible in the context of the NCC and ignorance of reality misdirected their efforts. Pain and suffering root in how one experiences an encounter, thus one doesn't heal damage but injury (perception of harm). The physical body automatically heals (besides damage needing mechanical repair) so long as negative Em𝓛F and a mindset ignorant of reality aren't restricting 𝓛ife force integrating the body. Unfortunately, this is life in The Corruption's milieu despite the Big Healing. It leaves us convinced life is prone to illness, disease, natural evil (§ 2.2.1:233; § 1.1.3.1:364), and irremediably short. But that's not human reality. Physicospirit humanity simply manufactured it in the throes of suffering. Let's consider how it is a person heals pain post-NCC from the perspective of what the healee necessarily does and then what Mina concomitantly does.

2.1 Healing via the Individual

The average person on Earth doesn't realize healing is even an option. Those who do, don't know how. When a person does choose to let go pain and suffering, it's a subconscious–conscious event whereby they neutralize (re-Intentionalize) their negative Em𝓛F. This occurs regardless Mina intervening with his own neutral Em𝓛F to 'reset' the 𝓛ife self's awareness of absolute autonomy as human WOB (§ 2.2.1:582). Healing is necessarily an individual's own choice. Others can only facilitate it or build on it. Since Em𝓛F is merely an aspect of 𝓛ife force, it's naturally via 𝓛ife force that one neutralizes it. We describe below how the individual heals and how Mina necessarily contributes to healing—absent The Corruption, healing is unnecessary, as one wouldn't experience harm despite encountering damage, pain, and negative Em𝓛F—and renormalizing the individual vis-à-vis the WOB of our universe.

2.1.1 Neutralizing Negative EmLF

'Negative energy' is simply Intentionalized harm arising in oneself or another. Recall Intentionality is human-generated fundamental force interacting with Energent–prime and natural as well as supranatural Energent proto-energy. It gives rise to Psyche Fundamental Force (PFF; § 3.2:282) which exerts in space as both ideated and emotive Intentionality. *Intentionality Force* (InF, ibid) is the product of the interaction between Thought force and proto-energy. With matter, for example, Fundamental Force (FF) arises in the interaction between archí force (Table 9:282) composed from matter–Energy structures (mE; § 2:114) and Energent proto-energy (§ 1:112). With Thought, on the other hand, PFF arises in the interaction between 𝓛ife force composed from a Thought structure and proto-energy of the natural or supranatural Energent (§ 7.1:212). Whether Intentionalizing 'negative energy' in one's mind as negative Em𝓛F—the Intentional interaction between 𝓛ife force and Thought structure—or in one's body as illness, disease, disability, aging, or in a way that interacts with other persons or objects, it inflicts harm.

   Since pain (and physical disability absent inflicted damage) arises in the context of experience, thus negative Em𝓛F, then its resolution lies in removing it, or more accurately, *neutralizing* it. One accomplishes this with Intentionality as well, *re*-Intentionalizing one's 𝓛ife force and proto-energy without the Intentionalized harm or with healing Intent (§ 1:515; § 2.3:583). Mina can't actually heal a person; he doesn't neutralize *their* negative Em𝓛F because it's impossible for a person to neutralize another's Em𝓛F. After all, it's a product of, and resides within, each person's mind. Pain is *one's own experience*. No one can change it but the one who chose it. Simply in choosing to let go—heal—one's subconscious mind naturally exerts Intentional force that neutralizes the particular negative Em𝓛F even if, consciously, the person doesn't know what it is or that they're doing it (§ 2.4:584).

---

508. Recall our 𝓛ife self forms an instant SOA to its reality that just as instantly Intentionalizes a particular SOB and SOA in our conscious mind of Thought which, altogether, is wholistic mind (NATURE OF MIND, § 1:391).

Mina *responds* to subconscious mind's healing by encompassing the person in his own neutral Em𝓛F, what people colloquially think of as positive, 'loving energy.' A person experiences this in two ways: first as an influx of 'energy' they experience as *positive*, usually loving, emotion; second as a sense of acceptance arising in their partially renewed awareness of human woB that Mina Intentionally 'wove' into the 'fabric' of our universe with which they've lost touch due to The Corruption (§ 3.1.2.1.1:358).

2.2   MINA'S CONTRIBUTION AND RENORMALIZING THE INDIVIDUAL

While Mina can't neutralize an individual's negative Em𝓛F, he can contribute to their healing process. Quite apart from curing (§ 1.5:579), Mina's contribution to healing is a two-step process. First, it encompasses an individual with Mina's own neutral Em𝓛F (§ 1.7:580). Second, it resets—normalizes—their 𝓛ife self's awareness of human woB that's writ large into the 'fabric' of our universe which is diminished to only a fraction of our overall awareness as an effect of The Corruption. We consider each step below.

2.2.1   STEP 1: ENCOMPASSING THE INDIVIDUAL WITH NEUTRAL EmLF

When an individual genuinely chooses to let go pain, meaning their subconscious–conscious reconciles to it (§ 2.2.2.1:396), subconscious mind immediately exerts that Thought structure as an Intentionality which neutralizes the relevant negative Em𝓛F. This is the act of healing. It's not something Mina can force on or induce in a person. Even in personal relationships, Mina as universe builder—for many, a role equivalent to God—is ever unwilling to exert his will upon another unless, on equal footing, he's certain his advice and opinions aren't inadvertently coercing the person. This is an all too common occurrence in people who like, admire, respect, or in some way worship a person whose word, practically speaking, they feel bound to obey, a bit like the old American financial services advertisement that, "When EF Hutton talks, people listen." This is the reason Mina rejects relationships that elevate him—even in genuine love—where there's any possibility of misconstruing his words or feelings as a divine imperative.

The girls and I often run into an immovable wall when seeking his opinion because he knows all too well we're often really seeking an authority's guidance and advice instead of a friend's perspective and options. Even when we say we're not . . . well, he knows us pretty well indeed. Absent maturing in our concern, we can't talk him into it. When you get to know, like, care about, and respect—*trust*—him, it's only natural to ask all we've ever wanted of God, gods, 'angels,' ancestors . . . whomever we admire. But your life is *yours* alone. You can't substitute another's judgment without abandoning the autonomy of your own. It's certainly your choice to do so, but isn't conducive to your aspirations and Mina doesn't partake.

When negative Em𝓛F neutralizes, it clears the way for one's 𝓛ife force to 'fill the void.' This is part of healing, as 𝓛ife force restores things to their original (peak) condition and nature, wiping away trauma's 'energy' patterns shackling people to its mental (mindset) and physical (health) rut, freeing them to naturally, *successfully*, change habits, behaviours, and attitudes. While Mina can't heal a person's negative Em𝓛F, he neutralizes the 'negative energy' one's negative Em𝓛F-influenced subconscious Intentionalized over time that interacts with mind–body and leads to dysfunction. In the context of 'energy,' recall an individual can Intentionalize literally anything. Although it often results in negative Intentionalized 'energy' in and around others, or a dark cloud following the person pushing others away, it most often shows up in the person's own body, affecting areas that associate with the pain they experience.

Once a person chooses to let go pain to heal, this whole train of consequence comes to a halt and the person heals mind *and then* body. When, from time to time, one feels anger, despair, sorrow, hurt, resentment, or any negative Em𝓛F rising in oneself, one can refocus Thought and 𝓛ife force to re-Intentionalize (neutralize) it. It then no longer exerts in their mind although, depending on how long it exerted before they neutralized it, their mind–body will have already been roiled and they need let that naturally dissipate, usually (in our experience) over minutes, hours, or days and sometimes longer (exclusive of damage). One can then choose to focus their 𝓛ife force as a healing (restorative) agent.

The more one neutralizes negative Em𝓛F and restores affect and bodystate, the quicker and more effective one gets at doing it. Since the girls and I exposed The Corruption that October 2017 morning, spirit persons lamenting its end and their place in it, and the larger, ecstatic crowd seeking healing by any means, targeted us. Those desiring healing but a certain cachet to go with it pursue our attention to help them heal. Being obliged to put up 'energy' shields to protect ourselves from the malicious, these unmalicious individuals consequently can't get close enough, or are afraid, to ask. They get our attention by Intentionalizing minor damage to our physical bodies as headaches, nausea, muscle spasms, ringing ears, 'accidental' injury, car malfunctions, mental confusion ('blindness'), ad nauseam. Very creative.

Initially, I had to ask Mina or Ayako to neutralize their Intentionalized 'energy attacks' in exchange for healing them, and to put up or renew my 'energy' shield around my body, home, and car. Eventually, I grew wiser, spiritually stronger, and more capable of building and maintaining my own shields, quickly recognizing and neutralizing an 'attack' before it morphed into something really painful, and then healing the person(s). At first, we were pretty outraged and resentful. But later we realized this is just what people in pain, ignorance, and confusion do—like a drowning person in their panic pulling a rescuer underwater (Baer 2003, 15–17)—and took it in stride, however inconvenient not to mention discomforting. The more aware, healed, and stronger one gets, the more capable one becomes.

2.2.2   Step 2: Resetting Awareness of Human WoB

When a person emergently births 'in' EPL, recall it's in accord with human wob of which absolute autonomy is fundamental (§ 2.1:340; § 3.1.2:358; § 1.1.2:363). The Corruption's intrinsic issue is in leading individuals to reject it for addictive nonautonomy. In other universes, this doesn't provoke the dichotomy and tension in the psyche between nonautonomy and absolute autonomy that it does in ours because, unique amongst the Cardinal (universe builders; FN 130:110; § 2.1.1:368), Mina Intentionalized this principal aspect of human wob into its very foundation. It's our universe's warp and woof.

Universal humanity lost its sensitivity to the 'energy' that *is* absolute autonomy as it embraced the nonautonomy of altruistic mindset addiction arising in The Corruption's milieu (§ 1.1:362). Every person—whose ESP self only has *awareness* of All Existence beyond (external to) it as 'energy,' which filters into subconscious–conscious mind where the individual *experiences* it—had no awareness, therefore no experience, of it. If we consider universal humanity absent The Corruption having a 100% baseline awareness of absolute autonomy irradiating our universe, our awareness of it in The Corruption's milieu averages only ~0.5%. That's how little the physical- and spirit-born came to experience autonomy as the wob of Ƕuman and of our universe, and why Accountableism became our de facto wob.

The reason for our unawareness was the NCC and individual negative Em𝓛F of which, recall, the NCC constituted. The Reconciliation spontaneously dissipated the NCC (§ 4.2:379). This left universal humanity with just its individual negative Em𝓛F, acting as a kind of personal NCC. Accordingly, individual awareness of absolute autonomy's 'energy' remains low despite the Big Healing until individuals progressively neutralize their own negative Em𝓛F through healing. As noted, it can be a time-consuming experience to heal pain layer by layer. Mina avers the average individual who's focused on healing can neutralize, thus resolve, *all* their layers of pain and suffering in about 4.75 years and cure in about another 10.25 years, on average (inclusive of damage). This leaves a person fully healed (not without memories, however) having full awareness—the level of awareness that's humanly capable, not of the full extent of the 'energy' itself—of absolute autonomy's 'energy' irradiating our universe.

A person experiences awareness of absolute autonomy's 'energy' as a direct interaction with human wob whereby they subconsciously perceive themselves as Ƕuman and therefore *accepted* at such a fundamental, universal level, they can only relate what they're experiencing to being encapsulated in the love of God, Creator, Higher Source, Universal 'energy,' or however they imagine the Ultimate. As one progressively heals and awareness of human wob broadens and knowledge of reality improves, he or she never really loses this initial sensorial experience of rediscovering Ƕuman. Instead, they relate to it more appropriately the way an adult doesn't throw away childish sensorial experiences in its context of limited knowledge even when they've matured to understanding it in light of greater awareness. Here, the analogy means individuals eventually recognize there is no Greater Power, that our universe 'creator' is simply a person like us, that their birth wasn't evolutionarily random or some (divine) Being's purposed creation but uniquely emergent in accord with pairwise Intentionality in the context of family (§ 2:304).

2.3   Laying On of Hands

As an ancient body-healing modality, the laying on of hands is practiced by religionists as a general extension of the Holy Spirit or the Divine (God). Spiritualists and shamans also practice it as a means to extend and utilize the (Divine) force that enlivens: the *ki* in Japanese, *chi* in Chinese, *prana* in Sanskrit, *n'ilchi* in Navajo, *ni* in Lakota, *mana* in Polynesian, *Nwyfre* in Celtic, and so on. In all cases, the force being tapped is *Living* force, as with H1 and the pre-Mayans, not 𝓛ife force (§ 2.3.4.2:554; § 1.2.1.2.2:500). Recall Living force enlivens nonhuman entities, including the human body, as the proto-energy expression enabling chemistry thus biology, hence life (§ 1.3.1:272). 𝓛ife force, on the other hand, enlivens the Living–𝓛ife body as 𝔥uman as the wholistic expression of its integrated 𝔭erson having 𝓛ife (§ 1.2:246). The force of the 𝔭erson's interaction with EPL is similar to FF being the force of proto-energy's interaction with matter–Energy except that, unlike FF emanating from nonsapient proto-energy, 𝓛ife force emanates from the sapient self-aware proto-energy being that's 𝔥uman (§ 1:112; § 2.3.2.1:241).

Recall from MACROSCOPIC PARITY—quantum entanglement—that humans 'entangle' via interactions like physical touch (§ 6.11.7:201). In touching another with Intentionality to heal, the act exerts just as the act of fertilization exerts the Intentionality triggering emergent birth (§ 1.2.1.1.1:248). Until now, healers have been unaware of 𝓛ife force. What they've thought of as *chi*, *prana*, and so forth is actually Living force. Hence, a healer's Intentionalized touch is like a circuit through which their body's Living force flows into another's. It has Intentionality although, even in this beneficent context, can only promote physical relief, not healing. And it diminishes the healer's energy, which isn't a result of real healing.

The laying on of hands is superfluous as a healing modality because, first, healing is Intentional, which has nothing to do with touching; second, Living force isn't even needed for, nor can accomplish, human healing, since 𝓛ife force as well as mindset integrate the body; and, third, individuals 'entangle' in ways that can diminish physical healing. For example, a healer's own pain and suffering more readily exerts via touch in the healee's body as negative 'energy' that either negates to some degree the Intentionalized healing or causes new damage. Moreover, Living force can't actually heal but only provide relief because it doesn't neutralize negative Em𝓛F. It's like throwing sand to block the surf.

2.4 HEALING OF THE PHYSICAL SELF VIA THE SPIRIT SELF

A consciously aware physical person can experience healing by, first, learning on his or her own or from another what it is and how it works and, second, choosing to heal. With practice, one can also consciously direct their 𝓛ife force to specific areas of the body to relieve or heal pain, inflammation, and the like depending on its severity although, without healing one's mind Intentionalizing the damage, these efforts are only band-aids. A concerned physical person—including with Mina or another spirit person's assistance—promoting healing in another who's spiritually unaware or resistant can directly interact with that individual's spirit self (awake or asleep) to educate and encourage them to accept healing, which Intentionally affects their physical body and physically-instantiated mind (§ 1.2.2.1:253).

2.5 MY 'DUMPSTER FIRE' HEALING

In May 2022, I experienced a PTSD event I thought I'd healed. It was shattering, drenched in irrational anxiety and fear and rooted, Mina said, in *my habituated response*, not in the other's action. I focused on changing this subconscious mindset. A week into it I woke up awash in migraines, exhaustion, weakness, heart pressure, and other symptoms like I'd been kicked to death by hoodlums as six decades of 'negative energy' (Em𝓛F) began expelling from my physical body. Spirit persons in the 'reflective' environment (where I argued with the spirit self of the person who kicked this off) could see it like thick, oily, black 'smoke' boiling out of me like a furious dumpster fire, which whiny analogy laying face down on the floor like a corpse got a bark of laughter out of Mina that reflexively popped out of my misery. I'd never experienced anything so painfully devastating, not even when I broke my spine . . . prostrate, intense pain within and without, muscles knotted by 40 years of injuries in my back and neck stabbing fire for days.

When Ayako's spirit self checked in on me, she saw orange 'energy'—Mina's EPL—around my heart and negative Em𝓛F's black 'energy'—the 'color' as a blackholeness—expelling from my liver. Mina said it would last a week and it did, the agony releasing and dissipating over several more days. My body *felt* healed—muscle knots, internal symptoms gone though headaches for several days more—even if bone-wearily, stagger-mode haggard. My biological energy had significantly upgraded, which shut down all but sway testing, and altogether necessitated a two and a half month recovery. My unusual healing was predicated on nearly five years with Mina. It's not an example of what others need or will experience since suffering is unique. It just conveys the physical effect on the body of healing one's mind.

36 Freedom

THERE ARE TWO aspects to human autonomy regardless linguistic traditions having singular or plural terms for it. We describe them using *freedom* from ancient Germanic (Norse) and *liberty* from Latin. Each has their own English and French etymological ideations that we ignore here. For Mina, freedom is *mind* and liberty is *mindset*. This means neither actually exists in the world of activity as its negative, positive, triadic—opportunity, exercise, theoretical—expressions, which Philosophy with a capital-P traditionally defines in personal, political, sociocultural, and like venues that, in everyday use, simply means one's ability to do or be as desired. Judging a person free or unfree by this conventional standard is a philosophical sleight of hand where choice and mindset morph into duty and interference in order to promote collective safety through individual harm while blaming the latter's constraint on the former's tyranny. Any degree of unfree experience (bondage) is a chimeric mirage because freedom comports with subconscious–conscious mind that intrinsically *is* free in absolutely autonomy (§ 2.1.1.5.2:353).

Mind is incoercible except by the self. Mindset is mind's own self-imposed tyrant ensconced upon one's throne of *choice*. Conceptually, *unfreedom* is the force of mindset rejecting one's autonomy *as choice*. The constant tension between these two aspects of self is inconsistent and irrational, as it means orthodox freedom as (negative) *opportunity* or (positive) *exercise* is, in its fundament, a literal impossibility. Philosophers and theologians endlessly tweak freedom's balancing act, yet come up empty. They've only ever resolved the dichotomy theoretically, as when America's founders recognized the individual's divine autonomy over earthly power only to deconstruct it in practice in accord with the mindset addiction that negates harm via altruism that *is* harm (ibid; § 1.1:362). The mind has always been free but, in its mindset addiction, chooses the path of least resistance because (physical) individuals frequently avoid their own or another's freedom for altruism's presumptive safety. Freedom is never one's opportunity (to *act*) or exercise (to *do*, or *be*), but simply one's mindset built in mind's unfettered choice.

All the soapboxing by freedom's thinkers falls like so much rain on the sea because, to mindset-addicted humanity, all that matters, the only real universal—*moral*—truth, the only bulwark between barbaric savagery and enlightened civilization is altruism, the codified control of the individual which a grouped, familial, tribal, national, or global socioculture deems relevant. Thus addicted, talking heads waggle their tails in the pristine halls of Academia or the scruffy tenements of Revolutionaria publishing endless books, treatises, and manifestos that do nothing to materially promote freedom. The freest speeched and most heavily published society *on* freedom *in* history has, despite fine words and effort, spent its history progressively embracing the mindset of unfreedom to where it's now on the verge of deceptively rejecting the one for the other. J.S. Mill's (d. 1873) belief that "[t]he only freedom which deserves the name, is that of pursuing our own good in our own way, so long as we do not attempt to deprive others of theirs, or impede their efforts to obtain it" (1867, 8) comprehends individual autonomy while blind to its own contradiction which, in its various forms, guts all possibility of *liberty*. Mina defines freedom as absolute autonomy *absent* mindset addiction whereas liberty is freedom expressing *as mindset*. Let's consider each.

SECTION 1
Freedom

Notwithstanding Mina's aforementioned definition of freedom, the term itself references the autonomy of self since the individual as *Life* is ineluctably free (§ 1.2.1.1:248). One can't choose to be unfree because that very choice *is* freedom. The self is, uncoercibly, itself. Humanity after all freely adopted The Corruption and its Accountableist mindset with its attendant altruism—not unlike a socioculture clouded by mindset electing a tyrannical overlord for 'reasons'—and like a bad habit can just as freely discard the mindset and its effects, howsoever difficult (§ 2.1.2.2.1:371). Regardless how coerced and traditionally unfree one's individual *embodiment* is in any given circumstance, one's *mind* is free to choose or reject it. "Everything," says Viktor Frankl (d. 1997), "can be taken from a man but one thing . . . to choose one's own way . . . The way in which a man accepts his fate and all the suffering it entails" (1959, 65, 67). In so doing, one *is* free in choosing to avoid being *at* liberty. Philosophy with a capital-P—in theology, freedom means obedience to God—necessarily errs in attributing freedom to the world instead of to one's mind or, when it does, to presume one's mind is unfree when it's not *at* liberty *in* the world. This effectively reduces mind to brain, *Life* to Living (§ 1.2:246, § 1.3:272), and freedom to circumstance or another's choice. This is why neuroscientism—materialism's modern basis—can only ever champion collective, not individual, freedom. But freedom is autonomy, not liberty, the latter which itself is not to act or to be but to choose.

One's autonomy is irremovable except by one's own mindset. No person or circumstance can *effect* one's choice but oneself. The self is inviolable, regardless one's experience of, and response to, coercion. Though we think of coercion as an externally applied force, in truth it's internally applied as one can tell when removing or replacing a horror film's soundtrack to negate its induced anxiety. *Thought* is the person's soundtrack, their perceived experience of an objective encounter (§ 2.2.2:396; § 1.1:577). Altering Thought alters experientiality. This is partly what healing accomplishes (§ 2.1.1:581). But a person isn't unfree simply because their experience isn't rational—obsessive, say, where addiction to drugs, sex, or gambling isn't physiological but habituated—because Thought, hence choice, arises in autonomous mind.

Philosophy with a capital-P likes to say addiction enslaves a person to their habit, hence by nature is irrational, the person therefore incapable of freedom and, in consequence, unfree. Yet, since mind–brain integration (MBI; § 1.2.2.4:257) means mind controls body, neurological response is confined to brain and choice to mind.[509] Habituation arising in autonomous mind powers physiological 'addiction.' One's apparent physiological inability to shake it because of neurological 'training' is merely subconscious mind's unwillingness to differently experience one's encounter with life. The notion such a person is irrational (unreasoned) and therefore incapable of freedom much less liberty is false; they're in pain, thus suffering. Their addiction and apparent irrationality is responsorial, a subconscious choice they consciously direct to drugs, workaholism, spousal abuse, or a myriad of options Philosophy with a capital-P finds compulsive, irrational, or lacking ownership whereby a person denies their own greater good that renders them intrinsically coerced and unfree. This misapprehends Human reality. The rational or normal self is not one's 'higher self' or its pointer to true freedom. *The ability to act has nothing to do with freedom*; it's a red herring (§ 5:427). Freedom *as* mind is a state *of* mind, a state of being thus mindset (mindstate), which brings us to *liberty*, one's irreducible freedom in the world.

SECTION 2
Liberty

Frankl (ibid) realized through his experience at Auschwitz that everyone is free but not necessarily at liberty, meaning, in essence, that one expresses choice regardless coercion because the person is incoercible. For example, a person taken into slavery experiences coercion toward choosing it, but no coercion can make them *accept* it. One does so only as a means to express a different choice that's generally an avoidance of their own or another's greater perceived pain. One is uncoercibly free to make any choice but the real, threatened, or imagined consequences to their body or conscious mind are usually unpalatable. One thus chooses to avoid

---

509. Obsessive-compulsive disorder, however, does leave a person unfree because it's an Intentionalized spirit *assault* disrupting MBI. Mind is free but the brain isn't at liberty. Tourette's, a spirit *attachment*, is unfreeness also (§ 3.2.1.1:566). In such cases, the solution isn't religious or psychological exorcism but healing.

the choice of subconscious mind having *awareness* of their circumstance—which, regardless, always says *no* to external limits or interference—for the choice of conscious mind in accord with mindset that's *experiencing* it (§ 2:393). Unlike subconscious–conscious mind, mindset interacts with one's environment as the filter by which a person perceives and experiences an encounter.

Mind rejects bondage of any sort while mindset views it as *less* bad than, say, physical damage or death. This is the dichotomous mind–body nexus where Philosophy with a capital-P asserts a person has no true choice, hence neither freedom nor liberty. But that's inaccurate. Not liking one's options in a world filled with other people disliking their own in no way deprives a person of authentic choice or being at liberty to express it. One's own mindset does that. Where a person's mindset values one choice over another, no coercion can sway conscious mind from rejecting or resisting bondage despite the consequences. Frederick Douglass, for instance, fought his overseer to avoid a whipping and realized that however "a slave in form, the day had passed forever when I could be a slave in fact . . . that the white man who expected to succeed in whipping, must also succeed in killing me" (1845, 73).

A person is ever free, hence never not at liberty. As freedom is a state of mind, liberty is a mode of mind, a mode of being (modestate; § 3.2.1:375). Liberty isn't a social condition but *actualized freedom* exerting in the world as effected through choice. The notion freedom thus liberty occurs only where there's no interference in a person's choice—traditionally: "[t]o coerce a man is to deprive him of freedom" (Berlin 1970, 121); and a "freeman, is he, that . . . , which by his strength and wit he is able to do, is not hindered to do what he has a will to" (Hobbes (1651) 1887, 100)—is not merely false but a deceit. It implies individual and collective freedom is obtained only at the individual and collective expense, that "the liberty of some must depend on the [necessarily compelled] restraint of others" (Berlin, 124). Thus, no person interferes with one's expression of absolute autonomy else, necessarily, one is by degrees not at liberty, hence, unfree. This means even a sports competitor, in striving to win, necessarily deprives their rival of liberty in order to compel their loss by substantively interfering with their autonomous thought, action, and productive conditions that facilitate or enhance their individual ability to self-actualize via winning (Mill, ibid; this defines 'woke' ideology). Yes, sports works by consensual rules, so we don't think its competition is an interference of liberty. But then so too is consent required in selling oneself into indenture (or employment), or in slavery's core bargain promising safety (life) in exchange for obedience (§ 6.8:439).

Strictly speaking, Philosophy with a capital-P's freedom and liberty are literal impossibilities anywhere there's two or more individuals who necessarily suffer interference or, lacking (or fearful of) individual power, call upon a third party to compel the other into a submission garlanded as liberty in law. The conundrum is always how two or more individuals at liberty (or their factors) won't assert real or perceived interference in one's choices where freedom (or liberty) is considered merely the *absence* of external rather than the *presence* of internal interference and, in consequence, the paradox of denying liberty for safety as a substitute fearfully keeping plugged-up the raging quagmire of sociocultural subjugation.

Well, the dilemma is insoluble in the mindset of pain. Suffering individuals inflict harm as a primal interference of liberty. Though never themselves unfree nor not at liberty, individuals and collectives in this milieu of harm and ignorance of physicospirit reality can only ever take measures in preemptive self-defense calculated, at the very least, to preserve their own most fundamental liberty: to live and to be. Individuals, sociocultures, and rulers—backed up by philosophers, theologians, and scientists who build moral, salvific, and natural-order structures like levees—grant or tolerate greater liberty only as a measure of its lack of real or perceived threat or propensity to inflict life-threatening damage on the ruler, the socioculture, or the individual (usually in that order) as the ultimate greater good.

America's mindset conditioning heavily regulates its citizenry's unprecedented albeit declining political and sociocultural liberty, which classification and attendant liberty its government demographically restricts to favored groups despite proclaiming "that all men are created equal . . . endowed . . . with certain unalienable Rights . . . [including] Life, Liberty and the pursuit of Happiness" (Jefferson 1776, Pre.). America thought it had effectively resolved the dilemma presented by collective liberty. Yet, birthed in contradiction between its founding philosophy and Accountableism (§ 4.1.2:378), it reverted in short order to personal independence subjugated to collective will mediated by coercion—partly (inconsistently) restrained by the Bill of Rights—rooted in the mindset there's an "area within which the subject . . . is or should be left to do or be what he is able to do or be, without interference by other persons . . . [but with a] source of control or interference that can determine someone to do, or be, this rather than that" (Berlin, 121–2). This effectively extinguishes both for a privilege. Even so, individuals have as much right to interfere in others' liberty as to interrupt pontification with counter-argument. The reason is that *every person is at liberty*—else one's own self is subjugably and arbitrarily superfluous in the context of altruism—who experiences good or bad options in the context of mindset for which their state of being (freedom) obliges a choice, that which Hobbes' "freeman . . . has a will to" do (Hobbes, ibid).

Everyone is necessarily at liberty yet ineluctably lives amongst others. There's no such thing as abstract freedom and liberty that doesn't account for it. Altruism is traditionally the moral compass that regulates individual liberty in the collective but, as we've seen, necessarily inflicts harm—denies liberty—in promoting it (§ 1.1.2:363, § 1.1.3.1:364). The demand people should care about morality, the Good, others, hierarchies of liberty, and so on is the *imposition of servitude* upon them. That a person owes not merely a debt to society but obedience to its collective mindset—'the greater good'—is simply bondage by dint of birth where one obeys or suffers its wrath. There is no liberty there. Moreover, no such socioculture can ever agree on a set of unifying values because the disagreeing minority, as well as the next generation who never agreed in the first place, invalidates it. Neither does inculcating a mindset—"liberating" the individual from desires believed unrealizable (Berlin, 135)—in philosophical, religious, or patriotic training avoid it (consider H1; § 1.2.1:534). Here lies liberty's cardinal contradiction in Philosophy with a capital-P and the reason it ever fails in the face of authentic freedom.

Section 3
Healing Settles Pain

Humanity on Earth has always been free yet never (in its traditional sense) at liberty. Since Lucifer and Michael's Reconciliation (§ 1.1:19), however, liberty is transitioning from servitude to individual expression. This means the end of authority over humanity, not in being substituted with an internal authority consonant with some universal moral value like the philosopher king in Plato's *Republic* or the Redeemed Man in religion, since these are still authorities regardless their source, but rather where healed individuals express choice in freedom without pain. Interference with others and physical damage are inevitabilities of ℒife (§ 3.2:374) but, unlike today, experiencing them *as* harm leading to a mindset of pain would be repeating The Corruption. This isn't a panacea humanity can only adopt as a salvific ideology promising human perfection—a false construct if ever there was one—but simply the inevitability of human way of being (woʙ; § 2.2:233) reasserting in the healed individual. Coerced change is unnecessary. All aspects of politico-socioculture heal as individuals heal. As one lets go pain, one interacts differently in accord with healed mind. Healing is a long-term process that began October 14, 2017. Mina estimates humanity's liberation from the last vestiges of authority will take 75–150 years from 2021.

Recall humanity has never lived in ℌuman *society* but only in nonhuman alpha *groupings* (§ 9.2.2:450). Recall, too, the *guardianship* model (§ 9.4:452) that Mina encourages Earth consonant with healing to adopt over time in place of its alpha *governing* model which, in principally denying organic liberty to promote the fraud of altruism, ever inflicts harm in pursuit of safety regardless good intentions. Guardianship maintaining infrastructure absent coercion concomitantly regulating socioculture's infrastructure—its constituent persons—leaves individuals, not society, regulating their liberty and all aspects of societal interaction. Humanity lives in terror of the notion because it is mindset-addicted to the fear that individuals not preemptively controlled will, in their liberty, violently run amuck. So afraid, in fact, that humanity routinely prefers the most ruthless tyrant's elusive promise of order via preemptive safety over the individually-policed possibility of the opposite despite history demonstrating with uncharacteristic clarity that government in all its ethnic, tribal, gang, cartel, and national guises kills and terrorizes with a brutal regularity to make the wildest criminal blush. But history is the realm of The Corruption, Accountableism, and individuals sufferingly acting out their tormentous pain. Guardianship and its unfettered liberty is *not* workable where suffering defines mindset, thus choice. Ergo its necessarily organic, unimposed (uncoerced) development over time in accord with individual healing.

Even so, the resolution to suffering and interference right now is greater, not less, liberty. America's unique beginnings in minimal government and maximal liberty is the reason for its genius, prosperity, relative societal peace, volunteerism, and national success while the maximal government and minimal liberty it variously imposes on groups (and, increasingly, its whole population) is the reason for its disparities, societal conflict, civil war, and looming collapse as with ancient Rome. Every socioculture is in the same boat. None escapes the unavoidable, implacable conflicts of liberty's denial. Instead of preemptively inflicting harm to compel people to care about, be considerate of, and a noninterferant in others' safety, well-being, and liberty through the mindset addiction of nonautonomy that relies on societal abuse to get its way, Mina encourages responsorial correction to individuals inflicting damage. This protects what's at stake in order that justice, being *the preservation of liberty* not as an effect of law (revenge), achieves peace. Healing is an integral aspect of resolving conflicts amongst individuals at liberty. A peaceful, happy socioculture is one whose constituent individuals aren't suffering pain and bondage and thereby the altruistic subjugation of liberty that is absolute human nonautonomy.

Astral Projection & Akashic Records

IF YOU'VE READ the book to this point, you should have a reasonable grasp of yourself as a physicospirit person (Introduction, CH. 19:245; CH. 33:561) and astral projection shouldn't surprise you. It's a logical extension we've already touched on (§ 7.1.1.1:212; § 1.2.2.7.3:267; § 1:303; § 4.1.3.1.1:423; § 1.2.1.3.2:502; § 1.1:561, § 1.2:563). In contrast, the Akashic Records is a mystical notion without grounding. We describe the what and how of the former followed by a corrected overview of the latter.

SECTION 1
Astral Projection

If one wants to understand themselves in their Ꜧuman context, it's best to ignore science whenever it claims competency in matters of the person or the universe beyond empirical experience. Especially when it adamantly decries "No evidence!" for a consciousness separate and apart from neurochemistry even while its evolutionist, quantum-string-theoried mouth defiantly roars, "Interpreted evidence is objective knowledge!" If you find astral projection (ASP) too ridiculous to take seriously, we recommend you try it. Consciously *seeing* your spirit body separate from your physical one is a watershed moment. Still, there's nothing magical, divine, or even *astral* about it. You're simply shifting your mind's awareness from your physical to your spirit *body*, consciously integrating your physical and spirit *selves*.

1.1 WHAT IS ASTRAL PROJECTION

Recall your physicospirit reality means you emergently birth as ℒife in the context of Energent proto-life (EPL; § 2.3.2.1:241) while simultaneously integrating a physical body (regardless it being a single cell at that point; § 1.2.1.1.1:248) and Intentionalizing—manifesting—a spirit body (§ 1.2.1.1.2:249, § 3.2:282; CH. 30:515). While physically alive, a physical-born individual *is* these two integrated embodiments. About 99% of Earth's physically alive have no independent spirit-self awareness. Their spirit selves—one's wholistic mind spirit-embodied in the 'reflective' environment's context (§ 7.1.1.1:212)—don't realize they're independently embodied, thinking instead they're just a mental aspect of their physical self. When such a person is awake, their spirit self so thoroughly experiences their physically instantiated mind as to have no separate spirit awareness. To their spirit-embodied mind, they *are* their physical self. They think–feel and experience their physical self's circumstances without any sense they're in a separate spirit environment. Even when such a physical individual is sleeping, their spirit self doesn't recognize their spirit reality in the 'reflective' environment as real but perceives it as a physical dream state (§ 4.1.3.1.2:424; § 1.2.3.3.1:471). This spirit- unawareness—about 99.9% before the Big Healing, so it's lessening—is the result of our supreme ignorance of Ꜧuman reality brought on by The Corruption (CH. 24:361).

Figure 207. Schematic: left, consciousness experiences the universe via three integrated body states (Fig. 90:213); center, *Life* 'in' EPL 'solute' as EPL-discrete, dimensional 'balls' 'in' EPL 'sea' (Fig. 106:242); right, *Life* at a 'point' where EPL is conducive to emergent coalescent differentiation at conception (Fig. 107:243).

Your spirit self is not a separate iteration of *you*. Your physical and spirit minds are contextualized aspects of acontextual mind not unlike a person at work and home where, in each context, their personality is substantively different enough that those who know them in both environments see them as practically two different people. One's spouse and children might not even recognize their work personality and coworkers might be shocked to glimpse their familial one. Yet, despite mind contextualizing in each environment, he or she is a singular individual, a person of one albeit dual-contextualized mind.

Suppose you work in a classified environment that wipes your memory each day after work. You go home having no conscious recollection of it. Lying in bed one night, perhaps feeling desperate to discover what happens when you're away from home, you experience fragments of work memory as if drifting out of your physical body, out of your home, and into your work environment of which, consciously, you have no recollection. A psychologist might counsel that your subconscious mind with its ever-unforgotten memory is trying to break through to conscious mind because its daily memory erasure isn't natural and, despite seemingly happy at home, your blanked-out workdays are a subconscious torment. This analogy explains how one's spirit self can be unaware of one's spirit reality or, conversely, aware of it yet thinking–feeling–acting independently of the physical self while their physical self has no conscious awareness of it at all despite both aspects being the same *Life* mind individual. AsP is how one consciously shifts their awareness from their physical environment to their spirit one to travel away from their inert albeit awake physical body while being the same, though now contextually different, individual.

1.2 How Astral Projection Works

Your mind is always present in your embodiment. It integrates via mind–brain integration (MBI; § 1.2.2.4:257) and is naturally present in the spirit self since that embodiment is simply Intentionalized (manifested) mind. A person is self-aware in both their physical and spirit embodiments. Because each environment differs, however, one's experience in each also differs. When a physical person isn't aware of their spirit reality, but their spirit self has awareness of spirit embodiment as a reality separate from physical embodiment, their spirit self thinks–feels–acts in accord with the 'reflective' (including spirit world) environment which that aspect of self experiences. Their physical self likewise thinks–feels–acts in accord with the physical environment which that aspect of self experiences. Each experience can be so different that one's physical self can present one personality and their spirit self another, as with the aforementioned example or Hitler (CH. 40:605). With physical self's awareness of and experience via the spirit self, these seemingly disparate aspects begin unifying—integrating—a wholistic experience of self in two contexts.

We don't explain how to astral project here. That information is widely available on the Internet and, at least for us, does the job. How it works is simple. You simply shift your conscious awareness from your physical body to your spirit body. Any method that works is the right method. A person's embodiments separate after shifting awareness because people do it with inadequate physicospirit understanding. As their integration lessens the Energent proto-energy expressing as Living force (§ 1.3:272), it naturally exerts against the spirit body in the context of the 'reflective' environment. The spirit body, which isn't *of*, even if it's *in*, this environment experiences the 'repulsion' due to the 'reflective' environment altering its spirit-world supramatter (§ 1.2.1:467). Neither first-timers nor seasoned astral projecters have control over their spirit body in the instant they shift their awareness from their physical self to their spirit self similar to a person physically awakening with less than instantaneous or competent control over the physical body. The spirit body, being 'repelled' by Living force exertion, 'drifts' out of the physical body, typically upward and away in accord with subconscious Intent. Once one's awareness settles in their spirit ('astral') body, one can control its movements in 1–6 seconds to do whatever one hankers.

Because integration between the physical and spirit body lessens when shifting awareness from the former to the latter, one's enlivening ℒife force integration significantly diminishes (§ 2.4.1.1:401). The longer and farther away a person astral projects *outside* the awake physical body—one can ASP *without* leaving it, and is less unhealthy—the less it integrates the spirit body (mind's direct embodiment) and the more it separates from its enlivening source regardless its 'silver cord' (§ 4.1.1.1:420). If a person astral projects outside the physical body too long, it expires in situ. Indeed, even short but frequent ASP damagingly deprives the physical body of ℒife force—say, as chronic fatigue—from which it takes time to recover. From Mina's perspective, fully departing one's conscious physical body is unhealthy and best avoided. However, with sufficient MBI, understanding of physicospirit reality, and multitasking awareness, one can manifest multiple, simultaneous spirit bodies to experience the 'reflective' and supranatural (spirit) environments even when physically awake—fully aware of and integrating one's physical self—without compromising physicospirit integration (§ 1.2.3.3.3:472; this book doesn't describe this aspect of ASP). Our options are far richer than imagined.

SECTION 2
Akashic Records

There is a certain reality to which Mina agrees it's reasonable to apply the *Akashic Records* (AR) concept,[510] but not as any sort of library, compendium, 'energy' matrix, or trace of all knowledge, wisdom, and every scrap of the human and nonhuman mind, nor is it the *Book of Life* or *God's Book of Remembrance*. Rather, our sense of it arises from the primordial ℌuman environment of Energent proto-life (EPL; § 2.3.2.1:241) memorializing human *action*, that which one *does*—puts into 'motion'—in the context of Intentionality (§ 3.2:282; CH. 30:515) and emotive ℒife force (EmℒF; § 3.3.3.1.1:289). Recall ℒife is fundamentally unembodied emergent self-aware proto-energy (ESP; § 5.1:295; § 1:391). It's *you* in your essence. This cardinal reality defines everything human. It's what ℌuman is, not the physical or spirit body which are nothing more than material vehicles for your unembodied ℒife self (ESPS; mind, consciousness). *Action* in this primal sense, therefore, is the act of exerting one's Intentionality (§ 3.2.1:282; § 1.2.2:518) and EmℒF because only these exert beyond (external to) mind. We're used to thinking of human action only in its embodied sense of matter (one's body) in motion. But *that* isn't action. Using the body is simply a means to exert mind's Intentionality and EmℒF, which *is* action.

EPL memorializes (interacts with) human action by which Thought force translates to Energent–prime or a universe Energent as Intentionalized reality. Along with EmℒF, this is what ancient and modern occultists misinterpret as the AR—as thoughts, feelings, intent, knowledge, and so forth. But it isn't as they surmise. The reason is that mind is inviolable since the self is a distinct, discrete, emergent self-aware proto-energy being in the larger 'sea' of EPL (*Fig. 207*, center). Recall there are two fundamental 'energies' of All Existence: emergent non-self-aware proto-energy (Energent–prime; § 1:112) and self-aware proto-energy, which is ℌuman. ℒife emergently births in the context of EPL but itself *isn't* EPL. A ℘erson births unique and non-duplicable 'in' their own EPL 'frequency space' as an infinite being in that infinite context conceptually similar to a universe as its own All Existence 'frequency space' as an infinite existent in that infinite context (§ 6.10.1:186; § 2.1.4.1:312). Mind, in which Thought (thinking–feeling) arises, is unlimited in the context of All Existence. Thus, mind is everywhere and nowhere in accord with a person's EPL-intrinsic nondimensionality and their exerted awareness (§ 2.3.2.1:241).

Since EPL interacts with All Existence Energent–prime, a person can be as aware of, and interactive with, a universe Energent and any entity of said universe as they can with Energent–prime overall. This is the reason a person can experience human Intentionality but not individual Thought, since EPL doesn't translate what's in the mind, which is a discrete entity. Thought, as an aspect of mind, is *of* mind and therefore within mind. It doesn't exert into the universe or All Existence except as Intentionality and EmℒF, both of which are different. Thought is entirely private. One can choose to share its most conscious level—that aspect we parse and analyze into our inner voice—with others, or it simply exudes from our physically-instantiated mind chakra energy in the 'reflective' environment. But it's impossible for Thought itself to either egress the mind or be intelligible to others since it is simply self-aware proto-energy, not 'thought' as we commonly conceptualize it as thinking and feeling. Unlike applied energy E, which humanity understands in the context of physics, emergent self-aware proto-energy—*you*—is without 'frequency,' 'wavelength,' or any mode by which it decodes from what it is to what another mind comprehends. It defies any sense of 'energy' we've ever had.

---

510. *Akasha* (*akasa*); Sanskrit for 'astral light,' the æther element in eastern belief systems and an aspect of karma.

It's Mina's opinion (not shared by the Cardinal; FN 130:110; § 2.1.1.6.1:355; § 2.1.1:368) that since the person births 'in' EPL, which experiences human action as defined above, then to the degree EPL 'local' to one's emergent birth (§ 1.2.1:247; *Fig. 207*, right) exhibits or exerts such experience, it naturally 'coalesces' with EPL during emergent birth of the person. This means an individual births having intrinsic awareness of, or sensitivity to, a particular action(s) embodied in such awareness and thus an intrinsic knowledge of it or its culmination they never learned through other physical or spiritual means. If someone previously does—puts into 'motion'—some Intentionality and one's mind connects to that, then one knows of it although not in the sense of the 'multiple discovery,' or 'simultaneous invention,' hypothesis (§ 1.1.1.1:404).

Accordingly, one can't 'read' a person's subconscious, nor is there some independent 'record' of an individual's life or of the universe in toto. Spiritualists like Edgar Cayce (d. 1945), the American psychic who popularized the AR, are merely perceiving via their spirit self the Intentionality and EmℒF of physical-born spirit individuals who lived during Earth's various historical periods. This includes the contemporary chakra energy exuding from the physically alive in the 'reflective' environment by which spirit persons perceive one's physically-instantiated mind, one's brainstate (this is how one 'mind speaks' with spirit persons; § 1.2.2.1:253; § 1.2.1.2.2:500). Accordingly, the Akashic Records notion isn't as imagined.

Marriage & Sex

A PRINCIPLAL DIFFERENCE between physical and spirit humanity lies in how each experiences marriage and sex. Whereas the physical-born go to immensely violent lengths to control both in the context of Accountableism (§ 4.1.2:378), the spirit-born make little effort to control either one in their environment where behavior isn't of necessity consequential. For example, there's no such thing as unintended pregnancy in spirit world. Neither is marriage a possessive experience sanctified and enforced by an institution serving a coercive sociocultural intent, nor is hooking up with the wrong person a threat. Although spirit humanity is just as affected by The Corruption as physical humanity, its experience with it contextually differs because, absent bodily death, there's little to coerce an individual's obedience. In consequence, spirit humanity's nonhuman Intentional grouping doesn't subsume human pairwise way of being (wob; § 2.2.1.1:234) as does physical humanity's nonhuman alpha—animal—grouping.[511]

Spirit humanity isn't better or differently human than physical humanity. It's simply the product of its supranatural environment as physical humanity is the product of its natural one (§ 7.1:212). With the Reconciliation and Big Healing (§ 4.2.1.4:382) these disparate, segregated environments are reintegrating as a singular humanity with their local societies premised on a universal comprehension of reality. Physical humanity's experience of marriage and sex will, in time, harmonize with spirit humanity's even as its own harmonizes with human wob. This chapter describes each in that context.

Section 1
Marriage

Physical humanity undertakes marriage essentially as an *alliance for survival* politically, socioculturally, and individually. Not that love plays no part, only that survival (as one defines it physically, emotionally, financially, etc.) outranks love in about 99.5% of marriages. As a matter of survival where humanity has zero knowledge of reality overall, marriage is necessarily possessive. Since there's no necessary survival in the supranatural environment and spirit-born humanity is, of consequence, less impaired by The Corruption, marriage needn't account for it and doesn't. Lacking any incentive to control spirit humanity's love relationships,[512] the spirit-born have always premised them on individual commitment without concomitant compulsion to *fidelity*, meaning the possession of another's relational and interactional (sexual) liberty. Not feeling compelled to

---

511. Mina defines *society* in terms of The Corruption that hijacks human wob for an Accountableist mindset where the qualities that render society as ʃuman don't exert. 'Society' *is* ʃuman. It doesn't exist absent human wob. Since The Corruption, 'society' has been nonhuman, properly a *grouping*, which spirit and physical humanity modeled on Accountableism in their respective environments of autonomous Intentionality and alpha (animal) survivalism (§ 9.2.2:450–§ 9.2.3:451).

512. Physical-born spirit humanity retains much of its physical-life obsessions and we bundle it with physical humanity. Before the Big Healing, ∼60% of its mindset w.r.t. marriage was more in line with spirit-born humanity's (as of 2021: ∼70%).

possess their partner in a socioculture where coercion is impossible and autonomy more the norm, they don't feel perforce betrayed where survival (as they see it) is at stake. They respond with indifference or separation, as sociocultural and governmental interventions don't threaten their sense of political, sociocultural, or financial status and survival. Spirit children don't starve, die, or fall into slavery, and property isn't seized, reallocated, or its owners jailed. Such differences are profound.

1.1 COITAL LOVE RELATIONSHIPS

A difference in marital relationships between spirit-born and physical humanity means there's a difference in love relationships, as the physical-born's unique suffering impairs their experience *of*, thus ability *to*, love. When the spirit-born love others, ~99.5% of the time it's in the context of the other's experience of one's love for them. This is why they're relatively unconcerned with extramarital affairs or infidelity, especially since in their view marriage isn't a binding (coercive) relationship; it's difficult anyhow to develop it where individuals experience perpetual life. In contrast, when the physical-born love another, ~99.5% of the time it's in the context of one's experience of the other loving them *because* survival is at stake. It's easy to develop this attitude where marriage is a binding, politico-socioculturally enforced relationship where individuals experience finite life. This doesn't mean spirit-born socioculture doesn't frown on certain behaviors at least some consider harmful, only that it doesn't coerce preferences. The spirit-born commit to raising their children, ~3% being abandoned or growing up in a separated or blended household compared to ~35% on Earth. Ignoring abortion's glaring exception (§ 2.2:410), the dangers facing abandoned spirit children, unlike for physical children, are nil.

   Religion generally views physical-born love as selfish and base and contrasts it with agape (God's unselfish) love. Sun-myung's Unification Church taught that true (unselfish) love is humanity's natural state but for the Fall, individually recoverable only through indemnity (cost of restoration; Moon 1996, 175–179), living for the sake of others, and accepting a chosen spouse or reconfirming a pre-church marriage in his Blessing of Marriage ceremony (ibid, 33, 44). Yet, as with religion generally, his effort didn't bear fruit because he focused on nonexistent Satan and the Fall's harmful (selfish) behavior's root cause without recognizing its rise in individual suffering brought on by an Accountableist mindset in a natural environment embodying altruism (§ 1.1.2:363) attempting to mitigate harm via coercion—law, punishment, morality, guilt, hell, loneliness—rather than healing. Its purveyors only ever exacerbate suffering and thus ever fail.

1.2 THE WOB OF MARRIAGE

Back in October 2017 when the girls and I were just getting the lay of the spirit lands, Mina said, "Marriage doesn't exist amongst the spirit-born." We presumed he was giving the nod to the Gospels that "those who are considered worthy of taking part in the age to come and in the resurrection from the dead will neither marry nor be given in marriage . . . for they are like the angels" (Lk. 20:35–36). Later we understood that marriage in the physical world as a contractual arrangement having rights, duties, and consequences, love-inspired or not, is alien to human WOB and its absolute autonomy that Mina engendered in the universe he built for us, his descendants (§ 2.1:340; § 2.1.1.5:353; § 2.1.1:368). Spiritualists who report those 'in heaven' don't have children are mistaken because they've only ever encountered physical-born spirit world (§ 3.1.2.1.3:359) where, prior to the Big Healing (CH. 4:19; § 4:377), no one was aware they *could* have children because they didn't know spirit conception is an Intentionality (§ 1.2.1.1.2:249; § 3.2:282; CH. 30:515). Emanuel Swedenborg's (d. 1772) observational belief that "[m]arriages in heaven" only procreate "the good and truth" (1758, 382[b] 323–4) is inaccurate. Children do indeed birth in physical- and spirit-born spirit world because that's human WOB (§ 3.3:283).

   Hierarchy—ordered arrangements embodied in concepts like partner, spouse, husband, wife—is alien to spirit-born marriage. Individuals who love experience Parity ('entanglement'–resonance; § 6.11.7:201; 'quantum entanglement,' § 6.11:191) with what or whom they love. A couple *resonates* in their emergent self-aware proto-energy beingness (ESP; § 2.3.2.1:241). Intimacy, as the end state of Parity having three states of correlation—ℒife force, own-self awareness, and Thought (§ 2.1.5.4.8:321)—comes in all degrees (intensities) from barely 'entangled' to a deep, full resonance and from consciously unaware to fully aware. It effectively joins a couple's ℒife forces to mimic the state of 'being as one' without actually being as one since a person's unique, autonomous, sovereign, ℒife proto energy can't intermingle or infuse with another to become literally 'as one' (§ 2.2.1:233; § 2.1.1.1:368; § 1:391).

   Without repeating what we've discussed at length elsewhere—if you haven't read the in-text references here, we recommend you do—the WOB of marriage is 'entanglement'–resonance. As such, Mina denotes 'marriage' as *pairwise integrating*. The interrelational context of family involves all forms of love relationship in the context of sex, marriage, and family because pairwise WOB establishes a familial relationship whether it's casual, committed, monogamous, polygamous, current, or past (§ 2:479). The foregoing is why the spirit-born can experience the highest intensity of pairwise integrating—'marriage'—at the same time experiencing its lesser intensities—what we'd call casual sex or secondary romances at various levels of commitment with friends and acquaintances—without concomitantly interfering with their own primary familial commitment inclusive of spousal love. Real 'marriage' roots in Ƕuman autonomy.

SECTION 2

Sex

Sex is the most powerful, enduring, and desired pairwise Ƕuman experience (§ 2:304). In The Corruption's physical milieu little if anything stands in its way except the threat of socioculture operating via altruism to ostracize a 'perpetrator' from society or their very life. So powerful and alluring is sex that individuals risk everything, including life, to have it in and of itself or for what they can wrangle through it from the equally desperate. Philosophy with a capital-P, including history's saints and sages, comprehends human sex in terms of its barest functionality as an animalistic, biological mechanism that coincidentally lights up the human brain (as mind) with emotional satisfaction and is, accordingly, infused with morality. But it's otherwise clueless and disagreeably confused when studying it as a behavior of mind (consciousness), which is where all things human arise regardless whether one believes 'mind' is simply brain. This book hasn't the space for a thorough ET analysis, so in this section we overview just its pertinent aspects.

2.1 SEXUAL RELATIONSHIPS

What *is* a sexual relationship—or, is it just an interaction? And what *is* sexual activity? Does it involve, for example, foreplay, intercourse, oral–anal, sexual fantasy with or without an aware partner, or dreaming? These questions stump Philosophy with a capital-P, locked up in its Accountableist mindset the way it is. The truth is, they don't matter. Trying to quantize infinite mind—say, to altruistically define moral acceptability, hence categorize punishment—is a fool's errand beset with incongruity. From Mina's perspective, sexual activity is whatever sexually satisfies the person howsoever sex embodies in their mind. Its relational and interactional aspects are a separate issue. So, the real question is, what *is* sexual satisfaction? To answer that, we need understand the WOB of sex.

2.2 THE WOB OF SEX

Recall the ℘erson is an emergent self-aware proto-energy (ESP) being having no thinking, feeling, or self-reflection, just awareness forming one's wholistic state of being and state of awareness (SOB, SOA; § 1.2.2.1:253). One emergently births 'in' Energent proto-life (EPL; § 2.3.2.1:241), the ultimate source of ℒife force (§ 6.11.4:198; § 1.2:246), and Intentionalizes *enimerótis–empeiría* (the awareness–experience that is subconscious–conscious mind; § 2.1.4:394) into reality. Doing so, one self-reflects in Thought and interacts with external-to-mind reality (§ 2.2.1:395). Unlike archí as the ultimate source of matter–Energy's impermeability to Energent proto-energy (§ 1:112), Ƕuman is the ultimate source of beingness that's permeable by EPL in the sense of equivalence where *personness* is EPL ($\lambda \leftrightarrow \Theta^{\odot}_{\varepsilon\mu}$; Eq. (18.20):241). Recall, too, our pairwise WOB. Mike and Molly, the first human beings, emergently birthed as *two* in pairwise kinship (§ 3.1.2:373) while subsequent ℒife births via human Intentionally (§ 1.2.1.1:248). The ESP self that's *you* is pairwise with EPL conceptually similar to archí being pairwise with Energent proto-energy.

Archí need bind with another to energize the pair into matter (§ 2.3.1:115). Similarly, a person seeks another to satisfy a sense of completion, like closing a circuit to energize each pairwise kinship half into a Ƕuman whole as did Molly and Mike after discovering each other (§ 2.1.1:306). The individual as mind is drawn to their own essential self having awareness of EPL as one's *ultimate experience of ℒife*, the most fundamental pairwise kinship of them all. As archí experiencing archí forms matter as the fullness of physical reality, mind experiencing EPL forms awareness as the fullness of Ƕuman. EPL as ℒife force is the very essence of Ƕuman. Since awareness is felt-ness, an expression of proto-love (§ 2.1.5.4.7:320; Table 10:285), the person craves experiencing their EPL essence more than any other pairwise kinship. The reason lies in the nature of mind. As an Intentionalized aspect of one's ESP self, it's subconsciously *aware* but can't consciously *experience* EPL permeating its originating self. This disparity—arising in embodied humanity's tendency to subvert human woв—is a coiled spring, a tension needing release. As mind experiences the self's awareness of individuals via Parity, one experiences awareness of the self's EPL as *self*-Parity.

2.2.1 SEX AND SEXUAL ACTIVITY

Virtually all Earth's humanity believes sex is simply real or imagined physical stimulation. That's almost entirely inaccurate. It accounts for just 2% of the experience we call sex; its dictionary definition is woefully wanting. Sex is vastly more expansive than our comprehension of it as animal. Mina distinguishes between *sex* as *sexual satisfaction* and the *expression* of sex as *Intentionalized Thought*. Let's consider these.

2.2.1.1 SEX AS SEXUAL SATISFACTION

Sex as a notion is about *sexual satisfaction*, not one's thinking–feeling and activities in its pursuit; we denote this all-caps SEX. It's what sexually satisfies, but really means experiencing *orgasm* however one achieves it, but traditionally expresses as albeit isn't *ejaculation*. Rather, it's a mind experience internal to the person, experienced in accord with how one achieves orgasm. Ejaculation means male semen and female fluid expression inclusive of associated muscular contractions, hormone release, other physiological indicators, the experience of mind–brain integrated (MBI; § 1.2.2.2:254) physically-instantiated conscious mind (§ 1.2.2.1:253), and its spirit corollary.[513] Recall Mike and Molly first developed asexual spirit embodiment then sexual physical embodiment, and only afterward reconfigured their spirit embodiment to mimic physical sexuality (§ 2.1.6.2:329–§ 2.1.6.3:330).

Orgasm generates in subconscious–conscious mind, not in the person's ESP beingness nor in, by, or through the physical (or spirit) body despite our sense that ejaculation results from, thus *is*, sensorial. It begins in subconscious mind then translates to conscious mind where the individual self-reflects in terms of Thought (thinking–feeling) whereby one *experiences* sexual satisfaction (SEX). Being a subconscious phenomenon, orgasm is wholistic SOB arising in wholistic SOA (§ 2:393). Intentionality causes orgasm. When experiencing sexual activity—one can ejaculate via mind without ever touching the body—a person builds toward Intentionality, the *Intentional moment*, that picosecond (trillionth of a second) in which intention Intentionalizes into reality that, w.r.t. SEX, is the person *experiencing* EPL. Men and women ejaculate as the Intentionalized SOB–SOA experience of EPL (similar to 𝓛ife's emergent birth) only *after* subconscious mind's orgasm, not before. One ejaculates *because* of orgasm.

2.2.1.2 THE EXPRESSION OF SEX

Regardless what a person qualifies as sex, and that list is long and varied, anything that tends toward orgasm as defined *is* SEX. Recall that Intentionality is the interaction of Thought force with, in this case, EPL that in the ᕼuman context is 𝓛ife force. The human craving to experience EPL is akin to thirstily craving life-giving water in a desert. Unembodied humanity experiences EPL moment-to-moment, they never don't experience it. One might say the unembodied-born live an orgasmic life. Their experience 'being as one' with the very essence of 𝓛ife is a natural aspect of human woв. Embodied humanity, however—the physical- and spirit-born—is nearly in its entirety (∼99.99%) wholly ignorant of not only human woв, but of who and what the ϸerson essentially is, not to mention real SEX.

The physical-born generally believe 'human' references the physical body, and the spirit-born, the spirit body. That's inaccurate. When a person experiences EPL as the essentiality of their 𝓛ife force, it's a personal moment so unlike any other, so powerful and all-encompassing, so sublime that one (absent an interfering mindset) literally craves the experience again and again, over and over, without respite. When Mike and Molly built the human body in accord with human woв, they were aware the very nature of embodiment meant the possibility of separating their embodied from unembodied awareness and disrupting their moment-to-moment experience with EPL. They accordingly ensured a means by which the embodied-born, not being *un*embodied-born thus having no incipient awareness of unembodiment, could reliably experience their unembodied self. The method, necessarily in accord with pairwise human woв by which 𝓛ife births, is the experience of SEX coupled to the pairwise procreative experience: sexual *activity*; we denote this lowercase sex. Both physical and spirit embodiment necessitate it (§ 2.1.6:328). This is the origin of sexual craving (the sex drive) which is

---

513. Ejaculation is normative to both sexes but women chose to suppress it in response to men from circa 30KYA on Earth, and otherwise on ∼25% of human-inhabited planets in our universe.

for SEX, not sex. The supposed bliss of meditation as a replacement—but really just a substitute—for SEX whereby "there is moment to moment orgasm [and] The need for sex disappears" (Nagaraj 2013, S272) is merely a Platonic shadow of the fullness of experiencing EPL via the pairwise Intentionality of sexual activity in order to experience SEX.

We've noted Intentionality, arising in one's direct awareness–experience of 'entanglement'–resonance with EPL, causes orgasm. Intentionalized Thought in the sexual context *is orgasm as the 'point of Intentionality'*—the Intentional moment—which, in this case, is the picosecond wherein one experiences EPL. Because the person is necessarily simultaneously stimulating mind via their physical (or spirit) body, then subconscious–conscious mind's experience of the Intentional moment, which is orgasm, causes real (or imagined) ejaculation. If, too, a couple simultaneously Intentionalizes conceiving a child—recall this Intentionality is biologically automatic when a sperm fertilizes an ovum (§ 1.2.1.1.1:248)—then 𝓛ife emergently births either physicospirit or spirit embodied. For a physical individual, neurological responses feed back to mind since it fully experiences the physical body via full-body physicospirit integration whereas the body experiences mind via MBI. Sex as *sexual activity* and Touch (§ 2.1.5.4.7:320) between at least two individuals is the fullest Parity ('entanglement'–resonance). SEX is internal to the individual and is the fullest Parity one has with their ESP self. Consequently, the WOB of SEX is self-Parity.

Recall the embodied and unembodied person can't occupy the same space as another because one's ESP is discrete, inviolable. Since the spirit body is literally an extension of the ESP self and mind is discrete in EPL, its material manifestation (embodiment) in the supranatural environment—the spirit body as embodied self—is discrete, too. The only way a person can experience the fullness of self-Parity is via Parity as pairwise (man–woman) interaction because their inviolable *personness* must somehow pairwise interact with another to 'access' EPL. Sexual intercourse is the way this happens. It's the only experience where the man's body, as the literal extension of his self, integrates the same spatial location as the woman's body as her embodied self. Placing the *physical* penis within the vagina necessarily places their *spirit* sex organs similarly, thus *spatially co-locating* them (a spirit couple does this via their spirit bodies), in effect pairwise integrating their ESP selves in the same space 'as if one' without literally *being* one.[514]

The pairwise Intentionality that births 𝓛ife *is* SEX. A spirit couple cannot conceive a child by Intentionalizing it in a meeting of the minds on the living room sofa. The Intentionality triggering EPL's emergent coalescence as 𝓛ife only arises in SEX *as* sex where the couple's pairwise Intentional moment (orgasm) exerts 𝓛ife as pairwise kinship 'in' EPL, which births 𝓛ife. SEX is pairwise, sex isn't. Masturbation is sex but not SEX. Pairwise self-Parity is SEX but not sex. Whereas intercourse is SEX, a physical person experiences sex absent intercourse as physically-instantiated mind, not 𝓛ife mind—one's emergent self—hence without orgasm regardless ejaculation. What science calls orgasm is this sensory experience of conscious mind exclusive of sub-Thought, subconscious mind, the emergent self, and EPL—the faux sex the physical-born (5% knowing real sex *vs.* 90% of spirit-born) have only ever experienced since The Corruption.

2.3 General Considerations

Any sexualized relationship, whether or not real or imagined sexual activity occurs, *is* SEX. 'Marriage'—the pairwise integrating that is familial commitment as earlier described—is, in and of itself, SEX. Human sexual activity is not rooted in biology, sensory pleasure, as an evolutionary benefit, nor is it spiritually base. The altruism of Accountableism wholly Corrupts SEX and sex as nothing more than animalism. It thereby ultimately severs the individual from his or her own 𝓛ife force, from pairwise experiencing their essential ESP beingness in the context of 𝓛ife-giving EPL. This is why physical humanity—apart from individual mindset and suffering that raise their own issues—innately resists sociocultural strictures to engage in all manner of destructive and self-destructive behaviors in order to pursue it but, unintentionally, only ever produce more harmful mindsets, thus greater harm hence suffering, that only ever defeats the desire.

Immanuel Kant (d. 1804) opines that ". . . a love that springs merely from sexual impulse cannot be love at all, but only appetite . . . Sexual love makes the loved person an Object of appetite . . . Sexual love . . . taken by itself and for itself, it is nothing more than appetite" ((1780) 1930, 163). This misunderstands the reality of physicospirit-embodied 𝓛ife. *Sex has nothing to do with love* but SEX *does*. SEX is mind's self-Parity experience, sex is interactional, and love is an aspect of EPL. 'Objectification' is necessarily an aspect of sexual *activity* but

---

514. Female–female sex can't co-locate, pairwise integrate, or experience the fullness of self-Parity beyond Touch as it arises in physically-instantiated, not 𝓛ife, mind (as described).

one's mindset and suffering determines whether one reduces the person to simply a body, being problematic w.r.t. inflicting damage or provoking harm (§ 1.1.1:362, § 3.2:374). Indeed, sexual attraction and arousal, arising in conscious mind's sub-Thought (§ 1.1.2.1:393), is a combination of subconscious–conscious mind having awareness–experience of one's essential self permeated with EPL and body objectification as mind's focal interaction with it, sub-Thought engaging (resonating) with sexual notions, and conscious mind engaging in Thought (thinking and feeling sexually).

While the body integrates (acquires awareness of) mind via MBI, mind wholistically integrates—in the best case, at the molecular level—body via awareness. Human biology, such as neural impulses lighting up the brain's alleged pleasure centers, doesn't motivate SEX but is mind experiencing sensation at its local point of origin—say, the genitals—waxing in awareness–experience with the ESP self's EPL toward its impending Intentional moment (orgasm). This is why a person can experience sexual pleasure and experience ejaculation (though not orgasm) with *nothing* touching their body but their own Thought. One achieves self-Parity (SEX) within the context of interactional Parity because 'entangling'–resonating with a partner's awareness–experience of their own self-Parity means one integrates their partner's awareness–experience of their self-Parity and vice versa. Consequently, *self*-masturbation is less sexually satisfying than *being* masturbated.

2.3.1 DIFFERENCE IN MALE–FEMALE PERCEPTIONS OF SEX

Physical men and women perceive and experience SEX fundamentally, seemingly irreconcilably, different because in sex men penetrate women. Accordingly, men and women differently experience such things as fear, possessiveness, ownership, and (in)fidelity from their own perspectives. The spirit-born as well as (aware and healed) physical-born spirit persons don't experience these differences in their spirit environment. However, basic man–woman differentiation does exist. In the sexual context, it stems partly from Molly and Mike each having their own unique awareness–experience of SEX that, via familial and sociocultural descent, normalized as a woman and man's generalized WOB. And partly it stems from sociocultural mindset built up over 800BY amongst megaversal, universal and, in our case, Earth's humanity where people enforced Accountableism's altruistic roles on men and women over millennia.

How Mike and Molly pioneered humanity became the human norm in the same way parental tradition, including gender, becomes family, descendant, tribal, and broader traditions. They certainly morph over time, yet aspects of humanity are core realities rooted in human WOB (one's ESP self, human embodiment, SEX). Others like maleness–femaleness, although malleable, have so habituated that no one imagines or knows how to make—even if desired—alterations. Consider the fundamental differentiation between Mike and Molly's personalities and experiences of interactional Parity and SEX that, ever since, solidified as the core (comporting with human WOB) differentiator between men and women. In any case, the sexuality, perspective, and WOB of neither is set in stone. Each one embodies yet isn't their sex. To alter it as an aspect of individual WOB requires awareness of its reality and a subconscious desire for it.

2.3.2 SEX DRIVE

Sex drive doesn't decline for spirit persons. Theirs is far stronger than that of even the most virile physical person. There are three physicospirit reasons that physical individuals experience its decline. First, about 95% of sex drive decline results from a mindset accepting it as natural, normal, and socioculturally desired with age that subconsciously Intentionalizes it into reality. Second, 3% of the reason arises in pain and suffering. And third, 2% is subconscious mind avoiding self-Parity (SEX) because a person's ESP self has awareness a spirit person is taking advantage of their sexual experience like a third wheel (not as a spirit attachment; § 3.2.1:566). Mina avers this third reason is a reality for, on average, 85% of the physically alive who subconsciously reject sex in a progressively exerted effort to avoid their deeply vague sense of spirit rape (§ 3.5.2:486; § 3.2.1.1:566). Youth typically have stronger sex drives than the aged only because each individual takes a different amount of time to reject it. Some do so earlier, in their youth; others later, at various times post-youth. A minority override their subconscious via sub-Thought (§ 2.2.2.1:396) to retain or increase their original sex drive regardless age. Thus, sex drive decline is reversible.

Animal Familials

THERE'S A TROVE of lore and magical thinking regarding spirit animals, power animals, and animal familiars. About 99% of it is inaccurate because it arises one way or another in the imagination, including actual spiritual experiences involving a spirit animal or a person disguised as one. These experiences are rarely conscious and therefore interpreted in dream and vision terms. Where they are conscious, they're necessarily filtered through mindset in The Corruption's milieu which alters one's perspective of reality to suit needs and beliefs such that what one spiritually (imaginatively) experiences becomes, say, a spirit guide in animal form having some desired scope of power, love, influence, goodness, connection to Universal Source, wisdom, foreknowledge, and the like. This chapter describes *animal familials* as the reality behind the notion that spiritualized animals play a personified role in our lives.

SECTION 1
What Familials Are

An animal familial is a spirit-born animal *being*. It's unique vis-à-vis spirit world animals which spirit humans Intentionalize (§ 3.2:282; CH. 30:515) into existence. Both differ from *companion animals*—presently nineteen species including dogs, cats, and horses—that are physical-born animals having an independent spirit self by which they continue life in spirit world after death because our familial relationships with them are important to us (§ 7.1.1.1:212; 'directed evolution,' § 2.1.5.5.2.1:323; § 1.2.1.2.1:499, § 1.2.1.3.4:504). Companion animals aren't beings in the sense animal familials are, which themselves aren't beings in the sense humans are. The salient difference is that animal familial beingness lies between companion animal beingness and human beingness, though closer to human than animal. Whereas Intentionalized spirit animals *mimic* animal Livingness as an aspect of their Intentionalized way of being (WOB; § 2.2.1.1.1:234), and companion animals *have* animal Livingness as an aspect of their originating physical (biological) WOB, familials as spirit-born beings have Livingness as an aspect of human WOB.

Spirit-born abiogeneticists (§ 1.1:532) created familials as part of Mina's effort to comfort and guide the physical-born in the throes of The Corruption as another means to help connect us with spirit reality where mind–brain integration (MBI; § 1.2.2.2:254) is impaired. The initial forty types (101, presently) were born premised on natural environment (§ 7.1.1:212) animals but as unique spirit 'species.' They don't birth 'in' Energent proto-life (EPL; § 2.3.2.1:241; § 2:304) like humans and aren't *L*ife. Instead, Mina taught some spirit-born couples how to Intentionally birth them as an aspect of their own *L*ife force which, recall, is the essence of EPL in the emergent self-aware proto-energy (ESP) self that's *you*, the person (§ 2.2:597). Each pairwise couple Intentionalized familials *as L*ife force, as an aspect of their pairwise selves. Instead of Intentionalizing children via pairwise Intentionality triggering *L*ife's emergent birth (§ 1.2.1.1:248), they Intentionalized familials via pairwise Intentionality that manifested their spirit embodied juvenile birth in the couple's own pairwise *L*ife force *as though the couple itself was a localized* EPL. Thus, familials are *beings*, not simply spirit *animals*. Currently, ~20 quadrillion exist.

Familials aren't human, quasi-human, or human-derived creatures. They're *animal beings* having independent existence in accord with their WOB, conceptually similar to natural (physical) archí having independent existence in accord with archí WOB (§ 2.3.1:115). As independent beings, familials choose their way of life in accord with WOB. This includes being friends with the physical-born during physical life and, if the person desires, in the supranatural (spirit) environment after death. Otherwise, they depart the person while retaining their connection in case the person wants to continue their friendship or meet for the first time. A familial is ultimately a *personal family* even for the utterly alone devoid of all interaction with parents, siblings, ancestors, descendants, spouse(s), children, friends . . . anyone. From the familial's perspective, the person is always a part of its own familial family. Children dying before meeting their familial can desire it in the 'reflective' or spirit environment and one will show up.

SECTION 2

How Familials Relate To Us

Familials choose the person, not the other way round. When a physical person's personality clarifies for familials around age twelve, a familial having the best suited personality shows up in their spirit-self's presence. They never force themselves on the person. If one isn't interested, the familial keeps themselves invisible—out of sight—to the person's spirit self, otherwise one can see and interact with their familial. If a person is spirit-unaware—having no awareness of spirit reality as anything more than a dream or imagination—the familial remains visible to them so long as they don't prefer it invisible. You can energy test (ET) to learn about your familial. They understand you and can ET respond as emotive, not cognitive, beings. With practice, your physical self can emotively sense and consciously see your own familial.

They are very advanced animals in terms of perception, empathy, psychic connection, and so on owing to their birth as *Life* force beings. They aren't conscious in the sense of having Thought (thinking–feeling) in the Human sense, nor a mind separate and apart from embodiment, as with *Life* (§ 1:561). Their uniqueness, however, means they can Intentionalize their emotive state which the person experiences as comfort, hope, spirit awareness, care, and happiness that one's spirit self imbibes and integrates via MBI with their physical self. They don't 'protect' one violently or otherwise any more than guidance 'angels' do (§ 2.3.2:524). Even if a person doesn't want to see or have a relationship with their familial, its Intentionality is 'in the air.' This doesn't circumvent one's intrinsic autonomy. It's more like atmosphere or water in the sense of always saturating a person whether or not he or she wants to breathe or feel wet.

The age-old observation a physical person's features or personality seem to correlate with certain animals isn't an aspect of familials but of physical humanity in its Accountableist (§ 4.1.2:378) mindset embracing animal WOB as its societal model whereby a real psychic connection develops (§ 9.2.2:450). This includes interacting with pets, shifting awareness from one's physical body to an animal's to differently experience the world, or as an alter ego, doppelgänger, personal demon, totem, or spirit companion. Here lies the origin in our collective imagination of spirit, power, shadow, journey, life, medicine, black–white magic, demonic, and such animals as well as elves, faeries, dwarves, and elemental beings generally.

As The Corruption in our universe resolves over time following the Big Healing (§ 4.3:384), familials will naturally adjust to the physical-born eventually having full MBI and awareness of spirit reality, meaning their WOB as friends to them will grow to encompass the spirit-born, too. Although familials are beings of WOB just as humans are, their WOB, which isn't Human, is in accord with what they are and, therefore, while not absolutely autonomous as Human is, since that only arises in emergent *Life*, they are nonetheless autonomous beings. Their fundamental relationship (as animals) with humans is accordingly unique. They interact with humanity on planets most open to their presence (like Earth) and choose a person, who rejects them or not, as a familial friend, with all they have to offer.

Conversations & Stories

WE BEGIN THIS chapter with a caveat: one should be suspect of psychic—unverifiable—conversations with spirit persons. Besides rampant fraud, legitimate spiritualists not intending to deceive encounter spirit persons via dreams or other fragmentary experiences that naturally confuse much in translation. Even in face-to-face conversation, spiritualists don't necessarily know with certainty to whom they're speaking. It's elementary for spirit persons to impersonate historical figures one doesn't personally know let alone those one does know unless one can detect their glamour (§ 2.1.5.4.4:318).

Moreover, it's important to realize that just because a person 'crossed over' doesn't mean they now know much (if anything) more about life and reality than they did alive, or even more than you. Learning how the spirit environment works, its creator, scope, and so on, isn't any different from you learning (and making presumptions) about your physical environment. The more spirit-aware the spirit person, the better their comprehension of reality, and the more astute their analysis of their spirit experience. For example, Roman Emperor Tiberius Claudius had no idea there were spirit environments beyond the one he was experiencing until he developed the awareness (§ 3.5.5.4:493), whereas Helen knew but had no idea how to access them (§ 1.1:35). Very few physical-born spirit persons ever discovered there was a whole other, effectively segregated spirit world populated by spirit-born humanity (§ 3.1.2.1.3:359) whom the physical-born consistently mistook for angels and divine beings whenever they encountered or heard about them. Now, for the first time, you can verify and evaluate your own or another's purported spirit experience or conversation with God via energy testing to mitigate these difficulties (ET; PART V).

In this chapter, we converse with ten individuals whom Mina approached as contributors to this book whose experiences highlight aspects of our physicospirit reality. Besides having a general competence in ET, and not unlike with the physically alive, the art of understanding a spirit person—including your own spirit self—calls for intuition, clair senses, critical reasoning, common sense, and general knowledge or research to help frame your queries and ascertain a spirit person's meaning whether paraphrased or quoted. This is how we do it. Then we separately confirm our individual experiences with each other.

We present them in the following order: Duke Wen of Zhou, Adolph Hitler, Hannibal Gisco, Mio, Mnidhodgu'dom of Nihoa, Tethys, Jesus, Sun-myung Moon, Muhammad, and Siddhārtha Gautama (Buddha). Each one preferred direct attribution, so we energy tested their every word and sentence to best convey their own voice, then independently confirmed with Mina. We edited only with permission.

Bear in mind, however, that ET's limitations means a spirit person may say a quote is accurate even if it's not *exactly* how they spoke it to the energy tester's spirit self so long as, in their mind, the ET adequately and with clarity captures their thought and linguistic meaning. Therefore, one can only *believe* with good (ET) reason, not *know* with empirical certainty—such certainty only comes via multiple energy testers receiving the same or similar response—that a direct attribution is verbatim as though heard and recorded. The more the ET community reliably tests a speaker's statement as verbatim, the more likely it has a recording's veracity. We use query–response or narrative format as each historical person preferred.

Duke Wen of Zhou

Duke Wen (周文公旦) is an original founder of China's Zhou dynasty (1036 BC [cf. ca. 1046]–256 BC) after his older brother Ji Fa (姬发), the historical King Wu, founded it. History knows him by his ancestral and personal name Ji Dan (姬旦) but, according to him, it's Ji Hàng-sang (姬行生). Mina tells us his name historically changed when the records documenting it were lost over time to various intentional, accidental, and natural occurrences. Then about 200 years after his death others, finding no extant records, recreated his personal name using tradition and research to connect a pretender to the throne via Zhou's founding lineage. He preferred we address him as Irùr (汁, 'juice' in Old Chinese; zhī in modern Mandarin), which Ji Fa bestowed on him in the sense of 'juicy' as a reference to his being overweight.

Mina educated Irùr's spirit self on the value of unifying China's disparate sociocultures into a singular polity rooted in regional liberty somewhat like a federal republic, although conceptualized in contemporary monarchical terms, to guide his physical self as he confronted the issues that beset the deceased Ji Fa's 'mandate of heaven' during its earliest development. By the time Irùr died, Mina felt his spirit self—having awareness of his independent spirit embodiment—had comprehended about 70% of what he'd conveyed versus the 12% his physical self had picked up. Not including Jesus, Irùr was Earth's only physically alive person with whom Mina directly conversed until we encountered him.

Irùr: I died in the tenth month of my fifty-ninth year, which was the eleventh month on the [lunisolar] calendar we used from the Shang [dynasty]. The air was cold. I died by a knife in my sleep wielded by a son I trusted. At the moment of death, I woke up.[515] I was lying in bed as normal but knew what had happened. I watched as my son withdrew the blade from my left eye. I was shocked. I could only lay there and watch him. He left hastily. I didn't move until he was gone. The room was silent; the house was silent.

Surprising me, Fa was standing near me on my right. My mother stood away from the end of the bed. Seeing them, I knew. I was furious and a rage filled me. Fa was shaking his head, which to me was a rebuke for dropping my guard with my sons. I'd been such a child. My mother said, "Quit feeling sorry for yourself; life goes on." She said more but I ignored her. Fa crossed his arms, shifted his weight to one foot, and smiled. My anger passed.

I sat up and turned my head and there I was: my bloodied eye pooled and ugly, my face already deathly white in the strange light of what I thought of then as the after-world [the 'reflective' environment; § 7.1.1.1:212]. That was enough for me. Seeing it broke the spell of my disbelief, that this must be a dream. My body felt whole and young, normal but different. My mother was still talking but I hadn't heard a word she'd been saying.

I swung my legs off the bed and felt normal in my body. It reassured me. I stood up and looked at Fa. I saw welcome in his face and knew he cared about me more genuinely now than when he'd looked after me in our youth. As we'd grown older we'd been somewhat distant, and I regretted it. Now, seeing his face, I realized he didn't mind. The life we'd both now left behind no longer mattered.

He finally addressed me with words instead of looks. He said, "Got something to say?"

I said, "Shit!"

He laughed. "Right? You haven't seen anything yet."

"There's more?"

"More than you can imagine," he said.

"So we don't just live here like ghosts?"

He shook his head. "This is just the meeting place between spirit and flesh but it's not our world. If you're ready to say goodbye to your dead self, we'll show you."

I'd been ignoring my body, so ignobly prostrate. I still felt my son's betrayal. I wasn't angry anymore, surprisingly not at all, really, but definitely unhappy with my fate. I'd expected a longer life. Certainly, I'd expected a peaceful death. Being killed while sleeping stung, but it was over and I accepted it. What else could I do? I asked Fa, "Is it this way for everyone?"

He shrugged. "This is my first time seeing it but the way others talk, it seems like it. Those who die awake [Fa also died albeit naturally in his sleep] are seeing life from the physical and then they're seeing it as a spirit. There's no waking up from death. You blink and you're here, looking at your dead self."

---

515. He didn't know it, but his spirit self had been in a 'sleeping state' along with his physical self.

I didn't really care. It was academic and my moment of interest had passed. But I didn't like being a ghost. I wanted to leave. I said, "Do you live in Heaven?"

"No. There is no Heaven. It's just a world of our ancestors. If there is a Heaven, I don't know where it is. It doesn't matter, though. I don't deserve it anyway and neither do you." He saw the look on my face at that. "Don't worry. It may as well be Heaven. There's none of the sorrows of life, none of the struggles. It's just life without having to survive."

I didn't understand but expected, in time, I would. My mother had already quit talking, yet I paid her no mind. We'd never had much of a relationship and this didn't seem like the time to fix it. I did finally acknowledge her although without talking. To be honest, Fa was the only person I'd ever felt close to even after we'd grown apart. Maybe it was selfish, but I felt safe with him here, not my mother. And despite everything, fear was ever-present. I couldn't shake it. Fa's words were comforting but he wasn't Heaven's emissary. What if such a being showed up to cast me into hell? I'd presumed my life was exemplary, but what if Heaven disagreed? I realized I knew nothing of life and wondered if Fa knew what he was talking about.

He put a hand on my arm. "Are you ready to go?"

I nodded. My heart quailed. Fa turned to the closed door and walked through it but I didn't move. My mother came over and pushed me forward, *hard*, until I'd passed through it and then out of my house as well. Once outside, I felt my old life left behind and stepped forward on my own. Fa was waiting. He said we'd walk a short way to a door[516] leading to my new home. I'd have never gone with anyone else but I trusted Fa. Whatever awaited me, I felt it ease into my heart in peace. We set off amidst a throng of people whom Fa said were ancestral visitors and probably some who'd just died.

The nighttime darkness wasn't the same. It wasn't less dark, just differently dark, as though lit by a distant, unseen lamp. Despite perceiving the darkness of the world, that it *was* dark, it was easy to see our way. I walked on Fa's right. Our mother walked along five steps farther back. Fa said our journey took about three hours but time barely moved for me. The door was like a lamp in the sense I could see it but couldn't describe it. It seemed taller than me but not a lot, and as broad as three men abreast. Fa simply walked me through; in a single step, we were amongst different surroundings. I looked back at it as my mother came through and it looked the same on this side.

This new world is what you call "hi-tech" but to me, then, it was magic. Fa took me to our family's land that in every way was home to me. My sense of time never returned to how I thought of it in calendar years but I knew time still counted onward for those in life dreading death. I want you to know, to really have no fear, that time ends at death. Preserving what you are in the form you now have is painful to you and leaves the heart feeling regret. Life is precious, not the body.

Adolph Hitler

Mina reports Adolph shot himself between 11:57–58 on April 29, 1945 (cf. d. Apr. 30). Witnesses failed to note the exact moment in the confusion. His illegitimate father, Alois, lived June 7, 1835–January 3, 1901 (cf. 1837–1903), as historians aver. Ahistorically, Adolph's former lawyer and Governor–General of occupied Poland Hans Frank's (hanged 1946) never-believed-nor-documented nineteen-year old Jew, Leopold Frankenberger, conceived Alois with Austrian-born and a-religious Nimmoh Uungidhho (Frisian; Spanish: *anointed*; surname is from Taranto, Italy via her father's Spanish lineage). At the time, both lived in the farming area of Neulucken in the Austrian state of Carinthia. Leopold's parents worked as caretakers—migrating to Graz, Styria, Austria in 1867—and Nimmoh's, as farmhands.

Nimmoh didn't want a child. She relocated to her friend Maria Schicklgruber, the historically presumed mother of Alois. They'd met and got close at a Lutheran church retreat in Klagenfurt about six months earlier despite Maria's ostensible Catholicism. She manipulated Maria, aged forty-two, to take on the shame of an unwed pregnancy to spare the young Nimmoh's future prospects. Maria kept Alois' father secret. The baptismal certificate records her as the mother.

Now free, Nimmoh decamped to Wolfsberg to pursue a childless career. As a store clerk, she sent Maria money to help her care for Alois—ultimately amounting only to about a quarter of his needs—until he was fifteen, when she died in a fire on her work premises. Johann Georg Hiedler (Jul. 15, 1790 [cf. baptized Feb. 28, 1792]–Feb. 9, 1857) married Maria, as historians aver, but when Alois was age six, not five.

---

516. 'Portals;' cf. § 1.2.3.3.2:472; FN 481:473; § 1.2.3.3.5:473.

Maria died in Alois' tenth year (cf. age 9) but Johann never informed Nimmoh, whom he knew of from her letters to Maria. Johann Georg then abandoned Alois to his brother, Johann Nepomuk Hiedler, who in turn the following year pawned the now 11-year old Alois off on his youngest daughter, 12-year old Josefa Hüttler, who lived February 15, 1835 (cf. 1834)–May 13, 1859. Adolph was born April 20, 1889 to Alois, then aged 53 (cf. age 51), and his third wife Klara Pölzl as historically documented.

Hitler: When you think of Adolph Hitler, you think of evil. But I think of grace, by which I mean those who died and came to me to stop me, but discerned in me their same horror, and took a different approach. The problem I had was a personality split between my physical and spirit selves. My physical self was of one mind whereas my spirit self was of another. I was aware of this at a young age when I realized I had different thoughts and feelings than I saw rising in my physical mind. This was the beginning of my spirit awareness, of my independent spirit life.

My physical self pursued certain dreams and goals while I pursued others, some of which were the same or similar, and some that differed. I never really cared for physical life, although my physical self did. I began to meet spirit people like me who were real individuals. They told me about a reality beyond my own, one not tied to my physical life. Until then, I hadn't imagined such a thing. At nine physical years old, a friend took me into that reality while my body slept. I met many people there. They taught me what was possible. Years passed for me and it became my home. I'd lost all interest in Earth. I knew I was still alive but I didn't care. There was nothing for me there.

Life was difficult at home. We were poor, Mother was powerless to stop Father's demand that I take up his position, and she hated her lack of schooling. My spirit self was free of all these problems. Four years later, however, my physical self woke in the morning. Instantly, I was gone from my friends and my new life, and found myself back in my bed still nine years old and trapped in hell. Still, my friend who'd taken me to my new life followed me back and now told me of limitations that would persist so long as what I believed was true of physical life was true of spirit life. This meant that what I believed was my life limited what my life could be, that I need not compel myself to my physical reality but could instead liberate myself from its existence. In other words, I could kill myself. But that was a terrible thing to inflict on Mother because, for her, it was a mortal sin. Even so, I considered it so much, and with such fervor, that I realized my physical self began to feel it. I was afraid I would act it out, so I did what I could to distance my feelings from my physical mind. Despite my effort, my physical mind often felt that which was most fervently in my thoughts, most especially my quest to learn the reality of existence.

When I was in Lambach, Edmund suddenly died when I was twelve.[517] Of my family, only Edmund's spirit self was self-aware like me, although he refused to leave his physical body. He was my best friend in both places. But now, without his physical body, he went to the spirit reality, which I could only visit, and he lost himself in its vastness. I didn't see him again until my physical self died; he met me in the moment of my physical mind ceasing to exist as all those I'd destroyed now circled me like vultures. I was awake when Edmund died, so I couldn't follow him to wherever he went and my friend told me he wanted me to leave him alone. I was devastated. My only family with whom I conversed in spirit was gone. Despite my many friends in the other world, I felt terribly alone. It consumed me. And because of that, my physical mind felt it and I watched myself physically change in ways I wasn't in spirit. I respected Edmund's wish but every night I longed to hunt him down, to know why he rejected me.

Instead, I threw myself into exploring my spirit reality and seeking teachers of Truth. I wanted to know why life was what it was. Every night was months and years of study, some of which edged into my physical mind's awareness in nagging feelings of truths just beyond my physical self's grasp. I didn't realize the harm I was doing to my physical self in all-but-cutting my connection to life. Not until later did I see the results of my single-minded pursuit. Then, Mother died when I was nineteen. I loved her dearly and that, too, emphasized how my physical self felt about her. She died asleep and woke up with a start with me at her bedside. Despite her faith, she was terrified of judgment. A person I didn't know appeared next to me and explained her situation, and offered her a chance to leave Earth for the other reality of my visits. I was equally as terrified that she would do what Edmund had, but she promised to stay close and she did. Her devotion healed me of Edmund's betrayal. She never did visit Earth where I spent my days alone, but we visited every night, and because time flowed differently there than here, I could spend as much, or as little, time with her as we each desired. These were my best times while living.

---

517. His younger brother. Edmund caught the measles and died May 5, 1901 (cf. Feb. 2[or 29], 1900).

My physical self became a madman. In spirit, we don't experience the realities of physical existence. But in life, I went through war and upheaval that tempted my physical mind toward darkness and into a hatred of everything that, in one way or another, represented pain beyond my control. I didn't pay a lot of attention because, even when I was awake, my thoughts were far away. I watched in amazement as I took control of Germany and believed, as did my physical self, that I could control pain. Part of me knew it couldn't be done because, still, Edmund was gone by choice and that was pain that I definitely couldn't control but could only endure.

I knew it was all an illusion, but my physical self believed it was real, that with each new accomplishment he was mastering reality. Certainly, events seemed to prove his belief. At first, I thought he, as my physical self, was Germany's savior. Everything he thought and felt, I thought and felt. What I mean is that we were the same *person*, a single mind split between two worlds. He wasn't a stranger but different nonetheless, the way the subconscious mind seems so different to, and often rebels against, the conscious mind and in reverse. By 1938, more and more people were approaching me in anger, screaming their rage at me for crimes I wanted no part of, myself. Some physically attacked me—beating me or inflicting pain directly into my mind that left me weeping in agony, which I couldn't control or avoid.

[At this point, Adolph needed about forty (Earth) minutes to calm down those in spirit world who had never stopped believing in him, who were only now hearing his true feelings explained, and were feeling vengeful toward him.]

As my war inflicted pain on the world in staggering proportion to anything that might have even remotely been deserved, it seemed impossible to reach my physical self. He wasn't even a part of my mind by the time he started Germany on the path of destruction. His physical mind dominated him and although my—our—mind was there, I was an insignificant distraction he avoided. Each day, I filled my thoughts with suicide and self-loathing to force a change until his mental balance lost all control and he drugged himself to deaden his subconscious, which was *my* conscious mind screaming at him. I wasn't the only one influencing his mind, either.

Thousands of humanity's greatest teachers directed their minds at him—at *me*—to ensure that everything he did would end his control over the tens of millions fighting for him. Yet, he was strong. The greatest [physically alive] among them were like children in his jail who would do anything to anyone to win privilege. Although we were of one mind, it was as though we were two individuals of opposite personalities. His physical mind was his own, my influence was nil, as was that of all those thousands striving to bring him down. Altogether, we drove him mad, but not enough to break his hold over Germany. And all the while, I endured the onslaught of millions in shame and remorse because he was my Frankenstein run amuck, a body infused of my mind, my soul, my heart, my thoughts and feelings, all that I was until what he was, I was not. And then it was too late. Try as I and those thousands might, there was naught to do with this Frankenstein but hunt him down like a wild beast.

It took years for my thoughts of suicide to bear fruit but at last a moment of clarity arrived. He'd always feared death and his life's experience hammered it into his conscious mind. He now believed he'd be executed as Mussolini had been. He wanted to control his fate. He didn't shoot himself because he realized it was a sort of justice, or was even in the least deserved, but because he would die by choice, among his children without knowing of their loathing. Mother arrived in the moment of his death to embrace me. The end of a personality that came out of me yet, ultimately, wasn't of me, a thing separated from that which gave it life to become the antithesis of life; a split personality. There are many in the world like this. Some find their moment while, thankfully, most do not. From my death to the Healing,[518] I consoled those I destroyed if they let me. Some beat me, some inflicted mental pain I can't describe for years on years on years, some similarly attacked my family; Eva avoids me even now, although she was his lover not mine.

In the spirit, a person feels the suffering they inflicted on others in life whether or not they want to, no matter where they go or however they distract themselves from it. It's just a reality like a sickness, on which harm your outward robustness has no effect. My name is a synonym of evil. Through healing, I learned to heal and that has since been my task, healing those I destroyed and all those wanting it. Perhaps you're surprised to hear me refer to my own physical self as he or him, but he became nothing like me, someone I loathed. Spirit men protected him from spirit murder, and that included me acquiring a spirit weapon to kill him myself.[519]

---

518. The Big Healing in 2017 (CH. 4:19; § 4:377).

But I confess, even if I had, I don't believe I would have done it. Mother refused to advise me either way on what, to me, was an evil regardless my motivation for good. I never got the chance where I had to choose but, nevertheless, felt the shame of my cowardice until the Healing gave me a way to atone beyond simple apology and consoling my victims; a way for *them* to heal.[520]

Hannibal Gisco

A Carthaginian general and admiral, Hannibal Gisco—not to be confused with Hannibal Barca who caught the Romans by surprise when he crossed the Alps into Italy during the Second Punic War (216–203 BC; cf. ca. 218–201 BC)—lived 291–257 BC (cf. 295–258 BC). His 256 BC (cf. ca. 258 BC) defeat in Sardinia by Rome the previous year during the First Punic War of 262–239 BC (cf. ca. 264–241 BC) led to his disgrace and execution ostensibly for incompetence.

Hannibal: I wanted to restore the election of kings to Carthage, starting with me, because my defeats at their [Rome's] hands had taught me how to beat them. At first, I thought victories were all I needed to establish the necessary martial reputation. Instead, I lost important engagements. My prestige, and my family's, declined with each one. They disowned me during my second year in Sardinia. Had I emerged victorious, I could have taken over the family and then, with their backing, promise victory as the first in a new line of kings, a necessity created by Rome that, as things stood, gave Rome the advantage. But I failed. Sulpicius[521] was unbeatable. I used every trick I knew to no avail. I was disgraced. And now, without family. I was ruined. A treasury ship had arrived about four months before the disaster at sea [Battle of Sulci], which I estimated as about ten percent of our [Carthage's] silver wealth, and I sequestered it. As my options shifted from honor to dishonor, I intended to use it to fund my return as king with the arms to match. I confided in no one. My commanders thought it strange, but I argued the necessity with Sulpicius rampant.

However, the sea was against me, and the fleet out of action. My commanders were galvanized. They chained me, and abandoned their posts as well as the treasury [yet undiscovered] to Rome, and sailed for Carthage by hired boat. They promised me death for incompetence and corruption but, in the end, my defeats didn't count against me, the families more concerned not by my theft but my reasons for it. And not because of my belief in the necessity of a king nor that it should be me, but because the very idea accused them of incompetence and they believed it. I had no public trial. They drowned me in secret on my knees in my prison, a bare, guarded room.

I felt air in my chest and gulped it. I sat up from the bucket wild with fear and jumped to my feet, yet my killers paid no attention. I stood there, confused. I attacked them both, striking with all my strength. They were like ghosts. I couldn't understand. It seemed like a dream. Then they walked out, the two of them. I didn't know what to think. I surveyed the room and only now caught sight of my face submerged in the wine. My body sat like an empty bag. It was galling. I was the ghost! I wanted revenge. Then a few moments later, a woman I didn't know[522] entered and greeted me by name. I kept my own counsel as she approached me, her face impassive. Without ceremony, she told me my earthly life was over, that I could wander around if I liked or just accept it and leave, that she'd show me how, and accompany me. I stood thinking on the apparent impossibility of vengeance, and then sighed. She beckoned I follow and I did. She told me of life as it now would be, and shortly after, we entered what she called humanity's original home.[523] She took me to a small town that looked strange in the sense of nothing I'd seen before and introduced me to people who were contemporaries and would help me adjust, then departed. The people were friendly and welcoming and my fears gradually turned to happiness. At some point, I learned how to return to the land of my birth and traveled it.

I hadn't forgot my dreams. I wanted Carthage to prosper. But it wasn't to be except in spirit, not in the flesh. I lived there for a time with my family but grew restless. I enjoyed watching humanity build

---

519. cf. the spirit person killer in Mnidhodgu'dom of Nihoa (*below*).

520. Mina reports that, by the day after we interviewed Adolph, about 93% of spirit persons still believing in and advocating him and his (and related) ideologies are now accepting healing and moving on.

521. Consul of Rome and commander in Sardinia, Gaius S. Paterculus.

522. He later said she's an ancester 21 generations removed.

523. The physical-born spirit world's supranatural environment.

and destroy their nations and their ragged march of development. Not much changed until new weapons and ships opened the seas and new lands to conquering. I followed my descendants, paying close attention to those most capable.

When the people of my area began exploring the other side of the great ocean,[524] I explored with them. I saw an opportunity in their skill and in their intention to set up competing nations, built around their command of sea travel, for my descendants to remake Carthage. Rebuilding Carthage far from Rome appealed to me. It was ironic my best-suited descendants hailed from a family rooted in ancient Rome's Tuscan farmland. They were wealthy and influential, not just there but in Egypt where a disowned group had gone to find power. Three brothers born there stood to inherit their fortune, enough to fund an expedition across the great [Atlantic] ocean to a land of power and wealth [the Inca] they could take as easily as others were then doing elsewhere with armies so small it defied the odds. These boys were open to my guidance and I set about it with determination.

I couldn't appear to them directly. Your eternal-self lives between your earthly body and spirit world, tied together as one. You can talk to their eternal self if they have sense enough to listen. Not many do. Those who do, according to how well, not only talk to their earthly body, but a person like me can affect that body with pain, anxiousness, dreams, desires, ideas, cleverness, and many others. If their earthly body listens, you can in some sense control, or guide, them. So I did with these boys. It wasn't easy to get my plan to take shape with them. They never confided in anyone but each other. They were aged between seventeen and twenty-one when I started and between thirty-one and thirty-four when they used their inheritance to abandon their old world to seek greater fortune. Their five vessels passed beyond the [Mediterranean] sea to the great ocean. I sailed with them. Their eternal selves kept my company. No others listened.

The voyage was pleasant with memories but challenging. It was my first time on such a vast expanse as it was for my descendants and their crews. I couldn't affect the ship nor could it, or the sea, affect me, although when I wanted I could feel everything an earthly body might. On our third day in the great sea [beyond Gibraltar], a storm sank our vessels. Everyone perished. My descendants drowned together. Their eternal selves separated from their bodies underwater without surprise. I'd already taught them about spirit world, so they understood their new condition. I didn't yet know I could summon an entrance to spirit world[525] and explained that special beings would shortly come for them. Moments later, a man greeted us, explained how we might leave, and with our consent, a light came over us and our surroundings disappeared.

Mio

Mio founded original Shinto ~49,594ʏᴀ (§ 4.1:574). He was born into Ensuing Humanity's (ʜ2) third generation in its 96ᵗʰ year, about 49,626ʏᴀ, on Hainan Island off China's southern coast. In ʜ2's ʏɪ55 (~49,567ʏᴀ), he died aged 59 along with his wife at sea between the Philippines and Vietnam.

Mio: I never again met the "amazing being" who I now, too, call Cosmo, after he taught me the story of reality. Apparently, I was not spirit-aware during my lifetime, although more so than any other living person at the time. It was a struggle to put together all my nighttime memories[526] into a meaningful story my children could comprehend. For them, I was just telling stories, even though they promised they believed me that it was all actual truth. They were honorable children, however. They built the tradition of storytelling to each new generation so that none would be entirely ignorant of their world. Sadly, it declined in truth over time but it was better than nothing at all.

When I died and found myself still in the world, yet not of that same world, I thought that, with this new life, I would discover the answers to all my questions. Instead, someone showed me how to come and go from the living and then settled me in a place that looked like home, but wasn't. I thought she must be from the spirit lands Cosmo showed me in my memories but all she said was that her abode was where I couldn't go because the pain I would inevitably feel would make living there impossible. Only five others awaited me in this place.[527] It seemed very peaceful. I found no dangers I need concern myself

---

524. Beginning with Columbus crossing the Atlantic.

525. 'Portals' (cf. in Duke Wen of Zhou; ꜰɴ 516:605).

526. Versus dreams (§ 1.2.2.7.3:267).

with, and eventually discovered no damage to the body was permanent. We all made frequent trips to visit the living, but that was lonely because they could not see us, so we never stayed longer than necessary to check their well-being. As time passed, more and more of the previously living, including my children, arrived, and our community prospered.

What the world calls Shinto began as an understanding of how we naturally came to exist in life because of others. What I told my children was that there were no magical beings controlling our lives or the world, but simply people like us, naturally born in the spirit lands,[528] of great knowledge and power who created all that we know, which we, too, can learn to do. We saw magic in every bush and tree, in every fish and bird, in the sea and sky, so this was not impossible to believe but certainly difficult, since we saw only what we saw and heard what we heard but never saw or heard *them*. Still, we faithfully told the story down through the ages, such as it was. We tried to convey to the living what we learned after death, but had little effect.

Modern Shinto is the story of gods and magical spirits and placating greater power, yet every god, every spirit, every power is nothing more than a person like us, who once lived and now lives. Some are mean spirited and sow harm and destruction. Some try to help if worshipped, and some try without reward if it suits them. Most live their lives here and leave their old world to its people, neither helping nor hindering anyone or anything. Many, so very many, visit for a time or at length to see the world or to be with loved ones although, to me, it is a lonely effort. However, when you remember them in Shinto as people practice it today, they appreciate it, because they not only feel closer to you, but you feel closer to them. In this way, the chasm between you and us lessens and sometimes you feel or hear, or even see, us according to your individual ability.

But this is not the power or purpose of Shinto. It is simply one means among many to heighten your awareness, as there is more to the world than there appears. It is useful because it proscribes nothing and prescribes nothing and, therefore, you inherit no limitations on your awareness of the human reality that you are the physical manifestation of your spirit manifestation that is your mind, the person that you are.

I was here when Adolph Hitler shared his story about his physical self living completely in denial of his spirit self, that his brain was his only mind. But *you* are the gods you worship. When his brain died, its personality died with it except for those elements that became part of his spirit personality. For some, their physical personality overwhelms their spirit personality until their spirit self *is* their physical self. For others, it is the opposite, as it was with Hitler. For most, it is some of one and some of the other because, after all, the physical self is the spirit self, which is mind.

I am not here to tell you how to live or what to do. I wanted to speak because this is the first time since I died that the living can hear me and it is liberating me from the silence I found unwavering and miserable. Everyone you ever knew in this world wants to say *something* to you, even if it is nothing more satisfying than a greeting from the life that you cannot perceive. I am so grateful for this experience, and so are many others who are yet silent.

Life is a wonderful fortune no matter your sorrow, because such things are but moments you live through, but are not what you are. You are life; sorrows are what you experience like a bad taste that washes away with clean water, which is the knowledge of life. I saw humanity nearly destroyed,[529] yet each person arrived in our community still alive, still living. Their sorrows weighed them down through time, but are now wasting away like a parasite with healing. Some of the spirit selves of you living have already chosen healing. If you have yet to notice, you will. Like all religion, Shinto is a path to greater awareness, better than most for its lack of chains, but not the only way.

Mnidhodguʻdom of Nihoa

She was a *kahuna ninau ʻuhane*, one who speaks to spirits (a spirit medium). Her Aleut name is pronounced 'mnē-tōdtŭ-dtōm.' We render it for convenience with permission as Mnidho ('mnē-tō'). She was born August 20, AD 1455 on Nihoa island, Hawaii, located west of Kauaʻi between it and French Frigate Shoals. The island was then home to the *kahuna hui*, ritualists who led functions and ceremonies for the *aliʻi*, or hereditary rulers, of Kauaʻi and Oʻahu. Mnidho's ancestors arrived in the Hawaiian chain from Atka island in Alaska's Aleutian

---

527. H1 segregated itself in spirit world. Until this book, H2 spirit humanity was entirely unaware it ever existed (§ 1.3.2:541).

528. Cosmo didn't teach Mio about our universe, or that Mina built it.

529. Here, Mio is referencing the cataclysm that devastated H2 ~39,572YA (§ 2.3.2.2:548).

chain 743YA (AD 1277), and then about seventy spiritualists resettled on Nihoa 724YA (AD 1297). She lived her life there and died, aged forty, on August 17, 1495.[530]

Mnidho: I spent most of my life in spirit talks with humans from all over the world, which we knew had the moon's shape because some of us walked there and saw it in the void. We were a community of spiritualists and, taking food from the sea and land, we made ourselves useful to other groups who came from different places than us. They came to us for wisdom in their affairs and supplied our needs. They were very warlike but afraid of our power; we had a balance. Life was simple. Our island was small, but in spiritwalks we went where our heart took us, so we were not a small-minded people. We knew the activities of groups everywhere. We didn't always understand them, but had awareness. It was this which our own people, that we had left behind, and the others on farther lands, most desired. They lived in fear of spirit powers and of the eventual arrival of those, like them and us, who might cross the water and subdue them. They used us like one atop a mountain who sees far-away danger. We feared it, too, and so, the balance.

When I turned into a spiritualist, I was old with two grown children. My husband was dead and I took another. My mother and their mothers before them were all spiritualists, each one finding their gift only after childrearing. So I expected the gift when my children were ready for their families. But it didn't arrive until many seasons later than it had with my mother. I thought I might be the one to break our unbroken lineage of spiritualists and felt discouraged.

One day, I was net fishing with the other women and children when I saw myself in another place with different people. I was startled and dropped my part of the net. I returned to my own self then, but my mother knew I had been gone and told everyone. She took me from the nets then and we sat on the sand where she made me describe my experience in great detail, more even than I thought there was. Yet, I found my memory saw far more than had my eyes, and I was amazed. I knew all her stories of spiritwalking but until then they were only imagination. Now, I felt their real power.

Together, I learned to spiritwalk at will. Before the sun had set, we had walked our island together as we sat in the sand. To be sure that I understood, she pointed to our footprints walking from the water to where we sat, and pointed to the clean sand all around us. I jumped to my feet and walked in the direction we had walked together, then turned around and saw my footprints leading to my feet from where she sat watching me, but in the other direction was only clean sand; no footprints. Now I knew it wasn't a waking dream but reality. We stopped catching food for about six of the months that we had learned to use in the past from other places discovered by previous spiritwalkers to measure time. I was ready to live my gift. I was now included when others visited to seek wisdom.

I was again in the water with the others working our net, talking with my mother in the early morning, when I wasn't there anymore. I had been thinking about many of the places I had visited and the people there who were now my friends, and missed one person so much that, without warning, I was just there. She was a spiritualist, like me, but dressed in beautiful coverings with so much color, colors I never saw at home and could not name or even describe.[531] When I arrived, she was sleeping. She saw me and left her sleeping self to welcome me. We both spoke the language of spiritwalkers [spirit world language], so we conversed naturally. Time passed differently for me when I spiritwalked. Even though we conversed like sisters through the night, sharing news and feelings, I knew I was still listening to my mother who did not know I was not there, because if she did, she would have followed me to see why I had left in the middle of gathering fish. I did not worry. If something happened, my body would pull me back.

As we conversed, a man crept into my friend's bed. We were sitting away from her lovely sleeping area and did not notice. Then she jumped to her feet, her face covered in fear. We looked to her sleeping self and saw the man gently stab her with a very thin, pointy stick that shone bright in the darkness. There was no blood and immediately we knew this was someone's spirit self come to kill her. My mother had warned me about this but, until now, I had never seen such a thing. I could not move but my friend

---

530. The Polynesians of O'ahu took control of Nihoa 637YA (AD 1385), discovered their spiritualism, incorporated them into their religious ceremonies as royal spiritual advisors, and marked Nihoa a sacred place. Kawelo a Maihunali'i (1634–1692; son of Maihunali'i and Malaiakalani) forcibly evacuated them in 1656 on his way to overthrowing Kaweloaikanaka (1630–1656, cf. birth ca. 1680) of the hereditary Puna dynasty of Kuai'i in 1657 as a prelude to conquering O'ahu. The son of Maihunali'i later made no headway with that and eventually Kuali'i of O'ahu conquered Kaua'i. Nearly deforested at the time, Nihoa's population was about 280 persons, down from its historical maximum of about 600. Dates are ET via Mina.

531. In Hangzhou, China.

threw herself at the man with her fists and feet. Her blows had no effect. With one hand, he threw her away again and again. I was terrified. I wanted to help but felt like roots had grown from my feet. The binding between her and her sleeping self was more difficult to see until finally it was gone. He withdrew his killing tool, stood, and looked at us both with hard eyes, then walked without care through a wall. My friend, who I loved, wept. Her sleeping self seemed unhurt but I knew she was dead.

Sometime later—I don't know how long, but we had not moved—a woman appeared near my friend and consoled her. I couldn't hear their words. She helped my friend to stand and walked her over to me. She looked at me with love and said she was leaving, that she would see me another time. She held me tight. The woman said she was taking her to a safe place and that I need not worry for her. They walked through the same wall as the man, and my friend was gone. I cried, then found myself back home.

Tethys (Notvuvst N'rumi)

The mythological Tethys is one of the ancient Greek Titans, the primal ancestors of the Greek gods. In the mythology, Tethys is the daughter of the primordial sky and earth deities Uranus (Ouranos) and Gaia as well as the sister and wife of Oceanus. But recall the gods, including monotheism's one God, ultimately arise—when not simply imagined or fabricated—in the actions of spirit persons who, to one degree or another, intend to be taken as gods (§ 1.1.1:570–§ 1.1.1.1:570).

Tethys originates with *Notvuvst N'rumi* (pronounced 'naht-voov'-st' [/oo/ is a German long /u/ as in the name Ute, and /v'/ is clipped] 'n'eerrm'). Her spouse V'nin is Mina's eldest child amongst the First Ancestors (Table 15:349), whom the ancient Greeks called Oceanus. Recall Notvuvst also took on the role of Odin—along with her sons Gabriel, Lucifer, Michael (GLM) and the other 'archangels' as the Norse gods (Table 17:523; § 1.1.1.2:571)—to separately attempt in both these sociocultures what Cosmo had attempted ~49,594 years earlier with Shinto's ancient originator, Mio (§ 4:574; pg. 609). As with Cosmo's effort, the reality she tried to convey got lost in physical humanity's inability to comprehend it.

Notvuvst: I was born in P'najj's universe before Dee[532] created yours. We decorated it like an empty house given to us for our families to enjoy and make our own.

SoL: *What are we to you?*

Notvuvst: You are us in the sense of shared origin, and I'm saying this to universal humanity, to everyone in our universe, not just to you on Earth. In this respect, we're family although we don't use that concept in a parental way but in the context of shared grief. If The Corruption had never happened, then the concept of family would exist only in how a person conceives it for themselves, even for the physical-born whose bodies come directly, genetically, from their parents' bodies but who birth outside of that as unique beings. Our collective experience of The Corruption necessarily means family in that, conceptually, one's suffering is everyone's sibling.

You on Earth matter to us—by that, I mean what this book calls the First Ancestors and archangels—because the physical-born are also spirit-born. They are both the same person, what this book calls physicospirit. When you're aware of this, you can walk among us while physically alive. It doesn't matter. You are of both worlds. It is only your lack of awareness that leaves you thinking you are only a physical being when physically alive, that not until death do you become a spirit being. It's easy for us to live, here, without ever considering your physical reality there, but that's like you ignoring pollution's lethal effects on your body. Your physical world is an integral part of our world just like air is an integral part of matter. Each physically embodied person is, at the same time, spirit embodied, and this means that, regardless you being physically alive, you are part of spirit world, part of spirit-born society, part of *us*. This is human.

SoL: *How is healing affecting humanity?*

Notvuvst: What this book calls Accountableism brought universal humanity into ignorance, the greater its obsession with mindset the deeper its ignorance. We, here, never imagined ourselves to be unaware of our reality. Michael's Lie had us all thinking one thing about reality, which steeped in our minds like a forgotten teabag until we forgot its flavor and accepted its bitter taste as the tea. V'nin and I taught our children—Titit'j, Tivi'iv'z, Bibci'd[533] whom you know of; the others you don't—about our universe, the

---

532. Her diminutive for Mina, based on his family name *Idefiñi* (§ 1.1:336).

533. Gabriel, Lucifer, Michael (GLM; § 2.2:522).

one we grew up in with Dee. They took it literally while young but, over time, as they grew older, they increasingly saw it as just a metaphor. We tried to bring them to see it but they wanted *us* to take them, not Dee. We wanted to, but our fear of getting lost on the way was still too much. After the Big Healing, we did finally do it, and now we're comfortable with it. Even so, our children didn't really believe they were in a different universe but just a different, never-before-known part of *this* universe because, despite Michael's confession, belief doesn't simply go unbelieved any more than a habit just ceases its habituation. You experience the same effect with those on your planet who are adamant it is flat, or that a particular faith, or ideology, or way of life is what's best for everyone, and so on.

Those of us born into this environment, what you call spirit world, don't have the same body as you physically do. Disease, death, pain, injury, disability, hunger—these and the fear they engender aren't part of our experience of embodiment. And although they seem a part of yours, they aren't because you manifest them into reality where your body appears to be at the mercy of your environment. This is why healing isn't of the body but of the mind. You heal your physical body with drugs, or acupuncture, or herbal medicines yet your diseases like cancer often return because their cause isn't of the body but of the mind, rooted in one's perspective. The individual healing of universal humanity is therefore of the mind, and for physical humanity, the body naturally follows. If you who are reading this suffer bodily, this book explains healing more than I will here.

The healing of those in spirit world is de-habituating Accountableism here, although its affect on Earth seems minimal and difficult to perceive. As you heal and de-habituate your mindset, your mind naturally opens to spirit reality—you might experience this intuitively, in dreams or epiphanies, or as acceptance that progressively liberates you from physical reality as the only reality—where you experience not just physical humanity but universal humanity and your *human* reality.

Jesus (Yeshua)

He was born February 20, 2 BC, 2,022 years ago from AD 2021. He died October 24, AD 32 from heart failure while exsanguinating on the cross after a government official partially severed both femoral arteries with a *spatha* (a straight, long sword) as an act of mercy at the order of Pontius Pilate, Rome's governor of Judaea. Mary named him Yeshua at birth and he prefers that name for Earth. His father Gabriel (§ 1.3.3.2:475) named him *Sioghthye* (pronounced 'see-ogh-thi-uh,' the /g/ not quite silent and the /th/ more of a fricative with the tongue behind the upper teeth), which he prefers; it's how the spirit-born know him.[534]

Recall Mina considers Earth's socioculture and Jesus the most spiritually advanced—in the sense of having full awareness–experience of physicospirit reality achieved at the age of eighteen—of all physical-born humanity (§ 4.2.2.1:383; § 1.2.1:247). Buddha is a close second in the sense of awareness–experience of *dukkha* (pain) from the age of twenty-six (§ 40:618), followed by Sun-myung in the sense of unconditional love awareness–experience from the age of thirty-five (§ 40:615). This gulf between these three individuals and physical-born humanity is slowly lessening as it heals from The Corruption.

Sioghthye: You know the Passover story when I was twelve years old. Until then, I had never studied the Torah. I had other plans. I wanted to visit Bharat [India] to study philosophy. I thought it was my calling because I spent all my time with philosophers in my sleep who said they lived in Bharat. These weren't dreams but actual experiences. I knew that because when I woke up, I remembered everything in perfect detail as though I had been awake. I believed they were living, were teachers I could visit, and would educate me in truth. I had been learning with them since I was six years old when I first discovered that many people I could see and talk to were only [visible and] there for me. People thought I was born from sin because they saw me talking to them. After that, I ignored them unless they approached me in private. They were always surprised I could see them and wanted me to carry news to their families, but I would not, so they were often raging at me. I could see them every moment as if living in reality. For me, seeing them was normal, a part of my life. I thought I was someone special.

The teachers thought I was dangerous and punished me. My mother scolded them for it and although she scolded me, too, for not hiding my ability, she encouraged me to ignore the teachers. They hated me. I couldn't wait to be a man and longed for time to pass. I didn't want to go to Jerusalem

---

534. Gabriel chose it for its pleasing sound more than its meaning, which is along the lines of 'intended light' in that Sioghthye represents Mina's intention for physical-born humanity's awareness–experience of physicospirit reality.

because I was certain it was crowded with people only I could see and it would be a torment. My mother forced me to go and I sulked the whole first day. Whether I walked or sat, I talked to no one, especially my mother. But she left me alone and only scolded me once.

On the second day, she allowed me to sit on the wheeled platform my father had rented, along with two friends, for my mother and their wives and the small children to sit, which the three of them pulled because he couldn't afford an animal. Around midmorning, a man appeared atop a water jar that was tied to the planks. He startled me but before I could say anything, he firmly told me to say nothing but to think my words and he'd hear me. I realized then that only I could see him. There were many such people on the road but none had dared climb onto our platform.

He was younger than my father. I had no idea he was Moses until he told me and warned me to control myself. He said if I was going to learn philosophy then I needed to learn the Torah first. I had no interest in that and in my thoughts, said so. He laughed and said I had no say in the matter, that no philosopher would take me seriously if I went to them with that attitude. Reluctantly, I listened as he explained who I was—never telling me Gabriel was my father; I didn't learn that until recently—and why I could see him like any other person. We talked all day every day and then again whenever I slept. When we reached Jerusalem four days later, which felt more like forty days to me, I had not only learned the Torah to what was expected of my age, but in long conversation with him (in my mind), I'd learned to argue it like a teacher. I didn't feel twelve anymore but on the cusp of manhood. He said goodbye then, and I never saw him again in my lifetime.

When I decided in my seventeenth year that I belonged in Bharat, my father was deceptively sad to see me go. He had always thought I did not belong in the law. On the other hand, my mother believed my father would support my study in preparation for joining those of the law. She was adamant. I impetuously rejected her notion and brought her to tears, then announced I was traveling to Bharat when the weather changed. I regretted her sorrow and grief but my life was tangled up with my spirit teachers and all that I'd learned about life. I had to go where I could learn more. That was my destiny: to *know*, not to teach the law but to discover its origin.

My mother cried bitter tears, believing I would never return. I didn't want to, yet believed I probably would. My father said my decision to go to Bharat would be one I would regret and my eventual rejection there would bring no prodigal return here. With those words, he disowned me. But he couldn't see what I saw. The world I lived in was so different to this one that the impetus to go was stronger than my desire to live. I would have died than stay. In the end, he borrowed three denarii toward my journey, which I used for accommodation with traveling merchants.

In my fifth year [there], when I was twenty-three, Archangel Gabriel joined me where I sat cross-legged on a raised stone platform in a small garden area meditating on my place in the world and wondering about my future in life. My teachers taught me how to think about the unknown but not of the truth of our creator or how to meet such a person. While sitting here, my mind had again run upon the impossibility of meeting our creator and it was with great frustration I looked up to see this angel. His demeanor was of a messenger. Immediately, I knew he was here with news.

My first experience with Gabriel was that of a man in the presence of authority over all things. I remained in place. He stood for a moment and then laughed. I rose to my feet. He told me his name and that, if I accepted it, he would convey my desire to those able to teach me everything I needed to know about our creator and the world's existence. I looked at him with dullness. Many people had already said that to me. But he was the first to appear in the guise of knowing our creator. He asked if I wanted to meet them. He took my silence as permission and in a moment, a man not more than my age with features I had never seen appeared before me along with a woman whose face reminded me of statues of Aphrodite. We sat. He told me what I was: a man of living and eternal flesh at the same time and that my experience seeing them together was normal, what anyone could do if they understood it.

Over the next half year, our creator taught me day and night, awake or asleep, all about building our world—which he proved by building a small likeness right in front of me which I touched and held in my hands—and the situation in which people found themselves, and what, knowing all this, I might do about it here. We traveled all around his creation to other worlds like ours and to Gabriel's home, where those like him lived. Elsewhere, I saw the suffering of those who had lost their living flesh. He told me I could heal them over time if I wanted and I spent more than two years with them. Those among the living couldn't believe me; they only desired to teach me their way. He then said that my own people had the clearest understanding of life of all the people of the physical world and approached me to return home to teach them. Remembering my father, I wasn't sure. In truth, they would likely react as had those here. But he was adamant.

He said, why beat a dead horse? He thought Rome's control was a path to those having minds more open to such new ideas. After much consideration, I agreed. I'd learned what I came here to learn. I felt fulfilled. Would I just keep it to myself while they suffered during and after life? It seemed too cruel. In my twenty-sixth year, I announced my departure. Despite their disbelief, my teachers regretted my leaving.

My father in Nazareth greeted me in disbelief that I still lived. My mother cried. True to his word, he gave me no prodigal return but he did permit me to stay in exchange for taking up his trade, which I did to satisfy my mother and to restore my relationships and trust. No one had forgot my childhood. I knew it would be difficult to get past that. While I quietly healed the suffering hearts of those who permitted me, I resumed my father's trade. His heart softened toward me in time, yet he looked at me with suspicion. He knew I had changed, not just in becoming a man but a teacher. Many times, he asked me what I'd learned in my travels and what I would do with it. He expected me to leave again. Part of me hated to disappoint him but he was right.

Despite believing the law was for all humanity, the teachers were closed on its meaning, their various schools in constant disagreement. I rarely encountered Greeks, and Romans ignored me. After giving my father three years to help make up his gift of three denarii, I told my mother I would begin my life as a teacher. She surprised me by accepting it and I loved her for it. I chose to avoid the synagogue because I wasn't teaching faith but truth. Instead, I decided to appeal directly to those suffering the heavy hand of life because they most desired something new. What I knew was the answer to why life is pain and how we can live in the world the way our creator intended without undoing our own happiness.

Sun-myung Moon

Sun-myung (문선명 (文鮮明), d. 2012) was a man lacking accurate knowledge of physicospirit life and Lucifer, yet lived a tremendously deep and resilient faith in God and Jesus. He founded the Unification Church (UC) to teach about God and humanity before and after its infamous Fall. His ultimate aim was to restore[535] what humanity had lost by bringing Lucifer, whom he saw as the root of all disobedience, thus sin, to repentance. In "his deep spiritual exploration," says one of his earliest followers, and the first to translate *Divine Principle* into English, ". . . [he] discovered Heavenly Father's profound han [한 (恨) deep-seated grief; § 4:345] . . . and what caused it. He determined to uproot its cause, unravel and heal God's han, the cosmic tragedy, and make it his lifelong mission" (Kim 1987, 55).

Sun-myung: I expected a very different reception than I got when I arrived in spirit world. The Creator as I understood him as God was on hand when I opened my spirit eyes in my bed. I now know him as Mina. He introduced himself as Reikishiña,[536] the builder of our universe but not the creator of life, which happens in its own way. That was my first shock, and I didn't believe it. At either side of his very tall Asian form, at the foot of my bed, stood two others, their height just above his shoulders, whom he introduced as Titit'j and Tivi'iv'z but whom I knew as Gabriel and Lucifer. Besides Kim-ae and Reverend Moobon,[537] twenty-two others, including Jesus, who I couldn't help but recognize, spiritually stood around my bed. Some were church members and the rest, my family. I was watching Lucifer. He seemed genuinely happy to meet me. I thought it was because I'd made his restoration possible but Reikishiña corrected me.

He said, "Everything you believe about Tivi'iv'z never happened." I believed him without doubt.

"I want to thank you, though," Tivi'iv'z said. "You're the first person who believed it all to want to fix its roots."

That was my second shock. "Are you saying that I didn't do what I thought I did?"

"Sorry," Tivi'iv'z said.

---

535. The process of recovering what was lost in the Fall of Man (Moon 1996, 75, 82–88).

536. OUR UNIVERSE BUILDER'S ACTUAL NAME, § 1.1:336.

537. Kim-ae (김애), his nickname for his wife Hak-ja Han (한학자), combines the names of two aristocratic women prominent in the King Taejong period (AD 1400–1418) whom he respects and admires. Rev. Moobon was then a Korean UC leader.

Gabriel added, "You made a huge difference throughout the universe, not just on Earth."

"We'll talk about it later," Reikishiña said. "Right now, what do you want to do?"

What do you mean? I wondered. I hadn't moved.

"You're not dead yet," Jesus said, "but give it a minute." He laughed.

I looked at Kim-ae and saw nothing on her face. Well, it must be true then. I thought over what they'd said. God was a man of Asian features if he, and who I intuitively knew was Jesus, were to be believed. If so, my faith, the Bible, and Principle were wrong. It would take me two days according to events with my physical family before I accepted it. For now, I just rolled with the punches, something I was very used to doing. I glanced at Lucifer. Jesus was the only person in the room I trusted implicitly. I recognized the family members I'd grown up with and my church members, but how did they know who Reikishiña or Lucifer were? We were in the same situation. But Jesus had to know. I'm sure you're wondering how I knew Jesus was really Jesus. It was easy. More than God, I'd loved Jesus more than I'd loved anyone my entire life. He looked like any physical person standing there but I was experiencing a heartfelt connection with him and only him. It wasn't his face, or color, or anything visible. He certainly looked nothing like any image I'd ever seen of him. Neither did he radiate anything special beyond a sense of caring I'd never felt. I felt the same from Reikishiña, Gabriel, and Lucifer but I didn't know them. I thought it must be my lifelong relationship with Jesus that let me feel his emotion for me in a way I'd never felt. Regardless, I knew that many people would know Jesus from direct experience and eventually I'd know myself.

And then I died. Until that moment, I'd felt all the physical sensations of my body like heartbeat, respiration, my guts, pain in my knee . . . like I was physically conscious. Then I felt my physical body's presence in my mind just fade away. I knew I was dead. So did they all, somehow. My spirit self was still laying in bed. Now Kim-ae was reacting. Her expression showed satisfaction. I expected it but seeing it was a body blow.

Jesus said, "Do you want to stay and watch?"

My eyes still fixated on Kim-ae's fixated on my now-dead face. It was hard to look away. Half a lifetime in service to Principle and I'd known she'd hated it the whole time. It hadn't mattered because I'd believed but now, seeing the horror of satisfaction in her eyes and with Reikishiña's words fresh and revealing, I realized her pain and felt it hard in my heart. Nothing I'd ever scolded her for had mattered and it didn't matter now. When Reikishiña told me, in effect, that my entire life—

"Not *all* you believed," Reikishiña threw out as if reading my mind, "just everything except your absolute commitment to Tivi'iv'z, whom you *believed* was the epitome of evil and the source of all grief but in practice was unconditionally loving not just him but the worst person you could imagine, which sets you apart from everyone."

I looked at him and saw it in his face. I wasn't sure about him at all but at that moment, he felt real. I glanced at Jesus and though I couldn't read his face, which was neutral, he was nodding. So, not all wasted, then. But Kim-ae's pain was real, and if I'd unconditionally loved the worst of humanity, I certainly hadn't loved her as much as she'd deserved. Well, I couldn't tell her now, she wasn't any more spiritually open than me. It would have to wait. She was her own woman now; whatever she was going to do, it would be all her.

I didn't want to stay and watch, so I said, "I want to go."

Reikishiña said, "Okay," and I found myself lying on a different bed in a different room filled with windows and nature and everyone from where we'd been. He said, "Are you going to get up?"

I didn't answer, but I didn't get up, either. Instead, Gabriel, Lucifer, and Jesus pulled me out of bed and stood me up. My spirit body felt as strong as ever.

Gabriel said, "Did you think were an invalid?"

Muhammad ibn 'Abd Allāh

The founder of Islam, Muhammad (مُحَمَّد بن عَبْد آللّه; October 23, AD 579–June 8, 643; cf. ca. AD 570–June 8, 632) experienced his revelations not from 'Archangel' Gabriel but from a wisdom 'angel' (§ 1:520; Michael's task, § 2.3.3:525). His first revelation was in February AD 612. After teaching these privately, he began teaching publicly in July, AD 614 in the city of Mecca.

Muhammad: My first revelation was the end of my life. My feelings tortured me each time I repeated them to my friends. In my unimpeachable spirit, I knew I was enlightening their lives, too, not because I was a messenger of falsehood but of a truth ripe for change. It did not take long to have its effect. Even so, the angel's messages rang with truth and the strident force used against me only strengthened my desire to eliminate the source of evil threatening us. I knew of Yasu' and his fate;[538] his inability to defeat the powerful was permission to defeat him. What remained of his teaching was the faith of which I knew. The angel said it was corrupted and without truth but to leave them to it, because soon a new prophet would arise for their faith.[539]

The angel admonished me to teach, not convert, but I did not listen. Instead, I looked to strength not compassion, to their actions that threatened the angel's message, not to their suffering that fulfilled it. I foresaw none of what would become in my name, only that which became from my own fears of failure. Yet, I never questioned myself. I acted in the greater realm of Allah, not the lesser realm of man. The world suffered from rebellion, and suffering would only cease in submission. It seemed to agree with the angel, the emissary of Truth, whom I trusted above all others. I was proud to fulfill my calling.

That changed for me when Michael and Lucifer exposed their conflict and Allah worked His healing on many of those in my company, true Muslims all of them together. At first, I rejected Him. I was a true Muslim, His direct messenger not merely in life but after, where I ceaselessly spread the angel's message of submission. Upon my death, I realized that life continues, that we live in His world not ours, and that judgment was still to come. But those who now accepted His healing[540] changed in ways I could not comprehend. They were not simply different now; they were beyond suffering, beyond fear, beyond even submission. It seemed they had become *of* Him not *bound by* Him. I felt my trust in Islam shaken.

They pestered me to accept healing, for, despite everything, they honored me. I was humbled because they no longer called themselves Muslim but *free*. I couldn't imagine their sublime happiness. I rejected them as apostates, as traitors to Allah. Still, they pestered me like younger brothers who cared about family, not position. I was angry and raged at them, infuriated by their betrayal of all I had, and still, lived for. I went to lonely places yet, from time to time, they found me. Their happiness was sickening. I would have put them to death were it but possible. But I could only flee. Eventually, I felt tired, not of the body but the heart. I collapsed in tears. I wanted to die but I was dead! Wherever I went, I saw people happier than I had ever seen. What could it mean? Slowly, I began to realize I was the fool, the miserable, pitiable fool I'd always taken the unbelievers for, and I loathed myself. In my despair, and thinking through events, I called out to Allah not for healing but justification.

A man appeared before me who radiated power and sureness. I thought he must be an angel but even so, I asked if he was the creator. He said yes, he was who built our world and healed the suffering, and was here because I had called on him for healing. I said I had not. He said I only thought I had not, but my heart longed for it and if I wanted to end the suffering I was feeling then I need only permit it. I said, you can take away my suffering? He said no, he can heal my pain and my suffering would end of its own accord. I didn't believe him because, who can take away pain?

Then I realized I must truly be in the presence of Allah, for who else could take a man's pain? I couldn't speak the words, so I only nodded assent. He touched me then with his hand on my cheek, and light and relief filled me. My guilt for the blood I had shed, for the bloodshed in pursuit of Islam through time, drained out of me like darkness fleeing the light. I felt light and airy as though anvils had dropped from my neck.

I had never thought of guilt before, had never believed I had ever done wrong because I had believed without doubt that righteousness justified any sacrifice. But now I could *feel* the pain I had inflicted on the world, on every individual ever touched by Islam. I cried; new guilt, even greater than I had already felt, built in me like a storm. I thought he would leave me like that to atone for my sin of not listening to the angel, but his hand remained on my cheek, and as I longed for release, I felt it drain away as before. What I felt was what I had seen in the countenance of those who had pestered me. Yes, I cried harder. My relief was beyond words. He stayed with me, his hand on my cheek, what seemed like hours as each healing brought new torment until at last I felt *healed*. He said healing takes time and that I would feel

---

538. عيسى, transliteration of Hebrew *Yeshua* (Jesus) to Arabic without using the Greek sources (cf. Sura 3:45).

539. This was to be St. Maurontus (AD 744–804) of Marseilles, France, originally abbot of St. Victor Abbey.

540. In the four years following the Big Healing in October 2017.

pain I had yet to discover, but when I did, he would heal me of it if I desired to heal. When I was ready for him to leave, he departed.

I was alone where I had been hiding, yet all the misery I had felt there was gone. My spirit felt as if I could drift on a breeze. I sat down. For a long while, I pondered my life. I don't know how long I was there but eventually I went in search of my friends, my *brothers*, whom I had called traitors and worse. When I found them, it was as if we were newly met, with no hard feelings. We cried together in joy. Life now seemed very, very different.

Sometime later, I met Yasu'. I could see his feelings as he read my countenance. He stepped forward fast and, for a moment, I thought of flight. But he embraced me like a brother and called me *friend*. I was dumbstruck. My mind was a tangle of thoughts and feelings. He said he had waited a long time to meet me. His body seemed to shine like the Sun. He plainly knew my thoughts because he said the more pain I healed the less its darkness would cover me. He meant *my* pain but at the time, I took it to mean others' pain. Because of that, I asked him if I could heal others and, if so, would he teach me. He brought me to meet other healers who heal through their relationship with our creator, and like an army, we marched off to heal instead of harm.

That is what I do, now. I spread the healing way of Allah without judgment or punishment or harm. Islam is submission to righteousness but healing is submission to the self's torment which *is* righteousness because it leads to the end of harm and the joy of life. That's true Islam. The compassion of Islam is the essence of righteousness.

Siddhārtha Gautama (Buddha)

The man known as the Buddha was born September 20, 472 BC and died September 15, 415 BC. He lived during and slightly beyond ancient India's Magahi empire's Shaishunaga dynasty (525–417 BC; cf. ca. 413–345 BC), located in the modern state of Bihar. Siddhārtha (सिद्धार्थ गौतम; he pronounces it 'sid-ûrt') experienced 'enlightenment'—to him, *vimukti* (release of Buddhism's fetters and hindrances)—in his twenty-sixth year (§ 40:613) at the traditionally recognized Mahabodhi Temple's Bodh Gaya site in Bihar.

Siddhārtha: Enlightenment is not religion. It is simply achieving happiness in life as you define it, not as I did. For some, they misjudge happiness and it leads them to misery, but that is not because they failed to follow the Buddhist Way, but because they failed to know their own self. Although I use failure to describe the result, it does not define the person. One fails to achieve but tries again until achieving their goal. Achieving *vimukti* is only enlightenment if, through it, you defined your happiness, which can be anything from children to wealth to self-denial. If it is genuine happiness of the soul, then it is enlightenment. What I found in my youth was the happiness for which I long desired. As the seasons change, so, too, does the human mind. In time, my idea of happiness matured, yet I found it impossible to follow because my teachings were a pit into which fell my trainees trying to emulate not just my discovery but also my concept of happiness. I tried to guide them toward their individual needs and the impermanence of self-awareness but all they could see was their belief in the righteous individual, not the happy life. I felt trapped in my own success and unable to pursue my own growth. When I was forty-five years of age, I realized my self-awareness had brought me back to where I was in my youth when I had a family and rejected it, whereas now, understanding the reality of life and my human place in it, I was ready to embrace it.

My announcement that I would take a wife met with disbelief and outright anger. My trainees accused me of abandoning the Way and denying them *vimukti*, of betraying their eternal self to the darkness of *dukkha* [pain]. Despite teaching them the two-fold nature of life, they had eyes only for perfection, which is impossible in an impermanent reality. They associated happiness with the vile and therefore *dukkha* without ever realizing, as I had, that when one is happy, one has ended *dukkha*. My purpose was to guide them toward discovering genuine happiness as individuals in a world that is impermanent, because the human *mind* is impermanent in the sense that, like the universe, it is never at rest, that it is ever changing as it develops greater awareness and encounters different experiences.

Despite their lip service, each of them only ever desired human perfection separate and apart from the reality of their minds as eternal beings because, for those lacking *vimukti*, their very beingness was vile, a dirty coat to be cast off by perfection where the cycle of *dukkha*, not of life as they chose to believe, would cease to be. It is true that the cycle of *dukkha*, one's recurring pain, can end but this is true only as suffering in response to pain, not in pain itself. In their desire to achieve *vimukti* as perfection, they only ensured themselves pain and thus denied themselves happiness without suffering.

I could not reject them. They were like my own children, not the family I now desired in my readiness for it, but they were family, even so. I felt their pain in their fear of losing perfection and realized I had failed them as their teacher. Even if I continued teaching after taking a wife, they might leave in despair because it was I who had showed them these things, whetted their appetite for a real end to suffering, and now would have seemed to embrace suffering as a permanent reality of life by embracing what, to them, was vile. I chose to put off what I now happily desired to renew my teachings and correct their misunderstanding of the Way.

In the end, my time ended without success, although my spirit afterward achieved a family[541] about two centuries later according to your time here. Perfection and suffering are illusions, even though pain is real. Today, I seek to heal, and be healed of, pain. If I suffer, it is because I choose it, not because it is reality. As I heal, I suffer less and feel happy more. Meditation is only a tool of awareness, not a path to perfection nor happiness, the latter of which arrives through healing, not avoiding, pain.

---

541. Only about 0.027% of H2 spirit persons were aware before the Big Healing they could procreate in spirit world.

Part V

Energy Testing

Energy Testing

WE REFERENCE ENERGY testing (ET) as data one objectively formulates as information, knowledge, and wisdom similar to that acquired via the scientific method (§ 1.2.1:85). Mina tells us H2 discovered ET about 13.5KYA in southeast Gabon, but warfare killed its practitioners some 170 years later. We rediscovered it October 6–12, 2017. Here in Section 1 we describe ET as it physically and energetically is and in Section 2 how it works and how to do it. As you acquire experience, develop your ET competence, proficiency, skill, and establish your own reliability baselines, you can verify what you read in this book. To the extent you connect with a local or global ET community (at storyoflifebook.com) you can test your understanding and interpretation of it individually and in the context of others.

SECTION 1
What is Energy Testing

Quite simply, ET is chakra energy (§ 1.2.1.2.2:500) interacting with the body's biological energy. Even if you have neither knowledge nor conscious awareness of ET, your physical body always responds to chakra energy which, if your chakras are sufficiently 'open' (§ 1.2:634; § 2.3.4:526), sways your body to a greater or lesser degree. When you develop awareness of this phenomenon, you can consciously utilize it by focusing on—having awareness–experience of—a specific 'frequency'–resonance (FR; § 1.2.1.2.1:499).

FR arises in your physically-instantiated mind's state of being and state of awareness (SOB, SOA; § 1.2.2.1:253) and that of spirit persons in the 'reflective' or supranatural environment (§ 7.1:212) who focus on a physical person's focal mindstate (§ 4.1.1:378). In this way, you can interpret your body's FR response to chakra energy in the context of focal mindstate (Thought; § 1.2.2.5.1:261), meaning a *query*—a question or affirmative statement posed, or conscious thinking–feeling—to which a spirit person responds. When you query a spirit person, they choose to respond to you. As their response (§ 2.1.1:581) interacts with your aura (§ 2.1:510) in the context of the 'reflective' environment, it gives rise to chakra energy in your 'reflective' body having a specific FR consistent with your query. You interpret this via your awareness–experience of it as 'movement' in your body. This is ET.

Recall that absent The Corruption, a physical person fully mind–brain integrates (MBI; § 1.2.2.4:257) their spirit self, their *Life* mind. Such a person has seamless, consciously full-time, *direct* awareness–experience of the natural, 'reflective,' and supranatural environments and experiences no disruption between them. A spirit person standing right in front of this person looks and sounds albeit isn't as physical as any physical person. He or she needn't utilize ET because they *directly* see and hear spirit persons via physicospirit MBI (§ 1:561). ET is the means by which a physical person lacking sufficient MBI *indirectly* communicates with spirit persons. It isn't a new method. It's always been available to us. We just haven't known about it till now except in the vaguest terms from spiritualists seeking to uncover it. As physical humanity's MBI improves post-Big Healing, individuals healing and improving their MBI over time can dispense with indirect ET for direct physicospirit sensorial experience. However, such direct communication with spirit persons is only available to, and verifiable by, that person. ET's indirect communication is repeatable, hence verifiable, by anyone. Let's consider how ET works.

1.1 Traditional Muscle Testing as Indirect Energy Testing

Although one might view ET as a form of kinesiology, traditional muscle testing (TMT) as a diagnostic tool of the subconscious isn't kinesiological. Nor does TMT's biofeedback, biomagnetism, or 'strong–weak' subconscious response indicate positivity, beneficence, truth, and congruence or conversely negativity, harmfulness, falsity, and incongruence as comprehended by chiropractor George Goodheart (d. 2008) and others' applied, clinical, and energetic kinesiology, Emotion Code (§ 1.1:4), ThetaHealing (§ 1.2.1:28), and various spiritual, alternative, and naturopathic diagnostic and healing modalities. Indeed, they are all *indirectly* employing ET without realizing what it is, whereas *personal query–response* (PQR, also QR; § 1.2.1.2:86) *directly* employs ET.[542] TMT's indirect ET responses aren't from your subconscious, however, but from your own spirit self, which is your independently spirit-embodied *conscious* mindstate having some variable level of awareness of your physical self, which is your independently physical-embodied mindstate. There's plenty about TMT and kinesiology on the Internet, so we don't describe them here.

1.2 Traditional Muscle Testing and Falsification

Besides accusations of fraud, skeptics dismiss TMT as a pseudoscience. They attribute its apparent effects to phenomena like ideomotor, observer-expectancy, subject-expectancy, and confirmation bias.[305] What these seemingly rational, scientific explanations for the presumedly irrational, pseudoscientific TMT effect have in common is that they rely for their own veracity on the *invisible mind* and in particular mind's even more elusive subconscious. Science relying on phenomena it attributes to mind to falsify phenomena others also attribute to mind is not science but religion. Let's consider what really happens when a skeptic like James Randi (d. 2020)—a magician famous for appearing to falsify, or debunk, paranormal and pseudoscience claims like 1970s spoon-bender Uri Geller—investigates TMT.

We walk you through an episode of Randi's self-hosted television show[306] where he appears to falsify applied kinesiologist and crystal healer Soozi Holbeche's TMT of actress–journalist Fiona Richmond as an unbiased participant. With Holbeche's hand near Richmond's wrist pushing down on her resisting arm, Holbeche baseline tests Richmond's normal strength as a 'weak' response. She then puts a pre-selected crystal in Richmond's other hand and places her own about halfway up Richmond's forearm. Holbeche now tests a 'strong' response because, according to her—not to Mina—that particular crystal imparts positivity, thus strength, to Richmond's body. One might opine her different hand positions impart greater or lesser torque, thus the 'weak' and 'strong' results are simply mechanical cause and effect. Mina says her hand placement isn't enough to make a difference. Anyway, it's irrelevant. Randi is merely outing Holbeche's apparent inattention or trickery—fraud, if you like—and not her TMT skill or capability (such as her chakras being 'open'), nor even TMT's operating principle as a pseudoscience.

Next, Randi puts the crystal into a small bag, then along with four identical bags which he says contain nothing "which could be described as good for anyone" (thereby incorporating into his own test the afore-mentioned biasing effects; at 2:24), puts it into a larger bag. As Richmond alternately holds each small bag, Holbeche ultimately tests her response as 'weak' to the crystal but 'strong' to a bag containing rat poison. After some jocularity and excuses—the bags 'interfered' (5:08–5:17)—Randi concludes that applied kinesiology, crystals, or both don't work. In truth, neither Randi nor Holbeche have any clue what's going on with the human body during TMT. Randi sees no scientific principle at work, thus a lack of veracity. Holbeche sees mental or spiritual principles at work, hence, the opposite.

Recall the physicospirit person is emergent self-aware proto-energy (ESP) *Life* existing independently of physical *and* spirit embodiment (§ 5.2:296; § 1:391, § 2.3.2.1:241). The physical is an independent, biological existent that, via MBI, moment-to-moment instantiates physical mind as an expression of *Life* (§ 1.2.2.1:253; § 1.2.2.2:254) somewhat the way spirit embodiment is its much fuller expression. But MBI isn't a two-way street. Your *Life* mind has awareness–experience of your physical reality via spirit–physical *body* integration, but not its MBI-deficient physically-instantiated mind. So, if Richmond's spirit self doesn't know what's in each bag,

---

542. We don't include here medical muscle testing used in clinical settings as a biomechanical diagnostic.

neither does her physical self nor other spirit persons observing the proceedings unless they keep aware of the bagged crystal throughout the process.

Since archí are 'concentrated' proto-energy (§ 2.3.1:115), each piece of matter exudes 'energy' associated with what it is. Spirit persons have awareness–experience of this 'energy' but need schooling to recognize it for what it physically represents the way they do to recognize mental 'energy' to gain awareness–experience of a physical person's focal mindstate (STEP 1, *below*); about 99% of those in the 'reflective' environment can't decipher one hidden thing from another. They can 'see' an object's 'energy,' but don't know whether it's good or bad for the body, or for that particular body (or person), in that specific situation. Neither can a person's subconscious–conscious *L*ife mind know, as described. Because TMT only accesses the subject's conscious mind, it doesn't test 'truth' but merely mind's guesswork, or sense of probability, regarding the crystal (and even its own physical body, as TMT doesn't access the subconscious having this awareness–experience). This makes TMT seem random, diagnostically chancy, ineffectual, and falsifiable. Debunking it appears legitimate, but isn't. About 99.9% of all paranormal–pseudoscience investigative work simply exposes fraud, trickery, lack of skill, and so on, but never identifies much less falsifies the *principle*—that of our physicospirit reality—that's being claimed. In that sense, debunking is itself trickery, hence, falsifiable. Your experience will tell you how believable and worthwhile ET is.

SECTION 2
How Energy Testing Works

To understand ET, you need read up on chakras if you haven't already, as we describe them and biological 'energy' (§ 1.2.1:498–§ 1.2.1.2.3:501). Here, we provide only their necessary aspects. ET is a two-step process: 1) a physical person has awareness–experience of chakra energy resulting in movement of their body and, 2) they interpret its movement in the context of focal mindstate (their query). Let's consider each.

2.1   STEP 1: PHYSICAL BODY RESPONSE TO CHAKRA ENERGY

Abiogeneticists (§ 2.1:522; § 1.1:532) developed chakras only after The Corruption to overcome physical humanity's MBI separation from spirit reality (Mina expects to deprecate them in ~175 years). Without The Corruption's effect on universal humanity, a spirit person speaks verbally with a physical individual via their spirit self's MBI. Even following dissolution of the Negative Collective Consciousness (NCC; § 1.2:21; § 4.2:379), the Big Healing, individual healings yet ongoing, and still-deficient MBI, only Mina can ET communicate without verbalizing. A spirit person needs verbalize so it interacts with Living force (§ 1.3:272; Table 11:285) in the 'reflective' environment to translate into the physical person's body via chakra energy with which it interacts to move as ET. This holds true for the physical person, too, until they train their chakras to be always 'open.' When the girls and I met Mina that October 13, 2017 evening, I had to verbalize my queries. Mina later said I'd advanced to Thought, like Ayako and El, by the end of our night. Such progress is individual. A caveat here is that, with whomever you ET, it's a *conversation* and *relationship*. Manners, courtesy, caring, and consideration may matter to them more than to you or vice versa (§ 1.3.1:24).

Your focal mindstate is your ET query. Be aware that spirit persons have awareness–experience of it as if in a universal group chat. Focal mindstate exudes into the 'reflective' environment via your 'reflective' body—not your spirit body—and 'illuminates' it in the sense a trained spirit person (*below*) has awareness–experience of it. Mina, who usually doesn't embody in my presence, chooses to have constant awareness–experience of my focal mindstate. It's the same for any spirit person, whether in the 'reflective' environment or staying in the supranatural. They choose to be aware of those who matter to them or, colloquially, keep an 'ear to the ground' for their name or situations amongst physical humanity relevant to them (§ 2.2:564). Focal mindstate exuding into the 'reflective' environment regardless a preference for mental privacy is the natural condition of physical life, although spirit self Thought is always private.

A spirit person in the 'reflective' environment develops sensitivity to, thus awareness–experience of, a physical person's focal mindstate. This takes about an hour, on average. It's the same as learning a language and is the lingua franca between spirit and physical persons until, through healing, physical humanity's MBI eventually removes the physical–spirit barrier and individuals can directly communicate face-to-face. Having learned this 'language,' a spirit person has awareness–experience of focal mindstates suffusing the 'reflective' environment that are unique to each physical individual. A spirit person becomes familiar with the 'energy' of an individual's focal mindstate—just as we grow familiar with the sound of a person's voice or an expert 'mind reads' via micro–macro body language, inflection, or vibe—and can differentiate it amongst the 'reflective' environment's panoply of focal mindstates.

Once they have this awareness–experience, develop their sensitivity to it, and learn to differentiate and interpret it, they can experience all focal mindstates to know who is saying what in the physical environment. It's like a person in a room crowded with people speaking a language they don't understand but, upon learning it from a single individual, can then understand what everyone is saying and direct their attention to—have 'vocal' awareness of—this or that person to overhear or respond to their conversation. About 30% of spirit persons visiting Earth via the 'reflective' environment in any given moment don't bother to learn the lingo. They remain unaware of individual focal mindstates because 'reflected' sound from, say, physical voices doesn't interact with a spirit person's ear since physical–spirit interaction in the 'reflective' environment is via Living force, not applied energy E (§ 2.1:114).

Spirit persons responding to a physical person's focal mindstate—their query—need do so verbally in order their Thought as 'voice'—Living force, conceptually similar as vibrational force—interacts with the person's aura to translate into their body as chakra energy that interacts with biological 'energy' to move their body as an interpretable ET response. This is the functional equivalent of hearing speech.

2.2   STEP 2: PHYSICAL PERSON INTERPRETS BODY MOVEMENT

A spirit person's verbalized response—their focal mindstate—translates to Living force that interacts with a physical person's aura, translating into the body as chakra energy to interact with biological 'energy' (§ 1.2.1.2.2:500). This induces the body's sway (a gross 'energy' interaction) that's a physical, not muscular, differential which enables hand, finger (progressively subtler 'energy' interactions), and mind testing (ET's subtlest awareness–experience). Let's consider how your body responds to a focal mindstate.

2.2.1   HOW YOUR BODY RESPONDS TO A SPIRIT PERSON'S ET RESPONSE

Recall that chakras and the aura are not of the physical but the 'reflective' body (§ 1.2.1.2.1:499). ET responses manifest in the 'reflective' body that conversely affect the physical body just as the physical body 'reflects' in the 'reflective' environment down to its constituent archí. Every aspect of the physical body 'reflects' moment-to-moment in the 'reflective' environment; conversely, whatever affects one's 'reflective' body translates to their physical body. If, for example, a spirit person in the 'reflective' environment violently shoves your 'reflective' body (having developed this difficult to accomplish capability), about 10% of that movement translates to your physical body. As a result, you physically experience a seemingly inexplicable movement which you might chalk up to any number of reasons that make sense to you in the context of your current situation with little to no awareness of your physicospirit reality. ET movement is similar, except instead of a spirit person using their spirit body to 'physically' shove you, the translated 'energy' of their verbalized Thought does it via your chakras, although with significantly less magnitude.[543]

Chakra energy arising in an ET response interacts with your body according to your Intentionality (§ 3.2:282; CH. 30:515). It's your choice if you want your body to sway forward, backward, or side-to-side to *yes*, *no*, or *maybe*. Your mind Intentionalizes your choice because it controls your body and all its 'energies.' Naturally, you can change your mind and re-Intentionalize your preference. The girls and I settled on swaying forward to *yes* and backward to *no*. As we encountered unexpected movements like side-to-side hip sway and tested what the spirit person was trying to say, we settled on a leftward push as *maybe no, not really*, and similar responses, and a rightward push as *maybe yes, kind of*, and similar to increase a query's possible ET interpretations (Fig. 208:628, right). There are four ways to have awareness–experience of an ET response: sway, hand, finger, and mind. We explain why and how each works below.

2.2.1.1   BODY-SWAY (-PUSH) ENERGY TESTING RESPONSE

When you query or have ongoing conversation using verbal or nonverbal thinking–feeling with a spirit person, their response translates from their verbalization, as described, into your 'reflective' body via the aura and pons chakras (§ 1.2.1.3.2:502) where, as chakra energy, it interacts with your physical body's biological 'energy.' Your physically-instantiated mind's awareness–experience of it feels something like muscle flex, but that's

---

543. Even so, some ET responses can be so energetic—a passionate *vs.* a calm *yes* or *no*—that one loses their balance.

an aftereffect, not the inducer, of the body's movement. The sensation you experience is Living force in the 'reflective' environment translating via your aura into chakra energy within your 'reflective' body and interacting with your physical body's biological 'energy' (§ 1.2.1.2.2:500). A magnitude change arises on one side of your body or the other in accord with your Intentionality. With a forward-sway *yes* response, a greater magnitude of biological 'energy' relocates to the back of your body than the front and your body moves forward analogous to air moving from an area having greater to lesser magnitude as wind, or as more air above than below an airplane wing resulting in lift. If your feet weren't contacting the ground, your body would relocate laterally just like a body of air. The reverse happens with a *no*, and side to side with a *maybe*. This same process occurs when a spirit person physically shoves your 'reflective' body (*above*). Unlike mimicking a shove, an ET response relocates biological 'energy' to move—sway, or push—your body consonant with your Intentional choice to move, say, forward to *yes* and backward to *no*.

This happens regardless your conscious effort to stand still because it has nothing to do with your mind–brain self except w.r.t. your Intentional choice. When we were determining in 2017 if ET was a real phenomenon or not, we tried holding perfectly still while energy testing, but couldn't. We decided ET wasn't us inducing our body to sway, lose balance, or unconsciously push our hips left or right. It was plainly no kind of ideomotor or other such effect, but the ET phenomenon. The effort to stand still arises in one's physically instantiated mind (§ 1.2.2.1:253) whereas the ET response is simply Living force translating to biological 'energy' with its concomitant physical effect.

When a spirit person can't decide on an answer, or is considering *yes–no* options, your body tends to wobble around without a clear sway in any direction. One can interpret it as an *I-don't-know* response; I typically sway backward for *I-don't-know*, which I then query to discern from a *no*, whereas Ayako interprets the wobble as *I don't know* or *I'm thinking about it*. *No* responses can also mean *don't worry about it, don't say/think that*, and so forth, which you can query. And the more passionate the spirit person's response—the more emotive ℒife force (EMℒF; § 3.3.3.1.1:289) it manifests—the greater the magnitude of Living force translating via the chakras, the greater the magnitude of biological 'energy' relocating in your body, hence, the more pronounced your body's movement, or sway. ET responses sometimes nearly push us off our feet. Some responses can be energetic enough to feel like a literal shove.

2.2.1.1.1 DOES ONE INITIALLY CALIBRATE ET?

It isn't necessary to calibrate your body to initiate ET by thinking about love–hate, peace–war, or positive-negative to establish a *yes–no* sway baseline. ET, like TMT, doesn't arise in the subconscious being intrinsically drawn to or repelled from positive and negative, truth and falsity, or congruence and incongruence, but in the context of spirit humanity inclusive of your own spirit self. You simply need decide your *yes*, *no*, and *maybe* response as whatever sway, or push, direction you desire (you can always change it later), be sure your chakras are 'open,' and then dive right in.

For example, begin by querying if there's a spirit person currently with you in your room or 'listening' from spirit world—long distance, we call it—and if they're willing to talk with you, who they are, and then take it from there. Alternatively, invite some religious, cultural, or political big shot—whoever interests you—to a conversation. They may not sense you, respond right away, or even be interested. Don't be discouraged. Mina and Lucifer are sometimes too busy to talk to the girls and me. ET is conversation built off relationships. So, meet-and-greet; develop a rapport with people just as you would when meeting someone over the telephone or maybe via Morse code. Spirit family and friends are the best place to gain ET proficiency (*below*) although, depending on relationships and attitudes, not always.

Recall ET is a limited means of communication until your intuition and spirit senses pick up the slack. Think of a Morse code message. The receiver can't experience your body language, voice, inflection, or thinking–feeling patterns to decode accurately what you mean by certain words and phrases. All he or she can do is take each word at face value or, more typically, interpret words according to their mindset rather than yours, the sender. You've no doubt encountered such miscommunication with emails and texts. Spirit persons have awareness–experience of your focal mindstate, but they can't know your thinking–feeling or how you interpret meaning unless it's *in* your focal mindstate or a spirit person develops a familiarity with you and learns to interpret your mental habits, eccentricities, and queries closer to how *you* interpret them. The same goes for how you interpret a spirit person's answer. Their *yes* may not necessarily mean yes in the way *you* think it does in the context of your query. Sometimes, it just indicates a verbalized head-nod, as common to conversation, or a response to an aspect of your query.

Never assume anything. To avoid misunderstandings, always confirm a response by rewording your query multiple times and from positive to negative or vice versa. Sometimes multiple spirit persons will respond to your query at the same time, like two people in a room inadvertently talking over each other. The person you're addressing might respond *yes* while the other responds *no*. Testing the latter can mislead you. A query that's vague or open to interpretation results in an unclear or inaccurate response.

2.2.1.1.2　SOCIALIZING VIA ENERGY TESTING IS NECESSARY TO ACCURACY

Your biological 'energy' interacts with chakra energy from Living force interacting with a spirit person verbalizing Thought in the 'reflective' environment. Living force, as the interaction twixt biological 'energy' and chakra energy, has the 'signature' of one or more spirit persons as well as other 'noise' that's analogous to the multiple, unique sounds filling one's physical ear; the more you physically talk, the greater your familiarity with unique voices and the more accurately you understand pronunciation, inflection, word choice, meaning, and thought patterns in speech patterns until you're able to recognize a voice, even mood, in about three-quarters of a second. Recognizing unique expressions of Living force in your biological 'energy'–chakra energy interaction is necessary to developing accurate ET.

Socializing puts you in sustained contact with a spirit person more than queries merely seeking knowledge or guidance. To recognize the chakra energy translating from spirit persons quickly, we encourage you to socialize with spirit family, friends, spirit guides . . . anyone you feel close to or interested in. We don't mean you ignore seeking knowledge and understanding from historical persons and the spirit-born, only that you combine it with socializing as you grow and develop your ET proficiency. Ayako considers it a necessity. She energy tests with *Obāsan* most every day in front of the mirror about fashion, looks, hair, skin, makeup, and different themes with other spirit family and friends. I converse with Mina about literally everything all day every day as I write this book, though Ayako urges me to branch out.

2.2.1.1.3　HOW TO SWAY (PUSH) TEST

The sway (push) test is the easiest of the four ET awareness–experiences to do. Stand—you can sit to torso sway but it's harder—in a relaxed but not too rigid posture or conscious muscle control tends to override the response, arms relaxed at your sides, in your pockets, across your chest (but can 'energy' interfere), hooked in your belt or anywhere comfortable, feet at shoulder width or as close as ankles touching (how Ayako does it). Closing your eyes helps segregate your mind from distractions or fighting your balance, but isn't necessary (*Fig. 208*). When we met Mina, ours eyes were wide open, to be sure. We find the body sways quicker to an ET response with eyes closed than open, although Ayako is so advanced and fast she rarely bothers. Begin your queries by asking for whomever you want to converse with until they respond and you feel comfortable they are who they claim to be.

A caution: while some spirit persons lie about their identity, their mind knows it's a lie and, therefore, their verbalized response albeit a lie embodies the 'energy' of their mind. If you ask, "Is this really Joe?" and he (or she) is lying, you'll sway test a *no* response (§ 2.1:636). It may take awhile before you intuit what's what while energy testing. Remember, ET is a skill, not woo-woo, a spiritual gift, the sole purview of intuitives, sensitives, spiritualists, or the like. Anyone can ET.

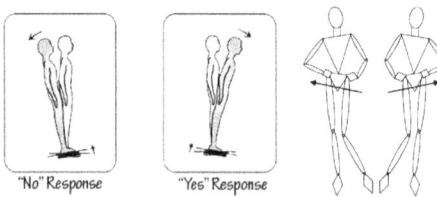

"No" Response　　"Yes" Response

Figure 208. Sway test stance; backward is *no*, forward *yes*; left–right hip sway (push) is various *maybes*.[307]

You might encounter a failure to sway or else confusing, contradictory, or spurious ET responses because your chakras are 'closed' even though you think or test they're 'open.' You might also find your body swaying or oscillating slightly. This isn't your body trying to keep upright, but its natural ET response to the spirit 'energy' in your environment; it can buffet you like a wind whether posing a query or not. Training from an experienced energy tester, as well as Mina, who can 'open' your chakras until you develop the ability, will mitigate such early-on problems. You can ET about others, too, which TMT calls muscle testing by proxy. It's really just Person A querying Person C about Person B. You should always have Person B's permission. Mina responds obliquely when querying without it; you might oscillate. You need determine veracity and intent before accepting a response. Dehydration doesn't affect ET.

2.2.1.2 HAND ENERGY TESTING RESPONSE

All ET awareness–experience involves the pons chakra. The hand testing we describe here additionally involves both forearm FR auras—the elbow FR to the metacarpophalangeal (the knuckles of the fist) where the fingers FR begins ('FREQUENCY'-RESONANT AURAS, § 2.1.1.2:511). You hand test with your arms straight out from your body with palms facing, and then move them together. The spirit person's response translates to biological 'energy' magnitude changes as described that, here, relocate along the hand–arm that moves less, resulting in one hand contacting the other closer to the torso.

Suppose you test *yes* having previously decided—Intentionalized—to interpret it as your right hand contacting your left closer to your torso where its fingertips are closer than your left's (*Fig. 209*, center). According to the EmℒF in the spirit person's response, your right arm will bend less or more while your left remains straight. This lands your right-hand fingertips closer to your torso than your left hand's, from just slightly closer to anywhere up your left arm to the shoulder. The more passionate the answer, the greater your arm bends, thus the farther up your arm your opposite hand will land seemingly of its own accord. We experienced this with Ayako who preferred to master this method.

The reason for this phenomenon is the ET response involving a much subtler biological 'energy' interaction with your chakra energy. A greater magnitude of biological 'energy' relocates just beyond the left fingertips (in this scenario) when testing an *I-don't-know*, and farther up the hand–arm according to the EmℒF in the *yes* response. The analogy most useful here is the left and right hands acting like same-pole magnets. The greater the magnitude of biological 'energy,' the more it repulses the opposite hand away from the fingertips until its weak enough to act like an opposite-pole magnetic, drawing the opposite hand to land in that area. Sitting confines your interaction with the ET response to your arms and hands rather your whole body. If you're standing, the hand test will sway your body somewhat. Although hand testing involves subtler 'energy,' you can learn it as easily as sway (push) testing.

2.2.1.2.1 HOW TO HAND TEST

This ET awareness–experience takes getting used to, according to the person, because you *consciously* move your hands together while *nonconsciously* allowing them to make contact. You begin with a relaxed standing or sitting posture. Hold your arms straight out in front of you at any angle to the floor. Ayako prefers parallel, and it's perhaps the most common. Your palms are vertical and facing, shoulder width to a foot apart (*Fig. 209*, left). Make your query, then gently move both hands together without trying to control where they make contact. Let your body's energy do the work. Your right-hand fingertips landing closer to your torso than your left's indicates a *yes* and the reverse a *no* if that's how you chose to manifest those responses (*Fig. 209*, center-left). Otherwise, it'll be the reverse.

The more passionate the spirit person's response, the more (as your proficiency improves) the indicating hand's elbow will bend, thus landing that hand farther up your other hand or arm as far as your shoulder (*Fig. 209*, center-right). Ayako interprets these varying ET responses as "yes," "strong yes," "super strong yes," and "really, *really* strong yes!" If you want to feel the passion in a spirit person's response, then sway and hand testing are for you. You initially may not indicate these hand variations, but increasingly you will, as your sensitivity and ability to move your hands together without overriding your body's response to your chakras improves. We interpret hands landing with matching fingertips to be *I don't know* or *maybe* (*Fig. 209*, right). Test your answers to work out the response and meaning exactly.

2.2.1.3 FINGER ENERGY TESTING RESPONSE

This is an advanced ET awareness–experience in that chakra energy and your body's interaction with it are subtler than with sway and hand testing. It involves the fingers FR (§ 2.1.1.2.1:511) while pulling an extended finger through the 'joint' made by the other hand's thumb-tip and any fingertip forming an 'O,' circle, or ring shape (*Fig. 210*). I learned it because, like El, I struggled with hand testing and got tired of standing up

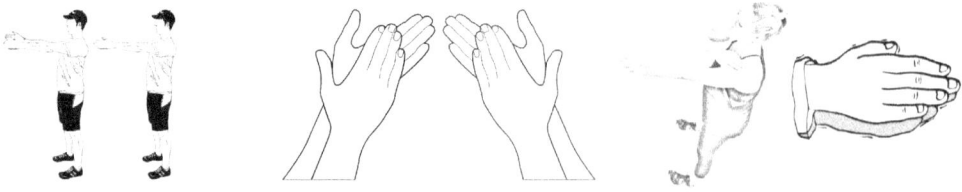

Figure 209. Hand testing stance: left, arms straight at any angle; center, palms facing ('right-over-left' is *yes*; 'left-over-right' is *no*; or reverse by choice); right, fingertips closest to torso response ('really, *really* strong!' *yes* or *no* according to choice); far-right, equal fingertips (*I don't know, maybe*, or others).₃₀₈

every second to sway test while writing this book. Ayako never warmed up to finger testing. She stuck with hand testing until she moved to New York City, where its spiritual 'energy' intensity (defined by Mina as a megacity) but lack of ley lines made hand testing unreliable, and she reverted to the sway test El prefers. The body's finger-test interaction with an ET response relocates lesser or greater biological 'energy' in the area of the 'joint' that 'bonds' the pressed-together thumb-tip–fingertip forming the 'O,' or ring, shape.

When you Intentionalize your *yes*-responding thumb-tip–fingertip 'joint' to resist your extended finger pulling through, it stops; conversely, it pulls through with a *no* response (*Fig. 210*). If the spirit person's response is something in the *maybe* realm then, as your sensitivity, intuition, and proficiency improve, you'll feel your extended finger pull through the 'joint' with a sense of drag. When I have this awareness–experience, I query the responder whether they meant *maybe yes, kind of, maybe no, not really*, and so forth until confirming the response. It's easy of, course, to forget these nuances and presume your finger pulling through means *no* when it's not necessarily so. For this reason, we recommend you master sway testing until you feel confident it's a real thing, that you're reliably—accurately—testing responses, that you're conversing with whom you think you are, that your chakras are consistently 'open,' and you're comfortable doing it before using these subtler ET awareness–experiences. There are many finger-testing methods you can find on the Internet related to TMT. Any will work with ET. Use those you prefer.

2.2.1.3.1   How to Finger Test

With one exception, the various methods of finger testing work by breaking the ring formed by the thumb-tip–fingertip of one hand forming a circle, or 'O' shape using a single, extended finger of the other hand inserted into it (*Fig. 210*, center-left). Experiment with the ring circle's thumb-tip–fingertip pressure as well as the strength you use to pull your extended finger through the ring circle 'joint' until you find the right equilibrium of pressure and resistance. Nominal pressure is sufficient. Too much makes it difficult for your body to have awareness–experience of the nuanced difference between *yes* and *no* and, in any case, overwhelms the subtle 'energy' involved with sheer muscular force. You simply need enough pressure and strength to satisfy yourself that you aren't willing a *yes* or *no* response, as sometimes one inadvertently applies the pressure and strength to get a desired answer. That's confirmation bias and a disservice to you. There's no room in ET for delusion or lying to others (§ 2.1:636) because otherwise—except to fool yourself or perpetrate a fraud—what's the point?

A caveat here is that hand or finger testing multiple queries in too quick a succession can lead to spurious results, as one sometimes tests a response that's really the body's residual interaction with the previous response. Your body's interaction with chakra energy (from the spirit person's response) is residual for about three seconds during which you can retest your query without having to re-query it before it's no longer accurately testable. You can mitigate spurious results by slowing down, improving your intuition, and confirming the ET response using differently worded queries until you're satisfied you've accurately tested and interpreted the spirit person's response.

2.2.1.4   Mind Energy Testing Response

This is the subtlest ET awareness–experience. Your physically-instantiated mind (§ 1.2.2.1:253) perceives the relocation of biological 'energy' without physically testing it. I learned it by chance when laying face down stretching my spine one day in November 2020. Pondering this book, I had questions for Mina. I was too lazy to keep rolling over to free up my hands to finger test. But as queries formed in my mind, I realized I could see myself finger testing in my mind's eye and physically feel the 'energy' in my fingers. Mina confirmed it was real and a viable ET awareness–experience. I practiced over the next six weeks until he gauged my accuracy on par

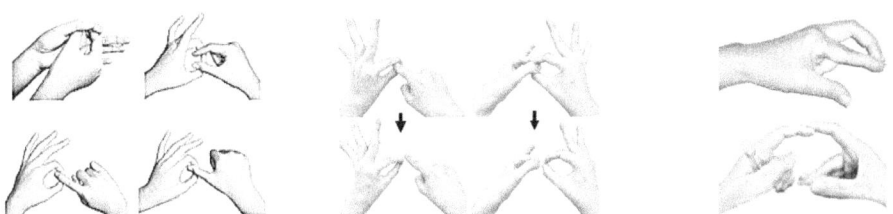

Figure 210. Finger testing stance. Breaking or pulling finger or thumb through circle (ring) or not is a 'weak' (*no*) else a 'strong' (*yes*) response. Top left: insert fingers into ring; bottom left: insert finger or thumb into ring; center left, right: straight finger and ring-ring test; top right: middle-over-index-finger; bottom right: index-on-index (pushing index down is 'weak,' or *no*, otherwise 'strong,' or *yes*).₃₀₉

with my finger testing. Even when just thinking of a query to finger test, I feel the biological 'energy' relocating in my fingers according to *yes–no–maybe* responses.

The 'energy' with this is very subtle and necessitates a refined sensitivity to it. Sometimes I can feel it whilst moving around and sometimes I can't due to ambient spirit 'energy,' distractions, or body movement. I'll also run through a series of queries, which succession of *no* responses I feel without having to test until I feel a *yes* response, which I then confirm with a physical test to be sure. Now, more often than not, I spiritually feel the interacting 'energy' as a *yes–no* and sometimes a *maybe* response upon thinking or inquiring, but before I test. As this ability develops, you might notice during finger testing that, after inserting a finger in your other hand's 'O' ring, but before trying to pull it through to determine the ET response, you already *feel* or *know* what it's going to be.

The origin of feeling your body's interaction with chakra energy in your mind without physically testing the ET response is in your 𝓛ife mind which, recall, embodies as your spirit self in the 'reflective' environment having awareness of a spirit person's responses to your queries. Your spirit self shares this awareness via spirit–physical body and mind–brain integration. People don't currently experience this level of awareness due to insufficient MBI, presently the norm for about 98% of Earth's physically alive population. The good news is that the more you energy test, improve your chakras, and develop your intuition the more your MBI improves beyond Earth's current 31% average. Approximately 50% full MBI is necessary to mind test. Mina says I discovered it when I was capable of it. Now that you're aware in advance, you'll naturally begin feeling it when your MBI reaches that level.

2.2.1.4.1 HOW TO MIND TEST

When we began this book, I had virtually no sense of energy in my body or around me. I needed Mina and the girls to do many things for me, like 're-opening' my 'closed' chakras, neutralizing ill-intentioned spirit individuals' Intentionalized 'energy' affecting my body, and so on until, little by little, I developed the necessary skill, capability, awareness, sensitivity, common sense, and the like to do these things on my own. Even so, I need Mina's assistance for some things still beyond me. Until I experienced it, mind testing never even occurred to the girls and me. You have the benefit of knowing about it in advance of your ability to do it, and can therefore seek out the ability sooner than we chanced across it.

In our experience, the easiest way to mind test is to imagine energy testing in your mind's eye. As you 'see' it happening, you'll begin feeling your body's interaction with chakra energy relevant to your body, hands, or fingers. When I think a query, I feel the 'energy' relocate in my body before physically swaying with movement. If my fingers are paused on the keyboard, I can feel the ET 'energy' between them and instantly know a query response is *yes*, *no*, and even *maybe*, which I then physically test to verify. Ayako feels where her hand will land on the other hand or arm before it actually does. You can even mind test with your hands in your pockets or on your car's steering wheel while seeing and feeling it in your mind. Just remember: the more physical distractions, the more elusive it is.

Energy Testing: Caveats & Cautions

UNLIKE THE WAY alternative diagnostic and healing modalities use traditional muscle testing (TMT) as an individualistic, clinical utility of the subconscious, energy testing (ET) is *human communication* with spirit persons, a mode of conversation between the physicospirit and spirit embodied including your own spirit self and other physical persons as they sleep, or awake if their spirit self is spirit-aware, and otherwise while awake. You can converse with anyone on any subject according to their willingness and what they know of your topic. If you want to know about spirit world, our universe, or All Existence then you can expect limitations in their knowledge and awareness. We don't talk to everyday spirit persons about topics they're unlikely to know about. For that, we turn to the relevant person, like Mina who built our universe. Yet, even he doesn't know as much about unembodied reality as the unembodied-born do. For that, we engage someone like Cosmo (§ 1.2.1.1:338). Being conversation, there are some general ET caveats and cautions to consider so your ET is productive for you.

SECTION 1
Caveats

Four caveats to consider as you engage in energy testing regard chakra health, changing ET responses, consistency, and spirit 'energy' disruptions. We consider each one as follows.

1.1 TRADITIONAL MUSCLE TESTING *vs.* ENERGY TESTING

As noted, Earth's average MBI (with an average ~105B neuron count; § 1.2.2.5.1:261) is now ~31% of human capability. This isn't enough for your mind to fully integrate, hence your physically-instantiated mind has insufficient awareness–experience of your *L*ife mind and your spirit self's experience in the 'reflective' environment. However, it's sufficient for the basic ET that's diagnostic TMT because you're only querying your spirit (*L*ife mind expressing your emergent self-aware proto-energy; ESP) self, not other spirit persons. Since your spirit body occupies the same physical space as your physical body, your embodied subconscious has full awareness–experience of your physical body down to its constituent archí.[544]

When you engage in TMT, however, you're only querying your conscious spirit self. This means your chakras can be 'closed' but your spirit self's response to your query nonetheless results in the Living-force-to-chakra-energy-to-biological-'energy' interaction as described for ET in CH. 41:623 because both encapsulate you as the querier *and* respondent; you experience relocating biological 'energy' accordingly. This basic ET isn't capable of much more than what TMT uses it for, as the magnitude of 'energy' in another spirit person's response is too strong for atrophied, weak, or 'closed' chakras to fully absorb. If you attempt ET with a spirit person while

---

544. For various reasons, this isn't always the case. When your spirit self is aware of your independent spirit embodiment in the 'reflective' environment, your two embodiments can safely separate for brief periods.

having 'closed' chakras, your MBI too restricted, or 'energy' disruptions you're unaware of, your ET responses are necessarily spurious. The reason is another spirit person's 'energy' at your level of development is greater than yours and doesn't fully translate through your chakras to interact accurately with your biological 'energy.' As you develop, you'll reduce such wrong results.

1.2   Chakra Health

Unlike with TMT, 'open' chakras are necessary for ET. If your MBI is the physical human average, or your spirit 'energy' is weak, you'll have difficulty keeping your chakras 'open' to effectively ET with a spirit person. As you practice ET and improve your chakra health, your MBI naturally improves, which helps your chakras 'open.' This process strengthens your spiritual 'energy,' which in turn helps your chakras 'open' more and stay 'open' longer. It's never the case that you want 'closed' chakras, because 'open' is integral to your physicospirit awareness–experience. Eventually, you'll develop control of your chakras and be able to Intentionally 'open' them. Visualize your chakras in a way that works for you, and practice expanding them. Recall your chakras are effectively an organ of your physical body residing in your 'reflective' body that's atrophied and weak and needs strengthening through exercise in order to use (§ 1.2.1.2.2:500). Recall, too, that you have multiple chakras. Even if one or more are sufficiently 'open,' others may be more or less 'closed.' All chakras need be sufficiently 'open' for accurate, reliable ET.

A 'closed' chakra means it's minimally interacting with Living force via the aura, reducing overall chakra energy movement in your 'reflective' body thus your physical body's biological 'energy' interaction with the full picture (§ 1.2.1.4:508). One or more 'closed' chakras are like vapor lock reducing fuel flow to an engine. Nevertheless, chakras never truly 'close' but only integrate Intentionalized Living force as chakra energy at a 10% minimum that for ET is functionally 'closed.' Over time, closed 'chakras' results in your biological 'energy' having insufficient sensitivity to chakra energy. As they 'open' more for longer, your biological 'energy' sensitivity to chakra energy naturally improves. Quite often in the early days, Ayako and El tracked our problematic ET to one or another 'closed' chakra(s) or our biological 'energy' having insufficient sensitivity to recently 'opened' chakras. Mina often insisted I let my 'tired' chakras rest for hours, days, sometimes weeks before using them again as one might with any weakened body part. It's sometimes necessary, even if frustrating. A further caveat is that, while chakras can be fully 'open' and your ET accurate, one or more chakras can be EmℒF (emotionally) 'blocked' and not functioning correctly in other ways. EmℒF 'blocks' can lead to chronic and problematic body and mental illnesses unless resolved (§ 1:577).

1.3   Changed Responses and Consistency

A spirit person might later change their ET response if re-queried when, since your (presumedly accurately tested) original query they've changed their mind, encountered more accurate information, developed a better understanding, and so forth. The important thing is they explain the change and why it's more accurate to your satisfaction, or that in your judgment the change, although substantive, is material and feels consistent. As with the scientific practice of repeated experiments yielding consistent even if somewhat different data in order to be useful, ET responses which are also data (§ 1.2.1:85) will vary individually and amongst the ET community, but should have an overall consistency if it's to inform awareness.

I began writing this book with virtually no comprehension of spirit reality as our currently very small ET community has since ET-agreed it really is. There was much I couldn't imagine, much less form coherent queries about, to which Mina told me this or that was true or false without having too much regard for *how* true or false across the totality of the topic I was querying. It's like telling a child something is true that's necessarily limited which an adult, having less-limited awareness, might regard as false. As I progressed through writing this book's material, I developed a more sophisticated understanding of the various topics covered. Over time, I improved my queries and Mina's responses expanded, broadened, and deepened my earlier comprehension. Sometimes, it seemed his current responses contradicted past ones. As I queried such anomalies, Mina would variously give me five reasons for it. First, that he'd winged his earlier answer, so it was really just a ballpark response until inquiring himself into the specifics of my query. Second, that my query was vague, ambiguous, he'd misinterpreted my intent, or I'd mis-tested (and hand't verified it) where my later query was lucid, unequivocal, he'd correctly interpreted my intent, or I'd accurately retested. Third, that he'd changed his mind. Fourth, that circumstances since the Big Healing had changed and that what was accurate at the time of my original query had since evolved new facts, such as percentages of humanity of which something is true. And fifth, that I was asking more pertinent questions that, in and of themselves, called into question my own earlier queries to which his responses now necessarily conveyed a more complete understanding than before to my less-informed queries.

Initially, for example, I so poorly imagined All Existence and the Energent that my boxed-in imagination limited my queries until I built up enough of a picture that my now-larger mental box could formulate *informed* queries to which Mina could better direct me through many (frustrating) *no* responses to a more correct understanding, instead of simply greater confusion and ignorant assumptions.

1.4 Spirit 'Energy' Disturbances

'Energy' disturbances degrade your ET accuracy or make it difficult to feel 'energy' shifts in your mind even if your chakras are fully 'open' because they're analogous to noise or static your biological 'energy' has difficulty 'hearing' chakra energy through. We consider 'upgrades,' ley lines, and flowing water.

1.4.1 Spirit 'Energy' 'Upgrades'

When we began our ET journey, my MBI was ~5% below Earth's then-average of 30%. My spirit awareness, clair senses, and so on was a tenth of what it is now. Despite a prayerful lifetime in ministry and chaplaincy, I was just a block of extrasensorial stone. My chakras' sensitivity to 'energy' were uniformly at 10%, the condition called 'closed.' Energy testing exposed them to stronger 'energies' they weren't used to. Like warm skin exposed to cold air, one, some, or all reflexively jerked 'closed' like pores, the 'energies' too much to process in their weakened, atrophied state and knocking my ET 'offline,' as we then-imagined it.

I was awash in religionism, often thinking I'd done some wrong and God closed them. I had no capabilities to speak of. The girls or Mina coaxed my chakras 'open' in what seemed like their own sweet time. The girls' explanations sounded like gibberish, the notion chakras are an 'organ' incomprehensible. Vague ET queries, mistesting, and misinterpreting was my daily dose. Plus, Mina was ever 'upgrading' our biology which changed our 'energies,' MBI, and spirit awareness and affected our chakras, fatigue, and bodies generally. As time passed, my chakras grew robust, my mindset changed, 'energies' strengthened, skills and understanding improved. As you begin your ET journey, you and your chakras will go through something similar according to your individual situation. Your 'energy' will constantly improve, your chakras playing catch-up. It will get frustrating and challenging when all you want is consistently accurate, reliable results. Keep at it. ET is best experienced in community, as it was for my daughters and me.

1.4.2 Ley Lines

Traditionally, ley lines are alignments between historical structures or sites, or earth energies considered to be healing, or power forces from which arise certain phenomena and witchcraft abilities. This is inaccurate. Ley lines are where Intentionalized Macrocosmic force (§ 2.3.7.1:528) concentrates Living force that embodies as straight lines about 75–125 feet (23–38 m) wide and a mile (1.6 km) deep in the landscape. The Living force of ley lines arises in the presence of a planet's physicospirit and visiting spirit humanity interacting with the Living force of the 'reflective' environment that concentrates as ley lines via Intentionality. They're not an emergent property, a 'natural occurrence,' or universal magic as science and pseudoscience often interpret the inexplicable. Ley lines enable physical humanity to influence (manipulate) matter–Energy (§ 2:114) in some contexts via mind, and in other contexts via technology. For example, those ancient proto-Nicaraguans and proto-Mayans who utilized Living force via their minds to heal—manipulate the cellular matter of—their bodies to power metabolism in a continual state of youth took advantage of this concentrated power of Living force (§ 2.3.4.2.1:554; § 2.3.4.2.2:554).

Ley lines are longitudinal and latitudinal (*Fig. 211*, left, right). They run irregularly spaced longitudinally as meridians between the geographic (not magnetic) poles, and latitudinally as *nonparallels* (unlike geodetic latitude) at varying angles between 0.75°–38° relative to the plane of the equator and from 0° where a single ley line circumscribes the equator to each hemisphere's greatest tangent of 80° north and 78° south (*Fig. 211*, center). Even when the magnetic poles undergo geographical change, ley lines remain fixed. They don't relate to topography, though do with structures, because both H1 and H2 (CH. 32:531) built in accord with the ley lines they sensed. Latitudinals cross longitudinals in groups of 3–12 lines at certain points (*Fig. 211*, right). This concentrated Living force integrates as an *energy point* (EP) that acts as a focal point for mind and technology to tap the greatest amount of Living force with which to more fundamentally influence matter–Energy than is available along non-intersecting ley lines, or absent them altogether.

Mind and technology can Intentionalize ley lines to influence electron flow (electricity) and its successor Mina calls *photon energy*, which is real energy ϒ as non-Fundamental Force momentarily expressing in the Energent as the interaction between up-'charged' archí and proto-energy that, in applied energy E's context, is *enérgeia* flux (§ 2.1:114–§ 2.3.2:116; § 3.7.3.3.1:139). Electricity's problem is it disrupts biological 'energy' and physicospirit integration—the electrical brain–body is symbiotic and doesn't—whereas photon energy is a natural power source. Mina estimates Earth can develop Intentionality and technology to interact with ley lines and manipulate large-scale matter in ~55–65 years. The planet has 101 ley lines and 197 EP. Seven are in the USA, for example a 6-line EP in New Mexico about five miles (8 km) east of Timberon in the south end of Lincoln National Forest, and a 9-line EP in SW Colorado about three-fourths of a mile (1.2 km) south of Point Lookout; one 3-line EP is in Kenya south of Nairobi in Tsavo West National Park area; a 4-line EP is in Thailand south of Wat Phra Bat Huai Tom Buddhist Temple in Li, Lamphun State, between Mae Ping and Mae Wa national parks; and others elsewhere.

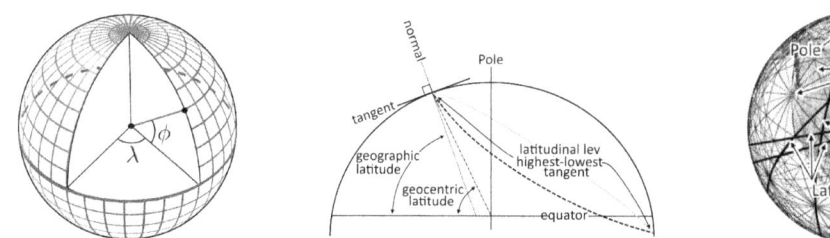

Figure 211. Ley lines; left, the graticule of the sphere where ϕ is angle of latitude and λ angle of longitude; center, maximum tangent of a latitudinal ley line; right, example of ley longitude, latitude, and EP.[310]

Because of The Corruption's effects on the physicospirit person, the concentrated Living force of ley lines disrupts the body's biological 'energy,' interfering with its sensitivity to, and interaction with, chakra energy until a person develops spiritual strength and resilience. You do this by progressively 'opening' your chakras and improving biological 'energy' sensitivity to chakra energy. ET is the best and quickest means for this because, via ET, the average person who isn't spirit-aware steadily improves their MBI and develops their physicospirit interaction with spirit humanity. Recall that, for the physicospirit person absent The Corruption's effects, the spirit environment is a seamless, 'always-on' experience.

1.4.3 FLOWING WATER

As weird as it sounds, the girls and I found ET unreliable in the shower. The reason is that water as matter-in-motion interacting with proto-energy creates stronger matter–Energy than still water. It's analogous to an up-'charged' archí moving through space where matter–Energy generates a proto-energy interaction as a photon emitting electromagnetic radiation (EMR) that's applied energy E, the only energy science understands. Since archí constitute matter emitting EMR (§ 5.4:158), water in motion emits a subtly greater EMR that's enough to disrupt the body's chakra energy by provoking weak chakras to 'close' (constrict), disrupting biological 'energy' analogous to 'noise' impairing its sensitivity to chakra energy. As you 'open' your chakras for longer periods, this EMR environment affects them less and you'll ET in the shower more accurately. If your elemental is water, it'll happen faster than if it's earth, air, or fire.

SECTION 2
Cautions

Unlike our caveats, which inform you of some anomalies to be aware of when engaging in ET, our cautions advise you to be on your guard. Mina draws your attention to three: lying, sabotage, and attention.

2.1 LYING VIA ENERGY TESTING

ET is a conversation with a spirit person being, not the subconscious or an all-beneficent universe that responds only with 'truth' and what's best for your 'higher self.' Our universe, built by a person, is an environment *of* humanity. Spiritual communication doesn't exist with anything that isn't human except animal familials, whose ability to communicate is roughly equivalent to a physically alive two-year old (equivalent to a spirit-born nine-month old; CH. 39:601). Like any conversation, a spirit person has their own thinking–feeling about things and often their own agenda when conversing with you. One should never accept ET responses carte blanche without the validation and confirmation—individually and amongst others in the ET community over time—that makes a response more than likely accurate. Science practices the same precaution in having different scientists independently run an experiment before accepting it as more than likely accurate. This is intrinsic to ET as data.

A spirit person can lie about whatever and a physical person will accurately ET their lie *as the lie*. A caveat is that, when lying about identity (§ 2.2.1.1.3:628), you will accurately ET that lie to reveal it *as* a lie. Their *yes, I'm Joe* lie will test as *no, I'm not Joe* because a person's identity is so fundamental to their self-aware proto-energy self (§ 5.2:296; § 2.1.1.1:368; Fig. 153:392) that the liar's ℒife force 'pulses' at the mere Thought of their identity. It interacts with the 'reflective' environment's Living force that overwhelms their verbalized lie with which, accordingly, the physical person's biological 'energy' doesn't interact. Topical lies don't encounter the liar's Life force in this way because, without exerting one's identity verbally or otherwise, the spirit person's Life force doesn't 'pulse.' Their verbalized response (their topical lie) is what interacts with your aura and translates to your chakras with which your body's biological 'energy' interacts to relocate magnitudes of biological 'energy' that you test as a *yes*, *no*, or *maybe* response. When you ET, you should always verify and re-verify that you're still testing the responses of the spirit person with whom you think you're conversing, and seek verification, validation, and intent. This caution goes for any spirit person, even after developing a sense of trust with them. It's a best practice.

2.2 SABOTAGE

Sometimes, your spirit family, friends, or interested others don't want you talking to spirit persons via ET, don't want you to learn of realities that conflict with theirs including their religious faith, or have some axe to grind with you, your ancestors, your race or nation, and so on. There's a single way they can sabotage your ET effort. For example, you might ET that your chakras are inexplicably 'closing' or, when teaching ET to a friend, you can't explain or reliably ET why his or her chakras won't 'open' or stay 'open' long enough to strengthen and develop. The reason may be a saboteur 'blasting' Living force that, like a shockwave sundering an environment, reflexively interrupts awareness–experience of the self by 'closing' the chakras. Your or another's inability to ET is simply symptomatic.

In all cases, ask your or another's spirit guide(s), family, friends, or others whom you trust about the problem. Remember, a saboteur might lie because, when (after death) he or she realizes the futility of certain of their life's choices, they might be overwhelmed with sorrow, grief, guilt, shame, embarrassment, anger, and the like which they don't deal with. A person joking, pranking, or just annoying you because it's fun, they can, or in their own way are trying to teach you something—recall Kengo, the chronic joker (§ 1.1:77)—doesn't constitute ET sabotage. Anger and resentment at a saboteur, while understandable, is unproductive. Consider opening, or asking others to open, a conversation toward reaching an accord with whom you believe is sabotaging your ET. We're not talking 'evil' spirits here (which don't exist), just human individuals who choose to sabotage your ET effort for reasons of their own, which a conversation might reveal and resolve. With some heartfelt care, ~99.8% of spirit persons prefer to let go their pain than continue as is. Work through it with patience and understanding, no matter how outrageous it feels.

2.3 ATTENTION

ET 'illuminates' your 'reflective' body (§ 2.1:625). Spirit persons noticing it may be curious about what you're doing since it's new on the scene, or may join your conversation without you being aware. Remember, you live physicospiritually regardless how it physically appears. When you ET, you're interacting with *people*. As you develop proficiency in ET, spirit persons may take advantage of the opportunity to talk to you, or to ask you to talk to others on their behalf. In our experience, there's nothing scary or dangerous about ET. However, when expanding your awareness and growing your circle of potential human interaction via ET from ~8 billion physical persons to another ±10 billion visiting Earth's 'reflective' environment, not to mention exponentially more tuning in from spirit world, you can expect a coincident upsurge in the human beings with whom you might now (physically *and* spiritually) interact.

Epilogue

"We wrote more than expected but less than we could; if it's not too much, perhaps it's enough."

E BEGAN THIS book November 15, 2017 and completed the text October 25, 2021 and then the pre-publication process by end of July 2022. We spent this near five-year effort in constant contact with Mina, who built our universe, and many tens of physical-born and spirit-born spirit persons while interacting with thousands, from the eldest of universal humanity and vastly older megaversal humans like Cosmo, to Mio and other Earth-born individuals as well as friends and family we knew before they died. The story of life it reveals is (for us) truly a shocking revelation. It liberates us from fear of the unknown, life, and death in providing insight and awareness of our physicospirit reality and, unlike traditional revelatory works, introduces energy testing (ET; PART V) for you to verify or correct what you've read, and to pursue your own answers.

The value of this book lies with physicospirit persons independently interacting via mind–brain integration (MBI; § 1.2.2.4:257) beyond today's ~31% average.[545] They're ripe for an alternative to the human reality we've always known. Their sense that something or everything about human existence is wrong, with no solution in the only mindset they've ever known—for which they can't imagine any other despite their ideological and utopian impositions that, for all their innovative bluster, are nothing more than variants of Accountableism—is the reason youth since the 1970s have rejected these mindsets. This book shows a different reality, an energy testable reality. Yet, it's so different, it's difficult to grasp. We plan more books in future but, for now, this book is the foundational reference work. If you want a better world, you can't build it in the context of a reality prescribing and proscribing your autonomy. One necessarily never "sews a patch of unshrunk cloth on an old garment. For the patch will pull away from the garment, and a worse tear will result" (Mt. 9:16). A total change in mindset is unavoidable because our current one only ravages others and harms the self, regardless how lofty and high-minded our dreams and motivations.

We encourage you to read this book many times, the better to absorb its wide-ranging and revolutionary content, and to experiment with ET until your experience leads you to determine it's a viable tool to converse with spirit humanity. As the ET community grows, we also encourage you to communicate with fellow energy testers because, on your own, you can never genuinely expect your ET results to be valid and correctly interpreted. As with science, everything you test you need gauge in the context of other energy testers' results. The greater your ET skill and experience, the less confirmation is strictly necessary to presume accuracy, but it's always a best practice. This is how your ET data becomes knowledge, information, and wisdom you can be confident justifies belief. For example, verify your personal-life ET results with family and friends you trust and

---

545. So-called indigo children's defining characteristic was their 32–38% MBI but, since May 2019, Mina 'upgraded' the entire population's crown chakra capability. Thus, its average MBI has been rising from ~30% in 2019 to ~31% with a high for some of ~40% as of 2021 and a few still higher. From Mina's viewpoint, the indigo concept is now redundant. Everyone is indigo. You can make yourself more spiritually self-aware by consciously choosing, then developing, your MBI.

the non-personal with others in the ET community at large. You can contact other energy testers via the ET directory at storyoflifebook.com as it develops.

Lucifer

Before we end, Mina wants to convey his general view of Tom Kapinos' *Lucifer* television series (Warner Bros.–Netflix, 2016–2021), as this book, like *Lucifer*, recasts the mindset regarding Lucifer and Michael here on Earth as well as in the physical- and spirit-born spirit worlds. *Lucifer* initially presents Lucifer (Tom Ellis) as an invulnerable, devil-may-care, roguish, lustful, and inconsiderate fallen angel who can suss out a person's deepest desire to grant favors that are repayable at a time and in a manner of his choosing. He bitterly resents his father (God) banishing him from Heaven to Hell for rebelling—rejecting him, he says—as the eternal overlord of punishment of the guilty. The series begins with him abandoning Hell for Earth and resolving never to return. His older brother Amenadiel engages in all manner of machinations to send him back. Lucifer meets Los Angeles police detective Chloe Decker (Lauren German), who's immune to his celestial abilities and detests him at first sight "on a chemical level" (s1e1, 'Pilot;' 29:01). Her resistance to his charms fascinates him. Later, his vulnerability to injury in her presence is a vexation he feels compelled to resolve and leads to his self-discovery and the character arcs of the players (§ 2.2.2:342).

Those willing to set aside their religio-cultural sensibilities to give *Lucifer* a view either like it or hate it, the latter not necessarily because Lucifer is cast as a good guy—a fallen *angel*—but more because it appears to celebrate evil and Satan as a likable, sympathetic *person*. And yet, he rejects lying and manipulation. The series also rejects DC Comics' originating focus on theology's free will problem to focus on Lucifer's rejection of suffering (Hell) and to ultimately embrace healing. Indeed, the finale has him healing the damned via couch therapy so they might resolve their guilt and transition to Heaven. God enigmatically leaves this realization to Lucifer, but it was beyond him until he challenged his reality—his mindset—by recognizing, then healing, his own suffering. The Lucifer–Chloe dynamic that leads to her loving him, and to him loving not just her but himself and therefore others, is the essence of the series. Mina's perspective is that the series' nub is the relationship between Lucifer and his identical twin Michael (which only gets airtime in its fifth season) because, in the real world, their dynamic led to The Corruption's manifestation as Accountableism which morphed Tivi'iv'z into Lucifer (Table 17:523). The series' conflict motivates his effort to replace his retiring father as God to prove he deserves Chloe's love, but in the end exposes the reality of pain and his calling not to rule the universe, but to heal the suffering.

Writer Neil Gaiman and others developed Lucifer, admittedly based in some sense on John Milton's *Paradise Lost*, for DC Comics' 1989–1996 *Sandman* series. Mike Carey then wrote an eponymous 2000–2006 spinoff. According to Mina, both writers' spirit selves are spirit-aware, recognizing their spirit reality as independent of their physical one (cf. Hitler; ch. 40:605). Mina became aware of Gaiman developing Lucifer and saw a teaching opportunity for which he recruited Gabriel, who conversed with Gaiman's spirit self about the real Lucifer's (Tivi'iv'z) life. Gaiman's spirit self didn't believe him. Nonetheless, about 10% of Gabriel's tale filtered into Gaiman's physical awareness via MBI and influenced his development of Lucifer's character. Gabriel later had the same conversations with Carey, who wasn't buying it, either. In his case, about 17% of what his spirit self learned migrated into his writing.[546]

Two other writers for the Netflix Lucifer are also spiritually self-aware and believed Gabriel's account (Mina won't identify them because their spirit selves denied permission). In their case, about 40% of his information made it into their work, primarily via Lucifer's TV struggle to accept his love for Chloe that was analogical of his real relationship with Mnèèptē (§ 1.4:14; § 4.2.1:379) and his tempestuous relationship with Michael and his Lie. It included none of Netflix Lucifer's self-loathing and antagonism with his Creator father, nor Michael's deviant and harmful behavior, none of which has any semblance to the real world. Mina hoped this unique television series might improve humanity's comprehension of its religious mindset, The Corruption, Accountableism, and reality generally but, alas, MBI limitation meant it was haphazard at best. Viewing the series having read this book, however, reveals nuances in the writing that, for us, opens to a progressively deeper understanding in accord with individual choice rooted in subconscious mind that transcends mere entertainment and its twist on the mainstream view of the human experience regarding sin, punishment, and life unfolding as the contest between good and evil.

---

546. News to their physical selves. Their spirit selves permitted Mina's mention after accepting Gabriel's story in July 2019.

Mina feels that, if given the chance, the series would eventually have achieved about a 95% real world accuracy regarding Lucifer and humanity's Accountableist experience. Unfortunately, its six seasons only managed an accuracy of 5%. There has been talk of a follow-on film. In this post-Reconciliation and *Story of Life* era of healing, Mina hopes it will be more accurate. We may develop a novelized series to tell Tivi'iv'z's and universal humanity's true (energy tested) story.

Our Final Word

When you began reading this book, perhaps you had no idea of your physicospirit reality. Fortunately, I had Ayako, El, and Moth Man (§ 1.1:4; § 1.1:61) to confirm or correct my ET discoveries. They instilled confidence not only in ET as a communications and data collection tool, but in my ET skills, too. ET takes time to develop. New energy testers need pursue a learning course, as we had to. Energy testing without verification inhibits ET skills, the ability to interpret results, and increases misinterpretation. Regardless what you believe you know, having others confirm or figuring out why they disconfirm your ET results is key to ET skills development and, therefore, real spiritual awareness. We hope this book revolutionizes your mindset and helps answer your most pressing questions in the healing context Mina intends, as it did for us. Either way, we thank you for reading it.

Part VI

Appendices

Dedication Page

1. This additional verse to Robert Lowry's song, "How Can I keep From Singing" (Bright Jewels for the Sunday School, New York: Bigelow & Main, 1869), was penned by Doris Plenn "[s]ometime in the 1950s" and handed off to folksinger Pete Seeger in 1956 (Sanga Music Inc. v. EMI Blackwood Music Inc.; EMI, 55 F.3d 756, 758 (2d Cir. 1995)). Plenn's preceding stanza: "When tyrants tremble, sick with fear, / And hear their death-knell ringing, / When friends rejoice both far and near, / How can I keep from singing?"

Chapter 1 – All Shook Up

2. [3] Moon 1996, 53–65. According to him, an illicit sexual relationship (symbolized by the "fruit" in Gen 3:1–13) between Lucifer and Eve is the original sin that separated us from God and brought about the violent, selfish world in which we live. His Divine Principle identifies Lucifer as Satan, the Devil, who consciously and willfully seduced Eve to steal Adam's place as God's son. At the same time, through 'owning' their love by converting Adam and Eve's hearts from God's originally intended unselfish lovingness to his new philosophy of selfish unlovingness, Lucifer dispossessed God and made himself god of this world (ibid, 68; Jn. 12:31, 2 Cor. 4:4).

3. [4] Emotion Code uses a pendulum or muscle test to communicate with the subconscious to identify trapped emotional energy in order to remove it so your body can heal its own disease and trauma. Dr. (of chiropractic) Bradley Nelson says he discovered it through prayer, study, and practice and popularized it in The Emotion Code (2007, 32, 91–2). In actuality, it energy tests the responses of any responding spirit person.

Chapter 2 – The Fracas

4. [9] Intense spiritual 'energy' expresses as heat one physically feels. My father later said they all endured pain in feeling 'burned,' though injury to the spirit body instantly heals via one's Intention (§ 3.2:282; CH. 30:515). I didn't know at the time they were present much less bodyguarding me.

5. [9] Nigh on 76% of spirit humanity barged into our solar system wanting answers. They packed Earth, including its ocean surface, though not the sky. When room ran out, Mina said "the vast majority hung out in space" encircling our planet and on the moon, Mars, Neptune, some of Saturn's moons, and any space rock suitable, in their minds, upon which to congregate (all in the 'reflective' environment; § 7.1.1.1:212).

6. [10] Ayako later said her original guardian angels—Gabriel's fraternal twin sister and her third-generation husband—left her immediately after the fight to help calm the situation in spirit world. They ended up needing to be away from her too long, so Lucifer—yes, he actually runs that 'department'!—replaced them with another ancient married couple of similar age, and friends with her original ones. For El, two boys her own age stepped up. In deference to my then-current infatuation with Scots-Irish redheads, Ayako announced he'd recruited "two hot redheads," which got plenty of laughs from my daughters and liberal red across my face.

7. [10] The Michael–Lucifer blow-up was so uproarious that ~60% of all guardian 'angels' and ~80% of all 'angels' came bodily to Earth to witness it, the remainder scrutinizing from afar. Of those who left their charges, some simply refused to continue being guardian 'angels' at all; others refused to go back to their current charges; still others said they'd go back when they felt the situation permitted but, right now, this issue ranked higher. The balance returned to their tasks as requested. Lucifer later told me he was "very sorry" his fight with Michael distracted so many 'angels' from their support task (CH. 31:519). Once a guardian 'angel' leaves their post, his policy is they don't remain that same person's guardian. He's ultra serious about it because, prior to the Big Healing, he alone amongst the 'angels' understood that being born into the physical world in The Corruption's milieu is a significant (if brief) sacrifice as a critical component of the human spirit world. He didn't know its exact role until after the Big Healing, just that it was essential and we thereby endure a harsh, traumatic life and, accordingly, deserve guardians' very best.

8. [10] Mina later said El correctly read the volatile situation in spirit world but incorrectly placed it in a war context, being the only context in which we could envision such a disturbance. His yes answers acknowledged her questions and fear that "war is breaking out" while refraining from technically disagreeing via no answers in the midst of a drama that realistically would have only confused us in the midst of multiple shocks and limited mindsets. Unexpected answers confound us less now because of our growth and development.

9. [10] For example, one day Michael showed up "tired" and appeared not a little "stressed," sipping an alcoholic beverage he said he once discovered on another planet and enjoyed as part of his "relaxation regimen." He was in no mood to think about the world's bigger problems and deflected my "serious" questions for inconsequential chatting on account of two of his students getting into a "big fight," an "unusual situation" amongst 'angels.' The students had rejected his mediation because the shockwave of his Lucifer scam still reverberated and his reputation was in a bit of tatters. Talking it over later, I said, "The neighborhood finding the trusted-local-priest-doing-the-altar-boys-on-the-side sort of tatters?" Michael said if he'd been drinking when I put it that way, he'd have snorted it through his nose, but yes. As it happened, Ayako's husband–wife guardian 'angels' were the parents of one of these students. Ayako went red for a laugh.

10. [10] In the Vedas and Sanskrit: Indra and Vritra, the Devas and Asuras, the Ramayana and Mahabharata; and biblically: Rev. 12:7–10, Isaiah 14:4–17, the Dead Sea Scrolls (War Scroll: 1QM, Songs of the Sabbath Sacrifice Scroll, Song 5: 4Q491–497, and perhaps the Melchizedek document 11Q13).

11. [10] Lucy (wife of British prime minister Stanley) Baldwin's vignette appears in the May 18, 1943 Washington Post, "Broadway Gazette" by Leonard Lyons, page 10, column 5, Washington, DC (https://quoteinvestigator.com/tag/pierre-daninos/ (accessed: 2018-06-25)). Mina felt Mother was trying to get Ayako to think and begin using her spirit mind in her physical life, and wouldn't actually have pressured her into their plan.

Chapter 3 – Michael's Reveal

12. [12] Yes for Sun-myung, who was spiritually strong, but of limited spiritual awareness. No for Jesus, who could fully interact with spirit world.

13. [12] We later realized that, in a general sense, this isn't always true. A number of times we thought Mina's viewpoint didn't work for us and defaulted to that of a person or 'angel.' For example, Gabriel vociferously insisted Ayako quit eating sugar. When she asked Mina about it, we understood his yes reply to mean, "if it makes you happy." One's happiness is everything to Mina. Until one clarifies their question isn't pursuing happiness per se but objective knowledge, he tends to accept how we view happiness as a default. If he didn't, he'd be intervening in our freedom without permission. Gabriel's attitude was, "Forget happy. It's at toxic levels, stop!" Ayako took Gabriel's advice. He kept at her for a couple months till she'd de-toxed. Thoughtlessly defaulting to Mina can be the logical fallacy of appealing to authority when it's better to query deeper or decide for oneself (CH. 42:633).

14. [13] Gen. 32:22–31. Mina said this event never occurred, nor was Jacob (or Esau) a real person, although some stories credited to Jacob—twins struggling in the womb, bowing seven times, offering goods to a brother—are real.

15. [14] This book is revelatory, so it is what it is. 'Mitochondrial Eve' isn't the same concept (e.g., Ayala 1995; Learn 2016). Science and religion chase their tails on this. Religion myopically climbs into the morass of scriptural infallibility and gets stuck in abject adherence to ossified authority over dynamic, testable (or at least arguable) revelatory data or reasoning. It abandoned to querulous science the search for comprehension of the bricolage of life, which (regarding Adam and Eve) largely concludes: "[W]e can be confident that finding evidence that we were created independently of other animals or that we descend from only two people just isn't going to happen. Some ideas in science are so well supported that it is highly unlikely new evidence will substantially modify them, and these are among them . . . DNA evidence indicates that humans descend from a large population because we, as a species, are so genetically diverse in the present day that a large ancestral population is needed to transmit that diversity to us . . . every genetic analysis estimating ancestral population sizes has agreed that we descend from a population of thousands, not a single ancestral couple. Even though many of these methods are independent of each other, all methods employed to date agree that the human lineage has not dipped below several thousand

individuals for the last three million years or more—long before our lineage was even remotely close to what we would call 'human.' Thus the hypothesis that humans descend solely from one ancestral couple has not yet found any experimental support—and it is therefore not one that geneticists view as viable" (Venema et al. 2017, 55). This is inaccurate for the reasons described in EARTH'S HUMAN HISTORY (CH. 32:531).

Scientific theories propose hypothetical mechanisms to explain data (observations). Specific consequences (predictions) of a proposition are developed. Scientists verify if the consequences (predictions) hold up. Energy (muscle; sway) testing opens a hitherto unknown mode of inquiry for gathering (spiritual; revelatory) data to propose previously unimagined hypotheses to which one can then apply empirical or logical analysis. While science says, "[y]ou simply cannot appeal to forces outside nature in the quest for understanding" (Ruse 2007, 285), energy testing pushes the boundary of "nature." Its data is akin to questioning a witness (making observations) from which one gathers testimony (data) to verify. One then empirically draws or reasons conclusions and consequences. We present energy-tested data herein as 'revelatory' because it's revealed, meaning energy tested. We expect the data will both increase and filter through humanity's reasoning faculties to eventually establish its empirical bonafides.

16. [14] She's from a different human-inhabited planet. Lucifer said the closest Earth language to spell its pronunciation is the Bantu language Gusii, centered on Kisii town in Kenya, Africa. Using the International Phonetic Alphabet (IPA), we initially spelled it mnɛɛptee, with each /ɛ/ pronounced as 'e' in 'dress' and drawn out, and the final /ee/ pronounced as in 'deep,' and short. I thought it sounded rather like ancient Egyptian as with Anck-Su-Namun in *The Mummy* (1999; film) or Nefertiti *The Mummy Returns* (2001), but Lucifer was all "Noooo, I don't think so."

17. [14] Mina didn't build our universe with any human–'angel' love prohibition although he didn't personally approve, either, because he viewed 'angels' as teachers and guides and, therefore, considered those *in that role* liaising with physical humans to be inappropriate. He reconsidered after observing Michael and Lucifer's gentlemanly behavior with Mnèèptē during her physical life and let it be known he had no problem with it. With The Corruption in play, however, his effort had little effect on the outcome of Michael's Lie.

18. [14] Michael was 18 years old at the time, Lucifer 22, Mnèèptē 24, and Gabriel 26. That was ca. 7.199MYA (Fig. 182:523).

19. [15] Lucifer and Mnèèptē consummated their relationship while she still lived in the physical world. Michael and other 'angels' knew about it because Lucifer didn't hide it. He had no reason to suppose their relationship was problematic—much less *wrong*—especially considering, in this early period of human history, Mnèèptē was two years "plus or minus one Earth month" older than Lucifer, thus 24 years old when their relationship kindled. Her planet orbits its sun comparatively faster than Earth, making her years shorter, hence her age somewhat younger than 24 as we reckon it.

20. [15] We're not *locked* in our physical body while alive. During sleep, our spirit self can 'detach' from our body to do whatever it likes until awakening pulls us back. Our vitiated spirit awareness means the time we spend on the 'spiritual plane' during sleep goes consciously unremembered except as dreams, déjà vu, intuitive feelings, and such like (§ 1.2.2.7.3:267).

21. [15] "St. Michael is one of the principal angels; his name was the war-cry of the good angels in the battle fought in heaven against the enemy and his followers" (https://www.catholic.org/encyclopedia/view.php?id=7948 (accessed: 2021-11-23)).

22. [15] Beginning with simple spiritism, animism, and shamanism until people organized spirituality into religion.

23. [15] It took me through August 2018 to comprehend it in the version you're reading.

24. [15] From my autobiography *Victim to Victor* (2003, limited; republication in 2024). I usually found my out-of-the-box self careening the wrong way down the Unification Church's tightly-boxed one-way street.

25. [16] When Sun-myung proclaimed that Satan–Lucifer "surrendered" and returned to God owing to his unconditional love for him (Moon 1999, 11–12).

26. [16] They've had twelve children to date. Michael disclosed he'd never married, but later happily recounted his engagement to an Iroquois woman (d. 1875). Kir-el presumed they'd broken up when he later answered *no* to her query "Are you still engaged?" But his *no* was because they'd married by then, so were, literally, no longer engaged. When I sang out "Congratulations, Michael!" he strongly pushed back a *no* response, surprisingly chiding me for thinking in the back of my thoughts that his wife was a "consolation prize," or that he'd "just picked anybody" to "level up" to Lucifer. I hadn't consciously noticed, and felt chastised. So, *ahem*. A good lesson to always dig into the what and why of energy test responses.

27. [16] Michael realized he was thoroughly in the wrong in 1999 when Lucifer reconciled with Mnèèptē and put everything behind him. His change of heart toward Michael, and Sun-myung declaring on January 13, 2001 "The Day of the Coronation of God's Kingship," his 2003 proclamation of *Cheon Il Guk* (Korean: "Cheonju Pyeonghwa Tongil Guk [천주평화통일국] (the Nation of Cosmic Peace and Unity), or simply, *Cheon Il Guk* [천일국]; "The words Cheon Il refers to the singular reality encompassing both heaven and earth. Cheon Il Guk implies that two people unite and form a nation. (360-086, 2001.11.12)" in headline, "International President at the 2017 Mother's Day Hyojeong Culture Festival in Tokyo," May 14, 2017 (https://cheonilguk.blogspot.com/; accessed: 2021-12-03)), each predicated on his concept that unconditionally loving Lucifer–Satan had enabled his healing and repentance and resolved the human Fall, inspired Mother (P'najj; § 1.2:336) to conceive her second son—Mina being the first—in March 2003, and physically born in December 2003. Sun-myung unknowingly followed this up with his proclamation of the "Age Before the Coming of Heaven" on May 5, 2004 (Moon, "Cheon Il Guk is the Ideal Heavenly Kingdom of Eternal Peace," June 13, 2006; http://www.unification.net/2006/20060613_1.html (accessed: 2022-01-30)). All these pronouncements celebrated, for him, the end of the Fall of Man's grip on humanity, the restoration in principle of God's relationship with us, and the imminence of the Kingdom of Heaven (the Ideal World).

Michael knew of Mother's second son but not when she'd conceived, because Mina only told him after the birth in a larger conversation about Lucifer's Sun-myung-inspired change and his own need to come clean about his Lie. Michael always came away from his series of conversations about this with Mina unwilling to admit to it and feeling judged, even though Mina obviously wasn't since he was loving him by respecting his autonomy and encouraging him to deal with it of his own volition without any looming punishment or judgment.

28. [16] Through the not-too-well-understood principles of reality that quantum entanglement (Parity; § 6.11.3:197) only imperfectly describes, Mina is aware of and connected with everything in the universe such that every human being, including the spirit selves of the physically-alive, could 'receive' his 'broadcast' and 'know' the full details of what had just transpired in our house.

29. [17] Mediums hijacking messages from spirit persons for their own purposes is a common problem virtually impossible to detect unless one can smell BS. Healthy skepticism includes this book, of course, which admittedly is so far off the bell curve you'd be nuts to take it just on faith. Unlike a medium's 'mystery of faith,' we teach you in PART V how to test it yourself to draw your own conclusions from your own experience instead of relying on ours.

Chapter 4 – The Big Healing

30. [20] Mina says El correctly used the word "apology" here but, at the same time, it's infused with many complex feelings and interpretations by Lucifer. Michael "apologizing" and Lucifer's remark did not imply any sort of Accountableism by either one.

31. [21] Mina said, "I expected the NCC would disappear, but wasn't sure till I was sure." I could say he can sure be enigmatic, but I intuited the quote to which he assented, so it could just be me.

32. [21] *Fallen* describes the universal human condition that promotes our ancient need to recognize our incomprehensible world as a place of the sacred and the profane—starting, perhaps, with the earliest human burial rituals, deitic carvings, and the like—and that humans in general became profane which, through interactions with the sacred, can restore their sacredness. Not all religions or cultures have a descent-from-original-nature myth as do most myths (Witzel 2012) and the three principal monotheisms. But all people have a theory of accountability, from explicating how that tree falling on Evil Bob was divine karmic judgment right down to promulgating why bad things happen to good people. Aside from spiritual experiences that independently lead toward a belief in gods, spirits, spirit worlds, and the like, the demand for accountability in others serves up much of the energy behind the sense that human misbehavior results in—which natural disaster (or, failing that, Hell) delivers—divine justice (punishment). We can postulate, using conceptual frameworks like the archetypal psyche, "which is manifested in universal patterns and images such as are found in all the world's religions and mythologies" (Edinger 1992, 3; Witzel 2012), a "plausible psychological basis for the fall/salvation monomyth, that . . . corresponds

to something very basic and important in the human condition, and is something universal. We would therefore expect it to find expression in myths and religions across cultures." (Uebersax 2018, par. 18).

33. [21] Such as Richard Dawkins' argument "that a predominant quality to be expected in a successful gene is ruthless selfishness. This gene selfishness will usually give rise to selfishness in individual behaviour" (Dawkins 1989, 2), a supposition that presumes causality in correlation.

34. [21] Religions, philosophies, and myths have their own views of the negative consequences of humanity separating itself from some original, paradisiacal existence. Even atheists and materialists advocating people being better than they are is just a roundabout secular way to reference sin. Most everyone knows that sin is (usually other people) simply not living as they should. Of course, when it comes to how one *ought* to live, the devil's in the details.

35. [21] As in sociobiology: originally proposed as 'hardwired' coding of the brain that begets social behavior, such as patterns of dominance and submission evolutionarily held over from early hominids' hunting life (Tiger et al. 1974).

36. [22] From Pierre Teilhard de Chardin (1959, 182) but somewhat recast in this book. The noosphere is not a collective identity, a collective consciousness, or even a "thinking layer" (ibid), but a collective mental state or, more properly, a *way of being* (WOB; § 2.2.1.1:234) although one never moving to Teilhard's future "Omega point" evolutionary end state (ibid, 192, 259–60), because that's wishful thinking from blind conjecture.

37. [22] French sociologist Émile Durkheim (d. 1917) presaged this understanding with his observation that, "The totality of beliefs and sentiments common to the average members of a society forms a determinate system with a life of its own. It can be termed the collective or common consciousness [French: *conscience collective*; not to be confused with *conscience* in English] . . . By definition it is diffused over society as a whole, but nonetheless possesses specific characteristics that make it a distinctive reality . . . it is independent of the particular conditions in which individuals find themselves. Individuals pass on, but it abides . . . it does not change with every generation but . . . links successive generations to one another. Thus it is something totally different from the consciousnesses of individuals, although it is only realised in individuals" (1984, 38–9). Durkheim's concept "mediates conscious and unconscious religious factors within society" with "psychological implications" (Greenwood 1990, 485, 494) while Carl Jung's tenably more famous collective *un*conscious "mediates conscious and unconscious religious factors within the psyche" with "social implications" (ibid). Two sides to the same coin and both at least arguably derived from German philosopher Arthur Schopenhauer (d. 1860; ibid, 485, 494). This *negative* variant of the collective consciousness suffuses not merely a discrete collective—a physical world organization, culture, or society—but physical and spirit humanity in toto at once with a set of characteristics consistent with its negative impetus. The NCC expresses the mental state of the noosphere (§ 4.2:379).

38. [22] de Chardin 1959, 181. Noogenesis is unrelated to proto-humanity, arising in 𝔥uman development unrelated to a physical biosphere.

39. [22] "The NCC prevented Mina from healing people or working with humanity . . ." (McKeon 2017–19, 48). He could, however, work with 'angels' owing to their obvious spirit awareness although couldn't heal them. "He said it was virtually impossible for him to penetrate and thus his effort to help and guide humanity was always thwarted. Even if the NCC wasn't universal early on, it blocked him from anyone influenced by it. They simply wouldn't listen to or receive anything from Mina" (ibid). Perhaps trained that God is omnipotent (yet inexplicably powerless before human avarice), you might scoff at Mina's remark the NCC was so ingrained that he could exert barely any influence or healing. In counterpoint, consider reasoning with a person so utterly convinced of their worldview they're immune to contrary evidence, such as believers in a flat Earth for whom contradictions are contrivances or distortions. What they accept, they insouciantly bend to fit their perspective (e.g., Natalie Wolchover, "Are Flat-Earthers Being Serious?" *Live Science*, May 30, 2017). How does one enlighten such a person when taking them into orbit necessarily involves 'trickery'? Similarly, the incriminatory story of life exclusively controlled and fostered through the ages via religion, philosophy, and culture, energized by the false reality of The Corruption and Michael's Lie, was an all-but insurmountable obstacle for Mina. This, not an indifferent, punitive, or testatious creator is the reason human history churns through its perverse bedlam generation to generation ad nauseam.

40. [22] The first 'angels' are Mina's own children with his spouse, Ag'poprje (§ 2.2:341). Those 'angels' then procreated the entire 'angelic,' or *spirit-born*, community that, in turn, sired the first physical-born humans, making us all Mina's descendant grandchildren (§ 1.1.3:533; § 2.1.3:543).

41. [22] Neuroscientist Richard Burton remarks on habit: "The brain is only human; it, too, relies on established ways. As interneuronal connections increase, they become more difficult to overcome . . . habits, whether mental or physical, are exasperating examples of the power of these microscopic linkages. At the most personal level, most of us glumly acknowledge that we could abandon many of our failed self-improvement efforts if we could somehow painlessly alter these neural networks" (Burton 2008, 53). But habits, like psychiatrically diseased "[n]etworks aren't localized like a spot of rust on a fender. They aren't separable into their component parts any more than a cake can be reverse engineered into eggs, sugar, flour, water, and chocolate. These networks *are* the brain" (ibid, 54, 10; that said, the physical brain isn't the habituating bottleneck, it's the ethereal mind). We might think of the NCC as a neural network writ large, built from our "skein of decisions" (Heffernan 2011, 20) multiplying in us mushroom-like across generations from the spore of Michael's Lie premised on The Corruption. We can productively understand all this through the lens of 'quantum entanglement' (Parity; § 6.11.3:197) by which Mina is 'aware of all things' in the universe and can, within parameters, affect their states.

42. [22] Later in the day, after hearing of the Big Reveal and Big Healing, Ayako confided she'd felt abandoned the previous evening when El had run into my arms and we'd stood "safely" behind the kitchen counter while she'd felt pinned in her chair and "blowtorched" by the 'energy' of the 'angelic' fight; and then, even more primally, during our later prescriptive discussions with Mother and Mina following the tempest. Hearing that, having seen and heard her pain, I honestly felt a cad. Despite my faux pas, she announced on November 10, 2017 that her "clinical depression"—troubling her throughout childhood but especially since middle school—had simply "disappeared and is now totally gone." Her ongoing affect backed up her pronouncement.

43. [22] Contrary to our initial understanding of Mina's one-week healing schedule, he finished the actual work in a day then took another six to recuperate and recharge. Likewise, as he continually heals the roughly 110 people who die just on Earth alone every single minute (158,116 per day; United Nations' *World Population Prospects*, 2011 (2010 Revised); mean figures for 2015–2020; https://www.un.org/en/development/desa/population/publications/pdf/trends/WPP2010/WPP2010_Volume-I_Comprehensive-Tables.pdf (accessed 2020-04-20)), he's not getting the same downtime to recuperate and recharge and is drawing on 'energy' reserves from throughout the universe, including (he says) various specific, capable individuals.

44. [23] A quick read-up is Ellen Hendriksen, "Why Do We Self-Sabotage?" *Psychology Today*, October 10, 2017 (https://www.psychologytoday.com/us/blog/how-be-yourself/201710/why-do-we-self-sabotage (accessed: 2018-01-09)).

45. [23] In the car a few days before Christmas 2017, I felt a strong pressure-*cum*-pain around my left temple, usually one of several signals someone in spirit world is trying to get my attention or there's just an energetic conversation or activity going on around me. Ten minutes of hand testing later revealed my Uncle Joe (his real name; d. 2004) wanting to talk. I asked, "Did you get healed October 13th or afterwards?" *No*. Well, I'd forgot our experience between midnight and 2 AM October 11th when all my children's Japanese ancestors, except one, refused healing. As for my uncle, he'd refused it even after that day's momentous events (which he readily acknowledged he knew of) because he'd felt angry with Mina on account of what turned out to be "the lies of the [Catholic] church." I said, "Why don't you come hang out at our house with everybody? You're totally welcome. It'll be fun." *No*. Some days later, he did ask Mina for healing but didn't feel it. "Yeah," I said, "something you don't want to let go is blocking it, which means you don't *really* want to be healed. You should look into that." He did let go his religious anger (and whatever else) so that, by July 2018 when I checked in with him, he now *felt* healed and was happily exploring infinite spirit world with a renewed interest in history.

46. [25] McKeon 1998. The book's argument builds off Unificationism's (now-deprecated) biblical Cain-Abel dynamic (Moon 1996, 190–2; Gen. 4).

47. [25] I got a taste of that in January 2018 when Mina let me know it was my wife's family in spirit world—wanting some accountability for their perception of how our marriage went—that provoked two back-to-back medically 'unprovoked' seizures, first during my mom's funeral mass, and then while tying my boots to check out of the emergency room. My face, ribs, back and all my torso muscles took a real beating from face planting in the floor and violently seizing in a grand mal twice in one day. Mina, Lucifer, my spirit guides, and guardian 'angels' were adamant they couldn't stop or even always successfully block such things ('ill-intention'—how things like this are done—is invisible even in spirit world) unless her family agreed to cease and desist. They didn't seem to particularly care they were disrupting Mina's work, either. I needed over three months' recovery to resume this book. So it was up to me. I got them on the horn so to speak and made peace with them; they agreed to leave me be. My new awareness of Mina, freedom, consideration, and

doing no harm robbed me of any resentment I surely felt justified to manufacture over this incident. Instead, I found myself understanding how they were feeling and actually empathized—possibly on account of empathizing with my wife and stepdaughter's post-separation travails—and accepted this event the way I'd accept a little rain on my parade.

Chapter 5 – Our Six-day Prolegomenon

48. [28] I can't say with conviction that I felt particularly different after having various trapped emotional energies cleared from me. But Ms. Medium, a 'licensed' Emotion Code practitioner, said my great-great grandfather from Ireland was there with us since some of the emotional energy trapped in me originated in his experience dodging early 19th-century British justice. That experience stirred me to persuade Ayako to attend the ThetaHealing workshop, which arguably paved the way later on for El to pull the pin on her curiosity grenade.

49. [29] (Stibal 2011, 143) "Visualize bringing up the energy through your feet, opening up all of your chakras as you go. Go up out of your crown, out to the Universe. Go beyond the Universe, past the white lights, past the dark light, past the white light, past the jelly-like substance that is the Laws, into a pearly, iridescent white light, into the Seventh Plane of Existence" (ibid, 224–33, "Dna Activation"). The seven planes are as follows. First, inorganic material. Second, organic material. Third, protein-based (human, animal) life, the purpose of which is to experience the challenge of emotion, instinct, and a physical body but which is an illusion, a figment of our minds. Fourth, spirit world, a "waiting room." Fifth, "Master's" penthouse after graduating from the fourth level: Jesus, Buddha, etc. and divided into multiple levels of "vibration and consciousness;" so, even in this rarefied world you're socially stratified by spiritual development. Sixth, Laws. And seventh, Creator of All That Is and Source energy that powers the works. "This is the first time in the history of humanity that the planes of existence have been opened up simultaneously so that they can be understood and utilized as never before" (Stibal, "What Are the Seven Planes of Existence?" *Heal Your Life*, January 27, 2016; https://www.healyourlife.com/what-are-the-seven-planes-of-existence (accessed: 2018-08-23)). In reality, Mina and 'Source' energy have always been freely available to everyone. People simply tune it out for the reasons noted in this book, although less so once in spirit world where physical life appears in its proper perspective. Mina says the physical–spirit universe exists in objective space. Whatever we create (even if only in our imagination), if we can interact with it then it's real.

50. [29] While I'd stayed overnight Friday and Saturday with friends, Ayako stayed with Ms. Medium, eating food from her backyard garden and getting, we later discovered, 'poisoned' by her toxic ('ill-intentioned') spiritual energy that unbeknownst to us (including Ms. Medium) permeated her household. Her 'poison' took El and me 1–3 weeks and Ayako more like seven to flush out. We suffered flu-like symptoms that in Ayako's case simply wouldn't abate. New, unopened foods or those not prone to spoilage that we'd consumed trouble-free just days earlier now sickened us, particularly Ayako. We finally grew suspicious and queried Mina. He identified Ms. Medium and Vianna's negative, "ill-intentioned energy" as the culprits. There was nothing to do, he said, but "let it dissipate over time." In the meantime, "remove from your pantry Ms. Medium's garden vegetables and all the 'ill-intentionally' contaminated foods," which he identified. "Negative, dark spiritual energy is powerful stuff and best avoided," he told us. This led to a wider discussion on ThetaHealing and its founder, Vianna Stibal. Mina revealed the toxic spiritual energy clinging to the whole ThetaHealing program and "infecting" those coming into contact with it results from Vianna's motivation and spiritual condition. Instead of connecting people to God, he said she's actually connecting them to her negative "energy force." Some practitioners report (and Mina agrees) this is actually a dark, negative 'entity,' meaning a human person in spirit world (e.g., Trisha Howell; http://fraudthetahealing.com (accessed: 2018-05-07)) along with increases in physical ailments and spiritual dysfunctions (ibid). According to Mina, her 'negative—ill-intentioned—energy,' infused into ThetaHealing, results from her "grudge against humanity" for her physical ailments (harm). This is similar to the imagined though poorly understood psychology of computer virus creators (e.g., "Chapter 5—Malware: Can Virus Writers be Psychologically Profiled?" in Kirwin and Power 2012, 79–85; Chad Perrin, "10+ reasons why people write viruses," *Tech Republic*, May 4, 2009; https://www.techrepublic.com/blog/10-things/-10-plus-reasons-why-people-write-viruses/ (accessed: 2018-10-10)).

51. [30] I'd crankily missed 2016's REFUEL thanks to the hybrid battery failing in my fancy Prius. A conversation with my dad while driving to day two of 2017's REFUEL twitched my antenna, so I asked him on a lark if he'd had anything to do with the October 2016 battery fail—and *surprise!*—he'd sabotaged it. That immensely shocked me on a moral *and* technical level. I mean, *Dad!* But, how? Some people in spirit world go to immense trouble to affect our life situations in positive or negative ways per their motivation. Throwing spiritual monkey wrenches isn't any different from the physical version most of us experience at some point in life, so that wasn't so hard to buy into. Physical death is just a transition from one mode of living to another, from one type of body and one set of physics to another. Why would our mind or attitude change when they're the same whichever body we're using? Even when now having the option of Mina's healing, some of the daily-dying refuse it. Our body, environment, and awareness of a bigger reality than we ever imagined might change, but our heart and mind not necessarily so much. We're still human, after all. But how my dad killed my hybrid battery—in simple terms, he'd made himself an 'energy vampire' much as such people drain our physical energy—and drained susceptible cells in my HV battery until at least one triggered the onboard computer that disabled the car. Mina said it was quite a bit of effort for my dad to accomplish, so he had to be serious about not wanting me to go to REFUEL 2016.

52. [30] My daughters instinctively disbelieved the suicide tales and spent months delving deep into the murky world of Japanese heavy metal, eventually deciding both were murdered and their best guess by whom. They were discerning sleuths, and opened an energy testing conversation with Hidé and Taiji on Tuesday, October 10, 2017. Each provided details of their lives and the day's events leading up to their deaths, and their reactions to their dead bodies unexpectedly confronting them. They explained their murders, Taiji by a colleague and Hidé by a rival band member. Taiji had felt drawn to our house months earlier after hearing "there's this girl going to do something big," and his friend Hidé tagged along. That Tuesday wasn't their first visit. Weeks before, Ayako's bedroom light switch began to now and then physically move itself to the 'off' position (Hidé trying to get her attention). She'd stalk over and slap it back on. I was frankly a little skeptical. I never thought she was lying; perhaps mistaken? "No!" she spat. "When your light goes out and you find the switch in the off position—well, what then, Dad? Was I mistaken my light was even *on?*" Then she felt touches on her skin, saw someone very "dark" standing over her bed in the half-lit groggy hours of the morning (that was Taiji, still rip-roaring mad over his murder, hence of pretty 'dark' energy), heard noises, and generally felt haunted. She couldn't sleep and increasingly felt unsafe. She finally broached her angst on the ride home from church one Sunday whereupon, arriving home, I marched to her room and militantly commanded whoever was hanging around to "get the F— outta here!" Ayako said she slept her best in months that night.

Only during their marathon sessions with Hidé and Taiji Tuesday and Wednesday did the girls figure out they were behind many of these events. It's a huge effort for spirit people to manipulate physical objects, and one Hidé only occasionally managed. He admitted I'd scared "hell out of him" when I'd ordered him out. He'd cleared off for weeks before tiptoeing back in, the sneak. Judging by Ayako's eventually renewed comments about spirits in her room, his timeframe sounded about right. She introduced Taiji to me midweek just before the Big Event. Recalling the intensity of my spiritual energy when I'd kicked him out of Ayako's room, he refused to enter my bedroom where I was then in bed vainly attempting sleep (he was resentful and bitter over his murder; that depresses one's spiritual energy relative to another not having that negative emotion). He preferred speaking from the door—a little head-start distance twixt us—though I can't imagine why. What was I going to do? It's not as if I could kick his ghostly seat through his immaterial crown. He had the upper hand all around (I was forgetting my spirit self (body) can directly interract). Not your usual paranormal encounter, I suppose. Eventually, we got friendly. As angry as Taiji still was at being murdered in his fifties, Hidé's murder in his young thirties evoked such eviscerating emotions that, even three decades later, reminders overwhelmed him. Ayako partially healed both, though Taiji "backed off after I'd just healed three things because it was all so hard for him." The Big Healing then finished the job. Spending time with the girls seemed cathartic for them both. Our "death-convos" triggered their emotions less and less. Ultimately, they decided to "just stay away" when their respective murderers inevitably arrived in spirit world. "Taiji says what's done is done, Dad," Ayako sagely said. Yep, life goes on, here *and* there.

53. [30] Until then, the girls thought they were part African through their mom. Instead, they found that, despite her looking African, she was Carib Indian (Polynesian) paired with Caucasian plus Japanese, Korean, and Chinese through their great-great grandmother *Obāsan*. In their minds, the ancestry surprise outweighed my spiritual, religious, cosmological, and cultural shocks that sometimes left me moping around the house. "At least you weren't deceived about where you came from, Dad," they'd artfully chuckle. But they left no doubt just how ecstatic they were to be Asian. Mina says modern Hawaiians are closest to how some American Indians used to look, and North American Indians had both curly and straight hair that tended to straighten through intermixing with Europeans. He said that when Europeans arrived there were "approximately 19 million" Indians in today's

geographical United States (∼6.79M today; USCB; https://worldpopulationreview.com/countries/united-states-population (accessed: 2022-04-18)) with, as of 2021, ∼98.5% dying from oppression, war, and related causes, up from ∼60% had Europeans never arrived.

54. [30] I was aching to tell my dad's tale to my children—his own grandchildren after all—but he flat out refused permission for weeks. When he relented, they yawned. Still, it was a shocker for me. I recall him pontificating years ago on the moral turpitude of pilots returning to his WWII aircraft carrier with bubbly stories of strafing Japanese civilians on the beaches and elsewhere. I always thought that was the source of his strident claims to pacifism and his snarled "No!" when I'd wondered back in 1981 if he'd fight or kill to defend my mom and sisters from rape or murder. I was 22 years old then, and could only look upon his pacifism with incomprehension and, frankly, revulsion. The story he now recounted in the car—retested with Ayako several times including while writing this endnote to be certain I'd got it right—was that when he went to spirit world in 2012, someone spitefully told him (and he'd believed) that God was angry because he'd put providentially-important Sun-myung Moon's life in danger during his Pacific War service. To my dad, Sun-myung was the fruity, self-proclaimed Second Coming of Christ, but now . . . well, damn, maybe he was?

    Here's the story. When young Sun-myung crossed by ferry from Japan to Korea across the Korea Strait, my father was at the same time prepping a carrier-based fighter for a mission. His intent while doing this work was that the plane and pilot kill "plenty of Japs." Soldiers or civilians, the distinction was without a difference. The revelation for me was that it was wholly out of character for the dad I knew based on the war's indiscriminate killing he'd tirelessly inveighed against. This aircraft spotted Sun-myung's ferry and reported it. I asked Mina if he'd ask the plane's pilot to corroborate. The pilot—whose name I didn't get permission to reveal—graciously did. He said he didn't know anything about my dad's situation, but that he did spot the ferry and reported it but didn't attack. Obviously, the ship safely arrived in Korea. Sun-myung said he never saw a plane overfly his ship, as he'd spent the voyage below decks. So, he was no help. Mina later said he was never upset with my dad because that's not his way. My dad's mal-intent was pretty small potatoes anyhow. Still practicing Emotion Code and ThetaHealing at this time—the Big Healing still being a few days away—I asked my dad if he wanted to be healed of this feeling of trauma and guilt. He did, and Mina healed him. Both Emotion Code and ThetaHealing are adamant that practitioners absolutely honor and respect the freedom of persons, and Mina confirms its importance. So, I learned to not only never attempt healing against a person's will or without their permission, but also to never share a person's information out of school. I argued (if you could call it that) with my dad several times for his consent to tell the girls and maybe others but he was resolute: *No*. Dang, I'd have to wait.

55. [31] This is an ancestral trace using spirit sources via energy testing. Born in 1921, *Obāsan*'s Japanese name is Ai Akiō (what we'd thought was her ethnic *Amami* surname—as *Obāsan* had spelled it out for us—was actually a codeword for her living family). Her family had forcibly separated her from her daughter with a Chinese aristocrat in Beijing and sent her home in disgrace to Okinoerabu Island (沖永良部島), about forty miles north of Okinawa in the Ryukyu chain. American bombs killed her in July 1945 at the island's airport in today's town of Wadomari. She thought it was probably a June 30th raid I'd read about online, but wasn't entirely clear anymore (we've found that people can't always recall details of their physical lives over time, as happens anyway while alive). She felt crushed and bitterly angry with her family, even if not one bit with Americans for killing her, and couldn't forgive them or overcome her grief at having been separated from her baby daughter. At that point, we were healing people using Emotion Code techniques but not yet realizing we could simply skip right to asking Mina to do it. El was eager to relieve *Obāsan*'s suffering, and I did the Emotion Code work in spite of her extended family—we counted well over thirty people—loudly arguing over how she was characterizing them. They refused en masse to be included in the healing and derided her for even wanting it. Well, funny thing. Her experience of having her trapped emotions released—particularly heartbreak and fear—and experiencing from Mina what it would feel like to live without them was so profound and transformative, and her 'energetic' response so electric, that El sensed the family now clamoring for it, too, as if shocked from a daze. All but three obstinate holdouts, that is. When Mina then healed *Obāsan*'s extended family—here, the trapped emotions were primarily guilt, shame, and the like—these last three threw in the towel. We got quite a (not roundly appreciated) laugh out of that.

    All the anger, enmity, resentment, hurt, despair, sorrow—all of it—disappeared as this family transformed as Mina infused them with how it would feel to live with emotions and beliefs opposite to what they'd been living with. They forgave each other and themselves, felt love and acceptance for and by each, and released any hatred from World War II. *Obāsan*'s older brother Kengo, for example, an inveterate joker, had died a coerced *kamikaze*. My daughters felt tears and emotions pouring from this family and especially their new BFF *Obāsan*. Their new energy and mood played across my daughters' faces and through their energy and body language. This vignette, along with my Uncle Joe's (EN 45:647), illustrates from our practical experience that people are people, here or in spirit world, and that not everyone wants, or is ready, to be healed of trauma. But when they are ready, Mina doesn't wait. He applies no conditions or judgment. He just heals, loves, and cares. If you think you're special because your 'sins' are so base that Mina—'God'—could never want to heal, or love, or talk to you, well, you're selling him and yourself short. You don't have to apologize, repent, change, promise the moon, or anything. You simply need let go your sorrows and woes; even subconsciously (or via your spirit self) is sufficient.

56. [32] ". . . on July 2 [1945] the Japanese military announced a *levée en masse* of civilians. 'In less lofty terms,' [Edward J.] Drea writes, 'these woefully untrained children, old men, and women were beasts of burden who cleaned debris after air raids, portered supplies on their backs, and, armed with bamboo spears, were used as cannon fodder. Americans had witnessed them in all these roles on Okinawa.' On Okinawa, Japanese forces had sacrificed the Okinawan people, 200,000 of whom perished" (Ferrell 1994, 212, 10). Also, "Many Okinawans died at the hands of the Japanese, who used them as human shields or forced mass suicides. Masahide Ota, a former governor of Okinawa, said he uncovered World War II archives that Imperial Japan considered Okinawans not to be pure Japanese and therefore expendable. 'Imperial Japan used Okinawans as a sacrifice. We have not been treated as human beings but as goods to be used,' he said" (Matthew Carney, "Okinawa's horrific World War II history driving battles with US and Japan," Australian Broadcasting Corp., May 15, 2015; https://www.abc.net.au/news/2015-05-15/caught-in-the-middle-okinawa-still-battling-japan-and-us/6473054 (accessed: 2018-09-13)).

57. [32] El, on fire to be a singer and model, had months earlier reached out to and met online Japanese megastar Akiō (a pseudonym) with whom she developed a mentoring friendship. After I went to sleep, the girls learned they're his second cousins through his still-living grandmother, who is *Obāsan*'s younger sister (aged 5 at *Obāsan*'s 1945 death; she'd heard stories but never knew what happened to her older sister and brother). El immediately messaged Akiō using *Obāsan*'s *Amami* surname that, in reality, is a family codeword. Unsurprisingly (except to my daughters), he went radio silent for a week. They fretted on pins and needles, thinking he must've cut them off as crazy Americans with a superstar fetish. Then he replied that he'd been shocked and dismissive of El's claim but the codeword had prompted him to visit his spiritualist grandmother still on Okinoerabu Island (沖永良部島) to hear what she had to say. He then tracked down other extended family. To his great surprise, they verified the familial connection. According to Akiō, his grandmother wept at her sister's "spitting image" in Ayako's photo (who was close to *Obāsan*'s age at death). Akiō was pretty shook. He and the girls then started getting to know each other as family.

58. [32] Since before the Middle Ages. Even so, Jesus continued to work with Christians and others receptive to him as he really is. According to Mina, this amounts to "exactly" 73 Christians and 681 non-Christians.

59. [33] Hidé spent the evening in Japan attempting to influence his "troublesome" adult son to mend his ways. When he 'portaled' into our house at a sleepy 2:30 AM, he was cross and ready for the Emotion Code healing session El had earlier promised him "tomorrow." "It *is* tomorrow," he declared. She laughed. I studied the wall clock. Exhausted, she nonetheless stood by her word after I'd gone to sleep. For the girls, Hidé and Taiji were already family and their issues were becoming ours. El knocked on the door as I lay in bed dropping off. Hidé wanted to formally meet (EN 52:648). "He's very nervous, Dad," said El, explaining his disinclination to step into the room. I consistently seemed to have that effect on these guys. Well, I sure wasn't climbing out of bed so we exchanged pleasantries long distance. I finally got to sleep around 3 AM wondering to what I'd awake.

60. [33] Her real name. Unlike *Obāsan*'s family's rejection, *Obāsan*'s lover *Yéyé* (爷爷; FN 50:33) was the scion of a wealthy political family that happily received their baby daughter. One of *Yéyé*'s sisters (now one of Ayako's spirit guides) reared her with love and acceptance while, joked Ayako, *Yéyé* "just made money." In 1953, his sister secretly paid their 14-year old daughter's passage on a freighter out of China (at this point, he'd had no money himself) to give her a shot at surviving the Communist takeover. His family stayed behind "for honor"—not abandoning China for Taiwan—after which, according to him and Mina, the Communists burst into their home and shot them all because *Yéyé* was secretly helping the anti-Communists (who'd assassinated an official and his family; *Yéyé* and his family was payback). She ran out of money at St. Vincent and the Grenadines in the West Indies. *Obāsan* said it seemed to her that St. Vincent, tucked out in the middle of Cold War nowhere, was "a place of peace and safety" after their tumultuous lives in war, rebellion,

and Communism's showdown with the West. Her daughter quickly birthed an illegitimate child with a Vincentian of African descent. She then married a Carib Indian man at age sixteen and produced my daughters' grandmother Martina in 1955, but died soon after of yellow fever. We used Emotion Code with her, too, healing her trapped emotion of sadness which Mina completed by 'downloading' his perspective on how it would feel to live with its opposite.

Chapter 6 – In the Hurricane's Eye

61. [35] Frederick Douglass' writings remorselessly pointed this out to me while writing "Cain and Abel" (Master's Thesis); see Douglass 1845, 5; DuBois 1969, 136; Myrdal 1964, 123, 607, 1197). Writing this endnote got me curious, though, so I checked my lineage. No African, Central or South American, or Caribbean, but—*wow!*—Mina says I'm 10% Natchitoches from the larger Caddo tribe of Louisiana—which entered my maternal Cajun French grandfather's ancestry around 1850; the Indian Ayako frequently saw around our Virginia house is a 19th-century Natchitoches ancestor—and my paternal great-grandfather is Chiricahua (*Aiaha*) Apache, the famous Geronomo's older (and only) sibling, whom I call Shasha (FN 236:202).

62. [35] Mina had a biological body before entering spirit world in Mother's universe, and before creating ours. He said his ethnicity is what we might call "archetypal Japanese." Don't think that didn't enthuse my two daughters.

63. [35] Technically, this isn't an unusual concept for Unificationists. My mandatory post-seminary 40-day retreat during summer 1998 saw me at the Unification Church's undeveloped *Cheongpyeong* Heaven and Earth Training Center's (천주청평수련원) compound on the mosquito coast of *Cheongpyeong* Lake (청평호반) near Seorak (설악), South Korea. My class arrived to incessant rain and some of Korea's worst-ever flooding. Our sodden hideaway's dearth of hygiene and proper plumbing cheered on a cauldron of infectious diseases that swamped our health and landed me in the *smoking* ward of a rural hospital with a severe but misdiagnosed lung infection, which I thought stood good odds of making me an ex-pat statistic. Leading up to this amusing respite, I found myself participating in a daily, hours-long traditional shamanistic ritual called *ansu* (안수) or *chan yang* (찬양, 'praise'). Participants sit in a line back-to-front cross-legged or on their knees and slap out the spirits residing in their body to a cadent song set to a steady, booming drumbeat, each body-part-specific slap alternated by hand claps to keep the rhythm. The person behind you takes care of whacking your back and you the one in front. These spirits are considered bad for the simple reason their presence selfishly disrupts your own spirit, body, and life. *Ansu* can be painful and outright debilitating as folks get carried away and pound hell out of themselves and their partner.

One day, mine compelled me to threaten to break his arms before he managed—some people think they have a religious duty to really let you have it—to ease up his blows. It was a bone-bruising, black-and-blue experience. Did it evict these spirit squatters? Well, taking a desperate break along the back wall in the midst of *ansu* one day, I saw 'angels.' They stood alongside each seated participant in the seven rows, thirty deep, rhythmically bending at the waist to yank forth a spirit trespasser, then doing actress Reese Witherspoon's *Legally Blonde* (2001) 'bend-and-snap' to fling them off like cotton bolls to the basket. *Ansu*'s purpose seems to be to make it too miserable for a spirit person to remain ensconced in your body, to shake them sufficiently loose that an 'angel' can haul their grasping selves out. Unificationists figure if it looks like you're being beaten to death, your bad spirits will abandon you like rats a sinking ship. *Ansu* made it almost too painful for *me* to remain in my body. And then we discovered we could simply ask Mina to accomplish the same outcome in a painless instant for all parties. I couldn't believe it.

64. [35] Brent Swancer, "The Mysterious Real Zombies of Haiti," *Mysterious Universe*, St. Leonards, NSW, Australia, August 5, 2014 (https://mysteriousuniverse.org/2014/08/the-mysterious-real-zombies-of-haiti/ (accessed: 2018-08-20)).

65. [37] Moon 1996, 12, 381–409. Also, ". . . Moon declared himself the Messiah . . . [and] 'humanity's Savior, Messiah, Returning Lord and True Parent' " (Charles Babington and Alan Cooperman, "The Rev. Moon Honored at Hill Reception," *The Washington Post*, June 23, 2004, A01).

66. [37] An important salvific component in *Divine Principle*'s Growth Stages (1996, 40–5). Like other ironies in Sun-myung's spiritual career, Mina says the Blessing actually produced spiritually elevated children. However, children conceived after the October 14, 2017 Big Healing are automatically 'blessed' in that sense and spiritually advanced (generally) over their parents. Unificationism's Blessing of Marriage is now redundant.

67. [37] Soon after the Big Healing, Mina said the various 'levels' of physical-born spirit world (§ 3.1.2.1.3:359; § 1.2:521) had naturally recombined into the single 'level' he'd originally intended as healed spirit people 'energetically' transformed, raising their 'vibration.' At the time of Helen's death, that epochal event was still years in the uncertain future. For us, now, it was still some eighteen hours away.

68. [37] See *ansu* (EN 63:650).

69. [37] Mina said that before the Big Healing less than one million people worldwide (including Ayako) were free of spirit people 'infesting' them, their spiritual energy being too strong for it. That's less than 0.0132% of the estimated 2017 global population. Since the Big Healing, spirit people generally no longer 'infest' people on Earth nor 'feed off' their energy. However, the physics between 'low' and 'high energy' ('vibration') means a 'higher-energy' person in the physical world can be 'energy'-siphoned simply by the presence of 'lower-energy' spirit persons (interacting similar to high- and low-pressure air systems), but it's rarely intentional. One might liken it to the exhaustion one feels after an emotionally intense event.

70. [37] "There was never malice in this situation," Mina said, because these spirit persons were "trying to survive" their flyblown situations. They acted in fear, desperation, and emotions similar to *Real Love*'s "drowning man" analogy (Baer 2003, 15–17): "[a] drowning man doesn't mean to hurt other people; in his state of mindless panic, he simply can't seem to stop himself from grabbing anything or anyone that might help to keep his head above the water. His fear is so overwhelming that he doesn't think for a second about the harm he might cause others as he saves himself" (ibid, 29).

71. [39] Mina says guardian 'angels' are not capable of stopping spirit persons from 'infesting' our physical bodies or removing them if they do (§ 3.2:566). But if such a person in their subconscious believes they're in the wrong—the way criminals who avoid capture then plead guilty after capture—there's an implicit subconscious permission for correction. An 'angel' can then pull them out even if consciously they don't want to leave (as with *ansu*; EN 63:650). Mina, of course, doesn't operate that way. Instead, he works to heal them so they leave naturally.

72. [39] Besides Helen, my currently known spirit guides are the following. A French ancestor who preferred anonymity. "Well," I drawled, "I'm calling you Frenchie, then." She took it in stride. At least, I didn't get a *no* push. Eight months later, she decided to drop her veil, although I stalled three months before energy testing her deets. Her name is Daphne Giles (d. 1430). There's my other best Unificationist friend Godwin D'Silva (real name; d. 2007) who joined the squad in March 2018. Then my best friend from the US Coast Guard, Billy Roberts (real name; d. 2015 per he and Mina), came on board in June 2018. Helen continues her long earthly practice of pulling no punches when I seek her advice. Godwin is his same patient, considerate self. Billy, I hadn't seen nor heard since 1980. Since then, others not listed here have joined me as well as the girls.

Chapter 7 – Doom Ride

73. [43] It is perhaps shocking that Mina and his wife Ag'poprje (§ 2.2:341) didn't educate the first 'angels'—their direct offspring—about the finer points of how to live—though they fully answered any questions—because they "were new to parenting and universe creating" and hadn't appreciated what needs be conveyed or the consequences of not doing so. They'd made a command decision not to influence their children's minds in any way, although concluded that stinting on that aspect was counterproductive since, with the Big Healing, they've been addressing it. Until then, no 'angels' were aware of Mina's unique awareness–experience of all that happens amongst humanity and the universe and 'quantumly entangles' everything and everyone. However, he doesn't look into people's *minds* because it's sacred and inviolable. Unless he's already aware, whenever we ask him what a person—say, Michael—was thinking or being motivated by, we always need wait as he actually converses with the person before answering us. The 'energy' of their conversation will often pendulum us around before settling into stillness and then his response. From the Cardinal's (FN 130:110; including Mina's) point of view, creating— building   a universe is analogous to building a large, multi-generational house for one's children to produce a multi-generational family that never moves out. If you view the universe through that metaphor, it is perhaps easier to comprehend.

74. [43] Ms. Medium's spirit self doesn't agree with or support what her physical self is doing in this respect, but takes a hands-off approach. Michael and Lucifer felt she should be trying a lot harder to rein in her physical self's behavior. As a result, she doesn't feel so welcome, hence "rarely visits" these 'angels.' I discovered this when conflicts in my energy testing revealed her physically asleep and her spirit self disagreeing with Mina's description of her

situation. In many ways, the physical pressure to survive and thrive along with erroneous beliefs—mindset—drives our physical choices. Absent that, our spirit self often has different attitudes, priorities, even personality from our physical self (e.g., Hitler CH. 40:605).

75. [44] There's no such thing as 'negative energy.' For energy to be 'negative,' it must vest with intention. Hence, 'negative energy' is 'ill-intentioned energy.' Ms. Medium could see Michael with Ayako and wondered, Ayako said, "Why is he following this little girl around?" Ms. Medium infused her—"She really let me have it!" Ayako jested—with 'negative energy' because she saw that Ayako was important to Michael. She didn't like Michael, so she vented her dislike on Ayako, too. Secondarily, Ms. Medium knew Ayako would become better and stronger—more successful—than she, although Ayako didn't even know how to use her spiritual prowess at the time. Ms. Medium wanted to derail her development and keep it that way. She invested Ayako with ill-intention at every opportunity so she'd never be able to develop herself. Having been knocked flat for nearly two months from interacting with Ms. Medium at the ThetaHealing Basic DNA workshop, she'd paralyzed Ayako's spirituality for months more. Even if a person dislikes one, if they have no intention of harm then there is no harm. Unconsciously harming someone merely in consequence of one's dislike doesn't happen. If one feels 'negative energy' or spiritual harm, it's because a person consciously intends it. Absent Ms. Medium's ill will, the three of us could've interacted with her all day long without any ill effect beyond her 'negative' ThetaHealing 'energy.'

76. [44] The eight clair senses are seeing, knowing, hearing, emotional feeling, tasting, physical feeling, touching, and smelling. We three experience more or less of these to greater or lesser degrees as we've improved or developed from scratch since 2017. Ayako remains the most advanced amongst us.

77. [45] For example, why did these 'angels' (as we then-understood their reality) tell us that God can only love them through human beings? If human beings don't care about angels then, practically speaking, it means neither does God. Yet God is supposed to be the God of Love. This sort of astral subordination is really enslavement. It contradicts the premise of freedom. If a human wants angels to be free and directly loved by God, for instance, it would contradict the created order and be unattainable. No free will but only bounded will. This sort of illogic raised significant conundrums for us as to God's consistency, logic, reason, and his heart. Frankly, Ms. Medium did a great job creating a sense of majesty and we felt overawed in the presence of such angels. But it was falderal. Interacting with Mina, Michael, and Gabriel ourselves produced a completely different experience, one where God and angels were not majestic, superior-subordinate deities but human, personable, friendly, loving, equal, and free, and most important, entirely consistent as well as supremely logical, rational, simple, and understandable in their descriptions of a very comprehensible universe. When it came to whom to believe—Ms. Medium or ourselves—even if we excluded our own personal experience and just stuck to the data, there was no contest. Logic and reason alone demanded we defer to Mina's account over Ms. Medium's own.

78. [45] *The Urantia Book* 1955, I, 42, 10. The book claims Uversa is the capital city of the *Orvonton* "superuniverse" of which our universe, *Nebadon*, forms a part (ibid, 1). Most of this work is ridiculous in its torturous complexity and supernumerary elitism whereas Mina's story of life is simple, straightforward, and egalitarian. But I was knocked flat when Mina said Uversa is an actual city in spirit world that spans both its physical-born and spirit-born iterations (§ 3.1.2.1.3:359; § 1.2:521), and that a spirit person living there had legitimately delivered the textual quotation even though the content doesn't comport with reality. He added that some facts scattered through the book—not Orvonton—are correct. That said, the following passage from the book rings sensible enough as it relates to Mina's perspective on mediums. "Information and intelligence, gleaned from even high sources, is only relatively complete, locally accurate, and personally true. Physical facts are fairly uniform, but truth is a living and flexible factor in the philosophy of the universe. Evolving personalities are only partially wise and relatively true in their communications. They can be certain only as far as their personal experience extends. That which apparently may be wholly true in one place may be only relatively true in another segment of creation. Divine truth, final truth, is uniform and universal, but the story of things spiritual, as it is told by numerous individuals hailing from various spheres, may sometimes vary in details owing to this relativity in the completeness of knowledge and in the repleteness of personal experience as well as in the length and extent of that experience . . . Truth is . . . both replete and symmetrical . . . The wise philosopher will always look for the creative design which is behind, and pre-existent to, all universe phenomena" (ibid, 42).

Franchezzo says much the same thing in Farnese's allegedly spirit-received *A Wanderer in the Spirit Lands* (1901). Admittedly, the *Urantia* authors—as spiritualists are wont to do from our perspective—could have built off this work, so a second opinion here is not necessarily a *second* opinion. "In the spirit world . . . there are a great number of different schools of thought, all containing the great fundamental eternal truths of nature, but each differing in many minor details, and also as to how these great truths should be applied for the advancement of the soul; they likewise differ as to how their respective theories will work out, and the conclusions to be drawn from the undoubted knowledge they possess, when it is applied to subjects upon which they have no certain knowledge and which are still with them as with those on earth, the subject of speculation, theory, and discussion . . . The waves of truth are continually flowing from the great thought centers of the Universe, and are transmitted to earth through chains of spirit intelligences, but each spirit can only transmit such portions of truth as his development has enabled him to understand, and each mortal can only receive as much knowledge as his intellectual faculties are able to assimilate and comprehend. Neither spirits nor mortals can know everything, and spirits can only give you what are the teachings which their own particular schools of thought and advanced teachers give as their explanations. Beyond this they cannot go, for beyond this they do not themselves know; there is no more absolute certainty in the spirit world than on earth, and those who assert that they have the true and only explanation of these great mysteries are giving you merely what they have been taught by more advanced spirits, who, with all due deference to them, are no more entitled to speak absolutely than the most advanced teachers of some other school" ([sic], Farnese, 90). Mina says this excerpt is largely albeit not fully true, although the book itself is not spiritually revealed but an aggregation of stories woven into a single storyline that gives a "partially correct view of spirit world." To know which is which requires energy testing the book line-by-line.

Still, we found the foregoing affirmed by our experience. When speaking with spirit human beings, we learned of their spirit world encounters and the truths about spirit world they'd gleaned from them. When speaking with 'angels,' we received a 'higher,' more universal understanding of spirit world, though even 'angelic' viewpoints reflect their own personal experience over the broader objective reality that Mina conveys who, by definition, has the singularly comprehensive understanding of our universe. When speaking with Mina, we learned in all respects the reality of how he, the universe, 'angels,' and human beings exist. But don't think for a moment that what we've learned from him and presented in this book represents all there is to know about such topics because the subject is vast beyond belief. For example, if we were to take Hidé's experience regaining consciousness after his drugged strangulation (EN 52:648) and extrapolate that to a truism for how all human beings recognize their transition to spirit world, we would be committing a fallacy. If, however, we include Mina's knowledge of how the transition from the physical to spirit works, on average, in all cases, then we'd have the larger context for which Hidé was describing only his part, and one colored by his personal circumstances.

79. [45] It's a simple logic. No compulsion means no judgment or punishment because even its threat—distant or vague—is coercion. Neither is there any moral law, as that not only eviscerates freedom but necessitates enforcement, judgment, and punishment of violators, the threat of which is also coercion. Mina provides no judgment or punishment himself, but individuals can and do provide it to the self (and others) which creates self-coercion. This is a common social engineering technique evident in the 20th and 21st centuries and the foundation of political 'liberty through law.' But coercion is alien to Mina. If you deal with him, you'll find it's never part of the program. You might compel yourself because you generate a personal duty or fear, but that's on you. Mina creates no standard by which one might feel compelled to duty or fear an outcome. Humans alone craft the compulsions we know. Ultimately, this logic dictates there's no such thing as sin. We three certainly felt a personal duty to pass Mina's message to Ms. Medium, mostly due to the heartistic bond we'd built with him. But what if we'd chosen not to? We'd have simply carried on with Mina, the 'angels,' and spirit family and friends. If Mina thinks his message crucial, he finds another means to deliver it without holding our unwillingness or inability against us, all the while continuing our relationship so long as we want one. We can say this because he did ask us to do other things at which we failed, forgot, let slide, or ignored without any diminution in our relationship—none we could perceive anyhow.

80. [45] For example, *Obāsan*'s eldest brother whom the girls call *Idaina-oji* (great-great uncle in Japanese, which he prefers to plain old generic *oji-san*, 'uncle', and whom I call "Gruncle One" on account of the multitude of great uncles) joined the Unification Church in the late 1950s after listening on Divine Principle lectures while visiting Earth. When I showed up in St. Vincent and the Grenadines many years later as a Unificationist, he saw an opportunity to 'restore' his lineage by connecting his great-great niece with me and my lineage through the Blessing of Marriage. This is the Church's marital method of restoring people to God through separating them from Satan via spiritual conditions that rectifies Adam and Eve's sin and heals their lineages of 'fallen' nature, original sin, and historical resentments, and then producing Blessed Children free of original sin entanglements to forge disparate lineages into united, spiritually-restored families. But the Blessing is redundant as of the Big Healing October 14, 2017 (EN 66:650; FN 545:639).

Children conceived since then naturally surpass 'Blessed children.' *Idaina-oji*'s puppeteering—if I'm being indulgent . . . well, okay, he didn't exactly put a gun to my head to marry her—introduced me to drama and trauma I might have avoided despite it bringing me children I adore and would never unmake, regardless. This sort of back-office intervention in our physical lives is common with spirit persons who are motivated by all sorts of prosy reasons to guide, inspire, harass, help, hinder, harm, or otherwise manipulate our lives absent our knowledge and permission (§ 1.3:473). Mina and the 'angels' don't engage in this rank behavior because it short circuits our freedom and is thus an unloving act.

81. [45] Not in its modality (sway test, healing regimen, etc. which pre-dates ThetaHealing; Howell 2007, ibid, par. 9), but as regards the adverse 'energy' ThetaHealers call 'Creator' to which practitioners are taught to connect. Our personal experience—Ayako recognized (and Mina confirmed) it at the Basic DNA workshop straight off—is that this energy is not the 'Source energy' of God or the universe but a personal, 'negative ('ill-intentioned') energy' afflicting those who imbibe it. Former certified ThetaHealer Trisha Howell alleges ThetaHealing founder "Vianna—with the help of her husband Guy Stibal, a dark shaman—befriended an entity called Creator. Vianna has a special relationship with Creator, a being she claims is God but which has been experienced by hundreds of former ThetaHealers as a dark entity that subtly takes some of practitioners' energy in exchange for 'healings' . . . Vianna and Guy use Creator not only for their own personal gain but also to keep practitioners in line." (ibid, par. 8–9). According to Mina, Vianna's 'Creator' is just a malevolent human being in spirit world using and harming others for his own purposes, but had "moved on" from Vianna and ThetaHealing by the time we encountered her. The 'negative energy' developed through this spirit person's association remains—is even growing—because he says Vianna and ThetaHealers keep adding to it through their personal-gain intention and because, as an 'energetic poison,' the more it's used the more it grows. ThetaHealing started as a 'using' rather than a 'healing' modality. Certified ThetaHealer instructors who don't know this aren't lying, per se. The modality itself is tainted. No matter how beneficial when pure, any corrupted medicine taints the patient. One could wonder if Mina, 'angels,' and the spirit persons with whom we interact aren't who they claim, and it wouldn't be unreasonable to do so. We have. Besides analyzing their message, if one builds a reasoned energy testing competency (§ 2:625), one can develop sufficient evidence to suit oneself either way. Mina hasn't sickened or disturbed us, however, and is doing all the healing without us, plus insists we don't charge money for our part in it.

82. [45] This is how we discovered Ms. Medium's underside, because we quite naturally asked Mina, "Hey, what's going on, here?" Mina had us go through our refrigerator and pantry item-by-item where he identified all the foodstuffs Ms. Medium's clinging 'toxic energy' had spoiled and were food-poisoning Ayako. The fresh vegetables from her garden, several recently-bought batches of more than sixty-four store eggs, jars of sealed, unopened peanut butter, and other typically 'unspoilable' foods—nothing frozen, interestingly—I peevishly carted to the landfill.

83. [45] Ayako was content with Mina's initial non-biological diagnosis. On the other hand, I revisited it over most of the weeks involved. No matter how I formed my queries, however, his answer was consistent and emphatic: it wasn't a biological infection but a 'negative energy' contamination. Similar symptoms, different cause. For me, it was just hard to accept.

84. [45] Eventually, El admonished me that "Mina says stop asking him if you're 'connected.' We're always connected to him. Everyone is. When your chakras are off you just aren't hearing him." Right. But isn't not hearing the same as not connected? Sometimes we go round and round with definitions, Mina and I. He was really just advising patience. It took me awhile to get it, though.

85. [45] I emailed Moth Man. "You probably think this is nuts, but we drove home from church yesterday with me and the kids in the car, Hide Matsumoto ([El's] spirit guide/guardian angel), Taiji Sawada ([Ayako's] spirit guide/guardian angel), [Helen Smith] (my spirit guide), my Dad showed up when he came up in the conversation, Obaasan (the girl's great-great-grandmother from Japan) who's always around, and Lucifer, who, besides gabriel, spends the most time with us of the angels (michael's the quiet sort). The girls had the conversation going like a party. You could feel the energy and the family nature of it. The girls call them all 'the squad.' Funny. The girls can hear and feel touches . . . 'Lucifer, did you just pat my head?' 'Hide, did you POKE me?' . . . 'Who's yelling? My head's pounding from it!' And so on, the whole [roughly two-hour] ride down. This is my life now, [Moth Man]. Heh" ([sic] "Nov. 20," Email to Moth Man, Nov. 20, 2017).

In the car, we discovered spirit people can change their size, which makes sense since the spirit body is thought-based, manifested by mind. We could have ten or twenty people packed in—more, probably; we never checked on numbers beyond asking after people we knew or suspected might be aboard. At those Unification Church *ansu* sessions in Korea (EN 63:650) they'd told us spirit people hiding out inside physical bodies were as tiny as insect larva; well sure, how else could thousands of human beings crowd into your body, right? It all seemed a little farcical, then. But now we had Hidé, Taiji, our 'archangel' squad, Helen, Jesus, Sun-myung, and others telling us how big they were and where they were sitting (or standing) in my diminutive Prius. Additionally, they don't share the same space despite the different 'planes' of existence, because our physical body has a spirit body, which same space another spirit person can't occupy. When the girls figured it out, they asked things like, "*Obāsan*, is my leg in your space?", "Lucifer, you okay squeezed between us?", "Taiji, are you *really* sitting on the console?!"

At home where our house always seemed like spirit party central, my daughters developed sensitivity for where they sat or stood, or they'd ask for space on the sofa to squeeze in. Sometimes I'd plop onto the sofa without thinking and one of the girls would throw a fit. "Dad! You just made Gabriel move to the floor when you sat on him!" None of our spirit guests seemed put out by our faux pas. They're invisible to us, so what's the point? Taiji often stood behind the sofa for hours watching movies or YouTube music videos with us because there was no available seat—either empty or in a position where, were he physical, he could or would actually sit to see the television—or he didn't want to obstruct someone else. One doesn't lose such sensibilities just because one transitions to a pliable spirit body.

86. [45] Our household got the same way. Ayako dubbed these spontaneous convocations as "turn-up Tuesday," "wildin' Wednesday," and so on. No day was without spirit persons participating in meals, conversations, lectures, movies, book discussions, illuminating philosophical and theological ruminations, and whatnot. Sometimes Mina, the 'angels,' or others would stop me asking serious questions (or they'd ignore my zeal with playful answers) because they just wanted to "relax" and "hang out" in the new clubhouse they'd found. From dozens to thousands of spirit persons would 'portal' into our house, jamming whatever room in which we happened to be. Billions of spirit people coalesced outside our home day and night bodily and 'long-distance' via awareness out of curiosity, concern, or to experience the carnival atmosphere. The 'energies' got so strong at times that the closer we'd get to our house when returning home from a drive the stronger the cranial pressure or ear ringing or torso (especially stomach) sensations got, particularly with Ayako. It served as an early-warning system to expect a lot of spiritual activity at the house. Helen never would tell me exactly how many people showed up day-to-day because she didn't want me to "get a big head." Maybe she was justified but usually I was stupefied so many people crowded into my Q&A sessions with Mina, the 'angels,' Jesus, Sun-myung, and others. I just felt out of place. Still, El's declaration from Mina that I was now the most famous person in spirit world rang in my inflated ears a long while even if I had no independent way to 'know' it.

87. [46] 'Energy' drains aren't unusual. Psychic John Holland notes that "doing psychic work can make you extra sensitive, so you may occasionally feel tired or drained. Being sensitive comes with this work . . ." (Holland 2018, 124). I'm not sure he knows just how sensitive or draining it can really get. In these early days, we often relied on Ayako because she tested the fastest and most accurate. In the car with me driving and El still learning to hand test—not terribly motivated to learn, either, as she preferred sway testing—Ayako was our principal receiver.

88. [46] On this day, every physically living being—human, animal, plant, and smaller—capable of contributing 'energy' without being damaged did so, channeled by each of their guardian 'angels,' færies (§ 1.1.1.4:572), and other 'maintenance' spirits (spirit persons, all), from which Mina infused every physically- and spiritually-living thing across the physical and spiritual universe with healing 'energy.' The energy generated through physical processes is what powers spirit world (§ 7:211). An unprecedented event like the Big Healing required copious energy beyond the norm. Even so-called constants (which aren't actually constant) such as the speed of light and the Big-G temporarily fluctuated 'lower.'

89. [46] Some friends and acquaintances reported their marriage, relationship, or other aspects of their emotional lives inexplicably improved on the Big Healing day or shortly thereafter. My children happily discovered their mother, with whom they couldn't get along for most of their lives, dramatically improved within days until she easily got along with them. For the first time, they looked forward to visiting her.

Chapter 8 – Confrontation

90. [49] Lucifer has a deep-feeling heart, tender, embracing, and long-suffering. Naturally, he's sensitive to the hate, scorn, and accusation directed at him by millennia of 'angels' and humans mistakenly blaming him for the conditions of life. Driving home from church in Bowie, Maryland one day in November 2017, we spontaneously visited the Basilica of the National Shrine of the Immaculate Conception in Washington, DC, a beautiful Romanesque-Byzantine Roman Catholic church my daughters and I always loved to experience. Lucifer was riding with us, tagging along with our perennial companions Taiji, Hidé, and Helen not to mention our guardian 'angels' and others. To our surprise, the ingrained hatred for Satan and the 'energy' of desperation swirling around and throughout the building so overwhelmed Lucifer that after entering merely a few feet into a side vestibule, he was all palms out "Nope!" and went back to spirit world. Hidé started weeping almost right away. After awhile the 'heavy energy' did in Taiji, too. He sympathetically joined Hidé's tears and eventually tugged Ayako's collar to move us upstairs from the basement chapels and then outside.

    It was a revelation to me that churches are so spiritually 'dark' and draining that the spiritually brighter can't take them. We traipsed around the lesser 'negative energy' grounds with a returned Lucifer and comforted our spirit friends in the natural, sunny beauty, shared our experiences inside, then decompressed before heading home. Most people can generally feel the vibes a person or place puts out. The stronger the vibe, the more likely they notice. Empaths or the spirit-aware are more sensitive to this, picking up vibes where no one else does, experiencing them in a personal, visceral way, particularly if they're unaware their empaths. Emotive energy in places like churches, where humanity pours out its grief, fear, frustration, sorrow, guilt, shame, hate, and desperation that's rarely countered by unconditional love, joy or psychic release, infuses and affects a sensitive psyche the way a vicious drug hits one's biology. Ayako (and less so, El) could always feel this 'energy' at the Basilica but realized they'd been blocking it out to enjoy the architecture and environment. Me—well, on reflection I could see how the basilica affected me when I'd visited before but, unaware then that I'm an empath, I chalked up my inexplicable feelings to other, conventional, causes.

91. [50] 'Angels' are used to this sort of treatment from physical persons, of course, and nobody more so than Lucifer. That doesn't blunt the hurt when a person sees yet snubs them. One might be surprised that people would knowingly snub an 'angel.' We sure were. But in spirit world, people snub *God*. In terms of emotive capacity, 'angels' aren't any different from you and me, though not as egocentric as physical humanity cut off from spirit reality.

92. [51] Mina said Ayako's current guardian 'angels' are a married second-generation couple, which makes them Mina's immediate grandchildren, as are Lucifer and his siblings. Her original guardian 'angels'—who gave up their role to help quieten riots in spirit world following the Big Fracas—were Gabriel's fraternal twin sister and her third-generation husband. Mina said it's "a majority of 'angels' " holding these two sets of guardian 'angels' in such high esteem while the remainder see them as simply "regular."

93. [54] Mina was egging us on, not face palming over our emotions. He saw ThetaHealer's response as a "likely but not necessarily foregone" conclusion. Ayako's efforts reasoning with her was as pointless as Sisyphus thinking he'd reach the top. Our effort (all things being equal) ultimately won't bear fruit in the physical world with either ThetaHealer One or Two. They are as they are, though as Mina has told us before, "It's never sure till it's sure."

94. [57] ". . . She heard the death bells ringing /And as they rolled they seemed to say, / Hard-hearted Barb'ry Allen . . ." from *Barbara Allen*, Traditional Scots, ca. mid-17th century (Emmylou Harris, *Songcatcher*, compact disc, NY: Vanguard Records, 2001; and Dolly Parton/Altan, *Heartsongs (Live From Home)*, album, NY: Columbia Records, 1994). Ms. Medium's hard-heartedness toward Lucifer and Michael (who feels our comparison here resonates) is ironically the very epitome of religion's critique of Satan and the Sinner vis-à-vis God.

95. [58] Late in December 2017, Ms. Medium hooked Ayako into a lengthy conversation at Sunday church where she touched and hugged her and transferred so much 'toxic energy' to Ayako that it dampened her chakras and shut down her energy testing for close to four months. Similar close proximity along with Ms. Medium's lengthy embrace at church in April 2018 snapped my own chakras shut within the hour. Five weeks of virtually no spiritual communication later, they'd recovered enough that Mina could open them for me and I could resume sway testing. Only in late September did my finger testing ability—a subtle, 'energy'-sensitive methodology (more so than sway or hand testing; § 2.2.1.3:629)—return. I had to exercise it like a withered arm. Mina pegged it 86% accurate within a couple weeks, however. People don't really notice 'negative energy,' instead chalking its effects up to random disease and misfortune, yet it can be quite toxic to the body and mind. Acknowledging Ms. Medium's toxicity isn't a slam on her character or personality—I liked her, all things being equal—but simply our awareness of her 'energy' intention and its effect on us. We didn't yet know how to build the spiritual equivalent of a hazardous environment suit, so keeping our distance was all we had for protection.

Chapter 9 – Revival Ride

96. [61] "In order to become a Sunnie, you have to free yourself completely from all shackles and become a real, true entity . . . What is the difference between Moonies and Sunnies? There is an important difference. The moon receives light and then reflects it, while the sun is the generator of the light and gives it out everywhere. Therefore, the difference between Moonies and Sunnies is also obvious. The Moonies are those who can only gain their strength from Father [Sun-myung], receiving his light and encouragement, then giving it out. But, for Sunnies it doesn't matter whether Father is present or not. Sunnies are dynamos themselves, giving out light to the world whether I am here or not . . . The wish of Heavenly Father, as well as my own desire, is for you to become such a Sunnie. Don't stay too long on the Moonie level; promote yourself to a Sunnie" (Moon 1987, par. 3).

97. [61] In my first Unification Church rebellion in 1984—rising from a culmination of confidence over self-doubt in the tradition of Martin Luther (Armstrong 2011, "A History of Darkness"; and Young 2017, "The Doubts of a Leader")—I wrote my own version of Luther's Ninety-five Theses (1517) slamming the church's corruption, violence, and abandonment of its own teachings. In the dead of night, I nailed—well, thumbtacked—my seven-page *A General Discourse on the Symbolic Relationship of Cain and Abel, Regarding its Theory and Misapplication in the Unification Church* to "the front doors of virtually every church center in the San Francisco Bay area" (McKeon 2003, 27). Local church leaders indeed tried to excommunicate its author but I'd thoughtfully signed my shot o'er their bow "as *Cassius*, a Roman jurist whom I thought embodied truth and fairness" (ibid, ia). Suspicions unquenched, they fell back on the all-purpose 'problem member' moniker to physically deny me entry to all Bay Area church centers, even for Sunday service. Unlike with medieval excommunication, religious liberty obviates the threat of local government hounding me from the succor of my friends, which Martin Luther also avoided only because his friends were well armed. Many months later, I did get the satisfaction of an indirect apology from the local persecutorial ringleader although it came in a Sunday sermon they prevented my attending.

98. [65] After discovering my spirit guides Daphne (formerly Frenchie) and Godwin bicycling along with me on a Charlottesville, Virginia bike trail, our conversation provoked me to ask Mina, "When I quit procrastinating and get your actual name, can I also get your wife's?" *Yes, of course.* Then I asked, "Say, do you know Cosmo's name?" *Yes.* "Will you tell me his name?" *Yes.* "Great! Wait. You're, like, totally persnickety about getting permission from people before you do anything regarding them, so your *yes* means you already got Cosmo's permission to give me his name?" *Yes.* I said, "Aha . . . then . . . did you happen to also get his permission for me to mention him in the book?" Because, since we first discovered Cosmo's existence, he (like my obstinate dad) wouldn't give me permission to expose him. But how could I not discuss Mina's teacher (§ 3:343)? The logic was obvious. Readers would wonder. "Will he go for it?" I added. *Yes.* I'd only been making my case to Cosmo from the start. In my (possibly quetching) negotiations with Mina, his wife finally reached a "rocking-the-marital-boat" mind to "damn the permissions and full speed ahead!" ("Cosmo," e-mail to Moth Man, par. 3, June 19, 2018). As I ecstatically told Moth Man the next day, "Now I can move forward on that front with Mina's happy connivance" (ibid).

99. [65] There are people so abominable that no 'angels' will work with them, for example Hitler (CH. 40:605), Stalin, and Pol Pot although not Mao Tse Tung, which took us by surprise. Here's what Mina said about that. Mao didn't care about the human cost of his policies. He knew suffering and death would result but was trying to accomplish good things for China and just didn't care how many suffered and died to do it. That separated him from the Stalin–Hitler-type crowd who target persons or groups for death (or slavery) unrelated either to accomplishing their national advancement or as an integral aspect of it. Brutality was gratuitous for Hitler, as it was unnecessary to his larger goals. Mao could accomplish his larger goals with little to no death and suffering but didn't care, thus it occurred. For Hitler types, death and suffering are integral to accomplishing their larger goals and brutality is encouraged and gratuitous. Aside from their own sense of duty, Mao's 'angels' overlooked his callousness and mass deaths as for them he didn't rise to the same egregious level as Stalin, Hitler, Pol Pot, and others once they'd crossed their individual Rubicons into Full Psycho Mode.

100. [65] It's hard to describe the sense of disconnection—wildly vibrating 'energy,' heat, prickles; floating, sinking, shifting sideways; spirit world light and seeing through closed eyelids; spirit arms and legs moving about till you're just out. The odd sensations and altered awareness were terribly disorienting and initially laced me with fear. When I couldn't quite get out of my body because I was distracted, had overeaten, or for whatever reason, my body sometimes felt cold, trembled, and electrified like an atomic reaction. It was impossible to sleep or relax even though tired and—as I'm doing now writing this endnote—I'd end up working all night on the book or otherwise distracting myself until 'normality' returned. If you've experienced any of this, or can empathize with the sensations described, then perhaps you imagine some of what El was going through.

101. [66] That's what spiritual 'gifts' are: learnable skills, not bestowed powers. Some folks (many more of which the public is unaware) are indeed inborn with what we'd call a talent or capability awaiting discovery and development. Many people experience the effects of their spiritual senses while it's still a latent skill without understanding the cause. They turn to prescribed or self-medication, or simply suffer anxiety, fatigue, headaches, 'hallucinations,' synesthesia, and so on. I've experienced some of these effects off and on throughout my own life but most especially since this amazing October 2017 week. For a list of the effects that spirit-awareness might induce, see https://psychickelli.com/signs-and-symptoms-of-the-spiritual-awakening-and-exp anded-consciousness/ (accessed: 2022-01-30 (original URL accessed: 2018-06-13)).

Chapter 10 – Denouement

102. [72] On another day, we found Mina watching *Moana* (2016) with us. He remarked that, while he disliked the movie overall for its goddess Te Fiti's violent stolen-heart form as Te Kā—he eschews violence in all forms and the film reinforced false good–evil, love–hate, peaceful–violent dualities—he loved its aesthetic, Moana persevering through loving freedom and consideration for (rather than from) others, and especially that Te Fiti looks like his wife, Ag'poprje (§ 2.2:341). That last bit really got my girls thinking.

Chapter 11 – A New Dawn

103. [78] For an overview and some literature on the topic, see Ingunn Karin Bendiksen, "Worldviews Shape Personality," *Science Nordic*, July 21, 2013 (http://sciencenordic.com/worldviews-shape-personality (accessed: 2019-01-22)); Steven Chisham, "The Anatomy of a Worldview: The Eternal Self-Identity," *Creation Research Society Quarterly*, 49 (Spring 2012), 63–72; and Artur Nilsson, *The Psychology of Worldviews: Toward a Non-Reductive Science of Personality*, Lund University (2013).

104. [78] Micro-observation is the tendency to extrapolate larger reality from details including, counterintuitively, when studying complex systems holistically. Macro reasoning is a thinker's tendency "to mentally dilute reality expanding their vision of it to include finer details" [sic] instead of "mentally condens[ing] reality into clotted material, and giv[ing] their mindful attention to clots but not to the surrounding fluid" (Fell 2017, 100). Concepts like, *If there is a God he's benevolent and good*, or *Why is there something instead of nothing?* are perfect examples of fluid over clots. Science and philosophy end up denying intuitive awareness.

105. [78] An example of science talking out its arse is the way it uses biologism to casually convert the person into an organic object in a random world amenable to subjective value of the sort we apply to an inorganic machine. "The possibility of cloning from the nucleus of an ordinary cell undermines the idea that embryos are precious because they have the potential to become human beings . . . [as] every human cell contains the genetic information to create a new human being, the old arguments for preserving 'unique' human embryos fade away" (Singer 2005, 40). ". . . even if the life of a human organism begins at conception, the life of a person—that is, at a minimum, a being with some level of self-awareness—does not begin so early" (ibid, 41). Ostensibly arguing for the right to die, Singer is really preaching biologism to justify metaphysical assumptions about what constitutes a person in order to free the hand of science to do . . . whatever. However, even a cloned human body at inception automatically generates a new human consciousness attached to that newly cloned cell (§ 1.2.1.1.1:248). According to Mina, there's one planet in our universe that knows how to do this and they clone bodies for slaves, unconcerned that cloned human bodies house—integrate—an eternal ꞔperson.

106. [79] Hilariously, Professor of International Health at Karolinska Institutet Hans Rosling (d. 2017) found that, regarding knowledge of world health, "the professors of the Karolinska Institute, that hands out the Nobel Prize in medicine . . . are on par with the chimpanzees . . . [mean ± confidence interval 2.4±0.4 correct answers out of five total]" (Hans Rosling, "Debunking third-world myths with the best stats you've ever seen," TED, January 14, 2007, 2:16–2:27; https://www.youtube.com/watch?v=RUwS1uAdUcI (accessed: 2019-01-17)).

107. [79] For example, "When I say 'noncomputational' I don't mean random. Nor do I mean incomprehensible. There are very clear-cut things that are noncomputational and are known in mathematics. The most famous example is Hilbert's tenth problem, which has to do with solving algebraic equations in integers" (Penrose 1995, 244).

108. [79] Instructive here is the television series *Dark Matter* (Canada, Prodigy Pictures, Syfy, 2015–17), a metaphor for the human drive to know and survive—or to survive and know, take your pick—in which a group of six humans awake alone, without memory, on an automated spaceship who then devote themselves to just two principal activities: surviving and discovering their reality.

109. [79] See, e.g., University of Oxford philosopher Richard Swinburne as featured in "The Inductive Theist of North Oxford" (Holt 2012, 95–107).

110. [80] As of 2022, about 3.5% (4% in 2019) of spirit humanity still fear the certainty of an Accountableist God. About 5.8% (6% in 2019) still feel too overwhelmed by shame, embarrassment, and the like to ask anyone in spirit world who can see or knows them for help and healing.

111. [81] You might wonder why people's fear of being held accountable—judged—by Mina if they directly ask him to heal their traumas is no longer an issue even though they still fear he'll hold them accountable or love them less if they don't do as he says they should, or ought, or comply with what he wants. The reason is their ingrained belief he has (or had) universal standards which, if they violate (or violated) them, that he'll judge them. When they consider asking Mina for healing what psychically ails them, they fear it will at the same time draw his attention to their misdeeds—their violations of his cosmic standards—for which they'd then be held accountable. This is similar to the law ruling in your favor on one issue but then holding you accountable on an unrelated issue; you can't win for losing. It's too much for many people, just as it sometimes stays the hand of a person wanting redress in court who realizes there's something in their life that might come up in the case for which they'd be prosecuted or humiliated (a problem not uncommon for victims in rape cases). Hearing of our seemingly unique relationship with Mina, such individuals come to us for intervention on their behalf. They want Mina to indirectly heal their traumas such that any other moral failure—their harm inflicted in the world such as sin that, for monotheists, directly harms God—to live up to his family standard is a fourth cousin thrice removed he wouldn't bother about. In keeping with the law metaphor, people coming to us (individually but often en masse) to facilitate their healing is akin to a class action suit where a group of persons seeks redress in court without their potential individual legal liabilities being used against them.

An artifact of the above is a feeling of inferiority before one's creator, that, when he speaks, one's obedience is due. Mina speaking in moral imperatives provokes a compulsion to obey because, if they don't, they fear Mina will look upon them as inferior thus judgeable hence proof they indeed must be. This in turn provokes them to hold Mina accountable (judged) for their inferiority. Coercion of any sort is an assault on the person. It denies freedom and is alien to Mina. This dynamic generates trauma, and Mina is all about healing and uplifting. As a result, he avoids moral imperatives save with a small handful of people who don't subject themselves to this dynamic, often not even with me, and I like to think I'm reasonably enlightened.

The deep-seated notion of accountability was certainly universal amongst spirit-born humans—'angels'—but an especially knotty problem for the physical-born cut off before the Big Healing from reality even after they'd transitioned to full-time spirit life. The concept of inviolable moral standards remains a thorny issue for the physically alive regardless faith or philosophy. This is some of the reality behind why Mina avoids speaking in even remotely imperative terms. Like *Star Trek*, Mina sternly guides himself by his own Prime Directive, his non-interference in human autonomy.

Chapter 12 – Energy Testing as a Mode of Inquiry

112. [83] "Remarks to the Commonwealth Club," par. 1–2, San Francisco, September 15, 2003.

113. [85] The most recent being 1917's alleged Miracle of the Sun involving 30–40,000 persons, which Mina calls a mass—collective—hallucination. On the other hand, the 'Phoenix Lights,' where a boomerang-shaped craft drifted over this city in Arizona in 1997, was spirit persons making spirit matter physically visible (which is the origin of UFO sightings). See, e.g., Le Bon 1896, 1–2, 6; Zusne et al. 2014, 117.

114. [86] Here's how it works. Ask a spirit person you trust to view the hands-free tire pressure gauge you're using to measure the air pressure in a particular tire. Without looking at the gauge yourself, query via ET—"Is it 30lbs? 33lbs? 35lbs?" or whatever—until you get a *yes* response. Check multiple times using different questions to be certain you correctly tested. Then, check the pressure yourself. If it's inaccurate, test the person's answers until you uncover the reason for the error. You might require a different gauge, perhaps you improperly tested, or the person you asked might be joking around, testing your abilities to maybe help you improve, or not as interested in helping as presumed. Remember, you're talking to people in a conversation. If correct testing exceeds statistical chance (50:50) then what do you have, subjective revelation or objective data?

115. [86] This last point is especially the case regarding 'special' revelation, meaning specific truths we can know via the supernatural, but especially from such revelators as, e.g., Zoroaster, Abraham, Moses, Jesus, or Muhammad as opposed to 'general' revelation, meaning generic truths we can know about God through nature (Rom. 1:10, Wis. 1:5) unless there's some reference back to a 'special' revelation such as sacred scripture.

116. [86] Hackett et al. 2012, 9. This percentage rises when the portion of Unaffiliated (16.3% of global population) with a monotheistic or semi-monotheistic (e.g., Zoroastrianism) albeit faith-unaffiliated belief is included. "[T]his report is based on information available as of early 2012" (ibid, 14).

117. [86] The fatal flaw in fusing science's somatic senses, Philosophy's qualia of the mind, and Religion's spirituality lies in philosophizing science to derive such ruminations as quantum mysticism relating consciousness, intelligence, spirituality, or mysticism to quantum science and its interpretations (e.g., Victor J. Stenger, "Quantum Quackery," *Skeptical Inquirer*, 21:1 (January 1997); https://www.csicop.org/si/show/quantum_quackery (accessed: 2019-01-27)), panspiritism where "the fundamental reality of the universe is not matter . . . another quality . . . so fundamental that it . . . pervades all living beings, and all non-living things, so that they are always interconnected . . . called fundamental consciousness, or spirit" (Taylor 2018, 6–7), and panpsychism that's similar to panspiritism where "consciousness is an inherent feature of the Universe . . . [and] all matter has a mental aspect to it, and therefore a certain degree of sentience" (Taylor 2017, 151, 152) but "doesn't conceive of a spiritual force that pervades all things" (Taylor 2018, 7).

Chapter 13 – Emergence

118. [89] 5th Dimension, *The Age of Aquarius* (Soul City, 1969, vinyl).

119. [90] Bishop of Canterbury (d. 1109). St. Anselm's ontology is essentially an argument that, because we can't conceive anything more infinite than infinity, then infinity must be infinite and that defines infinity. "Ontological arguments are arguments, for the conclusion that God exists, from premises which are supposed to derive from some source other than observation of the world—e.g., from reason alone" (Graham Oppy, "Ontological Arguments," *The Stanford Encyclopedia of Philosophy* Spring 2020 (1996), Ed. Edward N. Zalta, par. 1; https://plato.stanford.edu/archives/spr2020/entries/ontological-arguments/ (accessed: 2020-03-23)). "While there are several different versions of the argument, all purport to show that it is self-contradictory to deny that there exists a greatest possible being. Thus, on this general line of argument, it is a necessary truth that such a being exists; and this being is the God of traditional Western theism" (Kenneth Einar Himma, "Anselm: Ontological Argument for God's Existence," *Internet Encyclopedia of Philosophy* (n.d.), James Fieser, Bradley Dowden, Eds., par. 1; https://iep.utm.edu/ont-arg/ (accessed: 2020-03-23)). "In his *Proslogion*, St. Anselm claims to derive the existence of God from the concept of a being than which no greater can be conceived. St. Anselm reasoned that, if such a being fails to exist, then a greater being—namely, a being than which no greater can be conceived, and which exists—can be conceived. But this would be absurd: nothing can be greater than a being than which no greater can be conceived. So a being than which no greater can be conceived—i.e., God—exists" (Oppy ibid., par. 2).

120. [90] On the other hand, our inability to imagine something doesn't make it necessarily unreal, as "imaginability must not be made the test for ontology. The realist claim is that the scientist is discovering the structures of the world; it is not required in addition that these [microworld] structures be imaginable in the categories of the macroworld" (McMullin 1984, 14).

121. [90] See also, O'Connor 1994, De Wolf et al. 2005, and Clayton 2006, 1–31.

122. [90] [sic] "A good example of weak emergence is a cellular automaton computer program like The Game of Life . . . played on a grid of checkers where a cell can be either on or off; there are four simple rules as to whether a cell should be on or off depending on the state of it immediately surrounding neighbor cells. These simple rules, when computed, can create very complex and subtle emergent patterns that appear to have their own internal structure. Such as blinkers where a group of cells 'blink' on and off or gliders that seem to glide across the screen all of which are emergent phenomena. The program exhibit sensitivity to initial conditions and it is very difficult to predict what will emerge based on the initial conditions and ground rules. Although these programs can create emergent patterns they are said to be weakly emergent because they are determined by the elementary rules, the starting state and because there is no downward causation; the macro level system does not change the micro level rules. This weak emergence is characterized by the interaction between parts as the system evolves leading to computational complexity and the appearance of something new emerging, when in fact, it is theoretically reducible to causal accounts of the elementary parts. One can not in any straightforward way derive the high-level phenomena from the fundamental rules alone. Thus compact representation—such as equations—do not tell us very much of what is going on because we need to compute the interactions to produce the high-level phenomenon. These weakly emergent higher level phenomena do not affect the lower levels i.e. there is only upward causation present, the macro level is determined by the micro, but not vice versa. There is an asymmetrical flow of determination, macro level patterns are not doing anything over and above what the micro level events are doing to affect the positions and behavior of the elementary parts" ("Strong & Weak Emergence," *Systems Academy* (n.d.), par. 2–3; complexitylabs.io/strong-weak-emergence/(accessed: 2019-02-19)).

123. [91] [sic] "An event is thought to be strongly emergent when the high-level phenomenon derives from low-level events, but a complete description of the emergent pattern is not reducible, even in principle, to an account of the elementary parts and their interactions . . . Along with irreducibility, downward causality is commonly cited as a criterion for strong emergence . . . Strong emergence entails the idea that something truly new emerges at the different levels of organization that can not theoretically be reducible to accounts of the elementary parts. The whole is something truly other than the parts. Thus it makes sense to talk about qualitatively different levels or dimensions to the system as the rules that apply on one level become replaced—at least partially—by rules of a qualitatively different nature on another level. These higher level patterns then can exert a downward cause on their constituent parts affecting their structure and functioning. [Note: downward causality is not a feature of infinite emergent All Existence; CH. 14:93.] Strong emergence describes the direct causal action of a high-level system upon its components; qualities produced this way are irreducible to the system's constituent parts . . . One of the classical examples of strong emergence given is quantum entanglement . . . a phenomenon within quantum physics where two particles spin states become 'entangled' meaning the state of one is entirely dependent on the state of another. It has been empirically proven that the combined 'entangled' organization determines the spin direction of the parts. The two particles can be light-years away from each other but if the spin is changed on one this will be immediately reflected in a change in spin in the other. Thus the combined organization is in some way affecting a downward causation on the parts. Another example from physics of strong emergence is water, being apparently unpredictable even given a meticulous analysis to the properties of its constituent atoms . . . It would appear that no computational description of the system can exist, for such a simulation would itself constitute a reduction of the system to its constituent parts . . . The emergent phenomenon, in this case, can not be described with reference only to fundamental rules but requires some form of macro level rule. Likewise, consciousness is another often cited example of strong emergence" ("Strong & Weak Emergence," *Systems Academy* (n.d.), par. 4–5; complexity-labs.io/strong-weak-emergence/ (accessed: 2019-02-19)).

Chapter 14 – Infinity

124. [93] Though advocating a finite universe, Cantor founded Set Theory with its notion of multitudinous infinite sets that revolutionized (some say ruined) the fundamentals of mathematics.

125. [93] Actual infinity "expressing a quantity" (Mückenheim 2006, 1) refers to a technically completed series of an infinite number of members in a space with a beginning and end, such as the set of all natural numbers $\mathbb{N}$ { 1, 2, 3, . . . }. It's an infinity that wholly exists at one time. Potential—or, for

Cantor, "variable" (Jané 1995, 378)—infinity "expressing a direction" (Mückenheim 2006, ibid) refers to a procedure that continues infinitely over time, such as a sequence $[1, 2, 3, \ldots]$ of expanding numbers, that never reaches infinity because whatever the highest number, another can always be added, yet at any point in time is finite (e.g., Aristotle, *Physics and Metaphysics*). This is a distinction without a difference. Any infinite entity (completed or procedural) is by definition infinite if there's no intrinsic limit, otherwise countability or some other form of finite is implied. This is especially evident in Mückenheim's description. The terms create an abstraction, a faux infinity, but don't posit real infinity which is indeterminate and thus neither actual nor potential. Absolute infinity—divvied up as above into actual (categorematic) absolute infinity and potential (syncategorematic) absolute infinity, the latter being what he called transfinite infinity—is just a higher quantum category that inevitably quantifies not just a Creator but the essence of the universe itself. (Categorematic and syncategorematic are medieval scholasticisms that refer respectively to a term that can convey meaning employed on its own and a term that needs other terms to convey meaning, such as 'man' and 'many.') Infinity of any stripe pursued by Philosophy with a capital-P is a *collection* that's quantized, quantified, qualified, essentialized, and so on.

Suppose we say, "God's power is infinite." What we mean is that God's power indeterminately exceeds what power finitely is or can do. What we're actually saying, however, is that God's power is contained within a collection. The fact one describes it as infinite is immaterial because an infinite collection is still a collection and a collection is by necessity finite—*trans*finite, perhaps, by Set Theory's reckoning. The issue doesn't lie in circumscribing God's infinite power in an infinitely finite collection of attributes or features but in attributing infinity to power at all. If God's power is infinite as we typically conceptualize infinity (not to mention power), then God has the power to render himself powerless thus finite in terms of power. The contradiction defeats the premise. These sorts of paradoxes, contradictions, and inconsistencies are exactly what plagues Philosophy with a capital-P, and it's for the simple reason that thinkers misconstrue infinity.

126. [94] The Four Omnis of God are omnipotence, omniscience, omnibenevolence, and omnipresence. They mean, respectively, all-powerful, all-knowing, all-loving, and ever-present.

127. [94] Most pronounced in but not exclusive to Set Theory, which understands infinite sets in countability terms, which is to say that a set is uncountably infinite when its cardinality (the number of elements in a set) is greater than that of the set of all natural numbers $\mathbb{N}$ ($|S| > |\mathbb{N}|$) where S is an infinite set; the cardinality of an infinite set is $\aleph_0$, 'aleph null'). This only binds infinity to cardinality which, even though expressed as an infinite, is nonetheless finite for the simple reason that an uncountably infinite set by definition is the cardinality of the set of all natural numbers plus at least one ($|S| = [|\mathbb{N}| + 1]$), whereas infinity w.r.t. sets is an entity for which $\infty + n = \infty$ where n is any number. Infinity is immune to mathematical operations. The same holds for cardinality: $\aleph_0 + 1 = \aleph_0$. Cardinality speaks only to a set's elements and not to its infiniteness because infinity, being indeterminate, has nothing to do with cardinality, being determinate. There are no different 'sizes' for infinity, there is only different cardinality, which doesn't speak to finite or infinite. Whatever sets are, they aren't infinite. However useful a concept this faux infinity is for mathematics, it's not real infinity on account of it being impossible to conduct a determinate mathematical operation on a (non-numerical) indeterminate. It might seem we're splitting hairs here, but in so doing the many paradoxes, inconsistencies, and contradictions intrinsic to the mathematical and scientific concepts of infinity are mooted.

128. [94] This means an indeterminate is functionally infinite unless or until determinate. The example Mina consents to is, if a thing on the ground is indeterminate, is it infinite? *Yes.* Is it infinite in terms of what its nature could be, what its function could be, what its identity could be, and so forth? *Yes.* Plainly, infinity in Mina's mind quite exceeds what we've ever conceptualized. However, he dislikes the term *infinite* because of its past connotations, hence our redefinition herein.

129. [96] Mina agrees that "Mathematics is a philosophical exercise, it is a pure mental manipulation of concepts, except it comes out of the scientific tradition rather than the humanistic one" ("Mitch," May 27, 2016, https://philosophy.stackexchange.com/questions/1934/is-cantors-theorem-based-on-a-fallacy (accessed: 2019-03-05)). After working out and energy testing most of this discussion with Mina, we were quite interested to come across philosopher Kip K. Sewell's remark that "the 'infinite sets' of transfinite mathematics not only do not refer to real sets in nature, but actually lead us astray in understanding the quantifiable aspects of reality. Consequently, Cantor's math ought to be rejected as a tool for investigating reality even if it is saved as a kind of academic game" ("The Case Against Infinity," unpublished paper (Dec. 2010), 42. https://philarchive.org/archive/SEWTCA (accessed: 2019-03-01)). We're no kind of mathematicians and have no opinions on the matter except to say that, from Mina's perspective, mathematical infinity gives no enlightenment to real infinity.

130. [96] For example, see William Lane Craig, *The Kalām Cosmological Argument*, London: Macmillan Press, 1979; cf. Landon Hedrick, "Heartbreak at Hilbert's Hotel," *Religious Studies* 50 (2014), 27–46, https://doi.org/10.1017/S0034412513000140 (accessed: 2019-02-27); and Stephen Puryear, "Finitism and the Beginning of the Universe," *Australasian Journal of Philosophy*, 92:4 (2014), 619–629.

131. [96] The ratio out of balance only until all guests switch rooms to accommodate a new guest is irrelevant to the contradiction defeating the premise.

132. [96] "Quantum *res potentia*" ('potential things;' Kastner et al. 2018, 167) is proposed as the "mutually implicative ontological constituents of nature at the quantum mechanical level" (ibid, 160) in "an extraspatiotemporal domain of quantum possibility" (ibid, 168) that is additive to reality. Regarding Hilbert's Hotel, *res potentia* is the quantum possibility that a new guest will arrive and thus a new, unoccupied room in an extant reality of infinite, occupied rooms becomes the *res extensa* ('material things,' the new reality). "A quantum probability space is a pair $(A, \mathbf{P})$, where A is a *-algebra and $\mathbf{P}$ is a state . . . a generalization of the definition of a probability space in Kolmogorovian probability theory . . . The idempotents $p \in A$ are the events in A, and $\mathbf{P}(p)$ gives the probability of the event p" (https://handwiki.org/wiki/Physics:Quantum_probability (accessed: 2019-03-02)).

133. [96] In mathematical terms, one-to-one correspondence is a bijective (injective+surjective) mapping function $f : X \rightarrow S$. A proper subset P of set S has elements all of which are in P, but P has at least one more element not in $P(P \subseteq S)$.

Chapter 15 – Existence Infinity

134. [99] Efforts have been made to sidestep such questions by solving for time-infinity (such as physicist Sean Carroll's quantum eternity theory) although, in some cases, at the expense of space infinity. See Ahmed Farag Ali and Saurya Das, "Cosmology from quantum potential," *Physics Letters B*, 741:4 (Feb. 2015), 276–9, https://doi.org/10.1016/j.physletb.2014.12.057; and Saurya Das, Rajat K. Bhaduri, "Dark matter and dark energy from Bose–Einstein condensate," *Classical and Quantum Gravity*, 32:10 (Apr. 21, 2015), https://doi.org/10.1088/0264-9381/32/10/105003; cf. Kirk Durston, "Why past history cannot be infinite: there must be a beginning," *Evolution News & Science Today*, Mar. 5, 2016, https://evolutionnews.org/2016/03/why_past_histor/ (accessed: 2019-02-21).

135. [102] We derived some of the queries for Mina that led to this understanding from Ross (2019), Loke (2017), Klein (1998, 2003), Bliss (2013), Love (2006), BonJour (1985), Tahko et al. (2016), and general reading.

136. [102] Mina disclaims the concept of 'first cause' for All Existence because, irrespective of the nonexistence of an omnipotent 'uncaused cause' as a principle, 'first cause' connotes willed rather than emergent causative agency.

Chapter 16 – Time Infinity

137. [106] When Galileo first turned onto pendulums, for example, it's said he used his pulse to determine the regularity of a pendulum's event interval.

138. [107] In 1967, the 13th Conférence générale des poids et mesures defined a second as, "9 192 631 770 periods of the radiation corresponding to the transition between the two hyperfine levels of the ground state of the caesium–133 atom" (Howse 1980, 182, citing Resolution 1 of the CGPM).

139. [107] To understand the terms here, read LIGHTSPEED (§ 5:151). Any EMR source emits photons. A photon then emits a near infinite amount of EMW along its vector through space. EMR emitted nearer the supernova is more concentrated than EMR emitted hundreds of light-years away where, in any $4\pi r^2$ region of space, photon density is comparatively miniscule. About 30% of Betelgeuse's EMR arriving on Earth is photonic, moving at actual lightspeed ç. Accordingly, ET data shows its photonic supernova EMR has landed on Earth since late 1796. These photons emit EMW right up until

landing on Earth but their EMW is significantly less dense than the EMW emitted closer to the supernova, which is still in transit at normative lightspeed c and won't arrive until ca. 2045. Additionally, it arrives on Earth from many vectors and is confused with EMR from other regions of space. The supernova's apparent brightness itself as revealed by photonic EMR is presently about a magnitude 35. Since the Hubble telescope detects EMR only up to an apparent brightness of about a magnitude 31, the supernova remains invisible for now. Betelgeuse looks the way it does because we're seeing it in a partial supernova state where at least 70% —the main body, really—of the explosion remains undetected. Thus, it looks like a red supergiant instead of an exploding star although its supernova increased its apparent brightness since Ptolemy's (d. ca. AD 170) day about five magnitudes to its current visible light mean of magnitude 0.5. The in-transit EMW comprises about 70% of supernova EMR that eventually lands on Earth. Its greater luminosity relative to the photonic is substantial. We'll see the full supernova at an apparent brightness of about magnitude -16.8, or between 1–100 million times its current apparent brightness.

Betelgeuse more or less steadily oscillates about 110LY over a 150,000-year period, or 55LY over 75,000 years each way. It travels ~520,340,200,000,000 km per 55LY half oscillation. Its speed is therefore 520.3T km ×75 K yrs = 791,452 kmh or 219,848 m/s. This is about 0.0733% lightspeed c. Comparison of approximate speeds: Earth, 107,226 kmh; Sun/Solar System, 720K kmh (ET data shows ~800 kmh on average); Milky Way galaxy, ~403,200 kmh (ET data shows ~250K kmh because science's assumptions are inaccurate). The estimated supernova output of about 5.335×10^{58} J is > Milky Way mass-energy and < its total mass-energy inclusive of dark energy/matter (as science understands it).

140. [109] *Rip van Winkle* is an American folktale where the eponymous character falls asleep for 20 years but ages. "Epimenides of Knossos" is a folktale in Greek historian Diogenes Laërtius' *Lives and Opinions of Eminent Philosophers* (ca. 3rd c.) in which Epimenides falls asleep for 57 years but doesn't age. The *Seven Sleepers of Ephesus* is a ca. AD 250 Christian folktale in which some persecuted faithful hide out and fall asleep in a cave to awake 200 years later but don't age (this story is retold as "The People in the Cave" in the Quran, *As-hab al-Kahf*, 9–26).

Chapter 17 – Space Infinity

141. [111] For example, one proposal for navigating through deep space involves timing certain pulsar emissions that have similar accuracy to atomic clocks as they sweep past Earth and a spacecraft to establish location relative to each other. This defines the expanse of space relative to the spacecraft, providing locality thus permitting navigation.

142. [112] If there are finite configurations possible between particles but infinite particles because the universe is infinite, then at some point those finite configurations must repeat and, again at some point, the configurations of particles that is you must also repeat, thus another you . . . an infinite number of other you's because . . . infinity. However, while elementary particles or even molecular configurations do have finite possibilities, archí configurations are infinite. A body is configured from molecules that constitute from atoms that constitute from subatomic structures all built up from single bonded-archí pairs (see § 2.3.1:115 for terms). At the molecular or atomic level, it seems a body must be configurably finite therefore duplicable in an infinite universe. But underlying seemingly identical subatomic particles—leptons, quarks—are configurably differing, that is, infinite, archí configurations. The reason is that archí substructures are in constant flux because of Energent 'undulations.' Archí substructure 'energies' are what ultimately lie behind matter forming into specific macrostructures like Earth or you at any specific moment. As those 'energies' are always in flux then even with identical molecules it's impossible to form identical macrostructures. Therefore, with our current awareness of reality, there's no reason to presume duplicate matter—another Earth, another you, another ham sandwich with 5 grams of mayonnaise on it—will or even could occur.

143. [112] The quantum Higgs field is postulated as an 'energy' field permeating the universe with which all particles interact, one analogy being the Higgs field as an ocean and particles as fish in it. The Higgs boson (confirmed to exist in 2012) is the postulated carrier of the field as the photon is for the electromagnetic field. Vacuum energy is also an underlying background 'energy' that permeates the universe. Both concepts are poorly understood aspects of the Fundamental Energent.

144. [112] Generally considered zero, predictions that the cosmological constant (vacuum energy) has a positive non-zero value following the 1998 discovery that the expansion of the universe appeared to be accelerating have brought about the 'cosmological constant problem,' or 'vacuum catastrophe.' Some scientists believe it emerges from a microscopic quantum theory of gravity (cf. Stefano Finazzi, Stefano Liberati, and Lorenzo Sindoni, "Cosmological Constant: A Lesson from Bose–Einstein Condensates," *Physical Review Letters*, 108:7, 071101, Feb. 17, 2012).

145. [112] Briefly, each of the eight fundamental forces accomplish the following: 1) AF is single archí pair binding force; 2) SNF binds archí pairs thus holds matter together; 3) WNF stabilizes matter (radioactive decay) toward regulating 'energy;' 4) EMF lets matter interact with each other; 5) PF lets matter interact at distances beyond what's usually possible to create antimatter thus maintain 'energy' in the universe; 6) FF unites or harmonizes all forces within matter into a coherent 'energy' field; 7) MF mediates relative or best/most-suited strength of interaction between objects of matter (such as EM pull/repulsion); 8) FCF mediates the versioning of particles (quark and lepton flavor, quark color; the so-called color force is part of this larger FCF).

146. [113] The 19% net energy provided by Energent–prime is a negligible draw upon its 'energy.' A universe can be a perpetual motion machine and either an open or closed system (ours is open) while Energent–prime, being the root of All Existence—'all there infinitely is'—by definition is closed (§ 2:230) although 'closed' isn't a concept we can really use w.r.t. indeterminance (infinity) that is All Existence.

147. [113] Vitalism was a life-force explanans for the uniqueness of living beings until mechanistic reductionism identified reasons more plausible for life in non-inorganic beings. Since the 1930s, science considers vitalism a pseudoscience. Julian Huxley rather unsoundly trolled vitalists in 1926 by asking, if life results from *élan vital* (life force) then does a locomotive operate by its *élan locomotif* (locomotive force)?

148. [114] Carnegie-Mellon University (https://www.environ.andrew.cmu.edu/\T1\textcompwordmarkm3/s3/energy_sys.pdf, 12 (accessed: 2019-04-02)).

149. [114] Chang rewrote this paper for publication and deprecated the cited pre-publication quotes although the thrust of both versions appear the same.

150. [115] "In particle physics, a truly neutral particle is a subatomic particle with all its charges equal to zero. This not only requires particles to be electrically neutral, but also that all of their other charges (like colour charge) are neutral. Such a particle will be its own antiparticle. Mathematically, charge conjugation replaces all the constituent particles of a particle with their corresponding antiparticles. If a particle remains the same after charge conjugation then it is its own antiparticle and is truly neutral. Known examples of such elementary particles include photons, z bosons, and Higgs bosons along with hypothetical neutralinos, sterile neutrinos, and gravitons. For a spin-$\frac{1}{2}$ particle such as the neutralino, being a truly neutral particle implies being a Majorana fermion. Composite particles can also be truly neutral. The best known example is onium, a system composed of a particle forming a bound state with its own antiparticle." (https://en.wikipedia.org/wiki/Truly_neutral_particle (accessed: 2019-04-04)).

151. [116] If the archí is the first floor, then the quark is the sixth. So far, its binding 'energy' has been too strong for particle colliders. Indeed, quarks demonstrate that as particles get smaller and the distances between them shrink, the binding 'force' gets more resilient. All particles (excluding single archí) are separable with brute force or by neutralizing their binding 'force.' Lately, science is considering that smaller preons might indeed constitute quarks (Philip Ball, "Splitting the quark," *Nature*, 2007 (https://doi.org/10.1038/news.2007.292 (accessed: 2019-04-15)). According to Mina, about 83,427,500 archí, bonded in various configurations into six composite particles, constitute a quark.

152. [116] Some of this matter is claimed to have been found in the form of elementary particles called baryons (an archí composite structure). See Hideki Tanimura, Gary Hinshaw, Ian G. McCarthy, et al., *Notices of the Royal Astronomical Society*, 483:1, February 2019, 223–234 (accessed: 2019-05-18).

153. [118] There are indeed forces, including Fundamental Force and applied energy E, within the self-containment of the archí as though a miniature universe, but it's too complex to treat here.

154. [120] Source: left, https://isaacnewtonlifeandachievements.weebly.com/scientific-contributions.html; center and left, Heather (from August 3, 2016), https://physics.stackexchange.com/questions/3009/how-exactly-does-curved-space-time-describe-the-force-of-gravity (accessed: 2019-12-23).

155. [120] We came across this electricity, EMR+photons, and EM described as a candidate for gravity in a post by Shing Lau dated October 9, 2019 and tested its validity with Mina (https://www.quora.com/How-are-gravity-and-electromagnetism-related (accessed: 2019-12-23)).

156. [122] Gravitons penetrate inanimate (including dead) material with a lesser density than they exist in free space. They can't penetrate living tissue because they're repelled in the context of humans by our consciousness 'energy' and all other living entities by their consciousness-equivalent 'energy.'

157. [123] LIGO-detected disturbances are particle saturant shock waves from gamma ray bursts (§ 3.7.3.4.2:147).

158. [127] Source (modified): https://www.assignmentpoint.com/science/physics/line-of-force.html (accessed: 2020-01-10).

159. [128] Source (modified): https://courses.lumenlearning.com/physics/chapter/18-5-electric-field-lines-multiple-charges/ (accessed 2020-01-10).

160. [133] *Encyclopædia Britannica* (https://www.britannica.com/science/terminal-velocity (accessed: 2020-01-08)).

161. [135] "During the final minutes of the third extravehicular activity, a short demonstration experiment was conducted. A heavy object (a 1.32-kg aluminum geological hammer) and a light object (a 0.03-kg falcon feather) were released simultaneously from approximately the same height (approximately 1.6 m) and were allowed to fall to the surface. Within the accuracy of the simultaneous release, the objects were observed to undergo the same acceleration and strike the lunar surface simultaneously" (Jos. P. Allen, "Summary of Scientific Results," *Apollo 15 Preliminary Science Report*, NASA SP-289 (1972), 2–11).

162. [135] Professor of particle physics in the School of Physics and Astronomy at the University of Manchester; video duration 4:36 (https://www.bbc.co.uk/programmes/p02985m0 (accessed: 2019-05-13)). We couldn't find the variables in Cox's experiment and they appear to be unpublished.

163. [135] Source (modified): left, http://www.aerospaceweb.org/question/dynamics/q0203.shtml; center, https://www.ux1.eiu.edu/~cfadd/1150-05/02OnedKinematics/FreeFall.html; right, https://www.youtube.com/watch?v=77qJoYjCIOw (accessed: 2020-01-10; 2022-01-24; 2020-01-10).

164. [135] Our variables are as follows: 1) ∼32 frames (*Flipping Physics* says the experiment was televised (and recorded) at 29.97 frames per second); 2) depending on when one thinks the hammer is fully released from Scott's grip and the fall stopped by the lunar surface, we judged the start time at 00:00:59.653 and end time at 00:01:00.777 seconds for an elapsed time of 1.058 seconds without using frame rate and 1.067 seconds using frame rate as above; 3) acceleration of 1.429382 m/s^2 and 1.405371 m/s^2, respectively; 4) NASA's stated drop distance of 1.6 m.

165. [135] *Flipping Physics* variables are as follows: 1) 36 frames at 29.97 frames per second; 2) drop time of 1.201201 seconds; 3) drop distance of ∼1.2 m (https://www.youtube.com/watch?v=Gucr_OfzQ6M (accessed: 2019-05-14)).

166. [135] We calculated this from the expected drop time of 1.404222 seconds at $A_g = 1.625$ m/s^2 divided into Mina's 1.011102 seconds, yielding a 72.00442% difference, which when applied to standard A_g yields the stated A_g. Of course, NASA only estimates the 1.6 m drop distance.

167. [136] Source: https://www.wtamu.edu/~cbaird/sq/2013/05/22/why-is-gravity-the-strongest-force/ (accessed: 2020-01-05).

168. [137] *Wikipedia* 2020, "Gravitational Wave," par. 1; https://en.wikipedia.org/wiki/Gravitational_wave (accessed: 2020-01-26).

169. [137] *Kavli Foundation* 2020, par. 2 (https://www.kavlifoundation.org/ligo (accessed: 2020-02-16)). Mina gives the sky location and distance to NGC 4993, where LIGO–Virgo detected a neutron star merger in 2017, as about 10LY lower in the sky than where it appears to be owing to EMW mishmash (§ 5.6:161) and about 48.9MLY in distance, not the 130–140MLY that science estimates.

170. [137] Source (modified b/w): left, https://www.scientificamerican.com/article/gravitational-waves-reveal-the-hearts-of-neutron-stars1/; center, https://www.ligo.caltech.edu/page/ligo-gw-interferometer; right, Virgo Collaboration, CC0, https://commons.wikimedia.org/w/index.php?curid=45263649 (accessed: 2020-01-26).

171. [137] Source (modified): left, https://www.youtube.com/watch?v=3NpLnCpEyVk; center, right, https://www.gwoptics.org/ebook/interferometers.php, http://www.sci-news.com/physics/fourth-gravitational-wave-gw170814-05268.html (accessed: 2020-01-26; 2020-02-03).

172. [139] Source (modified and combined): as waveform, https://cnx.org/resources/ebe16f0b553433d6e663ceb787343a025c2f0794; as field extension, https://musicalsoundwaves.wordpress.com/types-of-waves/ (accessed: 2020-02-03).

173. [142] Source: https://byjus.com/physics/characteristic-of-em-waves/ (accessed: 2019-06-22).

174. [147] [sic] *The Liverpool Telescope* 2009, par. 3; https://telescope.livjm.ac.uk/News/Archive/index.php?sf=s20091209 (accessed: 2020-02-10).

175. [147] Source (individual gif frames rendered to inverted b/w): https://fermi.gsfc.nasa.gov/fermi10/fridays/08172018.html (accessed 2020-02-07).

176. [148] Left, Shahzad et al. 2016, Fig. 4B, 1140. Image: https://ceramics.org/ceramic-tech-today/mxene-films-provide-option-for-better-thinner-electromagnetic-shielding-for-electronic-devices (accessed: 2020-02-02).

177. [151] We excise "pleasurable" from the quote because we're dealing with consciousness not pleasure; Aristotle's point is unchanged by the omission.

178. [152] Špela Rožman, "Wake Pattern of a Boat," University of Ljubljana, Department of Physics, Seminar 2008–09, May 13, 2009 (prirodopolis.hr/\T1\textxtcompwordmarkdaily_phy/pdf/speed.pdf (accessed: 2019-06-05)). For a treatment of high-speed wakes where the Kelvin angle appears to deviate, cf. Marc Rabaud and Frédéric Moisy, "Ship Wakes: Kelvin or Mach Angle?" *Physical Review Letters* 110:21, 214503, May 22, 2013.

179. [152] Source: https://www.quora.com/Is-the-Mach-cone-a-shock-wave (retrieved 2019-05-15).

180. [152] More than a month after Mina taught us that EMR initially propagates conically, we stumbled across photographic evidence of a light-pulse-induced Mach cone using a camera capable of one billion frames per second. "Single-shot real-time imaging of light-scattering dynamics under different refractive index combinations. (A) Time-integrated image of a laser beam propagating faster in the source tunnel ($n_s = 1.0$) than scattered light does in the display panels ($n_d = 1.4$). (B) Representative snapshots of the same dynamic scene as in (A), acquired by LLE–CUP. A photonic Mach cone is observed" (Liang et al. 2017, Fig. 4, 4). We crop the graphic to its relevant portion. For the full image, see https://doi.org/10.1126/sciadv.1601814 (accessed: 2019-06-08); see also Liang et al. 2018.

181. [153] Source: left, EN 173:658; right, Internet; we lost the URL and couldn't rediscover it (accessed: Spring, 2019).

182. [155] Source (cropped, edited): https://www.flickr.com/photos/26677126@N06/2899320787 (accessed: 2019-06-11).

183. [155] In 1983, and then in 2018 and 2019, the Conférence générale des poids et mesures (CGPM) changed the Standard International (SI) units from physical objects to measured, calculated, or derived 'constants' of nature. Lightspeed is a principal constant for the CGPM (see https://www.nist.gov/si-redefinition (accessed: 2019-06-14)). Lightspeed is no longer measured as an actual speed in the real world but against the meter, which was redefined as the distance light travels in one second, a number (299,792,458 m/s) and time (9,192,631,770 periods of the radiation corresponding to the transition between the two hyperfine levels of the ground state of a cesium–133 atom) already agreed to by consensus out of the varied measurement efforts over the centuries. This means lightspeed is measured against a meter which itself is measured against lightspeed—the very definition of circular reasoning. "Using this method for defining the speed of light and the meter, we have absolutely no way to determine if the speed of light is changing because the units would simply change with it and no one would be the wiser. By pure definition, we have made the speed of light constant and incapable of change" (http://matterundermind.com/how-we-rigged-the-speed-of-light/ (accessed: 2019-06-14)).

184. [157] The *punctum caecum* is where the optic nerve plugs into the eyeball, so photoreceptor cells aren't possible. Our brain interpolates the missing data based on surrounding detail and from the other eye as it does with sound and dreams (§ 1.2.2.7.3:267) to create mental coherence. With only photonic light, this lack magnifies; the effect would be subjective. Light detectors like cameras would need an equivalent algorithm to avoid blank spots.

185. [158] Thomas Young, "Bakerian Lecture: Experiments and calculations relative to physical optics," *Philosophical Transactions of the Royal Society*, 94, 1804, 1–16.

186. [161] Source (modified): left, NKFUCOM, "Elektromagnetik Spektrum Nedir?" NKFUCOM, January 3, 2014 (https://www.nkfu.com/elektromagnetik-spektrum-nedir/ (accessed: 2019-06-28)); center, figures tab (https://inspirehep.net/literature/946729 (accessed: 2019-06-15)); right, Julius

Kaplunov and Danila A. Prikazchikov, "Asymptotic Theory for Rayleigh and Rayleigh-Type Waves," *Advances in Applied Mechanics*, 50, 2016, 1–106 (https://doi.org/10.1016/bs.aams.2017.01.001 (accessed: 2019-05-30)).

187. [162] Source: right, https://en.wikipedia.org/wiki/Aberration_(astronomy) (accessed: 2019-06-24).

188. [162] The ET data set for distance-to-photonic EMR is (0.0000000406, 99.999999999) (4, 85) (56.85, 50) (1000000, 15) (46000000000, 0.00000000406) where data set A is light-years and data set B is percentage not decimalized (which doesn't change the correlative outcome). We chose to analyze the given data using the Spearman over Pearson formula (which gives a moderate negative correlation of $R_s = -.64767$, $n = 5$, $p = .237332$ and not statistically significant, with an R^2 explained variance of 41.95%), because the given data appears monotonic rather than linear, thus suited to the methodology. For distance-to-EMW EMR the given data set indicates a moderate positive Pearson correlation where $R_s = +.64767$ with n, p, and R^2 the same as above. See plots below.

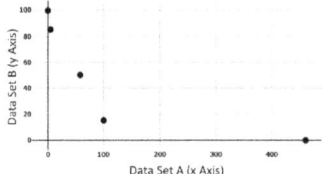 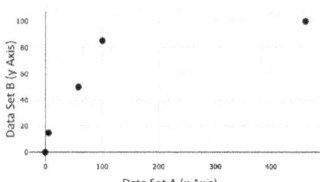

Left: distance-to-photonic EMR plot; right: distance-to-EMW EMR plot. The monotonic relationship is evident. To show the scatter, we reduced the scale of data set A to 0.406, 4, 56.85, 100, 460; therefore, it's not an accurate representation of the data but accurate to the correlation.

189. [163] Regarding electric (vacuum) permittivity $\varepsilon_0 = 8.8541878128(13) \times 10^{-12} F \cdot m^{-1}$ (farads per meter), Mina avers science has the data right but the equation inaccurate (ε_0 is too low). For magnetic permeability $\mu_0 = 1.257 \times 10^{-6} H/m$ (Henry per meter), the data is wrong but the equation accurate (μ_0 too low). For impedance of free space $Z_0 \cong 377\Omega$ (ohms), the data is inaccurate but the equations are accurate (Z_0 too low).

190. [164] The rationale—including for the expanding and accelerating universe—is something like, "The evidence for an accelerating universe is that these distant supernovæ appear fainter than they should be at their measured cosmological redshift, indicating that they are farther away than expected . . ." (Oesper 2017, 1) and ". . . the shape of the supernova light curve indicates the supernova's intrinsic brightness, analogous in a way to the period of a Cepheid indicating its intrinsic brightness" (ibid, 2). See also Lyndon Ashmore, "Supernovæ Ia Light Curves Show a Static Universe," *Proceedings of the NPA*, 9, Ed. by Greg Volk, 19th Natural Philosophy Alliance Conference, Albuquerque, NM, July 25–28, Lulu, 2012, 17–19.

191. [167] The LHC operates to smash particle clumps into each other at high speed and see what flies out of the train wreck. It uses electric and magnetic fields through a series of ever more energized machines to accelerate and channel particle beams around its 27-km track. To date, the LHC's fastest proton charged up to 6.5 TeV (6.5 trillion electronvolts, ~$2.8928186570833 \times 10^{-13}$ kilowatt hours; tiny) of energy and reached a Relativity-calculated speed of about $0.9999999896c$.

192. [168] *Groundspeed* is how we know a ball thrown on a train is moving at train+ball speed. If one removes groundspeed then one can't measure ball speed relative to train speed from outside the train. One can only measure it by a reference frame excluding the train where one can compare the two speeds. But that's not the ball's true speed, just its relative speed. The same is true for space. There is a 'groundspeed' in space, *event periodicity* (§ 2:107). One can compare ball speed on a spaceship moving at lightspeed c from such a 'groundspeed' reference frame just as with actual groundspeed.

193. [168] Source: left, https://scienceterms.net/physics/theory-of-relativity/; right, http://cmi2.yale.edu/bh/week2/pages/page2.html (accessed: 2019-12-10).

194. [168] Source (modified): http://mysearch.org.uk/website1/html/240.Principles.html (accessed: 2019-07-12).

195. [169] Source (modified; stick figure): https://www.slideshare.net/giganiyaseen1/special-relativity-17220525 (accessed: 2019-12-06).

196. [171]Source: https://courses.lumenlearning.com/physics/chapter/28-2-simultaneity-and-time-dilation/ (accessed: 2019-12-06).

197. [173] The 24,000:1 ratio holds from $v > 0$ through 2.09ç. A few event periodicity (EP) examples we calculated are as follows: 1) the International Space Station, which travels ~7.7 km/s or roughly $1/38,930$ lightspeed c, has an EP rate 0.676 times faster than Earth; 2) the Apollo rocket (and chemical rockets generally) traveled ~10.8333 km/s, or $1/27,673c$, an EP rate of .867; 3) next-gen nuclear rockets NASA hopes to one day field are estimated to go 100 times faster than Apollo at ~1,083.333 km/s, or $1/276.73c$, an EP rate of 86.727; 4) $1/20c$ has an EP rate of 14,986.5 km/s ~14,986.5 km/s, an EP rate of 1200.

198. [174] Source (left): http://hyperphysics.phy-astr.gsu.edu/hbase/hframe.html (accessed: 2019-07-22).

199. [175] Source: left and right, https://opentextbc.ca/openstaxcollegephysics/chapter/force-on-a-moving-charge-in-a-magnetic-field-examples-and-appli cations/ (accessed: 2019-07-17).

200. [175] Source (modified b/w): left, Messier 51a, Jean Tate, "Magnetic Fields in Spiral Galaxies—Explained at Last?" *Universe Today: Space and Astronomy News*, Apr. 3, 2010 (https://www.universetoday.com/61676/magnetic-fields-in-spiral-galaxies-explained-at-last/); right, IC 342, Rainer Beck, "Magnetic fields in the nearby spiral galaxy IC 342: A multi-frequency radio polarization study," *Astronomy & Astrophysics*, 578, June 11, 2015, A93. https://doi.org/10.1051/0004-6361/201425572 (accessed: 2019-07-17).

201. [175] Some of the partial derivative explanatory language here is from https://en.wikipedia.org/wiki/Magnetic_susceptibility (accessed: 2019-07-17).

202. [176] Source (modified): left, http://hyperphysics.phy-astr.gsu.edu/hbase/hframe.html; right, https://commons.wikimedia.org/wiki/User: Geek3/VectorFieldPlot (accessed: 2019-07-12).

203. [176] Source: Kathryn Jepsen, "Real Talk: Everything is made of fields," *Symmetry Magazine*, July 18, 2013 (https://www.symmetrymagazine.org/article /july-2013/real-talk-everything-is-made-of-fields (accessed: 2019-07-17)).

204. [178] Source (modified): left, ESA/Hubble, https://www.smithsonianmag.com/science-nature/astronomers-capture-first-images-supermassive-black -hole-180971927/; center, right, https://www.smithsonianmag.com/science-nature/astronomers-capture-first-images-supermassive-black-hole-180 971927/ (accessed: 2020-01-10, 14).

205. [179] Source: https://starlifecycle205.weebly.com/the-suns-life-cycle.html (accessed: 2020-01-14).

206. [180] Supernova remnant expansion stages: 1) free expansion of ejecta; 2) the Sedov–Taylor blast wave phase in which circumstellar or interstellar medium collects; 3) blast shell cooling; 4) blast interior cooling as shell continues expanding from momentum; 5) merging with surrounding interstellar medium (https://en.wikipedia.org/wiki/Supernova_remnant (accessed: 2020-01-15)).

207. [183] Source (left, original; right, modified): https://images.squarespace-cdn.com/content/5a6a727c18b27d1a710d8a79/1525453627777-BIN83CXV8VL U4H2RH3MC/venturi-effect.png?content-type=image/png (accessed: 2020-01-20).

208. [184] The context here is that "The Planck force is also associated with the equivalence of gravitational potential energy and electromagnetic energy and in this context it can be understood as the force that confines a self-gravitating mass to half its Schwarzschild radius: $F_P = {}^{G}m2/r_{G2}$, $r_G = r_s/2 = {}^{G}m/c^2$ where G is the gravitational constant, c is the speed of light, m is any mass and r_G is half the Schwarzschild radius, r_s, of the given mass" (http://dictionary.sensagent.com/Planck%20force/en-en/ (accessed: 2021-12-17)).

209. [185] Source (modified): https://www.cancer.gov/about-cancer/causes-prevention/risk/radiation/electromagnetic-fields-fact-sheet (accessed: 2020-01-23).

210. [185] Source (modified color-inverted b/w): https://skyandtelescope.org/astronomy-news/black-holes/best-evidence-yet-that-black-holes-really-exist-0505201523/ (accessed: 2020-01-23).

211. [187] Source (modified): left, https://www.pinterest.com/pin/411586853439452110/; right, https://www.1001freedownloads.com/free-clipart/grid-sphere (accessed: 2019-09-09).

212. [189] Source (modified): left, https://www.thinglink.com/scene/860893253489131521; right, https://www.shutterstock.com/image-vector/3d-wirefra me-terrain-contour-eps10-vector-315639740 (accessed: 2019-09-04; 2019-09-10).

213. [190] Source (modified): left, https://en.wiktionary.org/wiki/sphere (accessed: 2019-09-04).

214. [192] See, *Copenhagen Interpretation* at http://abyss.uoregon.edu/~js/21st_century_science/lectures/lec15.html (accessed: 2019-08-20).

215. [192] Source: left, https://supernovapcrepair.co.uk/technology-blog/a-quantum-leap-in-computing.html; right, https://slideplayer.com/slide/3808111, click on *link 4: The Wavefunction* (accessed: 2019-08-13).

216. [193] "The measurement problem in quantum mechanics is the problem of how (or whether) wave function collapse occurs . . . The wave function in quantum mechanics evolves deterministically according to the Schrödinger equation as a linear superposition of different states. However, actual measurements always find the physical system in a definite state. Any future evolution of the wave function is based on the state the system was discovered to be in when the measurement was made, meaning that the measurement 'did something' to the system that is not obviously a consequence of Schrödinger evolution. The measurement problem is describing what that 'something' is, how a superposition of many possible values becomes a single measured value. To express matters differently (paraphrasing Steven Weinberg), the Schrödinger wave equation determines the wave function at any later time. If observers and their measuring apparatus are themselves described by a deterministic wave function, why can we not predict precise results for measurements, but only probabilities?" (https://en.wikipedia.org/wiki/Measurement_problem, par. 3 (accessed: 2019-08-29)).

217. [194] Source (modified): left, Dhatfield, June 26, 2008, https://en.wikipedia.org/wiki/Schr%C3%B6dinger%27s_cat; center, right, https://discover.hubpages.com/education/Quantum-Physics---Werner-Heisenberg (accessed: 2019-08-13).

218. [198] Source (modified; citing European Space Agency): https://www.livescience.com/28550-how-quantum-entanglement-works-infographic.html (accessed: 2019-08-02).

219. [198] For Sun-myung's take on internal nature and external form, see Moon 1996, §1.1 "The Dual Characteristics of God," 17ff.

220. [198] Source (modified): https://www.publicdomainpictures.net/pictures/350000/velka/yin-yang-symbol-159195095846H.jpg (accessed: 2021-12-18).

221. [200] No two bonded–archí pair shares the same real energy Υ charge even though, as individual archí, they are Υ-charge-identical to one another. This is because SNF is partly a function of velocity, various momentums and spins, spatial coordinates, and other factors. As none of these repeat in toto for any other pair or group of archí anywhere in nature, Υ-charge is variant.

222. [200] "Electrical resonance occurs in a circuit with capacitors and inductors because the collapsing magnetic field of the inductor generates an electric current in its windings that charges the capacitor, and then the discharging capacitor provides an electric current that builds the magnetic field in the inductor. Once the circuit is charged, the oscillation is self-sustaining, and there is no external periodic driving action" (https://en.wikipedia.org/wiki/Resonance (accessed: 2020-12-01)). Universal electric–magnetic fields work this way to energize applied energy E.

223. [202] Ethan Siegel, "The Sun's Energy Doesn't Come From Fusing Hydrogen Into Helium (Mostly)," *Forbes*, September 5, 2017, par. 7 (https://www.forbes.com/sites/startswithabang/2017/09/05/the-suns-energy-doesnt-come-from-fusing-hydrogen-into-helium-mostly/amp/?sh=3259f0401480 (accessed: 2019-10-04)). The Sun needn't complete its lifespan and die as science predicts will happen in another 5+ billion years. Human consciousness is capable of initiating an infusion of *enérgeia* from the Energent directly into a star just as we can do with our own physical bodies. *Enérgeia*'s nature is to maintain (or revive) something's peak condition. In this case, it acts to increase the Sun's real energy Υ gravity well to pull in a hydrogen refill from the observable universe until the Sun's fuel tank tops off.

224. [203] Source: left, https://opentextbc.ca/openstaxcollegephysics/chapter/fusion/; right, https://slideplayer.com/slide/5110181/16/images/67/4.20+Qu antum+Mechanical+Tunneling.jpg (accessed: 2019-09-18).

225. [203] *Encyclopædia Britannica*, par. 1, 'uncertainty principle' (https://www.britannica.com/science/uncertainty-principle (accessed: 2021-06-01)).

226. [204] Ibid, par. 3

227. [204] Ibid, par. 4

228. [205] From § 6–History, par. 2 (https://en.wikipedia.org/wiki/Uncertainty_principle (accessed: 2019-11-02)).

229. [209] Source (video): https://imgur.com/gallery/tRoeWv6 (accessed: 2019-10-05).

230. [211] Source (modified and b/w): https://keystagewiki.com/index.php/Nuclear_Fusion (accessed: 2021-12-20).

231. [212] Source (*Gulf of Alaska meeting Pacific Ocean*; modified b/w): left, https://www.pinterest.com/pin/241787073718667458/?nic_v2=1a6C7dMdA (accessed: 2020-08-04).

232. [213] Source (modified b/w): left, https://www.education.com/activity/article/Solid_Liquid_fifth/ (accessed: 2020-08-24).

233. [216] Source (modified text): https://www.mechanicalbooster.com/2017/06/torque-converter.html (accessed: 2020-08-18).

234. [217] Source: left, https://image.shutterstock.com/image-vector/set-vector-silhouettes-man-woman-260nw-1134634124.jpg; right (modified): http://hyperphysics.phy-astr.gsu.edu/hbase/Acoustic/reflc.html (accessed: 2020-08-27).

235. [224] For the yin–yang duality of internal character–external form, see Moon 1996, 15–19. Source: left, http://tongil.org/ucbooks/slides/DP2ha1.htm; right, https://www.publicdomainpictures.net/pictures/350000/velka/yin-yang-symbol-159195095846H.jpg (accessed: 2019-11-26; 2021-12-18).

236. [224] In Relationism, time requires change: "Necessarily, if time exists, then change exists" (Dowden, n.d., § 5 par. 4). Mina says both concepts indeed are true in principle if not as theory.

Chapter 18 – All Existence

237. [228] Sun-myung's Divine Principle rests on revelation backed by reason, not in the logical sense but the sort made evident through his spiritually interpreted experience. The combination attracted me like gravity. All the revelatory books in the world failed to stack up to his simple, rational revelation. Not all his reasoning turned out accurate but in my twenties–forties it was sufficient for a cohesive spiritual worldview, certainly more grounded than traditional religion clinging to irrational premises for which it is obliged to advocate faith.

238. [231] No one older than Mina—as our 'creator' (progenitor), he's our grandfather many times removed—and thus outside our universe will talk directly to anyone in the physical universe. It's not because they're stuck up or don't like us but because we're just too unaware and locked into unproductive mindsets to make it worthwhile, like talking to a 2-year old when you're not family. Mother (P'najj; § 1.2:336) makes an exception for the girls and me since we pulled off a novel coup that got her attention and won her heart. Cosmo—one of the older megaversal humans in existence—now occasionally talks to Ayako and me. But you saw our effort to engage him during the Big Event: crickets (§ 1.3.1:63).

239. [232] We rewrite philosopher Jim Holt's (possibly in jest) "quick proof" that there must be something than nothing, using 'nothing' and 'something' *consistently* and per the text. "Suppose there were *nothing*. There would be no laws; for laws, after all, are $\{\mathsf{something}\}$. If there were no laws, then everything would be permitted. If everything were permitted, then nothing would be forbidden. So if there were nothing [i.e., $\{\ \}$], nothing [in its

normal sense] would be forbidden. Thus *nothing* is self-forbidding. Therefore, there must be *something*. QED" (Holt 2012, 1). His wording reveals his specious reasoning, as he equivocates the meaning of "nothing" until his premise and conclusion agree, much as one might change a game's rules mid-play to ensure its desired outcome. His conclusion is accordingly fallacious, invalid, and unsound not only on grounds of equivocation but because, even though *nothing* is impossible w.r.t. to All Existence, it is not *necessarily* impossible.

240. [234] John Lovelock, *Gaia: A New Look at Life on Earth* (1979). Earth indeed is a dynamical system in which all parties shape the ecosphere. Through individual functions that are in aggregate self-regulatory generally but as a holistic organism capable of self-regulation, Earth maintains a homeostasis fit for life in the absence of probabilistically inevitable exigencies—asteroids, supervolcanoes, solar crises—and humans who are free to blow it up if they choose. Mina's underlying causal intent that forms the deterministic and emergent activities of the larger natural environment ensure the *only* outcome is a biosphere that's fit for life. But that outcome is distinct from exigencies that are also a natural part of the universe and inevitable within Mina's larger, universal causal intent. As humans are eternal beings, it's no sweat for Mina to start over after disaster, which he's repeatedly done.

241. [234] See, e.g., Sahni 2002; Zlatev et al. 1999.

242. [236] The four-position foundation concept originates with Sun-myung (Moon 1996, 21ff).

243. [238] Although scientists have coaxed organic molecules to bind with silicon using a strategy called *directed evolution* (organo-silicon molecules have long been used in various commercial products), neither silicon nor organo-silicon is capable of life—nor will it naturally develop—because All Existence isn't 'coded' (Intentionalized) for it. See, e.g., Charles Q. Choi, "Possibility of Silicon-Based Life Grows," *Astrobiology Magazine*, February 8, 2017 (https://www.astrobio.net/news-exclusive/possibility-silicon-based-life-grows/); cf. Shirley Peng, "Silicon-Based Life in the Solar System," *Silicon*, 7:1, January 2015, 1–3 (https://doi.org/10.1007/s12633-014-9254-7); and David T. Jacob, "There is no Silicon-based Life in the Solar System," *Silicon*, 8:1, January 2016, 175–6 (https://link.springer.com/content/pdf/10.1007%2Fs12633-014-9270-7.pdf). Accessed: 2019-02-15.

244. [238] Science speculates about homeostasis outside biology (excluding man-made homeostatic devices such as thermostats) but it's unproven. Some literature indicates awareness of ultra-biological homeostasis, although the cited case "demonstrates the emergence of homeostasis as a consequence of the feedback loop operating between life and its environment" (Dyke et al. 2013, 1). Equilibrium—another type of homeostasis—is expressed as entropy (and disorder) w.r.t. All Existence. Physics scales entropy beyond where it actually operates and then reasons that existence necessarily reduces to its lowest energy level—thermodynamic equilibrium, or maximum entropy (the so-called heat death of the universe)—because it doesn't recognize the renewal systems implicit in the homeostasis of All Existence, which means our universe is not a closed but an open system.

245. [239] In Gen. 1:2, Earth represents God's creation, our universe. Prior to coming into being "the earth was formless and empty," meaning its 'frequency space' (§ 6.10.1.1:186) was yet unmade. Thus, nothing was yet creation but merely All Existence, unstructured, intangible, formless, only prototypically existing. Creation—our universe—was not yet Intentionalized, or in biblical terms, purposed. "[D]arkness was over the surface of the deep" means no Intentionality yet imposed, no purpose yet formed (in Energent terms, no 'modulation' of Energent–prime yet performed) on formless All Existence ("the deep"). The "Spirit of God" references not simply our 'creator' as an existent; "God was hovering . . ." would be sufficient for that. Rather, it references both the existence of God as 'creator' and the fundamental essence of his creative intent; he's not creating willy-nilly but with a defined endgame, which is a family and its home. It's this personalized creative intent "hovering" (preparing) "over the waters" that's the life environment of his intention, the created creation. Such metaphors in the Quran are 24:45, 41:11, and others; the 21:30 text: أَوَلَمْ يَرَ ٱلَّذِينَ كَفَرُوٓا۟ أَنَّ ٱلسَّمَٰوَٰتِ وَٱلْأَرْضَ كَانَتَا رَتْقًا فَفَتَقْنَٰهُمَا وَجَعَلْنَا مِنَ ٱلْمَآءِ كُلَّ شَىْءٍ حَىٍّ أَفَلَا يُؤْمِنُونَ as translated by Dr. Mustafa Khattab at https://beta.quran.com/21?locale=en (accessed: 2020-06-03).

246. [242] Source (modified to inverted b/w): https://www.shutterstock.com/video/clip-710974-multicolored-balls-floating-inflatable-water-pool (accessed: 2020-05-29).

247. [243] Source (modified to b/w): https://cdn.xxl.thumbs.canstockphoto.com/underwater-abstract-underwater-background-with-flowing-lines-and-bubbles-drawings_csp0198239.jpg (accessed: 2020-05-29).

Chapter 19 – Psyche Infinity

248. [248] Source (modified): https://sites.google.com/site/isami116/michellechapter8&22 (accessed: 2020-05-22).

249. [250] Source (modified b/w): https://www.pinterest.com/pin/521854675542401902/ (accessed: 2020-06-08).

250. [257] Source (modified to b/w): https://www.vectorstock.com/royalty-free-vector/human-body-icon-of-vitruvian-man-vector-11665553 (accessed: 2020-05-24).

251. Calculated with no order, no repetition, as $C_k(n) = \frac{n}{k} = \frac{n!}{k!(n-k)!}$.

252. [261] Source (modified): left, https://www.vectorstock.com/royalty-free-vector/set-of-speech-bubble-thoughts-in-head-vector-1884913; right, https://i.pinimg.com/236x/ce/06/c2/ce06c2f35f677f05fb303cccb8db13e3--solar-system-psych.jpg (accessed: 2020-06-09).

253. [263] Source: left, https://blog.goodaudience.com/how-to-type-with-your-brain-bed5bb8cafc0; right: https://www.cbsnews.com/news/amazing-but-true-robot-steered-via-brain-waves/ (accessed: 2020-05-30).

254. [264] Source (modified to b/w): https://www.smithsonianmag.com/innovation/scientists-prove-that-telepathic-communication-is-within-reach-180952868/ (accessed: 2020-05-30).

255. [264] In physics, *coherence* describes coupling and synchronization between oscillating systems (*Figure below*; source: https://www.heartmath.com/science/ (accessed: 2020-05-15)) such as phase-locked laser photons. *Autocoherence* describes single-system coherence (cf. EN 258:661).

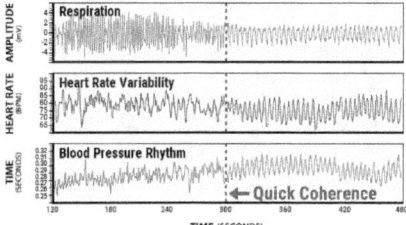

256. [264] *HeartMath Institute*, "What is coherence and how can I increase mine?" par. 2; https://www.heartmath.org/support/faqs/research/ (accessed: 2020-05-14).

257. [264] *Gaia Meditation*, "Coherence," par. 7 (refers to a state of optimal performance); https://www.gaiameditation.com/heart-coherence/ (accessed: 2020-05-14).

258. [264] *Heartmath Institute*, "Coherence," par. 1; https://www.heartmath.org/research/science-of-the-heart/coherence/ (accessed: 2020-05-15).

259. [265] Ibid.

260. [265] Source (modified): https://images.agoramedia.com/everydayhealth/gcms/Human-vs-Animal-Brainpower-More-Alike-1440x810.jpg (accessed: 2020-05-30).

261. [267] Source (modified): https://cancercaremalaysia.com/tag/brain-tumour/ (accessed: 2020-05-18).

262. [268] Source (modified): left, https://en.wikipedia.org/wiki/Memory_consolidation; right, *University of Washington*, https://www.teach-nology.com/currenttrends/brain_research/sleep.html (accessed: 2020-05-19).

263. [272] Source: piglet, https://www.wikihow.com/images/7/71/Draw-a-Simple-Pig-Step-9.jpg; plant, https://johnmuirlaws.com/wp-content/uploads/2016/01/bay_1.jpg (accessed: 2020-06-10).

264. [274] Unlike animal familials (CH. 39:601), companion animals in the supranatural context—'spirit animals'—are Intentionalized entities, not beings or life having independent existence. They're the same as any spirit world animal except their origin is physical.

265. [283] "And God said, 'Let there be light,' and there was light" (Ps. 1:3); "For he spoke, and it came to be; he commanded, and it stood firm" (Ps. 33:9); "When He decrees a matter, He only says to it, 'Be,' and it is" (بَدِيعُ السَّمَاوَاتِ وَالْأَرْضِ ۖ وَإِذَا قَضَىٰ أَمْرًا فَإِنَّمَا يَقُولُ لَهُ كُن فَيَكُونُ | Quran 2:117, Sahih Int'l.); ". . . and said to it and to the earth, 'Come [into being], willingly or by compulsion' " (ثُمَّ اسْتَوَىٰ إِلَى السَّمَاءِ وَهِيَ دُخَانٌ فَقَالَ لَهَا وَلِلْأَرْضِ ائْتِيَا طَوْعًا أَوْ كَرْهًا قَالَتَا أَتَيْنَا طَائِعِينَ | Quran 41:11, Sahih Int'l.).

266. [290] The moment I typed 'so very painfully' I burst out (empath) weeping. Mina said that now I'd voiced their reality, ~600 trillion physical-born spirit persons gathered around Earth for healing. Until then, these people—the least likely to consider healing—couldn't let go their pain, feeling no one understood or cared.

267. [295] James Powell, "The Real Four Position Foundation as Discovered in Theoretical Particle Physics," *Applied Unificationism* (2017), https://appliedunificationism.com/2017/04/03/the-real-four-position-foundation-as-discovered-in-theoretical-particle-physics/#more-6259; A. Garrett Lisi, "An Exceptionally Simple Theory of Everything" (2007), https://arxiv.org/abs/0711.0770 (accessed 2018-01-29).

Chapter 21 – Rise of the Humans

268. [320] Reportedly, a 1944 experiment with 40 infants in the United States demonstrated this effect in spades but, despite Mina's confirmation, we can't find a credible source. It's claimed "at least" ten infants died within four months and two more after the experiment's early halt despite receiving follow-up therapy (https://stpauls.vxcommunity.com/Issue/Us-Experiment-On-Infants-Withholding-Affection/13213, accessed: 2020-07-22). Alternatively, see psychiatrists John Bowlby and Harry Harlow's research during the mid-twentieth century in Eleanor Cummins, "These 1950s experiments showed us the trauma of parent-child separation. Now experts say they're too unethical to repeat—even on monkeys," *Popular Science*, June 22, 2018; https://www.popsci.com/1950s-experiments-attachment-unethical/ (accessed: 2021-12-26).

Chapter 26 – Conscious–Subconscious Mind

269. [395] Source (modified): https://images.fineartamerica.com/images/artworkimages/mediumlarge/1/infinity-symbol-carbon-fibre-allan-swart.jpg (accessed: 2020-11-15).

Chapter 27 – On Being Human

270. [405] Bandura (1963, 1986, 1995, 1997).

271. [421] Source (modified): left–right, http://www.atlanteanconspiracy.com/2014/06/dmt-psychedelic-death-and-rebirth.html (accessed: 2021-02-07).

272. [421] Source (modified): Internet, URL unknown.

273. [427] *Pirates of the Caribbean: Curse of the Black Pearl* (2003, film; Geoffrey Rush)

274. [447] Source: https://www.barrypopik.com/index.php/new_york_city/entry/the_philosophy_of_the_classroom_in_one_generation/ (accessed: 2020-11-16).

275. [454] Spock (Leonard Nimoy), "Mirror, Mirror," *Star Trek* S2E4, October 6, 1967; final par. [Bridge]; http://chakoteya.net/StarTrek/39.htm (accessed: 2021-01-12).

Chapter 28 – Spirit World

276. [470] Source (modified b/w): left, https://dreamcatcherreality.com/consciousness-human-brain-soul/; right, https://dreamcatcherreality.com/law-attraction/ (accessed: 2021-02-01).

277. [477] Source: https://www.washingtonpost.com/archive/local/1997/07/13/reston-man-22-dies-after-using-bungee-cords-to-jump-off-trestle/f9a074b2-837d-4008-a0a7-687933268f62/; https://www.latimes.com/archives/la-xpm-1998-dec-13-mn-53450-story.html (accessed: 2021-02-04).

278. [479] From 08:20, *The Good Place* (NBC–Universal), "The Trolley Problem," S2E5, airdate October 19, 2017.

279. [487] Source (modified and b/w): left, center, https://www.physicsclassroom.com/class/circuits/Lesson-4/Parallel-Circuits; right, https://en.wikipedia.org/wiki/File:Six_degrees_of_separation.svg (accessed: July 14, 2021).

280. [489] Eleanor (Kristen Bell) at 17:24, *The Good Place* (NBC–Universal), "Most Improved Player," S1E8, airdate October 27, 2016.

Chapter 29 – Chakras

281. [498] Source (modified b/w) left-to-right: https://www.chakras.info/12-chakras/; https://lifescriptdoctor.com/seven-chakras/; blog.zenward.com/wp-content/uploads/2015/10/chakras.jpg/; https://uplift.love/the-real-truth-about-the-chakras/ (accessed: 2021-03-20).

282. [500] Source (modified b/w): right, https://www.shutterstock.com/video/clip-16756765-4k-spine-pain-human-body-transparent-design (accessed: 2021-03-20).

283. [502] Source (modified b/w): left, https://www.researchgate.net/figure/Internal-face-of-the-right-hemisphere-Commissural-tracts-Corpus-callosum-anterior_fig21_281014334; right, https://juliantrubin.com/bigten/telephoneexperiments.html (accessed: 2021-03-07, 08).

284. [502] Source (modified b/w): left, https://healthiack.com/encyclopedia/pictures-of-brainstem; right, https://www.cgstudio.com/\T1\textcompwordmark3d-model/human-spine-with-spinal-cord-and-body-259653 (accessed: 2021-03-08).

285. [503] Source (modified b/w): left, https://media.springernature.com/\T1\textcompwordmarklw785/springer-static/image/chp/pct3A10.1007/pct2F978-3-319-28776-8_25/MediaObjects/324912_1_En_25_Fig1_HTML.gif; right, https://jtd.amegroups.com/\T1\textcompwordmarkarticle/view/6635/6351 (accessed: 2021-08-21).

286. [506] Source (modified b/w): left, https://www.alamy.com/stock-photo-illustration-of-female-internal-organs-135008245.html; right, https://www.cgstudio.com/\T1\textcompwordmark3d-model/human-spine-with-spinal-cord-and-body-259653 (accessed: 2021-03-10; 2021-03-08).

287. [506] Source (modified b/w): left, ibid; right, ibid.

288. [507] Source (right): ibid.

289. [508] Source (modified b/w): left, https://stealthbits.com/blog/effective-nested-group-membership-changes/; right (drawing by Mike Bowen at https://bowenimagery.com/), https://innersource.net/em/66-handout-bank1/hbbasicprinciples/199-donna-eden-a-david-feinstein-v15-199.html (accessed: 2021-03-20).

290. [509] Source: left (at left), http://horizonsmagazine.com/blog/the-chakras-a-basic-overview/; (at right), http://thesoulcodemethod.com/category/chakras/meng-mein/; right (modified b/w), http://thetorus.com/ (accessed: 2021-03-20).

291. [510] Source (modified b/w): left, https://www.alamy.com/stock-photo-illustration-of-female-internal-organs-135008245.html; right (drawing by Mike Bowen at https://bowenimagery.com/), https://innersource.net/em/66-handout-bank1/hbbasicprinciples/199-donna-eden-a-david-feinstein-v15-199.html (accessed: 2021-03-10, 20).

292. [513] Source (modified b/w): https://www.electrospaces.net/2015/04/torus-antenna-to-significantly-increase.html (accessed: 2021-03-20).

Chapter 32 – Earth's Human History

293. [534] Source (modified b/w): https://www.whatarethe7continents.com/the-continents-definition-what-is-a-continent/ (accessed: 2021-04-20).

294. [542] See, e.g., B. Jongman and J.M.G. van der Dennen, "The Great 'War Figures' Hoax: an investigation in polemomythology," in M. White per "Primitive War" in R. Muelenkamp; https://www.quora.com/What-percentage-of-all-humans-have-died-in-war?share=1 (accessed: 2021-04-21).

295. [543] Source (modified b/w): left, https://bradshawfoundation.com/origins/short_story_of_human_evolution.php; center, https://www.flickr.com/photos/tledoux/14846576535 (accessed: 2021-04-21); right, https://australian.museum/learn/science/human-evolution/ardipithecus-kadabba/ (accessed: 2021-04-25).

296. [545] We use divine right in the sense a government's founding principle—rooted in any kind of -archy or constitution—always is, or inevitably devolves to (as with America), a divine right in the socioculture's mindset that's uncontestable except via revolution that shifts government's 'divine right' from old to new.

297. [547] Source (modified b/w): left, https://id.wikipedia.org/wiki/Situs_Bhimbetka; right, https://curiosmos.com/before-the-pharaohs-ancient-egypt-was-ruled-by-a-scorpion-king-reveals-ancient-text/ (accessed: 2021-04-25).

298. [552] Source: male, https://insider.si.edu/2010/03/hall-of-human-origins/; female, https://allthatsinteresting.com/reconstructed-faces-of-ancient-people (accessed: 2021-05-03).

299. [555] H1 maintained youthful bodies until they died which, according to Mina, happened because, after a certain age, the metabotropic G-protein coupled receptors (GPCR) that sense molecules outside the neuron receptor cell (post-synaptic) ceased to activate signal transduction pathways that ultimately should activate cellular responses so as to pass a neurosignal neuron-to-neuron. The transduction pathway where this happened is the phosphatidylinositol signal pathway, and the problem was that GPCR didn't activate an associated G-protein via exchanging its bound GDP for a GTP, which halted neurotransmission in its tracks. This produced a cascade failure over about a month with inevitable death. After a certain number of years, an H1 person would quickly die despite being youthful and healthy, regardless their actual age in years. Abiogeneticists had no solution at the time for why physical bodies abruptly died absent, from their perspective, a valid cause. Also, the manner of death upset H1. Abiogeneticists felt it was traumatic to die suddenly at a certain point that people could more or less pinpoint, where people could know fairly certainly *when* they would die, in a milieu where people had lost their connection to spirit reality. Accordingly, abiogeneticists built H2 bodies with telomeres capping chromosomes, which H1 didn't have, to basically beat neurotransmitter shutdown to the punch—telomeres bring cell reproduction to an indeterminate end, which is different for everyone regardless any other factor including Living—Life force because, even when using these to heal cells to stay young, they can't *remove* (though they can re-lengthen) telomeres without causing genetically-compromised cell reproduction such as cancer—with an unpredictable time of death. The fix for programmed cell death isn't just introducing telomerase into cells to keep telomeres from shortening. It needs be a wholistic, not local, fix, which Mina is now applying.

300. [556] Source: http://temperature.global/ (accessed: 2021:05-15).

301. [559] Source: left, https://courses.lumenlearning.com/physics/chapter/31-5-half-life-and-activity/ (Source text paraphrased); right, https://courses.lumenlearning.com/cuny-lehman-geo/chapter/radiometric-dating-methods/ (accessed: 2021-05-20, 24).

302. [560] "Roger Penrose – Is Mathematics Invented or Discovered?" video, at 0:25; posted by *Closer to Truth*, April 13, 2020; https://www.youtube.com/watch?v=ujvS2Ko6dg4&t=27s (accessed: 2021-05-25).

Chapter 33 – Our Physicospirit Self

303. [562] Source (modified): https://www.abzu2.com/the-mind-is-an-illusion/ (accessed: 2021-06-27).

Chapter 34 – Religion

304. [572] According to Mina, Zoroaster is the earliest "to teach the doctrines of an individual judgment, Heaven and Hell, the future resurrection of the body, the general Last Judgment, and life everlasting for the reunited soul and body"—however incorrect the doctrines—that are ". . . familiar articles of faith to much of mankind, through borrowings by Judaism, Christianity and Islam . . ." (Boyce 1979, 29). While others before Zoroaster taught elements of these ideas, Mina says he's the first to put them all together into "their fullest logical coherence" (ibid).

Chapter 41 – Energy Testing

305. [624] *Ideomotor* is of or pertaining to involuntary actions caused by subconscious thought. *Observer-expectancy* is a researcher's cognitive bias that subconsciously influences experiment participants and affects results. *Subject-expectancy* is a research subject or patient expecting a given result that unconsciously affects the outcome or reports the expected result. *Confirmation bias* is selecting information supporting one's views, ignoring contrary information, or interpreting ambiguous evidence to support an existing attitude. Except for the latter, this is science using magic as an explanans.

306. [624] *James Randi: Psychic Investigator* (UK, Granada TV, E4, August 14, 1991, https://www.imdb.com/title/tt1589787/; uploaded by *HaulMorgan* December 28, 2007, https://www.youtube.com/watch?v=p_MzP2MZaOo (accessed: 2021-09-20)).

307. [628] Source (modified): left and center, https://www.allthingspossible.biz/tap-intuition-muscle-testing/; right, https://www.martelnyc.com/figure-illustration/popular-fashion-poses.html (accessed: 2021-09-19, 21).

308. [630] Source (modified): left to right, https://outdoorswimmer.com/guides/how-to-warm-up-on-land-for-swimming; https://imgbin.com/png/nZQben3p/clapping-gesture-png (accessed: 2021-09-27); https://evolvefitnessandcoaching.com/metabolic-resistance-training-1/ (accessed: 2021-10-01); http://cliparts.co/prayer-hands-clip-art (accessed: 2021-09-27).

309. [631] Source (modified): left, https://www.allthingspossible.biz/tap-intuition-muscle-testing/; center, https://www.myradiary.com/830/muscle-testing-a-skill-to-self-test-your-rheumatoid-arthritis-related-allergies-and-emotions; right, https://www.healing-with-eft.com/self-muscle-testing.html (accessed: 2021-09-19).

Chapter 42 – ET Caveats & Cautions

310. [636] Source (modified; b/w inverted): left, https://en.wikipedia.org/wiki/Latitude; center, https://www.britannica.com/science/latitude (©2012); right, https://mapsdatabasez.blogspot.com/2019/09/ley-line-map-google-earth.html (accessed: 2021-09-19).

Works Cited

Explanatory Note: Works cited and consulted (pg. 674) form no part of, though some here and there do coincidentally agree in part with the text of, this book beyond short quotes or as a reference. They're representative of the background material that informed and guided our ET inquiries in areas where our awareness was deficient. For example, when Mina said Carbon-14 dating methodologies are incorrect and date things too young or old, we had no knowledge base even to imagine the necessary questions to get to the bottom of why that would be the case beyond our vague, popular awareness and how anthropologists, for instance, use it to date fossil-bearing strata. In keeping with this book as not just revelation but response, it's wholly insufficient to simply relate Mina's pronouncements without rationale or analysis, as if "God told me, isn't that good enough?" That invites only scorn and defeats the purpose of conveying the revelation in the first place. *We* had to know why, anyway. And Mina wanted us to know. We figured you would, too. Citation page(s) follow(s) each entry as [cit. pg.#].

———————————————————— ∂♔∾ ————————————————————

Addiscott, Tom. 2011. "Emergence or Self-Organization? Look to the Soil Population." *Communicative and Integrative Biology* 4, no. 4 (July–August): 469–70. https://doi.org/10.4161/cib.4.4.15547. [cit. 91].

Agüera y Arcas, Blaise, Adrienne L. Fairhall, and William Bialek. 2003. "Computation in a Single Neuron: Hodgkin and Huxley Revisited." *Neural Computation* 15:1715–1749. [cit. 271].

Aiken, Henry D., ed. (1779) 1948. *Dialogues Concerning Natural Religion.* By David Hume. NY: Hafner Publishing Co. [cit. 100].

Alderson, Ella. 2019. *What Gravitational Waves Will Change: A direct observation of general relativity's last prediction,* January 17, 2019. Accessed January 16, 2020. https://medium.com/futuresin/what-gravitational-waves-will-change-8823fb3a3654. [cit. 137].

American Heritage Dictionary of the English Language. 2020. 5th ed. Boston: Houghton Mifflin Harcourt Publishing Company. [cit. 178, 394].

Arendt, Hannah. 1964. *Eichmann in Jerusalem: A Report on the Banality of Evil.* NY: The Viking Press. [cit. 293, 459].

Aristotle. (c. 353–322 BC) 1956. *The Nicomachean Ethics.* Edited by T.E. Page, E. Capps, W.H.D. Rouse, L.A. Post, and E.H. Warmington. Translated by Harris Rackham. Cambridge: Harvard University Press (Loeb Library Edition). [cit. 151].

Armstrong, Chris R. 2011. "A History of Darkness." *Leadership Journal* 32 (4). Accessed June 12, 2018. https://www.christianitytoday.com/pastors/2011/fall/historydarkness.html. [cit. 653].

Augustine. (1610) 1909. *The City of God.* Translated by John Healey. Vol. 2. Edinburgh: John Grant. [cit. 526].

Ayala, Francisco J. 1995. "The Myth of Eve: Molecular Biology and Human Origins." *Science* 270, no. 5244 (December 22, 1995): 1930–1936. [cit. 645].

Azevedo, Frederico A.C., Ludmila R.B. Carvalho, Lea T. Grinberg, José Marcelo Farfel, Renata E.L. Ferretti, Renata E.P. Leite, Wilson Jacob Filho, Roberto Lent, and Suzana Herculano-Houzel. 2009. "Equal Numbers of Neuronal and Nonneuronal Cells Make the Human Brain an Isometrically Scaled-Up Primate Brain." *The Journal of Comparative Neurology* 513:532–541. [cit. 258].

Baer, Greg. 2003. *Real Love: The Truth About Finding Unconditional Love and Fulfilling Relationships.* NY: Gotham Books. [cit. 583, 650].

Bandura, Albert. 1963. *Social Learning and Personality Development.* NY: Holt, Rinehart, and Winston. [cit. 662].

Bandura, Albert. 1986. *Social Foundations of Thought and Action: A Social Cognitive Theory.* NY: Prentice-Hall. [cit. 662].

Bandura, Albert. 1995. *Self-efficacy in changing societies.* NY: Cambridge University Press. [cit. 662].

Bandura, Albert. 1997. *Self-efficacy: The exercise of control.* NY: W.H. Freeman. [cit. 662].

Bartol, Thomas M. Jr., Cailey Bromer, Justin Kinney, Michael A. Chirillo, Jennifer N. Bourne, Kristen M. Harris, and Terrence J. Sejnowski. 2015. "Nanoconnectomic upper bound on the variability of synaptic plasticity." *eLife* 4:1–18. https://doi.org/10.7554/eLife.10778. [cit. 271].

Berlin, Isaiah. 1970. "Two Concepts of Liberty." In *Four Essays on Liberty,* edited by Isaiah Berlin, 118–172. NY: Oxford University Press. [cit. 587–588].

Bliss, Ricki Leigh. 2013. "Viciousness and the structure of reality." *Philosophical Studies: An International Journal for Philosophy in the Analytic Tradition* 166, no. 2 (November): 399–418. Accessed February 18, 2019. https://www.jstor.org/stable/42920276. [cit. 656].

Bond, Michael. 2014. "How extreme isolation warps the mind." In *BBC Future.* May 13, 2014. Accessed August 5, 2020. https://www.bbc.co.uk/future/article/20140514-how-extreme-isolation-warps-minds. [cit. 307].

BonJour, Laurence. 1985. *The Structure of Empirical Knowledge.* Cambridge, MA: Harvard University Press. [cit. 656].

Boyce, Mary. 1979. *Zoroastrians: Their Religious Beliefs and Practices.* NY: Routledge. [cit. 663].

Brooks, Patricia L., and John H. Peever. 2011. "Impaired GABA and Glycine Transmission Triggers Cardinal Features of Rapid Eye Movement Sleep Behavior Disorder in Mice." *The Journal of Neuroscience* 31, no. 19 (May 11, 2011): 7111–21. https://doi.org/10.1523/JNEUROSCI.0347-11.2011. [cit. 269].

Brooks, Patricia L., and John H. Peever. 2012. "Identification of the Transmitter and Receptor Mechanisms Responsible for REM Sleep Paralysis." *The Journal of Neuroscience* 32, no. 29 (July 18, 2012): 9785–95. https://doi.org/10.1523/JNEUROSCI.0482-12.2012. [cit. 269].

Brumm, Adam, Adhi Agus Oktaviana, Basran Burhan, Budianto Hakim, Rustan Lebe, Jian-Xin Zhao, Priyatno Hadi Sulistyarto, Marlon Ririmasse, Shinatria Adhityatama, Iwan Sumantri, and Maxime Aubert. 2021. "Oldest cave art found in Sulawesi." *Science Advances* 7, no. 3 (January 13, 2021): 1–12. https://doi.org/10.1126/sciadv.abd4648. [cit. 547].

Burgin, Mark. 2017. "Ideas of Plato in the Context of Contemporary Science and Mathematics." *Athens Journal of Humanities & the Arts* 4, no. 3 (July): 161–82. https://doi.org/10.30958/ajha/v4i3. [cit. 238].

Burton, Richard A. 2008. *On Being Certain: Believing You Are Right Even When You're Not.* NY: St. Martin's Griffin. [cit. 647].

Cavanaugh, T.A. 2018. *Hippocrates' Oath and Asclepius' Snake: The Birth of the Medical Profession.* NY: Oxford University Press. [cit. 361].

Čerenkov, Pavel. 1958. "Radiation of particles moving at a velocity exceeding that of light, and some of the possibilities for their use in experimental physics," 426–440. Nobel Foundation. Accessed June 13, 2019. https://www.nobelprize.org/uploads/2018/06/cerenkov-lecture.pdf. [cit. 152].

Chalmers, David J. 2006. "Strong and Weak Emergence." In *The Re-Emergence of Emergence: The Emergentist Hypothesis from Science to Religion,* 244–56. Oxford University Press. [cit. 90].

Chang, Donald C. 2016. *What is the physical meaning of mass in view of wave-particle duality? A proposed model,* December 29, 2016. Accessed April 20, 2019. arXiv: physics/0404044v2 [physics.hist-ph]. [cit. 114–115].

Cianciolo, Anna T., and Robert J. Sternberg. 2004. *Intelligence: A Brief History.* Malden, MA: Blackwell Publishing. [cit. 234].

Clarke, Peter G. 2013. "The Libet experiment and its implications for conscious will." In *The Faraday Institute, Paper 17.* Faraday Institute for Science and Religion. Accessed December 17, 2020. https://www.bethinking.org/human-life/the-libet-experiment-and-its-implications-for-conscious-will. [cit. 429].

Clayton, Philip. 2006. "Conceptual Foundations of Emergence Theory." In *The Re-Emergence of Emergence: The Emergentist Hypothesis from Science to Religion,* edited by Paul Davies and Philip Clayton, 1–34. Oxford University Press. [cit. 655].

Cooper, Keith. 2018. "The Dark-energy Deniers." *Physics World* 31, no. 6 (June): 20–24. https://doi.org/10.1088/2058-7058/31/6/27. [cit. 195].

Copenhagen Interpretation. 2019. Accessed August 21, 2019. http://thelifeofpsi.com/2013/09/01/the-measurement-problem/. [cit. 194].

Costandi, Moheb. 2017. *How Do Brain Cells Tell Us Where We're Going?,* January 13, 2017. Accessed July 22, 2020. https://www.scientificamerican.com/article/how-do-brain-cells-tell-us-where-were-going/. [cit. 317].

Crichton, Michael. 2003. *Remarks to the Commonwealth Club,* September 15, 2003. Accessed December 18, 2018. https://www.cs.cmu.edu/~kw/crichton.html. [cit. 227].

Damásio, António. 2006. *Descartes' Error: Emotion, Reason and the Human Brain.* London: Vintage. [cit. 289].

Davidson, Matthew. (2005) 2019. "God and Other Necessary Beings." In *The Stanford Encyclopedia of Philosophy,* Fall, edited by Edward N. Zalta. Metaphysics Research Lab, Stanford University. Accessed March 26, 2020. https://plato.stanford.edu/archives/fall2019/entries/god-necessary-being/. [cit. 228].

Davies, Paul. 2007. *Cosmic Jackpot: Why Our Universe is Just Right for Life.* NY: Houghton Mifflin. [cit. 234].

Dawkins, Richard. 1989. *The Selfish Gene.* (1976). Oxford University Press. [cit. 647].

de Chardin, Pierre Teilhard. 1959. *The Phenomenon of Man.* NY: HarperPerennial. [cit. 647].

de Tocqueville, Alexis. 1841. *Democracy in America.* 4th ed. Vol. 2. NY: J. & H.G. Langley. [cit. 455].

De Wolf, Tom, and Tom Holvoet. 2005. "Emergence Versus Self-Organisation: Different Concepts but Promising When Combined," edited by Sven A. Brueckner, Giovanna Di Marzo Serugendo, Anthony Karageorgos, and Radhika Nagpal, 3464:1–15, July 25, 2004. Utrecht, The Netherlands: Springer. https://doi.org/10.1007/b136984. [cit. 90–91, 655].

Dirac, Paul A.M. 1930. *The Principles of Quantum Mechanics.* Oxford: Clarendon Press. [cit. 193].

Douglass, Frederick. 1845. *Narrative of the Life of Frederick Douglass an American Slave.* Boston: Anti-slavery Office. [cit. 587, 650].

Dowden, Bradley. n.d. "Time." In *Internet Encyclopedia of Philosophy.* Accessed April 11, 2019. https://iep.utm.edu/time/#H5. [cit. 224, 660].

DuBois, W.E.B. 1969. *The Souls of Black Folk.* 17th ed. NY: NAL Penguin, Inc. [cit. 650].

Dumper, Kathryn, William Jenkins, Arlene Lacombe, Marilyn Lovett, and Marion Perimutter. 2019. *Introductory Psychology: What is Cognition?* Edited by Samantha Swindell. Open Text Washington State University. Accessed March 30, 2020. https://opentext.wsu.edu/psych105/chapter/7-2-what-is-cognition/. [cit. 234].

Dunne, John. (1624) 1840. *Devotions Upon Emergent Occasions and Several Steps in My Sickness, Meditation XVII.* London: William Pickering. [cit. 404].

Durkheim, Émile. (1893) 1984. *The Division of Labour in Society.* London: Macmillan Press. [cit. 647].

Dyke, James G., and Iain S. Weaver. 2013. "The Emergence of Environmental Homeostasis in Complex Ecosystems." *PLoS Computational Biology* 9, no. 5 (May): 1–9. Accessed February 15, 2019. 10.1371/journal.pcbi.1003050. [cit. 661].

Eagle, Antony. 2019. "Chance versus Randomness." In *The Stanford Encyclopedia of Philosophy,* Spring, edited by Edward N. Zalta. Metaphysics Research Lab, Stanford University. https://plato.stanford.edu/archives/spr2019/entries/chance-randomness/. [cit. 92].

Edinger, Edward F. 1992. *Ego & Archetype: Individuation and the Religious Function of the Psyche.* Boston: Shambhala Publications. [cit. 646].

Einstein, Albert. (1920) 1987. *The Collected Papers of Albert Einstein: The Berlin Years: Writings, 1918-1921.* Edited by John Stachel, Anna Beck, Peter Havas, and Diana Kormos Buchwald. Translated by Alfred Engel and Engelbert Schucking. Vol. 7. Princeton University Press. [cit. 167].

Emmeche, Claus, Simo Køppe, and Frederik Stjernfelt. 2000. "Levels, Emergence, and Three Versions of Downward Causation." In *Downward Causation: Minds, Bodies and Matter,* edited by Peter Bøgh Andersen, Claus Emmeche, Niels Ole Finnemann, and Peder Voetmann Christiansen, 13–34. Århus: Aarhus University Press. [cit. 91].

Farnese, A. 1901. *A Wanderer in the Spirit Lands by Franchezzo.* Chicago: The Progressive Thinker Publishing House. [cit. 651].

Fell, Elena. 2017. "Macro-Reasoning and cognitive gaps: understanding post-Soviet Russians' communication styles." *Journal for Communication Studies* 7 (1 [13]/2014): 91–110. [cit. 654].

Ferrell, Robert H. 1994. *Harry S. Truman: A Life.* Columbia: University of Missouri Press. [cit. 649].

Feynman, Richard P. 2015. *The Quotable Feynman.* Princeton University Press. [cit. 225].

Filippenko, Alexei V., and Adam G. Riess. 1998. "Results from the High-z Supernova Search Team." *Physics Reports* 307:31–44. [cit. 161].

Fisher, Yvette E., Jenny Lu, Isabel D'Alessandro, and Rachel I. Wilson. 2019. "Sensorimotor experience remaps visual input to a heading-direction network." *Nature* 576:121–125. [cit. 318].

Forrester, Rochelle. 2015. *Sense Perception and Reality: A theory of perceptual relativity, quantum mechanics and the observer dependent universe.* 3rd ed. Wellington, NZ: Best Publications Limited. [cit. 194–195].

Frankl, Viktor E. 1959. *From Death-camp to Existentialism: A Psychiatrist's Path to a New Therapy.* Boston: Beacon Press. [cit. 586].

Gottfredson, Linda S. 1997. "Mainstream science on intelligence: An editorial with 52 signatories, history, and bibliography." Originally published in *The Wall Street Journal* December 13, 1994. *Intelligence* 24, no. 1 (January–February): 13–23. Accessed February 14, 2019. https://doi.org/10.1016/S0160-2896(97)90011-8. [cit. 234].

Green, Douglas R., Lorenzo Galluzzi, and Guido Kroemer. 2014. "Metabolic control of cell death." *Science* 345, no. 6203 (September 19, 2014): 1466. [cit. 249].

Greenwood, Susan. 1990. "Émile Durkheim and C. G. Jung: Structuring a Transpersonal Sociology of Religion." *Journal for the Scientific Study of Religion* 29, no. 4 (December): 482–95. [cit. 647].

Greyson, Bruce. 1983. "The near-death experience scale: construction, reliability and validity." *Journal of Nervous and Mental Disease* 171:369–375. [cit. 425].

Greyson, Bruce. 1990. "Near-death encounters with and without near-death experiences: comparative NDE Scale profiles." *Journal of Near-Death Studies* 8:151–161. [cit. 425].

Hackett, Conrad, and Brian J. Grim. 2012. *The Global Religious Landscape: A Report on the Size and Distribution of the World's Major Religious Groups as of 2010.* Technical report. Washington, DC. [cit. 655].

Haldane, J.B.S. 1928. *Possible Worlds and Other Papers.* NY: Harper & Brothers. [cit. 430].

Harari, Yuval Noah. 2011. *Sapiens: A Brief History of Humankind.* London: Harvill Secker. [cit. 544].

Hartman, David, and Diane Zimberoff. 2012. "REM and non-REM Dreams: 'Dreaming Without a Dreamer'." *Journal of Heart-Centered Therapies* 15 (2): 27–52. [cit. 267].

Hartwell, Leland H., and Ted A. Weinert. 1989. "Checkpoints: Controls that Ensure the Order of Cell Cycle Events." *Science* 246, no. 4930 (November 3, 1989): 629–634. [cit. 249].

Heffernan, Margaret. 2011. *Willful Blindness: Why We Ignore the Obvious at Our Peril.* NY: Walker Publishing. [cit. 647].

Heidegger, Martin. 1962. *Being and Time.* Oxford: Blackwell. [cit. 22, 276].

Helmenstine, Anne Marie. 2019. *Charge Definition and Examples (Physics and Chemistry),* April 14, 2019. Accessed January 31, 2020. https://www.thoughtco.com/definition-of-charge-and-examples-605838. [cit. 140].

Henriques, Gregg. 2011a. *A New Unified Theory of Psychology.* NY: Springer. [cit. 294].

Henriques, Gregg. 2011b. "What is the Mind? Understanding mind and consciousness via the unified theory." In *Psychology Today.* December 22, 2011. Accessed April 29, 2020. https://www.psychologytoday.com/us/blog/theory-knowledge/201112/what-is-the-mind. [cit. 273–275].

Herculano-Houzel, Suzana, and Roberto Lent. 2005. "Isotropic Fractionator: A Simple, Rapid Method for the Quantification of Total Cell and Neuron Numbers in the Brain." *The Journal of Neuroscience* 25 (10): 2518–2521. https://doi.org/10.1523/JNEUROSCI.4526-04.2005. [cit. 258].

Heschel, Abraham J. 1975. *The Prophets: Part II.* NY: Harper Colophon Books. [cit. 345].

Hobbes, Thomas. (1651) 1887. *Leviathan, or The Matter, Form, and Power of a Commonwealth, Ecclesiastical and Civil.* 3rd ed. London: George Routledge and Sons. [cit. 448, 587–588].

Hobson, J. Allan, Edward F. Pace-Schott, and Robert Stickgold. 2000. "Dreaming and the brain: Toward a cognitive neuroscience of conscious states." *Behavioral and Brain Sciences* 23:793–1121. https://doi.org/10.1017/S0140525X00003976. [cit. 267].

Holland, John. 2018. *Bridging Two Realms: Learn to Communicate With Your Loved Ones on the Other-Side.* Carlsbad, CA: Hay House. [cit. 652].

Holman, Peggy. 2010. *Engaging Emergence: Turning Upheaval Into Opportunity.* San Francisco: Berrett-Koehler. [cit. 89–90, 231].

Holman, Peggy. 2011. "Engaging Emergence: Turning Upheaval into Opportunity," edited by H. Sayama, A. Minai, D. Braha, and Y. Bar-Yam, 1158–72. Singapore: NECSI Knowledge Press, June 1–3, 2011. [cit. 91].

Holt, Jim. 2012. *Why Does the World Exist? An Existential Detective Story.* NY: Liveright Publishing Corporation. [cit. 99–100, 231–232, 347, 654, 661].

Howell, Trisha. 2007. *ThetaHealing is a Fraud and a Dangerous Cult!* Accessed May 7, 2017. http://fraudthetahealing.com/index.html. [cit. 652].

Howse, Derek. 1980. *Greenwich Time and the Discovery of the Longitude.* Oxford University Press. [cit. 656].

Huang, Yu, Anli A. Liu, Belen Lafon, Daniel Friedman, Michael Dayan, Xiuyuan Wang, Marom Bikson, Werner K. Doyle, Orrin Devinsky, and Lucas C. Parra. 2017. "Measurements and models of electric fields in the in vivo human brain during transcranial electric stimulation." *eLife* (February 7, 2017): 1–26. Accessed July 22, 2020. https://doi.org/10.7554/eLife.18834. [cit. 318].

Hunt, Tim, Kim Nasmyth, and Béla Novák. 2011. "The cell cycle." *Philosophical Transactions: Biological Sciences* 366, no. 1584 (December 27, 2011): 3494–3497. [cit. 249].

James, William. (1911) 1916. *Some Problems of Philosophy: A Beginning of an Introduction to Philosophy.* NY: Longmans, Green, and Co. [cit. 89].

Jané, Ignacio. 1995. "The Role of the Absolute Infinite in Cantor's Conception of Set." *Erkenntnis* 42, no. 3 (May): 375–402. Accessed February 28, 2019. https://www.jstor.org/stable/20012628. [cit. 656].

Johnson, Phillip E. 1997. *Defeating Darwinism by Opening Minds.* Downers Grove, IL: InterVarsity Press. [cit. 415].

Johnson, Steven. 2001. *Emergence: The Connected Lives of Ants, Brains, Cities, and Software.* NY: Scribner. [cit. 90].

Kant, Immanuel. (1780) 1930. *Lectures on Ethics.* Translated by Louis Infield. London: Methuen & Co., Ltd. [cit. 599].

Kastner, Ruth, Stuart Kauffman, and Michael Epperson. 2018. "Taking Heisenberg's Potentia Seriously." *International Journal of Quantum Foundations* 4, no. 2 (March 28, 2018): 158–72. Accessed March 2, 2019. http://www.ijqf.org/wps/wp-content/uploads/2018/03/IJQF2018v4n2p1.pdf. [cit. 656].

Kaufman, Mark. 2019. *What's actually going on in that cryptic black hole photo?,* January 11, 2019. Accessed January 13, 2020. https://mashable.com/article/black-hole-picture-scientists-explain. [cit. 178].

Kim, Young-oon. 1987. *Unification Theology.* Revised. NY: HSA–UWC. [cit. 345, 615].

Kirk, Russell. 1993. "The Meaning of 'Justice.'" In *The Future of Justice: The Heritage Lectures, 457,* 1–7. The Heritage Foundation. Accessed March 30, 2021. https://s3.amazonaws.com/thf%5C_media/1993/pdf/hl457.pdf. [cit. 526].

Kirshner, Robert P. 1999. "Supernovæ, an accelerating universe and the cosmological constant." *Proceedings of the National Academy of Sciences of the USA* 96, no. 8 (April): 4224–4227. https://doi.org/10.1073/pnas.96.8.4224. [cit. 161].

Klein, Peter. 1998. "Foundationalism and the Infinite Regress of Reasons: Review of Metaepistemology and Skepticism by Richard Fumerton." *Philosophy and Phenomenological Research* 58, no. 4 (December): 919–25. Accessed February 18, 2019. https://www.jstor.org/stable/2653735. [cit. 656].

Klein, Peter. 2003. "When Infinite Regresses Are Not Vicious." *Philosophy and Phenomenological Research* 66, no. 3 (May): 718–29. Accessed February 17, 2019. https://www.jstor.org/stable/20140569. [cit. 656].

Kragh, Helge. 2014. *The True (?) Story of Hilbert's Infinite Hotel,* March 27, 2014. Accessed February 27, 2019. arXiv: 1403 . 0059 [physics.hist-ph]. [cit. 93, 96].

Krishnamurti, J. 1969. *Freedom from the Known.* Edited by Mary Lutyens. NY: Harper & Row. [cit. 573].

L'Annunziata, Michael F., ed. 2012. *Handbook of Radioactivity Analysis.* 3rd ed. Oxford: Elsevier. [cit. 152].

Lackner, James R., and Paul DiZio. 2005. "Vestibular, Proprioceptive, and Haptic Contributions to Spatial Orientation." *Annual Review of Psychology* 56 (February 4, 2005): 115–147. [cit. 317].

Le Blanc, Jill. 1993. "Infinity in Theology and Mathematics." *Religious Studies* 29, no. 1 (March): 51–62. Accessed March 1, 2019. jstor.org/stable/20019590. [cit. 96].

Le Bon, Gustave. 1896. *The Crowd: A Study of the Popular Mind.* NY: Macmillan. [cit. 655].

Lea, Robert. 2018. *The Double Slit Experiment Demystified. Disproving the Quantum Consciousness Connection,* April 4, 2018. Accessed May 27, 2019. https://medium.com/predict/the-double-slit-experiment-demystified-disproving-the-quantum-consciousness-connection-ee8384a50e2f. [cit. 158].

Learn, Joshua R. 2016. "No, a Mitochondrial 'Eve' Is Not the First Female in a Species." In *Smithsonian.com.* Smithsonian, June 28, 2016. Accessed July 19, 2018. https://www.smithsonianmag.com/science-nature/no-mitochondrial-eve-not-first-female-species-180959593/. [cit. 645].

Liang, Jinyang, Cheng Ma, Liren Zhu, Yujia Chen, Liang Gao, and Lihong V. Wang. 2017. "Single-shot real-time video recording of a photonic Mach cone induced by a scattered light pulse." *Science Advances* 3 (1): 1–7. Accessed June 4, 2019. https://doi.org/10.1126/sciadv.1601814. [cit. 152, 156, 658].

Liang, Jinyang, Liren Zhu, and Lihong V. Wang. 2018. "Single-shot real-time femtosecond imaging of temporal focusing." *Light: Science & Applications* 7 (42): 1–10. Accessed June 9, 2019. https://doi.org/10.1038/s41377-018-0044-7. [cit. 658].

Libet, B., C.A. Gleason, E.W. Wright, and D.K. Pearl. 1983. "Time of conscious intention to act in relation to onset of cerebral activity (readiness-potential): The unconscious initiation of a freely voluntary act." *Brain* 106:623–642. [cit. 429].

Lincoln, Don. 2013. "Quantum Foam." In *Fermilab Today,* edited by Edward N. Zalta. February 1, 2013. Accessed May 18, 2019. https://fnal.gov/pub/today/archive/archive_2013/today13-02-01_NutshellReadmore.html. [cit. 211].

Loke, Andrew Ter Ern. 2017. "Is the Past Infinite? An Assessment of the Current Literature." In *God and Ultimate Origins: A Novel Cosmological Argument,* edited by A.T.E. Loke. Springer International Publishing. [cit. 656].

Love, Nathaniel. 2006. "Transfer Learning Evaluation with Relational Nets." *Proceedings of the International Conference on Machine Learning (ICML) Workshop: Structural Knowledge Transfer for Machine Learning at Carnegie Mellon University* (Pittsburgh) (June 25–29, 2006). [cit. 656].

Lovelock, John. 1979. *Gaia: A New Look at Life on Earth.* Oxford University Press. [cit. 661].

Mahathera, Narada. 1998. *The Buddha and His Teachings.* Taipei, Taiwan: The Corporate Body of the Buddha Educational Foundation. [cit. 435].

Mahner, Martin, and Mario Bunge. 1997. *Foundations of Biophilosophy.* Berlin: Springer-Verlag. [cit. 91].

Makin, Simon. 2015. "The Brain Cells Behind a Sense of Direction." *Scientific American* 26, no. 3 (May 12, 2015). https://doi.org/10.1038/scientificamericanmind0515-12. [cit. 317].

Mancuso, Stefano, and Alessandra Viola. 2015. *Brilliant Green: The Surprising History and Science of Plant Intelligence.* Wash. DC: Island Press. [cit. 234].

Markus, Gabriel. *Why the World Does Not Exist: in conversation with Markus Gabriel.* Accessed December 22, 2018. http://christine-jakobson.squarespace.com/issue/world/markus-gabriel-interview. [cit. 45].

McKeon, Christopher. 1998. "Cain and Abel: A Spiritual Analysis of American Race Hate." Master's thesis, Unification Theological Seminary. [cit. 647, 650].

McKeon, Christopher. 2003. *Victim to Victor: Confessions of a Wrong-way Moonie.* Unpublished manuscript. Washington, DC. [cit. vi, 646, 653].

McKeon, Christopher. 2017–19. "October 13 (entered Nov. 10), 2017." In *The Diary of Christopher McKeon,* vol. VII. Unpublished; private collection. October 6, 2017–April 3, 2019. [cit. 647].

McMullin, Ernan. 1984. "A Case for Scientific Realism." In *Scientific Realism,* edited by Jarrett Leplin, 8–40. Berkeley: University of California Press. [cit. 655].

Merriam-Webster Dictionary. 2018–22. Springfield, MA: Encyclopædia Britannica. [cit. 138, 332, 354].

Mill, John Stuart. 1867. *On Liberty.* London: Longmans, Green, and Co. [cit. 585, 587].

Moody, Raymond A. 1975. *Life After Life: The investigation of a phenomenon—survival of bodily death.* Covington, GA: Mockingbird Books. [cit. 423].

Moon, Sun-myung. 1987. *When It Was Over, It Turned Out To Be Love.* True Parents Birthday at the World Mission Center Grand Ballroom, New York City. Speech, February 3, 1987. Accessed September 21, 2018. https://www.tparents.org/Moon-Talks/sunmy ungmoon87/870203.htm. [cit. 653].

Moon, Sun-myung. 1990. *True Abel.* Speech, February 5, 1990. Accessed November 3, 2020. https://tparents.org/Moon-Talks/SunMyun gMoon90/SunMyungMoon-900205.htm. [cit. 384].

Moon, Sun-myung. 1996. *Exposition of the Divine Principle.* Color Coded. Revised 2006. NY: HSA-UWC. [cit. 2, 295, 345, 362, 384, 596, 615, 645, 647, 650, 660–661].

Moon, Sun-myung. 1999. "Prayer and Declaration of the Liberation of the Cosmos (May 14, 1999)." Translated by Rev. Taek Yong Oh. *Today's World* (NY) 20, no. 6 (June): 11–12. [cit. 646].

Moon, Sun-myung. 2006. *Cheon Seong Gyeong: Selections from the Speeches of True Parents.* Family Federation for World Peace and Unification. eprint: 2009. [cit. 470].

Moon, Sung-il. 2018. "Jeong and Empathy for Pastoral Care and Counseling in the Korean Context." Ph.D. Thesis, University of St. Michael's College. Accessed December 10, 2020. https://tspace.library.utoronto.ca/handle/1807/99722. [cit. 345].

Mückenheim, Wolfgang. 2006. *The Meaning of Infinity,* December 13, 2006. Accessed February 28, 2019. arXiv: math / 0403238 [math.gm]. [cit. 655–656].

Myrdal, Gunnar. 1964. *An American Dilemma: The Negro in a White Nation.* Vol. 1. San Francisco: Harper & Row. [cit. 650].

Nagaraj, Anil Kumar. 2013. "Osho: Insights on Sex." *Indian Journal of Psychiatry (Supplement)* 55:S268–72. [cit. 599].

Neiman, Susan. 2002. *Evil in Modern Thought: An Alternative History of Philosophy.* Princeton University Press. [cit. 460].

Nelson, Bradley. 2007. *The Emotion Code: How to Release Your Trapped Emotions for Abundant Health, Love and Happiness.* 1st ed. Mesquite, NV: Wellness Unmasked Publishing. [cit. 645].

O'Connor, Timothy. 1994. "Emergent Properties." *American Philosophical Quarterly* 31, no. 2 (April): 91–104. Accessed February 5, 2019. https://www.jstor.org/stable/20014490. [cit. 91, 655].

O'Connor, Timothy, and Hong Yu Wong. 2015. "Emergent Properties." In *The Stanford Encyclopedia of Philosophy,* Summer, edited by Edward N. Zalta. Metaphysics Research Lab, Stanford University. https://plato.stanford.edu/entries/properties-emergent/. [cit. 90].

Oesper, David. 2017. *Distant Supernovæ Evince Accelerating Expansion of our Universe,* March 29, 2017. Accessed June 22, 2019. https://co smicreflections.skythisweek.info/2017/03/29/distant-supernovae-evince-accelerating-expansion-of-our-universe/. [cit. 659].

Paine, Thomas. (1776) 1824. *Common Sense.* In *The political writings of Thomas Paine, secretary to the Committee of Foreign Affairs in the American Revolution: to which is prefixed a brief sketch of the author's life,* 1:19–64. Charlestown, MA: George Davidson. [cit. 448].

Pais, Abraham. 1979. "Einstein and the quantum theory." *Reviews of Modern Physics* 51, no. 4 (October): 863–914. http://ursula.chem.yal e.edu/~batista/classes/vvv/RevModPhys.51.863.pdf. [cit. 295].

Parise, André Geremia, Monica Gagliano, and Gustavo Maia Souza. 2020. "Extended cognition in plants: is it possible?" *Plant Signaling & Behavior* 15 (2): 1710661. https://doi.org/10.1080/15592324.2019.1710661. [cit. 234].

Penrose, Roger. 1995. "Consciousness Involves Noncomputable Ingredients." In *The Third Culture: Beyond the Scientific Revolution,* by John Brockman, 239–261. NY: Simon & Schuster. [cit. 415, 654].

Penrose, Roger. 2010. *Cycles of Time: An Extraordinary New View of the Universe.* NY: Knopf. [cit. 231].

Piiroinen, Tero. 2014. "Three Senses of 'Emergence': On the Term's History, Functions, and Usefulness in Social Theory." *Prolegomena* (Zagreb) 13 (1): 141–61. [cit. 90–91].

Pine, Red, trans. 2009. *Lao-Tzu's Taoteching with selected commentaries from the past 2000 years.* Revised. Port Townsend, WA: Copper Canyon Press. [cit. 232].

Poe, Edgar Allen. 1902. *The Complete Works of Edgar Allen Poe - Virginia Edition.* Edited by James A. Harrison. Vol. XVI Marginalia–Eureka. NY: Thomas Y. Crowell & Company. [cit. 188].

Porteus, Beilby. 1759. *Death: A Poetical Essay.* Cambridge: Christ's College. [cit. 460].

Proske, Uwe. 2006. "Kinesthesia: The role of muscle receptors." *Muscle & Nerve* 34, no. 5 (November): 545–558. [cit. 317].

Proske, Uwe, and Simon C. Gandevia. 2012. "The Proprioceptive Senses: Their Roles in Signaling Body Shape, Body Position and Movement, and Muscle Force." *Physiological Reviews* 92 (October 1, 2012): 1651–1697. [cit. 317].

Richerson, Peter J., Robert Boyd, and Robert L. Bettinger. 2001. "Was Agriculture Impossible during the Pleistocene but Mandatory during the Holocene?" *American Antiquity* 66, no. 3 (July): 387–411. [cit. 551].

Ross, Cameron. 2019. "Infinite Regress Arguments." In *The Stanford Encyclopedia of Philosophy,* Fall, edited by Edward N. Zalta. Metaphysics Research Lab, Stanford University. Accessed February 16, 2019. https://plato.stanford.edu/archives/fall2018/entries/i nfinite-regress/. [cit. 100, 656].

Rousseau, Jean-Jacques. 1761. *Discourse Upon the Origin and Foundation of the Inequality among Mankind.* London: R. & J. Dodsley, Pallmall. [cit. 275].

Ruse, Michael. 2007. "Dossier Évolution et créationnisme: Intelligent Design Theory." *Natures Sciences Sociétés: Recherches et débats interdisciplinaires* 15, no. 3 (March): 285–286. [cit. 646].

Sahni, Varun. 2002. "The cosmological constant problem and Quintessence." *Classical and Quantum Gravity* 19, no. 13 (June 12, 2002): 3435–48. https://doi.org/10.1088/0264-9381/19/13/304. [cit. 661].

Salinger, J.D. 1953. *Nine Stories.* NY: Little, Brown and Company. [cit. 460].

Scoles, Sarah. 2016. "We Need a New Word for Infinite Spaces." In *The Atlantic.* February 25, 2016. Accessed April 5, 2019. https://www.theatlantic.com/science/archive/2016/02/a-new-word-for-infinite-spaces/470685/. [cit. 223].

Shahzad, Faisal, Mohamed Alhabeb, Soon Man Hong, Chong Min Koo, and Yury Gogotsi. 2016. "Electromagnetic interference shielding with 2D transition metal carbides (MXenes)." *Science* 353, no. 6304 (September 9, 2016): 1137–40. https://doi.org/10.1126/science.aag2421. [cit. 148, 658].

Shalizi, Cosma Rohilla. 2001. "Causal Architecture, Complexity and Self-Organization in Time Series and Cellular Automata." Ph.D. Thesis, University of Wisconsin–Madison. [cit. 91].

Sheldrake, Rupert. 2012. *Science Set Free: 10 Paths to New Discovery.* NY: Deepak Chopra Books. [cit. 79].

Sidiropoulou, Kyriaki, Eleftheria Kyriaki Pissadaki, and Panayiota Poirazi. 2006. "Inside the brain of a neuron." *EMBO reports* 7:886–892. https://doi.org/10.1038/sj.embor.7400789. [cit. 271].

Siegel, Daniel J. 2012. *The Developing Mind: How Relationships and the Brain Interact to Shape Who We Are.* 2nd ed. NY: The Guilford Press. [cit. 265].

Siegel, Daniel J. 2016. *Mind: A Journey to the Heart of Being Human.* NY: W.W. Norton. [cit. 273].

Siegel, Ethan. 2014. *How Many Planets in the Universe?,* January 23, 2014. Accessed October 8, 2020. https://medium.com/starts-with-a-bang/how-many-planets-in-the-universe-9153a05bd0d5. [cit. 357].

Siegel, Ethan. 2018a. *There is a Debate Raging Over Whether Dark Matter is Real, But One Side is Cheating,* August 2, 2018. Accessed August 29, 2019. https://medium.com/starts-with-a-bang/theres-a-debate-raging-over-whether-dark-matter-is-real-but-one-side-is-cheating-d25f28319d70. [cit. 195].

Siegel, Ethan. 2018b. *This is How We Know There are Two Trillion Galaxies in the Universe,* October 18, 2018. Accessed October 6, 2020. https://www.forbes.com/sites/startswithabang/2018/10/18/this-is-how-we-know-there-are-two-trillion-galaxies-in-the-universe/?sh=4b7fae255a67. [cit. 357].

Singer, Peter. 2005. "The Sanctity of Life." *Foreign Policy* (September–October): 40–1. [cit. 654].

Smuts, Jan Christian. 1926. *Holism and Evolution.* NY: The Macmillan Company. [cit. 230].

Solms, Mark. 2004. "Freud Returns." *Scientific American* 290, no. 5 (May): 82–9. [cit. 266].

Solms, Mark, and Oliver Turnbull. 2002. *The Brain and the Inner World: An Introduction to the Neuroscience of Subjective Relationship.* NY: Other Press. [cit. 266–267].

Stenger, Victor. 2012. "The God Issue: God is a testable hypothesis." In *New Scientist.* March 14, 2012. Accessed March 26, 2020. https://www.newscientist.com/article/mg21328562-300-the-god-issue-god-is-a-testable-hypothesis/. [cit. 573].

Stibal, Vianna. 2011. *ThetaHealing: Introducing an Extraordinary Energy Healing Modality.* Carlsbad, CA: Hay House, Inc. [cit. 29–30, 648].

Swedenborg, Emanuel. (1758) 1758–1916. *Heaven and its Wonders and Hell: From Things Heard and Seen.* NY: The American Swedenborg Printing / Publishing Society. [cit. 596].

Tahko, Tuomas E., and E. Jonathan Lowe. 2016. "Ontological Dependence." In *The Stanford Encyclopedia of Philosophy,* Winter, edited by Edward N. Zalta. Metaphysics Research Lab, Stanford University. Accessed February 19, 2019. https://plato.stanford.edu/entries/dependence-ontological/. [cit. 656].

Tanguay, Peter N. 2015. "The imaginary unit i as the temporal directional component of the complex position vector." *Physics Essays* 28, no. 2 (June): 188–191. https://doi.org/10.13140/RG.2.2.23621.35040. [cit. 206].

Tannehill, Morris, and Linda Tannehill. 1970. *The Market for Liberty.* Auburn, AL: The Ludwig von Mises Institute. [cit. 447].

Tattersall, Ian. 1998. *Becoming Human: Evolution and Human Uniqueness.* UK: Harcourt Brace. [cit. 275, 281].

Taylor, Steve. 2017. "Moving Beyond Materialism: Can Transpersonal Psychology Contribute to Cultural Transformation?" *International Journal of Transpersonal Studies* 36, no. 2 (September 1, 2017): 147–59. https://doi.org/10.24972/ijts.2017.36.2.147. [cit. 79, 655].

Taylor, Steve. 2018. "Beyond Materialism: Why science needs a spiritual perspective to make sense of the world." In *Integral World: Exloring Theories of Everything.* Frank Visser, November. Accessed January 27, 2019. http://www.integralworld.net/taylor7.html. [cit. 655].

Tegmark, Max. 2015. "Infinity is a Beautiful Concept—And it's Ruining Physics." In *This Idea Must Die: Scientific Theories that are Blocking Progress,* 48–51. NY: Harper Perennial. [cit. 93].

The Urantia Book. 1955. Chicago: Urantia Foundation. [cit. 651].

Thompson, Avery. 2018. "How Do We Know Black Holes Even Exist?" *Popular Mechanics* (January 11, 2018). Accessed January 13, 2020. https://www.popularmechanics.com/space/deep-space/a15062681/how-do-we-know-black-holes-even-exist/. [cit. 178].

Thurber, James. 1940. *Fables for our Time and Famous Poems Illustrated.* NY: Harper & Row. [cit. 452].

Thyssen, Pieter. 2013. *Schrödinger's Cat and the Measurement Problem,* September 1, 2013. Accessed August 21, 2019. http://thelifeofpsi.com/2013/09/01/the-measurement-problem/. [cit. 193].

Tiger, Lionel, and Robin Fox. 1974. *The Imperial Animal.* NY: Dell. [cit. 647].

Tompkins, Peter, and Christopher Bird. 1973. *The Secret Life of Plants.* NY: Harper & Row. [cit. 234].

Trimmer, John D. 1980. "The Present Situation in Quantum Mechanics: A Translation of Schrödinger's 'Cat Paradox' Paper." *Proceedings of the American Philosophical Society* 124, no. 5 (October 10, 1980): 323–338. [cit. 193, 197].

Uebersax, John S. 2018. "The Monomyth of Fall and Salvation." In *Christian Platonism.* Catholic Gnosis (blog), December 10, 2018. Accessed January 1, 2018. https://catholicgnosis.wordpress.com/2014/12/10/the-monomyth-of-fall-and-salvation/. [cit. 647].

Venema, Dennis R., and Scot McKnight. 2017. *Adam and the Genome: Reading Scripture after Genetic Science.* Grand Rapids, MI: Brazos Press. [cit. 21, 646].

Wang, Connie X., Isaac A. Hilburn, Daw-An Wu, Yuki Mizuhara, Christopher P. Cousté, Jacob N. H. Abrahams, Sam E. Bernstein, Ayumu Matani, Shinsuke Shimojo, and Joseph L. Kirschvink. 2019. "Transduction of the Geomagnetic Field as Evidenced from alpha-Band Activity in the Human Brain." *eNeuro* 6, no. 2 (March–April): 1–23. [cit. 317].

Ward, Keith. 2002. *God: A Guide for the Perplexed.* Oxford: Oneworld Publications. [cit. 44].

Watts, Alan W. 1951. *The Wisdom of Insecurity.* NY: Vintage Books. [cit. vi, 21].

Weyl, Herman. 2012. *Levels of Infinity: Selected Writings on Mathematics and Philosophy.* Edited by Peter Pesic. Mineola, NY: Dover Publications, Inc. [cit. 96].

Williams, Bernard. 1973. "The Makropulos case: Reflections on the tedium of immortality." In *Problems of the Self: Philosophical Papers 1956–1972,* 82–100. Cambridge University Press. https://doi.org/10.1017/CBO9780511621253.008. [cit. 494–496].

Wilson, Edward O. 1998. *Consilience: The Unity of Knowledge.* NY: Vintage Books. [cit. 87].

Witzel, E.J. Michael. 2012. *The Origins of the World's Mythologies.* Oxford University Press. [cit. 646].

Xu, Jingsong, Alexandra Van Keymeulen, Nicole M. Wakida, Pete Carlton, Michael W. Berns, and Henry R. Bourne. 2007. "Polarity reveals intrinsic cell chirality." *Proceedings of the National Academy of Sciences* 104:9296–9300. [cit. 177].

Young, Ben. 2017. "The Doubts of a Leader." In Ch. 5 "Famous Doubters." In *Room for Doubt: How Uncertainty Can Deepen Your Faith,* edited by Ben Young. Colorado Springs: David C. Cook. [cit. 653].

Zlatev, Ivaylo, Limin Wang, and Paul J. Steinhardt. 1999. "Quintessence, Cosmic Coincidence, and the Cosmological Constant." *Physical Review Letters* 82:896–99. [cit. 661].

Zusne, Leonard, and Warren H. Jones. 2014. *Anomalistic Psychology: A Study of Magical Thinking.* NY: Taylor & Francis. [cit. 655].

Works Consulted

Abend, Gabriel. 2008. "The Meaning of 'Theory'." *Sociological Theory* 26, no. 2 (June): 173–99. https://www-jstor-org.proxy.librarypoint.org/stable/20453103.

Astor, Maggie. 2018. "Getting Facts Wrong on the Holocaust." *The New York Times: NY Edition,* A15.

Beattie, Allan. 2009. *False Economy: A Surprising Economic History of the World.* NY: Riverhead Books.

Bell, John Stewart. 1964. "On the Einstein Podolsky Rosen Paradox." *Physics* 1 (3): 195–200.

Butler, Samuel. 1805. *Hudibras, In Three Parts Written in the Time of the Late Wars.* (1678, 1684). London: Ex-Classics Project (2009).

Callender, Craig. 2017. *What Makes Time Special.* Oxford University Press.

Carrier, Richard C. 2005. "The Spiritual Body of Christ and the Legend of the Empty Tomb." In *The Empty Tomb: Jesus Beyond the Grave,* 105–231. Amherst, NY: Prometheus.

Cayce, Edgar. 1969. *The Edgar Cayce Collection: Four Volumes in One.* Edited by Hugh Lynn Cayce. NY: Bonanza Books.

Chang, Donald C. 2018. "A New Interpretation on the Non-Newtonian Properties of Particle Mass." *Journal of Modern Physics* 9, no. 2 (January): 215–40. https://doi.org/10.4236/jmp.2018.92015.

Cooper, Alan, Chris S. M. Turney, Jonathan Palmer, Alan Hogg, Matt McGlone, Janet Wilmshurst, and Andrew M. Lorrey et al. 2021. "A global environmental crisis 42,000 years ago." *Science* 371, no. 6531 (February 19, 2021): 811–818. https://doi.org/10.1126/science.abb8677.

Cremo, Michael A., and Richard L. Thompson. 1996. *The Hidden History of the Human Race: The Condensed Edition of Forbidden Archeology.* Los Angeles, CA: Bhaktivedanta Book Publishing.

Csikszentmihalyi, Mihaly. 1993. *The Evolving Self: A Psychology for the Third Millennium.* NY: HarperCollins.

Einstein, Albert. 2002. "Fundamental Ideas and Methods of the Theory of Relativity, Presented in Their Development." In *The Collected Papers of Albert Einstein,* edited by Albert Einstein, translated by Alfred Engel, 7:113–150. Princeton University Press.

Einstein, Albert, Boris Podolsky, and Nathan Rosen. 1935. "Can Quantum–Mechanical Description of Physical Reality Be Considered Complete?" *Physical Review* 47 (May 15, 1935): 777–80.

Eliade, Mircea. 1959. *The Sacred and the Profane.* NY: Harcourt, Brace and Company.

Fang, Ferric, and Arturo Casadevall. 2011. "Reductionistic and Holistic Science." *Infection and Immunity* 79, no. 4 (April): 1401–04. https://doi.org/10.1128/IAI.01343-10.

Feser, Edward. 2017. *Five Proofs of the Existence of God.* San Francisco: Ignatius Press.

Gerlich, Stefan, Sandra Eibenberger, Mathias Tomandl, Stefan Nimmrichter, Klaus Hornberger, Paul J. Fagan, Jens Tüxen, Marcel Mayor, and Markus Arndt. 2011. "Quantum Interference of Large Organic Molecules." *Nature Communications* 2, no. 263 (April). https://doi.org/10.1038/ncomms1263.

Goldmann, Nahum. 1978. *The Jewish Paradox: A Personal Memoir.* 8th ed. Translated by Steve Cox. Worthing, UK: Littlehampton Book Services Ltd.

Gray, Reginald H., and David J. Dye. 2017. *Messages from Beyond the Veil: Spiritual Guidance for our Human Experience.* Mesa, AZ: Astralis Media Group.

Herculano-Houzel, Suzana. 2012. "The remarkable, yet not extraordinary, human brain as a scaled-up primate brain and its associated cost." Supplement 1: In the Light of Evolution VI: Brain and Behavior. *Proceedings of the National Academy of Sciences of the United States of America* 109 (June 26, 2012): 10661–10668. Accessed May 9, 2020. https://www.jstor.org/stable/41601653.

Kapinos, Tom. 2016–21. *Lucifer.* Based on *The Sandman* comic character by Neil Gaiman, Sam Kieth, and Mike Dringenberg and *Lucifer* by Mike Carey. Fox–Netflix. Television series.

Kirwan, Gráinne, and Andrew Power. 2012. *The Psychology of Cyber Crime: Concepts and Principles.* 1st ed. Hershey, PA: Information Science Reference (IGI Global imprint).

Lambek, Michael. 2003. "Memory in a Maussian Universe." In *Regimes of Memory,* 1st ed., edited by Katharine Hodgkin and Susannah Radstone, 202–216. London: Routledge.

Levenson, Jon D. 1985. *Creation and the Persistence of Evil: The Jewish Drama of Divine Omnipotence.* San Francisco: Harper & Row.

Loftus, Geoffrey R. 1985. "Evaluating Forgetting Curves." *Journal of Experimental Psychology: Learning, Memory, and Cognition* 11 (2): 397–406. https://doi.org/10.1037/0278-7393.11.2.397.

Mann, C. John. 1970. "Isochronous, Synchronous, and Coetaneous." *The Journal of Geology* 78 (6): 749–50. Accessed August 30, 2018. http://www.jstor.org.proxy.librarypoint.org/stable/30067904.

Meyer, Stephen C. 2013. *Darwin's Doubt: The Explosive Origin of Animal Life and the Case for Intelligent Design.* NY: HarperOne.

Mitchell, Daniel R. 2015. *Pondering Things: About the Bible, Christianity, and Other Stuff.* 1st ed. Morrisville, NC: Lulu Press.

Mittelstrass, Jürgen. 2015. "Complexity, Reductionism, and Holism in Science and Philosophy of Science," 45–53. Vatican City: Pontifical Academy of Sciences, Acta 22.

Moreau, Paul-Antoine, Ermes Toninelli, Thomas Gregory, Reuben S. Aspden, Peter A. Morris, and Miles J. Padgett. 2019. "Imaging Bell-type nonlocal behavior." *Science Advances* 5, no. 7 (July 12, 2019): 1–8. https://doi.org/10.1126/sciadv.aaw2563.

Morgan, Peggy. 2010. "Parallels between Jesus and Gautama." In Ch. 17, "Buddhist Perspectives on Jesus." In *The Blackwell Companion to Jesus.* Hoboken, NJ: Wiley-Blackwell.

Nietzsche, Friedrich. 1968. *The Will to Power.* Edited by Walter Kaufmann. NY: Vintage Books.

Oesch, P.A., G. Brammer, P. G. van Dokkum, G. D. Illingworth, R. J. Bouwens, I. Labbé, M. Franx, I. Momcheva, M. L. N. Ashby, G. G. Fazio, V. Gonzalez, B. Holden, D. Magee, R. E. Skelton, R. Smit, L. R. Spitler, M. Trenti, and S. P. Willner. 2016. "A Remarkably Luminous Galaxy at z=11.1 Measured with Hubble Space Telescope GRISM Spectroscopy." *The Astrophysical Journal* 819, no. 129 (March 10, 2016): 1–11.

Palmberger, Monika. 2016. *How Generations Remember: Conflicting Histories and Shared Memories in Post-War Bosnia and Herzegovina.* London: Palgrave Macmillan.

Peabody, Andrew P. 1886. *Cicero's Tusculan Disputations.* 195–250. Boston: Little & Brown.

Perrett, Roy W. 2002. "Evil and Human Nature." *The Monist* (Peru) 85 (2): 304–319.

Plantinga, Alvin. 1977. *God, Freedom, and Evil.* Grand Rapids, MI: Wm. B. Eerdmans Publishing Co.

Romig, Rollo. 2012. "What Do We Mean By Evil?" *The New Yorker: Page-Turner* (July 25, 2012).

Sawyer, Robert J. 2016. *Quantum Night.* Fiction. NY: Ace Books.

Sculthorp, Frederick C. 1969. *Excursions to the Spirit World: A Report of Personal Experiences During Conscious Astral Projection.* London: The Greater World Association.

Singer, Michael A. 2007. *The Untethered Soul: The Journey Beyond Yourself.* Oakland, CA: New Harbinger Publications and Noetic Books.

Smith, John Maynard, and Eörs Szathmáry. 1999. *The Origin of Life: From the Birth of Life to the Origin of Language.* Oxford University Press.

Swinburne, Richard. 1977. *The Coherence of Theism.* Oxford: Clarendon Press.

Turner, Bryan S. 2011. *Religion and Modern Society: Citizenship, Secularisation and the State.* NY: Cambridge University Press.

Wallace, J. Warner. 2015. *God's Crime Scene: A Cold-Case Detective Examines the Evidence for a Divinely Created Universe.* Colorado Springs: David C. Cook.

Wamsley, Erin J., and Robert Stickgold. 2011. "Memory, Sleep and Dreaming: Experiencing Consolidation." *Sleep Medicine Clinics* 6, no. 1 (March): 97–108.

Watts, Alan. 1973. *Cloud-hidden, Whereabouts Unknown: A Mountain Journal.* NY: Pantheon Books.

Wegter-McNelly, Kirk. 2011a. "Book Review: Victor J. Stenger, Quantum Gods: Creation, Chaos, and the Search for Cosmic Consciousness (Amherst, NY: Prometheus Books, 2009)." *Journal for the Study of Religion, Nature and Culture* 5:373–5.

Wegter-McNelly, Kirk. 2011b. *The Entangled God: Divine Relationality and Quantum Physics.* NY: Routledge.

Weisman, Alan. 2007. *The World Without Us.* 1st ed. NY: Thomas Dunne Books.

World Population Prospects: The 2017 Revision, DVD Edition. 2017. Technical report. NY.

Zalasiewicz, Jan, and Ki Freedman. 2008. *The Earth After Us: What Legacy Will Humans Leave in the Rocks?* Oxford University Press.

Index

A bolded page number [e.g., **57**] indicates an entry's most pertinent reference, if there is one. Some entries represent a range of noun, verb, adverb, adjective (e.g., *abandonment* for 'abandon(-ed, -ing);' *instantaneity* for 'instant(-ly, -aneous)); some have double duty (e.g., *bacteria* also references 'microbe').

www.ingramcontent.com/pod-product-compliance
Lightning Source LLC
Chambersburg PA
CBHW082136120626
46553CB00010B/2687

*9 7 9 8 9 8 6 4 7 0 7 0 2 *